Concentrated Acids and Bases

	Approximate weight percent in reagent grade	Molarity corresponding to wt %	mL of reagent needed to prepare 1.0 1 of 1.0-M solution
Acids			
Acetic	99.8	17.4	57.5
Hydrochloric	37.2	12.1	82.6
Hydrofluoric	49.0	28.9	34.6
Nitric	70.4	15.9	62.9
Perchloric	70.5	11.7	85.5
Phosphoric	85.5	14.8	67.6
Sulfuric	96.0	18.0	55.6
Bases			
Ammonia[*]	28.0	14.5	69.0
Sodium hydroxide	50.5[†]	19.3	51.8
Potassium hydroxide	52.0	14.2	70.4

[*]28.0% ammonia is the same as 56.6% ammonium hydroxide.
[†]Saturated solution at 20°C.

Prefix Notation

Exponential	Prefix name	Symbol
10^9	giga-	G-
10^6	mega-	M-
10^3	kilo-	k-
10^{-1}	deci-	d-
10^{-2}	centi-	c-
10^{-3}	milli-	m-
10^{-6}	micro-	μ-
10^{-9}	nano-	n-
10^{-12}	pico-	p-
10^{-15}	femto-	f-
10^{-18}	atto-	a-

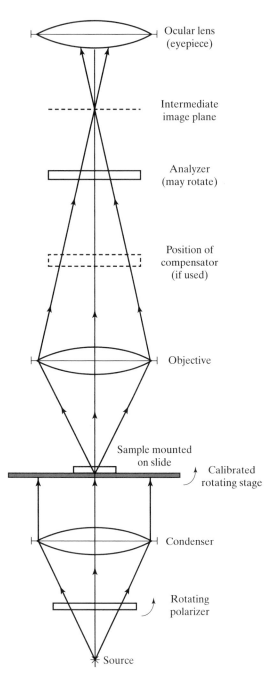

Ocular lens
(eyepiece)

Intermediate
image plane

Analyzer
(may rotate)

Position of
compensator
(if used)

Objective

Sample mounted
on slide

Calibrated
rotating stage

Condenser

Rotating
polarizer

Source

◀ *Optical path of a generic*
polarizing light microscope

Forensic Chemistry

Suzanne Bell
West Virginia University

PEARSON
Prentice
Hall

Upper Saddle River, New Jersey 07458

Library of Congress Cataloging-in-Publication Data

Bell, Suzanne.

   Forensic chemistry / Suzanne Bell.-- 1st ed.

     p. cm.

   Includes bibliographical references and index.

   ISBN 0-13-147835-4

  1. Chemistry, Forensic. 2. Chemistry, Analytic. I. Title.

   RA1057.B45 2006

   614'.12--dc22

2005011531

Executive Editor: Nicole Folchetti
Executive Managing Editor: Kathleen Schiaparelli
Assistant Managing Editor: Beth Sweeten
Editorial Assistant: Timothy Murphy
Project Manager: Kristen Kaiser
Production Editor: Donna King, Progressive Publishing Alternatives
Executive Marketing Manager: Steve Sartori
Senior Managing Editor, Art Production and Management: Patricia Burns
Manager, Production Technologies: Matthew Haas
Managing Editor, Art Management: Abigail Bass
Director of Creative Services: Paul Belfanti
Art Production Editor: Thomas Benfatti
Illustrations: Argosy
Director, Image Resource Center: Melinda Reo
Manager, Rights and Permissions: Zina Arabia
Manager, Visual Research: Beth Brenzel
Manager, Cover Visual Research & Permissions: Karen Sanatar
Photo Researcher/Image Permission Coordinator: Elaine Soares
Manufacturing Buyer: Alan Fischer
Manufacturing Manager: Alexis Heydt-Long
Illustration Art Director: Jay McElroy

© 2006 by Pearson Education, Inc.
Pearson Prentice Hall
Pearson Education, Inc.
Upper Saddle River, New Jersey 07458

Printed in the United States of America

10 9 8 7 6 5 4 3 2 1

ISBN 0-13-147835-4

Pearson Education Ltd., *London*
Pearson Education Australia, PTY. Limited, *Sydney*
Pearson Education Singapore, Pte. Ltd
Pearson Education North Asia Ltd, *Hong Kong*
Pearson Education Canada, Ltd., *Toronto*
Pearson Educación de Mexico, S.A. de C.V.
Pearson Education—Japan, *Tokyo*
Pearson Education Malaysia, Pte. Ltd

To my wonderful mentors, Dr. Robert Gaensslen and Dr. Gary Eiceman, and to my students past and present. Thanks for everything.

Contents

3   Multivariate Statistics, Calibration, and Quality Control   46

Part II: Essential Elements

4 Sample Preparation, Thin-Layer Chromatography, and Immunoassay   85

Part III: Drug Analysis

6 An Overview of Drugs and Pharmacology   212

Part IV: Chemical Analysis of Physical Evidence

9 The Chemistry of Combustion and Arson   384

The following appendices can be found at the Bell page on the Prentice Hall web site at: www.prenhall.com.

Preface

This is the only place the author (me) of a textbook is allowed to talk directly to the reader (you), so I will take advantage of this convention before fading into the background. It is also the section most skipped by readers, so I assume if you are reading this, you are a kindred spirit, one fascinated by this topic, or at least fascinated at the prospect of learning more. Forensic chemistry is one of the most interesting and integrative areas within chemistry, and I trust you will find it as challenging and rewarding as I have. I invite you to take advantage of the supplementary material that is available for this text, including the lab manual and Student Study Guide. The lab manual parallels the chapters and draws from the literature as well as from procedures used in most forensic laboratories. Suggestions for lab-based projects are provided.

If you are a student enrolled in a forensic chemistry course, it is probably safe for me to assume that you want to be doing so, and that you have selected forensic chemistry as a potential career path. Similarly, if you are working in a crime or toxicology lab, it is probably safe for me to assume you enjoy what you do and are seeking more knowledge, are involved in professional continuing training, or are preparing for a certification exam. Having been in all of those positions, I have framed my approach accordingly and have tried to serve the needs of such a range of audiences. I consider everyone in this audience as colleagues, and certainly we are all students of forensic chemistry even if we left college years ago.

For those taking a course using this book, it is likely not your first in forensic science and certainly not your first in chemistry.* It is probably the first time you have encountered these two areas as an integrated subject at the advanced level, but the combination is a natural one. Chemistry is the bedrock of modern forensic science. Sherlock Holmes was a chemist that Sir Arthur Conan Doyle modeled on a surgeon Doyle encountered while a student.[1] James Marsh, a distinguished English chemist, developed one of the earliest reliable tests for arsenic, a technique that marked the beginning of the end of poisoning as a common means of murder. Just as chemistry is referred to as "the central science," forensic chemistry can fairly be called the central science of forensic science. Certainly Sherlock Holmes saw it that way, and who are we to argue?

In this spirit, forensic chemistry is best described as applied analytical chemistry. It is distinguished from other types of analytical chemistry by the legal context in which the work is done, the types of samples and matrices, the variety of sample types encountered, and the extensive use of instrumentation. Suffice it to say that if you enjoy the challenges of analytical chemistry, you should find forensic chemistry a fascinating extension of your skills and experience. If you are a college student, this book can guide you in taking your first steps out of the student world into the professional one. If you are a working professional, this book will supplement your training and experience and provide a ready reference and review.

PREREQUISITES

This book is designed for juniors or seniors in a college chemistry program. Courses you need to have taken are first-year chemistry (majors) and organic chemistry,

---

*If this is your first course in chemistry, get out while you still can!

since the majority of analytes and compounds targeted in forensic chemistry are organic compounds. The content assumes this background, as do the problems at the end of each chapter.* A course in quantitative analysis or the equivalent such as analytical chemistry is strongly recommended, but a dedicated and resourceful reader can get by without it, particularly if your organic chemistry courses had a strong instrumental component. Background in biology and biochemistry is useful but not essential. Since this text targets upper-level chemistry students, a background in math and physics is assumed concomitant to a junior in chemistry.

It is helpful to have taken an introductory course in forensic science. If you have not, I strongly recommend having an introductory text available.[1,2] Background of legal aspects (the "forensic" in forensic chemistry) is addressed sparingly in the text. This is not to say it isn't important; rather, these topics are treated as prerequisite material, or at least material that can be quickly picked up outside of a chemistry course. In my experience, the *forensic* part of forensic chemistry is easier to master than the *chemistry* part, and the writing reflects this admitted bias.

STRUCTURE OF THE TEXT

Forensic Chemistry will introduce the principal areas of the field from the perspective of analytical chemistry. There are four sections:

- **Setting the Stage:** Chapters 1–3. This is foundational material that incorporates review material along with new material. Chemical concepts and practices are addressed from a forensic perspective, such as in Chapter 3 which delves into multivariate statistics and quality assurance/quality control (QA/QC). Applications and protocols used in working forensic laboratories are highlighted.

- **Essential Elements:** Chapters 4–6. With the foundational material in hand, this section will delve into aspects of analytical chemistry that are unique to forensic chemistry. Types of samples and how they are prepared is presented along with concepts such as acid/base chemistry of drugs, solubility, and preparations. Presumptive testing, a bedrock of forensic chemistry, is presented in detail. For those of you that have had a course in qualitative analysis (organic or inorganic), this chapter will have a familiar theme. For example, Chapter 5, *Instrumentation*, contains a detailed discussion of microscopy, a fundamental tool of the forensic chemist that you likely have not worked with extensively (or at all) as a student. If you have had quantitative and instrumental analysis, some of this material will be review, such as infrared spectroscopy. If you have not had such a course, it would be a good idea to have a quantitative analysis and/or instrumental analysis text available to reference.[3–5]

- **Drug Analysis:** Chapters 6–8. By workload and caseload, drug analysis is the largest subdivision of forensic chemistry. This section begins with an overview of drug and medicinal chemistry, metabolism, and other elements of what has come to be called forensic pharmacology. The forensic analysis of drug evidence is divided into two categories: physical evidence (pills, powders, plants, precursors, and paraphernalia—the five "P's") and biological evidence submitted to toxicology labs. The physical evidence portion is further divided into two chapters to present the material in

---

*The appendices have some background information, but for more detailed reviews of key topics such as organic reaction mechanisms and acid/base chemistry, consult organic chemistry or other appropriate textbooks.

manageable portions. The toxicological chapter builds on these previous chapters and discusses metabolites, half-lives, and other aspects critical to reconstructing the "crime scene"—the ingestion of a drug, poison, or mixture of the two. An organic textbook or the *Student Guide* is a helpful supplement for this section.

- **Chemical Analysis of Physical Evidence:** Chapters 9–14. The chapters in this section are application oriented and generally shorter than the preceding chapters. Following drugs, the largest part of forensic chemistry is devoted to the analysis of evidence related to combustion, be it firing of a gun, burning, or explosions. All are based on the same fundamental chemical reaction. Forensic chemists also are called upon to analyze polymers in many forms, be they synthetic fibers, plastic bags, or tapes. Recent advances in instrumentation make this an important aspect of forensic analytical chemistry. The forensic discipline of questioned documents is also delving more into the chemistry of paper and inks, the subject of another chapter. Paints and coatings are frequently encountered as evidence and although paints share many characteristics of ink, there are sufficient differences to warrant a separate chapter. As the resident chemist in a crime lab, you are likely to be asked about how these work at some point. The material is a natural complement to presumptive testing, but warrants separate treatment since it is somewhat specialized.

STRUCTURE OF THE CHAPTERS

Each chapter is structured with the following elements:

- **Overview:** This paragraph or two will orient you to the content and theme for each chapter. Case examples or anecdotes will show how the themes play out in professional practice. Words that are given in bold are considered important and potentially unfamiliar to the reader and defined either in the text or in the glossary.
- **Exhibits:** These provide interesting information related to the chapter content and emphasize the theme laid out in the overview. Contemporary and historical cases, developments, and concepts are provided to flesh out topics and link them to the professional world.
- **Example Problems:** Each chapter has a few example problems that are worked in detail. The aim of these examples is to reinforce learning and to provide guidance useful in working end-of-chapter problems.
- **Historical Evidence:** Rather than begin this book with a history of forensic chemistry, important historical developments are inserted in appropriate locations of the text. This makes the history relevant and interesting without distracting from fundamental chemical concepts.
- **Applying the Science:** Each chapter has several examples of applications drawn from the literature and from working forensic laboratories. The applications are associated with the relevant text area, but also are purposely selected because many integrate several aspects of forensic chemistry previously described and presented.
- **In Summary:** A wrap-up of the key concepts presented and a lead-in to the next chapter.
- **Key Concepts and Terms:** An extensive end-of-chapter term list serves as a review and learning check. All terms found in this list are highlighted in the text and defined in the glossary.

- **Problems:** Each chapter ends with a list of problems divided as follows:

  Chapter-based: These questions are drawn directly and exclusively from material described in the chapter.

  Integrative: Questions that go beyond text material and require review of other course materials or research. For practicing forensic chemists, these are the most important types of questions. Where feasible and appropriate, they are based on actual cases or experiences of those in the field.

  Food for Thought: More philosophical than technical, these questions are drawn from the experience of practicing forensic chemists and are meant to lead to contemplation and class discussion. There are no set answers. These questions could also provide material for presentations and seminars, particularly when integrated with the scientific and technical content of the chapter. For students, these problems and discussion points are especially important and are designed to guide the transition from student to working professional.

- **References and Further Reading:** Derived from books, edited books, journals, and from the Internet as appropriate. When web pages are cited, the http:// leader is omitted. Sites have been selected for inclusion only if they are deemed likely to persist.

There are a few footnotes, but these have been kept to a minimum. Each chapter is extensively referenced and a comprehensive bibliography and source of further reading is provided as part of the Appendices.

The above summarizes what the textbook is; now a few notes about what it is not. It is not meant to be a textbook in forensic toxicology, an enormous subject in which there are many fine books to choose from. Rather, the intent is to introduce this topic as a major aspect of forensic analytical chemistry. Nor is the book meant to cover advanced aspects of all the many forensic chemistry areas, each of which (glass, soils, fibers, paints, inks, drugs, and so on) have been addressed in specialized volumes. Having read this text, you will have the background to tackle these more advanced treatments.

Related to that, keep in mind that topic coverage is designed for budding or practicing forensic chemists, and I would urge you not to skip sections because they may appear to apply "only" to toxicology or only to crime laboratory chemists. Forensic chemistry is forensic chemistry, and foundational principles apply no matter what aspect of it you are interested in. Drug analysts should understand basic toxicology; toxicologists should know what diluents are; explosives chemists need to understand chemical microscopy.

Finally, as an advanced student or working professional, you should know where and how to obtain additional information as needed to supplement what the text provides. Suggestions have been provided but the doing is up to you. Resourcefulness and self-reliance are as much a prerequisite for forensic chemistry as organic chemistry. This course provides an excellent opportunity to hone these skills. If you have not already discovered it, you will soon learn that the best professors (hopefully you have one) and the best textbooks (hopefully you will feel this one is) can not teach you; only you can do that. The best I can hope for as an author and a professor is to help you in every way possible. In thermodynamic terms, the door is open, but it takes energy to walk through it. Learning is not a spontaneous process, but it is an enjoyable one.

REFERENCES

1. Nordby, J. J., and S. H. James, ed. *Forensic Science: An Introduction to Scientific and Investigative Techniques.* Boca Raton, FL: CRC Press, **2003**.
2. Saferstein, R. *Criminalistics. An Introduction to Forensic Science,* 8th ed. Upper Saddle River, NJ: Pearson Prentice Hall, **2004**.
3. Rubinson, K. A., and J. F. Rubinson. *Contemporary Instrumental Analysis.* Upper Saddle River, NJ: Pearson/Prentice Hall, **2000**.
4. Skoog, D. A., et al. *Analytical Chemistry: An Introduction,* 7th ed. New York: Saunders College Publishing/Harcourt College Publishers, **2000**.
5. Harris, D. C. *Quantitative Chemical Analysis,* 6th ed. New York: W.H. Freeman, **2003**.

ACKNOWLEDGMENTS

I am grateful for the help of many of my friends and colleagues who reviewed the manuscript, offered ideas and suggestions, and provided photos and other material. I am also indebted to my students who studied forensic chemistry from unpolished drafts of this work with admirable patience. The professionals at Prentice Hall, led by Nicole Folchetti, have my enduring thanks for helping a rookie textbook author through a first edition.

MANUSCRIPT REVIEWERS

Hongshik Ahn
Stony Brook University

Antje Almeida
University of North Carolina, Wilmington

Doug Barofsky
Oregon State University

John Baur
Illinois State University

Peter Bilous
Eastern Washington University

Avrom Blumberg
Depaul University

Simon Bott
University of Houston

Aaron Brudenell
Tuscon Police Department

Sharmaine Cady
East Stroudsburg University

Janis Cavanaugh
Rio Hondo College

Nadja Cech
University of North Carolina-Greensboro

Rose Clark
Saint Francis University

David Collins
Colorado State University-Pueblo

Charles Cornett
University of Wisconsin-Platteville

Scott Davis
Mansfield University

Brent Dawson
University of North Carolina-Greensboro

Salim Diab
Governor State University

Dennis Dillin
University of Mary Hardin-Baylor

Paul Flowers
University of North Carolina-Pembroke

Kenneth Furton
Florida International University

Terry Gallegos
Tuscon Police Department Crime Lab

Rhesa Gilliand
Drug Enforcement Agency Office of Forensic Science

Ray Gross
Prince George's Community College

Nancy Hayley
University of Rhode Island

Adam Jack
Waynesburg College

Mathew Johnston
Lewis-Clark State College

Thomas Keane
Russell Sage College

Steve Kornic
Wilfrid Laurier University

Doris Ingram Lewis
Suffolk University

Linda Lewis
Oak Ridge National Laboratory

Michael Lyman
Columbia University

Bruce McCord
The Ohio State University

David von Minden
University of Central Oklahoma

Andrew Morehead
East Carolina University

Keith Morris
West Virginia University

Layne Morsch
Depaul University

Khaled Nasr
Bay Path College

Walda Powell
Meredith College

Larry Quarino
Cedar Crest College

Faina Ryvkin
Emmanuel College

Mark Sabo
Catawba College

Heather Schafstal
Oklahoma Central Drug Laboratory

Howard Schindler
St. Paul's School

Jay Siegel
Indiana University-Purdue University Indianapolis

Bjorn Soderberg
West Virginia University

Ed Suzuki
Washington State Patrol

Charles Tindall
Metropolitan State College of Denver

Nanette Wachter
Hofstra University

Susan Wallace
Baylor University

Dale Wheeler
Appalachian State University

ACCURACY REVIEWERS

Charles Tindall
Metropolitan State College of Denver

Bjorn Soderberg
West Virginia University

Eric Person
Washington State Patrol Crime Laboratory

Wayne Rabablais
Lamar University

About the Author

Dr. Bell obtained her BS degree with a dual major in chemistry and police science (criminal justice) at Northern Arizona University a long time ago in a galaxy far far away. She went on to the University of New Haven and obtained an MS in forensic science. After an internship with the New Mexico State Police Crime Laboratory, she began work there in 1983. Her main duties were as a forensic chemist and she processed numerous crime scenes. She joined the Environmental Chemistry group at Los Alamos National Laboratory in 1985, where she stayed for eight years. Returning to school, she obtained her PhD at New Mexico State University in 1991 (chemistry) and completed a post-doctoral fellowship there. In 1994, she accepted a faculty position at Eastern Washington University where she worked with the Washington State Patrol to launch a forensic chemistry program.

She joined the C. Eugene Department of Chemistry at West Virginia University in 2003. She works in the forensic chemistry and forensic identification aspects of the WVU forensic science program at the undergraduate and graduate levels and has several doctoral students working with her. Projects underway in her lab include forensic microfluidics, fiber characterization, and post-mortem/decomposition chemistry. She maintains a website at www.wvu.edu/~forensic_chem/. She developed a forensic chemistry lecture and lab course (400-level) and chaired a workshop entitled, "Educating Forensic Scientists for the 21st Century: Instilling the Forensic Mindset" at the 2005 American Academy of Forensic Sciences (AAFS) meeting. Dr. Bell is a *Diplomat* of the American Board of Criminalistics (ABC) and a member of the AAFS and the American Chemical Society.

Her other books are the *Encyclopedia of Forensic Science* (2003) and the *Dictionary of Forensic Science* (2004) published by Facts-on-File (New York). She is series editor for the *Essentials of Forensic Science*, a seven-volume set due out in 2006 also published by Facts-on-File. She authored two of these books, *Drugs and Poisons* and *Fakes and Forgeries*. Her latest book project is entitled *The Science of Circumstance*, a history of forensic science to be published by Rutgers University Press in 2006.

Introduction

OVERVIEW AND ORIENTATION

Forensic chemistry exists where science and the law overlap. You might expect the marriage of science and the law to be an easy and natural one, but frequently it is not. The widespread perception is that science and the judicial system both exist to seek the truth, but that is an incomplete description. While tackling the definitions of scientific and legal truth is beyond the scope of this book, their intersection is at the heart of it, even when hidden behind chemical equations and reaction mechanisms. The term *forensic* refers to law enforcement, the judicial system, and the courts, and without *forensic*, there is no forensic chemistry. Accordingly, this brief chapter will provide you with the minimum legal context needed to explore forensic chemistry and the larger world of forensic science.

1.1 WHAT IS FORENSIC CHEMISTRY?

Forensic chemistry is applied analytical chemistry. If that were the extent of it, however, there would be no need for a separate course or textbook on the subject. What then makes forensic chemistry unique? Arguably, it is the same consideration that defines forensic science as a distinct discipline: the skill, art, and science of comparison. Analytical chemistry encompasses qualitative and quantitative analysis, but forensic chemistry adds comparative analysis to the task list. For example, spectroscopic analysis can quickly determine whether a fiber is made of nylon or a piece of plastic is polyethylene. These are analytical descriptors that answer analytical questions such as "What is it?" and "How much of it is there?" Analytical chemistry provides qualitative

Historical Evidence 1.1—The Origins of Science and Chemistry

Ancient chemistry was likely related to medicines and materials. Knowledge was based on experiment and experience and was passed on to a select few. Early humans used plant and animal products as treatments and learned from experience what worked and what didn't, but there was no understanding of natural laws (i.e., science) to guide them. The Greeks were the first to set forth the idea of science as a system or method of looking at the world, and this began to take shape 2500 years ago. By that time, chemistry was already well established in certain areas, including natural dyes, simple metallurgy, soapmaking, cosmetics, fermented beverages, and ceramics. The Greeks created a philosophy that allowed knowledge derived from experiment to be studied systematically and then extended logically to new situations.

Source: Salzberg, H. W. "Ancient Technology: The Roots of Chemistry," in H. W. Salzberg, *From Caveman to Chemist: Circumstances and Achievements*. Washington, DC: American Chemical Society, **1991**, 1–15.

and quantitative data that are required to answer forensic questions such as the following:

- "Where could this fiber have come from?"
- "Could this piece of plastic have come from this plastic trash bag?"
- "Was weathered gasoline used to start this fire?"
- "Did this paint chip come from that car"

Historical Evidence 1.2—"Those Who Live by the Poison Shall Die from the Poison."

The Greeks may have formulated the idea of science, but it was the practical Romans who formulated the first essential elements of forensic science. One of the most common, most feared, and most difficult crimes to detect in the ancient world was poisoning. A very early law outlawing this crime was set forth by Rome in 82 B.C. Nearly 250 years prior to that, the Romans had executed a number of women convicted of poisoning husbands, fathers, other relatives, and significant others. The women were executed by being forced to drink their own concoctions, leading to various versions of the preceding quote. The word *forensic* is tied to the Latin word *forum*, a place where the Romans conducted business and legal proceedings. To speak in the forum was to speak the truth (or so it was hoped or assumed), leading to the link between forensic and modern debate teams. However, the word also refers to speaking the truth in public, a good job description for forensic chemists.

When a forensic scientist works with an exhibit of evidence, generally there are three tasks to be accomplished. First is **identification**. In drug analysis, this incorporates qualitative identification and, sometimes, quantitative analysis. In other cases, such as fiber analysis, identification is the easy part. The next step is **classification** of the evidence. Is the fiber nylon 6 or nylon 66? Is it red, yellow, or blue? Has it aged? What is its cross section? The answers to these questions reduces the size of the class to which the fiber belongs. The smaller the class membership, the more meaningful is the evidence. Taken to its logical conclusion, classification results in placing the fiber in a class with only one member. This process is referred to as **individualization** or establishing a **common source**. The ideal situation, it is rarely possible in forensic chemistry.

Continuing with this example, assume that a fiber is found at a crime scene. The forensic analyst determines that it is a red nylon fiber with a circular cross section. A suspect wearing a red nylon windbreaker is arrested. Nylon fibers from the windbreaker (often labeled "K" for "known") are subjected to the same tests as was the fiber in question ("Q") from the scene, with similar results. The analysis demonstrated that Q and K belong to the same class, but this is not proof of a common source. In other words, the test fibers from the jacket and the fiber from the crime scene have not been individualized, and the analyst cannot assign a common source (the jacket) to Q and K. This does not mean that the evidence is useless, but it does limit what can be said with certainty. The jacket is not excluded as a possible source.

Drug analysis, both of physical and biological evidence, falls outside the traditional forensic framework of identification–classification–individualization. Analytical instrumentation, properly applied, nearly always allows for the unambiguous identification of a chemical compound, be it a drug or metabolite. Classification plays a role through presumptive testing and screening tests (Chapter 7), but identification follows classification rather than preceding it, as in the case of our hypothetical fiber. Regardless, identification, classification, and individualization are involved in forensic chemistry even if the order varies.

1.2 PRECEDENT IN CHEMISTRY AND THE LAW

Science exists to uncover a deeper understanding of the universe, guided by the principles of the scientific method. The tools used are experimentation and observation. Courts exist to settle disputes between individuals and the state (**criminal law**) or among individuals or entities (**civil law**). Courts are guided by the law, precedent, and function using an **adversarial system**. It would be mistaken to assume that the courts use a model similar to the scientific method. It would be equally mistaken to assume that science works on the basis of argument. There are elements of all in both systems, but to the forensic chemist, the differences are as important as the similarities (Figure 1.1).

Historical Evidence 1.3—The Origin of Law

The Greeks and the Romans could not have made their contributions to forensic science had it not been for a much earlier invention: the law. The first-known codified laws were put forth by the peoples who occupied the Tigris and Euphrates River valley areas in what were the earliest-known cities and civilization. The earliest-known laws and legal systems appeared around 2000 B.C. Arguably, the most famous was Hammurabi's code, named for the Babylonian king in power around 1700 B.C.

Both science and the courts are tasked with deriving information from evidence pertinent to the issue at hand. Science employs the scientific method to do so, whereas the courts employ the adversarial system, in which two opposing parties present arguments before the **trier of fact**. Scientific evidence and testimony may support or refute either argument. The relative

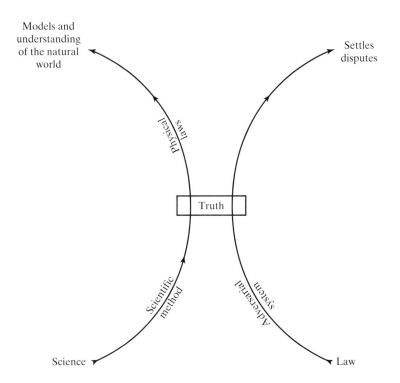

Models and
understanding
of the natural
world

Settles
disputes

Physical laws

Truth

Scientific method

Adversarial system

Science

Law

▶ **Figure 1.1** *Different paths toward similar, but not identical, destinations.*

strength of the arguments guide the court in settling the issue. Scientific knowledge and findings are part of that process, but only part. All scientists can and should do is produce the best science possible, followed by making the clearest presentation possible. How the data are used is for the courts to decide. Many such decisions are based on **precedent**, or that which has gone before. When a precedent is created, new rules or new applications of rules to decide a case or issue have been developed and used.[1] Precedent is a guide for decisions and is based on past lessons. In that sense, precedent is knowledge gained previously in similar settings. Science also invokes the concept of precedent, since new ideas are derived from previous observation and experiment.

1.3 KEY FORENSIC AND LEGAL CONCEPTS

This is a chemistry text first and foremost, but because it is a *forensic* chemistry text, brief mention of the discipline's legal foundation is in order. The central precepts applicable to forensic chemistry are summarized in the paragraphs that follow, and the sections titled "Further Reading" and "References" at the end of the chapter list additional resources.

1.3.1 CRIMINAL AND CIVIL CASES

Forensic chemists working in local, state, and federal laboratories are usually involved in criminal cases. Criminal law deals with crimes by a person or persons against the state, which can be any level of government, including cities, counties, states, and the federal government.[1] Civil cases arise from disputes that involve private rights or from disputes such as that between two people or two corporations. Cases referred to informally as lawsuits, wherein the complainant is said to be "filing suit," involve civil law.

1.3.2 ADMISSION OF EVIDENCE

The history of the admissibility of scientific evidence is surprisingly short, less than a century old. To date, standards of admissibility are founded on three court rulings, and which of the three is or are applied varies with the jurisdiction:

The Frye Rule ("general acceptance"): This standard of admission was established in a 1923 case heard in the District of Columbia Circuit Court: *Frye v. United States* (Frye v. United States, 293 Fed. 1013, 1014 (D.C. Cir. 1923)). Distilled to its essence, the court's ruling held that evidence produced by scientific analysis is admissible as long as the techniques are accepted as valid by the relevant scientific community.[2,3] In effect, the court said that if the test has passed through the rigor of the scientific method and peer review to reach the status of general acceptance, then it has already been tested and validated.[4] For example, if a new technique was developed for the chemical characterization of dyes in ink, the results of tests performed in accordance with that technique would not be admitted under the Frye rule unless the court determined that analytical and forensic chemists generally recognized the technique as useful and reliable. The Frye standard was predominant into the early 1990s and is still used in some jurisdictions.

The Daubert Decision: This ruling, handed down by the U.S. Supreme Court (*Daubert v. Merrell Dow Pharmaceuticals* (113 S.Ct. 2786 (1993))), was based on the Federal Rules of Evidence enacted in 1975. The case focused particularly on Federal Rule 702. The decision in *Daubert* gave judges what is referred to as a "gatekeeper role" in determining admissibility. The decision provided a list of criteria judges could use, such as error rate and peer review. Although this decision applied only to federal cases, several states have adopted the same approach to admissibility.

Daubert has had a significant impact on forensic science in the past decade, particularly in the realm of DNA evidence, which came of age under this decision. The rigor required for acceptance under *Daubert* and the role of *Daubert* in hearings determining admissibility are forcing a reexamination of forensic mainstays, such as fingerprint evidence. No doubt forensic chemistry will be affected as this situation evolves.

Kumho: *Daubert* was extended by the 1999 decision in *Kumho Tire Co., Ltd. v. Carmichael* (119 S. Cr. 1167 (1999)). This ruling extended scope of *Daubert* and the judge's gatekeeper role to *all* expert testimony, not just scientific. The decision also acknowledged that standards which would determine admissibility would be different, depending on the discipline in question.[3]

1.3.3 INCLUSIVE VERSUS EXCLUSIVE EVIDENCE

Often, forensic chemists produce scientific evidence that can be described as either **inclusive** or **exclusive**. Recall the red fiber example mentioned earlier in the chapter. In that example, successive classification based on analytical data demonstrated that the red fiber from a crime scene belonged to the same class as fibers from a suspect's red nylon jacket. This is an example of inclusive evidence: The jacket is included in the population of items that could have been the source of the fiber in question. Had the fibers from the jacket been found to have a cross section different from that of the fiber found at the scene, they would have been exclusionary evidence: The jacket could *not* have been the source.

1.3.4 DIRECT AND CIRCUMSTANTIAL EVIDENCE

Direct evidence is that which is known to a person by personal knowledge, such as eyewitness testimony. Such evidence, if found to be true, would prove a point in contention without requiring any additional analysis or inference.[3] Forensic scientists, by contrast, produce **circumstantial** evidence, or evidence that requires inference to move logically from the information provided to the answer to a question. For example, if blood is found on a knife, and DNA typing showed that the blood matched that of a suspect to 1 person in 6 trillion, the trier of fact must still infer that the blood came from the suspect, since the deposition of the blood was not directly witnessed. Contrary to popular belief, circumstantial evidence is not, by definition, weak evidence.

Applying the Science 1.1 The Power of a Common Source and Circumstantial Evidence

The Wayne Williams case was made without eyewitnesses, without DNA, and without fingerprints. In 1982, Wayne Williams was convicted of murdering 2 young boys in Atlanta, but he was likely responsible for at least 10 others. The key evidence in the case was fibers and dog hair that represented an accumulation of circumstantial evidence the jury could not ignore. In 11 of 12 fiber correlations, fibers found on the victims and in Williams's home or car were determined to be members of the same small class. Any one of these 11 correlations is inclusive evidence, but when they are considered together, the chances that 11 different fiber or hair types would be found both on the victims and in Williams's environment were too small for the jury to consider as coincidence.

From Deadman, H. A. "Case Reading: Fiber Evidence and the Wayne Williams Trial," in R. Saferstein, ed., *Criminalistics: An Introduction to Forensic Science.* Upper Saddle River, NJ: Prentice-Hall, **2004**.

1.3.5 CHAIN OF CUSTODY

The "chain" as it is called, is a paper form that tracks evidence from its creation or collection to its final disposal. A "cradle-to-grave" document that completely describes the history of a sample or an exhibit constituting evidence, the chain is initiated when the sample is collected or created and is updated each time the sample is transferred from one person to another. The chain ensures that the sample's history has no gaps and that the sample was in the direct control of one person at all times, though not always the same person. When a sample is in the laboratory, it either is stored in a secure, locked storage area or is being analyzed. Any break in the chain, no matter how innocent or inadvertent, raises the possibility that the sample could have been tampered with. Accordingly, painstaking steps are taken to ensure the integrity of all evidence. Among these steps are establishing security measures, guaranteeing controlled access to storage areas, and implementing specific protocols for opening, marking, sealing, and transporting evidence. Maintenance of the chain is a fundamental responsibility of any forensic analyst.

1.3.6 DESTRUCTIVE TESTING

If an exhibit of evidence is consumed in testing, the tests performed on it can never be repeated or verified. While this is not a limitation when the case consists of several milliliters of blood or a large bindle of white powder, other cases are not so simple. If the exhibit is a single fiber or one tiny paint chip, analytical options are limited. Solubility tests would be a poor choice for a single paint chip, but microspectrophotometry (nondestructive) would be ideal.

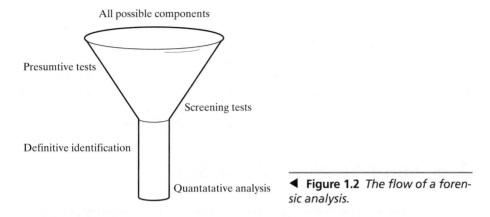

All possible components

Presumtive tests

Screening tests

Definitive identification

Quantatative analysis

◀ **Figure 1.2** *The flow of a forensic analysis.*

1.4 THE FLOW OF A FORENSIC ANALYSIS

A forensic analysis is usually a narrowing-down process as shown in Figure 1.2. Although the sample matrix may be known (Is it blood, urine, fire debris, etc.?), many samples are complex mixtures that require a systematic approach to characterize them. Generically, a forensic chemist relies on three groups of techniques: visual examination and inspection (both macroscopic and microscopic), organic chemical analysis, and inorganic chemical analysis. The sample or exhibit of evidence is often referred to as a **general unknown**, even though the analyst usually has some idea of what is or might be present in the sample.

Analysis starts with qualitative presumptive tests that narrow down the list of potential analytes and directs subsequent analysis. Presumptive tests belong to a family of analytical techniques referred to as **wet chemical methods**. Most are based on observing results when specific reagents are added to small portions of the samples. Color and crystal tests, as they are commonly called, are used in analyzing drugs, gunshot residues, and explosives. These tests will be discussed in detail in subsequent chapters.

Once presumptive tests have focused the analysis on a small set of potential components, the next step usually involves the separation and isolation of target components, either for screening tests or for definitive identification. Typically, such steps involve extraction and chromatography. Thin-layer chromatography (TLC) is often employed in the analysis of inks and drugs as follow-ups to presumptive tests, while toxicologists may use immunoassay to narrow the field of potential analytes. Chromatography can also be employed for sample cleanup and analyte isolation, as can solvent extractions, headspace methods, and solid-phase extractions. Confirmation of tentative identification follows, using instrumental techniques such as infrared spectrophotometry and gas chromatography–mass spectrometry (GCMS). The latter is particularly valued because of its capabilities in separating, identifying, and quantitating analytes, although the degree of quantitative analysis required varies. In toxicological analyses, GCMS is often the primary analytical instrument used, while for other purposes, such as analyzing fire debris and fibers, it may be less important or even inapplicable.

The majority of forensic chemical analyses do not require the complete characterization of a sample. For example, a small resinous cube of brown material may be found to contain heroin along with many other materials; however, analytical interest usually ends with the identification of the illegal drug or substances. Occasionally, the materials used as cutting agents (diluents) are identified, but that is usually the extent of the testing. Although a complete characterization could be invaluable for linking the resin to others and for determining origins, testing for such purposes is not routinely performed, given the time and expense required. Like all analytical chemists, forensic chemists balance the need for accuracy, precision, and completeness against the reality of limited time, money, and resources. The next chapter describes the acceptable compromises that yield useful, reliable, and legally defensible data.

1.5 THE FORENSIC MIND-SET

There is a core set of skills that any forensic scientist should cultivate as part of a forensic mind-set. The importance of comparison in forensic analyses imposes conditions on methods selected, how they are applied, and how the results are interpreted. Consider a case in which the forensic chemist is provided a tiny fragment of a thick, fibrous, silvery material with one adhesive surface. The evidence is the only remaining trace of the material that was used to bind a homicide victim. A suspect has been identified and a search of his house reveals three different rolls of duct tape. The forensic question is which roll, if any, could the fragment of tape have come from? The identification part of analysis is simple: A quick look through a stereomicroscope shows the material to be duct tape. The challenge is how to proceed, given that the evidence cannot be destroyed.

If the analyst is lucky, it may be possible to physically match the fragment to one of the rolls (identifying a common source, or individualization). If not, the tape can be examined microscopically and with microspectrophotometry. Careful study of the fiber pattern in the tape, combined with some database searching and phone calls, may narrow the possible manufacturers of the tape (classification). A trip to the library (a building or an electronic repository) may uncover an article in a forensic, analytical, or industrial journal (e.g., *Journal of Forensic Sciences, Forensic Science International, Canadian Journal of Forensic Science, Adhesives Age,* or *Adhesives and Sealants Industry*) that describes how others have approached similar problems. Experimentation with tapes unrelated to the case can further refine the approach.

Although this kind of case is not routine, it highlights the skills that constitute the forensic mind-set. Forensic scientists and forensic chemists should

- assume nothing.
- be resourceful. Finding at least two journals devoted to adhesives would be of significant help in the case and would take only minutes via an electronic search. Browsing articles could produce names of experts in adhesives to contact for assistance.
- think outside the discipline. Forensic science integrates many areas, chemistry being only one, but the core skills and principals of science are always the same. The analyst in this case would probably find reading adhesives journals easier than expected.
- be creative. Often, creativity is attributed to the arts (painting, music, etc.), but successful scientists and researchers must be creative as well. Creativity involves applying a novel approach to a problem or finding a novel application of existing tools and skills. All painters use paint, but there are an infinite number of ways to assemble the colors on a canvas. Similarly, all analytical chemists have access to the same set of tools; it is how they are applied that makes an approach creative. Challenging cases require creativity.

- build a big toolbox that never stops growing.
- know their limitations.
- be flexible. Just because something works in this case doesn't necessarily mean that it will work in the next one. The more knowledgeable and resourceful a scientist is, the more flexible he or she is.
- be persistent. The case described in this section might at first glance have seemed hopeless to the analyst, but it wasn't. Difficult is not the same as impossible; a good forensic scientist recognizes the difference.

1.6 FORENSIC CHEMISTRY TODAY

Analytical chemistry in the forensic field is generally divided into two areas: forensic toxicology and forensic chemistry. The divisions are somewhat artificial, but an understanding of them is important. Forensic toxicologists work with biological evidence and follow the trail of drugs and poisons ingested by humans or other organisms. Forensic toxicology is often associated with death investigation and the Medical Examiners or coroner's office, depending on the jurisdiction. Certainly, forensic toxicologists are also forensic chemists; the division between forensic toxicology and forensic chemistry and the use of those job descriptors are rooted in history and tradition.

Historical Evidence 1.4—The First Forensic Testimony

In truth, this may never be known. It has been reported that a surgeon who examined Julius Caesar's body was asked to testify as to which wound was fatal to the emperor. However, the first modern forensic testimony was given by a chemist, M. J. B. Orfila

◀ **Figure 1.3** *M. J. B. Orfila*

(1787–1853), in a poisoning case. Orfila, held by many to be the father of forensic toxicology, was a prominent toxicologist and skilled chemist when the case of Marie LaFarge crossed his path in 1840. Marie LaFarge was a young French widow who, at 24, remarried. Her second marriage, to Charles LaFarge (age 30), was reportedly not a happy one. In 1839, Charles died after eating cake made by his wife; the symptoms were consistent with arsenic poisoning. Marie was charged and chemical tests performed on the body, but the results were inconclusive. The court was unsatisfied and commissioned Orfila to journey from Italy to France to conduct a review of the

Historical Evidence 1.4—(Continued)

scientific work in the investigation. Orfila eventually had Charles's body exhumed. A skilled analytical chemist, Orfila was able to detect arsenic in the tissues. He also showed an appreciation for the need for control samples, testing the soil in which Charles had been buried and demonstrating that the arsenic did not originate from it. Marie was convicted and sentenced to involuntary servitude, during which time she wrote a book.

▶ **Figure 1.4** *Marie Lafarge*

Forensic chemists work with physical evidence and are often employed in what are often called "crime labs," although this term seems to be falling out of favor. In general, qualifications for employment in either type of laboratory (crime lab or toxicology lab) are a B.S. in a natural science (preferably chemistry) with an emphasis on analytical and instrumental methods. Entry-level toxicology positions may require additional training or experience in toxicology or pharmacology. The moniker "drug chemist" is sometimes used if the person works exclusively in that area, while some forensic chemists work in trace evidence and other forensic specialties. Forensic chemists also work with materials such as inks, dyes, fire debris, gunshot residues, dusts, explosives, polymers, paints, and glass. If there is physical evidence and it is amenable to, and benefits from, chemical analysis, a forensic chemist or someone trained in that area can be involved in analyzing that evidence.

1.7 BECOMING AND BEING A FORENSIC PROFESSIONAL

1.7.1 WHAT IS A PROFESSION?

Forensic science has evolved from an adjunct to medicine to a recognized profession—which raises the question of what defines something as a profession. A reasonable definition is that a profession is the practice of similar skills by a group of people who are paid to apply those skills in a more-or-less specified manner.[5] A profession is differentiated from a job in that there is a governing body that oversees, regulates, and ensures that practitioners of the profession adhere to standard guidelines and meet certain minimum requirements. In a true profession, this regulation is derived internally, not imposed by an outside entity that does not practice the profession. For example, the American Medical Association (AMA) dictates how medicine is taught and practiced. The AMA works in concert with medical schools, hospitals, and government agencies, but, fundamentally, doctors dictate how doctors work and what the public can expect from physicians. Thus, a profession requires the existence of professional associations that have recognized and accepted authority within the profession.

1.7.2 CERTIFICATION AND PROFESSIONAL ORGANIZATIONS

A profession defines what prerequisites one must have and what minimal educational standards one must adhere to in order to participate in it. In forensic science, there are a number of professional organizations. The largest is the American Academy of Forensic Sciences (AAFS, aafs.org), founded in 1947. The AAFS is organized into sections such as jurisprudence, toxicology, criminalistics, and engineering. Of most interest to chemists are the criminalistics and toxicology sections. The AAFS specifies membership requirements and three levels of membership, but does not certify individuals (although it is a partner in the process). The primary national professional organization for forensic toxicology is the Society of Forensic Toxicologists (SOFT, www.soft-tox.org). Certification of forensic toxicologists and accreditation of forensic toxicology laboratories is handled by the American Board of Forensic Toxicology (ABFT, www.abft.org).

There is no single organization or association that deals exclusively with forensic chemists in the same way that SOFT and ABFT do with toxicologists. The American Chemical Society (ACS, chemistry.org) is the largest scientific society in the world and has sections devoted to analytical chemistry and just about every other chemical discipline imaginable. There is a section called "Chemistry and the Law," but its scope includes things such as patent law—important, to be sure, but not directly forensic. The American Board of Criminalistics (ABC, criminalistics.com/abc/) offers certification of forensic scientists through a comprehensive examination called the General Knowledge Exam (GKE) and in specialty areas such as drug analysis, fire debris (arson), and trace-evidence specialties. General-service forensic science laboratories are accredited through the American Society of Crime Laboratory Directors LAB program (ASCLD, ascld.org). Certification of analysts and laboratories is discussed further in the next chapter.

SUMMARY

Forensic science and forensic chemistry are young professions distinguished from other sciences by their relationship to the legal system and by the importance of comparison in laboratory analysis. Forensic chemists need an understanding of the legal foundation of their chosen field, as well as a forensic mind-set, which relies on the fundamental precept of always being open to learning more and always adding tools to the toolbox. In that spirit, our journey into forensic chemistry can now begin.

KEY TERMS AND CONCEPTS

Adversarial system	Common source	Frye rule
Chain of custody	Criminal law	General unknown
Circumstantial evidence	Daubert	Inclusive evidence
Civil law	Direct evidence	Precedent
Classifications	Exclusive evidence	Trier of fact

PROBLEMS

From the chapter

1. Compare and contrast the adversarial system and the scientific method. List the strengths and weaknesses of both in the context of criminal and civil law.

2. During a *Daubert* hearing, what entity ultimately decides on admissibility?

3. What role does peer review play in science and in the law? Compare and contrast.

4. Describe how a preponderance of inclusive circumstantial evidence can become conclusive in the eyes of a jury.

Integrative

1. A great scientist can still be a terrible forensic scientist; a person who gives wonderful testimony can be a terrible forensic scientist. Comment on these observations and their implications for forensic chemistry.

2. Can jurors ask questions of expert witnesses? Comment on your findings regarding this issue.

Food for thought

1. Is the analysis of drugs with instruments such as mass spectrometers and infrared spectrometry based on comparison?

2. How important is the way in which scientific evidence is presented? Comment on the relative importance of content versus presentation. Why is learning how to testify such an important skill?

FURTHER READING

Gallo, M. A. "History and Scope of Toxicology," in C. D. Klaassen, ed., *Casarett and Doull's Toxicology: The Basic Science of Poisons*, 6th ed. New York: McGraw-Hill Medical Publishing Division, **2001**, 3–10.

Klinefelter, W. *Origins of Sherlock Holmes*. Bloomington, IN: Gaslight Productions, **1983**.

Lee, J. A. *The Scientific Endeavor*. San Francisco: Addison Wesley Longman, **2000**.

Moenssens, A. A., et al. *Scientific Evidence in Civil and Criminal Cases*, 4th ed. Westbury, NY: The Foundation Press, Inc., **1995**.

Saferstein, R. *Criminalistics: An Introduction to Forensic Science*, 8th ed. Upper Saddle River, NJ: Prentice Hall, **2004**.

Salzberg, H. W. "Ancient Technology: The Roots of Chemistry," in H. W. Salzberg, *From Caveman to Chemist: Circumstances and Achievements*. Washington, DC: American Chemical Society, **1991**, 1–15.

REFERENCES

1. Garner, B. A., ed. *Black's Law Dictionary*. St. Paul: West Publishing Group, **2001**.

2. Saferstein, R. *Criminalistics: An Introduction to Forensic Science*, 8th. ed. Upper Saddle River, NJ: Prentice Hall, **2004**.

3. Kennedy, D., and R. Merrill. "Assessing Forensic Science." *Issues in Science and Technology*, XX **2003**, 33–34.

4. Farley, M. A. "Legal Standards for the Admissibility of Novel Scientific Evidence," in R. Saferstein, ed., *Forensic Science Handbook, Volume III*. Upper Saddle River, NJ: Prentice Hall, **1993**, 1–23.

5. Kovac, J. *The Ethical Chemist*. Upper Saddle River, NJ: Prentice Hall, **2004**.

Statistics, Sampling, and Data Quality

2.1 Significant Figures, Rounding, and Uncertainty
2.2 Statistics for Forensic and Analytical Chemistry

OVERVIEW AND ORIENTATION

Data quality lies at the core of what forensic chemistry is and how forensic data are used. The goal of quality assurance and quality control (QA/QC) is to generate trustworthy laboratory data. There is an imperishable link between data quality, reliability, and admissibility. Courts should admit only trustworthy scientific evidence; ultimately, the courts have to rely on the scientific community for such evaluations. Rule 702 of the Federal Rules of Evidence states that an expert in a field such as chemistry or toxicology may testify about their results, "if (1) the testimony is based upon scientific facts or data, (2) the testimony is the product of reliable principles and methods, and (3) the witness has applied the principles and methods reliably to the facts of the case." Quality assurance practices are designed to define reliability in a concrete and quantitative way. The quantitative connection is found in statistics, the subject of this chapter. By design and necessity, this is a brief treatment of statistics. It is meant as a review and supplement to your existing knowledge, not as a substitute for material presented in courses such as analytical chemistry, quantitative analysis, and introductory statistics. We will discuss and highlight statistical concepts most important to a forensic chemist on a daily basis.

Quality assurance is dynamic, is evolving, and requires daily care and maintenance to remain viable. It is also a layered structure, as shown in Figure 2.1. At every level in the triangle, statistics provides the means for evaluating and judging data and methods. Without fundamental statistical understanding, there can be no quality management or assurance. Accordingly, we

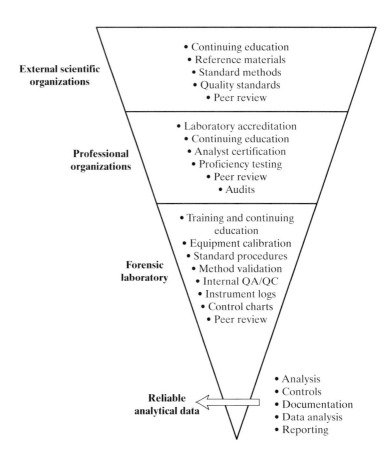

External scientific
organizations
- Continuing education
- Reference materials
- Standard methods
- Quality standards
- Peer review

Professional
organizations
- Laboratory accreditation
- Continuing education
- Analyst certification
- Proficiency testing
- Peer review
- Audits

Forensic
laboratory
- Training and continuing education
- Equipment calibration
- Standard procedures
- Method validation
- Internal QA/QC
- Instrument logs
- Control charts
- Peer review

Reliable
analytical data
- Analysis
- Controls
- Documentation
- Data analysis
- Reporting

▶ **Figure 2.1** *The layered structure of quality assurance. Statistics underlies each level and stage.*

will begin our exploration of quality assurance (QA) and statistics with a review of fundamental concepts dealing with uncertainty and significant figures.

You may recall working problems in which you were asked to determine the number of significant figures in a calculation. Forensic and analytical chemistry gives us a context for those exercises and makes them real. We will start there and quickly make the link between significant figures and uncertainty. The concepts of inherent uncertainty of measurement and random errors will lead us into a review of the statistical concepts that are fundamental to forensic chemistry. The last part of the chapter centers on sampling statistics, something that forensic chemists must constantly be aware of. The information presented in this chapter will take us in chapter 3 into a discussion of calibration, multivariate statistics, and quality assurance and quality control.

2.1 SIGNIFICANT FIGURES, ROUNDING, AND UNCERTAINTY

Significant figures become tangible in analytical chemistry. The concept of significant figures arises from the use of measuring devices and equipment and their associated uncertainty. How that uncertainty is accounted for dictates how to round numbers resulting from what may be a complicated series of laboratory procedures. The rules and practices of significant figures and rounding must be applied properly to ensure that the data presented are not misleading, either because there is too much precision implied by including extra unreliable digits or too little by eliminating valid ones.[1]

Exhibit A: Why Significant Figures Matter

In most states, a blood alcohol level of 0.08% is the cutoff for intoxication. How would a value of 0.0815 be interpreted? What about 0.07999? 0.0751? Are these values rounded off or are they truncated? If they are rounded, to how many significant digits? Of course, this is an artificial, but still telling, example. How numerical data are rounded depends on the instrumentation and devices used to obtain the data. Incorrect rounding might have consequences.

In any measurement, the number of significant digits is defined as the number of digits that are certain, plus one. The last digit is uncertain (Figure 2.2), meaning that it is an estimate, but a reasonable one. With the bathroom scale example, one person might interpret the value as 125.4 and another as 125.6, but it is certain that the value is greater than 125 pounds and less than 126. The same situation arises when you use rulers or other devices with calibrated marks. Digital readouts of many instruments may cloud the issue a bit, but unless you are given a defensible reason to know otherwise, assume that the last decimal on a digital readout is uncertain as well.

Recall that zeros have special rules and may require a contextual interpretation. As a starting point, a number may be converted to scientific notation. If the zeros can be removed by this operation, then they were merely placeholders representing a multiplication or division by 10. For example, suppose an instrument produces a result of 0.001023 that can be expressed as 1.023×10^{-3}. This demonstrates that the leading zeros are not significant, but the embedded zero is.

Trailing zeros can be troublesome. In analytical chemistry, the rule should be that if a zero is meant to be significant, it is listed, and conversely, if a zero is omitted, it was not significant. Thus, a value of 1.2300 grams for a weight means that the balance actually displayed two trailing zeros. It would be incorrect to record a balance reading of 1.23 as 1.2300. Recording that weight as 1.2300 is conjuring numbers that are useless at best and are very likely deceptive. If this weight were embedded in a series of calculations, the error would propagate, with potentially disastrous consequences. "Zero" does not imply "inconsequential," nor does it imply "nothing." In recording a weight of 1.23 g, no one would arbitrarily write 1.236, so why should writing 1.230 be any less onerous?

In combining numeric operations, rounding should always be done at the end of the calculation.[1] The only time that rounding intermediate values may be appropriate is in addition and subtraction operations, although caution must still be exercised. In such operations, the result is rounded to the same

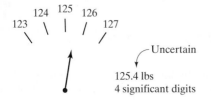

◀ **Figure 2.2** *Reading the scale results in four significant digits, the last being an educated guess or an approximation that, by definition, will have uncertainty associated with it.*

number of significant digits as there are in the contributing number with the fewest digits, with one extra digit included to avoid rounding error. For example, assume that a calculation requires the formula weight of $PbCl_2$:

$$Pb = 207.2 \text{ g/mole} \qquad\qquad 207.2|$$

$$+ \text{ } Cl = 35.4527 \text{ g/mole} \qquad 2(35.427) = 70.8|54$$

$$278.0|54 \text{ g/mole}$$

The correct way to round or report an intermediate value would be 278.0_5 rather than 278.1. The subscript indicates that one additional digit is retained to avoid rounding error. The additional digit does not change the count of significant digits: The value 278.0_5 still has four significant digits. The subscript notation is designed to make this clear.

The formula weight should rarely, if ever, limit the number of significant digits in a combined laboratory operation. In most cases, it is possible to calculate a formula weight to enough significant figures such that the formula weight does not control rounding. Lead, selected purposely for the example, is one of the few elements that may limit significant figure calculations.

By definition, the last significant digit obtained from an instrument or a calculation has an associated uncertainty. Rounding leads to a nominal value, but it does not allow for expression of the inherent uncertainty. To do this, the uncertainties of each contributing factor, device, or instrument must be known and accounted for. For measuring devices such as analytical balances, Eppendorf pipets, and flasks, that value is either displayed on the device, supplied by the manufacturer, or determined empirically. Because these values are known, it is also possible to estimate the uncertainty (i.e., potential error) in any combined calculation. The only caveat is that the units must be the same. On an analytical balance, the uncertainty would be listed as ±0.0001 g, whereas the uncertainty on a volumetric flask would be reported as ±0.12 mL. These are absolute uncertainties that cannot be combined as is, because the units do not match. To combine uncertainties, relative uncertainties must be used. These can be expressed as "1 part per ..." or as a percentage. That way, the units cancel and a relative uncertainty results, which may then be combined with other uncertainties expressed the same way (i.e., as unitless value).

Consider the simple example in Figure 2.3, in which readings from two devices are utilized to obtain a measurement in miles per gallon. The **absolute uncertainty** of each device is known, so the first step in combining them is to express them as "1 part per ..." While not essential, such notation shows at a glance which uncertainty (if any) will dominate. It is possible to estimate the uncertainty of the mpg calculation by assuming that the odometer uncertainty of 0.11% (the **relative uncertainty**) will dominate. In many cases, one uncertainty is much larger (two or more orders of magnitude) than the other and hence will control the final uncertainty.

Better in this case is accounting for both uncertainties, because they are within an order of magnitude of each other (0.07% vs. 0.11%). Relative uncertainties are combined with the use of the formula

$$e_t = \sqrt{(e_1^2 + e_2^2 + e_3^2 + \cdots + e_n^2)} \qquad\qquad (2.1)$$

For the example provided in Figure 2.3, the results differ only slightly when uncertainties are combined, because both were close to 0.1%, so neither overwhelms

Odometer   ($^+/-$ 0.2 miles)
183.4 miles   Absolute uncertainty

Fuel pump indicator 6.683 gallons
($^+/-$ 0.005 gallons)
Absolute uncertainty

MPG: $\dfrac{183.4 \text{ miles}}{6.683 \text{ gallons}}$ = 27.44 mpg

---

Uncertainties:

relative   % uncertainty

Odometer = $\dfrac{0.2 \text{ miles}}{183.4 \text{ miles}}$ = $\dfrac{1}{917}$ $\times$ 100 = 0.11%*

Pump = $\dfrac{0.005 \text{ gal}}{6.683 \text{ gal}}$ = $\dfrac{1}{1337}$ $\times$ 100 = 0.07%

Estimated: 0.11% of 27.44 mpg = 0.0302 = 0.30

Range = 27.44 $^+/-$ 0.030

= 27.41 — 27.47 mpg

Propagated:

$e_T = \sqrt{(0.0011)^2 + 0.0007)^2} = 0.0013 = 0.13\%$

0.13% of 27.44 = 0.0357 = 0.036

Range = 27.40 — 27.48 mpg

◄ **Figure 2.3** *Calculation of mpg based on two instrumental readings.*

the other. (Incidentally, the value e as given here is equivalent to a variance (v), a topic to be discussed shortly in Section 2.2.1.)

Equation 2.1 represents the **propagation of uncertainty**. It is useful for estimating the contribution of instrumentation and measuring devices to the overall potential error. It cannot take other types of determinate errors into account, however. Suppose some amount of gasoline in the preceding example overflowed the tank and spilled on the ground. The resulting calculation is correct but not reliable. Spilling gasoline is the type of procedural error that is detected and addressed by quality assurance, the topic of the next chapter. In turn, quality assurance requires an understanding of the mathematics of multiple measurements, or statistics.

2.2 STATISTICS FOR FORENSIC AND ANALYTICAL CHEMISTRY

2.2.1 OVERVIEW AND DEFINITIONS

The application of statistics requires replicate measurements. A replicate measurement is defined as a measurement of a criterion or value under the same experimental conditions for the same sample used for the previous measurement.

Example Problem 2.1

A drug analysis is performed with gas chromatography/mass spectrometry (GCMS) and requires the use of reliable standards. The lab purchases a 1.0-mL commercial standard that is certified to contain the drug of interest at a concentration of 1.00 mg/mL with an uncertainty of $\pm 1.0\%$. To prepare the stock solution for the calibration, an analyst uses a syringe with an uncertainty of $\pm 0.5\%$ to transfer 250.0 μL of the commercial standard to a Class-A 250-mL volumetric flask with an uncertainty of ± 0.08 mL. What is the final concentration and uncertainty of the diluted calibration stock solution?

Answer:

Commercial standard

$$\frac{1.00 \text{ mg}}{\text{mL}} +/- 1.00\%$$

Relative uncertainty
$= 0.010$

Syringe

Relative uncertainty

$$\frac{= 0.5 \text{ ul}}{100 \text{ ul}} = 0.005$$

Volumetric flask

Relative uncertainty

$$\frac{0.08 \text{ mL}}{250.0 \text{ mL}} = 0.0003$$

To calculate the concentration:

Concentrated   Diluted

$$C_1 V_1 \quad = \quad C_2 V_2$$

$\dfrac{1.00 \text{ mg}}{\text{mL}}$ 0.250 mL   ?   250.0 mL

$$C_2 = \frac{\left(\dfrac{1.00 \text{ mg}}{\text{mL}}\right)(0.250 \text{ mL})}{250.0 \text{ mL}} = \frac{0.00100 \text{ mg}}{\text{mL}}$$

$$C_2 = \frac{1.00 \text{ ug}}{\text{mL}} \times \frac{1000 \text{ mL}}{\text{L}} = 1000 \text{ ppb}$$

$$e_t = \sqrt{(0.010)^2 + (0.005)^2 + (0.0003)^2} = 0.01$$

Stock concentration = 1000 ppb $+/-$ 10 ppb

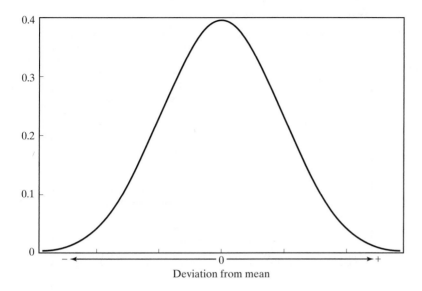

◀ **Figure 2.4** *A Gaussian distribution. Most measurements cluster around the central value (the mean) and the frequency of occurrence decreases as the value moves away from the mean. "Frequency" refers to how often a measurement occurs; 40% of the replicate measurements were the mean value, with frequency 0.4.*

That measurement may be numerical and continuous, as in determining the concentration of cocaine, or categorical (yes/no; green/orange/blue, and so on). We will focus attention on continuous numerical data.

If the error associated with determining the cocaine concentration of a white powder is due only to small **random errors**, the results obtained are expected to cluster about a central value (the mean), with a decreasing occurrence of values farther away from it. The most common graphical expression of this type of distribution is a **Gaussian curve**. It is also called the normal error curve, since the distribution expresses the range of expected results and the likely error. It is important to note that the statistics to be discussed in the sections that follow assume a **Gaussian distribution** and *are not valid* if this condition is not met. The absence of a Gaussian distribution does not mean that statistics cannot be used, but it does require a different group of statistical techniques.

In a large population of measurements (or parent population), the average is defined as the population mean μ. In most measurements of that population, only a subset of the parent population (n) is sampled. The average value for that subset (the sample mean, or $\bar{x}$) is an estimate of μ. As the number of measurements of the population increases, the average value approaches the true value. The goal of any sampling plan is twofold: first, to ensure that n is sufficiently large to appropriately represent characteristics of the parent population; and second, to assign quantitative, realistic, and reliable estimates of the uncertainty that is inevitable when only a portion of the parent population is studied.

Consider the following example (see Figure 2.5), which will be revisited several times throughout the chapter: As part of an apprenticeship, a trainee in a forensic chemistry laboratory is tasked with determining the concentration of cocaine in a white powder. The powder was prepared by the QA section of the laboratory, but the concentration of cocaine is not known to the trainee (who has a blind sample). The trainee's supervisor is given the same sample with the same constraints. Figure 2.5 shows the result of 10 **replicate** analyses (n = 10) made by the two chemists. The supervisor has been performing such analyses for years, while this is the trainee's first attempt. This bit of information is important for interpreting the results, which will be based on the following quantities now formally defined:

The sample mean ($\bar{x}$): The sample mean is the sum of the individual measurements, divided by n. Most often, the result is rounded to the same

True value		13.2% +/- 0.1%
	Trainee	**Forensic chemist**
Sample 1	12.7	13.5
2	13.0	13.1
3	12.0	13.1
4	12.9	13.2
5	12.6	13.4
6	13.3	13.1
7	13.2	13.2
8	11.5	13.7
9	15.0	13.2
10	12.5	13.2

	Trainee	**Forensic chemist**
% Error	−2.5	0.5
Mean	12.9	13.3
Standard (absolute) error	−0.3	0.06
Standard deviation (samples)	0.93	0.20
%RSD (CV) (sample)	7.2	1.5
Standard deviation (population)	0.88	0.19
%RSD (CV) (population)	6.8	1.4
Sample variance	0.86	0.04
Range	3.5	0.6
Confidence level (95.0%)	0.66	0.14
95% Cl range	12.2–13.6	13.2–13.4

▶ **Figure 2.5** *Hypothetical data for two analysts analyzing the same sample 10 times each, working independently. The chemists tested a white powder to determine the percent cocaine it contained. The true value is 13.2%. In a small data set (n = 10), the 95% CI would be the best choice to report uncertainty for reasons to be discussed shortly. The absolute error for each analyst was the difference between the mean that analyst obtained and the true value. Note that here, "absolute" does not mean the absolute value of the error.*

number of significant digits as in the replicate measurements.[1] However, occasionally an extra digit is kept, to avoid rounding errors. Consider two numbers: 10. and 11. What is the sample mean? 10.5, but rounding would give 10, not a terribly helpful calculation. In such cases, the mean can be expressed as $10._5$, with the subscript indicating that this digit is being kept to avoid or address rounding error. The 5 is not significant and does not count as a significant digit, but keeping it will reduce rounding error.[1] Having said that, in many forensic analyses rounding to the same significance as the replicates is acceptable and would be reported as shown in Figure 2.5. The context dictates the rounding procedures. In this example, rounding was to three significant figures, given that the known has a true value with three significant figures. The rules pertaining to significant figures may have allowed for more digits to be kept, but there is no point to doing so on the basis of the known true value and how it is reported.

Absolute error: This quantity measures the difference between the true value and the experimentally obtained value with the sign retained to indicate how the results differ. For the trainee, the absolute error is calculated as 12.9 − 13.2, or −0.3% cocaine. The negative sign indicates that the trainee's calculated mean was less than the true value, and this information is useful in diagnosis and troubleshooting. For the forensic chemist, the absolute error is 0.1 with the positive indicating that the experimentally determined value was greater than the true value.

% Error: While the absolute error is a useful quantity, it is difficult to compare across data sets. An error of −0.3% would be much less of a concern if the true value of the sample was 99.5% and much more of a concern if the true value was 0.5%. If the true value of the sample was indeed 0.5%, an absolute error of 0.3% translates to an error of 60%. To address this limitation of absolute error, the % error is employed. This quantity normalizes the absolute error to the true value:

$$\% \text{ error } = [(\text{experimentally determined value} - \text{true value})/\text{true value}]*100$$

(2.2)

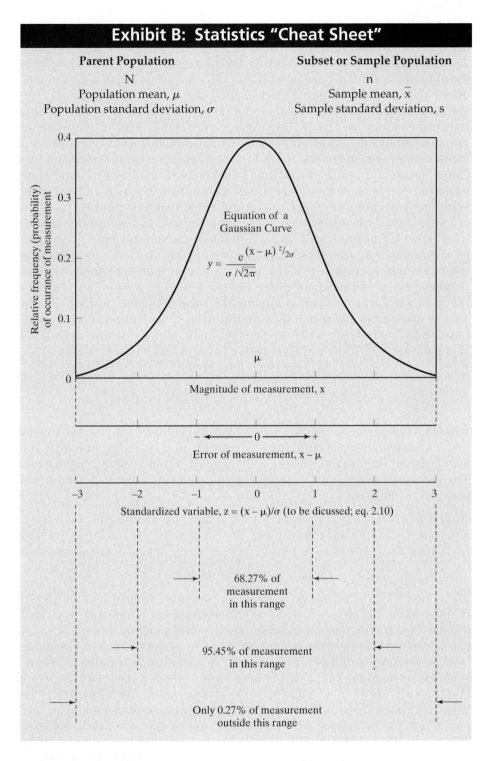

Exhibit B: Statistics "Cheat Sheet"

Parent Population

N

Population mean, μ

Population standard deviation, σ

Subset or Sample Population

n

Sample mean, $\bar{x}$

Sample standard deviation, s

Relative frequency (probability) of occurance of measurement

Equation of a Gaussian Curve

$$y = \frac{e^{(x-\mu)^2/2\sigma}}{\sigma\sqrt{2\pi}}$$

μ

Magnitude of measurement, x

$-$ 0 $+$

Error of measurement, $x - \mu$

Standardized variable, $z = (x - \mu)/\sigma$ (to be dicussed; eq. 2.10)

68.27% of measurement in this range

95.45% of measurement in this range

Only 0.27% of measurement outside this range

For the trainee, the % error is -2.5% whereas for the forensic chemist, it is 0.5%. The percent error is commonly used to express the accuracy of an analysis when the true value is known. The technique of normalizing a value and presenting it as a percentage will be used again for expressing precision (reproducibility), to be described next. The limitation of % error is that this quantity does not take into account the spread or range of the data. A separate quantity is used to

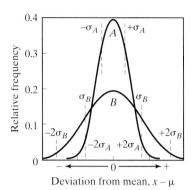

▲ **Figure 2.6** *Two Gaussian distributions centered about the same mean, but with a different spread (standard deviation). This approximates the situation with the forensic chemist and the trainee.*

characterize the reproducibility (spread) and to incorporate it into the evaluation of experimental results.

Standard deviation: The standard deviation is the average deviation from the mean and measures the spread of the data. (See Figure 2.6.) The standard deviation is typically rounded to two significant figures.[1] A small standard deviation means that the replicate measurements are close to each other; a large standard deviation means that they are spread out over a larger range of values. In terms of the normal distribution, ±1 standard deviation from the mean includes approximately 68% of the observations, ±2 standard deviations includes about 95%, and ±3 standard deviations includes around 99%. A large value for the standard deviation means that the distribution is wide; a small value for the standard deviation means that the distribution is narrow. The smaller the standard deviation, the closer is the grouping and the smaller is the spread. In other words, the standard deviation expresses quantitatively the reproducibility of the replicate measurements. The experienced chemist produced data with more precision (less of a spread) than that produced by the trainee, as would be expected based on their skill levels.

In Figure 2.5, two values are reported for the standard deviation: that of the **population** (σ) and that of the **sample** (s). The population standard deviation is calculated as

$$\sigma = \sqrt{\frac{\sum_{i=1}^{N}(x_i - \mu)^2}{n}} \tag{2.3}$$

where i is the number of replicates, 10 in this case.[†] As we will see, 10 samples in such a case is a very small subset or the parent population. The value σ is the standard deviation of the parent population. The use of σ with small sample sets underestimates the true standard deviation σ.[2] A statistically better estimate of σ is given by:

$$s = \sqrt{\frac{\sum_{i=1}^{n}\left(x_i - \overline{x}\right)^2}{n - 1}} \tag{2.4}$$

The value of s is the standard deviation of the selected subset of the parent population. Some calculators and spreadsheet programs differentiate between s and σ, so it is important to make sure that the correct formula is applied.

The sample standard deviation(s) provides an empirical measure of uncertainty (i.e., expected spread) and is frequently used for that purpose. If a distribution is Gaussian 68.3% of the values will fall between ±1 standard deviation (±1s), 95.4% within 2s, and 99.7% within ±3s from the mean. This concept is shown in Figure 2.7. This spread provides a range of measurements as well as a probability of occurrence. Most often, the uncertainty is cited as ±2 standard deviations, since approximately 95% of the area under the normal distribution curve is contained within these boundaries. Sometimes ±3 standard deviations are used, to account for more than 99% of the area under the curve. Thus, if the

---

[†]Although σ is based on sampling the entire population, it is sometimes used in forensic and analytical chemistry. One rule of thumb is that if n > 15, population statistics may be used. Similarly, if all samples in a population are analyzed, population statistics are appropriate. For example, to determine the average value of coins in a jar full of change, every coin could be included in the sampling and population statistics would be appropriate.

a.

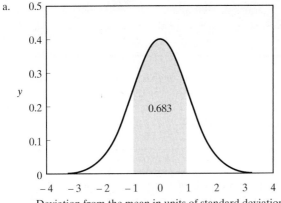

Deviation from the mean in units of standard deviation

b.

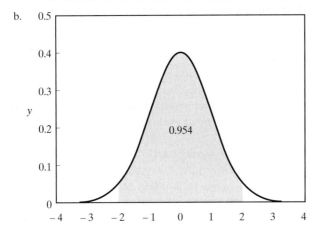

c.

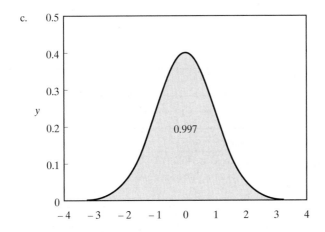

◀ **Figure 2.7** *Area under the Gaussian curve as a function of standard deviations from the mean. Within one standard deviation (a), 68.3% of the measurements are found; 95.4% (b) are found within two standard deviations, and (c) 99.7% are found within three standard deviations of the mean. The y-axis is frequency of occurence.*

distribution of replicate measurements is normal and a representative sample of the larger population has been selected, the standard deviation can be used to reliably estimate an uncertainty.

As shown in Table 2.1, the supervisor and the trainee both obtained a mean value within ±0.3% of the true value. When uncertainties associated with the standard deviation and the analyses are considered, it becomes clear that both obtained an acceptable result. This is also seen graphically in Figure 2.8. However, the trainee would likely be asked to practice and try again, not because of

Table 2.1 Comparison of Ranges for Determination of Percent Cocaine in QA Sample, True Value $\mu = 13.2\%$		
Calculation Method	Trainee, $\bar{x} = 12.9$	Forensic Chemist, $\bar{x} = 13.3$
Min–Max (range)	11.5–15.0	13.1–13.7
±1s	12.0–13.8	13.1–13.4
±2s	11.0–14.8	12.9–13.7
±3s	10.1–15.7	12.7–13.9
95% CI	12.2–13.6	13.2–13.4

the poor accuracy, but because of the poor reproducibility. In any laboratory analysis, two criteria must be considered: accuracy (how close the result is to the true value) and precision (how reproducible the result is). One without the other is an incomplete description.

Variance (v): The sample variance (v) of a set of replicates is simply s^2, which, like the standard deviation, gauges the spread, expected error, or variance within that data set. Forensic chemists favor standard deviation as their primary measure of reproducibility, but variance is used in analysis-of-variance (ANOVA) procedures as well as in multivariate statistics. Variances are additive and are the basis of error propagation, as seen in equation (2.1), where the variance was represented by e^2.

%RSD of coefficient of variation (CV or %CV): The standard deviation alone means little and doesn't reflect the relative or comparative spread of the data. This situation is analogous to that seen with the quantity of absolute error. To compare the spread (reproducibility) of one data set with another, the mean must be taken into account. If the mean of the data is 500 and the standard deviation is 100, that's a relatively large standard deviation. By contrast, if the mean of the data is 1,000,000, a standard deviation of 100 is relatively small. The significance of

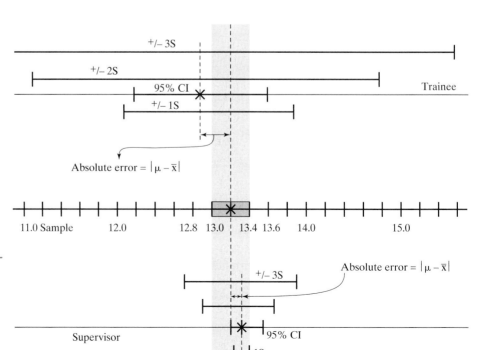

▶ **Figure 2.8** *Results of the cocaine analysis presented graphically with uncertainty reported several ways. The shaded region is the range around the true value of the sample.*

a standard deviation is expressed by the percent relative standard deviation (%RSD), also called the coefficient of variation (CV) or the percent CV:

$$\%RSD = (\text{standard deviation}/\text{mean}) \times 100 \qquad (2.5)$$

In the first example, $\%RSD = (100/500) \times 100$, or 20%; in the second, $\%RSD = (100/1{,}000{,}000) \times 100$, or 0.01%. Thus, the spread of the data in the first example is much greater than that in the second, even though the values of the standard deviation are the same. The %RSD is usually reported to one or at most two decimal places, even though the rules of rounding may allow more to be kept. This is because %RSD is used comparatively and the value is not the basis of any further calculation. The amount of useful information provided by reporting a %RSD of 4.521% can usually be expressed just as well by 4.5%.

Example Problem 2.2

As part of a method-validation study, three forensic chemists each made 10 replicate injections in a GCMS experiment and obtained the following data for area counts of a reference peak:

Injection No.	A	B	C
1	9995	10640	9814
2	10035	10118	10958
3	10968	10267	10285
4	10035	10873	10915
5	10376	10204	10219
6	10845	10593	10442
7	10044	10019	10752
8	9914	10372	10211
9	9948	10035	10676
10	10316	10959	10057

Which chemist had the most reproducible injection technique?

Answer: This problem provides an opportunity to discuss the use of spreadsheets—specifically, Microsoft Excel®. The calculation could be done by hand or on a calculator, but a spreadsheet method provides more flexibility and less tedium.

   Reproducibility can be gauged by the %RSD for each data set. The data were entered into a spreadsheet, and built-in functions were used for the mean and standard deviation (sample). The formula for %RSD was created by dividing the quantity in the standard deviation cell by the quantity in the mean cell and multiplying by 100.

Injection #	A	B	C	
1	9995	10640	9814	
2	10035	10118	10958	
3	10968	10267	10285	
4	10035	10873	10915	
5	10376	10204	10219	
6	10845	10593	10442	
7	10044	10019	10752	
8	9914	10372	10211	
9	9948	10035	10676	
10	10316	10959	10057	
Mean	10247.6	10408.0	10432.9	Function used: = average()
Standard deviation	379.14	340.79	381.57	Function used: = stdev()
%RSD	3.70	3.27	3.66	mean/stdev*100

Analyst B produced data with the lowest %RSD and had the best reproducibility. Note that significant-figure conventions must be addressed when a spreadsheet is used just as surely as they must be addressed with a calculator.

95% Confidence interval (95%CI): In most forensic analyses, there will be three or fewer replicates per sample, not enough for standard deviation to be a reliable expression of uncertainty. Even the 10 samples used in the foregoing examples represent a tiny subset of the population of measurements that could have been taken. One way to account for a small number of samples is to apply a multiplier called the Student's t-value as follows:

$$\text{confidence interval} = \frac{s*t}{\sqrt{n}} \tag{2.6}$$

where t is obtained from a table such as Table 2.2. Here, the quantity $\dfrac{s}{\sqrt{n}}$ is the measure of uncertainty as an average over n measurements. The value for t is selected on the basis of the number of degrees of freedom and the level of confidence desired. In forensic and analytical applications, 95% is often chosen and the result is reported as a range about the mean:

$$\bar{x} \pm \frac{s*t}{\sqrt{n}} \tag{2.7}$$

For the trainee's data in the cocaine analysis example, results are best reported as 12.9 ± 0.7, or $12.2-13.6_{(95\%CI)}$. Rephrased, the results can be expressed as the statement that the trainee can be 95% confident that the true value (μ) lies within the reported range. Note that both the trainee and the supervisor obtained a range that includes the true value for the percent cocaine in the test sample. Higher confidence intervals can be selected, but not without due consideration. As certainty increases, so does the size of the range. Analytical and forensic chemists generally use 95% because it is a reasonable compromise between certainty and range size.[3] The percentage is *not* a measure of quality, only of certainty. Increasing the certainty actually *decreases* the utility of the data, a point that cannot be overemphasized.

Table 2.2	Student's t-Values (Abbreviated); See Appendix 11 for Complete Table		
n − 1	90% confidence level	95%	99%
1	6.314	12.706	63.657
2	2.920	4.303	9.925
3	2.353	3.182	5.841
4	2.132	2.776	4.604
5	2.015	2.571	4.032
10	1.812	2.228	3.169

Exhibit C: Is Bigger Better?

Suppose a forensic chemist is needed in court immediately and must be located. To be 50% confident, the "range" of locations could be stated as the forensic laboratory complex. To be more confident of finding the chemist, the range could be extended to include the laboratory, a courtroom, a crime scene, or anywhere between any of these points. To bump the probability to 95%, the chemist's home, commuting route, and favorite lunch spot could be added. To make the chemist's location even more likely, the chemist is in the state, perhaps with 98% confidence. Finally, there is a 99% chance that the chemist is in the United States and a 99.999999999% certainty that he or she is on planet Earth. Having a high degree of confidence doesn't make the data "better": Knowing that the chemist is on planet Earth makes such a large range useless.

2.2.2 OUTLIERS AND STATISTICAL TESTS

The identification and removal of **outliers** is dangerous,[3] given that the only basis for rejecting one is often a hunch. A suspected outlier has a value that "looks wrong" or "seems wrong," to use the wording heard in laboratories. Because analytical chemists have an intuitive idea of what an outlier is, the subject presents an opportunity to discuss statistical hypothesis testing, one of the most valuable and often-overlooked tools available to the forensic practitioner. The outlier issue can be phrased as a question: Is the data point that "looks funny" a true outlier? The question can also be phrased as a hypothesis: The point is (is not) an outlier. When the hypothesis form is used, **hypothesis testing** can be applied and a "hunch" becomes quantitative.

Suppose the supervisor and the trainee in the cocaine example both ran one extra analysis independently under the same conditions and obtained a concentration of 11.0% cocaine. Is that datum suspect for either of them, neither of them, or both of them? Should they include it in a recalculation of their means and ranges? This question can be tested by assuming a normal distribution of the data. As shown in Figure 2.9, the trainee's data has a much larger spread than that of the supervising chemist, but is the spread wide enough to accommodate the value 11.0%? Or is this value too far out of the normally expected distribution? Recall that 5% of the data in any normally distributed population will be on the outer edges far removed from the mean—that is expected. Just because an occurrence is rare does not mean that it is unexpected. After all, people do win the lottery. These are the considerations the chemists must balance in deciding whether the 11.0% value is a true outlier or a rare, but not unexpected, result.

To apply a **significance test**, a hypothesis must be clearly stated and must have a quantity with a calculated probability associated with it. This is the fundamental difference between a hunch[†] and a hypothesis test—a quantity and a probability. The hypothesis will be accepted or rejected on the basis of a comparison of the calculated quantity with a table of values relating to a normal distribution. As with the confidence interval, the analyst selects an associated level of certainty, typically 95%.[3] The starting hypothesis takes the form of the null hypothesis H_0. "Null" means "none," and the null hypothesis is stated in such a way as to say that there is no difference between the calculated quantity and the expected quantity, save that attributable to normal random error. As regards to the outlier in question, the null hypothesis for the chemist and the trainee states that the 11.0% value is not an outlier and that any difference

---

[†]Remove the sugarcoating and a hunch is a guess. It may hold up under quantitative scrutiny, but until it does, it should not be glamorized.

a.

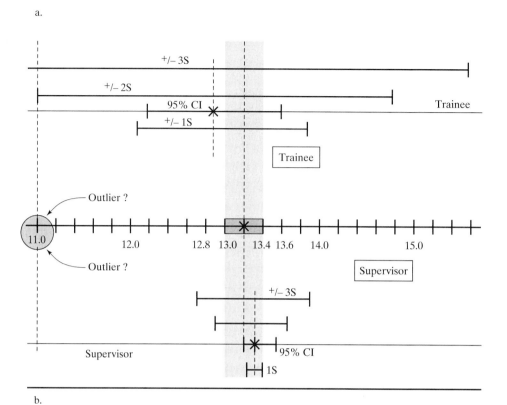

b.

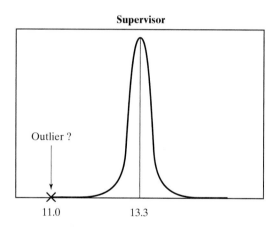

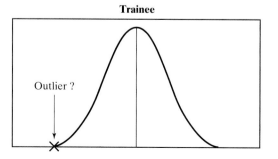

▶ **Figure 2.9** *On the basis of the spread seen for each analyst, is 11.0% a reasonable value for the concentration of cocaine?*

Table 2.3	Outlier Tests for 11.0% Analytical Results	
Test	**Trainee**	**Chemist**
Q test $Q_{table} = 0.444$	$Q_{calc} = \dfrac{[11.5 - 11.0]}{[13.3 - 11.0]} = 0.217$	$Q_{calc} = \dfrac{[13.1 - 11.0]}{[13.7 - 11.0]} = 0.778$
Grubbs test Critical Z = 2.34	$Z = \dfrac{\lvert 12.9 - 11.0 \rvert}{0.93} = 2.04$	$Z = \dfrac{\lvert 13.3 - 11.0 \rvert}{0.20} = 11.5$

between the calculated and expected value can be attributed to normal random error. Both want to be 95% certain that retention or rejection of the data is justifiable. Another way to state this is to say that the result is or is not significant at the 0.05 (p = 0.05 or α = 0.05), or 5% level. If the calculated value exceeds the value in the table, there is only a 1 in 20 chance that rejecting the point is incorrect and that it really was legitimate based on the spread of the data.

With the hypothesis and confidence level selected, the next step is to apply the chosen test. For outliers, one test used (perhaps even abused) in analytical chemistry is the **Q** or **Dixon test**:[3]

$$Q_{calc} = \lvert gap/range \rvert \qquad (2.8)$$

To apply the test, the analysts would organize their results in ascending order, including the point in question. The gap is the difference between that point and the next closest one, and the range is the spread from low to high, also including the data point in question. The table used (see Appendix 11) is that for the Dixon's Q parameter, two tailed.[3,†] If $Q_{calc} > Q_{table}$, the data point can be rejected with 95% confidence. The Q_{table} for this calculation with n = 11 is 0.444. The calculations for each test are shown in Table 2.3. The results are not surprising, given the spread of the chemist's data relative to that of the trainee. The trainee would have to include the value 11.0 and recalculate the mean, standard deviation, and other quantities associated with the analysis.

In the realm of statistical significance testing, there are typically several tests for each type of hypothesis.[4] The **Grubbs test**, recommended by the International Standards Organization (ISO) and the American Society for Testing and Materials (ASTM),[2,5,6] is another approach to the identification of outliers:

$$G = \lvert questioned - \bar{x} \rvert / s \qquad (2.9)$$

Analogously to obtaining Dixon's Q parameter, one defines H_0, calculates G, and compares it with an entry in a table. (See Appendix 11.) The quantity G is the ratio z that is used to normalize data sets in units of variation from the mean.

---

†Many significance tests have two associated tables: one with one-tailed values, the other with two-tailed values. Two-tailed values are used unless there is reason to expect deviation in only one direction. For example, if a new method is developed to quantitate cocaine, and a significance test is used to evaluate that method, then two-tailed values are needed because the new test could produce higher or lower values. One-tailed values would be appropriate if the method were always going to produce, for example, higher concentrations.

Example Problem 2.3

A forensic chemist performed a blind-test sample with high-performance liquid chromatography (HPLC) to determine the concentration of the explosive RDX in a performance test mix. Her results are as follows:

Laboratory data

56.8	57.2
57.0	57.2
57.0	57.8
57.1	58.4
57.2	**59.6**

Are there any outliers in these data at the 5% level (95% confidence)? Take any such outliers into account if necessary, and report the mean, %RSD, and 95% confidence interval for the results.

Answer: For outlier testing, the data are sorted in order such that the identifier is easily located. Here, the questionable value is the last one: 59.6 ppb. It seems far removed from the others, but can it be removed from the results? The first step is to determine the mean and standard deviation and then to apply the two outlier tests mentioned thus far in the text: the Dixon and Grubbs approaches.

$$\text{Mean} = 57.5_3 \qquad \text{Standard deviation (s)} = 0.8642 \qquad n = 10$$

Dixon Test (eq. 2.8)

$$Q = \frac{\text{gap}}{\text{range}} = \frac{(59.6 - 58.4)}{(59.6 - 56.8)} = 0.429$$

$$\text{Table value} = 0.477$$

$$Q_{calc} < Q_{table} = \text{keep}$$

Grubbs Test (eq. 2.9)

$$G = \frac{(59.6 - 57.5_3)}{0.8642} = 2.39$$

$$\text{Table value (5\%)} = 2.176$$

$$G_{calc} > G_{table} = \text{reject}$$

This is an example of contradictory results, and in such cases, ASTM recommends that the Grubbs test take precedence. Accordingly, the point is retained and the statistical quantities remain as is. The 95% confidence interval is then calculated:

95% confidence interval

$$\bar{x} \; +/- \; \frac{ts}{\sqrt{n}}$$

with $s = 0.8642$, $n = 10$

by Appendix 11
2.26

$$\bar{x} \; +/- \; \frac{(2.26)(0.8642)}{\sqrt{10}} = 0.618$$

$$57.5 \; +/- \; 0.6 \text{ or } 56.9 - 58.1$$

For example, one of the data points obtained by the trainee for the percent cocaine was 15.0. To express this as the normalized z value, we have

$$z = (15.0 - 12.9)/0.93 = 2.26 \qquad (2.10)$$

This value is 2.26s, or 2.26 standard deviations higher than the mean. A value less than the mean would have a negative z, or negative displacement. By comparison, the largest percentage obtained by the experienced forensic chemist, 13.7%, is 2.00s greater than the mean. The Grubbs test is based on the knowledge that, in a normal distribution, only 5% of the values are found more than 1.96 standard deviations from the mean.[†] For the 11.0% value obtained by the trainee and the chemist, the results agree with the Q test; the trainee keeps that value and the forensic chemist discards it. However, different significance tests often produce different results, with one indicating that a certain value is an outlier and another indicating that it is not. When in doubt, a good practice is to use the more conservative test. Absent other information, if one says to keep the value and one says to discard it, the value should be kept. Finally, note that these tests are designed for the evaluation of a single outlier. When more than one outlier is suspected, other tests are used but this situation is not common in forensic chemistry.[6]

There is a cliché that "statistics lie" or that they can be manipulated to support any position desired. Like any tool, statistics can be applied inappropriately, but that is not the fault of the tool. The previous example, in which both analysts obtained the same value on independent replicates, was carefully stated. However, having both obtain the exact same concentration should at least raise a question concerning the coincidence. Perhaps the calibration curve has deteriorated or the sample has degraded. The point is that the use of a statistical test to eliminate data does not, and should not, take the place of laboratory common sense and analyst judgment. A data point that "looks funny" warrants investigation and evaluation before anything else—chemistry before statistics. One additional analysis might reveal evidence of new problems, particularly if a systematic problem is suspected. A more serious situation is diagnosed if the new replicate shows no predictable behavior. If the new replicate falls within the expected range, rejection of the suspicious data point was justified both analytically and statistically.

2.2.3 Comparison of Data Sets

Another hypothesis test used in forensic chemistry is one that compares the means of two data sets. In the supervisor–trainee example, the two chemists are analyzing the same unknown, but obtain different means. The t-test of means can be used to determine whether the difference of the means is significant. The t-value is the same as that used in equation 2-6 for determining confidence intervals. This makes sense; the goal of the t-test of means is to determine whether the spread of two sets of data overlap sufficiently for one to conclude that they are or are not representative of the same population.

In the supervisor–trainee example, the null hypothesis could be stated as "H_0: The mean obtained by the trainee is not significantly different than the mean obtained by the supervisor at the 95% confidence level ($p = 0.05$)." Stated another way, the means are the same and any difference between them is due to small random errors.

[†]The value ±2 standard deviations used previously is a common approximation of 1.96s.

Example Problem 2.4

A toxicologist is tasked with testing two blood samples in a case of possible chronic arsenic poisoning. The first sample was taken a week before the second. The toxicologist analyzed each sample five times and obtained the data shown in the table below. Is there a statistically significant increase in the blood arsenic concentration? Use a 95% confidence level.

	Week 1	Week 2	
Possible arsenic poisoning	16.9	17.4	
Q: Has there been a statistically significant	17.1	17.3	**[As] ppb**
increase in the arsenic concentration?	16.8	17.3	**in blood**
	17.2	17.5	
	17.1	17.4	

Excel ⟶ **Use Tools → Data analysis → t test unequal variance**
p = 0.05, hypothesized mean = 0
Output:

t_{table}:
2.365

	Week 1	Week 2
Mean	17.02	17.38
Variance	0.027	0.007
Observations	5	5
Hypothesized mean difference	0	
df	6	
t Stat	−4.37	⟵ $t_{cal} = 4.37$
P(T<=t) one-tail	0.00	
t Critical one-tail	1.94	
P(T<=t) two-tail	0.00	
t Critical two-tail	2.45	

$t_{cal} \gg t_{table}$:

Null hypothesis that means are the same is rejected.

Answer: Manual calculations for the t-test are laborious and prone to error. The best way to work such problems is with Excel, as shown in the accompanying figure. The feature used is under "Data Analysis," found in the "Tools" menu. This analysis pack is provided with Excel, although it has to be installed as an add-in. (See Excel help for more information on installing it.)

Once the data are entered, the analysis is simple. Notice that it was assumed that the variances were different; if they had been closer to each other in value, an alternative function, the t-test of means with equal variances, could have been used. Also, the t-statistic is an absolute value; the negative value appears when the larger mean is subtracted from the smaller. For this example, $t_{calc} = 4.37$, which is greater than $t_{table} = 2.365$. This means that the null hypothesis must be rejected and that the concentration of arsenic has increased from the first week to the second.

The equation used to calculate the test statistic is

$$t_{calc} = \frac{|mean_1 - mean_2|}{s_{pooled}} \sqrt{\frac{n_1 n_2}{n_1 + n_2}} \qquad (2.11)$$

where s_{pooled}, the pooled standard deviation from the two data sets, is calculated as

$$s_{pooled} = \sqrt{\frac{s_1^2(n_1 - 1) + s_2^2(n_2 - 1)}{n_1 + n_2 - 2}} \qquad (2.12)$$

This calculation can be done manually or preferably with a spreadsheet, as shown in Example Problem 2.4. The result for the supervisor/trainee is a t_{calc} of 1.36, which is less than the t_{table} (Appendix 11) of 2.262 for 10 degrees of freedom. Therefore, the null hypothesis is accepted and the means are the same at the 95% confidence level or $p = 0.05$. This is a good outcome since both chemists were testing the same sample. Note that the t-test of means as shown is a quick test when two data sets are compared. However, when more data sets are involved, different approaches are called for. [4,7]

2.2.4 TYPES OF ERROR

One other set of statistical terms merits mention here, as they are often used in a forensic context. Whenever a significance test is applied such that a null hypothesis is proposed and tested, the results are always tied to a level of certainty, 95% in the example in the previous section. With the forensic chemist's data, the 11.0% data point was identified as an outlier with 95% certainty, but that still leaves a 1-in-20 chance that this judgment is in error. This risk or possibility of error can be expressed in terms of types. A **Type I** error is an error in which the null hypothesis is incorrectly rejected, whereas a **Type II** error is an error in which the null hypothesis is incorrectly accepted. Put in terms of the experienced chemist and the 11.0% value, H_0 states that that value is not an outlier, but the null hypothesis was rejected on the basis of the calculations for the Q test and the Grubbs test. If that were in fact a mistake, and the 1-in-20 long shot came true, throwing out the 11.07%. value would be a Type I error. In effect, the chemist makes a defensible judgment in rejecting that value, deciding that the harm done by leaving it in would be greater than the risk of throwing it out.

2.2.5 SAMPLING STATISTICS

Overview: One important application of statistics in forensic chemistry is in the selection of a defensible and **representative sample** n from a larger parent population. Each type of exhibit generates a different sampling challenge, from the barely detectable fragment of a synthetic fiber to the seizure of hundreds of packets of white powder. Regardless of the nature of the evidence, foundational principles of representative sampling apply, with the forensic caveat that the evidence should not be totally consumed in testing unless that is absolutely unavoidable. By definition, a defensible and representative sample is a random sample. It should not matter how, when, or where a subset or aliquot is drawn for analysis. If it does, further preparation and sorting are called for before samples are taken.

Neither the forensic literature nor the courts have provided concrete rules or definitions for what constitutes a representative sample. Partially this is due to the nature of forensic samples, and partly it has to do with the lack of consistent legal standards. [8,9] In general, the courts have emphasized the need for random and representative samples, but have not specified how those qualities are to be assured or quantified. [8] This gap between what is needed and how to satisfy that need should not be terribly surprising or troubling, given the infinite variety of evidence that enters forensic laboratories daily: In practical terms, it is far easier to identify a poor sampling plan than create the perfect one. In recognition of this fact, the treatment that follows is a general discussion of representative sampling couched in terms just introduced: normal distributions, probabilities, significance testing, and homogeneity.

If a sample is properly and thoroughly mixed, it will be **homogeneous** and the composition of any portion of it will be representative. Analysts thoroughly mix any sample before selecting an aliquot if such mixing is (1) applicable (one does not mix fibers purposely collected from different areas of a body), (2) possible (it's hard to mix a ton of green plant matter), and (3) appropriate (if several baggies of powder are seized, some tan and some black, they should not be mixed). Deciding when these conditions are satisfied relies on analyst judgment and the particulars of the case. In the discussion that follows, it is assumed that the analyst will, if necessary, ensure that the final subset or aliquot is drawn from a properly and appropriately homogeneous sample.

Consider an example in which a forensic laboratory receives evidence from a single case. Suppose the evidence consists of a hundred baggies, each full of white powder. Do all of the bags need to be tested, or can a representative subset suffice? A subset suffices if the powder in all of the bags is part of the same batch—in statistical terms, if all of the samples are part of the same population. So the forensic scientist has to answer the following question: Was some large shipment divided into these individual bags, or does this case represent several different original sources? In other words, does each of these n samples belong to a larger parent population that is normally distributed with respect to the variables of interest? If so, any difference between samples selected are due only to small random variations that would be expected of a normally distributed population. This argument should sound familiar; in a normally distributed population, there is a 68% probability that a randomly selected sample will be within $\pm 1s$ of the mean, a 95% probability that it will be between $\pm 2s$, etc. Although one sample does not completely describe the distribution, it isn't necessary to test all samples.

The previous paragraph is another window on the earlier sampling (n) versus parent population statistics discussion. The goal is to minimize the differences $|\bar{x} - \mu|$ and $|s - \sigma|$ and to be able to assign a level of certainty to the estimates. Selecting such a representative subset is called **probability sampling** or selecting an unbiased subset. When an unbiased subset is successfully chosen, n is a perfect snapshot of N. Designing a probability sampling plan is part and parcel of quality assurance and data integrity, yet forensic laboratories also have to balance cost and time considerations and allow room for analyst judgment.[5,10] This is particularly true in drug analysis, the area of forensic chemistry that deals with sampling issues the most often. As of late 2004, international forensic working groups such as the Scientific Working Group for the Analysis of Seized Drugs (SWGDRUG, swgdrug.org) were working on sampling guidelines to be recommended to the forensic community. Forensic chemists should monitor the progress of these groups and their findings, as they will likely define future sampling practices. The remainder of this discussion utilizes drug analysis to exemplify the principles introduced, which are applicable to all areas of forensic chemistry in which sampling plans are needed.

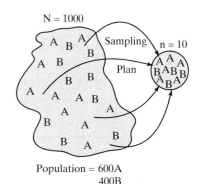

▶ **Figure 2.10** *Ideally, a subset of n samples will capture the composition of the larger parent population.*

Exhibit D: Statistics and Probability

Although the terms "statistics" and "probability" are often used interchangeably, they refer to different concepts. Statistics is based on an existing data set, such as that in the replicate measurement example of the supervisor and trainee used throughout this chapter. Based on knowledge of random populations and the Gaussian distribution, patterns observed in the smaller data set are extrapolated to the overall population. An example is the use of the sample standard deviation s as a starting point for determining a confidence interval. Thus, statistics is an inductive process wherein specific knowledge is extrapolated and applied generally. By contrast, probability is deductive and moves from general knowledge to a specific application. Describing the probability that a coin toss will yield three tails starts with the general knowledge that any one coin toss can give either a head or a tail. However, what statistics and probability do have in common is that they both describe uncertainty. A coin-toss question can be phrased in terms of the odds; the odds that three coin tosses in a row will produce three tails is $(1/2)^3$, or 1 in 8, meaning that, given a fair toss, one can expect three tails or three heads 1 time in 8, or 12.5% of the time. Nonetheless, that does not mean that if one replicates the three-toss experiment eight times, it is assured that one sequence will be three heads or three tails. There is still uncertainty associated with the outcome.

Source: Aitken, C. G. G., and F. Taroni. Statistics and the Evaluation of Evidence for Forensic Scientists, 2d ed. Chichester, U.K.: John Wiley and Sons, **2004**, p. 6.

A Working Example: Suppose a large seizure of individual baggies of white powder ($n = 100$) has arrived at the laboratory. Controlled substances in the powder are to be identified and quantitated in an expeditious and cost-effective manner. Clearly, a sampling plan is needed. The forensic literature and the standard (or at least common) laboratory practices furnish a starting point for the design of such a plan, and an illustrative example is provided in Table 2.4. According to recent data, most laboratories appear to use the first two methods listed in the table or variations of them, combined with presumptive and screening tests.[11] The latter phrase is an important qualifier and will be discussed shortly. Note that the number of samples tested to completion is not the sole criterion for judging the merit of a sampling plan; as mentioned earlier, it is usually easier to judge a bad approach than dictate the perfect one. Accordingly, there is nothing inherently wrong with a case-by-case approach to sampling; the key as always is to ensure that the plan is defensible.

Table 2.4   Comparison of Methods Used for Determining n

Formula for Determining n	N = 50, n = ?	N = 100, n = ?	N = 150, n = ?
$\sqrt{N}$	7	10	12
$N \times 0.10$ (10%)	5	10	15
$N \times 0.04$ (4%)	2	4	6
$\sqrt{\dfrac{N}{2}}$	5	7	9
Hypergeometric distribution	NA	12*	25*
$20 + 0.10(N - 20)$	23	28	33

Note: N = the total number of separate articles of evidence to be sampled; n = the size of the subset of samples. This table is based on one presented in Colon, et. al.[11] "NA" means that the value was not provided in the reference directly.

*For a 95% certainty that 80–90% of the entire collection is positive; assumes no negatives in presumptive testing.

An essential first step in sampling is visual inspection. Are the samples all the same color? Do they have the same granularity? If so, a hypothesis can be put forward that all of the samples are from the same batch or population and that any variation found within them is small and the result of an expected normal distribution. Next, a battery of presumptive tests or screening tests could be applied to each sample. Presumptive testing is described in detail in Chapter 7; suffice it for now to say that a positive result issuing from a screening test indicates that the substance is more likely than not to contain what it is suspected to contain. Suppose in this example that the screening tests all pointed to an identification of cocaine with similar characteristics, adding further confidence to the hypothesis that all the bags are part of the same population. Had either the visual or screening tests failed to support this assumption, the samples would then be placed into similar groups, each representing a new population.

The next step is the selection of n, the subset of the 100 exhibits that will adequately characterize the population with acceptable error (also called tolerable error) and acceptable uncertainty. Some methods available for selecting n are as follows:

ASTM E122-0[5]: This protocol is designed for articles within a batch or lot, a reasonable model for the hypothetical drug seizure. The equation used is

$$n = \left(\frac{3\sigma_0}{e}\right)^2 \tag{2.13}$$

where e is the tolerable error and σ_0 is the estimated standard deviation of the population. Since making such an estimate is somewhat difficult, an alternative based on the percent RSD expected or desired is

$$n = \left(\frac{3V_0}{e}\right)^2 \tag{2.14}$$

where V_0 is the CV (%RSD) and e is the allowable error, also expressed as a ratio or percentage. For our hypothetical case introduced above, assume that an error of 2% is acceptable (e = 2) and a %RSD of 5% (V_0 = 5) is expected, on the basis of the laboratory's previous experience. Then

$$n = \left(\frac{3 \times 5}{2}\right)^2 = 56.25 = 56 \tag{2.15}$$

If only the average value of a lot or batch is needed, the value of n can be further reduced with the use of the formula

$$n_L = \frac{n}{\left[1 + \left(\dfrac{n}{N}\right)\right]} = \frac{56}{\left[1 + \left(\dfrac{56}{100}\right)\right]} = 35.897 = 36 \tag{2.16}$$

where n_L refers to the size of a lot or batch.

Normal Distribution:[12] Another approach to selecting a subset is based on the assumption that variation in the subset is normally distributed. If so, then the sampling question can be rephrased to facilitate the selection of a reasonably sized subset n of a larger population N based on expectations or suspicions regarding how many items in the seizure are cocaine.[12] Suppose that 72 of the

Historical Evidence 2.1—ASTM International

The American Society for Testing and Materials, now known as ASTM International, was formed in 1898 to provide uniform standards for testing procedures used in science and engineering. The first "standard" (actually a written protocol), was called A-1 and covered stainless steel. The person most responsible for the founding of ASTM was the American Charles B. Dudley, a Ph.D. chemist. Over the years, ASTM formed committees and generated standards for many industries. ASTM's standards are based on consensus in that they are written by committees of practitioners in the appropriate field. Committee E-30, which concerned itself with forensic science, was formed in 1970; several of its standards are referenced in this text. ASTM publishes the *Journal of Forensic Sciences*.

baggies of powder contain cocaine and 18 do not. Then the value defined as θ is 72/100, or 0.72. Of course, the analyst does not know this prior to testing; rather, the goal is to select a random subset that provides an unbiased estimate of θ. This unbiased proportion can be represented as $p = z / m$, where m is the size of the subset chosen and z is as defined in equation 2.10.[12] On the basis of previous experience, the analyst expects the seizure to contain approximately 75% cocaine exhibits and the rest noncontrolled substances. The analyst's goal is to estimate the ratio of cocaine to substances that are not cocaine to within ±25%. On the basis of the normal distribution, one expression that can be used is[12]

$$m = \frac{4\theta(1 - \theta)}{0.25^2} = \frac{4 \times 0.75(1 - 0.75)}{0.25^2} = 12 \qquad (2.17)$$

In addition to assuming a normal distribution, this expression relies on the assumption that the selected subset's ratio of cocaine will lie somewhere between 0.75 ± 0.25 at a 95% confidence level. The analyst then would select 12 samples and analyze them. The results would allow the analyst to state with 95% confidence that the proportion of cocaine to substances that are not cocaine in the seizure is indeed greater than 50%. Why 50% and not 75%? The 50% figure arises from the range selected: 0.75 ± 0.25. Equation 2.17 can be useful for initial estimates, but a more flexible approach is one based on probabilities.

Hypergeometric Distribution and Related Techniques[9, 12–14]: The hypergeometric probability distribution is used in situations where samples are to be taken from a large population and not replaced. Consider a deck of cards, an example of a finite population. If 10 cards are drawn at random (and not replaced in the deck), a hypergeometric distribution could be employed to calculate the probability of drawing four queens in the 10 cards drawn. The hypergeometric mean is related to the **binomial distribution** used in forensic DNA analysis to calculate gene frequencies, and it applies to cases in which the outcome can be only one of two options. Flipping a coin is the classic example. To calculate the probability of getting 3 heads in a row, the individual probabilities are multiplied $0.5 \times 0.5 \times 0.5 = 0.125$. This figure can be expressed as approximately a 13% chance that three coin flips will produce 3 heads. The probability of getting 10 in a row is much smaller, namely 0.001, which can be stated as 1 chance in 1024. In the example of the bags of cocaine, the selection of any one bag can be considered an exclusive or (either/or) option—either it will contain cocaine or it will not. This is the reasoning behind the application of the binomial and hypergeometric distributions to selective sampling.

Example Problem 2.5

A seizure of 369 1-kilogram bricks of a tan powder is received in a crime laboratory. All of the bricks are carefully weighed, and it is determined that all weigh 1.00 kg $\pm$ 0.05 kg. The prosecuting attorney explains to the analyst that the penalty is more severe if controlled substances are found in the amount of more than 100.0 kg. Using the hypergeometric-mean approach, devise a reasonable sampling plan.

Answer: Enough samples must be tested to be sure that the amount of controlled substance found, if any, conclusively exceeds or does not exceed the 100.0-kg threshold. First, take into account the uncertainties of the weights. The worst possible case would be if every brick selected had a low weight. If so, more would have to be sampled to ensure that if all were found to contain the same controlled substance, the weight exceeded 100 kg. The determinative equation is

$$100.0 \text{ kg}/0.995 \text{ kg} = 100.53$$

Accordingly, to ensure that the weight threshold is exceeded, at least 101 of the bricks must be found to contain the same controlled substance. By contrast, $369 - 101 = 268$ bricks must be shown to contain no controlled substance in order to ensure that the threshold is not exceeded.

The Excel hypergeometric-mean function was used to generate the following table:

Initial random sample	No. positives observed	Population positives	% chance	Odds: 1 in . . .
10	10	10	8.77E-18	1.14E + 19
10	10	25	2.87E-11	3.49E + 12
10	10	50	9.01E-08	1.11E + 09
10	10	75	7.27E-06	1.38E + 07
10	10	101	1.68E-04	5.94E + 05
10	10	150	1.03E-02	9.75E + 03
10	10	200	0.2	508.0
10	10	250	1.9	52.1
10	10	260	2.9	34.9
10	10	270	4.2	23.8
10	10	280	6.1	16.4
10	10	300	12.3	8.2
10	10	350	58.5	1.7
10	10	360	77.9	1.3
10	10	368	97.3	1.0

Here it is assumed that the analyst decided to take 10 samples at random and test them completely. Suppose all came back positive for a controlled substance and were the same as far as the analysis showed. What are the odds that at least 101 would then be positive? The first line of the table shows that if there were 10 positives in the entire population of 369 kilos, the odds of selecting those 10 at random are on the order of 1 in 10^{19}. At the other extreme, if 360 of the 369 are positives, there is nearly an 80% chance that the first 10 selected at random will test positive. Assume that 101 are positive. If 10 samples are drawn from the entire 369 at random and are then found positive, that would be expected to occur only once in approximately 10,000 tries.

What does the latter statement mean for the analyst? If he or she samples 10, analyzes them, and finds that all are positive, then there is only 1 chance in 10,000 that less than 101 kilos contain the controlled substance. The advantage of using the spreadsheet function is that it allows for a "what if?" approach. Once the formulas are set up, the values for the initial random sample and other variables can be adjusted in accordance with different scenarios.

In the cocaine example, the question could be framed this way: If 5 baggies of white powder are selected from the hundred received and all test positive for cocaine, how many more would have to be sampled to be sure (within a defined probability range) that a selected portion of the remaining samples are also cocaine? To apply the hypergeometric distribution, the expression used is[†]

$$P_{x=i} = \frac{\binom{M}{i}\binom{N-M}{n-i}}{\binom{N}{i}} \quad i = 0, 1, 2, \ldots \tag{2.18}$$

where p is the probability of success (selecting a sample that is cocaine), M is the number of successes for selection event i, and N is the size of the population. Expressions of this form are solved with factorials. If N is 100 and $i = 5$, then

$$\frac{N}{i} = \frac{100!}{5!(100-5)!} \tag{2.19}$$

In the example of 100 baggies, assume that 72 contain cocaine and 28 have no controlled substance. What is the probability that the first 5 selected at random will be cocaine? Using the spreadsheet function produces a value of 0.19, so there is a 19% chance (approximately 1 in 5) of that occurring. If the seizure has 5 cocaine baggies and 95 samples that are not cocaine, the odds drop to about 1 in 300,000. Note that these are *probabilities*, not confidence levels. At this point, the treatment becomes more specialized and the interested reader is directed to excellent recent articles for detailed derivations of extensions of the hypergeometric distribution and probability theory to sample selection.[‡,12,14]

Finally, another article recommends a selection criterion based on the equation[11]

$$n = 20 + 0.10(N - 20), \text{ where } N > 20 \tag{2.20}$$

This equation has the virtue of simplicity and empirical support, although experiments were based solely on populations seen by the laboratory discussed in the article. The value of n is relatively large compared with that used in other approaches and has the virtue of being conservative.

2.2.6 SAMPLING AND QUANTITATION

Suppose a forensic chemist designs a sampling plan for the 100-baggie seizure that calls for presumptive testing of all 100 exhibits. All of the tests indicate cocaine, and a subset of 25 is selected for complete characterization. All 25 are confirmed to be cocaine. The analyst is then asked to determine the purity of the seizure. Once again, options abound: Should all 100 be quantitated? Each of the 25? A composite of the 100? A composite of 25? The answer will depend on the analytical results in hand. Once again, there is no single correct protocol.

If the presumptive, screening, and instrumental tests all indicate a similar composition, this supports the hypothesis that the bags are representatives of

---

[†]Microsoft Excel® has a built-in hypergeometric distribution function, HYPERGEOMDIST, that calculates probability.
[‡]Perhaps not surprisingly, another rich source of information on this approach, associated with gambling and lotteries, can be found on the Internet.

Historical Evidence 2.2—The Dreyfus Case

Alphonse Bertillon (French, 1853–1914), a pioneer in forensic science, was involved in an early case that employed probability-based arguments. Alfred Dreyfus was a French officer accused of selling military secrets. A document he admitted writing was seized as evidence against him. Using a grid, Bertillon analyzed the document and determined that 4 polysyllabic words out of 26 were positioned identically relative to the grid lines. Bertillon argued that such coincidence of positioning was highly unlikely with normal handwriting. Arguments were also made concerning the normal frequency of occurrence of letters in typical French versus those found in the questioned document. Subsequent analysis of the case and testimony showed that Bertillon's arguments were incorrect.

Source: Aitken, C. G. G., and F. Taroni. *Statistics and the Evaluation of Evidence for Forensic Scientists*, 2d ed. Chichester, U.K.: John Wiley and Sons, 2004, Section 4.2.

---

the sample population. If differences in composition are noted, then the samples should first be grouped. Perhaps half of the samples analyzed were cut with caffeine and half with procaine. All contain cocaine, but clearly two subpopulations exist and they should be treated separately.

Recall that the standard deviation is an expression of precision but that it is not additive. Variance, however, is additive and can be used as a starting point for devising a plan for quantitation. The overall uncertainty S_T in quantitative data will depend on two categories of uncertainty: that which arises from the analytical procedure (S_a) and that which is inherent to the sample (S_s):

$$S_T^2 = S_s^2 + S_a^2 \tag{2.21}$$

Given that methods used in a forensic laboratory will be validated and optimized, it is reasonable to assume that in most cases, the variance contributed by the analytical method will be significantly smaller than the variation arising from sampling. Thus, in most cases, S_a can be ignored. The goal of a sampling plan for quantitative analysis is to reduce the overall variance by reducing the sampling variance and confining it to acceptable ranges. The absolute error in any mean percent cocaine calculated from sampling several items can be expressed as the true value μ minus the calculated mean, or

$$\mu - \bar{x} = \frac{ts_s}{\sqrt{n}} \quad \text{or} \quad e = \frac{ts_s}{\sqrt{n}} \tag{2.22}$$

where e is the desired absolute error in the final result and t is obtained from the Student's t-table on the basis of the confidence level desired. Solving for n yields

$$n = \frac{t^2 s_s^2}{e^2} \tag{2.23}$$

In most cases, the difficulty is estimating S_s. If the initial assumption (that all samples are essentially the same or homogeneous) is correct, a smaller value would make sense; if appearance or other factors call this assumption into question, a larger value of S_s would be needed. Returning to the 100-baggie case, if a quantitative absolute error e of 5% is acceptable and a standard deviation of 7% is anticipated, the number of samples needed to obtain a mean with a 95% CI would be calculated iteratively, starting with the assumption that the number of degrees of freedom is infinite:

$$n = \frac{1.960^2(0.07)^2}{0.05^2} = 7.53 \approx 7$$

Now, the actual number of degrees of freedom is 6, and the calculation is repeated with the new value of t:

$$n = \frac{2.447^2(0.07)^2}{0.05^2} \approx 12$$

The process continues until the solution converges on $n = 10$. Notice that the number of pieces of evidence in the seizure (size of the larger parent population) is never given. The only consideration is the variance among the individual pieces. The weakness of the procedure is the estimation of S_s, but analyst experience can assist in such cases. This approach can also be used to select the size of a representative subset for sampling.

2.2.7 BAYESIAN STATISTICS

This topic is a proverbial hot potato in the forensic community. Whether one agrees or disagrees with how it has been applied, it hurts nothing to be familiar with it.[†] This section is meant only to provide a brief overview of a Bayesian approach to sampling statistics. For more information, Aitken's book (see "Further Reading" section at end of chapter) is highly recommended. Bayesian statistics formally and quantitatively incorporates prior knowledge into calculations of probability. This feature was touched upon in the 100-baggie example, in which the analyst used experience with similar cases to estimate the ratio of exhibits likely to contain cocaine to the total number of bags seized (ratio expressed as θ). Bayesian statistics can and has been used in many areas of forensic science and forensic chemistry, including sample selection and analysis. The controversy over its use centers on whether the introduction of analyst judgment is subjective rather than objective. As will be seen, applied with due care and thought, this method becomes another valuable tool with strengths and weaknesses akin to those of any other instrument.

The Bayesian approach is a logical addition to the hypergeometric distribution and binomial distribution techniques introduced earlier.[14] The idea behind the hypergeometric distribution is that, in a finite population such as a deck of cards or a drug seizure, a probability can be assigned to test results if there is knowledge of the possible outcomes. For a large drug seizure of N samples, a subset n can be removed and tested. For each test, the result is either positive or negative, so a fraction of positives in the subset can be calculated as m/n where m is the number of positives. A probability can then be assigned to the proportion M/N of positives in the parent population. This approach echoes the point made earlier that the better the selection of the subset n, the better the composition of n represents the composition of the parent population. Bayes's theorem can be invoked to rephrase this relationship in order to assist in selecting n and estimating M.[14]

[†]As evidence of the depth of feeling on this topic, one text (K. Inman and N. Rudin, *Principles and Practices of Criminalistics*, (Boca Raton, FL: CRC Press, 2001)) warns readers that "this approach should be viewed as a tool, not a religion" (p.143).

A Bayesian approach is based on a likelihood ratio that takes into account information that the analyst supplies. A generalized form of this ratio is[14]

$$\Pr(H_m \mid N, n, m) = \frac{\Pr(m \mid H_m, n, M)\Pr(H_m \mid N)}{\sum \Pr(m \mid H_m, n, N)\Pr(H_m \mid N)} \quad (2.24)$$

where Pr denotes probability and H_m is the hypothesis based on m. Although complicated, the expression essentially states that the probability of any one hypothesis being true depends on how likely that outcome is, given all other possible outcomes. Equation (2.24) can be solved with factorials[12] or, more conveniently, by the Excel function mentioned previously. With a set of hypotheses, the result is a set of probabilities that allow for the selection of a defensible sample size m. The prior probability is $\Pr(H_m \mid N)$, the probability of the hypothesis being true for sample size N before analysis.

The article by Coulson, et al.,[14] uses a spreadsheet to delve in detail into the implementation of this approach and provides an example of 100 exhibits similar to our 100 baggies example. In the example from this report the analyst first hypothesizes, on the basis of observation, that all exhibits are homogenous and represent the same population. That is, $\Pr(\text{hom}) = 0.99$. This means that all the exhibits will be positive or all will be negative. From experience (prior knowledge or posterior knowledge), the analyst also hypothesizes that 60% will be positive, or $\Pr(\text{pos} \mid \text{hom}) = 0.6$. If all of the exhibits were tested, there would be 101 possible outcomes: 100 positive; 100 negative; and 99 combinations running from $99:1, 98:2, \ldots, 1:99$. The method allows the probabilities of each of these outcomes to be calculated. If 5 exhibits are tested and are positive, the probability of all 100 being positive is 0.9973; if 50 are analyzed, the probability increases to 0.9998.

Applying the Science 2.1 Sample Selection for Weighing

The weights of exhibits are an important issue in some cases, and in large seizures it may be impractical to weigh each sample, just as it is impractical to test all the samples. The problem is that total weights must be reported to a reasonable degree of certainty. In Israel, the solution has been both legislative and scientific. The law defines the sampling protocol to be used, assuming that the samples all appear similar: According to this protocol, the sample size (n) from the total population (N) depends on the population size: 5 of a population up to 15 units, 6 between 16 and 50 units, and 7 if the population exceeds 51 units. Each randomly selected sample is weighed on a balance that is linked to a computer which calculates the mean S and a 95%CI for the weights, based on the weights of the random subset. The acceptance criterion is

$$\frac{1.96 \times 0.1}{\overline{x}} \times 100 \approx \leq 15\%$$

where 0.1 is the uncertainty expected for the mean weight. If the calculated value exceeds 15%, the analyst weighs more exhibits until all are weighed or the acceptance criterion is satisfied. As an example, if the mean were 3.0 g and the associated uncertainty at that weight were 0.3 g, the calculation would be $((1.96 \times 0.3)/3.0) \times 100$, or 19.6%. If this were the case, the examiner would have to weigh more exhibits.

To test the procedure, the laboratory evaluated approximately 1500 seized units in different ways to compare the estimated weights with the actual ones. The findings showed that, for about 88% of the exhibits, the actual weight was within the 95% CI, and a potential bias in sampling procedure was noted. Original estimates were lower than the true weight by approximately 0.7%, suggesting that the selection of individual exhibits for *n* may not be completely random or representative. The authors offered computerized random selection as a way to eliminate any analyst bias.

Source: Azoury, M., et al. "Evaluation of a Sampling Procedure for Heroin Street Doses." *Journal of Forensic Sciences*, 43 **1998**, 1202–1207.

SUMMARY

Statistics is a fundamental and quantitative component of quality assurance. Statistics is also a powerful tool for the forensic chemist, in that it can describe the accuracy and precision of data, assist in answering hypothesis-based questions, and identify trends and patterns in data. Statistics and the related tools of probability can be applied to direct sampling and provide a reasonable, defensible, and sensible sampling plan. With such a plan in hand, we are ready to move on to multivariate statistics, calibration, and the unification of these concepts under the umbrella of quality assurance and quality control.

KEY TERMS AND CONCEPTS

Absolute error	Mean	Sample size (N/n)
Absolute uncertainty	Normalization	Sampling statistics
Bayesian statistics	Outlier	Significance test
Bell curve	Population	Significant figures
Binomial distribution	Probability sampling	Standard deviation
Dixon's test	Propagation of uncertainty	Total quality management
Gaussian curve/distribution	Q test	Type I error
Grubbs test	Quality control	Type II error
Homogeneous	Relative error	Uncertainty
Hypergeometric distribution	Relative uncertainty	Variance
Hypothesis	Representative sample	z-transform

PROBLEMS

From the chapter

1. A standard of Pb^{2+} for a gunshot residue analysis using atomic absorption is prepared by first dissolving 1.0390 g dried $Pb(NO_3)_2$ in distilled water containing 1% nitric acid. The solution is brought to volume in a class-A 500-mL volumetric flask with an uncertainty of ± 0.20 mL. The solution is then diluted 1/10 by taking 10 mL (via an Eppendorf pipet, tolerance $\pm 1.3\ \mu L$) and diluting this in 1% nitric acid to a final volume of 100 mL in a volumetric flask with a tolerance of ± 0.08 mL. The balance has an uncertainty of ± 0.0002 gram.
   a. Using conventional rounding rules, calculate the concentration of the final solution of Pb^{2+}, in ppm.
   b. Determine the absolute and relative uncertainties of each value obtained in part a. Select the largest and report the results as a concentration range.
   c. Report the results as a range by the propagation-of-error method.
   d. Comment on your findings and why this case is somewhat unique.

2. If an outlier is on the low side of the mean, as in the example in the chapter, could a one-tailed table be used?

3. Find the following reference for Q value tables: Rorabacher, D. B. "Statistical Treatment for Rejection of Deviant Values: Critical Values of Dixon's 'Q' Parameter and Related Subrange Ratios at the 95% Confidence Level." *Analytical Chemistry*, 63 **1991**, 139–148. For the trainee/forensic chemist example used throughout this chapter, determine what the percent cocaine would have to be in the 11th sample for it to be eliminated at the following significance levels: 0.20, 0.10, 0.05, 0.04, 0.02, and 0.01. Present your findings graphically and comment on them.

4. Differentiate clearly between statistical and analytical errors.

5. Justify or explain the use of the factor 3 in equation 2.12.

6. The results of equation 2.14 blatantly ignore significant-figure conventions. Why?

7. a. A large seizure containing 1500 individually packaged units of a tan powder arrives at the laboratory. All units appear similar, and each weighs a kilogram. This is an unusual case unlike any seen before in this facility, and the laboratory staff has neither the time nor the resources to test all 1500 units. Design a sampling plan for qualitative analysis based on the methods described in the text. Summarize the outcome and justify a final value of n. As appropriate, note any assumptions made.
   b. The recommendation you made in part a is accepted, and the selected subset is tested and found to contain heroin, with all samples appearing to come from

the same batch. The federal prosecutor needs to know the average percent heroin in the seizure with an accuracy of ±5% (relative) and a precision of ±2%. Design a sampling plan for quantitation and defend the plan.

8. A small seizure consisting of 30 blotter papers of suspected LSD is submitted to the laboratory.
   a. Design a sampling plan, assuming that the contents of a minimum of three papers will be needed to obtain a sample sufficient for presumptive and confirmatory testing.
   b. After selecting n samples and testing them, you find that all are negative. Describe the next steps in the analysis.
   c. At what point in this analysis would it be appropriate to call the results negative for LSD?
   d. Assume that all samples tested are negative until four squares are left. Testing one gives a positive result. Using a flowchart, describe the next step(s) and any assumptions made.

   This problem will be seen again in a later chapter, where additional analytical information can be brought to bear on its solution.

9. An analyst proposes a new method for analyzing blood alcohol. As part of a method validation study, she analyzes a blind sample five times and obtains the following results: 0.055%, 0.054%, 0.055%, 0.052%, and 0.056%.
   a. Are there outliers in the data?
   b. On the basis of the results of the outlier analysis and subsequent actions, calculate the mean and the %RSD of the analyst's results.
   c. If the true value of the blind sample is 0.053% ±0.002% (based on a range of ±2s), is the mean value obtained by the analyst the same as the true value at p = 0.05?

Integrative

1. Use the Excel function for the hypergeometric distribution to calculate the probability of selecting five samples that will be positive for cocaine if a seizure contains 1000 baggies and past laboratory data suggest that 50% of such recent seizures are cocaine and the rest are not. Study the results and explain how the hypergeometric distribution is similar to a simple binomial distribution.

2. What is the difference between a confidence level and a probability?

3. A university instructs its professors to assign grades in the range from 0.0 for an F to 4.0 for an A+. The letter grade is not recorded; only the number grade is. When students' GPAs are calculated, they are reported to three decimal places. Can this be justified by the rules of significant figures?

4. Are random samples representative by definition? Are representative samples random by definition? What condition must exist for each of these questions to be answered affirmatively?

5. Why can there never be such a thing as a true value?

6. A government agency, the National Institute of Standards and Technology (NIST), provides certified reference materials to forensic laboratories. Research how NIST certifies a reference material, and comment on how this approach facilities reliability.

7. What is the difference between a hypothetical question and a hypothesis-based question?

Food for thought

1. If a laboratory receives a case containing 100 baggies of white powder, why not cut to the chase and test all of them?

FURTHER READING

Aitken, C. G. G., and F. Taroni. *Statistics and the Evaluation of Evidence for Forensic Scientists*, 2d ed. Chichester, U.K.: John Wiley and Sons, **2004**.

Billo, J. *Excel for Chemists: A Comprehensive Guide*, 2d ed. New York: John Wiley and Sons, **2001**.

Hair, J. F., et al. *Multivariate Data Analysis*, 5th ed. Upper Saddle River, NJ: Prentice Hall, **1998**.

Kanji, G. K. *100 Statistical Tests*. London: Sage Publications, Ltd., **2000**.

Moore, D. S., and G. P. McCabe, *Introduction to the Practice of Statistics*, 4th ed. New York: W. H. Freeman, **2003**.

Patniak, P. *Dean's Analytical Chemistry Handbook*, 2d ed. New York: McGraw-Hill, **2004** (Section 3: "Statistics in Chemical Analysis").

Ross, S. M. *Introduction to Probability and Statistics for Engineers*. New York: John Wiley and Sons, **1987**.

REFERENCES

1. "Standard Practice for Using Significant Digits in Test Data to Determine Conformance with Specifications," in *ASTM 14.02*. West Conshohocken, PA: ASTM International, **2004**,

2. Miller, J. N., and J. C. Miller. "Statistics of Repeated Measurements," in J. N. Miller and J. C. Miller, *Statistics and Chemometrics for Analytical Chemistry*, 4th ed. Upper Saddle River, NJ: Prentice Hall, **2000**, 80–90.

3. Rorabacher, D. B. "Statistical Treatment for Rejection of Deviant Values: Critical Values of Dixon's 'Q' Parameter and Related Subrange Ratios at the 95% Confidence Level." *Analytical Chemistry*, 63 **1991**, 139–148.

4. Kanji, G. K. *100 Statistical Tests*. London: Sage Publications, Ltd., **2000**.

5. "Standard Practice for Calculating Sample Size to Estimate, with a Specified Tolerable Error, the Average Characteristics of a Lot or Process," in *ASTM Standard E 122-00*, 14.02, ASTM International, **2004**,

6. "Standard Practice for Dealing With Outlying Observations," in *ASTM Standard E 178-02*, 14.02, ASTM International, **2004**,

7. Miller, J. N. and J. C. Miller, "Significance Tests," in *Statistics and Chemometrics for Analytical Chemistry*, 4th ed. Upper Saddle River, NJ: Prentice Hall, **2000**, 54–57.

8. Moenssens, A. A., et al. "Drugs and Their Control: Section V: Special Defenses, 14.25, Quantitative Considerations," in A. A. Moenssens, et al., *Scientific Evidence in Civil and Criminal Cases*, 4th ed. Westbury, NY: The Foundation Press, Inc., **1995**, 859–860.

9. Frank, R. S., et al. "Representative Sampling of Drug Seizures in Multiple Containers." *Journal of Forensic Sciences*, 36 **1991**, 350–357.

10. "Standard Practice for Probability Sampling of Materials," in *ASTM Standard E 105-58*, 14.02, ASTM International, **2004**,

11. Colon, M., et al. "Representative Sampling of 'Street' Drug Exhibits." *Journal of Forensic Sciences*, 38 **1993**, 641–648.

12. Aitken, C. G. G. "Sampling—How Big a Sample?" *Journal of Forensic Sciences*, 44 **1999**, 750–760.

13. Weisstein, E. W. "Hypergeometric Distribution." *Mathworld*, June 12, 2004. On the Internet at http://mathworld.wolfram.com.

14. Coulson, S. A., et al. "How Many Samples from a Drug Seizure Need to Be Analyzed?" *Journal of Forensic Sciences*, 46 **2001**, 1456–1461.

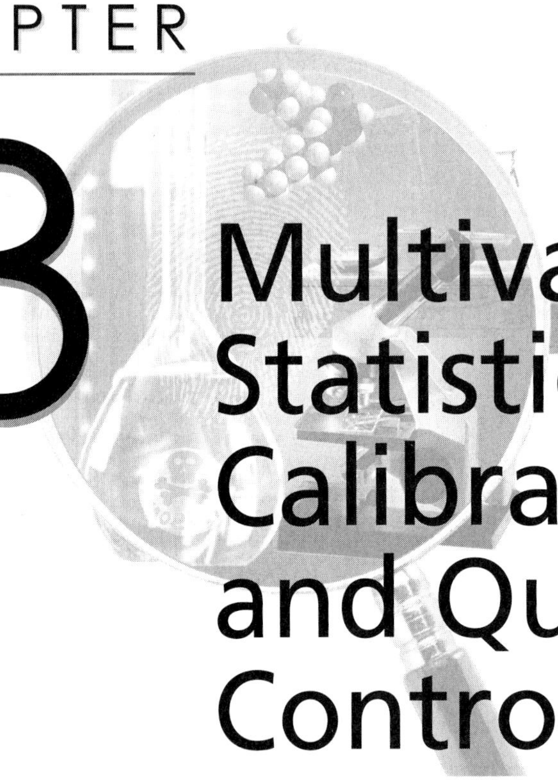

3

Multivariate Statistics, Calibration, and Quality Control

OVERVIEW AND ORIENTATION

Quality assurance (QA) is an all-encompassing, "cradle-to-grave" system that controls data generation. **Quality control (QC)** usually has to do with the procedures, policies, and practices designed to assure data quality. As shown in Figure 3.1, QA defines the triangle and QC populates it. Validated analytical methods, laboratory accreditation, blanks, replicates, and legally defensible documentation are all part of quality assurance. The system incorporates multiple reviews and can be viewed as an integrated, layered structure of redundant checks and protocols that relate directly or indirectly to data generated at the bench level. Quality assurance is dynamic, is evolving, and requires daily care and maintenance to remain viable.

The quantitative foundation of QA lies in (1) the presence of analytical data and (2) statistical tools and what they say about the **reliability** and **uncertainty** of the data. Statistics enables the analyst to evaluate and judge data and methods. We reviewed these essential concepts in the previous chapter, but before diving into QA/QC, we will delve briefly into multivariate statistics.

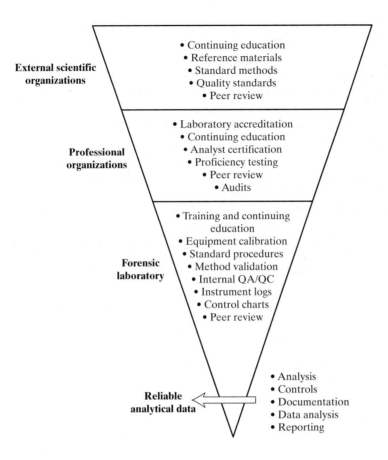

External scientific organizations
- Continuing education
- Reference materials
- Standard methods
- Quality standards
- Peer review

Professional organizations
- Laboratory accreditation
- Continuing education
- Analyst certification
- Proficiency testing
- Peer review
- Audits

Forensic laboratory
- Training and continuing education
- Equipment calibration
- Standard procedures
- Method validation
- Internal QA/QC
- Instrument logs
- Control charts
- Peer review

Reliable analytical data
- Analysis
- Controls
- Documentation
- Data analysis
- Reporting

◀ **Figure 3.1** *The layered nature of quality assurance. This chapter will discuss the specific elements shown in the layers.*

3.1 MULTIVARIATE STATISTICS AND CHEMOMETRICS

Chapter 2 focused on characteristics of single variables, both categorical and continuous. An analysis to determine the percent of a drug in a white powder sample yields a continuous variable since the value can lie anywhere between 0.0 and 100.0. Analysis of a fiber yields categorical data such as "red" and "nylon." Identification of green plant matter is another example of categorical data—either the sample is marijuana or it isn't.

Real analytical data are more complex and multivariate, even if other variables are not examined or used. If a white powder arrives at the laboratory, the following descriptors, among others, could be considered as variables: identity, weight, concentration, cutting agents, and concentration of each cutting agent. Some of these variables are continuous whereas others are categorical. In many cases, it is advantageous to study samples from the multivariate perspective. As with so many aspects of forensic chemistry, **multivariate statistics** (the application of statistics to data sets with more than one variable) is a separate field to which entire textbooks are devoted. Accordingly, this brief section will introduce the concepts most used in forensic chemistry and reported in the forensic literature; more detailed treatments can be found in the references and recommended readings. Our goal here is only to attain familiarity and, hopefully, whet your appetite for further study.

The tasks that require multivariate statistics can be divided into descriptive, predictive, and classification. The term "exploratory data analysis" (EDA) is sometimes used to describe such multivariate applications. The discipline within chemistry that focuses on the analysis of chemical data, EDA, and modeling is called **chemometrics**.

3.1.1 Predictive Modeling and Calibration

A good place to begin the discussion of multivariate predictive modeling is with a univariate model chemists are familiar with: linear regression. Regression lines are used to calibrate instruments and take the familiar form y = mx + b, where m is the slope and b is the y-intercept, or simply intercept. The variable y is called the **dependent variable**, since its value is dictated by x, the **independent variable**. All linear calibration curves share certain generic features, as shown in Figure 3.2. The range in which the relationship between concentration and response is linear is called the linear range and is typically described by "orders of magnitude." A calibration curve that is linear from 1 ppb to 1 ppm, a factor of 1000, has a linear dynamic range (LDR) of three orders of magnitude. At higher concentrations, most detectors become saturated and the response flattens out; the calibration curve is not valid in this range of higher concentrations, and samples with concentrations above the last linear point on the curve must be diluted before quantitation. The concentration corresponding to the lowest concentration in the linear range is called the **limit of quantitation** (LOQ). Instruments may detect a response below this concentration, but it is not predictable and the line cannot be extrapolated to concentrations smaller than the LOQ. The concentration at which no significant response can be detected is the **limit of detection**, or LOD.

The line generated by a least-squares regression results from fitting empirical data to a line that has the minimum total deviation from all of the points. The method is called **least squares** because distances from the line are squared to prevent points that are displaced above the line (signified by a plus sign, +) from canceling those displaced below the line (signified by a minus sign, −). Most **linear regression** implementations have an option to "force the line through the origin," which means forcing the intercept of the line through the point (0,0). This might seem reasonable, since a sample with no detectable cocaine should produce no response in a detector. However, forcing the curve through the origin is not

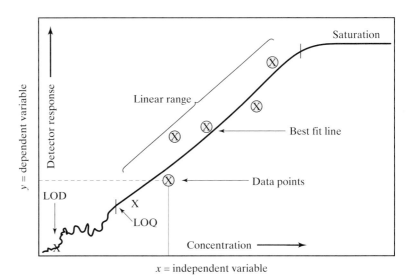

▶ **Figure 3.2** *General features of linear calibration curves.*

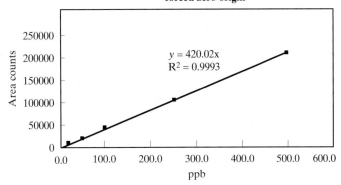

1. Cocaine calibration nonzero origin

ppb cocaine	Peak area
20.0	9599
50.0	21456
100.0	45326
250.0	102391
500.0	210561

Sample data:
Peak area = 72003
Concentration (1): 171.4
Concentration (2): 169.9

$y = 416.59x + 1213.7$
$R^2 = 0.9994$

2. Cocaine calibration forced zero origin

$y = 420.02x$
$R^2 = 0.9993$

◄ **Figure 3.3** *Problems associated with forcing a calibration curve through the origin. The bottom line includes the point (0,0) while the top line uses only empirical data. Calibration lines should not be arbitrarily forced through the origin, as shown by the two different values calculated for the sample.*

always recommended, since most curves are run well above the instrumental limit of detection (LOD). Arbitrarily adding a point (0,0) can skew the curve because the instrument's response near the LOD is not predictable and is rarely linear, as shown in Figure 3.2. As illustrated in Figure 3.3, forcing a curve through the origin can, under some circumstances, bias results.

The goodness of fit of the line is measured by the **correlation coefficient** or more frequently as its squared value (R^2):

$$R^2 = \frac{\left[\sum (x_i - \bar{x})(y_i - \bar{y}) \right]^2}{\sum (x_i - \bar{x})^2 \sum (y_i - \bar{y})^2} \tag{3.1}$$

The value of R^2 will range between -1 and $+1$ and is a measure of linearity of the points. If $R^2 = 1.0$, the line is perfectly correlated and has a positive slope whereas $R^2 = -1$ describes a perfectly correlated line with a negative slope (Figure 3.4). If there is no correlation, $R^2 = 0$. It is important to remember that R^2 is but one measure of the goodness of a calibration curve, and all curves should be inspected visually as a second level of control. More about calibration curves will be presented later in the chapter.

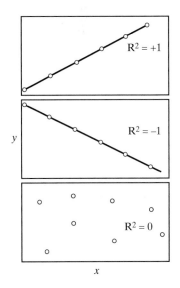

$R^2 = +1$

$R^2 = -1$

$R^2 = 0$

▲ **Figure 3.4** *Relationship of correlation coefficient (R^2) to linear fit. Typical calibration curves are at least "two nines," or 0.99. The value of (R^2) is an important criterion, but not the only one, for describing the goodness of the calibration curve.*

3.1.2 EXPLORATORY DATA ANALYSIS (EDA): PROFILING COCAINE

Linear calibration is a form of predictive modeling using a single dependent variable. Approached from a different perspective, one could explore a calibration

Exhibit A: Just Do It (Again)

There are a number of statistical tests and analyses that can be used to evaluate a calibration curve and to weigh the "goodness" of each calibration data point. As shown in the accompanying figure, one of the calibration points appears to be an outlier and including it would skew the calibration curve significantly. What is the best course of action? Clearly the point "looks funny," but, what should the next action be?

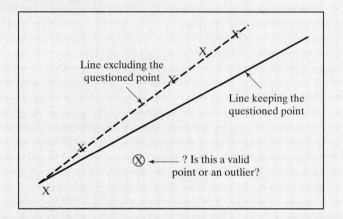

There is no justification for throwing the point away on a hunch. Of course it looks suspicious, but the question is, Why? Is it a symptom of an underlying problem, or is it just a fluke? There is only one way to resolve the issue, and it does not involve a calculation or a hypothesis test. The next step involves laboratory work. The suspicious solution would be rerun to see if the results are replicated. If so, then a fresh solution should be prepared and retested. Depending on the results, the entire calibration series may have to be prepared fresh and reanalyzed. Even then, though, the answer to this question has little to do with calculations, identifying outliers, or weighting the questionable point less than that of the other calibration points. Once again, it's a matter of *chemistry before statistics*.

Table 3.1 Hypothetical Data, Three Cocaine Seizures

Case ID	%Cocaine	%Procaine	%Caffeine
A1	34	16	7.2
A2	24	15	4.3
A3	20	15	4.3
A4	24	11	6.9
A5	29	14	4.1
A6	31	12	7.0
A7	21	15	6.9
A8	26	13	4.5
A9	30	13	4.4
A10	20	11	4.3
B1	14	26	6.3
B2	9	16	4.7
B3	7	20	5.0
B4	13	21	5.4
B5	8	20	4.1
B6	12	20	3.8
B7	8	16	5.0
B8	7	16	4.0
B9	11	19	4.0

Table 3.1	(Continued)		
Case ID	%Cocaine	%Procaine	%Caffeine
B10	6	16	3.2
C1	15	20	5.6
C2	9	16	3.6
C3	13	18	5.6
C4	11	18	3.3
C5	14	15	4.5
C6	7	17	4.2
C7	12	17	3.7
C8	12	20	3.9
C9	7	18	5.4
C10	7	15	3.3

dataset and quickly identify a linear relationship between concentration and response. One of the greatest utilities of multivariate analysis is in studying data and identifying relationships or patterns within the data, particularly within large data sets. In the discussion that follows, we consider a hypothetical example (Table 3.1). A laboratory receives three separate cocaine seizures, each containing 10 individually wrapped exhibits. Externally, all 30 powders appear similar. All contain cocaine, and all are diluted with a combination of procaine and caffeine, although in differing concentration ratios. The investigatory question is how the samples are related to each other beyond the obvious qualitative similarities. In other words, are there groups or patterns in the data?

Any EDA project must begin with an examination of the data and a thorough study of **correlations** and other relationships. In this simple example, the data are three dimensional and can be visually examined as shown in Figure 3.5. The plot indicates that case A appears different from case B and case C, which are grouped together. Furthermore, the distinguishing feature is the greater concentration of cocaine within A relative to B and C, which could indicate to the investigators that A had a source different from that of B or C or possibly that B and C are derivatives of A. The means, standard deviations, and uncertainty for each variable (Figure 3.6) show that the caffeine concentration is smaller and exhibits less variation than do the other two components.

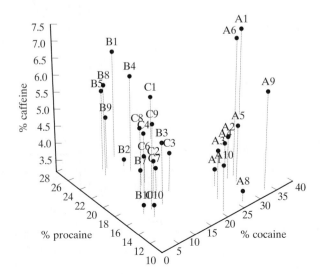

◀ **Figure 3.5** *Plot of the data from the three hypothetical cocaine seizures. Two groups can be distinguished: A and B + C.*

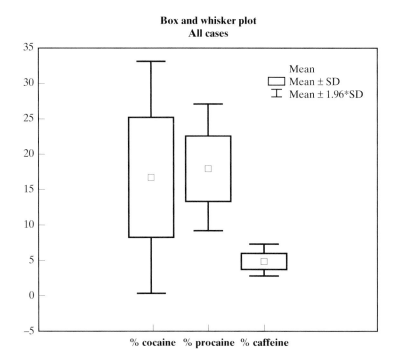

▶ **Figure 3.6** *The mean, standard deviation, and uncertainty (1.96 × SD) for each variable; N = 30.*

Correlations between the variables are next examined to see if there are any linear relationships among them. The scatterplots (Figure 3.7) hint at a correlation between cocaine and procaine; statistical analysis (Table 3.2) cements it. The table data shows that we can be 95% confident that there is a negative correlation between cocaine and procaine in the samples: as the cocaine concentration increases, the procaine concentration tends to decrease. This correlation implies that because one variable is correlated with the other, it may be possible to express the relationship by a linear equation.

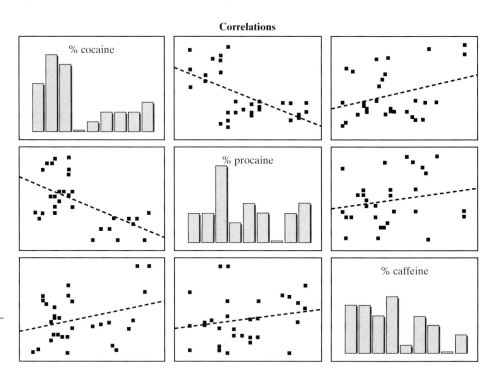

▶ **Figure 3.7** *Scatterplots of the three variables, along with histograms of each.*

Table 3.2	Correlation Matrix: r values		
	%Cocaine	%Procaine	%Caffeine
%Cocaine	1.00	−**0.59***	0.31
%Procaine	−**0.59***	1.00	0.19
%Caffeine	0.31	0.19	1.00

*Significant at $p < 0.05$.

Example Problem 3.1

The distributions shown in the histograms of Figure 3.7 indicate that the distribution of the variables %cocaine, %procaine, and %caffeine do not appear to be Gaussian. How will this affect the calculation of linear correlations and subsequent linear combinations?

Answer: A normal distribution of the variables is neither required nor assumed for linear correlation. Consequently, any applied techniques that are based on linear correlations and combinations will not be affected.

For statistical tests or analyses that do assume a normal distribution, there are tests that can be used to evaluate the distribution of the variables compared with a normal distribution. Two such functions are the kurtosis and the skewness, both of which are easily implemented with spreadsheet functions.

3.1.3 PRINCIPAL COMPONENT ANALYSIS (PCA)

When linear relationships exist among variables, PCA can be used to find groups and patterns within data by reducing the dimensionality of the data. For the current example, this might not seem a significant accomplishment, but consider a more complex example in which the cocaine samples are characterized by dozens of descriptor variables, such as the concentration of other alkaloids, trace impurities from processing, the concentrations of five or more diluents, etc. When the number of variables exceeds three, graphical data exploration is no longer feasible. Thus, combining variables to reduce the dimensionality of the data is an important step in simplifying and understanding more about the structure of the data set. In our hypothetical example, since a statistically significant linear correlation exists between cocaine and procaine, it should be possible to combine those two variables into a linear equation such that when the value of one is known, the value of the other can be predicted.

Formally, the purpose of PCA is to create or find such correlations and create linear combinations of variables that reduce the dimensionality of the data. In this example with three variables, three principal components exist:

$$Z_1 = a_{11}X_1 + a_{12}X_2 + a_{13}X_3$$
$$Z_2 = a_{21}X_1 + a_{22}X_2 + a_{23}X_3$$
$$Z_3 = a_{31}X_1 + a_{32}X_2 + a_{33}X_3 \tag{3.2}$$

Each principal component (Z) is a linear combination of all three variables (X), and the coefficients (a) are assigned such that the new variables ($Z_n, n = 1, \ldots, 3$) are not correlated and so that the first principal component accounts for the largest possible variance (V; see Chapter 2) in the data set, the second principal component the next-largest possible variance, etc. Each new variable Z_n refers to a new and previously hidden relationship among the original variables. The new variables are also referred to as **factors**.

A plot of the variance accounted for by the linear combination is shown in Figure 3.8. If there is sufficient correlation among variables such that the linear

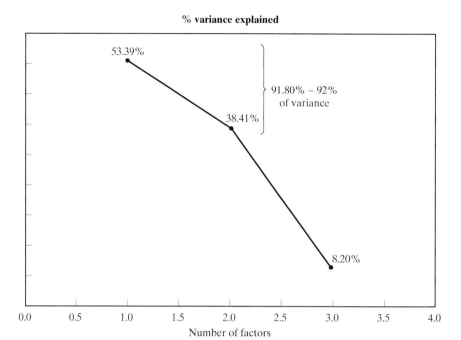

▶ **Figure 3.8** *The first two principal components account for nearly 92% of the total variance in the system and imply that a plot of the data points using the first two PCs will retain most of the information provided by the original three variables. The dimensionality has been reduced from 3 to 2.*

combinations can capture it, the end result can be a reduction in the dimensionality of the data. In this case, two new variables are able to capture the essential information nearly as well as three because 2 are linearly related.

When the data are plotted with the use of the loadings for the first two factors (the degree of correlation of each old variable with the two new ones Z_1 and Z_2, Figure 3.9), the pattern seen in Figure 3.5 is re-created, but in two dimensions rather than three. Set A is clearly different from the group consisting

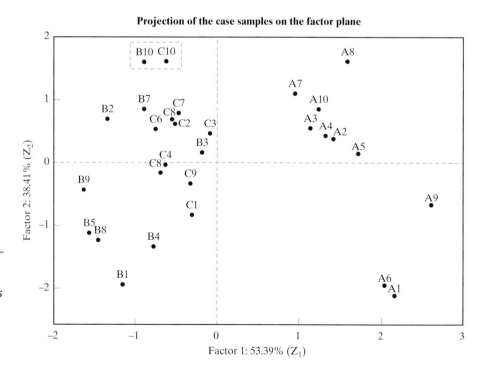

▶ **Figure 3.9** *The separation of A from BC is clear, as are some interesting relationships with the combined B and C group. The closeness of B10 and C10 is a point of interest for a later discussion.*

of sets B and C. Such a change might not be terribly exciting with small data sets, but it is a powerful tool with data sets with tens or hundreds of variables, which is not unusual in projects such as profiling drugs (Chapter 6). PCA is also used to reduce the number of variables prior to more advanced modeling and analysis.

Applying the Science 3.1   Narcotics Classification with Raman Spectroscopy and PCA

One of the strengths of PCA is its capability of reducing the dimensionality of data sets with very large numbers of variables. Spectra, be they infrared (IR), ultraviolet (UV), or Raman, consist of dozens or hundreds of variables that correspond to absorbances at given wavelengths. Since the responses at some wavelengths may be correlated, PCA can be helpful in exploring such data sets. In a recent report, PCA was applied to Raman spectra of 85 samples of various drugs and diluents in an attempt to distinguish and group the samples. Raman spectroscopy is described in detail in Chapter 5, but suffice it for now to say that it is a vibrational spectroscopy technique that complements IR and is based on scattered, rather than absorbed, radiation. The accompanying figure shows the variety of spectral response seen within the data set and points out the number of variables involved. The range covered is ~700 cm^{-1}; if the spectrometer has a resolution of 4 cm^{-1}, the 700 cm^{-1} corresponds to 175 data points per spectrum, or 175 variables, compared with the 3 variables in the example we just went through. Thus, compressing the dimensionality is essential to visualizing any relationships and, as was the case in this report, to visually discriminating among the different types of drug samples.

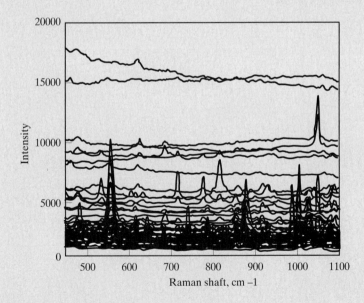

◀ *Raman spectra of the sample set illustrating the large spectral variations and complexity of vibrational bands. Figure reproduced with permission from the reference at end of box. Copyright 2002, ASTM International*

The author of this report noted that PCA on the spectra was at first unrevealing, but that, by taking the first derivative of each spectrum (normalized) and using that as the input data, PCA was effective even with just the first two principal components, which together accounted for 41% of the variance within the data set. The next two principal components were not helpful, which is not an uncommon occurrence. By weighting the wavenumber channels for the different drugs (cocaine, MDMA, and heroin), the technique also revealed patterns within each group. With this approach, the first two principal components accounted for 96% of the variance. The spectra illustrate the contribution of a diluent (sodium bicarbonate) and also indicate that spectra with similar response patterns, but different intensities (which can be related to relative concentrations), can be discriminated. This report is a good example of how multivariate methods are used for data exploration, to understand variables, and for practical identification and classification tasks.

Applying the Science 3.1 (Continued)

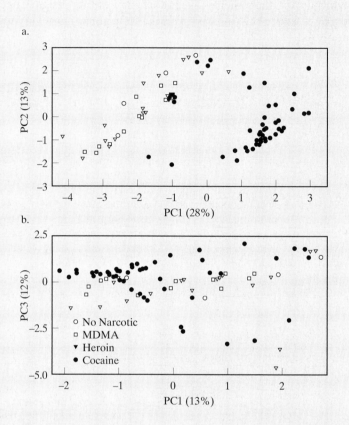

▶ Two-dimensional score plots from PCA model of 1st derivative of Raman spectra from 85 samples with all spectral variables showing: (A) partial separation of the cocaine (·) containing samples from the remainder along PC1 axis, and (B) no narcotic discrimination along PC2 or PC3 axes. Figure reproduced with permission from the reference at end of box. Copyright 2002, ASTM International.

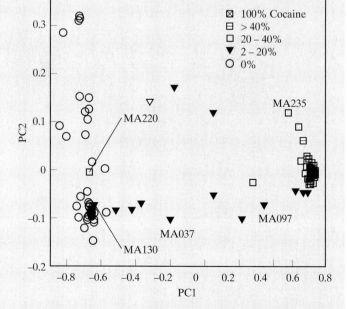

▶ Scores plot from a PCA model of 1st derivative Raman spectra with selective weighting of cocaine peaks, showing separation of the cocaine containing samples. MA130 and MA220 outliers are also marked. The explained x-variables is 94% for PC1 and 2% for PC2.

Applying the Science 3.1 (Continued)

a.

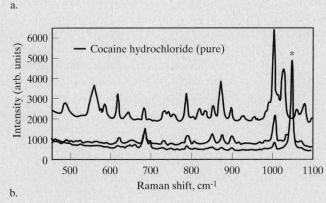

b.

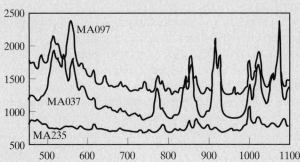

◀ *Raman spectra of outliers, MA130 (lowest) and MA220 (middle) with spectrum of cocaine hydrochloride (top) for comparison NaHCO₃, diluent peaks are marked by an asterisk. (B) Raman spectra of some of the discriminated samples. Figures reproduced with permission from the reference below. Copyright 2002, ASTM International.*

Source: Ryder, A. "Classification of Narcotics in a Solid Mixture Using Principal Component Analysis and Raman Spectroscopy." *Journal of Forensic Sciences*, 47 **2002**, 275–284.

3.1.4 CLUSTERING

Another versatile tool for EDA is cluster analysis. In this protocol, data points are considered to be points in a space called the "data space," regardless of the dimensionality of that space. Clustering can be performed on data with 10 variables as well as those with 3. Unlike PCA, the dimensionality is not reduced. Rather, the goal of clustering analysis is to identify like groups by measuring their separation in space, be this space 3-, 10-, or 100-dimensional, and to express the groups (clusters) in an interpretable graphical form. The units of the distances measured are defined by the variables and are not themselves important; what matters is the relative separation of the points.

Many metrics exist for measuring separation of data points in the so called "data space," the most common being the Euclidean distance

$$d = \sqrt{(x_1 - y_1)^2 + (x_2 - y_2)^2 + \cdots + (x_n - y_n)^2} \qquad (3.3)$$

where n is the number of variables. For example, the raw distance (i.e., when the data are not scaled) between points A1 and A6 (Table 3.1) can be calculated as

$$d_{A1-A6} = \sqrt{(34 - 31)^2 + (16 - 15)^2} = \sqrt{10} = 3.2$$

compared with the distance between A1 and B2:

$$d_{A1-B2} = \sqrt{(34 - 14)^2 + (16 - 24)^2 + (7.2 - 3.2)^2} = \sqrt{480} = 21.9$$

In practice, data may be normalized or scaled before cluster analysis is performed, since very large values will tend to overwhelm smaller ones. A common normalization is the **z-transform**, seen earlier in equation 2-9. To apply this transform, the mean and standard deviation of each column (each variable) are calculated. Each value within a column is then standardized by determining its separation from the mean and dividing by the standard deviation. An example for the cocaine variable normalization is shown in Figure 3.10. Such a transform becomes important when the range of variables covers approximately two or more orders of magnitude. Assume we add another variable to our example dataset, the concentration of a trace constituent of the cocaine leaf. Further assume that this percentage varies from 0.01% to 0.0001% or over 3 orders of magnitude, a factor of 1000. This variable could be essential in classifying our cocaine cases, but since 0.01% is far smaller in absolute terms than 1–100%, all this information will be lost unless the data is normalized. Similarly, standardization is essential if units are mixed. In the current example, all concentrations are reported as percentages, but if other units (e.g., absorbance, ratios, ppb), are used in variables, the "apples and oranges" comparison problem results. The z-transform of each variable eliminates this problem by scaling all values relative to the mean and standard deviation of each.

One approach to cluster analysis begins by assuming that each point is a cluster (Figure 3.11). The algorithm involved calculates the distance between each cluster and all the others. The individual clusters are consolidated stepwise into larger clusters of closely spaced groups. As with distances, there are several ways to accomplish this, the most common being single linkage. In a single-linkage algorithm, the two closest points are combined into a cluster, or "linked"

Sample number	Group	% cocaine (raw)	% cocaine (Z-transformation)
1	A	34	2.090
2	A	34	2.090
3	A	20	0.449
4	A	28	1.387
5	A	20	0.449
6	A	23	0.801
7	A	28	1.387
8	A	30	1.621
9	A	31	1.738
10	A	20	0.449
11	B	14	−0.254
12	B	8	−0.957
13	B	13	−0.371
14	B	9	−0.840
15	B	14	−0.254
16	B	12	−0.488
17	B	9	−0.840
18	B	11	−0.605
19	B	13	−0.371
20	B	6	−1.191
21	C	15	−0.137
22	C	12	−0.488
23	C	9	−0.840
24	C	10	−0.723
25	C	9	−0.840
26	C	12	−0.488
27	C	13	−0.371
28	C	8	−0.957
29	C	13	−0.371
30	C	7	−1.074
Mean		16.17	
Stdev		8.53	

$$z = \frac{x - \bar{x}}{s}$$

$$z = \frac{(20 - 16.17)}{8.53} = 0.449$$

$$z = 0.45$$

$\bar{x} = 16.1_7$

$x = 20$

$(-)z \qquad (+)z$

Deviation from the mean is positive and equal to 0.45s.

▶ **Figure 3.10** *The z-transform normalization applied to the cocaine variable for the data shown in Table 3.1. The mean value of this variable is 16.1₇ and each value can be expressed as a fraction of a standard-deviation unit displacement. Any value less than the mean will have a z-value less than zero, and any value greater than the mean will have a positive displacement.*

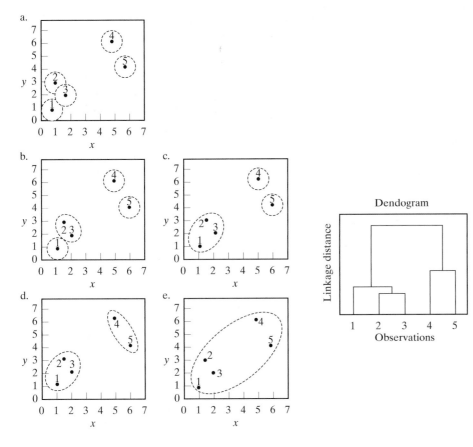

◀ **Figure 3.11** *Single-linkage clustering. (A) All points start as their own cluster. (B) 2 and 3, the two clusters closest to one another, are linked to make a new, larger cluster. This has the smallest linkage distance, as shown on the dendrogram. The process continues from C through E until all points are included in the cluster.*

to each other, and the linkage distance is recorded. Distances are recomputed, and for the newly amalgamated cluster, the distance between it and another cluster is considered to be that between the two nearest neighbors.

To determine which groups are clusters, one approach is to plot linkage distance as a function of step number, as shown in Figure 3.12. Initially, linkage distances should be small, since the data points should be close to each other in the data space. As the clustering nears completion, the distance between the two closest points in any two clusters should increase, because the linked objects are farther away. At the end, the increase is nearly exponential, and that fact can be used as a guide for what to call a cluster. The linkage pattern can be plotted as a dendrogram (tree diagram) as shown in Figure 3.13. In this example, the linkage distance jumps at around 5, and if a line is placed across the dendrogram, the data are indeed seen to be divided into two clusters, with some sub-structure evident in the larger, combined B and C cluster. Sample B10 is closer to C10 than it is to the other B samples, and in fact, C10 and B10 are the two closest points in the data set, as can be seen in a detailed examination of the figure. The information provided by cluster analysis is descriptive and qualitative, but is still useful, particularly when combined with other EDA techniques.

With this brief discussion of multivariate analysis and linear equations completed, we are ready to discuss the calibration of instruments. Often underemphasized, the reliable calibration of equipment and instrumentation is the foundation of data quality and reliability. Accordingly, before leaping into the topic of calibration, we must formally introduce quality assurance and quality control, which in turn will integrate the statistical concepts introduced here and in the previous chapter. The discussion that follows will provide our link between statistics, calibration, and data quality.

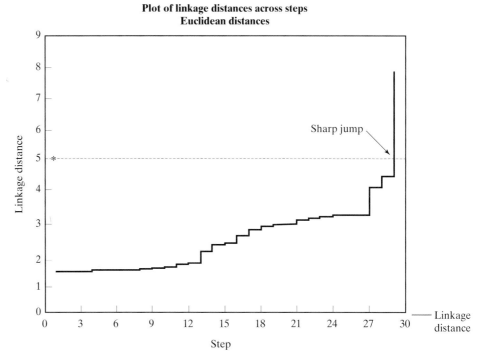

▶ **Figure 3.12** *The linkage distances early in the amalgamation process are small, but as the clusters get farther apart, the linkage distances increase until they take on an exponential appearance. This provides a reasonable breakpoint for the isolation of clusters. Here, the breakpoint is d ≈ 5.*

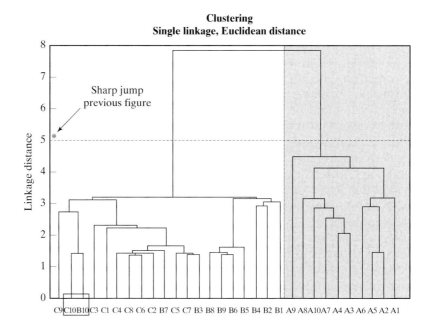

▶ **Figure 3.13** *A dendrogram of the example data. At d ≈ 5, the data fall into two distinct clusters, with substructures and relationships within the clusters. The closeness of B10 and C10 was also seen in Figure 3.9 when PCA was applied to the same problem.*

3.2 QUALITY ASSURANCE AND QUALITY CONTROL

3.2.1 OVERVIEW

Statistics and quality assurance are intimately and inextricably linked. Before exploring that link, however, we need to discuss quality assurance and quality control (QA/QC) as related to analytical and forensic chemistry. Typically, "quality assurance" refers to the philosophy and approach adopted to ensure the goodness of data, while quality control refers to the procedures, tests, and samples used to gauge that goodness. The recognition of the need for QA in forensic science and forensic chemistry is nothing new, given the nature, use, and potential consequences of the data.

As a systematic procedural approach, QA can be traced to the post-World War II years and to applications in the military and engineering.[1,2] Most quality management systems have a business orientation, but the philosophy is applicable to laboratory work. The International Standards Organization (ISO) states,

> "Quality management" means what the organization does to ensure that its products or services satisfy the customer's quality requirements and comply with any regulations applicable to those products or services.[2]

In a forensic context, the organization is the laboratory, the products and services are analytical data, and the customer is the justice system.

The practices and procedures used within an organization (the lower level of the triangle shown in Figures 2.1 and 3.1) such as a forensic laboratory are often referred to as **total quality management**, or TQM. TQM consists of the protocols used by the laboratory and involves everyone from the bench analyst through management. The structures and protocols within a TQM system are often adopted or adapted from external standardization and quality assurance entities. The ISO was formed in 1947 as a voluntary organization consisting of member groups. The American National Standards Institute (ANSI) is the U.S. representative in ISO. Also within ANSI, the American Society of Quality (ASQ) oversees issues of quality management.[3] These organizations are not regulatory bodies, nor are they industry or product specific.

Within the analytical and forensic communities, specific guidance for methods and procedures are provided by groups such as the American Society for Testing and Materials (ASTM International) and professional organizations, including the American Academy of Forensic Sciences (AAFS), the Society of Forensic Toxicology (SOFT), and the American Society of Crime Laboratory Directors (ASCLD). ASTM develops procedures called **standards** that are applicable to specific industries and processes.[†] The organization was formed by engineers and chemists in 1898 and has grown to cover everything from the manufacture of amusement rides to that of wood products. Standards are developed by committees of professionals in their field. Committee E30, currently with about 300 members, drafts and approves forensic science standards. A partial list of relevant ASTM standards relating to forensic science is given in Table 3.3.

Table 3.3 Partial List of ASTM Standards for Forensic Science	
Standard (year)	**Title**
E105-58(1996)	Standard Practice for Probability Sampling of Materials
E141-91(2003)	Standard Practice for Acceptance of Evidence Based on the Results of Probability Sampling
E620-97	Standard Practice for Reporting Opinions of Technical Experts
E1385-00	Standard Practice for Separation and Concentration of Ignitable Liquid Residues from Fire Debris Samples by Steam Distillation

[†]Analytical chemists usually associate the term "standard" with a solution or some other mixture, but in ASTM parlance, a standard is a practice, method, or procedure, not a chemical standard.

Table 3.3 (Continued)	
Standard (year)	**Title**
E1386-00	Standard Practice for Separation and Concentration of Ignitable Liquid Residues from Fire Debris Samples by Solvent Extraction
E1387-01	Standard Test Method for Ignitable Liquid Residues in Extracts from Fire Debris Samples by Gas Chromatography
E1388-00	Standard Practice for Sampling of Headspace Vapors from Fire Debris Samples
E1402-99	Standard Terminology Relating to Sampling
E1412-00	Standard Practice for Separation of Ignitable Liquid Residues from Fire Debris Samples by Passive Headspace Concentration with Activated Charcoal
E1413-00	Standard Practice for Separation and Concentration of Ignitable Liquid Residues from Fire Debris Samples by Dynamic Headspace Concentration
E1422-01	Standard Guide for Test Methods for Forensic Writing Ink Comparison
E1492-2(1999)	Standard Practice for Receiving, Documenting, Storing, and Retrieving Evidence in a Forensic Science Laboratory
E1588-5(2001)	Standard Guide for Gunshot Residue Analysis by Scanning Electron Microscopy/Energy-Dispersive Spectroscopy
E1610-02	Standard Guide for Forensic Paint Analysis and Comparison
E1968-98	Standard Guide for Microcrystal Testing in the Forensic Analysis of Cocaine
E1969-01	Standard Guide for Microcrystal Testing in the Forensic Analysis of Methamphetamine and Amphetamine
E2123-01	Standard Practice for the Transmittal of Evidence in Sexual Assault Investigation
E2124-01	Standard Practice for the Specification for Equipment and Supplies in Sexual Assault Investigations
E2125-01	Standard Guide for Microcrystal Testing in the Forensic Analysis of Phencyclidine and its Analogues
E2154-01	Standard Practice for Separation and Concentration of Ignitable Liquid Residues from Fire Debris Samples by Passive Headspace Concentration with Solid Phase Microextraction (SPME)
E2159-01	Standard Guide for Selection, Assignment, and Monitoring of Persons to Be Utilized as Assessors/Auditors or Technical Experts
E1459-2(1998)	Standard Guide for Physical Evidence Labeling and Related Documentation
E1488-02e1	Standard Guide for Statistical Procedures to Use in Developing and Applying ASTM Test Methods
E2224-02	Standard Guide for Forensic Analysis of Fibers by Infrared Spectroscopy
E2225-02	Standard Guide for Forensic Examination of Fabrics and Cordage
E2227-02	Standard Guide for Forensic Examination of Nonreactive Dyes in Textile Fibers by Thin-Layer Chromatography
E2228-02	Standard Guide for Microscopic Examination of Textile Fibers

Standardization and the adoption of standard methods and practices assure the comparability of analytical measurements. If one blood sample is submitted to 10 different laboratories, all of them should obtain the same result, within the range generated by small random errors and uncertainty. The odds of this happening increase dramatically if procedures are standardized. The concept of standardization is vital to ensure what informally is called data comparability. For example, instruments such as Fourier transform infrared (FTIR) spectrophotometers and GCMS systems are supplied with spectral libraries. Usually, the mass spectral library is provided by the National Institutes of Standards and Technology (NIST, www.NIST.gov). This library would be useless but for standardized instrument conditions. In mass spectrometry, instruments are adjusted (or "tuned") with the use of a standard compound such as perfluorotributylamine (PFTBA). This compound is introduced into the mass spectrometer, and instrument settings are adjusted, until the mass spectrum is comparable to one produced by standard specifications within specified tolerances. Analogous methods are used for other instruments.

A second advantage of standard methods is that they are optimized and validated. As the name implies, a validated method has been thoroughly tested and characterized. The performance limitations of the method are understood and quantifiable criteria for its satisfactory performance exist. As with mass spectrometers, tests can determine whether the method is working to specifications. If it is, then the data are comparable and reliable. Finally, because data generated by standard methods are comparable, it is possible to measure performance at the analyst and laboratory levels. The topics of analyst certification and laboratory accreditation will be addressed shortly.

3.2.2 NIST AND OTHER GROUPS

Unlike ANSI and ISO, NIST is an agency of the U.S. government. Founded in 1901, it is part of the Department of Commerce, but it does not have any regulatory functions. Rather, the role of NIST is to promote the standardization of weights and measures to serve the needs of industry, commerce, science, and technology. Forensically, one of the most important functions of NIST is the creation, maintenance, and supply of standard reference materials (SRMs). There are several types of SRMs, including certified SRMs (CRMs). According to NIST,[4] a certified reference value for an analytical parameter meets the following criteria:

> NIST Certified Value—Value and its uncertainty assigned by NIST in conformance with the NIST uncertainty policy. A NIST certified value is obtained by one or more of the following measurement modes:
>
> 1. A definitive (or primary) method using specialized instrumentation capable of high accuracy and precision and whose errors have been thoroughly investigated and corrected; or,
> 2. Two or more independent methods at NIST using commercial instrumentation that is calibration based and with differing sources of systematic errors; or,
> 3. Interlaboratory data from selected laboratories using multiple methods and NIST SRMs as controls.

A few NIST CRMs are used directly as QA samples in forensic science. For example, SRM 1511 (Figure 3.14) is freeze-dried urine containing drugs and metabolites. Other NIST materials are used for instrument verification and validation.

Consider infrared spectroscopy in which absorbance is plotted as a function of a wavenumber. Most users take for granted that if a peak appears at 1700 cm^{-1} on a screen or a printout, an actual absorbance of electromagnetic radiation with a frequency of 1700 cm^{-1} occurred. That assumption, however, rests on another: that the instrument has a reliable wavelength and frequency calibration. What if there were problems with the instrument, and a peak at 1700 cm^{-1} really represented the sample absorbing light at 1600 cm^{-1}? The only way to detect such a problem would be to obtain a spectrum with known and reliable absorbances of a material in which the frequencies of absorbance are certified. NIST provides

National Institute of Standards and Technology

Certificate of Analysis

Standard Reference Material 1511

Multi-Drugs of Abuse in Freeze Dried Urine

The Standard Reference Material (SRM) is intended primarily for verifying the accuracy used for the determination of morphine, codeine, cocaine metabolite (benzoylecgonine), marijuana metabolite (THC-9-COOH), and phencyclidine in human urine. SRM 1511 consists of three (3) bottles of freeze-dried urine with all of the analytes in each bottle. (See reconstitution procedure for reconstitution to 25 mL). There is no blank urine with this SRM.

Certified concentration: The certified values and uncertainties for the analytes, as free bases, are calculated and given in the table below. For benzoylecgonine, morphine, codeine, and phencyclidine, GC/MS and LC/MS data were used and the uncertainty is a 95% confidence interval for the mean. For the THC-9-COOH, the mean concentration was computed from GC/MS and GC/MS/MS measurements taken at NIST and the uncertainty is also a 95% confidence interval for the mean. However, this confidence interval also includes variability observed between NIST and five military labs which had been used to demonstrate the suitability of the material. It is assumed that systematic errors are very small compared to random errors.

	Concentration	
Analyte	**mmole/L**	**ne/mL**
Morphine	$1.08 \pm 0.07 \times 10^4$	309 ± 20
Codeine	$9.62 \pm 0.37 \times 10^4$	288 ± 11
Benzoylecgonine	$3.60 \pm 0.28 \times 10^4$	162 ± 8
THC-9-COOH	$4.09 \pm 0.23 \times 10^4$	14.1 ± 0.8
Phencyclidine	$9.74 \pm 0.33 \times 10^4$	23.8 ± 0.8

▶ **Figure 3.14** *Data sheet for traceable NIST standard reference material for forensic toxicology. Source: US Department of Commerce, National Institute of Standards and Technology (NIST). This and other data sheets are available from the NIST website, www.nist.gov.*

The certified concentration apply *only* to urine reconstituted as specified under "Reconstruction Procedure" and are based upon the concordant results from two different analytical methods for each analyte. Brief descriptions of the methods are given under "Analytical Methods." *Note:* This material also contains amphetamine and methamphetamine, but these analytes were not certified as analytical results that indicated probable degradation of these constituents with time.

The overall direction and coordination of the technical measurements leading to the certification of this SRM were performed by M.J. Welch of the Organic Analytical Research Division.

Analytical measurements were performed by R.G. Christensen, P. Elerbe, C.S. Phinney, L.C. Sander, and S.S. -C. Tai of the Organic Analytical research Division.

Statistical analysis was provided by K.J. Coakley if the Statistical Engineering Division.

such certified reference materials (CRMs). Laboratories that use those CRMs and obtain results comparable to NIST values can be confident that their spectrophotometers are calibrated sufficiently to produce acceptable spectra. Spectrophotometric data obtained on such instruments are comparable to each other and can be linked back to NIST. This linkage, called **traceability**, is a central premise of quality assurance.

Following is partial list of other organizations and concepts important in TQM within the forensic community

- *The American Board of Forensic Toxicology (ABFT)* is a professional organization that publishes laboratory guidelines and accredits forensic toxicology labs working in the areas of postmortem or human performance toxicology (blood alcohol) website: www.abft.org.
- *ASCLD/LAB* is a professional group within the American Society of Crime Laboratory Directors that publishes laboratory guidelines and accredits forensic labs website: www.ascld.org.

- *Good laboratory practice (GLP)* consists of federal regulations that govern practices in pharmaceutical (Food and Drug Administration, FDA) and environmental laboratories (Environmental Protection Agency, EPA). GLP guidelines address equipment, documentation, analyst training, and other aspects related to analytical laboratory work.
- *ISO-9000* is a group of standards created by members of ISO. These standards are generic quality management guidelines not specific to any industry, product, or process. ISO accredits organizations that meet the ISO-9000 quality guidelines website: www.iso.org.

3.2.3 TERMS AND MORE TERMS

With the basics of TQM, QA, and statistics behind us, we can introduce definitions of key terms that include aspects of all three:

- *Accuracy*: The closeness of a test result or empirically derived value to an accepted reference value.[5] Note that this is not the traditional definition invoking the closeness to a *true* value; indeed, the true value is unknown, so the test result can be reported only as existing in a range with some degree of confidence, such as the 95% CI. Accuracy is often measured by the error (observed value minus accepted value) or by a percent error (defined in Chapter 2).

Historical Evidence 3.1—M. B. Orfila and Quality Control

In Historical Evidence 1.4, the testimony of M. B. Orfila at the trial of Marie LaFarge was discussed. Being a consummate chemist, Orfila realized the need for quality control procedures long before these protocols were formalized. In the LaFarge case, Orfila took steps to ensure that the arsenic he detected in the tissues of the deceased husband originated from the exhumed body and not from the soil in which the remains had been buried. Such a course of action is not far fetched, since many soils have significant levels of arsenic. It would not have done any good to detect arsenic in the tissues, but not be able to eliminate the soil as the source. Orfila took the necessary analytical steps to guarantee the reliability *and* utility of the results: the guiding principles of quality assurance and quality management.

- *Bias:* The difference between the expected and experimental result; also called the total systematic error.[5] Biases should be corrected for, or minimized in, validated methods. An improperly calibrated balance that always reads 0.0010 g too high will impart bias to results.
- *Control chart:* A running graphical record of replicate measurements kept over time and designed to detect degradation in reagents, equipment failures, and similar problems. A control chart documents stability and reproducibility over time, as opposed to reproducibility within a batch.[5] Forensic labs use many control charts to monitor criteria ranging from the temperature of a refrigerator to concentrations of stock solutions. In most control charts, warning limits are set at $\pm 2s$ or $2s/\sqrt{n}$.[6] Control limits use 3s. Control charts differ from replicate measures in that they are spread out over time. An example control chart is shown in Section 3.3, Figure 3.19.
- *Interlaboratory comparisons:* Studies of the performances of several laboratories on the same sample.
- *Precision:* The reproducibility of a series of replicate measurements obtained under comparable analytical conditions. Precision is measured by %RSD.

Applying the Science 3.2 Interlaboratory Comparisons of Heroin

Drug profiling is an investigatory technique that will be discussed in Chapter 6. The goal of profiling is to identify and quantify compounds in a drug sample in order to facilitate comparisons between exhibits and seizures with the aim of identifying common links and sources. For widespread profiling to be effective, analyses must take place in several laboratories, an approach that, unfortunately, introduces interlaboratory variation. While inevitable, interlaboratory variation must be minimized if data analyzed in one setting can be fairly compared with data analyzed in another. The same sample analyzed with the same validated method should produce the same result, within normal expected uncertainties, regardless of where the analyses were undertaken.

In one case, three European laboratories participated in a project to evaluate and address interlaboratory variation arising from heroin profiling. GCMS analysis was used to profile

Variable no.	Old system	New system
1	9.8	4.2
3	3.5	1.9
4	3.2	2.0
5	19.0	6.8
7	2.4	0.9
9	8.5	6.9
10	9.6	4.8
11	–	–
12	3.2	2.5
14	11.6	4.0
15	6.2	2.5
16	12.7	7.4
18	9.6	5.7
19	24.0	5.7
20	13.5	5.8
25	5.8	3.7

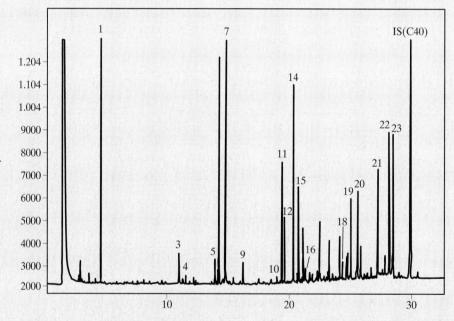

▶ The positions of the 16 selected reference peaks and the internal standard (IS) in the profile obtained with the 'BKA-standard' sample. Figures reproduced with permission from the reference cited below. Copyright 2000, Elsevier Science.

sample extracts, and 16 analytes were selected as shown in the chromatogram. Internal standard calibration was used, a topic to be addressed shortly. The compounds selected were minor constituents of a typical heroin exhibit, but the group of 16 did not include heroin. Using similar analytical protocols, each laboratory performed various repetitive analyses with a

standard, and the reproducibility of the results was a measure of the %RSD of the 16 components. The details of the analyses were compared and refined, and the experiment was repeated with the results shown in the figure above. Significant improvements in precision between the laboratories is clearly shown in the decrease in %RSD values.

Source: Stromberg, L., et al. "Heroin Impurity Profiling: A Harmonization Study for Retrospective Comparisons." *Forensic Science International* 114 (2000), 67–88.

- *Random error:* An inescapable error, small in magnitude and equally positive and negative, associated with any analytical result. Unlike systematic error, random error is unpredictable. Random error, which can be characterized by the %RSD (precision), arises in part from the uncertainties of

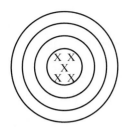

Ideal situation
- Accuracy acceptable
- Precision acceptable
- No bias
- Errors random

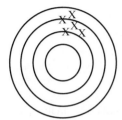

- Accuracy unacceptable
- Precision acceptable
- Bias present and predictable
- Errors systemic

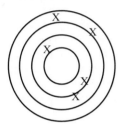

- Accuracy unacceptable
- Precision unacceptable
- Bias indeterminant
- Errors indeterminant

◀ **Figure 3.15** *Relationships among accuracy and precision, on the one hand, and random and systematic error, on the other.*

instrumentation. Typical micropipets have uncertainties in the range of 1–2%, meaning that, no matter how much care is taken, each use will produce a slightly different volume. The variation may be too small to measure, but it will be present. When all such discrepancies involved in a procedure are combined, the relative variation increases, decreasing reproducibility in turn and adding to random error. True random errors of replicate measurements adhere to the normal distribution, and analysts strive to obtain results affected only by such small random errors.

- *Systematic error:* Analytical errors that are the same every time (i.e., predictable) and that are not random. Some use this term interchangeably with "bias." In a validated method, systematic errors are minimized, but not necessarily zero, as illustrated in Figure 3.15.

- *Uncertainty:* A measure of variability associated with a measurement that takes into account bias and random error.[5] Uncertainty is most often expressed by a range of values value based on the standard deviation of replicates, but it can also be derived from method validation studies.

3.2.4 TRACEABILITY AND METHOD VALIDATION

In a nutshell, "traceability" means that analytical results, such as the concentration of a drug metabolite in urine, can be linked, related, or traced to an unassailable original source, such as an NIST SRM. Traceability is also interpreted more broadly to include the calibration of instrumentation and equipment. For example, analytical balances can be calibrated with certified weights that are traceable to NIST standard weights. Traceability can be thought of as a chain of custody for quality: Data that are traceable can be linked to reliable sources through what may be a long, but unbroken, documented chain of relationships and dependencies. Ideally, the calibration and performance of every piece of laboratory equipment

---

Example Problem 3.2

A toxicologist obtains the CRM urine shown in Figure 3.14, wherein the certified value for morphine is 309 ppb ± 20 ppb. The analyst carefully prepares the material and performs an analysis on three replicates. The following data are obtained:

$$\text{Trial } 1 = 286.2 \text{ ppb}$$
$$\text{Trial } 2 = 282.2 \text{ ppb}$$
$$\text{Trial } 3 = 280.9 \text{ ppb}$$

Calculate the percent error and state whether the analysis would be considered a success, assuming that no obvious errors occurred during the procedure

Answer: The mean of the data is 283.1 ppb. The resulting percent error is [(observed value − true value)/true value] × 100 = −25.9/309 × 100, or −8.3%.

This seems a significant offset, but uncertainty of the true value and the experimental value must also be considered. For the analyst's data, the 95% CI (equation 2-5) would be calculated as the mean: ±(4.303 × 2.762)/1.414, or 8.40. The 95% CI of the analyst's result spans the range from 283.1 ± 8.4, or 274.7–291.5. To match the number of significant figures on the CRM, this corresponds to a range of 275–292 ppb. The range of the certified reference value is 289–329 ppb. Thus, there is overlap—but is it statistically significant?

When the mean and standard deviation of two data sets are known, equations 2-10 and 2-11, the t-comparison of means, can be invoked. However, the CRM data sheet did not provide a value for the standard deviation s—only for the 95% CI. Therefore, in this case, using the tools introduced so far, the best that can be said is that the ranges overlap and that the means are comparable given the known margins of error.

---

and every instrument should be traceable to an unassailable standard, be it defined by a professional accreditation body or by NIST. The example given in the previous section referring to the wavenumber calibration of an IR spectrophotometer is typical of a traceability operation. According to laboratory policy, an IR spectrum used in routine drug analysis would be evaluated using a NIST SRM with certified values for wavenumbers and absorbances. If the instrument calibration falls within the uncertainty specified on the Certificate of Analysis, that fact would be documented and the instrument kept in service. Failure of the check would result in recalibration or repair, followed by another validation analysis, all documented. If the instrument passes a validation test, does it mean that every spectrum obtained on such an instrument is fully trustworthy? Not at all, because validation of the instrument is just one step in a long and complex analytical process. Traceability and quality management of the entire analysis ensures the ultimate reliability and utility of the spectrum and the data derived from it.

Traceability is also a foundation of method validation. When a method is validated, it means that, properly applied, the method will produce reliable and trustworthy data with a known performance and known limitations. This does not mean that each sample will be the same, but the analytical *protocols* will be, thereby ensuring optimal performance and comparability of data. Novel samples may require novel approaches, but a standardized and validated method will, at the very least, provide a starting point. Method validation is one of the key components of total quality management in a laboratory.

A validated method is intended to produce the best possible data for a given analyte or, more likely, group of analytes such that the data are acceptably accurate, precise, quantifiable, timely, and reliable.[7] The particulars of method validation are normally dictated by a professional association or accrediting body, such as SOFT, which publishes guidelines for the validation of toxicology methods.[8] Method validation involves many steps,[7,9] including (but not limited to) the determination of the following quantities:

- Instrument reproducibility. If 20 identical injections are made into a GCMS that will be used in the method, what is the %RSD of the peak areas? How do manual injections differ from those made by an autosampler? The variation contributes to the overall uncertainty.
- Interfering substances: What substances will cause false positives or false negatives? This parameter is also referred to as the **specificity** or **selectivity** of the method.
- Minimal error: What is the smallest error that can be observed? Typically, this is calculated via propagation-of-error techniques that were introduced in the previous chapter (Section 2.1).
- Accuracy and reproducibility (precision) of the method.
- Analyst variation.
- Characteristics of calibration curves (addressed in detail shortly).
- Stability over time.
- Limit of detection (LOD) of the method.
- Limit of quantitation (LOQ).
- Linear dynamic range (LDR).

3.2.5 ANALYST AND LABORATORY "VALIDATION"

Just as methods can be validated, so can laboratories and chemists. A standardized method is optimized, but the best analytical method can go terribly wrong if the analyst cannot perform it. As part of TQM, there has to be some way to ensure that the person on the bench and the organization he or she works for can perform the required analyses. Any mature profession, such as law or medicine, has professional organizations, and one of the roles of these organizations is to guarantee the ethics, responsibility, and trustworthiness of their members. This process is generically called **certification**. In the forensic context, **accreditation** refers to laboratories, but both functions are usually overseen by the same entity. This is an important distinction: Analysts are certified; laboratories are accredited.

The different areas of forensic science have different certification bodies, depending on the specialty, but most are coordinated by or affiliated with the American Academy of Forensic Sciences (AAFS). For forensic chemists working in drug analysis, arson, and trace evidence, accreditation is administered by the American Board of Criminalistics (ABC), which was founded in 1989. The ABC program is based on the General Knowledge Examination (GKE), as well as specialty examinations in trace evidence, fire debris, and drug identification. Forensic toxicologists seek certification through the American Board of Forensic Toxicology (ABFT).

Forensic laboratories are accredited by the American Association of Crime Laboratory Directors Laboratory Accreditation Board (ASCLD/LAB). Accreditation is an arduous multistep process that examines everything from the physical plant of a laboratory through its analysts and management structure. As of November 2003, 255 crime labs had earned this accreditation, which, like analyst certification, must be renewed periodically.

3.2.6 QUALITY CONTROL PROCEDURES

By now it should be clear that no sample stands alone and that every analysis is accompanied, directly and indirectly, by a multitude of quality assurance steps. These steps are themselves tested by means of quality control samples, procedures, and checks. Analytical quality control samples almost always accompany a sample run, and the collection (sample to be tested and quality control samples) is referred to as a **batch**. A batch cannot be broken apart without losing all relevance; it presents a snapshot of method, analysts, and sample, but only at a given moment in time. A picture taken a few hours or a few days later will never be the same. Similarly, analytical conditions vary with time, so a batch run on Monday will not be run under the same conditions as a batch run on Thursday. When validated methods and adequate quality assurance and quality control procedures are used, differences should be minimal, but not necessarily negligible.

What constitutes a batch depends on the type of samples being analyzed and whether quantitative, qualitative, or both types of data are required. At the very least, a batch should contain positive and negative controls. Even simple color tests (Chapter 7) should be performed alongside a sample that produces a positive result (**positive control**) and one that produces no result (**negative control** or **blank**). In a more complex example, suppose a stain suspected of being blood is found on a dark-blue bedsheet. Then another control that would be essential is a background or matrix control taken from an unstained portion of the sheet. Recall the overriding goals of quality assurance: reliability *and* utility. If something in the bedsheet itself produces a positive result, that presumptive test would be useless, indicative of absolutely nothing.

The number of control samples required per batch increases proportionately if quantitative information is sought. Consider a GCMS analysis of a drug sample extract that, based on initial presumptive tests and screening, is thought to contain heroin. Such a batch would likely include the following types of quality assurance samples:

Exhibit B: Trade-offs

Forensic chemists always balance the need for extensive quality assurance and quality control with more mundane limitations of time and money. For example, many students wonder why replicates are not done on known samples. After all, that would generate a measure of reproducibility which could be compared with that obtained from the unknown. Similarly, why are no replicates done on blanks? While such steps would provide useful information, they would require much more analysis time and reagents and would generate more waste. Thus, a trade-off is made: The quality assurance and quality control are acceptable and provide the necessary information without being excessive. This approach is further justified by performing a thorough method validation.

- *Blank samples* are used to make sure that glassware, equipment, and instrumentation are free of the analyte of interest and potential interferences. It does no good to analyze drinking water for trace amounts of acetone when laboratory glassware and procedures contribute 10 ppb per sample. Blanks provide information about the accuracy of the technique used and can help detect systematic errors such as a contaminated reagent or contaminated glassware.
- *Open controls or knowns:* These can be viewed as practice samples for the analyst that have known reliable values. In the drug screen example we are considering here, an open control could be a heroin standard prepared by the analyst from a reliable, but independent, source of heroin. The known provides a measure of expected accuracy and is usually gauged for accuracy by the percent error. Knowns are valuable for detecting and diagnosing systematic errors.
- *Blinds or blind controls:* These are samples in which the true value may be known to someone within the laboratory, such as the QA/QC officer, or to

someone outside or above the laboratory hierarchy, but not to the analyst. If no one in the laboratory knows the true value, the sample may be referred to as a "double blind." When forensic chemists go through proficiency testing, blind samples are used. In some cases, the blind sample may be disguised to be a case sample. The reason for this is to prevent any extraordinary care being taken with the sample, since handling the sample is, in a sense, a test. Double blinds such as this are often the only way to accurately gauge how routine samples are treated.

- *Calibration checks:* Using calibration curves, analyses are performed on calibrated instruments. Any calibration has a limited lifetime and thus should be checked regularly, either as part of each batch or on a time schedule, such as daily. A calibration check solution should be prepared from material that is completely independent of that used to prepare the calibration standards.

- *Replicates:* A replicate is a subsample, also occasionally referred to as an *aliquot*. Performing at least three replicates allows for simple statistics to be calculated (mean, s, %RSD). Often, time constraints within the laboratory dictate which samples are done in replicate. Replicates are frequently, but not always, analyzed at different times.[10]

- *Duplicates:* Duplicates differ from replicates in that a duplicate is a separate sample from a separate source. Replicates are aliquots taken from the same initial homogeneous sample. Duplicates are often taken in the field. For example, when urine samples are taken at sporting events, two separate containers are often filled and sealed for delivery to the laboratory. Since the containers arrive as two samples, they would be labeled as duplicates. A replicate would be a subsample created in the laboratory from one homogeneous sample. Replicates are sometimes referred to informally as aliquots. In practice, the three terms "duplicate," "replicate," and "aliquot" are sometimes used interchangeably, but technically there is a difference, as shown in Figure 3.16.

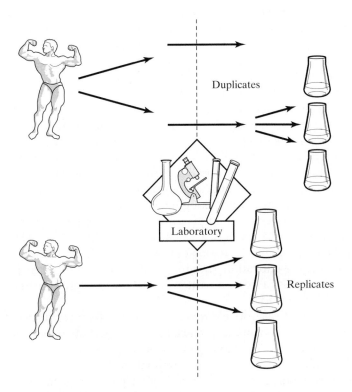

◀ **Figure 3.16** *"Duplicate" is the term used to describe samples collected outside of the laboratory, but from the same source or population. Suppose an athlete is required to take urine tests to check for the presence of banned substances. Replicates are taken either inside or outside the laboratory and are subsets of one sample, whereas duplicates are two separate samples. A duplicate can also be further divided into replicates in the lab.*

- *Spikes:* Spikes are compounds purposely added at known levels and used to gauge the recovery of an analyte from a specific matrix and sample. As a matrix, blood and urine are similar from person to person, so potential matrix effects, although significant, are nearly constant when the same matrix is used. However, when matrices vary, there is often a need for a quantitative assessment of their effect. Spikes are employed in this role.

  As an example, suppose a can containing fire debris is collected. Because the material is burned, the sample will contain significant levels of charcoal. Charcoal absorbs most organics, including accelerants such as gasoline, a complex mixture of hydrocarbons. Furthermore, each fire and each location within a fire will have different sample characteristics, depending on what was burned, how long it burned, how much accelerant was present, and more. Unlike the situation with blood and urine, the matrix effect for fire debris is neither consistent nor predictable. One way to measure how the matrix will influence the recovery of accelerant residues is to spike every sample with a known amount of a compound that is chemically similar to the components of gasoline. If the recovery of the spike compound is 90%, it implies that recovery of the accelerants will be high as well. A challenge with spikes is finding compounds chemically similar to the target analytes, yet that are unlikely to be found in the sample. When mass spectrometry is used as a detector for the analysis, deuterated compounds can be used. Deuterated benzene (benzene-d6) is chemically identical to benzene, but can be distinguished from it on the basis of mass. Consequently, deuterated compounds are frequently used as matrix spikes. Deuterated methods are described in more detail in Chapter 5.

3.2.7 TYPES OF ANALYTICAL ERRORS

The goal of TQM and QC is the reduction of errors to the absolute minimum, leaving only small random errors that can be addressed with the statistics discussed in Chapter 2. To fix errors, they must first be found and diagnosed. An overview of the different sources that contribute to analytic errors is shown in Figure 3.17. Errors associated with the matrix cannot be controlled, but they can be taken into account.

One way to divide errors is to separate them into two broad categories: those originating from the analyst and those originating with the method. The definitions are as the names imply: The former is an error that is due to poor execution, the latter an error due to an inherent problem with the method. Method validation is designed to minimize and characterize method error. Minimization of analyst error involves education and training, peer supervision and review, and honest self-evaluation. Within a forensic laboratory, new analysts undergo extensive training and work with seasoned analysts in an apprentice role for months before taking responsibility for casework. Beyond the laboratory, there are certification programs administered by professional organizations such as the American Board of Criminalistics (ABC) and the American Board of Forensic Toxicologists (ABFT). Requirements for analyst certification include education, training, professional experience, peer recommendations, and passing certain written and laboratory tests. Certification must be periodically renewed.

A second way to categorize errors is by whether they are **systematic**. As defined earlier, systematic errors are predictable and impart a bias to reported results. These errors are usually easy to detect by using blanks, calibration checks, and controls. In a validated method, bias is minimal and well characterized. **Random errors** are equally positive and negative and are generally small. Large random

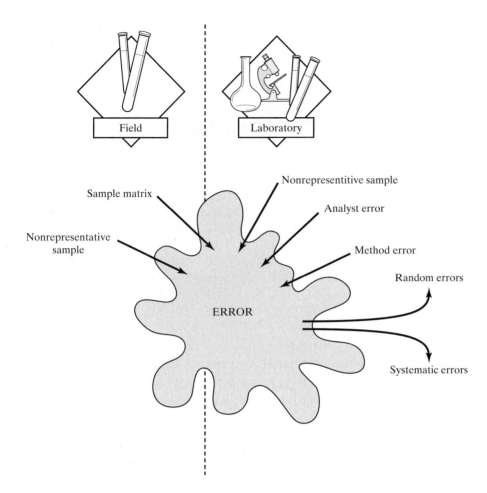

Sample matrix

Nonrepresentitive sample

Analyst error

Nonrepresentative sample

Method error

Random errors

ERROR

Systematic errors

Field

Laboratory

◀ **Figure 3.17** *Contributions to errors that lead to random and systematic errors in the data produced.*

errors are sometimes categorized as gross errors[†] and often are easy to identify, such as a missed injection by an autosampler. Small random errors cannot be completely eliminated and are due to uncertainties discussed in the previous chapter.

A whimsical example may help clarify how errors are categorized and why doing so can be useful. Suppose an analyst is tasked with determining the average height of all adults. For the sake of argument, assume that the true value is 5 feet, 7 inches. The hapless analyst, who of course does not know the true value, has selected a large subset of the population to measure, gathered data, and obtained a mean of 6 feet, 3 inches, plus or minus 1 inch. Clearly, there is error, but what type? The possibilities include the following:

- An improperly calibrated measuring tape that is not traceable to any unassailable standard. Perhaps the inch marks are actually more than an inch apart. This is a method error that is systematic. To detect it, an object of known height or length would be measured.
- The selected sample (n) included members of a professional basketball team. This is sample bias introduced by a poor sampling plan and is a case where n does not accurately represent the parent population.
- The tape was used inconsistently and with insufficient attention to detail. This is analyst error and would be classified as random. To detect it, the analyst would be tasked with measuring the height of the same person 10

[†]Large random errors are also known as OMG errors, for "Oh, my God!" or similar expressions that accompany their discovery.

times under the same conditions. A large variation (%RSD) would indicate poor reproducibility and would also suggest that the analyst take extensive training in the use of a measuring tape and obtain a certification in height measurement.

3.3 QUALITY CONTROL AND CALIBRATION

The process of calibration consists of linking an instrumental response or readout to performance. To calibrate instruments and devices, a trustworthy, traceable standard, procedure, or comparison is mandatory. Forensic laboratories calibrate equipment such as balances and pipets, as well as instruments, via calibration curves. All calibrations are transitory and must be repeated at intervals defined by **standard operating procedures** (**SOP**s) or known performance limitations. For example, an analytical balance might be calibrated weekly via NIST-traceable weights, while a calibration curve from a gas chromatograph might require recalibration or a calibration check every 12 hours. Calibration and calibration checks ensure that the device's output is reliable. Typically, the more complex the device, the more often and more detailed the calibration checking must be.

3.3.1 CALIBRATION OF EQUIPMENT AND USE OF CONTROL CHARTS

The calibration of analytical balances is one of many calibrations that must be done routinely in a forensic laboratory. Some laboratories contract out calibration services, but all are required to keep such records as part of total quality management. The accuracy and precision of such devices must be known and monitored. Devices requiring calibration include refrigerators, balances, pipets, syringes, pH meters, microscopes, and so on. In short, if the equipment provides a measurement that is related to generating data, it must be calibrated. In the case of a balance, the process is as simple as obtaining traceable weights, recording the displayed weight and certified weight, and seeing if the difference falls within the expected range, based on uncertainty and significant figures. With new equipment, manufacturers provide specifications that document the accuracy and precision of that equipment if it is used properly. If a balance fails the check, it must be taken out of service until it is repaired, which may be simple (cleaning and leveling) or may require a return to the factory.

Other devices, such as pipets or refrigerators, may be monitored with control charts, as described previously. Control charts identify failures and also predict and, ideally, diagnose such failures. There are a number of ways charts are implemented. The first step is the establishment or adoption of an expected range of variation. Once these limits are established, the chart is used to monitor the device's performance over time. Suppose an Eppendorf pipet arrives at the lab certified to deliver 200 μL $\pm$ 2.0 μL ($\pm$1%). The analyst immediately validates this performance by repeatedly pipetting what the device records as 200-μL aliquots into dried, tared containers on a calibrated analytical balance. By recording the water temperature and using a chart that relates density to temperature, the analyst converts the weight of water, in milligrams, to a volume delivered by the pipet. This example is illustrated in Figures 3.18 and 3.19.

A control chart usually has two sets of lines: warning limits and action limits. The ranges are calculated as $\pm$2 or 3s (if known) or 95% and 99.7% confidence intervals:[11]

$$\bar{x} \pm \frac{2s}{\sqrt{n}} (95\%) \tag{3.4}$$

Initial performance	
Stable water temperature	26.0°C
Date	2/2/2006
Analyst	S.H.
Pipette serial number	1098CX-3
Received	2/1/2006
Density H_2O	
CRC 2004	0.9967867

Trial	Weight	Volume (calc, uL)
1	0.2003	200.9
2	0.1995	200.1
3	0.2004	201.1
4	0.1993	199.9
5	0.2004	201.0
6	0.2007	201.3
7	0.1998	200.4
8	0.2003	200.9
9	0.2010	201.6
10	0.1999	200.5

Volume (calc, uL)	
Mean	200.8
Standard error	0.168
Standard deviation	0.531
Sample variance	0.282
%RSD	0.265
Range	1.7
Minimum	199.9
Maximum	201.6
Count	10
Confidence level (95%)	0.38

UWL: 201.1
LWL: 200.5
UAL: 201.3
LAL: 200.3

◀ **Figure 3.18** *Data used to determine the performance limits of the example pipet and to establish the warning and action limits of the control chart.*

$$\bar{x} \pm \frac{3s}{\sqrt{n}}\,(99.7\%) \tag{3.5}$$

The pipet is tested initially with 10 replicates and is found to meet the manufacturer's specifications and to have a %RSD of ~0.3%. On the basis of the variation observed, warning and action limits are established and performance is monitored. Whenever a warning line is crossed, a second test is made. If performance falls below the action limit, the pipet is removed from service. A close look at the control chart (Figure 3.19) presaged the failure; if a similar pattern is seen with other pipets, preventative action would be undertaken. Possible outcomes are summarized in Figure 3.20.

3.3.2 CALIBRATION OF INSTRUMENTS: CONCENTRATION AND RESPONSE

Some of the basics of calibration were presented in the discussion of linear regression earlier in the chapter. A good regression line is required for a valid and trustworthy calibration, but still is only one of many requirements. A calibration curve has a lifetime that is linked to the stability of the instrument and the calibration standards. A curve run Monday morning on an ultraviolet/visible-range (UV/VIS) spectrophotometer probably will not be reliable Tuesday. Therefore, procedures must account for the passage of time in considering the validity of a calibration curve. Modern instruments such as gas chromatographs and mass spectrometers can produce calibration curves that are stable over many days, but they must be tested periodically. Many instruments allow for automatic curve checks and updates, such as replacing the middle point of the curve with a fresh run every 12 hours.

Another aspect of curve validation is the use of calibration checks. The ideal calibration check (CC) is obtained from a traceable standard that is independent of the solutions used to prepare the calibration standards, as shown in Figure 3.21. This is the only method that facilitates the detection of a problem in the stock solution. Finally, blanks must be analyzed regularly to ensure that equipment and instrumentation have not been contaminated. Thus, four factors contribute to the validation of

Date checked	Volume (uL)	UWL	LWL	UAL	LAL	Nominal
2/9/2006	200.7	201.1	200.5	201.3	200.3	200.8
2/17/2006	200.8	201.1	200.5	201.3	200.3	200.8
2/25/2006	200.9	201.1	200.5	201.3	200.3	200.8
3/5/2006	201.1	201.1	200.5	201.3	200.3	200.8
3/13/2006	200.7	201.1	200.5	201.3	200.3	200.8
3/21/2006	201.0	201.1	200.5	201.3	200.3	200.8
3/29/2006	200.8	201.1	200.5	201.3	200.3	200.8
4/6/2006	200.8	201.1	200.5	201.3	200.3	200.8
4/14/2006	200.8	201.1	200.5	201.3	200.3	200.8
4/22/2006	200.9	201.1	200.5	201.3	200.3	200.8
4/30/2006	200.5	201.1	200.5	201.3	200.3	200.8
Dup 4/30/2006	200.6	201.1	200.5	201.3	200.3	200.8
5/16/2006	200.6	201.1	200.5	201.3	200.3	200.8
5/24/2006	200.4	201.1	200.5	201.3	200.3	200.8
Dup 5/24/2006	200.6	201.1	200.5	201.3	200.3	200.8
6/9/2006	200.4	201.1	200.5	201.3	200.3	200.8
Dup 6/9/2006	200.2	201.1	200.5	201.3	200.3	200.8
Dup 6/9/2006	200.1	201.1	200.5	201.3	200.3	200.8

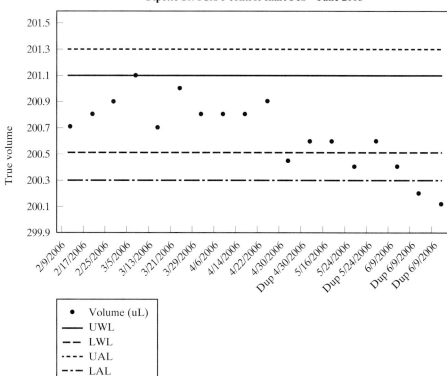

Pipette 1098CX-3 control chart Feb – June 2006

▶ **Figure 3.19** *Weekly control chart for the pipet. The data from June 9 were at the warning limit, and two duplicates fell below the action limit. The action (retesting) indicated that the pipet was no longer "in control" and would have to be taken out of service for repair or replacement.*

a calibration curve: correlation coefficient (R^2), the absence of a response to a blank, the time elapsed since the initial calibration or update, and performance on an independent calibration-check sample. These criteria should be met regardless of the type of curve being used, the most common of which are as follows:

- *External Standard:* This type of curve is familiar to students as a simple concentration-versus-response plot fit to a linear equation. Standards are prepared in a generic solvent, such as methanol for organics or 1% acid for elemental analyses. Such curves are easy to generate, use, and maintain. They

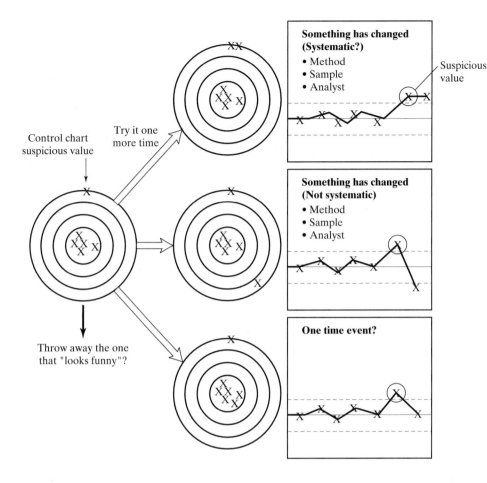

Control chart suspicious value

Try it one more time

Throw away the one that "looks funny"?

Something has changed (Systematic?)
• Method
• Sample
• Analyst

Suspicious value

Something has changed (Not systematic)
• Method
• Sample
• Analyst

One time event?

◀ **Figure 3.20** *Relationship of a control chart to the target analogy. If a sample exceeds warning or control limits, it should not be discarded arbitrarily, but rather be used to diagnose and correct problems. Once again, chemistry before statistics.*

are also amenable to automation. External standard curves work well when matrix effects are minimal. For example, if an analysis is to be performed on cocaine, some sample preparation and cleanup (the topic of the next chapter) is done and the matrix removed or diluted away. In such cases, most interference from the sample matrix is inconsequential, and an external standard is appropriate. External standard curves are also used when internal standard calibration is not feasible, as in the case of atomic absorption spectrometry.

• *Internal Standard:* External standard calibrations can be compromised by complex or variable matrices. In toxicology, blood is one of the more difficult matrices to work with, because it is a thick, viscous liquid containing large and small molecular components, proteins, fats, and many materials subject to degradation. A calibration curve generated in an organic solvent is dissimilar from that generated in the blood matrix, a phenomenon called **matrix mismatch**. Internal standards provide a reference to which concentrations and responses can be ratioed. The use of an internal standard requires that the instrument system respond to more than one analyte at a time. Furthermore, the internal standard must be carefully selected to mimic the chemical behavior or the analytes. This property is important, since internal standard calibration rests on the assumption that whatever happens to the analyte in a matrix also happens to the internal standard. However, as with spikes, the internal standard cannot be a compound that might occur in a sample. An example (Figure 3.22) illustrates how an internal standard protocol can correct for matrix effects or other problems.

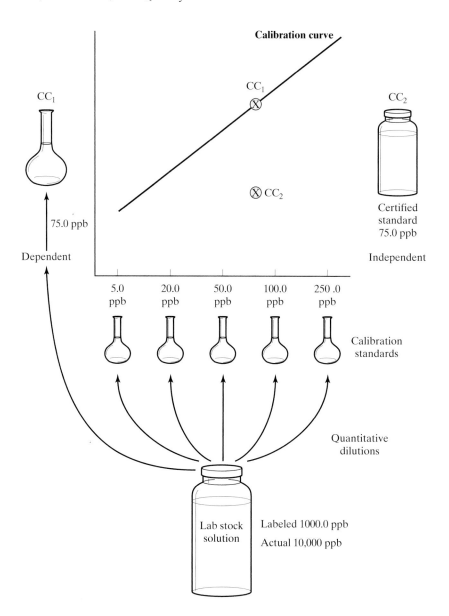

▶ **Figure 3.21** *The value of an independent calibration check (CC) solution. Any dilutions, be they calibration standards or test solutions taken from tainted stock, will be compromised. Only an independently prepared solution will identify the problem.*

Suppose an external-standard curve is generated for an analysis of cocaine. The calibration standards are prepared from a certified stock solution of cocaine in methanol, which is diluted to make five calibration standards. The laboratory prepares a calibration check in a diluted blood solution using certified standards, and the concentration of the resulting mixture is 125.0 ppb cocaine $\pm$ 1.2 ppb. When this solution is analyzed with the external-standard curve, the calculated concentration is found to be about half of the known true value. The reason for the discrepancy is related to the matrix, in which unknown interactions mask nearly half of the cocaine present. The mechanism could be protein binding, degradation, or a myriad of other possibilities, but the end result is that half of the cocaine in the sample is undetected. With external-standard methodology, there is no chance of identifying the loss or correcting for it, since the matrix is not accounted for in calibration.

External standard calibration curve

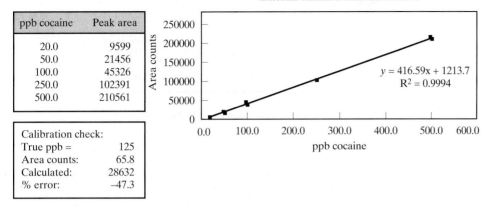

ppb cocaine	Peak area
20.0	9599
50.0	21456
100.0	45326
250.0	102391
500.0	210561

$y = 416.59x + 1213.7$
$R^2 = 0.9994$

Calibration check:	
True ppb =	125
Area counts:	65.8
Calculated:	28632
% error:	−47.3

◀ **Figure 3.22**
Demonstration of a matrix effect. The matrix reduces the response of the analyte cocaine by half, and as a result, the percent error is nearly 50%.

Example Problem 3.3

Given the following data, construct an internal-standard calibration curve and evaluate the results:

ppb codeine	Peak area	ppb internal standard	Peak area	[] ratio	Area ratio
15.0	9599	25.0	29,933	0.60	0.32
35.0	21,456	25.0	30,099	1.40	0.71
75.0	45,326	25.0	32,051	3.00	1.41
125.0	102,391	25.0	31,004	5.00	3.30
150.0	157,342	25.0	31,100	6.00	5.06
200.0	162,309	25.0	30,303	8.00	5.36

Calibration curve

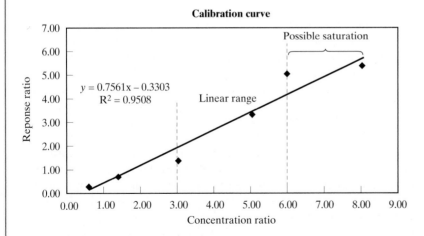

$y = 0.7561x - 0.3303$
$R^2 = 0.9508$

Possible saturation

Linear range

Answer: This calibration has problems that become clear when the curve is plotted. The response at the upper concentrations is flattening out, indicating detector saturation. At lower concentrations, there is what appears to be a linear relationship, but it differs from that in the middle of the curve. The LDR is approximately 35–150-ppb codeine; the calibration should be redone in this range.

Now consider an internal-standard approach (Figure 3.23). An internal standard of xylocaine is chosen because it is chemically similar to cocaine, but unlikely to be found in typical samples. To prepare the calibration curve, cocaine standards are prepared as before, but 75.0 ppb of xylocaine is added to each sample, including blanks, calibration solutions,

ppb cocaine	Peak area	ppb xylocaine	Peak area	[] ratio	Area ratio
20.0	9599	75.0	31063	0.27	0.31
50.0	21456	75.0	30099	0.67	0.71
100.0	45326	75.0	32051	1.33	1.41
250.0	102391	75.0	31004	3.33	3.30
500.0	210561	75.0	31100	6.67	6.77

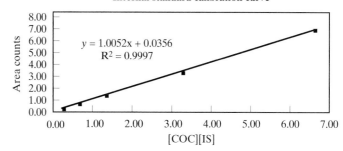

Internal standard calibration curve

$y = 1.0052x + 0.0356$
$R^2 = 0.9997$

Area counts (y-axis), [COC][IS] (x-axis)

True =	125
Area counts cocaine =	28832
Area counts IS =	16723
Area ratio (x)	1.712
Calculated [] ratio	1.668
Calculated cocaine:	125.1
% error:	0.1

▶ **Figure 3.23** *An internal standard corrects for the matrix effect as long as the internal standard is affected similarly to the way the analyte is affected.*

and other quality assurance/quality control samples. Since the added standard is always at the same level, the response should be the same, within expected uncertainties. Xylocaine is chemically similar to cocaine, so if half of the cocaine is lost to the matrix, half of the xylocaine will be lost as well. Area counts still decrease as with the external-standard curve, but here the *ratio* of the two will be unchanged, since both are reduced proportionally. Put another way, 8/4 is the same as 4/2 and 2/1—the individual numbers differ, but all three ratios equal 2. This is the principle of internal-standard calibration: *Ratios* of concentrations and responses are used, rather than uncorrected concentrations and responses. The improvement in performance, versatility, and ruggedness can be significant. As with external standards, internal-standard curves are easily automated and can be adapted to multi-analyte testing.

- *Standard Addition:* Although not widely used in forensic chemistry, the method of standard addition provides the perfect matrix match. To execute a standard addition, the sample is divided into four or five portions. Nothing is added to the first sample. Minute volumes of concentrated analyte are added in increasing increments to the remaining samples and the results plotted as shown in Figure 3.24. The *x*-axis intercept corresponds to the negative equivalent of the concentration.

Recall that the slope of any line, including a calibration curve, is defined as "rise over run." If the curve fit is good ($R^2 = 0.99$ or better), the rise over run is consistent and the rise (the offset from the origin) corresponds to

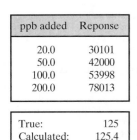

ppb added	Reponse
20.0	30101
50.0	42000
100.0	53998
200.0	78013

True:	125
Calculated:	125.4
% error:	0.3

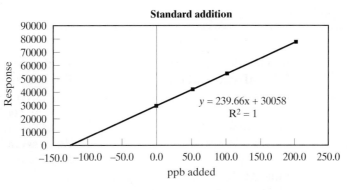

Standard addition

$y = 239.66x + 30058$
$R^2 = 1$

◀ **Figure 3.24** *Standard-addition calibration. The displacement along the x-axis to the left corresponds to the rise at x = 0.0; the equation is used to determine the associated concentration.*

the run along the *x*-axis. The rise along the *y*-axis in the first sample ("0 added") correlates with the run on the *x*-axis, or the concentration of the original sample. Two disadvantages of standard addition are the large amount of sample consumed and the difficulty in adapting the approach to routine analysis. It is also not amenable to quality control samples, such as blanks and calibration checks. However, for unusual cases with difficult matrices, standard addition is a ready tool.

- *Isotope dilution*: This relatively new calibration method is occasionally used in specialized forensic applications.[12,13] The method affords exceptional accuracy and precision, but is limited by the availability of suitable standards. Although the use of deuterated internal standards is sometimes equated with isotope dilution, the techniques are not the same. Isotope-dilution calibration is based on the addition of standards that contained enriched levels of stable isotopes of common elements such as ^{13}C. The enriched standard, referred to as the spike, is added to the sample and allowed to reach equilibrium. The sample is then analyzed via mass spectrometry.[14] Because the spike is chemically identical to the target analyte, the matrix correction is as good as that achieved with standard-addition calibration. However, until enriched stable isotope analogs of forensic analytes are available and affordable, isotope dilution will not be widely applied in forensic chemistry.

SUMMARY

Quality assurance and quality control are the unifying themes of this chapter as well as the previous one. Uni- and multivariate statistics provide the quantitative framework to measure reliability and uncertainty, two indispensable descriptors of any forensic data. Uncertainty and errors are inevitable in even the best-designed and validated method; quality control and statistics provide the methods to characterize and incorporate those errors into data analysis and reporting. If problems arise during an analysis, quality assurance and quality control procedures and practices serve to raise a red flag and allow the forensic chemist to take corrective action. Thus, QA/QC are as much a part of forensic chemistry as are stoichiometry, organic chemistry, and sample preparation.

This chapter concludes the first section of the text and has set the stage for our first forays into chemistry as applied to the world of forensic science. As with any analytical task, the first step is to understand and prepare samples, and this is the subject of the next chapter.

KEY TERMS AND CONCEPTS

Accuracy
Batch
Bias
Blank
Blind samples
Calibration
Calibration-check sample
Chemometrics
Cluster analysis
Control chart
Correlation coefficient
Dependent variable
Duplicates
EDA
Euclidean distance
External-standard curve

Independent variable
Internal-standard curve
Knowns
LDR
Least squared fit
Linear correlation
Linear regression
Linkage distance
LOD
LOQ
Matrix mismatch
Multidimensional data
Multivariate analysis
Negative control
PCA
Positive control

Precision
Product moment correlation
   coefficient
Quality control
Random errors
Regression line
Replicates
Spike
Standard addition
Standard operating procedure
   (SOP)
Systematic errors
Total quality management
Traceability
Univariate

PROBLEMS

From the chapter

1. Provide definitions of the reliability and utility of chemical data that could be presented on the witness stand. Why are both considered part of quality assurance?

2. A micropipet is certified by the manufacturer at 50.0 μL TD, $\pm$ 1.5% (95% confidence) An analyst performs a routine calibration check by pipetting a series of 5 aliquots of deionized water into a tared vial. The water is at a temperature of 25.0°C. The following data are obtained:

n	Weight (cumulative), g
1	0.0494
2	0.0997
3	0.1484
4	0.1985
5	0.2477

   Is the micropipet performing according to specifications? Cite sources.

3. In complex environmental samples such as soils, spikes are used to measure the matrix effect. The range of allowable recoveries for 1,2-dichloroethane-d4, a spike compound, is 80–120%. How is it possible to obtain a recovery greater than 100%? (*Hint*: This happens frequently, and it does *not* imply that the compound in question is in the sample.)

4. In Figure 3.13 which two points are physically the closest? Show the calculation for the distance. Which two points are the farthest apart? Show the calculation for *d*.

5. PCA is based on the assumption that variables can be linearly correlated. If this is not the case, how would it be diagnosed?

6. Does cluster analysis as described in this chapter assume a linear relationship among variables?

7. Why are deuterated compounds frequently used as internal standards?

8. If an analyst inadvertently generates a least-squared-fit calibration curve that is forced through the origin, what type of error would be introduced? Would accuracy or precision be affected? What types of quality assurance or quality control samples and procedures could identify this error?

9. In Exhibit A the point was made that a calibration result from the middle of a curve should never be arbitrarily thrown away. The same is not necessarily true of calibration points that define the upper and lower extremes of the curve. Why?

10. A toxicologist receives a blood sample thought to contain a low level of a new poison just identified. The quantitation is of paramount importance because the treatment can cause severe side effects if it is given to a healthy person. What would be the best calibration method for determining whether the sample contains the new poison?

Integrative

1. What levels of quality assurance are there in typical freshman chemistry laboratories? In organic laboratories?

2. Draw a diagram that employs two Gaussian distribution curves to illustrate the concept of bias. What does

the diagram have in common with the t-test of means introduced in the previous chapter? In what ways does it differ?

3. A forensic toxicologist receives a postmortem blood sample and performs a routine screening analysis followed by GCMS to confirm the presence of cocaine and its metabolites. The toxicologist also performs a quantitative analysis for these analytes. He writes his report and sends it through the laboratory system. The report arrives on the desk of the medical examiner. Identify at least 3 levels of peer review that would have occurred in this example. (*Hint*: Much of the applicable peer review would have occurred offstage and in the past.)

4. Obtain the following reference: Gardner, W. P., et al., "Application of Quantitative Chemometric Analysis Techniques to Direct Sampling Mass Spectrometry," *Analytical Chemistry* 73 (2001), 596–605. Using Table 1 as the input, perform a principal components analysis. Can the dimensionality of these data be reduced with this technique?

5. Research how NIST is able to apply the label "certified" and "standard" to CRMs and SRMs. What particular step is crucial and why does it lend such authority? Discuss this step in terms of error types as well as in terms of accuracy and precision.

6. Deuterated compounds are useful as internal standards, while isotopes such as ^{14}C and tritium are not. Why?

7. The following data are produced as part of a laboratory accreditation-check sample:

ppb codeine	Peak area	ppb internal standard	Peak area	[ ] ratio	Area ratio
15.0	9599	50.0	29,933	0.30	0.32
35.0	21,456	50.0	30,099	0.70	0.71
75.0	45,326	50.0	32,051	1.50	1.41
125.0	82,100	50.0	32,912	2.50	2.49
150.0	95,003	50.0	31,100	3.00	3.05
200.0	122,409	50.0	30,303	4.00	4.04
Blank:	3100	50.0	31,954		
Known (100.0 ± 1.0 ppb)	51,208	50.0	33,000		
Cal check (Independent, 125.0 ± 0.1 ppb)	74,912	50.0	32,844		

Critique these results. "[ ]" is the concentration.

Food for thought

1. Is there such a thing as a "true" value for the concentration of a prepared blind quality assurance sample?

2. Are standard desktop calculators traceable? Can a user be absolutely sure that every operation is correct, assuming that the key entry is?

FURTHER READING

Aitken, C. G. G. and F. Taroni. *Statistics and the Evaluation of Evidence for Forensic Scientists*, 2d ed. Chichester, U.K.: John Wiley and Sons, **2004**.

Billo, J. *Excel for Chemists: A Comprehensive Guide*, 2d ed. New York: John Wiley and Sons, **2001**.

Hair, J. F., et al. *Multivariate Data Analysis*, 5th ed. Upper Saddle River, NJ: Prentice Hall, **1998**.

Kanji, G. K. *100 Statistical Tests*, London: Sage Publications, Ltd., **2000**.

Moore, D. S., and G. P. McCabe. *Introduction to the Practice of Statistics*, 4th ed. New York: WH Freeman, **2003**.

Ross, S. M. *Introduction to Probability and Statistics for Engineers*. New York: John Wiley and Sons, **1987**.

ASTM Standards:

"Guide for General Requirements for Assessment and Accreditation of Certification/Registration Bodies: E 11905-97," in ASTM 14.02, ed. West Conshohocken, PA: ASTM International, 2004.

"Standard Guide for Evaluating Laboratory Measurement Practices and the Statistical Analysis of Resulting Data: E 1323-89 (Reapproved 2002)," in ASTM 14.02, ed. West Conshohocken, PA: ASTM International, 2004.

"Standard Guide for Proficiency Testing by Interlaboratory Comparisons: E 1301-95," in ASTM 14.02, ed. West Conshohocken, PA: ASTM International, 2004.

"Standard Practice for Use of the Terms Precision and Bias in ASTM Test Methods: E 177-90a," in ASTM 14.02, ed. West Conshohocken, PA: ASTM International, 2004.

REFERENCES

1. Hoyle, D. "What Is ISO 9000?" in *ISO9000 Quality Systems Handbook*, 2d ed. Oxford, U.K.: Butterworth-Heinemen, Ltd., 1995.

2. *In the Beginning: The Magical Demystifying Tour of ISO 9000 and ISO 14000*. International Organizations of Standards (ISO). Downloaded November 29, 2003. www.iso.org/iso/en/iso9000-14000/basics/general.

3. Kenkel, J. *A Primer on Quality in the Analytical Laboratory*. Boca Raton, FL: National Science Foundation/CRC Press, 2000.

4. *Standard Reference Materials: Definitions*. National Institute of Science and Technology, U.S. Department of Commerce. Downloaded November 30, 2003. www.nist.gov

5. ASTM, I. "Standard Terminology Relating to Quantity and Statistics," in *ASTM Standard E 456-02*,14.02, ed. ASTM International, 2003.

6. Miller, J. N., and J. C. Miller. "The Quality of Analytical Measurements," in J. N. Miller and J. C. Miller, *Statistics and Chemometrics for Analytical Chemistry*, 4th. ed. Upper Saddle River, NJ: Prentice Hall, 2000.

7. Green, J. M. "A Practical Guide to Method Validation." *Analytical Chemistry* 68 (1996), 305A–309A.

8. *Forensic Toxicology Laboratory Guidelines*. SOFT/AAFS. Downloaded December 3, 2003. www.soft-tox.org.

9. Malcolm, M. J., et al. "Internal Quality Control of a General GC Drug Screen in Forensic Toxicology: Experience, Questions, and Proposals." *Canadian Journal of Forensic Sciences* 28 (1995), 215–228.

10. "Standard Guide for Evaluating Laboratory Measurement Practices and the Statistical Analysis of Resulting Data: E 1323-89 (Reapproved 2002)," in *ASTM 14.02*, ed. West Conshohocken, PA: ASTM International, 2004.

11. Miller, J. N., and J. C. Miller, "Chapter 4: The Quality of Analytical Measurements," in *Statistics and Chemometrics for Analytical Chemistry*, 4th ed. Upper Saddle River, NJ: Prentice Hall, 2000.

12. McCooeye, M., et al. "Separation and Quantitation of the Stereoisomers of Ephedra Alkaloids Using Flow Injection–Electrospray Ionization–High Field Assymmetric Waveform Ion Mobility Spectrometry–Mass Spectrometry." Analytical Chemistry 75 (2003), 2538–2542.

13. White, S. A., et al. "The Determination of Lysergide (LSD) in Urine by High-Performance Liquid Chromatography–Isotope Dilution Mass Spectrometry (IDMS)." *Journal of Forensic Sciences* 44 (1999), 375–379.

14. Patniak, P. "Section 10.8: Isotope-Dilution Mass Spectrometry (IDMS)," in *Dean's Analytical Chemistry Handbook*, 2d ed. New York: McGraw-Hill, 2004.

Sample Preparation, Thin-Layer Chromatography, and Immunoassay

OVERVIEW AND ORIENTATION

The purpose of sample preparation is to isolate analytes from a matrix. Another term used for this operation is "sample cleanup," and the two terms are often used interchangeably. Sample preparation can range from a simple "dilute and shoot," in which a portion of the sample is dissolved in a solvent for subsequent introduction into an instrument to complex acid–base-neutral sequential extractions. In this chapter, we'll explore forensic separations and sample preparations that are used prior to instrumental analysis, which we delve into in the next chapter.

The heart of most sample preparation and cleanup methods is **partitioning**. For partitioning to occur, a phase boundary must exist; that is,

$$\text{Analyte}_{p1} \longleftrightarrow \text{Analyte}_{p2} \qquad (4.1)$$

where p_1 and p_2 refer to different phases. The two phases may be insoluble liquids (i.e., water and hexane) or a boundary between a solid and a liquid or a liquid and a gas. Partitioning relies on the analyte having a greater affinity for one phase over the other, due to charges, polarity, and other chemical properties. In many instances, **Le Châtelier's principle** is invoked to drive the equilibrium to one side or the other; the more complete this process, the more efficient is the separation. As we will see, the manipulation of equilibrium conditions is a cornerstone of extraction and partitioning.

Partitioning is also at the heart of chromatography, which is used in forensic chemistry for sample preparation, cleanup, screening tests, and as a first step in hyphenated instruments such as GCMS. Here, we will review chromatographic separations and discuss thin-layer chromatography (TLC) in some detail. The underlying principles extend into the discussion of chromatographic instruments in the next chapter. Finally, we'll explore **immunoassay**, a screening technique used extensively in forensic toxicology. For chemists, this topic can seem at first a bit alien, but immunoassay is also built on equilibrium and its applications.

4.1 GENERAL CONSIDERATIONS

The majority of forensic chemistry focuses on organic analytes such as drugs, poisons, and polymers. Inorganic analytes and metals are less common, but still important in areas such as gunshot residue, glass, and heavy-metal poisons. In general, samples are prepared for inorganic analysis through the utilization of acid **digestions**, which are effective at isolating elemental components, but which destroy the organic and biological components present in the matrix. Indeed, that is the goal: to attack and destroy everything but the metals or other inorganics of interest. In contrast, organic **extractions** pluck the analytes from the matrix (Figure 4.1). Aggressive techniques destroy most molecular compounds and so are rarely used in preparing organics. However, there are types of evidence, such as hair or insects (entomotoxicology), in which aggressive techniques are needed. Since these matrices are based on protein, enzymes are incorporated into the sample preparation scheme to digest proteins and other large biomolecules.

For qualitative analysis only, simple preparations and cleanups are adequate. If quantitative analysis is needed, rigorous techniques, quantitative extractions, and

▶ **Figure 4.1** *The difference between an extraction and a digestion. Most inorganic analyses, such as testing for arsenic in stomach contents, are based on aggressive digestion, which destroys the matrix in which the durable metal is contained. Preparations targeting organic analytes (A) are designed to remove (extract) the analyte from the matrix. Aggressive digestions such as those with acids, heat, or microwaves would destroy the molecules of interest along with the matrix.*

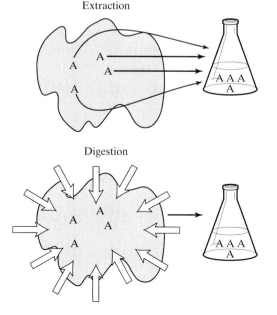

standardization are required. In such cases, the goal is to isolate the analyte from the matrix and to transfer the analyte quantitatively to the final analytical solution. As discussed in Chapter 3, quantitative analysis is the more challenging situation and requires additional quality control procedures to gauge and monitor the efficiency of extraction. Internal standards, surrogate spikes, and matrix spikes are among the tools available, all of which provide analogs for the analyte that can be tracked through the preparation of the sample. The earlier in the process the standards are added, the more realistically they will track the path of the analytes.

4.2 AN ILLUSTRATIVE EXAMPLE

Two conditions must be met to extract an analyte from a matrix. First, there must be an exploitable difference in a chemical or physical property between the matrix and the analyte. Second, there must be an equilibrium condition that can be manipulated (equation 4-1). Consider a sample preparation protocol based on differences in volatility. A headspace method can be used to determine blood alcohol concentration. The premise underlying the extraction is a difference in volatility between ethanol and the aqueous–biological matrix of blood. The system is illustrated in Figure 4.2. The equilibrium at the requisite phase boundary is

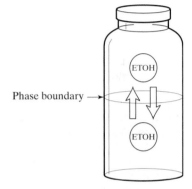

Phase boundary →

$$\text{ethanol (aq)} \longleftrightarrow \text{ethanol (g)} \tag{4.2}$$

As shown in Table 4.1, there is an exploitable difference in a physical property: The difference in volatility between ethanol and the matrix is sufficient to effect the desired separation and extract the ethanol from the matrix. Blood is thicker than water (literally as well as figuratively), and the components within blood do have different volatilities than water, but for first approximations, equating the vapor pressure of blood with that of water is reasonable.

▲ **Figure 4.2** *Simplified representation of the phase boundary and distribution equilibrium of ethanol in blood.*

   A small volume of blood is placed in a sealed container that has headspace above the surface of the sample. In a **headspace** analysis, **Henry's law** is employed. This law states that the partial pressure of the analyte above a liquid is proportional to its concentration in the liquid:

$$\underbrace{P_{A,g} \overset{K_H}{\longleftrightarrow} [A]_{aq};}_{\substack{\text{equilibrium to} \\ \text{exploit}}} \quad K_H = \frac{[A]_{aq}}{P_{A,g}}; \quad K_H{}^*P_{A,g} = [A]_{aq} \tag{4.3}$$

The partial pressure of ethanol above the blood, which is determined analytically by gas chromatographic analysis, can be directly related to the concentration of

Table 4.1	Relative Volatility of Ethanol and Water: An Exploitable Difference		
	Vapor pressure (atm)		
Temperature (°C)	**Ethanol**	**Water**	**Difference**
29	0.10	0.04	2.5
78	0.99	0.43	2.3

*Source: Handbook of Chemistry and Physics, 84th ed. Boca Raton, FL: CRC Press, **2004**.*

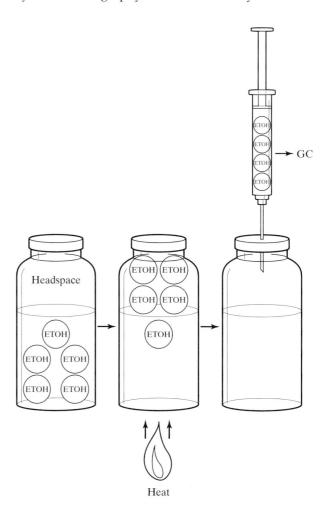

▶ **Figure 4.3** *The process of driving ethanol out of the aqueous (blood) phase into the gas phase, using gentle heating. The headspace above the blood is sampled, and the air, now enriched with ethanol, is transferred to a GC for quantitative analysis.*

alcohol in the blood as long as the Henry's law constant (the equilibrium constant K_H) is known. This law is the basis of many presumptive breath alcohol tests performed in the field. When applied in a portable testing method, the phase boundary between liquid and gas is in the lungs. The concentration of alcohol in the breath can be related through Henry's law to the concentration of alcohol in the blood, which in turn is related to the degree of intoxication. For the blood–air system, K_H is approximately 2100, meaning that the concentration of alcohol in the blood is about 2100 times as great as it is in the headspace above. Field instruments used to estimate alcohol intoxication detect the quantity of alcohol in exhaled breath. Blood alcohol concentration is estimated using equation 4.3, K_H, and by accounting for temperature. However, laboratory analyses rely not on K_H directly, but on calibration curves and internal standards, as discussed in the previous chapter.

Like all equilibrium constants, K_H depends on temperature:

$$\text{ethanol (aq)} + \text{energy} \longleftrightarrow \text{ethanol (g)} \qquad \Delta H = (+) \qquad (4.4)$$

According to Le Châtelier's principle, if the equilibrium is disturbed, the system will respond. In effect, heating the sample is like adding a reactant, favoring the products. As long as the calibration standards are analyzed under the same experimental conditions, quantitation should be acceptably accurate and precise.

The manipulation of equilibrium conditions is at the heart of most organic sample preparations.

Even in this straightforward example, there are caveats. As the blood is heated, water and any other volatile constituents will be driven inevitably into the headspace along with the ethanol. Reducing the heat reduces the water content, concomitantly reducing the ethanol concentration. Even under mild heating, other blood gases and volatiles will be introduced into the headspace, along with other compounds that might be present, such as acetaldehde (a byproduct of alcohol metabolism) and acetone. This situation is illustrated in Figure 4.4. A trade-off is made, the analytical compromise between sample and matrix that is always necessary and, fortunately, almost always manageable. In our blood alcohol example, it is not necessary that every last molecule of ethanol be transferred to the vapor phase. Rather, all that is essential is that sufficient amounts are transferred and that the transfer is reproducible. This need is met using standardized validated analytical methods.

Even under optimal conditions, ethanol will not be the only component of blood that is transferred to the vapor phase. No separation is 100% complete, nor does it have to be. As long as enough of the analyte is separated and the separation is reproducible, it can be used qualitatively and quantitatively. In the foregoing example, the chromatographic column in the gas chromatograph will be capable of sorting out the potential interferents from the ethanol. This is another reason to use validated methods, since common interferents are accounted for and their effects understood. The worst-case scenario, in which unexpected interferents coelute with ethanol, can still be mitigated by selecting the proper detector and implementing various types of quality assurance and quality control measures. Regardless, the analytical scheme is still fundamentally dependent on sample preparation and calibration.

4.3 THE SPECIAL K'S

4.3.1 EQUILIBRIUM CONSTANTS

The example in the previous section illustrates the importance of equilibrium in partition and separation processes. Before delving in detail into specific sample preparation considerations, a review of the more important of these in the forensic context is worthwhile. The generic expression of equilibrium for a reaction $aA + bB \longleftrightarrow cC + dD$ is

$$K_{eq} = \frac{[C]^c[D]^d}{[A]^a[B]^b} \tag{4.5}$$

This equation is a ratio of products to reactants, and some generalizations can be made. First, no matter what type of reaction is being studied, the form of the equation and the underlying equilibrium principles apply. The subscript on K denotes the type of reaction, such as acid (K_a)–base(K_b) or dissolution (K_{sp}), but equilibrium is equilibrium. This is a good point to keep in mind when facing seemingly complex systems, such as the dissociation of diprotic acids or competing equilibria. The generic equation 4.5 applies to *any* equilibrium. A second generalization is that relative values of K describe the balance of products to reactants. The ratio of the numerator to the denominator in equation 4.5 determines whether products or reactants predominate when the system is at equilibrium.

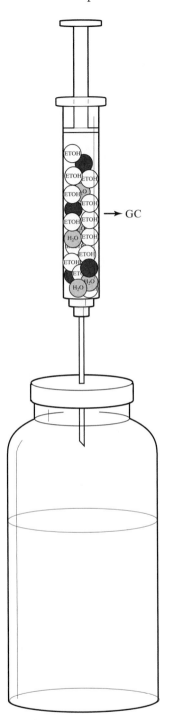

▲ **Figure 4.4** *A more realistic picture of the headspace sample. The heating will drive other substances—notably, blood gases, water, acetone, and so on—out of the blood sample. The separation is never complete, and these potential interferents must be accounted for and dealt with in subsequent analytical steps.*

For example, a small K value results when a small number is divided by a large number:

$$K_{eq} = \frac{1}{10} = \frac{small}{large} = 0.1 \longrightarrow \text{reactants "win"} \qquad (4.6)$$

By contrast, a large K value results when a large number is divided by a small number:

$$K_{eq} = \frac{10}{1} = \frac{large}{small} = 10 \longrightarrow \text{products "win"} \qquad (4.7)$$

Thus, if a K value is large relative to others in the same series (acid strength, water solubility, etc.), then the reaction favors the products. Certainly, any coefficients and exponents cannot be ignored, but the ability to glance at a K value and translate it to a likely chemical result is helpful.

Example Problem 4.1   Acid and Base Calculations

a. Rate the following acids from strong to weak on the basis of their pK_a values:
Phenylbutazone $pK_a = 4.40$
Ascorbic acid $pK_a = 4.10$
Arsenous acid (H_3AsO_3) $pK_a = 9.29$

Answer: The pK_a value is defined as the negative of the logarithm of K_a for the reaction $HA \longleftrightarrow H^+ + A^-$. The larger K_a, the stronger is the acid, as illustrated in equations 4.6 and 4.7. However, because of the negative sign, a large K_a corresponds to a small pK_a. In this example, ascorbic acid (vitamin C) is the strongest acid and arsenous acid is the weakest. The same logic applies to any such constant including K_b and K_{sp}.

b. Calculate the pH of a 2.00-M solution of amphetamine, a strongly basic drug with a pK_a of 9.8.

Answer: This problem requires that the equilibrium constant be expressed in terms of the base dissociation $B \longleftrightarrow BH^+ + OH^-$. With that value in hand, the calculation is straightforward.

$$pK_a = 9.8: K_a = 1 \times 10^{-9.8} \longrightarrow K_a = 1.58 \times 10^{-10}$$

$$K_w = K_a \times K_b \; so \; K_b = \frac{1.00 \times 10^{-14}}{1.58 \times 10^{-10}} = 6.33 \times 10^{-5}$$

Generically: $B \rightleftharpoons BH^+ + OH^-$
initially 2.00M   –   –
equilibrium 2.00 – x   x   x

2.00M >> than x because the K_b is relatively small (a weak base), so it can be ignored.

$$K_b = \frac{[BH^+][BH^-]}{[B]} = \frac{x^2}{2.00} = 6.33 \times 10^{-5}$$

$$x = 0.0113M = [OH]$$

$$pOH = \text{-log}\,[OH] = 1.95$$

$$pH + pOH = 14 \; so \; pH = 12.0$$

c. Calculate the pH of a 0.0025-M solution of amphetamine.

Answer: The only change from the previous calculation is that the dissociation can no longer be ignored and the quadratic equation must be used to calculate $[OH^-]$.

As with the previous calculation:

$$B \rightleftharpoons BH^+ + OH^-$$

initial 0.0025M   –   –
equilibrium 0.0025 – x   x   x

But x can't be ignored since it is much smaller than 2.00M. A rule of thumb is that if the difference between the initial concentration of a base is within ~ $+/- 10^3$ of the K_b, the loss from the initial concentrate should not be ignored.

$$\frac{x^2}{0.0025 - x} = 6.33 \times 10^{-5}: \text{use the quadratic equation}$$

$$x^2 = 6.33 \times 10^{-5} (0.0025 - x)$$

$$\overset{a}{\underset{}{\rightarrow}} x^2 + \overset{b}{6.33 \times 10^{-5}x} - \overset{c}{1.58 \times 10^{-7}} \quad x = \frac{-b +/- \sqrt{b^2 - 4ac}}{2a}$$

$$x = 3.67 \times 10^{-4} = [OH^-] \; pH = 10.56$$

Equilibrium constants are often presented as **pK**, values where p means "$-\log$ of", just as $pH = -\log [H^+]$. The negative sign has the effect of turning the relationships presented in equations 4-6 and 4-7 upside down; a large pK translates to a small K and reactants favored, a small pK to a large K and products favored:

$$K_{eq} = \frac{1}{10} = \frac{small}{large} = 0.1 \longrightarrow pK = -\log[0.1] = 1 \tag{4.8}$$

$$K_{eq} = \frac{10}{1} = \frac{large}{small} = 10 \longrightarrow pK = -\log[10] = -2 \tag{4.9}$$

Again, these relationships are approximations, but extremely useful ones.

4.3.2 SOLUBILITY EQUILIBRIUM CONSTANT K_{sp}

The solubility of drugs and other solids determines whether they can be placed into the aqueous phase. For drugs, water solubility is a critical consideration, since it correlates with bioavailability and toxicology. It is also important for sample preparation and cleanup, because most liquid–liquid extractions involve an aqueous phase in contact with an organic phase. The only unique aspect of solubility equilibrium is that, since one component is a solid, it is not expressed, because there is no aqueous concentration. The solubility is referred to as S and is obtained as shown in Example Problem 4.2.

The solubility of salts is an important criterion in sample preparation, as is the ionic character of drugs and larger molecules. One of the techniques used to increase the solubility of a drug is to convert the drug from an insoluble form to a soluble salt (more on this subject shortly). Common drug salts include sodium, calcium, sulfates, chlorides, tartrates, citrates, and lactates. The pH also plays a critical role in the water solubility of drugs and will be examined in detail momentarily. Soluble compounds are characterized as **hydrophilic** or **lipophobic**, for reasons to be discussed next.

Example Problem 4.2 K_{sp}

Calculate the solubility S of the solid Ag_2CO_3 with a K_{sp} of 8.1×10^{-12}.

Answers: The first step is to write the equation of the dissolution:

$$Ag_2CO_3(s) \longrightarrow 2\,Ag^+(aq) + CO_3^{2-}(aq)\ K_{sp} = [Ag^+]^2[CO_3^{2-}]$$

The solubility (S) of the compound is calculated by setting the carbonate concentration to S and the silver ion concentration to 2S:

$$S(2S)^2 = 8.1 \times 10^{-12} = 4S^3;\ S = 1.27 \times 10^{-4}\ mole/L$$

We use the symbol S to specify solubility, rather than the generic x notation used in other types of equilibrium calculations.

Historical Evidence 4.1—Analytical Separations

Without separations chemistry, it is hard to have any meaningful analytical chemistry. Historically, one of the driving forces behind the development of analytical separations was the need to isolate precious metals such as gold and silver from baser metals. Separations in turn require dissolution, a task that wasn't possible until the thirteenth century, when hydrochloric and nitric acids were created. This period also saw the introduction of *aqua regia*, a combination of these two acids that will dissolve gold. The interaction of acids with metals was put to use to detect counterfeiting. For example, when nitric acid reacts with copper, the copper dissolves and forms a distinctive green-colored complex. If a coin of "pure gold" showed a green color when nitric acid was dropped on it, the claim was false. This is an example of an early color-based presumptive test, a topic covered in Chapter 7.

Source: Salzberg, H. W. "Chapter 5: Medieval and Renaissance European Artisans," in H. W. Salzberg, *From Caveman to Chemist: Circumstances and Achievements*. Washington, DC: American Chemical Society, 1991.

4.3.3 Octanol–Water Partition Coefficient K_{ow} (Log P)

For drugs, solubility in fat is as important as solubility in water. Since drugs must cross a lipid membrane to enter a cell, solubility in octanol, a lipophilic alcohol, is often used to estimate fat solubility (**lipophilicity**). K_{ow} is the octanol–water partition coefficient and is calculated exactly as one would expect. This expression can be generalized as

$$P = \frac{[A_{org}]}{[A_{aq}]} \tag{4.10}$$

where P is the partition coefficient and the organic phase is octanol.[1] When other solvents are used, the equation

$$Log\ P' = a\,log\,P + b \tag{4.11}$$

can be employed (a and b are table values) to estimate solvent effectiveness.[1] Chloroform is widely used as an extraction solvent, so equation 4.11 is a useful relationship for converting K_{ow} values to partition coefficients in a chloroform–water system. Compounds with significant solubility in the organic phase are characterized as hydrophobic or lipophilic.

Applying the Science 4.1 Determining Hydrophobicity

The degree of fat solubility (lipophilicity) of a compound can be determined with the use of separatory funnels and instrumental techniques, but the process is tedious and time consuming. In the pharmaceutical industry, the ability to estimate K_{ow}/Log P values quickly is essential and has led to some innovative approaches. Researchers in the United Kingdom have reported a method that uses reversed-phase high-pressure liquid chromatography (HPLC) and correlation studies as a fast instrumental method for estimating hydrophobicity. They dubbed the resulting value the *chromatographic hydrophobicity index*, or CHI.

The theoretical basis of the chromatographic approach is fundamentally the same as for a separatory funnel method as described in the text—a phase boundary between a polar phase and a nonpolar phase. Octanol (nonpolar) can be used as a mobile phase with a polar stationary phase. A second option is to use a nonpolar stationary phase such as C18 (octadecylsilane) with an aqueous mobile phase. The researchers employed a gradient elution technique in which the composition of the mobile phase changed during the course of the analytical run from primarily organic (acetonitrile, nonpolar) to primarily aqueous buffer (polar), the pH of which depended on the drugs being evaluated. In chromatographic techniques such as gas chromatography or HPLC, the partition coefficient can be expressed as a capacity factor:

$$K_D = [\text{analyte, mobile}]/[\text{analyte, stationary}]$$

$$k'(\text{capacity factor or partition ratio}) = (t_r - t_m)/t_m$$

Here, t_r is the retention time of the analyte or drug of interest and t_m is the time it takes a portion of mobile phase to traverse the column (also called dead volume). The larger the capacity factor, the longer the analyte is retained in the column and hence the more like the stationary phase it is. Thus, in a reversed-phase system, the more hydrophobic the analyte is.

The researchers used HPLC and gradient elution, combined with a linear calibration method with substances of known K_{ow} values, to relate retention time to hydrophobicity. Their findings are summarized in the accompanying figures.

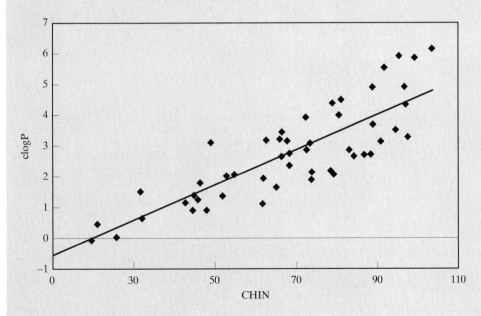

◀ CHI is the chromatographic hydrophobicity index, obtained experimentally via the calibrated HPLC system, here called CHIN for neutrals; C is an empirically determined constant. Figures reproduced with permission from the cited box reference. Copyright 1997, American Chemical Society.

Source: Valko, K., et al. "Chromatographic Hydrophobicity Index by Fast Gradient RP-HPLC: A High Throughput Alternative to P/logD." *Analytical Chemistry*, 69 **1997**, 2022–2029. As an interesting tidbit, this article has a comprehensive table of lipophilicity values that can be useful in designing extractions.

Applying the Science 4.1   (Continued)

a.
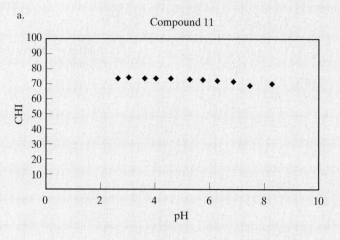

b.
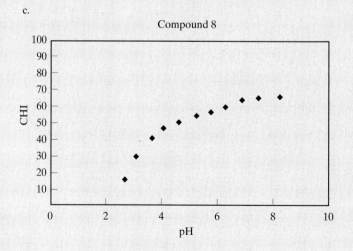

c.
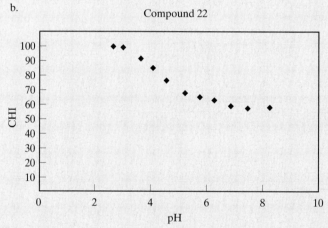

▶ *Compound 11 is indole; the other two compounds were not identified, except to note they were typical of the group represented. Figures reproduced with permission from the cited box reference. Copyright 1997, American Chemical Society.*

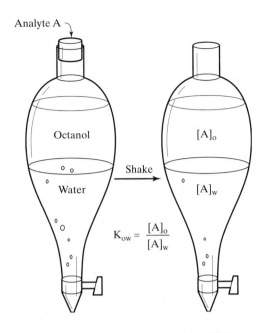

Analyte A

Octanol

Water

Shake

$[A]_o$

$[A]_w$

$$K_{ow} = \frac{[A]_o}{[A]_w}$$

◀ **Figure 4.5** *Determination of the octanol–water partition coefficient K_{ow} provides an estimate of fat solubility.*

Table 4.2   Values of *a* and *b* for Relating Solubility to K_{ow}

Solvent	a	b
Chloroform	1.13	−1.34
Diethyl ether	1.13	−0.17

Adapted from Thomas, G., "Chapter 3: Drug Solubility," in G. Thomas, *Medicinal Chemistry: An Introduction*. Chichester, U.K.: John Wiley and Sons, **2000**, p. 125.

4.3.4 PARTITION COEFFICIENTS

A partition coefficient K is established between two phases and an analyte that does not undergo any chemical changes when moving between one phase and the other. The use of headspace techniques to extract ethanol from blood is an example of a partition coefficient, defined here as K_H for the Henry's law constant. Ethanol undergoes a phase change, but not a chemical one, an important distinction. A liquid–liquid extraction using water and octanol is a partitioning as well. The analyte does not change chemically during the movement between the aqueous and organic phases. The generic form of the equilibrium constant for a partitioning is K_D, where "D" stands for distribution.

The value of K_D depends on the relative affinity of an analyte for each phase. The basis of that affinity may be any of the following properties:

- volatility (as discussed before in the blood alcohol example)
- polarity (like dissolves like)
- hydrogen-bonding interactions
- ion–ion interactions
- ion–dipole interactions
- dipole–dipole interactions

The concepts of distribution, partitioning, and **relative affinity** are central to chromatography and chromatographic separations. This topic will be discussed in detail in Section 4.5.

4.3.5 $K_a/K_b/K_w$

Acid–base chemistry plays a central role in drug chemistry and thus in drug analysis, toxicology, and sample preparation. Indeed, drugs are often classified as acidic, basic, or neutral. The functionalities in drugs that define their classes are amino groups (bases), phenolic groups (acids), and carboxyl groups (acids), all of which are weak acids or bases. It is not unusual for a drug molecule to have more than one acid or base group, each of which is called an **ionizable center**. When ionized, a drug molecule is soluble in water; when un-ionized, it is soluble in solvents such as octanol and chloroform. Accordingly, acid–base character is intimately related to solubility.

The key equations and expressions used in the forensic context are summarized in Figures 4.6 and 4.7. For drugs or other large molecules with a single weak-acid site, the relationship between pH and pK_a using the **Henderson–Hasselbalch** equation is derived. For large molecules with a single weak base (B), it is convenient to express the equilibrium in terms of the conjugate acid BH^+. Once the equilibrium is stated this way, all basic drugs may be described in terms of K_a. Thus, a drug's K_a value alone is not sufficient to define the drug as an acid or a base; knowledge of the structure and functional groups at the ionization centers is also needed.

The expressions shown in Figures 4.6 and 4.7 are useful for designing extractions. In general, equilibrium is considered to lie completely to one side or the other if the concentration of the product substance is at least 100 times greater than that of the reactant or vice versa.[†] In terms of the two equations presented, this corresponds to ratios of 100/1 or 1/100, depending on which form is desired. The corresponding logarithmic values are ±2 units. If an analyst desires to extract an acid drug into chloroform, for example, the drug must be in the un-ionized HA form. Suppose the drug has a pK_a of 3.5. To force the equilibrium to the fully protonated form and to a point such that [HA] exceeds [A⁻] by a factor of 100, the pH of the solution would need to be

$$pH = 3.5 + \log\frac{[A^-]}{[HA]} = 3.5 + \log\frac{[1]}{[100]} = 3.5 + (-2) = 1.5 \quad (4.12)$$

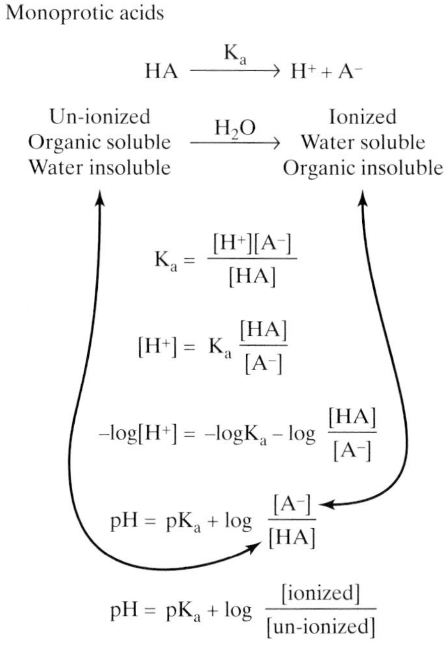

Monoprotic acids

$$HA \xrightarrow{\text{ } K_a \text{ }} H^+ + A^-$$

Un-ionized   Ionized
Organic soluble $\xrightarrow{\text{ } H_2O \text{ }}$ Water soluble
Water insoluble   Organic insoluble

$$K_a = \frac{[H^+][A^-]}{[HA]}$$

$$[H^+] = K_a \frac{[HA]}{[A^-]}$$

$$-\log[H^+] = -\log K_a - \log \frac{[HA]}{[A^-]}$$

$$pH = pK_a + \log \frac{[A^-]}{[HA]}$$

$$pH = pK_a + \log \frac{[\text{ionized}]}{[\text{un-ionized}]}$$

▶ **Figure 4.6** *Derivation of relationships used with monoprotic acid sites. Here, the generic term "organic" refers to a nonpolar solvent such as octanol.*

$$B \underset{H_2O}{\overset{Kb}{\rightleftharpoons}} BH^+ + OH^-$$

Weak base

or in acidic form:

$$BH^+ \underset{}{\overset{K_a}{\rightleftharpoons}} H^+ + B$$

Ionized
Water soluble
Organic insoluble

Organic soluble
Water insoluble

$$K_a = \frac{[B][H^+]}{[BH^+]}$$

$$[H^+] = \frac{K_a[BH^+]}{[B]}$$

$$-\log[H^+] = -\log K_a - \log \frac{[BH^+]}{[B]}$$

$$pH = pK_a + \log \frac{[B]}{[BH^+]}$$

$$pH = pK_a + \log \frac{[\text{un-ionized}]}{[\text{ionized}]}$$

◀ **Figure 4.7** *Derivation for large molecules with a single basic site. These molecules are called monobasic acids to indicate that the equilibrium is written as an acid dissociation.*

Exhibit A: The Elusive pK$_a$ Values

The pK$_a$ values for drug molecules, particularly those with multiple ionization centers, are not always easy to locate. The *Merck Index* is one source; *Clarke's Handbook* is another. Medicinal chemistry texts such as Thomas's[1] and pharmacology texts can be helpful. However, finding pK$_a$ values can be a quest.

This makes sense; to favor protonation, the concentration of protons in the solution should be high (the common-ion effect) in order to drive the reaction toward the reactant HA. The more acidic the solution, the less the HA will dissociate. Analogous arguments and calculations can be made for setting the pH to extract a basic solution.

| **Example Problem 4.3** | Simple Liquid–Liquid Extraction pH and pK$_a$ |

Propose a liquid–liquid extraction (LLE) scheme to separate a sample containing naproxen sodium (an analgesic) and codeine as the hydrochloride salt.

Answer: The first step in designing a separation is to obtain the necessary solubility data and pK$_a$ values. *Clarke's Handbook* and the *Merck Index* are two possible sources. A check of Clarke's Volume 2 provides the following data:

[†]You may recall this same approach from discussions of indicators used in titrations. Acid/base indicators change color over a range of 2 pH units; the reasoning is the same as described here.

Naproxen sodium: $pK_a = 4.2$; $\log P = 3.2$. Solubility of naproxen: insoluble in water, soluble 1 in 25 in ethanol, 1 in 15 in chloroform, and 1 in 40 in ether.

Codeine•HCl: $pK_a = 8.2$; $\log P = 0.6$. The HCl salt is soluble 1 in 20 in water, 1 in 180 in ethanol, and 1 in 800 in chloroform.

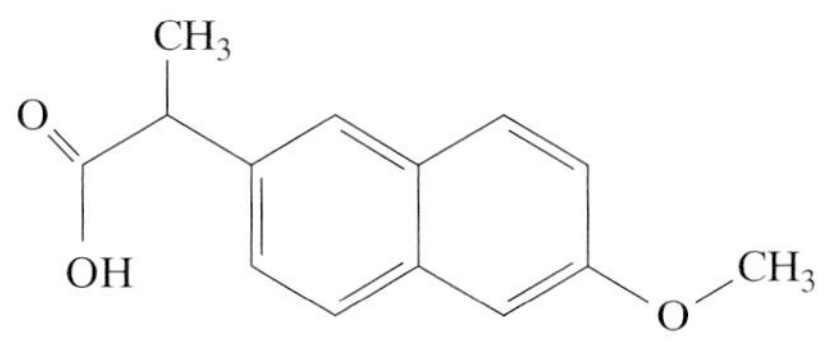

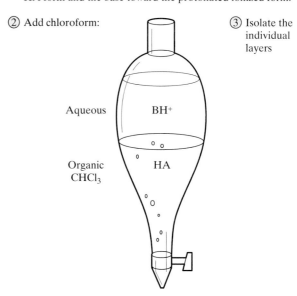

Naproxen structure 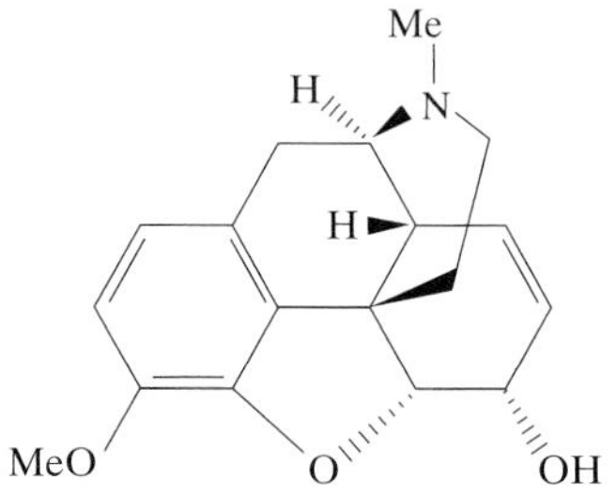   Codeine structure

The exploitable differences here are, first, the pK_a values and, second, solubility. Naproxen has an acidic ionization center and codeine has a basic ionizable center, affording relatively clean separation, as shown in the accompanying figure.

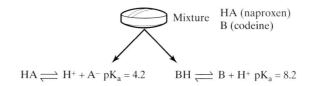

Mixture   HA (naproxen)
          B (codeine)

$$HA \rightleftharpoons H^+ + A^- \quad pK_a = 4.2 \qquad BH \rightleftharpoons B + H^+ \quad pK_a = 8.2$$

① Dissolve in dilute phosphoric acid such that the pH is 2.0 or lower. This will drive the acid toward the neutral protonated HA form and the base toward the protonated ionized form.

② Add chloroform:

③ Isolate the individual layers

Aqueous BH^+

Organic   HA
CHCl₃

Dilute phosphoric acid is a good choice in this case because, as mentioned in the text, phosphate salts tend to be less soluble in organic solvents such as chloroform than are the corresponding hydrochloride salts.

In general, the un-ionized form of a drug is lipophilic and will partition preferentially into the organic phase with relative polarities of the solvent and un-ionized form of the drug dictating the extent of solubility.

4.4 PARTITIONING

4.4.1 PARTITIONING WITH LIQUID PHASES: SOLVENT AND LIQUID–LIQUID EXTRACTIONS

Solubility is a function of relative polarities and is the basis of many separation techniques. In some cases, the separation is clean and simple, such as when a water-soluble drug like cocaine hydrochloride is cut (diluted) with an insoluble substance like cornstarch. It would be nice if that were the norm, but it rarely is in forensic laboratories. Simple or complex, "like dissolves like" is exploited to great effect in many forensic sample preparations. In the simplest case, an organic solvent such as chloroform is added to white powder to selectively extract drugs from diluents such as sugars. This procedure is referred to as a **dry extraction**. The next level of complexity is a liquid–liquid extraction (LLE) in which an analyte is separated from one liquid and transferred into the other by partitioning. The solvents used for these tasks in forensic chemistry include the usual suspects, shown in Table 4.3. From the table, a solvent can be selected that is suitable for dissolution of the target analyte solute. If the analyte is ionic or polar, water is an ideal choice for many reasons; if the analyte is nonionic or nonpolar, a solvent such as hexane or pentane would be a reasonable choice, with a caveat or two.

The extraction of arson samples with pentane provides an example.[†] The target analytes (accelerants) are mixtures of hydrophic hydrocarbons. Solvents such as toluene, hexane, and pentane make the first cut when solvents are considered, but toluene can be eliminated on the basis of its low volatility. (See the column headed "vapor pressure" in Table 4.3) Since the extraction involves a large volume of solvent that will subsequently be reduced by evaporation, a toluene extraction and concentration would take too long and would require aggressive heating to be completed in a reasonable amount of time. This heating would drive off lighter hydrocarbons that are crucial to a characterization of any accelerants that are present. Toluene is also a significant component of gasoline and other petroleum distillates used as accelerants, further disqualifying it.

Hexane might look promising on the basis of its volatility, but hexane could be found in the sample and it requires more heat to evaporate it than is desirable. Pentane, a solvent once used in many arson extractions, has a high vapor pressure and can be quickly driven off without sacrificing less volatile components. Pentane, too, is a component in gasoline, but an accelerant used in a fire will be weathered to some extent and will likely have lost most, if not all, of its original pentane component. The trade-off, however, in selecting pentane is its volatility. Precautions are needed to ensure that the pentane is not driven off too quickly, drying out the extract. Even with pentane, the lightest hydrocarbon components will be lost. In most arson samples, little of these lighter components remains, so the compromise is a reasonable one. Trade-offs are always made in any sample preparation. The goal is to make sure that these compromises are reasonable, manageable, reproducible, and understandable.

[†]Arson and its related chemistry are discussed in Chapters 9 and 10.

Table 4.3   Characteristics of Selected Solvents

Name	Structure	Molecular weight	Density	Vapor pressure	Dipole moment	Polarity	Solubility	Solvent group[2]
n-Pentane		72.15	0.626	420	0.00	0.0	0.04	1
Petroleum ether[1]	NA	NA	0.640	variable	NA	0.1	I	1
Hexane		86.18	0.659	124	0.08	0.1	0.01	1
Diethyl ether		74.12	0.713	442	1.15	2.8	6.89	2
Acetonitrile (methyl cyanide)		41.05	0.782	89	3.44	5.8	M	6
Isopropanol (2-propanol)		60.10	0.785	32	1.66	3.9	M	3
Ethanol		46.07	0.789	44	1.66		M	3
Acetone		58.08	0.790	185	2.69	5.1	M	6
Methanol		32.04	0.791	97	2.87	5.1	M	3
Toluene		92.14	0.867	29	0.31	2.4	0.05	7
N,N-Dimethylfor-mamide (DMF)		103.12	0.949	3	3.86	6.4	M	4
Pyridine		79.10	0.983	18	2.37	5.3	M	4
Water		18.02	1.000	18	1.87	10.2	NA	8
Methylene chloride (Dichloromethane)		84.93	1.326	350	1.14	3.1	1.60	5
Chloroform (Trichloromethane)		119.38	1.489	158	1.15	4.1	0.82	8

[1] Petroleum ether ("pet ether") is a mixture of hydrocarbons formulated to have a boiling point between 35 and 80°C. Pet ether contains no ethers. It is also called naptha, benzin, or petroleum benzin. Since the mixture varies, constants depend on the batch and the manufacturer.

[2] The solvent group is a classification based on similarity of behavior and solvent properties. It is useful for making generalizations and for selecting alternative solvents when safety, cost, or other constraints apply.

Note: NA = not applicable; M = miscible

Sources: Handbook of Chemistry and Physics, 84th ed. Boca Raton, FL: CRC Press, **2004**. *The Merck Index*, 13th ed. Whitehouse Station, NJ: Merck and Co., **2001**. "Solvent Information Website: Solvent Properties," Burdick and Jackson. Downloaded January 25, **2004**. www.bandj.com/BJSolvents/BJProperties.html. Snyder, L. R. "Classification of the Solvent Properties of Common Liquids." *Journal of Chromatography*, 92 (**1974**).

Other practical considerations are involved in selecting a solvent. Principal among these are safety and exposure concerns. Versatile solvents such as benzene, carbon tetrachloride, and the trichloroethanes are rarely used due to safety concerns. The use of chloroform and methylene chloride has also been reduced. The cost of disposal, often proportional to the safety risks, must also be weighed in laboratories that may consume liters of solvents weekly. The cost of the solvents is always an issue, and price increases with purity. It is not surprising that water is used whenever feasible. Finally, miscibility must be taken into account. There is no use attempting to separate analytes on the basis of their relative solubilities in ethanol and water, since ethanol itself is soluble in water. Most solvent separations are based on an aqueous phase and on solvents such as hexane, methylene chloride, or chloroform, which are insoluble in water. By comparing miscibility and polarity, an analyst can select candidate solvents for a separation LLE. If the analyte is appreciably more soluble in one liquid than in the other ($100 \times$ or more), partitioning can be successful. The relative densities of the solvents allow the analyst to predict which layer is which in a separatory funnel or similar vessel. Additional information on miscibility and solvents can be found in Appendix 3.

4.4.2 WATER SOLUBILITY AND PARTITIONING

With forensic analyses of toxicological and drug evidence, water solubility of the analytes is of paramount concern for sample preparation and extraction. Solubility is also important toxicologically, since it plays a role in determining how, where, and how quickly a drug is absorbed. The like-dissolves-like rule still applies but is broadened to include acid–base character and solubility of salts. Thus, target analytes may be ionic compounds, molecular compounds, or in the case of many drugs, salts like cocaine hydrochloride (cocaine HCl).

Neutral molecules with no significant acid–base character are soluble in organic solvents on the basis of polarity and according to like dissolves like. Salts such as cocaine hydrochloride are soluble in water according to their K_{sp}. In general, therapeutic agents are designed to be soluble in water under some set of physiological conditions, in order to facilitate their absorption into the bloodstream (more about this process in Chapter 6). As seen in Figure 4.8, the pH's in the digestive tract range from acidic to basic, and these differences are important in determining where a drug is likely to be soluble. If cocaine hydrochloride is swallowed,

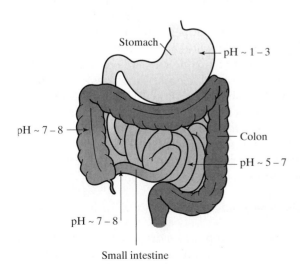

Stomach

pH ~ 1 – 3

pH ~ 7 – 8

Colon

pH ~ 5 – 7

pH ~ 7 – 8

Small intestine

◀ **Figure 4.8** *Approximate pH values at various locations in the digestive tract.*

Example Problem 4.4 **Where Drugs Are Absorbed**

In what locations of the digestive tract will the drug phendimetrazine tartrate (pK_a of phendimetrazine = 7.6) be most water soluble?

Phendimetrazine tartrate

Answer: In general, a drug is most soluble in the digestive tract, where it is most likely to be in the ionized form. The tartrate salt indicates that the drug is basic, a fact confirmed by examining its structure. A check of *Clarke's Handbook* reveals that the tartrate is freely soluble in water and thus in the digestive tract. Water solubility will be favored when the drug is in the ionized state, which, for a base, is the BH^+ form. Figure 4.16 is a useful reference in this type of problem, as is equation 4-12. At a pH of $7.6 - 2$, or 5.6, and below, the phendimetrazine will exist in the protonated ionized form, favoring dissolution. According to Figure 4.8, this pH exists in the stomach and portions of the small intestine.

---

it dissolves quickly to form the protonated cation ($cocaine-H^+$) and chloride ion. Cocaine is a weak base by virtue of an amine group, so its pH will dictate its further solubility. At more acidic pHs, the amine group will tend to protonate and be charged. If charged, it is an ion and water soluble. Under more basic conditions, the amine group will tend to deprotonate and lose charge. It then becomes a molecular compound with solubility dependent on polarity and related factors.

4.4.3 IONIZATION CENTERS

Many drugs and metabolites are acidic, basic, or amphoteric and can be protonated or deprotonated depending on their pH and pK_a values. An **ionization center** can produce a charged species and thus a water-soluble ion. Conversely, neutral molecules are soluble in organic solvents such as methylene chloride. Control and manipulation of the pH of an aqueous phase is exploited in LLEs and in solid-phase extractions (SPEs), to maximize separation efficiency.

A significant number of drugs and metabolites have acid-base character and measurable pK_a values. Many have more than one ionizable center and some, such as morphine, are amphoteric. The ionizable groups in drugs and metabolites include carboxylic acids (COOH), phenolic protons, hydroxyls, and amine groups. A range of drugs and their acid–base characters are illustrated in Figure 4.9. Meprobamate, an example of a neutral drug, is insoluble in water, but soluble in organic solvents according to relative polarities.

For example, when amphetamine is placed in water, the amine group picks up a proton, leading to a basic solution:

$$amphet - NH_2 \overset{H_2O}{\rightleftharpoons} amphet - NH_3^+ + OH^- \tag{4.13}$$

Conversly, acetylsalicylic acid (aspirin) is an acidic drug with one ionization center, a carboxylic acid group. When aspirin is dissolved in water, the general acidic dissociation equation $HA \longrightarrow H^+ + A^-$ applies.

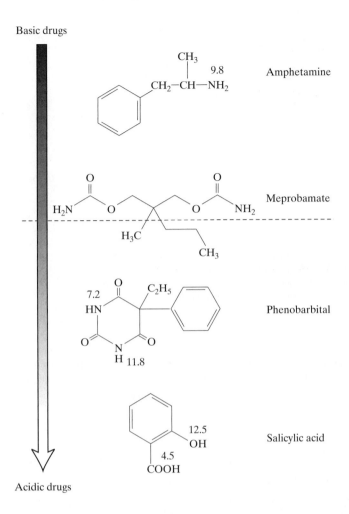

Basic drugs

Acidic drugs

Amphetamine

Meprobamate

Phenobarbital

Salicylic acid

◀ **Figure 4.9** *Examples of acidic, basic, and neutral drugs. The small numbers above the ionization centers are the pK_a values.*

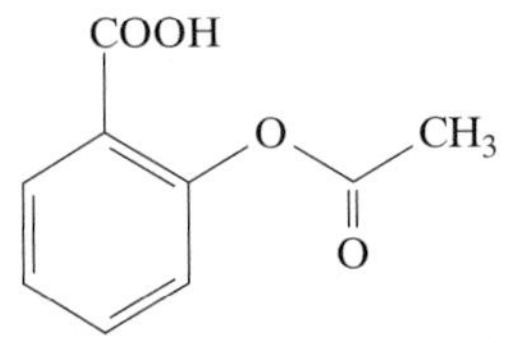

The picture is more complicated when a molecule has more than one ionizable center. Some drugs have two, three, and even four such centers,[2] and some are amphoteric. The two acidic drugs shown in Figure 4.9 have two acidic proton sites each, the model for these types of molecules is H_2SO_4. The relative values of the pK_a's reflect which site will deprotonate first. The larger the K_a, the stronger the acid is; the smaller the pK_a, the weaker the acid. Consequently, the site with the smaller pK_a value will dissociate first. To ensure that the molecules remain deprotonated and neutral for extraction, the smaller pK_a is the critical one. To extract phenobarbital, a pH of 5.2 is needed, whereas an extraction of salicylic acid requires a more acidic pH of 2.5. Similar arguments apply for dibasic molecules.

Amphoteric drugs present the greatest extraction and partitioning challenge. Consider morphine, an amphoteric drug with two ionizable centers, one an acidic phenol and one a basic amine. Selecting an extraction pH is more challenging than when a single ionization center is present because the two ionization centers, in effect, work against each other. To deprotonate the amino group, a high pH is needed. However, if the solution is too basic, the phenolic group deprotonates. Thus, it is not possible to find a pH such that the molecule will be neutral due to the lack of charged groups. It is possible, though, to isolate a pH at which the molecule is neutral due to balance of the positive and negative

▲ **Figure 4.10** *Aspirin, an acidic drug with one ionizable center, the carboxylic acid group. The pK_a of this group is 3.48.*

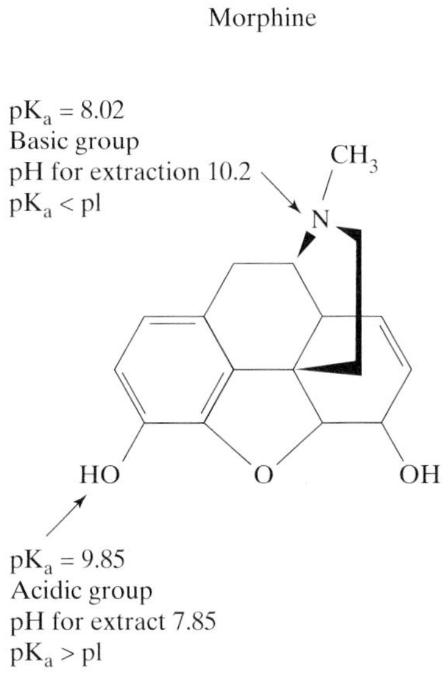

Morphine

pK$_a$ = 8.02
Basic group
pH for extraction 10.2
pK$_a$ < pI

pK$_a$ = 9.85
Acidic group
pH for extract 7.85
pK$_a$ > pI

▶ **Figure 4.11** *Morphine, an amphoteric drug. The pI is the isoelectric pH at which the positive and negative charges are balanced.*

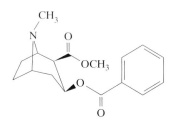

▲ **Figure 4.12** *The structure of cocaine, which has one ionizable center and a pK$_a$ of 8.6.*

charges. The di-ion is referred to as a *zwitterion* (German *zwitter* (hybrid), from *zwei* (two)). To determine the ideal pH for extraction, the average of the pK$_a$ values is calculated and is referred to as the **isoelectric point** or isoelectric pH (pI):

$$pI = \frac{pK_{a_1} + pK_{a_2} \cdots pK_{a_n}}{n} \quad (4.14)$$

For morphine, the isoelectric pH is the average of 9.85 and 8.02, or 8.94. Outside of this narrow pH around 8.9, the molecule is ionized and soluble in water.

Drugs with ionization centers can exist in a variety of forms. Cocaine, with a protonated amine is a cation that can associate with chloride to form what is known as cocaine hydrochloride, a water-soluble sparkling white powder that has lent it the slang term "snow." Crack cocaine ("freebase"), the unprotonated molecule shown in Figure 4.12 has an oily texture and is much less water soluble than the salt. Other forms of cocaine are a nitrate dihydrate and a sulfate salt, both of which are soluble in water. Morphine can be found as the hydrochloride salt, a monohydrate, an acetate trihydrate, a tartrate trihydrate, a sulfate salt, and a pentahydrate sulfate. Many of the hydrochloride salts of drugs have degrees of solubility in some organic solvents, such as chloroform.[3] The phosphate and sulfate salts tend to be less soluble in organic solvents, a property that can be exploited in designing separations. The use of alternative solvents is also called for under these circumstances.

Although there are occasions when a forensic chemist must devise an appropriate solvent extraction for a known or strongly suspected analyte, it is much more common to use a series of acid–base extractions to isolate components on the basis of their acid–base characteristics. Such acid–base–neutral acid-base (also called acid-base-neutral) extractions are widely used in analytical chemistry for screening and sample preparation. Figure 4.13 gives an overview of an acid–base LLE scheme. The first step is to acidify the sample and perform extraction with an organic solvent such as chloroform. The two layers, which can be distinguished by their density, are the organic layer and the aqueous layer. By initially setting the pH acidic, compounds that act as acids will remain protonated and uncharged and will partition preferentially into the organic layer. Ionized bases, water-soluble neutrals, other ions, and metals that are extracted

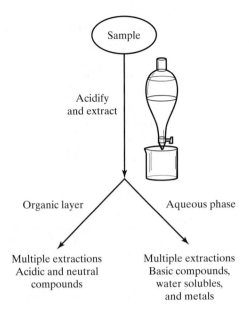

◀ **Figure 4.13** *An overview of an acid–base–neutral preparation. The series of Figures 4.13–4.15 is adapted from a scheme presented in Siek, T. J., "Specimen Preparation," in B. Levine, ed., Principles of Forensic Toxicology, 2d ed. (Washington, DC: American Association for Clinical Chemistry, 2003).*

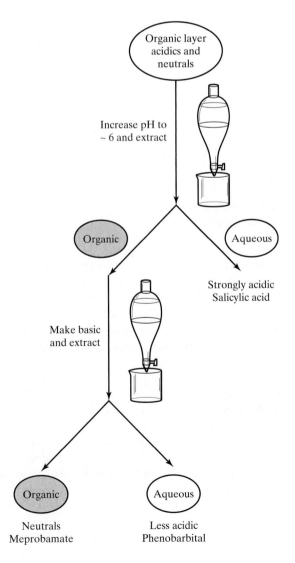

▶ **Figure 4.14** *The organic layer from Figure 4.13.*

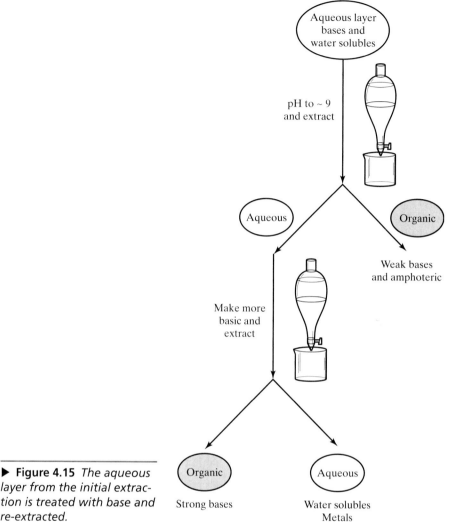

▶ **Figure 4.15** *The aqueous layer from the initial extraction is treated with base and re-extracted.*

by the acid will stay in the aqueous layer. Further manipulation of the layers is shown in Figures 4.14 and 4.15. The compounds described are from Figure 4.9.

Figure 4.14 illustrates the separation of the acid–neutral fraction. The organic layer containing the acids is made less acidic by addition of a buffer and is extracted again. Strong acids will remain ionized and in the aqueous phase, while weaker acids and neutrals will remain in the organic layer. The final step is to add a basic aqueous layer that will separate out the neutrals such as meprobamate from weakly acidic compounds that ionize only in the presence of a strong base. Processing of the aqueous layer from the original extraction (Figure 4.13) is shown in Figure 4.15. The aqueous layer from the initial extraction is made basic and re-extracted. Stronger bases will remain ionized and will partition into the aqueous layer, while weaker bases will be neutralized and will be extracted by the organic solvent. The last step is to make the aqueous layer even more basic such that strong bases will be neutralized and will partition into the organic solvent. The remaining aqueous layer will contain water-soluble materials.

To reiterate, water solubility of molecules with ionization centers is dependent on pH. The salts of drugs may be soluble in water, but once in solution, the solubility of such molecules depends on the pH. Neutral molecules can be extracted

	Acidic	**Basic**	**Amphoteric**
Functional groups	– COOH carboxyl – OH hydroxyl/phenolic	$-\overset{\mid}{\underset{\mid}{N}}$ amine	Both
Generic equations	$HA \underset{}{\overset{K_a}{\rightleftharpoons}} H^+ + A^-$ Soluable in organics LdL $\downarrow$ — Water soluable	$BH^+ \underset{}{\overset{K_a}{\rightleftharpoons}} B + H^+$ Water soluable $\downarrow$ — Soluable in organics LdL	Both
For extraction	$pK_a = pH + \log \dfrac{[A^-]}{[HA]} \dfrac{\text{aqueous}}{\text{organic}}$	$pK_a = pH + \log \dfrac{[B]}{[BH^+]} \dfrac{\text{organic}}{\text{aqueous}}$	Both
Water solubility curve	Solubility vs pH curve (pK_a); Acidic ← pH → Basic	Solubility curve (pK_a); Acidic → Basic	Solubility curve (pI); Acidic → Basic
Examples	Compound — pK_{a1} — pK_{a2} Salycilic acid — 4.5 — 12.5 Phenobarbital — 7.2 — 11.8 Acetaminophen — 10	Compound — pK_{a1} — pK_{a2} Caffeine — 0.6 Cocaine — 8.4 Quinine — 4.1 — 8.0 Amphetamine — 9.8	Compound — pK_{a1} — pK_{a2} Morphine — 8.02 — 9.85 Benzoylecgonine — 4.0 — 8.6

◀ **Figure 4.16** *Summary of acid–base–amphoteric solubility and extraction characteristics. Neutral molecules (not shown) are soluble in organic solvents according to like-dissolves-like (LdL) characteristics. The solubility curves depict trends in water solubility as a function of pH for the three different categories. In the ionic form (A^- or BH^+), drug molecules are water soluble.*

into organic solvents, to a degree dictated principally by relative polarities, while ionic forms partition preferentially into the aqueous phase. Figure 4.16 summarizes acid–base solubility and extraction characteristics for drugs and metabolites.

4.4.4 PARTITIONING WITH THE GAS PHASE: HEADSPACE METHODS

The discussion of headspace methods for blood alcohol and solid-phase micro extraction (SPME) in Section 4.2 introduced the concept of creating an enriched headspace above a sample. Headspace methods may be passive or active and may involve heating the sample. **Dynamic headspace** (DHS) methods, used in arson analyses, exploit the equilibrium at the liquid–sample interface by sweeping the headspace with a constant stream of gas, usually helium. DHS is also referred to as **purge-and-trap** (PT), although the latter can also mean a specific type of sample preconcentrator used in environmental analysis. The trap material can be thermally desorbed or desorbed with a solvent. The thermal method is preferred, but is not always possible. The choice of trapping or sorbent materials depends on the application; arson typically requires charcoal or charcoal combinations.

4.5 PARTITIONING WITH A SOLID PHASE

4.5.1 OVERVIEW

Recall the fundamental requirements of separation, that there must exist:

1. Equilibrium must exist across a phase boundary.
2. An exploitable difference in physical or chemical properties between analyte and matrix.

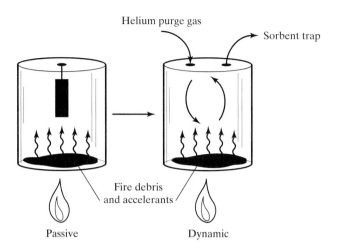

▶ **Figure 4.17** *Passive vs. dynamic headspace. In dynamic techniques, the headspace is swept constantly. As a result, the equilibrium*
$A(solid \ or \ aq) \longleftrightarrow A(g)$
is constantly disrupted and driven to the right, where the accelerants or other volatiles are driven into the vapor phase.

| Example Problem 4.5 | Propose a Method for Separating Procaine and Cocaine. |

Answer: This is a bit of a trick question in the context presented. The two compounds are so closely related that neither an LLE nor an SPE method will be sufficient for their separation. This is not a problem per se; gas chromatography affords easy separation. But the problem serves as a reminder that the separations performed during sample preparations don't have to be perfect.

If these conditions are met, selective partitioning between the phases is possible. If the difference is large, solvent extractions, liquid–liquid extractions, or LLE, pH and solubility-based extractions may be adequate if only qualitative data are needed. To separate a mixture of cocaine · HCl and cornstarch is an easy task since the drug salt is water-soluble and the cornstarch is not. This is an example of a straightforward dry extraction. It is not a simple matter to separate a mixture of cocaine (pK_a = 8.6 and log P = 2.3), procaine (9.0, 2.1), lidocaine (7.9, 2.4), and tetracaine (8.2, which are chemically similar. Differences exist, but are too subtle for a simple solvent extraction. When the exploitable differences among analytes are small, more discriminating and more frequent interactions are required to affect separation. These considerations are the basis of solid-phase separations and the natural extension of chromatography. Relatively small differences are amplified and expressed by facilitating a far greater number of interactions than is possible with solvent extractions and LLE protocols. Separation is accomplished not by changing the nature of the interactions, but by decreasing their scale and increasing their frequency.

4.5.2 SOLID-PHASE PARTITIONING

Solid-phase extraction and separation can be thought of in terms of a driving force and an opposing force. The analytes to be separated are dissolved in a solvent that moves past (the driving force) a stationary phase on which interactions occur. The more an analyte interacts with the stationary phase (the opposing force), the more its progress through the column is impeded. The less the interaction, the faster the analyte travels through the column. One way to express the degree of interaction is by considering the equilibrium and calculating a distribution coefficient K_D. A large K_D implies that a larger concentration of the analyte resides with the stationary phase at any given time than resides in the mobile phase.

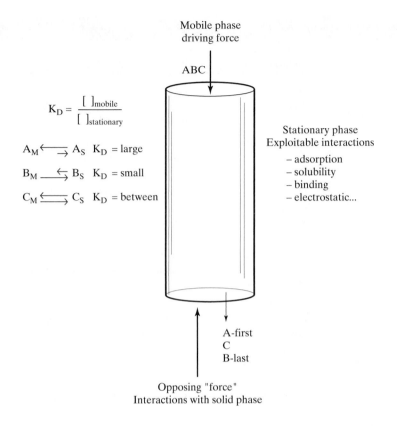

$$K_D = \frac{[\;]_{\text{mobile}}}{[\;]_{\text{stationary}}}$$

Mobile phase
driving force

ABC

$A_M \xleftarrow{\hspace{0.5cm}} A_S \quad K_D = \text{large}$

$B_M \xrightarrow{\hspace{0.3cm}\xleftarrow{}\hspace{0.1cm}} B_S \quad K_D = \text{small}$

$C_M \xrightleftharpoons{\hspace{0.5cm}} C_S \quad K_D = \text{between}$

Stationary phase
Exploitable interactions
  – adsorption
  – solubility
  – binding
  – electrostatic...

A-first
C
B-last

Opposing "force"
Interactions with solid phase

◀ **Figure 4.18** *Partitioning on a solid phase. A mobile phase is driven or forced past a solid phase on which multiple interactions can occur. The interactions slow the analytes and act as an opposing force.*

Applying the Science 4.2   True Racing Form

Performance toxicology is not limited to humans. Animal athletes—or rather, their trainers—must abide by rules that prohibit performance-enhancing substances. As with their human counterparts, these rules are broken and so must be enforced by toxicological monitoring. In one approach, basic drugs are converted to their cationic form $(-R-NH_3{}^+)$ by placing them in an acidic solution and then are introduced into a strong cation exchange (SCX) column. The drug cations displace less tightly associated cations such as Na^+ and are retained on the column by ion–ion and ion–dipole interactions. The columns are then rinsed with different solvents to eliminate interferents, after which they are flushed with a basic solution to remove the adsorbed basic drugs. This is accomplished by returning the drugs back to a neutral form that has little affinity for the SCX resin. In three trials, recoveries ranged from 70.1% ± 8.6% for caffeine, to 100.0% ± 2.3% for quinine, to 100.0% ± 1.0% for papaverine.

Source: Moore, C. M. "Solid Phase Cation Exchange Extraction of Basic Drugs from the Urine of Racing Greyhounds." *Journal of the Forensic Science Society*, 30 **1990**, 123–129.

The stationary phase provides a platform on which interactions and partitioning can occur. The interactions may be based on adsorption, solubility, binding, or electrostatic interactions, to name a few types. Fundamentally, most of these can be reduced to polarity-based interactions and even to like dissolves like. The stationary phase may be a solid or a liquid that is bound to a solid support. The selection of mobile and stationary phases can enhance the discrimination.

Solid-Phase Extraction (SPE): The generic structure of the solid phase in SPE is a small silica particle. A silica backbone extends away from the surface and is bonded to an active terminal "R" group. The beads have a porous surface, which increases the surface area available to interact with the analyte. R determines the affinity of the solid phase, while the chemical bonding to the silica ensures

Table 4.4   SPE Media

Name	Active group (R)	Surface characteristics	Binding type, conditions, and examples
Octadecyl	$(-C_{18}H_{37})$	Hydrophobic Nonpolar	Hydrophobic species from aqueous solutions (e.g., organics, peptides, oligonucleotides)
Octyl	$(-C_3H_{17})$	Hydrophobic	Hydrophobic species from aqueous solutions (less strongly held than C_{18})
Silica	$\overset{\displaystyle OH}{\underset{\displaystyle \mid}{}}\quad\overset{\displaystyle OH}{\underset{\displaystyle \mid}{}}$ $-O-Si-O-Si-O-$	Hydrophilic Polar Neutral	Species of low to moderate polarity from nonaqueous solutions (e.g., fat-soluble vitamins)
Florisil	Magnesium silicate	Hydrophilic Polar Slightly basic	Species of low to moderate polarity from nonaqueous solutions (e.g., fats, polychlorinated biphenyls)
Alumina A (acidic alumina)	OH OH $-O-Al-O-Al-O-$	Hydrophilic Polar Acidic Cation binding	Hydrophilic species in nonaqueous solutions (e.g., antibiotics, caffeine)
Alumina N (neutral alumina)	OH O^- $-O-Al-O-Al-O-$	Hydrophilic Polar Neutral	Hydrophilic species in nonaqueous solutions (e.g., petroleum)
Alumina B (basic alumina)	O^- O^- $-O-Al-O-Al-O-$	Hydrophilic Polar Basic Cation binding	Hydrophilic species in nonaqueous solutions (e.g., steroids, pesticides)
Aminopropyl	$-C_3H_6NH_2$	Hydrophilic Moderately polar Slightly basic Anion binding	Analytes in aqueous or organic solvents (e.g., phenols, petroleum, saccharides)
Cyanopropyl	$-C_3H_6CN$	Hydrophobic Nearly nonpolar Neutral	Analytes in aqueous or organic solvents (e.g., hydrophobic peptides, pesticides)
Diol	OH OH $-CH_2-CH_2-$	Hydrophobic Nearly nonpolar Neutral	Trace elements in water; proteins and peptides in aqueous or organic solvents
Styrene divinylbenzene		Hydrophobic Neutral	Organics in water (e.g., polyaromatic hydrocarbons, vitamin B_{12})
Anion binding (strong anion exchange)	$-CH_2CH_2-\overset{+}{N}(CH_3)_3$	Hydrophilic Anion binding	Anions in water or aqueous mixed solvents (e.g., Cl^-, $SO_4{}^{2-}$, $PO_4{}^{3-}$)

From Rubinson, J. F., and K. A. Rubinson, "Chapter 4: Sample Treatment, Interferences, and Standards," in J. F. Rubinson and K. A. Rubinson, *Contemporary Instrumental Analysis.* Upper Saddle River, NJ: Prentice Hall, **2000**, p. 106.

that the active groups cannot be stripped from the solid support. The common types of SPE media are summarized in Table 4.4.

SPE can be classified by relative polarity of the solid and mobile phases. A nonpolar solid phase that preferentially associates with nonpolar or slightly polar analytes is called **reversed phase**, and the solvents used as eluents are polar. **Normal-phase** SPE employs a polar solid phase and nonpolar solvents. Highly polar and ionizable solid phases are used in ion exchange, which can also be used as a form of analysis. The continuum of solid-phase sorbents runs from reversed-phase nonpolar such as C18, through moderately polar phases such as cyanopropyl, to strong anion and cation exchangers.

There are four general steps in SPE. After the appropriate column is selected, it is rinsed to condition it. Next, sample is loaded onto the column and flows or is drawn through by vacuum—the driving force of the mobile phase. The analytes of interest will be retained, as will some matrix components, while other matrix components will be eluted. The next step(s) are cleanups that may consist of altering the pH of the system, followed by the introduction of a solvent that will remove matrix components while leaving target analytes adsorbed to the solid phase. The last step is the elution of the target analytes. The cleanups are discarded while the final eluate is retained. Depending on the capacity of the column, large volumes of sample, such as several milliliters of urine or even a liter of water can be introduced; it is only the binding capacity and surface area of the solid phase that limits the volume. The more dilute the sample, the greater is the volume that can be introduced without saturating the active sites on the solid sorbent.

One of the advantages of an SPE preparation over solvent or LLE methods is that multiple solvents can be used to clean the sample before the final eluting solvent is added. The choice of solvents, as with LLEs, depends on the nature of the analyte. SPE can be performed with packed cartridges, disks, and syringe adapters. In addition, SPE can be automated to increase throughput.

Table 4.5   Solvent Strengths Relevant to SPE

Solvent	$e^{\circ*}$	Reverse phase eluting strength	Normal phase eluting strength
Pentane	0.00	Strong	Weak
Petroleum ether	0.01	↓	↓
Isooctane	0.01		
Carbon Tetrachloride	0.18		
Ethyl ether	0.38		
Chloroform	0.40	↓	↓
Methylene Chloride	0.42		
Ethyl acetate	0.58		
Acetone	0.56		
Acetonitrile	0.65	↓	↓
Isopropanol	0.82		
Methanol	0.95		
Water	large	Weak	Strong

*e° is a measure of solvent strength based on polarity. It is defined as the energy of absorption on a surface of alumina, a polar material.

Sources: 1. *A User's Guide to Solid Phase Extraction Reference #M2*, Alltech Associates, Inc., **1998**. 2. Rubinson, K. A., and J. F. Rubinson, "Chapter 14: Liquid Chromatography," in K. A. Rubinson and J. F. Rubinson, *Contemporary Instrumental Analysis*. Upper Saddle River, NJ: Prentice Hall, **2000**.

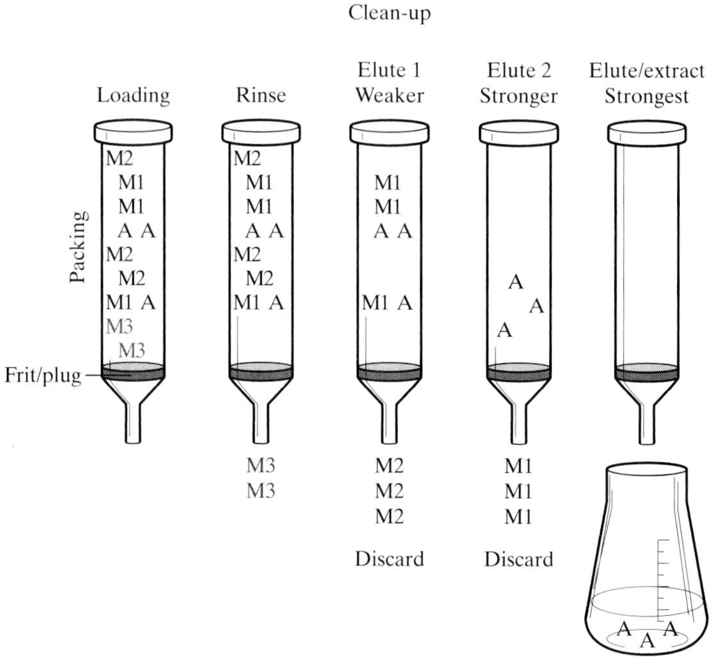

▶ **Figure 4.19** *Generic SPE using a column. The analyte A is separated and concentrated in the final elution by successive rinsings with weaker solvents. Some components of the matrix (indicated by M1 and M2) may also be left on the column.*

Applying the Science 4.3   Combined Acid, Neutral, and Basic Drug Sample Preparation with SPE

Blood and plasma are among the most difficult sample matrices to work with. Accordingly, SPE techniques have greatly improved sample preparation in forensic toxicology. Recently, vendors have introduced columns that facilitate isolation of the acid, basic, and neutral fractions using a single column. In one study, whole blood was spiked with 90 drugs and internal standards prior to its introduction into the Oasis® SPE column (Waters, Milford MA). The neutral and acidic drugs were eluted as one group separately from the basic drugs. Although problems were reported with benzodiazepines such as Valium®, traditionally challenging amphoteric drugs such as morphine were successfully eluted. The acid fraction was reported as "dirty." Overall, the authors reported that 75% of the test compounds were recovered and quantitative when therapeutic ranges of the drugs were studied.

Source: Yawney, J., et al. "A General Screening Method for Acid, Neutral, and Basic Drugs in Whole Blood Using the Oasis MCX^(TM) Column." *Journal of Analytical Toxicology*, 26 **2002**, 325–332.

For the extraction of drugs and metabolites with acid–base character, alumina phases are used. Many multifunctional columns have been developed to allow for the separate extraction of acids, bases, and neutrals that integrate an ion-exchange resin with relatively nonpolar functionality.[4–6] That way, different properties can be exploited sequentially by rinsing the column between elutions. In general, a buffered, slightly basic solution of the sample is introduced into the column. Following a water wash, an acidic solution is introduced. Acidic drugs will protonate and remain uncharged, allowing them to be eluted with an organic solvent, along with neutrals. The column is dried and then flushed with a basic solvent system to elute basic components. The two **eluants** are treated separately in subsequent analyses. When elution solvents are changed, the column must be rinsed and dried in between to avoid miscibility problems.

Example Problem 4.6 Propose an SPE Scheme for Cleaning a Sample Containing Heroin and Cocaine.

Answer: Cocaine has a pK_a of 8.6 and heroin has a pK_a of 7.6. Both are basic drugs that adhere to the generic relationship $BH^+ \longleftrightarrow B + H^+$. Heroin base is soluble in chloroform at a ratio of 1:1.5, but is not appreciably soluble in other organic solvents. Cocaine base is similarly soluble in chloroform, as well as in acetone, ether, and carbon disulfide. This solubility information can be used to select solvents for flushing the column of contaminants and for eluting the drugs at the final stage.

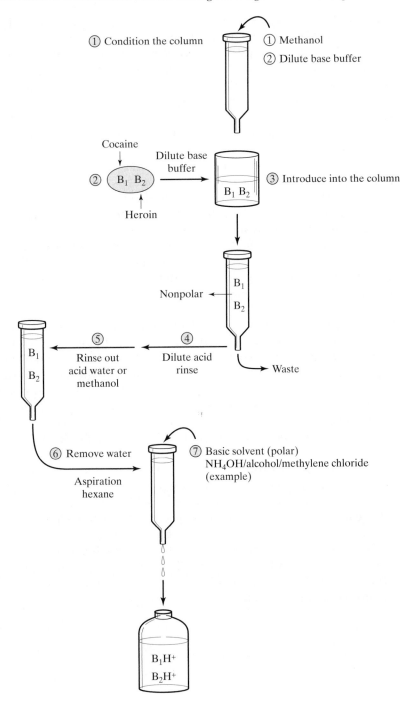

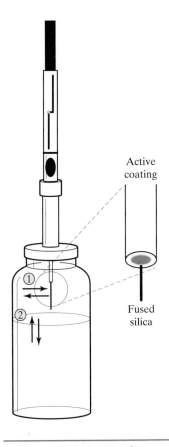

▲ **Figure 4.20** *SPME using coated fibers. The apparatus above the vial is a holder that protects the fragile fiber. The fiber is kept inside of the housing until it is ready to be exposed to the sample. Components in the headspace partition into the solid support and concentrate there. After the exposure, the fiber is withdrawn into the housing and removed.*

On the basis of the preceding data, the first step would be to dissolve the sample in dilute basic solution with a pH of ~11, which is 8.6 + 2 units, more than enough to ensure that both drugs are in the un-ionized base form. The solution would be introduced into the C18 column, where the un-ionized base will be retained. Since both drugs are basic, a weak acid wash of the column will flush out any acidic contaminants. A rinse with methanol will flush out the residual acid solution. To elute the basic drugs into an organic solvent, that solvent must be slightly basic. A moderately polar solvent mixture containing ammonia would be appropriate.

Solid-Phase Microextraction (SPME): A relatively new type of SPE is being used in drug and arson analysis. In this form, a small fiber holds the sorbent. **Solid-phase microextraction** (SPME) is versatile and particularly amenable to the extraction and preconcentration of volatile organics. The active material is bonded to a thin silica needle with dimensions similar to capillary GC columns (fractions of a millimeter). Coating materials are the same or similar to packing used in SPE, so the same types of analytes can be targeted. Although Figure 4.20 shows the fiber exposed to the headspace, fibers can be also be placed in the liquid.

SPME sample preparation begins with exposure of the fiber. Assuming a headspace application, variables such as height above the liquid, length of fiber exposed, and exposure time must be optimized. The coated fiber is fragile and so is usually kept in a protective housing until exposure. The housing also facilitate setting a constant and thus reproducible depth and height for the exposure. Depending on the volatility of the target analytes, the sample may be heated. Because the sorbent coatings are thin, overloading is a concern that must be addressed in method development and optimization. If used, internal calibration standards are introduced during this absorption phase.

At the end of the exposure period, the fiber is withdrawn into the housing and removed from the sample. Although some methods use a solvent to extract adsorbed materials in a way analogous to the elution of a solid-phase cartridge, more often the fiber is introduced directly into the heated injection port of a gas chromatograph or into the injector of a high-pressure liquid chromatograph. As in the absorption phase, the geometry of placement in the injector and time of desorption must be optimized. Automating SPME is more difficult than automating SPE, mainly because of the fragility of the fibers.

Forensic interest in, and applications of, SPME have increased, particularly since 2000. Arson analyses were the initial focus because, due to the nature of the absorption and desorption process, SPME fibers are ideally suited to the analysis of volatile material.[6–11] Less volatile components are also absorbed, but typically require greater heating and longer desorption times for effective removal from the fiber. In general, the more volatile the analytes, the less of a concern desorption is. Forensic applications of SPME have been reported for toxicology,[7–10] drug analysis[11,12] and toxicology,[13] drug analysis in hair,[14,15] explosives,[16,17] inks and currency,[18] and firearms.[19,20]

In arson, the target analytes are volatile hydrocarbons that are ideally suited for SPME. ASTM has published a standard method for screening fire debris for the presence of accelerant residues.[21,22] The specified fiber is coated with polydimethylsiloxane (PDMS), a nonpolar phase, and the sample is heated to 60–80°C for 20–30 minutes. Exposure time is between 5 and 15 minutes, depending on sample concentration. This method illustrates one of the limitations of SPME. Because the active coating is thin, it is easily overloaded with analyte. Once the fiber is saturated, no additional analyte can be absorbed. Qualitative results may not suffer, but quantitation becomes unreliable once this breakthrough occurs. Often, as described in the ASTM method (E2154), this limitation necessitates a trial-and-error approach to balance sample heating and desorption times. Furthermore, since the fibers are reused, it is essential that they be thoroughly purged of any residual sample before reuse. In turn, this means that a fiber blank must be analyzed. Consequently, any single use of a fiber generates the need for a second run to ensure that the fiber has been stripped clean and that there will be no carryover.

Solid Phase Stir-Bar Extraction: An innovative related technique, stir-bar solid-phase extraction (SBSE), has recently appeared in the forensic literature.[23–25] As the name implies, sorbent is coated on a stir bar that moves in solution, greatly improving mass-transfer characteristics from the solution to the solid phase. The mass transfer and larger surface area relative to SPME fibers are an advantage, as is the robustness of a stir-bar compared with a slender fused-silica support. For extraction, the stir bar can be placed in solvent, where vigorous mixing again aids in mass transfer. The stir-bar sizes can be adjusted as well.

Applying the Science 4.4   Hair Balls: A Sample Preparation Challenge

Hair provides a protected biological environment that can record the drugs and substances a person was exposed to and roughly when that exposure took place. Consequently, hair as a matrix is of increasing interest to forensic toxicologists. But as is typical with forensic samples, the matrix, in this case a complex protein mix, presents the analytical challenge, starting with how to collect a representative sample. Which kinds of hair should be collected? There are several, including head, pubic, body, and facial hair. Once collected, how should the hair be sectioned? In one-inch pieces? Two? These are the questions that must be addressed before chemistry even begins; if they are not answered correctly, any data that results are questionable at best.

Drugs and related compounds can be absorbed in hair as a result of being carried there by the blood supply feeding the root or by adsorption and absorption from the environment.

Accordingly, once a representative sample is collected, it is critical to clean and extract the sample thoroughly, since the compounds of interest are found inside the hair, originating from the blood supply source. Sample preparation methods must break down the protein without damaging the target analytes. The methods used are the by-now familiar ones that utilize acids, bases, and weak solvents. Enzymatic treatments have also been widely applied. Hydrolysis in base is effective in breaking up the protein in hair, for example, and is also the basis of the reaction that occurs when drains are unclogged with commercial products like Draino®. Drain clogs typically consist of fats and hair, so the reaction is effective if drastic. The enzymes used are proteolytic and also attack the matrix. Once the analytes are free of the matrix, the analysis itself is simple, using standard instrumentation and techniques.

Source: Chiarrotti, M. "Overview of Extraction Procedures." *Forensic Science International*, 63 (**1992**), 161–170.

4.6 EXTENSION OF PARTITIONING: THIN-LAYER CHROMATOGRAPHY

The leap from solid-phase extraction to chromatography is a natural and conceptually easy one. It is also a crucial one, given the central role of chromatography in forensic science, particularly forensic chemistry. Thin-layer chromatography (TLC, or planar chromatography) is used extensively as a screening technique; however, with the inclusion of multiple solvent systems, standards, and selective developing reagents, TLC can provide nearly conclusive identification of many analytes. TLC can be also be used preparatively.

TLC is carried out on a glass plate or other supportive backing coated with a solid phase. Common coatings for TLC are similar or identical to the many types of the phases described for SPE. The types of interactions are analogous (ion-dipole, dipole-dipole, etc.). The solvent systems used vary widely with the type of analyte; standard forensic references are used to select the appropriate system and solid phase for a particular analysis.[26,27] The most widely used solid phase is silica gel, in which the interaction is adsorption. Drugs associate with the Si–O moieties via ion–dipole interactions. The TLC "plates," as they are usually called, can be purchased impregnated with a compound that fluoresces when exposed to UV light. When the runs are complete, the final locations of the spots on the plates are visualized as dark areas against the fluorescent background. Sample solvent systems used with silica plates are ethyl acetate:methanol: 30% ammonia (17:2:3) and cyclohexane:toluene:diethylamine (75:15:10). In most applications, the TLC chamber is covered and equilibrium is established between the liquid and vapor phases before use. As illustrated in Figure 4.21, the sample is dissolved in a small portion of solvent, usually the system selected, and applied in small concentrated areas with the use of capillary tubes. The origin line is a few millimeters above the lower edge of the plate, high enough that the solvent will not cover the origin when the plate is placed in the tank.

Exhibit B: How to Talk to a Jury

Because TLC is used extensively in forensic chemistry, analysts are often called on to explain how it works to a jury. The goal is to present the basic concepts in terms that everyone can understand. Here, the forensic chemist can explain capillary action by telling the jury that this is what causes water from a puddle to soak into a paper towel when a corner is dipped into the puddle. Partitioning can be described with reference to two phases everyone is familiar with, such as oil-and-vinegar dressing or sugar in gasoline. The best explanations are visual and familiar; learning how to present them takes practice. Most forensic scientists develop a collection of such explanations.

Once the plate is in the tank, solvent is immediately drawn up the plate by capillary action. When the solvent front reaches the origin, partitioning begins. The process is analogous to what occurs in SPE. The TLC run is complete just before the solvent front reaches the top of the plate. At that point, the plate is removed and the solvent front is marked with a straightedge if retention values are to be calculated; this operation is illustrated in Figure 4.23. The plate is then allowed to dry or is heated until it is dry.

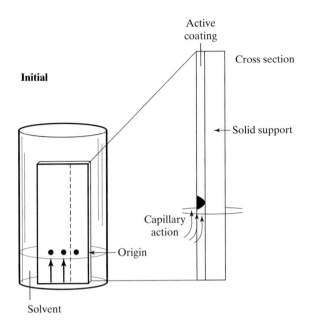

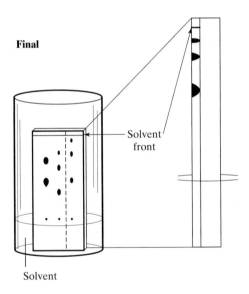

◀ **Figure 4.21** *Overview of TLC. The active phase is thinly coated on a glass plate with the sample placed at the origin line.*

Aside from the fluorescent background already mentioned, many other options exist for developing the plate to visualize components. Some analytes, such as LSD, fluoresce naturally and are easily visualized under UV light. Most drugs are visualized by the application of one or more developers, and the choice of these reagents can add significantly to the specificity of what an otherwise simple screening test displays. Iodoplatinate (acidified) is a near-universal developer for drugs,[28] reacting with alkaloids and amines to form dark-blue or black complexes. The reagent can be purchased ready-to-use or can be made from platinic chloride or potassium chloroplatinate and potassium iodide. Ehrlich's reagent (also a color test reagent for LSD) is used as a developer for LSD, mescaline, and related compounds. The Marquis and Mandelin presumptive test reagents can be used as developers as well.

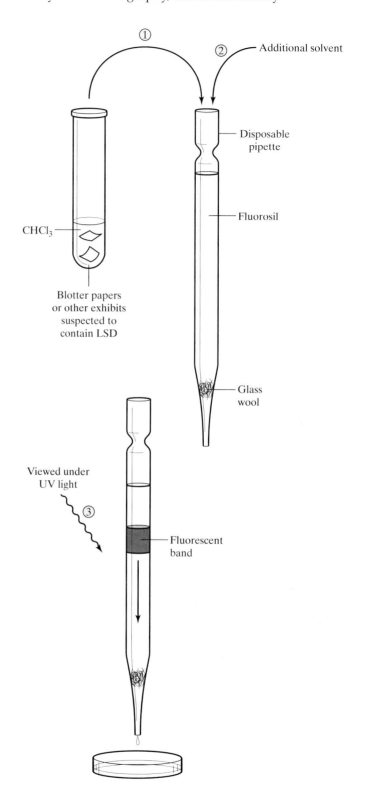

▶ **Figure 4.22** *A quick column cleanup of LSD blotter papers combining elements of SPE and TLC.*

The chemistry of the color-producing reactions for these reagents and many others is discussed in detail in Chapter 7.

Because TLC screening tests follow presumptive tests in the forensic analytical scheme, standards of suspected analytes are easily incorporated.

Historical Evidence 4.2—Chromatography

The word *chromatography* means "color writing," and the first chromatographic separations were of colored materials. By the middle of the 1800s, dyes and other colored materials were being separated on filter paper by placing a drop in the center. The components then separated by diffusing radially outward, forming a concentric ring pattern. The name most frequently associated with modern chromatography is that of a Russian, Mikhail Tsvett (1872–1919).[†] His work with pigments paved the way for techniques ranging from column chromatography to thin-layer chromatography.

[†]Interestingly, and appropriately, the word tsvet (ubet), in Russian, means "color."

Additional specificity is gained by using multiple solvent systems or different TLC stationary phases. A modified TLC–SPE approach is often employed to extract and clean up samples suspected of containing LSD. Since the drug fluoresces, it can be located on the TLC plate by placing it under UV light. For this application, a pipet is filled with Florisil® and the sample extract placed atop it. The fluorescent LSD (if present) moves down the column as additional solvent is added. The portion of the eluate containing the fluorescent band is collected for further analysis. The procedure is shown in Figure 4.22.

Spots developed on a TLC plate can be characterized by their **retention factor** (also called the retardation factor), or R_f value, given by

$$R_f = \frac{D_x}{(D_s - D_o)} \tag{4.15}$$

where D_x is the distance from the spot to the origin and $D_s - D_o$ is the distance the solvent front travels from the origin. The retention factor is analogous to the adjusted retention-time values reported for liquid and gas chromatography. A compound with an R_f of 1.00 travels with the solvent and does not interact with the bonded coating; conversely, an R_f of 0.00 (no movement) indicates that the analyte has no affinity for the solvent. R_f values are reported to two decimal places or, in some cases, multiplied by 100 and reported as values up to 100.[29] In forensic applications, R_f values are rarely cited to identify compounds, but they are useful for comparison purposes. A sample R_f calculation is shown in Figure 4.23.

TLC is an extension of sample preparation; hence, pH effects can play a role. If ionization is suppressed, the neutral compound will favor the less polar phase, typically the solvent in silica–gel TLC. If ionization is facilitated by pH, the compound will be charged and will interact much more with the charged silica gel moieties. Careful selection of solvent systems can facilitate separations based on small differences in pK_a values. As shown in Figure 4.24, the first solvent system incorporates methanol and acetone along with a small amount of ammonium hydroxide. The addition of the base ensures that basic drugs will remain un-ionized and thus have little affinity for the polar silica gel. Interaction still occurs on the basis of the polarity of the un-ionized molecules, but it is far less than the interaction for an ion. In the second case, where no base is added, the ionized drugs are absorbed onto the polar silica gel and stay near the origin. Consequently, resolution is poor. Further sample TLC analyses are shown in the color insert.

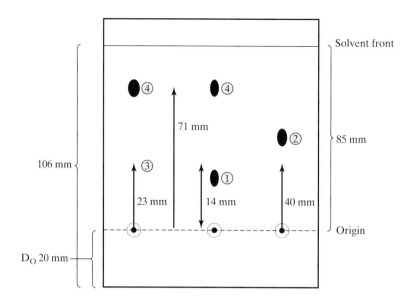

Figure 4.23 *Calculation of retardation (retention) factor R_f for TLC. In diffuse spots, the distance is measured from the line of origin to the center of the spot.*

$$R_{f_1} = \frac{14}{85 \text{ mm}} = 0.16 \qquad R_{f_3} = \frac{23 \text{ mm}}{85 \text{ mm}} = 0.27$$

$$R_{f_2} = \frac{40 \text{ mm}}{85 \text{ mm}} = 0.47 \qquad R_{f_4} = \frac{71 \text{ mm}}{85 \text{ mm}} = 0.84$$

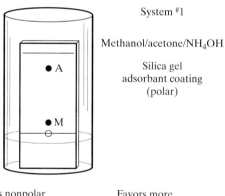

System #1

Methanol/acetone/NH$_4$OH

Silica gel
adsorbant coating
(polar)

Favors nonpolar   Favors more
phase   polar phase

$$B - NH_2 \xrightleftharpoons[]{H_2O} BNH_3^+ + OH^-$$

System #2

CHCl$_3$/methanol

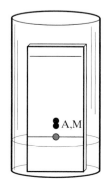

Figure 4.24 *The role of pH and ionization in TLC. With a polar stationary phase, nonpolar (un-ionized) forms of bases will partition preferentially into the mobile phase.*

4.7 IMMUNOASSAY

4.7.1 OVERVIEW

Immunoassay is to forensic toxicology what TLC is to forensic drug analysis: the key sample-screening technique. Not quite instrumental, but beyond sample preparation, immunoassay separates analytes on the basis of an **immunological reaction**. The technique was developed in the 1970s and has been refined to the point that automated immunoassay systems are a common sight in toxicology laboratories.

As with extraction and partitioning, equilibrium is involved:

$$Ab + Ag \longleftrightarrow Ab-Ag \qquad (4.16)$$

$$K = \frac{[Ab - Ag]}{[Ag][Ab]} \qquad (4.17)$$

In these equations, Ab is an **antibody**, Ag is an **antigen**, and K reflects what is called the **binding strength** of the antigen–antibody complex. In toxicology, the antigen is the drug or metabolite (or any number of other types of compounds) and the antibody is manufactured specifically against the drug or metabolite. This sounds simple enough, but under normal biological conditions, drugs do not have immunological activity. This property of drugs is a blessing since a drug that illicited an immune response would be quickly attacked and inactivated. However, the lack of immunological activity complicates the manufacture of the antibodies needed for immunological techniques.

To produce antibodies, the antigen is introduced into an experimental animal previously sensitized.[30] To induce an immunological response, the drug is combined with a protein. The drug molecule is sometimes referred to as the **hapten** portion of the complex. The drug molecule and the protein molecule are together called the **immunogen**. The protein portion is always larger than the drug molecule, often by a factor of a thousand or more. After the introduction of the immunogen into the animal and an incubation period, the animal is bled and the antibodies in the blood are isolated and purified to yield an antiserum. The stronger the reaction of the antiserum to the antigen (the drug immunogen), the stronger is the serum's **titer**. Under the conditions of a standardized immunological assay, an antiserum with a titer of 1:1000 would be active up to a dilution of 1 in 1000. Drug antisera have titers on the order of 1:500.[30]

Exhibit C: "Titering" on the Brink

For analytical chemists steeped in concentration units of molarity and ppm, titer is a difficult concept to grasp. An antiserum doesn't have a fixed or reproducible strength or concentration. The antiserum's strength (analogous, but not identical, to concentration) is relative rather than absolute. The higher the titer of an antiserum, the more strongly it binds to the antigen and the more dilute the antigen can be and still illicit the same response. But one does not walk into the stockroom, check out a 5-gm bottle of anti-amphetamine powder, and make a 1.00-M solution of it. Life should be so easy.

An antiserum produced this way is not pure, but rather is a mixture of different antibodies that respond to different areas of the large immunogen molecule. Such antisera have ranges of specificity, which means much the same in this context as it does in analytical chemistry. A specific reagent acts on or responds to one and only one substance. Similarly, an ideal specific antiserum will react with one and only one immunogen. However, because the immunogen molecules are large and spatially complex, such specificity is difficult to achieve with an in vivo technique. These antisera are called **polyclonal**, and they can vary from batch to batch even when obtained from the same animal.[30] However, this problem has been greatly reduced with the use of **monoclonal** techniques, illustrated in Figure 4.25.

Like the process of producing an ordinary antibody, the process of producing a monoclonal antibody starts with the injection of the antigen into an animal. Rather than bleeding, the animal is sacrificed and cells from the spleen are

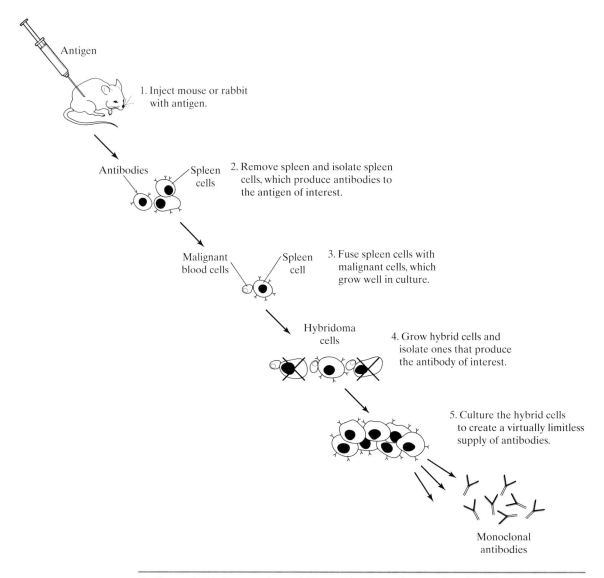

▲ **Figure 4.25** *An overview of the production of monoclonal antibodies.*

collected. These cells, which will produce the antibody, are then isolated and fused (hybridized) with cells from tumors, creating **hybridoma** cells. The next step is another isolation, in which the most productive hybridoma cells are kept and cultured (cloned), resulting in steady yields of high-specificity, high-titer antisera. However, even such highly purified antibodies can still react to some extent with antigenic molecules that have similar structures. This overlap of reactivity is similar to that seen with ion selective electrodes such as used in pH meters. A pH electrode is designed to respond only to H^+ ions, but high concentrations of Na^+ will also generate a response.

The same concept applies to antisera and is referred to as **cross-reactivity**. For example, the noncontrolled substances pseudoephedrine ("pseudofed"), ephedrine, and phenylpropanolamine react with antisera used in amphetamine–methamphetamine assays.[30] The result of cross-reactivity can be false positives, and it is this issue (among others) that leads to the classification of the immunoassay as a screening technique rather than a conclusive identification. However, with knowledge of potential cross-reactivity taken into account, immunoassay can be at least semiquantitative, something difficult to achieve with thin-layer chromatography. A typical immunoassay is used to determine whether the analyte of interest is likely present above a set threshold, a value referred to as the cutoff. Although there is wide variation in cutoff concentration, the detection limits of current assays are in the range of micrograms to nanograms per milliter of sample,[31,32] and many techniques allow for simultaneous screening of numerous drugs and metabolites.[32]

Exhibit D: Magic Brownies?

Cross-reactivity is a recognized limitation of immunoassays and is generally well characterized and well understood in forensic applications. However, new findings are always possible. In one case argued not long ago, a defendant maintained that a recent intake of a large amount of chocolate led to the in vivo production of cannabinoids that cross-reacted with the antibodies designed for marijuana immunoassays. An immunological experiment followed and debunked the idea, relegating the legal strategy to the "nice try" category.

Source: Tytgat, J., et al. "Cannabinoid mimics in chocolate utilized as an argument in court." *International Journal of Legal Medicine* 113 (2000), 137–139.

Although the discussion that follows uses drugs as examples, immunoassay is not restricted to drug and metabolite analysis. If an antibody can be made to a molecule, an immunological technique can be developed to detect that molecule. Immunoassays have long been used as field tests for polychlorinated biphenyls (PCBs), and there are immunoassays for explosives such as trinitrotoluene (TNT). Unlike thin-layer chromatography, immunoassays are amenable to automation. This is a boon to forensic toxicology laboratories that may have to screen tens or hundreds of samples in a variety of matrices on a daily basis.

4.7.2 TYPES OF ASSAYS

Immunoassay can be broadly categorized as **competitive** or **noncompetitive**. With noncompetitive methods,[33,34] also called immunometric methods,[34] the antibody is usually present in excess. In the competitive mode (Figure 4.26), antigens compete for a limited number of antibody binding sites. Initially, the

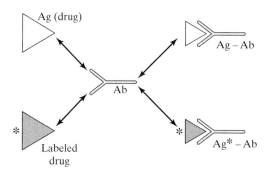

◀ **Figure 4.26** *Competitive binding in immunological reactions. Drug from a sample (the antigen Ag) will compete with the labeled drug for the limited available antibody (Ab) binding sites. The labeled sites are indicated by an asterisk *.*

antibody is bound to labeled antigen. The label is used in the detection scheme. The labels can be radioisotopes, species capable of fluorescence, or enzymes, to name the most common. Early assays used radioactive iodine (^{131}I; later, ^{125}I) as labels, and detection employed scintillation counting of emitted gamma (γ) radiation. Beta (β) particles are also used in certain techniques.[35]

The bound, labeled drug–antibody complex is coated on the inside of a tube and thus is immobilized. Suppose that the label is a radioactive material. Prior to the addition of sample, the equilibrium

$$\text{Ab–drug*(immobile/bound)} \longleftrightarrow \text{Ab(immobile)}$$
$$\text{+drug*(free, unbound)} \tag{4.18}$$

is established. A sample such as urine or blood is then added to the tube, and the system is allowed to incubate. If there is a high concentration of drug in the sample, it will eventually displace the bound and labeled drug. When the tube is rinsed, there will be little or no radioactivity associated with the bound or immobile antibody phase left behind. Concentration can be related to degree of displacement. The weaker the radioactivity in the bound phase, the more complete the displacement is and the more concentrated the drug is in the sample. Calibration curves can be established to make the assay quantitative. The method described in this example, in which the label is a radioactive material, is referred to as **radioimmunoassay** (RIA). RIA is a **heterogeneous** assay, meaning that the bound phase must be separated from the unbound phase before the detection method is employed. This process is shown in Figure 4.27.

4.7.3 HOMOGENEOUS ASSAYS

These elegant techniques do not require separation of the bound and unbound fractions prior to measurement of response. Such assays offer advantages by simplifying and eliminating a step, but are more prone to matrix effects. An example of a homogeneous assay is **fluorescence polarization immunoassay** (FPIA, Figure 4.28).[33]

Since there is no separation step, the sample and tube have the same total fluorescent signal before and after sample is added. However, when the labeled drug is bound to the antibody and immobilized, its movement is constrained

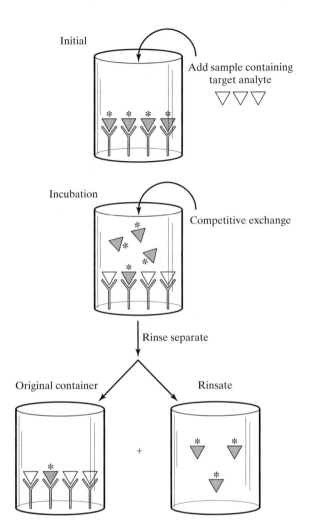

Initial

Add sample containing target analyte

Incubation

Competitive exchange

Rinse separate

Original container

Rinsate

+

◀ **Figure 4.27** *Example of a competitive binding heterogeneous assay using a labeled antigen.*

and, as a result, the light emitted will be strongly polarized. Light coming from unbound labeled molecules will not be polarized, because motion is not constrained and will be random over the collection. A high concentration of the drug in the sample will displace more labeled drug and decrease the polarization of the emitted light. Two other techniques used in forensic laboratories are enzyme-multiplied immunoassay technique and enzyme-linked immunosorbent assay.[33,34]

4.7.4 ENZYME-MULTIPLIED IMMUNOASSAY TECHNIQUE (EMIT, FIGURE 4.29)

This colorimetric technique is widely used to screen for drugs and metabolites. In EMIT, a complex between an enzyme and the target drug is created so that the enzyme retains its catalytic activity in a conversion reaction such as: NAD (colorless) $\longrightarrow$ NADH (colored).[34] The active enzyme complex can be inhibited by binding to an antibody molecule added to the system. This antibody can bind either with the drug or with the drug–enzyme complex.

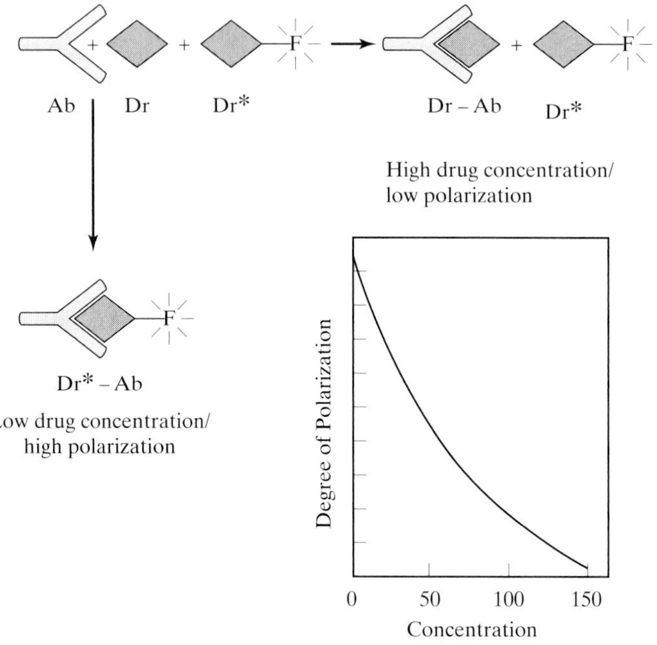

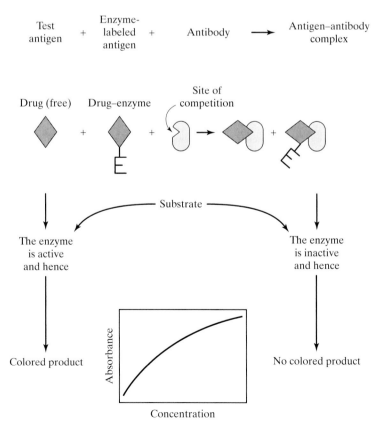

▶ **Figure 4.28** *Fluorescent polarization immunoassay (FPIA), a homogeneous assay. The -F indicates a fluorescing label.*

▶ **Figure 4.29** *EMIT.*

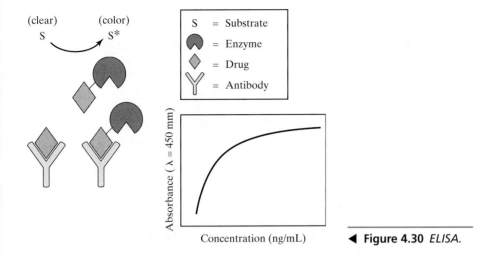

◀ **Figure 4.30** *ELISA.*

When there is excess drug antigen available, it will tend to displace the enzyme–drug complex from the antibody, and as a result, active enzyme will be available to catalyze the NAD $\longrightarrow$ NADH reaction. In turn, this will increase absorbance at 340 nm, λ_{max} of NADH. EMIT is a homogeneous assay.

4.7.5 ENZYME-LINKED IMMUNOSORBENT ASSAY (ELISA, FIGURE 4.30)

This is another colorimetric procedure which exploits unbound enzyme to catalyze a reaction that produces a color change. The label is the enzyme, and when labeled drug is displaced, the color-change reaction is catalyzed and the intensity of the color is proportional to the concentration of the drug. A darker color correlates with high displacement and high drug concentration in the sample, whereas faint or no color means that little of the enzyme has been liberated and thus little drug is available in the sample to displace it. ELISA is classified as a heterogeneous assay, but otherwise shares many characteristics with EMIT.

SUMMARY

From simple solvent extraction to RIA, sample preparation and screening tests share many common elements. The pivotal characteristics are (1) the existence of a difference in properties between the materials to be separated and (2) an exploitable equilibrium. An understanding of these ideas facilitates an understanding of partitioning and competitive equilibria. All of the sample preparation and screening procedures and protocols described in this chapter can be characterized by invoking some combination of these foundational principles. Furthermore, the theory behind TLC and immunoassay forms a bridge that leads naturally into a discussion of instrumentation, the subject of the next chapter.

KEY TERMS AND CONCEPTS

Active headspace method	**Antiserum**	**Digestion**
Antibody	**Competitive assay**	**Dipole-dipole interactions**
Antigen	**Cross-reactivity**	**Dry extraction**

Effluent	Hydrophobic	Passive headspace method
Eluant	Immunoassay	pK value
Eluent	Immunogen	Planar chromatography
Enzyme-linked immunoassay	Immunological reaction	Polarity
Enzyme-multiplied immunoassay	Ion-dipole interactions	Polyclonal antibody
	Ion-ion interactions	Purge-and-trap
Equilibrium constant	Ionization center	Quiescent solution
Extraction	Isoelectric point (isoelectric pH)	Radioimmunoassay
Fluorescent polarization immunoassay	K_a, K_b, K_w, K_{sp}	Relative affinity
	Le Chatelier's principle	Reversed phase
Hapten	Like dissolves like	Solid-phase extraction
Headspace	Lipophobic	Solid-phase microextraction
Henderson-Hasselbalch equation	Liquid-liquid extraction (LLE)	Solubility
Henry's law	$-$Log P/K_{ow}	Solvent extraction
Heterogeneous assay	Mobile phase	Solvent strength
Homogeneous assay	Monoclonal antibody	Stationary phase
Hybridoma cells	Noncompetitive assay	Thin-layer chromatography
Hydrophilic	Normal phase	Titer

PROBLEMS

From the chapter

1. Equation 4-2 expresses the relationship exploited by breath alcohol testing that is done in the field. Why is this test not considered accurate enough to determine blood alcohol concentration? In other words, why is the test considered to be presumptive rather than conclusive?

2. a. Without resorting to calculations, comment on the relative solubilities of the following compounds: silver bromate, $K_{sp} = 5.5 \times 10^{-5}$; silver sulfide, 6×10^{-51}; magnesium carbonate, 3.5×10^{-8}; $Mn(OH)_2$, 1.6×10^{-13}.

   b. Give the solubility product constant of each compound in part a in the form pK_{sp}.

   c. Calculate the solubility of each compound in part a.

   d. At what pH would manganese hydroxide precipitate out?

3. In Question 2, what other factor(s) must be considered in the case of the carbonate and the hydroxide?

4. a. Barium is a toxic metal, yet is given to patients in large quantities when X-rays of the stomach or intestines are needed. For such imaging, the patient is given a "milk shake" containing barium sulfate. Given the known toxicity of barium why is this "drink" safe?

   b. Comment on the implications of the barium test in part a for the toxicology of metals such as mercury, cadmium, lead, and antimony.

5. Aspirin (acetylsalicylic acid) has a pK_a of 3.5. The pH of the stomach is approximately 1, while the pH of the intestines is approximately 6. Calculate the fraction of aspirin that is ionized in each area (show your work), and use the results to predict where the drug is preferentially absorbed.

6. Repeat the calculation in Question 5 for caffeine, a weak base with a pK_a of 0.6.

7. Diazepam tablets are supplied in 2-, 5-, and 10-mg increments. Suppose several tablets are received in a laboratory as evidence and, using the *Physician's Desk Reference*, an analyst was able to tentatively identify them as Valium®, 10 mg. Suppose further that you learn that the tablets also contain anhydrous lactose, starches, dyes, and calcium stearate. Describe a method for isolating the active ingredient from fillers, using a LLE scheme. Justify and explain each step of the method.

8. Quinine $(C_{20}H_{24}N_2O_2)$ is a dibasic molecule with pK_a's of 5.1 and 9.7. It is encountered as a diluent (cutting agent) for heroin. To extract quinine from an aqueous solution, what pH should be used and why?

9. Devise a solvent extraction method that could be used to separate a mixture of powdered sugar, cornstarch, cocaine, and amphetamine. Justify each step and separation. Repeat, using SPE to effect the separation.

10. A case sample from a suspected arson fire is submitted to the laboratory. The fire was suppressed with large

volumes of water. The exhibit submitted consists of approximately 50 mL of this water, which appears dirty and has suspended solids and other visible debris in it. Propose an SPE method for cleaning the sample and isolating any residual accelerants, assuming that gasoline or another hydrocarbon was used.

11. List some practical limitations of RIA.

12. Would the enzymatic preparation of hair be classified as an extraction or a digestion?

13. Differentiate clearly between EMIT and ELISA.

14. Explain the patterns observed in Figure 1, Applying the Science 4.1.

Integrative

1. Diazepam (Valium®) is a member of the benzodiazepine family of drugs. This drug, at one time the most prescribed drug in the country, has a single ionization center, with a pK_a reported as 3.4. Answer the following questions about the drug:
    a. Draw the structure of diazepam or obtain it from a reliable referenced source. Indicate the location of the ionizable center.
    b. Is diazepam acidic, basic, or neutral? Justify your answer.
    c. What would be the pH of a 0.01-M solution of diazepam? Show your work.
    d. What would be an optimal pH to extract diazepam, using a simple solvent extraction?

2. For drugs supplied as salts, it is usually possible to determine whether the drug is acidic or basic by the chemical name. Explain and provide a list of three examples not in the chapter. (*Hint*: PDR.)

3. Review the list of solvents in Table 4.5, and find their material safety data sheets (MSDSs) and comparative pricing information. On the basis of your findings, suggest which solvents are likely and which are unlikely to be used routinely in a forensic laboratory.

4. TLC plates can be made in the laboratory, but it is recommended that they be purchased to ensure the uniformity of the solid-phase thickness. Comment on the role that

thickness would play, and illustrate how an uneven surface would affect the plates' performance and appearance.

5. For the minicolumn cleanup described for LSD, suggest other combinations of solid phase and solvent that might work as well. Based on the structure and chemical character of LSD, why is the method depicted a good one?

6. For each of the specific immunoassay techniques, draw a generic calibration curve and indicate whether the corresponding R^2 value would be positive or negative.

7. A relatively new type of immunoassay is based on the agglutination of coated latex particles. Research the procedure and summarize, in a few figures, how it works. What are some advantages and disadvantages of the technique?

8. A certain drug has a K_b of 3.2×10^{-6}. What is the corresponding K_a and pK_a?

9. Discuss the similarities of cation–anion exchange methods and competitive binding immunoassay techniques.

10. When SPE or related techniques are used to extract samples, internal standards are added before the sample is placed on the column. Why?

11. According to the Merck index, a 1% solution (wt/vol) of caffeine in water produces a pH of 6.9. Calculate the K_a and pK_a of caffeine.

Food for thought

1. If TLC with two different solid phases and several solvent systems is used to analyze a sample, will the results be considered conclusive? What about including standards and several developing reagents? At what point does a string of presumptive and screening tests become conclusive?

2. In relation to Question 1, comment on the analogy between the described scenario and the situation of combining circumstantial evidence to infer a fact.

3. Immunoassay is a staple of forensic toxicology, but is rarely used in the analysis of drugs as physical evidence. Comment.

FURTHER READING

Baltussen, E., et al. "Sorptive Sample Preparation—a Review." *Anal Bioanal Chem*, 373 (**2002**), 4–22.

Devlin, T. M., ed. *Textbook of Biochemistry with Clinical Correlations*. New York: Wiley-Liss, **1997**.

Harris, D. C. "Ch. 28: Sample Preparation," in D. C. Harris, *Quantitative Chemical Analysis*, 6th ed. New York: W.H. Freeman and Co., **2003**.

Holme, D. J. and H. Peck. *Analytical Biochemistry*, 3d ed. Edinburgh Gate, UK: Addison Wesley Longman, **1998**.

Patniak, P. *Dean's Analytical Chemistry Handbook*, 2d ed. New York: McGraw-Hill, **2004**.

Rubinson, K. A., and J. F. Rubinson. "Chapter 4: Sample Treatment, Interferences, and Standards," in K. A. Rubinson and J. F. Rubinson, *Contemporary*

Instrumental Analysis. Upper Saddle River, NJ: Prentice Hall, **2000**.

Rubinson, K. A., and J. F. Rubinson. "Chapter 14: Liquid Chromatography," in K. A. Rubinson and J. F. Rubinson, *Contemporary Instrumental Analysis.* Upper Saddle River, NJ: Prentice Hall, **2000**.

Siek, T. J. "Specimen Preparation," in B. Levine, ed. *Principles of Forensic Toxicology*, 2d ed. Washington, DC: American Association for Clinical Chemistry, **2003**.

Simpson, N. J. K., ed. *Solid-Phase Extraction: Principles, Techniques, and Applications.* New York: Marcel Dekker, Inc., **2000**.

Smith, M. A. "Chapter 8: Immunoassay," in B. Levine, ed., *Principles of Forensic Toxicology*, Vol. 1, 2d ed. Washington, DC: American Association of Clinical Chemistry, **2003**.

Thomas, G. *Medicinal Chemistry: An Introduction.* Chichester, U.K.: John Wiley and Sons, **2000**.

Wermuth, C. G., ed. *The Practice of Medicinal Chemistry.* London: Academic/Elseiver, 2003.

Websites

www.bandj.com/BJProductInfo.html. This is an excellent source for information regarding solvents used in extractions.

REFERENCES

1. Thomas, G. "Chapter 3: Drug Solubility," in G. Thomas, *Medicinal Chemistry: An Introduction.* Chichester, U.K.: John Wiley and Sons, 2000.

2. Box, K., et al. "High-Throughput Measurements of pK_a Values in a Mixed Buffer Linear Gradient System." *Analytical Chemistry* 75 (2003), 883–892.

3. Siek, T. J. "Chapter 5: Specimen Preparation," in B. Levine, ed., *Principles of Forensic Toxicology*, 2d ed. Washington, DC: American Clinical Chemistry Association, 2003.

4. Bogusz, M. J., et al. "Applicability of Various Brands of Mixed-Phase Extraction Columns for Opiate Extraction from Blood and Serum." *Journal of Chromatography B. Biomedical Applications* 683 (1996), 177–188.

5. De Zeeuw, R. A., and J. P. Franke. "Solid-Phase Extraction for Broad-Spectrum Drug Screening in Toxicological Analysis," in N. J. K. Simpson, ed., *Solid-Phase Extraction: Principles, Techniques, and Applications.* New York: Marcel Dekker, Inc., 2000.

6. Siek, T. J. "Specimen Preparation," in B. Levine, ed., *Principles of Forensic Toxicology*, 2d ed. Washington, DC: American Association for Clinical Chemistry, 2003.

7. Myung, S. W., et al. "Determination of Amphetamine, Methamphetamine and Dimethamphetamine in Human Urine by Solid-Phase Microextraction (SPME)–Gas Chromatography/Mass Spectrometry." *Journal of Chromatography B. Biomedical Science Applications* 716 (1998), 359–365.

8. Junting, L., et al. "Solid-Phase Microextraction (SPME) of Drugs and Poisons from Biological Samples." *Forensic Science International* 97 (1998), 93–100.

9. Fucci, N., et al. "Simultaneous Detection of Some Drugs of Abuse in Saliva Samples by SPME Technique." *Forensic Science International* 134 (2003), 40–45.

10. Benko, A., et al. "Determination of Amphetamine Derivatives in Urine with Solid Phase Micro-extraction (SPME)." *ACTA Pharmaceutica Hungarica* 68 (1998), 269–275.

11. Centini, F., et al. "Quantitative and Qualitative Analysis of MDMA, MDEA, MA and Amphetamine in Urine by Headspace/Solid Phase Micro-extraction (SPME) and GC/MS." *Forensic Science International* 83 (1996), 161–166.

12. Hall, B. J., and J. S. Brodbelt. "Determination of Barbiturates by Solid-Phase Microextraction (SPME) and Ion Trap Gas Chromatography–Mass Spectrometry." *Journal of Chromatography A.* 777 (1997), 275–282.

13. Mosaddegh, M., et al. "Application of Solid-Phase Microextraction Technology to Drug Screening and Identification." *Annals of Clinical Biochemistry* 38 (2001), 541–547.

14. Sporkert, F., and F. Pragst. "Use of Headspace Solid-Phase Microextraction (HS-SPME) in Hair Analysis for Organic Compounds." *Forensic Science International* 107 (2000), 129–148.

15. Lucas, A. C., et al. "Use of Solid-Phase Microextraction (SPME) for the Determination of Methadone and EDDP in Human Hair by GC–MS." *Forensic Science International* 107 (2000), 225–232.

16. Furton, K. G., et al. "Application of Solid-Phase Microextraction to the Recovery of Explosives and Ignitable Liquid Residues from Forensic Specimens." *Journal of Chromatography A.* 97 (2000), 419–423.

17. Furton, K. G., et al. "Optimization of Solid-Phase Microextraction (SPME) for the Recovery of Explosives from Aqueous and Post-explosion Debris Followed by Gas and Liquid Chromatographic Analysis." *Journal of Forensic Sciences* 45 (2000), 857–864.

18. Vu, D. T. "Characterization and Aging Study of Currency Ink and Currency Canine Training Aids Using Headspace SPME/GC–MS." *Journal of Forensic Sciences* 48 (2003), 754–770.

19. Andrasko, J., and S. Stahling. "Time since Discharge of Rifles." *Journal of Forensic Sciences* 45 (2000), 1250–1255.

20. Wilson, J. D., et al. "Time since Discharge of Shotgun Shells." *Journal of Forensic Sciences* 48 (2003), 1298–1301.

21. "Standard Practice for Separation and Concentration of Ignitable Liquid Residues from Fire Debris Samples by Passive Headspace Concentration with Solid Phase Microextraction (SPME)," in *ASTM Standard E 2154-01*,14.02, ed. ASTM International, 2003

22. Stauffer, E., and J. J. Lentini. "ASTM standards for fire debris analysis: a review." *Forensic Science International* 132 (2003), 63–67.

23. Tienpont, B., et al. "Stir Bar Sorptive Extraction–Thermal Desorption–Capillary GC–MS Applied to Biological Fluids." *Anal Bioanal Chem* 373 (2002), 46–55.

24. Tienpont, B., et al. "Stir Bar Sorptive Extraction–Thermal Desorption–Capillary GC–MS for Profiling and Target Component Analysis of Pharmaceutical Drugs in Urine." *Journal of Pharmaceutical and Biomedical Analysis* 32 (2003), 569–579.

25. Kawaguchi, M., et al. "Stir Bar Sorptive Extraction and Thermal Desorption–Gas Chromatography–Mass Spectrometry for the Measurement of 4-nonylphenol and 4-tert-octylphenol in Human Biological Samples." *Journal of Chromatography B. Analytical Technology Biomedical Life Science* 799 (2004), 119–125.

26. Rajananda, V., et al. "An Evaluation of TLC Systems for Opiate Analysis." *United Nations Office on Drugs and Crime: Bulletin on Narcotics* (1985), 35–47.

27. Galichet, L. Y., et al., ed. *Clarke's Analysis of Drugs and Poisons*. London: Pharmaceutical Press, 2004.

28. Blakesley, J., et al. "A Simplified Thin-Layer Chromatography System for the Detection of Commonly Abused Basic Drugs." *Annals of Clinical Biochemistry* 24 (Pt 5) (1987), 508–510.

29. Poole, C. F. "Thin-layer Chromatography," in L. Y. Galichet et al., ed. *Clarke's Analysis of Drugs and Poisons*, Vol. 1, London: Pharmaceutical Press, 2004.

30. Smith, M. L. "Immunoassay," in B. Levine, ed., *Principles of Forensic Toxicology*, Vol. 1, 2d ed. Washington, DC: American Association of Clinical Chemistry, 2003.

31. Hino, Y., et al. "Performance of Immunoassays in Screening for Opiates, Cannibinoids and Amphetamines in Post-mortem Blood." *Forensic Science International* 131 (2003), 148–155.

32. Yawney, J., et al. "A General Screening Method for Acidic, Neutral, and Basic Drugs in Whole Blood Using the Oasis MCX Column." *Journal of Analytical Toxicology* 26 (2002), 325–332.

33. Smith, M. A. "Chapter 8: Immunoassay," in B. Levine, ed., *Principles of Forensic Toxicology*, Vol. 1, 2d ed. Washington, DC: American Association of Clinical Chemistry, 2003.

34. Holme, D. J., and H. Peck. "Chapter 7: Immunological Methods," in D. J. Holme and H. Peck, *Analytical Biochemistry*, 3d ed. London: Addison Wesley Longman, 1998.

35. Chard, T. "Radioimmunoassay," in E. P. Diamandis and T. K. Christopoulos, eds., *Immunoassay*, Vol. 1. San Diego: Academic Press, 1996.

CHAPTER

5 Instrumentation

OVERVIEW AND ORIENTATION

In this chapter, we delve into the instrumental tools, techniques, and procedures utilized in forensic chemistry. The chapter is best thought of as akin to a *CliffsNotes*® of that enormous topic, a supplement to and summary of the many fine works listed in the "References" and "Further Reading" sections at the end of the chapter. For those who have recently taken an instrumental analysis course, much will be review; for those who have not, enough information is provided to understand how and why the instruments are used and to understand information presented in the chapters that follow. Mass spectrometry and infrared spectrometry often are covered in an organic chemistry course, at least to the level of detail assumed here. The depth and breadth of each treatment corresponds to how widespread its application is in forensic chemistry. For example, **inductively coupled plasma** mass spectrometry (ICP-MS) was introduced in the mid 1980s and is routinely used in many materials, environmental, and research laboratories. However, it is rarely applied to forensic chemistry and hence is omitted here. Conversely, microscopy is a staple of forensic science and is not frequently used in other analytical settings. The presentation of each method is necessarily concise and is meant to provide information requisite to an understanding of later topics; it is not meant as a replacement for an instrumental analysis course.

The first forensic science laboratory, founded in 1910 by Edmund Locard, reportedly had two instruments: a microscope and a spectrophotometer. The more things change, the more things remain the same: Forensic chemists have many procedures and devices at their disposal, but their core instruments are still spectrophotometers (hereafter, spectrometers), microscopes, and now, combinations of the two. Recently joining the arsenal are hyphenated systems incorporating chromatographic separation and advanced detectors. The selection of topics here does not reflect the most recent advances in instrumental analysis, and this is typical of forensic chemistry as a discipline. Scrupulous method validation, testing, and other constraints guarantee that forensic applications favor the tried and true.

The microscope has been associated with forensic science ever since Locard and Sherlock Holmes. The study of microscopy provides a foundation for study of spectroscopy. Simple microscopy is based on the interaction of visible light with matter, whereas spectroscopy is broadly defined as the interaction of electromagnetic energy with matter. Once visible light interacts with a sample, that light carries information about the physical and chemical characteristics of the sample. The same is true in all modes of spectroscopy. The detector in a microscope is the human eye and the characteristic that is most studied is color, but color is an expression of frequency and wavelength, characteristics exploited across the electromagnetic spectrum.

In forensic science, UV/VIS and IR spectroscopy are the most widely used types of spectroscopy. X-ray techniques are employed for elemental and structural analysis, often as a complement to **scanning electron microscopy** (SEM). **X-ray diffraction**, used to examine crystal structures, is much less common. On

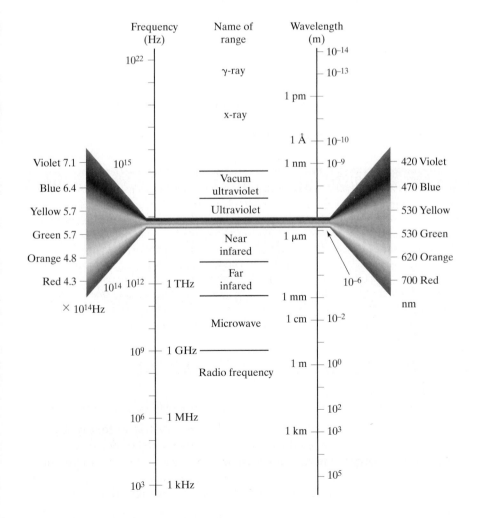

◀ **Figure 5.1** *The electromagnetic spectrum. Simple microscopy and colorimetry exploit the visible range. X-ray spectroscopy probes elements and crystal structure; UV spectroscopy focuses on molecular structure, while IR probes bonding through vibrational interactions.*

Example Problem 5.1

Calculate the following:

Green light has a wavelength of 550 nm.

① What is the frequency?

$$\nu = \frac{c}{\lambda} = \frac{3.0 \times 10^{10} \text{ cm/sec}}{550 \text{ nm} \times 10^{-7} \frac{\text{cm}}{\text{nm}}} = \frac{5.4 \times 10^{14} \text{ sec}^{-1}}{5.4 \times 10^{14} \text{ Hz}}$$

② What is the frequency in cm^{-1}, a unit used for IR spectroscopy?

$$\nu(cm^{-1}) = \frac{1}{\lambda(cm)} = \frac{10^7 \text{ nm/cm}}{\lambda(nm)}$$

$$\nu(cm^{-1}) = \frac{10^7 \text{ nm/cm}}{550 \text{ nm}} = 18,182 \text{ cm}^{-1}$$

③ What is the energy of the photon?

$$E = h\nu = \frac{hc}{\lambda}$$

$$E_{550} = \frac{(6.62 \times 10^{-37} \text{ KJsec})(3 \times 10^{10} \text{ cm/sec})}{550 \text{ nm} \times 10^{-7} \frac{\text{cm}}{\text{nm}}}$$

$$E_{550} = 3.61 \times 10^{-24} \text{ KJ (per photon)}$$

the other end of the spectrum, nuclear magnetic resonance (NMR) is occasionally used, but an NMR instrument is not a common sight in forensic laboratories. However, every forensic laboratory has at least one microscope, and it is with microscopy that we begin our exploration of instrumentation.

Exhibit A: What's Missing?

There is one broad class of instrumental methods yet to make inroads into forensic analytical chemistry: the electrochemical methods, such as ion-selective electrodes, coulometry, amperometry, and potentiometry. The relative inattention paid to these techniques is due to the nature of the analyses required and the kinds of matrices and target analytes with which forensic chemistry deals. Electrochemical techniques excel in applications such as the evaluation of reactions, kinetics, mechanisms, and other areas that are not usually of forensic interest. Ion-selective electrodes are generally good qualitative and quantitative tools, but they target ions and gases that are rarely involved in forensic work.

5.1 MICROSCOPES AND CHEMICAL MICROSCOPY

Microscopy was an established forensic tool by the 1890s.[1] In toxicology, microscopy was being used to evaluate crystals characteristic of poisons, not unlike the way microcrystal tests in modern drug analysis are used. Microscopes were also employed in the analysis of fibers.[1] To explore the principles of microscopy, the best place to begin is with the one instrument that symbolizes forensic science. A magnifying glass (Figure 5.2) consists of a single lens that creates a magnified image of the specimen on the retina of the person using it. The image is called a **virtual image**, because it exists only in the eye of the viewer (Figure 5.3). This kind of image cannot be projected onto a screen in the way a movie projector creates an image on the plane of the movie screen. The effect of using a magnifying glass is to make the object appear as it would if it were placed much closer to eye, but the image disappears when one stops viewing the sample through the lens; the image is not in real space.

The lens in the magnifying glass is made of glass, a substance that refracts or bends light. The refractive index (RI) of any material is given by

$$N_r = \lambda_{vacuum}/\lambda_{material} \tag{5.1}$$

where λ refers to the speed of light in a given medium. For air, the speed of light is assumed to be unity, and the speed of light in any other medium is less than this. The greater the difference in speed, the greater the refraction. Because a lens has two interfaces, two refraction events occur. The refraction angles θ_{air} and θ_{glass} are related through **Snell's Law** (Figure 5.4):

$$N_{r,air} \sin \theta_{air} = N_{r,glass} \sin \theta_{glass} \tag{5.2}$$

This relationship is also important in some types of spectroscopy, such as attenuated total reflectance (ATR), which is discussed in Section 5.2.5.

▲ **Figure 5.2**

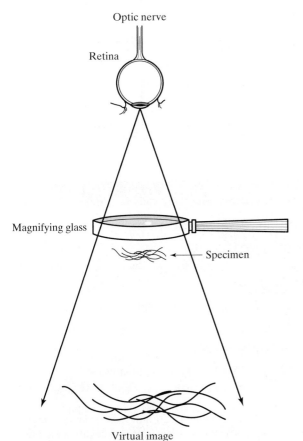

◀ **Figure 5.3** *A simple magnifying lens.*

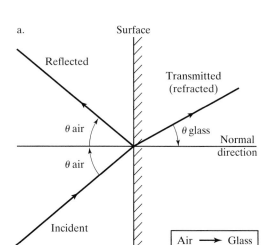

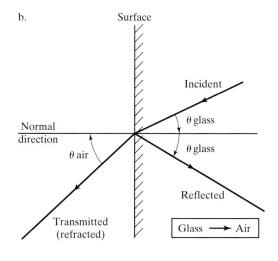

▶ **Figure 5.4** *Refractive index at an air–glass–air interface such as a lens. Differences in relative speed cause the light to bend when it is (a) reflected and (b) transmitted. In (a), the light enters the lens; in (b), it exits. Hence, there are two changes in speed and two refraction events.*

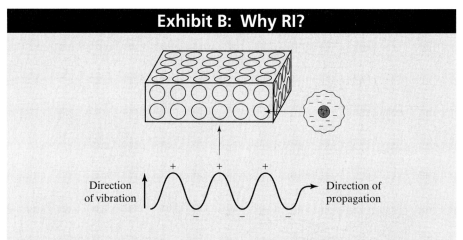

Exhibit B: Why RI?

What is responsible for the refraction of light in a material? Light is electromagnetic energy, which is an oscillating electromagnetic wave with positive and negative regions.

Exhibit B: (Continued)

These regions interact with atoms, which can be visualized as tiny concentrations of positive charges surrounded by a negatively charged electron cloud. When the oscillating electromagnetic wave interacts with these charges, it can distort them, resulting in an attenuation or modulation of the original electromagnetic wave. The refractive index (RI) is a measure of the ability of the material—or, more specifically, the electron clouds of atoms and molecules within the material—to alter incoming electromagnetic energy. One analogy is to imagine what happens when a small magnet is dragged through a sea of other magnets. Anyone holding the moving magnet would feel the forces asserted by the larger magnets and would sense the smaller magnet being moved and directed by those forces.

The RI of a material depends on the types and sizes of the atoms in the material, the nature of the bonds and how the atoms are arranged, the number of interactions between atoms (which depends on the density and crystal structure of the material), the thickness of the material, and the closeness of the wavelength of light in size to the size of the particles in the material. All of these factors influence the magnetic field environment encountered by light, which itself consists of oscillating electric and magnetic waves.

Recall that refraction is a function of wavelength as well, and applications of this phenomenon are referred to as **dispersion** techniques. A familiar example is the glass prism that disperses visible light into component wavelengths by exploiting the differences in their refractive indices. Gratings also disperse light by creating zones of constructive and destructive interference. Dispersion may play a role in microscope optics and is the basis of a technique called dispersion staining, which is useful in determining refractive indices of small particles.[2]

Lenses exploit the air–glass interface to magnify and focus light at predictable points, as shown in Figure 5.5. When light illuminates an object so that the light rays are parallel (rather than converging or diverging), the **principal focus** (p) is the point at which the light rays traveling out of the lens converge. The line that passes through the center of curvature of the lens is called the **optic axis**, and the distance on that line to the principal focus is the **focal length** (f). For the viewer to see an image of the object in focus, the principal focus must correlate with

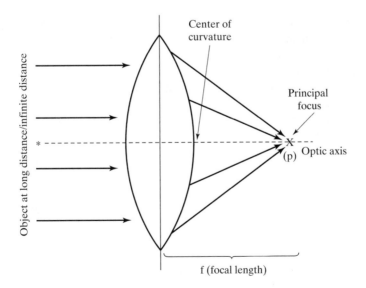

◀ **Figure 5.5** *Lens focusing light passing by an object far enough from the lens that the light illuminating it is travelling in parallel and not diverging rays as shown in the next figure.*

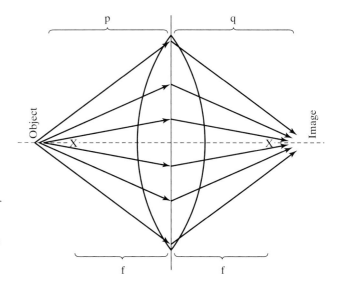

▶ **Figure 5.6** *Lens with closer object. The focal point moves away from the lens as the object moves closer.*

a point on the viewer's retina. Similarly, if the lens were in a movie projector, the image would be in focus at the focal length and the screen would correspond to the focal plane.

In cases where the light rays are not parallel and the object is not at an infinite distance, as in a microscope, the situation changes. The relationship of the points, as shown in Figure 5.6, can be summarized in the formula[3]

$$\frac{1}{f} = \frac{1}{p} + \frac{1}{q} \tag{5.3}$$

As the object moves closer to the lens (i.e., as p decreases), the point where the image is in focus moves away from the lens (i.e., q increases). The value of f, intrinsic to the lens, does not change. This relationship allows for calculation of the magnification as

$$m = \frac{p}{q} \tag{5.4}$$

If an object is placed such that p is twice the focal length, then q would also be twice the focal length and the magnification of the image that focuses at point q would be 2f/2f = 1 (no magnification).[3] At any other combination, the image is enlarged or reduced.

For example, consider a lens that has a focal length f of 25 mm, as shown in Figure 5.7. If an object is placed on the optic axis at a point 75 mm away, the image that comes into focus at q (37.5 mm) appears twice as large as the object itself:

$$\frac{1}{f} = \frac{1}{p} + \frac{1}{q}$$

$$\text{so } \frac{1}{25} = \frac{1}{75} + \frac{1}{q} \quad \text{and} \quad q = 37.5$$

$$m = \frac{p}{q} = \frac{75}{37.5} = 2$$

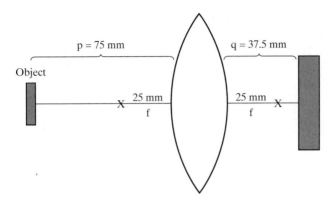

◀ **Figure 5.7** *Magnification of an image by a lens. The object comes into focus at point q and is magnified to appear twice as large as the real object.*

The image formed at q is called a **real image**, because it exists at a definable point in space and can be captured by placing a screen at the focal plane. Its existence does not depend on looking through a lens, as does that of a virtual image. The distance from the object to the lens and the distance from the lens to the focused image are critical in microscope and spectrometer design.

A compound, or binocular, microscope is constructed by creating a magnified real image and magnifying this image again to produce an image that is focused on the retina of the viewer. As shown in Figure 5.8, the sample is placed on a stage, and light is transmitted upward through it and into the first lens, or **objective lens**. The image comes into focus some distance away, inside the body of the microscope. This is a real image that can be viewed directly if desired. This real image is magnified again by the **eyepiece**, or **ocular lens**, to produce a virtual image seen by the viewer. The total magnification of the object is the sum of the objective and ocular lens magnifications, so if the ocular is 10× and the objective lens is 40×, the virtual image appears 400 times larger than the sample.

Historical Evidence 5.1—History of the Microscope

The microscope was conceived in the 1600s by Anton von Leeuwenhoek, who built the first workable magnifying device. Peering into a drop of pond water, he was able to see a variety of microscopic life-forms. Others, including Galileo and Robert Hooke, were also working on optics and magnification, leading to the production of serviceable, if primitive, devices. In the 1700s, microscopists learned to combine lenses to

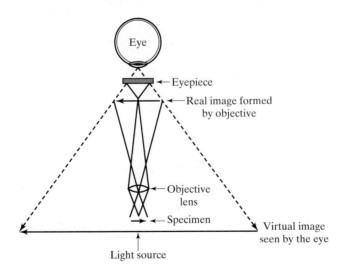

◀ **Figure 5.8** *A simple microscope. The viewer sees an image such as that produced by a magnifying lens; the difference is that what is magnified is not the object, but a magnified image of it. The dark arrows indicate the orientation of the sample and its images at different points in the light path.*

Historical Evidence 5.1—(Continued)

improve their performance, leading to the first compound microscopes. Modern designs emerged in the mid-1900s, and while components and designs continue to improve, the basic principles have changed little in over a century.

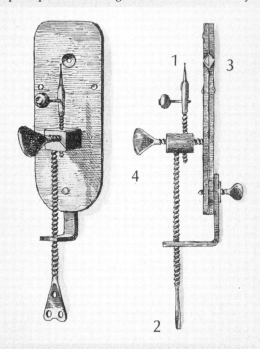

Source: Molecular Expressions™ website, "Optical Microscopy Primer." Available on-line at http://micro.magnet.fsu.edu/primer/anatomy/introduction.html. Downloaded November 2004.

Eyepiece (ocular)

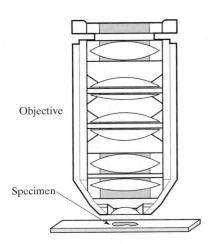
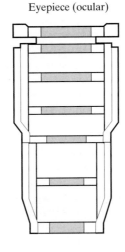

Objective

Specimen

◀ **Figure 5.9** *The objective and eyepiece lenses of a microscope are actually a series of lenses encased in a single housing.*

A compound microscope contains more optical components and lenses than just two simple lenses. In fact, the objective and the ocular are not single lenses, but rather a system of lenses, as shown in Figure 5.9. However, in the interests of clarity, we will treat them as if each were a single lens. There are two additional lenses, one that focuses light emerging from the source of illumination and one that condenses this light into a tight cone that passes through the sample. A simplified optical path of a compound microscope is illustrated in Figure 5.10. Light from the source lamp is focused into parallel rays by the lamp condenser (a) and is then condensed again into a tight cone of light by the substage condenser (b). Light passes through the sample (c) and into the objective lens (d), which forms a magnified real image in the body tube of the microscope (e). The ocular lens (f) creates the virtual image seen by the viewer (g). The spiral object represents the image of the lamp filament. Note that at three points a real image of the lamp filament is created. Although the filament is not viewed when a specimen is examined, its image is used to align the components of the microscope.

Example Problem 5.2

Why does the working distance decrease with increasing magnification?

Answer: Magnification, numerical aperture, resolution, and working distance are all related, and optimizing any one of them involves compromises with the others. To increase the magnification of a lens, the curvature must increase. The more curved a lens is, however, the less light it can collect. Yet a high numerical aperture is desirable in order to collect the largest cone of light emerging from the sample and to provide maximum resolution. The only way to compensate for the curvature of high-magnification lenses is to move the lenses closer to the sample, decreasing the working distance.

Figure 5.10 illustrates **Köhler** (pronounced "curler") **illumination**, the most common type of illumination utilized in forensic chemistry. To establish Köhler illumination, the image of the filament is used to align the lenses and to set **apertures** such that the field of view (the portion of the sample being examined) receives maximum illumination. The cone of light directed through the sample is adjusted to illuminate only the field of view and nothing more. The image of the filament is centered and focused with the **Bertrand lens**, which is

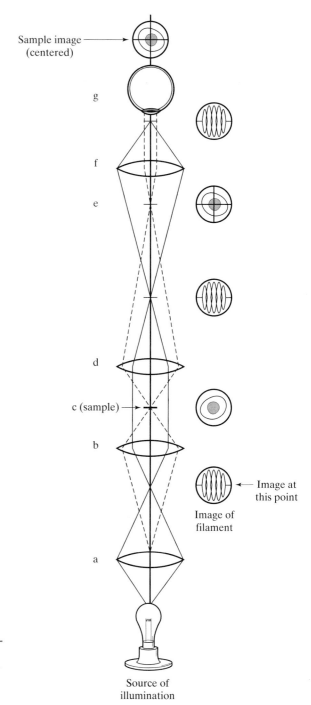

▶ **Figure 5.10** *The simplified optical path found in a compound microscope, transmission mode.*

inserted either inside the body of the microscope or near the ocular lens. Establishing Köhler illumination is analogous to aligning the optics in a spectrometer and setting slit widths.

Important measurements and considerations for microscopy are shown in Figure 5.11. Optimal imaging is attained when the objective collects the maximum possible amount of light passing through the sample. Ideally, the **angle aperture** (AA, or angle of acceptance) should match the ability of the objective lens

Historical Evidence 5.2—August Köhler (1866–1948)

Köhler developed the illumination pathway that is standard today in forensic microscopy. He worked extensively in the field of photomicrography, an infant science in the late 1800s. Köhler used the method of illumination now named after him to obtain full, even, and bright lighting of specimens that was essential for early photography.

Source: Murphy, D. B. *Fundamentals of Light Microscopy and Electronic Imaging.* Danvers, MA: Wiley-Liss, 2001, p. 9.

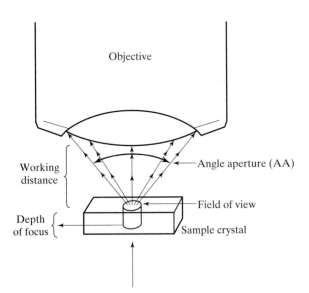

◄ **Figure 5.11** *Important characteristics and descriptors used in microscopy.*

to collect light transmitted through the sample. Objective lenses are characterized by their **numerical aperture (NA)**, expressed as $N\sin(AA/2)$, where N is the refractive index of any material between the condenser and the specimen. This calculation assumes that the sample is mounted on a glass slide.[3] The larger the NA, the more light is collected and the better is the image quality. As magnification increases, the NA of the objective lens increases also. The ability to resolve fine structure and detail in a sample depends on the quantity of light passing through it and is directly related to the NA of the objective lens. **Resolving power** is expressed as $0.6\lambda/NA$, where λ is the wavelength of illuminating light. Wavelength matters because, as mentioned previously, dispersion is a function of wavelength. This property is the basis light dispersion by a prism.

At low magnification, more of the sample area (the **field of view**) can be seen, and focus can be maintained throughout a deeper portion of the sample (**depth of focus**). As the magnification increases, both the field of view and the depth of focus decrease. Also, as the magnification increases, the working distance decreases. If a sample has significant depth, such as a sample containing fibers or a sample under a coverslip, short **working distances** can result in physical limitations. In such cases, the sample may not fit under the objective.

Forensic chemists use two other kinds of microscopes. The first is a stereomicroscope with magnification in the range of 40×. Stereoscopes are used for preliminary investigations and the sorting of fibers, soil, paints, glass, and for particles. The second kind of microscope is an adjunct to the compound microscope that incorporates polarized light. **Polarized light microscopy** (PLM) is central to forensic science and is used extensively in forensic chemistry and trace evidence analysis. Probing samples with polarized light reveals information about their crystal structure and organization and thus about their chemical structure. An overview of PLM is illustrated in Figure 5.12.

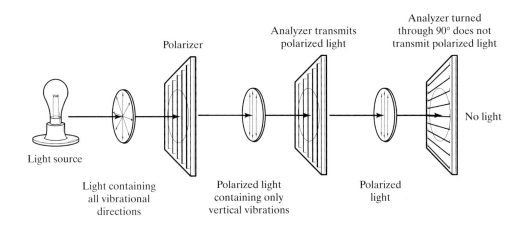

▲ **Figure 5.12** *The basis of PLM. A polarizing filter called the* polarizer *is positioned between the light source and the sample. The light emerging from the filter vibrates in only one plane. A second filter positioned perpendicular to the polarizer is placed in the light path, above the sample, but before the ocular lens. This filter is called the* analyzer. *If the sample does not change the direction of vibration of the light, the analyzer will block the light and the field of view will appear black.*

Visible light such as that from the sun or a lamp vibrates in all directions. When sunlight reflects off of a window, glare results. Polarized sunglasses reduce glare by blocking all vibrational directions except one. In a microscope, inserting the polarizer in the light path does not produce a color change. It is only when the analyzer is placed in the light path ("cross polars") that things get interesting. If the sample doesn't change the direction of vibration, the field of view appears black, because the analyzer blocks out the light. However, many samples alter the light path. These samples under crossed polars appear colored against a black background. Many materials that are crystalline or **pseudocrystalline** interacts with polarized light, and the observation and measurements of the interactions that take place reveal information about the chemical structure of the sample.

Example Problem 5.3

Under polarized light, starch grains have a distinctive appearance that is similar to the pattern produced when two synthetic fibers overlap. What does this pattern indicate?

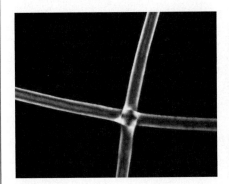 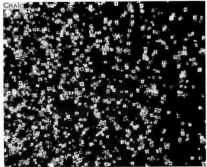

Answer: In both cases, what is observed is an interference pattern. Because the "crosses" appear only in polarized light, the pattern indicates that both starch and the fiber have an ordered, or pseudocrystalline, structure. Starch is a glucose polymer and the fiber is a synthetic polymer, so the appearance of interference is not surprising. Black areas are portions of the sample that completely block the polarized light (via destructive interference); the brighter locations are where constructive interference occurs. More about the microscopy of synthetic polymers and fibers is presented in Chapter 14.

Materials such as glass are not crystalline, and there is no order (in the sense of repeated and organized crystals) to the way in which their atoms are organized. Since there is no directionality to the internal organization, light that is polarized when it enters the glass remains polarized when it exits the glass. It doesn't matter how the light enters or exits, nor does it matter how the glass is oriented: Polarized light remains polarized after tranversing the crystal. This

Applying the Science 5.1   Glass Analysis and Refractive Index

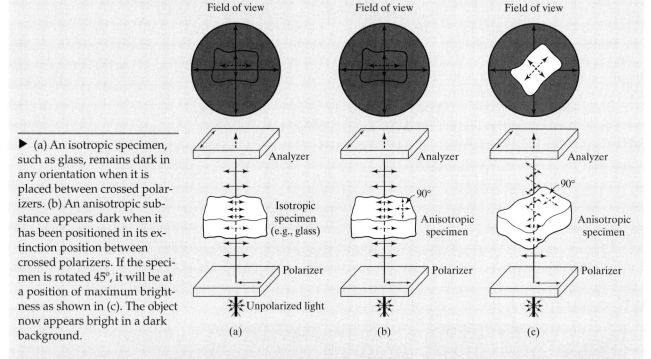

▶ (a) An isotropic specimen, such as glass, remains dark in any orientation when it is placed between crossed polarizers. (b) An anisotropic substance appears dark when it has been positioned in its extinction position between crossed polarizers. If the specimen is rotated 45°, it will be at a position of maximum brightness as shown in (c). The object now appears bright in a dark background.

One of best illustrations of how polarized light interacts with solid samples is found in the forensic analysis of glass. As shown in the figure, polarized light is not altered by an isotropic substance such as glass, and under crossed polars, the field of view appears black, since the analyzer effectively blocks all light that has passed through the glass. In contrast, anisotropic materials will appear black only when the optical axes in the samples are aligned with the polarizer or analyzer.

Source: Koons, R. D., et al. "Forensic Glass Comparisons," in R. Saferstein, ed., *Forensic Science Handbook*, Vol. 1, (2d) ed. Upper Saddle River, NJ: Prentice Hall, 2002.

characteristic is not to be confused with a material's refractive index. Because its speed changes when light enters and exits the glass, the light is refracted, even if it is polarized. There is no difference in refraction characteristics between polarized and unpolarized light. Glass and other such substances are referred to as *isotropic*, meaning that they have only one refractive index; the same is true of cubic crystals.

Crystals behave differently when polarized light passes through them, because they have a repeated structure, internal organization, and directionality. As shown in Figure 5.13, 5.14, and Applying the Science 5.1, light entering from one direction encounters a different organization of atoms than does light entering from the perpendicular direction. If, upon entering the crystal, polarized light vibrates in a plane parallel to a crystal axis, it is unaffected and the field of view remains dark. However, at orientations other than parallel, the polarized light is

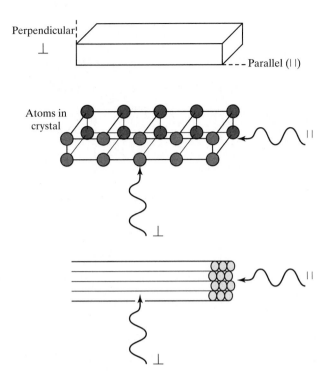

◄ **Figure 5.13** *Crystalline and pseudocrystalline materials. The ordered structure of the crystal means that light will "see" a different environment, depending on the orientation. Synthetic fibers (lower frame) show similar behavior, since their structure is ordered (pseudocrystalline).*

split into two components that vibrate perpendicular to each other along the axes. The two components are called fast and slow as shown in Figures 5.14 and 5.15. In one direction, the light encounters more atoms than in the other and thus is slowed to a greater extent than light that encounters fewer atoms in the other direction. Other factors, such as, size of the atoms also influence the degree of difference. In effect, the crystal acts as a beam splitter.[4] The two rays, one fast and one slow, emerge from the crystal now out of phase by a distance called the **retardation distance**. When the two rays enter the analyzer, they interfere with each other, producing interference colors that are seen even under crossed polars. These colors correlate to the crystal structure and thickness of the sample because the thicker the material, the greater is the retardation. (We will encounter this principle again later in the chapter in a discussion of **interferometry**.)

Materials that display **retardation** are **anisotropic**, meaning that they have more than one refractive index. If an anisotropic fiber or crystal is placed on a microscope stage under crossed polars and is rotated, there are two positions from which the fiber disappears from view. This phenomenon is called **extinction**, and it occurs when the light is propagating along a direction parallel to a crystal axis. At 45° between these extremes, maximum interference occurs, because that is the point where the difference between the fast and slow rays is the greatest. Because the sample is illuminated by white light and because dispersion is a function of wavelength, a range of vivid interference colors is observed, depending on the thickness and the degree of retardation of the material. Accordingly, PLM can be used to determine the thickness of anisotropic materials.

The numerical difference of the two refractive indices (parallel and perpendicular) is called **birefringence** (abbreviated B or Bi). Materials with low

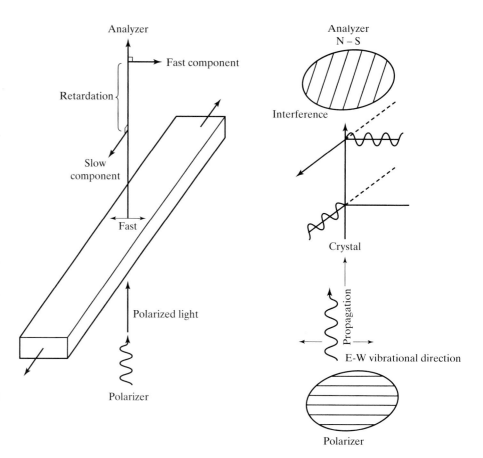

▶ **Figure 5.14** *Splitting of polarized light into two components by a birefringent sample. As light propagates upward through the crystal, its interaction with the sample alters the vibrational direction of the wave, which divides into two components, one that emerges quickly and one that lags behind due to the different interactions encountered. These two components vibrate perpendicular to each other. Once they reach the polarizer, they recombine and interfere, producing colors. The notations N-S and E-W stand for directions and are used to indicate when the analyzer and polarizer are at 90 degrees from each other.*

birefringence show small differences, whereas highly birefringent materials have large numerical differences.[5] In addition, light entering a thicker portion of a sample interacts more and undergoes a greater degree of retardation than light entering a thinner portion of the sample. As a result, a birefringent material often shows a banding pattern of repeating colors. This pattern is related to the thickness of the sample and can be thought of as a topographical map. The colors are correlated with thickness by means of a Michel-Levy chart (after Auguste Michel Levy, French geologist and crystallographer), which is shown in the color insert.

Related to, but distinct from, birefringence is **pleochroism**: variations in a material's absorbance of light, as opposed to variations in its refractive index. To determine if a sample is pleochroic, it is placed on the stage and illuminated as with polarized light, but not under crossed polars. Pleochroism can be visualized by rotating the stage and seeing if the sample changes color. If the color changes only at 90° angles of rotation and only two colors are visible, the sample is **dichroic**. Dichroism is common in fibers: When the fiber is oriented perpendicular, the color is different than when the fiber is oriented parallel.

Many other optical and crystalline properties are measured and explored with PLM. The interested reader is directed to any of the references listed at the end of the chapter for more information. One website deserves special mention: Nikon's "Microscopy University" (www.microscopyu.org). This site is a wonderful resource for learning about microscopes and microscopy and includes excellent figures and tutorials.

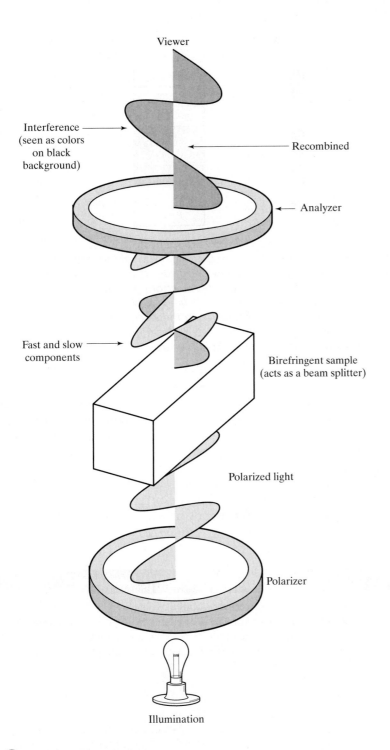

Viewer

Interference
(seen as colors
on black
background)

Recombined

Analyzer

Fast and slow
components

Birefringent sample
(acts as a beam splitter)

Polarized light

Polarizer

Illumination

◀ **Figure 5.15** *Another version showing the implementation of polarized light microscopy.*

5.2 Spectroscopy

Spectroscopy is the use of electromagnetic energy to probe matter and interpret the results in order to characterize chemical structure (Figure 5.16). When energy is absorbed by an atom, an ion, or a molecule, the energy is converted in accordance with the first law of thermodynamics. Absorption promotes the sample into an excited state, the exact form of which depends on the type of

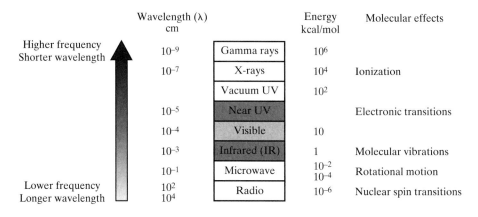

▲ **Figure 5.16** *The result of probing energy with matter depends on the energy involved. High-energy X-rays remove electrons from an atom, causing ionization; less energetic UV/VIS energy promotes electrons, but does not eject them from the atom or molecule; infrared energy and weaker forms are not energetic enough to promote electrons. Rather, absorption in these regions affects the kinetic energy of molecules by causing bonds to stretch (vibrational spectroscopy) or to rotate faster (microwave spectroscopy). At low energy, only the spin of the nucleus itself is affected (NMR spectroscopy).*

electromagnetic energy absorbed. Broadly speaking, spectroscopy can be divided into **atomic** (elemental) and **molecular** (having to do with compounds) spectroscopy, based on which transitions occur and where they occur. Regardless of the mode of energy conversion, the wavelength of light absorbed and the intensity of the absorption can be used to extract qualitative and quantitative chemical information. In forensic analytical chemistry, UV/VIS/IR and elemental spectroscopy is favored, whereas other kinds, such as nuclear magnetic resonance (NMR) spectroscopy and rotational spectroscopy are rarely employed.

Exhibit C: A Light Review

Electromagnetic energy is modeled as both a wave and a particle. In the wave model, frequency and wavelength are the descriptors and are related to each other through the speed of light, *c*. In the particle model, electromagnetic energy is visualized as a discrete massless particle carrying a discrete amount of energy. The two can be related through the frequency ν.

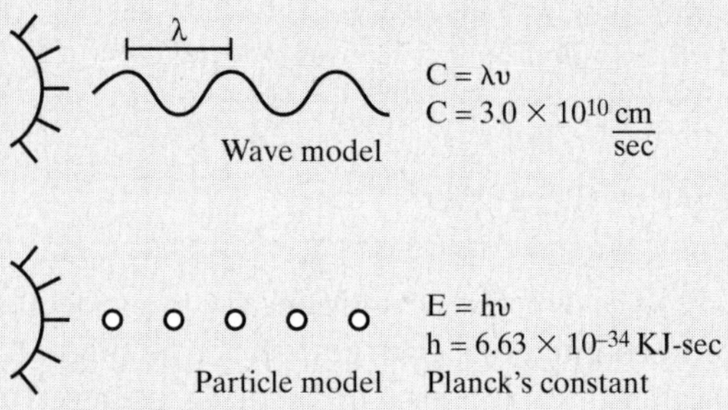

$$C = \lambda \upsilon$$
$$C = 3.0 \times 10^{10} \, \frac{cm}{sec}$$

Wave model

$$E = h\upsilon$$
$$h = 6.63 \times 10^{-34} \, \text{KJ-sec}$$

Particle model   Planck's constant

Exhibit C: (Continued)

$$C = \lambda \upsilon$$
$$E = h\upsilon$$
$$E = \frac{hc}{\lambda}$$
$$C = 3 \times 10^{10}\,\frac{cm}{S}$$
$$h = 6.626 \times 10^{-34}\,JS$$

Conversion matrix

	nm	Å	cm^{-1}	eV
nm		10	10^7	1.240×10^3
Å	0.1		10^8	1.240×10^4
cm^{-1}	10^7	-10^8		1.240×10^{-1}
eV	1.240×10^3	1.240×10^4	8.0655×10^3	
Spectrometric region	UV-vis	X-ray UV	Infrared	X-ray γ

Historical Evidence 5.3—Newton and Bunsen: The Road to Spectroscopy

None other than Sir Isaac Newton is credited with the crucial first steps towards spectroscopy, with his use of the prism to disperse sunlight. He also worked with different slits placed in the path of the dispersed light and observed that the more "pure" (monochromatic) the light, the lower was its intensity—a trade-off spectroscopists continue to grapple with. The first primitive flame emission experiments occurred in 1752, but infrared energy wasn't recognized as a form of energy until the early 1800s. The first device similar to spectrometers was reported during the same period, and the first true spectrometer was credited to two famous chemists: Bunsen (of burner fame) and Kirchhoff, who reported his findings in a paper published in 1860. Their device was a simple flame emission device. IR techniques were first developed in the 1880s, followed by X-ray analysis in the early part of the 20th century. Instrumentation for work across the spectrum improved continually, with the next big breakthrough coming in the 1950s with the development of atomic absorption. By that time, forensic chemists were using X-ray diffraction, UV/VIS, and IR spectroscopy. The next advance was the development of **Fourier transform** techniques, made possible by computers and lasers, both of which became widely available by the 1990s.

Source: Szabadváry, F. "Chapter XI: Optical Methods," in F. Szabadváry, *History of Analytical Chemistry*, tr. Gyula Svehla. Oxford, U.K.: Pergamon Press, 1966.

5.2.1 THE BASICS

Microscopy can be thought of as spectroscopy that uses visible light as the probing radiation and the human eye as a detector. There are many other parallels between the two techniques. As in microscopy, in spectroscopy light can be scattered, reflected, absorbed, and transmitted. The energy can be polarized or not; interference and scattering occurs and can be exploited even if it cannot be seen. It is not surprising that the first implementation of instrumental spectroscopy was based on color which is the visible manifestation of absorption of light in the visible range. As mentioned in the previous section, the absorption of a photon can trigger several events, depending on the energy of the photon. However, absorption is one of many phenomena that can be monitored to extract qualitative and quantitative information. As shown in Figure 5.17, a sample (denoted M) may absorb energy and consequently be promoted to some type of excited state

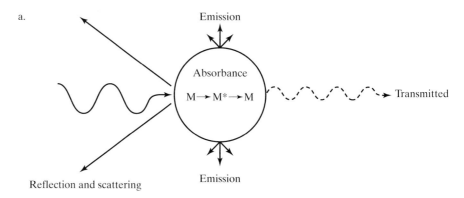

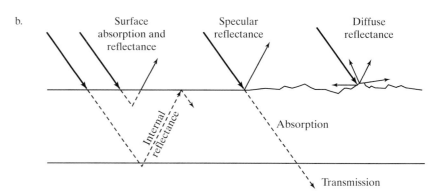

▶ **Figure 5.17** *(a) Some potential outcomes of the interaction of energy with matter. If emission results from the relaxation of M* ⟶ M, it will be in all directions. (b) Potential outcomes of interactions at a surface, particularly reflections.*

M*. As a result of the promotion, the transmitted signal is attenuated and reduced in proportion to the sample's concentration, the path length of the signal, and the molar absorptivity (in accordance with **Beer's law**) of the sample. The absorbance of the sample is given by the formula

$$A = Elc \tag{5.5}$$

where l is the path length and c is the concentration. Spectrometers are typically designed with a constant path length. For a given absorber at a given wavelength, E is a constant; therefore,

$$A = kc \tag{5.6}$$

which is a linear relationship of the form $y = mx + b$, where $b = 0$. Equation 5.6 represents a way of linking instrument response to the concentration of the sample. Note that with actual calibration curves, b (the intercept) is usually not zero.

Some relaxations M* ⟶ M result in the immediate or delayed emission of photons. Such emission is in all directions, not just in the optical path from the source to the detector. This is an important observation and is exploited to differentiate signals due to emission from signals due to absorption and transmittance. Regardless, emission spectroscopy is governed by Beer's law, and the linear calibration applies.

Other types of energy–matter interactions, such as reflection and scattering, can also occur. Both phenomena can be exploited to extract chemical information. **Specular reflectance** is simple reflectance from a surface, with no interaction between light and the surface and where the angle of reflection equals the angle of incidence. On rougher surfaces, such as powders, the reflection is diffuse because the angles of reflection are randomized. The difference is the same as that between looking in a shiny, polished mirror and looking in one with a scratched and scarred surface. The energy may penetrate a few microns into the material, undergo some absorptive interactions, and then reflect back, a phenomenon referred to as **surface absorption–reflection** (SAR). Such interactions may occur in diffuse reflection. Finally, certain materials can undergo internal reflections, a property that is used in attenuated total reflectance techniques in the infrared region. Fiber optics works on the basis of internal reflection that, in effect, traps the energy within the fiber.

All absorptive processes are governed by the first law of thermodynamics (energy is neither created nor destroyed; it only changes form), and all involve the excitation of a sample M in the ground state to a higher energy excited state M*. The energy absorbed, ΔE, must be sufficient to bridge the gap in energy between the two levels. The excited state could be the result of the ejection or promotion of an electron or a change in the electron's vibrational or rotational state. Regardless, the excited state is unstable and the system decays back to the more stable state. The process is shown in Figure 5.18. Excess energy can be dissipated by one of three generic processes. First, electrons can collide and convert their excess energy to kinetic energy, a process favored in solutions where molecular collisions are numerous and frequent. Because no electromagnetic radiation is emitted, these conversions are referred to as **radiationless transitions**, and this is how excited-state energy is dissipated in UV/VIS interactions. Second, the M* $\longrightarrow$ M transition can result in the emission of a photon with energy equal to the energy of the original absorbed photon if that is how the excited state was generated. This process is known as emission. Third, a combination of radiationless transmission and emission can occur, resulting in the emission of a photon of lower energy that corresponds to the smaller energy gap traversed in the relaxation. The emission of the photon may be immediate or delayed. In most instruments, the excitation M $\longrightarrow$ M* is instigated by electromagnetic energy ($E = h\upsilon$) or by thermal energy, such as that of a flame, a furnace, or plasma.

When a delayed emission of a photon occurs, either directly or with intermediate steps, the process is referred to as **fluorescence** or **phosphorescence** (Figure 5.19). The difference between fluorescence and phosphorescence is time: Phosphorescence is delayed relative to fluorescence and phosphorescence

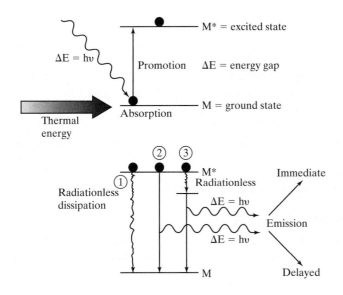

◀ **Figure 5.18** *The promotion of an atom, an ion, or a molecule to an excited state can be driven by the absorption of electromagnetic energy, thermal energy, or another form of energy, as long as the absorbed energy equals or exceeds the energy gap. Once excitation occurs, the system is unstable and tends to dissipate the excess energy. The small wavy line represents dissipation by conversion to kinetic energy (i.e., heat), while other relaxations involve the emission of a photon, the energy of which corresponds to the energy gap traversed.*

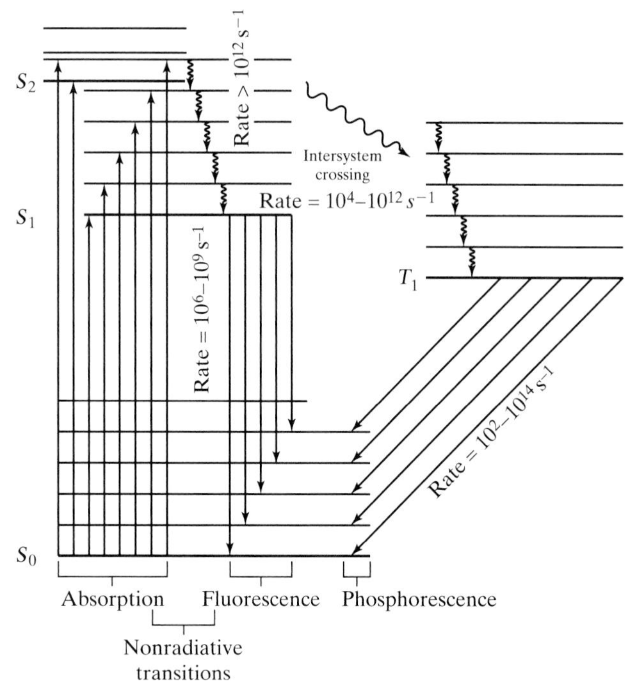

▶ **Figure 5.19** *Absorption and relaxation modes in emission spectroscopy. "S" refers to singlet states, or those states in which all electrons are paired with opposing spins ($\uparrow\downarrow$), whereas T refers to a triplet state in which two electrons are paired with the same spin ($\uparrow\uparrow$). The longer-lived states are referred to as* metastable *and are exploited in lasers.*

generally lasts longer. If the levels are vibrational levels exploited in infrared methods, the relaxation (dissipation by heat) is nearly instantaneous—on the order of a trillionth of a second (or a trillion relaxations per second). Fluorescence is exploited in many areas of forensic science, including DNA typing instrumentation and fingerprint visualization; however, traditional fluorescence spectroscopy is not frequently used.

A generic absorbance spectrum is a plot of the wavelength of electromagnetic energy interacting with the sample versus the degree of absorbance at a that wavelength. Absorbance is governed by Beer's law and depends on the molar extinction coefficient of each transition. In an idealized transition (Figure 5.20), the absorbance would be reflected in a single sharp peak at the wavelength corresponding to the energy gap. This situation can be approximated in some gas-phase techniques, such as atomic absorption spectrophotometry, but in other techniques and solution environments, the transitions are not singular or sharp. For any one lower energy level, there may be several possible excitations, although some are more likely than others. The more transitions possible, the broader the absorption peak becomes. In a solution matrix, interactions between analyte and matrix components further alter energy gaps such that even a simple transition is recorded as a broadened Gaussian peak as shown in Figure 5.21. If more than one transition is allowed, the picture is more complex, but such complexity is not inherently bad from an analytical point of view. The intricacy of infrared spectra facilitates the definitive identification of compounds. With other techniques, such as UV/VIS, the spectra are so general as to be nearly useless for identification of specific compounds.

5.2.2 Instrument Design

Most spectroscopic instruments contain the same generic components, but are designed according to the type of electromagnetic energy being probed and whether the energy is absorbed or emitted. This concept is illustrated in Figure 5.22. Both

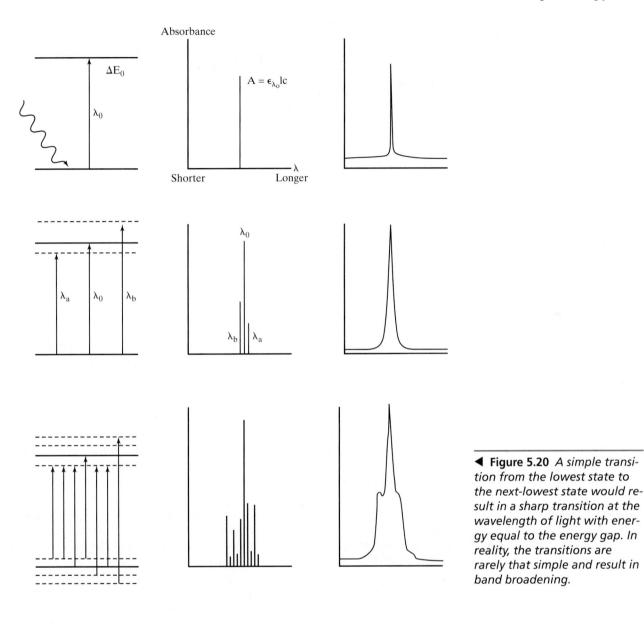

◀ **Figure 5.20** *A simple transition from the lowest state to the next-lowest state would result in a sharp transition at the wavelength of light with energy equal to the energy gap. In reality, the transitions are rarely that simple and result in band broadening.*

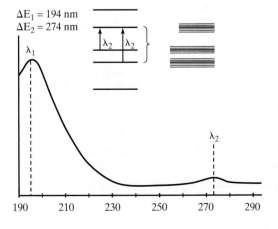

◀ **Figure 5.21** *When more than one transition can occur, the peak broadens even further. This example is a depiction of the UV spectrum of acetone, with two allowed transitions correlating with two broad absorption peaks.*

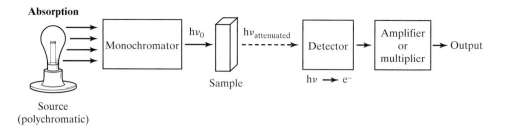

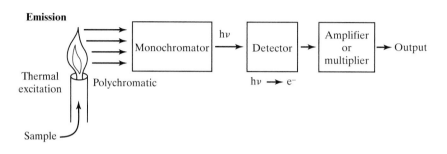

▲ **Figure 5.22** *Box diagram of an absorbance–transmittance spectrophotometer (top) and an emission spectrometer (bottom). Shared components are monochromators (typically gratings) and detectors (transducers) that convert photons into electrons and electrical signals.*

types of instruments use wavelength filters (monochromators) to obtain or isolate monochromatic energy (energy of a single wavelength, which translates into the best resolution possible) from a polychromatic source. Older **colorimeters** used prisms to break visible light into its component wavelengths, but modern instruments utilize dispersive gratings, which rely on geometry to establish predictable patterns of constructive and destructive interference. One or more slits further limit the range of wavelengths allowed to pass a given point at any given time. The smaller the slit widths, the lower is the intensity of the source, just as decreasing the size of an aperture in a microscope decreases the brightness of the viewed image. Because energy is physically separated by a grating, it is possible to simultaneously detect many wavelengths. Dispersive gratings can be divided into simultaneous and sequential types as shown in Figure 5.23. The other generic category of instruments is based not on dispersion, but on interferometry and the Fourier transform. Finally, some instruments, such as atomic absorption spectrophotometers, use monochromatic light, but as is discussed shortly, a monochromator is still required, though in a different place along the optical path.

The source of energy in a spectrometer is thermal or electromagnetic and depends on the type of interactions being probed. Increasingly, lasers are being used either as sources or as part of an interferometer that is coupled to the source. Regardless of the source or region of the electromagnetic spectrum being utilized, the role of the detector is the same across the spectrum; to convert photons into electrons as efficiently as possible. This device is sometimes referred to as a transducer, and it can consist of a semiconductor, a charged-coupled device, or some other design. In instruments in which the signal is not strong, such as microscopectrophotometers, the detector must be cooled to minimize noise.

a.

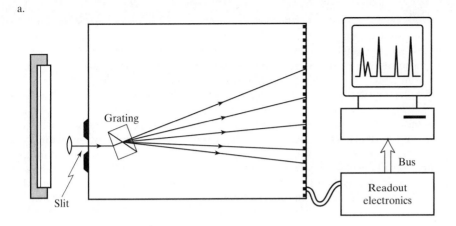

b.

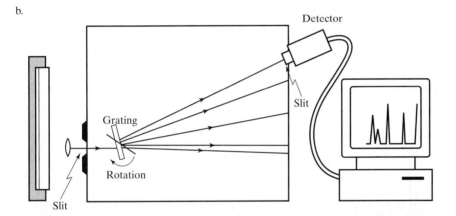

◀ **Figure 5.23** *(a) Use of a grating to disperse and detect all wavelengths of interest at once. This design is referred to as* simultaneous. *(b) In this approach* (sequential), *the grating is incrementally moved to direct one wavelength at a time on a fixed detector position. Such a design is also referred to as* scanning.

Exhibit D: Lasers

Lasers are commonly used as sources of intense monochromatic light for many types of spectroscopy. The word "laser" is derived from *l*ight *a*mplification by *s*timulated *e*mission of *r*adiation. Lasers can be based on electronic transitions in molecular systems (e.g., a CO_2 laser) or on atomic transitions such as that in a neodymium yttrium aluminum garnet (Nd:YAG). Laser light is monochromatic, coherent (oscillating in phase), plane polarized, and intense, properties that together make lasers ideal sources for spectroscopy. The beam can be tightly focused in small areas, making lasers ideal for microspectrophotometry as well. The drawbacks of lasers are their cost and somewhat limited lifetimes. Replacing a lamp as a source is cheap, whereas replacing a laser is a several-thousand-dollar proposition.

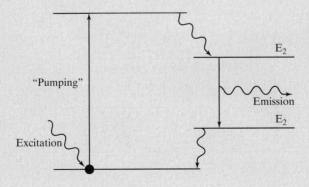

Exhibit D: (Continued)

A laser works by stimulation of the medium to a higher energy state through the input of electromagnetic or other forms of energy, such as thermal or even chemical energy. The system undergoes a radiationless transition to a metastable state (Figure 5.19, E_2) from which the photon-producing relaxation occurs. A population inversion, in which the population $E_2 > E_1$, is necessary for lasing to begin. Lasing is then perpetuated by a series of internal reflections of the photons emitted by this decay. A laser has four basic components: a medium that can be stimulated to emit light, a source of excitation, a feedback mechanism to perpetuate the excitation, and a means of directing the light out of the source (an output coupler). Different lasers have different mechanisms, but all are based on the foregoing principles. The Nd:YAG is a solid-state laser that emits in the near-infrared region (1064 nm), while a CO_2 laser is a gas laser that emits in the far infrared (10.6 μm). Helium–neon lasers emit red light at 632.8 nm.

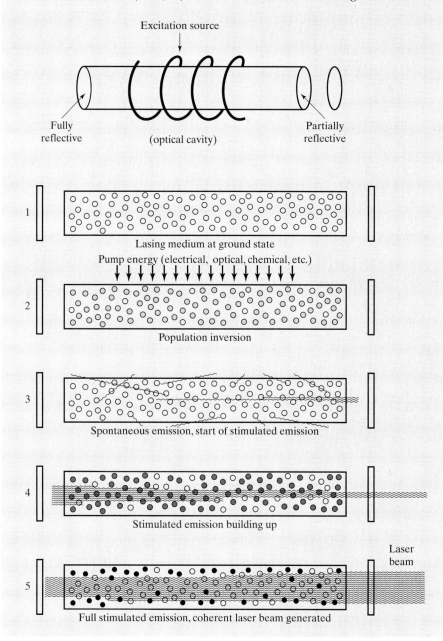

Excitation source

Fully reflective   (optical cavity)   Partially reflective

1   Lasing medium at ground state

Pump energy (electrical, optical, chemical, etc.)

2   Population inversion

3   Spontaneous emission, start of stimulated emission

4   Stimulated emission building up

Laser beam

5   Full stimulated emission, coherent laser beam generated

5.2.3 BANDWIDTH AND RESOLUTION

All spectrometers are designed to optimize the **bandwidth** of the source relative to the bandwidth of the transition that is targeted while maintaining maximum intensity of the source. Because electromagnetic radiation is a continuum, no light source is truly monochromatic. The *spectral bandwidth* is defined as the width of the radiation band from the source. The bandwidth depends on the source (if monochromatic) or on the slit width of the monochromator. The narrower the slit, the closer the energy is to the idealized monochromatic form; the trade-off is intensity. As the slit narrows, so does the strength of the signal. Figures 5.24 and 5.25 illustrate these concepts.

The ability of an instrument to differentiate between adjacent absorption or emission peaks is the resolving power of the instrument. Usually, this is defined as

$$\frac{\lambda}{\Delta\lambda} \tag{5.7}$$

where λ is the nominal wavelength of one peak and $\Delta\lambda$ is the difference between that peak and an adjacent one. The term **baseline resolution** refers to the situation in which both peaks are at the baseline as shown in Figure 5.26. The larger the resolution, the more complete is the separation of the peaks; the resolution in turn depends on the slit width, source bandwidth, and bandwidth of the transition.

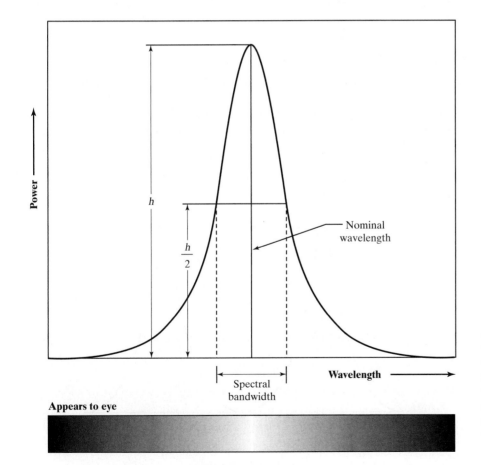

◀ **Figure 5.24** *Spectral bandwidth of a monochromatic source. Peak power is seen at the nominal wavelength, with detectable intensity on either side. The bandwidth is the full width at half maximum (FWHM) of this peak.*

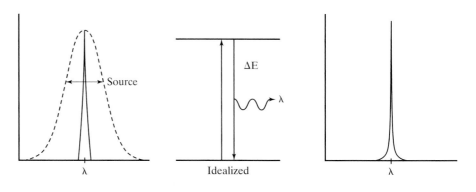

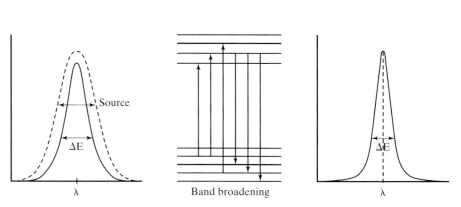

▶ **Figure 5.25** *Source emission bandwidth compared with absorption bandwidth. Ideally, the emission peak bandwidth is contained within the absorbance peak bandwidth; if not, poor resolution results. Monochromator bandwidth is also a critical consideration.*

5.2.4 UV/VIS SPECTROSCOPY

A UV/VIS spectrometer is a classic, but not the indispensable tool of forensic chemistry it once was. UV absorption is all but relegated to use as part of a detector system in instruments, whereas visible interactions are used as part of color analysis and characterization. Color is an important descriptor of presumptive

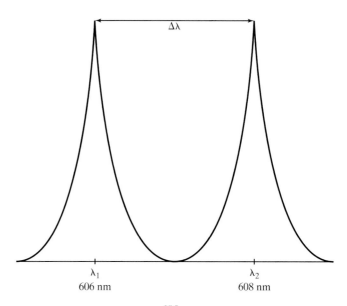

▶ **Figure 5.26** *Baseline resolution of two spectral peaks.*

tests, fibers, dyes, inks, and paints, all of which can be explored spectroscopically. However, traditional UV/VIS spectrophotometry and colorimetry are rarely used in forensic settings. A major reason for this neglect is the kind of chemical information the instrument provides and the need to isolate pure materials prior to recording a spectrum. However, recent advances in microspectrophotometry are leading to a revival of interest in this oldest of spectrophotometric techniques. (We address the topic in a later section.)

Absorbances in the ultraviolet and the visible ranges of the spectrum correlate with electronic transitions between molecular orbitals. Only two types of transitions can occur, as shown in Figure 5.27. As a result, only compounds that have π electrons have a UV/VIS spectrum. A UV spectrum provides information about double bonds and conjugation. Whereas this information is useful in many contexts, many UV spectra look similar to or even indistinguishable from one another and consequently cannot be used to definitively identify a given compound. UV/VIS instrumentation has been successfully adapted to liquid chromatography and capillary electrophoresis instrumentation, as both fixed-wavelength and scanning detectors.

5.2.5 INFRARED SPECTROSCOPY

The vibrational spectroscopy family is the most versatile in forensic chemistry. Unlike UV/VIS techniques, IR spectroscopy can provide unambiguous identification of isolated compounds, albeit after meticulous sample preparation. IR techniques are valued for drug analysis, fiber characterization, and other applications in which such identifications are essential. Applications of IR techniques

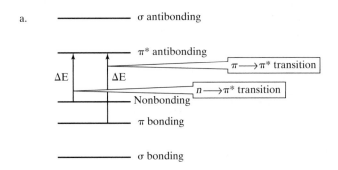

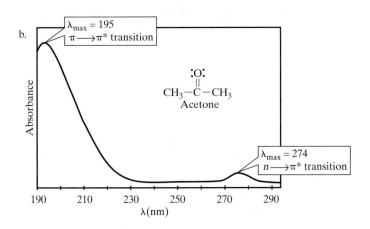

◀ **Figure 5.27** *(a) The only two types of transitions possible with the absorption of UV/VIS radiation. If a compound lacks π electrons, no absorption in that electromagnetic region is possible. (b) UV/VIS spectrum of acetone, showing examples of each.*

in forensic chemistry are exclusively qualitative; when quantitation is required, other techniques, such as GCMS, are used.

The infrared method most students are familiar with is absorption spectroscopy spanning the mid-IR range. The infrared region starts just above the visible one (~770 nm) and extends to approximately 3000 nm, which, by convention, is reported as a frequency in units of reciprocal centimeters (cm^{-1}) rather than in nanometers. The total IR range runs from about 13,000 cm^{-1} to 4000 cm^{-1} and can be divided into the near IR, from 780 nm to 2500 nm (12,820–4000 cm^{-1}); the mid-IR (4000 to 400 cm^{-1}); and the far IR (400–10 cm^{-1}).[6] All three regions can be exploited in forensic work, but midrange techniques dominate.

Several recent advances in instrument design have enhanced the applicability of mid-IR techniques. The first and most important was the replacement of dispersive IR with Fourier transform spectrometers (FTIR) (see Figure 5.28). Dispersive instruments utilized an infrared energy source and a monochromator such as a grating

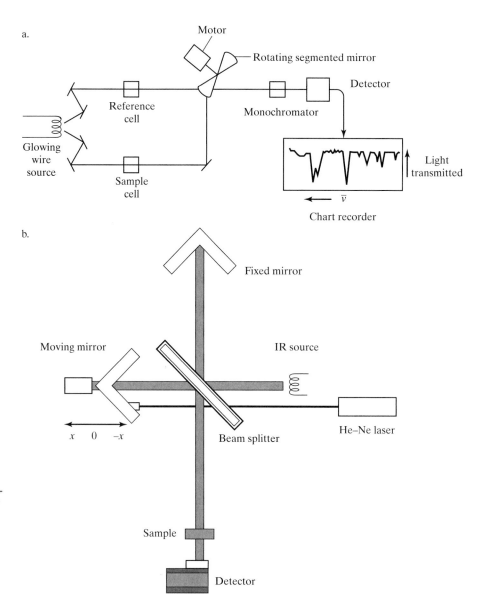

▶ **Figure 5.28** *(a) Box diagram of a dispersive IR instrument. (b) Box diagram of an FTIR instrument and the interferometer. The beam splitter creates two components that recombine at the detector.*

to separate the wavelengths. As mentioned before, isolation and the presentation of single wavelengths to a sample in sequence ("scanning") together cause an inevitable loss of intensity that limits the sensitivity of the spectrometer. To deal with this loss, FTIR instruments have a design that uses a "mathematical dispersion"[6] rather than a physical one. This approach is called **interferometry**.

Interferometry (Figure 5.29) may at first seem a difficult concept to grasp, but the general principles are the same as some we have already encountered in discussing polarizing light microscopy. Recall that in PLM light enters a birefringent sample which acts as a beam splitter, breaking the light into two components. The fast component emerges from the sample ahead of the slow component, which has undergone retardation. The thicker the sample, the greater is the retardation. When the components are recombined at the analyzer, visible interference patterns are created and interpreted by the eye on the basis of color (i.e., wavelength and frequency). An interferometer accomplishes the same thing in the infrared region.

Starting with a simple case of a single infrared wavelength, interference patterns are created by recombining beams split into two paths by the beam splitter. At the beginning of the cycle (Figure 5.30), the mirrors are equidistant from each other, so the two beams travel the same distance and are not shifted out of phase. When the mirror moves away to a point equivalent to one-fourth the value of the wavelength, the beam taking that path now travels the equivalent of $\frac{1}{2}\lambda$ farther, taking into account the trip to the mirror and back. In terms of the PLM analogy, this is the slow beam, retarded by a factor of $\lambda/2$. Retardation is given the symbol δ. Because the slow beam is half a wavelength out of phase, when the beams are recombined, the interference is destructive. When the offset is a full wavelength, constructive interference is restored. The distance moved by the mirror correlates with

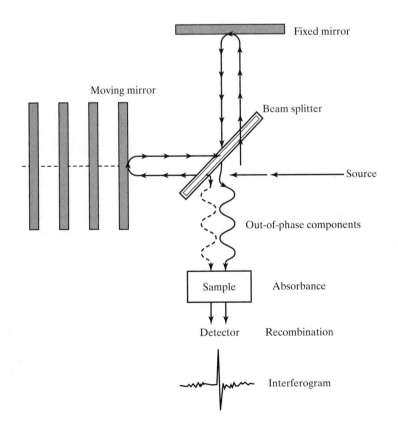

Fixed mirror

Moving mirror

Beam splitter

Source

Out-of-phase components

Sample   Absorbance

Detector   Recombination

Interferogram

◀ **Figure 5.29** *An interferometer. Beams are split into two components that when recombined, will be offset from each other an amount that depends on the different distances the beams travel.*

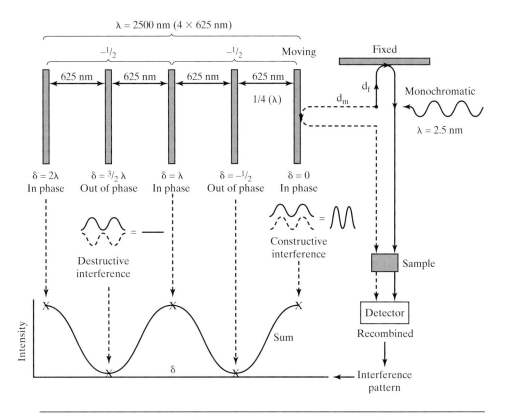

▲ **Figure 5.30** *How an interferogram is created with a monochromatic source at 2500 nm, which corresponds to 4000 cm⁻¹ in the infrared range. The sum of the two beams is plotted as the interferogram.*

the thickness of the sample, in PLM terms. Assuming no interaction with the sample, the interference pattern for a monochromatic source is in the form of a cosine wave. In an instrument, the signal is recorded over the range of the mirror's motion, producing the cosine curve, represented by the formula

$$I(\partial) = \frac{1}{2}I_0\left(1 + \cos\frac{2\pi\partial}{\lambda}\right) \tag{5.8}$$

The intensity is halved because half the light gets reflected back toward the source and does not contribute to the intensity of light reaching the detector. An interferogram represents a combination of these functions for each wavelength of interest; the Fourier transform separates the signal into the contributions from individual wavelengths.

In an FTIR, the source is not monochromatic, but spans the mid-infrared region. A He–Ne laser is used to measure distances and for calibration purposes. An interferogram is thus the combination of as many pairs of recombined wavelengths as are in the source. These signals are separated mathematically with the Fourier transform. The **interferogram** is a plot of mirror distance versus intensity and may be cast in terms of time because the mirror moves at a controlled speed. Such data are said to be in the time domain, and the Fourier transform is used to convert the data to the frequency domain, producing the familiar absorbance plot of intensity as a function of frequency (or wavelength in colorimetry). An example is shown in Figure 5.31. The spectral resolution of the

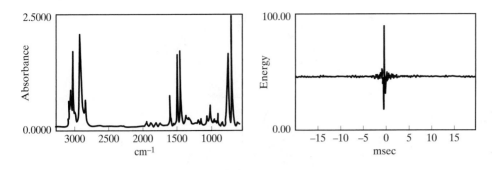

▲ **Figure 5.31** *An example of an interferogram and the corresponding IR spectrum displayed as absorbance.*

instrument depends on the quality of the optics and other factors, whereas the digital resolution depends on the maximum mirror movement. Data points on the interferogram are separated by a value of $1/\Delta$, the inverse of the maximum travel distance. If the mirror moves 1.0 cm, the optimal data point resolution is 1 cm^{-1}. Note that the signal which is recombined at the detector and deconstructed with the Fourier transform is a result of the source signal *minus* the sample signal. A background spectrum is still required (Figure 5.32). Because there is no scanning of wavelengths in FTIR, multiple spectra can be quickly collected and averaged, resulting in significantly improved signal-to-noise ratios and sensitivity.

Advances in FTIR and in computer-processing power have fundamentally changed infrared spectroscopy and its forensic applications. Infrared microscopy and **microspectrophotometry**, all but impossible with dispersive instruments, are becoming common in forensic laboratories. Finally, simplified sample preparation techniques allow for quicker analyses, always an advantage in busy forensic laboratories. The rest of this section summarizes the prevalent modes of FTIR.

Diffuse Reflectance: Diffuse reflectance, or diffuse reflectance infrared Fourier transform spectrometry (DRIFTS), exploits surface interactions and reflection. Although samples still are mixed with KBr, there is no need to press the mixture into a clear pellet. The technique is also more sensitive than traditional dispersive IR and requires less material than a pellet. The sample is mixed with KBr to create a dilute solid solution of reasonably uniform small crystal size. The mixture is placed in a small cup, and the IR beam is directed onto the surface, where

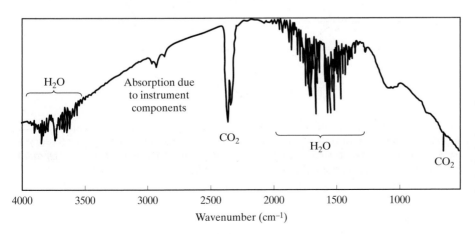

◀ **Figure 5.32** *A typical background of an FTIR instrument. Sample spectra are ratioed against the background to produce the final spectrum. FTIR spectra can be displayed in either the absorbance or the transmittance mode.*

▶ **Figure 5.33** *Simplified DRIFTS. The sample is mixed with KBr and placed in a cup in a DRIFTS accessory. Light from the interferometer hits the surface at an angle, and the specularly reflected light is blocked while the diffusely reflected light is captured by a curved mirror and directed toward the detector. The sample spectrum is ratioed against KBr.*

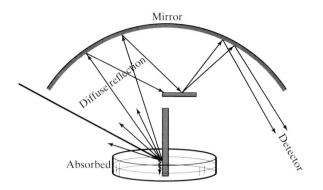

three interactions can occur: reflection, absorbance, and scattering. Specular reflection takes place when the angle of incidence is the same as the angle of reflection, whereas diffuse reflection is scattered. In DRIFTS work, the absorbed energy is measured indirectly by examining beams reflected diffusely. The difference between the characteristics of the input signal and those of the diffusely reflected signal is due to the absorbance of the sample. A DRIFTS accessory must contain some type of curved or spherical surface to ensure that all diffuse reflections are detected; typically, some type of stop is installed to preclude specular reflections from reaching the detector. A simplified depiction of DRIFTS is found in Figure 5.33.

Attenuated Total Reflectance: Although DRIFTS is simple and convenient to use, forensic laboratories are adopting another alternative for micro-IR analysis. Attenuated total reflectance (ATR) takes advantage of internal reflections within a sample to create the infrared absorbance spectrum of the sample. An ATR accessory (Figure 5.34) consists of a crystal (sometimes called a prism) made of

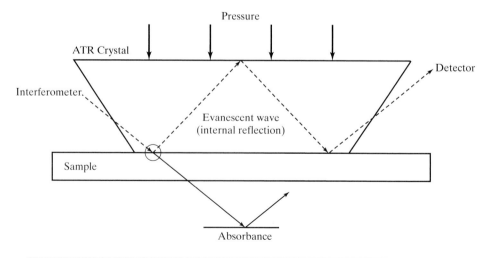

▲ **Figure 5.34** *Attenuated total reflection (ATR) as used as a sampling accessory for FTIR. A series of internal reflections provides multiple absorptive events similar to the multiple absorptions that occur off of different particles in DRIFTS.*

diamond, germanium, ZnS, ThBr, or ZnSe, all materials with high refractive indexes. The combination of the high refractive index and the geometry of the crystal facilitates a series of internal reflections, typically 10–50, and collectively referred to as an **evanescent wave** or multiple internal reflections (MIRs). When the crystal is pressed into tight contact with the sample, a tiny fraction of each reflection penetrates the sample, allowing interaction and absorption to occur. The more reflections, the more opportunities there are for absorption, the longer the effective pathlength is, and the stronger are the resulting signals.

ATR offers many advantages. The absorbance penetrates only about a micron or so of the sample, allowing very thin films and liquids, in addition to solids and powders, to be analyzed. There is no need to purge the sample area, because the IR signal never propagates through the air. In fact, the only destruction of note is the area of compression, which is very small. No KBr is needed, and sample preparation is minimal and nearly nondestructive. This is an issue only with samples such as fibers or tapes, in which the compression leaves a distinctive mark. ATR can be used for very small samples and is a common accessory to infrared microscopes. ATR may be performed in situ on very large objects such as soda cans and even car doors. As long as firm contact can be made between the crystal and the surface, the analysis is feasible. Several companies now offer micro-ATR as well as accessories for large samples. HATR is ATR accessories with a horizontal orientation. ATR accessories are now equipped with cameras to record the exact sampling location. Other designs allow viewing of the sample through a diamond element.

Selection of the type of crystal depends on the application. Diamond prisms are ideal for applying high pressures and ensuring good contact between the sample and the crystal. Diamond is also resistant to corrosive and other chemically aggressive samples. In addition, because diamond is so hard, excessive applied pressure may damage the sample before damaging the crystal. Diamond prisms are also expensive, and for many applications Ge, ZnS, or ZnSe crystals are acceptable. Because the crystal is an optical component in the instrument just like a lens or filter, selecting a crystal depends on what region of the IR spectrum is of interest. A list of crystal types is presented in Figure 5.35.

ATR is becoming a favorite tool in forensic chemistry, given its versatility, simplicity, small sample requirements, and nondestructive nature. However, it is important to note that spectra obtained by ATR are not directly comparable to transmission or reflection spectra. Although the energy–matter interaction is the same (absorption due to vibrational interactions), the locations of bands are shifted relative to transmission and reflection. Also, in transmission and reflection, the path length is fixed and is controlled by the thickness of the sample. In ATR, the depth of penetration, and thus the path length, is a function of wavelength, yet another manifestation of refractive index effects. The ATR crystal must have a high refractive index in order to establish the evanescent wave (Figure 5.34). However, the refractive index of the sample varies with wavelength; consequently, the depth of penetration varies across the spectral range. As the wavelength increases, so does the penetration, which in turn increases the path length and the resulting absorption signal. The influence of the refractive index on the depth of penetration also results in a generalized shift in the absorption to lower

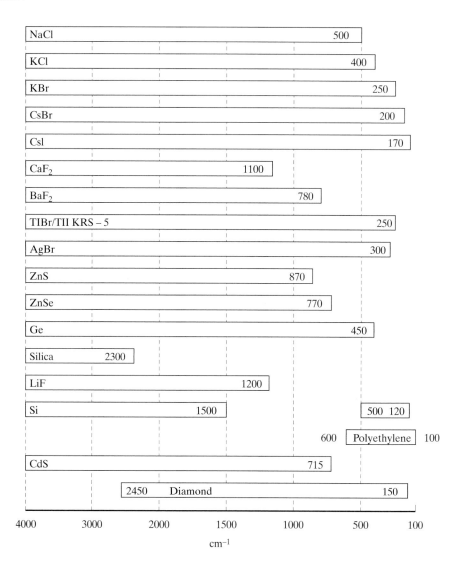

▶ **Figure 5.35** *Optical characteristics of materials in the IR range. ATR crystals are usually made of diamond, germanium, ZnSe, or ZnS.*

frequencies. Thus, correction algorithms are required to correct ATR spectra for these effects and to allow comparison with transmission IR spectra. Preferably, ATR spectra should be compared and evaluated against libraries and databases collected with ATR methods.

Near and Far Infrared Spectroscopy: The preceding discussion focused on the mid-IR range. The near infrared region has characteristics and properties that make it appealing in some forensic applications. Near-IR absorbance corresponds principally to overtones of primary absorbances of C—H, —OH, and N—H stretching vibrations found in the mid-IR ranges.[7–9] Absorbances in this region are generally less than in other regions of the spectrum due to lower molar extinction coefficients, but intensities are measurable because they depend on the sample's chemical environment. This allows not only for a pattern-matching

Applying the Science 5.2   Reconstructing the Past with NIR Spectroscopy

Environmental chemists are involved in reconstruction of the past in ways similar to forensic chemists. For example, it is important to understand environmental and climatic conditions in the distant past to estimate the magnitude of modern human impacts. The modern age has seen an increase in acid precipitation as a result of emissions of SO_2 and NO_2 released during combustion processes such as internal combustion engines and coal-fired power plants.

Both of these react with atmospheric components to form sulfuric and nitric acids. When these acids rain out, they drop the pH of natural waters which can have significant, even catastrophic impacts on the ecosystem. However, acid precipitation can occur from other natural sources and the question arises as to what the pH of a body of water such as a lake was 10, 20, 100, or 10,000 years ago. Near-IR spectroscopy applied to lake sediment cores has been proposed as one method of doing so.

When a core sample is taken, the deeper the layer in the core, the older it is. In many lakes, the mineral content of a core is derived from diatoms (algae) that lived and died in the lake and fell to the bottom to be covered. Any change in pH would have an impact on the biota of the lake and the material that fell to the bottom. Thus, pH conditions are reflected in the chemical composition of the core layers. Near-IR, which is effective for pattern recognition, is well suited for the task. By taking bottom and core samples of lakes with known pH and linking pH to the NIR spectrum via multivariate methods, researchers have reported some success in correlating pH to NIR spectra. As with much of forensic science, the goal was to recreate the past; the difference is the time-frame.

Source: Korsman, T., et al. "Near-Infrared Reflectance Spectroscopy of Sediments: A Potential Method to Infer the Past pH of Lakes." Environmental Science and Technology, 26, **1992**, 2122–2126.

spectroscopy targeting information such as moisture or alcohol content,[7,8] but also for the identification of bacterial species.[10] It does not permit information on specific functional groups or the identification of compounds. Near-IR techniques also are adaptable to fiber-optic probes, opening up possibilities for field-testing techniques. Because the bands seen in a near-IR spectrum do not correlate with functional groups per se, calibration is required to establish a correlation between the spectral features and the chemical characteristic of interest. For example, if moisture determination is the goal, a set of near-IR spectra from samples with known moisture content must be obtained. (Calibrations are discussed in detail near the end of the chapter.)

5.2.6 Raman Spectroscopy

Another vibrational technique, **Raman spectroscopy** is garnering attention for the forensic analysis of drugs and pharmaceuticals,[11,12] paints,[13] fibers,[14] and inks.[15,16] Raman techniques differ from traditional vibration IR in that scattered radiation, rather than absorbed radiation, is studied. Furthermore, Raman interactions are dependent, not on the existence of polar bonds, but instead on the existence of *polarizable* bonds as shown in Figure 5.36.

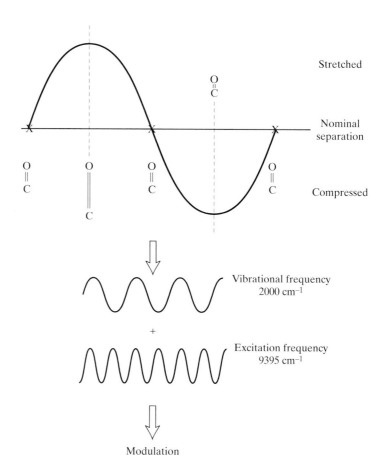

▶ **Figure 5.36** *Frequency of a hypothetical chemical bond vibration. This bond expands and contracts at a frequency of 2000 cm⁻¹. How polarizable the bond is will determine how it scatters incoming light. At the maximum stretch, the polarizability of the bond will not be the same as when the bond is at maximum compression, so polarizability has the same frequency as the vibration.*

A Raman spectrum is obtained by directing an intense laser onto the sample and examining the patterns of light scattered at higher and lower wavelengths relative to the wavelength of the incident laser beam. When scattering occurs, most of the photons are scattered at the same wavelength as the incident radiation, and this elastic scattering is called **Rayleigh** scattering. Interestingly, Rayleigh scattering contains no analytical information, but scattering on either side (inelastic scattering) of this band does. Excitation is with a laser in the visible or near infrared region, and the scattering signal is measured at 90° or 180° to the light path of the source. In general, the larger the atom, the more polarizable the element's electron cloud is. As a result, water can be used as a solvent, because oxygen and hydrogen are relatively small and the bonds in water are not easily deformed by interaction with visible light. Because visible light is used for excitation, samples can be mounted on or contained in glass.

Inelastic scattering can result from interactions with the polarizable bond that produce signals at the excitation wavelength, plus or minus the vibrational mode of the bond as shown in Figure 5.37. The Stokes signal is the stronger of the two, but it is still several orders of magnitude weaker than the Rayleigh line. Further problems can arise when higher energy excitation sources, such as those in the visible and UV range, are used. These sources can cause fluorescence (Figure 5.38), which may produce a signal that will swamp

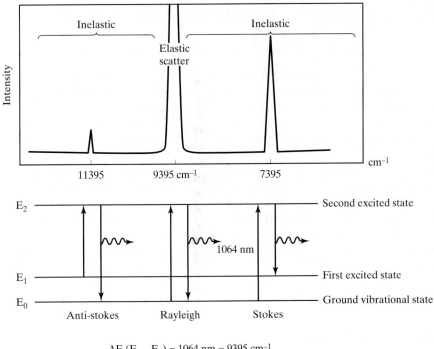

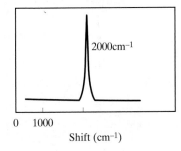

$\Delta E\ (E_2 - E_0) = 1064\ \text{nm} = 9395\ \text{cm}^{-1}$

$\Delta E\ (E_1 - E_0) = \text{Shift} = 2000\ \text{cm}^{-1}$

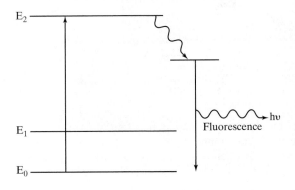

◀ **Figure 5.37** *A Raman spectrum of a sample bond in a system using a near-infrared laser as the excitation source. Elastic scattering or Rayleigh scattering dominates the spectrum, with inelastic scattering at wave numbers, plus or minus the equivalent of the vibrational frequency. The Raman spectrum can also be normalized and plotted as the shift in wavelength of the signal.*

the weak inelastic scattering signal. Despite these issues, Raman spectroscopy is finding a wider niche in forensic applications, given that it provides information that is complementary to absorptive IR and is generally nondestructive.

◀ **Figure 5.38** *The fluorescence problem. If the laser is at a wavelength with sufficient energy to promote the molecule to the next higher state, the molecule can decay to a metastable state and then fluoresce, producing a signal that will swamp the weak scattering signal.*

5.3 ELEMENTAL ANALYSIS AND ATOMIC SPECTROSCOPY

Infrared methods dominate forensic organic analysis and are suitable for some inorganic samples as well. For the detection of heavy-metal poisons and gunshot residue, other instrumentation is needed. In forensic laboratories, the methods that are widely used for elemental analysis are flame or **graphite furnace** (GF), atomic absorption spectrometry (AAS), and X-ray fluorescence (XRF), often associated with a scanning electron microscope. However, techniques based on inductively coupled plasma sources are starting to make inroads and within a few years may supplant AAS/GFAAS and XRF in many applications. The following discussion focuses on AAS/GFAAS and XRF, both of which are based on electronic transitions as compared to the molecular transitions we have been discussing. Elemental analysis is used for gunshot residue (GSR), paints, soils, and in toxicology. The oldest technique is flame emission a la Kirchhoff and Bunsen, which progressed to flame absorbance and then back to emission using inductively coupled plasma (ICP) as an excitation source.

Applying the Science 5.3   Raman Microscopy and the Vinland Map

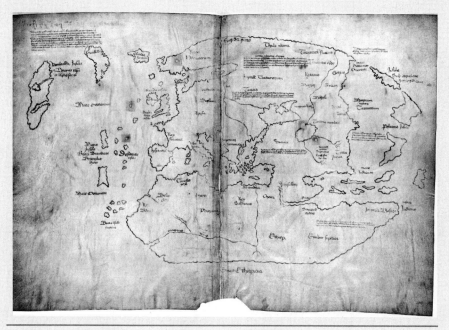

▲ Image courtesy of the Beinecke Rare Book and Manuscript Library, Yale University.

The Vinland Map surfaced in 1957. It appeared to be a map showing the coastline of North America and was purported to have predated Columbus's journey by 50 years. As with many objects of art and archaeology, the question of authenticity was immediately raised, but any chemical analyses undertaken had to be nondestructive. Raman

Applying the Science 5.3 (Continued)

analysis using a fiber-optic probe was one technique applied to the map, with results shown in the accompanying figures. Genuine medieval documents created with black inks often contain iron gallotannate, which slowly leaches from the ink into the parchment underneath. Over time, the migrating iron causes the parchment to yellow and become brittle, leaving a faint yellow border around black inks (Figure 2). In this case, however, the black ink was found to be carbon based, and the parchment showed no evidence of the damage expected from a iron gallotannate ink. Rather, it appears that a forger placed a yellow line on the parchment before overwriting with the black ink in an attempt to simulate the appearance of a nearly 500-year-old document.

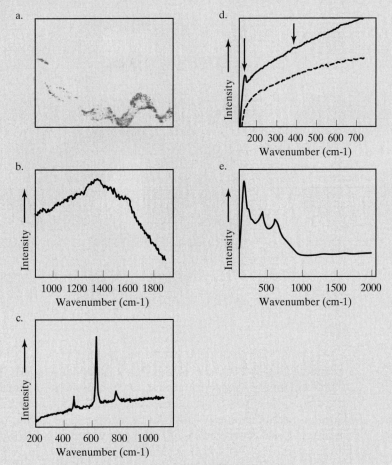

(a) Black ink with yellow under-layer, from the Vinland Map. (b) Black ink from the Vinland Map. (c) Chromite ($FeCr_2O_4$) from a specimen sample. (d) Anatase and plain parchment from the Vinland Map; solid line, anatase in yellow line; dotted line, plain parchment. (e) Ilmenite ($FeTiO_3$) from a specimen sample. Figures and captions reproduced with permission from the reference cited below, Copyright 2002, American Chemical Society.
Source: Brown, K. L., and R. J. H. Clark. "Analysis of Pigmentary Materials on the Vinland Map and Tartar Relation by Raman Microprobe Spectroscopy." *Analytical Chemistry* 74 (2002), 3658–3661. Copyright American Chemical Society 2002.

5.3.1 ATOMIC ABSORPTION (AA)

Electron transitions in atoms can be induced by thermal energy, such as that provided by a flame. Relaxation $M^* \longrightarrow M$ can result in the release of a photon of light in the ultraviolet or visible range, the basis of atomic emission spectroscopy. A flame matrix offers significant advantages over a solution. In such an energetic environment, most chemical bonds are broken and samples exist as free atoms or ions. Matrix interferences are minimized, as are collisional and other types

Historical Evidence 5.4—Practical Bunsen

Robert Wilhelm Bunsen (1811–1899), mentioned in an earlier *Historical Evidence*, was a true analytical chemist and would have no doubt made an excellent forensic chemist. He was nothing if not practical and was quoted as saying "A single determination of one fact is more valuable than the most beautifully constructed theory."

of interactions that can lead to broadened absorbance bands. The limitation with flame emission is sensitivity: Even at the temperature of most flames, only a tiny fraction of the atoms is promoted to the excited state. The **Boltzmann distribution** describes the ratio of atoms in the excited state to those in the ground state as a function of temperature and the energy gap involved in the transition:

$$\frac{N^*}{N_0} = \frac{g^*}{g_0} e^{\frac{-\Delta E}{kT}} \tag{5.9}$$

Here, T is the temperature in kelvins (K), ΔE is the energy gap in joules (J), and k is the Boltzmann constant, 1.381×10^{-23} J/K. The term g in the equation is the degeneracy of the transition and refers to the number of energy levels of equivalent energy. For example, if the transition is from an *s* orbital to a p orbital, the degeneracy term g^*/g_0 of the transition is 3/1, because there are three energetically equivalent *p* orbitals.

Sodium vapor lamps emit a yellow line at a wavelength of 589.3 nm for which ΔE is 3.371×10^{-19} J (per atom). This wavelength is also referred to as the sodium D line, and it appears bright yellow, the characteristic color of sodium vapor lamps. M has a degeneracy of 1, M* a degeneracy of 2. Thus, at room temperature (25°C, or 298 K), the ratio of atoms in the excited state to those in the ground state can be

Example Problem 5.4

Calculate the percentage of sodium atoms in the excited state at room temperature (25°C), at a typical flame temperature (2500 K), at plasma temperature (7500 K), and at sunlike temperatures of 10,000 K. Comment on the implications for elemental spectroscopy.

Answer: Focusing on the sodium D line at 589.3 nm, we can calculate the energy gap as shown. The degeneracies for this transition as 2:1, and the Boltzmann distribution (Equation 5.9) is used to calculate the ratio and percentage of sodium atoms in the excited state at the temperatures given. Even at the highest temperature, less than 1 in 5 sodium atoms is in the excited state. This implies that, in flames, emission signals will be too low to be of practical value and that only in plasma will emission be feasible.

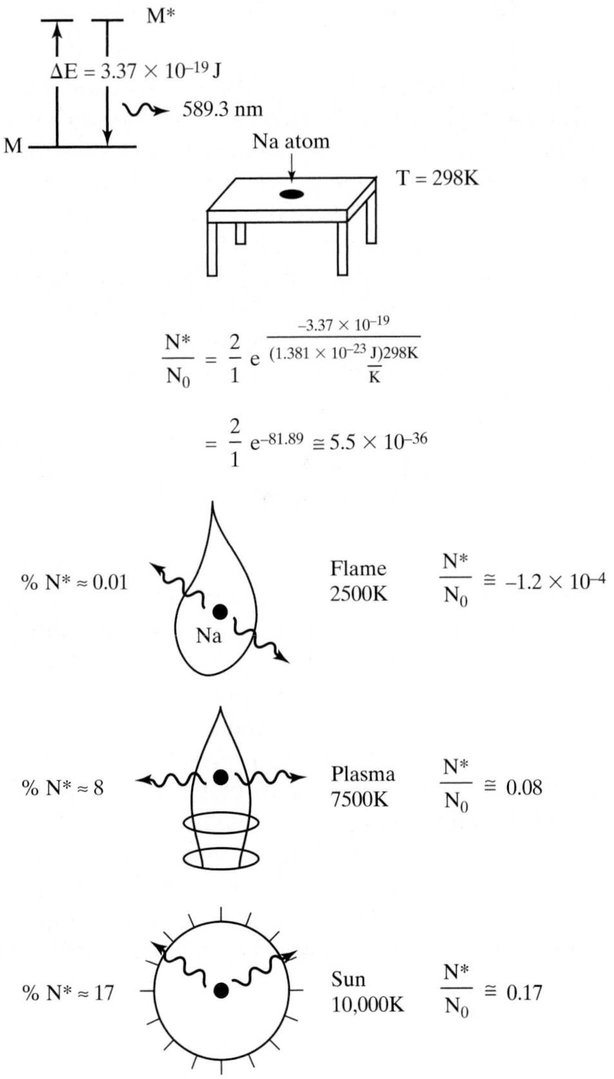

$$\frac{N^*}{N_0} = \frac{2}{1} e^{\frac{-3.37 \times 10^{-19}}{(1.381 \times 10^{-23} \, J)298K \frac{}{K}}}$$

$$= \frac{2}{1} e^{-81.89} \cong 5.5 \times 10^{-36}$$

% $N^* \approx 0.01$ Flame 2500K $\frac{N^*}{N_0} \cong -1.2 \times 10^{-4}$

% $N^* \approx 8$ Plasma 7500K $\frac{N^*}{N_0} \cong 0.08$

% $N^* \approx 17$ Sun 10,000K $\frac{N^*}{N_0} \cong 0.17$

calculated with the Boltzmann distribution. At room temperature, less than one atom per mole is in the excited state. This calculation fits with the observation that sodium does not glow in the dark. At flame temperatures the ratio increases, but the atoms capable of emitting a photon constitute less than 1%

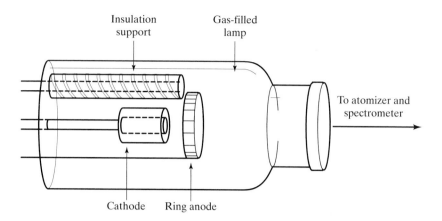

▶ **Figure 5.39** *A hollow cathode lamp. The cathode consists of the metal of interest, so it will emit the proper wavelength(s) for absorption.*

of the population. Accordingly, if a flame is to be used for quantitative spectroscopy, the only realistic option is to target absorbance rather than emission.

The breakthrough that facilitated the study of ground-state atoms was the **hollow cathode lamp** (HCL, vs HCl for hydrochloric acid). As shown in Figure 5.39, the cathode of an HCL is coated with the metal of interest, so, for a copper analysis, a copper cathode is used. The lamp is sealed and evacuated, save for ~1–5 Torr of argon, helium, or neon. When a potential is applied across the anode and cathode, it is sufficient to ionize some of the filler gas. The cations are accelerated and collide with the cathode surface, ejecting atoms into the gas phase. This process is called **sputtering**. Collisional interactions drive some of the atoms into the excited state, and relaxation results in the emission of a photon that corresponds exactly to one or more transitions in the target element. The operation of an HCL is shown in Figure 5.40.

Aside from the HCL, an AA spectrophotometer contains familiar components as shown in Figure 5.41. A peristaltic pump draws sample into the **nebulizer**, where it is converted to a fine mist. Fuel and oxidant gases such as acetylene and air are added, and the flow is directed into the flame, which is long and thin (called a slot-type flame) to provide an optimum path length for absorbance measurements. Light from the HCL enters the flame, interacts with it, and passes to the detector. A monochromator is placed between the flame and the detector to filter out flame emission signals.

Modifications and variants on AA include multielement lamps and alternative thermal excitation methods, such as furnaces. Graphite furnace AA utilizes a small graphite cell for sample introduction and heating. The sample is placed on a shelf called the **L'vov platform** inside the furnace (Figure 5.42). Graphite conducts, so when current is applied, the furnace rapidly heats and volatilizes the sample via electrothermal vaporization. A graphite furnace uses much less sample than a flame and allows for finer control of temperature.

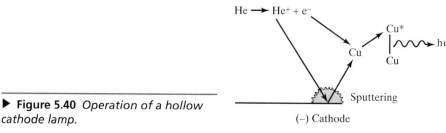

▶ **Figure 5.40** *Operation of a hollow cathode lamp.*

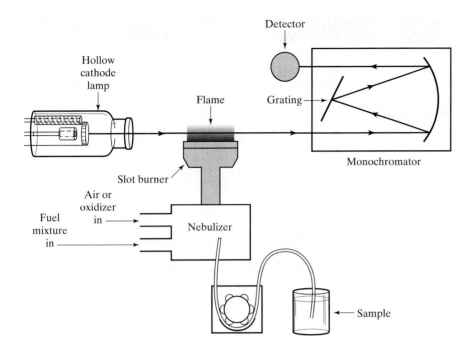

◀ **Figure 5.41** *Box diagram of a flame AA instrument.*

Example Problem 5.5

What would be the best choice for a calibration method for AAS?

Answer: An external standard. In typical AAS instrument configurations, only one element can be analyzed at a time, necessitating either an external standard or the standard addition method. Because standard addition is time consuming and sample intensive, it would be selected only if the sample matrix was particularly difficult to manage.

Exhibit E: The Problem with Mercury

Mercury is one of the primary heavy-metal poisons targeted by toxicologists and also one of the more difficult to analyze instrumentally. Mercury has three oxidation states (0, +1, and +2), and the metal form has a high vapor pressure. Traditional AA methods for mercury are too insensitive to detect the levels in tissue associated with poisoning. The solution has been to exploit this volatility as a means of separating mercury from the matrix and preconcentrating it in the sample path. When a sample—be it blood, tissue, hair, or some other material—is received for analysis, it is treated with acid to ionize mercury and prevent evaporative loss. It is then treated with a strong oxidant, such as potassium permanganate, to ensure that all mercury is in the +2 state. A reducing agent

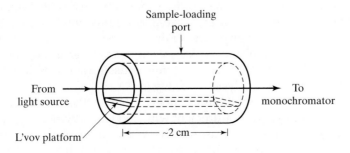

◀ **Figure 5.42** *A graphite furnace showing the L 'vov platform.*

Exhibit E: (Continued)

such as tin (II) chloride is then added, and the reaction rapidly produces gaseous mercury metal that is introduced into the light path. Since the mercury is placed en masse into the light path and without any matrix, the sensitivity of the testing method is greatly improved by several orders of magnitude over flame AA. To further preconcentrate the mercury, a bed of gold-coated beads can be placed in the sample path. Metallic mer-

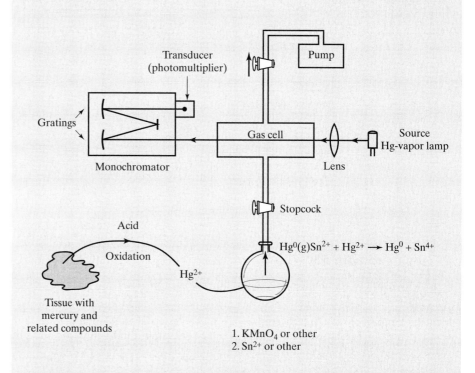

cury is adsorbed onto the gold, so the reaction can be allowed to proceed over a longer time with larger samples. The beads are flash heated to a few hundred degrees celsius to desorb the mercury. Finally, atomic fluorescence methods can be used. The instruments involved are essentially AA systems in which a detector is placed off of the axis of the light path to detect the photons released by the relaxation $M^* \longrightarrow M$. Such methods can detect mercury in the low parts-per-billion to parts-per-trillion range.

5.3.2 ATOMIC EMISSION AND INDUCTIVELY COUPLED PLASMA TECHNIQUES

Atomic absorption remains a staple of forensic chemistry, given its low cost, simple operation, and easy maintenance. The limitations are related to versatility. Unless multielement lamps are used, only one element can be tested for at a time, and each element requires a separate lamp and instrument optimization. For small target lists such as a list of barium, antimony, and lead for GSR, this is not onerous, but still is inconvenient. Limits of detection are in the low-ppm to high-ppb range for most elements. As a result, a few forensic laboratories have turned to inductively coupled plasma **atomic emission spectroscopy** (ICP-AES) for additional elemental analysis capability.

Plasmas operate several thousand degrees hotter than a flame and are hot enough to allow emission measurement with good sensitivities, typically in the low-ppb ranges for most elements. An ICP-AES system is composed of a nebulizer, plasma torch (Figure 5.43), monochromator, and detector. A sequential

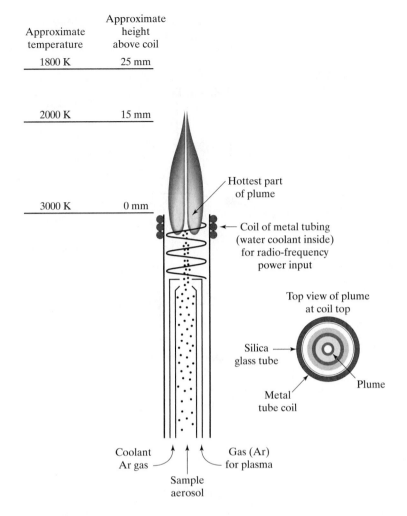

Approximate temperature

Approximate height above coil

1800 K — 25 mm

2000 K — 15 mm

3000 K — 0 mm

Hottest part of plume

Coil of metal tubing (water coolant inside) for radio-frequency power input

Top view of plume at coil top

Silica glass tube

Plume

Metal tube coil

Coolant Ar gas

Gas (Ar) for plasma

Sample aerosol

◀ **Figure 5.43** *A plasma torch for ICP. A radio-frequency generator ionizes argon in the tube and accelerates the ions, maintaining heat by sustained collisions. Once the generator is off, the plasma stops forming.*

instrument scans the emitted wavelengths, whereas a simultaneous instrument uses a grating or other device to physically disperse the output light such that all wavelengths are detected simultaneously. The latter uses less sample, but is more expensive. ICP-AES is a true multielement technique, but the cost of the systems is high relative to that of AA instrumentation. As the price falls, the improved accuracy and precision of these techniques compared with older elemental methods will undoubtedly facilitate more extensive forensic use of them.

5.3.3 X-Ray Fluorescence (XRF)

ICP methods are **bulk methods**, in that sample has to be dissolved or otherwise digested and prepared before being introduced into the instrument. Consequently, the elemental composition represents the bulk of the sample, as opposed to an isolated section or area thereof. Such preparation is also destructive and requires a significant amount of sample. Analytical instruments that exploit the X-ray region of the electromagnetic spectrum offer an alternative that is usually non- or minimally destructive and that targets the surface of the sample, as opposed to its bulk. X-ray techniques are also easily integrated into scanning electron microscopes, a topic covered in a later section of this chapter.

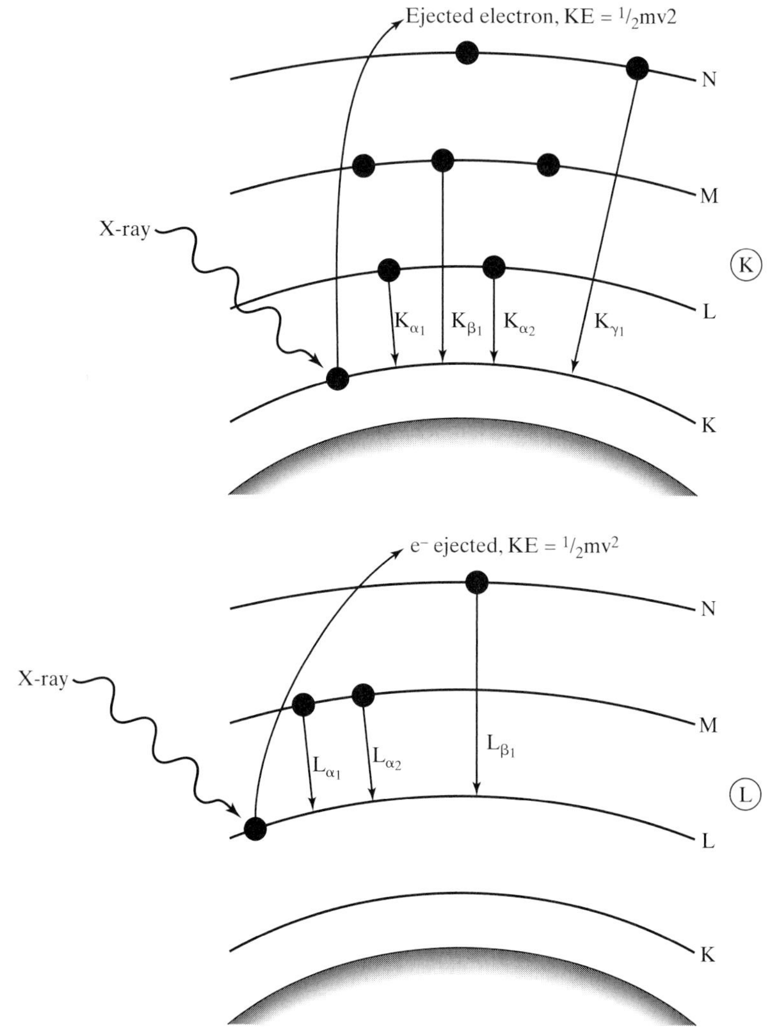

▶ **Figure 5.44** *Process that generates an XRF spectrum.*

X-ray energy is far more energetic than that in the ultraviolet range. If an X-ray photon has an energy that exceeds the ionization energy of an electron, absorption of that photon can eject the electron outright. Furthermore, the ejected electrons are from core levels—those closest to the nucleus. In terms of quantum numbers, these levels correspond to n = 1, 2, and 3, which are usually referred to with the older shell notation K, L, and M. When an inner-shell electron is ejected, an outer-shell electron "falls" to fill the vacancy and release X-ray photons (fluorescence) in the process as shown in Figure 5.44.

Because electrons may fall in a cascading fashion, the spectrum can contain several lines that are related to a transition, as shown in the figure. The letter refers to the quantum level to which the electron falls, whereas the α, β, γ notation refers to how many levels the electron falls. Because more than one electron per level may fall, the transitions are numbered. An $L_{\alpha 2}$ transition refers to an electron that falls into the L level from one level above (α) and is the second electron to do so from that same level. Most transitions are to an inner shell (K or L).

X-ray spectrometry is a family of related techniques for elemental and crystal structure analysis that derive information from emitted radiation and from the ejected electrons XRF can be based on the energy of the emitted photons (energy-dispersive spectrometry, or EDS) or on the wavelengths emitted

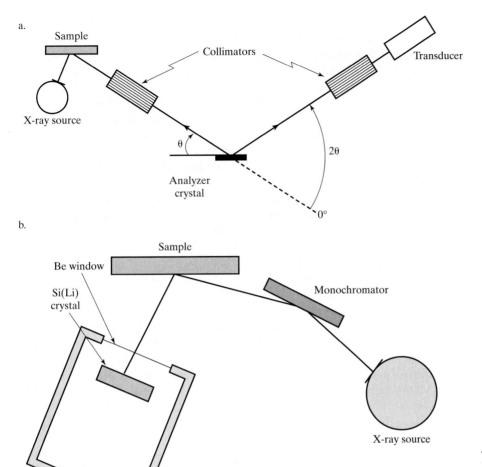

a.

b.

◀ **Figure 5.45** *(a) A box diagram of a WDS X-ray spectrometer. (b) A box diagram of an EDS spectrometer.*

(wavelength-dispersive spectrometry, or WDS). Both techniques are illustrated in Figure 5.45.

Wavelength-dispersive XRF operates much as does any emission method in which emitted light is physically dispersed by a grating to isolate individual wavelengths. Because the wavelengths of X-ray energy are so small, it isn't feasible to construct a grating. Instead, crystals with predictable geometries are used to generate constructive and destructive reinforcement patterns analogous to those generated by a grating. EDS does not use a monochromator, but rather calculates the energy of the X-rays that strike the detector and converts those energies to equivalent wavelengths.

Other X-ray techniques include X-ray diffraction (XRD), which reveals information about crystal structures. It is used less frequently than XRF in forensic science. Other related techniques, such as Auger spectroscopy, have yet to find significant applications in forensic chemistry.

5.4 MICROSPECTROPHOTOMETRY

Microscopes and spectroscopes both use electromagnetic energy to probe matter, so why not use a microscope as the source of energy so that very small samples such as single fibers can be easily studied? Until recently, the roadblock was technological. Because the amount of energy directed through a microscope is so small, the intensity of that energy is limited. Accordingly, the development of suitable detectors was one of the keys to implementing practical microspectrophotometry (MSP), particularly for the infrared range. In the last 15 years, MSP has come of age and is beginning to displace traditional macrospectroscopy in the forensic laboratory. Any spectroscopy can theoretically be adapted to microspectroscopy. Molecular and atomic methods are now available, and the instruments that perform such analyses are an increasingly common sight on the forensic bench. Most MSP tests are nondestructive or minimally destructive, and the instruments are now more affordable for forensic labs. In some cases, such as UV/VIS spectroscopy, microspectrophotometry is reviving interest in techniques that had been marginalized or nearly abandoned in forensic chemistry.

The marriage of a microscope, designed to work with visible light, and colorimetry is the simplest proposition, because the optics of both operate in the same spectral range. Thus, glass lenses, objectives, and other optical components can be made of the same material. The situation is more complex when a visible microscope is combined with a spectrophotometer that operates outside of the visible region, such as the IR or UV. In these cases, optics must be capable of focusing and directing energy in all applicable ranges of wavelength. The realization that mirrors could be used in lieu of or in combination with lenses was a pivotal advance for MSP. A **Cassegrain system** uses highly polished stainless-steel mirrors to focus rays of UV, VIS, and IR energy and thus serves as an objective "lens" across many spectral regions. Reflection, transmission, and ATR modes can be accommodated by this design, as shown in Figures 5.46 and 5.47. The design also provides a large numerical aperture and can have large working distances, topics previously discussed in Section 5.1.

Another factor constraining microspectrophotometry was the intensity of the source. The trade-offs among intensity, slit width, and energy are amplified when energy must be focused on a very small portion of the sample. As a result, intense light sources such as lasers or extremely bright lamps are required. Lasers have the added advantage of being tightly focused. The final consideration is the detector, which, as all transducers do, converts photons to electrons, but with extraordinary efficiency. Because analytical signals are so small, background

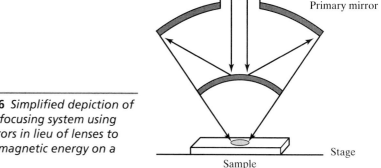

▶ **Figure 5.46** *Simplified depiction of a Cassegrain focusing system using polished mirrors in lieu of lenses to focus electromagnetic energy on a sample.*

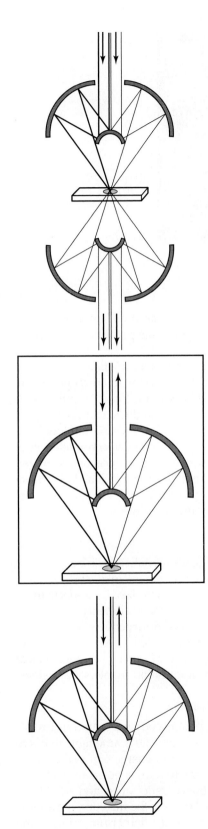

◀ **Figure 5.47** *Cassegrain lens in transmission mode (upper frame), reflection mode, and as part of an ATR system (lower frame).*

▶ **Figure 5.48** *A commercial microscope base with a UV/VIS/NIR spectrophotometer detector and imaging system. Photo courtesy of Dr. Paul Martin, Criac Technologies.*

noise must be minimized. Many MSP detectors are based on semiconductors, and a number of them are cooled either by electrothermal processes or with liquid nitrogen.

Early microspectrophotometers were designed as adjuncts to an existing spectrometer. Energy from the source was directed into the microscope, where it interacted with the sample and then traveled back to the bench and the existing detector. This approach had the advantage of dual use (bench and scope), but typically optimized the macrospectroscopy rather than the micro. Newer instruments are stand-alone devices with microscope bases and spectrometers supplied as integrated components. One common accessory is a precision motorized stage that allows for computer control of sample positioning, which is crucial when the size of the image is as small as a few microns. Computerized stage controls also facilitate automated surface mapping of samples.

5.4.1 UV/VIS MICROSPECTROPHOTOMETRY

The availability of UV/VIS spectrophotometers has revitalized the examination of evidence for characteristics associated with color. Fibers, inks, and paints in particular can be examined nondestructively and characterized by a spectrum as well as the analyst's judgment of their color. Prior to the availability of UV/VIS MSP, obtaining a visible spectrum of a fiber involved destructive extraction followed by colorimetry. Large numbers of fibers were needed, and potentially useful inter- and intrasample variations in color were lost. (Particular applications of MSP to color determinations are addressed in the application chapters that follow.)

5.4.2 IR AND RAMAN MICROSPECTROPHOTOMETRY

As with macroscopic work, microvibrational spectroscopy has found its broadest use in forensic chemistry. FTIR techniques are particularly amenable to micro applications, given the ability to simultaneously collect energy across the wavelength range and average a large number of scans to reduce noise and enhance sensitivity. All modes of IR, including transmittance, reflectance, and ATR, have been adapted to FTIR microscopy. Detectors used include the mercury–cadmium–tellurium (MCT) design, which requires cooling, and the deuterium–triglycerine sulfate (DTGS) design, which does not. Some designs have adapted a novel diamond ATR objective through which the user can sight and obtain an IR spectrum. In many forensic laboratories, micro-FTIR, and particularly micro-ATR, are replacing bench FTIR for applications such as drug and paint characterization, given the ease of ATR, the small sample size needed, and the nondestructive nature of the test. Raman microspectrophotometry has also proven valuable, particularly for ink and pigment analysis, although it is still not considered a routine forensic procedure.

5.4.3 MICROELEMENTAL ANALYSIS

XRF is readily adaptable to microscopic platforms and is used for surface mapping applications. Forensically, the most important micro-XRF method is that associated with scanning electron microscopy (SEM), which uses electron beams as opposed to photon beams to visualize a sample. Consequently, X-ray emission is a natural and exploitable byproduct of this interaction. The prevalent adaptation for forensic work is the SEM-EDS configuration illustrated in Figure 5.49. Electrons are emitted from a filament or other source and are focused onto the sample, whereupon the beam scans the surface. There are instruments that target transmitted electrons (transmission electron microscopy, or TEM), but they are not widely used forensically.

Electrons are scattered analogously to photons, with heavier elements scattering more electrons relative to lighter ones. In the output display, scattering correlates with increased brightness. Because electrons are exploited for imaging, but photons are not, there is no color information in the signal, although false coloring can be added to the image. The sample must be conducting and is usually coated with a thin layer of gold. Secondary electrons are those emitted when the incident electrons eject an inner-shell electron, resulting in X-ray fluorescence. These electrons are ejected at angles and energies correlated with surface shapes and features. The resulting image can be magnified by a factor of a

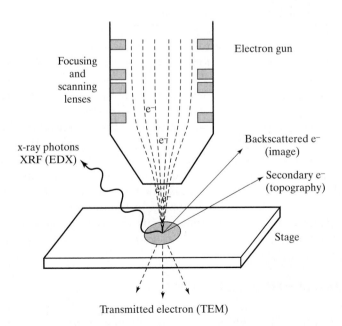

◄ Figure 5.49 *Simplified SEM-EDS. Scattered electrons create the image, ejected electrons relate to topography, and the wavelength of the photons correlates with an element.*

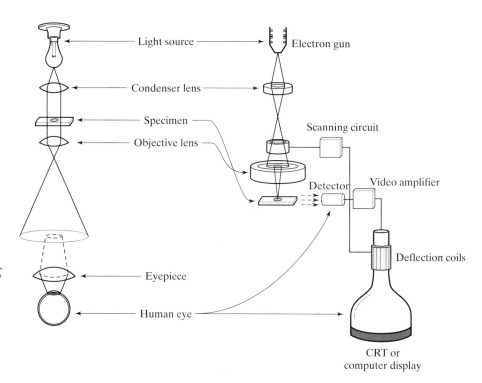

▶ **Figure 5.50** *SEM and optical microscopy share the same generic features, including a source, focusing lenses, and a detector. The optical path of the microscope is inverted for comparison.*

million or more compared with a few hundred times in conventional microscopy. The added benefit of identifying topography and elemental composition is critical in the forensic identification of gunshot residue, a topic to be addressed in detail in a later chapter. SEM-EDS is also used in analysis of trace evidence, such as paint chips, bullets, and glass.

5.5 DIVIDE AND CONQUER: HYPHENATED AND 3D TECHNIQUES

Hyphenated instruments consist of an inlet that separates and preconcentrates analytes prior to their introduction into an integral detector. A hyphen can be used to separate the two components when the name is written in abbreviated form—for example, GC-MS. The separation module is the GC and the detection module is the MS. As hyphenated instruments became more common, the hyphen often was dropped, and that is the convention used in this book (i.e., GCMS rather than GC-MS). Separations alone, such as in thin layer chromatography, are not instrumental methods in the traditional sense, but mating a separation technique to a detector creates an instrument that is capable of what is called a hyphenated technique. The basis of most separation modules is selective partitioning, a topic discussed in the previous chapter. However, there is a group of hyphenated instruments in which separation is achieved with electrochemical methods, an increasingly important topic in forensic chemistry.

5.5.1 ELECTROPHORETIC INSTRUMENTS

Once the exclusive purview of biologists, biochemists, serologists, and DNA analysts, electrophoresis is entering the realm of small-molecule separations and consequently now plays a role in forensic chemistry. **Ion mobility spectrometry** is a gas-phase form of **electrophoresis** that has become the workhorse of field-deployable forensic instrumentation for detection of drugs and explosives.

Electrophoresis separates ions and molecules on the basis of differences in their size-to-charge ratios, which in turn dictate how fast they move through an electrical field. The velocity of a charged particle or an ion in an electric field is given by

$$V = \mu_e E \qquad (5.10)$$

where μ_e is the mobility of the ion and E is the electric field strength, determined by the voltage applied across the region through which the ions move. As charged species, ions move under the influence of the field, based on the charges they carry, tempered by the friction created by the ions as they move. Electrophoresis was originally used to separate proteins on the basis of the charges that can be acquired by protonation and deprotonation of the amino, carboxyl, and other groups. The pH of the solution determines the charge on a protein. The gel provides resistance to flow proportional to the size of the ion, and separation is based on the balance between friction and induced movement in the electrical field. The process is illustrated in Figure 5.51.

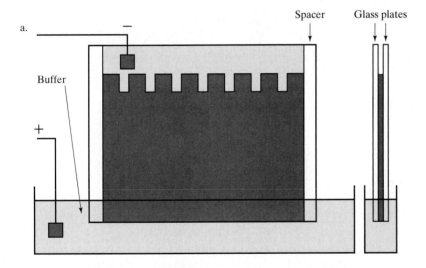

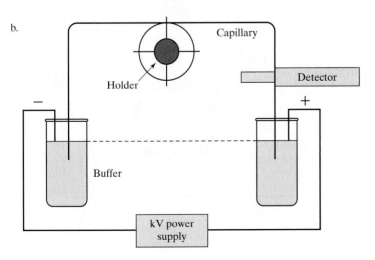

◄ **Figure 5.51** *(a) Slab-gel electrophoresis. A power supply generates the electric field, and the buffer ensures that the pH remains constant. (b) Electrophoretic separation in a capillary tube.*

Capillary Electrophoresis: Slab-gel techniques were used in forensic serology until the late 1980s to separate and detect polymorphic serum proteins found in blood and body fluids. Around the time that DNA began to supplant traditional blood group typing in forensic serology, capillary electrophoresis (CE) was introduced to separate small molecules. Ironically, by the turn of the century, CE-based instruments dominated DNA typing.

Applying the Science 5.4   CE and XRF

The detectors used in CE are typically electrochemical or spectrochemical, relying on UV absorbance or fluorescence. XRF has been reported as a novel detection system that expands the applications of CE. Using an elemental detector facilitates the detection of organometallic compounds such as vitamin B_{12}, which contains cobalt. As seen in the figure, the $K\alpha$ transition for cobalt was used in this study, with iron and copper being examined in others.

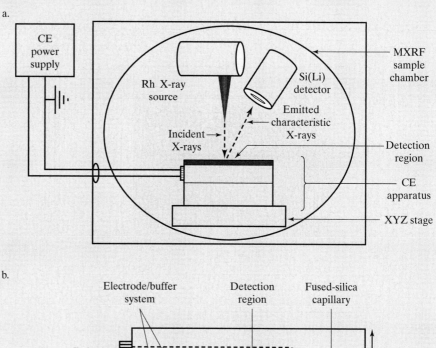

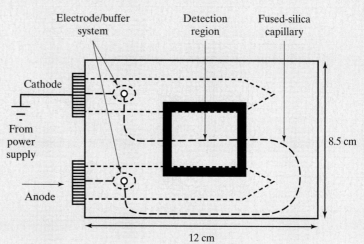

▶ (a) CEMXRF interface. (b) Top view of CE apparatus.

Applying the Science 5.4   (Continued)

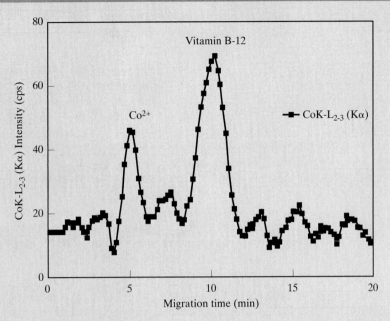

Electropherogram of the separation of 0.2 mg/mL Co^{2+} and 14 mg/mL cyanocobalamin in deionized water. Buffer conditions: 75 mM Trizma run buffer, pH 8.0. Separation conditions: 4-s hydrodynamic injection via suction at 1/2 ambient pressure (380 mbar) and 10-kV run potential. Spectral acquisition rate, 0.1 s^{-1}.
Sources: Mann, S. E., et al. "Element Specific Detection in Capillary Electrophoresis Using X-ray Fluorescence Spectroscopy." *Analytical Chemistry* 72 (2000), 1754–1758. Miller, T. C., et al. "Capillary Electrophoresis Micro X-ray Fluorescence: A Tool for Benchtop Elemental Analysis." *Analytical Chemistry* 75 (2003), 2048–2053. Figures and captions reproduced with permission from Miller et. al., copyright American Chemical Society 2003.

One of the advantages of CE systems is their simplicity. A capillary tube (composed of SiO_2) is placed with both ends in a buffer system so that separation will take place within the capillary rather than in a slab. The mode of separation is altered as well, to exploit an electroosmotic flow generated within the tube. As shown in Figure 5.52, polar sites attract a layer of hydrated cations at the tube's inner surface. These cations are attracted to the cathode and flow regardless of what is introduced into the capillary. As a result, neutral species as well as positive can be detected. Even negatively charged small ions are eventually dragged to the detector by the electroosmotic flow. Modifications to the surface of the tube, to the pH, to the electric field, and to other experimental parameters impart unmatched flexibility to CE.

CE can be operated in several modes. The approach described in the previous paragraph is referred to as **capillary zone electrophoresis**, or CZE. A variant called capillary gel electrophoresis uses a capillary tube filled with gel, essentially a miniaturized version of slab-gel techniques. The third variant, and the one of most forensic significance, is **micellar electrokinetic chromatography** (MEK or MECK). MEK is a modification designed to improve the separation of neutral species, which are easily separated from cations and anions, but not well separated among themselves.

MEK achieves improved separation by adding another discriminating interaction. **Micelles** (Figure 5.53) form when surfactant molecules such as soaps and detergents are added to water. Soap is a molecule with a hydrophobic hydrocarbon

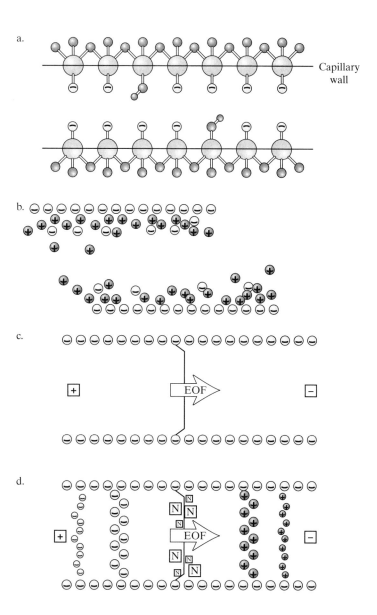

▶ **Figure 5.52** *Generation of electroosmotic flow. (a) Exposed Si—O— groups on the capillary wall attract hydrated cations (b) and form a layer along the capillary wall. When the potential is applied, the positive layer migrates (c) toward the cathode (−). This flow is strong enough to move neutrals and anions at different rates while accelerating the movement of any analytical cations in the system.*

portion and a hydrophilic ionized end. When soap is added to water at a sufficient concentration, micelles form. Neutrals can interact and associate with (i.e., selectively partition) the micelles, which themselves are charged and move with the electroosmotic flow according to that charge. If a micelle is negatively charged, it moves slowly toward the detector—more slowly than the neutrals do. However, because the neutrals interact with the micelles, the progress of the neutrals is impeded in proportion to their degree of association with the micelles. This is another form of chromatography in which separation is based on differences in partitioning between two phases, and MEK is often described as a hybrid of CE and chromatography. The micelle is like a "column" on which the solute is retained; the longer the retention, the slower the migration. This process is illustrated in Figure 5.54.

The detector module of a CE system is usually spectroscopic. Hence, its sensitivity is a function of path length, which introduces one of the fundamental problems of linking a flowing separation system to a detector designed for

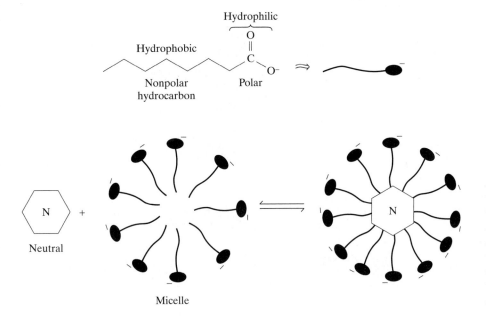

◀ **Figure 5.53** *Soap is surfactant molecule that can form micelles in water; neutrals can move in and out of a micelle, with the degree of association dependent on factors such as the size and polarity of the neutral.*

static measurements. The volume used in CE is on the order of nanoliters, and that already minuscule volume is constantly moving. The simplest detectors are those based on UV absorption and are implemented by "burning" a clear window into the capillary at the point where detection is to occur. By creating a Z-shaped bend in the tube (Figure 5.55), the path length can be increased, as long as the path is not so long as to allow more than one separated component into the detection zone. Laser excitation and fluorescence is another more sensitive option and is used for DNA typing. However, the complexity of such systems has limited more generalized applications.[17,18] Electrochemical detectors have been used, as has mass spectrometry, but UV modes dominate forensic implementations.

Because of its versatility, CE is making inroads into forensic laboratories. Instrumentation is also fairly inexpensive and easy to maintain, a prerequisite for the wide adoption. Toxicology in particular has embraced CE for drugs and analytes,[17] which can be acidic, basic, or neutral, and hydrophobic or hydrophilic.

Gas-Phase Electrophoresis: Ion Mobility Spectrometry (IMS): In airports, seaports, and border crossings, ion mobility spectrometry (IMS) has become a standard field screening method for explosives and drugs. Although the instrument operates in the gas phase at atmospheric pressure, the basis of separation is the size–charge ratio. In fact, one of the original names for the technique was *gas-phase electrophoresis.* IMS instruments (Figure 5.56) are best known to the public as handheld detectors

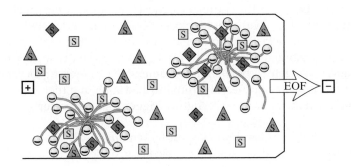

◀ **Figure 5.54** *Separation in MEK, using micelles to carry neutrals along. S = sample.*

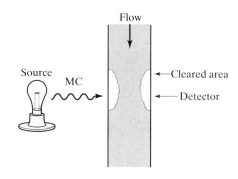

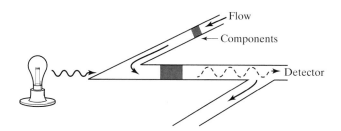

▶ **Figure 5.55** *Use of a Z-shaped flow cell to increase the path length for spectrophotometric detection in CE. The same principle has been applied to detectors in liquid chromatography.*

for chemical weapons. The instrument operates at atmospheric pressure and requires small amounts of power, important criteria for any portable system.

As sample enters the inlet, it is ionized through a complex series of reactions. The first step is ionization of N_2 by [63] Ni, a β emitter. Because the instrument runs at ambient pressures, there exists a reservoir of reactant ions of the form $H(H_2O)_n^+$ that surrenders protons to M^+ ions, depending on relative proton affinities. What enters the drift region is a complex mixture of M^+ and other cluster ions that move toward the detector under the influence of an applied electric field, analogous to the situation in gel electrophoresis. In IMS, an opposing drift gas flow collides with the clusters, impeding the progress of the larger ones more than that of the smaller ones. The drift gas acts as the gel does, resisting migration in proportion to size. The smaller charged species arrive at the detector before the larger ones. The same process occurs in the negative mode, but with a different group of reactant ions, such as O_2^- and Cl^-. Fundamentally, IMS measures the collisional cross-sectional area of the ions and ion–molecule clusters.

The output of the instrument is a plot of signal intensity versus drift time. **Mobility spectra** are information poor in much the same sense that UV/VIS spectra are. A mobility spectrum cannot definitively identify compounds alone, but linkage to libraries and databases allow for the range of potential analytes to be reduced to a small population. In screening applications, this is an acceptable trade-off, as long as false negatives are minimized. At airports, IMS is used to screen baggage for explosives and is found at security checkpoints. Attendants may wipe a pad over luggage or computers and place the pad in the instrument to obtain a fast negative-mode scan for potential explosives. Recently, IMS has been combined with gas chromatographs and with time-of-flight mass spectrometers to create hyphenated instruments. The newest generation of IMS instruments has been significantly miniaturized such that the portion of the instrument shown in Figure 5.56 is slightly bigger than a quarter.

Chromatographic Inlets: Gas chromatography remains a workhorse inlet of forensic chemistry, be it for drug analysis, toxicology, or accelerants. High-pressure

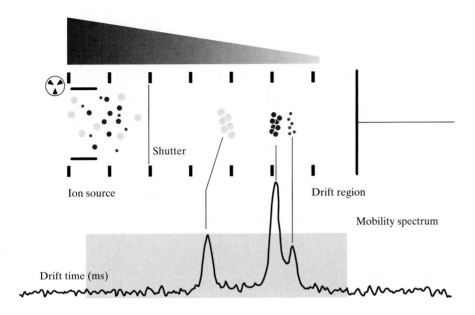

◀ **Figure 5.56** *An ion mobility spectrometer and mobility spectrum. Ion molecule clusters move toward the detector and separate on the basis of size and charge. Ion drift time is recorded in milliseconds (ms). Image courtesy of Dr. G. A. Eiceman, New Mexico State University.*

liquid chromatography[†] is finding a home in toxicology, particularly when the technique is linked to a mass spectrometer. As inlets, both methods effect separation by selective partitioning, the theory of which was covered in the previous chapter. In gas chromatography, analytes are volatilized and introduced into an inert carrier gas stream that is directed through a capillary tube[††](Figure 5.57). The tube is coated with a material in which the analytes partition (usually) on the basis of their relative polarities and boiling points. Just as more interactions with micelles slow the progress of neutrals in MEK, more interaction with the stationary phase means a longer retention time in the column. Capillary columns provide large surface areas for interaction, facilitating excellent separation and resolution. The principal limitation is in the capacity of the column. With thin films, it is easy to saturate the solid phase.

In a separations module employing a flowing system, the goal is to separate or resolve each component of a complex mixture into a discrete and pure packet separated in space and time from all other components. Doing this requires a tightly packed grouping with maximal separation between groups, expressed by the resolution or efficiency of the column. Figure 5.58 shows a mixed sample introduced into the flowing system. Partitioning and separation take place in the column. The ideal situation (Figure 5.58b) occurs when the separated groups of molecules are tightly packed together and the separation between groups is large. The resulting chromatogram will have narrow peaks with baseline resolution (Figure 5.58c). Tight groups, but little separation (Figure 5.58d), or broad groups both lead to overlapping peaks and mixtures entering the detector.

The most frequently cited measure of column efficiency is the number of theoretical plates, given by

$$N = 16\left(\frac{t_{r_i}}{w_i}\right)$$
(5.11)

[†]HPLC generically, meaning high *performance* or high *pressure* liquid chromatography.
[‡]Forensic GC is capillary based; packed-column applications are rare.

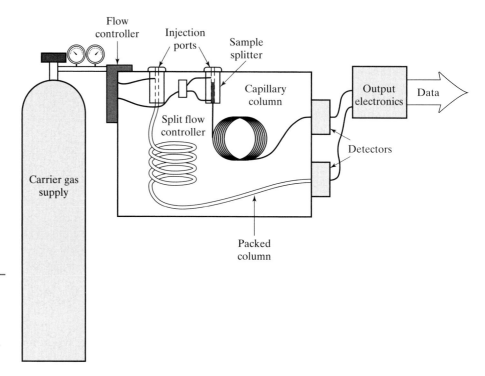

▶ **Figure 5.57** *A gas chromatograph with packed and capillary columns shown for purposes of illustration. Forensic applications are capillary-column based.*

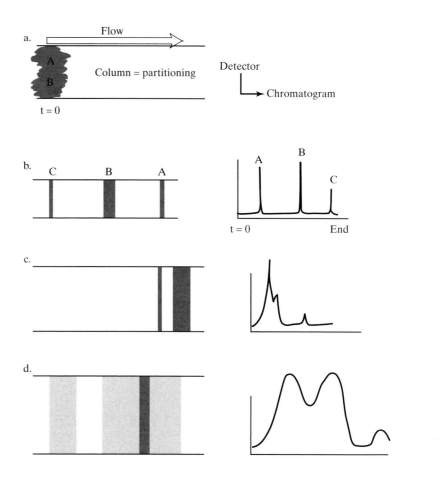

▶ **Figure 5.58** *Separation of a complex mixture.*

where t_r is the retention time of the peak being used and w is the width of that peak at the baseline; larger is better, and capillary columns can have N values of 10,000 or greater. Also used is the height equivalent of a theoretical plate (HETP),

$$H = \frac{L}{N} \tag{5.12}$$

where L is the length of the column.

Although a detailed review of GC and HPLC is beyond the scope of the present treatment, a brief review of the key relationships is appropriate. The **van Deemter curve**, shown in Figure 5.59, is a plot of efficiency (HETP, equation 5.12) as a function of mobile phase velocity (the flow rate). Three terms contribute to determining the shape of the curve. The minimum point is the flow rate that

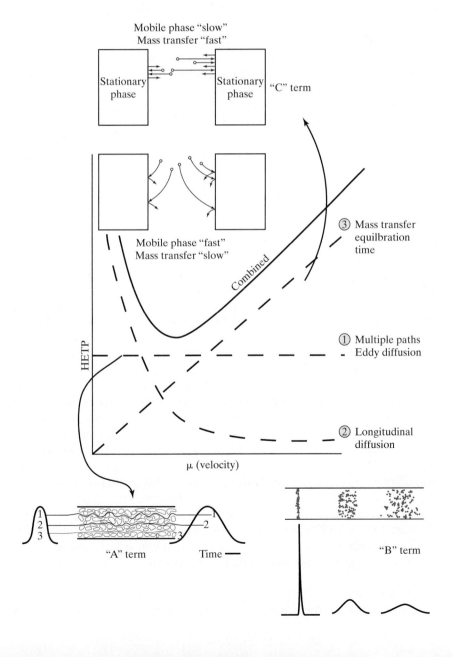

◀ **Figure 5.59** *The three factors that contribute to band broadening and efficiency of a chromatographic separation, plotted as a function of velocity (μ) of the mobile phase, be it liquid or gas.*

gives the best separation efficiency for a given mobile phase. Note that curves for different gases have different minima, but a similar shape. The first factor that causes peaks to spread is diffusion. When analyte travels through the column, molecules follow different paths and a Gaussian distribution of spreading results. In a capillary GC column, where stationary phase is coated on the walls of the column rather than on beads packed into it, this term (A) drops to negligible values and has the effect of dropping the curve toward the *x*-axis. The second term is longitudinal **diffusion**, in which any concentrated mass of material naturally spreads out over time. As the flow rate increases, time in the column decreases, as does the contribution of this factor to band broadening (B/μ).

The third term that adds to band broadening is the time allowed for equilibration between the mobile and stationary phase ($C\mu$). Partitioning requires an analyte to associate with the stationary phase:

$$\text{Analyte (mobile)} \longleftrightarrow \text{Analyte (stationary)} \tag{5.13}$$

The kinetics of this interaction is important. If the transfer of the analyte to the stationary phase and back (**mass transfer**) occurs quickly relative to the flow rate, the analyte has many opportunities to interact without being left behind in the stationary phase. If the flow is rapid (the mobile phase is "fast" in Figure 5.59), some of the analyte associated with the stationary phase is left behind the solvent front, leading to band broadening. Accordingly, this type of broadening is worsened by increasing the flow rate, since that would slow equilibration. The combined expression—the Van Deemter equation—is

$$\text{HETP} = A + \frac{B}{\mu} + C\mu \tag{5.14}$$

and it can be applied in analogous forms to any chromatographic or electrophoretic separation.

The liquid-phase analog of GC is high-pressure liquid chromatography (HPLC), in which small volumes of solvent are directed through a column tightly packed with beads coated with the stationary phase. As the name implies, the system operates at high pressure, which facilitates the tight packing and high surface area for interaction. HPLC is ideal for analytes that do not volatilize easily, such as large polymers and sugars. Thermally unstable compounds, including the drug LSD, formaldehyde, and many explosives, are amenable to HPLC without derivatization. The ability to combine solvents, which can include aqueous solutions and buffers in the mobile phase, adds to the versatility of HPLC. Unlike what happens in capillary GC, band broadening due to different paths is significant, but the expression for efficiency is still based on theoretical plates and HETP.

HPLC techniques cover a larger range of analytes than GC does, as shown in Table 5.1. The interactions should be familiar; they are drawn from the same group of interactions as previously described for solid-phase extraction (Section 4.5.2), with some additions. Gel permeation techniques are valuable for separations of large molecules such as polymers and proteins. Ion-pairing interactions will be introduced in Chapter 7 in the context of presumptive testing; suffice it for now to describe these as electrostatic (ion–ion) interactions. Chiral separations, invaluable in drug analysis, will be discussed shortly.

Detector Systems: GC: In any hyphenated instrument, a critical design concern is the interface between the separations module and the detector. The issue was

Table 5.1	**HPLC Separation Modes**	
Separation Mode	**Separation Mechanism**	**Application**
Normal Phase (NP)	Partitioning between a polar stationary phase and a less polar mobile phase	Organic-soluble polar analytes and water-soluble nonionic analytes; usually of a molecular weight <2000
Reversed Phase (RP)	Partitioning and/or adsorption between a nonpolar stationary phase and a more polar mobile phase	Organic-soluble nonpolar analytes and water-soluble polar nonionic analytes; usually of a molecular weight <2000
Hydrophobic Interaction (HI)	Adsorption between a nonpolar stationary phase and an aqueous mobile phase	Aqueous-soluble, denatured proteins and peptides
Ion Pairing (IP)	Interactions between a nonpolar stationary phase and a more polar, usually aqueous, mobile phase containing an ion-pairing reagent	Aqueous-soluble ionic analytes
Ion Exchange	Interactions between cationic and/or anionic stationary phase and aqueous mobile phase	Aqueous-soluble ionic analytes
Gel Permeation Chromatography/Gel Filtration Chromatography/Size Exclusion Chromatography (GPC/GFC/SEC)	Size sieving of analytes through or around pores in either a polymeric or a bonded silica stationary phase	Organic-soluble analytes, typically MW >2000, but not exclusively
Chiral	Physical interaction with an optically active stationary phase	Optically active analytes

hinted at in the previous section with the discussion of the "Z" **flow cell** for capillary electrophoretic systems. The task is simplified for GC relative to HPLC, because there is no solvent to contend with, yet the overall issue of flow out of the column, either too much or too little, must be addressed. All detectors have a characteristic selectivity and sensitivity; inescapable trade-offs are involved. The selectivity of a detector refers to the analytes it detects, whereas the sensitivity refers to the LOD of the detector for detectable analytes. In forensic chemistry, three detectors are widely used: a **flame ionization detector** (FID) for arson cases and screening applications; a **nitrogen–phosphorus detector** (NPD) for drugs and metabolites; and mass spectrometry (MS). **Mass spectrometers** are the only detectors that provide qualitative and quantitative data and, accordingly, are interfaced to nearly all kinds of separations modules, including electrophoretic and HPLC. The interface to the GC is the simplest and hence the most rugged and affordable.

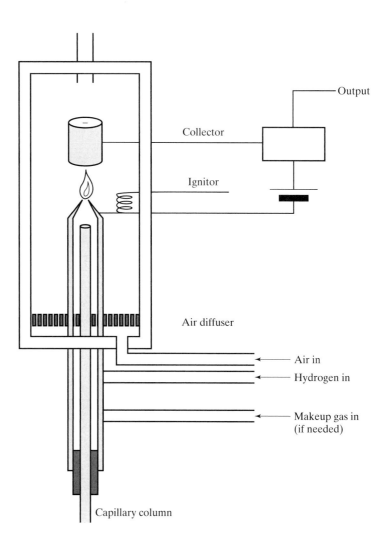

▶ **Figure 5.60** *Schematic of an FID.*

The flame ionization detector (FID, Figure 5.60) is sensitive to compounds that contain C—H bonds, and the more of these bonds, the stronger is the response. In forensic science, an FID is used for the analysis of fire debris to detect the presence of accelerants such as gasoline. GCFID is also employed for other screening applications and for developing methods. The flow of carrier gas and analytes exiting the column is supplemented with a supply of hydrogen and air (O_2) that is ignited, resulting in the production of free radical cations such as CHO·. Some free radicals are positively charged and so are attracted to the cathode (collector). The detector output is a plot of the current generated by the detector as a function of the run time. With capillary GC systems, a makeup gas such as nitrogen is often needed to maintain the optimum fuel–oxidant ratio for efficient combustion. The nitrogen–phosphorus detector (NPD) is a variant of the FID with comparable sensitivity, but greater selectivity. A small heated bead of an alkali salt such as rubidium sulfate is used to generate ions, a process that is at maximum efficiency in the presence of nitrogen- and phosphorus-containing compounds. Forensic toxicologists employ NPD in screening tests because most drugs and metabolites contain nitrogen.

The FID and NPD are used in screening applications because they are not specific detectors. A peak in a chromatogram indicates a detector response, and

Example Problem 5.6

Of the solvents pentane, hexane, and carbon disulfide, which would be the best choice for analyzing arson debris with GCFID?

Answer: All three solvents are acceptable for the extraction of nonpolar gasoline components, since all three are themselves nonpolar. If the extract is to be analyzed by GCFID, carbon disulfide is the best choice, because the FID detector is not very sensitive to this solvent. The other two contain C—H bonds, and as a result, the solvent peak could mask the response to materials found in the fire debris. Finally, CS_2 is unlikely to be found in the sample, whereas pentane and hexane would possibly be if the fire debris does contain an accelerant.

the population of molecules that could have produced that peak is limited. However, even the NPD detector responds to thousands of compounds. Analytical conditions used in sample preparation and instrument operation further constrain the possibilities, as does the retention time and the use of traceable standards for comparison. Peak areas combined with retention times are used for quantitative purposes, but definitive identification, particularly of unknown peaks, is not possible using a single column and single detector. Clearly, a detector that provides quantitative information as well as qualitative is ideal; in analytical chemistry, that detector is the mass spectrometer.

The name **mass spectrometer** is somewhat of a descriptive misnomer. Mass spectrometry works on the basis of separation, but not separation of electromagnetic energy into component wavelengths. Rather, a mass spectrometer disperses mass fragments, the pattern of which is sufficient to definitively identify a compound in most cases. In this sense, "spectrometer" is a reasonable analogy since the output is a spectrum of masses across a range of masses. A good way to visualize a mass spectrometer is as a mass filtering device, as shown in Figure 5.61. When this device is coupled to a GC, the outlet flow is directed into a vacuum region, where the sample is ionized and broken apart. The ions are then introduced into a filtering device that separates them on the basis of their mass-to-charge ratio (as opposed to size-to-charge ratio). Ions arrive at the transducer and are converted to electrons. The signal is amplified by an electron multiplier and then recorded.

There are many types of ionization modes and mass separation filters, the discussion of which is beyond the scope of this book. In forensic science applications, the most common design is an **electron impact ionization/quadrupole** mass filter (Figure 5.62) interfaced to a capillary GC. The small flows of the capillary column, on the order of 1 mL/minute or less, are managed by a simple vacuum system, allowing for a direct insertion of the column into the ionization region. Ionization and fragmentation are achieved by the collisions between

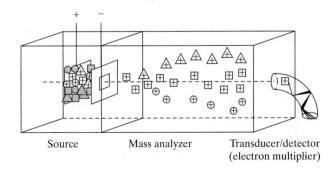

Source   Mass analyzer   Transducer/detector
(electron multiplier)

◀ **Figure 5.61** *A generic mass spectrometer, which does with mass fragments what a grating does to light: filters it and separates it into individual components.*

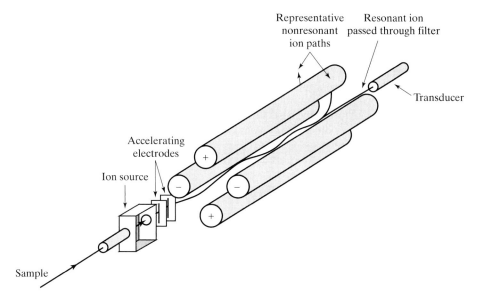

▶ **Figure 5.62** *A quadrupole mass spectrometer, the most common type of mass spectrometer used in forensic GCMS systems. Alternating DC and radio frequencies applied to the quadrupoles dictate ion paths. At any given setting, only one mass will get through and this is called the resonant mass.*

molecules from the sample and electrons generated by a filament, as shown in Figure 5.63. Few collisions result in ionization, but enough to generate both positive and negative ions, with positive ions usually being the polarity of interest. The positive ions are pushed into the focusing lenses by a repeller plate kept at a positive potential. The degree of fragmentation depends on the electron energy; standard values are 70 eV. The vacuum is necessary to prevent secondary collisions and combinations. Ions are focused into a tight stream by a series of electron lenses and introduced into the quadrupoles, where alternating DC and radio-frequency currents determine the field and thus the ion pathways. At a given setting, only ions with a particular mass transit the quadrupoles safely, whereas all others collide with the quadrupoles or are ejected.

A typical capillary GC peak spans a few seconds, which means that there is a limited time to collect mass fragmentation patterns from each component (Figure 5.64). To collect an adequate number of scans across a peak (three or more),

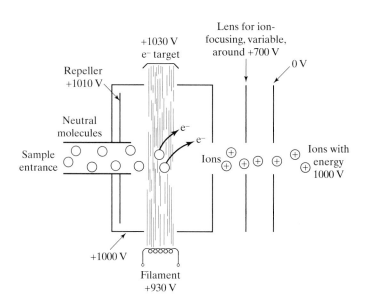

▶ **Figure 5.63** *The inlet, ionization region, and lens stack of a typical mass spectrometer.*

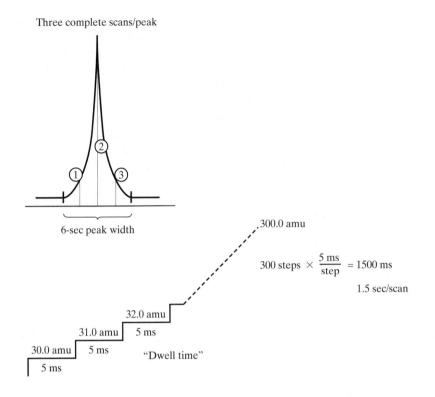

Three complete scans/peak

6-sec peak width

300.0 amu

$$300 \text{ steps} \times \frac{5 \text{ ms}}{\text{step}} = 1500 \text{ ms}$$

1.5 sec/scan

32.0 amu

31.0 amu   5 ms

30.0 amu   5 ms

5 ms   "Dwell time"

◀ **Figure 5.64** *The scan time–mass range trade-off. The time spent collecting ions from a given mass is called the* dwell time.

the scan time must be balanced against the mass range scanned. The larger the range covered, the less time can be spent at each mass and the lower is the overall sensitivity of the instrument. The high resolution of capillary GC columns exacerbates this situation because peaks are narrow. The mass range scanned is typically as small as possible, given the range of analytes expected under the experimental conditions selected.

Compounds are identified through the mass fragmentation pattern, library matches, and traceable standards. Key to identification is reproducible and controlled instrumental conditions. Electronics must be set such that patterns are reproducible in and across instruments. This is done by an internal calibration or tuning procedure in which a standard compound, usually perfluorotributylamine (**PFTBA**), is introduced into the mass spectrometer and settings are adjusted or tuned until the resulting mass spectrum meets the required criteria of masses detected and relative abundances. The standard forensic library is the NIST/EPA/NIH Mass Spectral Library, which was acquired under instrumental conditions for PFTBA. Because the electronic settings alter mass intensities, if an instrument is out of tune (i.e., if it cannot produce a PFTBA spectrum with the required mass peaks and intensities), any calibration curves obtained under those tuned conditions have to be redone. Therefore, an instrument must be tuned to produce a standard PFTBA spectrum within tolerances before any calibration curve is obtained. In some cases—chiefly environmental applications—other tuning compounds are used, but the same principles apply. The sum of all the ion signals produced generates a signal much as an FID does. When total ion signal is plotted as a function of time, the chromatogram is called a total ion Chromatogram or TIC. Quantitation by mass spectrometry is usually based on extracted ion chromatographs rather than the TIC.

Detector Systems: HPLC: Similar detectors are used for capillary electrophoresis and HPLC, with many of the same design considerations and limitations. Three detectors are common: UV single wavelength, UV/VIS **photodiode array** (PDA), and mass spectrometry. HPLCMS (or simply LCMS) is a more complicated proposition, given the nature of the interface and the need to remove large amounts of solvent that may include buffers. Currently, electrospray interface designs are popular. A surface charge and evaporation combine to remove solvent efficiently. Unlike conditions in a capillary GC interface, the pressure difference is large and requires a staged or differential pumping system using lenses and skimmer cones to reduce the flow into the mass analyzer to a level that is controllable by the vacuum system. LCMS is used mostly in forensic toxicology.

The two other detectors are based on absorbance. The fixed-wavelength UV detector essentially is a marriage of a flow cell and a UV/VIS spectrophotometer. Absorbance at one wavelength at a time can be detected, but most such detectors can operate at more than one wavelength. A photodiode

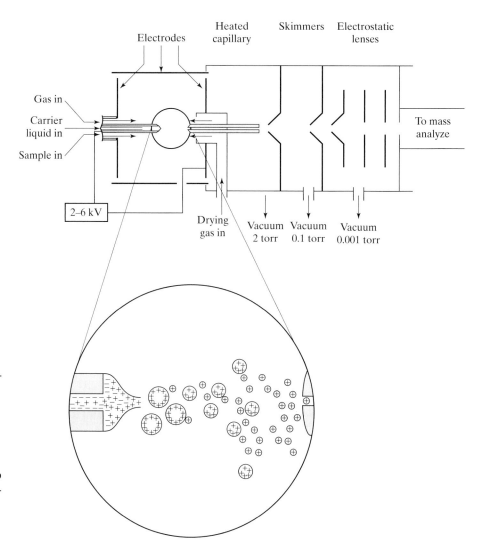

▶ **Figure 5.65** *An electrospray interface from an LC column to an MS detector. A charge is imparted to the surface of the solvent drop, which is then heated. As solvent evaporates, the charges are drawn closer to each other until repulsion causes the drop to disperse. The process is repeated until most of the solvent is removed.*

array detector uses a grating to disperse the light that is transmitted through the sample onto a grid of photodiodes placed such that the location of each photodiode correlates with the spot where a given wavelength is found. In practice, two gratings are used to provide not just linear, but two-dimensional, dispersion. As with a mass spectrometer, the diodes must be scanned, requiring a finite amount of time that is always at odds with a flowing system design. The advantage is being able to obtain a full UV/VIS scan for each component, rather than just absorbance at one wavelength, analogous to the comparison of an FID and MS.

5.5.2 THREE-DIMENSIONAL DATA

The ability to collect a mass spectrum or a UV/VIS spectrum from one analyte of many in a complex mixture is an example of multidimensional data (Applying the Science 5.5). In a GCMS analysis, retention time data and the mass spectrum yield the qualitative information, whereas the peak height or area (the total and selected ion signals) provides quantitative information. A recent trend in instrumentation is stringing together both separation modules and detectors to increase the dimensionality and information density obtained from each analysis. For example, mass spectrometers can be linked to break up the fragments and provide additional information; GC $\times$ GC is being used in arson investigations, and IMS is being linked to MS in field applications. A number of these methods are introduced in subsequent chapters. Although they are not yet common, the trend is worth watching.

5.6 MISCELLANEOUS SAMPLE PREPARATION AND INSTRUMENTAL ANALYSIS TECHNIQUES

5.6.1 DERIVATIZATION

As described in the previous sections, HPLC and CE techniques are among the most versatile in terms of the types of analytes that can be analyzed. However, most forensic laboratories still rely on gas chromatographic techniques for the majority of their routine analyses. To be amenable to GC, analytes must be appreciably volatile in the temperature range of the instrument, typically up to 350°C. Analytes must also be stable in this range and not subject to thermal degradation. They must be detectable with the detector used. Finally, analytes must have acceptable chromatographic characteristics, meaning they must form narrow peaks. While a large group of analytes meet these requirements, many do not. One way to address the inherent limitations of GC is to convert analytes to derivatives with improved chromatographic characteristics under a given set of GC conditions. Derivatives can also be prepared for other reasons, such as improving detection. For example, in HPLC and CE, it is not uncommon to derivatize a compound by adding a fluorophore such that the derivatized compound can be detected by exploiting fluorescence. In fact, that is the basis of automated DNA typing systems; however, this discussion will focus on derivatives used in gas chromatography. In GC applications, derivatization is employed to improve chromatographic behavior (i.e., improve peak shape by minimizing tailing), to make an otherwise nonvolatile substance volatile under GC conditions, or to modify a compound such that it will not degrade under GC conditions.

Applying the Science 5.5

An example of three-dimensional data is data obtained from an analysis of gunshot residue by a capillary electrophoresis separation module coupled to a photodiode array UV detector. The electropherogram is a plot of absorbance versus retention time, with the third dimension of data provided by the UV spectrum at each collection point.

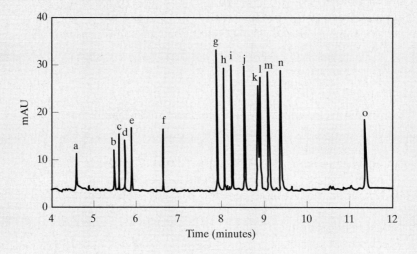

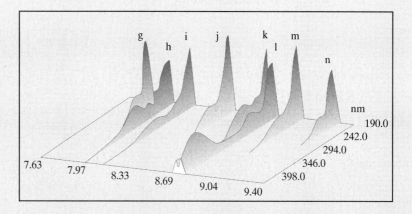

MECK separation of gunshot residue standards (10^{-4} M). Analytes are (a) nitroglycerin, (b) 2,4-dinitrotoluene, (c) 2,6-dinitrotoluene, (d) 3,4-dinitrotoluene, (e) 2,3-dinitrotoluene, (f) 2-naphthol (internal standard), (g) diethylphthalate, (h) diphenylamine, (i) N-nitrosodiphenylamine, (j) methylcentralite, (k) 2-nitrodiphenylamine, (l) 4-nitrodiphenylamine, (m) ethylcentralite, (n) dibutylphthalate, (o) styphnic acid.

Source: Northrop, D. "Forensic Applications of High-Performance Liquid Chromatography and Capillary Electrophoresis," in R. Saferstein, ed., *Forensic Science Handbook*, (2d) ed., Vol. 1. Upper Saddle River, NJ: Prentice Hall, 2002.

A variety of derivatizing agents are commercially available, most of which fall into three general categories summarized in Table 5.2.[19, 20] Derivatization reactions typically target hydrogen atoms that can interact with chromatographic stationary phases. For example, the H on a carboxyl group (COOH) may form hydrogen bonds with stationary phases, thereby affecting mass transfer (Figure 5.59) and result in tailing of peaks. Hydrogen-bonding interactions can also increase boiling points, decrease volatility, and make it impossible to analyze a compound via GC. Finally, some derivatives are used to facilitate the separation and identification of optically active isomers.

Table 5.2   Selected Derivatizing Agents for GC

Example reagents*	Chemical reaction	Example structure	Used for
BSTFA, TMS, TMCS	Silylation	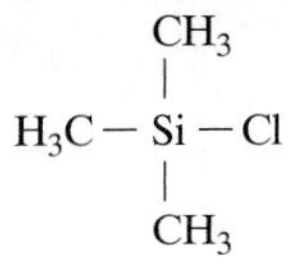 $H_3C - Si - Cl$ with two CH_3 groups **TMCS**	Acids and alcohols
MSTFA	Acylation	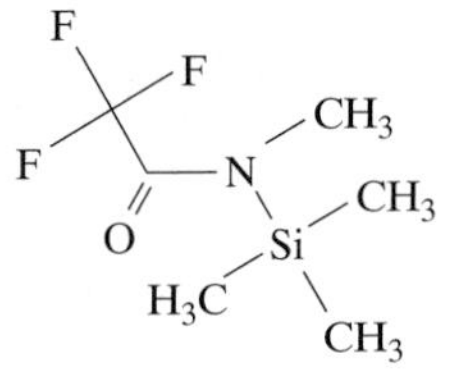 **MSTFA**	Drugs and drug–HCl salts
TMAH	Alkylation	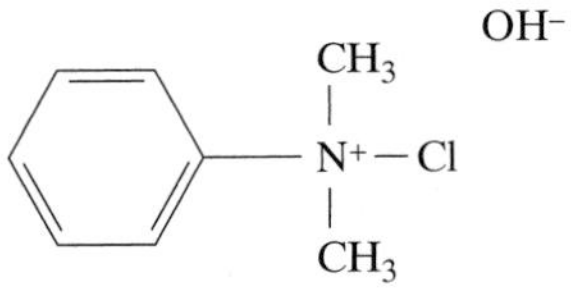 OH^- **TMAH**	Drugs and fatty acids

*: BSTFA = N,O-bis(trimethylsilyl)trifluoroacetamide
TMS = trimethylsilane
TMCS = trimethylchlorosilane
MSTFA = *N*-methyl-*N*-trimethylsilyltrifluoroacetamide
TMAH = *N, N, N*-trimethyl-benzenaminium

5.6.2 CHIRAL SEPARATIONS

The stereochemistry of organic analytes is an important consideration in forensic toxicology and drug analysis. Recently, specialized chromatographic techniques have emerged that allow for the separation of stereoisomers. These techniques separate isomers on the basis of selective partitioning with chiral phases. Chirality and stereoisomerism are reviewed in detail in Chapter 8; for now, recall that a chiral atom is an atom with four different groups attached to it and that a chiral compound is not superimposable on its mirror image. It is not possible to separate a pair of isomers such as D-methamphetamine and L-methamphetamine from each other using traditional partitioning techniques. One solution is to implement partitioning via a chiral stationary phase, and this has been achieved in GC, HPLC, MEKC, and TLC.[17, 21–23]

The bases of many chiral phases are cyclodextrins, which are glucose polymers that possess a hydrophobic cavity. The glucose is the D(+) form, which allows for interactions based on chirality. The three most commonly used cyclodextrins (Figure 5.66) are the α, β, and γ-cyclodextrins, with the α having the smallest cavity and γ-cyclodextrin having the largest. A cyclodextrin is usually depicted as a washerlike shape with the opening wider than the base.

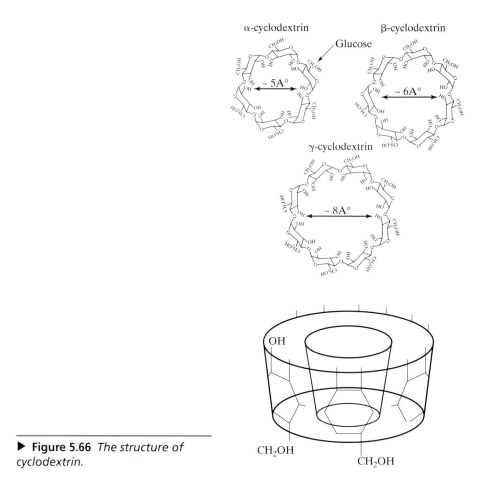

▶ **Figure 5.66** *The structure of cyclodextrin.*

When a racemic mixture is introduced into a chromatographic system containing cyclodextrin, the two isomers will have a different affinity for the chiral phase, affording what is called the **enantioselectivity** of the cyclodextrin phase. Finally, one other approach to the separation of enantiomers that has been applied in forensic work is enantioselective derivation.[24] Rather than using an optically active stationary phase, this technique achieves separation by derivatizing the chiral compounds with chiral agents resulting in different selectivities for chiral molecules.

SUMMARY

This chapter has presented a whirlwind tour of the instruments employed in forensic chemistry. These instruments are usually not the newest, nor do they necessarily reflect the cutting edge of analytical instrumentation—and there is good reason for this. First, analytical techniques must prove their worth and exhibit a good cost–benefit ratio as applied to forensic casework, a process that takes years of testing and research. Second, instruments and methods must be rigorously tested and validated to meet legal requirements. Third, cost and intercomparability of those results are essential.

Instruments must be rugged and suitable to heavy use and automation. Finally, the cost of obtaining and maintaining the instruments must fit into constrained budgets. In the forensic context, "elegant and exotic" doesn't always translate to practical or feasible. The emphasis remains on the tried and true, which is why we discuss AAS in the age of ICP-MS.

Hyphenated instruments have come to play a central role in forensic analytical chemistry, taking their place alongside of microscopy and spectroscopy as the primary instruments of the modern laboratory. As mentioned at the beginning of the chapter, the microscope and the spectrometer were the pillars of the first forensic laboratory; add to that a GC-MS, and a modern forensic chemistry laboratory takes shape. The most important advancement in recent years has been the development of reliable and affordable IR microspectrophotometers, hyphenated instruments, and capillary electrophoresis.

KEY TERMS AND CONCEPTS

Angle aperture
Anisotropic
Anti-Stokes scattering
Aperture
Atomic emission spectroscopy
Bandwidth
Baseline resolution
Beer's law
Bertrand lens
Birefringence
Boltzmann distribution
Bulk method
Capillary electrophoresis/CZE
Cassegrain lens
Colorimeter
Condenser/condenser lens
Depth of field
Dichroic
Diffuse reflectance
Diffusion
Dispersion
Electron impact ionization
Electronic transition
Electroosmotic flow
Electropherogram
Electrophoresis
Enantioselectivity
Evanescent wave
Eyepiece
Field of view
Flame ionization detector

Flow cell
Fluorescence
Focal length
Focal plane
Fourier transform
Graphite furnace
Hollow cathode lamp
Hyphenated instrument
Inductively coupled plasma
Interferogram
Interferometry
Ion mobility spectrometry
Isotropic
Kohler illumination
L'vov platform
Mass spectrometer
Mass transfer
MEK
Micelles
Microspectrophotometry
Mobility spectrum
Molecular transition
Monochromator
NA
Nebulizer
Nitrogen phosphorus detector
Objective lens
Ocular lens
Optic axis
PFTBA
Phosphorescence

Photodiode array
Pleochroic
Polarizable bonds
Polarized light
Polarized light microscopy
Principal focus
Pseudocrystalline
Quadrupole
Radiationless transition
Raman spectroscopy
Rayleigh scattering
Real image
Resolving power
Scanning electron microscopy
  (SEM)
Sequential
Simultaneous
Snell's law
Specular reflection
Stokes scattering
Surface absorption-reflection
Surface method
Theoretical plates
Three-dimensional data
Transducer
Van Deemter curve
Virtual image
Working distance
X-ray diffraction (XRD)

PROBLEMS

From the chapter

1. What is the best wavelength to use to examine the smallest visible samples? Why?

2. On the basis of the information presented in Sidebar 2, explain why blue light bends more (is refracted to a larger degree) than red light.

3. Draw a box diagram of a simple microscope next to that of a simple spectrophotometer. Trace the light paths and show common components and features. On the basis of your drawing, how would you expect a polarizing IR microscope to function? Draw a schematic.

4. Why are fluorescent and phosphorescent emissions always redder than the source used to stimulate the emission?

5. How would a gas-phase UV spectrum of acetone compare with one obtained in the liquid phase? From a forensic point of view, would this provide any additional information or value?

6. If the resolution of an FTIR depends on the distance the mirror travels, why aren't relatively long moving distances such as 2 or 4 cm used? What is the trade-off?

7. Why would the electron clouds of bonds made with larger atoms be more polarizable than those from smaller atoms?

8. Why can't an atomic absorption instrument be designed like a simple UV/VIS instrument, where a lamp is the source and a monochromator isolates the wavelength of interest, such as 589.3 for sodium?

9. In AA, does it matter if the target atom is ionized? What about in ICP-AES? Explain.

10. Is an HCL the same thing as a laser? Compare and contrast the two.

11. Using the Boltzmann distribution, explain why the Stokes lines are always more intense in a Raman spectrum than the anti-Stokes lines.

12. A large N value is not the sole criterion for selecting a GC column for a given separation. What other factors must be taken into account?

13. Which of the three contributing factors to band broadening in chromatography is independent of the flow rate? Explain why.

Integrative

1. Suppose a sample of urine contains quinine, a molecule that can be excited by visible light and that fluoresces strongly. How would the design of a simple colorimeter–spectrometer have to be modified to detect the fluorescence and not the transmitted light coming from the excitation source?

2. The development of the technology for micro-Raman methods has been much more difficult than for traditional IR methods. What factors contribute to this difficulty?

3. The light from a hollow cathode lamp is intense at discrete wavelengths, but not necessarily monochromatic. Explain. Is this an advantage, disadvantage, or neither?

4. In the case of the assassination of President John F. Kennedy, a key piece of forensic evidence was provided by the analysis of bullets and fragments recovered. Research this case, describe how the elemental analysis was done, and discuss some of the limitations of the instrumental technique used. How would such an analysis be accomplished today?

5. Use the concepts of scattering and polarizability to draw links between atomic and molecular scattering, the refractive index, and Raman spectroscopy.

6. The calibration of spectroscopic methods is based on Beer's law and a linear relationship of the form $y = mx + b$. Theoretically, b should be zero, but usually it is not. Why?

7. Most manufacturers send test runs of 5–10 peaks with new GC columns and calculate the number of theoretical plates for each peak rather than just for the first one. Why?

8. One way to dramatically increase the sensitivity of a quadrupole mass spectrometer is to use a technique called selected ion monitoring (SIM). Explain how this technique works and why it improves sensitivity. Forensically, why is SIM rarely used? Is there a compromise between a wide range of masses scanned and SIM? Explain.

9. Discuss and explain why the intensity of the source in any type of spectroscopy fundamentally controls the instrument's LOD and LOQ. Why does interferometry change this control?

10. There is a form of MS that utilizes the Fourier transform. Research this technique, explain how it works, how it is used, and what the advantages and disadvantages are. Are there any incentives for forensic laboratories to adopt FTMS over existing quadrupole designs?

11. Spectroscopy in the UV/VIS range produces broad bands for reasons discussed in the text. In addition, rotational and vibrational modes contribute to band broadening even though these quantum states and transitions are not targeted. Explain. Would performing the analysis in the gas phase alter the contribution of these modes? Would any additional forensic information be gained?

Food for Thought

1. Although the Michel-Levy chart is easy to use, there are difficulties associated with it and its applications. What might those difficulties be? In what other areas could this be an issue in forensic analysis?
2. a. For the elemental analysis of bullets, what would be "better," a surface analysis technique such as XRF or a bulk analysis method such as ICP-AES? Explore each and discuss their pros and cons.
   b. Research how the bullets involved in the assassination of John F. Kennedy were analyzed, and critique the procedures and results.
   c. A recent report commissioned by the FBI and published by the National Research Council discusses the use of elemental analysis and "chaining" as a method of analysis and interpretation of the composition of bullets. Find this report, read it, and describe what chaining is and how it is used. Critique the method and offer alternatives, keeping in mind the typical forensic laboratory capabilities and time pressures.
3. Does an HPLC-PDA instrument provide the same level of qualitative and quantitative information as a GCMS?

FURTHER READING

Bogusz, M. J. "Liquid Chromatography–Mass Spectrometry as a Routine Method in Forensic Sciences: A Proof of Maturity." *Journal of Chromatography B*, 748 **2000**, 3–19.

Chamot, E. M., and C. W. Mason. *Handbook of Chemical Microscopy: Volume II: Chemical Methods and Inorganic Qualitative Analysis*, Chicago: McCrone Research Institute, **1989**.

Cooke, P. M. "Chemical Microscopy." *Analytical Chemistry*, 72 **2000**, 169R–188R.

De Forest, P. R. "Foundations of Forensic Microscopy," in R. Saferstein, ed., *Forensic Science Handbook*, Vol. 1, 2d ed. Upper Saddle River, NJ: Prentice Hall, **2002**.

Eiceman, G. A., and Z. Karpus. *Ion Mobility Spectrometry*, Boca Raton, FL: CRC Press, Inc., **1994**.

Eyring, M. B. "Visible Microscopical Spectrophotometry in the Forensic Sciences," in R. Saferstein, ed., *Forensic Science Handbook*, Vol. 1, 2d ed. Upper Saddle River, NJ: Prentice Hall, **2002**.

Harris, D. C. *Quantitative Chemical Analysis*, 6th ed. New York: W.H. Freeman, **2003**.

Holland, L. A., et al. "Capillary Electrophoresis in Pharmaceutical Analysis." *Pharmaceuticals Research*, 14 **1997**, 372–387.

Holme, D. J., and H. Peck. *Analytical Biochemistry*, 3d ed. London: Addison Wesley Longman, **1998**.

Ingle, J. D. J., and S. R. Crouch. *Spectrochemical Analysis*. Upper Saddle River, NJ: Prentice Hall, **1988**.

Jenkins, R. "X-ray Techniques: An Overview," in R. A. Meyers, ed., *Encyclopedia of Analytical Chemistry*. Chichester, U.K.: John Wiley and Sons, **2000**.

Kneipp, K., et al. "Ultrasensitive Chemical Analysis by Raman Spectroscopy." *Chemical Reviews*, 99 **1999**, 2957–2975.

Lambert, J. B., et al. *Organic Structural Spectroscopy*. Upper Saddle River, NJ: Prentice Hall, **1998**.

Landers, J. P., ed. *Handbook of Capillary Electrophoresis*. Boca Raton, FL: CRC Press, **1996**.

McHale, J. L. *Molecular Spectroscopy*. Upper Saddle River, NJ: Prentice Hall, **1999**.

McLaughlin, R. B. *Special Methods in Light Microscopy*. Chicago: Microscope Publications, Ltd., **1977**.

Mulvaney, S. P., and C. D. Keating. "Raman Spectroscopy." *Analytical Chemistry*, 72 **2000**, 145R–157R.

Murphy, D. B. *Fundamentals of Light Microscopy and Electronic Imaging*. Danvers, MA: Wiley-Liss, **2001**.

Northrop, D., "Forensic Applications of High-Performance Liquid Chromatography amd Capillary Electrophoresis," in R. Saferstein, ed., *Forensic Science Handbook*, Vol. 1, 2d ed. Upper Saddle River, NJ: Prentice Hall, **2002**.

Petraco, N., and T. Kubic. *Color Atlas and Manual of Microscopy for Criminalists, Chemists, and Conservators,* Boca Raton, FL: CRC Press, **2004**.

Rubinson, K. A., and J. F. Rubinson. *Contemporary Instrumental Analysis.* Upper Saddle River, NJ: Prentice Hall, **2000**.

Saferstein, R. "Forensic Applications of Mass Spectrometry," in R. Saferstein, ed., *Forensic Science Handbook*, Vol. 1, 2d ed. Upper Saddle River, NJ: Prentice Hall, **2002**.

Skoog, D. A., et al. *Analytical Chemistry: An Introduction*, 7th ed. New York: Saunders College Publishing/Harcourt College Publishers, **2000**.

Slayter, E. M., and H. S. Slayter. *Light and Electron Microscopy.* Cambridge, U.K.: Cambridge University Press, **1992**.

Szaloki, I., et al. "X-ray Spectrometry." *Analytical Chemistry,* 74 **2002**, 2895–2918.

Tagliaro, F., et al. "Capillary Electrophoresis: Principles and Applications in Illicit Drug Analysis." *Forensic Science International,* 77 **1996**, 211–229.

Terabe, S. "Micellar Electrokinetic Chromatography." *Analytical Chemistry* **2004**, 241A–246A.

Viney, C. *Transmitted Polarised Light Microscopy.* Chicago: McCrone Research Institute, **1990**.

Zadora, G., and Z. Mucha-Bozek. "SEM-EDX—a Useful Tool for Forensic Examinations." *Materials Chemistry and Physics*, 81 **2003**, 345–348.

REFERENCES

1. Stoney, D. A., and P. M. Dougherty. "The Microscope in Forensic Science: Forensic Microscopy in the 1890s and the Development of the Comparison Microscope," in R. Saferstein, ed., *More Chemistry and Crime: From Marsh Arsenic Test to DNA Profile*. Washington, DC: American Chemical Society, **1997**.

2. McLaughlin, R. B. "Chapter 4: Sample Characterization," in R. B. McLaughlin, *Special Methods in Light Microscopy*, London and Chicago: Microscope Publications, Ltd., **1977**.

3. De Forest, P. R. "Foundations of Forensic Microscopy," in R. Saferstein, ed., *Forensic Science Handbook*, Vol. 1, 2d ed. Upper Saddle River, NJ: Prentice Hall, **2002**.

4. Robinson, P. C., and M. W. Davidson. "Plane Polarized Light Microscopy," Nikon Microscopy U, http://www.microscopy.com, March 7, 2004.

5. Petraco, N., and T. Kubic. *Color Atlas and Manual of Microscopy for Criminalists, Chemists, and Conservators*. Boca Raton, FL: CRC Press, 2004.

6. Suzuki, E. M. "Forensic Applications of Infrared Spectroscopy," in R. Saferstein, ed., *Forensic Science Handbook*, Vol. 3. Upper Saddle River, NJ: Prentice Hall, **1993**.

7. Cavinato, A. G., et al. "Noninvasive Method for Monitoring Ethanol in Fermentation Processes Using Fiber-Optic Near-Infrared Spectroscopy." *Analytical Chemistry*, 62 **1990**, 1978–1982.

8. Laasonen, M., et al. "Fast Identification of *Echinaxea purpurea* Dried Roots Using Near Infrared Spectroscopy." *Analytical Chemistry*, 74 **2002**, 2493–2499.

9. Choquette, S. J., et al. "Identification and Quantitation of Oxygenates in Gasoline Ampules Using Fourier Transform Near-Infrared and Fourier Transform Raman Spectroscopy." *Analytical Chemistry*, 68 **1996**, 3525–3533.

10. Saona-Rodriguez, L. E., et al. "Rapid Detection and Identification of Bacterial Strains by Fourier Transform Near-Infrared Spectroscopy." *Journal of Agricultural and Food Chemistry*, 49 **2001**, 574–579.

11. Bugay, D. E., and P. A. Martoglio Smith. "Raman Spectroscopy," in L. Y. Galichet et al., ed., *Clarke's Analysis of Drugs and Poisons in Pharmaceuticals, Body Fluids, and Postmortem Material*, Vol. 1. London: Pharmaceutical Press, **2004**.

12. Ryder, A. "Classification of Narcotics in a Solid Mixture Using Principal Component Analysis and Raman Spectroscopy." *Journal of Forensic Sciences*, 47 **2002**, 275–284.

13. Suzuki, E. M., and M. Carrabba. "In-Situ Identification and Analysis of Automotive Paint Pigments Using Line Segment Excitation Raman Spectroscopy: I. Inorganic Topcoat Pigments." *Journal of Forensic Sciences*, 46 **2001**, 1053–1069.

14. Miller, J., and E. Bartick. "Forensic Analysis of a Single Fiber." *Applied Spectroscopy*, 55 **2001**, 1729–1732.

15. Mazzella, W. D., and A. Khanmy-Vital. "A Study to Investigate the Evidential Value of Blue Gel Inks." *Journal of Forensic Sciences*, 48 **2003**, 419–424.

16. Claybourn, M., and M. Ansell. "Using Raman Spectroscopy to Solve Crime: Inks, Questioned Documents, and Fraud." *Science and Justice: Journal of the Forensic Science Society*, 40 **2000**, 261–271.

17. Tagliaro, F., et al. "Capillary Electrophoresis: Principles and Applications in Illicit Drug Analysis." *Forensic Science International*, 77 **1996**, 211–229.

18. Holland, L. A., et al. "Capillary Electrophoresis in Pharmaceutical Analysis." *Pharmaceuticals Research*, 14 **1997**, 372–387.

19. Holme, D. J., and H. Peck. "Chapter 3: Separation Methods," in D. J. Holme and H. Peck, *Analytical*

Biochemistry, 3d ed. London: Addison Wesley Longman, 1998.

20. Patnaik, P. "Section 5.1.5: Derivatization Reactions," in P. Patnaik, *Dean's Analytical Chemistry Handbook*, 2d ed. New York: McGraw-Hill, 2004.

21. Nielen, M. W. F. "Chiral Separations of Basic Drugs Using Cyclodextrin-Modified Capillary Zone Electrophoresis." *Analytical Chemistry*, 65 **1993**, 885–893.

22. Ward, T. J. "Chiral Separations." *Analytical Chemistry*, 76 **2004**, 4635–4644.

23. Ward, T. J., and D. M. Hamburg. "Chiral Separations." *Analytical Chemistry*, 74 **2002**, 4635–4644.

24. Shin, H.-S., and M. Donike. "Stereospecific Derivatization of Amphetamines, Phenol Alkylamines, and Hydroxamines and Quantitation of the Enantiomers by Capillary GC/MS." *Analytical Chemistry*, 68 **1996**, 3015–3020.

CHAPTER

6 An Overview of Drugs and Pharmacology

6.1   What Is a Drug?
6.2   Classification and Categories
6.3   Drugs as Evidence
6.4   Turbo Pharmacology
6.5   Online Resources for the Forensic Chemist and Toxicologist

OVERVIEW AND ORIENTATION

This chapter covers a diverse set of topics that must be introduced before we delve into any comprehensive discussions of drugs and drug families. Because classification is a prelude to identification, we'll start with classification. Forensic scientists are classifiers. Those who work with body fluids classify a red material first as a biological fluid, next as blood, then as human, and finally by DNA type. Fingerprint analysts begin their work by classifying the major features of a fingerprint as a loop, an arch, or a whorl. From there, fine features are used to locate a fingerprint within an increasingly smaller group. Thus, classification is the process of placing an exhibit of evidence into successively smaller categories. Ideally, classification results in a category that contains only one member. When this happens, the evidence has been individualized to a reasonable degree of scientific certainty. For example, there are millions of people with loops and whorl patterns in their fingerprints, but you are the only one with your unique combination of features on ten fingers.

Forensic chemists are also classifiers. Is the evidence biological or physical? Answering that question allows analysts to assign the evidence to a smaller category. We saw in Chapter 4 that drugs can be classified as acidic, basic, or neutral, but that is just one of many ways drugs are categorized. The first part of the current chapter discusses the many ways in which drugs are categorized and how these categorizations overlap and interact.

The classification of a drug directs subsequent analysis and investigation. One of the most valuable investigative tools that a forensic chemist can provide is a detailed profile of drug evidence. As we'll see, profiling is an extension of classification, and some of the "Applying the Science" demonstrate how this kind of classification is visualized using the tools of multivariate statistics covered in Chapter 3. Profiling is informally referred to as "chemical fingerprinting," and as with real fingerprinting, the more detailed the characteristics and the more descriptors that can be identified, the more useful will be the fingerprint.

Finally, we'll investigate the basics of forensic toxicology. How do drugs and poisons get into a person's systems? What happens to a drug when it is ingested, and how long does it take to make itself felt in the body? How does one's metabolism alter a drug or poison? How can the toxicologist use all of this information to re-create the ingestion event? The underlying process and principles are the same ones used to reconstruct a crime scene: examining evidence available in the present to re-create the past. Any forensic chemist, even those who do not work as toxicologists, should be familiar with the basics of toxicology included herein.

6.1 WHAT IS A DRUG?

A **drug** is a substance that, when ingested, is capable of inducing a physiological change. There are many modes of ingestion, including swallowing, injection, inhalation, and absorption through the skin. All drugs are toxic; it is the dose that differentiates a therapeutic drug from a poison. Drugs are used to treat or prevent disease, to alleviate pain, to promote sleep, or to induce other physiological responses. Medicines are combinations of drugs and inert ingredients, but the terms "drug" and "**medicine**" are often used interchangeably. Aspirin is a drug, but if it is part of a preparation used to treat a cold or the flu, that preparation is called a medicine. An example is shown in Figure 6.1.

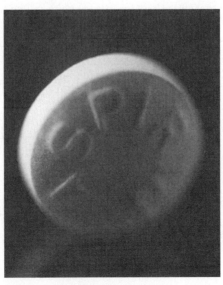

◀ **Figure 6.1** *Aspirin by itself is a drug, but when aspirin is combined with other active ingredients, such as in a cold preparation, that preparation is a medicine.*

Historical Evidence 6.1—The Dose Makes the Poison

"All substances are poisons; there is none which is not a poison. The right dose differentiates a poison from a remedy." Paracelsus (1493–1541).

M. B. Orfila is considered the father of forensic toxicology, but the title "father of modern toxicology" could belong to Paracelsus. Among his many contributions was the reintegration of the emerging science of chemistry with medicine, something not seen since the age of the Greeks. Paracelsus heralded the coming Renaissance, during which science and, eventually, forensic science would arise. A physician and alchemist, Paracelsus appreciated the value of the scientific method and experimentation. He also realized that what is a beneficial medicine at a low dose can become a toxin at a higher dose. The use of mercury as a treatment for syphilis was his suggestion—and not such a bad one, based on the limited knowledge of the time. Like all poisons, mercury, by definition, has antimicrobial properties.

Source: Gallo, M. A. "History and Scope of Toxicology," in C. D. Klaassen, ed., *Casarett & Doull's Toxicology: The Basic Science of Poisons*, 6th ed. New York: McGraw-Hill Medical Publishing Division, **2001**, 3–10.

Drugs can also be abused, but the definition of what constitutes drug abuse changes over time and differs among societies. Cocaine was an ingredient in Coca Cola®, LSD and a compound related to methamphetamine (Ecstasy or MDMA) were used in psychotherapy and methamphetamine was used by American soldiers from World War II through the first Gulf War in 1991.

Marijuana and related preparations were used medicinally in ancient times, and the active ingredient in the drug has been found to be useful in treating glaucoma, anorexia, and the nausea associated with chemotherapy. In fact, the active ingredient in marijuana is now prepared synthetically and marketed as the drug Marinol®. While these social and historical considerations may not affect how the forensic chemist performs an analysis, they do dictate what the target analytes are.

Exhibit A: What a Difference a Century Makes

The original formula for Coca-Cola® was invented by chemist John S. Pemberton, who wanted to create the perfect medicinal drink. He had heard about extracts of the coca

▲ *An early advertisement for Coca-Cola®. The "vim and vigor" came from cocaine; now it comes from caffeine.*

plant and knew of its purported stimulant and aphrodisiac effects. His first concoction was "Pemberton's French Wine Cola," launched in 1885. It sold particularly well in Atlanta, the city that became the corporate headquarters of the Coca-Cola® company. He continued working on the beverage, striving to make a "temperance drink" based on coca extracts and the kola nut, but without the bitter taste typical of alkaloids. The addition of sugar and corn syrup helped, along with some citric acid to counter any oversweetening. The name Coca Cola® came from the two key ingredients: the kola nut and cocaine. Pemberton sold the company when he became ill with cancer, but work continued on the formula. By the turn of the century, public sentiment was turning against cocaine, given its potential for addiction, and cocaine had been removed from the formula by 1929.

Exhibit A: (Continued)

▲ *John Pemberton, chemist and inventor of the original Coca-Cola® formula.*

Sources: "Drug Enforcement Administration Historical Interviews: James McGivency, Tape No. 162," downloaded March 14, 2004, http://www.usdoj.gov/dea/deamuseum/transcripts/jamesmcgiveney_11042003.pdf.

Other sources: "John Smyth Pemberton," from cocaine.org, cocaine.org/coca-cola/, downloaded March 14, 2004.

Urban Legends Reference Page: Cokelore, www.snopes.com/cocklore/cocaine.asp, downloaded March 14, 2004.

6.2 CLASSIFICATION AND CATEGORIES

6.2.1 BY ORIGIN AND FUNCTION

As was discussed in Chapter 4, drugs can be classified on the basis of their acid–base character. While this approach is useful and meaningful to chemists, it is one system of many and not a common one in the legal context. A drug can also be classified by origin (i.e., by how it was obtained). This classification system includes the categories **natural product, semisynthetic**, and **synthetic**. **Alkaloids**, for example, are extracted from seed plants and are natural products. Because these compounds are basic, they have an alkaline character, leading to the name. A large number of drugs are alkaloids, including the opiate alkaloids (derived from the opium poppy) and compounds such as caffeine. Other plant-derived drugs include cocaine, aspirin, opiates, and tetrahydrocannibinols (active ingredients of marijuana.) Heroin is a semisynthetic compound that is made by the acetylation of morphine. Hormones and steroids are obtained from or synthesized by animals, humans, or genetically engineered bacteria and are also semisynthetic. Compounds like diazepam (Valium®) are synthetic. Details of the chemical structure and chemistry of these and many other drugs will be presented in the next two chapters.

Compounds that once were obtained only from plant matter, such as Δ^9-tetrahydrocannabinol (THC), can now be synthesized. **Dronabinol** is synthetic THC and the active ingredient in Marinol®. As a result of the new ability to synthesize drugs, classifying drugs by origin has become problematic.

6.2.2 BY GENERAL EFFECT

In addition to classifying drugs by their acid–base character, forensic chemists often categorize drugs on the basis of the physiological consequences of ingesting them. This scheme leads to five groups: analgesics, depressants, hallucinogens, narcotics, and stimulants. Note that drugs may fall into more than one category; for example, narcotic drugs are also CNS depressants.

Analgesics: These are drugs that relieve pain. Among the common analgesics are aspirin, ibuprofen, naproxen sodium, and morphine. Aspirin and related drugs

---

Exhibit B: Aspirin

The history of aspirin (acetylsalicylic acid) is typical of that of many other drugs and starts with folk knowledge. As early as 400 B.C., the Greek physician Hippocrates recommended that his patients chew on willow bark when they had a fever or pain. It is likely that the use of aspirin-based folk remedies predates even this ancient practice, perhaps by centuries. It took nearly two thousand years for chemists to enter into the story and synthesize the active ingredient of aspirin. By the 1800s, salicylic acid, closely related to acetylsalicylic acid and also found in willow bark, was available. The drug often produced stomach pains, a side effect also associated with aspirin. A German chemist, Felix Hoffman, is generally credited with the first synthesis of acetylsalicylic acid. Hoffman performed his work at a company with a familiar name: Bayer. This company, the name of which has become synonymous with aspirin, was not active in pharmaceuticals until the 1890s. Many of the firm's early drugs were actually byproducts of making dyes, a complex chemical process and not far removed from drug synthesis. Aspirin hit the market in 1899, and by 1915 it was available over the counter. Still, it wasn't until the 1970s that scientists unraveled the mechanism of the drug. Although aspirin was originally sold as an analgesic, by 2003 most people taking aspirin did so to lower their likelihood of suffering a heart attack or for related reasons, not to relieve pain.

Aspirin
Acetylsalicylic acid   ◀ *Structure of aspirin, acetylsalicylic acid*

are nonsteroidal anti-inflammatory drugs (NSAIDs), which stop pain by reducing fever and inflammation. This is accomplished by blocking the function of prostaglandins, fatty acid derivatives found associated with cell membranes. Prostaglandins affect many processes, including inflammation. The NSAID drugs prevent the synthesis of prostaglandins, thereby reducing inflammation and the pain associated with it. Aspirin also inhibits pyrogens, which play a role in the fever response. Specifically, pyrogens ("fire starters") are released by white blood cells in response to injury or infection. Pyrogens act on the hypothalamus and stimulate both the release of prostaglandins and heat-producing processes in the body. This physiological cycle describes the mechanism of action of aspirin.

Morphine and other opiates reduce pain by a different mechanism. Although the complete mechanism is not fully understood, morphine appears to reduce pain by attaching to sites called opiod receptors scattered throughout the **central nervous system** (CNS) and also in the gastrointestinal tract. By binding to sites in the CNS, opiates such as morphine block the transmission of nerve impulses that relay the sensation of pain to the brain. Because morphine can bind to multiple sites, the side effects of pain relief include sleepiness and a sense of well-being. Morphine also interacts with the sites in the brain associated with pleasurable sensations—sites that are activated by endorphins found in the brain. (Interestingly, the term "endorphin" means "endogenous morphine.") As a result of its mimicry of endorphins, morphine can produce pleasurable sensations and euphoria.

To summarize and simplify, aspirin reduces pain by inhibiting the pain-inducing event, whereas morphine intercepts the pain signal after it is produced (Figure 6.2). The different mechanisms help explain why morphine is addictive and aspirin is not. Aspirin stops inflammation and pain, but it does not produce euphoria

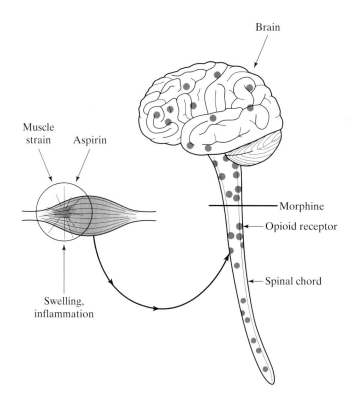

▶ **Figure 6.2** *Both aspirin and morphine treat pain, but they stop it by two different mechanisms. Aspirin attacks the cause of the pain, while morphine blocks the nerve impulse that signals pain.*

▲ **Figure 1.** *A sink in which blood evidence was disposed of. Note the reddish material in the lower right corner.*

▲ **Figure 3** *A solution of Δ^9-THC to which a few drops of the Duquenois color test reagent has been added.*

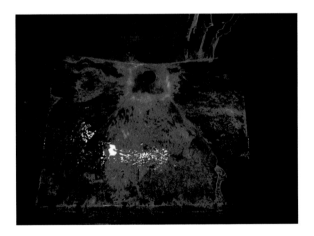

▲ **Figure 2** *The same sink treated with luminol, a presumptive test reagent for blood. Interestingly, the material that appears as blood to the eye is not. Luminol reacts with hemoglobin and produces chemoluminescence rather than a color change. These two photos courtesy of Amy Richmond, WVU.*

▲ **Figure 4** *The full Duquenois-Levine color test. Note the purple compound that has extracted into the lower chloroform layer.*

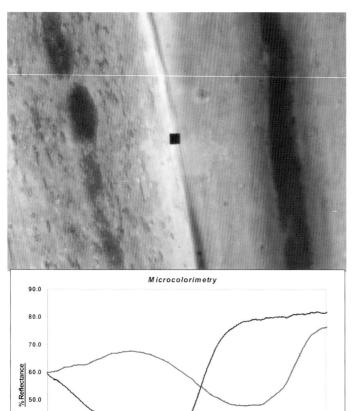

▲ **Figure 6** *An example of intaglio printing in which there is depth and texture in the surface of the currency shown here. This photo courtesy of Amy Richmond, WVU Department of Chemistry.*

▲ **Figure 5** *Two fibers viewed side-by-side under a UV/VIS microspectrophotometer. The spectra for each in the visible range are shown below. The small box in the upper frame is the aperture of the microspectrophotometer.*

▲ **Figure 7** *The color version of Figure 9.31 in which the smoke plume and burning propellant grains are visible. Image courtesy of Aaron Brudenell, Firearms Examiner, Tucson Police Department Crime Laboratory.*

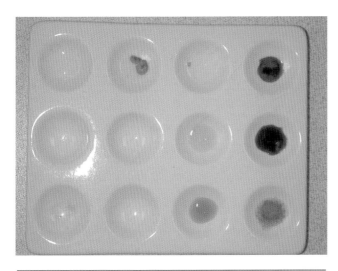

▲ **Figure 8** *Examples of presumptive color tests for drugs. The pink reagent is cobalt thiocyanate and in the lower right is this reagent combined with cocaine. Note the shiny solid that forms, an ion/pair complex. The upper tier of tests consist of the Marquis reagent added to methamphetamine (right) and amphetamine (left). The middle well in the right column contains oxycodone and Marquis reagent.*

▲ **Figure 9** *The clandestine synthesis of methamphetamine using the Birch method (Chapter 8) yields solvated electrons and a deep blue color. Here this color is evident along the stirbar and in the tope of the beaker. Image courtesy of Aaron Brudenell, Firearms Examiner, Tucson Police Department Crime Laboratory.*

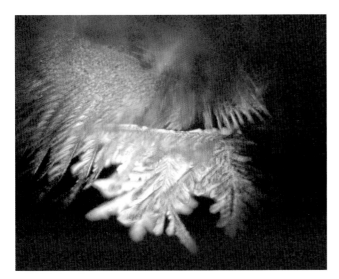

▲ **Figure 10** *An example of a microcrystal test for drugs; here produced by cocaine and gold chloride in an agar matrix. The image was taken under polarized light and interference colors are visible in the blades. This photo courtesy of Rebecca Hanes, WVU Department of Chemistry.*

▲ **Figure 11** *A second type of drug crystal showing a serrated blade appearance under polarized light. This photo courtesy of Rebecca Hanes, WVU Department of Chemistry.*

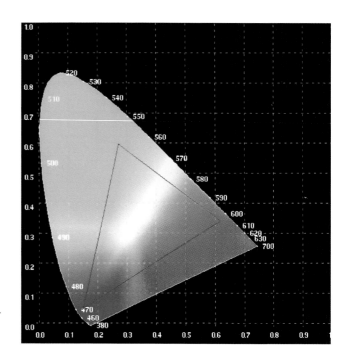

▶ **Figure 12** *A plot of the chromaticity parabola showing locations of colors.*

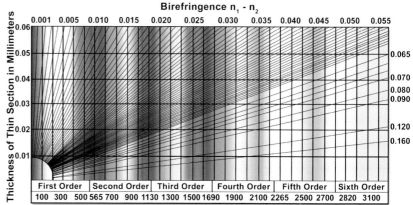

▶ **Figure 13** *The Michel-Levy chart used in polarized light microscopy.*

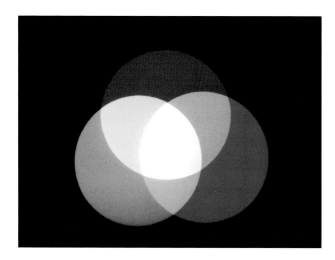

▲ **Figure 14** *Additive colors. Where all three colors combine, white is perceived. This is also called the RGB system.*

▲ **Figure 15** *Subtractive colors where the combination of all three produced black. This is also called the CMY system or CMYK system.*

along with the pain reduction. Conversely, morphine can cause feelings of deep relaxation and euphoria as a side effect of pain relief. The side effects of morphine create more potential for abuse and lead it to be classified also as a **narcotic**.

Depressants: These are a class of drugs that depress functions of the CNS generally, resulting in a slowed heartbeat, a reduction in anxiety, and, in some cases, the promotion of sleep. Barbiturates, tranquilizers, sleep aids, and ethanol are depressants. The benzodiazepine family of synthetic drugs, introduced in the 1960s, has become one of the largest classes of prescribed drugs and includes familiar brand names such as Valium®. As a mechanistic example, this group of drugs works by interacting with gamma amino butyric acid (GABA) receptors in the brain.[1] The GABA receptors are the most common inhibitory neurotransmitter in the brain and central nervous system; the benzodiazepines are able to bind with GABA receptor sites and generate the inhibitory response, resulting in depression of the CNS.

Hallucinogens: These are drugs that alter the perception of time and reality, a difficult effect to quantify. Movement, thought, perceptions, vision, and hearing are also affected. LSD, mescaline, and marijuana are examples of hallucinogenic drugs. A number of stimulants, such as methamphetamine, are hallucinogens at high doses. The pharmacology of this class is complex and cannot easily be summarized,[2] but some generalizations can be made. There are two classes of hallucinogens: those based on the phenethylamine molecular skeleton and those based on tryptamines. Hallucinogens create their effect by interacting with receptors in these two neurotransmitter systems, but the delineation is not as clean as the structures suggest.[2] Methamphetamine and ecstasy (MDMA, related to amphetamine) are phenethylamines, while psilocybin, derived from psilocybin mushrooms, is a tryptamine.

Table 6.1 Hallucinogens

Molecular Basis	Example Drug	Neurotransmitter

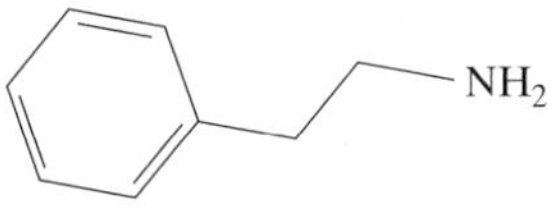

Phenethylamine — MDMA (ecstasy) — Dopamine

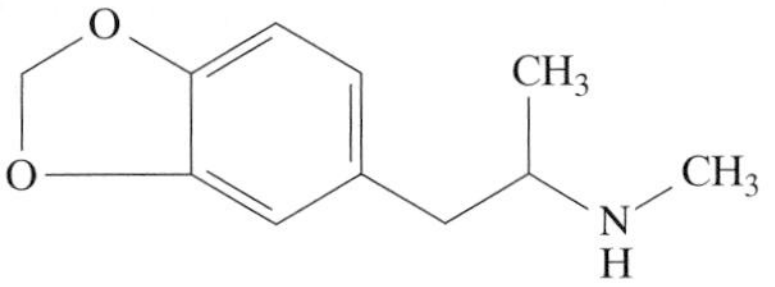

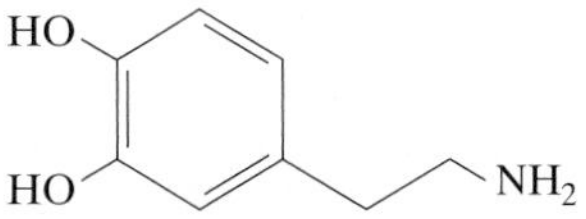

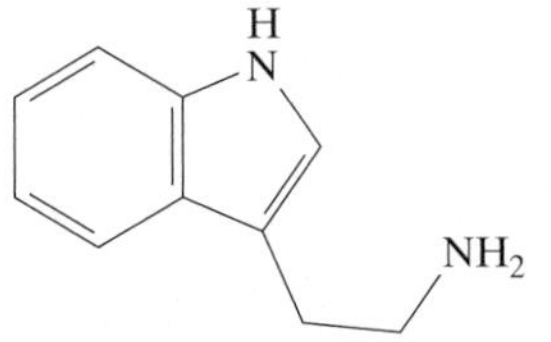

Tryptamine — Psilocybin — Seratonin

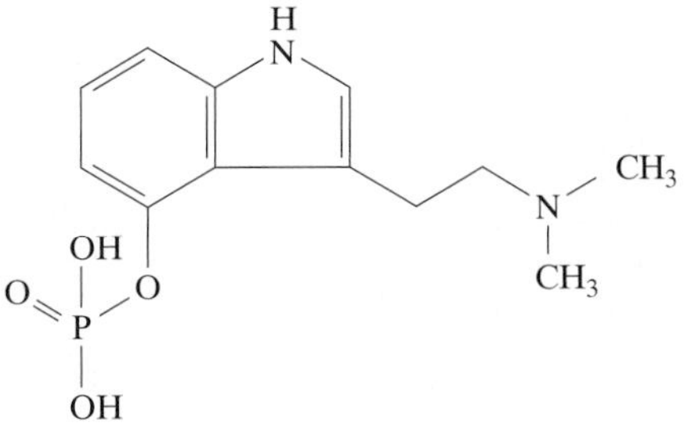

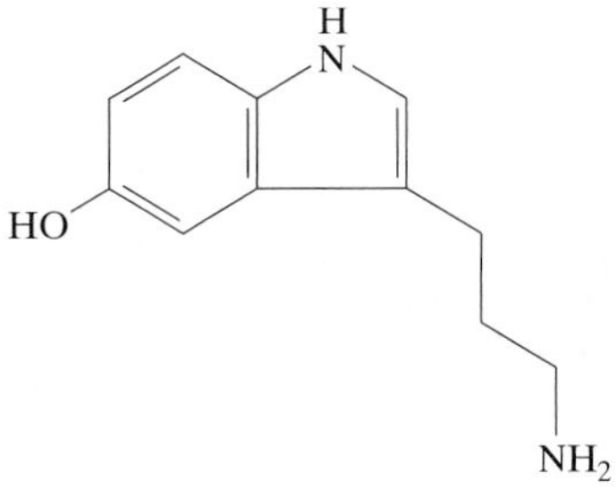

Applying the Science 6.1 Toolmarks in Drug Analysis

When commercial tablets are made, they are often marked by a machine called a *tablet press*, which incorporates a die that presses letters, symbols, or logos into the tablet's surface. As a consequence, toolmarks are created by the die in the surface of the tablet. Illicit chemists often use tablet presses to accomplish the same thing, especially with tablets of MDMA (ecstasy).

In some cases, these toolmarks can be useful in profiling counterfeit preparations. In a recent paper, researchers used near-infrared spectroscopy to evaluate commercial tablets that

▶ *A clandestinely produced ecstasy tablet. The butterfly pattern was likely created with a tablet press as described here.. Image courtesy of Aaron Brudenell, Tucson Police Department Laboratory.*

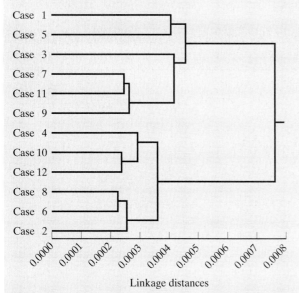

contained caffeine. The study also employed statistical and cluster analysis to group the data. The spectra taken from the front of the tablet (the compressed face) were distinguishable from those taken from the opposite face. To address this discrepancy, the authors averaged the two spectra to create a representative near-infrared spectrum for each tablet.

Sources: 1. Geradts, Z., and J. Bijhold. "Content Based Information Retrieval in Forensic Image Databases." *Journal of Forensic Sciences*, 47 **2002**, 285–292.

2. Laasonen, M., et al. "Development and Validation of a Near-Infrared Method for the Quantitation of Caffeine in Intact Single Tablets." *Analytical Chemistry*, 75 **2004**, 754–760.

▲ *Dendrogram for the hierarchical analysis of second-derivative spectra of t he front (case with odd numbers) and back face (case with even numbers) of a 58.82% caffeine tablet. Reprinted with permission from source 2, copyright 2004 American Chemical Society.*

Narcotics: Narcotic drugs have analgesic effects and tend to depress the CNS and promote sleep. Opiate alkaloids (drugs derived from the opium plant) are the best-known narcotics and include morphine, codeine, heroin, hydromorphone, oxycodone, and hydrocodone.

Stimulants: In contrast to narcotics and depressants, this group of drugs stimulates functions of the CNS, induces alertness, and interferes with sleep. Common stimulants include cocaine, amphetamine, and methamphetamine. At high doses, many stimulants are hallucinogenic. The mechanisms of action within the class vary widely. Cocaine, for example, can block the absorption (called reuptake) of dopamine, serotonin, and norepinephrine, leading to generalized stimulation and potential hallucinogenic responses.[3]

6.2.3 BY USE

Some drugs are grouped together on the basis of how they are used and how they are abused. Within a group, the chemical structures are typically similar, as are the physiological effects. Most of these substances will be discussed individually later. Four examples of classes based on use and abuse are predator drugs, club drugs, human-performance drugs, and inhalants.

Predator Drugs: Also known as date-rape drugs and drug-facilitated sexual assault (**DFSA**) agents, these substances are used to incapacitate a woman for sexual purposes. Current date-rape drugs, aside from alcohol, are ketamine, Rohypnol® (flunitrazepam), and gamma hydroxybutyrate (GHB) and related compounds. When the drug is mixed in a drink, the effects can range from disorientation to unconsciousness and loss of short-term memory. Victims may awaken several hours after an assault with no memory of the event or the few hours leading up to it. Consequently, they may delay seeking treatment until the drug and metabolites are no longer detectable by traditional toxicological methods.

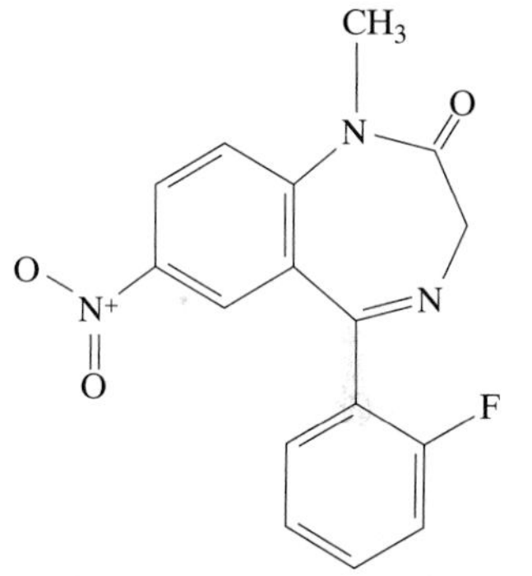

▲ **Figure 6.3** *The structure of Rohypnol®.*

Club Drugs: These are drugs used at parties and clubs frequented by young people;[4] many are also predator drugs. In addition to the compounds listed as predator drugs, ecstasy (MDMA) is a club drug. Other hallucinogens, such as LSD and psilocin mushrooms, are sometimes included, as are the stimulant–hallucinogens phencyclidine (PCP) and methamphetamine. One apparent reason for their popularity is the misconception that the club drugs are less dangerous than drugs such as cocaine and heroin.[4]

Human-Performance Drugs: These drugs consist of substances that improve or impair one's performance, most notably anabolic steroids and alcohol. Anabolic steroids include dozens of drugs, mostly acquired by prescription, based on **testosterone**. These drugs are abused by athletes in attempts to increase their muscle mass and decrease the recovery time after strenuous training and competition. Abuse has been found at the high school level.

Inhalants: Unlike the other groups of drugs listed in this section, inhalants are substances that are inhaled to produce their desired effects. Most inhalants are not intended to be used as drugs. Examples of inhalants are paint thinners, nitrous oxide (laughing gas), gasoline, cleaners, and nail polish. Any substance that has a volatile component can be used as an inhalant, and in general, these substances have depressant effects similar to those of alcohol.

Exhibit C: Toxicological Samples from Athletes

Sample analysis for banned substances in athletes is similar to forensic analysis for controlled substances. Urine is the primary matrix, but blood may also be collected. The National Collegiate Athletic Association (NCAA) stipulates how urine is to be collected and maintains a list of banned substances for college athletes. Not all of these substances are illegal.

The procedure for collecting urine starts when the athlete arrives at a collection station, where he or she selects a beaker. The athlete must deliver 85 mL of urine while being watched by a crew chief; until that volume is obtained, the athlete stays at the collection station. If a single urination event fails to deliver the needed volume, the athlete can be given approved beverages only from sealed containers. The urine collected must have a pH between 4.5 and 7.5 and a specific gravity of above 1.005; a lower value suggests the possibility of dilution. Once the urine sample meets these requirements, it is divided into two containers, with approximately 60 mL in "A" and the balance in "B." Both the crew chief and the athlete witness all steps, including the creation of the chain-of-custody forms.

Note that drugs can be classified under multiple systems. Rohypnol® (flunitrazepam, Figure 6.3), for example, is a basic drug, a benzodiazepine, synthetic, a depressant, and a predator drug. It is also a federally controlled Schedule IV drug, a categorization based on legislative, rather than chemical or physiological, characteristics, the topic of the next section.

6.2.4 CLASSIFICATION BY SCHEDULE: THE CONTROLLED SUBSTANCES ACT AND LISTED CHEMICALS

For the forensic chemist, the legal categorization of a drug is nearly as important as the chemical and physiological one. The term "drugs of abuse" applies to drugs and related compounds that are subject to regulations and laws because of their potential to be abused and to cause harm. Abused drugs are usually addictive, causing physiological dependence, psychological dependence, or both. Physical addiction is traceable to a biochemical or physiological change caused by repeated use of the substance. In the case of morphine, for instance, repeated regular use can lead to a decrease in the number of active opioid receptors in the brain and CNS. Since fewer receptors are active, the user can't simply stop taking the drug without feeling symptoms of withdrawal. Ever-increasing doses are needed to elicit the desired effect, a phenomenon referred to as tolerance, which accompanies physical addiction. Psychological dependence does not have a direct physiological cause, but rather is rooted in emotional needs and responses.

In the United States, drugs are federally regulated under the **Controlled Substances Act**, passed in 1970. The act divides drugs into categories called "Schedules" on the basis of their medical uses and potential for abuse. For violations, the act specifies criminal penalties ranging from 0 to 20 years in prison and $1,000,000 in fines for the first offense (Schedule I) down to a maximum of 1 year

Historical Evidence 6.2—The Government Steps In

In the United States, the first "recreational" drugs were the opiates, such as morphine and opium, introduced by Chinese immigrants in the mid-1800s. San Francisco was the first city to pass a law regulating drugs, in 1875. The first federal law regarding drugs was the Pure Food and Drug Act of 1906, which required labeling on patent medicines. The first federal agency with a responsibility for drug control, the Bureau of Revenue, was formed in 1915. This organization was a precursor to the Drug Enforcement Administration (DEA).

	Table 6.2	**Controlled Substances and the Controlled Substances Act**				
Schedule	**Medical Use**	**Controls on Prescriptions**	**Required Security**	**Potential for Abuse**	**Addiction Potential**	**Examples**
I	None accepted	None; used only for research	Vault or safe	Highest	Severe	LSD, heroin, MDMA (ecstasy), marijuana, GHB
II	Some accepted uses with restrictions	Written prescription with no refills	Vault or safe		Severe	Morphine and many related opiates, cocaine, amphetamine and methamphetamine, most barbiturates, oxycodone
III	Accepted uses	Written or oral (phone in), limits on refills and time	Secured area		Moderate to low	Ketamine, anabolic steroids, some codeine preparations
IV	Accepted uses	Written or oral (phone in), limits on refills and time	Secured area		Limited	Benzodiazepines such as valium, mild sleep aids
V	Accepted uses	Over the counter, written, or oral (phone in), limits on refills and time	Secured area	Lowest	Limited	Selected preparations of codeine

Source: United States Drug Enforcement Administration, http://www.dea.gov/pubs/csa.html and http://www.dea.gov/pubs/scheduling.html. Accessed March 13, 2004. Appendix 10 contains a list of most controlled substances and listed chemicals.

and $100,000 for a first offense involving a Schedule V substance. The federal **Anti-Drug Abuse Act** of 1986 expanded the list to include "designer drugs," synthetically produced analogs of controlled substances. A list of controlled substances (as of May 2004) is provided in Appendix 10.

While substances such as cocaine and heroin require extensive extraction and chemical processing before they are ingested, drugs such as PCP, GHB, and methamphetamine are relatively simple to make, requiring little more than basic chemistry skills and access to the Internet. An effective tool for minimizing illicit production is to limit access to the precursors. Accordingly, the Controlled Substances Act has been modified to include many of the key precursor chemicals needed for making methamphetamine and other clandestinely produced drugs, such as the hallucinogen PCP. Rather than list all precursors as controlled substances, the **Chemical Diversion and Trafficking Act (CDTA)** was passed in 1988 and amended in 1993. This legislation created two lists of regulated chemicals that are controlled to deter diversions of these compounds for clandestine synthesis. (The lists are also found in an appendix). Notable among the chemicals on List I are "ephedrine, its salts, optical isomers, and salts of optical isomers," as well as "phenylpropanolamine, its salts, optical isomers, and salts of optical isomers." All of these precursor substances used in the synthesis of amphetamine and methamphetamine. Note the inclusion of "all salts and isomers," typical wording in the regulations. Compounds such as iodine, sulfuric acid, and diethyl ether are on List II. These are necessary ingredients for many clandestine drug syntheses, but have legitimate uses. The federal **Methamphetamine Anti-Proliferation Act** (MAPA) of 2000 placed limitations on the availability of pseudoephedrine and phenylpropanolamine (PPA) in over-the-counter medication; PPA was withdrawn from the market by an unrelated FDA action in 2000. As of mid-2005, efforts were underway nationwide to limit access to pseudoephedrine.

6.3 DRUGS AS EVIDENCE

6.3.1 PHYSICAL EVIDENCE: THE FIVE P'S

The analysis of materials suspected to be or to contain controlled substances represents the largest portion of the workload in most forensic laboratories. When suspected controlled substances are submitted as physical evidence (**exhibits**), the forensic chemist must identify and, in some cases, quantify the controlled substances present. The most common forms of drug evidence seen can be summarized as the "**five P's**": *p*owders, *p*lant matter, *p*ills, *p*recursors, and *p*araphernalia. **Powders** include colored powders from crystalline white to resinous brown, and many, such as heroin and cocaine, are derived directly or indirectly from plants. Many powders are oily and odiferous, while some can be described (unofficially and informally) as goo. Hashish, a concentrated form of marijuana, lies between plant and powder. Typical **plant matter** exhibits are marijuana, mushrooms, and cactus buttons. As biological evidence, plant matter must be stored properly to prevent rotting and degradation prior to analysis; failure to do so can generate the aforementioned goo.

Exhibit D: GPLM

Like any discipline, forensic chemistry has unique acronyms and conventions. GPLM—"green plantlike material"–is a generic description of evidence suspected to be marijuana. A laboratory report might state something like "Exhibit 1: One small plastic bag containing green plantlike material. Laboratory analysis showed the presence of marijuana with a weight of 0.87 ounce." Another shorthand term is GVM (green vegetable material). Solids ranging in consistency from resinous goo to bricks are often described as "amorphous solids."

Pills, such as prescription medications or clandestinely synthesized tablets, are common forms of physical evidence. In cases where the evidence is or appears to be commercially manufactured (over the counter or prescription) drugs, tentative identifications can be made visually, using references such as the *Physicians' Desk Reference* (**PDR**).[5,6] In other cases, the pills may have different markings, such as crosses or other imprints. Amphetamines, methamphetamine, and LSD are often sold in pill form, although typically the pills are cruder than those produced commercially.

Precursors are compounds or materials used in the clandestine synthesis of drugs such as methamphetamine. Some precursors are controlled and listed on Schedules while others are not. For example, 1-phenylcyclohexylamine (PC) and 1-piperidinocyclohexanecarbonitrile (PCC) are listed on Schedule II, as are precursors used in the synthesis of PCP. (PCP is listed on Schedule II as well.) Illicit methamphetamine was once predominantly made starting from phenyl acetone (phenyl-2-propanone, or P2P), now listed on Schedule II. Methamphetamine is now usually made starting from pseudoephedrine, an ingredient in over-the-counter cold and allergy remedies. Lysergic acid and lysergic amide, precursors of LSD, are listed on Schedule III. Other precursors are not necessarily controlled, but must still be identified as part of investigations of clandestine synthesis. **Immediate precursors** are those requiring only one or two simple steps to convert to the controlled substance; **distant precursors** require additional steps.

Drug **paraphernalia** are the implements and equipment used in the preparation and ingestion of drugs. Typical items include syringes (a significant biohazard to the analyst) and cookers used to prepare heroin and other drugs; pipes and bongs (water-filled vessels used in smoking marijuana); and razor blades, mirrors, and straws, used for snorting cocaine. Such items present both a sampling challenge and an analytical challenge, since only traces of material may remain. Typically, the items are rinsed with a solvent to extract the residues. While effective, this is a destructive step that significantly alters the evidence. If this step is unavoidable, the analyst should adhere to any laboratory or legal requirements regarding the preservation of extracts.

Of the five P's, the cases most frequently submitted are those in which the exhibits are plant matter suspected of being or containing marijuana. Methamphetamine, cocaine, and heroin round out the "top four," although the mix and numbers vary across regions and states.[7] Over the past ten years, there

▶ **Figure 6.4** *A roach clip, used to hold a marijuana cigarette. Image courtesy of the Oklahoma State Bureau of Investigation.*

◀ **Figure 6.5** *A lightbulb modified as a crank bulb, used to smoke methamphetamine. Image courtesy of the Oklahoma State Bureau of Investigation.*

has been increasing concern over predator drugs, methamphetamine, and MDMA (ecstasy or XTC), while cocaine and heroin abuse appear to have leveled off. Different states and regions deal with differing problems, however. States such as Hawaii and West Virginia are hot spots of marijuana production, Washington state grapples with over a thousand clandestine methamphetamine laboratories, and border states north and south struggle to stem the flow of smuggled drugs.[7]

Forensic chemists also are called upon to analyze other types of evidence that is not easily categorized. For example, phencyclidine is a controlled substance that is often seized in liquid form, usually a greenish-colored solution with an overwhelming smell. Other unusual exhibits might include spray cans, bags, or rags soaked with inhalants. Apples, candy bars, and fruit are often submitted soon after Halloween.

▲ **Figure 6.6** *A pipe made from a bottle cap. Image courtesy of the Oklahoma State Bureau of Investigation.*

6.3.2 Cutting Agents

In addition to identifying and quantitating a target drug, drug chemists often must identify **cutting agents** (also called **diluents**) added to many drug exhibits. A similar term, **excipients**, is used in a similar vein, referring to inactive ingredients in commercial preparations. Cutting agents are used to stretch the supply of a controlled substance and maximize profits. Cutting agents are chosen on the basis of their physical and chemical similarity to the controlled substance. Cocoa powder can be used to cut powders that have a tan or brown appearance, while cornstarch (Fig. 6.7) has a dry, powdery appearance that is ideal for cutting drugs with a similar morphology.

The taste of a cutting agent is a crude measure of its chemical similarity to a target drug. For example, heroin, which is an alkaloid, has a bitter taste that is mimicked by the cutting agent quinine. Similarly, cocaine is a topical anesthetic that is used in eye surgery, so it should be no surprise that cocaine is often cut with local anesthetics such as procaine, lidocaine, or tetracaine. Other common cutting agents include sugars, such as mannitol, inositol, and sucrose (table sugar); baking soda; and caffeine. The identification of diluents is an important part of drug profiling, a topic to be introduced shortly.

The convention we will use to categorize cutting agents is one seen in the literature.[8,9] Diluents (**thinners**) are substances that are not drugs and that have no pharmacological properties. Baking soda and sugars fall into this category. **Adulterants** are active and typically (but not always) have effects that are grossly similar to the target drug's effects. Caffeine added to cocaine is an example in which both the drug and the adulterant are stimulants.

In forensic toxicology, the term "adulterant" has a different meaning. An adulterant is something added to a urine sample to mask or otherwise defeat the detection of another substance. Bleach is a common adulterant that will cause many screening tests to fail. As a result, it is sometimes necessary to test a sample for the presence of adulterants as well as for the presence of target analytes.

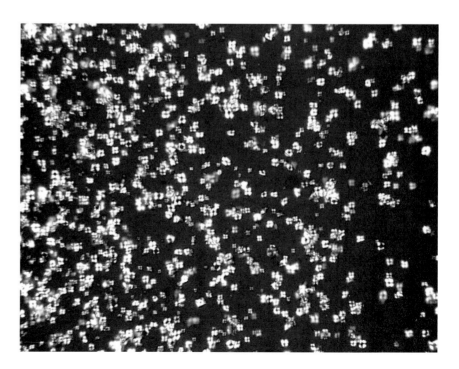

▶ **Figure 6.7** *Grains of cornstarch viewed under polarized light, showing the distinctive cross pattern. Starches such as cornstarch are common diluents—pharmacologically inactive fillers.*

Impurities are materials found with the drug (if it is a natural product) or added to it inadvertently during processing. Cocaine and heroin are drugs that originate from plant matter and thus are usually accompanied by a number of impurities. Codeine, for example, is found in the opium poppy and is frequently an impurity in heroin. Contaminants, a subcategory of impurities, are substances that find their way into the sample by accident. If heroin is extracted with the use of lime $(Ca(OH)_2)$ contaminated with barium, the barium that ends up in the heroin is a contaminant that originated as a contaminant in the lime.

6.3.3 PROFILING

Informally referred to as "chemical fingerprinting," profiling a drug sample involves analyzing the sample's composition beyond simple identification and quantitation of the controlled substance(s) present. Profiling data is used to categorize drug samples into similar groups to provide investigative information, such as learning that the samples have a common origin.[†] Additional goals of profiling can include any or all of the following:

- Elucidation of the synthetic pathway or extraction method used
- Identification of diluents, adulterants, and impurities
- Identification of the drug's geographic origin for plant-derived exhibits

The road from the fields or the clandestine laboratory to the street and to the forensic laboratory has many steps, each of which can add its own distinct variations to the sample batch. Figure 6.8 provides an example based on a common heroin preparation method called the lime method.[10] This procedure begins with a nonselective hot-water extraction of the opium poppy.[‡] Calcium hydroxide (the lime) is added and the material is heated and filtered. Already the sample contains characteristics of the batch of opium poppies, as well as residuals from the water and the lime used. The filtrate is brought to a boil and ammonium chloride is added. The morphine base is captured as the solid while the filtrate is discarded. To convert morphine to heroin (diacetylmorphine), the morphine base and other constituents associated with it are treated with acetic anhydride and heated, after which carbonate is added to produce the basic form of heroin. Acetone is added to the solid and the solution is acidified, precipitating the hydrochloride salt of heroin. The solid is then subjected to further processing, such as grinding or bleaching, and is diluted with adulterants, diluents, or both. Each step introduces components into the product that reflect the process and reagents used and that can be considered characteristic of that batch. Once the batch is broken, additional changes and contamination can occur, but some characteristics will remain consistent. Many of the added constituents are at the trace level, making profiling more complicated. Even so, profiling is finding increasing use as an investigatory tool.[10–12]

[†]In drug analysis, profiling a drug and identifying its source does not individualize evidence or identify a common source in the same sense as DNA and fingerprints may. Rather, finding a common source might indicate that several samples came from the same processing laboratory.

[‡]A detailed discussion of heroin and the opiate alkaloids, including their extraction, preparation, synthesis, and chemistry, is presented in Chapter 8.

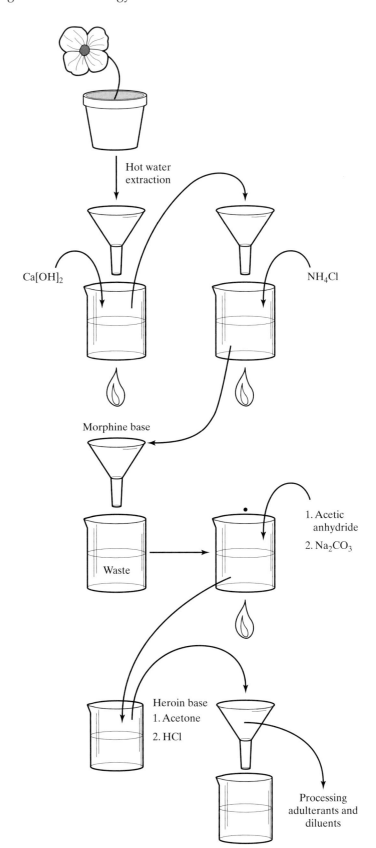

▶ **Figure 6.8** *Simplified depiction of one common method of preparing heroin from opium. The morphine base filtered out in the second step will contain many related alkaloids, which can be partially or fully acetylated along with the morphine. Each step in the process contributes constituents that can be useful in profiling and linking a sample to a batch.*

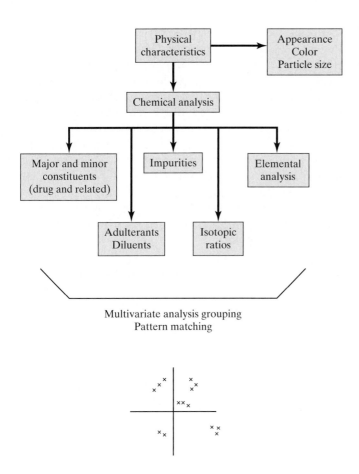

◀ **Figure 6.9** *Aspects of profiling a drug sample. Not all profiling involves all of the steps shown; for example, elemental analysis is infrequently used, while analysis of adulterants and diluents may be incorporated into a laboratory's standard protocol. Pattern matching and chemometrics can be used to identify groups or clusters of like samples.*

Overview: Profiling a drug sample (Figure 6.9) includes physical examination and organic and inorganic analysis. Continuing with the heroin example, the first step is often an examination of the color and appearance of the sample (sparkling powder vs. oily appearance), and a microscopic characterization of diluents such as starches or sugars. Analysis of particle sizes has been employed as part of physical characterization as well.[13] Organic analysis of major and minor constituents reveals information about the drug and also the chemical methods used to process and prepare it. With heroin and other plant-based drugs, **isotopic ratios** (ratios of stable natural isotopes in plant tissues—also called **stable isotope ratios**) can be related to the environmental conditions prevailing at the time and location when and where the poppies were cultivated. Plants draw nutrients such as nitrogen from the soil, along with calcium, magnesium, and other elements, so relative amounts of these elements can be informative. Finally, when all the data from the various characterizations are pooled, statistical grouping and categorization methods such as those described in Chapter 3 can be employed for data analysis. Often, the most useful variables in grouping arise from the organic analysis and the stable isotope ratios.

Stable Isotope Ratios: Measurements of stable isotope ratios (stable because their ratio in nature is relatively constant) have long been used in ecological, hydrological, geochemical, and botanical research. Variations of those ratios (compared with a standard) can provide useful information. Such variations arise from biological (biotic) or abiotic processes referred to as fractionation. Given that isotopes are chemically identical, fractionation is based on differences in behavior that can be traced to differences in mass. For example, ^{18}O is a stable isotope that constitutes approximately 0.2%, on average, of any sample of oxygen. If ^{18}O is incorporated into a water molecule, that water will be slightly heavier than a molecule containing the more common ^{16}O isotope. In the form of a liquid, the heavier water will require slightly more energy to be transported into the gaseous state in the form of water vapor. Similarly, precipitation favors heavier isotopes over lighter ones. These are examples of abiotic fractionation processes which have much in common with partitioning. Biotic processes also lead to fractionation, although the basis of this fractionation remains physical and not chemical. For example, when water evaporates from the surface of a leaf, water molecules incorporating lighter isotopes will evaporate preferentially to molecules containing heavier isotopes, so the leaf becomes enriched in the heavier isotopes. Similar cycles and interactions can be identified for nitrogen, a key nutrient for plants.

The isotopic ratios within a plant are the result of numerous and complex fractionation processes that are unique to a region and that depend on that region's climate, temperature, precipitation, elevation, soil, and so on, including the season. For plant-derived drugs, isotopic ratio analysis can provide information on the geographical region of origin, but with some caveats. First, to link the isotopic signature of a plant to a region, trustworthy samples from that region which adequately represent the expected values and uncertainties are essential. Second, seasonal variations in rainfall, as well as other climatic factors, must be accounted for. Finally, each step in processing (see Figure 5.6) can influence the ratios, complicating the interpretation of the information obtained.

Results of ratio analysis are reported in delta notation ($\delta‰$), which relates the experimentally derived ratio of the isotopes to that of a reference material. The relevant formula is

$$\delta‰ = \left(\frac{R_s}{R_r} - 1 \right) \times 1000 \tag{6.1}$$

where R is the ratio of the number of atoms of ^{13}C in a sample to the number of ^{12}C atoms, r is the reference sample, s is the sample, and the symbol ‰ is per mill, analogous to the % notation.[†] Isotopes of elements other than carbon can be used, with the heavier of the two isotopes acting as the numerator. A negative $\delta‰$ indicates that the sample has a lower heavy–light ratio than the standard. The standards used include $CaCO_3$ from a deposit in North Carolina called Pee Dee belemnite (PDB carbon), and the atmosphere for nitrogen.[14,15] For PDB carbon, the value of $R_r = 0.0112372$, and most samples analyzed against this standard will have a negative $\delta‰$ value.[15]

Isotopic abundances can be determined with isotope ratio mass spectrometry (IRMS), an instrument described in Chapter 5. To analyze the stable isotope ratios of carbon and oxygen, the instrumental procedure incorporates a conversion of all organic carbon to CO_2, followed by the introduction of that compound into the mass spectrometer.[11] The fragments of interest have amu's of 44 ($^{12}C^{16}O_2$), 45 ($^{13}C^{16}O_2$ and $^{12}C^{17}O^{16}O$), and 46 ($^{12}C^{18}O^{16}O$, $^{13}C^{17}O^{16}O$, and $^{12}C^{17}O_2$).[11,16] Since both carbon and oxygen have stable isotopes, calculations to isolate the ratios of carbon isotopes ($^{13}C/^{12}C$) from the oxygen isotope ratios are complicated and involve ratios of the mass intensities detected at 44 and 45 amu, as well as the use of accepted constants and oxygen ratio values.[16,17] NIST maintains a

---

[†]One part per hundred is 1%; 1 part per million is 1‰.

Example Problem 6.1

A plant sample is analyzed by isotope ratio mass spectrometry (IRMS) and is found to have a δ‰ value of -21.3 relative to PDB for carbon. What is R_s for this plant sample?

Answer: Starting from equation 6-1, we substitute the known value to obtain

$$-21.3‰ = \left(\frac{R_s}{R_r} - 1 \right) \times 1000$$

For PDB, the value of R_s is given as 0.0112372. The foregoing expression then simplifies to

$$-0.0213 = \left(\frac{R_s}{0.0112372} - 1 \right)$$

$$0.9787 = \left(\frac{R_s}{0.0112372} \right)$$

so that

$$R_s = 0.0110$$

Web-based calculator at www.cstl.nist.gov/div837/837.01/outputs/ standards/algorithm/algorithm.html to assist investigators in performing these calculations.

Four isotopic ratios have been used in drug profiling:[11,18] $^{13}C/^{12}C$, $^2H/^1H$, $^{15}N/^{14}N$, and $^{18}O/^{16}O$, with the nitrogen and carbon ratios having garnered the most attention. In one study examining heroin and cocaine,[18] material obtained from four different regions could be distinguished. An example of profiling by isotope ratio is shown in Figure 6.10. Using caffeine, an extractable alkaloid, as an example, Table 6.3 gives an example of how such data can be combined.

Unquestionably, stable isotope ratio analysis is a powerful tool for classifying and grouping forensic samples. Some authors have gone further, referring to stable isotope ratio analysis as analogous to DNA typing.[15] For example, two white

Table 6.3   Stable Isotope Ratios and Caffeine

Caffeine	Origin	Region	^{13}C, δ‰[a]	^2H SMOW, δ‰[a]	^{18}O SMOW, δ‰[a]
	Laboratory stock	N.A.	-35.8 (0.2)	-237.1 (1.7)	13.0 (0.3)
	Coffee	Jamaica	-28.8 (0.6)	-132.5 (3.8)	9.6 (1.8)
		Kenya	-29.8 (0.6)	-136.5 (3.5)	3.6 (0.6)
		Brazil	-28.2 (0.2)	-157.3 (3.9)	4.9 (0.7)
	Tea	Sri Lanka	-31.7 (0.8)	-223.6 (2.8)	1.8 (0.02)
		Darjeeling	-29.6 (0.2)	-195.9 (2.5)	-4.3 (0.8)
		China	-32.4 (0.6)	-226.8 (4.1)	1.2 (0.3)

N.A. = not applicable. SMOW is an ocean water standard.
[a] Uncertainty in parentheses.
Adapted from Dunbar, J., and A. T. Wilson. "Determination of Geographic Origin of Caffeine by Stable Isotope Ratio Analysis." *Analytical Chemistry*, 54 **1982**, 590–592.

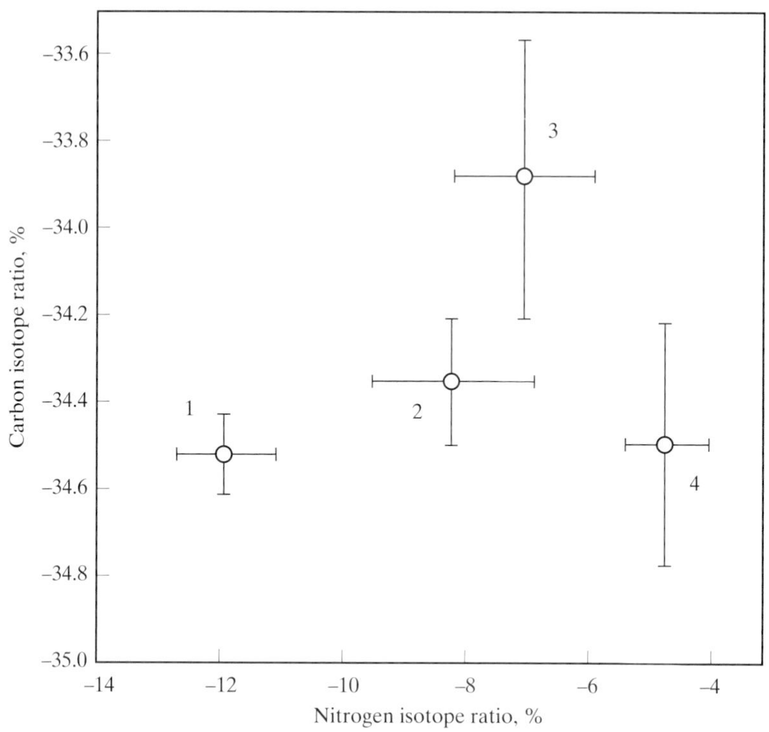

▶ **Figure 6.10** *Example of the use of isotope ratios for geographical profiling. A plot of the nitrogen-vs.-carbon ratios, with error bars included, clearly differentiates four groups.* Reproduced with permission from Ehleringer, J. R., et al. *"Geo-location of Heroin and Cocaine by Stable Isotope ratios."* Forensic Science International, *106* **1999**, *27–36.* Reproduced with permission, Elsevier Science, copyright 1999.

powders can both be identified as cocaine in the same sense that two red liquids can be identified as human blood. The role of stable isotope ratio analysis in this correlation would be to individualize a cocaine sample to a common source by using multiple isotopic ratios in the same way that DNA typing of multiple genetic loci can individualize a blood sample to one person.[†] While a great deal of work remains before this concept becomes reality, real DNA can be part of drug analysis. For example, marijuana DNA allows for the typing and grouping of samples as well as the definitive identification of the species, something that chemical tests cannot achieve.[19–21]

Coextracted Components: With plant-derived drugs, alkaloids are extracted along with the drug or its precursor. In the case of opium, morphine is the target compound and precursor to heroin, but other alkaloids are inevitably carried throughout processing. Codeine, thebaine, papaverine, noscapine, and other trace alkaloids will be extracted along with the morphine and will interact and react along with morphine as the process continues. These ratios of opium alkaloids and chemical derivatives are similar within a batch, but variable outside of that batch. In addition, because of the chemical similarity of the aforementioned compounds, analytical methods such as TLC, GCMS, or HPLC optimized for heroin or cocaine usually will also separate and identify those impurities. As a result, impurities can be analyzed simultaneously with the necessary evidentiary analysis.

Impurities: Each stage of processing introduces impurities into a batch, much as any laboratory analysis can be contaminated by impure reagents, dirty glassware, etc. Acids and bases can be contaminated with trace metals and ions, as can water.

[†]To a reasonable degree of scientific certainty.

Applying the Science 6.2   Stable Isotope Ratios and Wine Identification

Wine is derived from grapes and can be classified by stable isotope ratio analysis. In a 2004 report, researchers employed ^{13}C isotope enrichment values for glycerol and ethanol to categorize wines. Glycerol forms naturally during fermentation by the degradation of sugars from grapes. Fermentation also produces ethanol and CO_2. Four countries, two vintage years, and two wines (rosé and red) were characterized, and the δ‰ for ethanol was plotted against that of glycerol. Differences among countries are evident in the slopes and axis values of the plots. PDB was used as the reference standard.

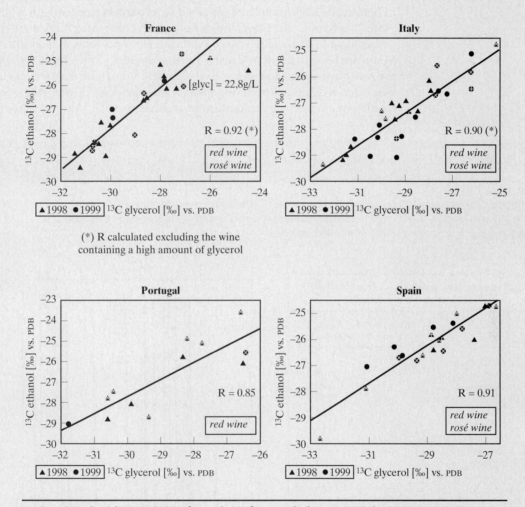

(*) R calculated excluding the wine containing a high amount of glycerol

▲ *Reprinted with permission from the reference below, copyright 2004 American Chemical Society.*

Source: Calderone, G., et al. "Characterization of European Wine Glygerol: Stable Carbon Isotope Approach." *Journal of Agricultural and Food Chemistry,* **2004**, Web Release August 28, 2004.

Solvents can carry organic contaminants or can be themselves contaminants. Residual solvents and any characteristic impurities contained within them can be occluded within the crystal matrix of the final salt product. The use of different solvents at different processing stages adds to residuals. Because residual solvents are likely to be found in higher concentrations than trace contaminants of reagents, they have become part of profiling methodologies.[22,23] Results from one study, summarized in Table 6.4, illustrate the potential usefulness of residual solvent techniques for categorizing and grouping substances. Except in unusual cases, testing for residual solvents requires a separate analysis, typically involving headspace methods and gas chromatography.

Adulterants and Diluents: Adulterants and diluents added to a batch can provide useful information regarding batches and groups. Common adulterants in heroin are acetaminophen (referred to as **paracetamol** outside of the United States), caffeine, and lidocaine, all of which chromatograph well and can be detected simultaneously with the heroin. Diluents tend to be highly variable. Many are hard to identify during routine analysis, since some are removed in the sample preparation steps. Even if a diluent can be isolated, its identification often requires more time than can be spared in routine cases. Sometimes a quick microscopic examination of residues is sufficient to identify starches

Applying the Science 6.3   Occluded Solvents and Impurities in Cocaine and Heroin Samples

A 1997 report in *Science and Justice: Journal of the Forensic Science Society* illustrates the value of organic characterization using GCMS. In this study, the authors employed a static headspace method to evaluate impurities and occluded solvents found in cocaine and heroin exhibits.

Solvent	Retention time (min)	Relative retention time
Formaldehyde	5.0	0.32
Acetaldehyde	7.0	0.45
Methanol	7.6	0.49
Ethanol	10.0	0.64
Acetone	11.6	0.74
Isopropanol	12.4	0.79
Diethylether	13.2	0.85
Dichloromethane	14.0	0.90
Methylacetate	14.2	0.91
Carbon disulphide	15.6	1.00
Methylethylketone	18.0	1.15
Ethylacetate	19.2	1.23
Hexane	19.4	1.24
Chloroform	19.6	1.26
2-butanol	20.2	1.29
Benzene	22.8	1.46
Methylisobutlketone	25.2	1.62
Toluene	28.4	1.82
M,p-xylene	33.0	2.12
O-xylene	34.2	2.19
N-decane	37.6	2.41
1, 2, 3-trimethylbenzene	39.0	2.50

Retention time data for the solvents detected and employed in this study.

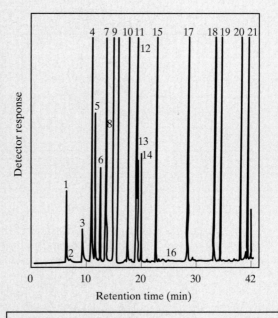

Figure 1 Chromatagram of solvent standards identified in cocaine and heroin samples in this study. Elution order: 1, acetaldehyde; 2, methanol; 3, ethanol; 4, acetone; 5, isopropanol; 6 diethylether; 7, dichlorolethane 8, methylacetate; 9, carbon disulphide; 10, methylethylketone; 11, ethylacetate; 12, hexane; 13, chloroform; 14, butanol; 15, benzene (from carbon disulphide); 16, methylisobutylketone; 17, toluene; 18, m& p-xylene; 19, o-oxylene; 20, m-decane (internal standard); 21, 1, 2, 3- trimethylbenzene.

Applying the Science 6.3   (Continued)

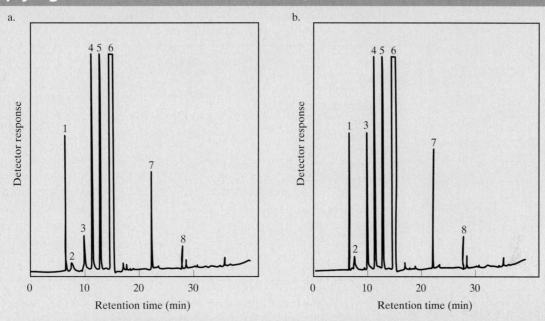

Figure 2 Occluded solvents identified in cocaine samples (a) 95/90.2; (b) 95/90.3 1: chloroform; 2: methanol; 3: ethanol; 4: acetone; 5: diethylether; 6: carbon disulphide; 7: benzene (from carbon disulphide); 8: m and p-xylene.

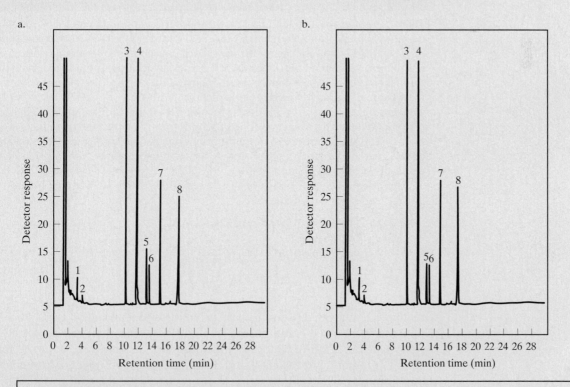

Figure 3 Impurities found in cocaine samples (a) 95/90.2; (b) 95/90.3.
1: ecogonine methyl ester-TMS; 2: ecogonine-TMS; 3: heneicosane (internal standard); 4: cocaine; 5: benzoylecgonine-TMS ; 6: norcocaine-TMS; 7: cis-cinnamoylegonine methyl ester-TMS; 8: trans-cinnamoylegonine methyl ester-TMS.

Source: Cartier, J., et al. "Headspace Analysis of Solvents in Cocaine and Heroin Samples." *Science and Justice: Journal of the Forensic Science Society,* 37 **1997**, 175–181. Figures reproduced with permission, the Forensic Science Society, Copyright 1997.

Table 6.4 Residual Solvents in Cocaine Exhibits: Percentage Occurrence			
	United States	Canada	Switzerland
Toluene	59	7	46
Acetone	52	62	44
Diethyl Ether	52	62	37
Methylethylketone (MEK)	65	54	24
Isopropanol	—	—	17
Methylene chloride	41	3	17
Methanol	—	—	13
Chloroform	—	—	11
Isobutanol	—	—	7
Ethanol	—	—	6
Acetaldehyde	—	—	4
Benzene	55	12	—
Hexane	61	—	—
Xylene	31	—	—
Cyclohexane	27	—	—

— = nothing detected

Adapted from Cartier, J., et al. "Headspace Analysis of Solvents in Cocaine and Heroin Samples." *Science and Justice: Journal of the Forensic Science Society,* 37 **1997**, 175–181.

Exhibit E: That's a Lot of Bunk!

"Bunk" is a slang term that refers to concoctions of legal drugs and other substances designed to mimic controlled substances and to command the same price on the street. Some of these mixtures even mimic the expected responses to screening tests. There is also a growing problem with counterfeit drugs, which is not surprising, given that some modern drugs are literally worth their weight in gold. The federal Food and Drug Administration reported recently that the number of counterfeit-drug cases it is pursuing has quadrupled since the 1990s. Counterfeit preparations usually have less active ingredients than a genuine street sample does, or no active ingredients at all. Currently, Mexico is the source for most counterfeit drugs entering the United States. Other drugs are ordered by organizations such as nursing homes, and the unused excess is diverted to the shadow market. One method suggested to combat counterfeiting is a "drug pedigree," similar to a chain of custody, to ensure that a preparation is genuine and has not been diverted.

Sources: 1. Hileman, B. "Countering Counterfeits." *Chemical and Engineering News,* November 17, **2003**, 36–43.
2. Hileman, B. "Counterfeit Drugs." *Chemical and Engineering News,* November 10, **2003**, 36–43.

or sugars. However, materials such as baking soda are not so easily tackled. There are specialized columns and methods for HPLC that can be applied to sugars, but the limiting factors in most forensic laboratories are not technology or equipment, but caseload and time. Finally, profiling generates an enormous amount of data and descriptors for each sample. This information must be stored and analyzed with the use of multivariate methods such as cluster analysis and principal-component analysis. (Both methods were introduced in Chapter 3.) For these reasons, profiling is typically performed by national entities in their respective countries.

Synthetic and semisynthetic drugs such as amphetamine and methamphetamine can be profiled, although isotopic abundances are not useful in the same way as described in this chapter. With synthetic and semisynthetic drugs, profiling is used to identify the synthetic method and reagents used and to link samples to batches and groups.

6.3.4 Biological Evidence

The Controlled Substances Act defines the principal target analytes for the drug analyst, with adulterants, diluents, and impurities forming a subset that receives lesser attention. For the forensic toxicologist working with biological evidence, there is an analogous situation. Toxicologists must answer specific questions and reconstruct a specific event: the ingestion of a controlled substance or a poison. To reconstruct the event, specific questions are posed:

Was a drug or substance ingested?
If so, what drug, drugs, or substances?
When?
How much?

Historical Evidence 6.3—Albertus Magnus Isolates Metallic Arsenic (∼ 1250).

Whether Albertus Magnus (~1208–1280 A.D.) was or was not actually the first to isolate metallic arsenic, this feat of separations chemistry is often attributed to him. Arsenic compounds were known as both poisons and medicines as early as Hippocrates (~400 B.C.). "Sulfur of arsenic" (As_2S_3) was recognized as a treatment for many ills due to its antimicrobial and general antibiotic activities, as long as doses were kept low. Poisonous arsenic compounds were known from at least early Roman times sometime before prior to the Christian era. Arsenic was also a common ingredient in cosmetics and paint.

The work done by Magnus was notable and notably difficult given the primitive tools available at the time. Prior to the 1600s, there were no mineral acids available. These acids (sulfuric, phosphoric, and hydrochloric acids) are needed to dissolve metals and minerals, a necessary step in any separation of an element from a solid matrix. The alternative was a technique based on flame pyrolysis in which extreme heat was used to selectively melt or volatilize elements. The method was crude at best. However, heating was an integral part of the Marsh test, the first method that was successful in isolating arsenic from tissues.

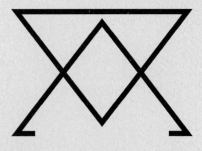

▲ *The symbol for arsenic used in alchemy.*

In the forensic sense, the ingestion event is like a crime scene. The toxicologist analyzes the biological trail of evidence to determine what happened and when it happened. This means that not only is the ingested material of interest, but so are the products of the biotransformation that occurs after ingestion. This dual interest makes the list of target analytes much larger than the list of scheduled and controlled substances. By contrast, there are fewer types of sample matrices for toxicology, reducing the complexity and facilitating standardized methods.

Matrices of Toxicological Samples: One way to divide forensic toxicology is into two categories: **postmortem** toxicology and **human-performance** toxicology, the latter focusing on blood alcohol. Workplace or other types of drug screening are often included in this definition.[24] The category of forensic toxicology dictates what samples (blood, urine, etc.) are collected and can be subdivided into what could be called routine or typical matrices and unusual or atypical matrices. Samples for postmortem toxicology are collected during the autopsy and include the specimens listed in Table 6.5.[24–26]

Less Typical: Cases arise in which the usual biological materials are not sufficient to answer the pertinent forensic questions. The type of toxin suspected, the mechanism of action, and the state of the body dictate which atypical materials would be submitted. If exposure to a volatile toxin might be involved, a sample of lung tissue would be useful. If a body is decomposed or burned, hair, bone, or insects associated with it may be all that is available for analysis.[†] Other materials, such as muscle tissue,[27] have been studied, but these samples would not be the first choice in many cases.

   Ideally, samples are collected near the time of death and before burial. However, on occasion, samples have been obtained from decomposing or exhumed bodies. The **embalming** process eliminates blood, a medium that provides a feasting ground for microorganisms involved in decomposition. Other tissues remain, but in intimate contact with the embalming fluids, which contain a significant concentration of formaldehyde (CH_2O). Formaldehyde is a reactive aldehyde that acts as a disinfectant and a preservative, two functions naturally linked. Disinfection kills microorganisms that drive the decomposition process. The formaldehyde also causes proteins to cross-link, "fixing" the tissue and stopping any further cell wall lysis. There is a small, but significant, body of research examining the effect of formaldehyde or formaldehyde-based preservation on drug residues,[28–31] and it is not surprising that embalming tissues with these compounds does affect subsequent forensic analysis. Formaldehyde is toxic and is being phased out; however, whatever substitutes are used will inevitably influence toxicological analysis.

[†]Entomotoxicology is a relatively new area of death investigation in which toxicologists analyze insects found on or near a body. If the insects fed upon the tissues of the deceased, any toxins contained in the ingested materials will be ingested by the insects.

Table 6.5 Postmortem Samples and Typical Amounts Needed

	Specimen	Amount
Typical	Blood (heart)	25 mL
	Blood (drawn peripherally)	10 mL
	Urine	all
	Vitreous humor	all
	Gastric contents	all
	Bile	all
	Brain	100 g
	Liver	100 g
	Kidney	50 g
	Hair	
Atypical	Spleen	Variable ↓↓
	Fatty (adipose) tissue	
	Lung	
	Muscle tissue	
	Insects (forensic entomology)	
	Bone marrow	
	Intestine	

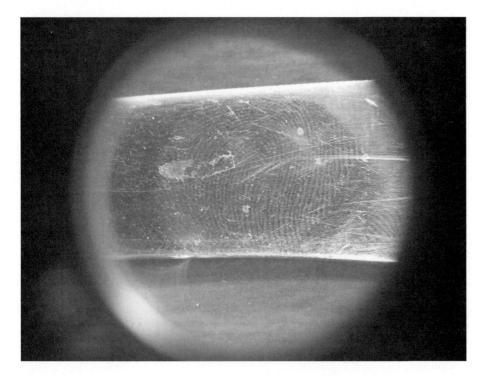

◄ **Figure 6.11** *Formaldehyde cross-links proteins by linking collagen chains. A similar procedure is involved in developing fingerprints using cyanoacrylates (Superglue). The cyanoacrylates cross-link the proteins found in fingerprint residue, forming a white polymer that marks the fingerprint residues.*

6.4 TURBO PHARMACOLOGY

Pharmacology is the study of drugs and medicines. Two aspects of pharmacology are **pharmacokinetics** and **pharmacodynamics**. Broadly defined, pharmacodynamics is the study of effects of drugs over time and is concerned with the interaction of a drug with its target. Of more immediate concern in forensic applications is pharmacokinetics, the study of the movement of a drug and its metabolic products through the body. The process begins at ingestion and ends with final disposition, be it elimination, storage, or a combination of the two. The process is outlined in Figure 6.12.

Although a detailed discussion of pharmacokinetics[†] is beyond the scope of this text, basic pharmacokinetics is an important part of forensic chemistry. The foundations of pharmacokinetics are familiar chemical principles of kinetics and equilibrium applied to a biological environment. Toxicokinetics involves multiple partitioning steps, solubility considerations, protein-bound complexes, and an enzymatically facilitated metabolism that converts the original drug or toxin into new compounds.

6.4.1 PHARMACOKINETICS

Pharmacokinetics studies the movement of a drug or foreign substance (a **xenobiotic**) by dividing it into the stages of absorption, distribution, metabolism, and elimination, a process referred to by its initials, ADME.[32] The simplified flowchart shown in Figure 6.12 disguises a complex chain of events that begins with the entry of the drug into the body. The method by which this occurs is the **mode of ingestion** (Figure 6.13), of which there are several. Drugs and drugs of abuse can be swallowed, injected, or snorted (absorbed through the nasal membranes), but

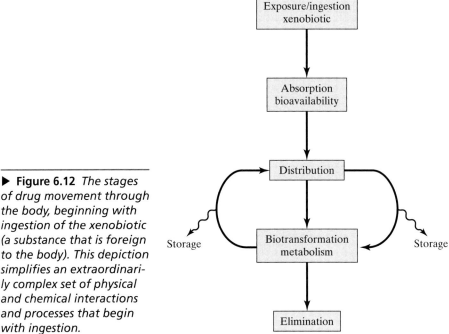

▶ **Figure 6.12** *The stages of drug movement through the body, beginning with ingestion of the xenobiotic (a substance that is foreign to the body). This depiction simplifies an extraordinarily complex set of physical and chemical interactions and processes that begin with ingestion.*

[†]The term "toxicokinetics" is also used and refers to dosage events in which toxic effects, as opposed to therapeutic effects, result.

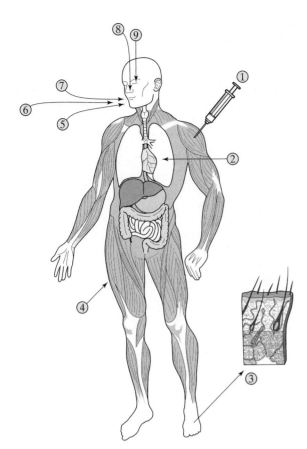

◀ **Figure 6.13** *Modes of ingestion. (See Table 6.6 for the legend.)*

there are other routes of exposure and some of these may be incidental or unintentional. Poisonous gases such as CO and HCN enter the bloodstream by way of inhalation, and many substances can be absorbed through the skin. Drugs delivered by suppository are absorbed in the lower intestine. Injections can be introduced directly into a blood vessel (**intravenous** injection), just below the skin's surface (**subcutaneous** injection), or into a muscle (**intramuscular** injection). The mode of ingestion affects how and when a drug appears in the bloodstream, an event that must occur before the substance can be distributed to various tissues in the body. Although any mode of ingestion is possible in forensic casework, the discussion that follows concentrates on the oral and intravenous routes.

Table 6.6	Modes of Ingestion: Numbers Correspond to Notation in Figure 6.13
Number	**Mode**
1	Injection into the tissue under the skin
2	Injection into a vein (intravenous)
3	Absorption through the skin (dermal)
4	Injection into a muscle
5	Inhalation or aspiration (inhalation of liquid)
6	Ingestion into the stomach
7	Dissolution below the tongue (sublingual)
8	Absorption through the mucous membranes of the nose
9	Absorption through the eyes

Exhibit F: Fatal Skin Absorption

Toxicologists played an important role in the investigation of the illness and death of Professor Karen Wetterhan of the Dartmouth College Department of Chemistry in February 1997. Dr. Wetterhan, 48, was using dimethyl mercury (CH_3—Hg—CH_3) in her research. She was working in a fume hood and wearing latex gloves when the incident occurred. While transferring the dimethyl mercury from one container to another, she apparently spilled a tiny amount (perhaps even a single drop) on the back of one of the gloves. She reported removing the gloves and giving the incident no further thought. Later studies proved that the organic liquid quickly penetrated the latex gloves, delivering a lethal dose via skin absorption. The fume hood likely protected her from incidental inhalation exposure.

Symptoms appeared months later, when she reported numbness, tingling, and difficulty speaking. Given the symptoms and her area of research, mercury poisoning was suspected. The suspicion was confirmed by further testing, including hair analysis. Mercury levels in her urine were recorded at 234 ppb and in her blood at 4000 ppb (4 ppm) months after the exposure. Despite therapy, she died 10 months after the incident. It is thought that the long delay in the appearance of symptoms was due at least in part to the lipophilic nature of dimethyl mercury.

Source: U.S Department of Labor, Occupational Safety and Health Administration Hazard Information Bulletin 19980309. Available on-line at www.osha.dov/dts/hib/hib_data/hib19980309.html. Downloaded March 14, 2004.

Kinetics and Compartments: An Overview: Pharmacokinetic studies can be divided roughly into two segments, the first consisting of absorption and distribution and the second of metabolism and elimination (summarized as ADME). The overall path is depicted in Figure 6.14. In this approach, the dividing line is that time after ingestion at which the concentration C_p (plasma, specifically) in the bloodstream reaches a maximum.[†] For an intravenously injected drug, this happens quickly, since no phase barriers must be crossed. For an orally ingested drug, the picture is more complex, because a lipophilic membrane is involved. (The particulars of this absorption and distribution process will be discussed shortly.)

Once the drug is distributed in the plasma, it can be delivered to tissues, where metabolism and elimination processes begin. It is important to note that metabolism is elimination in the sense that the parent molecule is converted to a new substance, causing C_p of the parent to decrease. The rate of removal of the drug, sometimes referred to as the **clearance rate**, usually follows first-order kinetics.

In any first-order process, the rate of the reaction depends only on the concentration of the drug. The half-life is derived by starting with the general equation for a **first-order process:**

$$t = \frac{1}{k}\ln\frac{C_0}{C_t} \tag{6.2}$$

where k is the elimination rate constant, C_0 is the initial maximum blood concentration of the drug, and C_t is the concentration at some time t. After one half-life, the concentration $C_t = \frac{1}{2}C_0$ and

$$t_{1/2} = \frac{1}{k}\ln\frac{C_0}{0.5C_0} \tag{6.3}$$

[†]The C is generic and can represent the concentration in any body fluid, such as whole blood, urine, etc. The current discussion focuses on C_p.

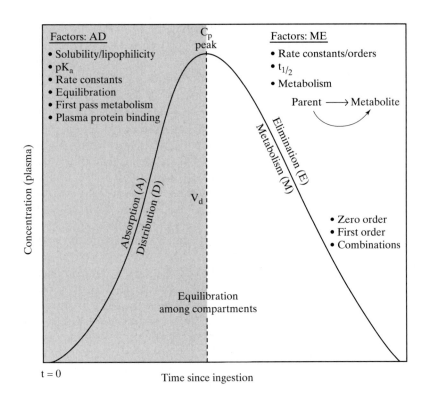

◀ **Figure 6.14** *The path taken by a xenobiotic substance from ingestion to elimination or clearance; the ADME process. Metabolism and elimination can take place even as concentrations build toward peak values. However, for simplicity, we will assume that significant elimination begins when C_p is reached. For our purposes, this is reasonable.*

$$t_{1/2} = \frac{1}{k} \ln 2 \tag{6.4}$$

$$t_{1/2} = \frac{0.693}{k} \tag{6.5}$$

The half-life should carry a descriptive label, such as $t_{1/2 \, plasma}$, for clarity. This notation is also important because a decrease in plasma concentration does not

Exhibit G: Kinetics: A Speedy Review

Kinetics is the study of the speed of a chemical reaction or process and is a critical element in toxicology. Most processes described in the discipline follow zero- and first-order kinetics. Recall that rate laws are employed to determine concentrations as a function of time. Although there are other variables and factors, the elimination of a xenobiotic substance from the body is fundamentally dependent on the kinetics of the reactions involved. Elimination processes often involve catalysts (enzymes), the role of which is central in determining the overall speed of the elimination, since a catalyst reduces the energy of activation, E_a.

Concepts of mechanism and rate-limiting steps apply as well, as can be illustrated with a simplified view of the metabolic processing of ethanol:

1. $C_2H_5OH \longrightarrow C_2H_4O \quad k_1 = slow$
2. $C_2H_4O \longrightarrow C_2H_3O_2^- \quad k_2 = fast$

Net: $C_2H_5OH \longrightarrow C_2H_3O_2^-$, rate-limiting step = first necessarily mean that a drug has been removed from the body. A decrease in concentration in the plasma "compartment" may correlate partly or exclusively with a concomitant increase in concentration of the same substance or a metabolite in a different compartment. How those compartments are linked is critical information for the toxicologist.

Compartment Models and Pharmacokinetics: When a drug is ingested orally, the plasma concentration does not peak immediately. Even when the drug is injected, adsorption and distribution do not occur instantaneously. As absorption and distribution occur, elimination may have already begun. This requires that the relative speed of competing processes be taken into account if tissue concentrations are to be used to re-create dosage events. Toxicologists employ compartment models to facilitate such calculations.[33,34] A compartment does not necessarily correlate with a single, isolated place in the body, such as a finger or a lung. A compartment is better thought of as a barrier or partition over which equilibrium must be established before the plasma concentration reaches a steady state.[34]

A one-compartment model (Figure 6.15) is based on a single compartment—here, the plasma—also referred to as the central compartment. A first-order rate constant k_a determines how fast the drug is absorbed into the bloodstream, while the first-order elimination rate constant k_{el} describes the speed at which the drug is removed. A logarithmic plot of plasma concentration versus time is linear with a slope of $-k_{el}/2.303$. The plasma concentration as a function of time is described by the relationship:

$$C = C_0 e^{-k_{el}t} \tag{6.6}$$

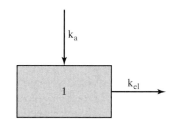

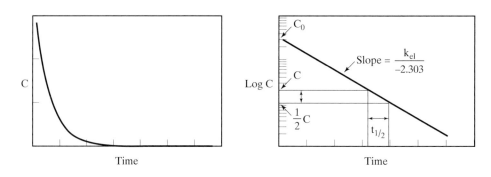

▲ **Figure 6.15** *A one-compartment model with first-order elimination. The rate constant and half-life can be derived from the logarithmic plot of the concentration as a function of time (above left).*

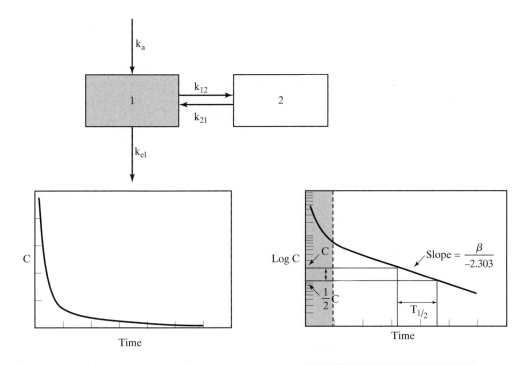

▲ **Figure 6.16** *A two-compartment model in which the central compartment is linked to another compartment with speed of movement described by new rate constants.*

Note this is the same equation used to derive the first-order-rate half-life described in equations 6-2 through 6-5. The rate constant is specified as the elimination rate constant k_{el}. The first-order rate law can be restated as follows to allow the calculation of concentration as a function of time:

$$\ln(C_t) = -k_t + \ln(C_0) \qquad (6.7)$$

If not given, the rate constant can be derived from the half-life and equation 6-5. A single-compartment model is based on the assumption that an injected drug is instantaneously distributed in the plasma and tissues.[34] Such a model is a good starting point and applicable in many situations.

In many cases, the logarithmic plot of concentration vs. time is a curve, indicating more than one stage of elimination. In turn, this implies the existence of more than one compartment that the drug must move through. In these situations, a two-compartment model (Figure 6.16) can be invoked.[33,34] Not surprisingly, even the two-compartment model is sometimes inadequate. To cope with the complexity involved, physiological models are invoked.[34] These are more realistic and flexible, but are beyond the scope of the introductory material presented here. Even so, a cursory glance at Figure 6.17 shows that such models retain the components of partitioning, distribution coefficients, and rate constants. These models also are based on the fundamental steps of ADME, which can now be discussed in detail.

Absorption (A) and Distribution (D): When a drug is injected directly into the bloodstream peak plasma concentration C_p is quickly established. We will assume that C_p becomes C_0 in the first order elimination process (Eq. 6.7). When a drug is taken orally, several factors control how long it takes for the compound to establish the peak initial value of C. The absorption of a drug in the gastrointestinal tract first requires that the drug be soluble, a topic addressed in Chapter 4. Solubility of the

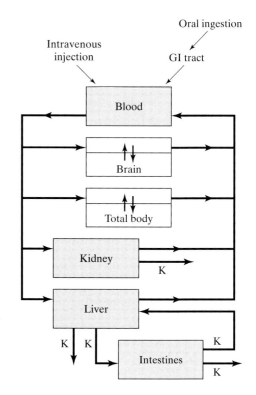

▶ **Figure 6.17** *An example of a physiological model with many compartments, partitions, equilibrations, and rate constants.*

preparation is also a factor, because time-release formulations or tablets are coated to control when or where in the gastrointestinal tract dissolution occurs.

Once a drug is solubilized, pH dictates when and where the drug will be absorbed (Figure 6.18). Recall that the pH of the gastrointestinal tract progresses from acidic in the stomach (pH 1–3) to basic in the small intestine and colon (pH 7–8), so the pK_a values of ionizable drugs determines where the drugs will be charged and where they will be neutral. Like the gastrointestinal tract, the bloodstream is an aqueous system, so similar considerations apply once the drug arrives in the blood. Before entering the bloodstream, drug molecules must traverse a membrane containing lipids. The membrane represents a partitioning between phases, similar to partitioning in the context of chromatography. In general, neutral forms of weakly acidic or basic drugs will be preferentially absorbed when the pH drives the equilibrium toward the neutral form,[35] since that form is lipophilic relative to the ionized form. The relative lipophilicity of a drug is gauged by the LogP value discussed in Chapter 4. In addition, small water-soluble molecules may pass through the membrane via small water-filled pores that bypass the partitioning step.[36] Ethanol is absorbed this way, principally in the top portion of the small intestine.[24] The driving force of the movement from the gastrointestinal tract to the bloodstream is a concentration gradient. Other factors that play a role in absorption include the surface area of the absorbing region and the blood flow.[35]

In contrast to injected drugs, orally administered drugs pass through the liver before entering the general circulation[34] and are subject to **first-pass metabolism**. These processes occur before the drug is generally available and before pharmacological effects are observed. To account for the changes that occur, the bioavailability (F) can be used. Bioavailability is defined as the ratio of drug that would be available after injection, compared with that available after oral administration. F is expressed as a percentage, and the higher the F value, the smaller is the loss of the active form of the drug to first-pass metabolic changes.

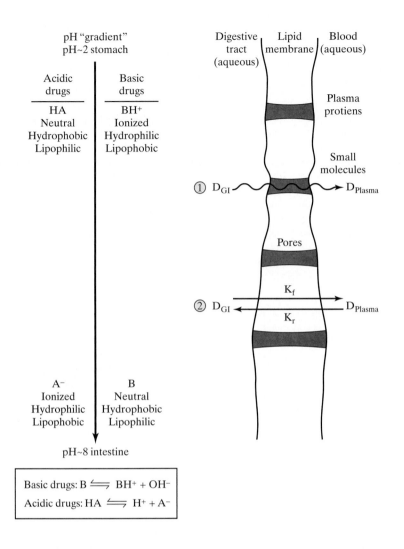

◀ **Figure 6.18** *Factors related to the absorption of a drug (D) in the gastrointestinal tract. The pH gradually increases from strongly acidic in the stomach to basic in the small intestine, affecting the solubility of many drugs. Absorption across membranes is favored when the drug is un-ionized, but small water-soluble substances can pass directly through pores in the membrane. The concentration gradient drives the diffusion.*

Other modes of ingestion follow the same basic steps of ADME, but the specific processes and mechanisms differ. For example, substances introduced intravenously can immediately be distributed, since there is no barrier to cross for the drug to enter the bloodstream. Gases entering the lungs are also nearly in direct contact with the blood. Xenobiotics on the skin must move through seven layers of the outer epidermis before contacting capillaries and blood,[36] making skin a good protective barrier against many toxic agents.

The distribution of a drug in tissues is determined by considerations similar to those governing absorption. Depending on these factors, a drug may preferentially reside in the blood, in fatty tissues, or in other locations, such as the liver. The volume of distribution is a quantitative expression of this distribution and is given by

$$V_d = \frac{D}{(C_p \times k)} \tag{6.8}$$

where D is the dose of the drug; C_p is the plasma concentration once equilibrium has been reached in the plasma, but before elimination of the drug has begun; and k is the person's body weight in kilograms. Although the plasma concentration is used here, V_d can be calculated for any body fluid and should be specified.

Applying the Science 6.4 Partitioning Across the Blood–Brain Barrier

Drugs that affect the brain, such as morphine, must first penetrate it by crossing the blood–brain barrier. This barrier is not a wall per se, but a complex membrane that is not fully understood. The partitioning coefficient between the bloodstream and the brain, C_{brain}/C_{blood}, is based on the same factors discussed in Chapter 4, and the quantity of the drug involved can be expressed as a logarithmic value called the logBB (for brain barrier).

Given the difficulties associated with experimental determinations of the LogBB, there has been much interest in alternative approaches. One tactic that has been proposed employs molecular modeling techniques to calculate the free energy of solvation of the drug in water and in a nonpolar solvent such as hexadecane.

Recall from basic thermodynamics that a process with a negative ΔG is spontaneous and the product—here, the solvated state—is favored relative to the unsolvated state. The authors of the study proposing this alternative approach derived a relationship that exhibited a reasonable correlation with measured values of LogBB. Some values obtained for $\Delta G°_w$ were −5.00 for ethanol (freely water soluble) and 2.08 for hexane; for $\Delta G°_{HD}$ the values were −0.16 and −3.45, respectively, for the same compounds. Caffeine, a water-soluble basic drug, had calculated values of −15.27 and −9.31, respectively. The difference in the $\Delta G°$ values suggests that caffeine is more stable when it is solubilized in water than in a lipophilic medium. In the case of caffeine, the calculated LogBB value of 49.5 compared reasonably well with an experimental value of 40.3.

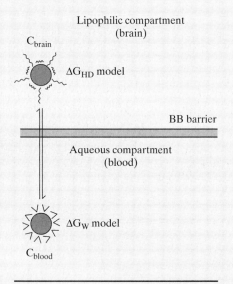

▲ The solvation of a drug molecule by water and by an organic solvent.

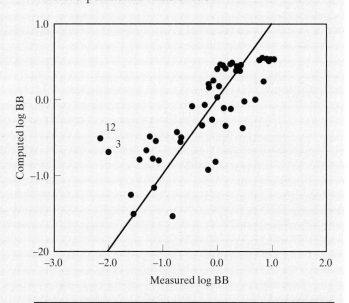

▲ The correlation of calculated and measured ratios of concentration of target analytes in the brain and blood. Compounds 12 and 3 were identified by the authors as outliers. Reprinted with permission from the reference below. Copyright 1996 American Chemical Society.

While work remains to be done, the study presented here provides a quantitative value which could ultimately be applied to physiological models that incorporate the brain, such as the model shown in Figure 6.17.

Source: Lombardo, F., et al. "Computation of Brain–Blood Partitioning of Organic Solutes via Free Energy Calculations." *Journal of Medicinal Chemistry,* 39 **1996**, 4750–4755.

The volume of distribution is not a physical volume, but rather a quantitative expression calculating how a drug is distributed in compartments of the body. For this reason, it is referred to as the **apparent volume of distribution**.[34,37] In general, the higher V_d, the more lipophilic the drug is. If the drug is administered orally, the value of C_p has to be adjusted on the basis of the bioavailability. The value of V_d depends on the lipophilicity of a drug, the degree of ionization (pK_a), the association of the drug with proteins, and many other physical and chemical parameters.[38–40] V_d provides a measure of the relative partitioning of the

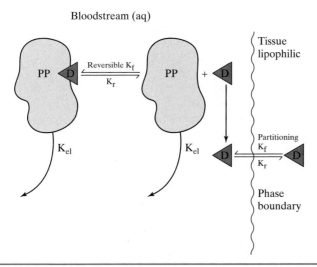

▲ Figure 6.19 *Distribution into the tissues. To move into tissue, a drug must be free from any bound plasma proteins (PP). Competing processes, such as elimination, are also possible.*

Example Problem 6.2

The desired therapeutic concentration of morphine for a man weighing 180 lb is 0.05 mg/L. Assuming that V_d for morphine is 4L/kg and the bioavailability is 25%, calculate the oral and injected doses needed to obtain the desired plasma concentration.

$$V_d = \frac{D \longrightarrow ?}{C_p\, k}$$

$$\frac{4L}{kg} \qquad \frac{0.05\ mg}{L} \qquad \begin{array}{c} kg\ 81.65 \\ 180\ lbs \end{array}$$

$$D = \frac{4\cancel{L}}{\cancel{kg}} \cdot \frac{0.05\ mg}{\cancel{L}} \cdot 82\ kg\ =\ 16.4\ mg\ =\ 16\ mg$$
$$\text{(injected)}$$

For an oral dose, $F = 25\%$ meaning that
$^3/_4$ of the dose is lost to first pass metabolism
Thus, the oral dose must be larger:

$$0.25D = \frac{4\cancel{L}}{\cancel{kg}} \cdot \frac{0.05\ mg}{\cancel{L}} \cdot 82\ kg$$

$$F = 25\% \qquad D = 65.6\ mg\ =\ 66\ mg\ oral$$

drug between the plasma and other tissues. If two compounds experience roughly the same degree of binding to plasma proteins, the compound with the greater affinity for association with the tissues will have a larger V_d relative to the compound with more affinity for the plasma. Compounds that are lipophilic also tend to have higher V_d values.[40] Note that calculations of V_d combine all tissues together and consider them as one unit.[39,41]

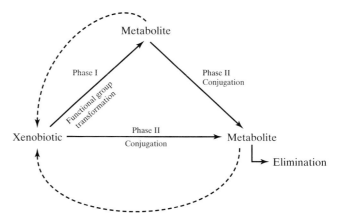

▶ **Figure 6.20** *General flow of metabolism. Not all metabolic pathways go through Phase I, and at each step, metabolic byproducts may reenter the cycle as new xenobiotics.*

As mentioned in the previous paragraph, drugs in the bloodstream may bind with plasma proteins such as albumin, sometimes irreversibly. Binding is dependent on many factors, including the concentration of the drug and the relative affinities of the drug and protein for each other, as well as their affinities for other substances found in the plasma. The drug must be in the unbound form to cross into the tissue,[35] so protein binding can be useful in controlled-release applications. Protein binding affects V_d, since binding prohibits crossing into tissues. The more a substance binds with a plasma protein, the more it will tend to stay in the plasma. Forensic toxicologists can use V_d values to estimate the total amount of a drug that is present. The following equation gives the dose D (mg/kg) of a drug present in the plasma in terms of it's volume of distribution V_d, and a blood-test measurement of the concentration C_p of the drug:

$$D = V_d \times C_p \tag{6.9}$$

Metabolism (M): Typically, once a drug enters the target tissue, the intended pharmacological effect begins; this is also the point at which most metabolic processes begin (Figure 6.20). The major tissue site of metabolism is the liver. The biological goal of metabolism is deactivation and elimination of the xenobiotic substance, and in general, the more lipophilic a compound is, the more likely it is to be metabolically altered.[40]

Exhibit H: Toxic Metabolites

The metabolite produced from a drug or some other exogenous substance is often pharmacologically active. Such substances are referred to as active metabolites. In some cases, active metabolites are responsible for toxic effects which exceed that of the parent substance. Methanol, ethylene glycol, and DDE are examples of active toxic metabolites. Methanol (wood alcohol) can be ingested accidentally or intentionally. Methanol is metabolized similarly to ethanol, via a two-step oxidation to an aldehyde (formaldehyde) that is converted to an acid (formic acid). The acid causes toxic effects such as acidosis and impaired cell respiration, while the penetration of methanol into the vitreous humor can lead to blurred vision and blindness.

Ethylene glycol (antifreeze) has a sweet taste that makes it attractive to animals and children, resulting in frequent accidental poisonings. Although the metabolic process is more complicated, active toxic metabolites of the corresponding aldehyde and acids are produced. Particularly insidious is the formation of crystals of calcium oxalate (K_{sp} (hydrate), $\sim 10^{-9}$), which may be detected as crystals in the urine.

Drug metabolism typically occurs in two phases. Phase I metabolism involves an alteration of a functional group on the molecule, while Phase II is a conjugation with a substance found naturally in the body (an **endogenous substance**). Some metabolic pathways do not require a Phase I conversion prior to conjugation. Enzymes are involved in both phases, and common Phase I reactions include hydrolysis and dehydrogenation. The most common Phase II transformations result in the formation of conjugates of glucuronic acid.[42] Metabolic processes can produce unintended consequences, such as the creation of metabolites that are more toxic than the parent molecule. Complex metabolic pathways can produce many **metabolites** and result in multiple cycles of distribution, metabolism, and storage.

Table 6.7	Examples of Illicit Drug Metabolites
Drug	**Metabolites**
Cocaine	Benzoylecgonine, ecgonine methyl ester
Codeine	Morphine
Heroin	6-Monoacetylmorphine
THC	9-carboxy-11-nor-Δ^9THC

The final step is excretion of the drug and metabolites from the body. Water-soluble materials are excreted in the urine and in sweat. If a metabolite is a gas, such as CO_2, or has appreciable vapor pressure, as does ethanol, the metabolite can be eliminated by exhalation. Excretion in feces, tears, and any other body fluid is also possible.

Table 6.8 shows selected toxicological parameters for two sample compounds from earlier in the chapter: aspirin and morphine. The pK_a values

Table 6.8	Example Toxicological Factors	
	Aspirin	**Morphine**
Structure	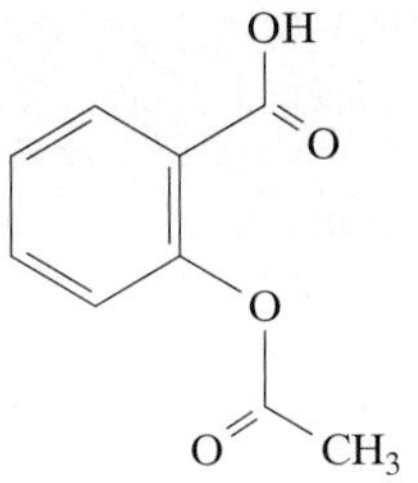	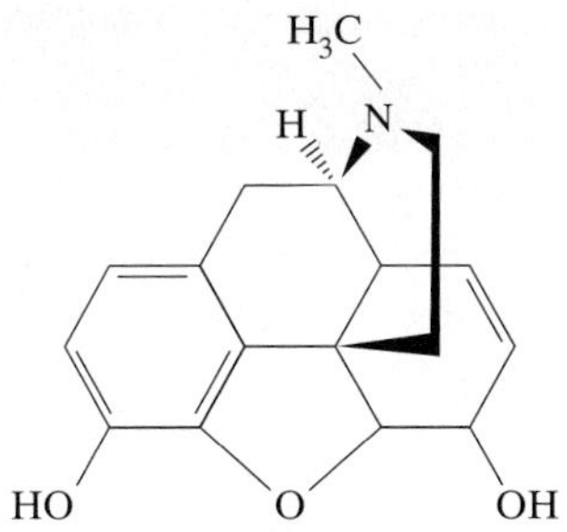
pK_a	3.5	8.0, 9.9
Log P	−1.1	−0.1
$C_{theraputic}$	100 mg/kg	0.01–0.07 mg/L
F%	N.A. (oral administration only)	20–30%
$t_{1/2\ plasma}$	17 min	2–3 hours
V_d	0.15 L/kg	3–5 L/kg
Protein binding	90%	20–35%

N.A. = not applicable.

and logP values help predict characteristics of absorbance if the drug is taken orally. Aspirin, with the more negative logP, is hydrophilic and lipophobic compared with the amphoteric morphine. The loss that results from oral ingestion is reflected in F; none is reported for aspirin, since it is delivered orally rather than by injection. Morphine can be delivered by either route, although the price paid at first-pass metabolism is significant. The V_d and protein-binding data provide information about how the drug partitions between the central plasma compartment and other tissues, quantities that also relate back to the logP value, which measures lipophilicity. Not surprisingly, the more lipophilic morphine has a higher V_d value and a longer half-life in plasma, likely due to its stronger association with lipophilic tissues that result in its lingering in the plasma longer than does aspirin, which is rapidly hydrolyzed to salicylic acid.

Elimination (E): The half-life of a drug or other substance in the plasma represents the amount of time it takes for half of the original concentration to disappear. Half-life does not take into account why or how that concentration is consumed, only that it is no longer present in the plasma compartment. The "missing" concentration may be attributed to metabolic changes, but it may also be due to binding with tissues such that it is no longer detected in the plasma. A more inclusive term is the clearance rate, which does take into account other processes and factors, such as metabolism and volume of distribution, along with the half-life. In general, the more lipophilic a compound is, the more likely it is to be subject to metabolic processes that in turn can increase the clearance rate relative to a less lipophilic entity.[40] A number of variables affect the actual clearance rate in an individual, as seen by the large ranges shown in Table 6.9.

Estimates of time since the administration of a drug are made easier when there is more than one substance present in the blood, urine, or other tissue sample. Recall that metabolism produces metabolites that are also subject to elimination. The concentration of the drug in blood or another compartment will decrease as metabolism progresses and the concentration of the metabolite increases. If the metabolite is subject to further biological transformations, it, too,

Table 6.9 Sample (Approximate) Half-Lives of Drugs of Abuse, Typical Dose		
Drug	**Half-life Range, Blood (hours)**	**Detectable in Urine (days)**
Methamphetamine	7–34	1–2
Cocaine	0.7–1.5	1–2
Valium	21–37	Several
Heroin	1–1.5	2–4
Cannabinoids (marijuana)	20–57	Several

Source: Benjamin, D. M. "Forensic Pharmacology," in R. Saferstein, ed., *Forensic Science Handbook,* Volume 3. Englewood Cliffs NJ: Prentice Hall, **1993**.

Example Problem 6.3

A woman weighing 135 lb takes two codeine tablets of 20 mg each as directed by her dentist to alleviate the pain associated with minor dental surgery. Assuming that the peak plasma concentration is reached in 1 hour, V_d of codeine is 3.0 L/kg, F = 50%, and $t_{1/2}$ for codeine in plasma is 3.0 hr, complete the following tasks:

1. Sketch the ADME curve.
2. Calculate the peak plasma concentration C_p
3. Calculate the plasma concentration 2 hours after the woman took the pills. Note any assumptions.
4. Determine when the plasma concentration of codeine will become too small to be detected by a mass spectrometry method with an LOD/LOQ of 1.0 ppb. Assume that the blood sample is injected directly into the instrument.

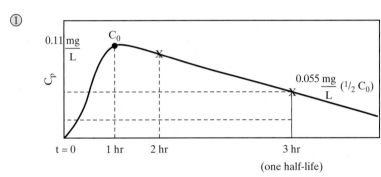

①

②
$$V_d = \frac{D}{C_p \cdot kg} \qquad C_p = \frac{D}{V_d \cdot kg}$$

$$C_p = \frac{40 \text{ mg}}{3.0 \text{ L} \cdot 61.2 \text{ kg}} = \frac{0.22 \text{ mg}}{L}$$

but must be correct for bioavailibility;
50% is lost to first pass metabolism

$$C_p = \frac{0.11 \text{ mg}}{L}$$

③ We will assume that the peak plasma concentration C_p is the nominal value of C_0 for the elimination calculations. 2 hours after ingestion is 1 hour after peak plasma concentration is reached, as seen on sketch.

$$\ln C_t = -Kt + \ln C_0$$

Use $t_{1/2}$ to find K:

$$t_{1/2} = \frac{0.693}{K} \qquad K = \frac{0.693}{t_{1/2}} = \frac{0.693}{3 \text{ hr}}$$

$$K = 0.23 \text{ hr}^{-1}$$

$$\ln C_t = (-0.23 \text{ hr}^{-1})(1 \text{ hr}) + \ln(0.11)$$

$$\ln C_t = -2.44 \text{ hr}^{-1} \qquad C_t = 0.087\frac{mg}{L}$$

(4) $\quad LOQ = 1.0 \text{ ppb} = \dfrac{1.0 \text{ ug}}{L} = \dfrac{0.001 \text{ mg}}{L}$ units must match C

$$\ln(0.001) = -0.23 \text{ hr}^{-1} \text{ t} + \ln(0.11)$$

$$\ln(0.001) - \ln(0.11) = -0.23 \text{ t}$$

$$-4.70 = -0.23 \text{ t}$$

$$t = 20.4 \text{ hours}$$

So undetectable after ~21 hours of ingestion.

will decrease as the next metabolite increases, and so on. At certain times, all three may be present, while at others, only the drug or the final metabolite may be detectable. Knowing the metabolic pathways and reaction rates is critical to determining the time of ingestion.

In the example shown in Figure 6.21, injected heroin is rapidly metabolized to 6-monoacetylmorphine (6-MAM). A slower, but still quick, conversion occurs to morphine, which has a much longer plasma half-life. A blood sample drawn even an hour after the initial injection might show no heroin, but a distinctive ratio of 6-MAM and morphine that could be used to estimate the size and time of the initial injection.

Finally, toxicologists must consider different tissues or fluids in which a drug or metabolite may end up. As shown in Figure 6.22, as a drug is processed and excretion begins, concentrations of the drug and metabolites may be detectable in more than one tissue. If a compound enters the hair, it is protected from further changes or alteration, so there is increasing interest in hair as a sample matrix in toxicology. Figure 6.22 illustrates a generic model for distribution, and the picture is again complicated with the addition of metabolites that may also partition among different fluids and tissues.

An Integrative Example: Consider the simplified pharmacokinetics of a familiar small water-soluble molecule shown in Figure 6.23. Ingestion via the oral

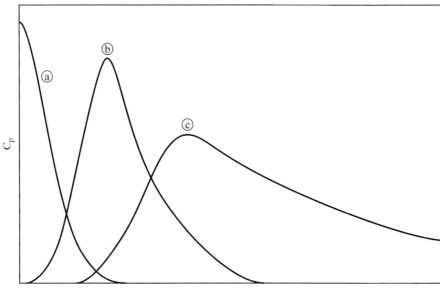

▶ **Figure 6.21** *If a drug is metabolized, a drop in the concentration of the parent corresponds to an increase in the concentration of the metabolite. Here, a represents the plasma concentration of heroin ($t_{1/2} \sim 3$ min), b is the metabolite 6-monoacetylmorphine ($t_{1/2} \sim 20$ min), and c is morphine ($t_{1/2} \sim 2.5$ hr).*

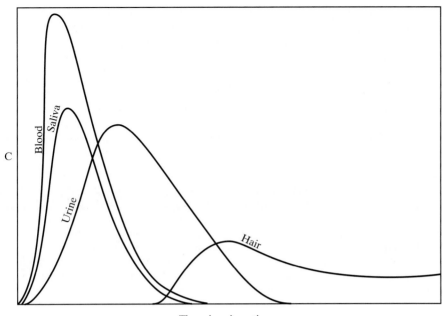

◀ **Figure 6.22** *The concentration of a drug or metabolite may fall in one tissue and rise in another.*

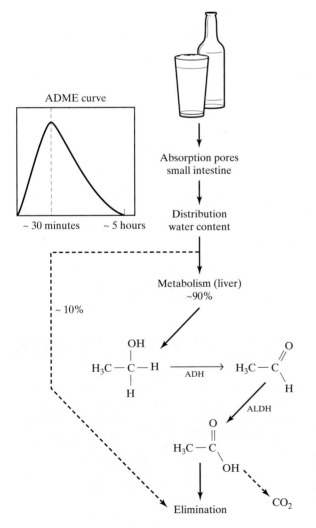

◀ **Figure 6.23** *Simplified ADME pathway of ethanol. After ingestion, peak blood concentrations are reached in half an hour.*

route leads to absorption taking place primarily in the top portion of the small intestine, as mentioned earlier. Peak ethanol blood concentration occurs roughly half an hour after ingestion, assuming that the subject stops at one dose. Ethanol distributes into tissues on the basis of their water content. The solubility of the molecule also means that a portion (~10%) of the dose will be excreted unchanged while the remaining portion is metabolized in a two-step process. Overall, the elimination of ethanol is an interesting example in kinetics because the order of the elimination depends on the ethanol concentration. At lower concentrations, on the order of 0.01g/dL, the elimination follows first-order kinetics.[24]

Applying the Science 6.5   The More Things Change . . .

Some of the best chemists in the ancient world were brewers. The Sumerians appeared to favor beer, the Egyptians wine, but both cultures had mastered brewing thousands of years ago. Making alcoholic beverages generally requires an understanding of two chemical processes: fermentation and distillation. In the investigation of archaeological samples, tartaric acid is considered a good marker for the presence of wine.

More challenging than detecting traces of ancient wine is determining whether the wine once held in a container was a red wine or a white wine. Not surprisingly, the reds are attributable to dyes, a topic covered briefly in the next chapter and extensively in Chapter 9. Older brewing methods were also an unintended source of lead poisoning, since lead was widely used to line pots and other distillation equipment. One early chemist offered this commonsense safety tip for distilling oils ("oyls"):

You must be very careful that the ashes and pot do not wax too hot, for if the oyl within takes fire it will break the vessels and flie up, that it can hardly be quenched, and reach the very ceiling; so that it is best to operate upon oyls in arched rooms.

Sources: 1. Egloff, G., and C. D. Lowry. "Distillation Methods, Ancient and Modern." *Industrial and Engineering Chemistry,* 21 **1929**, 920–923.

2. Gauasch-Jane, M. R., et al. "Liquid Chromatography with Mass Spectrometry in Tandem Mode Applied for the Identification of Wine Makers in Residues from Ancient Egyptian Vessels." *Analytical Chemistry,* 76 **2004**, 1672–1677.

3. Wittmers, L., et al. "Archaeological Contributions of Skeletal Lead Analysis." *Accounts of Chemical Research,* 35 **2002**, 669–675.

To begin the elimination, alcohol dehydrogenases (ADHs) catalyze the conversion of ethanol to acetaldehyde, a compound thought to play a role in the symptoms of a hangover. This step is the rate-limiting step in the process.[24] Fortunately, the subject in this example drank responsibly and stopped at one dose, so suffering will be minimal. Aldehyde dehydrogenases (ALDHs) convert the acetaldehyde to acetate ion and acetic acid. Carbon dioxide is the final metabolic product and is eliminated via exhalation. The clearance rate of ethanol is about 0.016 g/dL per hour,[24] leading to elimination of the initial dose in a few hours.

Exhibit I: Drug Recognition Experts (DREs)

The acronym "DUI" is commonly known to mean "driving under the influence," but intoxication and impaired functioning can result from the ingestion of many substances other than ethanol. Laboratory analysis is essential to determine which substance caused intoxication, but the work requires time. Rarely can it be completed while the subject is still intoxicated. To assist police officers in determining the likely source of intoxication, drug recognition experts (DREs) can be called. Certified DREs use a battery of tests and examinations, including interviews, physical examinations, and evaluations of vital signs, to offer an opinion as to which intoxicating agents are present. Blood and urine are also collected.

Historical Evidence 6.4—Hangover Remedy

One of the earliest-known examples of writing is a stone tablet with cuneiform symbols written by a Sumerian pharmacist (or the ancient equivalent) several thousand years ago. The prescription described the treatment for a hangover.

6.4.2 DOSAGE CONSIDERATIONS

Unlike simple chemical reactions taking place in a beaker, biotransformation rates and effects vary with the person and the dose. While the former is a function of genetics, general health, age, and many other variables, the latter is easier to quantify and describe. Drugs are taken in order to invoke a therapeutic physiological effect. The range of a dose, again variable depending on the person, is referred to as the effective dose (ED), and to obtain it, repeated administration is often called for. The goal in these cases is to establish a steady level of C_p.

Since there will be a range of effective doses within a population, one way to report the effective dose is as the **ED_{50}**, the dose that will lead to the desired response in 50% of the test population. In toxicology, where a death is likely involved, the same concept is used, but is reported as the **LD_{50}**, which is the dose that causes death in 50% of a test population (Figure 6.24). In a test population, typically laboratory animals, there will always be individuals that are sensitive and susceptible to drug effects and those which are tolerant and resistant. This variability is due to genetic factors, health, and other parameters. Even at low doses, some individuals will show a response or, in the case of a poison, will die. The values are also specific to the test population, and if that is a group of laboratory animals, there is no guarantee that the data will

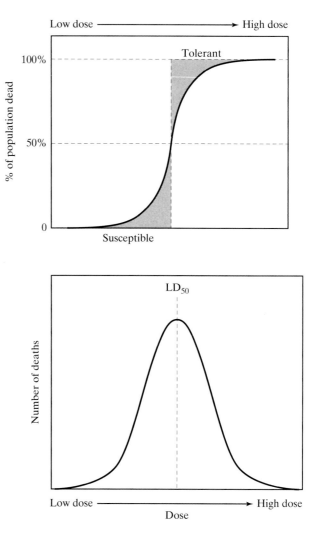

▶ **Figure 6.24** *Two graphical representations of the* LD_{50}/ED_{50} *concept.*

extrapolate to humans. The ability to extrapolate is important in the case of poisons, for which the body of research on human test populations may be small or nonexistent.

6.5 ONLINE RESOURCES FOR THE FORENSIC CHEMIST AND TOXICOLOGIST

For any given drug, the forensic drug chemist or toxicologist needs to be able to locate specific information relevant to his or her analysis. Much of that information will be in-house in some form, but there will be many occasions where the chemist will have to find reliable information elsewhere quickly. For example, a pK_a value may be needed to fine-tune an extraction, or a half-life of a metabolite may be necessary to estimate the time of ingestion of a drug. The logical place to turn for such information is the Internet, which has become a terrific resource for the prudent and skeptical forensic chemist. The two qualifiers are important ones. Government websites are preferred, since there is a level of control and review associated with the data posted. Such sites tend to be updated frequently and are considered (unless noted otherwise) as public domain.

Some commercial sites are also useful, but should be taken with the appropriate grain (i.e., 64.8 mg) of salt.

Among government agencies, the U.S. Drug Enforcement Administration (DEA) has a website (www.dea.gov) that provides a centralized repository of information, including current trends and summaries of existing and emerging drug problems. Forensic chemists are well advised to bookmark and visit this site frequently. The DEA also publishes an electronic journal called *The Microgram* that is loaded with solid, timely, and practical information for laboratory scientists. The *Microgram Journal* is published quarterly, the *Microgram Bulletin* monthly. Both can be found at the DEA website, and subscriptions are available to those working in forensic laboratories. The publication *Illegal Drug Price and Purity Report*[43] gives current information on the subject stated in its title, while the *State Fact Sheet*[7] describes current national trafficking trends as well as offering state summaries. An often-unappreciated gold mine of information can be found in an international online journal similar to the *Microgram* and entitled the *Bulletin of Narcotics* (http://www.unodc.org/unodc/en/bulletin_on_narcotics.html). The *Bulletin* is published by the United Nations Office of Drug Control. The online keyword index quickly links to articles covering a variety of analytical and general topics, some from the 1950s. At first glance, this publication might seem dated, but there are occasions when such archived information can be invaluable. In fact, the *Bulletin* is often underappreciated as a source of reliable and referenced information on an array of analytical and scientific topics.

Review articles allow even the busiest forensic chemist the opportunity to find summaries of current research. The journal *Analytical Chemistry* publishes a semiannual review of forensic science that emphasizes forensic analytical chemistry.[44-46] This publication contains extensive and current research in drug analysis, as well as in many other aspects of forensic chemistry. For drug analysis, the DEA has published a recent extensive review of articles covering 1992–2002.[47] As part of the *Microgram Journal*, this review is available online.

Another good source of general information is the National Institute of Drug Abuse (NIDA; www.nida.nih.gov). While focusing more on health and abuse as opposed to providing analytical information, NIDA is the place to go for statistical information. Finally, chemical and toxicological information, including structures in two- and three-dimensional format, can be found on the databases of the National Library of Medicine (NLM; http://www.nlm.nih.gov/). Chemical information such as structures, classifications codes, and synonyms can be quickly found. For toxicological data, the NLM site has a gateway to several useful databases, such as ToxNet and the Hazardous Substances Data Bank (HSDB). Most of the structures discussed or shown in this chapter were obtained via searches performed at the NLM site. For chemical information, the National Institute of Standards and Technology research library ("Virtual Library"; nvl.nist.gov).

SUMMARY

Drug evidence, like all evidence in forensic science, has characteristics that can be used to describe and categorize it. The first division used by forensic scientists reflects the type of drug analysis needed. For physical evidence submitted to a crime laboratory (pills, powders, plant matter, paraphernalia, precursors, or related evidence), the central forensic question is "What controlled substance is present?" Secondary questions relate to how much and to what else might be there, such as adulterants, diluents, and contaminants. Exhaustive analysis may be used to further categorize drug samples into batches. The forensic toxicologist receives biological evidence and answers the forensic question "What substances (drugs or poisons) where taken and when were they taken?" Knowledge of pharmacology is essential to this reconstruction, as are chemical and physical data that increasingly are available online if sources are properly vetted. With this conceptual framework in hand and with the available resources, the next step is to delve into the detailed chemistry of the various classes of drugs, beginning with drugs as physical evidence.

KEY TERMS AND CONCEPTS

Adulterant	Excipients	Pharmacodynamics
Alkaloid	First-order process	Pharmacokinetics
Analgesics	First-pass metabolism	Pharmacology
Biotransformation	Five P's	Postmortem toxicology
Central nervous system	Half-life	Precursors
Chemical Diversion and	Human performance toxicology	Predator drugs
Trafficking Act	Inhalants	Profiling
Classification	Intramuscular	Prostaglandin
Clearance rate	Intravenous	Pyrogens
Controlled Substances Act	Isotopic ratio	Semisynthetic
Cutting agent	Lime method	Stable isotope ratio
Depressants	Medicine	Stimulants
DFSA	Metabolites	Subcutaneous
Diluent	Mode of ingestion	Synthetic
DRE	Narcotics	Testosterone
Drug	Natural drug or product	Thinner
Embalming	NSAID	Volume of distribution
Endogenous substance	Paracetamol	Xenobiotic
Entomotoxicology	Paraphernalia	

PROBLEMS

From the chapter

1. Why is it increasingly difficult to classify drugs as natural, semisynthetic, or synthetic?

2. From a regulatory and analytical perspective, why would immediate precursors be of more concern than distant precursors?

3. For over-the-counter preparations, inactive ingredients are called fillers. Are these the equivalent of diluents, adulterants, impurities, contaminants, or thinners? Why or why not?

4. How is the process of fractionation similar to partitioning?

5. How would the presence of sugar as a diluent affect isotope ratio determinations of a heroin or cocaine sample? What does this behavior imply for sample preparation for such determinations?

6. What practical reasons could explain the fact that oxygen and hydrogen ratios are not as commonly used to profile plant-derived drugs compared with nitrogen and carbon ratios?

7. Could isotope ratios be used to determine whether a heroin or cocaine sample was synthesized, as opposed to having been extracted from a plant? Justify your answer.

8. Would a profile based on residual solvents be useful in locating the geographic origin of a sample? Why or why not?

9. Based on material presented in this chapter, what would be the expected metabolic elimination pathway for isopropyl alcohol?

10. Why is it more effective to administer morphine by injection than by oral ingestion?

11. A woman weighing 60 kg drinks the equivalent of 60 g of ethanol. Her peak plasma concentration was found to be 1.91 g/L.
    a. What is the value of V_d for ethanol in this example?
    b. Assume that the woman's weight is 55% water. How do the weight of water in her body and the value of V_d compare? What does this mean in terms of the distribution of ethanol?

12. When administered orally, the predator drug Rohypnol® (flunitrazepam) has a bioavailability F of 70%. A woman arrives unconscious in the emergency room with signs that a sexual assault may have occurred within the last hour. She weighs 120 lb, and a blood analysis reveals a C_p of flunitrazepam of 0.50 mg/L. Estimate the size of the initial dose in milligrams, assuming that the concentration found is the peak concentration. Is it conceivable that a dose of this size could be administered surreptitiously in an alcoholic beverage?

13. According to the *CRC Handbook of Chemistry and Physics* (84th edition), the accepted natural isotopic abundance of ^{13}C is cited as 1.07% of all carbon. What would be the δ‰ value of a 1.00-g sample of carbon that had this isotopic ratio?

Integrative

1. Photosynthesis is the key partitioning process for fractionation of carbon in plants. Illustrate the process, and determine which isotope of carbon would be preferentially fractionated by this fixation.

2. Consider the following data regarding aspirin:

pKa	t$_{1/2}$ plasma	Principal metabolic reaction:	Conjugates with	~LD$_{50}$
3.5	17 min	hydrolysis	glucuronic acid	225 mg/kg

Source: Galichet, L. Y., et al., ed. "Aspirin," Clarke's Analysis of Drugs and Poisons. London: Pharmaceutical Press, **2004**, p. 652.

Answer the following questions:
a. What is the reported lethal dose for an adult female (130 lb), in number of tablets of aspirin, each of which typically contain 325 mg of aspirin?
b. Can the plasma half-life be used to determine how long aspirin will remain in the tissues? Explain.
c. Assuming a first-order process and rapid absorption, what would be the concentration of aspirin in the woman an hour after she took two 325-mg tablets?
d. Show the hydrolysis of aspirin and the expected product.
e. At what stage (ADME) does conjugation play a role?
f. Where in the gastrointestinal tract is aspirin absorbed preferentially? Justify your answer with calculations.

3. The following data apply to the drug Rohypnol® (flunitrazepam), FW 313.39/mole

Log P	pKa	Structure	t$_{1/2}$ plasma	t$_{1/2}$ elimination	Elimination
2.1	1.8		3 hr	16–35 hr	1% unchanged urine; 10% feces and the rest metabolites in urine

Source: Galichet, L. Y., et al., ed. *Clarke's Analysis of Drugs and Poisons, Vol. 2.* London: Pharmaceutical Press, **2004**.

Answer the following questions:

a. Where in the gastrointestinal tract is flunitrazepam absorbed preferentially? Justify your answer with calculations.

b. Assuming a typical dose of 1 mg, what would be the expected concentration of unchanged drug in a urine sample of 25 ml?

c. If the LOD/LOQ for this drug in a mass spectrometer is 2.5 $\mu g/L$, how long after the dose will it be possible to detect the unmetabolized drug in urine?

d. Propose a sample extraction scheme for flunitrazepam from blood.

e. The four major peaks in the mass spectrum of this drug are 312, 285, 266, and 238. Propose fragment losses to explain this distribution of peaks.

f. Based on the structure of the drug, what distinctive IR spectral features might be expected?

4. Find out the chemical structure of mescaline, a potent hallucinogen derived from the peyote cactus and one of the oldest-known hallucinogens. Is this hallucinogen a tryptamine or a phenethylamine?

5. Using Table 6.3 and a statistical or scientific graphing program, create a 3D scatterplot of the data as might be prepared for court. Prepare a second such plot that incorporates error bars. Comment on their importance.

Food for thought

1. Is caffeine an addictive substance? If so, is it psychologically addictive, physiologically addictive, or both? What about chocolate? Bubble gum? How are such distinctions made?

FURTHER READING

Ehleringer, J. R., et al., ed. *Stable Isotopes and Plant Carbon–Water Relations*. San Diego: Academic Press, **1993**.

Fenton, J. J. *Toxicology: A Case-Oriented Approach*. Boca Raton, FL: CRC Press, **2002**.

Klaassen, C. D., ed. *Casarett and Doull's Toxicology: The Basic Science of Poisons*. New York: McGraw-Hill Medical Publishing Division, **2001**.

International Atomic Energy Agency, (IAEA). *Reference and Intercomparison Materials for Stable Isotopes of Light Elements*. *IMAEA-TECDOC-825*, **1993**. Available online at www.iaea.org.

Levine, B., ed. *Principles of Forensic Toxicology*. Washington, DC: American Association of Clinical Chemistry, **2003**.

REFERENCES

1. Levine, B. "Chapter 11: Central Nervous System Depressants," in B. Levine, ed., *Principles of Forensic Toxicology*, 2d ed. Washington, DC: American Association of Clinical Chemistry, **2003**, 3–13.

2. Shulgin, A. T. "Basic Pharmacology and Effects," in R. Laing, ed., *Hallucinogens: A Forensic Drug Handbook*. San Diego: Academic Press, **2003**, 67–138.

3. Isenschmid, D. S. "Chapter 13: Cocaine," in B. Levine, ed., *Principles of Forensic Toxicology*, 2d ed. Washington, DC: American Association of Clinical Chemistry, **2003**, 3–13.

4. Drug Enforcement Administration. *Club Drugs: An Update*, **2001**.

5. *Physicians' Desk Reference for Nonprescription Drugs and Dietary Supplements*, 22. Montvale, NJ: Medical Economics-Thomson Healthcare, **2001**.

6. *Physician's Desk Reference*, 58th ed. Montvale, NJ: Thomson PDR, **2004**.

7. *State Fact Sheet*, U.S. Drug Enforcement Administration, Downloaded March 19, 2004, http://www.dea.gov/pubs/state_factsheets.html.

8. Gomez, J., and A. Rodriquez. "An Evaluation of the Results of a Drug Analysis." *United Nations Office on Drugs and Crime: Bulletin on Narcotics*, **1989**, 121–126.

9. Remberg, G., and A. H. Stead. "Drug Characterization/Impurity Profiling, with Special Focus on Methamphetamine: Recent Work of the United Nations International Drug Control Programme." *United Nations Office on Drugs and Crime: Bulletin on Narcotics*, 51 **1999**. Available on-line, www.inodc.orglunodclen/en/bulletin_on_narcotics.html

10. Dams, R., et al. "Heroin Impurity Profiling: Trends throughout a Decade of Experimenting." *Forensic Science International*, 123 **2001**, 81–88.

11. Besacier, F., et al. "Comparative Chemical Analyses of Drug Samples: General Approach and Application to Heroin." *Forensic Science International*, 85 **1997**, 113–125.

12. Esseiva, P., et al. "A Methodology for Illicit Heroin Seizures Comparison in a Drug Intelligence Perspective Using Large Databases." *Forensic Science International*, 132 **2003**, 139–252.

13. Holt, P. J. "Particle Size Analysis of Six Illicit Heroin Preparations Seized in the U.K." *Forensic Science International*, 81 **1996**, 17–28.

14. International Atomic Energy Agency. *Reference and Intercomparison Materials for Stable Isotopes of Light Elements. IMAEA-TECDOC-825*, **1993**.

15. Meier-Augenstein, W., and R. H. Liu. "Forensic Applications of Isotope Ratio Mass Spectrometry," in J. Yinon, ed., *Advances in Forensic Applications of Mass Spectrometry*. Boca Raton, FL: CRC Press, **2004**, 149–180.

16. National Institute of Standards and Technology, *Report of Investigation: Reference Materials 8562, 8563, 8564*, **2003**.

17. Santrock, J., et al. "Isotopic Analyses Based on the Mass Spectrum of Carbon Dioxide." *Analytical Chemistry*, 57 **1985**, 1444–1448.

18. Ehleringer, J. R., et al. "Geo-location of Heroin and Cocaine by Stable Isotope Ratios." *Forensic Science International*, 106 **1999**, 27–36.

19. Coyle, H. M., et al. "Criminalistics—Technical Notes—a Simple DNA Extraction Method for Marijuana Samples Used in Amplified Fragment Length Polymorphism (AFLP) Analysis." *Journal of Forensic Sciences*, 48 **2003**, 343–347.

20. Alghanim, H. J., and J. R. Almirall. "Development of Microsatellite Markers in *Cannabis sativa* for DNA Typing and Genetic Relatedness Analyses." *Analytical and Bioanalytical Chemistry*, 376 **2003**, 1225–1233.

21. Linacre, A., and J. Thorpe. "Detection and Identification of Cannabis by DNA." *Forensic Science International*, 91 **1998**, 71–76.

22. Cole, M. D. "Occluded Solvent Analysis as a Basis for Heroin and Cocaine Sample Differentiation." *Forensic Science Review*, 10 **1998**, 113–120.

23. Cartier, J., et al. "Headspace Analysis of Solvents in Cocaine and Heroin Samples." *Science and Justice: Journal of the Forensic Science Society*, 37 **1997**, 175–181.

24. Levine, B., and Y. Caplan. "Chapter 10: Alcohol," in B. Levine, ed., *Principles of Forensic Toxicology, Vol. 1*, 2d ed. Washington, DC: American Association of Clinical Chemistry, **2003**, 3–13.

25. Poklis, A. "Analytic/Forensic Toxicology," in C. D. Klaassen, *Casarett and Doull's Toxicology: The Basic Science of Poisons*, 6th, ed. New York: McGraw-Hill Medical Publishing Division, **2001**, 1089–1108.

26. *Forensic Toxicology Laboratory Guidelines*, SOFT/AAFS, **2002**. Downloaded December 3, 2003, www.soft-tox.org.

27. Langford, A. M., et al. "Drug Concentrations in Selected Skeletal Muscles." *Journal of Forensic Sciences*, 43 **1998**, 22–27.

28. Tracy, T. S., et al. "Stability of Benzodiazepines in Formaldehyde Solutions." *Journal of Analytical Toxicology*, 25 **2001**, 166–173.

29. Rohrig, T. P. "Comparison of Fentanyl Concentrations in Unembalmed and Embalmed Liver Samples." *Journal of Analytical Toxicology*, **1998**, 253.

30. Gannett, P. M., et al. "In Vitro Reaction of Formaldehyde with Fenfluramine: Conversion to *N*-Methyl Fenfluramine." *Journal of Analytical Toxicology*, 25 **2001**, 88–92.

31. Alluni-Perret, V., et al. "Determination of Heroin after Embalment." *Forensic Science International*, 134 **2003**, 36–39.

32. Benjamin, D. M. "Forensic Pharmacology," in R. Saferstein, ed., *Forensic Science Handbook*. Englewood Cliffs, NJ: Prentice Hall, **1993**, 253–286.

33. Medinsky, M. A., and J. L. Valentine. "Toxicokinetics," in C. D. Klaassen, ed., *Casarett and Doull's Toxicology: The Basic Science of Poisons*, 6th ed. New York: McGraw-Hill Medical Publishing Division, **2001**, 3–10.

34. Drummer, O. H. "Pharmacokinetics and Metabolism," in L. Y. Galichet, ed., *Clarke's Analysis of Drugs and Poisons in Pharmaceuticals, Body Fluids, and Postmortem Material, Vol. 2*, 3d ed. London: Pharmaceutical Press, **2003**, 173–188.

35. Spiehler, V. "Hair analysis by immunological methods from the beginning to 2000." *Forensic Science International*, 107 **2000**, 249–259.

36. Rozman, K. J., and C. D. Klaassen, "Absorption, Distribution, and Excretion of Toxicants," in C. D. Klaassen, ed., *Casarett and Doull's Toxicology: The Basic Science of Poisons*, 6th ed. New York: McGraw-Hill Medical Publishing Division, **2001**, 107–132.

37. Fenton, J. J. *Toxicology: A Case-Oriented Approach*. Boca Raton, FL: CRC Press, **2002**.

38. Spiehler, V., and B. Levine. "Pharmacokinetics and Pharmacodynamics," in B. Levine, ed., *Principles of Forensic Toxicology*. Washington, DC: American Association of Clinical Chemistry, **2003**, 47–63.

39. Lombardo, F., et al. "Prediction of Volume of Distribution Values in Humans for Neutral and Basic Drugs Using Physicochemical Measurements and Plasma Protein Binding Data." *Journal of Medicinal Chemistry*, 45 **2002**, 2867–2876.

40. Lombardo, F., et al. "ElogPoct: A Tool for Lipophilicity Determination in Drug Discovery." *Journal of Medicinal Chemistry*, 43 **2000**, 2922–2928.

41. Lombardo, F., et al. "Prediction of Volume of Distribution Values in Humans for Neutral and Basic Drugs. 2. Extended Data Set and Leave-Class-Out Statistics." *Journal of Medicinal Chemistry*, 47 **2004**, 1242–1250.

42. Levine, B., and V. Spiehler. "Chapter 4: Pharmacokinetics and Pharmacodynamics," in B. Levine, ed., *Principles of Forensic Toxicology, Vol. 1*, 2d ed. Washington, DC: American Association of Clinical Chemistry, **2003**, 47–63.

43. *Illegal Drug Price and Purity Report*, U.S. Department of Justice Drug Enforcement Agency, **April 2003**. Downloaded March 20, 2004.

44. Brettell, T. A., et al. "Forensic Science (Review)." *Analytical Chemistry*, 73 **2001**, 2735–2744.

45. Brettell, T. A., et al. "Forensic Science (Review)." *Analytical Chemistry*, 71 **1999**, 235R–255R.

46. Brettell, T. A., et al. "Forensic Science (Review)." *Analytical Chemistry*, 75 **2003**, 2877–2890.

47. Klein, R. F. X., and P. A. Hays. "Detection and Analysis of Drugs of Forensic Interest, 1992–2001; a Literature Review." *Microgram Journal*, 1 **2003**, 55–153.

Forensic Drug Analysis I

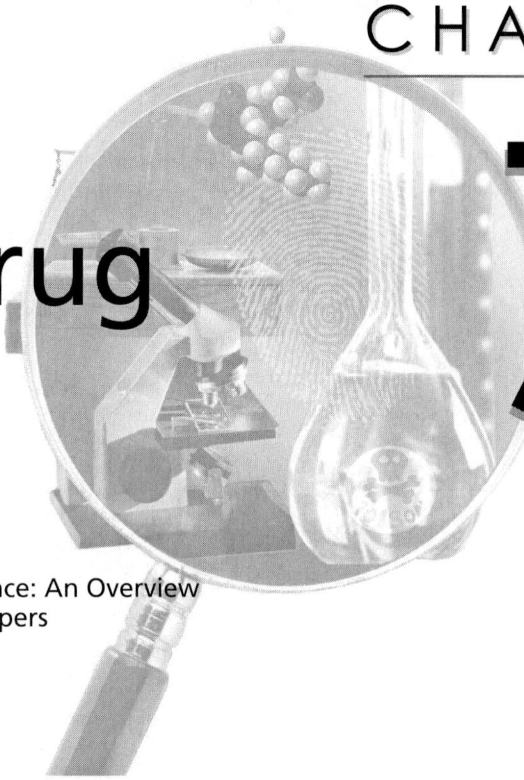

OVERVIEW AND ORIENTATION

This chapter will examine the nuts and bolts of forensic drug analysis, starting with **presumptive** color and precipitate (**microcrystal**) **tests**. These tests trace back to early qualitative organic chemistry. To investigate their mechanisms is to take a trip through the history of analytical chemistry, **functional group** chemistry, condensation reactions, and the nature of color. Effective ways to categorize drugs are classification by functional group or by chemical properties. The former, while useful in discussions of presumptive tests, becomes cumbersome, given that many drugs have multiple functional groups. Consequently, the approach we'll use here is one introduced in Chapter 4: classification by acidity, basicity, and neutrality. Secondary classifications, such as by the general effect of the drug (is it a narcotic, a stimulant, and so on) and the drug's schedule are also noted. Neutrals are a relatively small group and so will be discussed case-by-case. More attention will be paid to lipophilic drugs and oils, for which solubility becomes a more important defining characteristic than acidity or basicity.

Acids and lipophilic neutrals will be the first drug classes described in detail. The fundamentals presented in this chapter will set the stage for the next, in which we'll tackle the basic drugs. Although relatively small by comparison, the acidic drug group includes arguably the star of the forensic chemistry show: marijuana. Exhibits of marijuana, of drugs suspected to be marijuana, or of drugs related to marijuana typically make up the largest caseload of forensic laboratories that have drug sections. Indeed, marijuana exhibits make up the largest single category of forensic science casework. Chemically, the active ingredient THC is atypical in that it is a nonalkaloid plant extract that is acidic and lipophilic. Another interesting acidic drug, gamma hydroxybutyrate (GHB), is also one of the smallest in size. In addition, given its propensity for interconversion between an open and closed molecular form, it is one of the more difficult to extract and to analyze.

The focus of the discussions on drugs in this chapter and the next is not the analyses, but rather, fundamental chemistry, given that the latter defines and

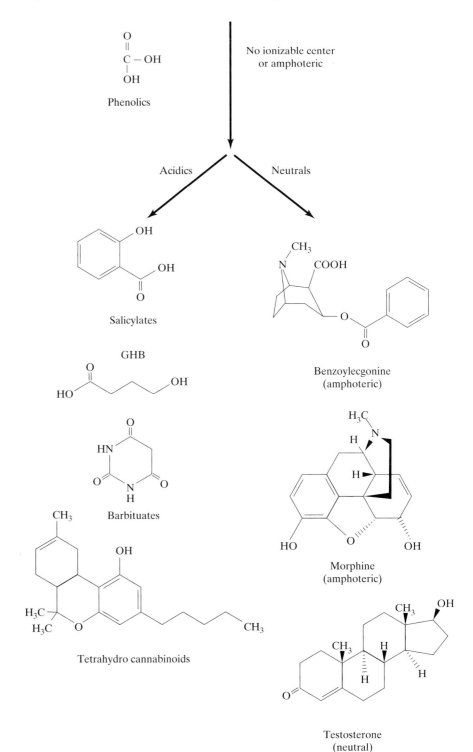

▶ **Figure 7.1** *Acidic and neutral drugs are the drug classes addressed in this chapter. Neutral drugs consist of those with no ionizable center, such as testosterone and related steroids, and those which are amphoteric, such as morphine and benzoylecgonine, a metabolite of cocaine.*

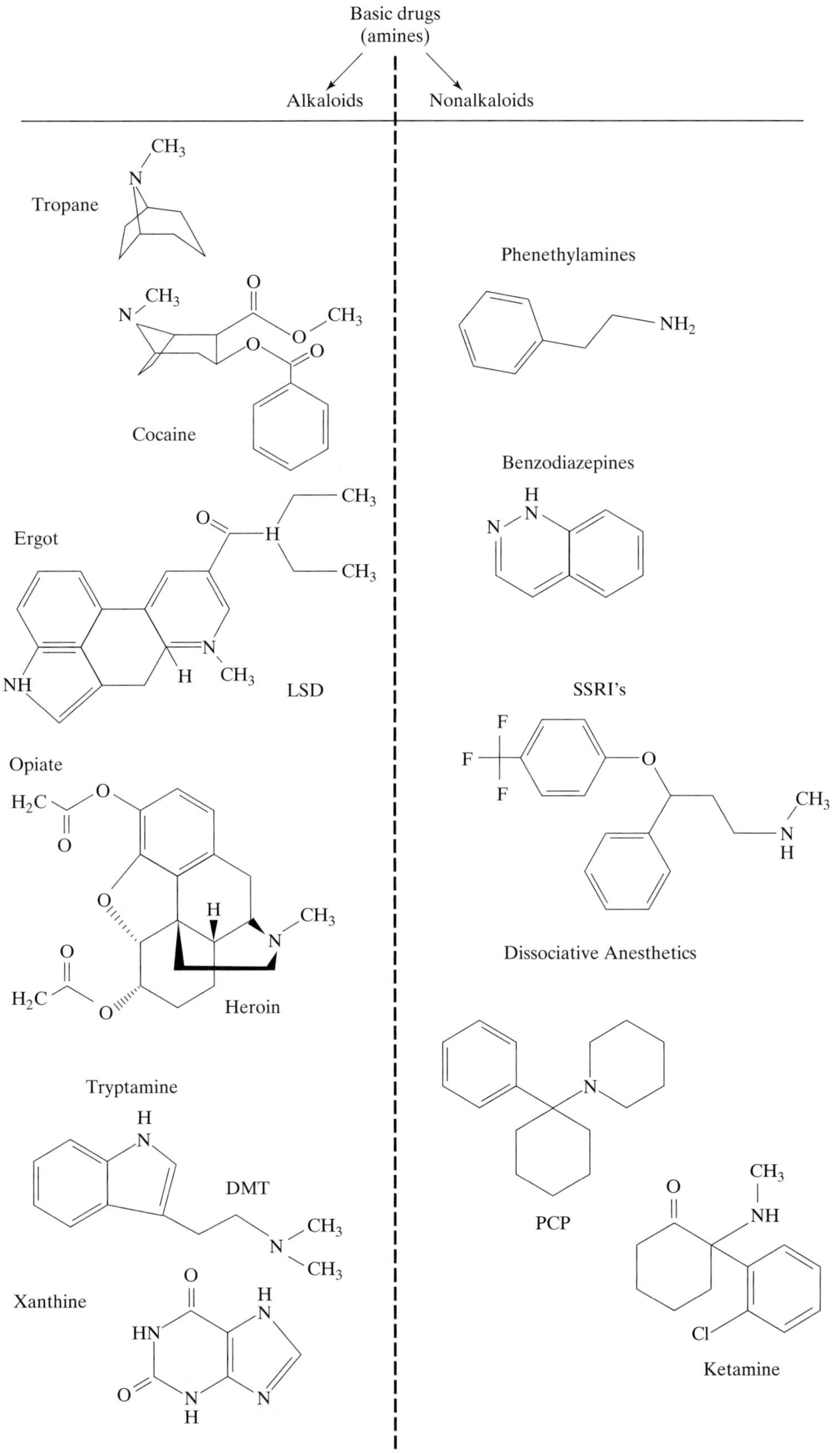

Basic drugs (amines) → Alkaloids | Nonalkaloids

Tropane

Cocaine

Ergot

LSD

Opiate

Heroin

Tryptamine

DMT

Xanthine

Phenethylamines

Benzodiazepines

SSRI's

Dissociative Anesthetics

PCP

Ketamine

◄ **Figure 7.2** *Basic drugs and classes, the largest subgroup in the acid–base classification scheme. The alkaloids are (or at least once were) derived from plant matter, while nonalkaloids are generally synthetic or semisynthetic. Tropane alkaloids include cocaine, while tryptamines include mescaline and psilocyn. Caffeine and theophylline are xanthine alkaloids. The selective serotonin reuptake inhibitors (SSRIs) include the second-generation SSRI antidepressants. Prozac® (fluoxetine, shown) and Paxil® belong to this class. Valium® is an example of a benzodiazepine. The basic drugs are the subject of Chapter 8.*

drives the former. Laboratory methods and protocols applied to drug analysis fill several volumes, and discretion being the better part of valor, no attempt will be made to reproduce that material here. For analytical references, *Clarke's Analysis of Drugs and Poisons* and the *Merck Index* are recommended as supplements to a laboratory's procedure manual.[1, 2]

7.1 THE ANALYTICAL APPROACH TO DRUG EVIDENCE: AN OVERVIEW

The analytical approach to drug analysis is the forensic approach: narrowing down possibilities until the drug is identified. With physical evidence, the initial screening is a visual examination, followed by presumptive and screening tests such as TLC. The final step is a definitive identification of the controlled substance or a determination that the sample does not contain one at detectable levels. This step usually necessitates instrumental analysis, such as GCMS or infrared spectrometry. Other instruments that have been employed are HPLC-MS, NMR, Raman spectrophotometry, and CE, but the emphasis here is on techniques that are routinely used and are available to the crime laboratory chemist or toxicologist. The method of choice for extraction and sample preparation is determined from the results of initial presumptive tests based on simple color changes.

7.2 PRESUMPTIVE COLOR TESTS AND TLC DEVELOPERS

7.2.1 OVERVIEW

Drug analysis and, to a lesser extent, toxicology utilize traditional color-based presumptive testing, targeting both drugs and diluents.[3] In a recent survey, 86% of responding laboratories reported using **spot testing** (another term used to describe presumptive testing) for drug analysis. The most frequently used color tests were the **Duquenois–Levine** (for marijuana), **cobalt thiocyanate** (for cocaine and related drugs), **Marquis** (for opium derivatives, amphetamines, and other alkaloids), and **p-DMAB** (p-dimethylaminobenzaldehyde, for **LSD**) tests.[4] Presumptive color tests arose from organic qualitative analysis dating back to the 1800s, and many are still used in courses incorporating organic qualitative analysis. The appearance of color or a change in color is evidence that a chemical reaction has occurred, and a simple color change is often evidence of a complex chemical reaction.

Color tests target the type of compound and functional groups. Drugs of interest in forensic chemistry are characterized by a relatively small number of functional groups, the most important of which are phenols, aromatic rings, and basic nitrogens (primary, secondary, or tertiary amines). Since many drugs have more that one active moiety, color testing is more complicated than the simple identification of the drug's functional group. In general, presumptive tests have detection limits from 1 to 50 μg, discounting complicating factors such as diluents.[4] The time of contact is an important consideration in color testing; Leaving samples in the reagents, many of which contain strong acids, can lead to colors unrelated to the presence of the target analyte. Finally, most color-test reagents can be used as developers for TLC and vice versa.

Section 7.2 Presumptive Color Tests and TLC Developers **271**

When an unknown powder, plant matter, or some other substance arrives at the laboratory as physical evidence, a series of color tests is performed, assuming that the amount of sample is sufficient. Most tests require a few milligrams, but the response depends on the concentration of the target analyte and may be influenced by the presence of other substances, such as the diluents. Analyst judgment rather than a set flowchart usually dictates which tests will be used and in what order. If green plantlike material is submitted, there would be little point in performing a test targeting cocaine or heroin, at least initially. Brownish tarry material suggests **hashish or heroin**, while tan powders often contain heroin, methamphetamine, and related controlled substances. Blotter papers, gel windows, or tiny tablets are common dosage forms of LSD. Evidence consisting of tan or whitish powders or pills is most suited to an extensive battery of color tests. As has been noted, when powders are encountered, the two tests used most frequently (initially) are the cobalt thiocyanate test for cocaine and the Marquis test for a variety of alkaloids. Some color tests are also precipitation tests in which the new solid accounts for the color change, but this is not universally true. The Duquenois (also Duquenois–Levine) test results in the formation of a colored solute that is selectively partitioned into a chloroform layer.

Spot tests are usually performed with a **spot plate** (glass or ceramic) or a disposable test tube. Disposable surfaces are preferred, to eliminate carry-over or cross-contamination from earlier tests. Results are easier to see with a white background, although a few spot tests work better on a black spot plate. To perform the test, a small amount of the questioned powder is placed in a well of the plate and reagent is added. For tests that require successive reagents or a liquid–liquid extraction, test tubes are used. As presumptive tests, all will react with more than one substance, but to an experienced chemist, subtle differences are usually apparent. Control samples that include a blank or negative control (a reagent only in the spot plate or test tube) and a known sample or samples should be analyzed in parallel with the questioned material.

7.2.2 What Is Color?

A color change is the outward evidence of a chemical reaction, just as the evolution of a gas indicates chemical decomposition. Appearance or change of color points to an alteration in chemical bonding that accompanies a reaction. This change is manifest by some surprisingly complex reaction chemistry. **Colorants** are substances or materials that can absorb or emit electromagnetic energy in the visible range; two types of colorants (**dyes** and **pigments**) are of particular interest in forensic chemistry. Many of the color changes observed with presumptive-testing reagents are the result of dye formation, a subject that will be addressed shortly.

Exhibit A: A Light Review

Electromagnetic radiation can be described as a particle and as a wave; the key equations are as follows:

In the wave model, $c = \lambda \nu$, where λ is the wavelength, ν is the frequency in Hz (s^{-1}) and c is the speed of light, $3.0 \times 10^8 \text{ ms}^{-1}$. In the particle model, $E_{photon} = h\nu$, where h is Planck's constant $= 6.63 \times 10^{-34}$ Js. The bridge between the two models is $E = hc/\lambda$, derived by combining the foregoing expressions.

Exhibit A: (Continued)

In UV-VIS spectroscopy, the energy of an absorbed photon drives the molecule into an excited state via the promotion of an electron in accordance with the relationship $M + h\nu \longrightarrow M^*$. The energy is dissipated via collisions in solution. In order for a photon to be absorbed, its energy must match that of the energy gap to be traversed, such as the HOMO-LUMO gap discussed in this chapter.

For example, the natural colorant β-carotene consists of a conjugated system of double bonds and a λ_{max} of 455 nm. As a consequence of absorbing this blue light, the compound appears orange (the complementary color). The energy gap is calculated by first converting the wavelength to meters (to match units of Planck's constant) and then substituting:

$$455 \text{ nm} * \frac{1 \text{ m}}{10^9 \text{ nm}} = 4.55 \times 10^{-7} \text{ m}$$

$$\Delta E = \frac{6.63 \times 10^{-34} \text{ Js} * 3.0 \times 10^8 \text{ ms}^{-1}}{4.55 \times 10^{-7} \text{ m}} = 4.37 \times 10^{-19} \text{ J per photon}$$

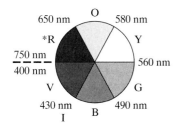

▲ **Figure 7.3** *An artist's color wheel showing the relationship between complementary colors. If a molecule absorbs, for example, orange light, it will appear blue, the color directly across the circle. Starting from red (R*) and moving clockwise, spectral colors are shown. The acronym ROYGBIV stands for red, orange, yellow, green, blue, indigo, and violet, in that order. These colors are also called Newton's colors.*

Molecular Orbital Transitions: A reasonable place to begin a discussion on color is to relate human vision to the spectrophotometric detection of visible light. Molecular compounds are covalently bonded, meaning that atomic orbitals combine to form **molecular orbitals**, denoted as σ, π, and so on. If a sample powder appears white, it is reflecting all wavelengths of visible light in the 400–700-nm range. In other words, none of the energy gaps in the molecular orbital structure correlate with visible energy. No visible light is absorbed and no color is observed.

If, upon the addition of a few drops of Marquis reagent, a red color appears, red light is being reflected and the complementary color of light is absorbed by the sample. Since absorption in the UV/VIS range correlates to an electronic transition between molecular orbitals, it follows that the electronic structure and bonding arrangement were altered by the addition of reagent. The change may be to the ingredients in the reagent, the sample, or both. The rearrangement of molecular orbitals means that blue light is now matched with some energy gap between the orbitals, a gap that did not exist before the Marquis reagent was added to the white powder. The color change indicates that a chemical reaction occurred.

Light from the sun or some other type of broad-spectrum light source emits a mix of the visible wavelengths and is referred to as white light. If a substance or surface reflects the light diffusely or at random angles, the light appears

▶ **Figure 7.4** *Superimposed spectra of the spectral colors by wavelength. If all are absorbed equally, a viewer will perceive black; if all are reflected equally, a viewer will perceive white. If all wavelengths are partially absorbed in equal proportion, a viewer will perceive gray.*

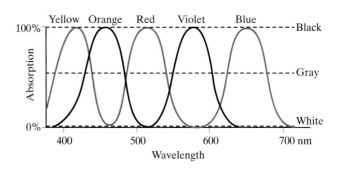

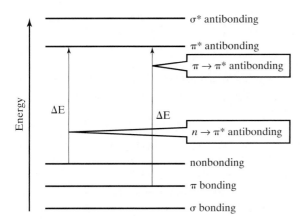

◀ **Figure 7.5** *The two electronic transitions feasible with UV/VIS radiation, ranging from 200 nm to 700 nm.*

white. By contrast, if the material absorbs all wavelengths, it will appear black. Between these extremes is the color gray, which is what is seen if some constant percentage of intensity at all wavelengths is absorbed. White, gray, and black are referred to as **achromatic**—literally, lacking color. If a specific color is perceived, the light is **chromatic**.

Absorption of energy in the visible range is governed by Beer's law,

$$A = \varepsilon_\lambda bc \qquad (7.1)$$

where A is the absorbance, ε is the molar extinction coefficient of the sample at wavelength λ, b is the path length, and c is the concentration of the sample. Many dyes have high extinction coefficients, in the range of 10^4–$10^5\,\mathrm{M}^{-1}\,\mathrm{cm}^{-1}$, and as a result are intensely colored.[5] This is important in color testing, since the more intense a color, the easier it is to perceive and the smaller the amount of the sample required.

UV/VIS light is of relatively low energy and capable of exciting only two kinds of electronic transitions. The $\sigma \longrightarrow \pi^*$ transition is shorter (has a smaller energy gap) and involves a lower energy, or "redder," photon than the $\pi \longrightarrow \pi^*$. If, in a given molecule, an energy gap corresponds to red light of 650 nm, the sample will reflect all light but 650 nm. In other words, red light will be subtracted from the white light, and what the eye then perceives is the complementary blue-green color, as shown in Figure 7.3. Note that an organic compound must have π electrons if there is to be any possibility of absorption of a UV/VIS photon. Finally, recall that in solution there are no single sharp transitions. Even for one discrete energy gap, a Gaussian distribution defines the possible transitions. Add to that more gaps and more distributions, and what results is an endless variety of colors as perceived by the eye.

The portion of the molecule capable of absorbing a photon is called the **chromophore**. This term is generic in the sense that even a UV absorber can be

Exhibit B: A Hundred Thousand Shades of Green

It is estimated that the average human visual system can discriminate about a million different colors. If we assume the seven basic colors of red, orange, yellow, green, blue, indigo, and violet (ROYGBIV), then the human eye perceives roughly 142,000 shades of green alone.

called a chromophore, although the human eye cannot detect any color resulting from a UV transition. To generate color, the transitions require lower energy photons corresponding to smaller energy gaps. One way to decrease the size of the gaps is through **conjugation** (Figure 7.6). Because the gaps are smaller, visible light has enough energy to promote electrons through absorption, imparting color. The more conjugation in the system, the longer is the wavelength of light absorbed and the darker is the perceived color.

Another method of altering transitions and imparting color is via the addition of other functional groups. An **auxochrome** is a group that is not by itself a chromophore, but a group that will alter the wavelength or intensity of the chromophore. Oxygen and nitrogen contain unshared electrons and possess π electrons that are available to interact with the aromatic system. This property decreases the energy gap and increases the wavelength of absorbed light. When these unshared pairs are removed, as in the case of the anilinium ion, λ_{max} drops back to the value it has for unsubstituted benzene. Changes to absorption maxima can be characterized as shown in Figure 7.7. When the wavelength of absorption increases, the energy of the light absorbed decreases, or becomes "redder," corresponding to a "blueshift" in the observed color. This kind of shift is referred to as a **bathochromic** shift, while the opposite, a shift to absorbance of bluer light and a redshift in appearance, is called a **hypsochromic** shift. Increasing the intensity (increasing ϵ_λ) correlates with a hyperchromic shift, and decreasing it corresponds to a hypochromic shift. These shifts are summarize in Figure 7.8.

▶ **Figure 7.6** *The effect of conjugation is to reduce energy gaps. As a result of conjugation, the photon energy required to promote an electron is less than it would be in the absence of conjugation. If there is sufficient conjugation, the electron can be promoted with visible light.*

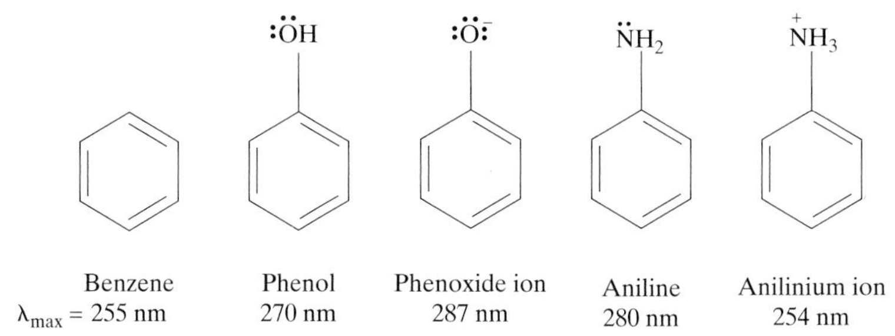

▶ **Figure 7.7** *The effect of auxochromes on absorbance. Auxochromes change the electronic character of the molecule, including the π-electron availability. The combination of auxochromes and conjugation is important in generating the visible colors characteristic of many color tests.*

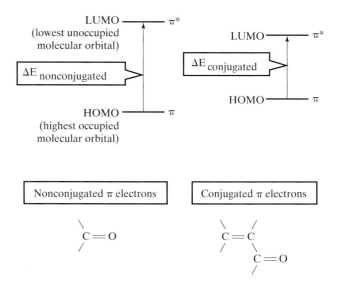

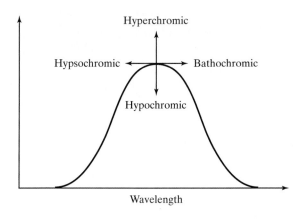

Hyperchromic

Hypsochromic ← → Bathochromic

Hypochromic

Wavelength

◀ **Figure 7.8** *The addition of an auxochrome can affect the absorbance of a chromophore by altering the wavelength, intensity of absorptivity, or both.*

For relatively simple conjugated systems, the Woodward–Fieser rules can be utilized to estimate λ_{max}. As seen in Table 7.2 in particular, the prediction of absorption from structure is complicated, and a more detailed discussion is beyond the scope of this text. For example, solvents may play a role in dictating

Table 7.1   Woodward–Fieser Rules for the Calculation of Absorption Maxima of Dienes and Polyenes (good to about ±3 nm)[*]

	$\lambda(nm)$
Parent chromophore	214
Each alkyl substituent (at any position) add	5
Each exocyclic double bond add	5
* Exocyclic to ring B only	
Each additional conjugated double bond (one end only) add	30
Each homoannular (rather than acyclic or heteroannular) add	39
° Homoannular (same ring)	

Note: In cases for which both types of diene systems are present, the one with the longer wavelength is designated as the parent system. Do *not* count the double bond as a substituent, since this effect is included.

Each polar group	
—O—acyl	0
—OR	6
—SR	30
—Cl, $_y$—Br	5
—NR$_2$	60
Solvent correction	0

[*] From R. B. Woodward, *J. Am. Chem. Soc.*, **63**, 1123 (1941); **64**, 72, 76 (1942); L. F. Fieser and M. Fieser, *Natural Products Related to Phenanthrene*, Reinhold, New York, 1949. Reproduced with permission from J. B. Lambert et al., *Organic Structural Spectroscopy*. Copyright 1998 Prentice Hall, Inc.

Table 7.2	**Rules for the Calculation of the Position of $\pi \longrightarrow \pi^*$ Absorption Maxima of Unsaturated Carbonyl Compounds**[†]

β α R $\quad\mid\quad\mid\quad\mid$ $\beta-C=C-C=O$ and	δ γ β α R $\mid\quad\mid\quad\mid\quad\mid\quad\mid$ $-C=C-C=C-C=O$	λ(nm)
Parent α, β-unsaturated carbonyl compound		
(acyclic, six-membered, or larger ring ketone) R=alkyl		215
(5-membered ring ketone)		202
(aldehyde) R=H		207
(acid or ester) R=OH or OR		193
Each alkyl substituent:		
α add		10
β add		12
If other double bonds, for each γ, δ, etc., add		18
Each exocyclic carbon–carbon double bond add		5
Each extra conjugation add (do not count double bond as		
substituent, as this effect is included)		30
Each homoannular add		39
Each polar group		
—OH	α	35
	β	30
	δ	50
—O—Ac	α, β, or δ	6
—OR	α	35
	β	30
	γ	17
	δ	31
—SR	β	85
—Cl	α	15
	β	12
—Br	α	25
	β	30
—NR_2	β	95
Solvent correction		0
Ethanol, methanol		0
Chloroform		1
Dioxane		5
Diethyl ether		7
Hexane, cyclohexane		11
Water		−8

[†] From R. B. Woodward, *J. Am. Chem. Soc.*, **63**, 1123 (1941); **64**, 72, 76 (1942); L. F. Fieser and M. Fieser, *Natural Products Related to Phenanthrene*, Reinhold, New York, 1949; A. I. Scott, *Interpretation of the UV Spectra of Natural Products*, Pergamon Press, New York, 1964. Reproduced with permission from J. B. Lambert et al., *Organic Structural Spectroscopy*. Copyright 1998 Prentice Hall, Inc.

absorbance and color, as can configurations and steric effects.[6,7] Also, more than one transition often is involved in producing the perceived color of a solution. Central to the present discussion and color-based presumptive tests is an understanding that, in general, place in italics for emphasis. The latter results from a change in λ_{max}, which in turn changes the perceived color in accordance with the law of complements. The benzene ring chromophore is a common element in many colored structures, and substituents on the rings can have dramatic effects on absorbance.[7] When a substituent adds unshared electron pairs to an aromatic

Example Problem 7.1

Lycopene is the red colorant responsible for the color of ripe tomatoes. Use the Woodward–Fieser rules (Table 7.1) to predict λ_{max}, and compare your result with the actual value.

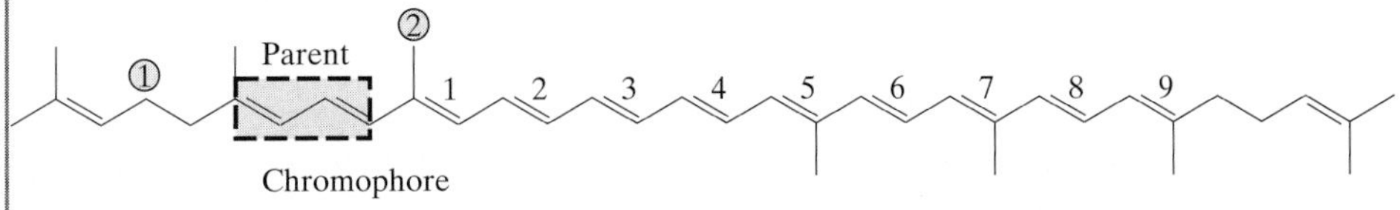

Lycopene
λ_{max} = 474 nm

Answer: The parent chromophore is highlighted and provides the base absorbance of 214 nm. Two alkyl substituents at points 1 and 2 contribute $2 \times 5 = 10$ nm, to reach a base of 224 nm. Nine additional conjugated double bonds contribute $9(30) = 270$ nm, to yield a predicted λ_{max} of 464 nm, which is a reasonable estimate of the true value of 474 nm.

system, as in the case of —OH and amine groups, the effect can be significant and can depend on the pH, since protonation–deprotonation changes the electronic characteristics of the chromophore. Finally, absorption characteristics and color are affected by the presence of electron donor and acceptor moieties. To simplify, whenever two electrons are added or donated to a molecule, a new energy level and potential transition results. Example donor groups are those with unshared electron pairs such as amines. Acceptor groups are those that stabilize the added electrons via resonance structures; examples are nitrate and carbonate. Keeping these fundamentals in mind, we can usually understand color changes caused by presumptive-test reagents and can interpret the results in a general sense. Given that the tests are presumptive, this level of understanding is sufficient.

Example Problem 7.2

The indicator phenolphthalein is colorless under basic conditions and an intense pink color under acidic conditions. It is also used as a presumptive test for blood. What accounts for the color change?

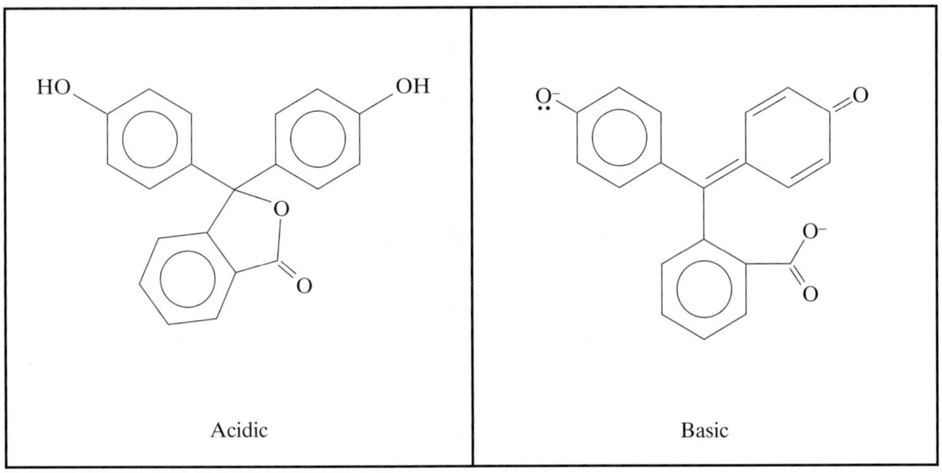

Acidic

Basic

Answer: Under acidic conditions (pH at least 2 pH units below the pK_a), the two phenolic groups are protonated. Under basic conditions, these deprotonate become a donor/acceptor pair that increases conjugation, decreases the existing energy gaps, and allows for absorption in the blue range. This produces the perceived pinkish red color. Note also that under basic conditions the ring opens and another unshared pair is donated to the conjugated structure.

Dyes and Dye Formation: A number of presumptive tests generate color through dye formation. Like pigments, dyes are colorants, but the two terms are often confused.[5] A *pigment* is a suspension of insoluble materials in a solvent, whereas a *dye* is a solution of the colorant. Colorants can be organic, inorganic, natural, or synthetic, but it is solubility that differentiates a dye from a pigment. For purposes of presumptive testing, the distinction is not crucial, but it becomes so in other areas of forensic interest, such as paint and ink analysis. Much more about dyes and pigments in these contexts will be presented in Chapter 9.

Historical Evidence 7.1—Drugs and Dyes

These two families of compounds have much more in common than might first be expected, and both are, and continue to be, important in forensic chemistry. Many drugs and dyes have an acid–base character, and many are based on similar structures, such as aromatic and other amines. The drug and dye industries came of age in the mid-1800s, and the first synthetic dye, mauve (aniline purple), arose from an attempt to make quinine to treat malaria. In 1856, an 18-year-old-chemist named William Henry Perkin was studying at the British Royal College of Chemistry when he accidentally created the dye from a mixture of aniline and toluidines. He left school and founded what was to become one of the largest segments of the chemical industry: the production of dyes and pigments.

In 1863, the company that was to become Bayer (of aspirin and pharmaceutical fame) was founded in Germany by Friedrich Bayer (1825–1880) and Johann Friedrich Weskott (1821–1876), both of whom were dye makers. The pharmaceutical group was not formed until 1881. Aspirin, developed by Bayer chemist Felix Hoffman, was commercialized in 1899, a year that marked the initial emergence of the drug industry as a separate entity.

Out of the many reaction pathways that can lead to dye formation, four are central in presumptive color testing:

- *Di- and triarylmethines.* These dyes are characterized by systems of two or three linked substituted phenyl rings (**aryl** groups). Common functionalities attached to the phenyl rings include dimethylamine, OH, and O^- groups. Some of these molecules can exist as cations. There are also multiple-linked ring dyes in this class, characterized by an **aza** linkage —N= between the substituted phenyl rings.
- *Azo dyes, diazonium salts, and azo coupling.* **Azo** dye chemistry is one of the most important subjects in colorant chemistry. The defining characteristic of azo dyes is the azo linkage, of the form —N=N—. The reactions in which groups are linked through the azo group are called *coupling reactions.* Like the arylmethines, these dyes can exist as cations and can form salts, called diazonium salts. An example is Fast Blue B, a diazonium cation that was once widely used as a spray reagent for TLC and as a color test for the active ingredients in marijuana. Due to concerns about

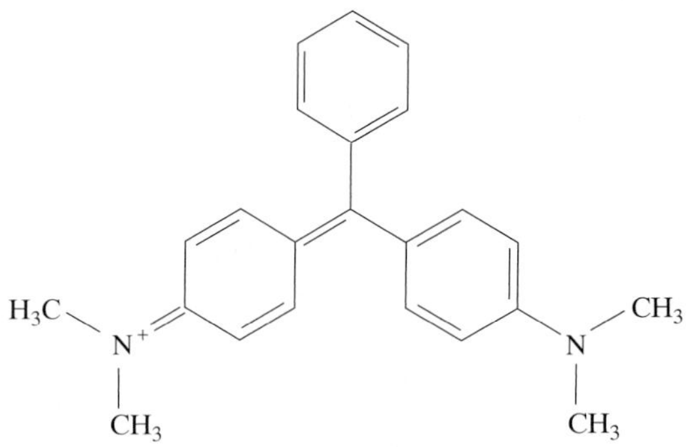

◀ **Figure 7.9** *Malachite green cation, a triarylmethine dye characterized by three phenyl rings.*

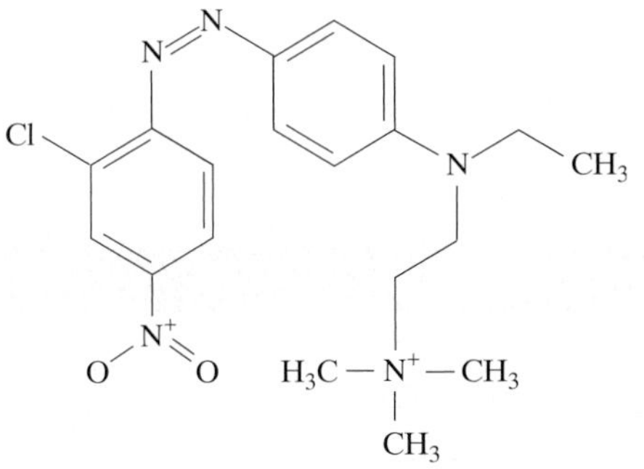

Malachite green, cation form

Basic red 18

◀ **Figure 7.10** *Basic Red 18, an azo dye.*

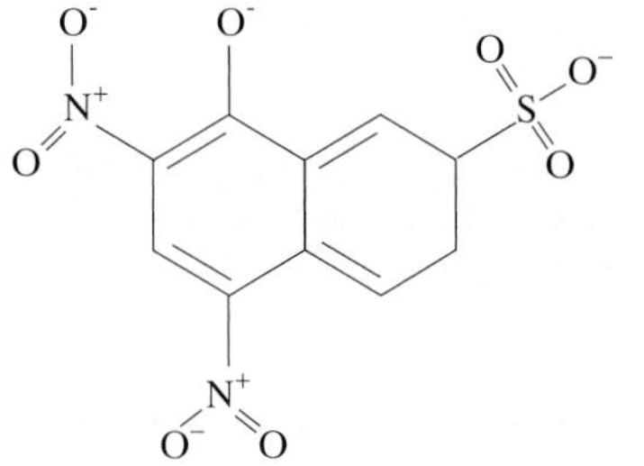

◀ **Figure 7.11** *Acid yellow dye, also called naphthol yellow. This is a nitroso dye.*

its carcinogenicity, it is rarely used now, but substitutes work in accordance with comparable principles.

- *Nitro and nitroso dyes*. These are dyes that contain NO_2 functionality.
- *Carbonyls*. These are dyes that contain the carbonyl group. A large number are based on the structure of anthraquinone.

Other Structural Features: The colored products of presumptive testing frequently contain carbonium ions. Alternatively called carbocations and carbonium ions, these ions have a positively charged carbon atom in their structure. A carbocation that is highly substituted or found within a conjugated system, this carbon atom can be quite stable. A number of proposed structures for colored products include carbocations.

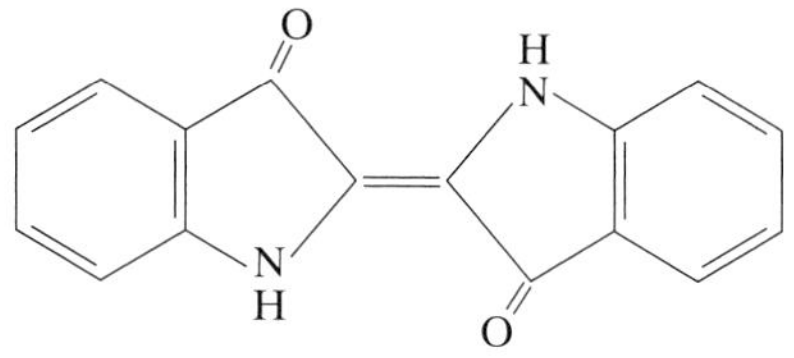

Indigo

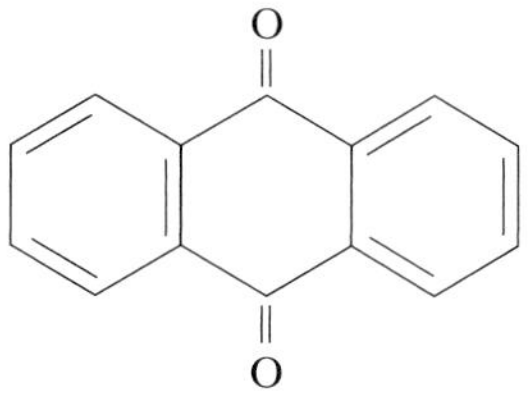

▶ **Figure 7.12** *Indigo is one of the oldest natural dyes known and is deep purple in color. It is a carbonyl dye, many of which are based on or related to the structure of anthraquinone.*

Anthraquinone

Exhibit C: Carbocations

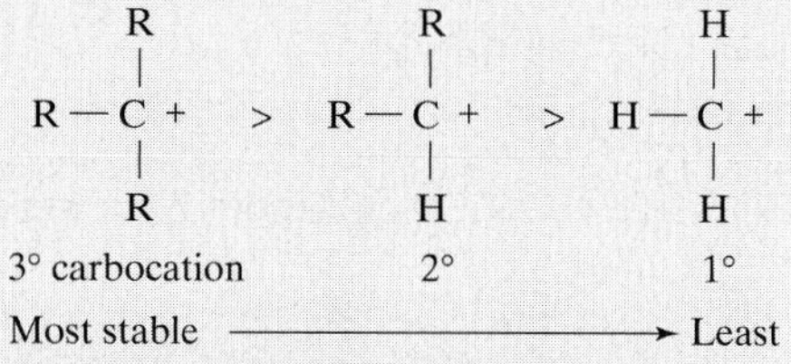

$$
\begin{array}{ccc}
\text{R} & \text{R} & \text{H} \\
| & | & | \\
\text{R} - \text{C} + \;>\; \text{R} - \text{C} + \;>\; \text{H} - \text{C} + \\
| & | & | \\
\text{R} & \text{H} & \text{H} \\
3° \text{ carbocation} & 2° & 1°
\end{array}
$$

Most stable ————————————→ Least

Recall from organic chemistry that carbocations are encountered as intermediates in many reactions. Since these compounds are electron-deficient species, they are strongly electrophilic and generally reactive. Carbocations are stabilized by substitution, and highly substituted carbocations may be stable enough to remain as carbocations and to be isolated as products of a reaction. Conjugation, the key to producing color, also stabilizes carbocations through resonance structures. If a carbocation is sufficiently stable, it can form salts, just as any cation can.

Carbocations should not be confused with free radicals or carbanions. A free radical is similar to a carbocation in that it has three bonds, but rather than having a deficit of two electrons, a free radical has one unshared electron and, as a result, is highly reactive. A carbanion has an unshared pair of electrons in addition to three bonds and carries a negative charge. A carbene carbon has two bonds and one unshared pair of electrons. Carbenes are rarely isolated, because of their propensity to react with one another to form dimers.

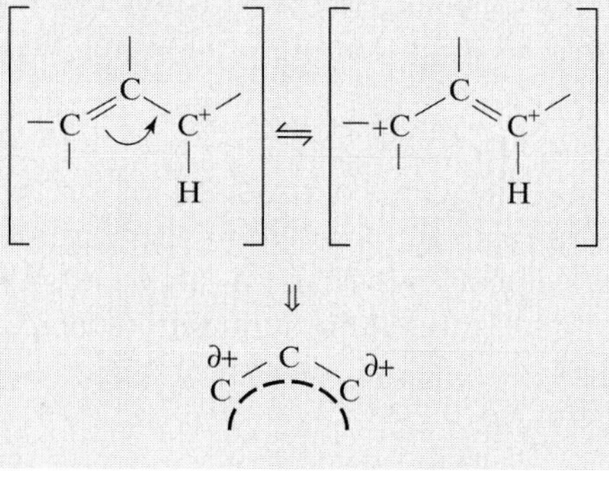

Example Problem 7.3

The following dye is used as indicators in acid–base titrations:
Rationalize the color changes.

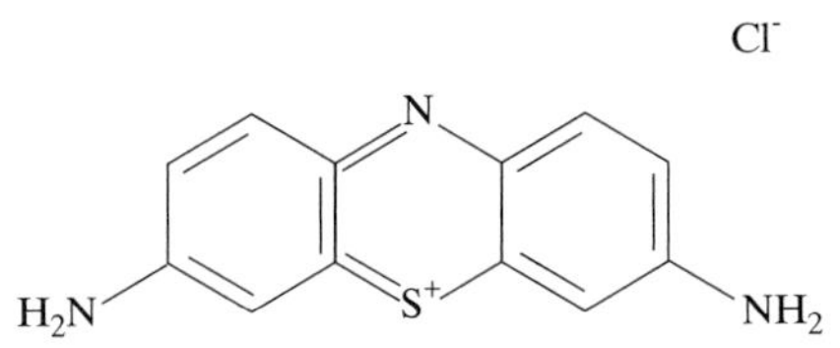

Color change
of colorless to violet in the
pH range of 7-8

Answer: The amine groups are protonated under acidic conditions and deprotonated in neutral-to-mildly-basic color ranges. Deprotonation has the same effect here as it did with phenolphthalein, allowing unshared pairs of electrons to interact with the aromatic system. Under acidic conditions and protonation, there is less conjugation than under basic and unprotonated conditions. The indicator is cyanine.

7.2.3 EXAMPLES OF PRESUMPTIVE COLOR TESTS

The Marquis Test: This test is arguably the most versatile and widely used color test in drug analysis (Figures 7.13 and 7.14). Its chemistry is complex and not completely understood.[8] The color produced is apparently the result of a relatively stable **carbocation**[9,10] formed through the action of formaldehyde,[8] although a **free-radical** mechanism has also been suggested.[11] The first step is addition of the formaldehyde to an aromatic ring that has an amine group in a side chain. The intermediate product of this reaction is an alcohol that is available for later reactions. The carbocation can then be attacked by nucleophiles such as the alcohol or the electrons in the double bond of the original structure. The product is a dimer of the original molecule with more conjugation that in some cases can be revealed by the appearance of a color. Analysis using low-temperature NMR has shown that the reagent will react with some aromatics to form carbonium ions,[9,12] and a comprehensive spectral analysis employing UV, IR, and NMR spectroscopy pointed to a polymerization step. However, these reports are dated, and structures and mechanisms are best considered as proposed rather than confirmed.

The Marquis reagent reacts with amphetamine and methamphetamine to produce the orange-red product shown in Figure 7.14 and in the color insert.[8] The proposed mechanism involves an attack of the amine on the carbonyl of formaldehyde, although the path from there to the products proposed is debatable.[13] The orange color produced by amphetamine and methamphetamine is distinctive, but to differentiate amphetamine (a primary amine) from methamphetamine (a secondary amine), an additional color test is needed. The Simon test, described shortly, is employed to differentiate the two compounds.

Example Problem 7.4

Explain how the Marquis reagent (formaldehyde and sulfuric acid) would likely react with a substituted aromatic compound. One of the earliest synthetic polymers, called Bakelite, was made from formaldehyde and phenol in an analogous process.

Answer:

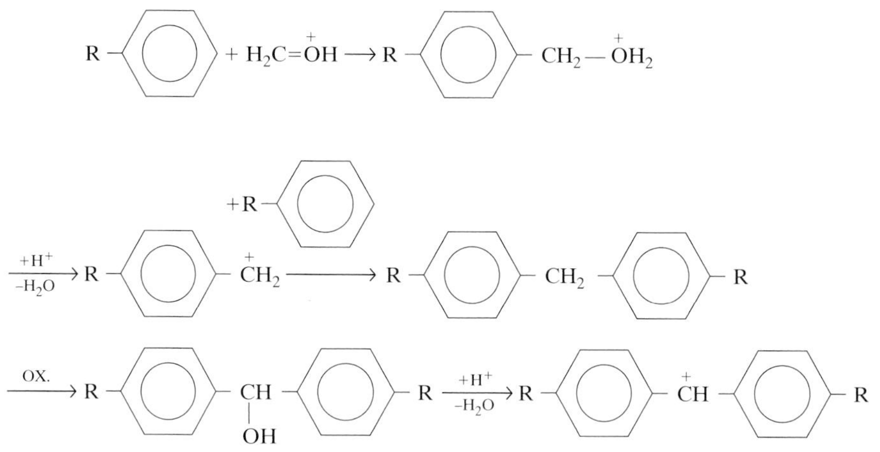

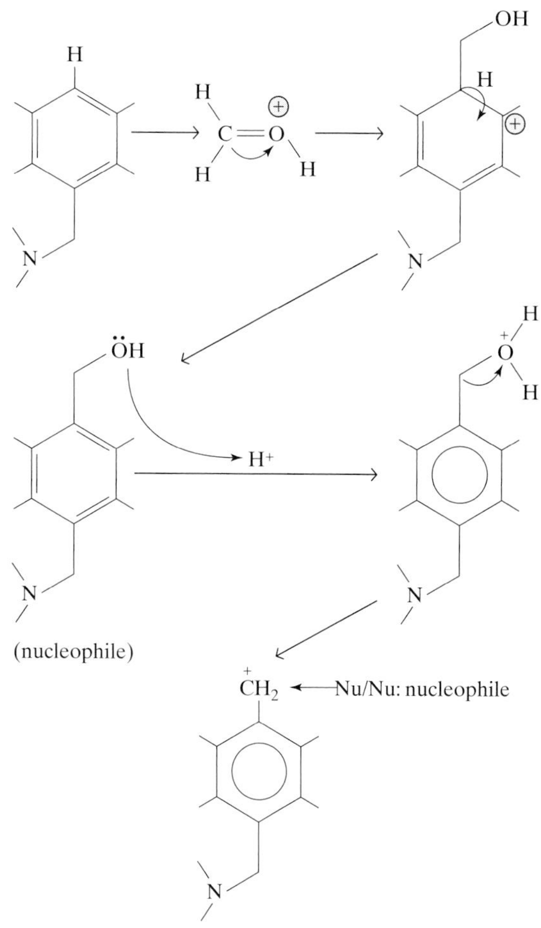

▶ **Figure 7.13** *(a) The first step in the reaction of formaldehyde and an aromatic ring with an amine subsistuent. A carbocation is created that can react with other nucleophiles, including the alcohol produced as an intermediate.*

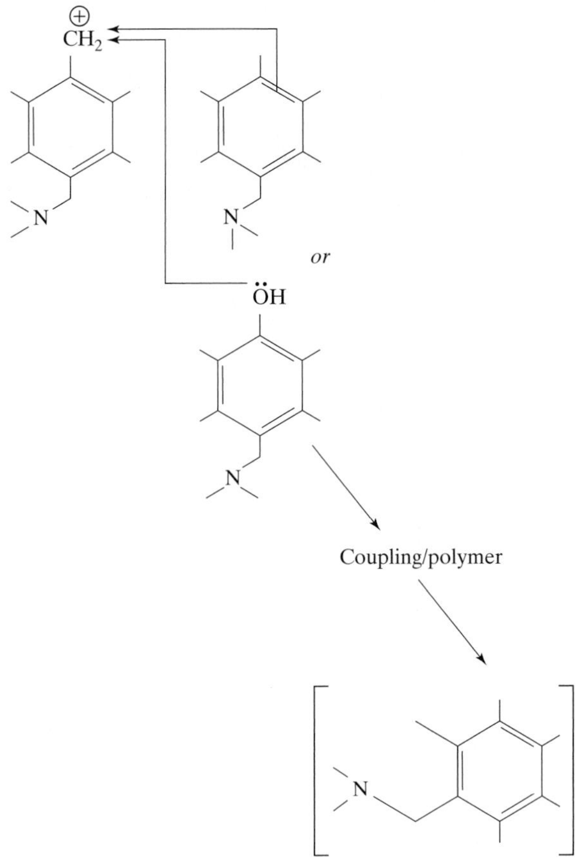

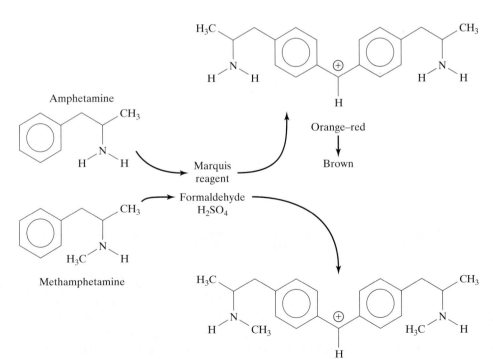

◀ **Figure 7.13b** *(b) Two possible nucleophilic attacks that could produce a polymer.*

◀ **Figure 7.14** *The reaction of the Marquis reagent with amphetamine and methamphetamine.*

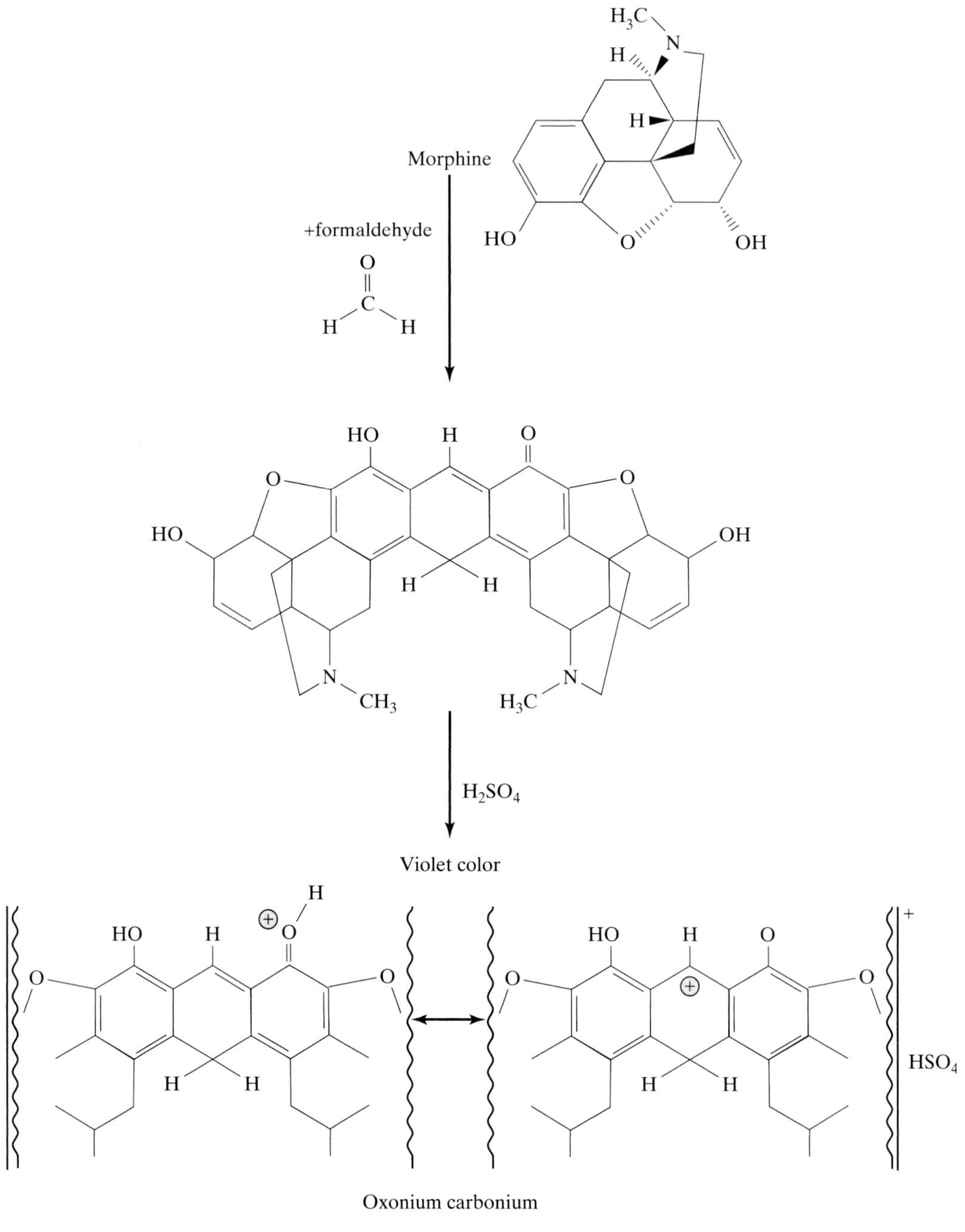

▲ **Figure 7.15** *The likely steps involved in the reaction of morphine with the Marquis reagent leading to formation of a colored product. Adapted from Auterhoff, H. and D. Braun. "Die Farbreaktion des Morphins nach E. Marquis."* Arch. Pharrmaz. (Weinheim), *306 1973, 866–873.*

In the case of the Marquis reagent and morphine, a linked oxonium carbonium ion has been suggested as the source of the violet-colored product via an intermediate linked structure.[9] The mechanism is analogous to the amphetamine–methamphetamine pathway: an attack on formaldehyde by the amine, the linkage of two drug molecules, and formation of the colored carbonium under acidic conditions.

Ehrlich's Test: Ehrlich's reagent, p-dimethylaminobenzaldehyde (p-DMAB) in ethanol with HCl, works through the formation of a stable carbocation or ion by **condensation** (Figure 7.16).[10,14–17] This reagent is used principally for the detection of LSD, as well as for **indole** alkaloids, for which the test is highly sensitive. This sensitivity is necessary, given that the individual dosage unit of LSD is in the low microgram range.

The Liebermann Test: The **Liebermann** test, also known as the Liebermann nitroso test (Figure 7.17), is another presumptive test that incorporates a coupling reaction

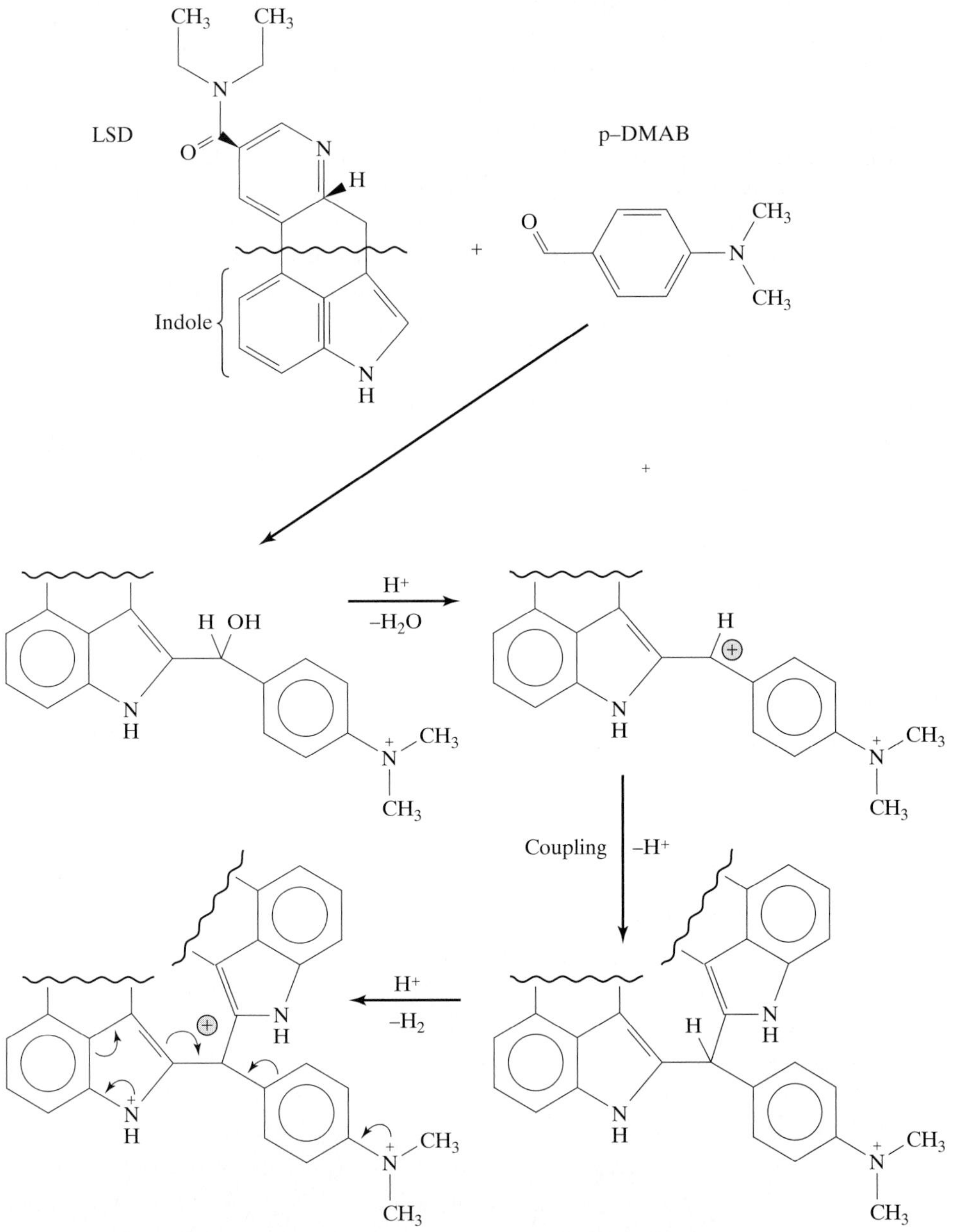

▲ **Figure 7.16** *The proposed reaction for LSD (an indole) and Ehrlich's reagent. Adapted from "United Nations Scientific and Technical Notes,"* Chemistry and Reaction Mechanisms of Rapid Tests for Drugs of Abuse and Precursor Chemicals, *1989.*

to form the colored product. The Liebermann reagent will react with phenols and amines, both of which are common in drug molecules. The reagent consists of KNO_2 dissolved in sulfuric acid, forming nitrous acid (HONO). Two steps are involved in color formation: nitration of the substrate drug (step 1 in Figure 7.17) and coupling to form a quinone imine (step 2). The coupling begins with a dehydration step promoted by the sulfuric acid, followed by diazonium coupling to yield a colored product. The resulting compound possesses characteristics of an indicator, since the color is pH dependent; not surprisingly, many acid–base indicators, such as methyl red and methyl orange, are diazonium based.

The Simon Test: The **Simon** test (Figure 7.18) is one of the more intriguing color tests that combines elements of dyes (diazonium ions), transition metal complexes (discussed in detail shortly), and carbocations.[18–20] The Simon test is a variation of the sodium **nitroprusside** test that has been utilized in organic qualitative analysis for decades; the typical formulation used in forensic testing is a nitroprusside solution containing acetaldehyde,[4] with a second reagent consisting of 2% Na_2CO_3. This two-step test is used to differentiate methamphetamine from amphetamine, which both give a similar orange color when treated with the Marquis reagent (Figure 7.14). Both compounds will be discussed in detail in the next chapter; for now, note that amphetamine is a primary amine of the generic form RNH_2 and methamphetamine is a secondary amine of the form R_2NH.

The generic reaction of nitroprusside with bases such as the amines is[19]

$$[(NC)_5FeNO]^{2-} + B^n \longleftrightarrow [(NC)_5\ FeN(B)O]^{-2+n} \qquad (7.2)$$

For methamphetamine (a secondary amine), the inclusion of acetaldehyde in the reagent facilitates an addition–condensation reaction to form an enamine and an

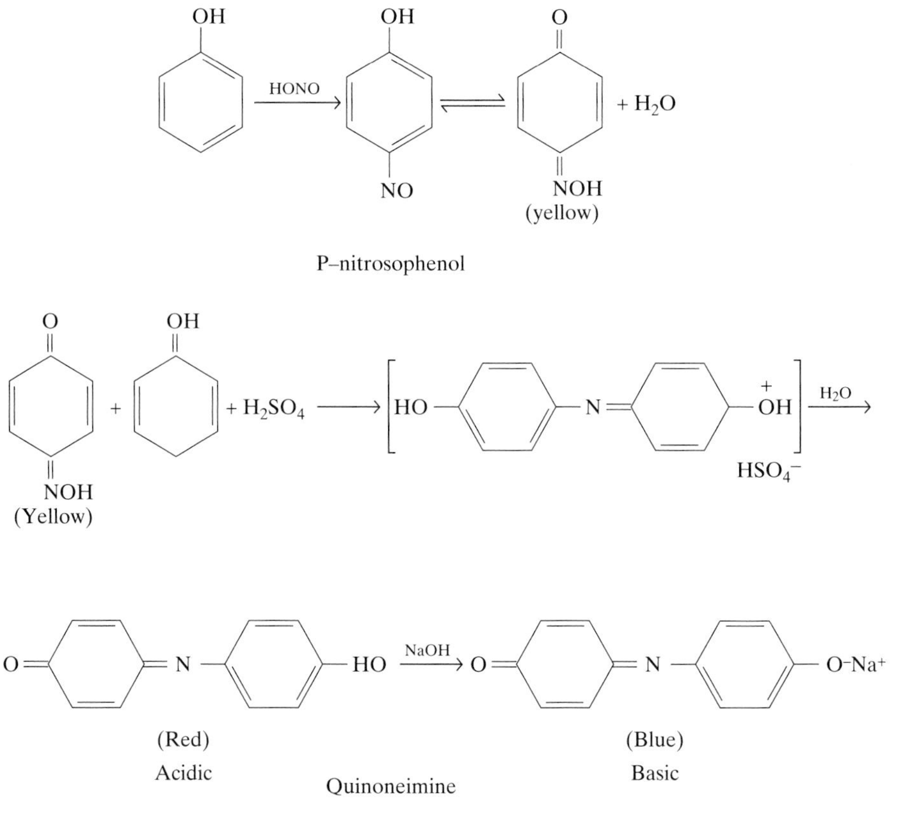

▶ **Figure 7.17** *The reaction of nitrous acid from the Liebermann reagent with phenol, resulting in a pH-sensitive colored product.*

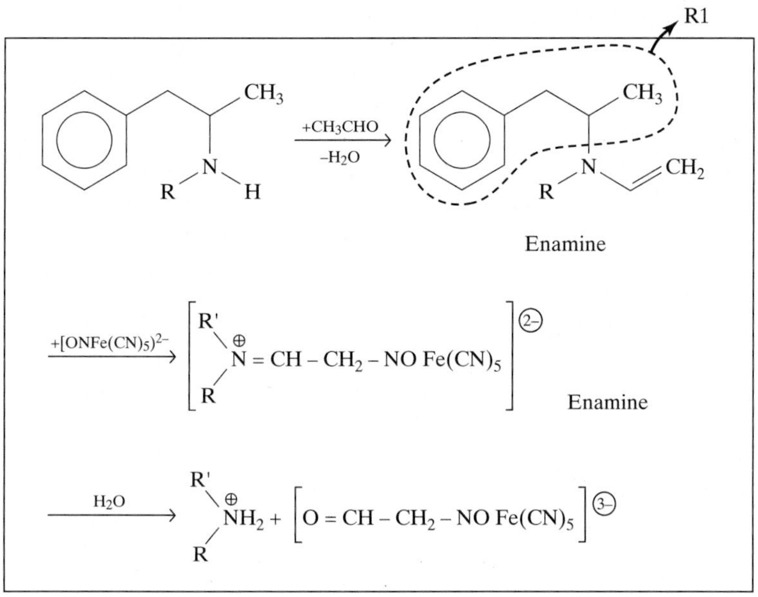

◀ **Figure 7.18** *Proposed reaction of methamphetamine with Simon's reagent. Adapted from "United Nations Scientific and Technical Notes,"* Chemistry and Reaction Mechanisms of Rapid Tests for Drugs of Abuse and Precursor Chemicals, *1989.*

intermediate that further reacts with water to form a blue complex, as shown in Figure 7.18.[8] This complex is sometimes referred to as the Simon–Awe complex.[8]

Tests for Marijuana: The Duquenois reagent (Duquenois or Duquenois–Levine test) involves a condensation reaction leading to creation of a purple chromophore (Figure 7.19) with the active ingredient **tetrahydrocannabinol**.[21, 22] Marijuana analysis frequently includes TLC using Fast Blue BB salt (or a similar

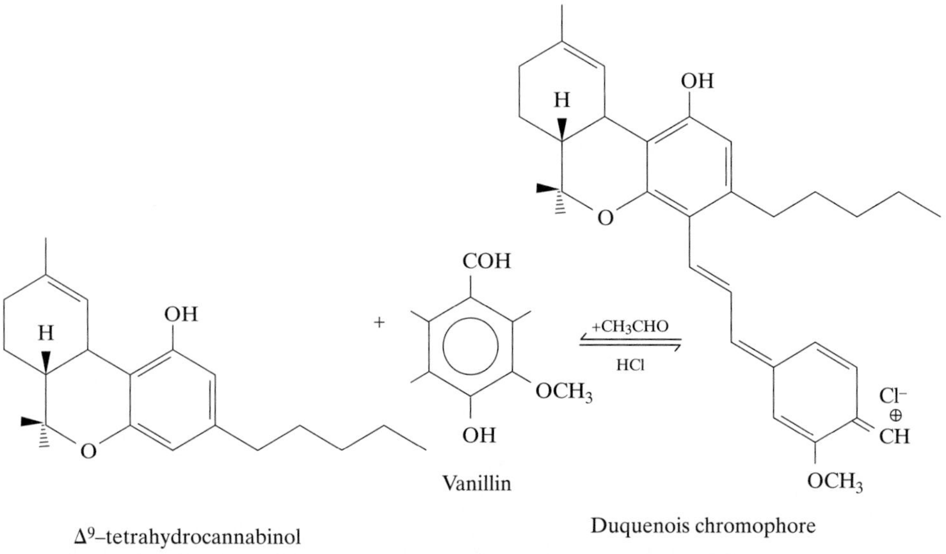

▲ **Figure 7.19** *The Duquenois reaction for THC in marijuana. The acid drives the condensation of THC with vanillin and acetaldehyde to form a resonance-stabilized and conjugated chromophore. This purple material can be extracted into chloroform. Adapted from Forrester, D. E., The Duquenois Color Test for Marijuana: Spectroscopic and Chemical Studies. Doctoral dissertation, Georgetown University, Washington, DC: 1997.*

replacement) as the developer. This reagent is useful in that it produces a different color with THC[8] and the two other cannabinoids of interest in the plant extract. These will be discussed in detail later in the chapter; for the purpose of the present discussion, this reaction provides an example of diazonium coupling.

Transition Metal Complexes: Related to the Simon test is a family of color-producing reactions based on transition metal complexes (coordination complexes) and tightly associated ion pairs. **Coordination complexes** arise from a **Lewis acid–base** interaction between a metal cation, such as cobalt, and an atom with unshared electrons, such as water or, in the case of drugs, basic nitrogen found in alkaloids and amines. Metals that have been used in these reagents include copper, vanadium, bismuth, and cobalt. Cobalt, as part of two common reagents (cobalt thiocyanate and **Dilli–Koppanyi**) is perhaps the most versatile. Cobalt has an electron structure of $3d^7 4s^2$, while the cation has a $3d^7 (2^+)$ or $3d^6 (3^+)$ structure.

In aqueous solution, the cobalt ion typically has a light pink appearance as a result of the complex formed with water (Figure 7.21). The same is true of copper, which is light blue in solution due to a water complex. In both cases, the

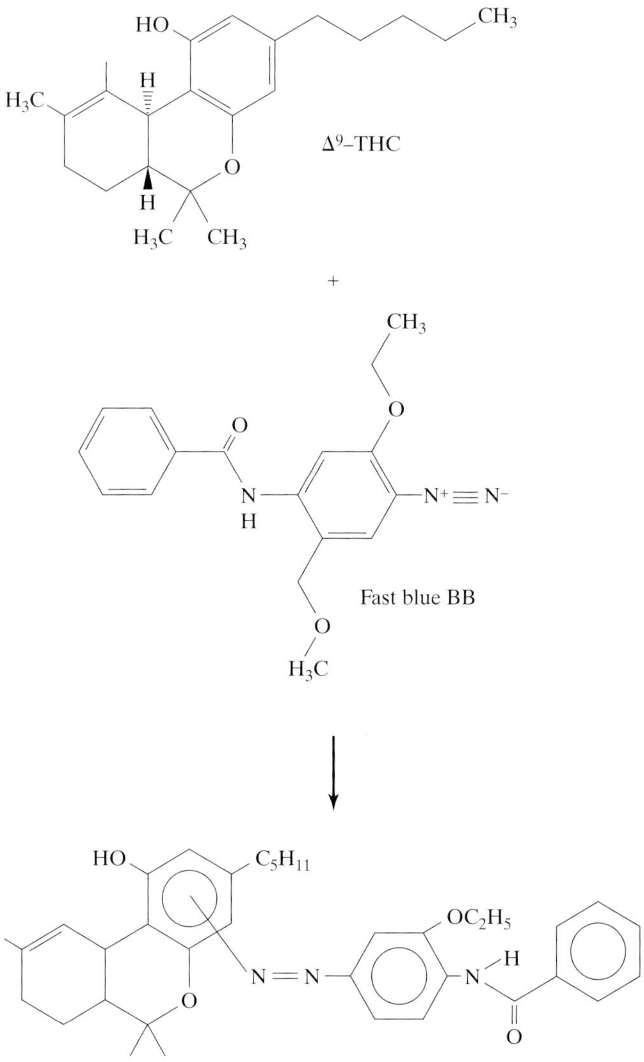

▶ **Figure 7.20** *Reaction of the TLC developer Fast Blue BB with THC, the active ingredient in marijuana.*

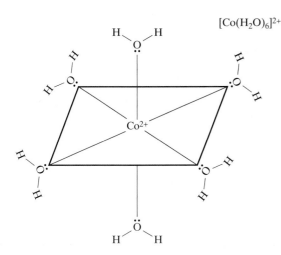

$[Co(H_2O)_6]^{2+}$

◀ **Figure 7.21** *Hydrated cobalt ion, a coordination complex with an octahedral structure. The unshared pairs of electrons on the oxygen are attracted to the metal cation via a Lewis acid–base interaction.*

water ligands are arranged in an octahedral pattern around the central metal cation. If a color is observed, electronic transitions are taking place, which can occur only if there is some disparity in the energy of the outermost orbitals with electrons. In the case of transition metals, these are the d orbitals, which, under normal conditions, are degenerate (all of equivalent energy). **Ligand field theory (LFT)** allows for an explanation of d-orbital alterations, color, and magnetism of transition metal complexes. LFT represents a merging of **crystal field theory (CFT)** and molecular orbital theory, invoking principles such as orbital overlap, bonding–nonbonding interactions, and orbital splitting.[23]

To greatly simplify LFT, as a **ligand** approaches and forms an association with a metal ion, it will be acted upon by two different electron density environments as illustrated in Figure 7.22. The approach along an axis will be impeded by two of the five d orbitals, with the electron density repelling the electrons of the approaching ligand. The other three d orbitals have a zero electron density along the axis and present an easier approach for a ligand, since the repulsion is weaker. Because the three orbitals are symmetric, their energy is degenerate and lower than that of the other two. Put another way, an unshared pair of electrons on oxygen that reside in the metal's $d_{x^2-y^2}$ orbital will be repelled significantly more from metal ion electrons than would an oxygen residing in the d_{x-z} orbital. Since a gap is created, d electrons can be promoted if the energy of the incoming photons is sufficient. All that is required for promotion is a vacancy in the upper d orbitals.

The degree of d-orbital splitting depends on the relative strength of the ligand, described in the spectrochemical series. This abbreviated series is $CO, CN^- > NO_2^- > NH_3 > H_2O > OH^- > Cl^-$, with NH_3, H_2O, and Cl^- being of most interest in forensic chemistry and presumptive color testing. CO and CN are the strongest ligands and create the largest splitting. Any charge on the metal ion will also affect splitting. All else being equal, an octahedral ammonia complex will have a larger gap than a water complex of the same structure around the same central atom. A larger gap means that light of higher energy (more blue) will be absorbed, leading to a more reddish appearance. However, there are complicating factors that exceed the scope of this discussion. Suffice it to say that there are also square planar and tetrahedral complexes with four ligands ($[CoCl_4]^-$, for example) in which the splitting is not as straightforward. Also, with many d electrons, such as those in cobalt, the distribution of electrons will depend on the gap distance, leading to what are called

a.

d–orbitals electron density

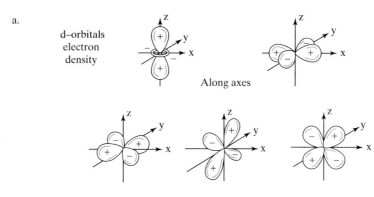

Along axes

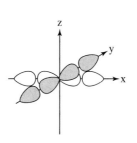

Between axes

b.

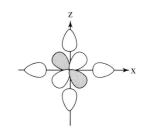

Bonding interaction between two ligand orbitals and metal d_{z^2} orbital

Bonding interaction between four ligand orbitals and metal $d_{x^2-y^2}$ orbital

Nonbonding (no interaction) four ligand orbitals and metal d_{xy} orbital

▶ **Figure 7.22** *(a) Unlike s and p orbitals, d orbitals are not all symmetric. The d_{xz}-axis, for example, has lobes that project out into the x–z plane; there is no electron density along the axes, only between them. (b) Where overlap occurs with the orbitals of ligands, bonding interactions occur; nonbonding interactions occur where there is no electron density and no overlap.*

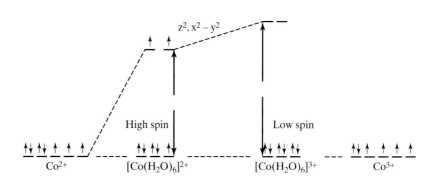

z^2, x^2-y^2

High spin

Low spin

Co^{2+} $[Co(H_2O)_6]^{2+}$ $[Co(H_2O)_6]^{3+}$ Co^{3+}

▶ **Figure 7.23** *Effect of ligand and metal ion charge. High-spin complexes, with unshared electrons, are favored when weak field ligands generate smaller energy gaps than strong field ligands do. Similarly, for the same ligand, increasing the charge on the metal ion increases the energy gap, favoring low-spin complexes.*

z^2, x^2-y^2

High spin

$[Fe(H_2O)_6]^{3+}$ Fe^{3+}

$[Fe(CN)_6]^{3-}$ xy, xz, yz

Low spin

high-spin and **low-spin complexes** (Figure 7.23). High-spin complexes have unshared electrons, while low-spin complexes have paired electrons.

Key to the current discussion is the ability of transition metals to form charged complexes. As charged and relatively stable entities, complex ions can act as cations or anions and form coordination compounds or tightly associated ion pairs. These ion pairs may be solids, or they may form stable neutral species that can be extracted into an organic solvent such as chloroform. This is indeed the basis of the cobalt thiocyanate test for cocaine, in which a pink solution of aqueous cobalt thiocyanate is added, along with hydrochloric acid, to the unknown powder. If cocaine or a related substance, such as procaine, is present, a blue color results. In one modification of the test, this blue ion pair is extracted into a chloroform layer as further evidence for the formation of a tightly associated ion pair.[4,24–29]

As an alkaloid and a tertiary amine, cocaine is basic, with a pK_a of 8.6 (26). To extract it into an organic solvent in the base form, the pH of the aqueous layer must be adjusted to approximately 11. The cocaine remains neutral and thus extractable. However, in acidic aqueous solutions, cocaine behaves as any other nitrogenous base and will exist in the protonated form BH^+. Once ionized, the BH^+, equivalent to the protonated cocaine, can form the ion pair according to the reaction

$$2\,NHR_3^+ + [Co(SCN)_4]^{2-}(\text{pink, aq})$$

$$\longrightarrow (NHR_3)_2[Co(SCN)_4](\text{blue solid}) \qquad (7.3)$$

where the product is a neutral compound that will extract into chloroform. This ion pairing is one of many that can be used for simple color testing, as well as in quantitative assays and atomic absorption spectrophotometry.

As with most complexation and drug solubility situations, pH is a critical variable. Cocaine base is not soluble in water, and if the drug is in this form rather than a soluble salt, no reaction occurs. Acid is needed to ensure that the cocaine is in the water-soluble ionic form to allow for the formation of a complex. The color is the result of an **ion-pair compound** formed from the cationic cocaine and the anionic cobalt complex. As with all amine bases, such as ammonia, the base becomes protonated in acidic solution. The pK_a of the base determines the ratio of the protonated, ionized form to the neutral form. It is possible to add too much HCl, because cobalt forms a water-soluble pink complex with chloride $[CoCl_4]^{2-}$. The pH can also influence the type of complex and ion pair formed. Under acidic conditions, the ion pair favored is $[Co(\text{cocaine})_2](SCN)_2$ (which is pinkish and soluble in water), while in the neutral-to-basic ranges, the ion pair is assigned the structure $[\text{cocaine-}H^+]_2\,[Co(SCN)_4]$ (which is a blue solid and soluble in chloroform).[30,31] The important points of the cobalt thiocyanate reaction with cocaine are summarized in Figures 7.24–7.26.

The Bottom Line: Drug analysts and toxicologists use many more color tests, far too many to list and discuss in this chapter. Table 7.3 gives a summary of the more common color tests, and forensic practitioners who use color tests usually adapt a battery of personal favorites. A good laboratory reference for color tests is L. Y. Galichet et al., eds., *Clarke's Analysis of Drugs and Poisons, Vols. 1 and 2* (London: Pharmaceutical Press, **2004**). Some references provide flowcharts,[27] but there is no one correct protocol for presumptive color testing. The important point is that analysts understand the reagents and reactions, the methods, and their strengths and limitations.

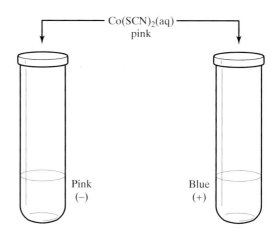

▶ **Figure 7.24** *An acidic solution is required for the cobalt thiocyanate test, since the cocaine must be soluble.*

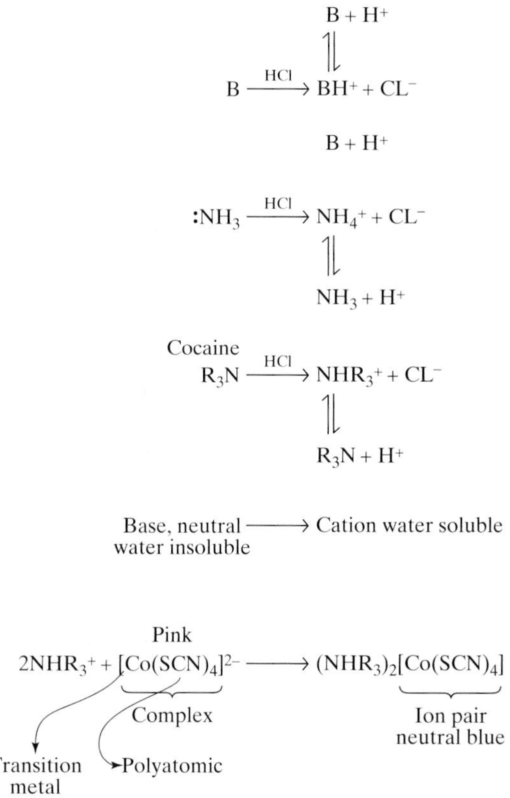

$$B + H^+$$
$$\upharpoonleft\downharpoonright$$
$$B \xrightarrow{\text{HCl}} BH^+ + CL^-$$

$$B + H^+$$

$$:NH_3 \xrightarrow{\text{HCl}} NH_4^+ + CL^-$$
$$\upharpoonleft\downharpoonright$$
$$NH_3 + H^+$$

Cocaine
$$R_3N \xrightarrow{\text{HCl}} NHR_3^+ + CL^-$$
$$\upharpoonleft\downharpoonright$$
$$R_3N + H^+$$

Base, neutral ⟶ Cation water soluble
water insoluble

Pink
$$2NHR_3^+ + [Co(SCN)_4]^{2-} \longrightarrow (NHR_3)_2[Co(SCN)_4]$$

Complex

Transition Polyatomic
metal

Ion pair
neutral blue

▶ **Figure 7.25** *The addition of acid ensures that the base is soluble. The overall reaction illustrates several interactions and bonding types.*

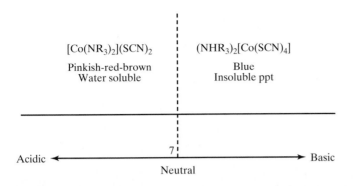

$[Co(NR_3)_2](SCN)_2$
Pinkish-red-brown
Water soluble

$(NHR_3)_2[Co(SCN)_4]$
Blue
Insoluble ppt

Acidic ← 7 → Basic
Neutral

◀ **Figure 7.26** *Additional pH effects that can occur in the cobalt thiocyanate reaction.*

Table 7.3   Common Color (Presumptive) Tests and TLC Developers for Drugs

Name	Other Names or Variants	Reactive Species	Use or Targets	Likely Mechanism
Dragendorff	Kraut's	$Bi^{3+}I^-$	Alkaloids, cholines, TLC developer	Ion pair with BI_3^- complex
Dilli–Koppanyi		Co^{2+}	Barbiturates	Colored complex
Ferric chloride		Fe^{3+}	Salicylates (aspirin family), phenols	Colored complex
Froedhe	Frodhe (older literature)	Mo^{3+} acidic	Alkaloids	Colored complex
Iodoplatinate		I^-, Pt	Alkaloids, amines, general developer for TLC	Colored complex
Mandelin's	Ammonium vanadate	V cation	Steroids, alkaloids, aspirin	Colored complex
Zwikker		Cu^{2+}, pyridine in chloroform	Barbiturates	Colored complex

7.3 MICROCRYSTAL TESTS

Some controversy and debate surround the use of microcrystals (**crystal tests**) in drug analysis, but this shouldn't be the case. Properly employed, crystal tests are powerful extensions of color tests. Specificity is derived chiefly from appearance and behavior of crystals under polarized light. The catch—and there usually is one—is the user's ability to identify crystal forms. However, there is a subjective element in all judging colors in all color tests, which is addressed by controls, literature validation,[4] experimentation, and experience. The same is true of crystal tests. In fact, prior to the wide availability of instrumentation, crystal tests were considered to be one of the most specific and selective tests available for many drugs.

Exhibit D:

"The best chemical color tests form a natural partnership with the microcrystal tests, in which each kind not only adds to the other but does so when most needed, making good some of the other's inevitable deficiencies. ... Any 'controversy' over which is 'better' is absurd, since both should be used."

Source: Charles Fulton in *Modern Microcrystal Tests for Drugs* (New York: Wiley-Interscience, **1976**), p. 3.

To give a refined definition, crystal tests are presumptive precipitation tests in which crystal morphology lends specificity. Consequently, the analyst's experience is an important part of interpreting results of crystal tests. Heroin, cocaine, and amphetamine are the most frequently targeted analytes for crystal tests, and procedures using gold and platinic chlorides and bromides have been standardized by ASTM.[32–34] A recent study supports microcrystal testing as a viable tool for the forensic chemist.[35] The authors note that, although a battery of presumptive color tests produced false positives for cocaine among a number of drug powders, the inclusion of crystal tests to the regime allowed for the elimination of false positives that might have been observed during color testing. Microcrystal tests are also valuable for differentiation of isomers such as d-amphetamine/d,l-amphetamine and d-cocaine/l-cocaine.

Microcrystal tests are simple to perform: A reagent is added to a speck of homogeneous sample on a microscope slide, and the result is observed under transmitted light microscopy. Variations in methodology take advantage of solubility and volatility. For example, the freebase forms of amphetamine and methamphetamine have appreciable vapor pressure at room temperature and can be driven into the vapor phase. The drop of reagent hanging above the sample contains acidified gold chloride in which the characteristic crystals will form if the drugs are present. This simple, but elegant, separation leaves behind diluents such as sugars and starches, making the crystals easier to see and study. Photomicrographs of crystal tests can be found in the color insert to Figure 7.27.

The basis of most crystal tests for alkaloids involves protonation of basic nitrogen to form a charged cation and precipitation as an ion-pair salt. In fact, many of the most widely used reagents for crystal tests also are or were at one time used in presumptive color tests. Examples include ion pairs formed between the cationic alkaloid base and anion complexes such as $BiI_3{}^{3-}$ (**Dragendorff test**) or $HgI_4{}^{2-}$ (an older color test called **Mayer's** test). Currently, the most commonly used forensic microcrystal tests involve complexes incorporating gold, platinum, and halogens, principally chloride and bromide.[32–34] The gold standard for crystal tests is described in a book written by Fulton and published in 1969.[36] Unfortunately, this reference is now difficult to obtain.

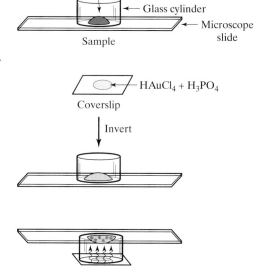

▶ **Figure 7.27** *A volatility-based separation and crystal test for amphetamine and methamphetamine. The precipitating reagent is placed on a coverslip and inverted over a small portion of the sample to which a strong base is added. Amphetamine and methamphetamine in the freebase form have sufficient vapor pressure to evaporate and condense in the reagent. Nonvolatiles are effectively removed from the sample. See the color insert for photos of this test.*

7.4 SCREENING AND INSTRUMENTAL ANALYSIS

Many forensic laboratories use TLC as the bridge between presumptive and confirmatory tests. TLC is particularly valuable in toxicology laboratories, where color and crystal tests are less feasible in the biological sample matrices. TLC, discussed in detail in Chapter 4, can now be coupled to an understanding of developing reagents. In drug analysis, TLC is used to narrow down the list of candidates provided by the presumptive tests. The level of specificity arises from the number of separate solvent systems employed, from standards, and from developing reagents. *Clarke's Analysis of Drugs and Poisons*[1] lists over 20 TLC solvent systems, along with a variety of spray-developing reagents, including familiar names such as Ehrlich's reagent. *Clarke's* also lists combinations of developers that can be used to increase specificity and selectivity. The variety of available thin-layer systems is in sharp contrast to the number of instruments actually used for positive identification of the controlled substances and other materials of interest in a sample. Two methods are currently used: mass spectrometry (predominately GCMS) and infrared spectroscopy. These techniques were discussed in Chapter 5 and will be revisited as appropriate in sections that follow.

7.5 WHAT IS DEFINITIVE IDENTIFICATION?

Before moving on into specific drug classes, it is worth reflecting on a uniquely forensic question: What constitutes a definitive identification? How much data and what combination of tests are adequate to identify a white powder as cocaine or as something else? This is both a scientific and, a legal question and, for any forensic chemist, not a trivial one. When M.B. Orfila analyzed the exhumed remains of Charles Lafarge, his analysis was at the cutting edge of analytical chemistry in 1840, but it is unlikely that his results and testimony would be accepted today. This is not Orfila's fault, but the inevitable result of the evolution of chemical science, instrument technology, and legal precedent. Less than a hundred years ago, forensic chemists identified drugs on the basis of their color and microcrystal tests; there were no mass or infrared spectrometers readily available, as they are today.

As instrument capability and availability has improved, courts have come to expect instrumental confirmation of identification in drug cases. The one common exception is marijuana (discussed shortly), but for nearly every other type of controlled substance, instrumental identification is expected, be it confirmation of other testing, such as presumptive and screening tests, or as stand-alone data. The specific requirements for a complete analysis vary by jurisdiction, but most forensic laboratories follow some form of the model presented in Section 1.4. A given laboratory may utilize color tests, TLC with standards, and GCMS. At the other end of this spectrum, another laboratory may employ only GCMS and IR analyses. Both protocols, if performed with the appropriate controls and procedures, can provide definitive identification and exceed what would be required in many other contexts. For example, environmental analysis for most organic pollutants relies on GCMS; such data also are subject to legal scrutiny.

Analytical chemists usually accept chromatographic retention-time data combined with mass spectral data as sufficient to identify most compounds. The legal question involves the degree of certainty of such identification. Could there conceivably be a compound that has the exact same retention time as cocaine on a given chromatographic column and exactly the same mass spectrum? Of course there could; the question is, How likely is it that such a compound exists? This question is unanswerable and is addressed by adding confirmatory testing. The more testing added to the protocol, the less likely a false positive becomes. Is it conceivable that a compound has *identical* (not just similar) behavior and responses to color testing, crystal testing, TLC using multiple solvent systems and standards, gas chromatography, mass spectrometry, and infrared spectrophotometry? Conceivable perhaps, but the probability is vanishingly small. It is in this context that a forensic chemist operates. The phrasing is something such as "identified as x to a reasonable degree of scientific certainty."

One final question merits attention: At what concentration is a drug considered to be present in a sample? The scientific answer relies on concepts introduced in Chapter 2. The LOD and LOQ of any validated analytical protocol are known and documented. Suppose, for example, that a solid-phase extraction/GCMS analysis of a resinous powder is capable of reliably detecting a heroin concentration of 12 ppb $\pm$ 2%. This concentration may extrapolate to only a few micrograms of heroin in a powder, a value that may in turn represent a weight percentage of far less than 0.01% in the original material. If the method was properly performed and all other data remained consistent, the analyst can indeed be confident that heroin was present to a reasonable degree of scientific certainty. Is this amount of heroin, even though it is detectable, a sufficient amount to warrant judicial action? This is where analytical chemistry ends and legal debate begins.

The issues raised in this discussion are as much philosophical questions as they are legal and scientific ones. There are no single correct answers, but there are accepted scientific and legal guidelines used to frame them. For example, color tests are not, by themselves, sufficient to identify a drug. This is why such tests are called presumptive. Arguments continue as to whether color tests combined with crystal tests can provide unambiguous identification. The question is less important in the instrumentation age, but it raises yet another question: Is GCMS or IR alone sufficient to identify a substance? The discussion has come full circle, and the forensic community has generally taken the position that if there is any reasonable doubt as to identification, additional confirmatory testing is added to the protocol. At what concentration levels is a drug considered present in the eyes of the law? That varies; all the chemist can do is follow laboratory protocols, be aware of jurisdictional standards, and report the best scientific data possible.

7.6 APPLICATIONS: ACIDIC DRUGS

7.6.1 GHB AND GBL

Gamma hydroxybutyric acid (GHB) and gammabutyrolactone (GBL, Figure 7.28) are among the most analytically challenging abused drugs. GHB is a small, polar, water-soluble molecule capable of extensive hydrogen bonding. It is a

Table 7.4 GHB/GBL	
Source:	Synthetic from GBL and strong base
Form/morphology/exhibits:	Aqueous solutions, beverages
Classification:	Schedule I, nonalkaloid, predator drug, club drug
Medical uses:	None
Color test:	Indicators
Microscopic/Crystal tests:	Cu/Ag ion salts reported
Other tests:	TLC, GCMS as derivates, HPLC

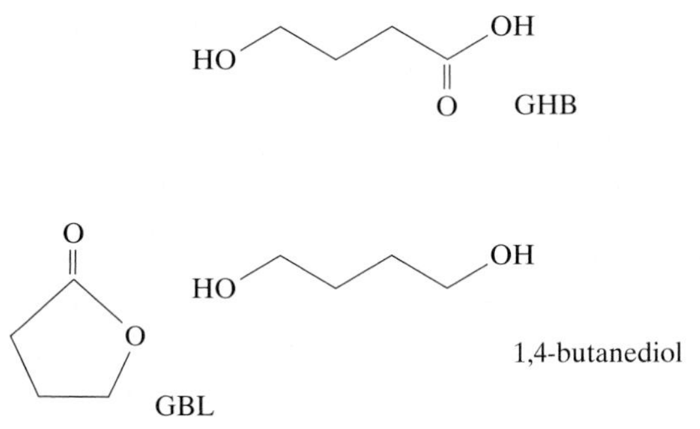

◀ **Figure 7.28** *Structures of 1.4-butanediol, GHB, and GBL, the corresponding lactone. Conversion between GHB and GBL depends primarily on pH.*

club and predator drug originally designed to treat narcolepsy; now it is encountered principally in cases of drug-facilitated sexual assaults (DFSAs). Analogs of GHB relevant in forensic analysis are 1,4-butanediol and GBL.

GHB has been used as a hypnotic and as an anesthetic agent; during the 1980s, it became popular as a bodybuilding supplement. It was banned by the Food and Drug Administration in 1990, around the time it began being used as a club and predator drug. In 2000, GHB was added to Schedule I. GBL and 1,4-butanediol found increasing use, since these substances are converted to GHB in the body.[37] As a predator drug, GHB is typically spiked surreptitiously into a beverage at concentrations in the range of approximately 0.5%.[37]

The effects and toxicology of GHB are somewhat unusual. Ingested GHB is converted to the lactone and quickly eliminated via urine. The peak plasma concentration C_{max} occurs within an hour and induces sedative effects. A dose of approximately 50mg/kg is required to induce unconsciousness. Ethanol has a synergistic effect, increasing the anesthesia. The half-life of GHB is 20–60 minutes, and nearly all of the compound is converted to GBL; less than 5% of the unchanged drug is found in the urine.[38] As a consequence of the short half-life, traces of the drug are undetectable in blood within 8 hours of dosing and undetectable in urine within 12 hours of ingestion.[26,38] Unfortunately, one of the effects of GHB is a loss of short-term memory, and as a result, victims of sexual assault may not seek medical attention until after the drug has been cleared from their system. In the worst cases, they do not seek help at all. Adding further to the complexity, GHB is found naturally in the body in concentration ranges of 5 mg/L, although this concentration increases significantly postmortem.[26,38]

Exhibits suspected to contain GHB or related substances are often received as a liquid, either a suspect beverage or in concentrated form. Powders may

Applying the Science 7.1   GHB as an Anesthetic

The anesthetic power of GHB was illustrated in a recent case reported in the *Journal of Forensic Sciences*. When paramedics arrived at the home of a couple, they discovered the woman bleeding from the mouth. Both residents were chronic abusers of GHB. At the home, the responders found 18 teeth that had been removed from the woman's mouth with a pair of bloody pliers also found at the scene. Later interviews were unable to confirm who had done the extraction, but both individuals reported that they believed the female had been possessed by a demon. At the hospital, the wounds were sutured. Fortunately, despite the lack of dental training by either party, the extraction was done with no additional damage to bone. The male was charged with assault, but was acquitted when the jury was unable to decide which party had done the actual extraction.

Source: Pretty, I. A., and R. C. Hall. "Self-extraction of Teeth Involving Gamma-Hydroxybutryic Acid." *Journal of Forensic Sciences,* 49 **2004**, 1069–1072.

also be encountered. Given the chemistry of the substance, the submission of liquid samples presents significant analytical challenges.[39–43]

Analytical Approach and Interconversion: Under mildly acidic conditions, GHB undergoes an internal condensation via Fischer esterification to produce a stable **lactone**. This involves two steps: cyclization, followed by the elimination of water. The reverse reaction, the hydrolysis of GBL to GHB, can be driven in the presence of a strong base, which is the method used clandestinely to make GHB (Figure 7.29). The reverse reaction can occur in solution when GHB is spiked into a drink, many of which are slightly acidic.[41] However, once equilibrium between the acid and the lactone form has been reached, no significant losses of GHB appear in typical exhibits over the time frame of days or weeks.[37]

The starting points for GHB analysis are presumptive tests, including many of the color tests based on acid–base indicators such as phenol red or the formation of a colored complex with cobalt.[26] Crystal tests using copper and silver nitrates have also been reported,[39] and TLC has been employed as well. The significant analytical challenges arise at the stage of instrumental confirmation, and they are due to the tendency toward interconversion and the polarity of the molecule.

One crude analytical approach would involve driving the equilibrium to one extreme or the other by adjusting the pH, thereby driving the equilibrium to strongly favor a single form. Two problems arise: First, the analysis of the sample will not reflect the ratio of GHB to GBL, an important legal and analytical consideration, and second, driving the equilibrium to either extreme does not solve the fundamental analytical problem related to polarity. If the pH is set to 12, hydrolysis is favored and the lactone is rapidly and completely converted to the free acid form. However, sample preparation and cleanup are complicated, since a liquid–liquid extraction is difficult.[42,43] The extracting solvent must be sufficiently polar to extract the polar GHB, yet the solvent itself cannot be soluble in water. A solvent such as *n*-butanol is a possibility, but the low vapor pressure of this alcohol makes it difficult to concentrate extracts.[43] Ethyl acetate has been recommended,[43] because it can extract the free acid form in sufficient purity to obtain an IR spectrum. However, problems with water and hydrogen bonding persist.

The alternative method, setting the pH to acidic conditions, might seem a better option, but also fails. At a pH of 2, the esterification of GHB takes

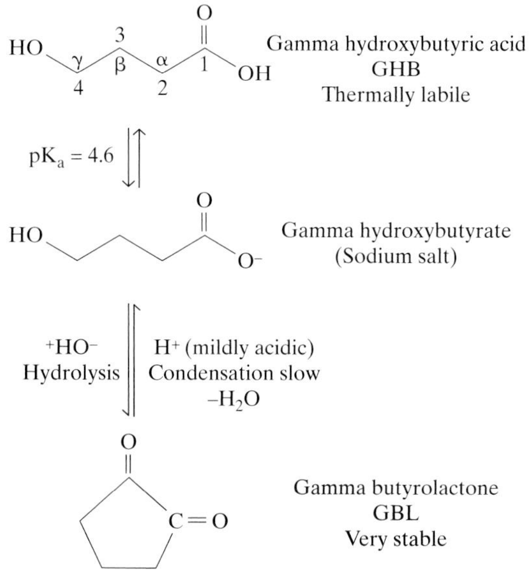

▶ **Figure 7.29** *Interconversion of GHB and GBL.*

hours or longer, only to reach equilibrium with GBL rather than complete conversion.[41] Even though the lactone form can be extracted with an organic solvent, the link to the original sample concentration is further muddied, with no discernible gain for the trouble. Direct injection of the sample into a GCMS is not an option, because GHB is thermally labile. HPLC is an alternative, but unless the system is equipped with a mass spectrometer, definitive identification is not possible. One method used successfully in some laboratories is derivatization of GHB (described in Chapter 5), using (**BSTFA**),[44] followed by GC or GCMS. Derivatizaion using **TMS** and an on-fiber SPME approach has also been reported.[40,41] A recent article described a screening method utilizing micellar electrokinetic chromatography applicable to spiked beverages.[37] When solid samples are received or made, ATR (infrared spectroscopy) has also been used.[44]

7.6.2 TETRAHYDROCANNABINOLS: MARIJUANA AND HASHISH

In terms of caseloads, marijuana represents the bulk of the work in most forensic chemistry sections and the largest number of case submissions to most full-service forensic laboratories. It is also the most widely available, most widely used illegal drug in the United States, where one-third of the population has reportedly tried it.[45] Marijuana (also spelled "marihuana") is

Table 7.5	Marijuana and Hashish
Source:	Plant, *Cannabis sativa* L.
Active ingredient:	Cannabinoids
Form/morphology:	Plant matter, resin (hashish)
Classification:	Schedule I Hallucinogen, nonalkaloid
Medical uses:	Antinausea, antiglaucoma (Marinol®)
Color test:	Duquenois–Levine (modified)
Microscopic:	"Bear claws" (cystolythic hairs)
Other tests:	TLC; GCMS occasionally for THC

usually defined as all parts of the plant *Cannabis sativa* L., excluding the stalk and sterilized seeds. *Cannabis sativa* is a weed also known as **hemp**, cultivated for use as a fiber. Some jurisdictions use a more generic definition that lists any plants of the genus *Cannabis*. This approach circumvents legal questions about species that have been raised in the past. **Hashish** and hash oil are derivative products of the marijuana plant. Hashish is the resinous material derived from the flowering tops, while the oil is a potent solvent-extracted form. Sinsemilla is a particularly potent form of marijuana plant in terms of its psychoactive ingredients. At one time, Colombia was the principal source of smuggled marijuana, but that country was supplanted by Mexico by 1990.[45] Domestically, the top states for outdoor marijuana cultivation in 2004 were California, Hawaii, Kentucky, and Tennessee, while California, Florida, Oregon, Washington, and Wisconsin topped the list for indoor cultivation.[45]

The active ingredients of marijuana and its derivatives are the cannabinoids, summarized in Table 7.6. Two naming conventions (Figure 7.35) can be used for these compounds, so names can be a source of confusion. The

▶ **Figure 7.30** *A leaf of a marijuana plant showing the distinctive serrated leaves. Image courtesy of the Oklahoma State Bureau of Investigation.*

dibenzofuran method is more common in the forensic context and will be used throughout this text. All cannabinoids are oily and insoluble in water, but soluble in solvents such as chloroform and petroleum ether. They are unusual among plant-derived controlled substances in that none contain nitrogen; thus, none are alkaloids. However, marijuana plant and extracts do contain a variety of alkaloid bases, as is typical of any plant extract.[46]

The principal active ingredient of concern in marijuana is Δ^9-tetrahydrocannabinol (Δ^9 THC, or just THC). THC is acidic and has an ionizable center and a pK_a of 10.6. THC also has a logP value of 6.97, which reflects the insolubility of oils in water. The typical concentration of THC in the leaves is between 1 and 5%, and much higher values are found in the oily resin on the flowering

▶ **Figure 7.31** *Marijuana plant seeds. Note the distinctive mottled appearance. Image courtesy of Aaron Brudenell, Tucson Police Department Crime Laboratory.*

◀ **Figure 7.32** *A roach (hand-rolled cigarette) of marijuana, along with plant matter and seeds. Image courtesy of the Oklahoma State Bureau of Investigation.*

◀ **Figure 7.33** *"Blunts," currently a popular form of marijuana for smoking. Image courtesy of the Oklahoma State Bureau of Investigation.*

tops. Marijuana growers have also taken the lessons of selective breeding to heart. The concentration of THC has increased steadily since 1980, with values reaching as high as 13.2% in sinsemilla.[45] Hashish and hash oil are much more potent, with a THC content ranging from 2 to 30%.[47] Δ^8 THC is found in much smaller quantities, while CBD and CBN are found in larger amounts; all are

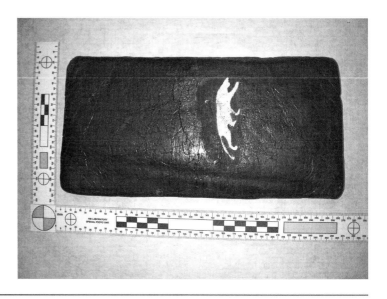

▲ **Figure 7.34** *Hashish. This batch has a dry, taffylike consistency, but hash can be much oilier. Note the distinctive jaguar imprint. Image courtesy of Heather Campbell, Idaho State Patrol Forensic Laboratory.*

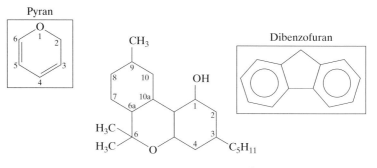

▶ **Figure 7.35** *Two naming conventions used for the cannabinols. The top frame shows the dibenzofuran–dibenzopyran method that is more common in forensic usages, although the monoterpenoid system (bottom frame) is also encountered. Δ^9-THC in the dibenzofuran method is the equivalent of Δ^1-THC in the monoterpenoid system, which is based on a skeleton of 10 carbon atoms as shown.*

much less psychoactive than THC. Δ^9-Tetrahydrocannabinolic acid is similar, but can be converted to THC by smoking.[48] In fact, Δ^9-tetrahydrocannabinolic acid is the major component in freshly cut marijuana plants, and most of the THC is created as a result of the decarboxylation of this acid as the leaves dry.

Table 7.6 Cannabinoids	
Name[a]	**Structure**[b]
Δ^9-Tetrahydrocannabinol, also generically referred to as tetrahydrocannabinol or "THC"	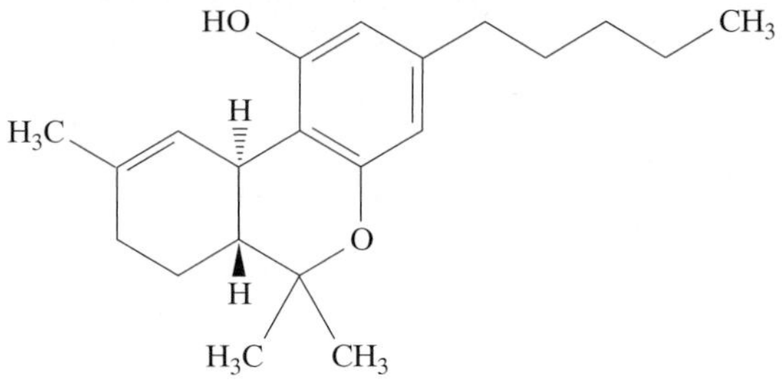
Δ^8-Tetrahydrocannabinol	
Cannabinol (CBN)	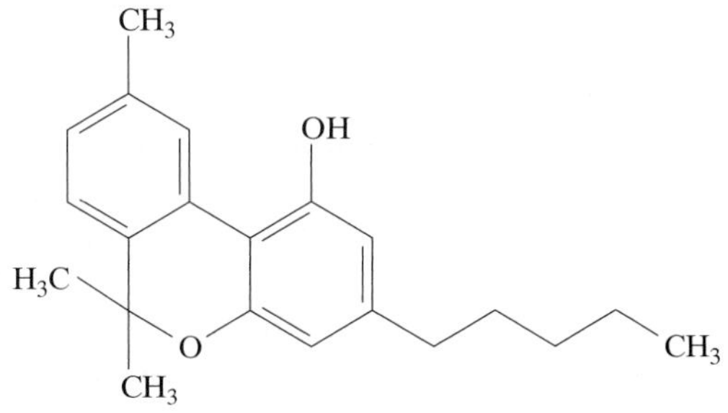
Cannabidiol (CBD)	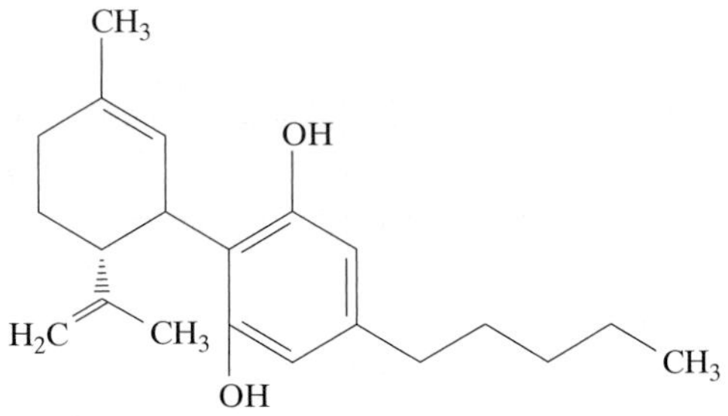

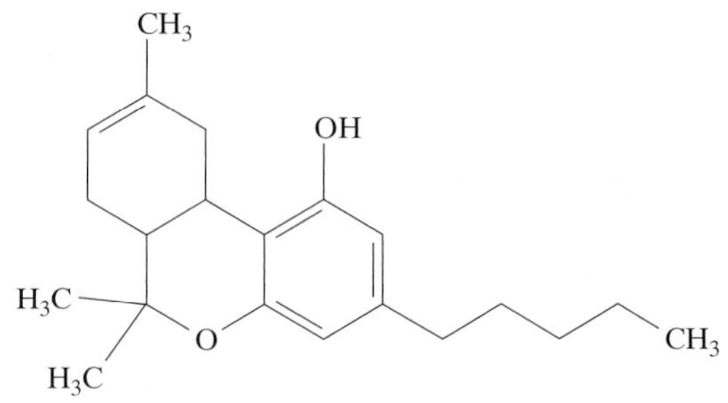

Table 7.6 (Continued)	
Name[a]	**Structure**[b]
Δ^9-Tetrahydrocannabinolic acid	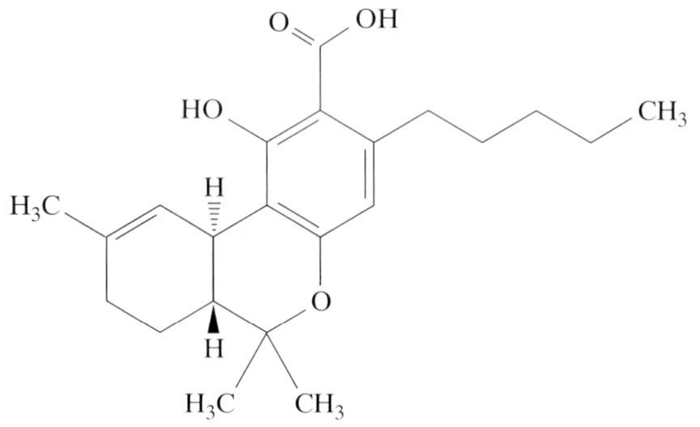

[a] Using the dibenzopyran–dibenzofuran naming convention.

[b] Source of the structures for this table and for all compounds in this chapter:The National Library of Medicine (National Institutes of Health) chemical information database, http://sis.nlm.nih.gov/Chem/ChemMain.html.

Acceptable, but limited, medical uses have been found for THC. The pharmaceutical company Unimed manufactures Marinol®, currently the only manufactured drug containing a synthetic isomer of THC (**dronabinol**) in its formulation. **Marinol**® is listed on Schedule III. The medicine is used to stimulate the appetite in AIDS patients and to treat nausea and vomiting associated with chemotherapy.[49] The synthesis of THC and cannabinols is difficult and complex;[46] thus, there is little reason to expect clandestine synthesis to be a factor in the restricted legal use of marijuana.

The last few years have seen an influx of consumer products manufactured from hemp. Since the plant is hardy and grows well in many types of soil, marijuana is easy to cultivate without a great deal of care. Products made from hemp include fiber, clothing, rope, paper, and consumer products such as shampoo, which contains oil extracted from seeds. These legitimate uses of hemp products led the Drug Enforcement Agency (DEA) to issue clarifications to existing regulations governing marijuana. In essence, the clarifications state that such products are exempt from provisions of the Controlled Substances Act if the products are in a form in which the THC is unavailable, unsuitable, or unlikely to be used for human consumption and abuse. For example, it is hard to image anyone attempting to get high on hemp-derived shampoo; the THC content is minute, and any extraction would not be worth the time or the effort. In many countries, varieties of hemp that are low in THC content are grown for purposes of manufacturing hemp products.

Analytical Approach: The analysis of marijuana begins with an examination of the plant's morphology. A microscopic examination is also required, as the leaves have characteristic (but not definitive) features. The most important of these are "**bear claws**," or **cystolithic hairs**, found on the dorsal leave surface. These features are seen in Figure 7.36. The shape is distinctive, and the information to be gained is enhanced by adding a small amount of a dilute acid to the sample and observing the results under the microscope. The $CaCO_3$ that makes up the **cystolith** will dissolve and produce bubbles. Bear claws are actually one

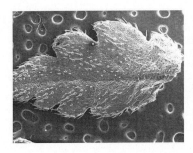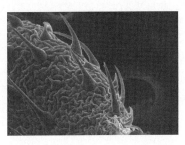

Figure 7.36 Scanning electron micrographs of the marijuana plant, showing the cystolithic hairs from the side (right frame) and above (left frame). Image courtesy of the Oklahoma State Bureau of Investigation.

◀ **Figure 7.36** *Scanning electron micrographs of the marijuana plant, showing the cystolithic hairs from the side (right frame) and above (left frame). Image courtesy of the Oklahoma State Bureau of Investigation.*

of a group of surface features referred to as *trichromes*. The others are unicellular trichromes and glandular trichromes. Unicellular trichromes are thin hairs found on the ventral leaf surface, while glandular hairs are topped with a bulb. Even in ground material or hashish, trichromes may be microscopically identifiable.

The presumptive color test for marijuana is the Duquenois–Levine test. A portion of the sample is extracted with petroleum ether and transferred to a test tube. The Duquenois reagent is added, followed by hydrochloric acid. A bluish-purple color is indicative of cannabinoids. Several drops of chloroform are added to the test tube, and it is shaken until the purple color drops into the chloroform layer. Depending on the concentration of cannabinoids, this transfer can be complete, leaving the top layer in the test tube nearly clear. Potential false positives occur in the presence of some coffees and other oils, but, as with most color-based presumptive tests, an experienced analyst will often recognize a false positive as being subtly different from a true positive. See the color insert for photos of the Duquenois test.

In some laboratories, the analysis stops with the Duquenois–Levine test, but many add TLC with standards as the final step, using the dye Fast Blue B (which is carcinogenic), or Fast Blue BB or the Duquenois reagent as a developer. Fast Blue B gives the constituents distinctive colors: Δ^9-THC turns red, **CBN** purple, and **CBD** orange. The combination of microscopy, the Duquenois–Levine test, and TLC with standards is considered conclusive identification for marijuana. Quantitation of THC is currently not required in the United States. Derivatization techniques can be used for GC, but HPLC is better suited to such analyses.

On the Stand (Legal Issues and Questions): Since the severity of the crime and applicable penalties depend on the weight of the marijuana seized, the issue of total weight (aggregate weight) is central. The stalks of the marijuana plant are not always controlled; definitions vary by state. Similarly, wet or rotting plant matter will have a higher weight than the same material fresh or dried. To date, there is no consistent guidance from the courts on this question;[50] thus, laboratory policy and procedures, (including proper notation in laboratory notes and reports as appropriate) tempered by applicable local statutes, if any, should be followed.

Although species is less an issue today than 20 years ago, a forensic chemist may still be asked on the stand if the plant matter that he or she identified as marijuana was from *Cannabis sativa* L. rather than some other *Cannabis* species, such as *Cannabis indica*. Unless also an expert in *Cannabis* botany, the chemist is not qualified to answer such questions and should unequivocally say so. Many jurisdictions have adopted a definition that mentions the genus without specifying the species to address this ambiguity.

Applying the Science 7.2 The Importance of the Visual Examination

At first glance, the candy bar might seem innocent, but closer inspection of the label and contents reveal that this is no ordinary confection. Note the label "For medicinal use only." Images courtesy of the Oklahoma State Bureau of Investigation.

Another question posed to chemists during their testimony deals with the lack of a mass spectral or IR identification of THC. The issue is raised in part because many attorneys who work on drug cases are familiar with those techniques and are accustomed to seeing some form of instrumental data to accompany visual, color, and TLC testing. A proper and defensible reply to such challenges is that, to a reasonable degree of scientific certainty, there is no plant save marijuana that possesses the combination of microscopic morphology, response to the Duquenois–Levine test, and TLC behavior documented, assuming that appropriate quality control procedures are followed. Finally, since marijuana does have limited acceptable medical use, this has been employed as a defense. Again, the forensic chemist should testify only to his or her area of expertise: The *reason* for possession or use is not related to analytical chemistry.

7.6.3 HUMAN-PERFORMANCE DRUGS: ANABOLIC STEROIDS

The analysis of drugs abused in sports—particularly toxicological analysis—has evolved into a discipline of its own. Because many of the banned substances are not controlled (caffeine above a threshold concentration is a violation), the chemistry and analysis are unique. Once anabolic steroids and other performance-enhancing substances were added to the Controlled Substances Act in 1991, what had principally been a toxicological concern became a drug analysis issue as well, since physical evidence could now be seized and submitted to crime laboratories.

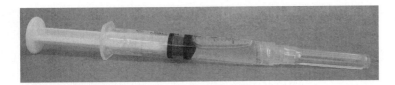

◀ **Figure 7.37** *A syringe exhibit containing mestanolone testosterone propionate. Image courtesy of the Oklahoma State Bureau of Investigation.*

Steroids are a class of biological compounds that include hormones. Steroids contain large fused ring structures classified as simple fats, which means that, unlike other fats, they will not undergo hydrolysis. The fused ring structure is grossly similar to that of THC, in that there are no nitrogen groups and both are oily substances. Some subgroups of steroids are not of forensic concern. The corticoids (andrenocorticals), for example, secreted by the adrenal cortex, are referred to as the cortisones or simply "cortisone." These substances are used to treat itching and inflammation, and pain. Aspirin also reduces inflammation, but is classified as a nonsteroidal anti-inflammatory drug (NSAID); cortisone is a steroidal antiinflammatory drug. Other drugs in this category include prednisone and hydrocortisone.

The bodybuilding steroids include testosterone and related anabolic steroids. Anabolic substances promote secondary male sex characteristics that improve athletic performance by increasing muscle mass and promoting a fast recovery between workouts. Illicit steroids can be synthesized or diverted and are available via mail order on the Internet. Since these substances are sex hormones, abuse can lead to excessive aggression ("'**roid rage**"), the development of male characteristics in females, liver damage, sterility, acne, and increased cholesterol levels.

The analysis of steroids is complicated by the similarity of the drugs' structures, but can be achieved with standard forensic analysis tools.[51,52] Color tests with ammonium vanadate (Mandelin's reagent) has been reported to be the

◀ **Figure 7.38** *Tablets containing methandrostanolone. Image courtesy of the Oklahoma State Bureau of Investigation.*

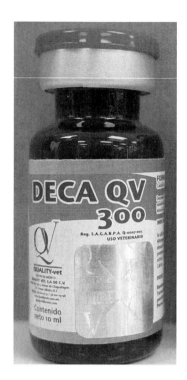

▶ **Figure 7.39** *Nadronlanolone decanoate solution, an example of a diverted drug. This solution is a veterinary preparation likely from Mexico. Image courtesy of the Oklahoma State Bureau of Investigation.*

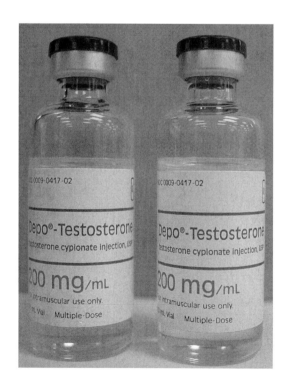

▶ **Figure 7.40** *Solutions of injectable testosterone ciprionate. Image courtesy of the Oklahoma State Bureau of Investigation.*

◀ **Figure 7.41** *Solutions of testosterone enanthate. Image courtesy of the Oklahoma State Bureau of Investigation.*

Applying the Science 7.3   Drug Testing at Athens

The 2004 Summer Olympic Games took place in Athens, Greece. In homage to the first Olympics, some events were held at the same location as events of the first games two thousand years ago. One uniquely modern concern was that of banned performance-enhancing drugs and other substances, including many of the steroids. The World Anti-Doping Agency (WADA) is charged with regulating and enforcing antidoping rules in Olympic sports, and the first systematic testing began at the 1972 games in Munich.

Athletes who place first through fourth were tested for banned substances, as were others (teams and individuals) selected at random. Most samples were urine, but some testing required blood. Typical sample preparation involved liquid–liquid and solid-phase extraction methods.

The turnaround time was 24–72 hours, depending on the substances targeted. Instruments used were GCMS and GC with a nitrogen–phosphorus detector (NPD). The mass spectrometers included quadrupole, time-of-flight, and isotope ratio systems. Isotope ratios of $^{13}C/^{12}C$ were used to differentiate endogenous anabolic steroids from synthetic versions. LC-MS-MS was also employed. Samples were divided into two aliquots, the first subject to screening and the second for confirmatory results if the initial sample tested positive. The cost of laboratory operations during the games was estimated at $6 million. The drugs of particular concern were the anabolic steroids, including stanozolol, methandienone, testosterone, and nandrolone, as well as new synthetic steroids.

Source: Ritter, S. K. "Drug-Testing Lab Stands Ready." *Chemical and Engineering News*, August 9, **2004**, 26–29.

most versatile,[53] but the form of the exhibit and the matrix, such as an oil or a cream, can complicate preliminary testing. A hexane–methanol extraction of the oil-based steroidal preparations has been reported to be a useful method of sample preparation.[52]

7.6.4 OTHER ACIDICS OF NOTE

Had this text been written 15 years ago, an entire section would have been devoted to the barbiturates, which are sedatives and hypnotics derived from barbituric acid. However, the introduction of benzodiazepines, tricyclic antidepressants (TCAs), and SSRIs such as Paxil® and Prozac® has reduced the

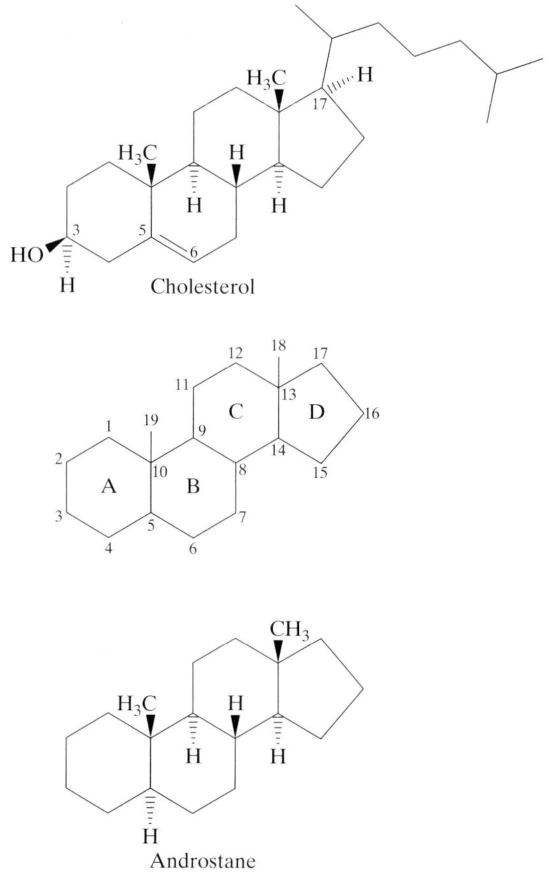

Cholesterol

▶ **Figure 7.42** *Steroids are biologically derived from cholesterol, and the ring-numbering scheme used to describe these compounds is shown. Androstane is an example of a steroid molecule with a methyl group at the C19 position, an important position for classification.*

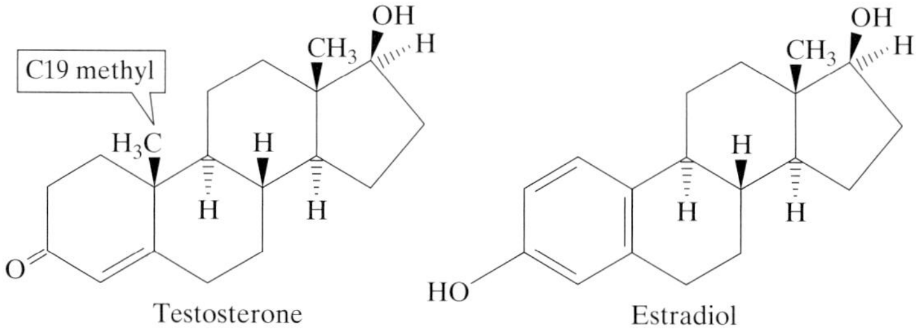

Androstane

▶ **Figure 7.43** *The male sex hormone testosterone and the female sex hormone estradiol. Bodybuilders use testosterone or other steroids that encourage male secondary sex characteristics, such as increased muscle mass.*

Testosterone

Estradiol

Exhibit E: Designer Steroids and Bad Apples

The term "designer drugs" refers to drugs that are clandestinely synthesized to form new structures that mimic the effects of controlled substances. Today, there are designer steroids. In 2003, a person described as a prominent coach in the track-and-field arena delivered a syringe to the U.S. Anti-Doping Agency, the entity that regulates which medications and substances are permitted and which are banned in amateur athletics. The source of the sample was purported to be BALCO, a laboratory in the San Francisco area that has supplied many prominent athletes with supplements.

Exhibit E: (Continued)

Analysis identified a steroid, tetrahydrogestrinone, in the sample, one that would not have been detected in a routine laboratory screening method. According to the CEO of the United States Anti-Doping Agency (USADA), "What we have uncovered appears to be intentional doping of the worst sort. This is a far cry from athletes accidentally testing positive as a result of taking contaminated nutritional supplements. Rather, this is a conspiracy involving chemists, coaches, and certain athletes. . . . "

Source: USADA Statement (October 16, 2003), United States Anti-Doping Agency, *usantidoping.org.*

Table 7.7   Selected Steroids Encountered as Physical Evidence

Compound	Structure
Boldenone	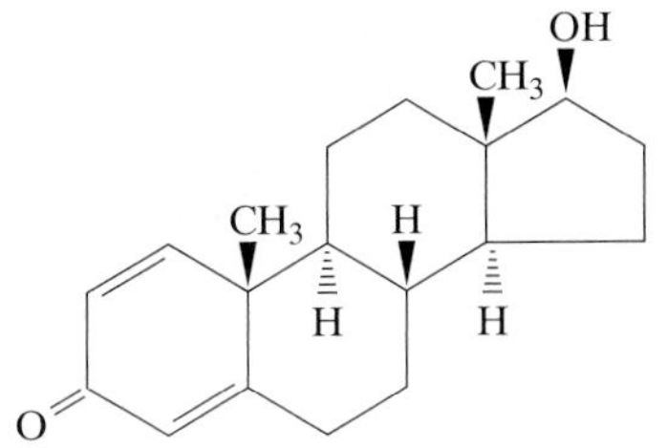
Danazol	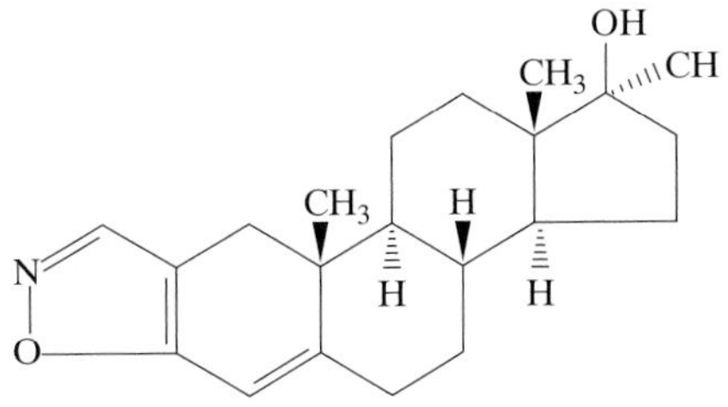
Methandrostenolone	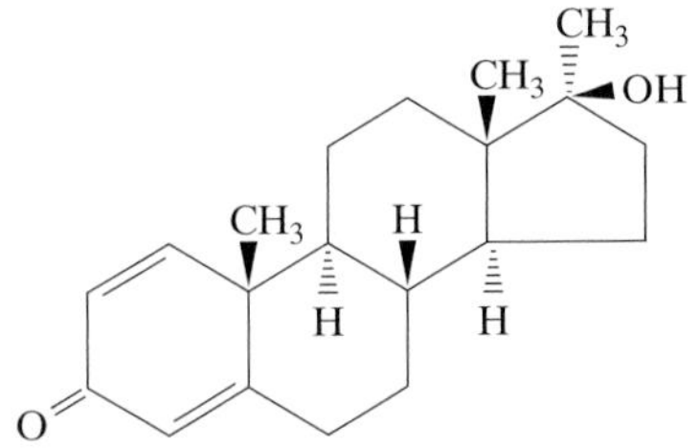
Nandrolone	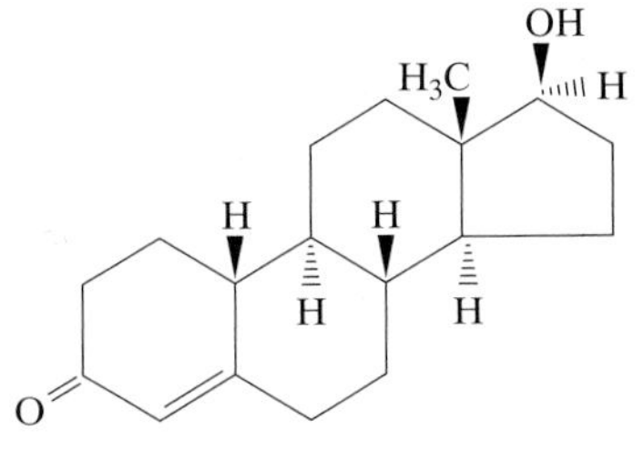

Table 7.7 (Continued)

Compound	Structure

Nandrolone decanoate

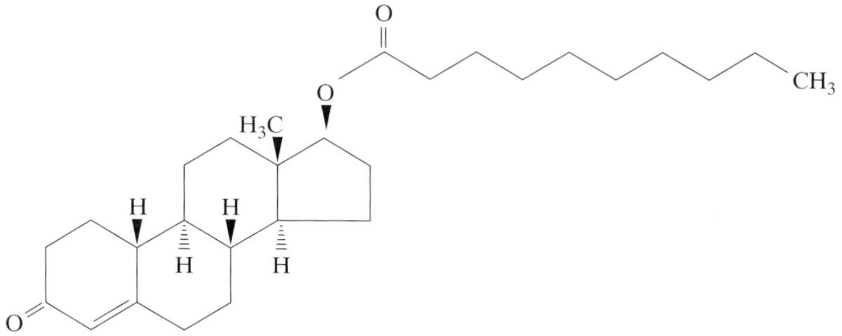

Methandriol

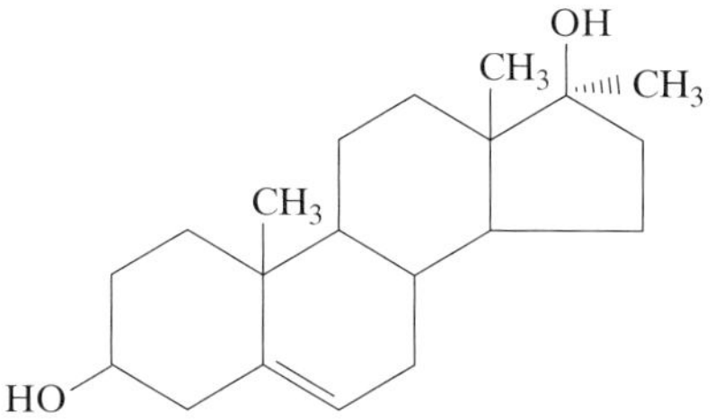

Oxandrolone

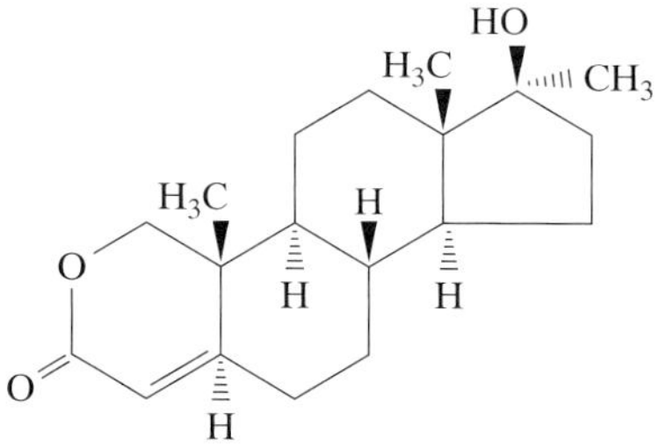

Oxymetholone

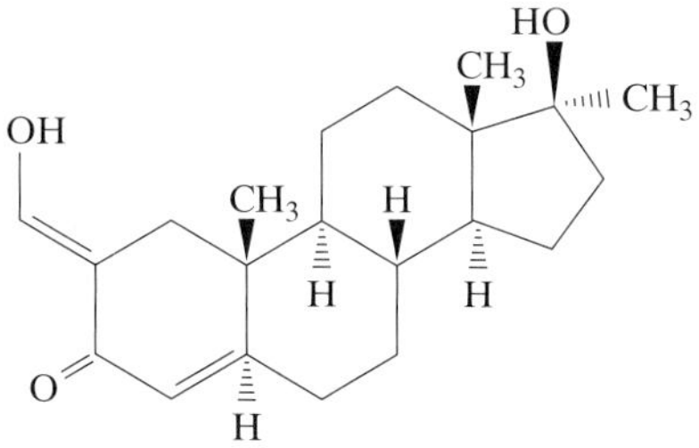

Stanozolol

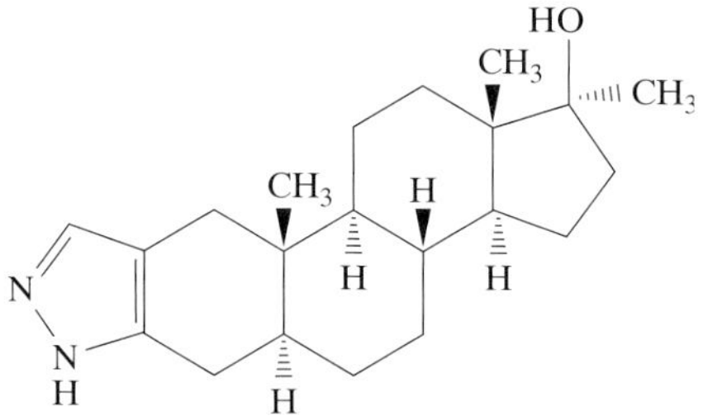

Table 7.7 (Continued)

Compound	Structure
Fluoxymesterone	
Methyltestosterone	
Testosterone enanthate	
Testosterone cypionate	
Testosterone propionate	

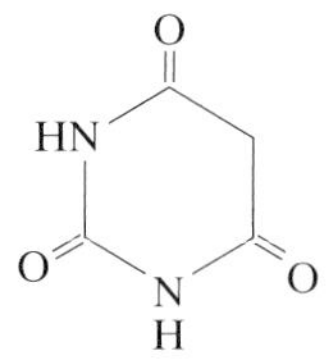

Barbituric acid

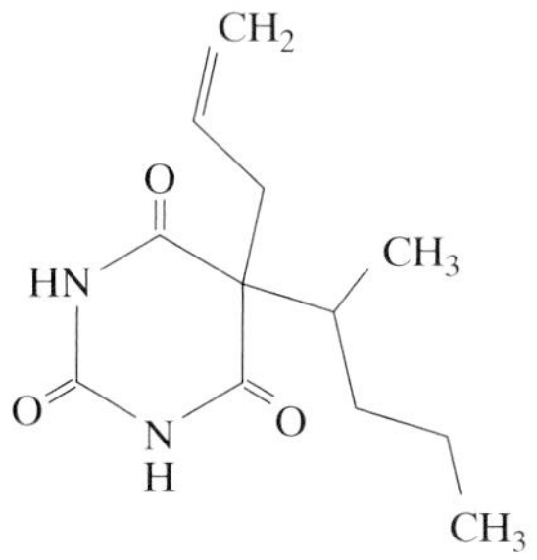

Secobarbital

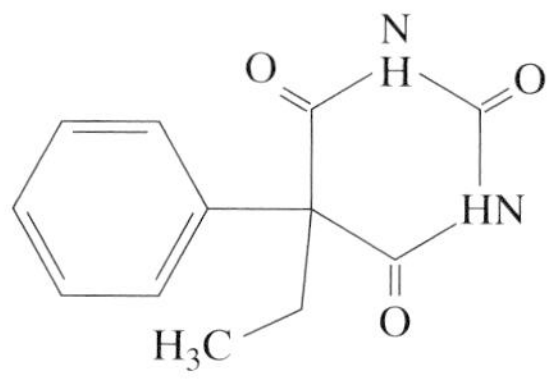

Phenobarbital

▶ **Figure 7.44** *Barbituric acid forms the skeleton of the acid barbiturates. Also shown are secobarbital and phenobarbital.*

use and abuse of the barbiturates. The other class of acids the forensic chemist can expect to see includes salicylates (aspirin) and other analgesics with acid functionality, such as acetaminophen and ibuprofen. These are not controlled substances, but are encountered as fakes and adulterants. Structures of key acidics in these groups are provided in Table 7.7 and Figures 7.42 to 7.45.

Summary

The foundation of forensic drug analysis, historically and practically, is presumptive testing. Presumptive color tests underlie initial sample screening, as well as the choice of developing reagents for thin-layer chromatography. Understanding the fundamental chemistry is important not only in recognizing positives and negatives, but also in diagnosing unusual responses. Color tests are not specific, but they can provide significant information to the forensic chemist who understands how and why they work. Color testing also provides the foundation for preliminary investigations of dyes, a topic that will be revisited in detail in Chapter 11. The underlying common themes of color tests include acidification, the use of aldehydes such as formaldehyde and acetaldehyde, coupling and polymerizations, and carbocations. All colored products incorporate large conjugated systems.

The solubility of a substance, together with its characteristic acidity or basicity in aqueous solution, allows drugs to be separated into acidic, basic, and neutral categories. Acidic and lipophilic drugs illustrate many of the fundamentals described in this chapter and in previous ones and lay important groundwork. These drugs also represent two extremes among controlled substances: the large and nearly insoluble cannabinoids of

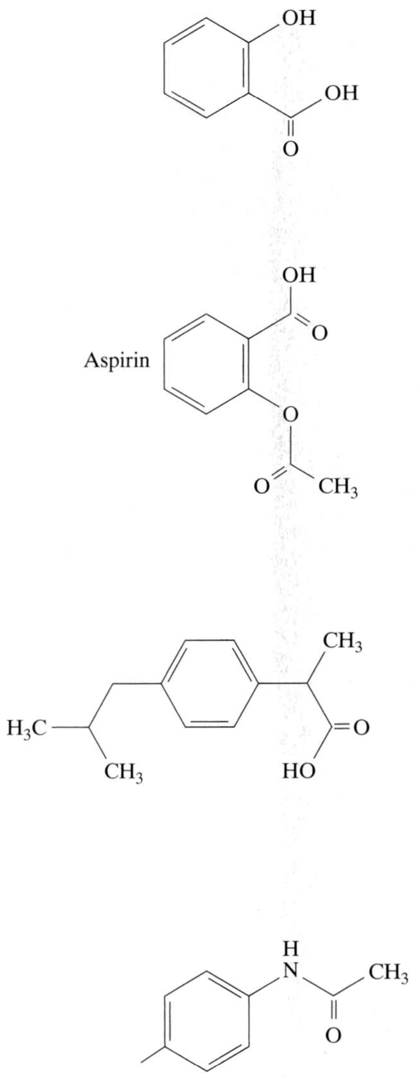

◀ **Figure 7.45** *Salicylic acid, aspirin (acetylsalicylic acid), ibuprofen, and acetaminophen.*

marijuana and the small, polar, and highly soluble GHB family of predator drugs. The next chapter will tackle the largest group within the acid–base–neutral classification system: those which are basic.

KEY TERMS AND CONCEPTS

Achromatic	Barbiturates	Colorant
Anabolic steroids	Bathochromic shift	Condensation reaction
Androgens	Bear claw	Conjugation (conjugated system)
Aryl group	CBD	Crystal field theory (CFT)
Auxochrome	CBN	Crystal test
Auxochromes	Chromophore	Cystolith
Azo	Cobalt thiocyanate	Cystolithic hair
Azo/aza linkages	Color test	Diazo coupling

Diazonium salt	Hemp	Pigment
Diffuse reflection	Hyperchromic shift	Presumptive test
Dilli-Koppanyi	Hypochromic shift	'roid rage
Dragendorff test	Hypsochromic shift	Salicylates
Dronabinol	Ion pair	Simon test
Duquenois-Levine	Law of complements	Sodium nitroprusside test
Dye	Liebermann reagent or test	Spot plate
Dye	LSD	Spot test
GBL	Marinol	Tetrahydrocannabinol
GHB	Marquis	THC
Hashish	p-DMAB	Vehicle

PROBLEMS

From the chapter

1. Summarize the mechanisms by which color can be created with a color-test reagent.

2. Why are reagents based on the formation of diazonium ions and salts used almost exclusively for alkaloids and bases?

3. What would happen if the Liebermann reagent was added to a sample of cocaine HCl? Why? Give a defensible chemical explanation.

4. The nitroprusside reaction will not work (i.e., it will not produce colored products) with primary and secondary amines if the pH is acidic. Why?

5. Related to the previous question, why would NaOH be a poor choice for the base, as opposed to sodium carbonate?

6. In reference 17, the following statement is made: " . . . when a chloroform solution of indole is treated with dilute acid (up to approximately 12 percent) and Ehrlich's reagent the color remains in the chloroform, but if the test is made with stronger hydrochloric acid the color is transferred to the aqueous phase. If the acid is too concentrated, the color may be inhibited or destroyed." Explain this statement.

7. Name the functional group(s) in THC. What presumptive color or crystal tests could be useful, aside from the Duquenois–Levine test? Why are crystal tests of limited use with plant extracts?

8. Resorcinol gives a false positive with the Duquenois–Levine test. Why?

9. One test occasionally performed on aqueous solutions containing a mixture of GHB and GBL is a test for elevated concentrations of K^+ or Na^+. Why?

10. Give the specific mechanism of the conversion of GHB to GBL. Would a mix of products be expected?

11. Name a presumptive test or test series that could distinguish between testosterone and estradiol. Justify your selection.

12. Explain what is meant by the term "undetectable" in referring to a designer steroid. Obviously, it is a misnomer if taken literally, since such compounds have been identified.

13. The following colors are obtained in presumptive testing:

Steroid	Liebermann's	Mandelin's
Testosterone	Light violet	Orange red
Testosterone cypionate	Orange brown	Dark brown
Testosterone enanthate	No reaction	Orange red
Testosterone propionate	Orange brown	Orange brown

Explain or justify these observations.
Source: Chiong, D. M., et al. "The Analysis and Identification of Steroids." *Journal of Forensic Sciences,* 37 **1992**, 488–502.

Integrative

1. Calculate the minimum and maximum frequencies and energies of a photon capable of promoting an electron with UV/VIS radiation.

2. Set up a spreadsheet and use it to determine the ratio of protonated to unprotonated cocaine at the following pH values: 1.0 (as if concentrated HCl were used), 2.0, 4.0, 6.0 (typical of laboratory-distilled water used in preparing reagents), 6.6 ($pK_a = -2.0$), 7.0, 8.6 ($pK_a = +2.0$), 9.0, 10.0, 10.6, and 12. Make the spreadsheet as generic as possible so that other compounds and other pK_a values can be substituted. Graph the results showing the concentration of the two species as a function of pH.

Using the preceding data, information from the chapter, and supplementary information as needed, answer or explain the following:

a. A "one-well" approach is a variation of the cobalt thiocyanate test. In it, the cobalt thiocyanate reagent is dissolved in 98 mL of water to which 2 mL of con HCl is added. When the solution is first prepared, it

turns blue, but no precipitate is formed. The color eventually reverts to pink. Explain and discuss the implications of this test for field-test kits.
Source: Deakin, A. L. "A Study of Acids Used for the Acidified Cobalt Thiocyanate Test for Cocaine Base." *Microgram Journal,* 1 **2003**, 40–44.

b. In an experiment similar to that described in part a, it was observed that if 0.1 N HCl was used instead of con HCl, no transitory color change was observed and the test worked as expected with cocaine. Explain this observation.
Source: Deakin, A. L. "A Study of Acids Used for the Acidified Cobalt Thiocyanate Test for Cocaine Base." *Microgram Journal,* 1 **2003**, 40–44.

c. Cocaine can hydrolyze in solution when exposed to strong acids or bases, but the process typically requires hours. Give equations or reactions for the hydrolysis under both conditions and state the likely products.

d. The Scott variant of the cobalt thiocyanate consists of a cobalt thiocyanate solution that is prepared in 1:1 water and glycerin. When this solution is added to a sample of cocaine, the characteristic blue precipitate forms. The test continues by the addition of HCl until a precipitate-free pink solution is observed. The solution is extracted with chloroform. The bottom layer is blue, the top pink. Explain. What is the likely function of the glycerin?
Source: Schlesinger, H. L. "Topics in the Chemistry of Cocaine." *United Nations Office on Drugs and Crime: Bulletin on Narcotics,* **1985**, 63–85.

e. What other transition metals might work as ion-pair reagents? List two or three, and discuss the considerations and experiments that would be needed to use them.

3. One colored species proposed for some stable carbocation color change reactions is a tropylium ion. Why would a tropylium ion be expected to be colored a different color than the starting material?

4. Fast Blue B has been used as a spray reagent developer for the TLC of marijuana samples and as a color-test reagent. Due to its carcinogenic properties in that form, the Fast Blue BB salt has replaced it in most uses. Find the formula for Fast Blue BB and postulate how it reacts with THC, CBN, and CBD. Why are the colors developed with Fast Blue B different for the three cannabinoids? Which two would you expect to be the most similar?

5. Describe an extraction scheme to separate testosterone and estradiol.

6. Of the compounds shown in Table 7.7, several are generally provided in solution for injection. What would the solvent likely be and why?

7. Using one of the references for finding chemical structures presented in the previous chapter, locate the structure of gentian violet, also called crystal violet. This dye is a widely used biological stain.

a. Into what class of dye does the structure of gentian violet fall in the four groupings presented in this chapter?

b. Using the guidelines given in Appendix 5 for estimating the color of a structure, rationalize the color of gentian violet.

Food for thought

1. A common scene in movies and TV programs shows the detective tasting a suspected drug powder to determine its identity. In addition to being poor laboratory practice, it is a really bad idea. Discuss and explain.

2. How important is it for a forensic chemist to understand why heroin turns the Marquis reagent purple or why cocaine forms a blue precipitate with the cobalt thiocyanate reagent?

FURTHER READING

Chamot, E. M., and C. W. Mason. *Handbook of Chemical Microscopy: Volume II: Chemical Methods and Inorganic Qualitative Analysis.* Chicago: McCrone Research Institute, **1989**.

Chang, R. "Chapter 22: Transition Metal Chemistry and Coordination Compounds," in R. Chang, *Chemistry,* 8th ed. Boston: McGraw Hill, **2005**.

Gibbs, H. D. "Phenol Tests I: A Classification of the Tests and a Review of the Literature." *Chemical Reviews,* 3 **1926**, 291–319.

Lagowski, J. J., and C. H. Sorum. *Introduction to Semimicro Qualitative Analysis,* 7th ed. Englewood Cliffs, NJ: Prentice Hall, **1991**.

Lambert, J. B., et al. *Organic Structural Spectroscopy.* Upper Saddle River, NJ: Prentice Hall, **1998**.

Maunder, M. J. d. F. "The Rapid Detection of Drugs of Abuse." *Medicine, Science, and the Law,* 14 **1974**, 243–249.

Miessler, G. L., and D. A. Tarr. *Inorganic Chemistry,* 3d ed. Upper Saddle River, NJ: Prentice Hall, **2004**.

Schlesinger, H. I., and R. E. Palmateer. "Studies on Complex Ions III. The Relative Stabilities of the Halogenplatinates." *Journal of the American Chemical Society,* 52 **1930**, 4316–4331.

Sen, N. R., and N. N. Sinha. "Condensations of Aldehydes with Resorcinol and Some Other Aromatic Hydroxyl

Compounds." *Journal of the American Chemical Society*, 45 **1923**, 2984–2996.

Shriner, R. L., et al. *The Systematic Identification of Organic Compounds*, 8th ed. New York: John Wiley and Sons, **2004**.

United Nations Scientific and Technical Notes. *Chemistry and Reaction Mechanisms of Rapid Tests for Drugs of Abuse and Precursor Chemicals*, 1989.

Wermuth, C. G., ed. *The Practice of Medicinal Chemistry*. London: Academic/Elsevier, **2003**.

Wesp, E. F., and W. R. Brode. "The Absorption Spectra of Ferric Compounds: I. The Ferric Chloride–Phenol Reaction." *Journal of the American Chemical Society*, 56 **1934**, 1037–1042.

Zollinger, H., ed. *Color Chemistry: Synthesis, Properties, and Applications of Organic Dyes and Pigments*. Zurich: VHCA/Wiley-VCH, **2003**.

REFERENCES

1. Galichet, L. Y., et al., eds. *Clarke's Analysis of Drugs and Poisons, Vol 1*. London: Pharmaceutical Press, **2004**.

2. *The Merck Index*, 13th. Whitehouse Station, NJ: Merck and Co., **2001**.

3. Velapoldi, R. A., and S. A. Wicks. "The Use of Chemical Spot Test Kits for the Presumptive Identification of Narcotics and Drugs of Abuse." *Journal of Forensic Science*, 19 **1974**, 636–656.

4. O'Neal, C. L., et al. "Validation of Twelve Chemical Spot Tests for the Detection of Drugs of Abuse." *Forensic Science International*, 109 **2000**, 189–201.

5. Zollinger, H., ed. *Color Chemistry: Synthesis, Properties, and Applications of Organic Dyes and Pigments*. Zurich: VHCA/Wiley-VCH, **2003**.

6. Lambert, J. B., et al. "Chapter 12: Structural Analysis," in J. B. Lambert et al., *Organic Structural Spectroscopy*. Upper Saddle River, NJ: Prentice Hall, **1998**, 304–344.

7. Lambert, J. B., et al. "Chapter 11: UV–Vis, CD, and ORD," in J. B. Lambert et al., *Organic Structural Spectroscopy*. Upper Saddle River, NJ: Prentice Hall, **1998**, 274–303.

8. United Nations Scientific and Technical Notes. *Chemistry and Reaction Mechanisms of Rapid Tests for Drugs of Abuse and Precursor Chemicals*, 1989.

9. Auterhoff, H., and D. Braun. "Die Farbreaktion des Morphins nach E. MARQUIS." *Archiv der Pharmazie (Weinheim)*, 306 **1973**, 866–873.

10. Auterhoff, H., and J. Oswald. "Die Farbreaktion des Meprobamats mit 4-Dimethylaminobenzaldehyde." *Archiv der Pharmazie (Weinheim)*, 307 **1974**, 887–888.

11. Ueda, T., et al. "Reaction of Naphthylamine with the Marquis Reagent." *Yakugaku Zasshi*, 92 **1972**, 661–664.

12. Rehse, K., and H. G. Kawerau. "Mechanism of the Reaction of Aromatic Compounds with Formaldehyde in Sulfuric Acid (Marquis Reagent)." *Archiv der Pharmazie (Weinheim)*, 307 **1974**, 934–942.

13. Soderberg, B, Bennett Department of Chemistry, West Virginia University, personal communication, 2004.

14. Mattocks, A. R. "Spectrophotometric Determination of Unsaturated Pyrrolizidine Alkaloids." *Analytical Chemistry*, 39 **1967**, 443–447.

15. Knowlton, M., et al. "Use of a Modified Ehrlich's Reagent for Measurement of Indolic Compounds." *Analytical Chemistry*, 32 **1960**, 666–668.

16. Mauzerall, D., and S. Granick. "The Occurrence and Determination of d-Aminolevulinic Acid and Prophobilinogen in Urine." *Journal of Biological Chemistry*, 219 **1956**, 435–446.

17. Chernoff, L. H. "Quantitative Determination of Indole." *Industrial and Engineering Chemistry: Analytical Edition*, 12 **1940**, 273–274.

18. Maltz, H., et al. "Reaction of Nitroprusside with Amines." *Journal of Organic Chemistry*, 36 **1971**, 363–364.

19. Wolfe, S. K., et al. "Kinetic Studies of the Pentacyanonitrosoylferrate(2-)-Azide and –Hydroxylamine Reactions." *Inorganic Chemistry*, 13 **1974**, 2567–2572.

20. Ford, P. C., and I. M. Lorkovic. "Mechanistic Aspects of the Reactions of Nitric Oxide with Transition-Metal Complexes." *Chemical Reviews*, 102 **2002**, 993–1017.

21. Kovar, K. A., and M. Keck. "Zur Kenntnis der Duquenois-Reacktion auf Haschisch und Marihuana." *Archiv der Pharmazie (Weinheim)*, 321 **1988**, 249–252.

22. Forrester, D. E. *The Duquenois Color Test for Marijuana: Spectroscopic and Chemical Studies*. Doctoral dissertation, Georgetown University, Washington, D.C: **1997**.

23. Miessler, G. L., and D. A. Tarr. "Ch. 10: Coordination Chemistry II: Bonding," in G. L. Miessler and D. A. Tarr, *Inorganic Chemistry*, 3d ed. Upper Saddle River, NJ: Prentice Hall, **2004**, 337–378.

24. Deakin, A. L. "A Study of Acids Used for the Acidified Cobalt Thiocyanate Test for Cocaine Base." *Microgram Journal*, 1 **2003**, 40–44.

25. Eisman, M., et al. "Automatic Continuous-Flow Method for the Determination of Cocaine." *Analytical Chemistry*, 64 **1992**, 1509–1512.

26. Galichet, L. Y., et al., ed., *Clarke's Analysis of Drugs and Poisons, Vol. 2*. London: Pharmaceutical Press, **2004**.

27. Jungreis, E. "Forensic Applications of Spot Test Analysis," in *Spot Test Analysis: Clinical, Environmental, Forensic, and Geochemical Applications*, 2d ed. New York: John Wiley and Sons, **1997**.

28. Nerin, C., et al. "Indirect Determination of Alkaloids and Drugs by Atomic Absorption Spectrometry." *Analytical Chemistry*, 57 **1985**, 34–38.

29. Travnikoff, B. "Semiquantitative Screening Test for Cocaine." *Analytical Chemistry*, 55 **1983**, 795–796.

30. Schlesinger, H. L. "Topics in the Chemistry of Cocaine." *United Nations Office on Drugs and Crime: Bulletin on Narcotics*, **1985**, 63–85.

31. Elsherbini, S. H. "Cocaine Base Identification and Quantification." *Forensic Science Review*, 10 **1998**, 32–34.

32. "Standard Guide for Microcrystal Testing in the Forensic Analysis of Phencyclidine and Its Analogs," in *ASTM Standard E 2125-01*, 14.02, ASTM International, **2004**.

33. "Standard Guide for Microcrystal Testing in the Forensic Analysis of Methamphetamine and Amphetamine," in *ASTM Standard E 105-58*, 14.02, ASTM International, **2004**.

34. "Standard Guide for Microcrystal Testing in the Forensic Analysis of Cocaine," in *ASTM Standard E 105-58*, 14.02, ASTM International, **2004**.

35. Swiatko, J., et al. "Further Studies on Spot Tests and Microcrystal Tests for Identification of Cocaine." *Journal of Forensic Science* 48 **2003**, 581–585.

36. Fulton, C. C. *Modern Microcrystal Tests for Drugs*. New York: Wiley-Interscience, **1976**.

37. Bishop, S. C., et al. "Micellar Electrokinetic Chromatographic Screening Method for Common Sexual Assault Drugs Administered in Beverages." *Forensic Science International*, 141 **2004**, 7–15.

38. Elliot, S. "The Many Faces of Gamma-Hydroxybutyrate (GHB)." *Syva Drug Monitor: The Journal of Dade Behring Limited*, 4 **2003**, 9–12.

39. Andrera, K. M., et al. "Microchemical Identification of Gamma-Hydroxybutyrate (GHB)." *Journal of Forensic Sciences*, 45 **2000**, 665–668.

40. Blair, S., et al. "Determination of Gamma-Hydroxybutyrate in Water and Human Urine by Solid Phase Microextraction–Gas Chromatography/Quadrupole Ion Trap Spectrometry." *Journal of Forensic Sciences*, 46 **2001**, 688–693.

41. Ciolino, L. A., et al. "The Chemical Interconversion of GHB and GBL: Forensic Issues and Implications." *Journal of Forensic Sciences*, 46 **2001**, 1315–1323.

42. Chew, S. L., and J. A. Meyers. "Indentification and Quantitation of Gamma Hydroxybutyrate (NaGHB) by Nuclear Magnetic Resonance Spectroscopy." *Journal of Forensic Sciences*, 48 **2003**, 292–297.

43. Chappell, J. S., et al. "The Extraction and Infrared Identification of Gamma Hydroxybutyric Acid (GHB) from Aqueous Solutions." *Journal of Forensic Sciences*, 49 **2004**, 52–59.

44. Brudenelle, A., Tucson Police Department, personal communication, 2004.

45. *State Fact Sheets*, U.S. Drug Enforcement Agency, downloaded March 19, 2004. http://www.dea.gov/pubs/states/hawaii.html.

46. Mechoulam, R., et al. "Recent Advances in the Chemistry and Biochemistry of Cannibis." *Chemical Reviews*, 76 **1976**, 75–112.

47. Cole, M. D. "Chapter 4: Cannibis Sativa and Products," in Michael D. Cole, *The Analysis of Controlled Substances*. Chichesterm, West Sussex: Wiley, **2003**, 49–72.

48. L. Y. Galichet et al., eds., "Cannibis," in L. Y. Galichet et al. eds., *Clarke's Analysis of Drugs and Poisons, Vol. 2*. London: Pharmaceutical Press, **2004**, 740–741.

49. *Physician's Desk Reference*, 58th ed. Montvale, NJ: Thomson PDR, **2004**.

50. Moenssens, A. A., et al. "Drugs and Their Control: Section V: Special Defenses, 14.25, Quantitative Considerations," in A. A. Moenssens et al., *Scientific Evidence in Civil and Criminal Cases*, 4th ed. Westbury, NY: The Foundation Press, Inc., **1995**, 859–860.

51. Lurie, I. S., et al. "The Determination of Anabolic Steroids by MECC, Gradient HPLC, and Capillary GC." *Journal of Forensic Sciences*, 39 **1994**, 74–85.

52. Chiong, D. M., et al. "The Analysis and Identification of Steroids." *Journal of Forensic Sciences*, 37 **1992**, 488–502.

CHAPTER

8

Drug Analysis II: Basic Drugs

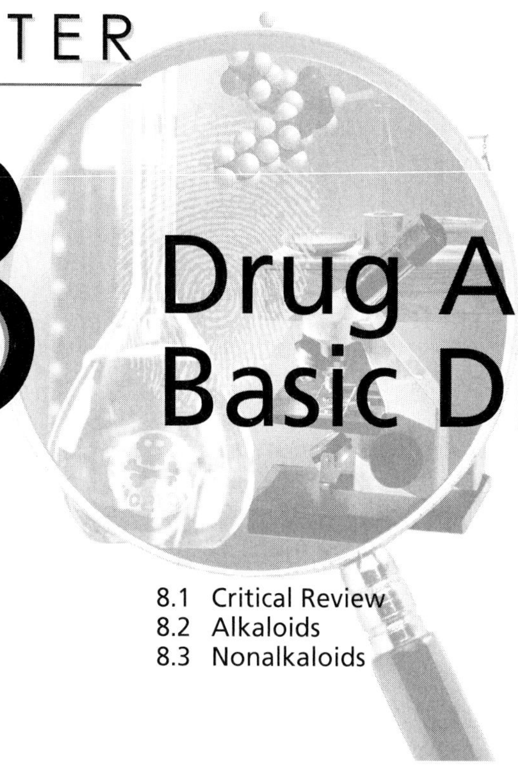

8.1 Critical Review
8.2 Alkaloids
8.3 Nonalkaloids

OVERVIEW AND ORIENTATION

In this chapter we cover basic drugs (Figure 8.1), an enormous category of substances, most of which are derived from plant matter. These alkaloids include the oldest-known hallucinogens, cocaine, opiate alkaloids, and familiar constituents of tea, coffee, and chocolate. The remaining category—basic drugs not derived from plant matter—includes methamphetamine, amphetamine, and a collection of widely prescribed antidepressants and tranquilizers. However, the lines between natural, synthetic, and semisynthetic drugs is blurry at best in an age of molecular design, advanced organic synthesis, and automated drug discovery. For example, methamphetamine either can be made from ephedrine, which is obtained from the *ephedra* plant, or can be synthesized from precursor chemicals, yet the drug is generally considered to be synthetic rather than semisynthetic. Rather than get bogged down in semantics, we will focus instead on core chemical concepts such as extractions, synthetic methods, products, and byproducts produced when a basic drug is obtained or synthesized.

Basic drugs elicit a variety of physiological effects. Stimulants such as methamphetamine can act as hallucinogens at higher doses, while the opiate alkaloids are analgesic and promote general depression of the central nervous system. Many natural products, such as cocoa leaves, peyote, and khat leaves, have been used for hundreds of years. Some—for example, LSD and mescaline—are associated with religious explorations or celebrations.

A large contingent of the basic drug family consists of stimulants, which humans have been using for centuries. Their desirable effects include the ability to work longer and harder with increased alertness. Many would give just those reasons for drinking their morning cup(s) of coffee or tea, and what student has not pulled an all-nighter fueled by some form of caffeinated beverage? Like caffeine, many stimulants have a history of accepted use, and some,

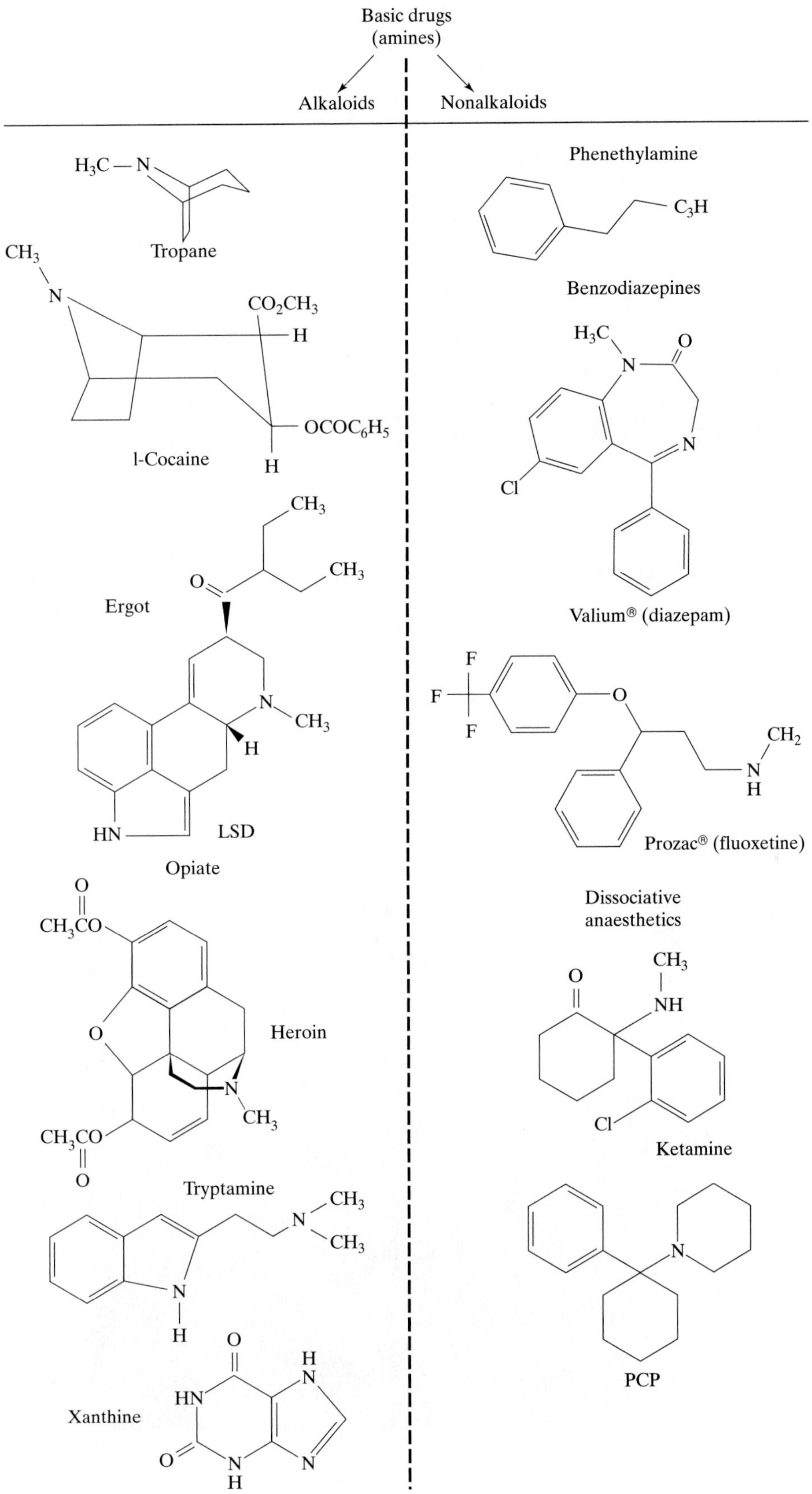

Basic drugs (amines)

Alkaloids | Nonalkaloids

Alkaloids:

Tropane

l-Cocaine

Ergot

LSD

Opiate

Heroin

Tryptamine

Xanthine

Nonalkaloids:

Phenethylamine

Benzodiazepines

Valium® (diazepam)

Prozac® (fluoxetine)

Dissociative anaesthetics

Ketamine

PCP

◄ **Figure 8.1** *Just your basic drugs in this chapter.*

such as khat, are integrated into cultures. Structurally, stimulants such as the amphetamines, mescaline, and the **tryptamines** (psilocin and psilocybin) are similar to the **neurotransmitters** dopamine and serotonin as shown in Table 8.1. Many stimulants produce a continuum of effects, beginning with increased alertness, passing through elevated heart rates and agitation, and ending in hallucinations. Some, such as methamphetamine and PCP, are easily synthesized by amateur chemists; hence, we will delve in detail into how clandestine chemists prepare these substances and their precursors. Before diving into the rich and complex categories of basic drugs, however, we will set the stage for our explorations with a brief review of two core concepts: base chemistry and stereochemistry.

Exhibit A: "One Person's Coffee Is Another's Dope"

In a previous chapter we noted that the definition of a dangerous drug depends as much on social, political, and economic factors as it does on pharmacology and chemistry. One recent example is the drug khat, which is discussed in this chapter. Khat is a leaf that is chewed, much as coca leaves (the source of cocaine) once were, to provide energy. In parts of Africa and the Middle East, khat is socially accepted just as caffeine is accepted in the West. Both caffeine and khat can be abused; however, at present, coffee has not been placed on the list of controlled substances, whereas the ingredients of khat are on the list. As different nationalities and ethnic groups migrate to the West, substances that are illegal and rarely encountered now will become more common as they filter out of migrant communities and into the general population. Thus, khat, a negligible problem 20 years ago in the United States, is now a controlled substance of concern. An analogy would be for an American to emigrate to a country where coffee and tea are illegal. The situation with khat emphasizes the social and cultural aspects of drug control.

Table 8.1 **Neurotransmitters**

Dopamine

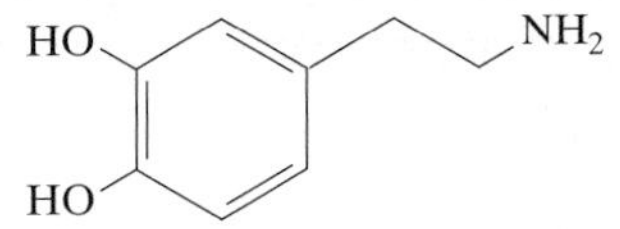

Serotonin

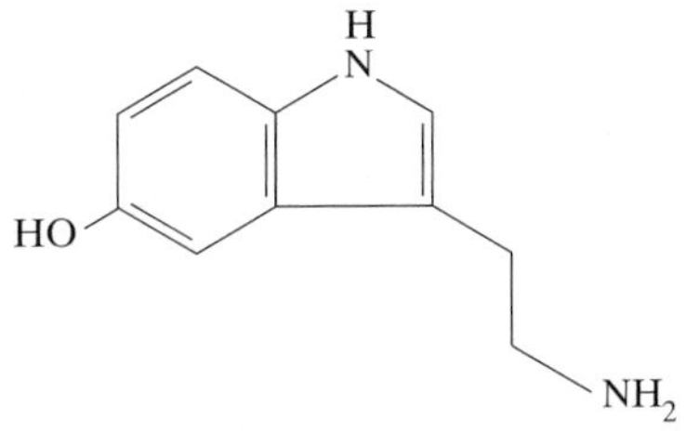

8.1 CRITICAL REVIEW

Recall that drugs possessing basic character are described by their pK_a values for the generic expression

$$BH^+ \longrightarrow B + H^+ \qquad (8.1)$$

where B represents a large structure and the basic group is an amine of the type RNH_2, R_2NH, or R_3N. Basic drugs often exist as soluble salts such as hydrochlorides or sulfates; once these drugs are ingested, their solubility and absorption are dependent on the factors described in Chapter 6.

Knowledge of the stereochemistry of basic drugs, particularly the tropane alkaloids and the methamphetamine family, is essential to understanding synthesis, precursors, and legal questions. A summary of terms is given in Figure 8.2; for a detailed review, refer to a textbook on organic chemistry, such as any of those listed in "Further Reading" at the end of the chapter.

An asymmetric carbon (also called a chiral carbon) is a carbon atom bonded to four different groups. The presence of an asymmetric carbon lends a molecule chirality, and the asymmetric carbon is referred to as the chiral center. Nitrogen atoms, which are key atoms in basic drugs, can also be chiral centers. To describe the arrangement of groups around a chiral atom, the Cahn–Ingold–Prelog convention assigns priorities to the groups bonded to the chiral atom. The lowest-priority group is oriented so that it points away from the viewer (Figure 8.3) and the direction of a curved arrow drawn through the groups determines the rotation of the group. Appendix 7 details the rules used to assign priorities in accordance with this convention. If the direction of rotation is clockwise, the chiral center is assigned the R (Latin *rectus*, for "right") designation. If the rotation is counterclockwise, then the chiral center is designated S (Latin *sinister*, for left).

The R and S nomenclature is related to, but not synonymous with, two complementary nomenclatures used to describe chiral centers. When polarized light (Chapter 5) propagates through media containing chiral atoms, the plane of rotation shifts slightly. Enantiomers of the same compound will shift the rotation in different directions, a property that provides a laboratory technique for differentiating among enantiomers. For this reason, enantiomers are referred to as optical isomers. A polarimeter is used to measure the direction of rotation, which is designated as d or + for dextrorotatory (to the right) or as l or − for levorotatory (to the left) enantiomers. Many syntheses produce mixtures of d and l isomers, which are

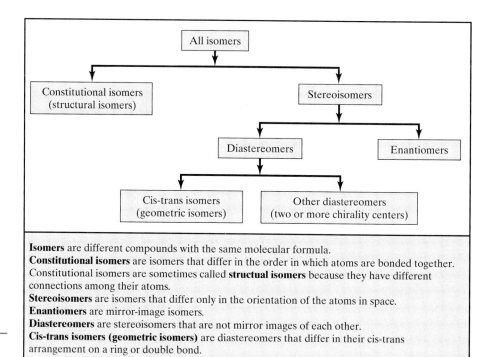

Isomers are different compounds with the same molecular formula.
Constitutional isomers are isomers that differ in the order in which atoms are bonded together.
Constitutional isomers are sometimes called **structual isomers** because they have different connections among their atoms.
Stereoisomers are isomers that differ only in the orientation of the atoms in space.
Enantiomers are mirror-image isomers.
Diastereomers are stereoisomers that are not mirror images of each other.
Cis-trans isomers (geometric isomers) are diastereomers that differ in their cis-trans arrangement on a ring or double bond.

▶ **Figure 8.2** *Definitions and flowchart for stereochemistry.*

referred to as racemic mixtures. It is common for optical isomers of drugs to have different activities and effects. For example, the dissociative anesthetic ketamine, discussed in a later section, has an R and an S form; the R isomer tends to cause hallucinations, while the S form has anesthetic properties.

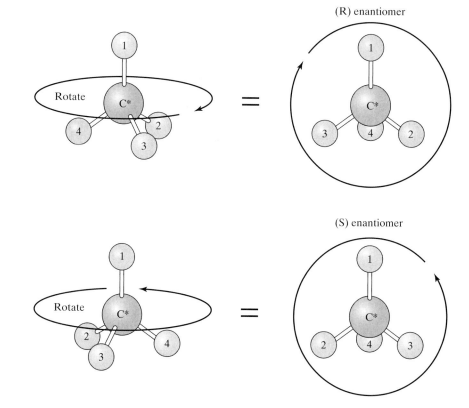

▶ **Figure 8.3** *The R,S naming conventions, shown in three dimensions. The numbers refer to the priority of the substituent. (See Appendix 7 for more details on how priorities are assigned.)*

Example Problem 8.1

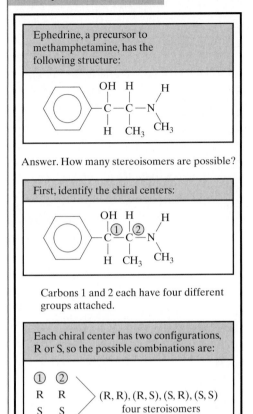

Ephedrine, a precursor to methamphetamine, has the following structure:

Answer. How many stereoisomers are possible?

First, identify the chiral centers:

Carbons 1 and 2 each have four different groups attached.

Each chiral center has two configurations, R or S, so the possible combinations are:

① ②

R R ⎞
     ⎬ (R, R), (R, S), (S, R), (S, S)
S S ⎠ four stereoisomers

One other notational convention is used in describing enantiomers: the D,L convention, which is distinct from the dl system just presented. The D,L convention describes the configuration of groups around a chiral center relative to another molecule, rather than in absolute terms as is done in the R,S system. The D,L system is still used to describe sugars (carbohydrates) and amino acids. Most natural sugars are of D form, while most amino acids are of L form. Briefly, to determine the D,L configuration of a carbohydrate or an amino acid, the molecule is drawn by means of the Fischer projection method (Figure 8.4) with the terminal carbonyl group oriented upwards. The D,L designation is assigned on the basis of how substituents are arranged when the molecule is drawn in accordance with the Fischer projection method. An example is shown in Figure 8.5.

COOH
H——OH
HO——H
COOH

L−(+)-tartaric acid
(2R, 3R)-tartaric acid

H   O
 \\ //
  C
H——OH
HO——H
H——OH
H——OH
CH₂OH

D−(+)-glucose

COOH
H₂N——H
CH₃

L−(+)-alanine

HC = O   HC = O

H ►C◄ OH   H————OH

HO ►C◄ H   HO————H

H ►C◄ OH   H————OH

H ►C◄ OH   H————OH

CH₂OH   CH₂OH

Wedge-and-dash   Fischer projection
structure

◄ **Figure 8.4** *The "wedge-and-dash" representation of the groups around a chiral carbon indicates where each group points in space. The Fischer projection is used to orient a carbohydrate molecule such as a sugar. Both projections can be used to derive the R,S configuration.*

▲ **Figure 8.5** *Examples of compounds drawn as Fischer projections and indicating R,S, D,L, and d,l (+,−) directionality. Note that the R,S configuration does not dictate how a molecule will rotate plane polarized light.*

Applying the Science 8.1 Separation of Enantiomers

The stereochemistry of drugs and precursors can be vital in determining synthetic routes. However, since enantiomers are nearly chemically identical, standard chromatographic methods cannot separate them. To effect a chromatographic separation of enantiomers, stereospecific interactions have to be incorporated. As described in Chapter 5, the use of chiral stationary phases is one method of discriminating enantiomers; while capillary electrokinetic chromatography (MEKC) using chiral cyclodextrins is another. Both of these protocols have been applied to methamphetamine and related compounds and precursors, substances that will be discussed in detail later in the chapter.

Cyclodextrin is a chiral molecule with a small cavity into which molecules partition as the mobile phase moves. The degree of partitioning is partially controlled by chirality, so enantiomers can be separated as long as there is sufficient contact time between analytes and the cyclodextrin and as long as the concentration of cyclodextrin is optimized. While the separation via MEKC is impressive, the problem of detection remains. The great advantage of GCMS is its ability to separate and provide definitive identification, a capability that is absent in traditional MEKC detection devices. Combining data from both methods is possible, but MEKC has yet to make significant inroads into forensic laboratories.

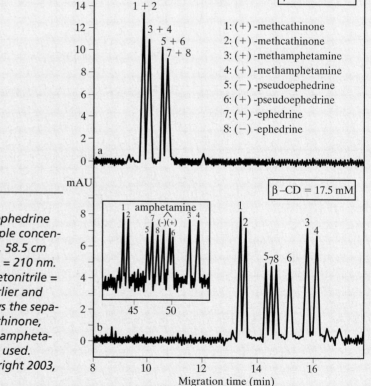

▶ UV electropherograms of (±)-methamphetamine, (±)-methcathinone, (±)-ephedrine and (±)-pseudoephedrine standards. The sample concentrations were 25 ppm. CE conditions: capillary, 58.5 cm (50 cm to detector); detection wavelength, l_{ab} = 210 nm. Running buffers: (a) 150 mM H_3PO_4; water:acetonitrile = 95:5 (v/v); (b) the same buffer as described earlier and the addition of 17.5 mM b-CD. The inset shows the separation of (±)-methamphetamine, (±)-methcathinone, (±)-ephedrine, (±)-pseudoephedrine and (±)-amphetamine standards when and 80 cm capillary was used. Reprinted from reference 3 cited below, copyright 2003, with permission from Elsevier.

Sources: (1) Liau, A. S., et al. "Optimization of a simple method for the chiral separation of methamphetamine and related compounds in clandestine tablets and urine samples by beta-cyclodextrine modified capillary electrophoresis: a complementary method to GC-MS." *Forensic Science International,* 134 **2003**, 17–24. (2) Cheng, W.-C., et al. "Enantiomeric Separation of Methamphetamine and Related Analogs by Capillary Zone Electrophoresis: Intelligence Study in Routine Methamphetamine Seizures." *Journal of Forensic Sciences,* 47 **2002**, 1248–1252. (3) Al-Dirbashi, O., et al. "Achiral and Chiral Quantification of Methamphetamine and Amphetamine in Urine by Semi-micro Column High Performance Liquid Chromatography and Fluorescence Detection." *Journal of Forensic Sciences,* 45 **2000**, 708–714.

Application the Science 8.1 (Continued)

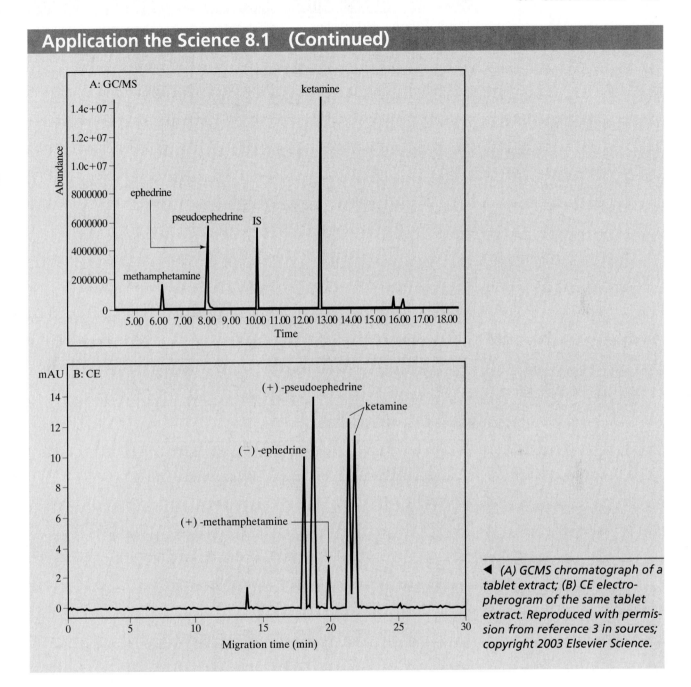

(A) GCMS chromatograph of a tablet extract; (B) CE electropherogram of the same tablet extract. Reproduced with permission from reference 3 in sources; copyright 2003 Elsevier Science.

Note that the configuration around a chiral atom (in R,S or D,L notation) does not define the direction in which polarized light will be rotated. In other words, a D configuration does not necessarily correlate with d (or +) rotation of polarized light. The direction of rotation is a physical property, not a description of the bonding around the chiral center. Molecules may have more than one chiral center, complicating both the notation and the interaction of the molecule with polarized light. Finally, stereochemical aspects of syntheses can be important in forensic chemistry, as will be emphasized when we discuss the methamphetamine family. An example is shown in Figure 8.6.

Exhibit B: Polarimetry

The direction in which a substance rotates plane polarized light is a physical property that can distinguish isomers from one another. The rotation is measured by a device called a polarimeter, which is based on the same concepts discussed in Chapter 5 in relationship to polarized light microscopy. A polarimeter uses an intense light source, such as a sodium lamp. The light is polarized with a polarizing filter (corresponding to the polarizer in a PLM scope) that orients the light so that it is vibrating in only one plane. The polarized light interacts with the sample, and the plane of rotation may be altered to the left or right. A slotted plate is rotated such that the light signal is the same as the original polarized light beam, and the angle of rotation is read. If there is no interaction with the sample, the plate does not have to be turned at all.

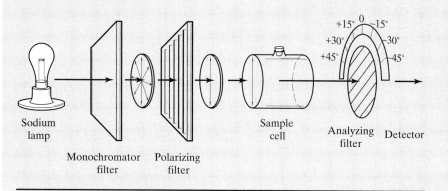

Sodium lamp   Monochromator filter   Polarizing filter   Sample cell   Analyzing filter   Detector

▲ *Operation of a polarimeter.*

Example Problem 8.2

Below is the pharmacologically active stereoisomer of ephedrine.

What is its designation?

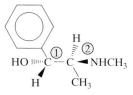

Answer
To answer this question, use the priority assignment and rules reviewed in Appendix 7. Around each chiral carbon, assign priorities to attached groups. H is the lowest priority in both cases.

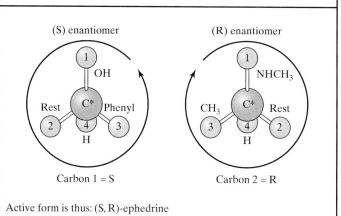

Active form is thus: (S, R)-ephedrine

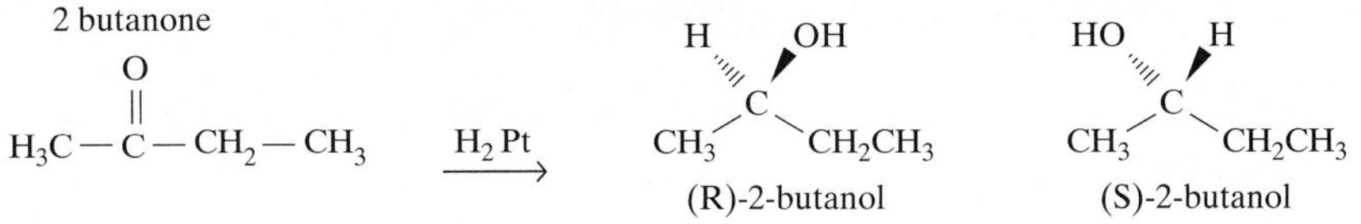

2 butanone

$$H_3C - \overset{\overset{\displaystyle O}{\|}}{C} - CH_2 - CH_3 \quad \xrightarrow{\text{H}_2 \text{ Pt}}$$

(R)-2-butanol

(S)-2-butanol

◀ **Figure 8.6** *Example of how a reaction can create a racemic mixture.*

8.2 ALKALOIDS

8.2.1 OPIATE ALKALOIDS AND HEROIN

Table 8.2 Heroin	
Source:	Semisynthetic from morphine (opium extract)
Form/morphology:	Opiate alkaloid as free base or salts
Classification:	Schedule I Narcotic, semisynthetic alkaloid
Medical Uses:	None
Color tests:	Marquis, purple; Mecke, green
Microcrystal:	Gold and platinic chloride
Other tests:	TLC, GCMS, IR

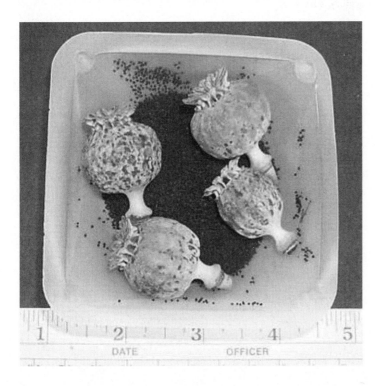

◀ **Figure 8.7** *Opium poppies and poppy seeds. Image courtesy of the Oklahoma State Bureau of Investigation.*

The **opiate alkaloids** are a mix of semisynthetic and synthetic compounds derived from or related to the extract of the unripe seed pods of the opium poppy *Papaver somniferum*. Specifically, the alkaloids are obtained from the **latex**, or milky, exudates of the seed pod that appear when it is cut or sliced. The liquid contains about 10% morphine and about 1.5% codeine, with various amounts (~0.2–8%) of papaverine, thebaine, and noscapine (Table 8.3). The

Table 8.3 Opiate Alkaloids	
Compound	**Structure**
Morphine	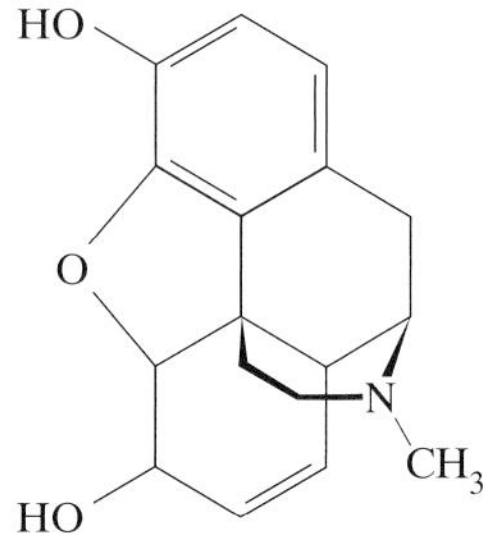
Codeine	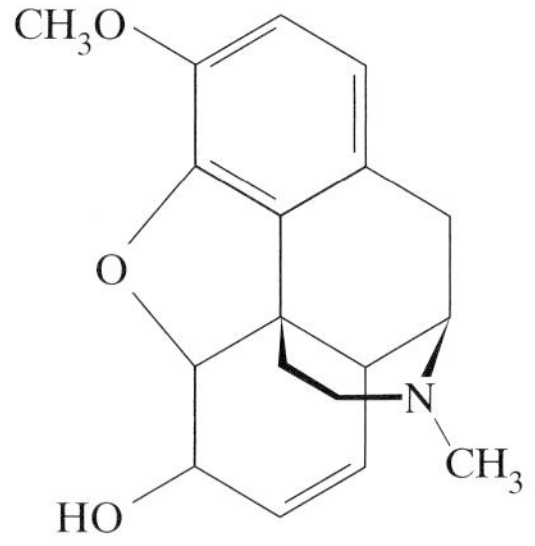
Acetylcodeine	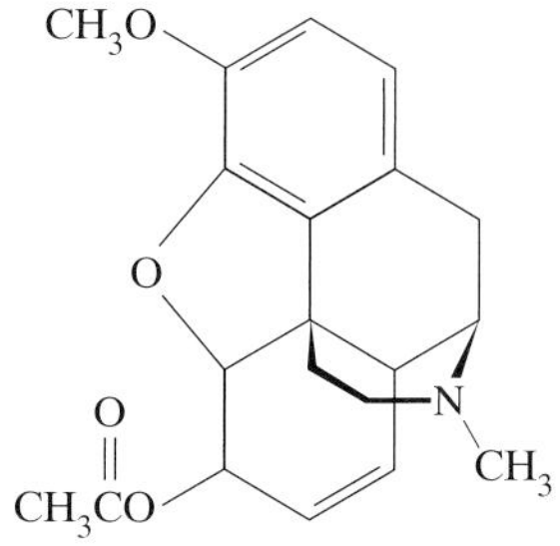
6-O-Monoacetyl morphine (6-MAM) 3-O-MAM is analogous	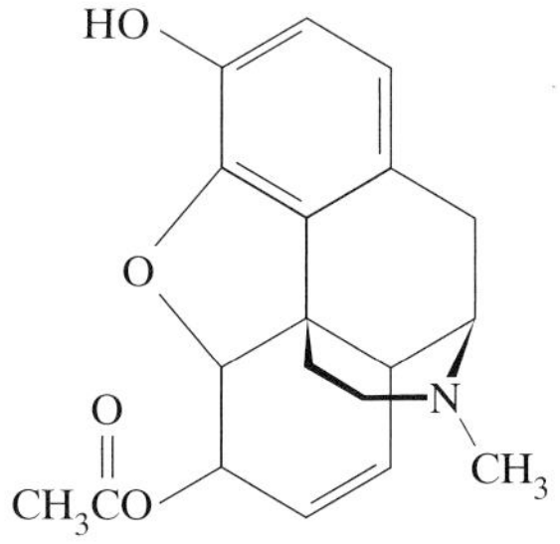
Diacetylmorphine (heroin)	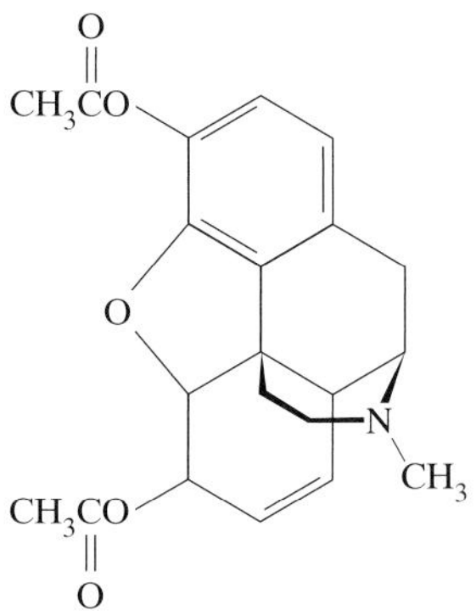

Table 8.3   (Continued)

Compound	Structure

Thebaine

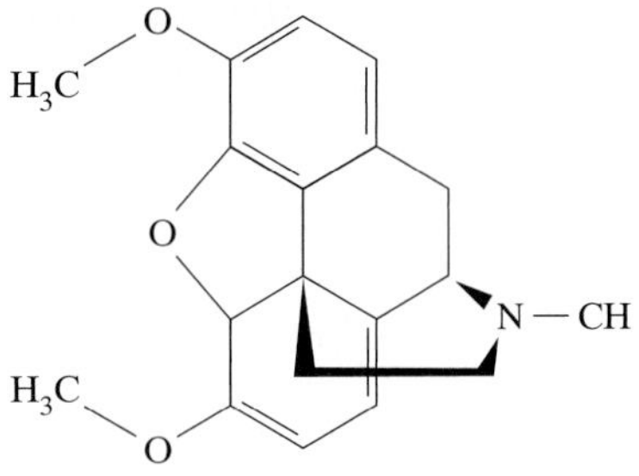

Papaverine

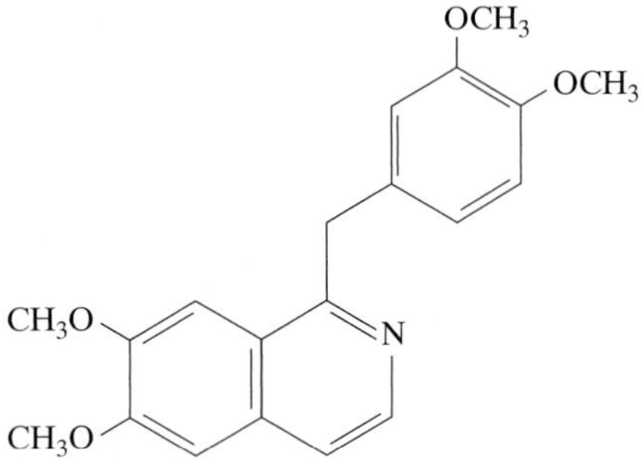

Noscapine

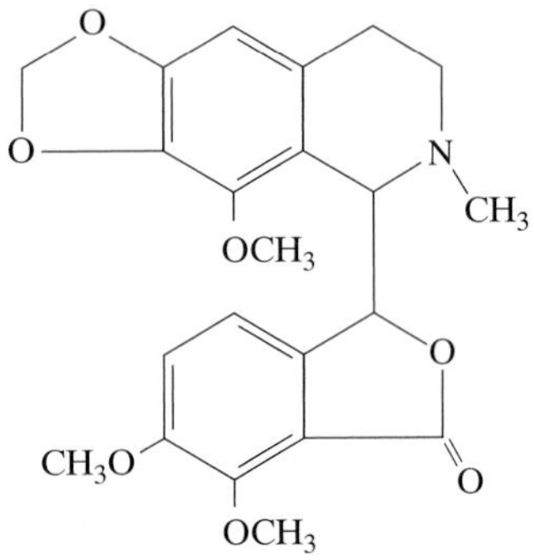

Oxycodone

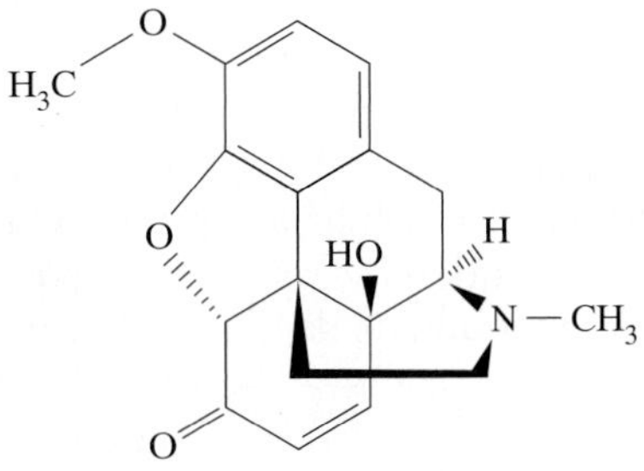

Table 8.3 (Continued)	
Compound	Structure
Hydromorphone	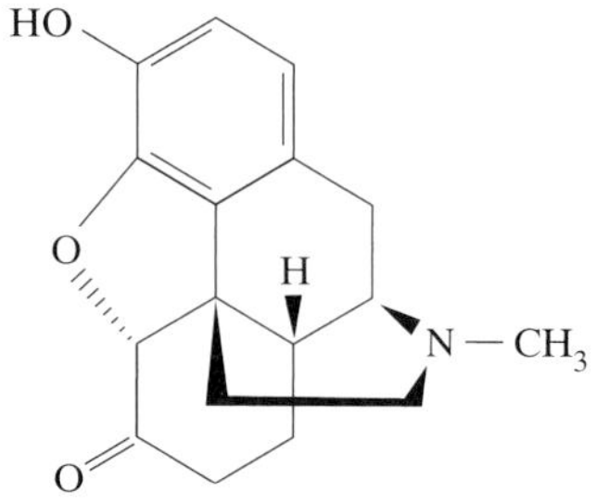
Hydrocodone	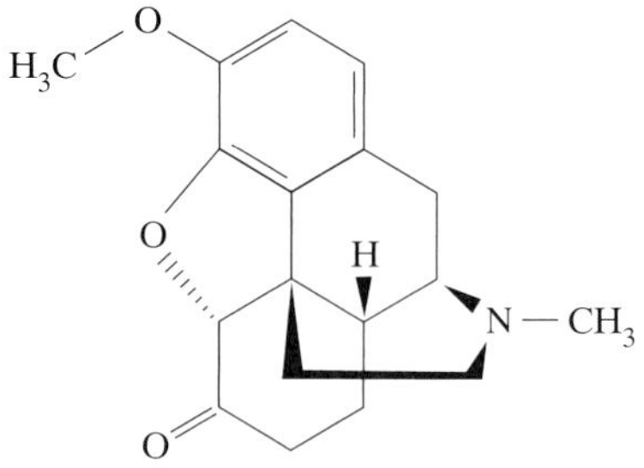
Methadone	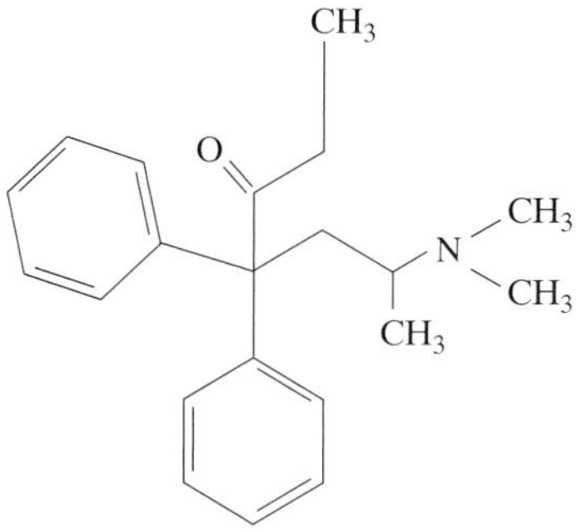

majority of the family has the character of both a base and a phenol, leading to interesting and complex chemistry (Figure 8.8). The hydroxide associated with carbon 3 is more active than that associated with carbon 6, a property that is useful in profiling, synthesis, and degradation studies.[1] The poppy plant is also the source of poppy seeds used in baking.

Morphine has a long history of use and abuse. It was the first so-called vegetable base drug isolated, an event recorded in 1805.[2] Because morphine is basic, an early quantitation method was titration with an acid. Morphine is subject to oxidation, so the morphine content of an extract can decrease after harvest. Similar degradation issues arise with the stimulant khat. **Codeine**, the 3-methyl ether of morphine, whose first extraction was recorded in 1832, is also found in the raw opium extracts.[2] Opiates are used principally for pain relief; **thebaine** is the oddball of the opiate alkaloid family, classified as a stimulant. The primary use of thebaine is as a starting point for the synthesis of oxycodone and other related semisynthetic compounds. Thebaine was also used as a poison.

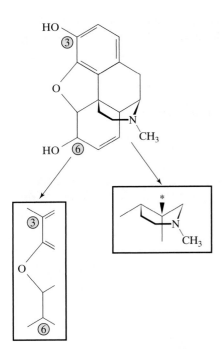

◀ **Figure 8.8** *The functional groups and atoms of opiate alkaloids. The number-three carbon is more important in terms of chemical reactivity than the number six, and the carbon with the asterisk is the site that differentiates oxycodone from other family members.*

The opiate alkaloids of the greatest forensic interest are **heroin (diacetylmorphine** or **diamorphone**, Schedule I), codeine (II and IV), morphine (II), hydrocodone (Lortab®/Vicodin®, II), hydromorphone (Diluadid®, II), and oxycodone (Percoset®, OxyContin®, II). Thebaine (II) is a precursor to these substances. As a group, the opiate alkaloids are analgesics (painkillers), depressants, and narcotics; all are addictive to varying degrees. Their mechanism of action is related to their chemical similarity to the class of endogenous compounds known as **endorphins**, *endo*genous m*orphin*es. Endorphins are large molecules compared with the opiate alkaloids and proteins involved in the transmission of nerve impulses (neuropeptides). Unlike aspirin and related analgesics, the opiate alkaloids do not act on the cause of the pain, but rather interfere with the transmission of the pain impulses to the brain.

Morphine is one of the strongest analgesics known and is used to treat otherwise intractable pain, such as that associated with cancer. As a manifestation of its depressant characteristics, morphine overdoses cause death by interfering with breathing. Heroin has no acceptable medical uses in the United States, while codeine is used as an analgesic and cough suppressant. Formulations of codeine and analgesics are widely prescribed for short-term pain relief. The synthetic opiate alkaloids hydrocodone, hydromorphone, and oxycodone (Figure 8.9) are also considered strong pain relievers; a time-release formulation of **oxycodone (OxyContin®**, Purdue Pharma) has become one of the most commonly abused prescription drugs. Abusers crush the tablets to obtain an immediately large dose that can be fatal.[3] The opiate alkaloids are commonly available as sulfate or hydrochloride salts. Among the controlled opiate alkaloids, heroin is typically the most commonly encountered as physical evidence, morphine the least, a fact that is likely due to the relative simplicity of the conversion of morphine to heroin.

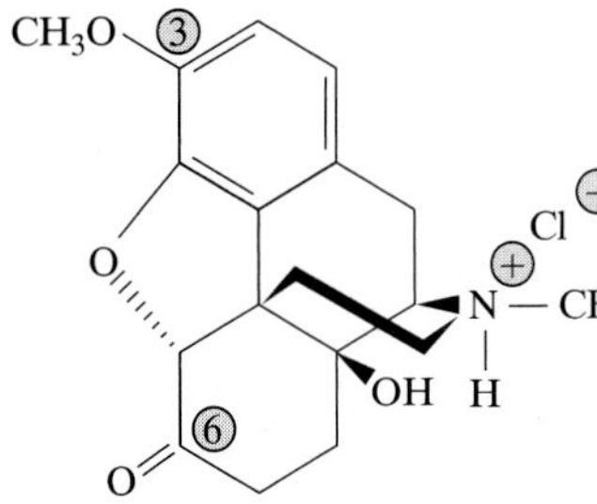

Chemistry: The first step toward making heroin is extracting morphine from the opium plant extract. The lime method, introduced in Chapter 6, Section 6.3.3, and shown in Figure 6.8, is a common extraction protocol that yields morphine

▲ **Figure 8.9** *Oxycodone as a hydrochloride salt. The shaded numbers are as in Figure 8.8.*

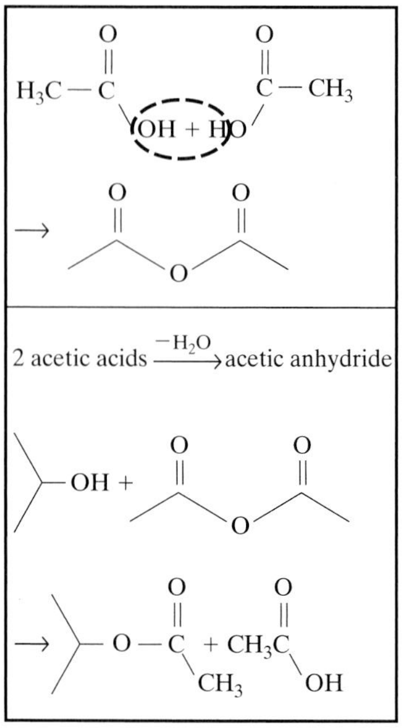

▲ **Figure 8.10** *Acetic anhydride is formed when two acetic acid molecules combine. Water is lost in the reaction. Acetic anhydride will esterify alcohol functional groups as shown, producing acetic acid.*

base along with other related alkaloids. Morphine base is the immediate precursor of heroin. The conversion of morphine to heroin involves acetylation of the hydroxyl groups on carbons 3 and 6. The most common method uses acetic anhydride and heating for this purpose.[4]

Historical Evidence 8.1—Morphine

The name of the drug morphine is derived from *Morpheus*, the God of dreams in Greek mythology. Morpheus is the son of *Hypnos*, the God of sleep, who is the namesake of the hypnotic drugs. Morphine was isolated around 1805, but as late as 1947 the molecular structure was still not clear. The debate in those years related to the group at the C6 position. The question was settled in 1952, with the first reported synthesis of morphine.

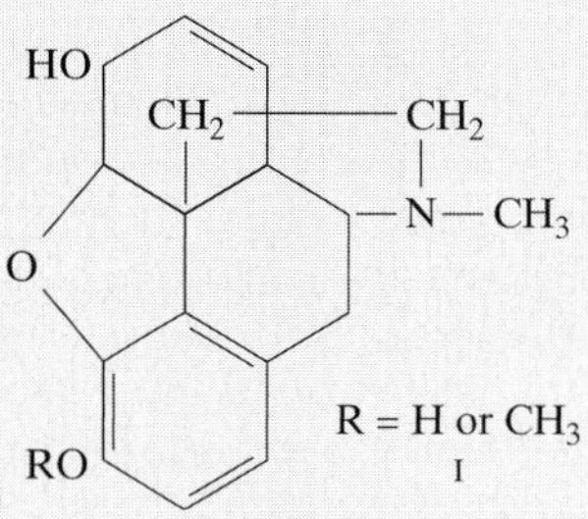

◀ *The structure of morphine as understood in 1947.*

Source: Holmes, H. L., and C. C. Lee. "A Possible Route to the Location of the Nitrogen Atom in Morphine I." *Journal of the American Chemical Society,* 69 **1947**, 1996–1997.

Acetic anhydride (Figure 8.10) is produced by the linkage of two acetic acid molecules, with water lost during the reaction. Anhydrides are versatile synthetic reagents that will react with alcohols and —OH groups, such as those found in morphine, to form an ester and acetic acid. Once the heroin is produced, the solution is made basic in order to precipitate heroin base. A series of re-crystallizations and purification steps, coupled with the addition of HCl, yields the hydrochloride salt of heroin.

The —OH group attached to the number 3 carbon is more reactive than that associated with carbon number 6. Accordingly, the number-3 carbon reacts first. By contrast, when degradation occurs, it generally occurs at the number-6 carbon site.[1] Another site of variation is central in the molecule; an OH group in this position is found in oxycodone. An examination of Table 8.3 shows that, with the exceptions of papaverine and noscapine, chemical reactivity and transformations occur at these three molecular sites. The 3 and 6 positions typically follow the chemistry of alcohols.

Starting from morphine, heroin can be made in good yields (typically 50% or greater) by acetylation, using acetic anhydride and heat. The process is illustrated in Figure 8.11. Acetylation can be accomplished by **refluxing** or direct ignition.[1] The hydroxyl group on carbon 3 is preferentially acetylated, yielding 3-O-monoacetylmorphine, which is usually found in heroin manufactured this way. Also present will be residuals of codeine, acetylcodeine, papaverine, noscapine, thebaine, and acetylthebaol.[4,5] Once the heroin has been made, a small portion will partially degrade via deacetylation to form 6-O-**monoacetylmorphine (MAM)**.[4] Codeine has also been used as a starting point to make heroin.[1,6–8] For illicit purposes, the starting point is typically medicines combining codeine and such analgesics as aspirin or acetaminophen.

Example Problem 8.3

Give the mechanism for the acetylation of the —OH groups in morphine.

Answer:

General mechanism:

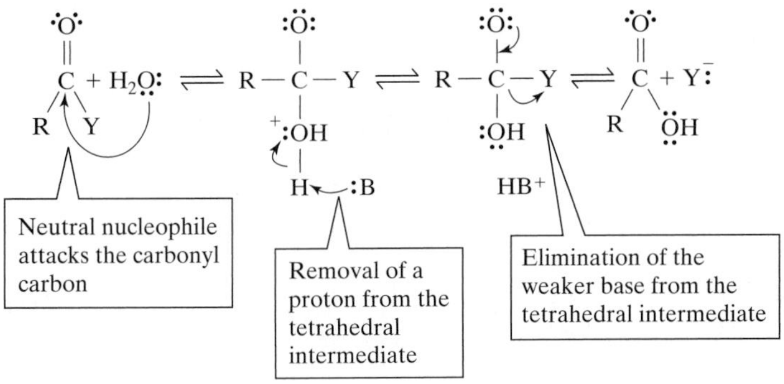

Neutral nucleophile attacks the carbonyl carbon

Removal of a proton from the tetrahedral intermediate

Elimination of the weaker base from the tetrahedral intermediate

with an alcohol / – OH site: R = morphine molcule

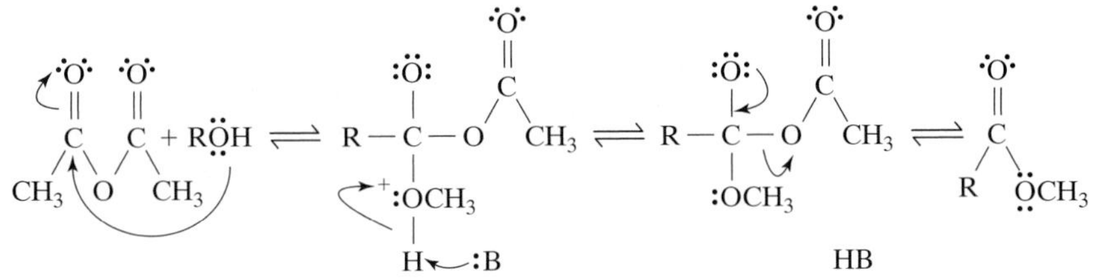

Although heroin is often injected, another mode of ingestion is inhalation, accomplished by placing powder on a piece of foil and heating it until vapors are released.[9] Under these conditions, most of the heroin is degraded to 6-MAM and associated by-products, with 6-MAM being fairly stable and 3-MAM unstable.[4,9] This behavior mirrors the natural degradation of heroin that can occur even when exhibits are refrigerated, a situation that merits attention when quantitative analysis is needed. Recent data compiled for methanolic solutions revealed a degradation of ~60–90+% of the original heroin content, even when the solution was refrigerated.[10] Solid refrigerated samples lost ~20% of their heroin content over an eight-week period.

Profiling: The approach to profiling described in Chapter 6 evolved out of profiling heroin and cocaine exhibits. Depending on the laboratory and case requirements, profiling can be as simple as examining diluents and adulterants, which, for heroin, include acetaminophen, **lidocaine, procaine, caffeine, theophylline** and **phenacetin, papaverine, phenobarbitone**, and **noscapine**.[11–13] Sugars, starches, and quinine are also observed.[14] Acetaminophen is apparently added because it will increase the volatility of heroin base,[4] which can lead to a more intense response when the drug is smoked. Procaine is a local anesthetic related to cocaine and may be included as a cutting agent to numb the site of an injection.[4]

The first distinguishing characteristic noted for heroin samples is their physical state and appearance, ranging from dry, white powders to black resins. Particle size analysis has been employed for purposes of differentiation.[12] Some

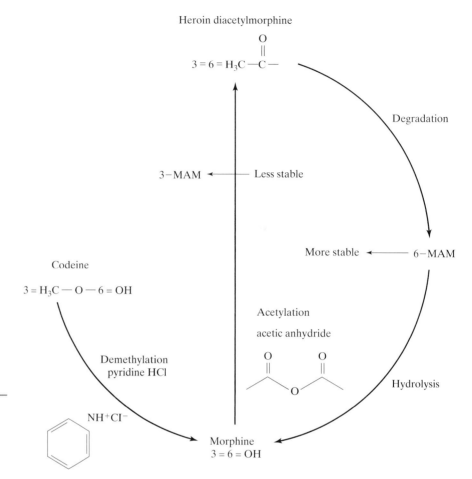

Heroin diacetylmorphine

$$3 = 6 = H_3C - \overset{\overset{\displaystyle O}{\|}}{C} -$$

Degradation

3–MAM ← Less stable

More stable ← 6–MAM

Codeine

$3 = H_3C - O - 6 = OH$

Acetylation
acetic anhydride

Hydrolysis

Demethylation
pyridine HCl

NH^+Cl^-

Morphine
$3 = 6 = OH$

▶ **Figure 8.11** *The chemistry of morphine–codeine–heroin, showing synthesis and degradation paths. Numbering as per Figure 8.8.*

▲ **Figure 8.12** *Two heroin exhibits showing the extremes of solid forms. Image courtesy of the Oklahoma State Bureau of Investigation.*

Example Problem 8.4

Explain how to separate a mixture containing heroin as the hydrochloride salt, dextrose (glucose), and cornstarch.

Answer:

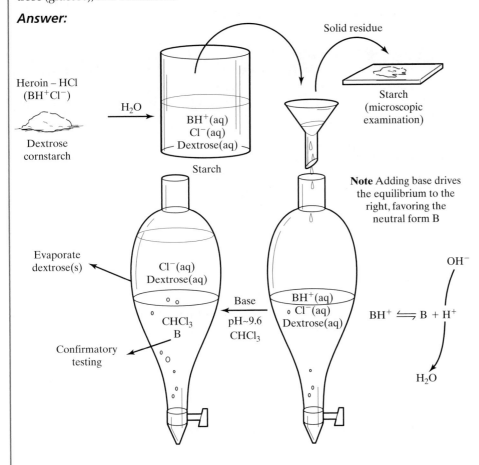

particles are finely ground powders, while others are more amorphous and irregular; the particle size distribution may be characteristic of a batch, although the technique is not widely used.

A simple solvent extraction, such as dissolution in chloroform, can separate starches and sugars for microscopic identification. The organic extract is then analyzed using GCMS and, if necessary, other hyphenated chromatographic techniques. At this stage, the constellation of morphine constituents (typically heroin, MAMs, and morphine) and related opiate alkaloids can be identified and quantitated as needed. For example, noscapine is found in opium extract in quantities exceeding that of codeine and is frequently seen as a component of heroin samples.[13] Ratios of compounds such as 3MAM/6MAM may be employed at this stage.[11] Since the preparation of heroin from opium involves extractions and conversions, detection of these residuals is useful. Headspace methods are also employed for this purpose and are able to target methanol, ethanol, ketones, toluenes, and chlorinated solvents.[15] Degradation products can be identified as well.

In some instances, elemental analysis has been used to examine heroin, with limited success;[16] however, as with cocaine, isotopic ratios have proven to be powerful profiling and sourcing techniques.[17,18] The ratios of $^{13}C/^{12}C$, $^{15}N/^{14}N$, $^{18}O/^{16}O$, and $^2H/^1H$ in a plant-derived sample reflect the environment in which the sample was grown. Ratios such as carbon–carbon may be further altered by chemical processing.[17] Nitrogen ratios have been shown to be particularly useful for isolating heroin or morphine to a geographical region.[18]

Exhibit C: Where Drugs Are Hidden

The drugs described in this chapter are frequently smuggled into the United States on planes, in cars, on ships, and via many other methods. In cars, hidden compartments are referred to as "traps." These hidden compartments are not illegal, except in California, Illinois, and Michigan. Small traps are often ingeniously designed and hard to locate. Larger compartments can hold up to 50 kg and may be found in naturally empty places behind dashboards, inside the frame, or inside the fuel tank. For the largest loads of contraband, railroad tanker cars, large trucks, buses, and SUVs have been altered to contain smuggled goods.

Source: U.S. Drug Enforcement Administration, *Drug Intelligence Brief: Common Vehicle Concealment Methods in the United States,* **2003**.

Analytical Approach: Heroin samples follow the typical flowchart approach from presumptive tests to confirmation by instrument, usually by GCMS, since the presence of other alkaloids makes it difficult to purify the sample sufficiently for IR. Thin-layer chromatography can be particularly useful in separating components of a complex heroin sample and, coupled with the appropriate standards and developers, can assist in identification of specific compounds. Marquis and Dragendorff reagents are commonly used for the purpose.

8.2.2 TROPANE ALKALOIDS AND COCAINE

Cocaine is a **tropane** alkaloid (characterized by a bridge structure) obtained by extraction from leaves of the *coca* plant. It is an addictive CNS stimulant listed on Schedule II. Coca leaves have been chewed by people for thousands of years and, cocaine was considered to have therapeutic benefits until early in the 1900s. Although the drug can be synthesized, the overwhelming majority of cocaine that is seized is obtained by extraction from **coca paste**. Like other alkaloids, cocaine exists as the freebase, which ranges from a colorless solid to a tan to off-white and slightly oily material. The drug also exists as a salt, usually the hydrochloride. Cocaine HCl is a white powder, known on the street as "snow," among many other monikers. "Crack," or crack cocaine, usually refers to the

Table 8.4	Cocaine
Source:	Extracted from coca leaves (*Erythroxylon coca*)
Form/morphology:	Alkaloid base or salts
Classification:	Schedule II stimulant, natural product, alkaloid
Medical:	Topical anesthetic for the eye
Color tests:	Cobalt thiocyanate blue; Scott and Ruybal variants
Microcrystal:	Gold and platinic chloride
Other tests:	TLC, GC/MS, IR

Table 8.5

Compound	Structure

Cocaine (d- and l-isomers)

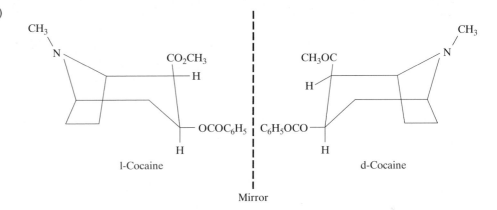

Pseudococaine
(Diastereoisomer of cocaine)

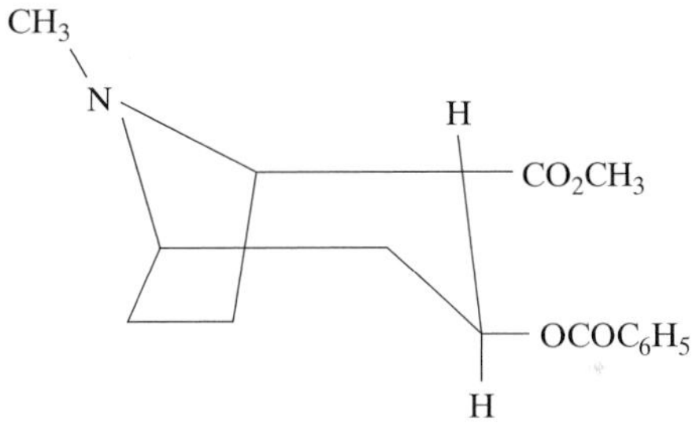

Allococaine
(Diastereoisomer of cocaine)

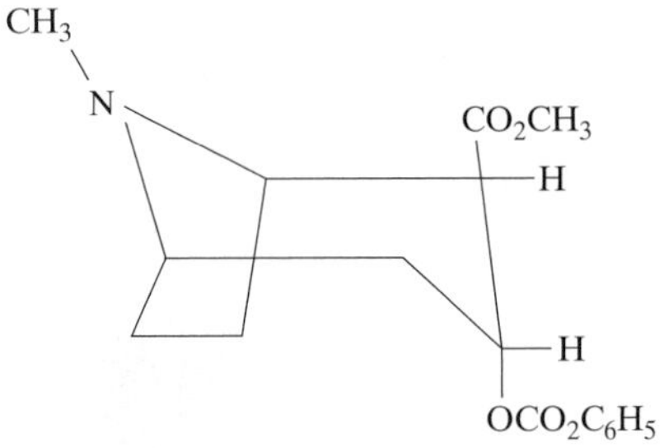

Pseudoallococaine
(Diastereoisomer of cocaine)

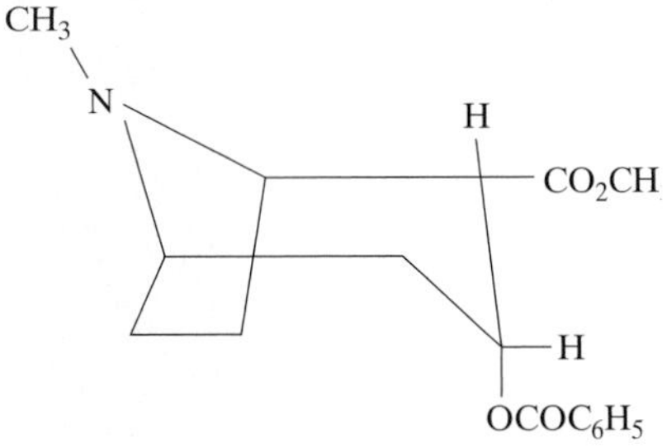

Table 8.5 (Continued)	
Compound	**Structure**
Lidocaine	
Procaine (Procaine HCl = Novocaine)	
Benzocaine	
Tetracaine	

▶ **Figure 8.13** *Cocaine powder found inside a shaving cream can. Image courtesy of the Oklahoma State Bureau of Investigation.*

◀ **Figure 8.14** *Large bricks of cocaine. Image courtesy of the Oklahoma State Bureau of Investigation.*

freebase, smokable form of cocaine often sold in small quantities packaged in vials. Recent estimates are that 1% of the U.S. population uses cocaine.[19] Mexico and Colombia are the principal sources of the drug.

Cocaine is extracted from coca leaves by crushing the leaves into a mush, making the solution basic, and extracting the drug with an organic solvent such as kerosene. Bubbling HCl through the solution is an effective method for converting the base to the hydrochloride salt. The salt can be converted back to the base, to be sold as crack cocaine. Pretreatment of the leaves to convert related alkaloids to cocaine has also been noted.[14,20] One possibility is treating the leaf extract with acid to hydrolyze it to ecgonine. Esterification yields ecgonine methyl ester, which can be further treated to yield cocaine.

Exhibit D: Drug Money

A large percentage of the paper currency in circulation today carries detectable amounts of drugs, principally cocaine. This fact has complicated forfeiture proceedings in which a government appropriates cash that is related to drug crimes. In analytical terms, the blank is contaminated. In forensic terms, drugs on cash can be viewed as evidence of transfer. Money that is in the presence of large amounts of drugs will inevitably pick up residuals of those compounds. Similarly, rolled bills are employed by drug users to sniff substances such as cocaine, which will leave a significant residue on the currency. However, this type of evidence degrades as the money moves physically and temporally farther away from the time and place of initial contact. The same is true of trace evidence such as fibers: The fibers found on a person at any given time most accurately reflect their most recent environment. Accordingly, the quantity of drugs found on cash becomes important in determining whether the money really was part of illegal drug activity or innocent residue. Good analytical practice calls for the use of a representative population of currency from a given area to determine what the "natural background" amounts of illegal substances are.

Sources: Jenkins, A. J. "Drug contamination of US paper currency." *Forensic Science International,* 121 **2001**, 189–193. Sleeman, R., et al. "Drugs on Money." *Analytical Chemistry,* June 1, **2000**, 397A–403A.

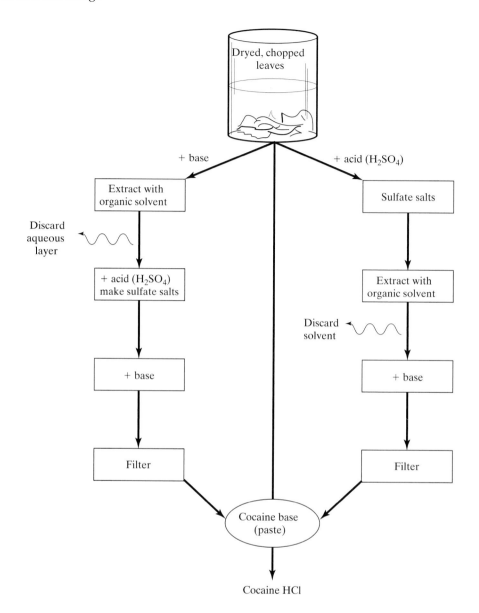

Dryed, chopped leaves

+ base

+ acid (H₂SO₄)

Extract with organic solvent

Sulfate salts

Discard aqueous layer

+ acid (H₂SO₄) make sulfate salts

Extract with organic solvent

Discard solvent

+ base

+ base

Filter

Filter

Cocaine base (paste)

Cocaine HCl

▶ **Figure 8.15** *Two methods used to extract cocaine from coca leaves.*

Cocaine seized in dosage-size units is typically cut with diluents such as caffeine, sugars, procaine, or lidocaine. Like cocaine, the latter are topical anesthetics and produce a numbing sensation on the tongue and mucus membranes. In fact, cocaine is listed on Schedule II because it is still used as a local anesthetic. Other cutting agents frequently seen are sugars (glucose, mannitol, inositol, etc.); starches, including flour and baking soda; lactose; and caffeine.[21]

Cocaine can be profiled with some success for categorization and **provenance** determinations.[21] Cutting agents and other trace chemical constituents, such as residual extraction solvents, impurities, contaminants, cutting agents, and a chemical profile of the plant material, can all be used for this purpose. **Bleaching agents** added to improve the coloration are also useful in profiling. One recent report described finding predominantly ethyl acetate and n-propyl acetate, a mixture consistent with commercial paint thinners.[21]

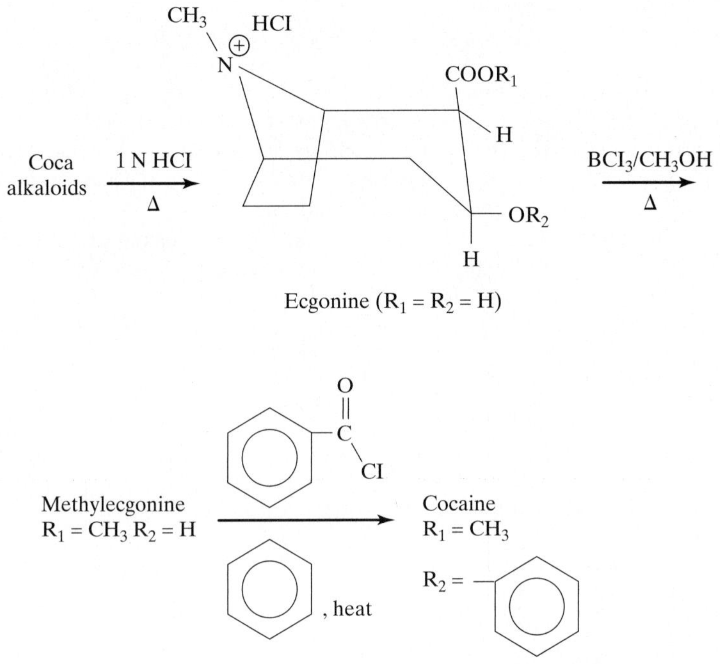

Ecgonine ($R_1 = R_2 = H$)

◀ **Figure 8.16** *Yields of cocaine-content pastelike plant extract can be increased by treating it with hydrochloric acid to hydrolyze the extract to ecgonine. Treatment with boron chloride in methanol produces methyl ecgonine, which is converted to cocaine by the addition of benzoyl chloride and benzene.*

Example Problem 8.5

Assume a sample is delivered to the lab that is suspected to contain cocaine, lidocaine, benzocaine, and procaine. What would be the best method of sample extraction and preparation?

Answer: Actually, little sample preparation is needed. All four compounds are related and have similar structures, so a LLE or SPE extraction to separate them from each other is neither feasible nor necessary. A rudimentary sample preparation, such as a dry extract, would be sufficient to allow for TLC with standards and GCMS.

This problem is a reminder that sample preparation does not have to separate every analyte from every other one. Rather, sample preparation should extract the analytes from the matrix. If GCMS or other hyphenated techniques will separate the analytes, that capability should be exploited. Exhaustive isolation should be undertaken when necessary.

Analytical Approach: The analysis of cocaine exhibits is straightforward and employs color tests and instrumental methods. Cocaine is amenable to crystal tests[22] using gold and platinic chloride and can be analyzed using a number of TLC systems. Since the penalty in some jurisdictions (e.g., federal cases) are based on purity, cocaine samples are often quantitated. The compound and related species chromatograph well on nonpolar or slightly polar stationary phases. GCMS, along with appropriate standards, provides definitive identification of cocaine; IR spectra can also be used for the purpose. Because many cocaine samples are quantitated, GCMS is more widely used, as it can accomplish both tasks.

On the Stand (Legal Issues and Questions): Aside from the usable-quantity question, there are no common legal challenges to identification. In the 1970s and 1980s, questions often arose concerning the isomers and diastereoisomers of cocaine, as shown in Table 8.6. However, legislative wording has generally been changed to include all (optical and geometric) isomers, enantiomers, and salts thereof.

Applying the Science 8.2   Raman Spectroscopy for Mixtures with Diluents

IR spectroscopy is rarely used for quantitative purposes, particularly when a mixture is involved, principally because of the method's low sensitivity. In addition, IR is not well suited in forensic applications, so samples are purified prior to confirmatory instrumental analysis with FTIR. GCMS is a better technique for mixtures, providing separation, identification, and quantitation. However, sometimes GCMS is not the first choice, due to thermal instability or other problems. A recent report suggests that Raman spectroscopy (described in Chapter 5) can be applied to some types of mixed samples, allowing for rapid analysis, minimal preparation, and nondestructive analyses.

A Raman spectrum of cocaine and glucose shows characteristic peaks for cocaine that increase with increasing

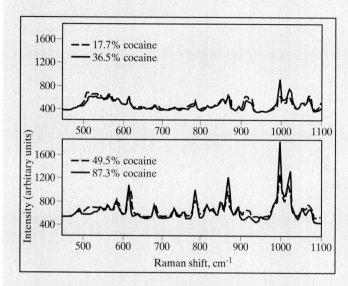

◄ *Raman spectra of cocaine and glucose mixtures using 785 nm excitation. The spectra have been smoothed and the MSC common offset function applied. Reproduced with permission from the reference cited, copyright 2000, ASTM International.*

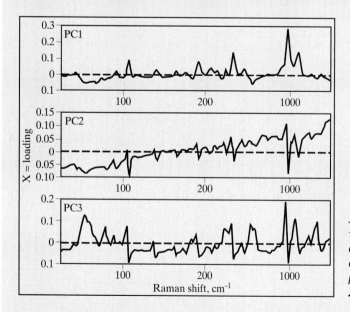

◄ *X-loading plots for the three principal components of the PCA model for the cocaine/glucose mixtures. Reproduced with permission from the reference cited, copyright 2000, ASTM International.*

Source: Ryder, A. "Classification of Narcotics in a Solid Mixture Using Principal Component Analysis and Raman Spectroscopy." *Journal of Forensic Sciences,* 47 **2002**, 275–284.

Applying the Science 8.2   (Continued)

concentration. When principal-component analysis (Chapter 3) is applied to the data, the factor loadings illustrate that most of the variance in spectra can be accounted for by the first three principal components as shown. The negative regions of the loading plots correspond to glucose spectral features, the positive to spectral features associated with cocaine. The authors suggest that the stronger response of cocaine may be due to the two crystal structures: Cocaine is more crystalline than glucose and would be expected to give a stronger reflection.

Once the regions of variance were known, a partial least-squares (PLS) algorithm was used to generate calibration data. The second—and better—model resulted from removing outliers and produced a viable calibration curve.

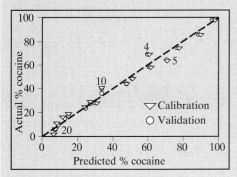 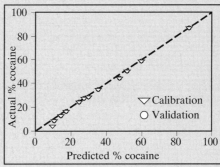

◀ *PLS regression models (M1 and M2) for predicting the % cocaine (by weight) dispersed in solid glucose from the Raman spectra in the 450–1100 cm⁻¹ range. Reproduced with permission from the reference cited, copyright 2000, ASTM International.*

8.2.3 ERGOT AND TRYPTAMINE ALKALOIDS AND HALLUCINOGENS

The hallucinogens are among the most dangerous of abused drugs. Some, such as PCP ("angel dust"), are synthetic; others, such as **lysergic acid diethylamide (LSD)**, are semi-synthetic; and the remainder are derived from plants. The dissociative drugs, such as ketamine and PCP, are not hallucinogenic in the same sense as LSD, but create dissociative feelings described by some as "out-of-body" experiences. These two compounds are or have been used as anesthetics for this reason. Recently, MDMA (Ecstasy) has joined the ranks of widely abused hallucinogens. (See Section 8.3.1, which covers the amphetamine family.) LSD, while no longer a common form of hallucinogen, is arguably the most infamous. It was synthesized by Albert Hoffmann in 1938.

LSD is a derivative of a class of compounds called **ergot alkaloids**. These chemicals are compounds that are extracted from a fungus (*Clavica purpurea*) that grows on cereal grain plants, principally rye. The fungus is the source of toxins as well as the hallucinogens. The effects of **"ergotism"** (ergots as poisons) have been documented since the 10th century.[23] The immediate precursor of LSD is **lysergic acid**, the synthesis of which is a complex, multi-step procedure; thus, the synthesis of LSD is much more difficult than that of methamphetamine. The final conversion of lysergic acid to LSD is accomplished by converting the carboxylic acid functional group into an amide via a more reactive carboxylic acid derivative intermediate. One procedure uses sulfur trioxide as shown in Figure 8.17.[24] Because of the difficulty of the synthesis, LSD laboratories tend to be larger, more centralized, and harder to find, compared with those which produce methamphetamine and PCP (discussed shortly).

Table 8.6   LSD

Source:	Semisynthetic from lysergic acid
Form/morphology:	Ergot alkaloid, semisynthetic or synthetic
Classification:	Schedule I Hallucinogen
Medical:	Briefly used in psychotherapy
Color tests:	Ehrlich's purple; UV-induced fluorescence
Microcrystal:	None
Other tests:	TLC, IR

Table 8.7   Psilocyn and Psilocybin

Source:	Mushroom *Psilocybe mexicana* and others
Form/morphology:	Whole mushroom, tryptamine alkaloid, natural product
Classification:	Schedule I Hallucinogen
Medical:	None
Color tests:	Marquis yellow; Froehde's green; Mandelin's green
Microcrystal:	None
Other tests:	TLC, GC/MS

Table 8.8   Mescaline (Peyote)

Source:	Peyote (*Lophophora williamsii* Lemaire)
Form/morphology:	Cactus "button" or extracted HCl salt, tryptamine alkaloid, natural product
Classification:	Schedule I Hallucinogen
Medical:	None
Color tests:	Marquis orange; Froehde's yellow-green
Microcrystal:	None
Other tests:	TLC, GC/MS

In addition to marijuana (described in the last chapter), another form of plant-based drug exhibit seen in crime labs contains **mescaline**. This hallucinogen is obtained from the peyote (peyotl) cactus (*Lophophora williamsii*). Psilocyn (**psilocin** is also an accepted spelling) and **psilocybin** (**psilocybine**), are obtained from the mushroom *Psilocybe mexicana*, and are members of the indole

Table 8.9 Hallucinogens and Precursors

Compound	Structure

Lysergic acid diethylamide (LSD)
Schedule I

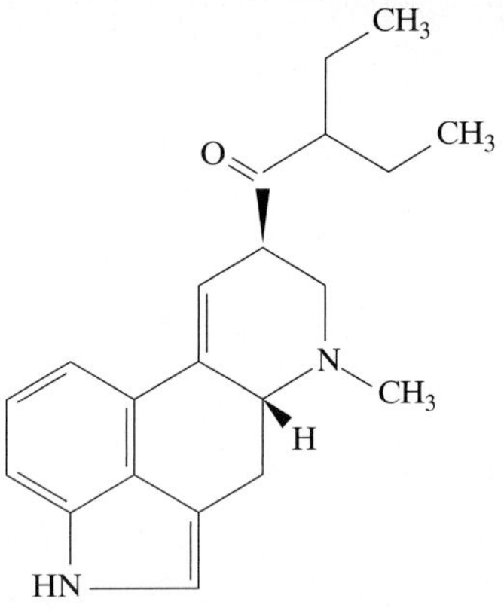

Lysergic acid Schedule III

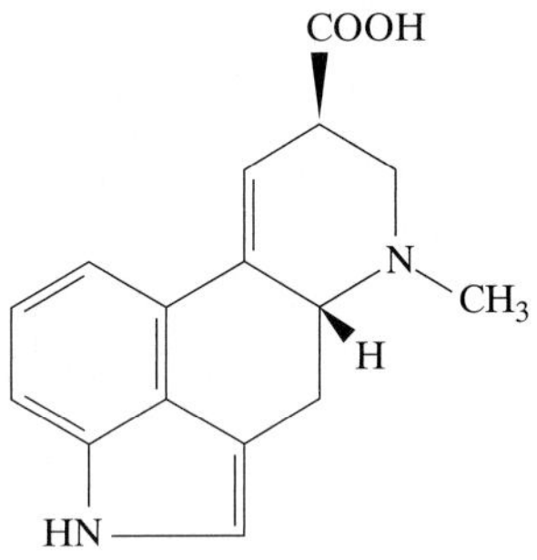

Lysergic acid amide Schedule III

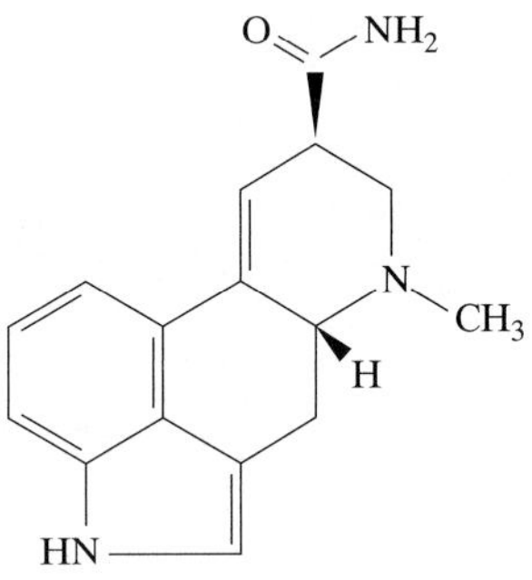

Ergotamine Schedule III

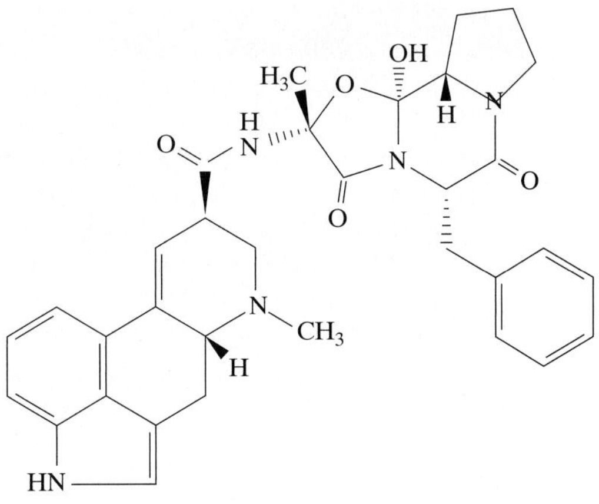

Table 8.9 (Continued)	
Compound	Structure

Psilocybin Schedule I

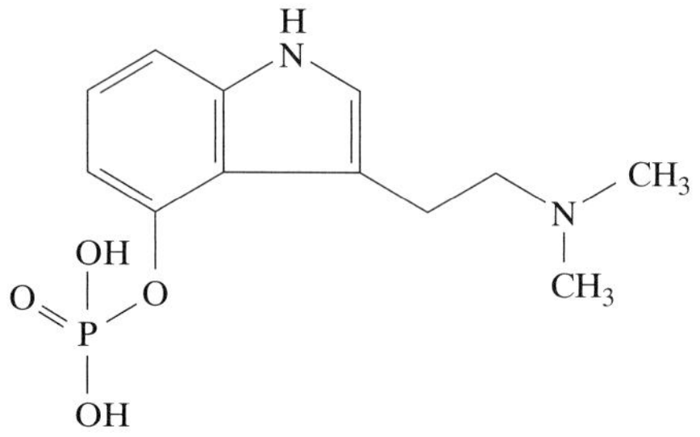

Psilocyn (or psilocin) Schedule I

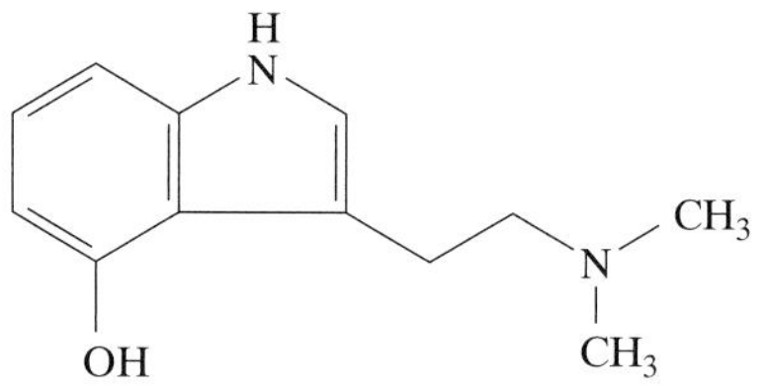

3,4,5-Trimethoxyphenethylamine
Mescaline Schedule I

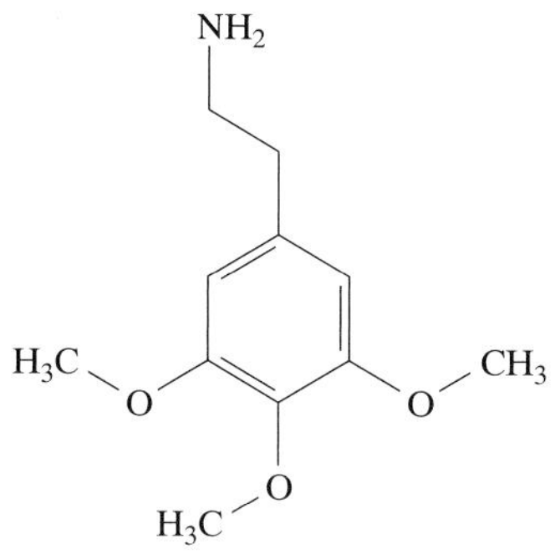

Exhibit E: Purple Haze

Few drugs have had the impact on popular culture that LSD had in the 1960s and 1970s. Dr. Albert Hoffmann, the discoverer of LSD, inadvertently took the first known "trip" in 1943. Intrigued, he performed a self-experiment, ingesting 250 μg. The typical street dose tops out at around 50 μg. Hoffmann experienced hallucinations and what he termed a "severe crisis." He described out-of-body type experiences and "demonic transformations." He later coined LSD his "problem child." It was subsequently embraced (secretly) by intelligence agencies in the 1950s and early 1960s, but the experiments they performed were eventually abandoned. In the late

Exhibit E: (Continued)

1950s, Timothy Leary, a Harvard psychologist, began experimenting with the drug as an aid to therapy. He became its most vocal and, eventually, most famous advocate. The nature of the "trip" was touted to have religious and spiritual overtones much as those taken in older cultures by other psychedelics, such as mescaline. The LSD fad had peaked by the 1970s, but left cultural icons in its wake; the songs "Lucy in the Sky with Diamonds" (the Beatles) and "Purple Haze" (Jimi Hendrix) and other works by artists such as the Grateful Dead and Bob Dylan have been linked to the drug, even if speculatively. The novel *One Flew over the Cuckoo's Nest* was penned by a man who had been part of a government study on LSD.

amine family referred to as tryptamines. The structure of psilocin in particular is similar to that of dopamine.

Peyote is an interesting case in that it is legal for use by members of the Native American Church. Although mescaline can also be prepared synthetically, most evidence submitted to laboratories is in plant form. Psilocin mushrooms have the longest-known history of use; they were first noted as part of religious ceremonies, a common theme for the hallucinogens.[24] Psilocin is the physiologically active ingredient, but the body converts psilocybin to psilocin via dephosphorylation after ingestion.

Analytical Approach: LSD as physical evidence is submitted in forms such as blotter papers, gelatin windows, candies, mints, and, less frequently, pills. The potency of the drug creates both analytical challenges and safety concerns,

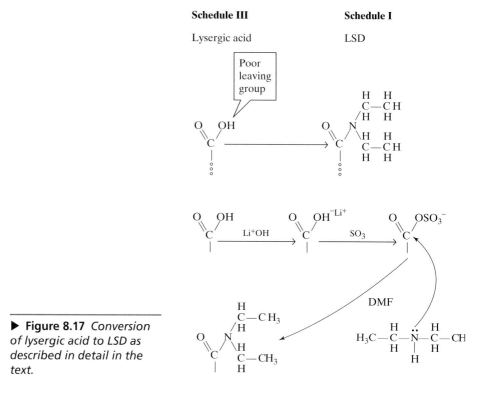

▶ **Figure 8.17** *Conversion of lysergic acid to LSD as described in detail in the text.*

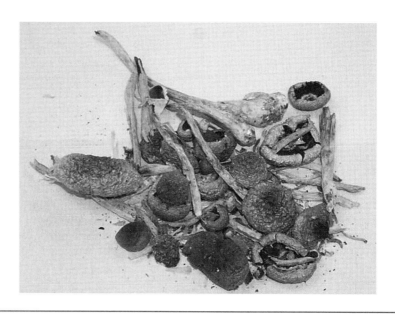

▲ **Figure 8.18** *Mushrooms (psilocybin and psilocin). Image courtesy of the Oklahoma State Bureau of Investigation.*

Applying the Science 8.3   Good, Not Perfect

GCMS is central to forensic drug analysis because analytes are separated and definitively identified by the combination of their retention time and mass spectrum. Unfortunately, there are compounds that have nearly identical mass spectra. A partial list of compounds of forensic interest includes the following:

Compound 1	Compound 2	Notes
GHB	GBL	Heat causes GHB → GBL
Psilocin	Psilocybin	Heat causes dephosphorylation
Cathine	Phenylpropanolamine	
Ephedrine	Pseudoephedrine	Diastereoisomers

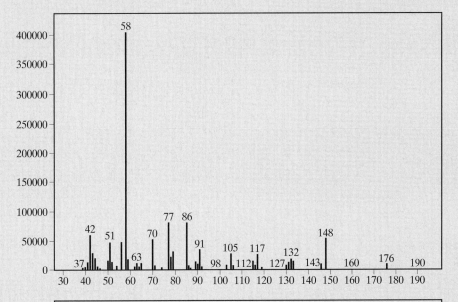

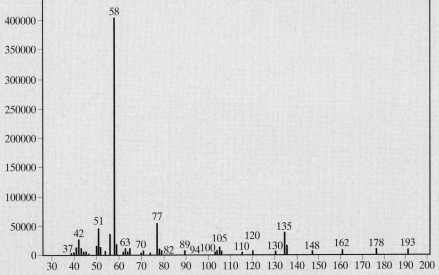

▲ *Original spectra for pseudoephedrine and MDMA. Reproduced with permission from the reference cited, copyright 2004 ASTM International.*

Applying the Science 8.3 (Continued)

As noted in Applying the Science 8.1, there are separation techniques that will discriminate between enantiomers, but the mass spectra do not definitively differentiate them. As a result, instrumental confirmation of identification can be lengthy and complicated without a definitive mass spectrum. However, there is another option for some compounds, and it has to do with how mass spectra are mathematically processed.

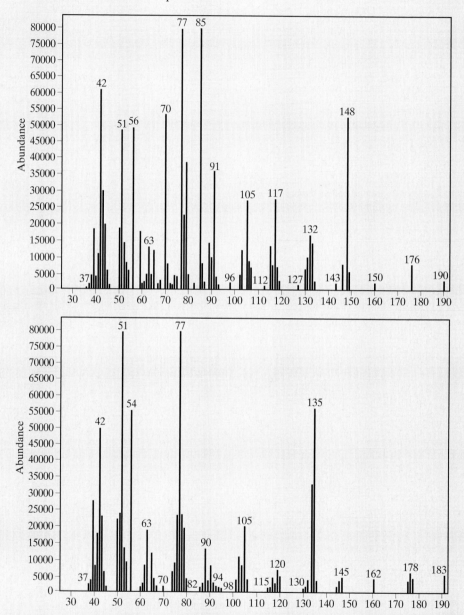

► Normalized spectra for pseudoephedrine and MDMA. Reproduced with permission from the reference cited, copyright 2004 ASTM International.

The most abundant ion peak in many compounds in the methamphetamine family is found at 58 amu. Mass spectra are processed by assigning the largest peak (called the base peak) a value of 100 and scaling all other peaks to that value. Consequently, many minor peaks may be all but lost. Removing the base peak and renormalizing the remaining ion peaks has shown promise in visualizing otherwise small differences in related spectra. While this protocol will not work with enantiomers, in many other cases such renormalization may be useful in distinguishing similar mass spectra that are dominated by the same base-peak ion.

Source: Steeves, J. B., et al. "Normalization of Residual Ions after Removal of the Base Peak in Electron Impact Mass Spectrometry." *Journal of Forensic Sciences,* 45 **2000**, 882–885.

since the effective dose of LSD is quite small. One of the useful characteristics of LSD and related compounds is their strong fluorescence under UV light, which provides a quick presumptive test, as well as a useful property for sample preparation and cleanup. This fluorescence property also makes spectrofluorometry useful, although such instrumentation is not common in forensic labs. Hyphenated methods incorporating fluorescence based on HPLC, capillary electrophoresis (CE), and related methods are appearing in the literature, but it is unlikely that these methods will find routine use in laboratories in the near term.[25,26] Between HPLC and CE, the latter is likely the most promising, given cost considerations and general utility. Ehrlich's reagent provides a good color test, but dyes in the pills or papers may obscure the results. The reagent is useful as a TLC developer for LSD samples. Gas chromatography of LSD is difficult, given low concentrations and reactivity issues, although slow-temperature ramp methods can be employed. HPLC–MS holds more promise, but such instrumentation is not as widely available as GC in forensic laboratories. This leaves IR as the preferred confirmatory technique when a sufficiently large sample can be extracted to produce a good spectrum.

IR requires a pure sample, necessitating cleanup and often composite sampling of LSD exhibits (Figure 8.19). If sufficient papers or pills are available, a cleanup procedure can be used that employs an acid–base extraction scheme to remove excipients and dyes. The final chloroform extract can be placed directly into a mortar and allowed to evaporate before the addition of KBr. This technique also allows for examination of the mortar under UV light; the degree of fluorescence indicates how successful the extraction has been in concentrating LSD. Smaller IR pellets (7–10 mm) are preferred for these applications. Alternatively, the extract may be spread on a KBr surface to allow for micro-ATR IR. Indeed, IR microspectrophotometry is an ideal approach for analytes present in such minute quantities. For example, samples can be run with TLC, the plates dried, spots marked under UV light, and the marked areas analyed using micro-infrared spectrometry. This process is outlined in Figure 8.20.

A second cleanup method, useful when only a few dosage units are available, employs a pipette filled with fluorosil, an acidic absorbent. An extract of the exhibit is placed on the top of the column, which is then inserted into a light box under UV light. The analyst can monitor the movement of the LSD via movement of the fluorescent band and place the mortar under the pipette at the appropriate time to catch the LSD. The process is shown in Figure 8.21.

Unlike the situation noted for marijuana, the morphology of mushrooms and peyote is normally not used as part of their identification, due to the more complex botanical challenge. The plant-matter matrix of peyote and psilocin mushrooms makes the use of color tests impractical, unless the tests are applied to the extract. In most cases, ethanol or methanol is the extraction solvent of choice for dried plant matter. Some laboratories heat the methanol prior to extraction. The peyote button, and sometimes mushrooms, must be ground with coffee grinders or similar equipment or must be macerated prior to extraction. Cleaning these appliances between uses is crucial to prevent cross-contamination. The extracts are then amenable to TLC and instrumental confirmation by GCMS.

There is one caveat when mushroom extracts are analyzed by GC or GCMS: In many cases, the injector temperatures are hot enough to facilitate the dephosphorylation of psilocybin to psilocin. This problem can be addressed by

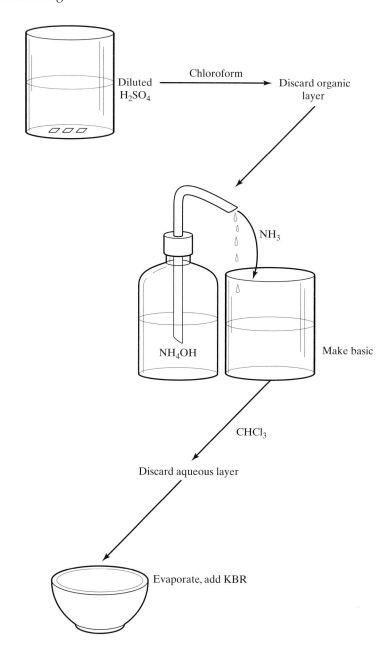

▶ **Figure 8.19** *Acid–base cleanup of LSD exhibits for IR.*

reporting the results as "psilocin and/or psilocybin" or by derivatization with a reagent such as BSTFA. LCMS is an option when psilocin and psilocybin must be differentiated, as are TLC and CE.

On the Stand (Legal Issues and Questions): The primary issue related to LSD analysis relates to the small dosage units, particularly when few are submitted. Instrumental confirmation may require most or all of the exhibits to be consumed, a situation that always demands special consideration, planning, and documentation.

8.2.4 Xanthines

Like the salicylates mentioned in the previous chapter, **xanthine alkaloids** (Figure 8.22) are of forensic interest not because they are controlled, but because

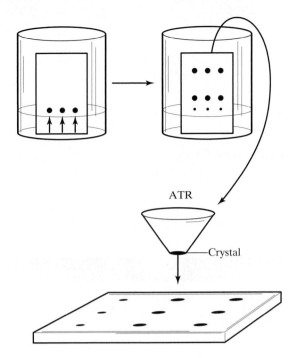

ATR

Crystal

▶ **Figure 8.20** *The combination of TLC and microspectrophotometry is ideal for the isolation and identification of LSD. The chromatography separates the components into small bands that are amenable to analysis by attenuated total reflectance (ATR) IR spectroscopy.*

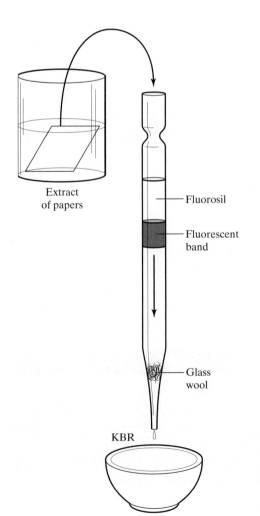

Extract of papers

Fluorosil

Fluorescent band

Glass wool

KBR

▶ **Figure 8.21** *A homemade Fluorosil column and UV light box can be used to extract small samples of LSD for IR spectroscopy.*

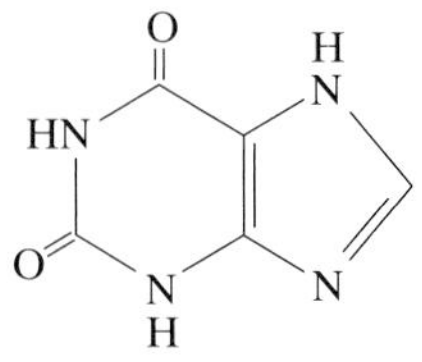

Xanthine

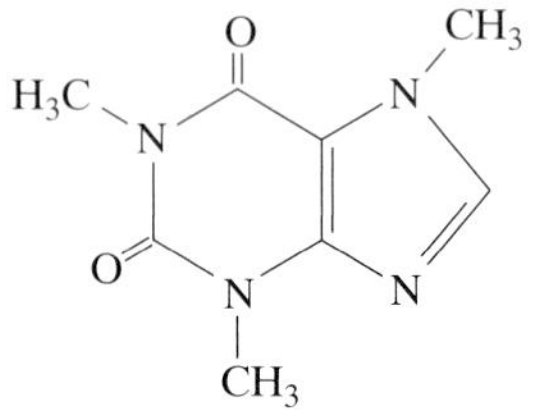

Caffeine

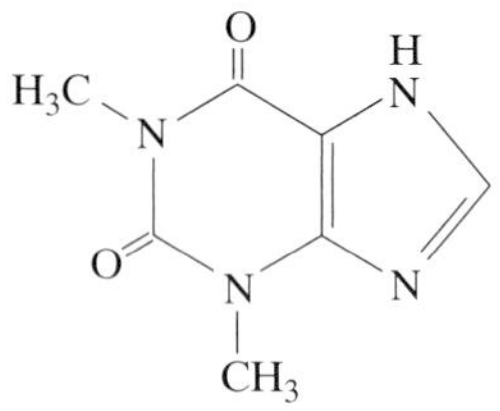

Theophylline

▲ **Figure 8.22** *Representative xanthine alkaloids. Theophylline is found in many teas, in chocolate, and, occasionally, as an adulterant, although caffeine is much more common.*

they are frequently encountered as adulterants. Fortunately, these substances chromatograph well and with high sensitivity with standard GCMS methods.

8.3 NONALKALOIDS

8.3.1 PHENETHYLAMINES: AMPHETAMINE FAMILY

Stimulants related to amphetamine, particularly methamphetamine, have nearly supplanted cocaine as the second most abused controlled substance in the United States. Methamphetamine is highly addictive and easy to make from readily available materials, a combination that has proven hard to defeat or control. Clan-

Table 8.10 Methamphetamine	
Source:	Synthetic; based on phenylethylamine skeleton
Form/morphology:	Alkaloid base or salts
Classification:	Schedule II Stimulant
Medical:	Weight loss, antisleep
Color tests:	Marquis orange; Mandelin's green; Nitroprusside (Simon's test)
Microcrystal:	Gold and platinic chloride (55)
Other tests:	TLC and IR

Table 8.11 Amphetamine	
Source:	Synthetic; based on phenylethylamine skeleton
Form/morphology:	Alkaloid base or salts
Classification:	Schedule II Stimulant
Medical:	Weight loss, antisleep
Color tests:	Marquis orange; Mandelin's green
Microcrystal:	Gold and platinic chloride
Other tests:	TLC and IR

Table 8.12 MDMA (Ecstasy)	
Source:	Synthetic; based on phenylethylamine skeleton
Form/morphology:	Alkaloid base or salts
Classification:	Schedule II Stimulant
Medical:	Weight loss, antisleep
Color tests:	Marquis orange to black; Mandelin's green
Other tests:	TLC and IR

destine synthesis can start from organic chemicals or (semisynthetic) plant extracts. The methamphetamine family (Table 8.13) consists of phenylalkylamines based upon on a **phenylethylamine** skeleton.

Amphetamine was synthesized in Germany in 1887 and later marketed under the trade name Benzidrine®, the origin of the older street slang term "bennies." **Methamphetamine** (trade name Methedrine®) was synthesized in Japan in 1919 and was used as a decongestant, much as pseudoephedrine is now. Amphetamine and methamphetamine were once widely prescribed as appetite suppressants and antisleep medications. The military issued methamphetamine to soldiers during the Second World War and amphetamines to troops in Vietnam. Long-haul truckers and athletes started using methedrine, causing the drug to increase in both popularity and abuse.

◀ **Figure 8.23** *A tablet of Ecstasy (MDMA). Image courtesy of the Oklahoma State Bureau of Investigation.*

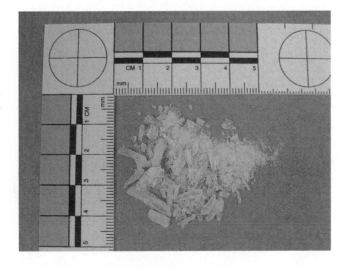

◀ **Figure 8.24** *"Ice," a purified and recrystallized form of methamphetamine. Image courtesy of the Oklahoma State Bureau of Investigation.*

Table 8.13 Amphetamine Family

Compound	Structure
Phenylethylamine (phenethylamine) Skeleton	
Phenyl-2-propanone (P2P) Precursor, Schedule II	
Ephedrine (precursor)	
Pseudoephedrine (precursor)	
Phenylpropanolamine (precursor for amphetamine, OTC*) *Recently voluntarily removed from most products due to concerns about increased risk of stroke.	
Amphetamine (Schedule II)	
Methamphetamine (Schedule II)	

Table 8.13   (Continued)

Compound	Structure
3,4-Methylenedioxymethamphetamine (MDMA; Ecstasy, Schedule I)	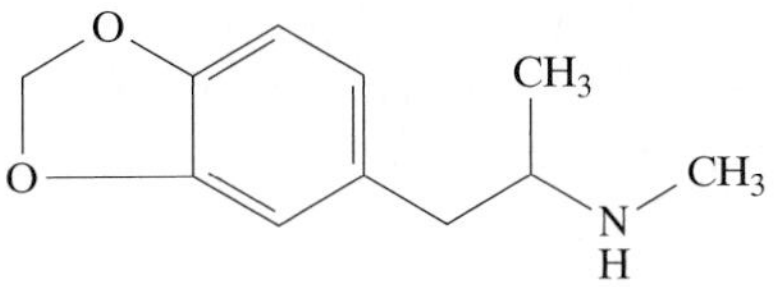
3,4-Methylenedioxyethylamphetamine (MDEA, Schedule I)	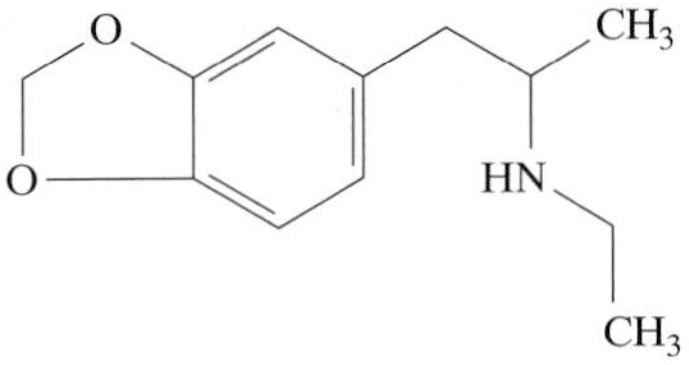
3,4-Methylenedioxyamphetamine (MDA, Schedule I)	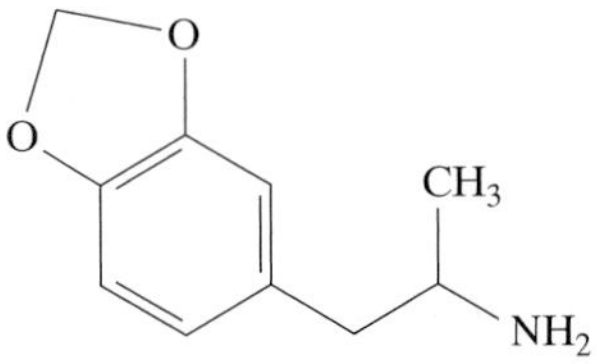
Cathine (Norpseudoephedrine)	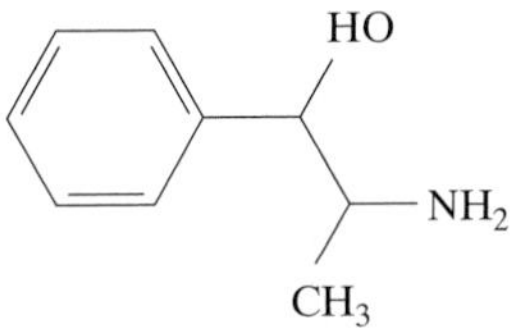
Cathinone	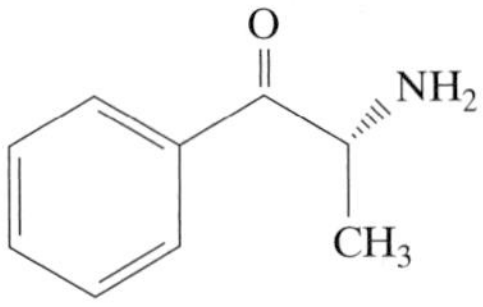
Methcathinone (Cat)	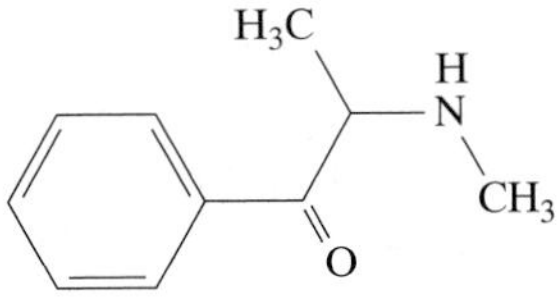

Methamphetamine was listed on the CSA in 1970. Large-scale domestic clandestine production of methamphetamine is most prominent in California, but small laboratories are ubiquitous. Most of the smuggled supply originates in Mexico.

Methamphetamine is found as pills and powders and commonly, as a hydrochloride salt. Ingestion is via swallowing, injection, snorting, or smoking. "**Ice**" is a potent form of methamphetamine named for its appearance. Its crystalline appearance is the result of purification and recrystallization. Smoking produces the quickest absorption and effects, which can last for several hours. Users may stay awake for days, followed by days of sleeping to recover. Methamphetamine is physically and psychologically addictive.

There are many other controlled drugs based on the same phenylalkylamine skeleton. Of greatest current concern is MDMA (**Ecstasy**) which has become a significant problem principally because of its use as a "**club drug**" or a party drug. As with most stimulants, MDMA has hallucinogenic properties. In acute high doses, the drug can produce serious psychotic events. One insidious side effect of MDMA is that it can cause users to ignore symptoms of dehydration that may arise during marathon parties. This, combined with high-energy activities associated with CNS stimulants, has led to several deaths by dehydration and hyperthermia. Conversely, users who are knowledgeable about this issue may drink far too much water and may even die as a result. MDMA has no legitimate medical uses and is listed on Schedule I. It is usually supplied in tablet form, often with designs stamped onto the surface. MDMA is typically synthesized in Europe and smuggled into the United States, but domestic seizures of MDMA clandestine laboraties have occurred. Two other drugs closely related to amphetamine and MDMA are MDA (3,4-methylenedioxyamphetamine) and MDEA (3,4-methylenedioxyethylamphetamine).

Precursors and Clandestine Synthesis[†]: Methods of synthesizing methamphetamine have changed in response to the control of precursors. No doubt these methods will continue to evolve, so forensic chemists must work to stay abreast of current developments. All common methods are based on reductions[‡] or reductive amination (the addition of an amine group) to a molecule having the phenethylamine skeleton. Our discussion will focus on methamphetamine; however, chemical methods for synthesizing the phenylalkylamines are generally analogous. Note that dozens of methods have been and are used in clandestine laboratories, as have dozens of variations of those methods under different experimental conditions. Accordingly, a detailed discussion of all synthetic procedures is beyond the scope of the text. Instead, this section will highlight current methods while providing the basis for further study. The DEA, through its *Microgram* and *Intelligence Brief* publications, provides timely updates. Although a bit dated, an excellent review of these methods is also available.[27]

Clandestine synthesis begins with precursors, either immediate or more distant. An immediate precursor is defined as a precursor that is converted directly to the final product, although that conversion sometimes involves more than one step. Another way to think of it is that a direct precursor can be converted to the controlled substance from readily available items and reagents. As shown in Figure 8.25, methamphetamine has two immediate

---

[†]Some may question the wisdom of showing these syntheses in the detail presented. The emphasis here is on the chemistry and on mechanisms, not recipes and instructions. The information is drawn from the open literature and is available to anyone armed with a library card, an Internet connection, and sufficient motivation. No secrets are revealed in these sections.

[‡]Here, oxidation and reduction are best thought of in their organic context, wherein oxidation is the addition of oxygen or loss of hydrogen while reduction is the gain of hydrogen or loss of oxygen. This is an older definition, but a useful one in the current context.

Applying the Science 8.4   Methamphetamine and Nicotine

The value of derivatization in chromatography has been mentioned several times. However, derivatization can be utilized in field-deployable instrumentation as well. Ion mobility spectrometry, described in Chapter 5, is widely used as a field detection device for basic drugs and explosives. IMS has many advantages for field use, but one disadvantage is its lack of specificity: Many compounds exhibit the same drift time, such as nicotine and methamphetamine. The latter is of obvious forensic interest, and IMS can be used to help locate clandestine laboratories and uncover smuggling operations. Unfortunately, clandestine laboratories and those who use or smuggle methamphetamine are frequently associated with copious amounts of cigarette smoke and nicotine.

To address the nicotine interference problem, derivatization has been proposed. Propyl chloroformate will react with methamphetamine, but not with nicotine, significantly increasing the mass of the methamphetamine. Given that IMS separation depends on the size-to-charge ratio of the molecules, this increase in mass is sufficient to differentiate two otherwise indistinguishable signals. In the figures, "RIP" stands for the reactant ion peak, which is naturally present. As sample is introduced, charge transfer occurs, decreasing the RIP intensity while the product ion peaks appear. The derivatized methamphetamine is more massive than the underivatized form and takes longer to traverse the drift tube. The increase in drift time is sufficient to separate the nicotine and methamphetamine signals.

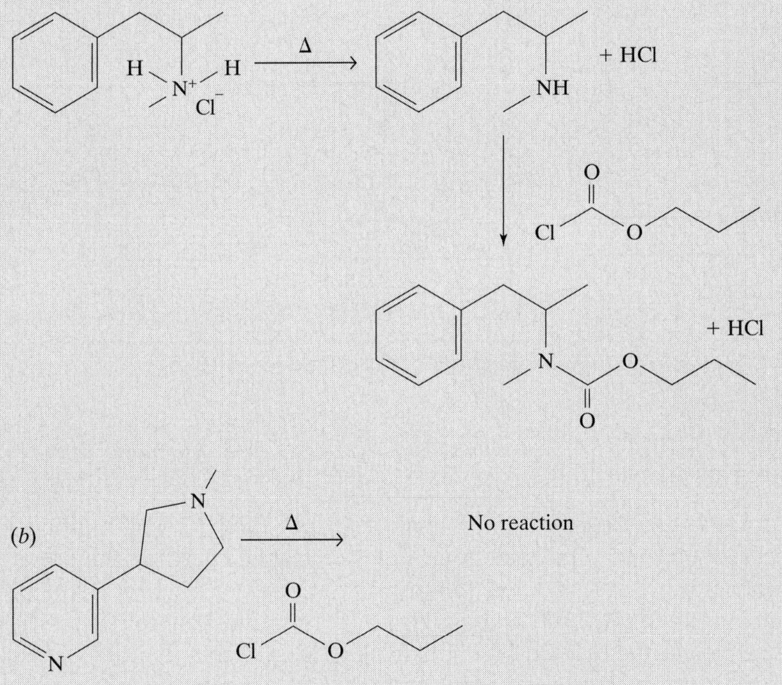

◄ *Schematic of derivatization reactions. (a) Proposed pathway of methamphetamine hydrochloride derivatization. After thermal decomposition, the salt was converted to the free base, which was successfully derivatized with propyl chloroformate. A hydrogen atom in the methamphetamine molecule has been replaced by a propyl ester moiety. (b) Nicotine (tertiary amine) does not have any replaceable hydrogen atoms; hence, no products were observed. Reproduced with permission from the reference cited, copyright 2004 American Chemical Society.*

precursors: phenyl-2-propanone (also called P2P, phenyl acetone, and benzyl methyl ketone) and ephedrine or pseudoephedrine. Starting with P2P, the clandestine chemist must effect reduction of the carbonyl group, the addition of a methyl group, and the addition of an amine group. The term **reductive amine** describes the process. The route from ephedrine or pseudoephedrine is simpler, requiring only the reduction.

Myriad synthetic routes starting from P2P and ephedrine or pseudoephedrine will yield methamphetamine. Most of these are summarized in Figure 8.26.

Applying the Science 8.4 (Continued)

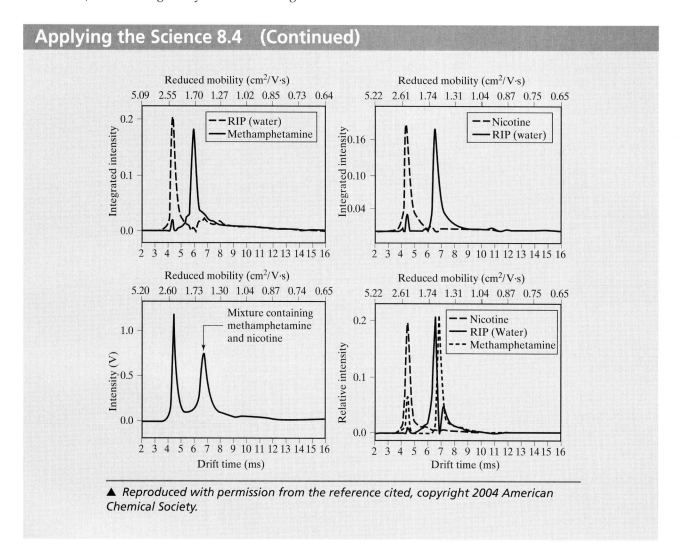

▲ *Reproduced with permission from the reference cited, copyright 2004 American Chemical Society.*

Three routes—the Leuckart, red P cook (HI), and Birch "Nazi" methods—will be discussed in detail. An analogous situation exists regarding the preparation of amphetamine and related phenylethylamines. The precursor phenylpropanolamine (PPA) used to be a common ingredient in cold remedies, but that is no longer the case. In 2000, the FDA requested that manufacturers reformulate their products to reduce or eliminate PPA after studies showed that the compound could increase the risk of strokes. Immediate precursors such as PPA and P2P can be made from distant precursors. In the case of P2P, several distant precursors are used to make P2P, but as in all syntheses, clandestine or not, the more steps and products produced, the less efficient, more expensive, and time consuming is the process. Consequently, **cooks** prefer to work with the immediate precursor. The P2P/PPA synthetic routes are summarized in Figures 8.27 and 8.28.

Until the last 10–20 years, domestic clandestine methamphetamine laboratories employed P2P, a common and versatile solvent with many legitimate uses. It and related compounds have also potent smells that can betray the location of a clandestine facility. The most common P2P synthesis is based on the **Leuckart reaction**, in which nucleophilic nitrogen attacks a carbonyl carbon, forming an intermediate that is reduced to methamphetamine or amphetamine

Applying the Science 8.4 (Continued)

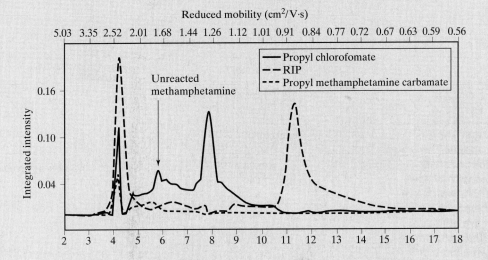

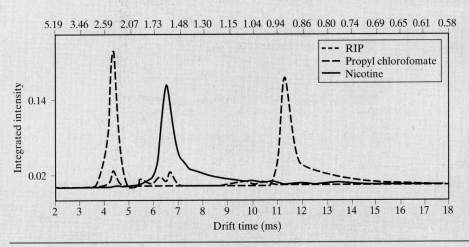

▲ *Reproduced with permission from the reference cited, copyright 2004 American Chemical Society.*

Source: Ochoa, M. L., and P. B. Harrington. "Detection of Methamphetamine in the Presence of Nicotine Using in-Situ Chemical Derivitization and Ion Mobility Spectrometry." *Analytical Chemistry*, 76 **2004**, 985–991.

as shown. The final product is the base, which is converted to the hydrochloride salt by bubbling HCl gas through an organic solution of the product. This synthetic route is illustrated in Figure 8.29.

In response to the widespread clandestine synthesis of methamphetamine by this method, the DEA added P2P to Schedule II of the controlled substances list as part of the **Chemical Diversion and Trafficking Act** (CDTA) of 1988. The legislation was aimed at impeding clandestine laboratories by cutting off the necessary precursors for methamphetamine as well as other drugs. The act also placed controls on some of the equipment needed for making drugs. For a few years, the number of methamphetamine laboratories that were seized decreased, but the decrease was short lived. Clandestine operations

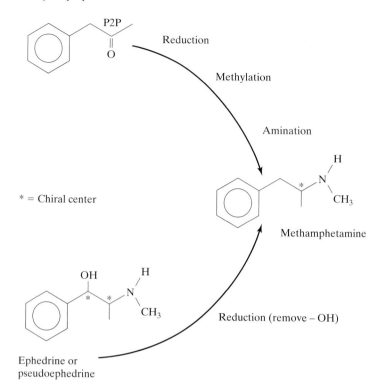

► **Figure 8.25** *Precursors of amphetamine and methamphetamine. Older synthetic methods started with phenyl-2-propanone (P2P), which is reduced to amphetamine or subjected to reductive amination to produce methamphetamine. When P2P became more difficult to obtain, pseudoephedrine, which can be reduced to methamphetamine, became the precursor of choice.*

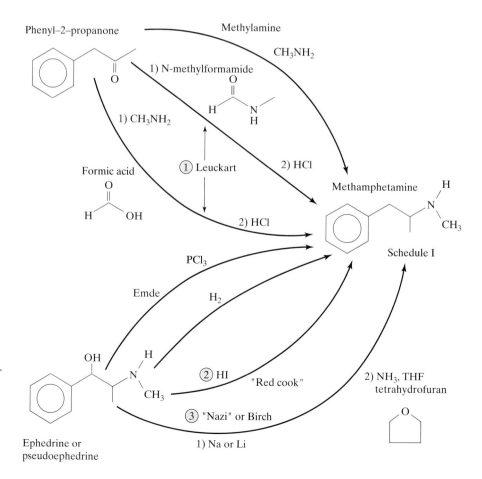

► **Figure 8.26** *A selection of the specific routes to the synthesis of methamphetamine. The Leuckart process (1), HI (2), and Birch methods (3) are described in the text.*

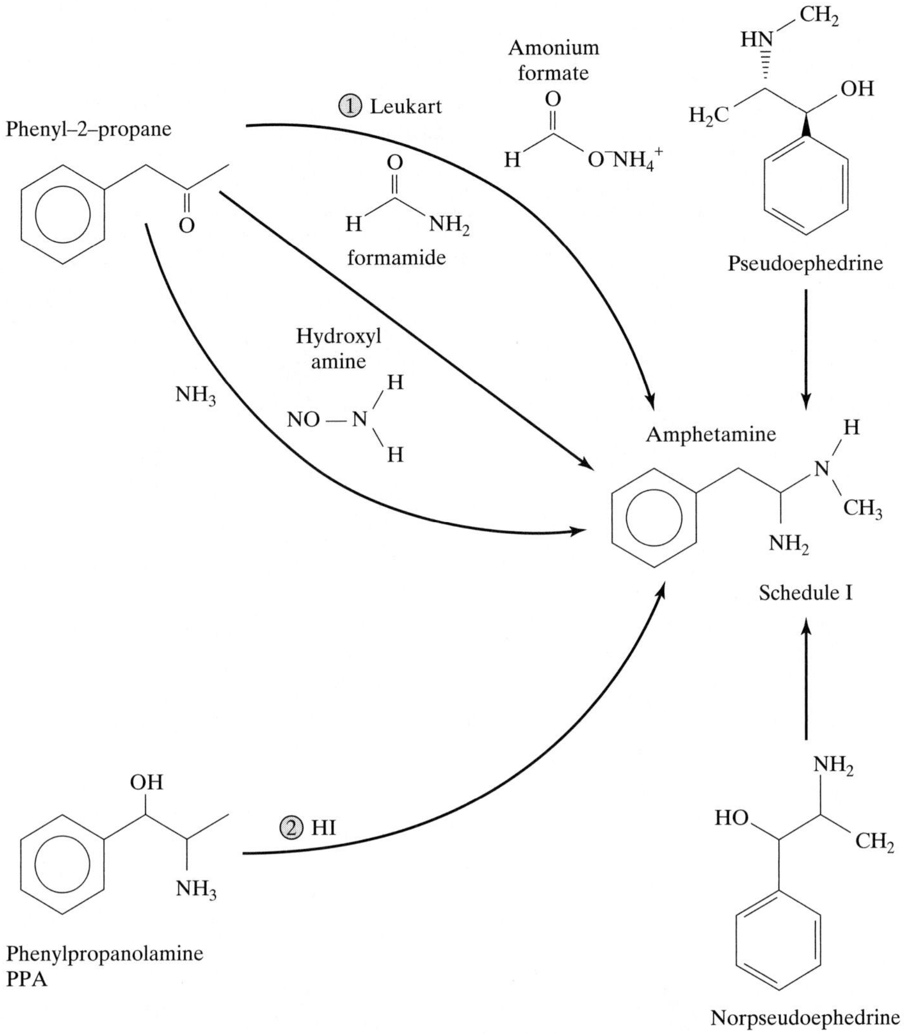

◀ **Figure 8.27** *The routes leading to the synthesis of amphetamine are analogous to those leading to the synthesis of methamphetamine. Pseudoephedrine and norpseudophedrine can also be used. Although the text focuses on methamphetamine, the principles are easily extrapolated to amphetamine.*

turned to ephedrine or pseudoephedrine, common ingredients in cold and allergy medicines, as a precursor. Many over-the-counter (OTC) products contain only ephedrine as the active ingredient, simplifying the job of the clandestine cook. Soon after the development and dissemination of ephedrine synthetic methods, those medicines were being stolen, diverted, or purchased in large quantities for clandestine laboratories.

Currently, the two favored routes for converting ephedrine to methamphetamine are the **Birch method (Nazi method)** and a red-phosphorus "cook" method. The latter is based on reduction of the alcohol group to hydrogen via an alkyl halide, is reasonably quick, produces high yields, and can be carried out via a "one-pot" method. Two variants of this approach are encountered, one involving reflux and another in which the reactant is "cold" or mildly heated. Generally, hydroiodic acid is used in conjunction with red phosphorus obtained from matches or road flares. The cold-cook method differs in that the reactants are not heated as aggressively (or not at all) and the process uses HI that is generated from iodine (I_2), water, and red phosphorus. With reasonable skill, clandestine cooks can achieve yields of 50–75%.[28] Figures 8.30 and 8.31, outline the two cook methods.

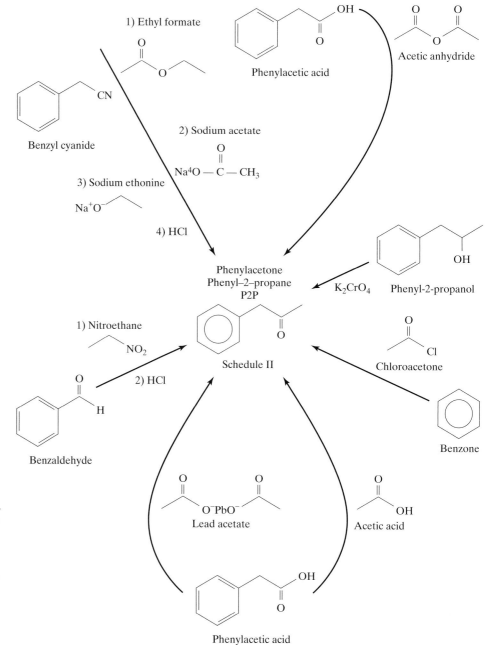

▶ **Figure 8.28** *Clandestine laboratories can also work with distant precursors that are used to make immediate precursors such as P2P. Each method introduces a unique set of contaminants and by-products.*

The refluxed red-phosphorus method may produce phosphine gas (PH_3), which can be deadly to the cooks or to first responders:[29]

$$3I_2 + 2P \longrightarrow 2PI_3 \tag{8.2}$$

$$2PI_3 + 6H_2O \longrightarrow 6HI + 2H_3PO_3 \tag{8.3}$$

$$4H_3PO_3 + O_2 + heat \longrightarrow 3H_3PO_4 + PH_3 \tag{8.4}$$

Phosphorous acid (H_3PO_3) is produced as a byproduct of the first reaction and, under continued heating, is converted to phosphoric acid and phosphine gas.

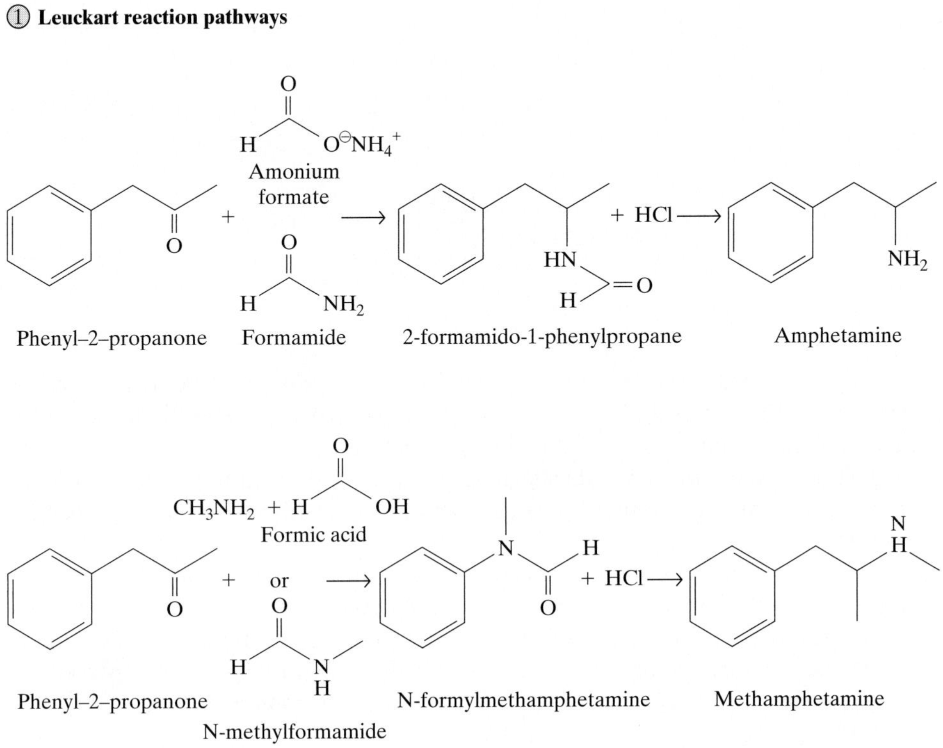
① Leuckart reaction pathways
H O⊖NH4+
Amonium formate
+ HCl
HN
=O
H
NH2
O
H NH2
Phenyl–2–propanone
Formamide
2-formamido-1-phenylpropane
Amphetamine
CH3NH2 + H OH
Formic acid
or
N H
+ HCl
N H
H N H
Phenyl–2–propanone
N-methylformamide
N-formylmethamphetamine
Methamphetamine

◀ **Figure 8.29** *The Leuckart method (1 in Figure 8.26) for synthesizing amphetamine and methamphetamine.*

The second common synthetic route is called the **Birch method**, Birch reaction, or Birch reduction. The reaction is not a traditional Birch reduction described in organic text and reference books in which a benzene ring is reduced, resulting in two double bonds rather than three. Rather, the name "Birch" may have arisen

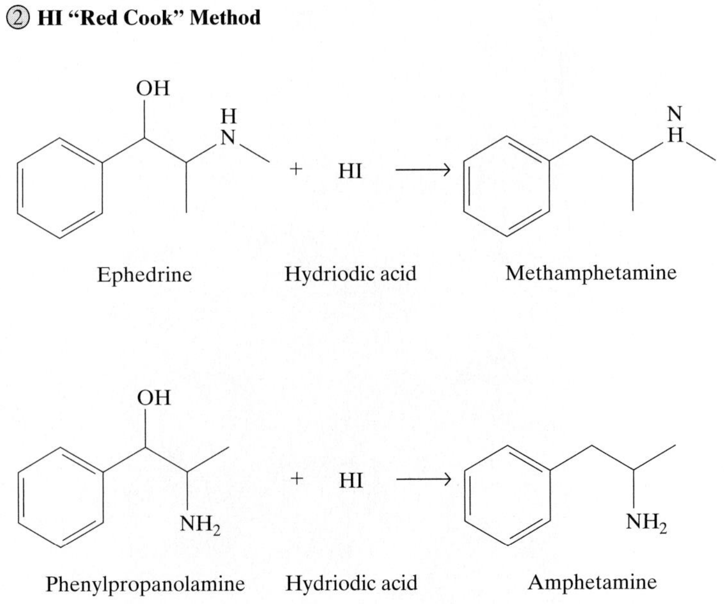
② HI "Red Cook" Method
OH
H N
+ HI
N H
Ephedrine
Hydriodic acid
Methamphetamine
OH
+ HI
NH2
NH2
Phenylpropanolamine
Hydriodic acid
Amphetamine

◀ **Figure 8.30** *Overview of the HI (red P cook) method (2 in Figure 8.26) for producing amphetamine and methamphetamine.*

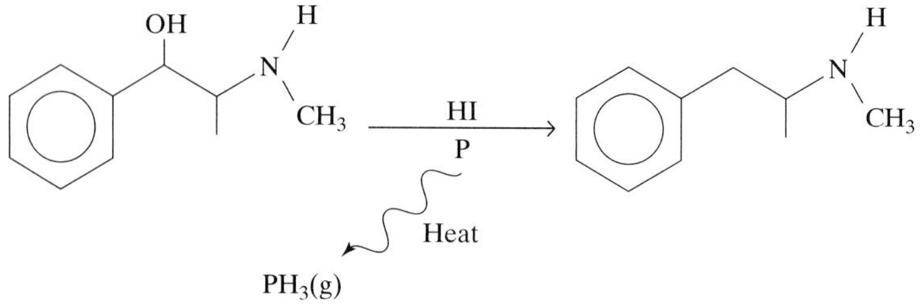

▶ **Figure 8.31** *A stepwise breakdown of the HI method. The first step displaces the —OH and replaces it with an I. The reduction follows. If the mixture is heated excessively, phosphine gas can be produced.*

from the reactants used in the procedure. The descriptor "Birch reduction" is still seen, but "Birch method" or "Birch reaction" is preferred. The Birch method is also referred to informally as the "Nazi" method, although there are conflicting reports as to why this name has been adopted. Thus, the naming of this synthetic method couldn't get much more confusing, even if the chemistry is clear (or rather, blue . . .).

As shown in Figures 8.32 through 8.35, synthesis begins when ephedrine, dissolved in THF, is combined with lithium metal (usually from batteries and anhydrous ammonia, a chemical used as fertilizer). The ammonia can also be generated in situ from lye and ammonia fertilizer products. Once ammonia is present, the solution turns blue due to solvated electrons that are generated by the lithium metal:

$$Li(s) + NH_3(anhydrous) \longrightarrow Li+ + e^-(solvated, deep blue) + :NH_2^- \quad (8.5)$$

▶ **Figure 8.32** *A step in the Birch reduction method being performed in the laboratory. More images can be found in the color insert. Image courtesy of Aaron Brudenell, Tucson Police Department.*

Applying the Science 8.5   Phosphine Gas Fatalities

Phosphine gas is a highly toxic substance produced by the "red-cook" method of clandestine methamphetamine synthesis. The gas itself is odorless, but associated by-products lend a fishy garlicky odor to the solution, detectable in the concentration range at which toxic effects are manifest. Death has been reported within 30 minutes at concentrations in the range of 400 ppm, with toxic effects noted at much lower concentrations. In one documented report, three individuals working in a motel room died while making methamphetamine; this and similar incidents have led to increased concern and awareness among first responders concerning the dangers of phosphine.

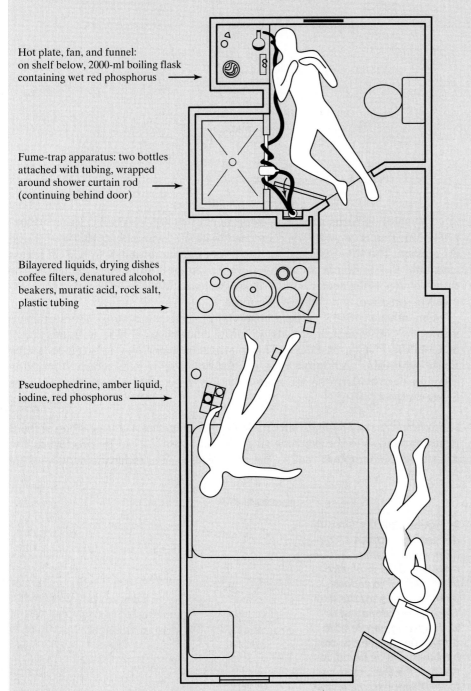

Hot plate, fan, and funnel:
on shelf below, 2000-ml boiling flask
containing wet red phosphorus

Fume-trap apparatus: two bottles
attached with tubing, wrapped
around shower curtain rod
(continuing behind door)

Bilayered liquids, drying dishes
coffee filters, denatured alcohol,
beakers, muratic acid, rock salt,
plastic tubing

Pseudoephedrine, amber liquid,
iodine, red phosphorus

◀ *Diagram of the Carlson, California motel room, showing the locations of victims in relation to chemicals and clandestine laboratory apparatus. Reproduced with permission from the reference cited, copyright 2000, ASTM International.*

Source: Willers-Russo, L. J. "Three Fatalities Involving Phospine Gas, Produced as a Result of Methamphetamine Manufacturing." *Journal of Forensic Sciences,* 44 **1999**, 647–652.

③ **Nazi or Birch Method**

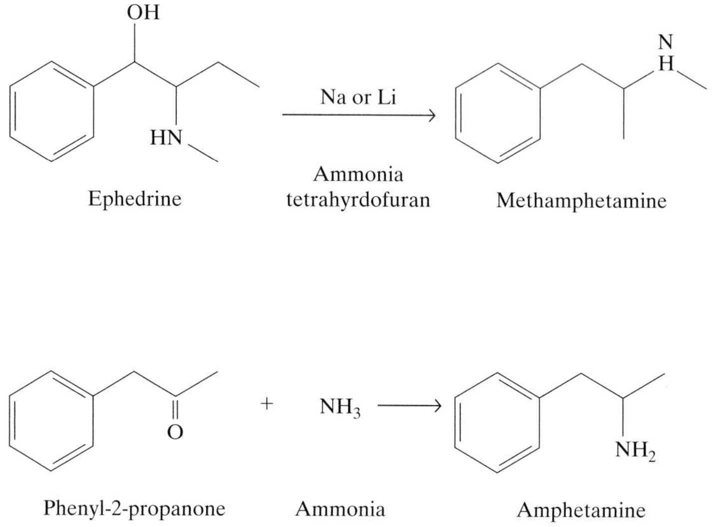

Ephedrine → (Na or Li, Ammonia tetrahyrdofuran) → Methamphetamine

▶ **Figure 8.33** *Overview of the Birch method (3 in Figure 8.26) for producing methamphetamine. In an analogous process, P2P can be reduced to amphetamine.*

Phenyl-2-propanone + Ammonia (NH_3) → Amphetamine

The solution turns a grayish color as the reaction proceeds. The methamphetamine that is generated is converted to its salt by bubbling HCl(g) through the solvent. The advantages of the Birch method are its ability to boil off excess ammonia and its simple decomposition of residual lithium metal by water. The disadvantage is the need for anhydrous ammonia, which can be hazardous, explosive, corrosive, and difficult to handle.

One other synthetic method observed in some clandestine laboratories involves the conversion of ephedrine to the chlorinated analog with the use of $SOCl_2$, PCl_5, $POCl_3$, or PCl_3.[30] This method is sometimes referred to as the **Emde synthesis**.[31] A byproduct is an **aziridine** (Figure 8.36) which, if found in a sample or in evidence seized from a clandestine facility, is characteristic of the Emde method.

Stereochemistry and Profiling: Since methamphetamine has a chiral carbon at the β position relative to the benzene ring, d- and l-isomers can be produced. The d-form of methamphetamine is the more active, so clandestine syntheses are

Birch Reduction

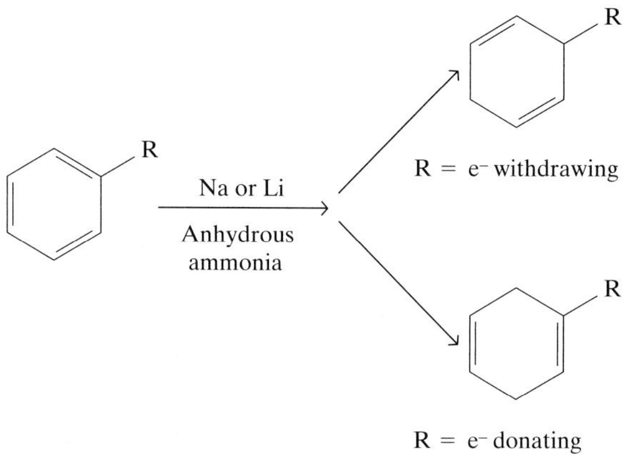

▶ **Figure 8.34** *The Birch reduction. Anhydrous ammonium and sodium or lithium metal are used in an alcoholic solution to reduce (add hydrogen to) the ring. The electron donating or withdrawing nature of R determines where the double bonds will be found. Notice that the Birch method for methamphetamine synthesis does not affect the phenyl ring.*

R = e⁻ withdrawing

R = e⁻ donating

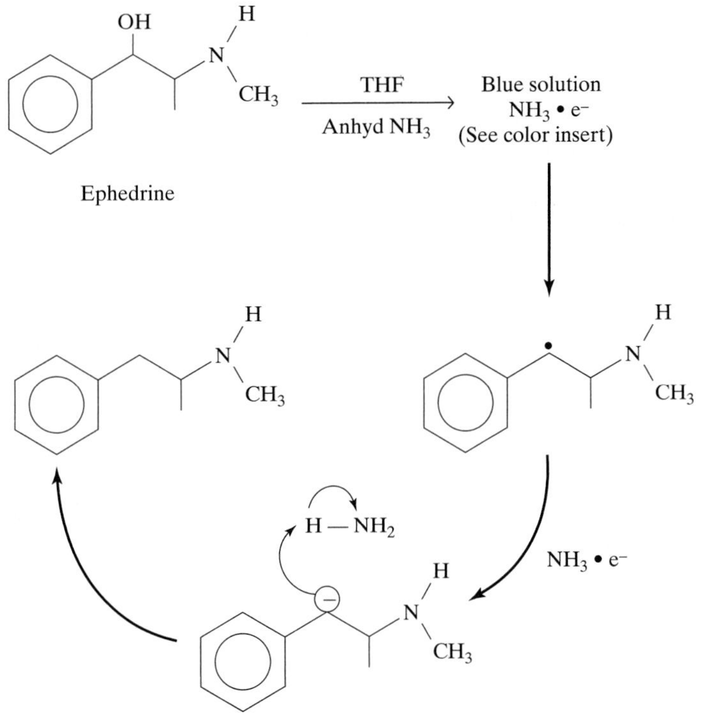

Ephedrine

THF
Anhyd NH₃

Blue solution
NH₃ • e⁻
(See color insert)

H — NH₂

NH₃ • e⁻

◀ **Figure 8.35** *The Birch method applied to ephedrine to produce methamphetamine. The progress of the reaction can be monitored by observing the disappearance of the blue color and the appearance of a grayish color associated with the product, methamphetamine. See the color insert for photos of the reaction process.*

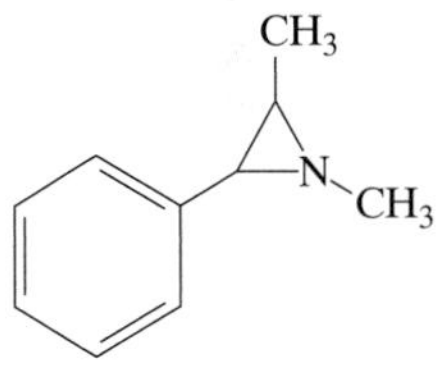

geared to favor d-methamphetamine (also referred to as (+) methamphetamine, the S enantiomer). The mechanism used dictates the stereochemistry of the products. The Leuckart method, starting with P2P, yields a racemic mixture of d- and l- ((+) and (−)) methamphetamine, while reductive methods, starting with ephedrine or pseudoephedrine, are controlled by the form of the ephedrine or pseudoephedrine.[32] The Birch and iodide methods yield (+) methamphetamine if the starting material is either (−) ephedrine or (+) pseudoephedrine.[28,33] The stereochemical aspects of the Emde method are more complex.[30] A few of the stereochemical considerations are summarized in Figure 8.37.

The plethora of synthetic methods and conditions used to create methamphetamine facilitates profiling investigations. Because of the stereospecificity of the Birch method versus the Leuckart method, stereochemistry can be a valuable profiling aid. A method for profiling in which a basic extraction into ethyl acetate is used has been published by the United Nations (35);[34] an SPME approach has also received attention and appears to work as well or better.[31] Such extractions often yield a large number of chromatographic peaks and identifications of compounds, not all of which are easily explained. Some may be contaminants of original ingredients, while others may be byproducts created by less than stringent attention to experimental conditions. In one recent study, 1,2-dimethyl-3-phenyl-aziridine (typical of an Emde chloroephedrine intermediate) was identified with the SPME method, as were a number of other compounds, such as caffeine (a diluent) and vanillin, likely added for flavoring.[31]

Profiling provides useful investigative information, such as the likelihood that evidence seized separately may have come from the same batch or from the same cook or, more generally, that similar or dissimilar synthetic methods were used. Thus, it is often the pattern of byproducts and contaminants—the so-called "chemical fingerprint"— that provides the most useful information. Profiling was useful in identifying ephedra as a precursor in clandestine syntheses as early as 1995.[35] **Ephedra** is a grass (*Ephedra sinica*) that contains **pseudoephedrine**

Azridrine

▲ **Figure 8.36** *An aziridine that forms as a by-product of the Emde method for methamphetamine production.*

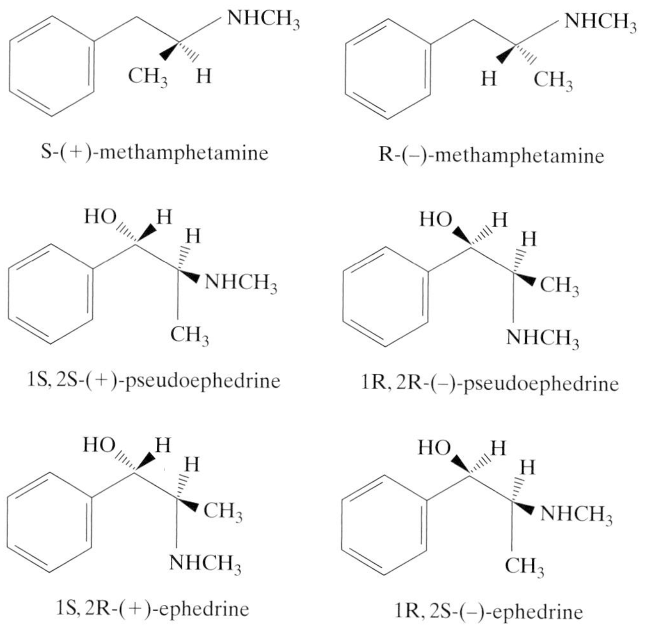

S-(+)-methamphetamine   R-(−)-methamphetamine

1S, 2S-(+)-pseudoephedrine   1R, 2R-(−)-pseudoephedrine

1S, 2R-(+)-ephedrine   1R, 2S-(−)-ephedrine

▶ **Figure 8.37** *The optical iso-mers of methamphetamine and its precursors. Ephedrine has two chiral carbons—α and β—to the phenyl ring, but the α carbon is reduced to $-CH_2$, leaving only one chiral center.*

(1R, 2S)-(−)-ephedrine
(1S, 2S)-(+)-pseudoephedrine ⟶ (S)-(+)-methemphetamine

(1S, 2R)-(+)-ephedrine
(1R, 2R)-(−)-pseudoephedrine ⟶ (R)-(−)-methemphetamine

and ephedrine, as well as other related compounds, such as norephedrine (which leads to amphetamine) and *N*-methylephedrine.

MDMA (Ecstasy): MDMA is a member of the methamphetamine–amphetamine class of drugs and is unusual in that it is chemically similar to mescaline, a hallucinogen. MDMA has become popular among young adults as a club drug or rave drug. Unlike methamphetamine, it is supplied mostly by foreign laboratories that smuggle their product into the United States.[36] Europe and Israel are the centers for this activity, and the drug is often supplied as a pill with a logo stamped into the surface. The synthesis of MDMA typically begins with MDP2P (also called 3,4P2P) in a method analogous to the synthesis of methamphetamine via P2P. MDP2P is in turn made from piperonal or safrole obtained from sources such as sassafras oil.[36] As with methamphetamine, there are dozens of variants of this approach, and profiling can be useful in determining the method and ingredients used.[24,37,38] Finally, MDA can also be made from isosafrole.[37] The synthetic routes to MDMA are summarized in Figures 8.38 and 8.39.

Khat got your Tongue?: **Khat**, a plant-derived stimulant popular in Africa and parts of the Middle East, is an emerging problem in the United States, likely due to increasing emigration from those regions. The two active ingredients in khat are **cathinone** (Schedule I) and **cathine** (Schedule IV). Like many controlled substances, khat is socially acceptable in large parts of the world, giving many countries little incentive to limit its use or cultivation. For example, a third of the gross national product of Yemen is related to khat.[39] The major

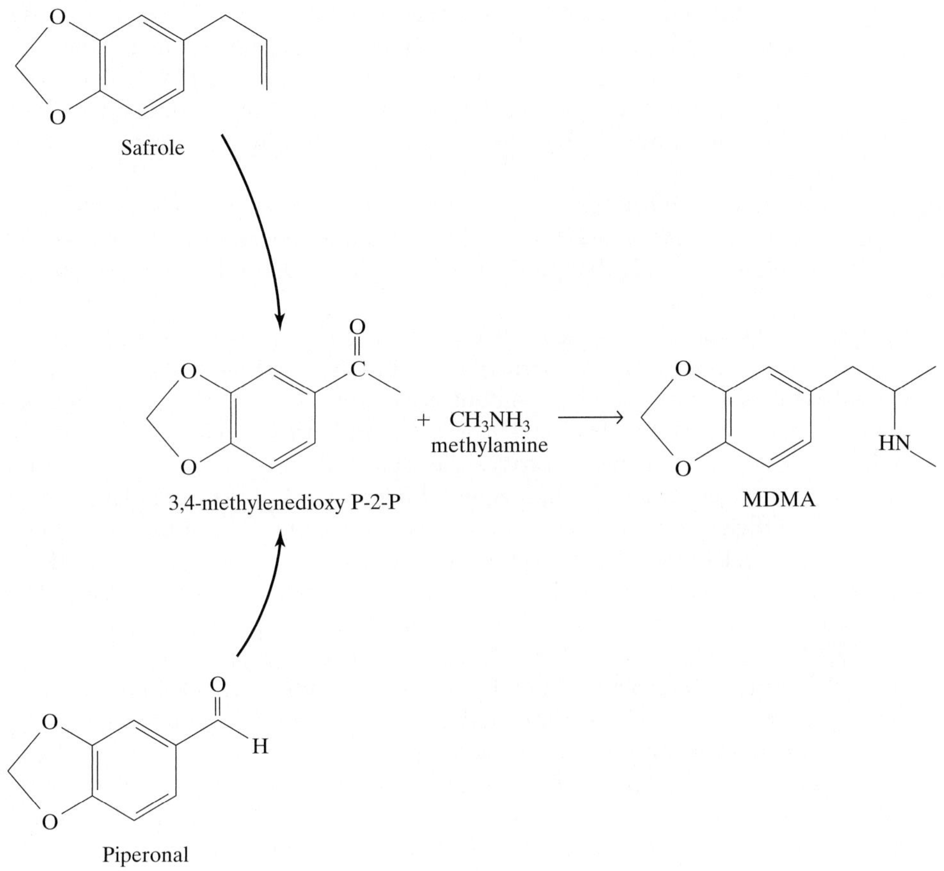

◀ **Figure 8.38** *One of many methods that can be used to manufacture MDMA. Most of the methods are analogous to those available and used to make methamphetamine. Here, the 3,4-methylenedioxy P2P is analogous to P2P.*

sources of khat coming into the United States are Ethiopia, Yemen, and Somalia. Khat evidence is collected in the form of plant matter. The drug is ingested by chewing the plant matter, and, like most stimulants, it can be hallucinogenic in high doses. Khat is chemically related to ephedrine and therefore to

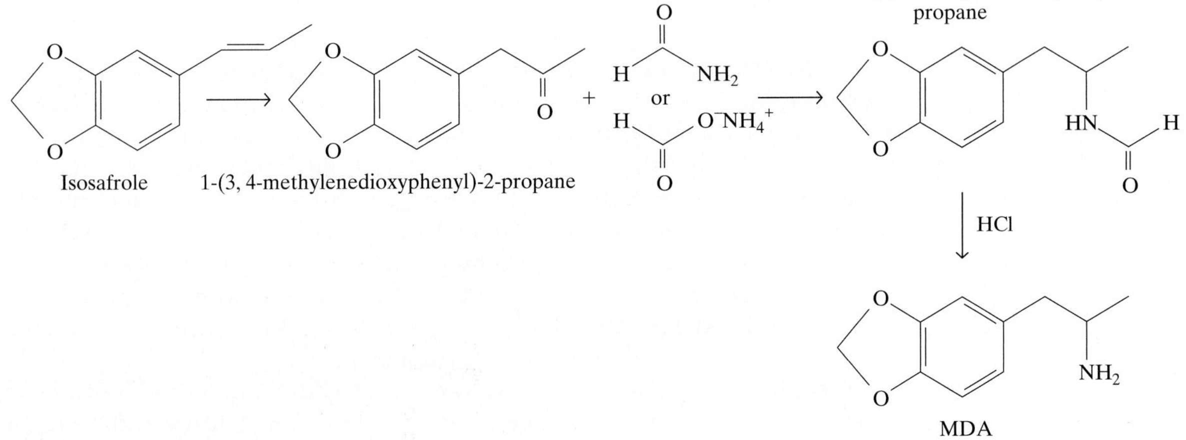

▲ **Figure 8.39** *A pathway leading to the production of MDA, another phenylethylamine.*

amphetamine, methamphetamine, and other ephedrine preparations. Analysis requires an initial extraction similar to that required for marijuana, peyote, and mushrooms. While no good color or crystal tests are known, TLC has been reported as useful, followed by confirmatory instrumental methods, including GCMS and NMR, although the latter is of limited use in forensic laboratories, since few have NMR instruments.[40–45]

A newcomer on the stimulant scene is a drug called cat, which is not the same drug as khat. "Cat" is the street name for methcathinone, another member of the methamphetamine family that produces similar effects and is listed on Schedule I.

Analytical Approach: The analysis of the phenylalkylamine stimulants follows the typical path of color tests to confirmation by instrumental methods, typically IR. Because of the structural similarity among the members of this drug family, special attention has to be paid to distinguish them. Controls are essential, and, in the case of GCMS, retention time data is a critical element of identification, since the spectra are similar. Longer capillary columns with high theoretical plate counts and high separation efficiency are of value in separating compounds seen in phenylalkylamine samples. Enantioselective techniques such as derivatization, as well as chiral chromatographic columns based on cyclodextrins, have also been employed to separate the many enantiomers that can be found in this type of evidence.[46]

GCMS is clearly useful for quantitative purposes and profiling, but IR spectroscopy is often preferred for identification in cases where that technique is feasible. Extraction is usually required, although not necessarily a quantitative one. Because methamphetamine and related compounds are amines, they are weak bases and are extracted from a basic solution as the un-ionized amine compound into an organic solvent such as chloroform. Bubbling HCl through the chloroform converts the base to the corresponding salt. Identifying enantiomers is a more difficult challenge. Recent advances in chiral separations using chiral stationary phases allows for enantiomeric differentiation; however, the most promising method for routine use may be capillary electrophoresis (CE), which has the added advantage of allowing for chiral separations using cyclodextrins.[47,48]

An identification problem arises in the analysis of khat in that cathinone will begin to degrade to cathine as soon as the khat is harvested. The analytical window is about two days from that time.[49] In addition, the electron impact mass spectrum of cathine is identical to that of phenylpropanolamine, an amphetamine precursor.

On the Stand (Legal Issues and Questions): In methamphetamine and similar cases in which diluted samples are encountered, the forensic chemist may be asked about "**usable quantity**." In some jurisdictions, the prosecution is required to prove not only that the defendant had a controlled substance, but that the amount possessed was usable.[50] This concept is also referred to as "**measurable quantity**." Since quantitation of the methamphetamine family is not routinely performed, a concentration or percentage value of purity is not always available. The defense may argue that the amount present was so small as to be negligible or harmless. Because exhibits are received with low concentrations of the controlled substance, this is a reasonable question.

There is no uniform standard addressing measurable quantity from a legal perspective. The prevalent position requires the amount to be sufficient for analysis or enough to be accurately weighed.[50] The forensic chemist should be prepared to estimate this quantity on the basis of the limits of detection used in the analysis. As discussed in Chapter 3, determination of the limit of detection (LOD) is an intrinsic part of validating the method. Ideally, the LOD should be expressed as both a traditional chemical unit, such as ppm, ppb, or M, and a percentage, since non-scientists understand percentages.

The other questions that may arise deal with the method of synthesis. If the sample was part of a clandestine laboratory seizure, this type of question should be anticipated. However, if the sample is not directly obtained from such a facility, the method of synthesis may not be a relevant issue. Whether it is is for the courts and investigators to decide. If it is not clear what method was used, or if profiling is not requested or conducted, a forensic chemist should answer such questions accordingly.

8.3.2 DISSOCIATIVE ANESTHETICS

Phencyclidine (PCP) and **ketamine** are synthetic dissociatives that are usually categorized as hallucinogens. Once a significant problem, PCP has faded as a concern, although there is some evidence of a revival in its use.[51] PCP is 1-(1-phenylcyclohexyl) piperidine, and the abbreviation is thought to have come from the moniker

Table 8.14 Dissociative Anesthetics and Analogs

Compound	Structure
Phencyclidine (PCP) Schedule II	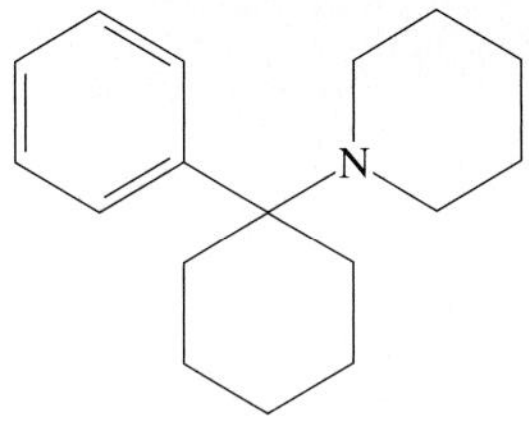
1-Phenylcyclohexalamine Schedule II	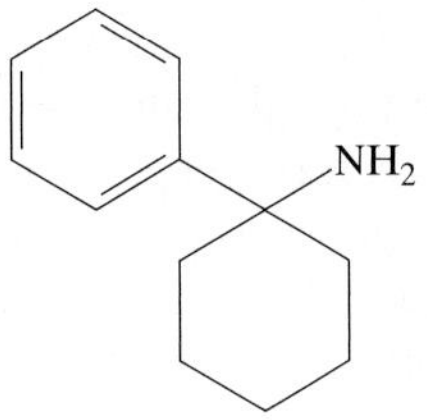
1-Piperidinocyclohexane carbonitrile (PCC) Schedule II	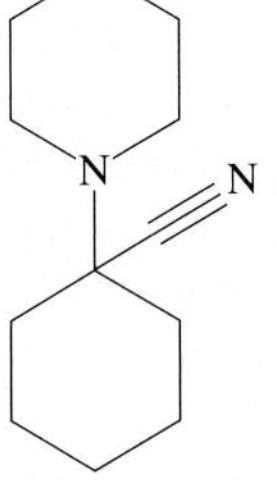
1-(1-Thiophenecyclohexyl)piperidine (TCP)	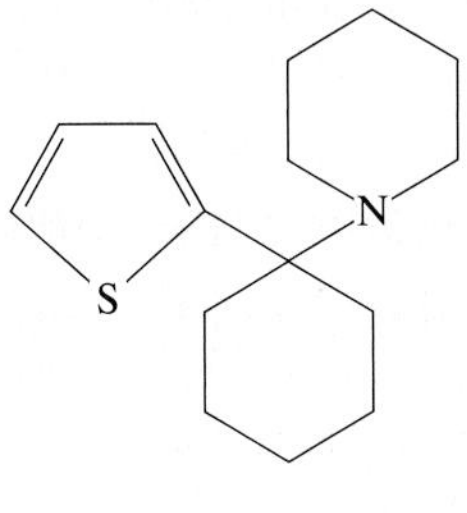

Table 8.14 (Continued)	
Compound	**Structure**
1-(1-Phenylcyclohexyl)ethylamine (PCE)	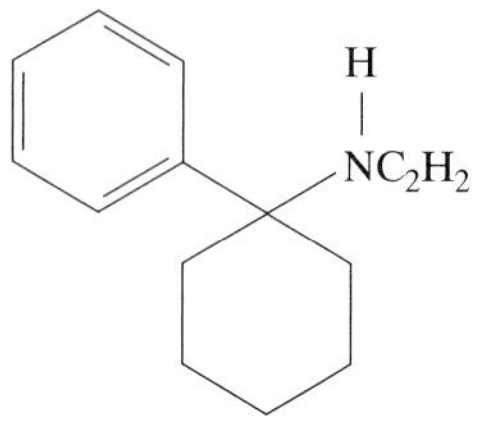
1-(1-Phenylcyclohexyl)pyrrolidine (PHP)	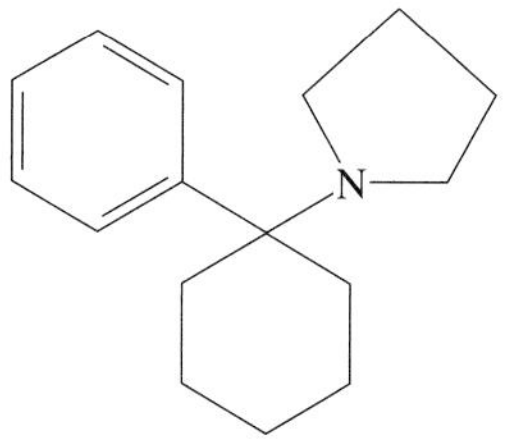
Ketamine	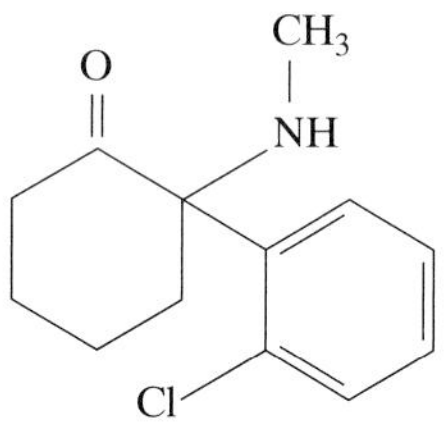

"*peace p*ill." Aside from methamphetamine, this is the drug most likely to involve clandestine laboratory synthesis on a small scale. The synthesis of PCP is also dangerous compared with even the Birch method for synthesizing methamphetamine. Due to its uses as a veterinary anesthetic (Sernyl), PCP was originally listed on Schedule III, but unpredictable effects and abuse prompted a move to Schedule II. As evidence, it is frequently found as a liquid in which cigarettes of marijuana, mint, or other plant matter are dipped. The salt form is referred to as angel dust. PCP evidence usually has a distinctive and strong solvent odor. Like PCP, ketamine is a veterinary anesthetic. Diversion and theft from clinics and pharmacies is the primary source of ketamine, which is used primarily as a club drug.

Compared with the synthesis other drugs, that of PCP is relatively simple, via a Grignard reagent (Figure 8.40). Several PCP analogs are easily prepared and are listed on Schedule I. The analysis of PCP is similar to that used for mescaline and related hallucinogens. The liquid form, particularly when applied to cigarettes, makes presumptive testing more difficult. Once extracted, PCP chromatographs well in both TLC and GCMS. Ketamine is also amenable to chromatographic analysis, as well as IR spectroscopy. The analysis is simplified considerably if evidence is seized when still in commercial packaging.

8.3.3 BENZODIAZEPINES AND SELECTIVE SEROTONIN REUPTAKE INHIBITORS

The **benzodiazepines** were among the first class of drugs developed as a result of targeted modern drug discovery techniques.[52] Drugs used specifically to treat psychological problems and mental illnesses are relatively new compared

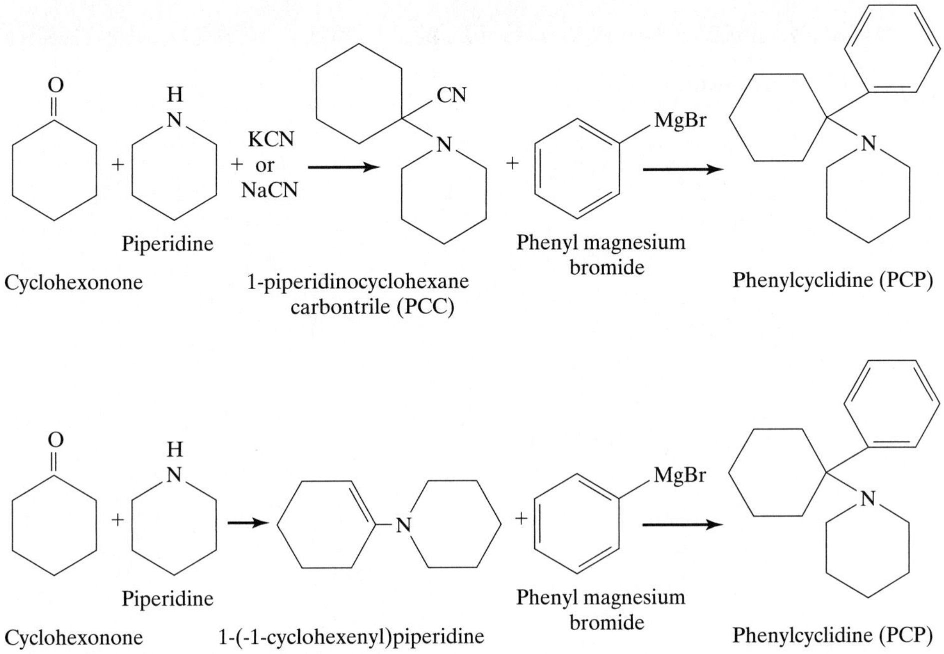

▲ **Figure 8.40** *Examples of synthetic routes to PCP using a Grignard reagent to add the phenyl group. As a strong nucleophile, the Grignard reagent attacks the carbonyl carbon in the top route to add the phenyl group, while a conjugate addition occurs in the other route.*

Table 8.15   Examples of Benzodiazepines and SSRIs

Valium® (diazepam)

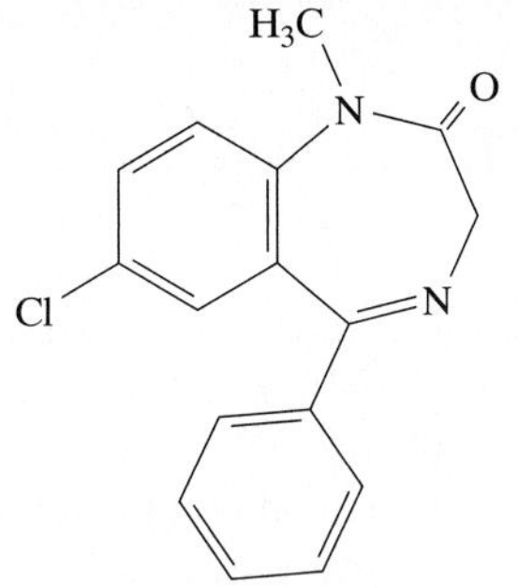

Xanax® (alprazolam)

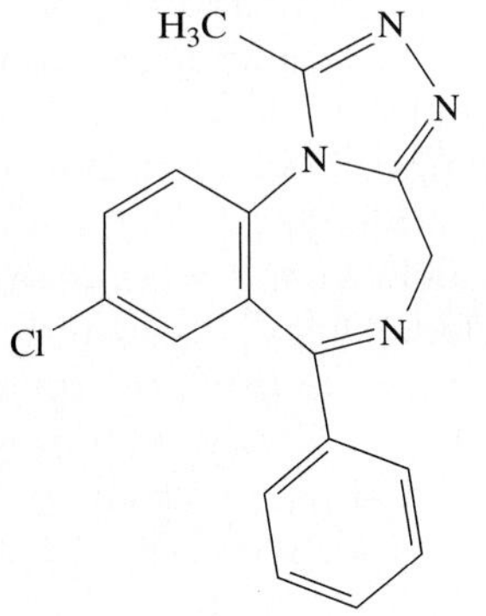

Table 8.15 (Continued)

Elavil® (amitriptyline)

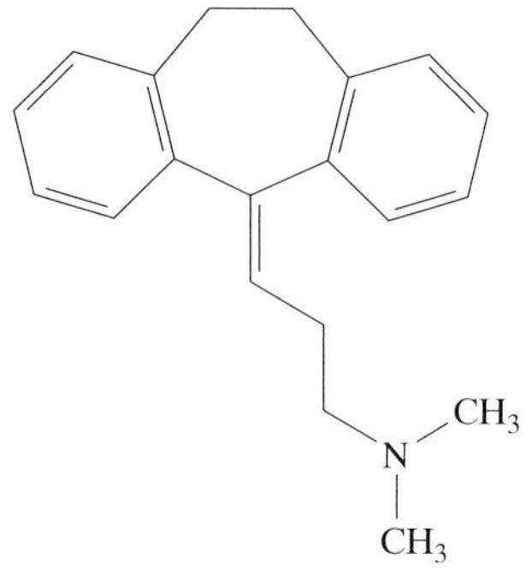

Paxil® (Paroxetine hydrochloride)

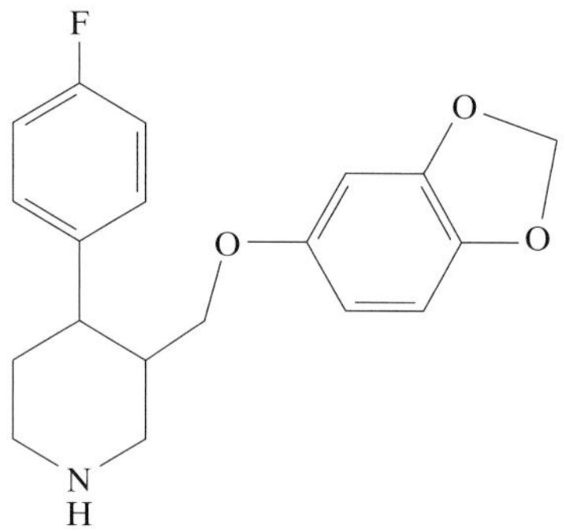

Prozac® (Fluoxetine)

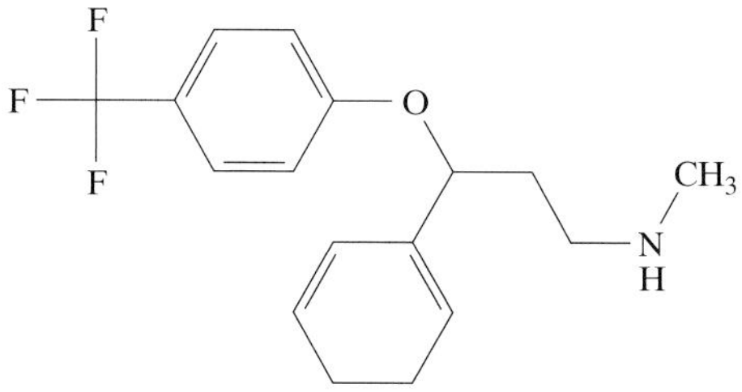

with narcotics and stimulants, which trace back to the introduction of lithium carbonate in 1948 as a treatment for bipolar disorder. In the 1950s, monoamine oxidase inhibitors (MAOIs) were introduced. These drugs function by blocking enzymatic processes that degrade neurotransmitters. As a group, they were effective, but were plagued by side effects and interactions with other medications and food. To address these limitations, as well as those of barbiturates in treating anxiety and depression, a group at Roche Pharmaceuticals undertook research that led to some of the most widely prescribed drugs in the world.[52]

The first of the benzodiazepines was **Valium**® (diazepam), introduced in 1963. A number of related compounds, including Dalmane® (flurazepam) and Ativan® (lorazepam), were developed over the next two decades. More recent entries include Xanax® (alprazolam), an antianxiety drug with additional ring structure. Another group of prescription antidepressants is the tricyclic amines (TCAs), such as Elavil. Finally, with drug discovery and expanding knowledge of brain chemistry and neurotransmitter function, a new class of antianxiety–antidepressants—the selective serotonin reuptake inhibitors (SSRIs)—was produced. This class includes fluoxetine (Prozac®), introduced in 1987, which was followed by many others (e.g., Paxil®) that are consistently among the most widely used and prescribed drugs in the world.

Forensically, these drugs are encountered as diverted pharmaceuticals, simplifying the analysis. In such cases, and in any case in which commercial labeling or marking remains, the first step is usually a check of the *Physician's Desk Reference* (PDR) to determine the likely identity and constituents of the preparation.[53] Rather than identifying a complete unknown, the task then becomes one of confirmation with instrumental techniques. In effect, the PDR becomes a presumptive test. While there are cases in which commercial preparations are faked, such cases are rare. Fortunately, abuse of these new-generation medications is far less prevalent than was abuse of earlier medications, such as the barbiturates.

SUMMARY

Drugs with basic character are the largest subgroup of illicit drugs and, with the exception of marijuana, represents the majority of target analytes. Drugs derived from plants (either directly or indirectly) cover the gamut, from narcotic CNS depressants such as heroin to dangerous stimulants and hallucinogens such as MDMA and LSD. While some—for example, LSD—are difficult to synthesize, methamphetamine is easily made; thus, drug chemists can expect to be dealing with illicit samples and synthetic schemes for the foreseeable future. An understanding of drug chemistry is essential to answering questions concerning how a given sample was made and is critical information for those who respond to clandestine laboratory crime scenes. Even commercially prepared pharmaceuticals find their way to the crime lab, in which case the analysis reverts to a confirmation. This chapter concludes the drug chemistry section of the text. Next we move into the hot topics of combustion, arson, and explosives.

KEY TERMS AND CONCEPTS

Amphetamine	Enantiomers	Methamphetamine
Aziridine	Endorphins	Morphine
Benzodiazepines	Ephedra	Nazi method
Birch method	Ephedrine	Neurotransmitter
Birch reduction	Ergot alkaloid	Noscapine
Bleaching agent	Ergotism	Opiate alkaloids
Caffeine	Heroin	Optical isomers
Cahn-Ingold-Prelog convention	Hydrocodone	Oxycodone
Cathine	Hydromorphone	Oxycontin
Cathinone	Ice	Papaverine
CDTA	Ketamine	PCP
Club drugs	Khat	Peyote
Coca paste	LAMPA	Phenacetin
Cocaine	Latex	Phenethylamines
Codeine	Leuckart method	Phenobarbitone
Cook	Lidocaine	Procaine
Diacetylmorphine	LSD	Provenance
Diamorphine	Lysergic acid	Pseudoephedrine
Dissociative anesthetics	MAM	Psilocin
Ecstasy	Measurable quantity	Psilocybin
Emde method	Mescaline	Quinine

Reductive amination
Refluxing
Tetracaine
Thebaine

Theophylline
Tropane alkaloid
Tryptamines
Usable quantity

Valium
Xanthine alkaloids

PROBLEMS

From the chapter

1. Would a sample of heroin containing significantly more 3-MAM as opposed to 6-MAM be noteworthy? Why? What could this indicate?

2. For any given molecule of heroin, what percentage of the carbon originates from morphine and what percentage is traceable to acetic anhydride, assuming that is the reagent used in the conversion.

3. On the basis of your answer to Problem 2, and using chemical equations and diagrams, explain how the acetylation of morphine will alter the $^{13}C/^{12}C$ ratio of a sample. From the perspective of profiling, is this alteration the source of potentially useful information, or does it merely confuse the situation? Justify your answer.

4. One of the difficulties in profiling plant-derived drugs is obtaining reliable standards. Elaborate on this statement.

5. Caffeine is an alkaloid base with a bitter taste that is cheap and easy to obtain. It is frequently used as an adulterant of cocaine, but is rarely used as an adulterant of heroin. Why?

6. What is the difference between aggregate weight and usable quantity?

7. What is a key structural feature seen in the benzodiazepines and SSRIs that is not seen in any other drugs discussed so far?

8. One method used to remove the alkaloids papaverine and noscapine from extracted morphine is to scatter the powder in water and adjust the pH to 6.4. After a time, the pH is made basic (9.0) and extracted with an organic solvent. Explain how and why this works.

9. The following data are obtained from the PDR regarding an elixir:

   Tylenol® with Codeine (Ortho-McNeil)
   tablets CIII
   (acetaminophen and codeine phosphate)
   Contains:
   Codeine Phosphate   12 mg
   Acetaminophen   120 mg

   a. Assuming that the elixir is a syrupy aqueous solution, suggest a method to isolate the two active ingredients from the syrup by using SPE.
   b. Make the procedure you suggested in part a quantitative for a GCMS analysis. Assume that the linear

dynamic range of the curve for both drugs is 10.0–200.0 ng/mL and that the recovery of your method will be within 95–105%. Assume further that the injection volume is 1.0 μL. (*NOTE*: There is more than one correct answer, just as there are many preparations that could work. Select one that is reasonable.

   c. Could this sample be extracted with an organic solvent such as chloroform and directly injected into the GCMS system as described? Why or why not?

Integrative

1. Why are the functional groups attached to carbon 3 in morphine more active than those attached to carbon 6?

2. Suggest two alternative reagents that could be used for simple (one- or two-step) conversions of lysergic acid to LSD. Show the reaction(s).

3. The active ingredients of khat are shown in Table 8.13. Cathinone loses its potency quickly once the plant is harvested; cathine does not. Provide a defensible explanation for this difference in chemical behavior.

4. Postulate a mechanism and explanation for the formation of the aziridines during the Emde method of methamphetamine synthesis.

5. Research and briefly explain how dopamine and serotonin work. Using structures presented in this chapter, postulate how and why these substances produce their characteristic effects.

6. What byproducts would you expect if the Birch method is used to prepare methamphetamine from ephedrine?

7. One sign that the Birch or "Nazi" method has been used to synthesize methamphetamine is an empty propane tank like those used for barbecue grills. Such tanks have a blue patina around the valve. What could account for this sheen?

8. On the basis of the fundamental characteristics of abused substances, what are some reasons for the relatively limited abuse of modern antianxiety and antidepressant drugs relative to those they have replaced?

9. This question was presented in Chapter 2 (question 9). Compare the approach that is possible now by using presumptive tests and screening tests, compared with the initial response and comment on the role these tests play in sample selection.

   a. A small seizure of suspected LSD is submitted to the laboratory and consists of 30 blotter papers. Design a sampling plan, assuming that the contents of a minimum of three papers will be needed to obtain a sample sufficient for presumptive and confirmatory testing.

b. After selection and testing, all results are negative. Describe the next steps in the analysis.

c. At what point in this LSD analysis would it be appropriate to call the results negative for LSD?

d. Assume that all results are negative until four squares are left. Testing one gives a positive result.

Using a flowchart, describe the next step(s) and any assumptions made.

Food for thought

1. If designating precursors, such as P2P, as controlled substances or listed chemicals, has been successful in eliminating the method of synthesis, why not add ephedrine to Schedule I of the Controlled Substances Act?

FURTHER READING

ASTM International. "Standard Guide for Microcrystal Testing in the Forensic Analysis of Methamphetamine and Amphetamine," in *ASTM Standard E 105–58*, 19.02, ed. ASTM International, **2004**.

Bentley, K. W. *The Chemistry of the Morphine Alkaloids.* Oxford, U.K.: Clarendon Press, **1954**.

Bentley, K. W. "II: Morphine and Its Isomers," in K. W. Bentley, *The Chemistry of the Morphine Alkaloids.* London: Oxford University Press, **1954**.

Bentley, K. W. "IV: Codeine and Its Isomers," in K. W. Bentley, *The Chemistry of the Morphine Alkaloids.* London: Oxford University Press, **1954**.

Bentley, K. W. *The Alkaloids (Volume I).* London: Oxford University Press, **1957**.

Bentley, K. W. *The Alkaloids (Volume II).* London: Oxford University Press, **1965**.

Bruice, P. Y. *Organic Chemistry*, 4th ed. Upper Saddle River, NJ: Pearson Education, Prentice Hall, **2004**.

Christian, D. R. *Forensic Investigation of Clandestine Laboratories.* Boca Raton, FL: CRC Press, **2004**.

Cole, M. D. *The Analysis of Controlled Substances.* Chichester, U.K.: John Wiley and Sons, **2003**.

Laing, R., and J. Hugel. *Hallucinogens: A Forensic Drug Handbook.* Boston: Academic Press, **2003**.

Physician's Desk Reference, 58th ed. Montvale, NJ: Thomson PDR, **2004**.

Seigel, J. A. "Forensic Identification of Controlled Substances," in R. Saferstein, ed., *Forensic Science Handbook, Volume II.* Upper Saddle River, NJ: Prentice Hall, **1988**, 69–160.

Sternbach, L. H. "The Benzodiazepine Story." *Journal of Medicinal Chemistry*, 22 **1979**, 1–7.

Wade, L. G. *Organic Chemistry*, 5th ed. Upper Saddle River, NJ: Pearson Education, Prentice Hall, **2003**.

REFERENCES

1. Bedford, K. R., et al. "The Illicit Preparation of Morphine and Heroin from Pharmaceutical Products Containing Codeine: 'Homebake' Laboratories in New Zealand." *Forensic Science International*, 34 **1987**, 197–204.

2. Bentley, K. W. "IV: Codeine and Its Isomers," in K. W. Bentley, *The Chemistry of the Morphine Alkaloids.* London: Oxford University Press, **1954**, 57–97.

3. *Physicians' Desk Reference*, 58. Montvale, NJ: Medical Economics–Thomson Healthcare, **2004**.

4. Dams, R., et al. "Heroin Impurity Profiling: Trends throughout a Decade of Experimenting." *Forensic Science International*, 123 **2001**, 81–88.

5. Cole, M. D. "Occluded Solvent Analysis as a Basis for Heroin and Cocaine Sample Differentiation." *Forensic Science Review*, 10 **1998**, 113.

6. Raport, H., et al. "The Preparation of Morphine-N-methyl-C14." *Journal of the American Chemical Society*, 73 **1951**, 5900–5901.

7. Raport, H., and R. M. Bonner. "Delta-7 Desoxymorphine." *Journal of the American Chemical Society*, 73 **1951**, 5485.

8. Lawson, J. A., and J. I. DeGraw. "An Improved Method for O-Demethylation of Codeine." *Journal of Medicinal Chemistry*, 20 **1977**, 165–166.

9. Brenneisen, R., and F. Hasler. "GC/MS Determination of Pyrolysis Products from Diacetylmorphine and Adulterants of Street Heroin Samples." *Journal of Forensic Sciences*, 47 **2002**, 1–4.

10. Wijesekera, A. R. L., et al. "Studies on the Degradation of Heroin." *Forensic Science International*, 67 **1994**, 147.

11. Zhang, D., et al. "Component Analysis of Illicit Heroin Samples with GC/MS and Its Application in Source Identification." *Journal of Forensic Sciences*, 49 **2004**, 1–6.

12. Holt, P. J. "Particle Size Analysis of Six Illicit Heroin Preparations Seized in the U.K." *Forensic Science International*, 81 **1996**, 17 (12 pages).

13. Klemenc, S. "Noscapine as an Adulterant in Illicit Heroin Samples." *Forensic Science International*, 108 **2000**, 45 (46 pages).

14. Seigel, J. A. "Forensic Identification of Controlled Substances," in R. Saferstein, ed., *Forensic Science Handbook, Volume II*. Upper Saddle River, NJ: Prentice Hall, **1988**, 69–160.

15. Cartier, J., et al. "Headspace Analysis of Solvents in Cocaine and Heroin samples." *Science & Justice: Journal of the Forensic Science Society*, 37 **1997**, 175–181.

16. Bora, T., et al. "Levels of Trace and Major Elements in Illicit Heroin." *Journal of Forensic Sciences*, 47 **2002**, 959–963.

17. Besacier, F., et al. "Comparative Chemical Analyses of Drug Samples: General Approach and Application to Heroin." *Forensic science international*, 85 **1997**, 113–125.

18. Ehleringer, J. R., et al. "Geo-location of Heroin and Cocaine by Stable Isotope Ratios." *Forensic Science International*, 106 **1999**, 27 (10 pages).

19. Substance Abuse and Mental Health Services Administration, *Summary of Findings from the 2000 National Household Survey on Drug Abuse*, September 2001. Available on-line: URL: www.health.org/govstudy/bkd405/Downloaded January 2005.

20. Cole, M. D. "Chapter 6: Cocaine," in M. D. Cole, *The Analysis of Controlled Substances*. New York: Wiley, **2003**, 113–125.

21. *Selected Intelligence Brief: Cocaine Signature Program Report*, U.S. Drug Enforcement agency, January 2003. Available online, URL: www.dea.gov.

22. "Standard Guide for Microcrystal Testing in the Forensic Analysis of Cocaine," in *ASTM Standard E 105–58*, 14.02, ed. ASTM International, **2004**.

23. Mann, J. "Chapter 2: Murder," in J. Mann, *Murder, Magic, and Medicine*, 2 ed. New York: Oxford University Press, **2000**, 7–59.

24. Beyerstein, B. L., and M. Kalchik. "Chapter 1: History of the Psychedelic Experience," in R. Laing, ed., *Hallucinogens: A Forensic Drug Handbook*, Boston: Academic Press, **2003**, 1–36.

25. Frost, M., and H. Köhler. "Analysis of Lysergic Acid Diethylamide: Comparison of Capillary Electrophoresis with Laser-induced Fluorescence (CE-LIF) with Conventional Techniques." *Forensic Science International*, 92 **1998**, 213–218.

26. Bergemann, D., et al. "Determination of Lysergic Acid Diethylamide in Body Fluids by High-performance Liquid Chromatography and Fluorescence Detection—a More Sensitive Method Suitable for Routine Use." *Journal of Forensic Sciences*, 44 **1999**, 372–374.

27. Allen, A., and T. Cantrell. "Synthetic Reductions in Clandestine Amphetamine and Methamphetamine Laboratories—a Review." *Forensic Science International*, 42 **1989**, 183–199.

28. Skinner, H. F. "Methamphetamine Synthesis via HI/Red Phosphorus Reduction of Ephedrine." *Forensic Science International*, 48 **1990**, 128–134.

29. Willers-Russo, L. J. "Three Fatalities Involving Phosphine Gas Produced as a Result of Methamphetamine Manufacturing." *Journal of Forensic Sciences*, 44 **1999**, 647–652.

30. Allen, A. C., and W. O. Kiser. "Methamphetamine from Ephedrine I: Choroepherines and Aziridines." *Journal of Forensic Sciences*, 32 **1987**, 953–962.

31. Koester, C. J., et al. "Criminalistics—Technical Notes—Optimum Methamphetamine Profiling with Sample Preparation by Solid-phase Microextraction." *Journal of Forensic Sciences*, 47 **2002**, 1002–1006.

32. Noggle, F. T. J., et al. "Liquid Chromatographic Determination of the Enantiomeric Composition of Methamphetamine Prepared from Ephedrine and Pseudoephedrine." *Analytical Chemistry*, 58 **1986**, 1643–1648.

33. Liau, A., et al. "Optimization of a Simple Method for the Chiral Separation of Methamphetamine and Related Compounds in Clandestine Tablets and Urine Samples by Beta-cyclodextrine Modifed Capillary Electrophoresis: A Complementary Method to GC–MS." *Forensic Science International*, 134 **2003**, 17–24.

34. Remberg, G., and A. H. Stead. "Drug Characterization/Impurity Profiling, with Special Focus on Methamphetamine: Recent Work of the United Nations International Drug Control Programme." *United Nations Office on Drugs and Crime: Bulletin on Narcotics*, 51 **1999**.

35. Andrews, K. M. "Ephedra's Role as a Precursor in the Clandestine Manufacture of Methamphetamine." *Journal of Forensic Sciences*, 40, no. 4, **1995**, 551–560.

36. "US Drug Enforcement Agency: Drug Intelligence Brief: MDMA-Ecstasy." June **1999**, U.S. Drug Enforcement agency. Available online, URL: www.dea.gov.

37. Christian, D. R. *Forensic Investigation of Clandestine Laboratories*, Boca Raton, FL: CRC Press, **2004**.

38. Cheng, W. C., et al. "Chemical Profiling of 3,4-Methylenedioxymethamphetamine (MDMA) Tablets Seized in Hong Kong." *Journal of Forensic Sciences*, 48 **2003**, 1249–1259.

39. *Drug Intelligence Brief: Khat*, U.S. Department of Justice, Drug Enforcement Agency, **June 2002**. Downloaded March 18, 2004.

40. Cole, M. D. "Chapter 7: Products from *Catha edulis* and *Lophophora williamsi*," in M. D. Cole, *The Analysis of Controlled Substances*. New York: Wiley, **2003**, 113–125.

41. Lehmann, T., et al. "Rapid TLC Identification Test for Khat (*Catha edulis*)." *Forensic Science International*, 45, no. 1–2, **1990**, 47–51.

42. El-Haj, B. M., et al. "The Use of Cyclohexanone as a "Derivatizing" Reagent for the GC–MS Detection of Amphetamines and Ephedrines in Seizures and the Urine." *Forensic Science International*, 135 **2003**, 16–26.

43. Lebelle, M. J., et al. "Gas Chromatographic–Mass Spectrometric Identification of Chiral Derivatives of the Alkaloids of KHAT." *Forensic Science International*, 61 **1993**, 53–64.

44. Sporkert, F., et al. "Determination of Cathinone, Cathine and Norephedrine in Hair of Yemenite Khat Chewers." *Forensic Science International*, 133 **2003**, 39–46.

45. Dawson, B. A., et al. "Nuclear Magnetic Resonance Identification of the Phenylalkylamine Alkaloids of Khat Using a Chiral Solvating Agent." *Journal of Forensic Sciences*, 39, no. 4, **1994**, 1026.

46. Shin, H.-S., and M. Donike. "Stereospecific Derivatization of Amphetamines, Phenol Alkylamines, and Hydroxamines and Quantitation of the Enantiomers by Capillary GC/MS." *Analytical Chemistry*, 68 **1996**, 3015–3020.

47. Cheng, W.-C., et al. "Enantiomeric Separation of Methamphetamine and Related Analogs by Capillary Zone Electrophoresis: Intelligence Study in Routine Methamphetamine Seizures." *Journal of Forensic Sciences*, 47 **2002**, 1248–1252.

48. Nielsen, M. W. F. "Chiral Separations of Basic Drugs Using Cyclodextrin-modified Capillary Zone Electrophoresis." *Analytical Chemistry*, 65 **1993**, 885–893.

49. Schafstall, H. Personal communication, Oklahoma State Bureau of Investigation.

50. Moenssens, A. A., et al. *Scientific Evidence in Civil and Criminal Cases*, 4th ed. Westbury, NY: The Foundation Press, Inc., **1995**.

51. Drug Enforcement Adminstration (DEA), *Drug Intelligence Brief: PCP: The Threat Remains*. Available on-line, www.dea.gov. 2003.

52. Sternbach, L. H. "The Benzodiazepine Story." *Journal of Medicinal Chemistry*, 22 **1979**, 1–7.

CHAPTER

9

The Chemistry of Combustion and Arson

9.1 The Combustion Continuum
9.2 Four Aspects of Combustion
9.3 Combustion, Deflagration, and Detonation
9.4 Deflagration and Fires
9.5 Explosives

OVERVIEW

This and the next chapter will tackle the second most important work area (behind drug analysis and toxicology) in forensic chemistry. We'll begin with an exploration of the fundamentals of combustion, a specialized type of oxidation--reduction that spans candle flames to powerful and destructive explosions. The important differences between a fire and a bomb are the speed at which the combustion occurs and the degree to which is it confined. As we'll see, combustion is a continuum. Forensically, combustion is the process at the heart of arson, bombing, and, perhaps less obviously, gunshot residue. In this chapter, we'll cover the fundamental principles that underlie these three types of forensic cases and evidence. In Chapter 10, we'll delve into the analysis of combustion evidence.

9.1 THE COMBUSTION CONTINUUM

Combustion is an oxidative decomposition in which oxygen (the oxidant) oxidizes a fuel. The different manifestations of combustion (Figure 9.1), ranging from a gentle candle flame to a violent military explosive are part of a continuum that includes the **propellants** used in firearms. What is normally described as "burning"— that which is associated with a flame—is defined as **deflagration**, whereas explosions are **detonations**. The dividing line between the two is the

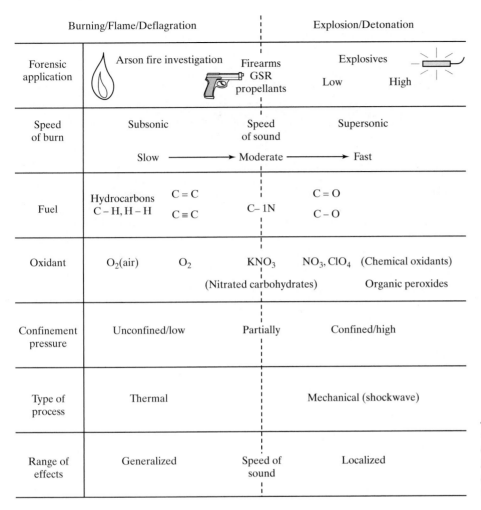

	Burning/Flame/Deflagration		Explosion/Detonation	
Forensic application	Arson fire investigation	Firearms GSR propellants	Explosives Low High	
Speed of burn	Subsonic	Speed of sound	Supersonic	
	Slow ⟶	Moderate ⟶	Fast	
Fuel	Hydrocarbons $C-H, H-H$ $C=C$ $C\equiv C$	$C-1N$	$C=O$ $C-O$	
Oxidant	O_2(air) O_2	KNO_3 (Nitrated carbohydrates)	NO_3, ClO_4 (Chemical oxidants) Organic peroxides	
Confinement pressure	Unconfined/low	Partially	Confined/high	
Type of process	Thermal		Mechanical (shockwave)	
Range of effects	Generalized	Speed of sound	Localized	

◀ **Figure 9.1** *The continuum of combustion. The dividing line between deflagration and detonation is the speed at which the reaction front propagates.*

speed at which the combustion wave, or reaction front, moves. In deflagration, the flame front moves slower than the speed of sound, while in a detonation, the reaction front moves faster than the speed of sound.[†] As the front's speed increases, oxygen from the atmosphere is incapable of sustaining it, and additional oxygen must come from another source such as potassium nitrate (KNO_3, or saltpeter). The fuel must also change as the energy derived from it increases.

Combustion is an exothermic reaction in which reactants are converted to principally gaseous products. Because the reaction is exothermic, the product gases heat up and expand. In a fire, such as arson, this expansion generates plumes with predictable behaviors that leave distinctive markings at the crime scene. In contrast, propellants rely on expansion of hot gases to drive a projectile forward, while explosives confine the expansion as long as possible to generate a destructive shock wave. Because of this confinement, a detonation is a

[†]In air at 0°, the speed of sound is 331.3 m s^{-1}, or ~741 miles per hour. The speed of sound depends on the nature and density of the medium through which it passes. Formally, $V = \sqrt{E/\rho}$ where E is the modulus of elasticity of the medium and ρ is the density. For comparison, the speed of sound in water at 25° is approximately 3350 miles per hour and in glass at 20° is over 11,000 miles per hour. *Source:* Daintith, J., and J. O. E. Clark, *The Facts on File Dictionary of Physics*, 3d ed. New York: Facts on File, 1996.

mechanical process, whereas deflagration is a thermal one. This critical distinction will be discussed in detail in the next section.

Historical Evidence 9.1— Salt, Peter?

An older name for the salt KNO_3 (potassium nitrate) is saltpeter (also spelled salt Peter and salt peter), which is used as a chemical oxidant in gunpowder and explosives. Saltpeter is a mineral that forms when organic material such as waste, decaying plants, and animal manure is placed in contact with soil high in alkali content (such as limestone). Saltpeter is found on the earth's surface as well as in caves and is easily collected and mined. The first recorded mention of saltpeter was from a Taoist alchemist writing and working in the ninth century. Although the mineral was once used for medicinal purposes, demand "skyrocketed" with the invention of gunpowder and explosives. Lammont du Pont, of the famous du Pont family of chemists, was able to patent a method of making blasting powder without saltpeter, a much more economical approach. Unfortunately, he died in 1884 while experimenting with dynamite and sulfuric acid. Du Pont and several of his assistants were literally blown apart in the accident.

Sources: Harmon, M. B. "Gunpowder, Ingenuity, Madness, and Murder: The Saga of the du Ponts." *Biography*, November 2002, 92.

Morrison, P., and P. Morrison (October 1999). "Nitrogen: The Dark Side." *Scientific American*, **281**: 125–126.

Combustion requires reactants and enough energy to exceed the energy of activation (E_a) required to initiate the reaction. The reaction profile shown in Figure 9.2 illustrates the exothermic nature of a combustion, reaction, as well as the need for enough energy to initiate it. Once initiated, enough energy is produced to supply the necessary E_a to sustain the reaction until one of the reactants is exhausted. With a simple flame, the fuel is exhausted first, since the oxidant is atmospheric oxygen. When chemical oxidants are employed, either fuel or oxidant may be the limiting reagent.

The energy released in a combustion reaction results from the increased stability (lower potential energy) of the products relative to the reactants. The

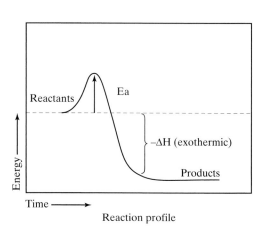

▶ **Figure 9.2** *A generic reaction profile for combustion, along with a simple example of a combustion reaction. Combustion is a specialized type of redox reaction.*

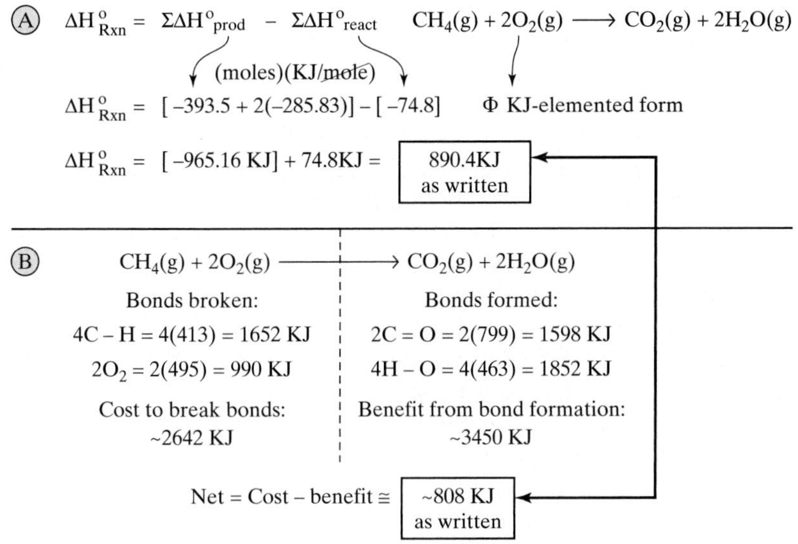

(A) $\quad \Delta H^{o}_{Rxn} = \Sigma \Delta H^{o}_{prod} - \Sigma \Delta H^{o}_{react} \quad CH_4(g) + 2O_2(g) \longrightarrow CO_2(g) + 2H_2O(g)$

$\quad\quad\quad\quad\quad\quad \overset{\text{(moles)(KJ/mole)}}{\searrow} \quad\quad\quad \downarrow$

$\Delta H^{o}_{Rxn} = [-393.5 + 2(-285.83)] - [-74.8] \quad \Phi$ KJ-elemented form

$\Delta H^{o}_{Rxn} = [-965.16 \text{ KJ}] + 74.8 \text{KJ} = \boxed{\begin{array}{c} 890.4 \text{KJ} \\ \text{as written} \end{array}}$

(B) $\quad\quad CH_4(g) + 2O_2(g) \longrightarrow CO_2(g) + 2H_2O(g)$

Bonds broken:	Bonds formed:
$4C - H = 4(413) = 1652$ KJ	$2C = O = 2(799) = 1598$ KJ
$2O_2 = 2(495) = 990$ KJ	$4H - O = 4(463) = 1852$ KJ
Cost to break bonds:	Benefit from bond formation:
~2642 KJ	~3450 KJ

Net = Cost − benefit ≅ $\boxed{\begin{array}{c} \text{~808 KJ} \\ \text{as written} \end{array}}$

◀ **Figure 9.3** *Two methods of estimating how much energy is released by a combustion reaction. In the top frame (A), ΔH° is calculated from table values while in (B), the energy balance between bonds broken and bonds formed is used.*

energy (ΔH) released can be estimated with the two methods shown in Figure 9.3. The first method is based on table values (found in Appendix 13) of thermodynamic quantities under standard conditions of temperature and pressure (STP, 25°C and 1 atm). The second method calculates how much energy is required to break the chemical bonds in the reactants and form the bonds of the products. As shown in the figure, this result should be relatively close to that determined from the table values; however, the quantities calculated are only used as starting points, because the combustion reactions encountered in forensic chemistry are complex and rarely occur close to STP.

Some readers may be familiar with the fire triangle which is one way of summarizing the requirements for a combustion reaction. Such a triangle is divided into three regions, identified as fuel, oxidant, and heat (the last of which supplies E_a). Building on the concept of the triangle, we will consider the requirements for combustion to be

1. Fuel and oxidant in appropriate quantities and concentrations.
2. A source of E_a.
3. Sufficient contact time for the energy source to initiate the reaction.

The absence of any one factor prevents combustion, and we will delve into the particulars of each in the pages ahead.

Example Problem 9.1

Does a combustion reaction such as a burning candle have a negative or positive value for the change in free energy?

Answer: Recall that any spontaneous reaction (in the forward direction, as written) has a negative ΔG value and that ΔG depends on the change in enthalpy (ΔH) and entropy (ΔS, disorder). The relationship between these three quantities is

$$\Delta G = \Delta H - T\Delta S$$

where T is the temperature. A combustion reaction is exothermic (negative ΔH) and also increases disorder (positive ΔS) by generating gaseous products at high temperatures. These factors combine to drive ΔG to large negative values. The reaction is spontaneous, but still requires that enough energy be input to exceed E_a.

The first requirement, fuel and oxidant in proper proportions, illustrates key points and unmasks common misconceptions. Wood does not burn; rather, what burns are the vapors emanating from heated wood. Gasoline in a can will not explode because the proper fuel–air mixture does not exist. A cigarette tossed into a pool of gasoline usually smothers before it has a chance to ignite the vapor above it. Similarly, the Hollywood staple of exploding gas tanks in cars is more fiction than fact. Deflagration can occur, but only when the gas tank is ruptured, the contents leak and vaporize, and the proper air–fuel vapor mixture is created at the same time and place as a source of ignition that stays in contact long enough to spark the reaction.

These foregoing three requirements can be further restated and categorized into manageable topics that will be addressed next. We will attack combustion from four complementary aspects, starting with thermodynamic considerations. Then we'll discuss the kinetics (the relative speed of combustion), which depends on the mechanism of the reaction. How heat is transported is critical in determining burn patterns and direction, while how mass is transferred can dictate when a fire will burn and when it will not.

9.2 FOUR ASPECTS OF COMBUSTION

Consider a simple model of combustion: burning wood (Figure 9.4). Once the fire is burning, heat must be transferred efficiently to the wood to vaporize reactants. Heat transfer is also needed to ensure that E_a is overcome and the reaction is self-sustaining. Specifically, the activation energy must be sufficient to form free radicals, the heart of combustion reaction mechanisms. Oxygen must move into the reaction zone via transfer and the rate of this transfer directly affects the reaction. Think of blowing across a smoldering fire, an action that increases the efficiency of mass transport of oxygen and speeds the reaction by supplying more oxidizing agent. The kinetics (speed) of combustion depends on the rate of formation of free radicals in the flame flickering above the wood. The reaction speed also depends on multiple rate constants and reactant concentrations in multiple connected chain-reaction pathways. The heat evolved, favored pathways, and the balance of products will all depend on thermodynamic considerations, including stoichiometric ratios and equilibria. Thus, while we'll address each of these topics individually, all act and interact to control and define the complex process of combustion.

9.2.1 THERMODYNAMICS

Thermodynamics relates to concepts of energy flow, enthalpy (H), entropy (S), free energy (G), and equilibrium.[†] The first law of thermodynamics can be roughly stated as energy is neither created nor destroyed, but only changes form. In combustion and in explosions, potential energy in chemical bonds (chemical energy) is converted to heat and work. Energy is defined as the ability to do work and can be categorized by the type of work done. For example, there is chemical energy, potential energy, mechanical energy, and kinetic energy. The second law of thermodynamics relates to entropy and (again, roughly) states that, in any spontaneous process, the disorder of the universe increases. Entropy increases during combustion because gaseous products are formed and

[†]Equilibrium is defined as the point at which $\Delta G = 0$.

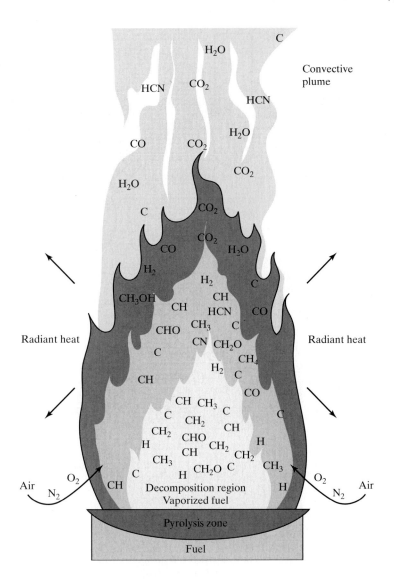

◄ **Figure 9.4** *The combustion of wood (fuel), illustrating the four aspects described in the text. Note the complexity of what would at first seem to be a simple chemical reaction.*

heat is released by the exothermic reaction. Molecules move faster at higher temperatures relative to molecules at lower temperatures, resulting in increased disorder.

The free energy change of any reaction, including combustion, is defined by enthalpy and entropy:

$$\Delta G = \Delta H - T\Delta S \tag{9.1}$$

As shown in Example Problem 9.1, the combination of an exothermic reaction with increasing disorder leads to a large negative value for the change in free energy (ΔG). ΔG also is a measure of how much work can be done by a system in a spontaneous reaction. Work can be divided into two components: actual work (w) and heat (q). Both aspects come into play across the combustion continuum.

In chemical applications, the most common type of work is pressure–volume work. Examples are shown in Figure 9.5. The top frame illustrates how the evolution of a gas (H_2) in a spontaneous process is used to do PV work in a system

a.

b.

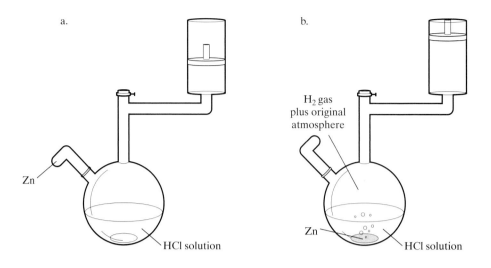

H$_2$ gas
plus original
atmosphere

Zn

HCl solution

Zn

HCl solution

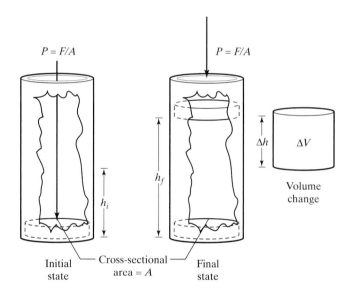

$P = F/A$

$P = F/A$

h_i

h_f

Δh

ΔV

Volume
change

Initial
state

Cross-sectional
area = A

Final
state

▶ **Figure 9.5** *Two illustrations of PV work. In the top frame, zinc metal is dropped into acid and pressure exerted by the evolving gas raises the piston. In the lower frame, pressure is defined as force per unit area (F/A), but the concept is the same and the PΔV term can be calculated geometrically by using the volume of a cylinder. For the piston to move, work of quantity −PΔV must be done by the system. An example of this mechanism is gasoline burning in the cylinder of an internal combustion engine.*

in which heat is a minor contributor. The lower frame depicts the relationship between PV, work, and force. To move the piston, work—specifically, PV work—must be done and the force acting inside the cylinder must exceed the force exerted by atmospheric pressure.

Forensic examples involving energy and illustrating how work is done are shown in Figures 9.6 and 9.7. In Figure 9.6, a bullet is propelled out of a gun by PV work done by expanding gases produced by the burning propellant. Here, the bullet is analogous to the piston, (Figure 9.5) which is moved as a result of the production of gas. In the gun, primer ignites when struck by the hammer, provides the initial E_a spark, and initiates combustion, which produces heat and hot expanding gases. The bullet is held in the cartridge by compression and friction, but the joint is designed to give way once sufficient pressure builds up. The result is movement of the bullet down the barrel, just like movement of the piston shown in Figure 9.5, except that the force must overcome the compression and friction forces holding the bullet in place. As gas expansion continues, much of the energy is transferred to the bullet as kinetic energy. The energy

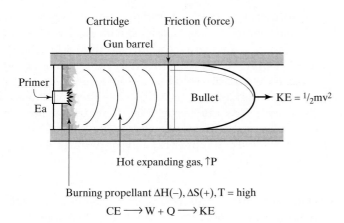

KE = $\frac{1}{2}mv^2$

◀ **Figure 9.6** *How a combustion reaction is used to create sufficient energy to do the work of moving a bullet out of a gun barrel.*

trace of a gun firing can be summarized as a mechanical energy (hammer striking primer) $\longrightarrow$ chemical energy $\longrightarrow$ heat and work (heat and mechanical) $\longrightarrow$ kinetic energy. This progression can be simplified to ME $\longrightarrow$ CE $\longrightarrow$ ME (and heat) $\longrightarrow$ KE.

For a crude pipe bomb (Figure 9.7) made of galvanized steel pipe and gunpowder, the energy pathway is the same. What differs is that no joint is designed to fail as was the case with the gun firing. A pipe bomb is a mechanically stronger containment device that allows pressure to build until it exceeds the strength of the container at its weakest point. The pipe shatters and ejects sharp shrapnel in all directions. In contrast, a gun is designed to focus and direct the gas expansion and work in order to impart the most kinetic energy to a single projectile traveling in one direction.

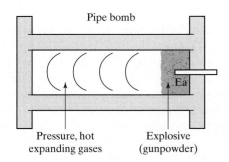

KE = $\frac{1}{2}mv^2$

◀ **Figure 9.7** *A pipe bomb is designed to rupture and not to fail at a specific joint. The result is catastrophic destruction of the container and the ejection of sharp shrapnel moving at high speed.*

Before going further, we should introduce terminology to eliminate the negative–positive sign confusion often associated with the heat of reaction and the release of heat. All combustions are exothermic, all release heat, and all have a negative value for $\Delta H°_{reaction}$. The heat released by the system is absorbed by the surroundings and is always positive. In the examples just discussed, the system is the burning propellant or the detonating explosive. These reactions release heat to the surroundings, such as the gun barrel. For this discussion, heat released will be referred to as Q, in keeping with traditional thermochemical notation. In combustion, Q is always positive and numerically the opposite of $\Delta H°_{reaction}$:

$$Q = -(\Delta H°_{reaction}) \tag{9.2}$$

We will also assume that combustion is **adiabatic** combustion—that is, that the heat released is used only to heat the products and that there is no heat exchange to the surroundings. Again, using the gun example, if the firing process is adiabatic, it means that all of the heat evolved is consumed by heating of the products created by the combustion reaction. Of course this is only an approximation, but a useful one.

Heating the products also increases their kinetic energy. This heating causes pressure to increase as per the ideal-gas law:

$$PV = nRT \tag{9.3}$$

This law shows that temperature is directly proportional to pressure and volume. In the case of an explosive, the higher the pressure generated, the more powerful is the explosive. The power of an explosive can be defined as VQ, where V is the volume of gaseous products and Q is the heat evolved.[1] Thus, the most powerful explosives (per gram) are those which create the largest number of moles (n) of gas at the highest temperatures. A common way to express this relationship is via a modification of the ideal-gas law[1]:

$$F = nRT_e \tag{9.4}$$

where F is force of the explosive, n is moles of gas produced, and T_e is the temperature of the resulting product mix.

The value of Q (used to heat the products to T_e) is central to explosive power. Figure 9.3 illustrated two methods of calculation of the heat of reaction, but of more interest here is gauging the relative heat generated per gram of fuel. Also, the calculations shown in that figure assume that the fuel and oxidant are in stoichiometric equivalence, meaning that the balance of concentrations of fuel and oxidant exactly match the stoichiometric balance. In the case of methane combustion (Figure 9.2), if 1.0 mole of methane was present when the reaction started, then, at stoichiometric equivalence, there would be exactly 2.0 moles of O_2 present. This situation, however, is rarely encountered, and as a result, both the products of the reaction and the heat evolved will be affected. Therefore, a brief discussion of the **stoichiometric ratio** is warranted.

Φ is defined as the oxidant–fuel ratio in a combustion mixture, divided by the oxidant–fuel ratio at stoichiometric equivalence:

$$\Phi = \frac{\left(\dfrac{F}{O}\right)_{SYS}}{\left(\dfrac{F}{O}\right)_{STE}} = \frac{\left(\dfrac{M_F}{M_O}\right)_{SYS}}{\left(\dfrac{M_F}{M_O}\right)_{STE}} \tag{9.5}$$

Example Problem 9.2

Assuming that conditions are such that methane (CH_4) and methanol (CH_3OH) combust via an explosion, which is the more powerful per gram detonated?

Answer: To answer this question, the value of heat released (Q or ΔH) for each compound is needed, as well as the number of moles of gas produced. Use the thermodynamic values provided in Appendix 13 to determine Q per mole combusted. Some assumptions are necessary, but for a rough comparison, this approach is acceptable.

$$CH_4 + O_2 \longrightarrow CO_2(g) + 2H_2O(g)$$

$\dfrac{\Delta Hg}{KJ/mole}$	-74.8		-393.5	-241.82	
moles	1.0		1.0	2.0	(3.0 total)
g	1.0				
moles per gram	0.063		0.063	0.125	(0.19 total per gram)

$$\frac{0.19 \times 22.4L}{mole} \cong 4.3L/g$$

$$\Delta H^{\circ}_R = [-393.5 + 2(-241.82)] - (-74.8)$$

$$= -802.3KJ \qquad = \frac{-50.1KJ}{mole\ CH_4} \qquad \frac{}{gCH_4(g)} \cdot Q \cong \frac{50KJ}{gCH_4}$$

$$CH_3OH(g) + 3O_2 \longrightarrow 2CO_2(g) + 4H_2O(g)$$

2 moles $\longrightarrow$ 6 moles gas

$$\frac{moles}{g} \quad 0.0313 \longrightarrow 0.0313\ moles + 0.0625\ moles$$
$$\text{or calculated as above,} \quad \frac{2.1L}{gCH_3OH}$$

$$\Delta H^{\circ}_{Rxn} = [2(-393.5) + 2(-241.82)] - (-238.6)$$

$$\Delta H^{\circ}_{Rxn} = \frac{-1032KJ}{2\ mole\ CH_3OH} = \frac{-516KJ}{mole} \cong \frac{16KJ}{gCH_3OH}$$

$$\frac{QV_{CH_4}}{g} \cong 50 \times 4.3 = 215 \qquad QV_{CH_3OH} = (16)(2.1)$$
$$\text{Difference is} \sim \text{a factor of 6} \qquad \approx 34$$

Notice that, in balancing the equations, clearing the fractions was not necessary, since the oxygen does not contribute to Q. The combustion of a gram of methanol produces about half the gas volume as does the combustion of methane.

where F is the fuel, O is the oxidant, STE is the ratio at stoichiometric equivalence, SYS is the ratio of the system of interest, and M is mass.

As Φ decreases below 1.0, the amount of fuel relative to the amount of oxidant decreases and the mixture becomes **lean**. In chemical terms, the system is overoxidized, and, if the fuel concentration drops too low relative to the oxidant, combustion cannot take place. When Φ is greater than 1.0, there is more fuel relative to the oxidant, the mixture is **rich**, and the system is underoxidized, which can also be taken to an extreme at which combustion is impossible. An underoxidized system favors production of the less oxidized product and releases less heat.

The calculation of Φ is an important one and can assist in determining such properties as potential flammability of mixtures. Returning to the combustion of methane as our example, the molar ratio of methane to oxygen in a balanced equation at stoichiometric equivalence is 1:2 respectively. Since the types of combustion of interest here take place in air, additional corrections are required. Assuming that the atmosphere is 21% oxygen, the number of moles of air supplied must be adjusted upward. A mole of air will contain 0.21 moles of O_2; to obtain one mole of O_2, we need to multiply this by 4.76(0.21 * 4.76 = 1.0). One last adjustment is to multiply this value by 2 since the complete combustion of one mole of methane requires 2 moles of oxygen. This is easily converted to a mass ratio using the formula weight of methane $(16.0 \text{ g mol}^{-1})$ and the weighted average mass of air generally taken to be 28.85 g mol^{-1}:

$$\left(\frac{M_F}{M_O}\right)_{STE} = \frac{(16.0 \text{ g mol}^{-1})(1 \text{ mole})}{(2.0 \text{ moles O}_2)\left(\frac{4.76 \text{ moles air}}{\text{mole O}_2}\right)\left(\frac{28.85g}{\text{mole air}}\right)} = 0.0583 \quad (9.6)$$

Thus, at stoichiometric equivalence, the mass ratio F/O is 0.0583.

Now consider an example in which 5.0 grams of methane is released into a container of air with a volume of 20.0 L at a temperature of 25°C. To determine if the resulting mixture is combustible, rich, or lean, the mass ratios of fuel to air are calculated and compared to the ratio at STE just calculated. The first step is to obtain mole ratios via partial pressures and the ideal gas law:

$$P_{CH_4} = \frac{nRT}{V} = \frac{\left(\frac{5.0 \text{ g}}{16.0 \text{ g mol}^{-1}}\right)\left(0.0821 \frac{\text{Latm}}{\text{mol k}}\right)(298 \text{ k})}{20.0 \text{ L}} = 0.38$$

therefore, $P_{air} = 0.62$ (9.7)

These mole fractions are converted to mass using formula weights:

$$M_{CH_4} = M_F = (0.38 \text{ moles})(16.0 \text{ g mol}^{-1}) = 6.08 \text{ g}$$

$$M_{air} = M_O = (0.62 \text{ moles})(28.85 \text{ g mol}^{-1}) = 17.89 \text{ g} \quad (9.8)$$

The last step is to determine Φ using equation 9–5:

$$\Phi = \frac{\left(\frac{M_F}{M_O}\right)_{SYS}}{0.0583} = \frac{\frac{6.08 \text{ g}}{17.89 \text{ g}}}{0.0583} = 5.83 \quad (9.9)$$

The mixture in the container is rich and would be plotted as a point to the right of the peak in Figure 9.8.

Staying with our methane example, Figure 9.9 illustrates how rich and lean mixtures alter the heat evolved. The heat released at stoichiometric equivalence was previously calculated (Figure 9.3); note that the heats of formation for water (in gas or liquid form) and methane are constants in this combustion and the contribution of elemental O_2 is zero. As a result, the expression for calculating $\Delta H°$ in order to compare the three reactions depicted in the figure can be simplified as:

$$\Delta H°_{reaction} = X_{CO}\Delta H°_{CO(g)} + X_{CO_2}\Delta H°_{CO_2(g)} \quad (9.10)$$

$$\Delta H°_{reaction} = X_{CO}(-110.5 \text{ KJ mol}^{-1}) + X_{CO_2}(-393.5 \text{ KJ mol}^{-1}) \quad (9.11)$$

where X_i represents the mole fraction of each species produced. The most negative value (the largest Q) occurs when only CO_2 is produced. Any carbon monoxide produced decreases the heat released, since the overall heat of the reaction becomes more positive ($\Delta H°_{reaction}$ becomes less negative). Thus, underoxidized systems, which favor CO production, release less heat than do systems at stoichiometric equivalence. However, if there is excess oxidant, some of the heat evolved is diverted to heat that oxidant, rather than just the products, as we assumed in the adiabatic combustion model. As a result of heat diversion, Q decreases from the maximum produced at stoichiometric equivalence, at which Q is used only to heat products.

The discussion becomes more interesting when we examine reactions in which the oxidant is not atmospheric oxygen or in which the source of oxygen is chemical, as in the case of explosives such as TNT or nitroglycerin (Figure 9.10). With these explosives, part of the oxidant is supplied by the molecule, part is supplied by the atmosphere, and the ratio is expressed as the **oxygen balance**. As shown in Figure 9.11, nitroglycerin has a positive oxygen balance, meaning that when the explosive decomposes to gaseous products, the explosive molecule itself can supply all the needed oxygen, with some to spare. The reverse is true for explosives such as TNT, which require oxygen from the atmosphere or another chemical source. When the oxygen balance is negative and relatively large, CO will form in preference to CO_2. In other words, the system is underoxidized and lean. The oxygen balance can also be expressed as a weight-percentage-like quantity derived from the ratio:

$$\frac{\text{mass O released or consumed}}{\text{mass of explosive}} \quad (9.12)$$

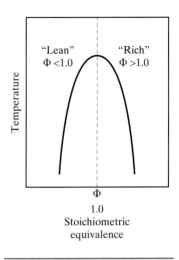

▲ **Figure 9.8** *Temperature of a flame as a function of stoichiometric ratios.*

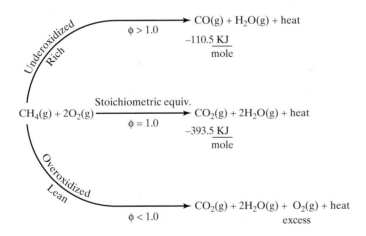

◀ **Figure 9.9** *How underoxidation and overoxidation affect heat released.*

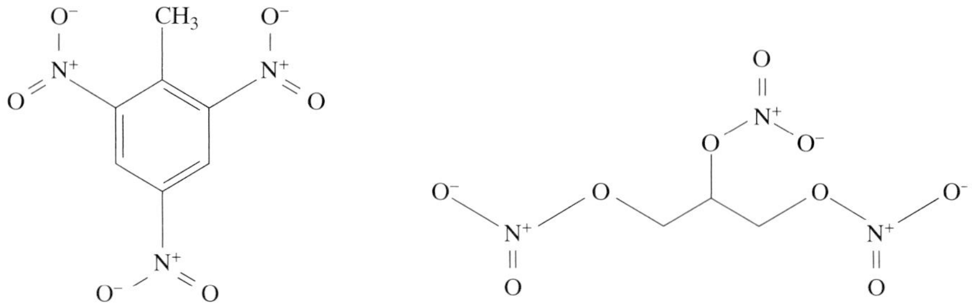

▶ **Figure 9.10**   Trinitrotoluene (2,4,6 TNT) $C_7H_5N_3O_6$ Nitroglycerin $C_3H_5N_3O_9$

Example Problem 9.3.

For combustion of a hydrocarbon such as methane or ethane, is the oxygen balance positive or negative?

Answer: Always negative. There is no oxygen in the molecule.

Nitroglycerin: $C_3\,H_5\,N_3\,O_9$

$$C_3\,H_5\,N_3\,O_9 \longrightarrow 3CO_2 + {}^5/_2H_2O + {}^3/_2N_2$$

$$9 \text{ oxygen} \longrightarrow 6 + 2.50 = 8.50$$

$$C_3\,H_5\,N_3\,O_9 \longrightarrow 3CO_2 + 5H_2O + {}^3/_2N_2 + {}^1/_2O_2$$

Positive oxygen balance

TNT: $C_7\,H_5\,N_3\,O_6$

$$C_7\,H_5\,N_3\,O_6 \longrightarrow 7CO_2 + {}^5/_2H_2O + {}^3/_2N_2$$

$$6 \text{ oxygen} \longrightarrow 14 + 2.5 = \underline{16.50}$$

▶ **Figure 9.11** *Sample oxygen balance calculations for explosives.*

$$C_7\,H_5\,N_3\,O_6 \longrightarrow 7CO_2 + {}^5/_2H_2O + {}^3/_2N_2 - 10.5O_2$$

which, for TNT, would be calculated as

$$\frac{10.5 \times 16}{227} \times 100 = -74\% \tag{9.13}$$

The $(-)$ sign means O_2 is consumed; a $(+)$ sign means O_2 is released.

Table 9.1 gives the oxygen balance of some representative explosives.[1]

The concept of oxygen balance is analogous to the definition of a rich or lean mixture of fuel vs. oxidant. The difference is that the oxygen balance is internal to

Table 9.1 Oxygen Balance of Representative Explosives

Explosive	Oxygen Balance
Ammonium nitrate	+20%
Nitroglycerin	+4
Picric acid	−45
TNT	−74

the fuel molecule; in other words, the molecule supplies both fuel and at least part of the oxidant. Because the oxygen ratio is related to stoichiometric ratios, it also relates to the heat release Q. When a given explosive is the only material combusted, the more positive the oxygen balance, the greater is the heat released. By itself, TNT does not generate as much heat as a compound such as nitroglycerin. However, explosives are often combined in a manner that their combined oxygen balance approaches zero, which corresponds to $\Phi = 1.0$, or stoichiometric equivalence. For example, suppose an explosive mixture consists of TNT and nitroglycerin. To maximize Q, the combined oxygen balance should be as close to zero as possible. TNT has a large negative oxygen balance, while nitroglycerin has a small positive balance. Clearly, then, the mixture should contain a little TNT and lots of nitroglycerin. The calculation is shown in Figure 9.12.

9.2.2 KINETICS OF COMBUSTION

Kinetics is the study of the speed of reactions and their mechanisms. Combustion is a complex free-radical process in which many reactions can occur and in which a complex mixture of products forms. The pathways favored and resulting products depend on which reactions are favored under the given conditions. In turn, the speed of a reaction is the key in differentiating deflagration from explosion.

Two components: $x =$ fraction NG
$1 - x =$ fraction TNT

$$4x + \underbrace{(1 - x)(-74)}_{\text{negative}} = 0$$

(+) Oxygen balance

$$4x + 74x - 74 = 0$$
$$78x = 74$$
$$x = 0.95 \qquad 95\% \text{ NG}$$
$$1 - x = 0.05 \qquad 5\% \text{ TNT}$$

$$4(0.95) + 0.05(-74)$$
$$\Downarrow \qquad \Downarrow \qquad \approx 0$$
$$3.8 \qquad -3.7$$

▲ **Figure 9.12** *Oxygen balance calculations when a mix of explosives is used.*

Combustion processes can be described with the collisional model of reactions, an idea based on kinetic molecular theory, which also underlies the ideal-gas law. In this model, three criteria must be met for a reaction to occur:

- There must be a collision between the species that will react.
- This collision must have sufficient energy to overcome the activation energy barrier E_a.
- The collision must occur with the reacting species in the proper orientation.

If these conditions are met, the reaction proceeds at a given rate k described by the Arrhenius equation

$$k = Ae^{\frac{-E_a}{RT}} \tag{9.14}$$

where k is the rate constant, A is the frequency factor that describes the likelihood of a successful collision, R is the gas law constant, and T is the temperature. A incorporates orientation considerations. As the temperature increases, the value of the exponent will become less negative and the rate constant will become larger. The frequency factor is temperature dependent, but this dependence is relatively small. Consequently, A is assumed to be a constant. The reasons temperature increases reaction rate are related to the aforementioned three requirements. The hotter the system, the faster the molecules are moving. This faster motion increases their energy and also the overall frequency of collisions, thus increasing the rate. Consequently, the greater the value of Q, the faster the reactions will proceed.

Combustion does not involve simple single-step collisions between a fuel molecule and an oxidant. Rather, the reactions that occur during combustion are based on free radicals. In a free-radical[4] mechanism, three generic steps take place:

- *Initiation*, in which the first free radicals are formed
- *Propagation*, in which reactions among radicals produce more radicals
- *Termination*, which results from the combination of two free radicals to form a neutral species.

Exhibit A: It's a Radical Difference

Radicals form when a bond such as H—H in H_2 is cleaved homolytically: $H_2 \longrightarrow 2\,H\cdot$. A heterolytic cleavage would send two electrons to one atom and none to the other: $H : H \longrightarrow H^+ + H:^-$. That which causes the formation of the free radical is called the initiator, which may be a chemical species or energy such as UV light. In forensic situations, peroxides (ROOR) are frequently encountered as free-radical initiators: $ROOR \longrightarrow 2\,RO\cdot$. The relative stability of radicals is comparable to that of carbocations, with tertiary free radicals being the most stable and primary the least.

Because radicals react with neutrals to create new radicals, a chain reaction results. Each step in a generic free-radical reaction has an associated rate constant. One of these steps will be the slowest and is termed the rate-limiting step. Just as the slowest member of a relay team limits its performance, the rate-limiting step limits the speed of the chemical reaction. The rate-limiting step is generally the step with the highest energy of activation. Partial and simplified steps for the combustion–oxidation of hydrogen is shown in Figure 9.13.

$CO + O_2 \longrightarrow CO_2 + \cdot O$	Initiation
$\cdot O + H_2O \longrightarrow \cdot OH + \cdot OH$	Propagation
$CO + \cdot OH \longrightarrow CO_2 + \cdot H$	
$\cdot H + \cdot OH \longrightarrow H_2O$	Termination

◀ **Figure 9.13** *Sample free-radical reactions that occur in a flame.*

The combustion of even a simple hydrocarbon such as methane is extraordinarily complex. A recent count revealed 277 known elementary reactions for this well-studied combustion involving 49 different chemical species.[3] Compare this with the combustion of an accelerant such as gasoline, itself a complex mixture of hydrocarbons, and the task of modeling the combustion becomes impossible. Fortunately, in forensic chemical applications, the most important point is that complex and competitive free-radical pathways lead to a mixture of products.

9.2.3 HEAT TRANSFER

Heat transfer and heat flow in combustion begins with the premise that all the heat Q evolved in the process goes into heating the products and raising their temperature.[†] In other words, we assume an adiabatic flame. Excess oxidant (a lean mix) reduces temperature, because Q must be distributed to excess reactant as well as to the products. There are other places heat can and must flow to sustain combustion, some of which were seen in Figure 9.4 and which are also shown in simplified form in Figure 9.14. Heated air is less dense than cooler air, and as a result, much of the radiant heat produced in a simple combustion like a burning candle is carried away in rising air and gases. This kind of combustion is also called a *buoyant flame*. Heat is required as well for phase transitions, as shown in Figure 9.15. In the candle, the wax must first be melted to liquid and vaporized before combustion occurs. For

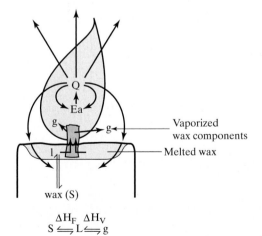

Vaporized wax components

Melted wax

wax (S)

$$S \underset{\Delta H_F}{\overset{}{\rightleftharpoons}} L \underset{\Delta H_V}{\overset{}{\rightleftharpoons}} g$$

◀ **Figure 9.14** *Simplified heat flow paths in a candle flame.*

[†]Our discussion here will focus on heat transfer via convection (matter transport), but heating by conduction and radiation also take place.

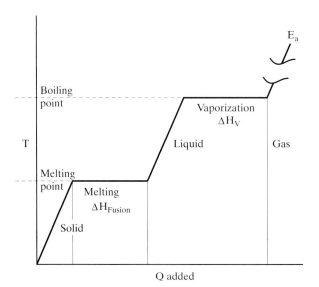

▶ **Figure 9.15** *Some of the heat generated by the combustion is consumed in the necessary phase transitions of the fuel.*

some heavier hydrocarbons, the melting point and heat needed to vaporize them can be quite high. If Q dwindles, so will the supply of vaporized fuel.

Heat transfer to the substrate has interesting effects on fire behavior and arson investigation. As shown in Figure 9.16 (top frame), heat may reach deep into a substrate such as wood even when oxygen cannot. The result is **pyrolysis** ("fire cutting") or decomposition in a reducing environment. We discussed pyrolysis in Section 5.5.2 in the context of an inlet to a gas chromatograph, and the same principles apply here. The products of pyrolysis are different from those of

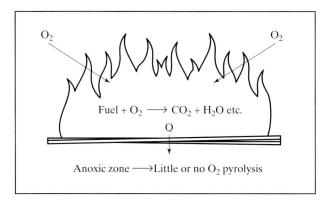

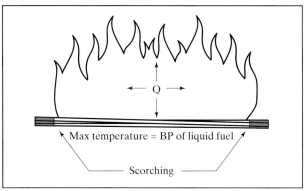

▶ **Figure 9.16** *Burn patterns reflect heat flow as well as the presence or absence of oxygen.*

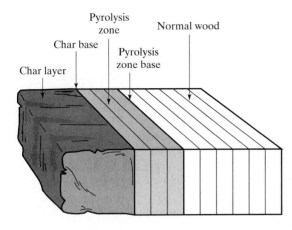

Char layer

Char base

Pyrolysis zone

Pyrolysis zone base

Normal wood

◀ **Figure 9.17** *Intense heat reaches the interior of the wood, but oxygen does not, creating a zone where pyrolysis can occur.*

oxidation and, as shown in Figure 9.17, can be identified as a layer in burned wood. Notice that the pyrolysis zone is some distance below the burned surface. The layer is defined by oxygen and by the depth to which heat can penetrate.

The bottom frame of Figure 9.16 illustrates a situation seen in many arson cases: A liquid accelerant such as gasoline is poured over a surface and ignited. If the pool is deep enough, it insulates the substrate below and limits the temperature increase. Just as the temperature of liquid water (not steam) cannot exceed 100°C, the temperature of the liquid accelerant cannot exceed its boiling point. Consequently, the pattern of burning and scorching at the edge of the pool and away from it will be different from the patterns directly beneath.

Heat transfer is directly related to the concept of mass transfer. Q is used to heat products of the reaction, which, on a molecular level, means that the greater Q is, the more kinetic energy is transferred to the product molecules. This kinetic energy can be transferred to other molecules via collision. However, for that transfer to occur to key molecules such as those found in the vaporized candle wax, the energy has to be delivered, via fast-moving molecules, to the right place. That movement of mass is called *mass transfer*.

9.2.4 MASS TRANSFER

Figure 9.4 shows one aspect of mass transfer: the movement of atmospheric O_2 and N_2 to the combustion zone. This diffusion is driven by a concentration gradient, a process aided by rising heated gases. As the heated products rise, surrounding air moves in to fill the void. As these molecules approach the reaction zone, they collide with molecules heated by the combustion increasing the velocity of those heated molecules. This is a simple view of how heat is conducted in the combustion zone.

Mass transfer and diffusion are also important considerations in evaluating how well the fuel and oxidant mix. In a quiescent (quiet and not mixing) solution of water, a drop of food coloring added will diffuse over time until it is equally distributed throughout the liquid. This is another example of diffusion driven by a concentration gradient. The same will happen in the gas phase. However, in combustion, the process is more complex and dynamic. Consider the simple systems shown in Figure 9.18. Heat transferred to the fuel imparts the energy needed to vaporize the fuel or its pyrolysis products. These vapors diffuse away from the surface, a zone of high concentration. In the combustion zone, the fuel is consumed, as is oxygen, which diffuses inward toward the combustion zone. Figure 9.19 illustrates two simple combustions and the

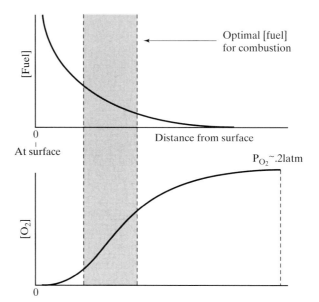

▶ **Figure 9.18** *Concentration gradients of fuel and oxidant as a function of distance. The [ ] notation refers to the concentration.*

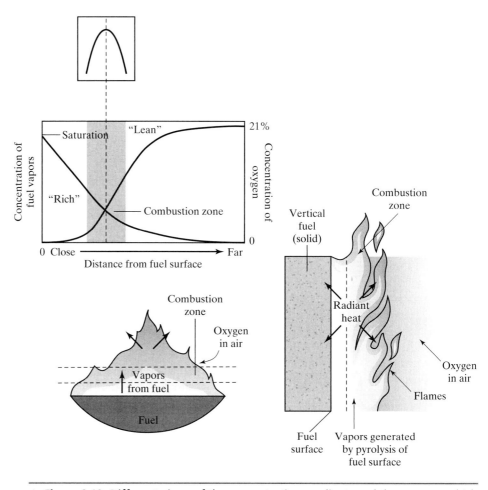

▲ **Figure 9.19** *Different views of the concentration gradients and the zones at which the concentrations of the fuel and the oxidant support combustion. Figure 9.8 is superimposed for reference; the ratio Φ defines rich, lean, and optimal combustion.*

gradients created. The combustion zone approximates the concentration ratios shown in Figure 9.8. The right frame shows a fire burning on a vertical surface such as a wall, and the lower frame shows a "pool fire," which would occur in an arson in which gasoline was used as an accelerant.

Finally, in cases involving a poured liquid accelerant, mass transport of the fuel occurs in a lateral direction, controlled by the characteristics of the surface. Gasoline on a nonporous surface like concrete will diffuse easily, while gasoline on a porous surface like wood or carpet will tend to be absorbed. As a result, porous and semiporous surfaces should be sampled in depth, since the chances of finding residual accelerants is increased in such cases.

9.3 COMBUSTION, DEFLAGRATION, AND DETONATION

With some basic combustion concepts in hand, our discussion returns to the combustion continuum of Figure 9.1. All of the factors discussed in Section 9.2 (Q, pressure, mass transfer, heat flow, and oxygen balance) are needed in examining and classifying combustion reactions. Confinement is also an important variable. For our purposes, it is convenient to divide the combustion continuum into four categories: flames, propellants, low explosives, and high explosives. The reaction rate in flames is the slowest of these and explosives the fastest. Flames produce copious quantities of hot expanding gases, but these gases are minimally—if at all—contained; thus, pressure does not build rapidly compared with the buildup in explosions. Propellants burn rapidly, but in succession, from one particle to the next. The burn rate has to be carefully controlled to ensure that the work done (e.g., imparting kinetic energy to a projectile) is maximized. Too fast a burn, and an explosion results; too slow, and the bullet will move slowly. Low explosives are easily detonated and are frequently used to detonate high explosives.

When a flame front moves, it travels at less than the speed of sound (subsonically), whereas a detonation occurs when a combustion wave moves at supersonic speeds. Both are sustained by Q, but in a detonation, a compressive shock wave is created. When a potentially explosive mixture exists (conditions to be addressed shortly), the factors that determine whether a detonation or deflagration occurs are the fuel–oxidant mixture, the degree of confinement, and the source of the ignition. For now, note that an explosion does not require a chemical reaction to sustain it. For example, when the concrete roof was blown off the reactor building during the Chernobyl accident in 1986, the explosion was the result of the rapid vaporization of water (a steam explosion). However, it was not a chemical detonation, since no chemical reaction drove the expansion, pressure buildup, and catastrophic structural failure.

9.4 DEFLAGRATION AND FIRES

9.4.1 FLAMES

A common type of fire or flame is a **laminar flame**, meaning that the flame has definable layers or regions. Within the laminar category, there are two familiar examples: a candle and a Bunsen burner, shown in Figures 9.20 and 9.21. In a Bunsen burner, gaseous methane is mixed with air and injected into the combustion zone. Hot gaseous products diffuse away, while atmospheric oxygen

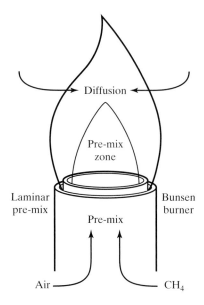

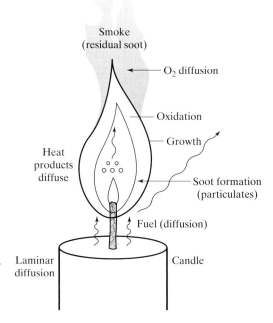

▶ **Figure 9.20** *A Bunsen burner and a candle are examples of laminar flames.*

diffuses inward, creating a second region in which the fuel–air mixture is no longer in the same proportions as in the premix zone. In a candle, fuel is vaporized and diffuses upward as oxygen diffuses inward. As shown in Figure 9.21, different regions in the candle flame are defined by temperature. Pyrolyzed waxes form particulates (soot) that grow and rise. Partial oxidation occurs, and any residual soot diffuses upward and outward as smoke. In both cases, the flame is self-sustaining once ignited and burns until the fuel is exhausted.

A visible combustion wave is created if the fuel and oxidant gases are stationary, as shown in Figure 9.22. A flame front is visible when, for example, a large puddle of gasoline is ignited at one end and the flames propagate

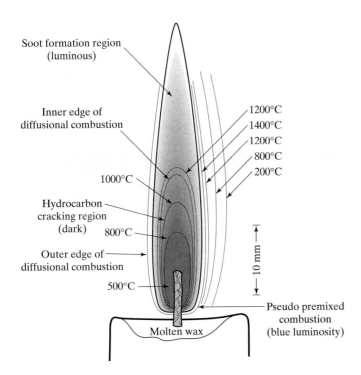

Soot formation region
(luminous)

Inner edge of
diffusional combustion

1200°C
1400°C
1200°C
800°C
200°C

1000°C

Hydrocarbon
cracking region
(dark)   800°C

Outer edge of
diffusional combustion

500°C

Molten wax

10 mm

Pseudo premixed
combustion
(blue luminosity)

◀ **Figure 9.21** *Candle flame with zones delineated by temperature.*

across the surface much as waves on a pond propagate from the point where a stone is dropped into the water. Typical flame velocities for a mixture of methane and air are in the range of approximately 15 to 45 cm/sec, depending on factors such as the fuel–oxidant ratio Φ^4. In a candle or Bunsen burner, the wave front is stationary because the gases are moving into and out of the combustion zone. The combustion wave remains stationary because the unburned gas molecules are moving away at a rate equal to the burn rate.[5] In simple combustion (deflagration), the combustion wave never exceeds the speed of sound.

As long as the fuel–air mixture is in the combustible range, the flame will be self-sustaining. The events that bracket the flame "event" are initiation (ignition) and quenching or suppression. The range of combustibility is referred to as the *flammable range* and is defined as the fuel–oxidant ratios that permit steady propagation of the flame. The lower end of the scale is called the **lower flammability limit** (LFL) or the lean limit, whereas the upper range is the **upper flammability limit** (UFL) or rich limit. The terms "lower explosive

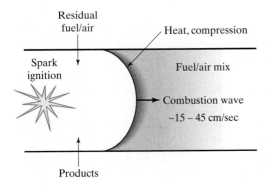

Residual
fuel/air

Spark
ignition

Heat, compression

Fuel/air mix

Combustion wave
~15 – 45 cm/sec

Products

◀ **Figure 9.22** *A visible combustion wave generated in an enclosed tube containing fuel and oxidant.*

limit" and "upper explosive limit" (LEL and UEL, respectively) are also used. For a mixture of propane and air, the lean limit is approximately $\Phi = 0.5$ and the rich limit is approximately $\Phi = 2.8$.

The explosive limits of some common materials are given in Table 9.2. The reference cited there, the *NFPA Fire Protection Handbook*, contains a comprehensive list of these values. The NFPA website (www.nfpa.org) has a wealth of information,

Table 9.2	**Explosive Limits**				
	Explosive Limits (in air, wt%)		Ignition Temperature Range (Minimum)		Minimum Ignition Energy
Fuel	Lower	Upper	°C	°F	mJ
Natural gas	4.5	15	482–632	900–1,170	0.25
Propane (commercial)	2.15	9.6	493–604	920–1,120	0.25
Butane (commercial)	1.9	8.5	482–538	900–1,000	0.25
Acetylene	2.5	81[a]	305	581	0.02
Hydrogen	4	75	500	932	0.01
Ammonia (NH_3)	16	25	651	1,204	—

Source: NFPA Fire Protection Handbook, 17th ed. Quincy, MA, 1991, Table 3-7c. and *SFPE Handbook*, 2nd ed., Table 3-16.2. Quincy, MA, 1995.
[a] Higher concentrations (up to 100 percent) may detonate.

including publications and software of use to forensic chemists and fire investigators. The relationship of the explosive limits to the air–fuel mixture ratios is illustrated in Figure 9.23. As demonstrated and discussed already, many other variables will alter these limits. Since the fuel and oxidant are gases, pressure and temperature are critical. For example, the higher the temperature, the wider is the flammable range. In arson cases, homogeneous mixtures rarely exist, and the relative densities of materials become critical factors, as shown in Figure 9.24.

The weighted-average formula weight of air is taken to be approximately 29 g/mole. The relative weight of hydrogen (H_2; formula weight FW ~ 2) is therefore 2/29, or about 0.07. If hydrogen is released into the air, it rapidly dissipates upward and away from the release point. Conversely, gasoline vapors tend to sink. If gasoline is crudely represented by n-octane (C_8H_{18}, FW ~ 104), the weight ratio relative to air is 104/29, or ~ 3.6. Therefore, in a quiescent or nearly quiescent environment, fuel vapors disperse according to their weight and density. This phenomenon is illustrated in Figure 9.24. Methane from a natural-gas leak will tend to accumulate higher in the room than will gasoline vapors, for example.

Two other important quantities are reported in Table 9.2: ignition temperature and **ignition energy**. The presence of vapors within the explosive limits is a necessary condition for combustion to occur, but it is not a sufficient one. The initial E_a barrier must be overcome, and the energy to do so is supplied by an ignition source that must have sufficient energy available and that must remain in contact with the flammable mixture long enough to ignite it. In arson investigations, the ignition source is called an **incendiary device**, such as a match, a cigarette, or a more sophisticated apparatus. As demonstrated in Figure 9.24, this device must also be in the right place at the right time. The energy needed to ignite a mixture is usually thermal. Kinetic

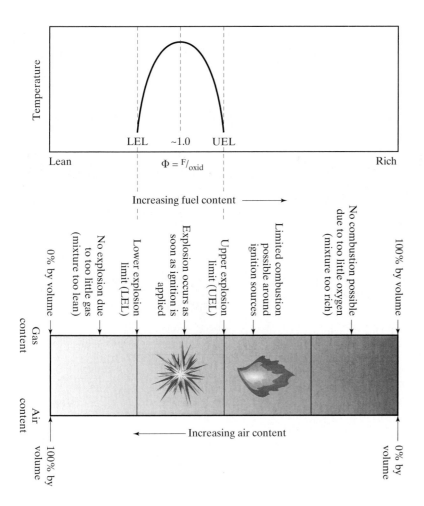

◀ **Figure 9.23** *Flammability limits correlate with* Φ.

energy is transferred to the reactants via collisions among the molecules of the mixture. The collisions may be instantaneous, as in the case of someone using a striker and spark to ignite a Bunsen burner, but even the biggest spark won't ignite a mixture that is too rich or too lean. In other cases, ignition takes much more time, as when a smoldering cigarette is placed between the cushions of a couch. With explosives, pressure can provide sufficient energy for combustion.

Another useful quantity related to fuels is their **flash point**, which is the lowest temperature at which an ignitable mixture is capable of combustion. The flash point is loosely similar to the concept of the boiling point; at the flash point, the vapor pressure of a fuel in air corresponds to Φ at the LEL. The flash points of materials used as accelerants in arson cases are summarized in Table 9.3. In Table 9.2 the final column is the **minimum ignition energy**, a quantity also referred to as the spontaneous ignition energy. In chemical and molecular terms, this is the energy transferred to the fuel by molecules in the environment to overcome E_a and begin the reaction.

9.4.2 FIRE DYNAMICS

A fire is a time-dependent event that has definable phases and dynamics. After ignition, a fire will grow until it reaches a steady state that depends on the amounts of fuel and oxidant available in the given environment. In the steady

a.

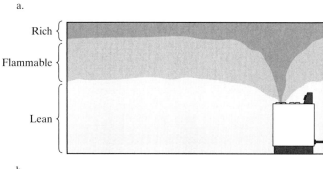

b.

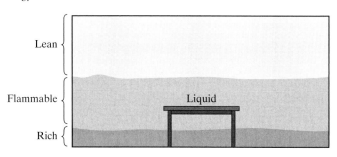

c.

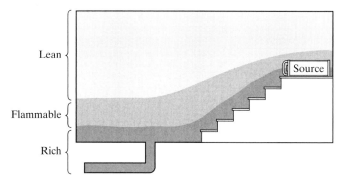

▶ **Figure 9.24** *In a quiescent or nearly quiescent environment, the density of the fuel relative to the atmosphere will dictate the places where fuel vapors accumulate and the zones where combustion is supported.*

Table 9.3	Representative Flash Points
Compound or Mixture	**Flash Point (Closed Container), °C**
Acetone	−20
Kerosene	38
Diesel oil	52
Gasoline	−45
Toluene	4

Source: DeHann, J. D. "Chapter 4: Combustion Properties of Liquids and Gaseous Fuels," in *Kirk's Fire Investigation*, 5th ed. Upper Saddle River, NJ: Prentice Hall, 2002. These data can also be obtained from MSDS sheets and from the *NFPA Fire Protection Handbook*.

Example Problem 9.4

A propane cylinder used with an outdoor barbecue is stored in a small shed of dimensions $4 \times 4 \times 6$. The cylinder contains 2.5 pounds of propane. If the tank ruptures in the shed and forms a homogeneous mixture, is it flammable? Assume that the temperature is 25°C and the pressure is 1 atmosphere.

Answer: To solve this problem, calculate Φ and see if it falls within the flammable limits. Here, $\Phi \approx 2.2$, which lies within the flammability limits. However, realize that there are many other factors to consider. For example, a homogenous mixture is unlikely to form, since the shed is not leakproof and propane is heavier than air. Similarly, air could leak in as propane leaks out, creating localized areas in which the mixture is not flammable. These types of calculations are best viewed as useful approximations and as starting points for further study and investigation.

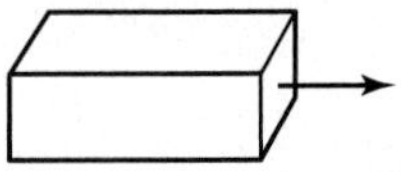

$$4' \times 4' \times 6' = 96 \text{ ft}^3$$
$$96 \text{ ft}^3 = 2718.4 \text{ L} = 2718 \text{L}$$

With volume, we can use the ideal gas law to obtian mole fractions

$$PV = nRT \; ; \; P_{propane} = \frac{nRT}{V}$$

$$2.5 \text{ pounds C}_3\text{H}_8 = \frac{1134\text{g}}{44 \text{ g/mole}} \cong \frac{25.8 \text{ moles}}{\text{C}_3\text{H}_8}$$

$$P_{propane} = \frac{nRT}{V} = \frac{(25.8 \text{ moles})(0.0821 \frac{\text{L atm}}{\text{mole K}})(298\text{K})}{2718 \text{ L}}$$

$$P_{propane} = 0.23\text{atm} \qquad X_{propane} = \frac{0.23 \text{ atm}}{1.0 \text{ atm}}$$

$$X_{propane} = 0.23$$

$$X_{air} = 1 - 0.23 = 0.77$$

Weighted average mass air

$$\Phi = \frac{(0.77)(28.85)}{(0.23)(44)} \cong 2.20$$

* On-line or calculator conversions are helpful.

Exhibit B: TWA Flight 800

This accident marked a historical milestone in forensic science and its interface with forensic engineering and homeland security. TWA Flight 800 departed from John F. Kennedy International Airport in New York at eight o'clock on the evening of July 17, 1996, bound for Paris. At 8:31 P.M., the plane exploded as it climbed to 13,000 feet and was reduced to flaming debris and wreckage, littering a 12-square mile area off the coast of Long Island. Two hundred three people died. The accident lit up the sky before hundreds of witnesses on the ground, on the water, and in the air.

Eyewitness accounts of fiery streaks heading upward in the sky before the explosion led credence to the theory that a shoulder-launched missile had brought down the huge plane. Later, the discovery of traces of high explosives on parts of the recovered

Exhibit B: (Continued)

▲ *The reconstructed fuselage of TWA Flight 800. Image courtesy of the Federal Emergency Management Agency (FEMA).*

wreckage supported the theory of a missile or a bomb. Despite the preponderance of early evidence pointing toward a criminal act, investigators from the National Transportation Safety Board (NTSB) converged on the site. The NTSB would assume responsibility for the investigation if no criminal activity was involved.

As the investigation proceeded, it quickly became evident that the cause of the crash was an explosion in the center fuel tank, but the reason for the explosion was not clear. On the night of July 17th, the center fuel tank of Flight 800, a massive hollow space the size of a garage, contained only 50 gallons of fuel. Complicating the matter was the heat of an east-coast summer day, which meant that air-conditioning units below the tank were running nonstop while the jet was on the ground. These units generated considerable heat, some of which was transferred to the fuel tank. The hotter the jet fuel becomes, the more of it vaporizes, and the more vapor, the more explosive is the atmosphere. The flash point of jet fuel is close to 100°F, a temperature easily reachable in the tank, although a source of ignition would still be required.

Bombs and missile impacts leave distinctive traces on aircraft, such as characteristic structural damage and explosive residues. Structural damage would still be detectable even after the wreckage was submerged for some time, but explosives residues were another matter. A study conducted as part of the investigation revealed that explosives, which are somewhat water soluble, are quickly dissipated by immersion in salt water. However, a quick recovery of the debris was impossible, as it was scattered over an area approximately 4 miles by $3\frac{1}{2}$ miles at a depth of 120 feet. The area was divided into three "debris fields," and wreckage recovered was assigned a color code based on the field from which it was recovered. Computer models were used to reconstruct the last few seconds of Flight 800 and to account for the pattern of dispersal of the wreckage. Simulations indicated that the section of the plane where the center fuel tank was located was the first to separate from the fuselage, further evidence that the initial catastrophic event took place there. Seconds later, the front portion of the plane, including the cockpit, was ripped away, falling to the sea farther east. The rear of the plane, including the wings and engines, considerably lighter with the loss of the other two sections, apparently shot upward in flame until the engines exhausted their fuel. This, investigators felt,

Exhibit B: (Continued)

could explain many of the eyewitness accounts of flaming streaks ascending in the sky. The wreckage continued to break apart and plummeted to the sea far away from the airport.

At the wreckage site, visibility in the water was poor and the water temperature at various depths was cold and grew colder as recovery work moved into the fall. As the underwater recovery effort was getting under way, the FBI organized hundreds of agents to interview witnesses and chase down leads. Early speculation that a "friendly fire" accident involving American armed forces was discounted, as was the possibility of large missiles. A smaller, shoulder-launched missile remained a possibility, but an increasingly remote one, as the FBI learned more about the limitations of such a weapon. At the altitude the plane was when the explosion occurred, nearly 14,000 feet, only a missile fired from a boat directly under the plane would have a chance to hit the target, and even then the odds were slim. In addition, anyone below on the water would have been showered with flaming debris and fuel. Thus, despite the convincing and numerous eyewitness accounts of flaming streaks in the sky, the investigation turned more toward the possibility of a bomb.

Bombs that had been used to bring down aircraft before—for example, the Pan Am 103 bomb—were composed of chemical compounds such as RDX, residues of which investigators hoped would remain on materials that were near the detonation. However, the long immersion times concerned everyone and made the task of detecting, confirming, and interpreting findings exceedingly difficult. As wreckage was recovered and delivered to the hangar, forensic chemists and explosives experts from the FBI and ATF used dogs and portable equipment to comb the pieces for any traces of explosives. Promising pieces of debris were swabbed or transported whole to the FBI laboratory in Washington, DC, for further testing. Explosives were found, but were traced to a dog-training exercise months earlier. As the investigation continued and more pieces of wreckage were recovered, no structural or metallurgical evidence of a bomb or missile had been found. Similarly, the FBI probe had not uncovered definitive evidence of criminal activity. The NTSB began leaning toward an accidental cause of the explosion in the center fuel tank and pursued forensic engineering tests to examine possible accident scenarios.

Diving operations ended in November 1996, but since a full reconstruction of the plane had been approved, trawling operations were conducted until April 1997. When those operations ended, an amazing 98% of the aircraft had been retrieved from the bottom, wreckage that was transported to the hangar, examined, tested, and eventually reconstructed. No convincing evidence of a bomb or missile was found, either in the form of chemical residues or characteristic structural damage. This, coupled with other evidence and the flammability of the vapors in the center tank, led to the investigation's closing within a few months. The NTSB listed the probable cause as ignition of these vapors, but even after months of work, the agency was not able to pinpoint the source of the spark or flame that ignited the vapors.

Sources: Milton, P. *In the Blink of an Eye: The FBI Investigation of TWA Flight 800.* New York: Random House, 1999.

National Transportation Safety Board, *In-Flight Breakup over the Atlantic Ocean, Trans World Airlines Flight 800, Boeing 747-131, N93119, Near East Moriches, New York, July 17, 1996.*

Aircraft Accident Report NTSB/AAR-00/03. Washington, DC. Notation 6788G, August 23, 2000. Available online at www.ntsb.org.

state, the fire triangle requirements of fuel–oxidant–heat are met and the fire burns steadily. As one or more of the key ingredients dissipates, the fire begins to decay and is eventually quenched, although destruction and residual heat linger after the flame itself goes out. Of course, the behavior of any given fire will be more complex even while it follows this general model. How a fire behaves during its lifetime has important consequences for the fire investigator and the forensic chemist. The dynamics of a fire will depend on all the factors described so far, which combine to make each fire event unique, although some generalizations can be made.

In an arson fire, there are one or more **points of origin** for the fire, and an understanding of fire dynamics is essential to locating these points. As noted earlier, conventional fires are diffusion types in which heated gases move upward and outward from the combustion zone. Such flames are also referred to as **buoyant flames**, since the heated gases are less dense, and thus more buoyant, than the unheated gases. Consequently, flames burn in plumes that can leave distinctive physical and chemical evidence. A simple buoyant flame is shown in the top frame of Figure 9.25. Since the hot gases are moving upward and outward, a V-shaped burn pattern on adjacent surfaces is often observed. Given that a fire usually burns the longest at the point of origin, the V pattern often marks this spot. If the fire burns in an enclosed room, a ceiling jet will form in which the hot gases and smoke are forced outward.

If the fire is sufficiently intense, flashover may occur. In a fire in an enclosed room, for example, flashover is the point at which all of the flammable vapors in the room ignite. A fire started in a corner could generate enough heat and vapors from furniture, paint, and flooring that the entire room erupts in flame and what was a fire burning in one or more isolated locations becomes generalized. Flames extend out through openings, and windows can be broken out by the sudden creation of hot gaseous combustion products. If the room is tightly enclosed, flames may subside to a smoldering state that can erupt again if a door or window is suddenly opened, allowing oxygen in. A similar situation can result if a fire only smolders in an enclosed space, depleting

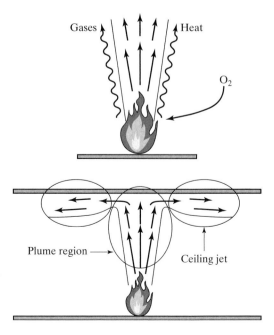

▶ **Figure 9.25** *Examples of fire dynamics that produce distinctive patterns.*

oxygen over time without the telltale flames. A door opened in this situation can cause immediate flashover in a room rich in fuel vapors. Flashover is a significant danger to firefighters and first responders to fire scenes.

9.5 EXPLOSIVES

Although phenomena such as forest fires and flashovers are sometimes described as explosive, this description is technically incorrect. However, under certain conditions, flammable mixtures can explode or, more accurately, detonate. Recall the discussion of a flame front as a propagating wave, illustrated in Figure 9.22. Detonation occurs when the speed of this flame front exceeds the speed of sound. The example shown in that figure is a combustion initiated in a closed tube. If the tube is long enough, the compression wave created by combustion can accelerate sufficiently to become a detonation wave.[6] As shown in Figure 9.26, compression waves can catch up with earlier waves, surpass the speed of sound, and establish a **detonation wave**.

A detonation wave results from a positive feedback cycle of increasing acceleration. When simple combustion begins (Figure 9.22), the first event generates heat and a wave of hot compressed gases that propagates outward. Increasing the pressure increases the heat, and as a result, more of the energy released is available, since less is needed to pre-heat the reaction mixture. This process establishes a positive feedback such that each new pressure wave

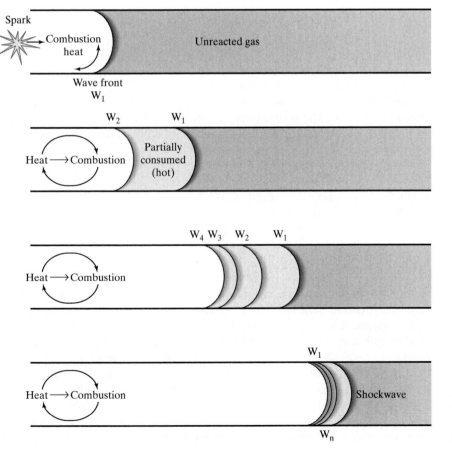

◀ **Figure 9.26** *How a confined deflagration can progress to a detonation.*

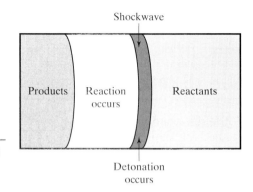

▶ **Figure 9.27** *The detonation zone is the zone where combustion is initiated by mechanical pressure.*

moves faster than the previous one because the gases produced in successive combustions are hotter. Eventually, one of the waves exceeds the speed of sound and passes the initial wave at supersonic speed. This shock wave ignites the fuel–air mixture and sustains the detonation via extreme compression.[6] As material is compressed under high pressures, adiabatic heating of the mixture occurs and provides sufficient energy to overcome E_a for the process. A snapshot of a detonation is shown in Figure 9.27.

The speed of propagation of an explosion is in the range of 1500 to 9000 m/s.[7] The speed of sound depends on the medium through which the pressure wave is propagating and the temperature, since temperature influences density. The relationship is

$$V = (331.4 + 0.6T)\text{m s}^{-1} \qquad (9.15)$$

V is the speed of sound and T is the temperature in °C. At 25°C in air, V = 347 m/s. However, during detonation, the wave is propagating, not through air, but through the reaction mixture and through the solid explosive, both of which are denser than air. The greater the density of the propagating medium, the faster the sound propagates. Similarly, the denser the explosive, the faster the detonation wave propagates. Table 9.4 summarizes the detonation speeds and structures of some common explosives.

Among the common structural features of explosives are carbon, oxygen, hydrogen, and nitrogen. Because an explosion is a combustion, the principal products of the reaction are familiar (CO_2, H_2O), with some additions such as N_2. Unlike typical deflagration fuels, most explosives contain oxygen, but many (such as TNT) are oxygen deficient. Others, such as the azides, contain no oxygen. Other sources of oxygen for explosive mixtures include chlorates (ClO_3^-) and perchlorates (ClO_4^-).

Some explosives are classified as **molecular explosives**, which mean that, in pure form, they detonate relatively easily. It also means that they are unstable and difficult to handle safely. Consequently, most commercial and military explosives are mixtures of materials (fuel and oxidants) combined with components called sensitizers. The role of the sensitizer is as the name implies, although different sensitizers are sensitive to different stimuli. One may impart shock sensitivity, while another creates sensitivity to electrical currents or heat.

As with all things forensic, the classification of explosives is an important part of understanding and analysis. Figure 9.28 classifies explosives into three groups—low, high, and propellants—a division that makes forensic sense, given the importance of propellants in firearms. **Low explosives**

Table 9.4 Detonation Speeds and Structures of Selected Explosives (m/s)

Explosive	Structure	Density (g/cm^3)	Speed	Power Index
Low				
Mercury fulminate	$Hg(C \equiv N - O)_2$	1.25	2300	14
		3.07	3925	14
Lead styphnate	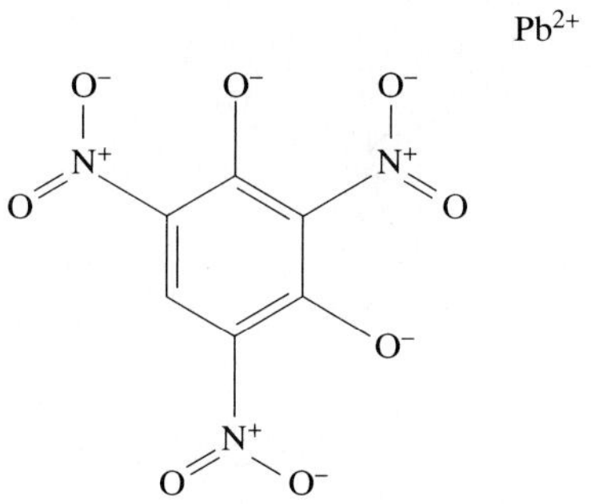 Pb^{2+}	2.9	5200	21
Lead azide	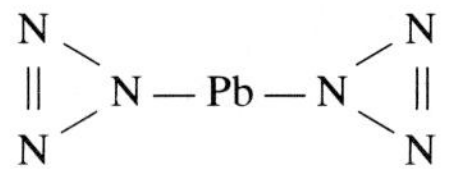	3.8	4500	13
High				
Nitroglycerin primary high explosive	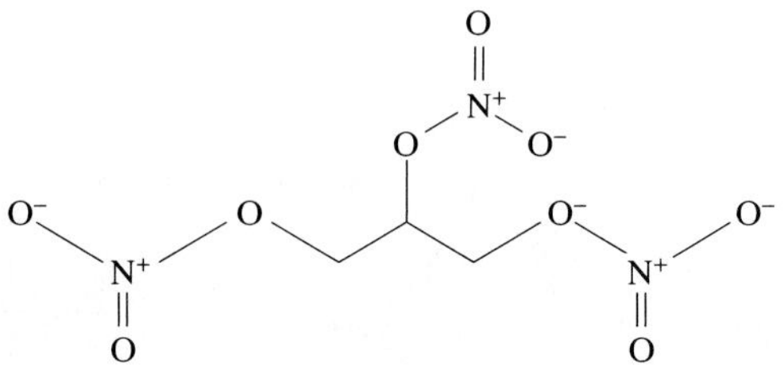	1.60	7750	171
Picric acid primary high explosive	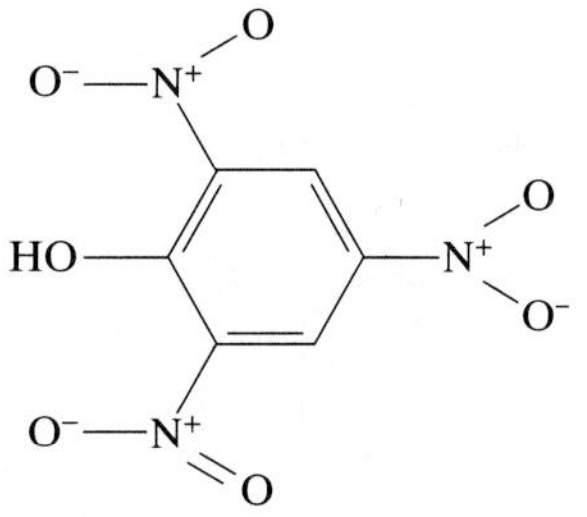	1.60	7900	100
TNT 2,4,6-Trinitrotoluene Secondary high explosive	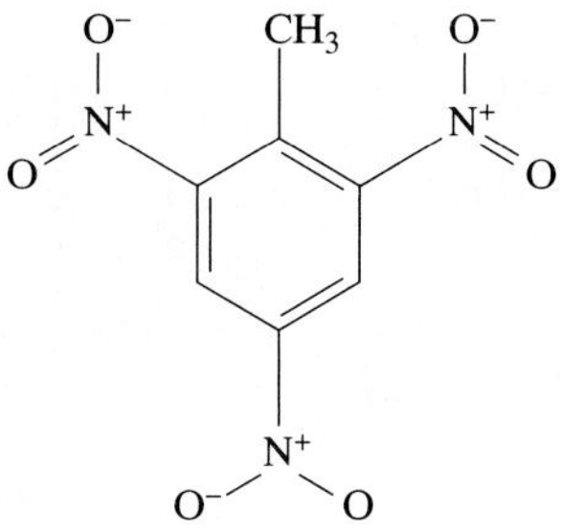	1.55	6850	331.2

Table 9.4 (Continued)

Explosive	Structure	Density (g/cm^3)	Speed	Power Index
HMX Octogen; cyclotetramethylenete-tranitramine	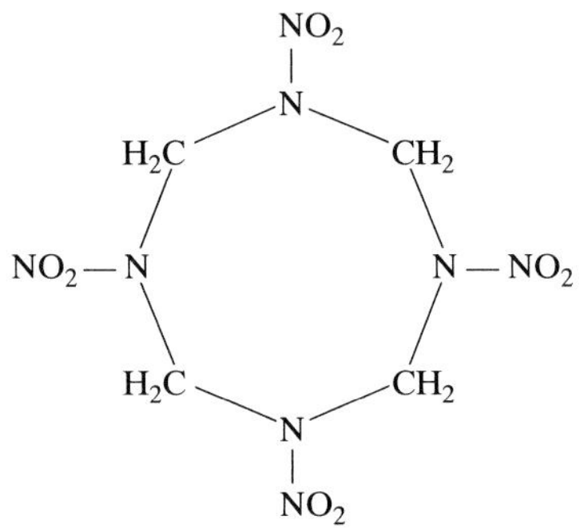	1.89	9100	455
RDX Hexogen; cyclotrimethylene-trinitramine	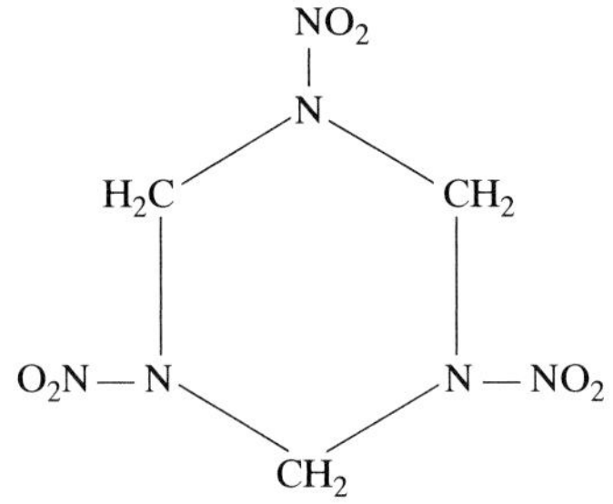	1.70	8440	457
Nitrocellulose Nitrated cellulose; —NO$_3$ replacing —OH groups	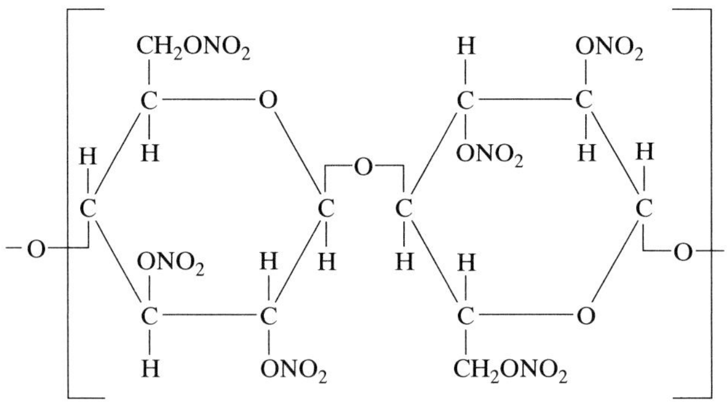	1.15	7300	variable
Tetryl 2,4,6-trinitrophenyl-methylnitramine	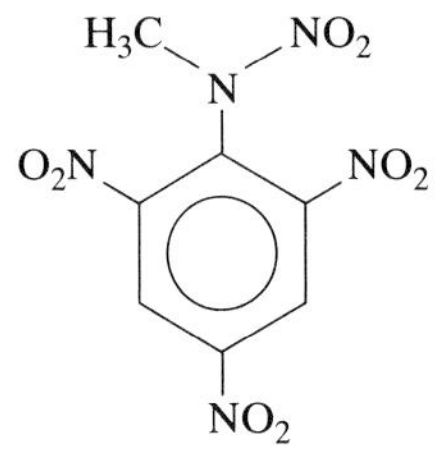	1.55	7080	355
PETN Pentaerythritol tetranitrate	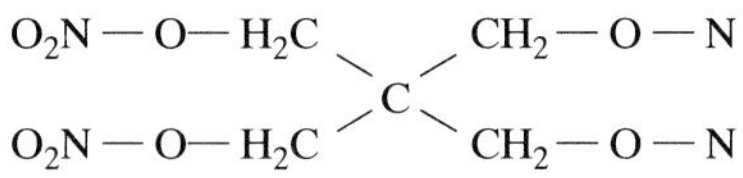	1.60	7920	452

Table 9.4 (Continued)				
Explosive	Structure	Density (g/cm³)	Speed	Power Index
TATB 1,3,5-triamino-2,4,6-trinitrobenzene		1.88	7760	273

Source: Akhavan, J. "Ch. 3: Combustion, Deflagration, and Detonation," in J. Akhavan, *The Chemistry of Explosives,* Cambridge, U.K.: Royal Society of Chemistry, 1998.

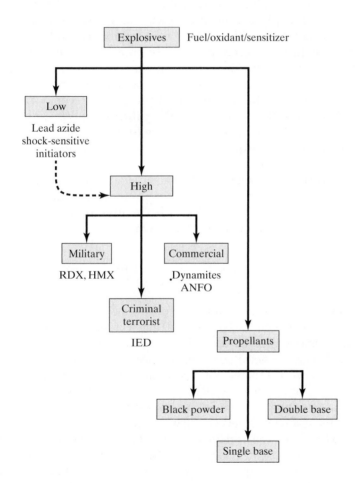

◀ **Figure 9.28** *A scheme for classifying explosives. Low explosives are linked to high explosives because low explosives are often used to detonate high explosives. "IED" stands for "improvised explosive device."*

are deflagrating explosives that only detonate when confined. The detonation of a low explosive is frequently used to detonate a high explosive which is relatively insensitive and stable. **Primers** used to ignite propellants in ammunition are primary explosives. **High explosives** are not sensitive and require an initiator for their detonation. High explosives are detonating explosives that produce high pressure shock waves and are generally more powerful than low explosives. High explosives are further categorized as primary or secondary. Primary high explosives such as nitroglycerin are shock and spark sensitive and easily detonated. Secondary high explosives are stable and usually require a detonator to initiate detonation. In Table 9.4, the first three entries are low explosives; note the difference in detonation velocity between these materials and the high explosives making up the remainder of the table. Because the reason for using explosives is to generate a destructive pressure wave (blast wave), explosive power will be discussed in detail.

9.5.1 EXPLOSIVE POWER

The destruction associated with explosives depends on the pressure and speed at which the blast wave moves. High explosives have higher shattering power, also called **brisance,** compared with low explosives. Low explosives generate what is often called pushing power. Consider a pipe bomb as an example, with explosive materials confined within. The detonation of a low-explosive bomb would produce few fragments, and the blast wave might displace heavy objects nearby. By contrast, a high-explosive pipe bomb would demolish the pipe, create showers of sharp shrapnel, and shatter objects nearby. A bomb's shatter power depends on the pressure created by the shock wave, behind which is the blast wave of hot, compressed gaseous products of the combustion. The different effects are illustrated in Figure 9.29, in which the shock wave is seen to shatter the container and eject shrapnel away from the explosion, while the hot, expanding gas creates the crater in the soil beneath.

The explosive power of a bomb depends fundamentally on the heat evolved (Q) and the volume of gaseous products produced (V) and is expressed as the product of these two quantities.[†] The relative power of one explosive compared with another is obtained through the power index

$$PI = \frac{QV_{explosive}}{QV_{picric\ acid}} \times 100 \tag{9.16}$$

The **explosive index** of some common explosives is given in Table 9.4; typically, the index is calculated on the basis of 1.00 gram of material.

We have already touched upon the heat produced (Q), in a reaction, determined by ΔH of the reaction, the oxygen balance, and the pressure involved. In our discussion of flames, we started with the assumption that the flame was adiabatic and that all of the heat evolved went into heating the gaseous products. In the context of arson, this first-pass assumption is reasonable, since the question usually asked of the forensic chemist relates to the presence or absence of an accelerant. For explosives, a bit more detail is required, given the role of heat in determining blast damage which can be useful in identifying the components of explosives.

Like all combustion, explosives produce a complex mixture of gaseous products. Part of the heat evolved is absorbed by these products as a function of their heat capacities (C). In turn, heat capacity depends on temperature, so the temperature must be taken into account. This process—the creation of products, followed by the liberation of heat and the subsequent absorption of heat—determines the

[†]This discussion relies principally on material from Akhavan's book: Akhavan, J., "Ch. 5: Thermochemistry of Explosives," in *The Chemistry of Explosives*, Cambridge, UK: Royal Society of Chemistry, 1998. This is an excellent pocket reference to explosives.

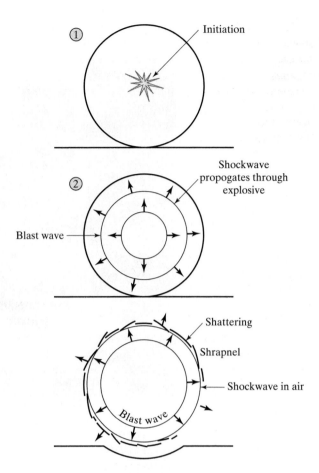

◀ **Figure 9.29** *Effects of the detonation of a bomb. Note the shrapnel and compression of the soil beneath the bomb; these constitute the crater created by the expanding hot gases.*

maximum obtainable temperature of the explosion (T_e). The relationship between the heat evolved and the change in temperature can be stated as

$$Q = \text{mass} \times \text{specific heat} \times \Delta T \tag{9.17}$$

or

$$\Delta T = \frac{Q}{\text{mass} \times C_v} = T_f - T_i \tag{9.18}$$

where C_v is the specific heat of one of the gaseous products. To take into account *all* of the product gases, equation 9–21 can be further simplified to the form

$$T_f = \frac{Q}{\overline{C}_v} + T_i \tag{9.19}$$

where the term $\overline{C}_v$ is the weighted average of the heat capacities of the product gases.[†] Equation 9–23 still does not afford a simple calculation, because the heat

---

[†]The subscript v on C_v refers to the heat capacity at constant volume, which can be converted to C_p, heat capacity at constant pressure. C_v is a reasonable choice over the very short time that an explosion occurs.

Applying the Science 9.1   Oklahoma City: ANFO

ANFO is a high explosive made from *a*mmonium *n*itrate and *f*uel *o*il. This is the type of explosive Timothy McVeigh used to attack the Murrah Federal Building in Oklahoma City on April 19, 1995. It is composed of ammonium nitrate and 6% fuel oil. A similar mixture of urea nitrate and other materials was used in the first attack on the World Trade Center in 1993.

▶ *Image courtesy of the Federal Emergency Management Agency (FEMA).*

capacity is proportional to the temperature. Accordingly, we are back to the point that the heat produced is one of two key variables, the other being the volume of gas produced.

How, then, do we know which gases are produced and in what amounts? Once again, we turn to approximations. As noted in our discussion of combustion, the products are not just CO_2 and H_2O, and for explosives containing nitrogen, additional complexity results. To address this complexity, a series of rules is used to predict products on the basis of the molecular composition of the explosive. Examples include the Kistiakowsky–Wilson rules and modifications thereto and the **Springall Roberts rules**. The latter are summarized in Table 9.5. An application of these rules is illustrated in Example Problem 9-5. Note that the rules approximate the composition of the gaseous components, not predict them with certainty.

Table 9.5   Springall Roberts Rules for Determining the Gaseous Products of Explosives

1. C is converted to CO.
2. Any O remaining after the implementation of rule 1 is incorporated into water.
3. If any O remains after the implementation of rule 2, CO from rule 1 is converted to CO_2.
4. N is converted to N_2.
5. One-third of the CO formed is oxidized to CO_2.
6. One-sixth of the original amount of CO (prior to the implementation of rule 5) is converted to C and water.

Example Problem 9.5

Assume that 1.00 gram of nitroglycerin is detonated.

a. Predict which gaseous products are produced and in what quantities. Use the rules given on the previous page.

Answer:

a. Nitroglycerin: $C_3 H_5 N_3 O_9$

   Rule:
   1. $3CO$ takes up 3 oxygens, leaving $6O$
   2. $5H \rightarrow {}^5/_2 H_2O$, 1 oxygen left
   3. $1CO \rightarrow CO_2$. Now we have $2CO + 1CO_2$
   4. $3N \rightarrow {}^3/_2 N_2$

   Equation so far:

   $$2CO + CO_2 + {}^5/_2 H_2O, + {}^3/_2 N_2$$

   Clear fractions for easier conversions multiply by 2:

   $$4CO + 2CO_2 + 5H_2O, + 3N_2$$

   5. $4CO \xrightarrow{{}^1/_3} {}^4/_3 CO \rightarrow$ hard to balance; multiply all by 2:

   $$12CO + 6CO_2 + 15H_2O + 9N_2$$
   $$12CO \xrightarrow{{}^1/_3} 4CO \rightarrow 2C + 2CO_2$$

   Leaves:

   $$8CO + 6CO_2 + 15H_2O, + 9N_2 + 2C + 2CO_2; \text{ Collect terms}$$
   $$8CO + 8CO_2 + 15H_2O, + 9N_2 + 2C$$

   6. Original amount of $CO = 12CO$

   $$12CO \xrightarrow{{}^1/_6} 2CO \rightarrow 2C + 2H_2O$$

   This requires $4H$ (from $2H_2O$)

   $$2CO + 4H \rightarrow 2C + 2H_2O, \text{ so net water produced in unchanged.}$$

   Final form of equation:

   $$6CO + 8CO_2 + 15H_2O, + 9N_2 + 2C + 2C + 2H_2O$$
   (2 used in step 6)

   $$6CO(g) + 8CO_2(g) + 15H_2O(g), + 9N_2(g) + 4C(\theta)$$

   Total # atoms: $C = 18$
   $H = 30$
   $N = 18$

   $2 \times 3 (C_3 H_5 N_3 O_9) = 18C$
   $30H$
   $18N$

   Two multipliers used
   to clear fractions

b. Calculate the number of moles of gas released per gram detonated.

c. What volume would the number of moles you found in part b correspond to at STP?

Answer:

b. If 1.00g is detonated, convert to moles:

$$C_3 H_5 N_3 O_9 = \frac{227g}{mole}$$

$$= 0.0044 \text{ moles}$$

Applying to above (a) results.

$$6(0.0044)CO + 8(0.0044)CO_2 + 15(0.0044)H_2O + 9(0.0044)N_2$$

$$= 0.184 \text{ moles} = 0.18 \text{ moles total gas for } 1.00g$$

---

c. $0.18 \text{ moles}\left(\dfrac{22.4 \text{ L}}{\text{mole}_{STP}}\right) \cong 4L$

The detonation of 1.00 g of nitroglycerine produces about 4L of gas, if the conditions are at STP. As we will see, this is only an approximation.

9.5.2 Low and High Explosives

Low explosives are easier to detonate than high explosives and are less powerful (gram for gram) than high explosives. These trends are evident in Table 9.4. Many low explosives will detonate with applied friction or with impact. As with any combustion, enough energy has to be input over a long enough time and over a wide enough area to overcome the E_a of the reaction and generate sufficient heat for the reaction to be self-sustaining. The ignition of an explosive does not automatically mean that it will detonate; recall that the mixture must be confined such that combustion can become detonation.

Mechanisms of igniting a low explosive include thermal (a simple fuse or spark), an electrical current or spark, friction, and impact. Consider the ignition of an impact-sensitive low explosive such as lead azide in the primer of a cartridge of ammunition. When the trigger of the firearm is pulled, a firing pin is driven into the primer. The surface area of the primer is very small, so that the force of the impact is high in the localized area of the primer that is struck. This force compresses the explosive and the gases trapped within its matrix, generating high heat. In addition, particles and crystals are moved forcibly against each other, producing friction heating. If sufficient in energy and duration, these localized heating events will ignite the low explosive. Note that ignition is not the same as detonation: When an explosive ignites, it burns; when it detonates, it explodes. The former is a thermally driven event and the latter a mechanically driven one.

Low explosives are used in propellants (described in Section 9.5.3) and to ignite high explosives. Many bombs, such as pipe bombs, are made from low explosives. High explosives are on the order of 10 to 100 times less sensitive to friction and 10 times less sensitive to impact than are low explosives. Typically, they will not ignite or detonate without the high-pressure compression associated with a shock wave. To detonate a primary explosive, devices such as a detonation cord and blasting caps are needed. These devices incorporate primary and secondary explosives in what is referred to as an explosive train, in which ignition or detonation of the primary explosive is used to detonate the high explosive, which in turn creates a shock wave capable of detonating the charge. The devices are called detonators rather than igniters because they produce a shock wave and detonation, not just simple ignition and deflagration.

The first high explosives appeared in the 1800s, beginning with nitroglycerin, an oily substance produced when glycerol is treated with nitric acid, replacing the —OH functionality with —NO$_2$ groups. In discussions of explosives, the abbreviation NG is often used for nitroglycerin. NG was embraced by the mining industry, but was found to be unstable and dangerous to work with. Alfred Nobel, a Swede and founder of the prize named after him, combined the oily NG with diatomaceous earth to make a much safer product called dynamite, although the modern formulation contains other ingredients. The most common high explosives seen in forensic investigations are summarized in Table 9.5.

9.5.3 PROPELLANTS

Propellants used in firearms integrate many aspects and concepts of combustion, both deflagration and detonation. Because a cartridge of ammunition (Figure 9.30, top) has a joint designed to fail, the energy of the combustion reaction is transferred to the bullet, which leaves the barrel at high speed (Figure 9.31; see also color insert). The bottom frame of Figure 9.30 shows a burning "ring" of gases exiting the barrel. This is a combustion wave that forms similarly to an exhaled smoke ring or bubble ring made under water. It is interesting to note that some of the propellant particulates have overtaken the bullet after both have exited the barrel. If the bullet exceeds the speed of sound, a cracking sound is heard due to the shock wave produced. However, it is important to

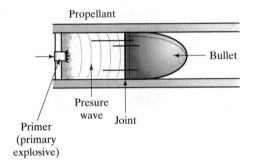

Progressive burn end-to-end

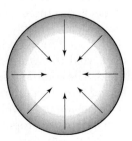

Outside in

◀ **Figure 9.30** *The use of propellants to propel a projectile (bullet) from a weapon. The propellant, primer, and bullet are contained in a cartridge of ammunition. The middle frame illustrates the end-to-end burning of propellant granules. The lower frame shows a propellant granule burning from the outside in, called degressive burning.*

▶ **Figure 9.31** *A high-speed camera image of a gun firing. Smoke, bullet, residue, burning propellant, and a combustion wave can be seen. This image is shown in color in the insert. Image courtesy of Aaron Brudenell, Firearms Examiner, Tucson Police Department Crime Laboratory.*

understand that the propellant is not exploding; it is deflagrating. The shock wave heard in this instance is due to the bullet's movement through the air and is generated in exactly the same way a high-speed jet produces a shock wave when it exceeds the speed of sound. Similarly, the primer ignites the propellant powder used in the ammunition, but does not detonate it.

Because the propellant is used to accelerate a projectile to high velocity, the volume of gas produced (V) is the key variable. The rate of gas production is also important. Ideally, gas will be produced at a rapid, but steady, rate to accelerate the bullet smoothly. If gas is produced instantaneously or too fast, the initial acceleration cannot be supported and the bullet will slow down before exiting the barrel. If the gas is produced too slowly, the bullet will be gone before all of the propellant is converted to gas. Consequently, the burn pattern and burn rate must be controlled. The middle frame of Figure 9.30 shows the progressive burning, or end-to-end burning pattern, typical of propellant particles. The particles burn from the outside in as well. Thus, the burn rate is controlled by the physical characteristics of the propellant (size, shape, etc.) and by surface coatings that speed or inhibit combustion. The composition of propellants will be described in detail shortly.

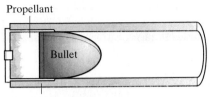

Propellant

Bullet

Cartridge case

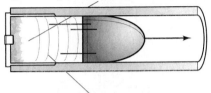

Impact of firing pin
ignites the primer, which ignites the propellant

Pressure waves of hot expanding gas

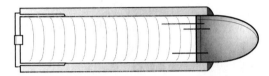

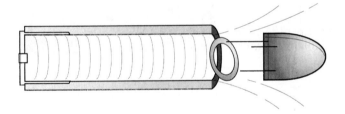

◀ **Figure 9.32** *Drawing corresponding to the photos in Figure 9.31.*

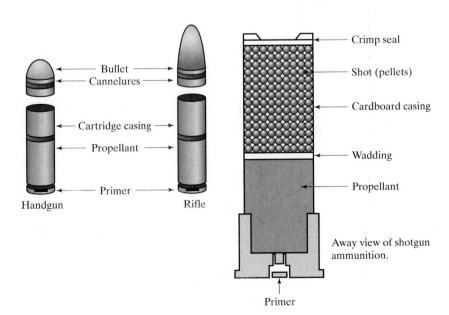

Bullet
Cannelures

Cartridge casing

Propellant

Primer

Handgun

Rifle

Crimp seal

Shot (pellets)

Cardboard casing

Wadding

Propellant

Away view of shotgun ammunition.

Primer

◀ **Figure 9.33** *Different types of ammunition.*

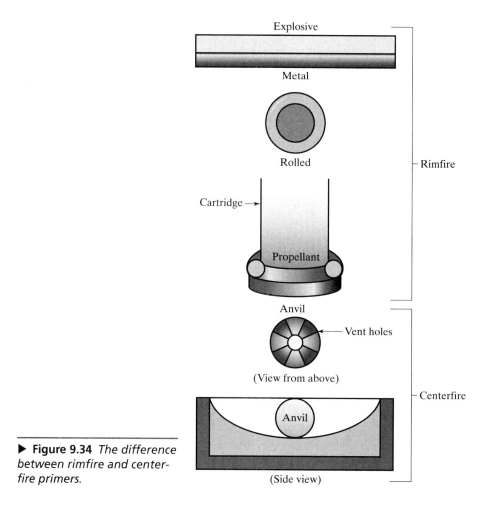

▶ **Figure 9.34** *The difference between rimfire and centerfire primers.*

Ideally, all of the chemical energy Q released by the propellant is imparted to the bullet of mass m_b and is converted to kinetic energy:

$$Qm_p = \frac{1}{2}m_b v^2 \tag{9.20}$$

Here, Q is the heat evolved per gram of propellant (derived from the heat of reaction) and m_p is the mass in grams of the propellant. Rearranging this equation yields an estimate of the velocity of the projectile when it leaves the barrel of the gun (the **muzzle velocity**):

$$V = \sqrt{\frac{2m_p Q}{m_b}} \tag{9.21}$$

The final modification is to add a factor η to account for the inevitable inefficiency of the energy transfer:

$$V = \sqrt{\frac{2m_p Q \eta}{m_b}} \tag{9.22}$$

As we have seen many times in this chapter, this equation gives only an estimate, but it provides a starting point for determining propellant loads and muzzle velocities.

A cartridge of modern ammunition (pistol and rifle) consists of a cartridge case, a primer, propellant, and the projectile. Primers for small-caliber guns, such as 0.22 **caliber**, are rimfire designs, whereas larger caliber ammunition is center fire. The difference between the two is shown in Figure 9.36. Early primers were simple sparks. Flintlock muskets used a flint to generate a spark that ignited black powder propellants. The first chemical explosives used were compounds such as mercury fulminate and potassium chlorate ($KClO_3$). Modern primers contain percussive explosives such as lead azide, lead styphnate, tetracene, and compounds of barium and antimony. Primer residues are forensically important constituents of gunshot residue.

Shotgun ammunition differs in several ways from rifle and pistol cartridges. In a shotgun, the cartridge case is made of plastic or cardboard and is crimp sealed at the top. The projectiles are small lead or steel pellets, the size of which reflects the **gauge** of the weapon. The pellets are separated from the propellant by wadding that can be made of paper or plastic. This wadding material can provide important evidence relating to the manufacturer and gauge of the ammunition.

From the chemical point of view, the components of ammunition of the most interest are the propellant and the primer. Combined, these are the primary source of gunshot residue evidence. It is possible to perform an elemental analysis of a bullet with the use of inductively coupled plasma and laser ablation methods, although these tests are not routinely performed in forensic laboratories and will not be discussed further here. The first propellant used in firearms was black powder (now called gunpowder), the invention of which is generally credited to the Chinese. Gunpowder is a simple formulation of charcoal ($\sim$15% w/w), sulfur ($\sim$10%), and **saltpeter** ($\sim$75%, potassium nitrate, KNO_3). This powdered formulation burns to produce nitrogen and carbon dioxide gases:

$$8C(s) + 3S(s) + 10KNO_3(s) \longrightarrow 3K_2SO_4(s)$$
$$+ 2K_2CO_3(s) + 6CO_2(g) + 5N_2(g) \tag{9.23}$$

The two salts formed (ideally) are solids and contribute to the copious smoke associated with black powder.

Variations of the preceding formula were used for crude cannons and pyrotechnics (fireworks) until the mid-1800s, when several important products were invented. One of these was the guncotton, in the 1830s. **Guncotton**, also called nitrocellulose (NC) or cellulose nitrate, is produced by treating cotton with nitric and sulfuric acids. This treatment parallels that with NG, in that —OH groups are nitrated, but in guncotton the conversion is not complete. Guncottons are rated according to their degree of nitration, which, expressed as a percentage, falls into the range of 12–14%. The first gunpowder using guncotton was introduced to the French Army in the late 1880s and was made with thick guncotton gelatin that used ethanol and ether. The slurry was extruded into flat sheets that were allowed to dry and then chopped into small grains for use in ammunition. This simple nitrocellulose-based propellant is called **single-base smokeless powder**. Alfred Nobel played a role in the development of propellants by introducing **double-base smokeless powder** in 1888.[8] The additional ingredient was nitroglycerin. **Triple-base powders** included a third explosive: nitroguanidine. Triple-base powder is used in very large caliber weapons not typically encountered in forensic contexts.

Exhibit C: Caliber and Gauge

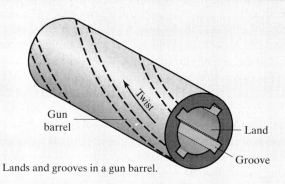

Lands and grooves in a gun barrel.

The *caliber* of a gun originally referred to the diameter of the barrel of a rifled pistol or rifle; however, the term can also refer to the size of cartridges used in firearms. Caliber is measured from the tops of the lands and is given in hundredths or thousandths of an inch or in millimeters. Common calibers include .22, .38, .40, .45, and 9 mm for pistols and .22 and .30–06 for rifles. The caliber of a gun is considered to be a nominal measurement, meaning that the actual barrel diameter may vary slightly from the caliber measure used to describe it.

Originally, the gauge of a pellet referred to how many pellets of a given size (the same as the barrel diameter) were needed to reach a weight of 1 pound. Twelve-gauge pellets weighed approximately $\frac{1}{12}$ of a pound each and would fit in the barrel of a 12-gauge shotgun. Now the term *gauge* is similar to *caliber* and describes the size of the shotgun barrel. Higher gauge numbers mean smaller barrels, so a 12-gauge shotgun has a barrel of larger diameter than does a 16-gauge shotgun, just as 12-gauge shot is larger than 16-gauge shot.

Historical Evidence 9.2—Gunpowder

The invention of gunpowder (black powder) has been attributed to many cultures, including the Greeks and the Chinese. Although gunpowder has been used for centuries, on a battlefield the copious smoke either quickly obscured the view or gave away the position of those firing. Smokeless powder was developed for use by the French Army in 1876 and has replaced black powder in commercial ammunition, although the latter is still used by collectors and hobbyists. Smokeless powder contains cellulose nitrate and organic stabilizers and is manufactured to carefully control the size of the grains. Powder does not explode when ignited (it is considered a low explosive), but rather burns very rapidly, and since burning occurs at the surface of particles, the size of those particles dictates how much surface area is available and how fast the burning will occur. The term "gunpowder" now commonly refers to smokeless powder.

Modern firearms—at least the type seen most frequently in forensic laboratories—employ double-base powder formulations. Typical ingredients and their function are summarized in Table 9.6. The shape of the propellant grains is an important variable and a key consideration for use in ammunition. As noted earlier, the burn time has to be controlled in order to impart the maximum kinetic energy to the projectile. The rate of burn is adjusted by adding deterrents and by shaping of the powder particles as illustrated in Figures 9.35 and 9.36. So-called ball powders are manufactured by creating spheres in an emulsion that dries to form spherical granules of propellant.[9]

Figure 9.30 illustrates powder granules burning end to end and outside in, but this is not the only burn pattern employed. Powders that burn from outside

▲ **Figure 9.35** *Micrograph of double-base powders.*

Table 9.6 Double-Base Propellant Ingredients

Ingredient	Function
Nitrocellulose	Combust to form a large volume of hot gases
Nitroglycerin	Combust to form a large volume of hot gases
Diphenylamine	Stabilizer–preservative

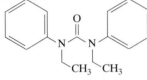

Ethyl Centralite (N,N′-Diethylcarbanilide)	Deterrent, gelatinizer and texture control, and hygroscopicity reducer
Plasticizers	Texture control
Graphite	Lubricant

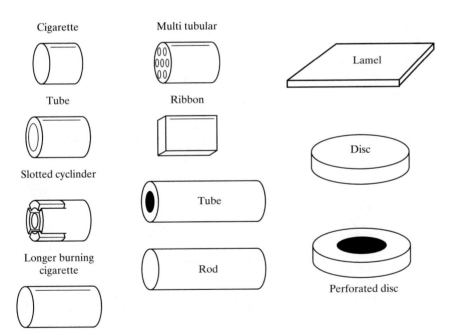

Cigarette

Tube

Slotted cyclinder

Longer burning cigarette

Multi tubular

Ribbon

Tube

Rod

Lamel

Disc

Perforated disc

◀ **Figure 9.36** *Powder granules are shaped to optimize the surface area for given applications. See also the photo in Figure 9.35.*

to inside are categorized as **degressive-burning** powders, whereas **neutral-burning** powders burn evenly. Neutral burning is accomplished by creating holes and pores in the powder granules, exposing more of their surface. A **progressive-burning** powder results from coating the propellant with a **deterrent**. At first, burning is inhibited, but it increases in speed as the deterrent is consumed.[9]

   The act of pulling a trigger initiates a set of linked combustion events (explosion and deflagration) that generates a complex mixture of compounds. This residue is seen in Figure 9.31 as the cloud of smoke and burning particle ejected from the weapon. Collectively, these products are called gunshot residue, the chemical analysis of which will be described in the next chapter. Gunshot residue is distance and, to some extent, time, dependent; it is most pronounced within 6″ of the target, and little is transferred to a target more than 18″ from the muzzle of the weapon. Because it is particulate based, gunshot residue, like any transfer evidence, can be dislodged from a surface.

SUMMARY

From flame to bomb, the underlying chemistry of combustion is the same: a rapid oxidative decomposition that produces large volumes of hot expanding gases. A slower reaction front produces deflagration, while a rapid and confined mixture can explode. Combustion can be understood by looking at four of its aspects: thermodynamics, kinetics, heat transfer, and mass transfer. All four are intimately involved across the combustion continuum. Any combustion produces physical evidence, the analysis of which is the subject of the next chapter.

KEY TERMS AND CONCEPTS

Adiabatic combustion
Buoyant flame
Caliber
Deflagration
Degressive-burning propellant
Deterrent
Detonation
Detonation wave
Double-base powder
Explosion
Explosive power index
Flash point
Gauge
Guncotton
High explosive

Ignition energy
Incendiary device
Laminar flame
Lean mixture
Low explosive
Lower flammability limit (LFL)
Minimum ignition energy
Molecular explosive
Muzzle velocity
Neutral-burning propellant
Oxygen balance
Percussive explosive
Point of origin
Primary explosive
Primers

Progressive-burning propellant
Propellant
Pyrolysis (combustion reactions)
Rich mixture
Saltpeter
Secondary explosive
Single-base powder
Spontaneous ignition
  temperature
Springall Roberts rules
Stoichiometric ratio
Triple-base powder
Upper flammability limit (UFL)

PROBLEMS

From the chapter

1. Suppose that 1.00 gram of nitroglycerin is used in a firearm as a propellant. Suppose also that combustion is 100% efficient and that 65% of the chemical energy is transferred to a bullet that weighs 115 grains. How fast will the bullet be moving? Will it exceed the speed of sound?

2. How is a shotgun like a pipe bomb in terms of energy conversion? How is it different?

3. ANFO is a powerful explosive mixture containing ammonium nitrate and fuel oil. It was used in the 1995 bombing of the Alfred P. Murrah Federal Building in Oklahoma City. Optimal power, related to Q, is obtained with a mixture of about 94% NH_4NO_3 and 6% fuel oil. What is the approximate oxygen balance of fuel oil?

4. Determine whether reactions 9-14 through 9-18 are exothermic or endothermic under standard conditions. For each reaction, predict how the system will respond to

  a. a decrease in volume.
  b. a decrease in pressure.
  c. a decrease in temperature.
  What assumptions have to be made? Critique them.

5. a. Methane explosions can destroy homes. Assume that a natural-gas furnace is located in an enclosed basement room of dimensions 8′ × 6′ × 8′. A leak begins and methane is introduced into the room at a rate of 100 grams per hour. The flammability limits of methane are approximately 0.5 to 1.6. If the pressure in the room is 1 atmosphere and the temperature is 18°C, how long will it be before the methane concentration reaches a flammable stage?

  b. The same scenario as in part a occurs in a home located in the mountains of New Mexico, where the atmospheric pressure is approximately 0.89 atmosphere. How does this change the situation? Justify and explain your answer.

c. Based on material shown in Figure 9.27, what additional considerations play into your interpretation of the data?

6. Two common solvents used in clandestine drug laboratories are diethyl ether and acetone. Being less than vigilant in laboratory and safety practices, clandestine chemists often work with leaky equipment. If a person were brought to the emergency room under suspicious circumstances, where would you predict the burn patterns on the person's body to be most pronounced if he or she was injured by a fire or explosion at a clandestine laboratory?

7. A temperature above the flash point of a fuel is a necessary condition for combustion, but is it a sufficient one?

8. Based on the results of part a of Example Problem 9-5, comment on the oxygen balance of nitroglycerin.

9. a. Use the Springall Roberts rules (Table 9-5) to predict the products of an explosion of TNT.
   b. If 1.00 gram of TNT is detonated, what is the total volume of gas produced?
   c. How much heat is produced?

10. Crude bombs can be made from dry ice. How do they work and, what type of chemical evidence would be left behind if one were used?

Integrative

1. Triacetone triperixide, (TATP, $C_9H_{18}O_6$) is an extremely powerful and sensitive explosive first made in the late 1800s.

2. a. Find the structure of TATP.
   b. Calculate the value of $\Delta H°$ for the complete combustion of TATP at stoichiometric equivalence.
   c. How many moles of gaseous products would be produced by the explosion of 10.0 g of TATP?
   d. What would the IR spectrum of TATP look like (roughly)? Assign bands and intensities. What features common to other explosives are noticeably absent?

2. How do silencers work? Would the use of a silencer impart changes to the physical evidence left by firing it, compared with a nonsilenced weapon?

Food for thought

1. Hydrogen is billed as "the fuel of the future" for automobiles. A popular misconception, mostly due to films of the *Hindenburg* disaster, is that cars which store hydrogen as fuel will be more likely to explode in an accident than current cars that use gasoline. Why is this a misconception?

FURTHER READING

Akhavan, J., "Ch. 5: Thermochemistry of Explosives," in J. Akhavan, *The Chemistry of Explosives*. Cambridge, U.K.: Royal Society of Chemistry, 1998.

Almirall, J. R., and K. G. Furton, eds. *Analysis and Interpretation of Fire Scene Evidence*. Boca Raton, FL: CRC Press, 2004.

DeHann, J. D., *Kirk's Fire Investigation*, 5th ed. Upper Saddle River, NJ: Prentice Hall, 2002.

Glassman, I. *Combustion*, 3d ed. San Diego: Academic Press, 1996.

Kelly, J. *Gunpowder: Alchemy, Bombards, and Pyrotechnics: The History of the Explosive That Changed the World*. New York: Basic Books, 2004.

Turns, S. R. *An Introduction to Combustion*, 2d ed. Boston: McGraw-Hill, 2000.

REFERENCES

1. Akhavan, J. "Ch. 5: Thermochemistry of Explosives," in J. Akhavan, *The Chemistry of Explosives*. Cambridge, U.K.: Royal Society of Chemistry, 1998.

2. Turns, S. R. "Ch. 2: Combustion and Thermochemistry," in S. R. Turns, *Introduction to Combustion: Concepts and Applications*, 2d ed. Boston: McGraw-Hill, 2000.

3. Turns, S. R. "Ch. 5: Some Important Chemical Mechanisms," in S. R. Turns, *Introduction to Combustion: Concepts and Applications*, 2d ed. Boston: McGraw-Hill, 2000.

4. Turns, S. R. "Ch. 8: Laminar Premixed Flames," in S. R. Turns, *Introduction to Combustion: Concepts and Applications*, 2d ed. Boston: McGraw-Hill, 2000.

5. Gamboa, J. A., et al. "Rate Controlling Factors in a Bunsen Burner Flame." *Journal of Chemical Education* 80 (2003), 524–528.

6. Glassman, I. "Chapter 5: Detonation," in I. Glassman, *Combustion*, 3d ed. San Diego: Academic Press, 1996.

7. Akhavan, J. "Ch. 3: Combustion, Deflagration, and Detonation," in J. Akhavan, *The Chemistry of Explosives*. Cambridge, U.K.: Royal Society of Chemistry, 1998.

8. Hopler, R. B. "Ch. 1: The History, Development, and Characteristics of Explosives and Propellants," in A. Beveridge, *Forensic Investigation of Explosives*. London: Taylor and Francis, 1998.

9. Rowe, W. F. "Ch. 8: Firearms Identification," in R. Saferstein, *Forensic Science Handbook*. Upper Saddle River, NJ: Prentice Hall, 1988.

10

Combustion, Part II: Forensic Analysis of Physical Evidence Associated with Combustion

10.1   Arson and Fire Investigation
10.2   Gunshot Residue
10.3   Explosives

OVERVIEW

Next to drug analysis, physical evidence related to combustion events makes up the second-largest category of forensic chemistry casework. To describe the forensic analysis of combustion-related evidence, we will use the same continuum as that employed in Chapter 9. We'll begin with a discussion of deflagration in arson cases. The forensic chemist is concerned principally with testing fire debris for the presence of liquid accelerants, so that is where we will concentrate our efforts. Next, we'll move into propellants and gunshot residue, which involves both deflagration and explosions. We'll wrap up the chapter with a discussion of the forensic analysis of low and high explosives both in the field and in the laboratory.

10.1 ARSON AND FIRE INVESTIGATION

In 2002, an estimated 44,500 fires were intentionally set in buildings and about 41,000 fires were intentionally set in vehicles such as cars and boats.[1] Total property loss was about $1.1 billion, and the fires caused at least 350 deaths. In structures, about 8.6% of the fires were intentionally set, whereas for vehicles, the percentage was 12.4%. Intentionally set fires, or arson, usually involve an **accelerant** of some type, as well as an **incendiary device** used to ignite it, and these two components create the physical evidence forensic chemists work with. Arson fires are also referred to as incendiary fires, which are ignited by an incendiary device.

One of the challenges of fire investigation is the classification of a fire as natural, accidental, or incendiary (arson). Fire investigators utilize evidence at the scene, as well as forensic analysis, to make such determinations. One of the most important pieces of information required in making a determination of arson is the location of the point or points of origin of the fire. Multiple points of origin are strongly indicative of an intentionally set fire, whereas a point of origin at an electrical outlet suggests an accidental fire. As discussed in Section 9.4, the behavior of a fire creates predictable damage that is useful in locating a point of origin. While such fire and fire scene investigations are critical in determinations of arson, we will focus on the chemical analysis aspects of fire and arson investigation. The former is fire investigation; the latter is forensic chemistry.

10.1.1 ACCELERANTS AND INCENDIARY DEVICES

An **accelerant** is anything that is intentionally placed at a scene to start and sustain a fire. Accelerants can be solids (wood, paper, road flares), liquids (gasoline), or gases (natural gas, propane). Although a gaseous accelerant will not leave chemical residues, there will always be physical evidence related to the container used to hold or deliver it. For example, if bottled propane is used to start a fire, the bottle will remain even though the propane will not. As with any type of combustion, fuel, oxidant, and a source of ignition are required for combustion, and the forensic chemist will be concerned with two of these three: the fuel, such as an accelerant, and the incendiary device. The latter can be as simple as a match, a candle, or a smoldering cigarette. More complex devices are also seen; however, we will focus on the analysis of accelerants, since they represent the bulk of the casework seen by forensic chemists. The most common accelerants are liquid petroleum distillate products. Also frequently seen as physical evidence are gasoline, kerosene, and diesel fuel.

As the name implies, **petroleum distillates** are extracted from crude oil by distillation. The process shown in Figure 10.1 is one of many available, but for our purposes, it is the most useful because of the parallels between distillation and gas chromatography.[†] As shown in the figure, crude oil is introduced into the cracking tower and heated to about 350°C, volatilizing much of its content. The vapors rise, cool, and condense, whereupon they are collected on plates and removed. The heavier fractions, such as diesel and kerosene, are collected lower in the tower than are gasolines and fuel gases. The separation is not complete,

---

[†]Recall that one measure of the efficiency of a chromatographic column is the number of theoretical plates. This analogy is drawn from distillation: The more collection plates in the column, the more effective is the separation. The maximum number of plates (N) is achieved when the distance between them (i.e., the smallest possible height of a plate, HETP) is minimized.

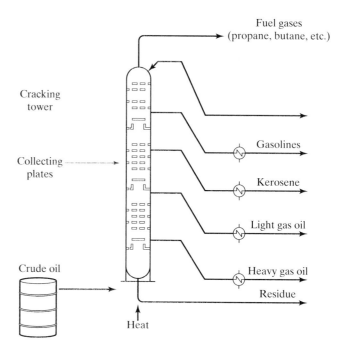

▶ **Figure 10.1** *Thermal distillation, crude oil. The oil is heated, volatilizing most of the components, which then condense as they cool. Fractions are collected that consist of a mix of hydrocarbons with similar boiling points.*

and each fraction collected consists of a mixture of hydrocarbon components with similar boiling points. This separation is re-created on a small scale when samples are analyzed by gas chromatography, which separates components on the basis of their volatility and preferential partitioning with a solid phase.

10.1.2 FORENSIC ANALYSIS OF FIRE DEBRIS

The most frequently encountered accelerants are readily available petroleum distillates such as gasoline, jet fuel, and kerosene. ASTM has published a classification for ignitable liquids that is widely used as part of the forensic analysis of fire debris; a summary is presented in Table 10.1. Each class is further

Table 10.1 Classification of Ignitable Liquids (after ASTM)			
Class	Light (C_4–C_9)	Medium (C_8–C_{13})	Heavy (C_8+)
Gasoline	Primarily C_4–C_{12}		
Petroleum distillates	Pet ether	Charcoal starter fluids	Kerosene, diesel oil
	Lighter fluids (butane)		
Isoparaffinics	Aviation gas (av gas)	Paint thinners, copier toners	Specialty solvents
Aromatics	Toluenes and xylenes, degreasers	Degreasers, specialty cleaning agents, fuel additives	Industrial cleaning solvents
Naphthenic paraffins	Cyclohexane-based solvents	Lamp oils	Lamp oils, industrial solvents
n-Alkanes	Solvents to heptane	Candle oils	Copier toners
De-aromatized distillates	Camp stove fuels	Some paint thinners	Odorless kerosenes
Oxygenated solvents	Ketones, lacquers	Metal cleaners	
Miscellaneous	Blends	Turpentines	Specialty products

Source: ASTM Standard E 1618, "Test Method for Ignitable Liquid Residues in Extracts from Fire Debris Samples by Gas Chromatography–Mass Spectrometry."

subdivided into three groups based on carbon chain length, which correlates with volatility. As we will see shortly, volatility plays an important role in laboratory analysis.

Fire debris evidence is collected in coated paint cans of various sizes with a predrilled hole sealed with a septum. The debris is placed loosely in the can, leaving plenty of headspace above. Like all paint cans, the can is closed by pounding the lid into the metal lip. This creates an airtight seal that traps vapors, including any residual volatile accelerants. Table 10.2 and Figure 10.2 summarize existing ASTM-recommended protocols for fire debris preparation and analysis. They also summarize the evolution of sample preparation methods over the past decades. The first protocols used involved steam distillation. Fire debris (slightly wet) is transferred to a distillation apparatus, and heat is applied. As the vapors rise in the distillation column, they are cooled and condense, dropping into a collection thimble. Any petroleum products collect as a layer atop water. This approach is effective in separating and concentrating accelerants, but is time consuming and relatively aggressive, meaning that more volatile components can be lost.

The next development in sample preparation was solvent extraction of fire debris with pentane and carbon disulfide (CS_2). Solvent is added to the evidence, collected, and concentrated into a small volume (about 1–5 mL). Both pentane and CS_2 are nonpolar and well suited to solvation of petroleum hydrocarbons, but both also have limitations. Pentane is extremely volatile, so care must be taken to ensure that the solvent extract does not go to dryness. If it does, the lighter fractions will be lost along with the pentane. Carbon disulfide is not as volatile, but it is relatively toxic and has a foul odor. Additionally, solvent extraction, like steam distillation, is relatively aggressive and can result in a loss of the more volatile fractions of residual accelerants.

Currently, the favored methods of sample preparation are based on headspace (Chapter 4, Section 4.4). The headspace may be heated or unheated,

Table 10.2 ASTM Standards Relevant to Fire Debris Analysis	
Number (E-)	**Title and Subject**
1385	Standard Practice for Separation and Concentration of Ignitable Liquid Residues from Fire Debris Samples by Steam Distillation
1386	Practice for the Separation and Concentration of Ignitable Liquid Residues from Fire Debris Samples by Solvent Extraction
1387	Test Method for Ignitable Liquid Residues in Extracts from Fire Debris Samples by Gas Chromatography
1388	Practices for Sampling of Headspace Vapors from Fire Debris Samples
1389	Cleanup of Fire Debris Samples Extracts by Acid Stripping[a]
1412	Practice for Separation of Ignitable Liquid Residues from Fire Debris Samples by Passive Headspace Concentration with Activated Charcoal
1413	Practice for Separation and Concentration for Ignitable Liquid Residues for Fire Debris Samples by Dynamic Headspace Concentration
1618	Test Method for Ignitable Liquid Residues in Extracts from Fire Debris Samples by Gas Chromatography Mass Spectrometry
2154	Practice for Separation of Ignitable Liquid Residues from Fire Debris Samples by Passive Headspace Concentration with Solid Phase Microextraction

[a] Used to remove nitrogenous and oxygenated species from a prepared extract.

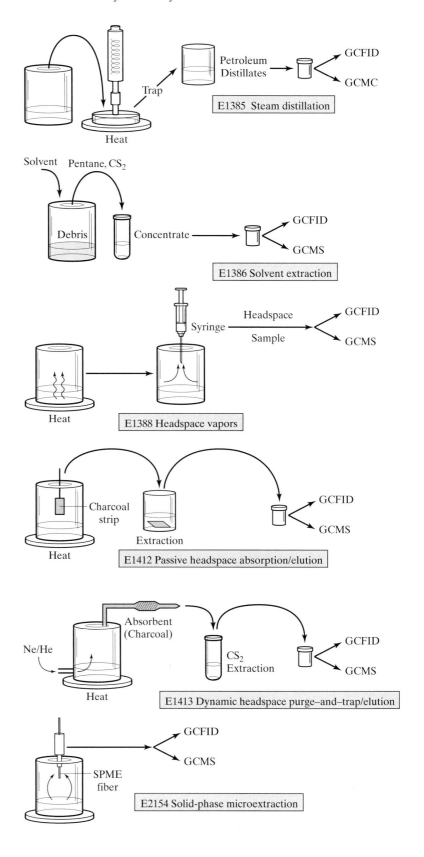

▶ **Figure 10.2** *Depiction of the sample preparations used in analyzing fire debris.*

Historical Evidence 10.1—Crude-Oil Distillation

Distillation is one of the oldest techniques used by chemists, but using it to refine crude oil began when the first crude-oil well was drilled in 1859. The site of this well was Titusville, Pennsylvania. The reserve tapped was called "rock oil," and it led to the construction of stills that operated on the same principle as the distillation towers described in the text. Demand for petroleum products soared after the turn of the century, with the invention of the internal combustion engine and the wide availability of cars. Thermal distillation techniques predominated until the 1930s, when catalytic techniques emerged.

Source: "Petroleum Refining." *Encyclopedia Britannica Online*. Accessed February 15, 2005. URL: http://search.eb.com/eb/article?tocId = 9110685.

▲ **Figure 10.3** *The types of containers used to collect fire debris samples.*

passive or active. All headspace methods involve concentrating volatiles into a solid phase by absorption. The effect is the same as a solvent extraction: Target analytes are extracted from the fire debris matrix and concentrated on the adsorbent. Generically, this protocol is called trapping, and in the case of fire debris, the trap is made of charcoal. In simple passive methods, a polymer strip coated with charcoal is dangled above the fire debris and the evidence can be resealed. Gentle heating drives the volatiles into the vapor phase, from which they move via diffusion to the charcoal, where they are absorbed. At the end of the heating time, the charcoal strip is removed and extracted with a solvent such as CS_2. Active or dynamic headspace (DHS) is also called purge-and-trap, a methodology widely used in environmental analysis. In DHS, an inert gas constantly flows through the heated container, carrying volatiles downstream to a trap. Because the equilibrium analytes (debris) $\rightleftharpoons$ analytes (vapor) is constantly disturbed by removal of product, the volatiles are efficiently extracted and trapped. Solvents are used to desorb the sample traps. DHS methods are particularly effective with low concentrations of residual accelerants.

Another passive method of vapor preconcentration is solid phase microextraction (SPME). The procedure is much like that used for the charcoal strip, except that other adsorbents are used to coat the silica needle. The needle can be directly introduced into the gas chromatograph for thermal desorption, or a solvent extraction can be employed.[2] An added advantage of SPME is versatility: The fiber can be immersed in an aqueous matrix if the fire debris is waterlogged. Currently, ASTM lists as a screening technique standard E 2154-01, but high sensitivity and a solventless approach make the SPME method increasingly attractive. A chromatogram of the same sample prepared by different methods is presented in Figure 10.4. Note the peak to the far left on the lower two frames, attributable to the CS_2 used in the extraction. Detection was with an FID, and the sample was gasoline on charred carpet.

No matter what sample preparation method is used, discrimination occurs and there are inherent limitations. Analyses of fire debris samples are designed to detect a wide range of compounds and, as a result, are not optimized for any one compound. Headspace methods will be biased toward the more volatile materials, even under conditions of gentle heating. Excessively aggressive heating can drive off the more volatile fractions, so heating temperature is limited and typically falls into the range of approximately 70°C. The efficiency of a solvent extraction, like any partitioning, will depend on the relative polarities of the solutes and solvent; in a complex hydrocarbon mixture, discrimination is inevitable and some compounds will be desorbed more efficiently than others. Similarly, not all components of an accelerant will be absorbed with equal efficiency

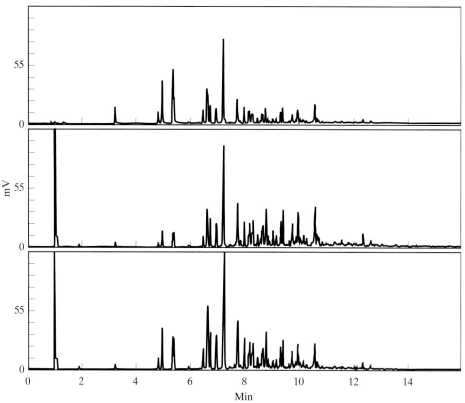

▶ **Figure 10.4** *Comparison of recovery by 3 heated headspace enrichment methods. Sample: Fire debris sample, gasoline on a charred matrix of carpet and carpet padding (Instrument 1). Top: SPME, Carboxen/PDMS fiber (70°C, 3 min extraction). Middle: Static headspace enrichment (90°C, 16 h extraction). Bottom: Dynamic headspace enrichment (80°C, 15 min extraction). Reprinted with permission from Ren, Q., and W. Bertsch, "A Comprehensive Sample Preparation Scheme for Accelerants in Suspect Arson Cases," Journal of Forensic Sciences 44 (1999), 504–515. Copyright 1999, ASTM International.*

onto charcoal or other solid phases.[3] These caveats do not mean that the methods are fatally flawed, but they do mean that the limitations of each technique must be understood and that validated methods are essential. In the case of fire debris, the conditions that are optimal for the collection of gasoline components are likely not optimal for heavy distillates, and vice versa; the discrepancy is even more critical when nonpetroleum products, such as methyl ethyl ketones or industrial cleaning solvents, are involved. However, keep in mind that the transfer (from debris to instrument) does not have to be 100% efficient for every compound that might be in the matrix. Rather, the transfer of each target compound must be in an acceptable range and also must be reproducible. The analysis of fire debris is qualitative, not quantitative, and is based on pattern matching, not the presence or absence of any one component.

Regardless of the type of sample preparation, the instrumental method employed for fire debris analysis is gas chromatography, coupled to either a flame ionization detector or a mass spectrometer. Unlike other chromatographic methods used in forensic chemistry, the primary goal (in most cases) is to recognize patterns rather than identify specific compounds. The pattern of gasoline (Figure 10.4) differs significantly from the pattern of diesel (Figure 10.5, bottom frame), which is composed of heavier and less volatile hydrocarbons. With the use of mass spectrometry, the patterns can be further analyzed to identify significant groups of compounds within a sample, such as aromatics, alkanes, and branched alkanes.[4–6] In addition to recognizing patterns and groups of compounds, the analyst must consider environmental factors. Accelerants undergo weathering and their composition changes over time. The changes are predictable in that the more volatile a compound is, the more quickly it will be lost. For gasolines, then, weathering is more of an issue than it is for diesel. Understanding weathering and the analysis of weathered samples is essential to interpreting analytical results.

Mineral Spirits

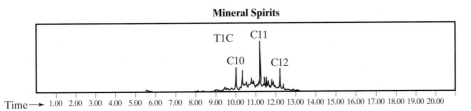

Tung Oil Furniture Polish

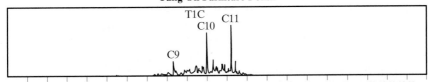

Paste Shoe Polish

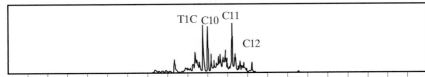

WD 40 Spray Lubricant

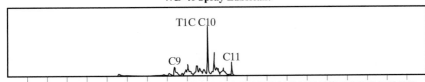

Raid Insecticide

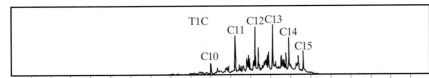

Lemon Oil Furniture Polish

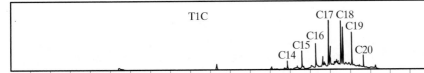

Diesel Fuel

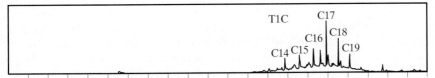

◀ **Figure 10.5** *An illustration of why control samples are critical in fire debris analysis. Many of the patterns shown here are similar to accelerant patterns. Total ion chromatograms of common household products compared with mineral spirits and diesel fuel. Reprinted with permission from Lentini, J. J., et al., "The Petroleum-Laced Background," Journal of Forensic Sciences 45 (2000), 968–989. Copyright 200, ASTM International.*

Also essential in any fire debris analysis is the collection and analysis of background samples (**matrix controls**).[7,8] For example, if debris suspected of containing an accelerant is collected on a carpet, samples of undamaged carpet should be collected as well, if at all possible. Carpeting is manufactured from synthetic fibers (Chapter 12), the raw materials of which are polymers, many derived from petroleum products. As seen in Figure 10.5, many common materials produce patterns that could be confused with accelerants. The data shown in this figure were collected by means of passive headspace–charcoal strips and heating at 80°C for 16 hours. The instrument used was a GCMS, but the patterns of the total ion chromatogram (TIC) are comparable to patterns that would be obtained from a GCFID. The figure illustrates the vital nature of controls in fire debris analysis.

Example Problem 10.1

An officer submitting fire debris requests that you analyze it for the presence of gasoline with ethanol. Would you use GCFID or GCMS?

Answer: GCMS. The FID detector would respond to ethanol (it is widely used for blood alcohol analysis), but the response is not specific. Since a complex pattern of peaks would be expected from such a sample, it would be difficult to definitively identify one as ethanol, although it would likely be one of the earliest eluting peaks. A mass spectrometer could provide definitive identification of ethanol via the compound's mass spectrum.

Whereas identifying residual accelerants is a well-developed forensic protocol, classifying an accelerant beyond gasoline, diesel, and the like is a difficult or impossible task. Part of the difficulty is attributable to **weathering** and environmental factors, part to the mass-production nature of distillates such as gasoline. Attempts have been made to allow for greater discrimination by targeting compounds other than hydrocarbons such as oxygenates. For example, ethanol is added to many gasoline formulations on a seasonal basis, so identifying ethanol in a solvent mixture could provide valuable investigatory information. Oxygenates are added to gasoline for similar reasons, to increase the oxygen balance and improve the efficiency of combustion. The main oxygenates in gasoline are shown in Table 10.3. In addition to GC methods, spectroscopy protocols have been studied in this role.[9] Other techniques that have been studied for fire debris analysis are two-dimensional gas chromatography[10] and GCMS–MS.[11]

Applying the Science 10.1   Spontaneous Combustion? Human Candles

One of the more persistent urban myths of forensic science is the belief that the human body can somehow erupt into flame and rapidly burn down to ashes with no discernible ignition source and nearly no peripheral burning. The material discussed in Chapter 9 concerning heat and mass transfer, fuel–air ratios, flammability limits, and the conditions that must be met for successful ignition are sufficient to debunk any ideas of spontaneous human combustion, but the myth persists.

To combat misperceptions, a series of experiments was conducted and the results recently reported in the *Journal of*

Forensic Sciences. The author noted that, in most cases of spontaneous human combustion, a source of ignition can be located, with cigarettes being one common culprit. The mystery centers on how a body can burn with such ferocity (a large Q value) and become incinerated while nearly all the furniture—even furniture the victim is sitting on—is barely damaged. One theory is the "wick effect," in which the fat in a body supplies a wick consisting of clothing to facilitate a long burn of a victim such that most of the body's mass is consumed as fuel, leaving little but small amounts of bone behind. The author of the article cited here conducted experiments and monitored the heat of

Applying the Science 10.1 (Continued)

combustion of biological materials, including and fat, tissue, bone, and an amputated leg. The results supported the theory of the wick effect of human combustion, but not spontaneous human combustion.

Source: Christensen, A. M. "Experiments in the Combustibility of the Human Body." *Journal of Forensic Sciences* 47 (2002), 466–470.

Table 10.3   Oxygenates in Gasoline

Ethanol	 H_3C ⌃ OH
Methyl-tert-butylether (MTBE)	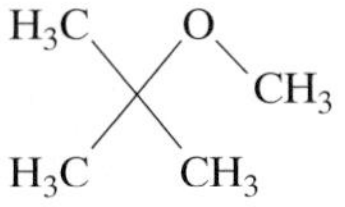
Ethyl-tert-butylether (ETBE)	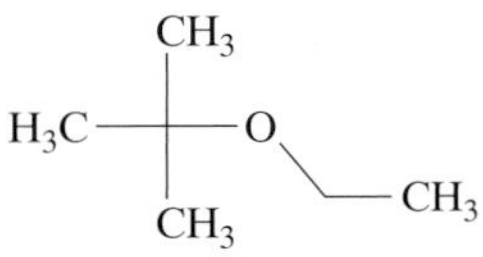
Tert-amyl-methyl ether (TAME)	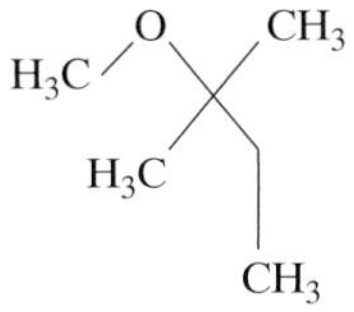

10.2 GUNSHOT RESIDUE

When a gun is fired and a bullet strikes and passes through a target, several forms of evidence are transferred, as shown in Figure 10.6. If the muzzle is extremely close to or touching the target, burn patterns may be evident. A dark ring called *bullet wipe* is created by lubricants and other foreign matter transferred from the bullet to the target as the bullet enters. Grains of unburned or partially burned propellant can adhere to the target as well, as do organic and inorganic combustion products and byproducts. However, the term **gunshot residue** (GSR) refers to residues traceable to the primer used to ignite the propellant.[12] Like any combustible mixture, the primer contains fuel and oxidant as well as a shock sensitive initiator. Lead styphnate is a typical initiator that detonates when struck by the firing pin. The typical fuel in primers is antimony sulfide (SbS), while the oxidant is barium nitrate $(Ba(No_3)_2)$. The three metals are the principal ingredients in GSR.

As seen in Figure 9.31 and Figure 10.7, GSR travels a significant distance from the muzzle of the gun, but a distance that is still measured in inches. In general, GSR is expected to be found when the muzzle is within a foot or so of the target. Beyond about 18″, the amount of GSR transferred to a target falls dramatically to undetectable levels. Variables of importance include the caliber of the weapon, the ammunition, and wind conditions. Figure 9.31 illustrates how GSR and other products of the firing event propagate outward in a cone-shaped zone away from the muzzle of the gun. Particulates settle out of the plume based on their morphology and weight. When larger particles of unburned powder or other

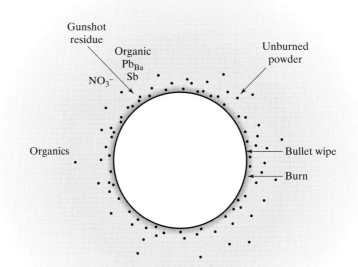

▶ **Figure 10.6** *The different types of physical evidence produced by firing a gun into a target at relatively close range.*

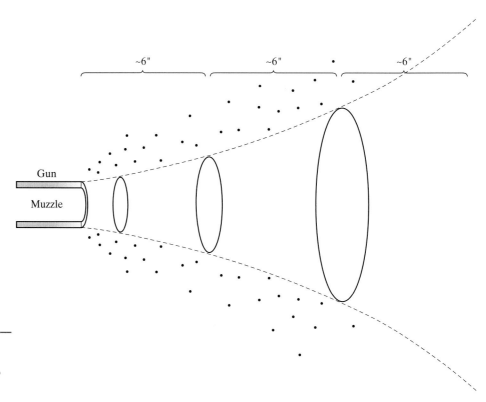

▶ **Figure 10.7** *The cone-shaped dispersal of GSR as a function of distance from the muzzle.*

Historical Evidence 10.2—Guns

It's not surprising that the culture credited with inventing gunpowder engineered the first guns. The Chinese were utilizing gunpowder to hurl projectiles at their enemies. Their original designs, called fire lances, were used as crude flamethrowers, with small projectiles added in. Later versions were optimized into what could be called crude shotguns. One version was called "Nine-Arrow Heart-Piercing Magic Poison Thunderous Fire Erupter."

Source: Kelly, J., "Ch. 1: Fire Drug," in J. Kelly, *Gunpowder: Alchemy, Bombards, and Pyrotechnics: The History of the Explosive That Changed the World.* New York: Basic Books, 2004.

residue are found associated with a bullet hole, they indicate a short distance between the muzzle and the target. Determining the distance between a shooter and a target is an important application for the chemical detection of GSR.

10.2.1 Elemental and Inorganic Analysis

Although no longer frequently employed, analyses targeting anions (nitrates and nitrites) were once routinely used as tests for GSR. Nitrates are found in the oxidizers of fuels and propellants and are easily detected with the use of simple reagents. However, nitrates are nearly ubiquitous, being found in cosmetics, fertilizers, and numerous commercial products. Nitrites are less common in the environment. Reagents used for presumptive tests for nitrates include diphenylamine (DPA) and naphthylamine (Figures 10.8, 10.9). The paraffin test, or dermal nitrate test, involved dipping a suspect's hand in warm wax and allowing it to set. The peeled wax was then treated with diphenylamine or similar reagents to reveal deposition patterns of nitrates. This test has largely been abandoned due to excessive false positive rates. The **Walker** test used in distance determinations is based on naphthylamine–sulfanilic acid-impregnated photographic paper. The target surface—typically clothing—is placed in contact with the paper. An iron is used to press the fabric into the paper, resulting in reddish patterns marking nitrite deposits.

Another presumptive test for nitrates is the Griess test. The **Griess** reagent consists of sulfanilamide and naphthylamine in acidic solution, although there are many variations of the recipe. Elemental zinc or cadmium may also be present. The Griess reagent reduces NO_3^- to NO_2^-, and the nitrite reacts with the reagents to form the characteristic azo dye as shown in Figure 10.10.[13] Lead and barium residues are detected using sodium rhodizonate

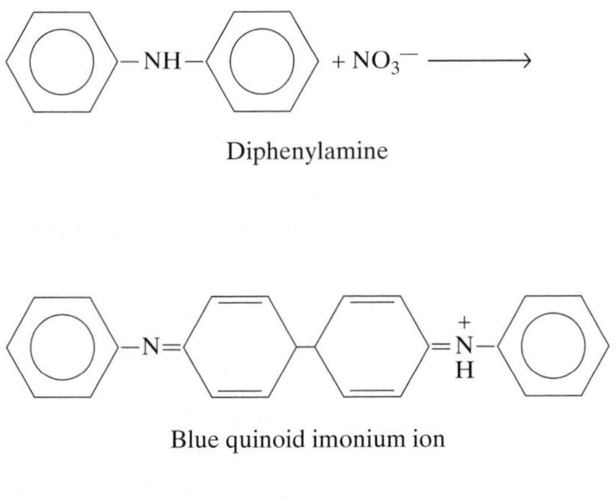
NH
+ NO3−
Diphenylamine
N=
=N
H
Blue quinoid imonium ion

◀ **Figure 10.8** *The reaction with diphenylamine and nitrate to produce a blue color.*

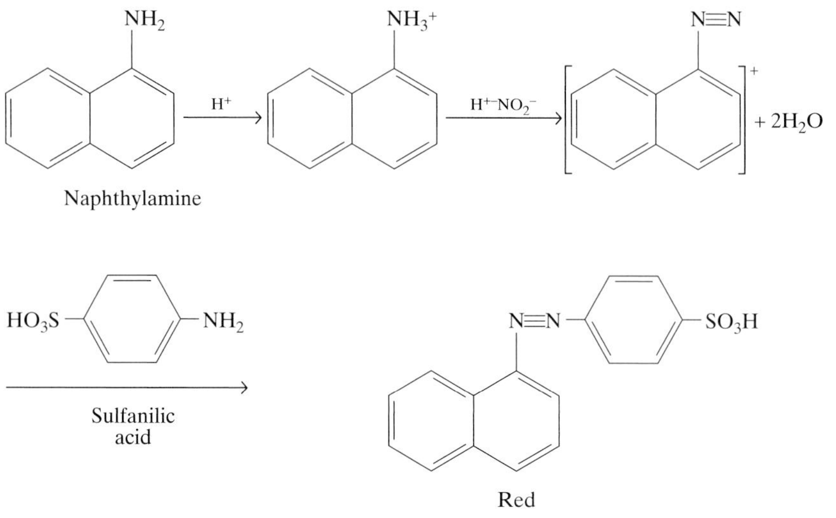

▶ **Figure 10.9** *The naphthyl-amine test.*

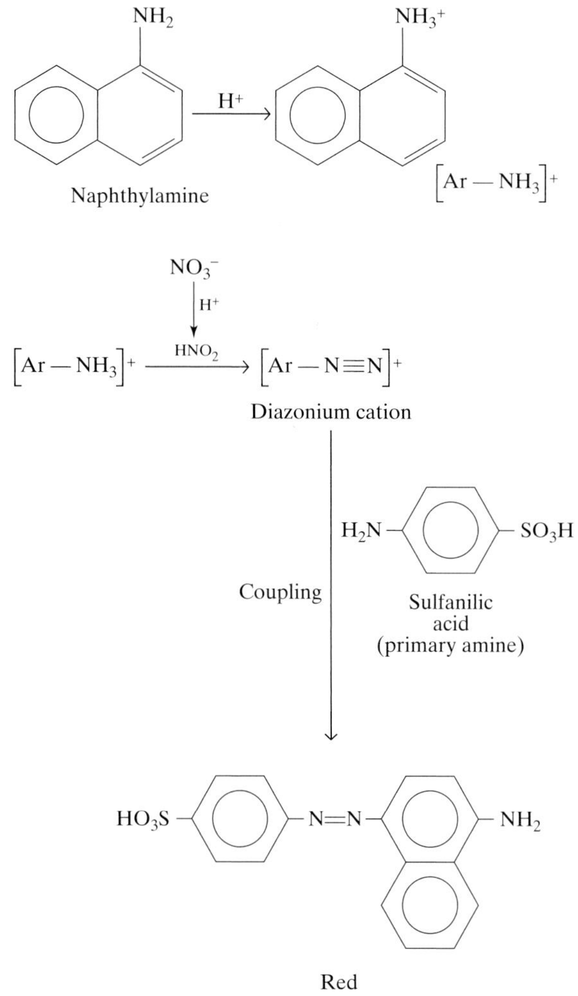

▶ **Figure 10.10** *The Walker test.*

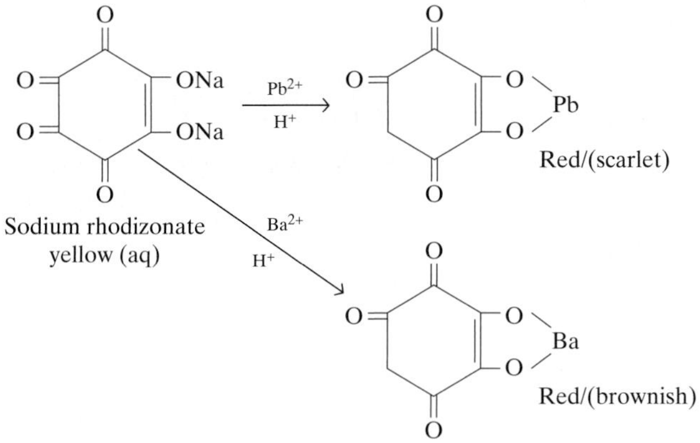

◄ **Figure 10.11** *The sodium rhodizonate test. An example is shown in the color insert.*

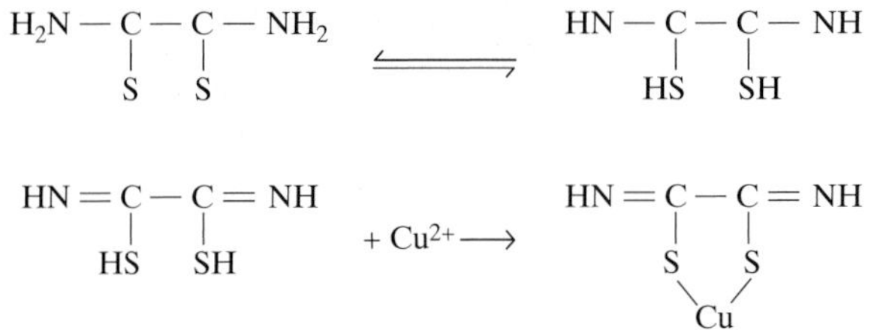

◄ **Figure 10.12** *Rubeanic acid and its reaction with copper.*

(Figure 10.11). Concerns about lead toxicity have led to the introduction of lead-free primers, making the rhodizonate test less useful when such ammunition is employed. An alternative is rubeanic acid, which will react with copper.[14] The copper originates from the cartridge casing, bullet, or primer casing, but not from the chemical compounds in the primer.

The compounds that definitively identify material as GSR are particulates containing lead, antimony, and barium. The morphology of the particulates is also important. These distinctive particles are not simply unburned residues of the primer, but particulates that form under the unique combustive and explosive environment created when the primer is detonated by the impact of a firing pin.[12,15] As the primer detonates or deflagrates, gases are released into a hot, high-pressure environment. Elemental metals are vaporized and condense with cooling, resulting in particulates ranging in size from about 10 to 100 μm. Many, but not all, of these are spherical. Just as occurs in solution, smaller particles can aggregate to form larger ones that will appear lumpy and irregular. The key feature is that these particles are condensates, a fact that defines their morphology.[15] Currently, particulates containing Pb–Sb–Ba are considered characteristic of GSR,[12,16,17] as are those containing Sb and Ba together.[16] Other combinations are considered to be consistent with GSR, but not uniquely identificatory; these combinations include elements such as Ca, S, and Si.

Lead-free primers, created in response to environmental concerns, complicate the identification of GSR; however, such particulates retain the physical characteristics of condensed metals. Table 10.4 summarizes key analytical findings relating to lead-free primers. Another alternative to lead styphnate as an initiator are mercury compounds, such as mercury fulminate[†] (Table 9.4). Not surprisingly, little mercury residue is found in the GSR, due to the volatility of mercury.[18]

[†]From an environmental perspective, even worse than lead.

Example Problem 10.2

Assume that a plume of GSR is hot enough to melt all compounds and reduce metals to their elemental gaseous state. Predict the layering of a spherical condensate.

Answer: The elements of interest are Pb, Sb, and Ba, with the following characteristics:

	Mass (g/mole)	Melting point (°C)
Ba	137.34	727
Sb	121.75	631
Pb	207.2	328

Assuming a uniform temperature gradient, barium will condense first, lead last.

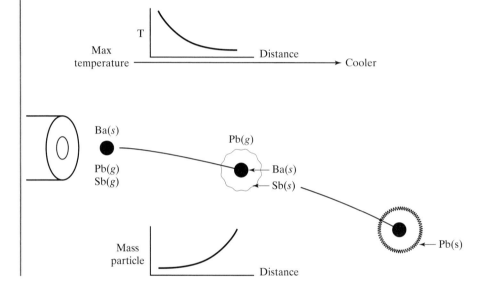

Exhibit A: Bullet Lead

GSR is the most common subject of chemical analysis applied to firearms, but it is not the only one. Bullets can be characterized with inorganic analysis methods such as inductively coupled plasma mass spectroscopy (ICP-MS). As with many other characterization protocols described in this text, one aspect of interest is comparing surface characterization with bulk characterization. For example, a paint chip can be studied layer by layer, or the whole chip can be analyzed by means of pyrolysis GC. Both approaches have advantages and disadvantages, strengths and limitations. A recent report noted work using laser ablation ICP-MS applied to bullets for an elemental characterization, with the goal of categorizing bullets more effectively on the basis of their elemental profiles. This technique is loosely comparable to the drug-profiling methods discussed in Chapter 7.

Recent applications of bullet profiling have been controversial. Forensic chemists have employed elemental data to link bullets to boxes of ammunition and to original batches of smelted lead. The controversy swirls around an issue we have seen and will see again in this text: The characterization of inter- and intrasample variation in mass-produced items. Bullets are such items; in the article cited at the end of this exhibit, it was noted that about 100,000 pounds of lead are used to make millions of bullets. The lead contains many minor and trace constituents that could conceivably be used to characterize each batch of bullets. However, to date few data are available concerning what are normal expected variations in these trace and minor

---

Exhibit A: (Continued)

constituents in bullets. This type of data is obtained by repetitive measurements with validated methods that yield defensible mean values as well as the critical uncertainties. As we discussed in Chapter 3, knowing the range of expected values (the uncertainty) is essential before data sets can be compared. Without this foundational database, the utility of bullet analysis will remain problematical.

Source: Smith, W. D. "Controversy Over Forensic ICPMS Method." *Analytical Chemistry—"A" Pages* (2002), 411A.

Table 10.4   Characteristics of Lead-Free Primers

Elements in Primer	Primer Residues	GSR Findings
Strontium	Sr, Al,[a] Cu,[b] spherical particulates with Sr and trace Ba	Pb–Sb–Ba; Pb–Ba, Pb–Sb, Pb, Sr, Sr–Pb–Sb–Ba
Zinc and titanium	Zn, Ti	Particulate with TiO_2 core with various elements as coating; Ti; Zn

[a] Component of casing.
[b] Component of bullet.

Source: Summarized and adapted from Romolo, F. S., and P. A. Margot, "Identification of Gunshot Residue: A Critical Review," *Forensic Science International* 119 (2001), 195–211.

Methods of analysis for GSR have evolved along with the instrumentation available for elemental analysis. Prior to the advent of scanning electron microscopy–energy-dispersive X-ray (SEM–EDX) techniques, (flame and graphite furnace) atomic absorption was the principal analytical technique employed. Suspected GSR was collected with the use of wipes or swabs moistened with 1% nitric acid, and the residue collected was introduced into the instrument. Less frequently used were neutron activation analysis (NAA), anodic stripping voltammetry, and photoluminescence techniques.[17] ICP methods (AES and MS) appear promising, but have not been widely used to date for GSR.

Given the importance of particulate morphology, it is no surprise that SEM–EDX is the preferred method for GSR analysis. The disadvantages of the technique are high cost and limited availability. SEM facilitates examination of the particulates under high magnification, whereas EDX allows for elemental analysis. ASTM has published and recently reapproved a GSR standard (E 1588) for SEM–EDX. As shown in Figure 10.13, the morphology of condensed, mostly spherical, particulates is distinctive under SEM imaging conditions. Samples for SEM can be collected using tape or other adhesives. Advances in SEM techniques in recent years are the advent of automated GSR particulate searches and research into elemental ratios to further classify ammunition.[19,20] However, given the dearth of components in GSR particles and the relative scarcity of instrumentation, improved discrimination of GSR is likely to come from the organic components that are present.

10.2.2 ORGANIC ANALYSIS

Organic compounds are found in all smokeless powders and are used as fuel, as deterrents to control burn rate, and as ingredients to control consistency. A

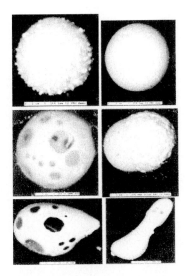

▲ **Figure 10.13** *Typical spheroid forming GSR as seen through electron microscopy. Reprinted with permission from Lebiedzik, J., and D. L. Johnson, "Handguns and Ammunitions Indicators Extacted from the GSR Analysis," Journal of Forensic Sciences 47 (2002), 483–489. Copyright 2002, ASTM International.*

Exhibit B: Not So Fast?

A recent article in the *Journal of Forensic Science* identified a possible source of particulates with the same elemental composition (Pb–Sb–Ba) as GSR. The authors noted that brake linings are a source of such particles, although the particles often also contain additional elements, such as iron and sulfur, not typically found in GSR. However, the authors also noted that the morphology of the brake-lining particulates was not consistent with that of GSR, emphasizing the necessity of looking at both the physical and chemical characteristics of any particulate before making definitive statements as to its origin.

Source: Torre, C., et al. "Brake Linings: A Source of Non-GSR Particles Containing Lead, Barium, and Antimony." *Journal of Forensic Sciences* 47 (2002), 494–504.

---

number of these compounds were listed in Table 9.6; they can be classified generically as propellants (P), stabilizers (S), and plasticizers, and the P/S ratio has been used to further classify organic gunshot residues (OGSR).[†] Other types of OGSR are summarized in Table 10.5.

OGSR is less persistent than particulate inorganic GSR. Detectable amounts have been shown to be recoverable only within the first hour or so of firing. However, false positives are minimal, a significant advantage.[21] Analytical techniques that have been applied to OGSR analysis are micellular correct as electrokinetic capillary electrophoresis (MEKC, Section 5.5.1)[21–24] and mass spectrometry,[25] with MEKC garnering the most attention. An example of an electropherogram is shown in Figure 10.14. Sampling and analytical protocols employ specialized extractions based on solvents, ultrasound, and supercritical fluid methods.[21–24,26] Some researchers have employed propellant-to-stabilizer (P/S) ratios to further classify and distinguish OGSR.[22,27] Figure 10.15 shows an example of P/S ratios from two different powders. The analysis of the bulk powders is compared with the analysis of single particulates under different experimental conditions. NG refers to nitroglycerine, Σ DPA to the sum of the diphenylamines, and EC to ethyl centralite. These experiments involved sequential firings of two different types of ammunition, and in this case little carryover in OGSR was noted from firing to firing.[22]

10.3 Explosives

According to the most recent data available from the Bureau of Alcohol, Tobacco, Firearms, and Explosives (www.atf.gov), there were 386 actual or attempted bombings in the United States in 2003 that injured 55 people and killed 7. Property damage was estimated at about $5.5 million. The forensic analysis of explosives has more in common with the analysis of propellants than it does with the analysis of arson evidence, but elements of both aspects exist. There are two broad categories of explosives analysis: techniques applied in the laboratory and those used in the field—for example, to screen airline passengers as part of pre-flight security. We will discuss both, emphasizing laboratory methods. As we saw with the analysis of fire debris, knowledge of background and matrix

---

[†]The abbreviation OGSR is sometimes used to distinguish these materials from GSR, an abbreviation used to describe particulates formed by condensation and containing the elements Pb–Sb–Ba or other combinations described.

Table 10.5 Representative Components of Organic Gunshot Residue

Name	Function	Formula
Dinitrotoluenes (DNT) 2,4; 2,6, etc.	Propellant	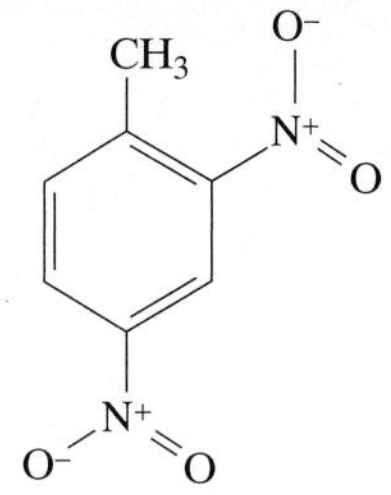
2,4,6-Trinitrotoluene (TNT)	Propellant	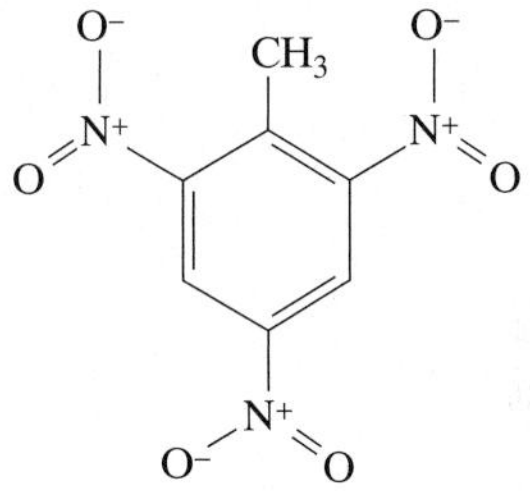
Nitroglycerine	Propellant	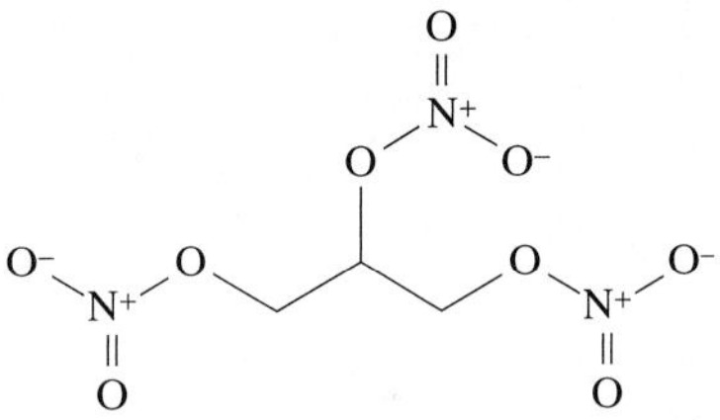
Nitrocellulose	Propellant	Various degrees of nitration
Triacetin	Plasticizer	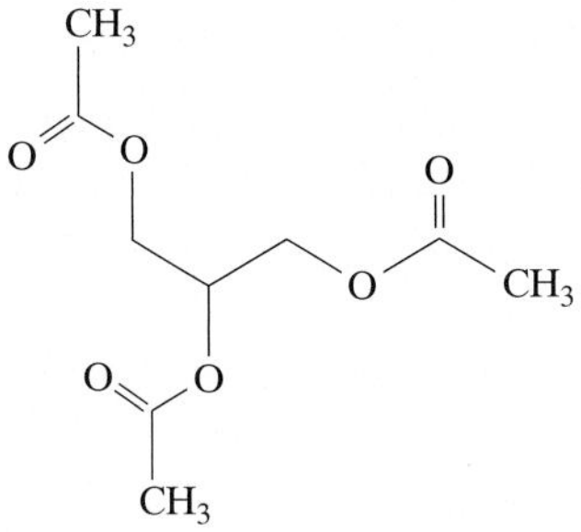
Dibutylphthalate	Plasticizer	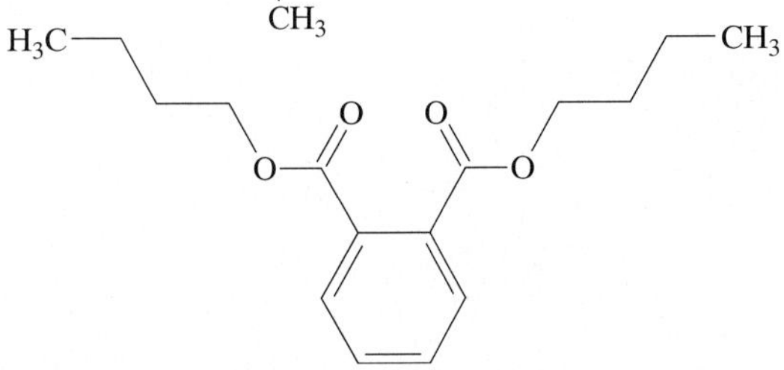
Camphor	Plasticizer	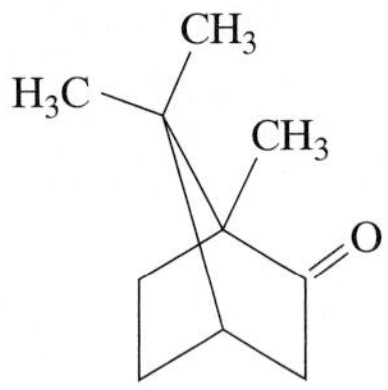

Table 10.5 (Continued)

Name	Function	Formula
Dioctylphthalate	Plasticizer	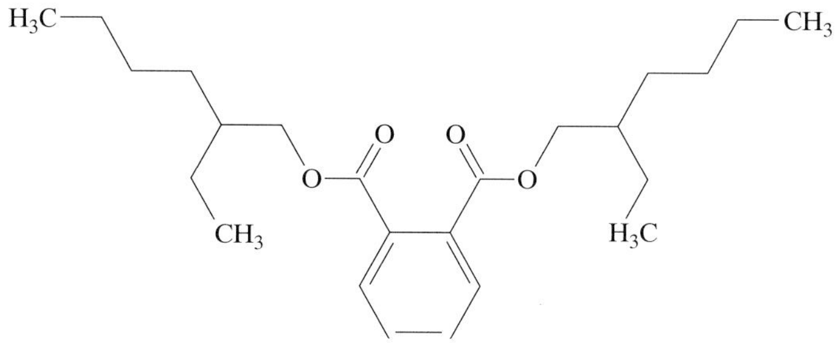
Diphenylamine	Stabilizer	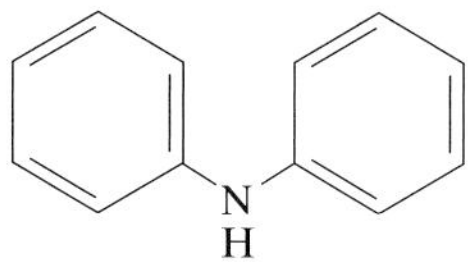
Methyl centralite (Centralite II) N,N'-dimethyl-N,N'-diphenyl -urea	Stabilizer	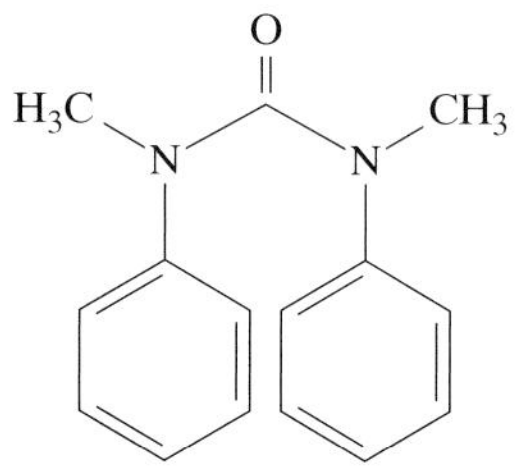
Ethyl centralite (Centralite I) N,N'-Diethylcarbanilide	Stabilizer	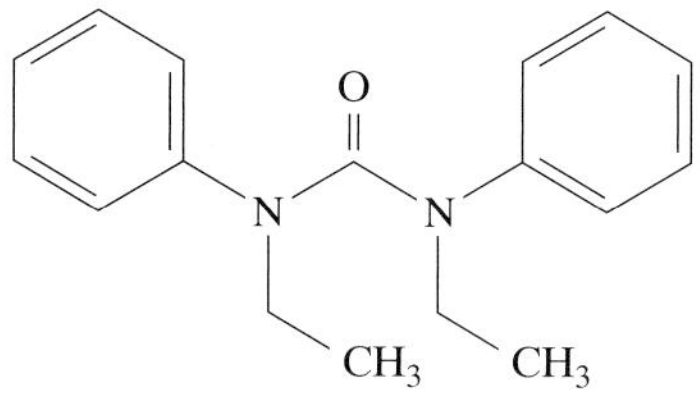
4-Nitrodiphenylamine	Reaction by product of stabilizer	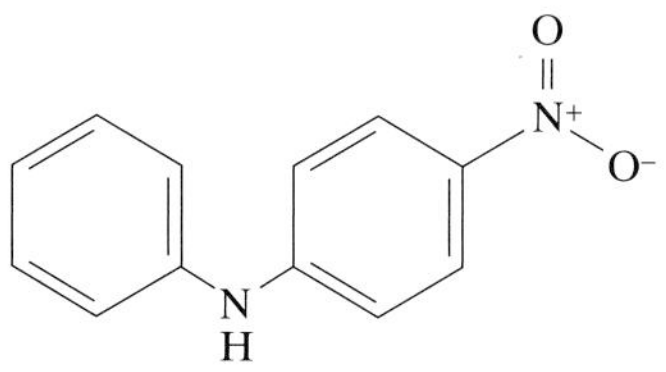
2-Nitrodiphenylamine	Reaction by product of stabilizer	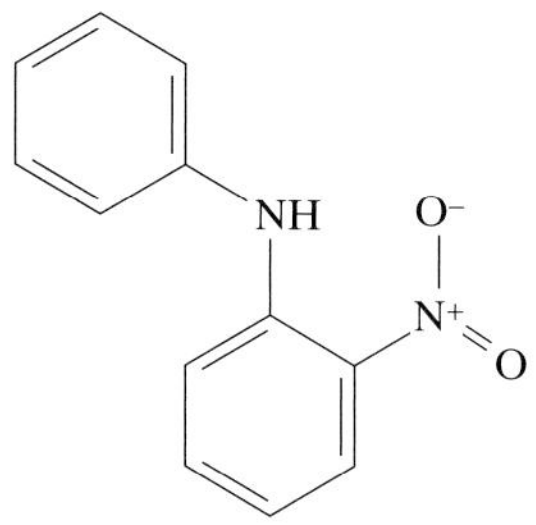

Table 10.5 (Continued)		
Name	**Function**	**Formula**
N-Nitrosodiphenylamine	Reaction by product	

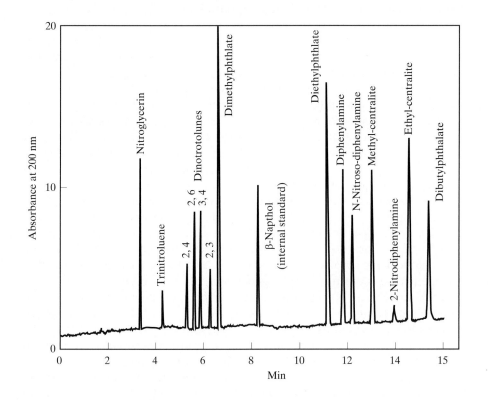

Sources: MacCrehan, W. A., et al. "Sampling Protocols for the Detection of Smokeless Powder Residues Using Capillary Electrophoresis." *Journal of Forensic Sciences* 43 (1998), 119–124. MacCrehan, W. A., et al. "Investigating the Effect of Changing Ammunition on the Composition of Organic Additives in Organic Gunshot Residue (OGSR)." *Journal of Forensic Sciences* 46 (2001), 57–62. Northrop, D. "Gunshot Residue Analysis by Micellar Electrokinetic Capillary Electrophoresis: Assessment for Application to Casework" (Parts 1 and 2). *Journal of Forensic Sciences* 46 (2001), 549–572.

◀ **Figure 10.14** *Electropherogram of the standard mixture of analytical targets under study conditions: 75 μm bare silica column, 15 mmol/L phosphate buffer (pH of 7.0), 25 mmol/L sodium dodecyl sulfate, electrokinetic injection (5 s, 2 kV), 25 kV applied for 15 min, absorbance detection with a deuterium lamp set at 200 nm. Reprinted with permission from MacCrehan, W. A., et al., "Sampling Protocols for the Detection of Smokeless Powder Residues Using Capillary Electrophoresis," Journal of Forensic Sciences 43 (1998), 119–124. Copyright 1998 ASTM International.*

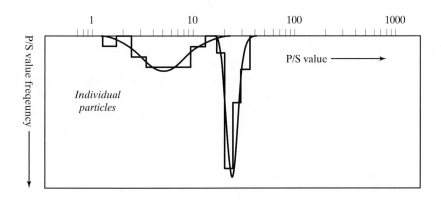

◀ **Figure 10.15** *Propellant-to-stabilizer ratios in GSR particulates obtained from two different propellants. The portion of the figure. Reprinted with permission from MacCrehan, W. A., et al., "Associating Gunpowder and Residues from Commerical Ammunition Using Compositional Analysis," Journal of Forensic Sciences 47 (2002), 260–266. Copyright 2002, ASTM International.*

contributions is critical. For example, the residuals of many explosives contain simple anions and cations, such as nitrates, phosphates, sodium, and sugars (used as oxidants). The aim of forensic detection is not so much to detect these ions, but to detect them above expected background levels. One recent report noted that sugars such as glucose and fructose were detected in many interior locations, while ions such as perchlorates and ammonium were less common.[28] Residues of high explosives have so far not been found as background materials, but only small data sets have been reported,[29,30] so further testing is worthwhile.

10.3.1 FIELD SCREENING METHODS

Ion mobility spectrometry (IMS, Section 5.5) is the most common instrument used in the field detection of explosives. At airports, IMS is utilized to screen devices such as portable computers; a swiped sample obtained by wiping a sample pad over the case is inserted into the instrument, producing an alarm–no-alarm response. IMS can also be used in a laboratory as part of a GCIMS or IMS–MS system, but to date its forensic applications have been outside the laboratory. IMS is also used at border crossings and ports to detect smuggled drugs.

IMS works by separating ion–molecule clusters on the basis of their size-to-charge ratio, and the instrument can operate in the positive- or negative-ion mode. Most explosives detection work is conducted in the negative-ion mode, in which nitrates or nitrate groups are targeted. Explosives such as nitroglycerin (NG), RDX (cyclonite), and pentaerythritol tetranitrate (PETN) are electronegative and amenable to analysis by IMS. Typically, such systems employ methylene chloride as the "doping agent," which functions as a source of dopant ions that increase selectivity and reduce background interference.[31–34]

When a sample is introduced into an ion mobility spectrometer, a soft ionization occurs via interactions with beta particles emitted by a ^{63}Ni source.[†] Molecules in air form clusters of ions or molecules, and in the negative-ion mode, these are usually species such as $O_2^-(H_2O)_n$ where n, the number of associated water molecules, depends on the humidity and other factors. These ions are referred to as reactant ions, because they always exist under atmospheric conditions. The components of the clusters are associated with each other, but can undergo further exchange reactions when a sample (generically, M) is introduced. The reactions can be complex, involving proton abstraction, fragmentation, and charge transfer[32] and creating products such as M^-, $(M - 1)^-$, and NO_2^-. When methylene chloride is present as the dopant, Cl^- ions are also present and participate in the reactions as well. The pool of potential product ions is reduced to species such as $M \cdot Cl^-(H_2O)_n$. For example, if the explosive TNT is present, the ion produced would be $C_5H_7(NO_2)_3Cl^-$ or $(TNT)Cl^-$. This ion is introduced into the drift region of the instrument, where it will separate from others based on the time it takes it to reach the detector, which is held at a positive potential to detect negative ions. Mobility spectra of two explosives are shown in Figure 10.16. Note that the RDX cluster is much farther to the right, corresponding to the longer drift time of the $RDX \cdot Cl^-$ cluster relative to the nitrate. PETN dissociates and shows a nitrate peak, but not an $M \cdot Cl^-$ peak. A recent advance in IMS is the development of a microfabricated device about the size of a 50-cent piece, but the device has not been widely deployed in field applications.

Intense interest has arisen in developing microchip-based sensors and chemical "noses" to supplement IMS instrumentation and bomb-sniffing dogs.[35–38] Because small quantities of analytes are involved, detection modes are usually,

---

[†]This is the same technique used to create ions in an electron capture detector (ECD). There are other ionization methods used in IMS, but ^{63}Ni currently is used in most field-deployable instruments.

Applying the Science 10.2   Human Heat Plumes

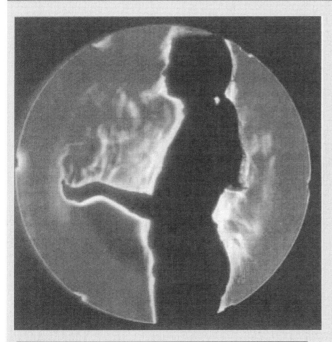

▲ *Schlieren photo of human thermal convection.*

Airport screening for explosives has taken on new urgency after September 11, 2001. To facilitate rapid and noninvasive screening, walk-through portals or other "no-touch" systems are preferred. Systems that use techniques such as ion mobility spectrometry detect explosive vapors and work well when the explosives have a high vapor pressure. These systems are more problematical, however, when the explosives have low vapor pressures, as does RDX. To enhance the efficiency of portal detection, it is imperative to maximize the transfer of residuals from the person to the sampling inlet and detection system. Because our bodies are warmer than their surroundings, a heat plume surrounds us, as shown in the accompanying figure. Just as buoyant flames produce a rising column of heated air that carries soot upward, the heat plume of the human body can do the same, albeit on a much smaller and less dramatic scale. Explosive residues clinging to skin or clothing can be caught in this plume, so the more completely the plume is sampled, the lower are the limits of detection and the more effective is the screening. In the report cited here, researchers studied the effect of clothing, motion, room temperature, and other variables on the detectability of TNT and RDX from patches worn by volunteers as they stood in a portal. Among the interesting findings were significant variations from person to person. Findings regarding explosives are applicable to other portal screening devices targeting other materials, such as drugs.

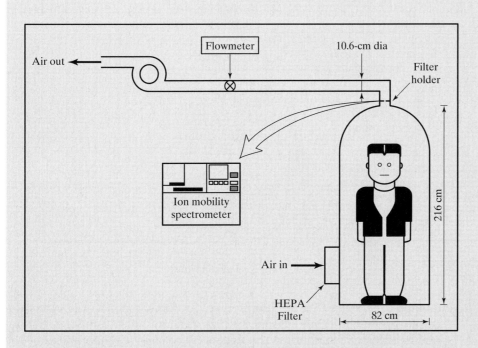

◀ *Dispersal chamber and associated apparatus.*

Source: Gowadia, H., and G. S. Settles. "The Natural Sampling of Airborne Trace Signals from Explosives Concealed upon the Human Body." *Journal of Forensic Sciences* 46 (2001), 1324–1331. Figures and captions reproduced with permission from this source; copyright 2001, ASTM International.

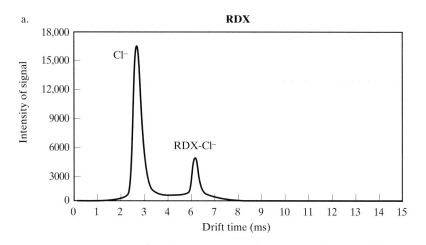

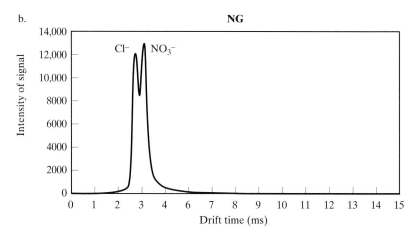

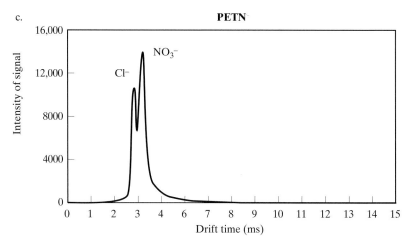

▶ **Figure 10.16** *⁶³Ni IMS spectra of 100 ng of (a) RDX, (b) NG, and (c) PETN. Spectra were obtained at 200°C with methylene chloride as dopant. Reprinted with permission from Tam, M., and H. H. Hill, "Secondary Electrospray Ionization–Ion Mobility Spectrometry for Explosive Vapor Detection," Analytical Chemistry 76 (2004), 2741–2747. Copyright 2004 American Chemical Society.*

but not exclusively, based on fluorescence. To mimic a dog's nose, many designs incorporate multiple sensors, such as different films or coatings that respond to different compounds. The signals are collated and interpreted by the associated electronics. A recent review in *Analytical Chemistry* provides an overview of numerous designs.[38] For chip-based detection, separation is incorporated into the process, just as it is in chromatographic and electrophoretic hyphenated instruments. Electrochemical and spectroscopic detection methods are employed in these devices, which are fabricated out of glass or polymeric materials. An element common to all of the devices is the frequent use of electrophoretic separations, and, as we will see in the next section, these separation techniques are ideally suited to explosives analysis.

10.3.2 LABORATORY METHODS

Prior to the wide availability of instrumentation, explosives were analyzed by color tests, TLC, and microscopy. Polarizing light microscopy has been used in many cases to identify explosives based on their crystal morphology.[39–43] SEM–EDX, the workhorse instrument for gunshot residue, has also been used for the microscopic examination of explosives.[44] Not surprisingly, the particulates created during detonation are spherical since the heat present during an explosion is sufficient to melt and vaporize most components of the explosive. However, unlike the analysis of GSR, no distinctive elemental signature of pyrotechnic residue has been identified.

Applying the Science 10.3   Immersed Explosives

The crash of TWA Flight 800 (Chapter 9, Exhibit B) raised the critical issue of how immersion in water affects analyses of explosives. The results of recent experiments show that the persistence of explosives residues depends on the type of explosive and the surface on which it was deposited. PETN (Table 9.4) was shown to be the most persistent of the explosives studied; RDX dissipated within a few hours.

Source: Kamyshny, A., et al. "Water-Soaked Evidence: Detectability of Explosive Traces after Immersion in Water." *Journal of Forensic Sciences* 48 (2003), 312–317.

Given the variety of explosives, it is no surprise that chromatography is central to their analysis. Techniques that are or have been used include TLC, GC, HPLC, ion chromatography, CE, MEKC, supercritical fluid extraction, and size exclusion chromatography.[45] Samples can be prepared for chromatographic analysis with simple solvents using water, acetone, and the like. SPME is also used to preconcentrate samples, particularly when the explosives must be extracted from an aqueous environment.[46,47] SPME can be adapted to HPLC to avoid thermal degradation issues that commonly arise in explosives. Another approach is to derivatize the explosives directly on the fiber such that the derived substance can be analyzed by means of GC.[46]

The types of detectors used in GC are primarily mass spectroscopes and thermal energy analyzers (TEAs). The latter are specialized detectors that are sensitive to nitrates and nitroso groups and that work on the basis of chemoluminescence (Figure 10.17). GCTEA is selective and widely used as a screening test for explosives and explosive residues; GCFID is also used in this role.[45] For confirmation, GCMS is the technique of choice when matrices and analytes permit its use. Limits of quantitation obtained from electron impact ionization MS have been reported in the range of 10 ng.[48] The main limitation to GCMS and other heat-based techniques is the inherent thermal liability of many explosive compounds, which results in thermal degradation in the injector port or at other heated zones in the instrument. HPLC is a versatile alternative, particularly when coupled to detectors such as mass spectrometers or photodiode arrays. The latter provides a UV/VIS scan for each data collection point in the chromatogram, analogously to the collection of mass spectra in GCMS.

Ion chromatography is a valuable tool for explosives analysis, although the associated instruments are not found in most forensic laboratories.[49] Target

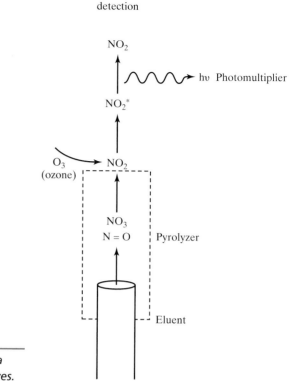

Thermoluminescense detection

▶ **Figure 10.17** *Schematic of a TEA detector used for explosives.*

analytes for IC include nitrates, nitrites, ammonium, potassium, thiocyanate, monomethylamine, chlorate, and perchlorate. IC is now being supplanted by CE methods for the detection of ions in explosive residues.[50–53] CE facilitates the detection of all ions and does not require complex suppression systems. As seen in Figure 10.18, the complete separation of common explosives is feasible

▶ **Figure 10.18** *CEC separation of 14 explosive compounds. Column: 30 cm x 75 μm i.d., 17 cm packed with 1.5-μm nonporous ODC II particles. Mobile phase: 15% methanol, 85% 10 mM MES. Running potential: 12 kV (550 V/cm in packed portion). Injection: 1 s at 2 kV of 50 mg/L (each component) sample. Reprinted with permission from Bailey, C. and C. Yan, "Separation of Explosives Using Capillary Electrochromatography," Analytical Chemistry 70 (1998), 3275–3279. Copyright American Chemical Society, 1998.*

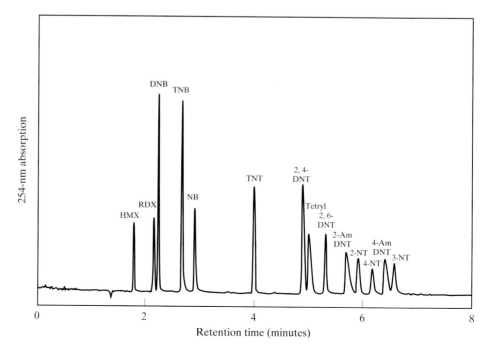

with this technique. It is also easily implemented on a small scale and so is used in prototype chip designs that were mentioned in the previous section. It is likely that GSR and explosives constitute an area of forensic chemistry in which capillary electrophoretic techniques will be widely adopted.

SUMMARY

Combustion is a continuum of the same fundamental reaction: a rapid oxidative, exothermic decomposition that produces copious quantities of hot expanding gas. The physical evidence produced by the various types of combustion is different and distinctive, requiring specialized approaches. Accelerants and fire debris are tackled with gas chromatography, while explosive residues require a wider range of tools, depending on the compounds involved. Gunshot residue is characterized by the morphology and elemental profile of particulates formed by heating and condensation. Thus, while the fundamental reactions are similar, the forensic approach to them is quite different.

This concludes the combustion portion of the text. Next we move into the world of colorants—pigments and dyes. These compounds, are the key ingredients in paints, inks, and dyes, and will lead us into an exploration of questioned documents and the world of trace evidence such as fibers.

KEY TERMS AND CONCEPTS

Accelerant	Incendiary device	Stabilizer
Cracking	Matrix controls	Walker test
Griess test	Petroleum distillate	Weathering

PROBLEMS

From the chapter

1. Is SPME destructive or nondestructive? Justify your answer.
2. Is the environment surrounding brake linings similar to that which produces GSR? Why or why not? How would you respond on the witness stand to a challenge to GSR identification based on the possibility of a false positive?

Integrative

1. Comment on the similarities between the presumptive tests for GSR shown in Figures 10.10–10.12 and those described for drugs in Chapter 7. What are the common threads?

Food for thought

1. Can you make a bomb using only dry ice? How? Does it detonate or explode?

FURTHER READING

Almirall, J. R., and K. G. Furton, eds. *Analysis and Interpretation of Fire Scene Evidence*. Boca Raton, FL: CRC Press, 2004.

DeHaan, J. D. *Kirk's Fire Investigation*, 5th ed. Upper Saddle River, NJ: Prentice Hall, 2002.

Lewis, R. J., et al. "The Analysis of Fire Debris for the Presence of Propan-2-ol Using Dynamic Headspace Concentration and Gas Chromatography with Flame Ionization Detection." *Journal of Forensic Sciences* 44 (1999), 1061–1064.

McCord, B., and K. A. Hargadon. "Explosives Analysis by Capillary Electrophoresis," in J. Yinon, ed., *Advances in the Analysis and Detection of Explosives*. Dordrecht, The Netherlands: Kluwer Academic Publishers, 1993.

Midkiff, C. R. "Ch. 9: Arson and Explosive Investigation," in R. Saferstein, ed., *Forensic Science Handbook, Vol. 1*, 2d ed. Upper Saddle River, NJ: Prentice Hall, 2002.

Rowe, W. F. "Ch. 18: Firearm and Toolmark Examinations," in S. H. James and J. J. Nordby, eds., *Forensic Science: An Introduction to Scientific and Investigative Techniques*. Boca Raton, FL: CRC Press, 2003.

Schwoeble, A. J., and D. L. Exline. *Current Methods in Gunshot Residue Analysis*. Boca Raton, FL: CRC Press, 2000.

REFERENCES

1. Karter, M. J. *Fire Loss in the United States during 2002.* National Fire Protection Association (NFPA), 2003; on the Internet at www.nfpa.org.

2. Harris, A. C., and J. F. Wheeler. "GC–MS of Ignitable Liquids Using Solvent-Desorbed SPME for Automated Analysis." *Journal of Forensic Sciences* 48 (2003), 41–46.

3. Lloyd, J. A., and P. L. Edmiston. "Preferential Extraction of Hydrocarbons from Fire Debris Samples by Solid Phase Microextraction." *Journal of Forensic Sciences* 48 (2003), 130–134.

4. Dolan, J. A., and Stauffer, E. "Aromatic Content in Medium Range Petroleum Distillate Products—Part I: An Examination of Various Liquids." *Journal of Forensic Sciences* 49 (2004), 992–1004.

5. Gilbert, M. W. "The Use of Individual Extracted Ion Profiles versus Summed Extracted Ion Profiles in Fire Debris Analysis." *Journal of Forensic Sciences* 43 (1998), 871–876.

6. Wallace, J. R. "GC/MS Data from Fire Debris Samples: Intepretation and Applications." *Journal of Forensic Sciences* 44 (1999), 996–1012.

7. Lentini, J. J. "Persistence of Floor Coating Solvents." *Journal of Forensic Sciences* 46 (2001), 1470–1473.

8. Lentini, J. J., et al. "The Petroleum-Laced Background." *Journal of Forensic Sciences* 45 (2000), 968–989.

9. Choquette, S. J., et al. "Identification and Quantitative of Oxygenates in Gasoline Ampules Using Fourier Transform Near-Infrared and Fourier Transform Raman Spectroscopy." *Analytical Chemistry* 68 (1996), 3525–3533.

10. Frysinger, G. S., and R. B. Gaines. "Forensic Analysis of Ignitable Liquids in Fire Debris by Comprehensive Two-Dimensional Gas Chromatography." *Journal of Forensic Sciences* 47 (2002), 471–482.

11. De Vos, B.-J., et al. "Detection of Petrol (Gasoline) in Fire Debris by Gas Chromatography/Mass Spectrometry/Mass Spectrometry (GC/MS/MS)." *Journal of Forensic Sciences* 47 (2002), 736–757.

12. Schwoeble, A. J., and D. L. Exline. "Ch. 2: Explanation of Gunshot Residue," in A. J. Schwoeble and D. L. Exline, *Current Methods in Gunshot Residue Analysis*. Boca Raton, FL: CRC Press, 2000.

13. Jungreis, E. "Ch. 3: Applications of Spot Tests in Clinical Analysis," in E. Jungreis, *Spot Test Analysis: Clinical, Environmental, Forensic, and Geochemical Applications*, 2d ed. New York: John Wiley and Sons, 1997.

14. Jungreis, E., "Forensic Applications of Spot Test Analysis," in E. Jungreis, *Spot Test Analysis: Clinical, Environmental, Forensic, and Geochemical Applications*, 2d ed. New York: John Wiley and Sons, 1997.

15. Basu, S. "Formation of Gunshot Residue." *Journal of Forensic Sciences* 27 (1982), 1–20.

16. "Standard Guide for Gunshot Residue Analysis by Scanning Electron Microscopy/Energy-Dispersive Spectroscopy," in *ASTM Standard E1588-95 (Reapproved 2001)* ASTM International, 2004.

17. Romolo, F. S., and P. A. Margot. "Identification of Gunshot Residue: A Critical Review." *Forensic Science International* 119 (2001), 195–211.

18. Wallace, J. S. "Discharge Residue from Mercury Fulminate–Primed Ammunition." *Science and Justice* 38 (1997), 7–14.

19. Lebiedzik, J., and D. L. Johnson. "Handguns and Ammunitions Indicators Extacted from the GSR Analysis." *Journal of Forensic Sciences* 47 (2002), 483–489.

20. Mucha-Brozek, Z., and A. Jankowicz. "Evaluation of the Possibility of Differentiation between Various Types of Ammunition by Means of GSR Examination with SEM/EDX Method." *Forensic Science International* 123 (2001), 39–47.

21. Northrop, D. "Gunshot Residue Analysis by Micellular Electrokinetic Capillary Electrophoresis: Assessment for Application to Casework. Part 2." *Journal of Forensic Sciences* 46 (2001), 560–572.

22. MacCrehan, W. A., et al. "Investigating the Effect of Changing Ammunition on the Composition of Organic Additives in Organic Gunshot Residue (OGSR)." *Journal of Forensic Sciences* 46 (2001), 57–62.

23. MacCrehan, W. A., et al. "Sampling Protocols for the Detection of Smokeless Powder Residues Using Capillary Electrophoresis." *Journal of Forensic Sciences* 43 (1998), 119–124.

24. Northrop, D. "Gunshot Residue Analysis by Micellular Electrokinetic Capillary Electrophoresis: Assessment for Application to Casework. Part 1." *Journal of Forensic Sciences* 46 (2001), 549–559.

25. Wu, Z., et al. "The Utilization of MS–MS Method in Detection of GSRs." *Journal of Forensic Sciences* 46 (2001), 495–501.

26. Reardon, M., and W. A. MacCrehan. "Developing a Quantitative Extraction Technique for Determining the Organic Additives in Smokeless Handgun Powder." *Journal of Forensic Sciences* 46 (2001), 802–807.

27. MacCrehan, W. A., et al. "Associating Gunpowder and Residues from Commerical Ammunition Using Compositional Analysis." *Journal of Forensic Sciences* 47 (2002), 260–266.

28. Walker, C., et al. "An Environmental Survey Relating to Improvised and Emulsion/Gel Explosives." *Journal of Forensic Sciences* 46 (2001), 254–267.

29. Crowson, A., et al. "A Survey of High Explosive Traces in Public Places." *Journal of Forensic Sciences* 41 (1996), 980–989.

30. Cullum, H. E., et al. "A Second Survey of High Explosive Traces in Public Places." *Journal of Forensic Sciences* 49 (2004), 684–690.

31. Eiceman, G. A. "Ion Mobility Spectrometry in National Defense." *Analytical Chemistry* (2004): 392A–397A.

32. Eiceman, G. A., et al. "Separation of Ions from Explosives in Differential Mobility Spectrometry by Vapor-Modified Drift Gas." *Analytical Chemistry* 76 (2004), 4937–4944.

33. Lawrence, A. H., and P. Neudorfl. "Detection of Ethylene Glycol Dinitrate Vapors by Ion Mobility Spectrometry Using Chloride Reagent Ions." *Analytical Chemistry* 60 (1988), 104–109.

34. Tam, M., and H. H. Hill. "Secondary Electrospray Ionization–Ion Mobility Spectrometry for Explosive Vapor Detection." *Analytical Chemistry* 76 (2004), 2741–2747.

35. Medintz, I. L., et al. "Self-Assembled TNT Biosensor Based on Modular Multifunctional Surface-Tethered Components." *Analytical Chemistry* 77 (2005), 365–372.

36. Wallenborg, S. R., and C. Bailey. "Separation and Detection of Explosives on a Microchip Using Micellular Electrokinetic Chromatography and Indirect Laser-Induced Fluorescence." *Analytical Chemistry* 72 (2000), 1872–1878.

37. Wang, J., et al. "Single-Channel Microchip for Fast Screening and Detailed Identifcation of Nitroaromatic Explosives or Organophosphate Nerve Agents." *Analytical Chemistry* 74 (2002), 1187–1191.

38. Yinon, J. (2003). "Detection of Explosives by Electronic Noses." *Analytical Chemistry "A-pages"* (March 1, 2003): 99A–105A.

39. Hopen, T. J. "Dr. Walter C. McCrone's Contribution to the Characterization and Identification of Explosives." *Journal of Forensic Sciences* 49 (2004), 275–276.

40. McCrone, W. C., et al. "Identification of Organic High Explosives." *The Microscope* 41 (1993), 161–182.

41. McCrone, W. C., et al. "Identification of Organic High Explosives, II." *The Microscope* 42 (1994), 61–73.

42. McCrone, W. C., et al. "Identification of Organic High Explosives III." *The Microscope* 47 (1999), 183–200.

43. Skidmore, C. B., et al. "Microscopical Examination of Plastic-Bonded Explosives." *The Microscope* 45 (1997), 127–136.

44. Kosanke, K. L., et al. "Characterization of Pyrotechnic Reaction Residue Particles by SEM/EDS." *Journal of Forensic Sciences* 48 (2003), 531–537.

45. McCord, B., and E. C. Bender. "Chromatography of Explosives," in A. Beveridge, ed. *Forensic Investigation of Explosives*. London: Taylor and Francis, 1998.

46. Brown, H., et al. "New Developments in SPME Part 2: Analysis of Ammonium Nitrate–based Explosives." *Journal of Forensic Sciences* 49 (2004), 215–221.

47. Furton, K. G., et al. "Optimization of Solid-Phase Microextraction (SPME) for the Recovery of Explosives from Aqueous and Post-Explosion Debris Followed by Gas and Liquid Chromatography." *Journal of Forensic Sciences* 45 (2000), 857–864.

48. Sigman, M. E., and C.-Y. Ma. "Detection Limits for GC/MS Analysis of Organic Explosives." *Journal of Forensic Sciences* 46 (2001), 6–11.

49. McCord, B., et al. "Forensic Analysis of Explosives Using Ion Chromatographic Methods." *Analytica Chimica Acta* 288 (1994), 43–56.

50. Casamento, S., et al. "Optimization of the Separation of Organic Explosives by Capillary Electrophoresis with Artificial Neural Networks." *Journal of Forensic Sciences* 48 (2003), 1075–1083.

51. Hilmi, A., et al. "Development of Electrokinetic Capillary Electrophoresis Equipped with Amperometric Detection for Analysis of Explosive Compounds." *Analytical Chemistry* 71 (1999), 873–879.

52. Klapec, D. J., and D. Ng. "The Use of Capillary Electrophoresis in the Detection of Monomethylamine and Benzoate Ions in the Forensic Examination of Explosives." *Journal of Forensic Sciences* 46 (2001), 1168–1173.

53. McCord, B., and K. A. Hargadon. "Explosives Analysis by Capillary Electrophoresis," in J. Yinon, ed., *Advances in Analysis and Detection of Explosives: Proceedings of the 4th International Symposium on Analysis and Detection of Explosives, September 7–10, 1992, Jerusalem, Israel*. Dordrecht, The Netherlands: Kluwer Academic Publishers, 1993.

11

The Chemistry of Color and Colorants

OVERVIEW AND ORIENTATION

This chapter returns to a subject we touched upon in Chapter 7: color. There, we briefly discussed color in the context of screening tests for drugs. Now we'll build on that foundation and talk about color quantitatively and analytically. Colorants (substances that impart color) of forensic interest are dyes and pigments, and they are applied to or are part of a wide range of evidence, including fibers (discussed in Chapter 14), inks, and paint. There are numerous chemical structures in this chapter, but don't be daunted or overwhelmed. The underlying theme is color.

11.1 COLOR: A QUANTITATIVE VIEW

In Section 7.7.2, basic elements of color chemistry were introduced in the context of spot tests. When we move into evidence such as inks, paints, and fibers, a quantitative description of color is essential. The problem, however, is that color is a difficult concept to quantify or describe in a common language. For example, one person's perception of "red" may be different from another person's. A descriptor such as "fire-engine" red or "stop-sign" red makes it easier to imagine a color, but each person still perceives color differently. One person may be a bit more sensitive to reds and less sensitive to blues than another, so what the eye sees and what the brain registers are different and inherently impossible to describe with words. Some people are partially or completely colorblind. Color can be quantitated on the basis of spectral characteristics, removing the viewer's subjectivity from descriptions of color.[†]

11.1.1 CIE System

To convert a perceived color into a standardized quantitative equivalent, three elements are needed:[1] a sample, such as an ink; a source of illumination; and an observer. Samples such as an ink spot are viewed under white light, and color is perceived in accordance with which spectral components are reflected and which are absorbed. The procedure for processing a perceived color into standardized components is outlined in Figure 11.1, using a reflectance spectrum of ink as an example (top frame), a set of standard weighting factors for the contribution of red (R), blue (B), and green (G) are selected based on the illumination (white light source) and viewing angle. As shown in frame 3, the reflection value at each wavelength in the spectrum is expressed as a weighted contribution of RGB $(\bar{z}, \bar{y}, \bar{x})$. To obtain these **tristimulus** values XYZ, the individual $\bar{x}\,\bar{y}\,\bar{z}$ values are summed over the spectral range. In this example,

$$X = \sum_{l=400}^{700} \bar{x}.$$ The tristimulus value X can be thought of as the total blue component of the perceived color. The final step is to normalize XYZ to chromaticity coordinates that can be plotted in two dimensions (frame 5). Each step of the process outlined in Figure 11.1 is described in further detail in the following paragraphs, beginning with the source of illumination.

Not all light sources are equivalent and colors are perceived differently under different illumination. Daylight has a different spectral spread of wavelengths and intensities than does an indoor fluorescent lamp. Different spectral intensities affect absorbance, reflectance, and color perception. Thus, either a standardized light source must be used, or, more practically, results must be normalized to a standard. Several standard illuminate spectra are shown in Figure 11.2.

One method of standardizing illumination is to consider it relative to the radiation released by an object called a **blackbody radiator**. Blackbody radiation correlates with the spectral emission profile of a perfect blackbody radiation source when it is heated to a given temperature. The term "white hot" is taken in the same vein: If an object such as an iron rod is heated sufficiently, it glows red, then yellow, and then, at the hottest, white to blue. When light has the same spectral spread as a blackbody emitter at a given temperature, the light is said to have that **temperature**. Here, "temperature" is a descriptor, but it

---

[†]Note that many of the grayscale figures in this chapter are also shown in the color insert.

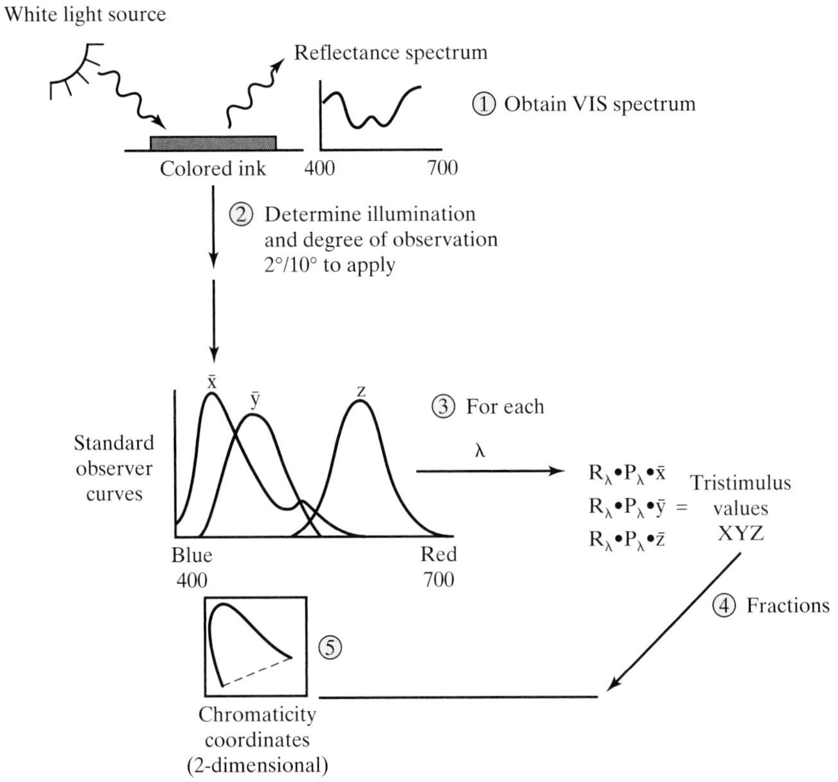

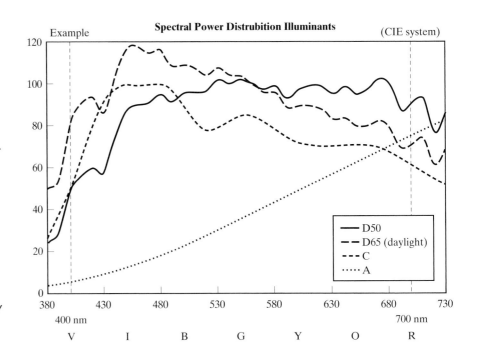

White light source
Reflectance spectrum
① Obtain VIS spectrum
Colored ink
400
700
② Determine illumination and degree of observation 2°/10° to apply
x̄
ȳ
z̄
Standard observer curves
Blue 400
Red 700
③ For each λ
$R_\lambda \bullet P_\lambda \bullet \bar{x}$
$R_\lambda \bullet P_\lambda \bullet \bar{y}$ =
$R_\lambda \bullet P_\lambda \bullet \bar{z}$
Tristimulus values XYZ
④ Fractions
⑤
Chromaticity coordinates (2-dimensional)

▶ **Figure 11.1** *The steps involved in converting a color to a numerical description that can be plotted in "color space." This flowchart describes the CIE system presented in the text.*

Spectral Power Distrubition Illuminants
Example
(CIE system)
120
100
80
60
40
20
0
380
430
480
530
580
630
680
730
400 nm
700 nm
V I B G Y O R
D50
D65 (daylight)
C
A

▶ **Figure 11.2** *The spectral power of some illumination sources used in the CIE system. The range extends slightly beyond the standard visible range of 400 nm–700 nm since electromagnetic radiation in that range can influence perceived color. D65 is the CIE standard illuminant for daylight. A is a standard blackbody radiation spectra with a temperature of 2854K.*

does not have any physical correlate. A filament in a lightbulb is hot, but the actual temperature of the filament is not the same as the temperature of the emitted light. Some example temperatures are 1500K for candlelight, 3400K for a tungsten lamp, and 5500K for noon on a sunny day.

To standardize the observer contribution to color perception, more elaborate methods are used, as shown in Figure 11.3.[1] A viewer (observer) is assumed to be looking at a white screen inside of a box protected from stray light. A light source, such as a tungsten lamp, illuminates an image on a screen. The image is colored, such as a simple projected circle of colored light. On the opposite side of an opaque partition, three lamps emitting the primary colors illuminate another image on the same background screen. The viewer controls the intensity of the three colored lamps and adjusts the contribution of each until the observed color on both sides of the barrier appears identical. In some cases, this requires alteration of the source light. As long as the alteration is known (for example, adding red to the source), it can be accounted for in the final calculations. Images with different colors can be illuminated and their color appearance matched. An examination of the source light spectral characteristics compared with the three combined light spectra allows the observed color to be broken down into three components as shown in Figure 11.4. The three curves are referred to as the **standard observer curves**. For example, assume that a purple circle is projected onto the screen and that you are the observer. You would adjust the intensity of the 3 lamps to match the purple you perceive. Likely, you would turn the green lamp intensity to zero and adjust the red and blue to approximately equal proportions since purple is a mixture of red and blue. In terms of RGB (ZYX), Z and X would be large and approximately equal while Y would approach zero. Since only 3 lamps are used to create the color, the sum can be scaled to 1.0. In our purple example, X would be ~0.5, Y ≈ 0,

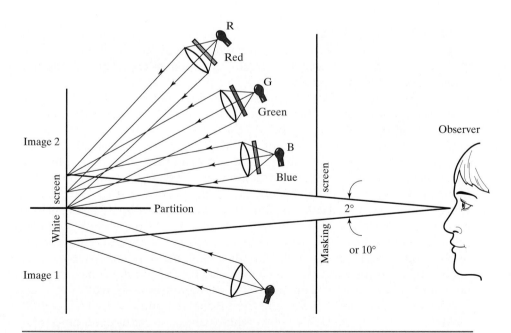

▲ **Figure 11.3** *Use of mixtures of illuminants to match the appearance of white light. This approach is the conceptual foundation of the CIE color quantitation system. The observer adjusts the contribution of each lamp until the color on both sides of the partition is perceived to be identical.*

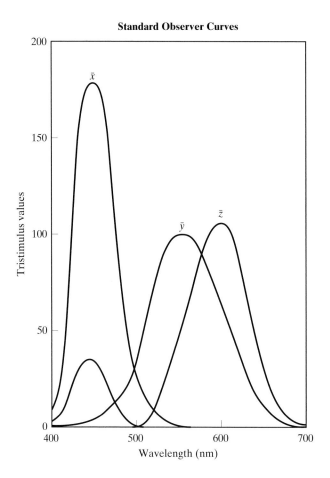

▶ **Figure 11.4** *Standard observer curves. Weighted contributions from each curve are used to recreate spectra. The red contribution (R) is represented by z̄, green (G) by ȳ, and blue (B) by x̄.*

and Z ≈ 0.5. Similarly, if you were shown a white spot, you would adjust each lamp to approximately equal levels since white is a mixture of all colors. In this case, X ≈ Y ≈ Z ≈ 0.33 each. Combining projected colors results in additive color, a topic we'll revisit shortly.

The system for standardizing and quantifying color was first formalized in 1931 by the International Commission on Illumination (Commission International d'Eclairage, CIE).[1] Using standard illuminants, such as daylight (designated D65) and A (the equivalent of 2854K blackbody emission), the CIE specified methods for calculating quantities X, Y, and Z, called tristimulus values, which are derived from standard observer curves and considerations of illumination. This system allowed for a normalization of a spectrum such that it was possible to express a color in a uniform way. In 1964, the CIE also specified a 10° angle of viewing as an option in the calculation. The tristimulus values are calculated for each wavelength by taking the reflectance value and multiplying by the product of the power of the illuminant and the standard observer curve values at the specified wavelength (symbolized Px̄, Pȳ, and Pz̄), which are standard table values that are set on the basis of the illumination equivalent selected.

For example, using the daylight illuminant D65 and a 10° viewing angle yields Table 11.1. Figure 11.5 is a plot of these values, shown as a smoothed line, as seen previously in Figure 11.4 with a different *y*-axis label. The more blue a color appears, the higher is the weighting factor applied to Px̄ and the less weight is given to the red and green contributions. If the conditions of illumination change the table values change as well. The table values are multiplied

Table 11.1	Tristimulus Weighting Factors (Normalized to $P\bar{y}$ = 100)		
—	$P\bar{x}$	$P\bar{y}$	$P\bar{z}$
400	0.251	0.023	1.090
420	3.232	0.330	15.383
440	6.679	1.106	34.376
460	6.096	2.620	35.355
480	1.721	4.938	15.897
500	0.059	8.668	3.997
520	2.184	13.864	1.046
540	6.810	17.355	0.237
560	12.165	17.157	0.002
580	16.467	14.148	−0.002
600	17.233	10.105	0
620	12.894	6.020	0
640	6.226	2.587	0
660	2.111	0.827	0
680	0.573	0.222	0
700	0.120	0.047	0

Source: Laden, P. J., "Colorimetry and the calculation of color difference," in P. J. Laden, ed., *Chemistry and Technology of Water Based Inks,* London: Blackie Academic and Professional/Chapman and Hall, 1997.

by the reflectance value at each wavelength to obtain the tristimulus values. For example, assume an example that reflectance spectrum of a green paint sample has a percent reflectance of 0.145 (14.5%) at 400 nm and that the illuminant equivalent selected is D65 at a 10° angle of observation. Then the corresponding values at 400 nm are calculated as follows:

$$P\bar{x} \times R = 0.145 \times 0.251 = 0.364 \tag{11.1}$$

$$P\bar{y} \times R = 0.145 \times 0.023 = 0.0033 \tag{11.2}$$

$$P\bar{z} \times R = 0.145 \times 1.090 = 0.158 \tag{11.3}$$

This calculation is repeated for every wavelength in the spectrum to yield the total tristimulus values:[†]

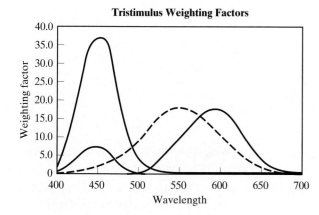

Tristimulus Weighting Factors

◀ **Figure 11.5** *Weighting factors for each standard observer curve.*

[†]Wavelength ranges other than 380–760 nm, such as 400–700 nm, can be used.

$$X = \sum_{\lambda=380}^{760} P\overline{x}_{\lambda}R_{\lambda} \tag{11.4}$$

$$Y = \sum_{\lambda=380}^{760} P\overline{y}_{\lambda}R_{\lambda} \tag{11.5}$$

$$Z = \sum_{\lambda=380}^{760} P\overline{z}_{\lambda}R_{\lambda} \tag{11.6}$$

where R is the reflectance value at each wavelength and $P\overline{x}$, $P\overline{y}$, and $P\overline{z}$ are the weighting factors for RGB and illumination derived from a table. By means of a normalization procedure, X, Y, and Z can be further manipulated to allow a two-dimensional depiction of the data:

$$x = \frac{X}{X + Y + Z} \tag{11.7}$$

$$y = \frac{Y}{X + Y + Z} \tag{11.8}$$

$$z = \frac{Z}{X + Y + Z} \tag{11.9}$$

A chemical analogy is the calculation of mole fractions in a mixture of 3 components; the sum of the mole fractions is always equal to 1.0. As a result, one degree of freedom is eliminated, and if x and y are known, z is also known. The problem has gone from three degrees of freedom to two and can be plotted in two dimensions. Consequently, a visible spectrum representing the color of an ink or some other material is reduced to two points that can be plotted and compared with others.

Example Problem 11.1

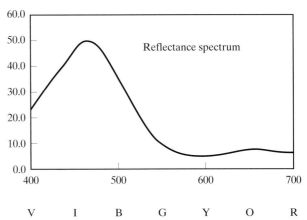

Calculate the tristimulus values for the following spectrum based on a 10° observer angle. Determine the chromaticity coordinates. What color is the sample?

Answer: Working this problem requires tables of standard values for the normalization constants, which are available from references such as K. Nassau, *The Physics and Chemistry of Color: The Fifteen Causes of Color*, 2d ed. (New York: John Wiley and Sons, 2001). For this problem, assume the 1931 values and a 2° observer angle for purposes of illustration. The first step is to multiply the reflectance values for each wavelength by the normalization constant from the CIE tables (RGB contribution and illumination) as per equations 11.1–11.3. The corrected values are then summed over all wavelengths in accordance with equations 11.4–11.6.

These calculations provide the data needed to calculate the chromaticity coordinates x and y. The sum $X + Y + Z$ is 80.90 (14.26 + 14.31 + 51.52), so $x = 14.26/80.90 = 0.176$, and similarly, $y = 0.177$. The quantity z is not plotted, but can be calculated $= 0.637$. This color corresponds to a grayish blue, with which the reflectance spectrum is consistent; note that the blue ranges are reflected strongly, while others are absorbed. These calculations are executed by software, but it is a valuable exercise to go through the process to solidify the idea of reducing a spectrum to a location on a two-dimensional plot.

Calculations:

—	%R	$P\bar{x}$	$P\bar{y}$	$P\bar{z}$	$P\bar{x} \times R$	$P\bar{y} \times R$	$Pz \times R$
400	23.3	0.00044	0.01	−0.00001	0.00	0.00187	0.04
420	33.0	0.02926	0.97	0.00085	0.03	0.14064	4.64
440	41.7	0.07680	3.20	0.00513	0.21	0.38643	16.11
460	50.0	0.06633	3.32	0.01383	0.69	0.38087	19.04
480	47.2	0.02345	1.11	0.03210	1.52	0.19464	9.19
500	36.5	0.00069	0.03	0.06884	2.51	0.05725	2.09
520	24.0	0.01193	0.29	0.12882	3.09	0.01450	0.35
540	13.5	0.05588	0.75	0.18268	2.47	0.00365	0.05
560	7.9	0.11751	0.93	0.19606	1.55	0.00074	0.01
580	6.0	0.16801	1.01	0.15989	0.96	0.00026	0.00
600	5.5	0.17896	0.98	0.10684	0.59	0.00012	0.00
620	6.0	0.14031	0.84	0.06264	0.38	0.00003	0.00
640	7.2	0.07437	0.54	0.02897	0.21	0.00000	0.00
660	8.2	0.02728	0.22	0.01003	0.08	0.00000	0.00
680	7.4	0.00749	0.06	0.00271	0.02	0.00000	0.00
700	7.0	0.00175	0.01	0.00063	0.00	0.00000	0.00

Sum X = 14.26   **Sum Y = 14.31**   **Sum Z = 51.52**

The chromaticity diagram (Figure 11.6) conveys significant information about a color in a concise and easily interpretable way. The chromaticity coordinate of a color (x,y) describes the color but do not distinguish light and darkness of that color. A dark red and light red, as long as the base red hue is the same, will have identical chromaticity coordinates. The more saturated a color, the closer to the edge of the parabola it will fall, whereas paler colors plot more interior. The depth of color (light vs. dark) is not the same as the saturation. One way to think of it is in terms of applying watercolors to a piece of paper. If you start with a tube of color and apply one layer, it may appear light but application of subsequent layers of the same color from the same tube will make the color darker. The hue does not change since the same tube of paint is used, but the color becomes darker with each application, increasing the saturation.

When the illuminant source is taken into consideration, even more information can be extracted. Figure 11.7 is the same as 11.6 with the addition of the incandescence curve superimposed over the chromaticity chart. The curve shows the temperature of the illuminant and a few of the available CIE standard illuminants such as D65 (daylight 6500K equivalent). The white point W is also called achromatic since it consists of equal amounts of RGB and is perceived as white. Utilizing the incandescence curve and the chromaticity coordinates, additional information and descriptors of a color can be obtained.

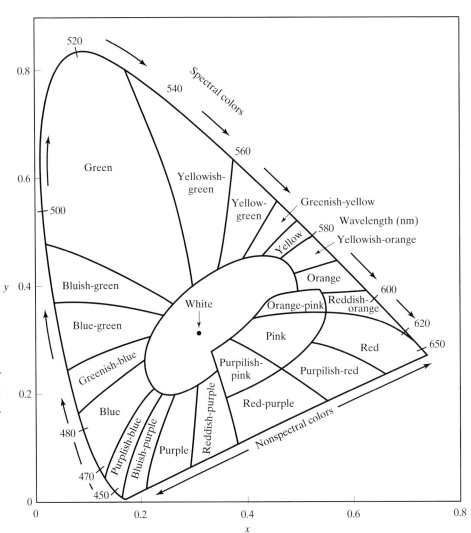

▶ **Figure 11.6** *Chromaticity diagram or chart. Color as encoded in a VIS spectrum is described by plotting the chromaticity coordinates x and y points on the chart. The outer band contains spectral colors (ROYGBIV), and the connecting line consists of nonspectral colors, such as pink and purple. A colored version is found in the color insert.*

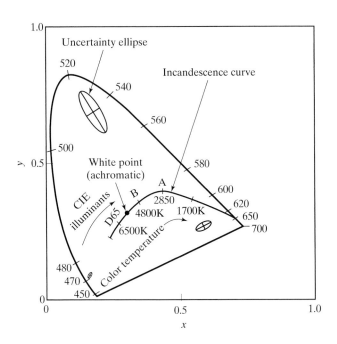

▶ **Figure 11.7** *The chromaticity chart with the incandescence curve added. The temperature of the illuminants are indicated in K. D65, B, and A are standard CIE illuminants.*

Exhibit A: Human Color Vision and the Tristimulus System

The tristimulus system is based on the mechanism by which humans perceive color. The eye contains receptor cells called rods and cones. The rods respond to all wavelengths of light and are quite sensitive and so are utilized in night vision and peripheral vision. They are not sensitive to different colors and so if a person had only rods, they would see the world in shades of black, white, and gray. The cones are far less sensitive but do respond to color via the reaction of light with pigments. The cones contain three different light sensitive pigment complexes that correlate with the RGB of the tristimulus system. Although the physiology and chemistry of vision is complex, the key to color perception is a simple photo-induced change in pigment molecules from the *cis* to the *trans* form. The so-called blue cones respond optimally to a wavelength of ~420 nm, the green cones to ~530 nm, and the red cones to ~560 nm. When we perceive a mixed color such as orange, both the red and green cones are stimulated, the balance of which determines the shade of color we see such as yellow (little green contribution) to deep orange (strong green contribution). If all three types of cones stimulated equally, you see white.

The goal of the CIE and tristimulus system is roughly to recreate the pattern of cone stimulation in the eye of a standard observer under controlled conditions of illumination and viewing angle. Humans sense color by perceiving mixtures of RGB simultaneously whereas the CIE system employs a reflectance spectrum broken down sequentially by wavelength. The RGB contribution is determined for each wavelength and then summed to obtain the total overall contribution of RGB, expressed as the chromaticity coordinates xyz. This is why the center of the chromaticity diagram (Figure 11.6) is white; it is the point at which RGB contributions are equal.

Source: Marieb, E. N., Chapter 15, "The Special Senses," in *Human Anatomy & Physiology* 6th ed. Upper Saddle River, NJ: Pearson Benjamin Cummings, 2004, pp. 554–602.

As useful as the chromaticity diagrams are, they have their limitations. Because the chromaticity parabola is asymmetric, calculations and comparisons of color differences are not uniform. Consider, for example, two pairs of inks, one pair blue and one pair red. Suppose that the perceived color difference between the two blue inks is the same as the perceived difference between the reds. If the chromaticity diagram were uniform, then, when the x and y values were plotted for the four samples, the Euclidean distance between the two blues would be the same as the distance between the two reds. The problem is illustrated in Figures 11.7 and 11.8. The elliptic regions are drawn around a point centered on a standard color, and the region around the point is that region in which an x–y plot of colored sample would be perceived as identical to the central color. The region represents the zone in which the eye can't perceive a difference. The zones are not uniform and distortion is introduced.

To address the distortion, a transformation is applied. The algorithm begins with considering color from the perspective of how someone would describe its characteristics and then relate those characteristics to chromaticity. Before discussing how distortion is corrected, we need to formalize terms as illustrated in Figures 11.9 and 11.10. **Saturation** of a color refers to how much pure spectral color it includes. The terms **shade** and saturation are sometimes used interchangably but as shown in Figure 11.10, this description is technically incorrect.[3] Shade relates to hue (spectral color) and degree of black. Saturation is also called **chroma**.

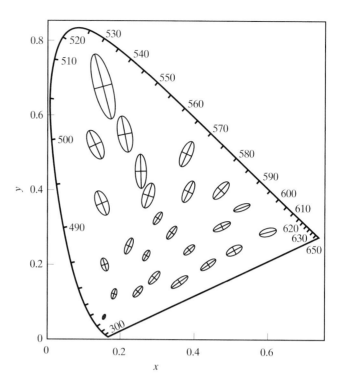

▶ **Figure 11.8** *Regions of uncertainty are not uniform in the chromaticity diagram. Within any given ellipse, the color is indistinguishable. For greens, the uncertainty ellipse is large; for blues small, and between the two extremes for the reds. The CIELAB mapping addresses this asymmetry.*

To map the asymmetric space of the chromaticity parabola into a symmetrical color space in which the regions of variability are comparable, three descriptors are used. These variables are hue, lightness, and chroma:

- **Hue**: The color itself, such as red, blue, green. The hue corresponds to a color that would appear on a color wheel; in other words, the spectral colors that form the parabola of the chromaticity diagram.
- **Lightness**: The depth of the color, rated on a scale from darkest (black) to lightest (white). The term **value** is sometimes used in this context. A color that reflects more white light is brighter than one that reflects less.
- **Chroma**: The deviation of the color from gray. Pure spectral colors such as red and violet have high saturation. Saturation refers strength of the dominant wavelength or hue. Pink and red have the same hue but differing saturation.

Distance between points in the **CIELAB**[†] color space (corresponding to a color difference) can be calculated with the use of a Euclidean distance

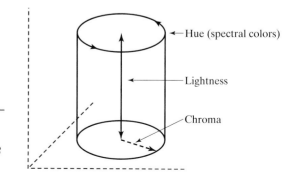

▶ **Figure 11.9** *The hue-lightness-chroma color space (HSV) that underlies the CIELAB modification to CIELAB.*

[†]The terms CIEL*a*b and CIELAB are interchangeable; the latter version is used in this text.

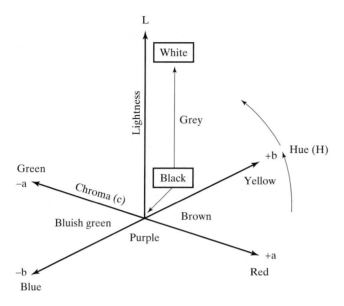

Color difference:

$$\Delta E = \sqrt{(\Delta L)^2 + (\Delta a)^3 + (\Delta b)^2}$$

◀ **Figure 11.10** *Limits and labels of the axes in CIELAB space. Color differences are expressed based on Euclidean distances. Another way to think of a is as measuring the "redness" of a color with a negative value indicating less red and more green. An analogous interpretation for b is of "blueness."*

(Eq. 3-3), a concept introduced in Section 3.1.5 in the context of cluster analysis. This technique, introduced in 1976, uses the tristimulus values X, Y, and Z as inputs and converts these to the corresponding L, a, and b coordinates in the uniform color space. The distance between two points in the CIELAB system can be calculated as[†]

$$\Delta E = \sqrt{(\Delta L)^2 + (\Delta a)^2 + (\Delta b)^2} \tag{11.10}$$

In some cases, only two of these criteria need be considered. For example, if the lightnesses of two colors A and B are the same, the ΔL term is zero and is not needed to calculate distances. This concept is shown in Figure 11.12.

The transformations used to convert tristimulus values to the CIELAB equivalent are as follows:

$$L^* = 116\left(\frac{Y}{Y_n}\right)^{\frac{1}{3}} - 16 \tag{11.11}[‡]$$

$$a^* = 500\left[\left(\frac{X}{X_n}\right)^{\frac{1}{3}} - \left(\frac{Y}{Y_n}\right)^{\frac{1}{3}}\right] \tag{11.12}$$

$$b^* = 200\left[\left(\frac{Y}{Y_n}\right)^{\frac{1}{3}} - \left(\frac{Z}{Z_n}\right)^{\frac{1}{3}}\right] \tag{11.13}$$

[†]Chemists may find the use of *E* confusing in this context, because the same symbol is used to describe the energy gap in atoms and molecules. In turn, absorption by energy in the visible range occurs when the energy gap correlates with the color of the photon; thus, the two E's are related to colors. Context is the best guide as to which interpretation of E applies.

[‡]Eq. 11-12 applies to those cases where $\frac{Y}{Y_n} > {\sim}0.01$. A slightly modified form is used for smaller values.

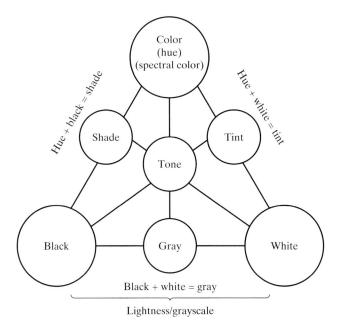

▶ **Figure 11.11** *Terms used to describe color and their relationship.*

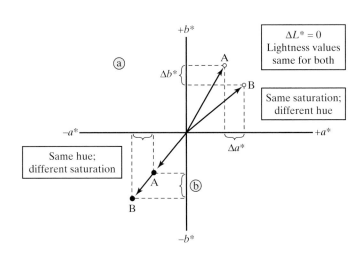

▶ **Figure 11.12** *Two examples showing colors that have the same lightness coordinate but different values of hue (A) and saturation (B).*

▶ **Figure 11.13** *Elliptical region around a point plotted in CIELAB space. The region defines the uncertainty or tolerance; an observer would perceive no difference in color among spectra that plot within the ellipsoidal region.*

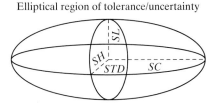

The values X_n, Y_n, and Z_n are a reference white color and vary with the illumination selected. This color space also has some inherent distortion,[1,4] but far less than that of Figure 11.8. The CIELAB system is widely used in forensic analyses to describe color and color differences.

Table 11.2	Reference White Factors	
	D65	**D50**
X_n	96.422	95.047
Y_n	100.0000	100.0000
Z_n	82.521	108.883

D65, D50 refer to standard CIE illuminants and their temperature equivalent. D65 is daylight, 6500K

One final and critically important consideration is uncertainty in color measurement, which here has a concrete and easily "visualized" meaning in the present context. Assume that three values are used to represent a color in the CIELAB system. The uncertainty associated with that color could be expressed as the magnitude that each of those coordinates can change before an observer would perceive a difference in the color. Because color vision varies with the individual, there is no NIST standard reference material that can solve this particular analytical challenge. However, it is possible to assign reasonable regions of uncertainty around a point; because the space is three dimensional, the uncertainty space is elliptical. The Colour Measurement Committee (CMC) of the Society of Dyers and Colourists developed a formula, also referred to as CMC, that constructs the elliptical area on the basis of a standard and taking into account relative differences in hue–saturation–lightness and the distortions in the color space. The calculations are beyond the scope of this discussion; however, many software packages exist, some built into spectrophotometers, that are capable of producing a variety of quantitative color measurements and outputs. For interested readers, a detailed worked example starting from a typical reflectance spectrum through the CIELAB system is found in the Appendices.

11.1.2 MUNSELL SYSTEM

The **Munsell color system** is conceptually similar to the CIELAB system, but with some significant differences. The Munsell system was conceived by the American painter Albert H. Munsell in 1905 with subsequent revisions and variations.[2] The three variables used to describe colors in the system are hue, brightness (similar to lightness in CIELAB), and saturation (similar to chroma; also called value). As shown in Figure 11.14, the color space is cylindrical. The hue is divided into 100 equal spaces around the circle that forms the cross section of the cylinder, while the y direction is the brightness, scaled from 0 to 18. The x-axis is the saturation, scaled from 10 to 18. Munsell charts and collections are used in the forensic analysis of paints and soils. Because books and samples of color are used for color comparison, the Munsell color space is sometimes referred to as a catalog system. An example application is in soil analysis in which soil particles can be seived, sorted, and grouped by their Munsell color.

11.1.3 OTHER SYSTEMS AND CONVERSIONS

Two other color systems encountered in forensic applications are the CMY (cyan–magenta–yellow) system used in printers and the RGB (red–green–blue) used in monitors. We have seen additive colors (Figure 11.16) already in the context of the standard observer, and combining spectral colors. Additive colors

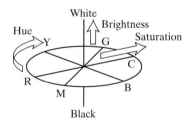

▲ **Figure 11.14** *Munsell color space. The hue circle is divided into 100 equally spaced regions.*

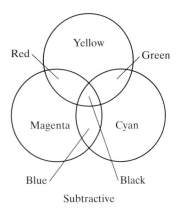

Subtractive

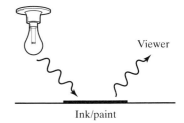

▶ **Figure 11.15** *The CMY subtractive colors such as used to create colors with inks, paints, and other coatings. The surface interacts with white light and subtracts wavelengths to create the perceived reflected color. See the color insert.*

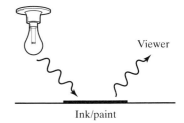

Projected light

▲ **Figure 11.16** *The RGB additive colors. See the color insert.*

require projected or transmitted light. The CMY system is referred to as a **subtractive system**, as illustrated in Figure 11.15. Subtractive colors are produced by reflection interactions. Consider a printing system such as a color computer printer that uses different inks to create a color on paper. The goal is to combine the different inks such that when the printed combination is viewed by an observer, the perceived color faithfully reproduces the desired color. Inks are combined in ratios such that the resulting mixture reflects the desired wavelengths to the observer. This approach can be thought of as subtractive in the sense that, by absorbance, the mixture of ink subtracts wavelengths from the source of illumination such that the reflected light has the desired color. The CMY system is limited by its inability to faithfully reproduce black, so, in practice, a black ink is usually supplied in the printer and the system is referred to as a CMYK system, with K representing the contribution of black. In contrast to the CMYK system, the RGB color system is additive and is used in applications, such as computer monitors and televisions, where an image is projected.

11.1.4 COLOR CONUNDRUMS

Mention was made of **pleochroism** in Chapter 5. Recall that a dichroic material appears to have a different color when viewed at different orientations due to the crystal structure of the material. Similarly, different colorants, such as a dyed fabric, can appear to be a different color, depending on the illumination. This property is called **metamerism**, and often the effect is produced deliberately. It results from a change in illumination, one of the three components required to measure color. It can also change with a change in observer although to a lesser extent. Metamerism is not the same thing as dichroism, which depends on orientation, not illumination. It is also worth mentioning that the same perceived color can be produced in more than one way. For example, the color orange can be created by using a dye that reflects all orange light or by combining dyes that absorb combinations of yellow and red. The colors may be very difficult to distinguish by visual inspection, but are easily separated by colorimetry. Similarly, the perceived reflected color of black, such as used in the ink found on this page, can be created by many different combinations of colorants.

11.2 COLORANTS

The two colorants of forensic interest are **dyes** and **pigments**, both of which are encountered in many types of forensic evidence. Although these terms are sometimes used interchangeably, this is incorrect. Contrary to a common misconception, the difference does not have to do with organic versus inorganic constituents, nor is it based on a natural versus synthetic origin. The fundamental difference between dyes and pigments is *solubility*: Dyes are soluble in the solvent they are carried in, whereas pigments are suspended particulates. Both dyes and pigments can be found in the same matrix, such as in an ink, but the distinction between them is a fundamental, important one and it is illustrated in Figure 11.17.

Example Problem 11.2

Can a substance be a dye and a pigment?

Answer: Yes. The difference between the two is solubility, a parameter that depends on the solute (pigment or dye) and the solvent. For example, "permanent" marker inks contain water-insoluble pigments that dissolve in pyridine.

Analytical chemists work routinely with dyes even if they are unaware of it. Most acid–base indicators are dyes, as are a number of products of presumptive tests discussed in Chapter 7. Histological stains used in biological disciplines are also dyes. As mentioned, dyes are organic compounds that are soluble in the media they are contained in (such as ink or paint). Dyes also have an affinity for the substrate they are being placed on (such as paper). Pigments, by contrast, are typically metallics or organometallics that contain a

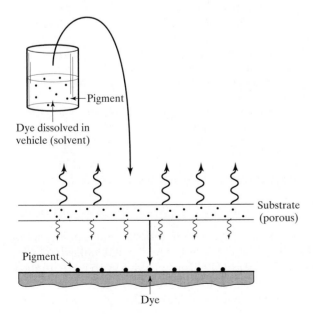

◄ **Figure 11.17** *The feature that distinguishes a dye from a pigment is solubility. The dye penetrates with the solvent while pigment particles remain on the surface.*

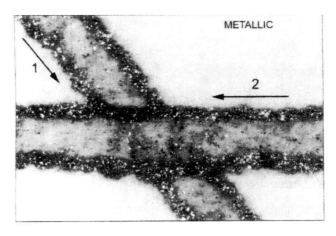

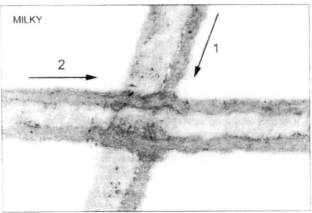

▶ **Figure 11.18** *Intersecting lines of metallized ink; the order of drawing can be deduced from the layering. Figure reprinted with permission from Mazzella, W. D., and A. Khanmy-Vital, "A Study to Investigate the Evidential Value of Blue Gel Inks,"* Journal of Forensic Sciences *48 (2003), 419–424, Fig. 1. Copyright 2003, ASTM International.*

Exhibit B: Why a Ruby Is Red

The gemstone called a ruby is another manifestation of color due to transition metals, in this case chromium (Cr^{3+}). A ruby is composed of the mineral corundum, familiar to chemists as alumina (Al_2O_3) with bonds possessing ~60% ionic and ~40% covalent character. The resulting crystal structure is such that six oxygens are arranged in a distorted octahedron around any given aluminum ion. This packing arrangement generates an electrostatic field around the aluminum, since there is an excess of negative charge relative to the +3 on the aluminum. When the crystal lattice contains a small amount (~1%) of Cr_2O_3, the chromium atoms occupy the same crystal location as aluminum atoms. The distorted shape and electrostatic field splits the *d* orbitals in chromium and results in an energy gap corresponding to a photon in the visible range. A ruby absorbs light in the blue and yellow or green regions. The resulting transmission of red and some purple light gives the ruby its distinctive color.

Source: Nassau, K., "Ch. 5: Color Caused by Transition Metals in a Ligand Field," in K. Nassau, *The Physics and Chemistry of Color*, 2d ed. New York: John Wiley and Sons, 2001.

transition metal, but organic pigments are becoming more common. Pigments are suspended or dispersed in a solvent, but not dissolved in it. Unlike dyes, pigments do not have an affinity for their substrate. Thus, if a dye in an ink is applied to paper, the dye penetrates into the paper to the extent that the solvent does, whereas pigments in paint dry atop the paper. In other words, pigments must be affixed to the substrate. Dyes can be natural or synthetic, organic or inorganic. As a result of these various possibilities, there is a plethora of dye materials.[5] Dyes were also one of the first modern industrial chemicals, as well as one of the earliest chemical commodities. The types of forensic evidence in which dyes and pigments are seen include questioned documents (inks and colorants), paints, and fibers among others.

Historical Evidence 11.1—The Color of Kings

Ancient purple

Purple is a color (hue) often associated with royalty. The history of this association traces back to the early Babylonians and the later Phoenicians and is related to one of the earliest commercial products, a natural dye extracted from mollusks and called Tyrian Purple, Royal Purple, Imperial Purple, or Ancient Purple (6,6-dibromoindigo). The name *Tyrian* refers to the city of Tyre in Lebanon, where production was centered. The preparation of the dye was labor intensive and required the extraction of tiny amounts of precursor chemicals from thousands of mollusks. Because of labor and material costs, the dye was literally worth more than gold; thus, Kings were the only ones who could afford it.

Sources: Florence, D., "Spectral Comparison of Commercial and Synthesized Tyrian Purple," *Modern Microscopy*, November 18, 2003.

Zollinger, H., *Color: A Multidisciplinary Approach*. Zurich: Wiley Verlag, 1999.

Pigments may be simple inorganic compounds such as TiO_2 or complex organics such as the phthalocyanines. Dyes can be converted into pigments by chemical means such as making a salt from a cationic or anionic dye. An older term used to describe such a solid was "lake." Because pigments coat a surface, an observer's perception of the resulting color depends on chemical and physical properties of the pigment. It is also determined subtractively as in the CMYK system shown in Figure 11.15. Because the pigment is a particulate, scattering also occurs. The more light that is scattered off the pigment, the better the hiding power of the paint. Scattering is optimal when the pigment particles are about half the size of the wavelength of incident light. When an ink or paint dries, the pigment is encased in a matrix of the binder, the refractive indices of the binder and the pigment must also be considered when describing the apparent color. Optimal hiding power (maximum opacity) is favored when reflection and scattering are maximized. In turn, this situation is favored when the difference between the refractive index of the matrix and that of the pigment is large.[6] Thus, appearance and hiding power depend on the composition of the pigment, its strength, the size of the particulates, and their refractive indices compared to the binder.

Example Problem 11.3

The pigment particles in most white paints are between 0.2 and 0.4 μm in size. Why?

Answer: This size corresponds to 200–400 nm. Scattering is maximized when the particle size is approximately half their wavelength, so these particles will effectively scatter light in the 400–800-nm range, the range of visible wavelengths.

Applying the Science 11.1   Pigments in Wine

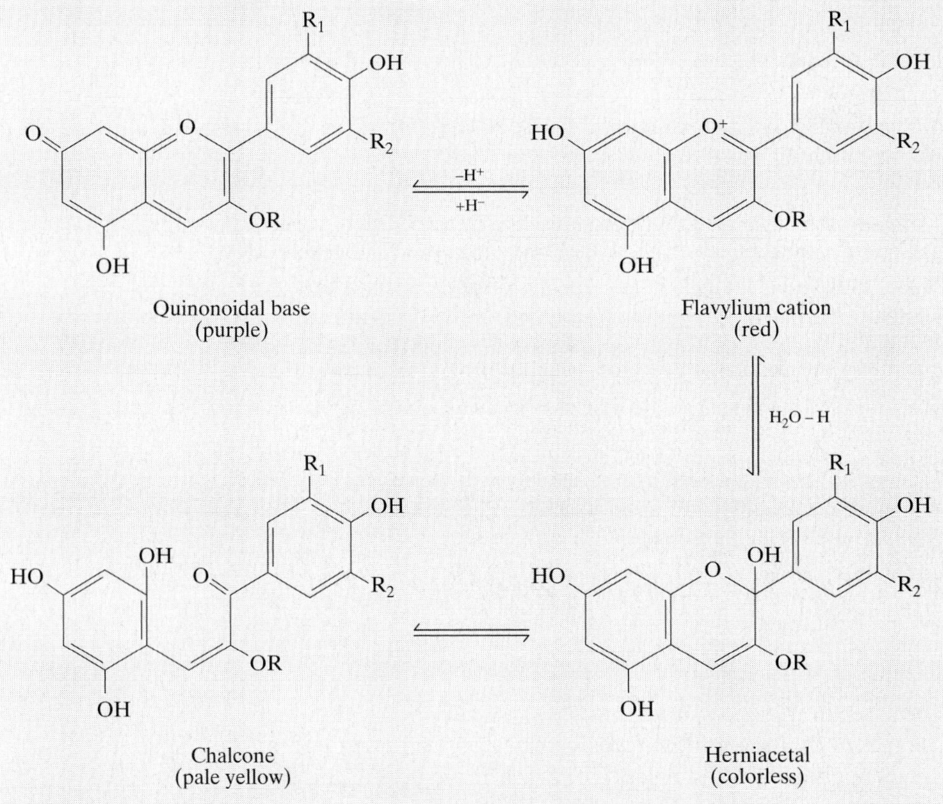

▲ **Figure 1.** *Reproduced with permission from source 1, copyright 2002 American Chemical Society.*

Colors associated with red wines are of considerable interest to the wine industry as well as to historians. The colors are due to complex pigment structures that may change as the wine ages. The primary class of pigments found in wine consists of anthocyanins. These compounds exist in forms dictated by their pH, which, for wines, is in the range of 3–4. Anthocyanin compounds range from yellow to red to purple, with malvidin-3-glucoside being the primary anthocyanin responsible for color in "young" wines. The polymerization of these pigments is postulated as the mechanism of color change as the wine ages. Archaeological chemists have exploited modern knowledge of wine chemistry to determine the likely colors of ancient Egyptian wines. The researchers started with a brown material found in a wine jar recovered from the tomb of King Tutankhamum and treated it with an alkaline solution as shown in the figure. An extraction of this solution was introduced into an HPLC coupled to a tandem mass spectrometer system (LC/MS/MS). The identification of syringic acid as a breakdown product of the polymerized pigment was strong evidence that the ancient wine was a red one.

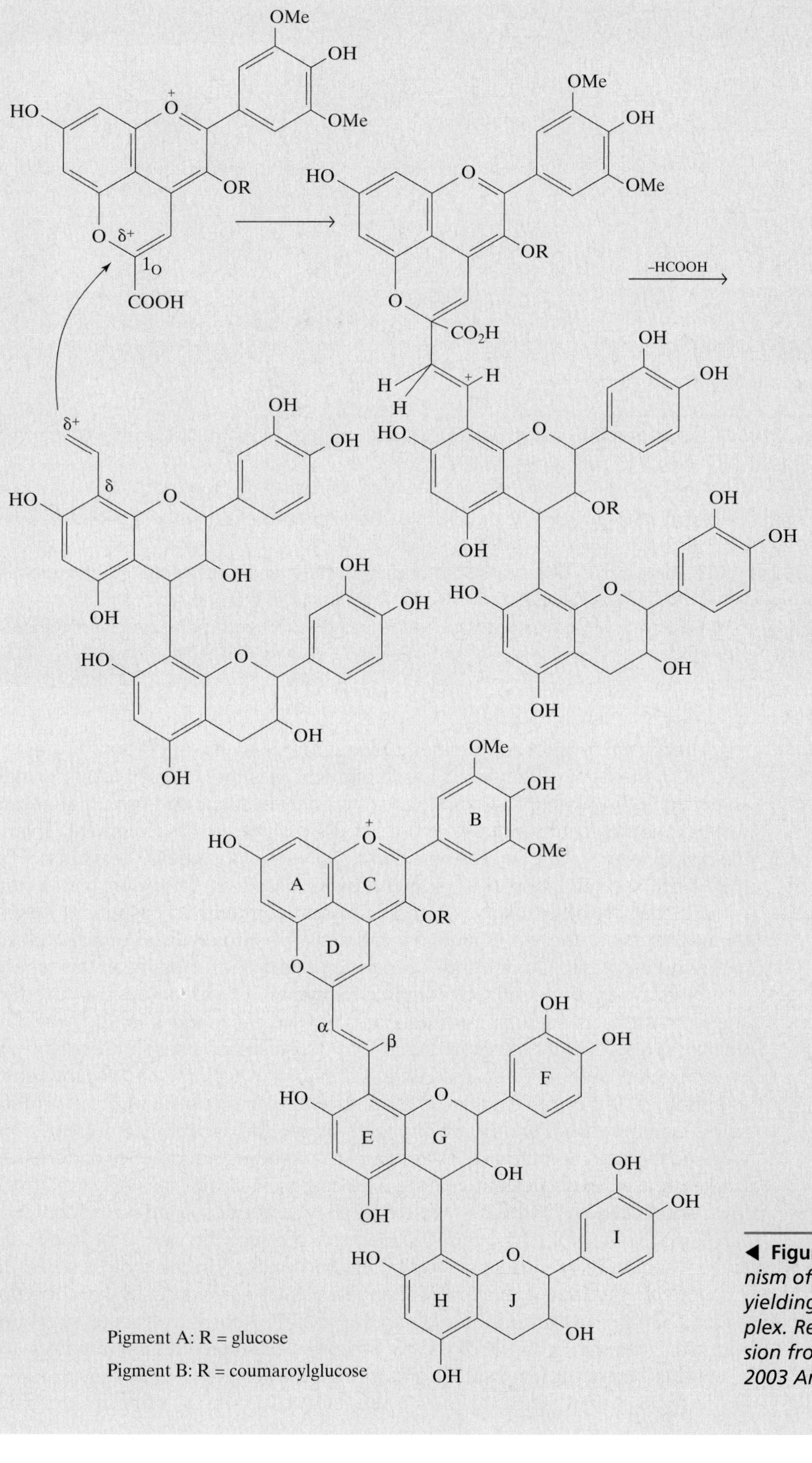

Pigment A: R = glucose

Pigment B: R = coumaroylglucose

◀ **Figure 2.** *Proposed mechanism of pigment polymerization yielding a blue pigment complex. Reproduced with permission from source 2, copyright 2003 American Chemical Society.*

479

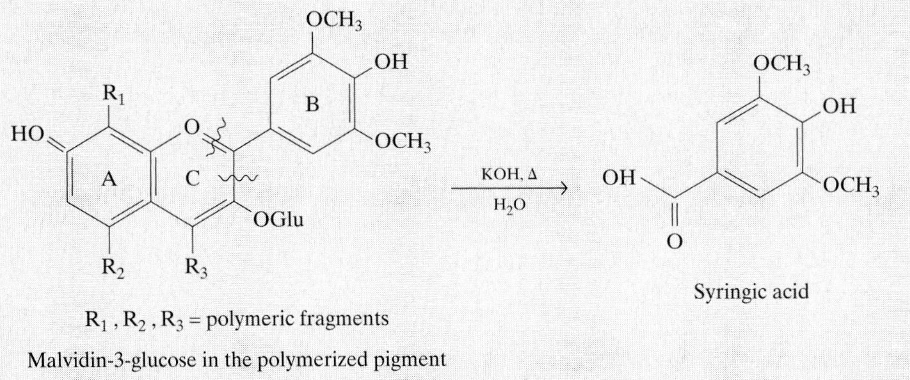

▲ **Figure 3.** *Degradation of the residue of a polymeric pigment to form syringic acid. Reproduced with permission from source 3, copyright 2003 American Chemical Society.*

Sources: 1. Darias-Martín, J., et al., "Effect of Caffeic Acid on the Color of Red Wine," *Journal of Agricultural and Food Chemistry* 50 (2002), 2062–2067.

2. Gauasch-Jane, M. R., et al., "Liquid Chromatography with Mass Spectrometry in Tandem Mode Applied for the Identification of Wine Makers in Residues from Ancient Egyptian Vessels," *Analytical Chemistry* 76 (2004), 1672–1677.

3. Mateus, N., et al., "A New Class of Blue Anthocyanin-Derived Pigments Isolated from Red Wines," *Journal of Agricultural and Food Chemistry* 51 (2003), 1919–1923.

The crystal form of simple inorganic pigments is also important. For example, TiO_2, the most widely used white pigment, has three crystal forms[7]: rutile, anatase, and brookite. The first two are tetragonal in shape and have high refractive indices whereas brookite does not. Brookite is not used as a pigment. The rutile crystal form of TiO_2 has the best hiding power but anatase is the whiter of the two. Until recently, inorganic pigments were based on transition metal compounds that are also toxic, lead and cadmium compounds prominent among them. The use of these pigments has fallen as substitutes were found, both organic and inorganic. Compounds of titanium and zinc are notable in this regard.

Other types of specialized inorganic pigments include those which produce specialized effects such as luminescence, pearlescence, and metallic sparkling (metal flakes). Luminescent pigments may fluoresce or phosphoresce and are used in paints and inks. Luminescent paint marks evacuation and escape routes in buildings, for example, whereas luminescent inks are useful in some printing and consumer inks. Pearlescent pigments mimic the appearance of pearls and work on the basis of internal reflection and the resulting interference patterns. An approach used to create pearlescence is to coat mica, a mineral with a relatively low refractive index, with TiO_2, which has a higher refractive index. Incident light can undergo multiple internal reflections and produce the muted pearl appearance. A similar technique was described in Section 5.2.5 in the context of the design of the sampling device for attenuated total-reflectance IR spectroscopy (ATR). Similar manipulations of coated metallic particles create sparkling pigments. Another group of pigments is used as **extenders** (fillers) in paints and inks. These compounds produce a coloring effect, but typically, they are present to reduce manufacturing costs by stretching the supply of more expensive

Table 11.3 Ink and Paint Pigments

Class	Pigment Group	Colors*	Example
Organic	Azo and metallicized azos	ROY	

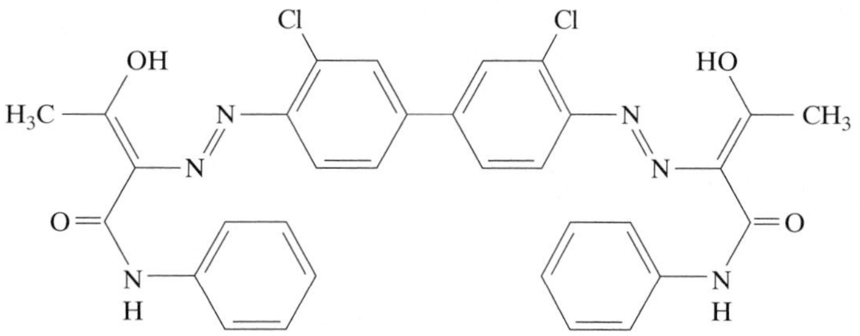

Benzidine yellow

Pigment yellow 12

| | Phthalocyanines (copper) | BG | |

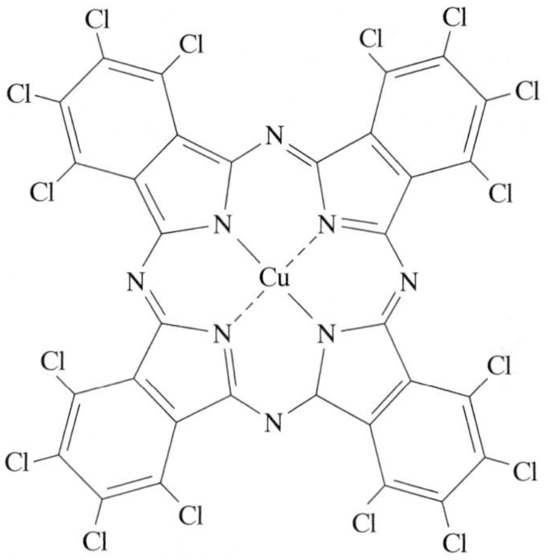

Phthalocyanine green

| | Anthraquinones | Many | |

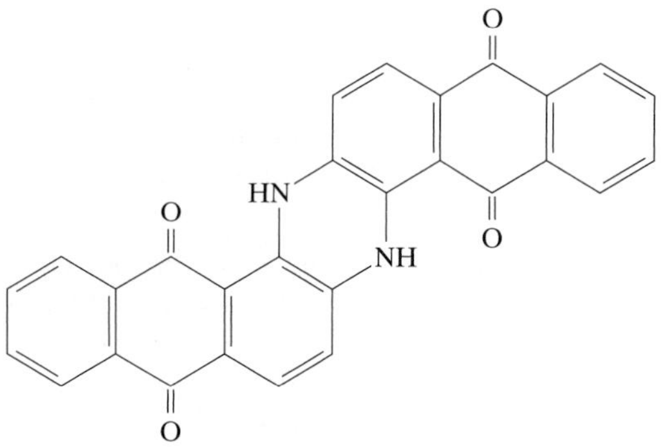

CI blue pigment 60
Indanthren blue

Table 11.3	(Continued)		
Class	**Pigment Group**	**Colors***	**Example**
	Quinacridones	RV	
			Pigment violet 19
			Linear quinacridone
Inorganic	Transition metal oxides	Many	TiO_2 (white)
	Graphite (carbon black)	Black	
	Metallic	Shine	Al, Cu, Zn, and alloys
	Transition metal sulfides	Many	Cadmium sulfoselenide (R)
	Chromates	YO	$ZnCrO_4$ (Y)
	Ferrocyanides	BR	$Fe[Fe(CN)_6]$ Prussian blue

*Spectral colors ROYGBIV (red–orange–yellow–green–blue–indigo–violet).

pigments. Extender pigments include compounds such as $CaCO_3$, gypsum, talc, diatomaceous earth, quartz, mica, barium sulfate, silicates, and clay materials.

The oldest organic pigments are the azo type ($-N=N-$).[7] The copper phthalocyanines are now widely used in inks and paints. Numerous systems are utilized to classify and describe dyes and pigments; two are particularly useful in forensic contexts. The first is by application method or mode, and the second is by chromophore (Table 11.3). Regardless of how dyes are classified, all contain long conjugated bond systems. Many pigments do as well; exceptions are materials such as zinc oxide and TiO_2, widely used white pigments. Dyes bond or affiliate themselves with a substrate via the familiar mechanisms: ionic bonding, covalent bonding, and hydrogen bonding.[5] Dyes may be anionic, as in the case of acid dyes, or cationic, as in basic dyes. Reactive dyes form covalent bonds with the substrate, typically a fiber. In many cases, mixed bonding modes are seen.

Forensically, dyes are typically classified by their chemical structure or method of application (Table 11.4) or by their chemical dye class (Table 11.5). Quantitative description and classification of dye color is most commonly done with the Color Index (Colour Index) or CI number, although use of the CI number is limited by the application of the dye. The Color Index is compiled by joint efforts of the Society of Dyers and Colourists (SDC, www.sdc.org.uk) and the American Association of Textile Chemists and Colorists (AATCC, www.aatcc.org). The CI number system is similar to the CAS numbering system used for chemicals, in that it provides a common reference and numerical key that unambiguously identifies a dye or pigment regardless of other names applied to it. For example, indigo, a natural dye, has a CAS number of 482-89-3 and a CI constitution number of 73000. The constitution number contains five digits and refers to the time the dye was registered; the lower the number, the older is the registration. The first two to three digits code for the chemical class. The notation *dye* or *pigment* is included, and if appropriate, the salt form can be noted. For example,

Table 11.4 **Dyes and Pigments Categorized by Functional Behavior or Application Method***

Class	Description	Example
Acid	Dyes used under acidic conditions; ionic interactions with substrate; anionic in solution; most are sulphonic acid derivatives	Acid red 33
Azo	Dyes created by coupling reactions to create diazonium salts or the like	Solvent red 1
Basic (cationic)	Dyes that form cations in solution; tribenzene (trimethine) structural element is common	Gentian violet/Basic violet 3

CI Pigment Red 48 (12070) is available as several salts, including the calcium (CI Pigment Red 48:2) and manganese (CI Red Pigment 48:4) salts. Many dyes and pigments also have common names, such as Tyrian Purple. Appendix 13 contains tables showing the names and structures of dyes and pigments commonly encountered in forensic chemistry grouped by color.

Table 11.4 (Continued)		
Class	**Description**	**Example**
Direct	Dyes that are applied directly to cellulose (as in cotton fibers or cellulose component in paper). Also called substantive dyes	

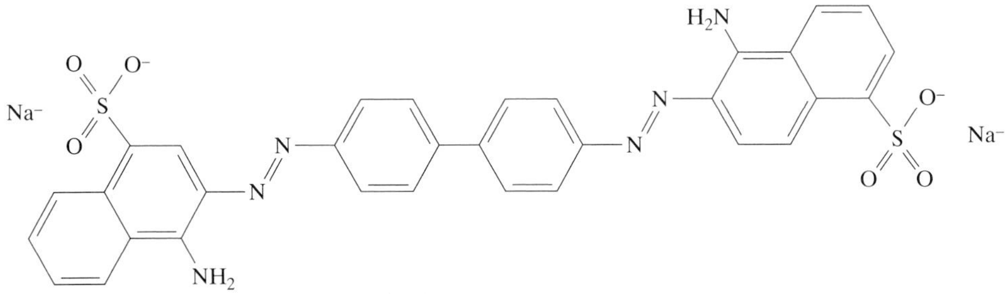

Direct red 28 (congo red)

Natural	As the name implies; Tyrian Purple is an example	

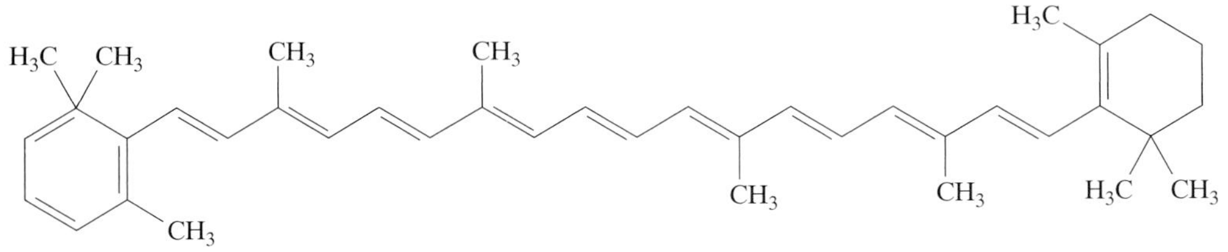

Natural yellow 26 (β carotene)

Solvent	Dyes that are molecular as opposed to ionic and that dissolve in nonpolar solvents	

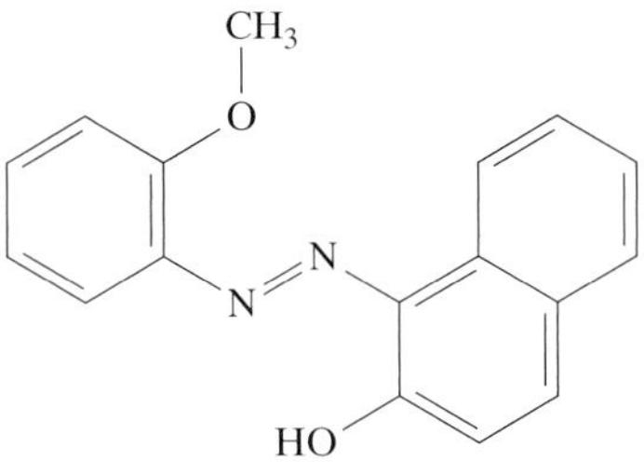

Solvent red 1

*Note that more than one classification can apply.
Sources: Eklund, D., and T. Linstrom, *Paper Chemistry: An Introduction*. Grankulla, Finland: DT Paper Science, **1991**.
Hunger, K., ed., *Industrial Dyes: Chemistry, Properties, and Applications*. Kelkheim, Germany: Wiley-VCH, **2003**.
Zollinger, H., ed., *Color Chemistry: Synthesis, Properties, and Applications of Organic Dyes and Pigments*. Zurich: VHCA/Wiley-VCH, **2003**.

Table 11.5 Dyes and Pigments Grouped by Chromophore

Chromophore	Structure	Example
Anthraquinone	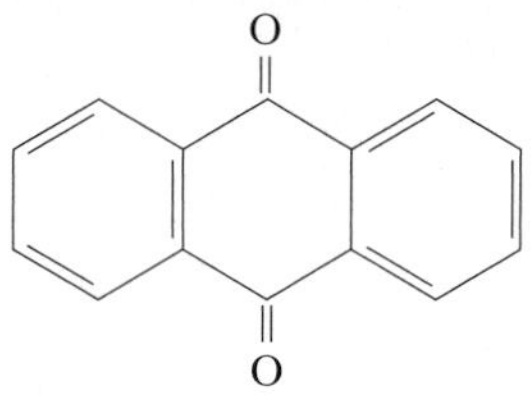	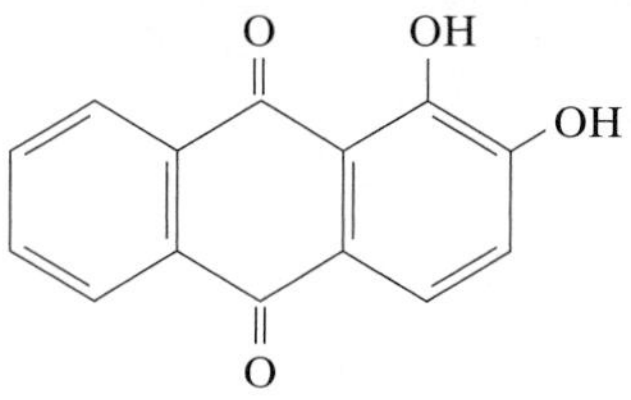 Alizarin (dye)
Azo	$-N{=}N-$	Methyl orange (dye) Yellow 13 (pigment)
Carbonyl	Conjugated C=O system	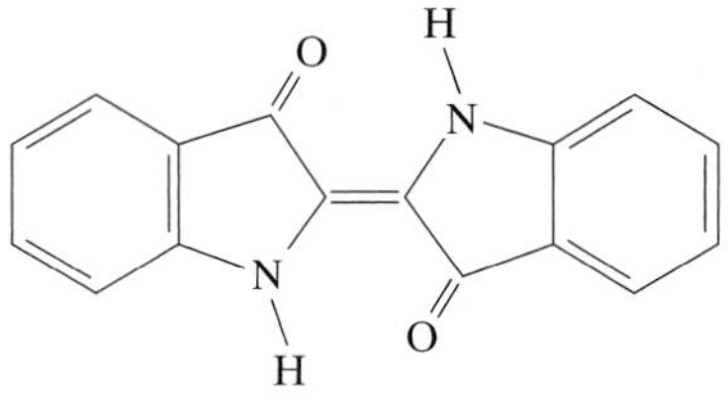 Indigo

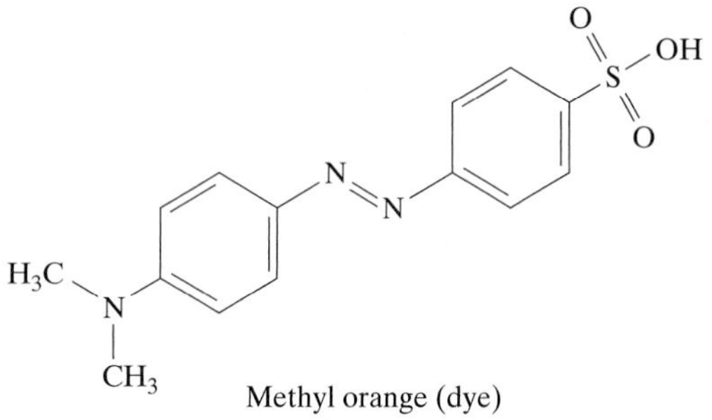

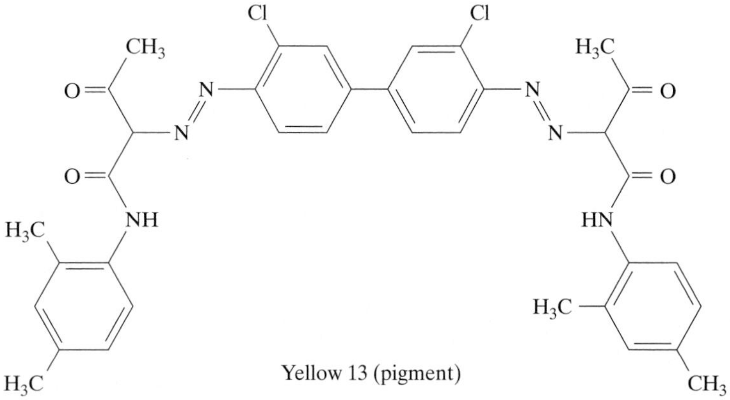

Table 11.5 (Continued)

Chromophore	Structure	Example
Cationic	R_4N^+	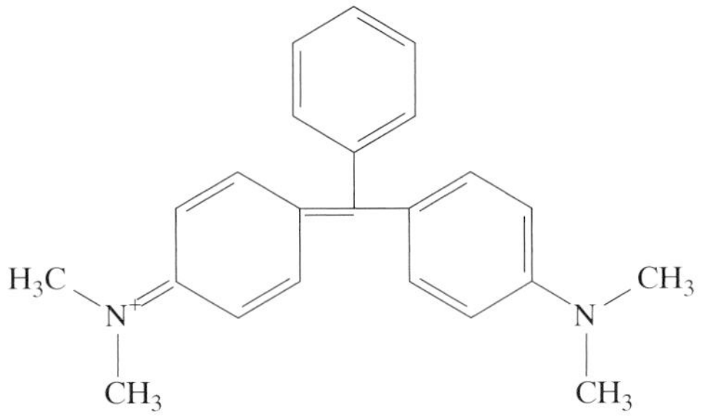 Malachite green
Indigoid	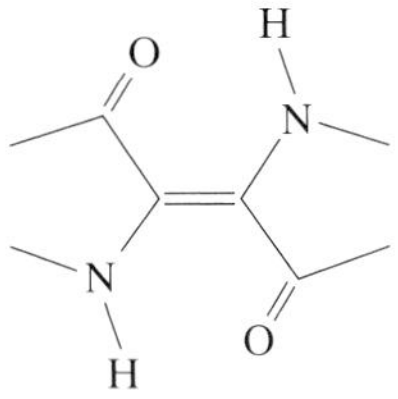	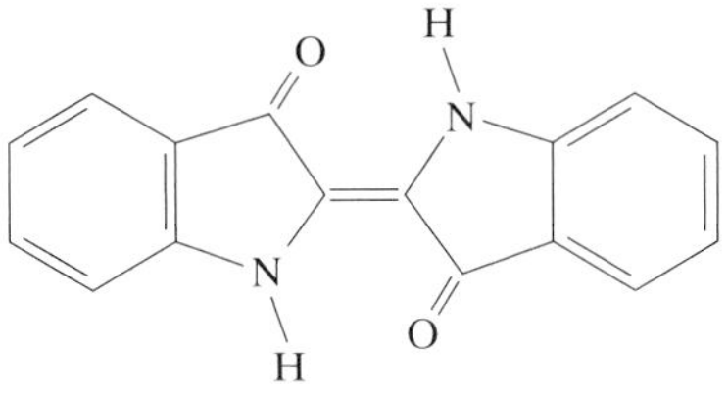 Indigo
Metal complexes	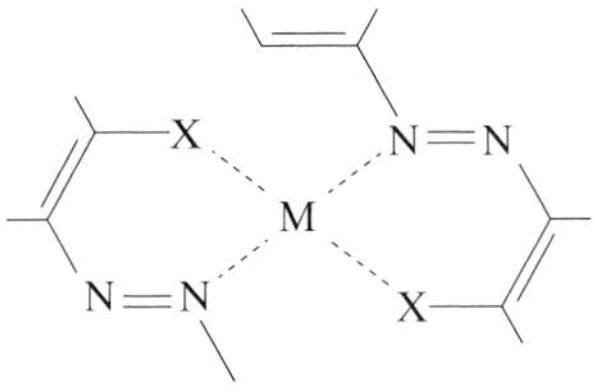 $M - Cu^2, Ni^2, CO^2$ $X - O, NH$	

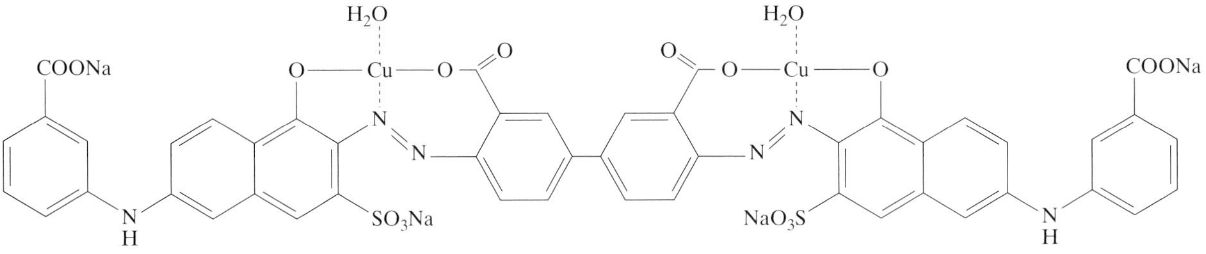

C.I. direct blue 93

| Nitro and nitroso | 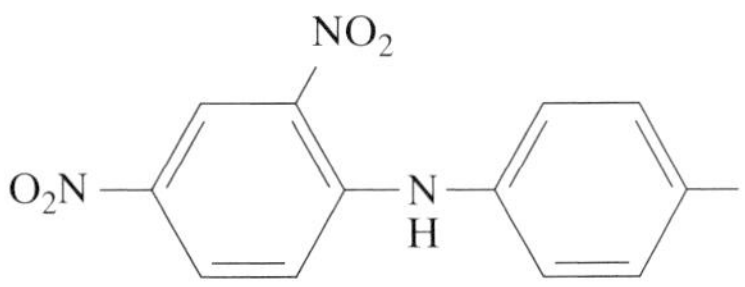 | 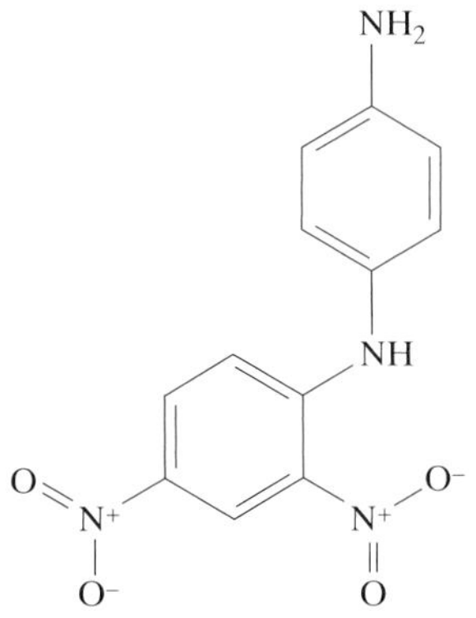 C.I. Dispersive yellow 9 |

Table 11.5 (Continued)

Chromophore	Structure	Example
Phthalocyanine	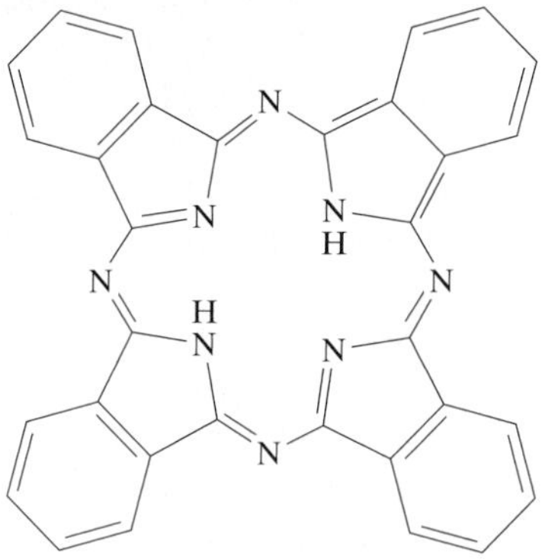	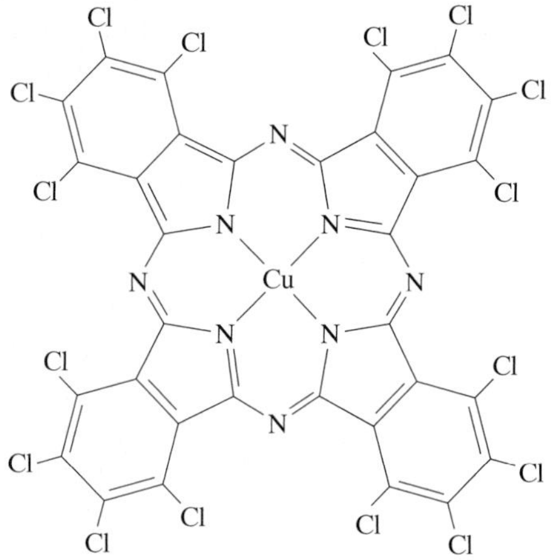
Polymethine	Long chain of conjugated double bonds terminated by e⁻ donor and e⁻ acceptor

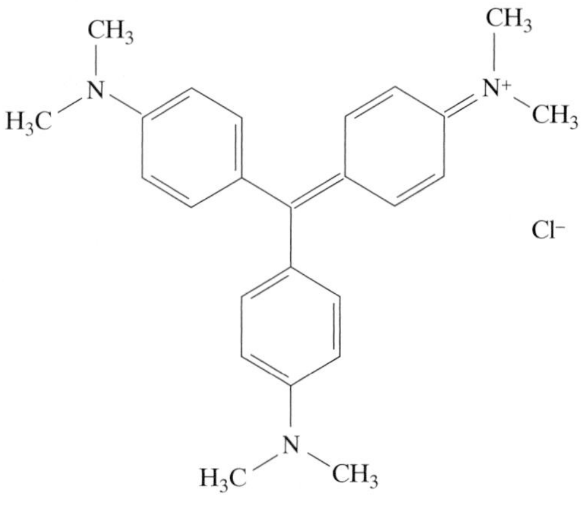

Gentian violet |

Sources: Hunger, K., ed., *Industrial Dyes: Chemistry, Properties, and Applications.* Kelkheim, Germany: Wiley-VCH, **2003**.
Zollinger, H., ed., *Color Chemistry: Synthesis, Properties, and Applications of Organic Dyes and Pigments.* Zurich: VHCA/Wiley-VCH, **2003**.

Historical Evidence 11.2—Drugs and Dyes

Drugs and dyes have historical as well as chemical properties in common. The dye industry began with the synthesis of mauve (aniline purple) by William Henry Perkins in 1856. Perkins, then an 18-year-old chemist, was attempting to make quinine to treat malaria. Bayer Pharmaceuticals, a German company famous for aspirin, was a dye-manufacturing company well into the 20th century.

11.3 APPLICATION OF COLORANTS: INKS

Inks consist of a solvent called a **vehicle**, colorants (dyes, pigments, or both), and other additives to control the flow, thickness, and appearance of the ink when dry, as well as other qualities. The ingredients in an ink are optimized on considerations pertaining to the marketplace and the production facility. For example, ballpoint pen ink must be pumped into a cartridge that is inserted into the pen. The ink must flow well, clean up easily, and not foam. Accordingly, the ink manufacturer might include a defoaming agent in the formulation to address the needs of the pen maker, not the desires of the consumer. This knowledge is important in interpreting analytical results. Ballpoint-pen inks are arguably the most frequently encountered ink evidence,[8] but the market changes constantly, and newer types, such as felt-tip pens with soft application surfaces and gel ink pens, are now common. Inks are involved in questioned document cases such as forgery and counterfeiting. Chemical analysis is used to answer such forensic questions as "Was all the writing on this page done with the same writing instrument?" "When was the writing placed on the paper?" and "In what order was the writing done?" The last question may be of importance in determining whether a pen stroke has been added atop an existing stroke, but this is usually sorted out microscopically. See Table 11.6 for other relevant terms.

Example Problem 11.4

Two inks are submitted to a forensic chemist for comparison, one a dark blue and one a light blue. How would the chromaticity values be expected to differ?

Answer: For the first part of the question, refer to the chromaticity space plot shown in the color insert. The darker the color, the farther the point will be toward the periphery of the parabola; the lighter the color, the closer to the center it will be. CIELAB values would be the best choice for expressing the color difference quantitatively.

Inks and paint (to be discussed shortly) are similar in many respects. Both are designed to deliver a colorant to a substrate such that the resulting coloring is evenly distributed and has the desired characteristics once it is dry. As solutions, each consists of (water or organic) solvents and solutes. If a colorant is a dye, it is dissolved in the solvent; if the colorant is a pigment, it is suspended in the solvent. Other solutes include adhesives, finishing agents, viscosity control agents, antimicrobials, antifoaming agents, extenders, and a myriad of other materials. All ingredients in the complex ink solution can yield important analytical information to the forensic chemist. Ink formulations have changed dramatically since the 1970s as environmental concerns related to the manufacturing of ink increased.[9] A similar development occurred in the paint field. Solvents and binder compositions in particular have evolved significantly, moving toward more water-based products and ether solvents.

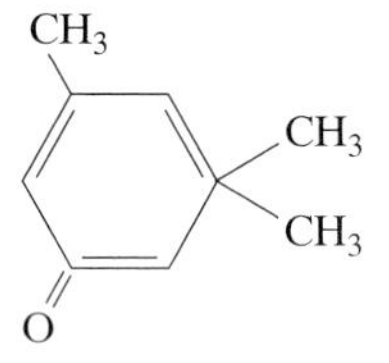

Solvents common in ink formulations (in addition to water) are methyl ethyl ketone (MEK), isophorone, and the glycol ethers such as ethylene glycol,

Isophorone

▲ **Figure 11.19**

Applying the Science 11.2   The Vinland Map

The Vinland map (mentioned and shown previously in Chapter 5, Applying the Science 5.3) has been controversial from the day it surfaced in 1965. The map appears to show the outline of Canada and North America—no great surprise, except that the parchment on which the map is drawn has been dated to the period 1411–1468. This dating, calculated from ^{14}C techniques, is not disputed. Columbus sailed to the New World in 1492, but Vikings had discovered and settled in North America hundreds of years earlier, another fact not contested. However, the authenticity of the map has been questioned on the basis of the ink and techniques used to create it. Modern forgeries created on old parchment are not uncommon, but it is difficult to forge the types of pigments that would have been used on an authentic map. This is the heart of the controversy.

The map was donated to Yale University in 1965, and at the request of the university, Dr. Walter McCrone, the famed microscopist and chemist, examined it. Using PLM and other techniques, he concluded that a clever forger had first drawn a yellowed outline on the paper with a yellowish anatase (TiO_2) pigment to simulate ink diffusion and fading. The forger then drew a darker line down the center of the yellowed region to complete the ruse. As evidence of this technique, McCrone maintained that the anatase he found was too finely ground and had other characteristics that only a modern anatase, produced after 1917, could have.

Dr. Jacqueline Olin, a retired chemist from the Smithsonian Institution, countered by creating a black ink starting from the mineral ilmenite ($FeTiO_3$). This ink, she argues, could explain the observed pattern. Another possibility is that the anatase could have come from kaolin, which is still used as an additive in colorant formulations. Instrumental analyses have produced conflicting results: A 1987 analysis using particle-induced X-ray emission lent support to those arguing for authenticity, while another study using Raman spectroscopy supported McCrone's assertions concerning the anatase. In addition to being an interesting historical mystery, the Vinland map case illustrates the need for deep knowledge of chemistry and formulations of inks as part of the investigative process.

Source: Graham, R., "Vinland: An Inky Controversy Lives," *Analytical Chemistry* "A" pages November (2004), 407A–412A.

a family of related compounds formed by the reaction of alcohols and ethylene oxide. As with alcohols, the longer the hydrocarbon chain, the less water soluble is the glycol. The terms **cellusolve** and **carbitol** are used to describe many of these compounds, which can be synthesized as shown in Figure 11.20.[10] The longer the alcohol chain, the less water soluble is the ether produced. However, having ether functionality increases the hydrogen-bonding capability of the ether. These solvents are also called alcohol–ethers because of their mixed functionality.

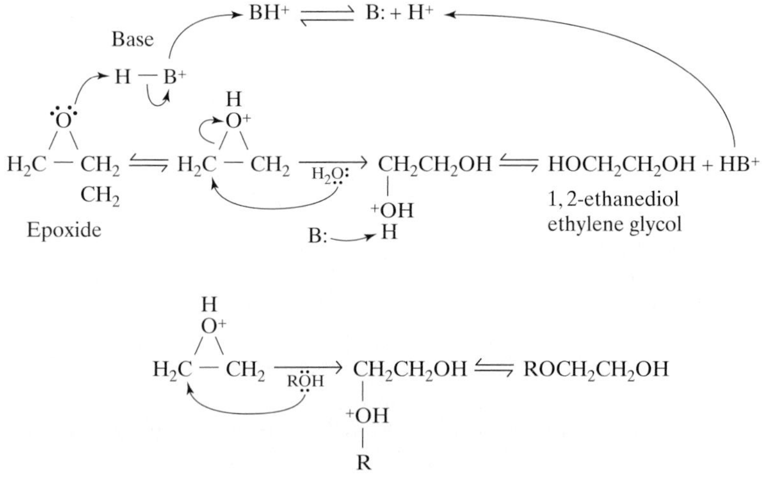

◀ **Figure 11.20** *Synthesis of common ink solvents using epoxides. Epoxide and water form ethylene glycol. Alcohols react analogously to the water.*

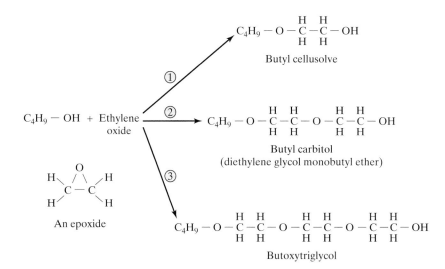

The reaction mechanism for producing cellusolve and related ethers is illustrated in Figure 11.21 by the production of ethyl glycol, another important
solvent in inks. Epoxides are extremely reactive. Once the epoxide is protonated, even relatively poor nucleophiles such as water (shown) or alcohols can
open the ring and add to it. Altering the stoichiometric ratio of alcohol to epoxide dictates which ethers are produced.

Pigments in ink are not dissolved; accordingly, the particles have to be
ground finely and dispersed as evenly as possible. Because many pigments are
charged, the electrostatic interactions can be exploited to improve the dispersion of fine particulates. The solution is treated to prevent the formation and
growth of particles.[†] Stabilizing the double layer (Figure 11.22) maintains electrostatic repulsion between pigment particles and prevents agglomeration of
the fine dispersion into unevenly distributed globs. One approach to stabilization is to use a surfactant, as illustrated in Figure 11.23. In this example, the

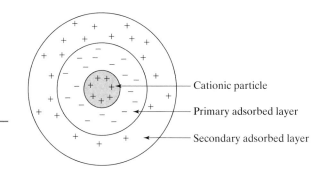

▶ **Figure 11.22** *The double layer surrounding a
charged particulate.*

Cationic particle

Primary adsorbed layer

Secondary adsorbed layer

[†]Readers may recall performing gravimetric analysis as part of an analytical chemistry
or quantitative analysis course. A successful gravimetric analysis requires that particle
formation be encouraged and that the electrical double layer be disrupted and decreased in size. This is the exact opposite of what is desired for optimal dispersion. The
particles are treated to insure that they don't clump together in solution.

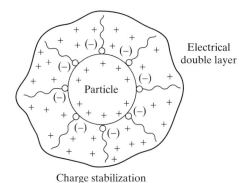

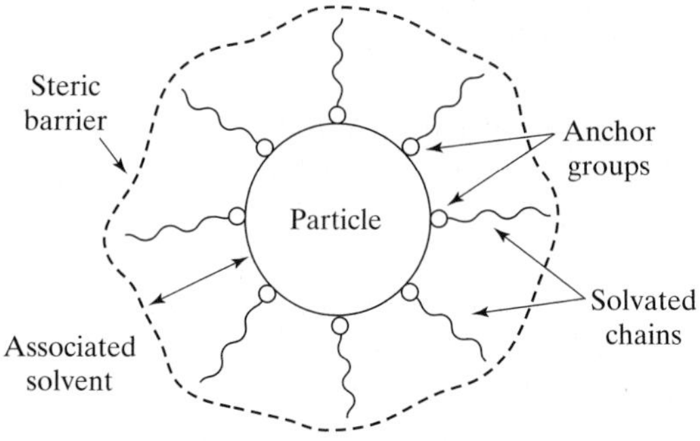

Charge stabilization

Electrical double layer

Particle

Steric barrier

Particle

Anchor groups

Solvated chains

Associated solvent

◀ **Figure 11.23** *Methods of stabilizing the double layer using surfactants. The anionic group of the surfactant associates with the cationic particle and stabilizes the double layer which in turn prevents particulates from aggregating and settling out of solution.*

surfactant has an anionic end that associates with the particle. A similar construct was introduced in Section 5.5.1 (capillary electrophoresis), in the discussion of micelles. Here, it is important that the surfactant–particle complex remain soluble in the ink's vehicle, such as water. A similar approach is based, not on stabilization of the double layer, but on physically blocking the particle surface. This method is referred to as steric hindrance.[11]

In addition to pigments, many printing inks are metallized, such as metallized azo pigments.[11] Among the various applications of metallized pigments are printing on boxes and on currency. Some consumer ink formulations incorporate metal flakes, as is seen in Figure 11.18. Dyes are also used as colorants for inks, with the key criterion being solubility. Dyes penetrate the paper matrix to the

Exhibit C: Why Metals Are Shiny

The characteristic shine of metals is related to their ability to conduct electricity. In a simplified explanation, the bonding in a metal such as copper differs from that in covalent compounds such as H_2 in that the valence shell electrons are shared by all of the metal atoms in a contiguous piece of the pure metal. The electrons are completely delocalized and move easily within the valence-bond bands that are available. When a photon of the appropriate wavelength is absorbed, an electron is easily promoted. The extinction coefficient for the transition is strong, and as a result, photons do not travel far into the metal. The absorption of a photon—a packet of electromagnetic energy—causes an electrical current to flow in the metal and emits a photon at the same wavelength. The collection of photons emitted is perceived by an observer as "shine" or luster.

Source: Nassau, K., "Ch. 5: Color Caused by Transition Metals in a Ligand Field," in K. Nassau, *The Physics and Chemistry of Color*, 2nd Ed. New York: John Wiley and Sons, 2001.

degree the solvent does and may associate with the cellulose matrix on the basis of ion–dipole interactions. Dyes that would not otherwise adhere to cellulose can be modified to afford such association as desired. Other ingredients in inks include adhesives, resins, agents to control viscosity, and varnishes. Adhesives and varnishes are often used to bind pigment particles to the paper surface.

There are numerous types of inks, such as printing ink, ballpoint-pen ink, gel-pen ink, and inks used in printers and typing ribbons. Formulations vary with the application and the differences are useful in chemical characterization and interpretation. One of the oldest inks, and one still in use, is carbon ink, also called India ink. The composition is as it sounds: ground carbon black suspended in glue or some other adhesive material to enable the particulates to adhere to the substrate. Modern uses of India ink are in fountain pens, printing inks, and drawing inks.[12] Until the mid-1900s, fountain pens were widely used, with inks consisting of iron gallotannate formulations or mixtures of dyes. Interestingly, there are few truly black dyes, and almost all black inks consist of mixtures of dyes that work in accordance with the subtractive color principle described earlier.

Iron gallotannate inks are made by suspending iron salts in solutions containing tannic acid (MW 1701), a polyphenol used to stain wood. Tannic acid functions as a **mordant**, or binding or bonding agent, for pigments and dyes. In this capacity, tannic acid is used to prepare cellulose fibers to receive dyes; as is discussed in the next chapter, cellulose is the primary ingredient in papers and in cotton fibers. The name originated from one of the earliest applications of tannic acid: the dyeing of leather, which is also called tanning. Iron gallotannate inks penetrate, bind to cellulose fibers, and can be removed only by physical means.[12] These inks are also interesting in that, when first applied, they have little color, acquiring color with oxidation.[12]

The ballpoint pen, introduced in the United States around 1943, is based on the delivery of ink to a small metal ball that rolls over the paper's surface. The inks used are relatively thick and may contain dyes and pigments. Because the writing process involves mechanical actions, ballpoint-pen ink contains additives to lubricate the ball. Other additives range from adhesives to viscosity control agents, resins, and drying agents.[12] Common solvents include ethylene glycol, glycerin, and related compounds. Among the colorants currently favored are metallized phthalocyanines, such as those shown in Tables 11.3 and 11.5.

Another group of ink delivery devices consists of those which operate via capillary action. Fiber-tipped pens, also called "felt tips" deliver inks with solvent bases that are aqueous, glycol based, or xylene based.[12] The inks are generally less viscous than ballpoint inks. Recently introduced gel pens are increasing in popularity and, as the name implies, deliver colorants via a gel rather than a comparatively thin solution. Colorants are primarily pigments, and once dry, the inks are virtually insoluble.[12] As a result, forensic analyses are more complex, but still feasible, as is discussed later in the chapter.

Example Problem 11.5

Two inks are to be compared, one extracted from a ransom note and one obtained from a pen recovered from a suspect. Both inks are a light-blue color. A reflectance spectrum of one reveals a single broad peak for one ink, while the spectrum of the other shows two peaks. Are the inks differentiated?

Answer: Yes. The spectra indicate that, although they appear similar, the colors are produced by two different compositions. The first is likely a single colorant, the second a mixture. The inks are not from a common source.

Table 11.6	Paint and Coatings Terminology
Additives	Materials added to a paint or coating in small amounts and with varying purposes.
Binder	Substance that binds pigment particles to each other and the substrate. May also be the solvent or vehicle of a colorant solution
Drying oils	Triglyceride compounds that form a coating via oxidation; also used as precursors to varnishes
Extender/extender pigment	A pigment added to a colorant to alter its final appearance as well as reduce manufacturing costs
Hiding power	The ability of a coating to cover what is below it.
Lacquer	A protective topcoat that dries by evaporation of the solvent. Lacquers do not polymerize but they may be polymers.
Latex	Emulsion of colorant in an aqueous solution.
Modifier	A substance added in small amounts to alter physical or chemical characteristics of a coating.
Opacity	Degree of clearness of a coating. Topcoats should have minimal opacity and be nearly clear; colorant layers should be highly opaque to cover what is below.
Plasticizer	Substance added to a polymeric material to soften it and increase its flexibility.
Primer	The first coat placed on a surface; used to prepare the surface for receiving subsequent layers and binding them to the substrate.
Resin	Component that polymerizes from solution.
Sealant	Coating designed to seal a porous surface; can be used as a primer or topcoat
Shellac	A varnishlike material derived from insects.
Stain	Colorant that penetrates a surface rather than drying upon it. Stains lack binder components and are similar to inks.
Varnish	A protective topcoat that may contain oils, resins, and solvents.
	Polyurethane varnish is an example of a varnish that polymerizes after it is delivered to the substrate.
Vehicle	Binder and solvent and colorants, usually a synthetic resin.

Sources: Ryland, S. G., "Infrared Microscopy of Paints," *Practical Spectroscopy* 19 (1995), 163–243.
"Standard Guide for Forensic Paint Analysis and Comparison," in *ASTM Standard E 1610-02* 14.02, ed. ASTM International, 2004.
Thornton, J., "Ch. 8: Forensic Paint Examination," in *Forensic Science Handbook, Volume II*, R. Saferstein, ed., 2d ed. Upper Saddle River, NJ: Prentice Hall, 2002.

11.4 APPLICATIONS OF COLORANTS: MECHANICAL AND COMPUTER PRINTING

In addition to writing devices such as pens, a plethora of mechanical printing devices also deliver inks. Two decades ago, the term *mechanical printing* would have referred principally to one device: the typewriter. Computer technology has changed this situation, and now mechanical (as opposed to handwritten) documents have become much more important in society and consequently much more common as forms of physical evidence. For the forensic chemist however, the common theme remains inks, dyes, and pigments. This section approaches mechanical printing from this perspective.

11.4.1 COMPUTER PRINTING

One of the first computer printers available, and one still widely used for printing forms and checks, is the dot matrix printer. Like a typewriter, a dot matrix printer uses an impact method to create letters by striking paper through an inked ribbon. The letter is formed by a series of dots mounted on a printing

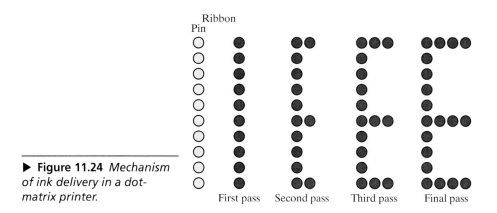

Ribbon
Pin

First pass Second pass Third pass Final pass

▶ **Figure 11.24** *Mechanism of ink delivery in a dot-matrix printer.*

head. Multiple printhead passes coupled to selective activation of the pin generates the letters. The printhead consists of a single row of pins as shown in Figure 11.24. To make a capital E, all pins are active and strike the ribbon on the first pass, creating the "|" backbone. On the second, third, and fourth pass, pins 1, 6, and 10 are active. Any common letter, number, or symbol can be formed by a dot matrix printer.

Laser printers, photocopiers, and ink jet printers employ non-impact printing technologies. Ink jet printers work on much the same principle as dot matrix printers except that ink is sprayed from the print head onto the paper in tiny target areas. Laser printers and copiers work on a different principle, as shown in Figures 11.25 and 11.26. At the start of the print cycle, a rotating drum surface is charged electrostatically in a fine grid pattern. A laser selectively scans the grid, discharging any grid square that it strikes. This creates a pattern that corresponds to lines from the image on the drum called the latent image.

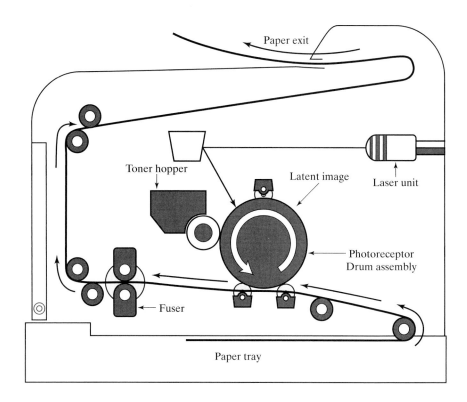

Paper exit

Toner hopper

Latent image

Laser unit

Photoreceptor
Drum assembly

Fuser

Paper tray

▶ **Figure 11.25** *Operation of a typical laser printer or copier. More details are found in the text.*

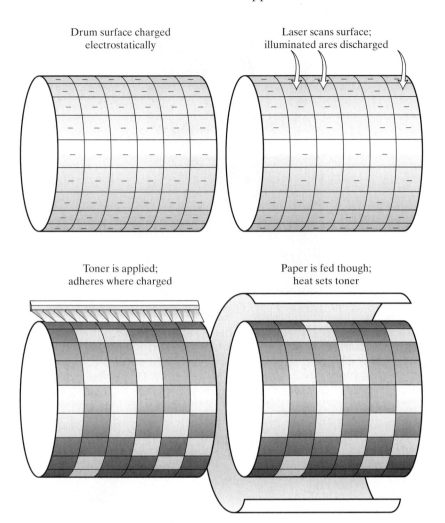

Drum surface charged
electrostatically

Laser scans surface;
illuminated ares discharged

Toner is applied;
adheres where charged

Paper is fed though;
heat sets toner

◀ **Figure 11.26** *How toner is applied to the drum to form the latent image in a laser printer.*

The next step is to apply color, either black and shades of gray, or color using toners. As shown in Figure 11.27, the difference between letters made by a laser printer and an ink jet printer can be distinguished microscopically.

Toner is a dry material that feels like powder but that contains waxy plastic in addition to the colorant. Finer grain sizes of toner allows for sharper lines and resolution in the printed image. The toner grains have a plastic consistency that melts much as wax when an image is fixed to paper in the fuser. Each color of toner is kept in a separate toner cartridge. Color copiers usually have three in addition to black: yellow, magenta (a light rose red), and cyan (a bluish purple) which is often abbreviated as CMY, the subtractive color system. The abbreviation CMYK is sometimes seen if a separate black toner cartridge is used in the printer. These colors can be combined to create thousands of other colors as was discussed earlier in the chapter. Toner that is negatively charged is applied to the drum and adheres wherever the charge remains. Paper, also given an electrostatic charge, is rolled on the drum, transferring the toner from the drum to the surface of the paper. The toner is fused to the paper by heat, which melts the waxy toner so that it adheres to the paper. The final step in the process is to remove the latent image from the drum by means of a discharge lamp. The drum is then ready to receive the next image.

Thermal transfer printing, similar to the laser and ink-jet printing technologies, has existed since the 1930s[13] and is used in relatively specialized applications,

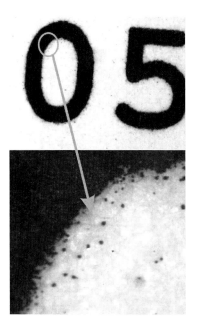

▶ **Figure 11.27** *Upon magnification, residual toner particles are visible and evidence of printing using a laser jet process. Image courtesy of Amy Richmond and Jennifer Wiseman, WVU Department of Chemistry.*

such as graphic arts, bar-code printing, tape label printing, commercial labeling such as that for CDs, and some fax machines. There are two common forms of thermal transfer printers, as shown in Figure 11.28. Dye diffusion operates by resistive heating. As more heat is applied, more dye is vaporized and delivered

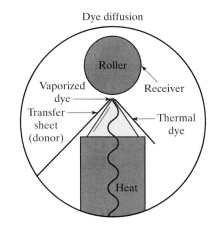

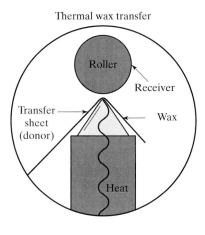

▶ **Figure 11.28** *The two common mechanisms of thermal transfer printing.*

to the substrate. In thermal wax transfer, contact is made between the heated print element and the substrate. Dye diffusion is similar to ink-jet printing, and wax transfer is similar to laser printers, but the differences are significant enough to result in different ink compositions.

11.4.2 MECHANICAL PRINTING

Many types of documents are still printed mechanically. Of principal forensic interest are commonly forged documents, such as currency and stamps. Mechanical processes deliver ink to a substrate by mechanical pressure applied against an ink-coated metal plate. As an example, consider the process used by the U.S. Treasury Department's Bureau of Engraving and Printing (www.moneyfactory.com). The first step in making paper currency is to create an engraving that is called the master die. This is done by hand via a painstaking process, but the die can be used for years. For example, the portrait of Lincoln on the $5 bill was originally carved in 1869. The master die must next be duplicated exactly on a plate that produces 32 bills each time it is used. The complex process involves the creation of a cast of the die made in plastic and then combined with the other elements of the bill. The plastic relief, called an alto, is placed in an electrolytic bath that forms the foundation of the plate. Careful inspection follows. If the alto is deemed acceptable, it is used to make the final metal plate.

For printing, the plate is coated with ink and wiped down, so that ink remains in the grooves in the plate. Special paper is rolled across the plates under extremely high pressure that forces the paper into the inked areas on the plates and transfers it to the paper surface. Because the paper is pressed into the grooves, the bill acquires texture such as fine ridges and grooves. This process of pressing is referred to as **intaglio printing**, and the texture created by pressing the currency cannot be easily re-created by counterfeiters using any other process. An example of intaglio printing is shown in the color insert. Because of the importance of deterring and detecting counterfeiting, the inks used in currency are unique and have features not found in typical consumer inks. This is an important consideration; most counterfeit bills are made with computer scanners and color printers. This aspect of ink analysis is discussed shortly.

Historical Evidence 11.3—Making Money (Literally)

"Money" can be described as a physical object of little intrinsic value that nonetheless represents wealth. The dollar bill is ink on paper and not worth much; it can't be used for anything other than as a token to be exchanged for something else. Early human business interactions, such as exchanges of material or services, were based on bartering. The earliest forms of money were not coins or notes, but food such as cows, sheep, and crops. The most widely used form of early money, still seen today, is a small shell called a cowrie shell. The Chinese adopted it as early as 1200 B.C. Within a few hundred years, the Chinese were also using metal coins of copper and bronze. Many of these coins were made with holes in the middle to allow them to be strung together like beads, a widespread practice. Native Americans were using chains of clamshells on strings by the middle of the 16th century. These were called wampum. Coins of silver appeared in the West around 500 B.C. and took a form that is recognizable today: rounded and with figures and scenes stamped into them. These coins could also be made of gold and other precious metals, but many were made of the

---

Historical Evidence 11.3—(Continued)

less expensive and less valued "base metals." Modern American coins used in general circulation are made of base metals.

The Chinese also pioneered paper money, with the first examples appearing around 800 A.D. In a problem often repeated since, so much money was printed that its value fell and prices soared, a situation referred to as inflation. The problem became so severe that the Chinese abandoned paper currency in the 15th century, and it was only in the 1700s that paper money was seen on a large scale again. The first paper currency in the United States was issued in 1690 by the Massachusetts Bay Colony. After the Revolutionary war, states continued to issue their own currency into the 1800s. Anticounterfeiting features were incorporated from the beginning, including very fine engraving, signatures, and elaborate patterns that are difficult to recreate. The Bureau of Engraving and Printing was established in 1877 and continues to be responsible for printing paper currency. The Bureau also prints stamps for the U.S. Postal Service. Each day, the Bureau produces approximately 37 million bills.

11.5 APPLICATION OF COLORANTS: PAINT

Like inks, paints are solutions that deliver colorant to a substrate. However, the term "paint" has come to refer to the generic field of coatings. Most coatings contain three elements: a solvent (organic or water), a colorant (typically, a pigment), and a binding agent that polymerizes during a curing stage. The solvent ensures that the pigment suspension and polymer-forming molecule are evenly spread over a surface; once the solvent evaporates sufficiently, the polymerization begins. Paint may cure unassisted or be accelerated by heat or irradiation with UV or other ranges of electromagnetic energy. Ancient paints used materials such as beeswax and fats as the binding agent. Tempera paints, made from egg yolks, are used today as artists' and children's paint; they were among the most common types of paint from ancient times until the Renaissance. Around the 16th century, oil-based binders such as linseed oil, still widely used today in oil painting, became popular. They dissolved in turpentine or a similar liquid. The oils in these paints polymerize slowly by oxidation to form a clear, resilient matrix binding the pigment particles to the surface and to each other.

Paints can be placed on porous surfaces, such as wood or paper, or on non-porous materials, such as metal. Paints are also frequently incorporated into a layered system, each layer representing a different type of coating and different forensic and analytical characteristics. As shown in Figure 11.29, a typical paint system consists of three generic layers: a layer that coats and prepares the substrate (the primer); the colorant layer or layers, in which the dyes and pigments are found, and a protective layer such as a varnish or clearcoat. Not all systems include all layers, but this model is a reasonable place to begin the discussion of paints. Table 11.6 summarizes the common terms used in such a discussion. When a coating is applied to a surface, a chemically complex process occurs. Consider the simple example of a paint containing pigment and a binder in a solvent (Figure 11.30). Once the paint is applied, two processes occur: solvent evaporates and the binder polymerizes to bind pigment particles to each other and to the substrate. The time required may be referred to as the curing time, depending on the application. The colorants are usually chemically passive in this process, which depends on the actions and interactions among the solvents and binders in a given paint formulation.

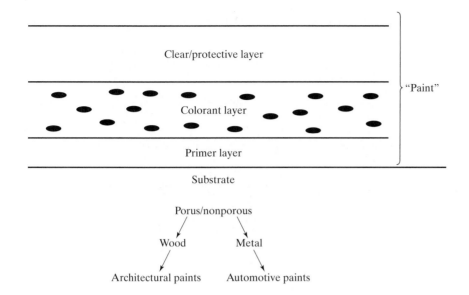

◀ **Figure 11.29** *Paint is often found in layers. The primer prepares or seals the surface, the colorant layer delivers the pigment or dye, and the protective layer seals out moisture and protects from weathering.*

11.5.1 SOLVENTS

Solvents in paint function as do ink solvents. The solvent must ensure that the colorant is homogeneously suspended (in the case of pigments) and delivered evenly to the substrate. Once the colorant and the associated additives are in place, the solvent evaporates and, in doing so, allows the curing and film-building polymerization process to begin. As with inks, environmental concerns have driven paint manufacturers to an increasing use of water as the solvent where that is feasible. Latex paints are water based and illustrate some of the challenges introduced when water is the solvent. Many of the binders and resins used in paints are not water soluble, but can be made so by using micelles. As illustrated in Figure 11.31, the micelles surround and dissolve the monomers, which then polymerize. The resulting suspended aggregate is called a **latex particle** and remains suspended in an emulsion. Once a latex paint is applied to a substrate, the water evaporates and allows the polymerization to come to completion.

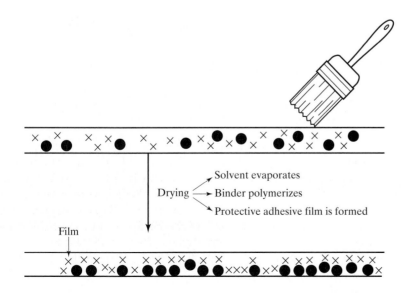

◀ **Figure 11.30** *The drying of paint involves both evaporation of solvent and polymerization of the binder. This step is also called film formation.*

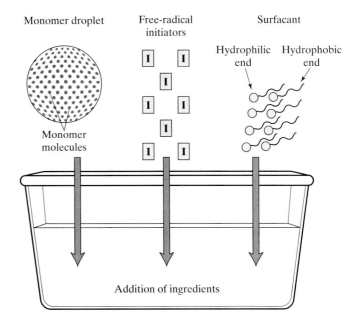

Monomer droplet

Free-radical initiators

Surfacant

Hydrophilic end   Hydrophobic end

Monomer molecules

Addition of ingredients

Emulsion before polymerization

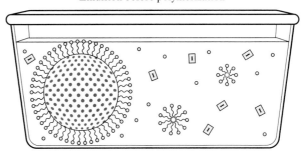

Polymerization to form latex particles

Polymer

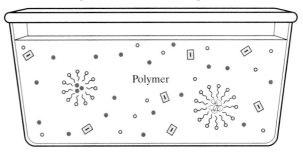

▶ **Figure 11.31** *Formation of a latex emulsion. A micelle is created around the monomers which partially polymerize within the micelle. The micelle remains suspended in the aqueous solution until the paint is delivered to the substrate.*

In addition to water, oxygenated hydrocarbon solvents are generally preferred whenever the formulation allows them. This is also due to environmental considerations. Types of solvents used include alcohols, esters, ketones, and the alcohol ethers associated with inks. Some paints still use hydrocarbon solvents such as turpentine and kerosene, and there a few instances of chlorinated hydrocarbon solvents, such as trichloroethylene, being used. Finally, there are solventless delivery systems such as electrodeposition used in some applications such as automotive coatings.

11.5.2 BINDERS OR RESINS

The role of the vehicle in paint is to form an adhesive film over the pigment granules that is optically clear, glossy (reflective) or matte (diffusely reflective) as desired, and protective. In this section, the term **binder** is used collectively to represent all similar compounds and components. Because of their function, binders may be referred to as **film-forming agents**, and they function in concert with the solvent system. Film formation, or curing, occurs by several mechanisms:[14,15]

- **Polymerization**, wherein resins polymerize as the result of heating or a catalyst.
- **Oxidation**, in which reactions between C=C sites in drying oil (discussed shortly) and oxygen lead to polymerization.
- **Solvent evaporation**, in which evaporation allows film-forming agents to coalesce.
- **Coagulation**, wherein dispersed solutions of particulates coalesce into a networked structure. Latex paints are aqueous dispersions that cure by this mechanism.

Binders, vehicles, or resins may be of several types. Alkyd resins are among the most common and are composed of polymers of alcohols and acids—thus the term **alkyd** (*-alc* from alcohol, *-yd* standing for acid). Acrylic resins are based on polymers of methacrylate and methyl methacrylate (esters, Figure 11.32); similarly, vinyl resins are derived from vinyl chloride. Urethanes (polyurethanes) and some silicon-based resins are also encountered. Watercolor paints use gum arabic as a binder. This material is obtained from the sap of the acacia tree and, when dry, forms a clear, water-soluble polymer matrix.

Polyurethane resins are used as protective coatings, both as binders in paint or as separate protective clear coatings without colorant. Polyurethanes are made by linking existing polymer units possessing —OH end groups with a di-isocyanate.[14] The process is outlined in Figure 11.33. The choice of the existing polymer and di-isocyanate dictates the characteristics of the film that results. Some polyurethanes are used in two-part systems much like epoxy glues, wherein a separate hardener is added to initiate polymerization.[15] In light of this, it is not surprising that there are epoxy binders as well, but they are not as common as the polyurethanes.

The polymerization of the binders may be speeded up by the addition of catalysts and drying oils and agents. The term is a misnomer, in the sense that the oils don't evaporate. Rather, they catalyze and speed film formation,

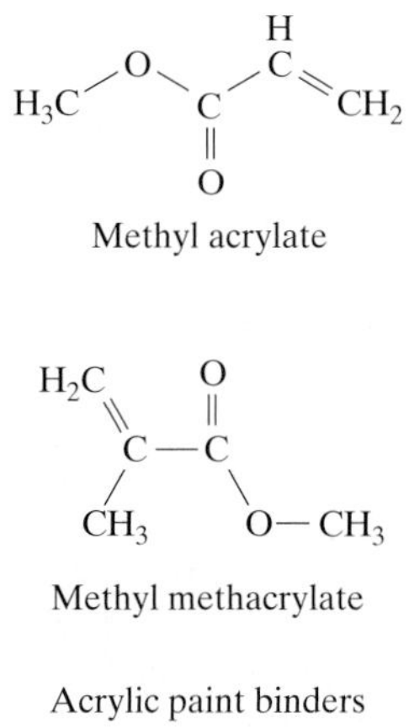

▲ **Figure 11.32** *The monomers used in acrylic paints. Polymers and polymerization is discussed in detail in Chapter 13.*

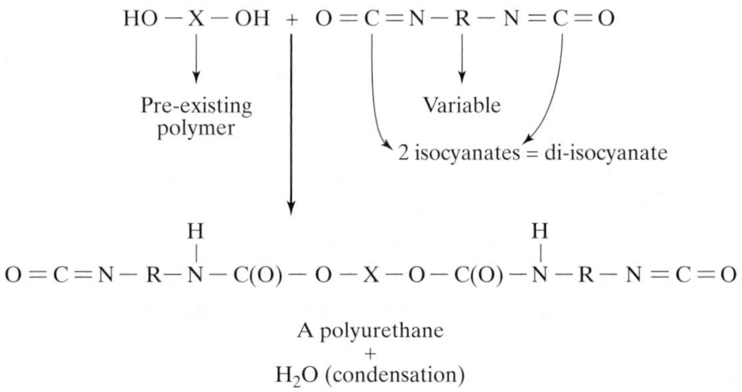

◄ **Figure 11.33** *Formation of a polyurethane polymer. "X" and "R" can be varied to control the characteristics of the final polymer.*

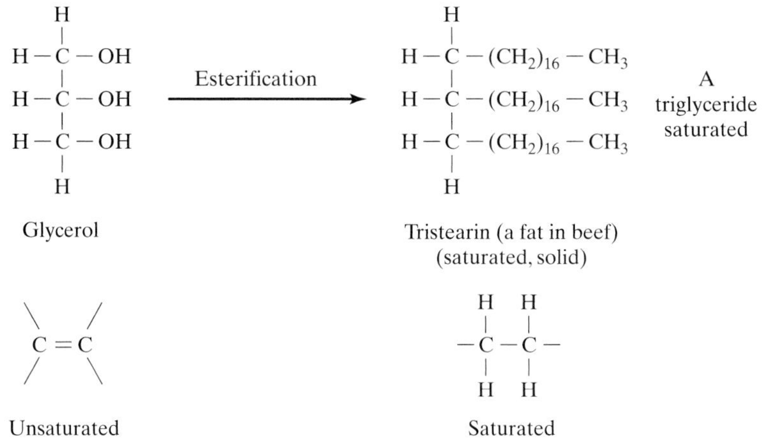

▶ **Figure 11.34** *Esterification of the tri-alcohol glycerol yields a triglyceride. A saturated fat is maximally "saturated" with hydrogen and has no C=C reactive sites. Saturated triglycerides are waxy solids while unsaturated triglycerides tend to be liquid oils.*

which appears as drying. Perhaps the best-known drying oil is linseed oil, but fish and vegetable oils can be used. **Drying oils** are grouped on the basis of their drying characteristics; linseed oil is a drying oil, safflower oil is semidrying, and cottonseed oil is nondrying. All of these oils are triglyceride oils with varying degrees of saturation. As saturation increases, the number of hydrogens bonding to the carbons in the hydrocarbon chain increases with a decrease in the number of $C=C$ bonds. Lard, which contains highly saturated fats, is a waxy solid, whereas less saturated fats, such as vegetable and seed oils, are viscous liquids. The more saturated an oil is, the less active it is in drying.[15] This relationship can be understood in light of reactivity: A $C=C$ bond is reactive toward oxygen, a key component in the drying process. A $C—C$ bond is not reactive to any comparable extent, and $C—C$ bonds dominate saturated systems since a single $C—C$ bond allows for more $C—H$ bonds to exist.

The process that leads to the polymerization of oils is the same reaction that causes oils and foods containing high unsaturated fat content to go rancid. As shown in Figure 11.35, the double-bond sites can be oxidized by a free-radical mechanism (Chapter 9) which becomes a chain reaction that continues until polymerization is complete. In the case of paints, polymerization involves cross-linking to form a strong binding matrix for the pigments. The curing and polymerization process requires the loss of some solvent by evaporation: Because the role of the solvent is to suspend and dissolve the colorants and polymerizing materials, some solvent must be removed to bring the polymerizing species into close enough proximity for the reaction to proceed. Additional drying agents, such as metals, may be added to speed the process. Examples include iron and cobalt, typically in the form of metal soaps[15] that form when the cation associates with the anionic end of the ionized fatty acid. This salt catalyzes both the formation of free radicals and the drying process.

11.5.3 ADDITIVES

Inks and paints contain small amounts of additives that may be of forensic interest. The drying agents already described are one example. Other additives, including plasticizers such as phthalates, are inserted into resins to impart flexibility to the polymerized mixture. These additives lessen brittleness and cracking. Antifoaming agents are also found in paints; recall the use of micelles

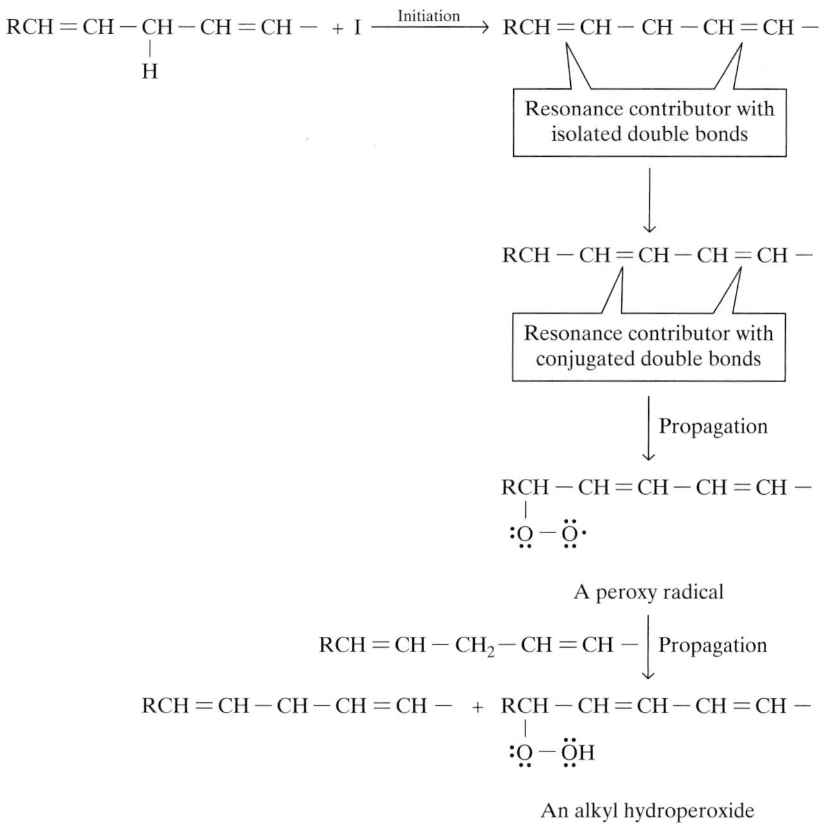

$$RCH=CH-\underset{\underset{H}{|}}{CH}-CH=CH- \; + \; I \xrightarrow{\text{Initiation}} RCH=CH-CH-CH=CH-$$

Resonance contributor with
isolated double bonds

$$RCH-CH=CH-CH=CH-$$

Resonance contributor with
conjugated double bonds

Propagation

$$RCH-\underset{\underset{:\ddot{O}-\ddot{O}\cdot}{|}}{CH}=CH-CH=CH-$$

A peroxy radical

$$RCH=CH-CH_2-CH=CH- \Big| \text{ Propagation}$$

$$RCH=CH-CH-CH=CH- \; + \; RCH-CH=CH-CH=CH-$$
$$\underset{:\ddot{O}-\ddot{O}H}{|}$$

An alkyl hydroperoxide

◀ **Figure 11.35** *Polymerization of an unsaturated fat via a free radical reaction.*

to stabilize particulates in emulsions and in colloidal suspensions. Stabilization is frequently achieved by adding surfactants to paint (generically called **dispersing agents**). Surfactants, however, can cause foaming, which is undesirable because foam bubbles can form and mar the painted surface. Foaming is also undesirable from the manufacturing point of view, so antifoaming agents are used to control this tendency when it occurs. Finally, water-based paints such as latexes contain antimicrobial agents to prevent fungus, mildew, and other forms of microbial degradation.

11.5.4 AUTOMOTIVE PAINTS

Among the most common types of paint evidence exhibits, automotive paint is worthy of brief mention. Cars are painted in a complex layering system that itself can be highly informative. Often, the layering pattern is sufficient to differentiate two automotive paint samples. Each layer has a specialized function and distinctive chemical characteristics. Exterior surfaces of cars are made of steel, plastics, and composite materials and are coated to protect against moisture and UV light. For steel, corrosion protection is required. The simple layering system presented in Figure 11.29 provides the starting point for more complex systems seen in the industry. That three-layer application is referred to generically as the clearcoat–base-coat system, which may have one or two primer layers.[14] Examples of other systems are illustrated in Figure 11.36. The coatings on automobiles are designed to be smooth and glossy, another distinctive feature relative to household and other architectural paints.

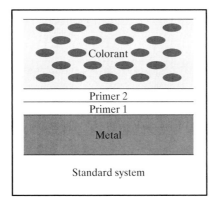

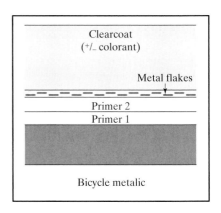

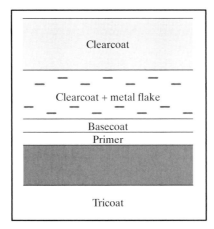

▶ **Figure 11.36** *Three generic coating layer systems.*

Steel surfaces of a car are protected from corrosion by **galvanization** with zinc. Galvanization prevents corrosion of the iron in steel via anodic protection. Because of its standard half-cell potential, metallic zinc surrenders electrons and oxidizes preferentially to iron, becoming the anode in the corrosion redox reaction. The principle of anodic protection, illustrated in Figure 11.37, is of forensic interest because elemental analysis of galvanized surfaces will indicate that zinc is not associated with a pigment or other coating element. Applications of coatings are accomplished by spraying, dipping, baking, electrodeposition, and powder sprays, the last of which are increasingly used and are affixed by an imparted charge of static electricity to the part that is grounded. When a portion of the part is evenly covered, it no longer attracts the particulates, assuring a uniform layer. The coating is fixed in place with the use of heat, UV radiation, or other methods.[15] Powder spray application can be used for any layer.

Exhibit D: Paint Stratigraphy

The discussion of paint in this chapter focuses on chemical aspects, but the layering is an important source of information that can be uncovered with microscopic examination. In some cases, the layer structure is so distinctive that further examinations are unnecessary. The architectural paint sample shown here is almost like geological layering of soils (stratigraphy), and within the layers may be decades of history unique to the house or other structure from which it came. Photo courtesy of William Schneck, Northwest Microvision.

Exhibit D: (Continued)

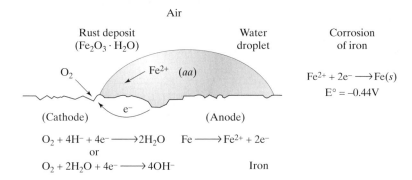

Air

Rust deposit
$(Fe_2O_3 \cdot H_2O)$

Water droplet

Corrosion of iron

O_2

Fe^{2+} (aa)

$Fe^{2+} + 2e^- \longrightarrow Fe(s)$
$E° = -0.44V$

(Cathode)

e^-

(Anode)

$O_2 + 4H^- + 4e^- \longrightarrow 2H_2O$
or
$O_2 + 2H_2O + 4e^- \longrightarrow 4OH^-$

$Fe \longrightarrow Fe^{2+} + 2e^-$

Iron

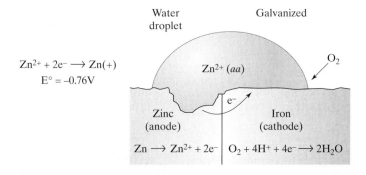

Water droplet

Galvanized

$Zn^{2+} + 2e^- \longrightarrow Zn(+)$
$E° = -0.76V$

Zn^{2+} (aa)

O_2

Zinc
(anode)

Iron
(cathode)

e^-

$Zn \longrightarrow Zn^{2+} + 2e^-$ | $O_2 + 4H^+ + 4e^- \longrightarrow 2H_2O$

◀ **Figure 11.37** *Use of zinc to prevent corrosion. In the absence of zinc, iron reacts with atmospheric oxygen and moisture to form rust. On a galvanized surface, the zinc acts as the cathode and thus protects the iron from corrosion.*

Exhibit E: Sunscreens

The purpose of a sunscreen, be it a lotion for people or a coating for a car, is either to reflect or to absorb and dissipate UV energy before it reaches the substrate. Pigments such as zinc oxide reflect the energy, but, for a clear coating, this approach is impractical. The first commercial sunscreen available in lotion form was PABA (p-aminobenzoic

Exhibit E: (Continued)

acid). The chromophore formed by a benzene ring in conjugation with a carbonyl group (benzophenone) is frequently used in sunscreen formulations. When a UV photon is absorbed, the energy is dissipated by collision and does not reach the substrate.

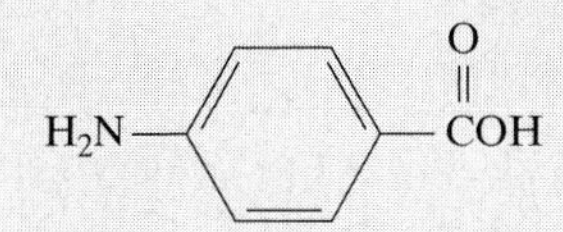

para-aminobenzoic acid
PABA

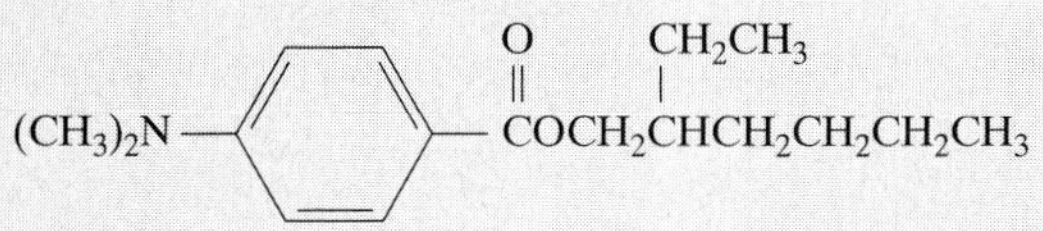

2-ethylhexyl 4-(dimethylamino)benzoate
Padimate O

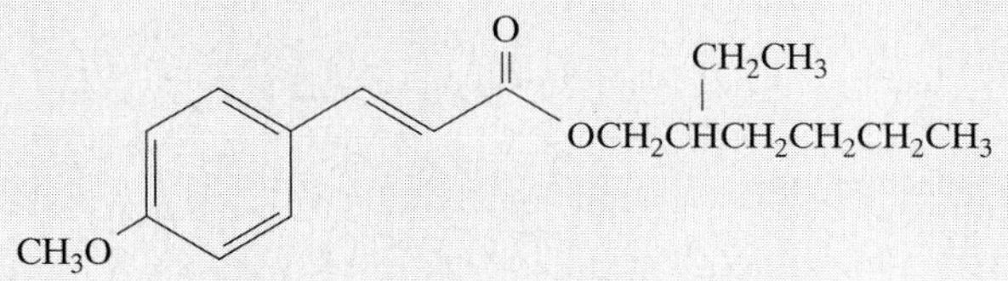

2-ethylhexyl (*E*)-3-(4-methoxyphenyl)-2-propenoate
Giv Tan F

Summary

This chapter completes our discussion of color fundamentals. We have covered which chemical structures create color, why they do so, and how they do it. Using color spaces, we have described how color, an inherently subjective property, can be described quantitatively. The next chapter will explore the principal types of evidence that involve colorants: inks and paints. The final chapter of the text will revisit colorants briefly in the context of fibers.

Key Terms and Concepts

Additive color system
Alkyd
Binder
Blackbody emitter
Carbitol
Cellusolve
Chroma
Chromaticity diagram
CIELAB

Coagulation
Dispersing agent
Drying oils
Extenders
Film-forming agent
Galvanization
Hue
Intaglio printing
Latex particle

Metamerism
Munsell color system
Resins
Standard observer values
Subtractive color system
Temperature (color)
Thermal transfer printing
Toner
Tristimulus values

Problems

From the chapter

1. Methyl orange is a dye and acid–base indicator. Locate the structure and classify this dye on the basis of the systems presented in this chapter.

2. Examine Table 11.2 and rationalize the values in light of their definitions.

3. What is the difference between solvent evaporation, curing, and drying?

4. What is the core structure of a Rhodamine colorant?

5. Given the following data for a visible spectrum of an ink, derive the tristimulus values:

–	R (%)
400	10.0
420	12.0
440	8.0
460	12.0
480	19.0
500	65.0
520	75.0
540	65.0
560	65.0
580	22.0
600	12.0
620	10.0
640	5.0
660	4.0
680	6.0
700	2.0

What color is the ink? What dyes or pigments shown in the tables in this chapter might be responsible for the color, assuming that a single colorant is used?

6. Review the structures of some of the dyes and pigments presented in this chapter and in the Appendices. Are there any that would *not* show some absorbance in the IR range?

7. Melamine polymers are becoming more common in paints and inks. What are they and how do they form a protective film? What else are these polymeric materials used for?

8. Applying the Science 11.1 discusses the polymerization of pigments in wine.
   a. How do the structures shown in the text compare with those given in Table 11.9?
   b. Refer back to the Marquis test discussed in Chapter 7 and comment on the similarities.

Integrative

1. Why are the orange and red dyes typically smaller molecules than the blue dyes? Relate your answer to the fundamental principles of color.

2. Drugs and dyes share at least two general similarities as a group of compounds. Discuss.

3. Locate the structure of chlorophyll and categorize it. Might this substance be found in items of physical evidence? Suggest an analytical scheme to identify it.

4. An older resin system used in automotive paints exploited cellulosic-based resins such as nitrocellulose. What are the components of this resin system? How does the film form?

Food for thought

1. Why are white boards (dry-erase boards) nonporous? For writing on such boards, what type of dyes or pigments and solvents would be best? Would special additives be needed? For what purpose? Justify your answer.

2. What do tristimulus values and principal component analysis (Chapter 3) have in common?

FURTHER READING

Bentley, J., and G. P. A. Turner. *Introduction to Paint Chemistry and Principles of Paint Technology*, 4th Ed. London: Chapman and Hall, 1998.

Ellen, D. *The Scientific Examination of Documents*. London: Taylor and Francis, Ltd., 1997.

Green, F. J. *The Sigma–Aldrich Handbook of Stains, Dyes, and Indicators*. Milwaukee: Sigma Aldrich Chemical Company, **1990**.

Laden, P., ed. *Chemistry and Technology of Water Based Inks*. London: Blackie Academic and Professional/Chapman and Hall, 1997.

Lubs, H. A., ed. *The Chemistry of Dyes and Pigments*. New York: Reinhold Publishing Corporation, **1955**.

Nassau, K. *The Physics and Chemistry of Color: The Fifteen Causes of Color*, 2d ed. New York: John Wiley and Sons, 2001.

Nickell, J. *Detecting Forgery: Forensic Investigation of Documents*. Lexington, KY: University of Kentucky Press, 1996.

Ryland, S. G. "Infrared Microscopy of Paints." *Practical Spectroscopy* 19 (1995), 163–243. This chapter has an excellent introductory portion that covers (pun intended) paint thoroughly, but concisely, and includes several useful tables.

REFERENCES

1. Laden, P. J. "Colorimetry and the calculation of color difference," in P. J. Laden, ed., *Chemistry and Technology of Water Based Inks*. London: Blackie Academic and Professional/Chapman and Hall, 1997.

2. Zollinger, H. "Chapter 4: Colorimetry," in H. Zollinger, *Color: A Multidisciplinary Approach*. Zurich: Wiley Verlag, 1999.

3. Thornton, J. "Visual Color Comparison in Forensic Science." *Forensic Science Reviews* 9 (1997), 37–57.

4. Cousins, D. R. "The Use of Microspectrophotometry in the Examination of Paints." *Forensic Science Reviews* 1 (1989), 1–141.

5. Green, F. J. *The Sigma–Aldrich Handbook of Stains, Dyes, and Indicators*. Milwaukee: Sigma Aldrich Chemical Company, 1990.

6. Nassau, K. "Ch. 13: Colorants of Many Types," in K. Nassau, *The Physics and Chemistry of Color*, 2d ed. New York: John Wiley and Sons, 2001.

7. Kunjappu, J. "Pigments in Ink." *PCI—Paints and Coatings Industry Feature Article* (www.pcimag.com) September (2000).

8. Andrasko, J. "HPLC Analysis of Ballpoint Pen Inks Stored at Different Light Conditions." *Journal of Forensic Sciences* 46 (2001), 21–30.

9. Laden, P., ed., *Chemistry and Technology of Water Based Inks*. London: Blackie Academic and Professional/Chapman and Hall, 1997.

10. Holshue, T., and H. Gaines. "Chapter 6: Solvents," in P. J. Laden, ed., *Chemistry and Technology of Water Based Inks*. London: Blackie Academic and Professional/Chapman and Hall, 1997.

11. Durgan, C., and E. Reich. "Chemistry and Technology of Water Based Inks," in P. J. Laden, *Chemistry and Technology of Water Based Inks*. London: Blackie Academic and Professional/Chapman and Hall, 1997.

12. Brunelle, R. L. "Ch. 13: Questioned Document Examination," in R. Saferstein, ed., *Forensic Science Handbook, Volume II*. Englewood Cliffs, NJ: Prentice Hall, 1982.

13. Ryland, S. G. "Infrared Microscopy of Paints." *Practical Spectroscopy* 19 (1995), 163–243.

14. Allcock, H. R., et al. "Ch. 1: The Scope of Polymer Chemistry," in H. R. Allcock et al., eds., *Contemporary Polymer Chemistry*, 3d ed. Upper Saddle River, NJ: Prentice Hall, 2003.

15. Thornton, J. "Ch. 8: Forensic Paint Examination," in R. Saferstein, ed., *Forensic Science Handbook, Volume II* 2d ed. Upper Saddle River, NJ: Prentice Hall, 2002.

Forensic Analysis of Inks and Paints

12.1 Analytical Methods
12.2 Aging and Dating

OVERVIEW AND ORIENTATION

In the last chapter, we studied the fundamental chemical principles of colorants. Now we can delve into the types of physical evidence that contain colorants. The two types of evidence we will focus on are inks and paints, which have much in common. Both contain dyes or pigments dissolved or suspended in a complex solvent system that, when delivered to a substrate, undergoes predictable chemical changes as the mixtures dry and cure. An understanding of those processes is essential to understanding analytical results and to classifying the inks and paints encountered.

12.1 ANALYTICAL METHODS

Inks and paints offer the forensic analyst many characteristics to work with. Aside from their invaluable physical characteristics, such as layer structure and markings, inks and paints are amenable to all three general analytical techniques (optical, organic, and inorganic) that are useful for the analysis of colorants. Older destructive tests are rapidly giving way to nondestructive microspectrophotometric techniques, but with sufficient sample, all can be useful. Libraries, databases, and other collections are vitally important for the analysis of colorants. The Royal Canadian Mounted Police maintains the **PDQ (Paint Data Query) database** of infrared spectra of automobile paints. A Munsell color chart for paints is useful, as are reference spectra of dyes and pigments obtained by using a variety of instrumental techniques. For microscopy, a reference set of pigments is indispensable.

There are two ASTM standards (along with referenced standards within) dealing with paint and ink analysis. E1422-01 deals with ink analysis, and E1610-02 outlines recommended procedures for paint analysis. Figure 12.1 combines the methodology for analyzing inks with that used to analyze paints for the purposes of the discussion that follows. Notations in the figure

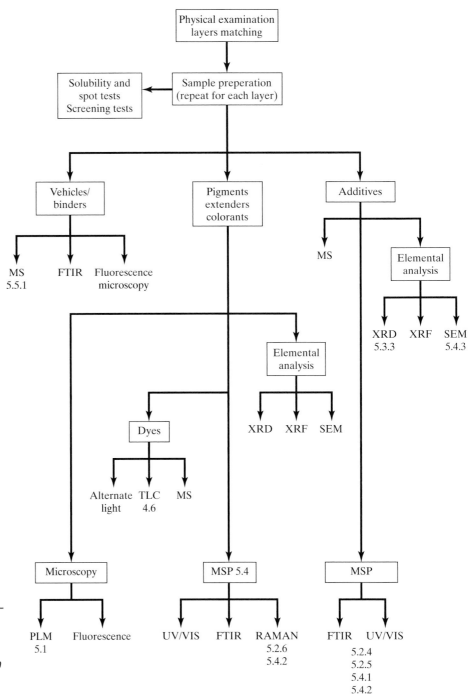

▶ **Figure 12.1** *A flowchart for the analysis of coatings and colorants. The small numbers refer to appropriate sections in previous chapters describing the techniques.*

refer to sections in Chapters 4 and 5 relevant to the analytical technique discussed. The figure is not meant to imply that paint and ink examinations are identical, but rather that they share many characteristics. Analysis of paints and inks begins with visual examination and comparison. It may be possible to perform a physical match of paint chips or to classify an automotive finish on the basis of its layer structure and a comparison with commercial databases and information. Further analysis, if needed, is where the flowchart of Figure 12.1 begins.

◀ **Figure 12.2** *Two examples of obliterated writing made visible using near and mid-IR illumination and imaging. Images courtesy of Foster & Freeman USA.*

12.1.1 OPTICAL MICROSCOPY

When a colorant is a pigment and thus particulate, optical microscopy and PLM are a critical part of any analytical scheme.[1,2] Microscopy can include microchemistry and solubility tests, as well as direct observations of layers and pigment particles. In the case of inks, microscopic examination will reveal the presence of metallic particulates and other solids that are part of the formulation (Figure 11.18). Skilled microscopists may be able to identify pigments on the basis of their optical properties and crystalline form. Microscopy of documents is useful for differentiating printing methods. As seen in Figure 11.27, toner particles from a laser printer are visible under low magnification and differentiate toner-based printing from ink-jet-type printing. Fluorescence microscopy, although somewhat specialized, is also useful for screening and analyzing paints and inks. In such applications, an excitation wavelength in the UV range is used to stimulate emission in the visible range and to create a fluorescence spectrum.

12.1.2 ALTERNATIVE LIGHTING

UV and IR lighting is a common nondestructive tool used in the analysis of questioned documents. The principle behind most of these techniques is fluorescence. Many inks fluoresce in the visible region or infrared region of the spectrum when they are exposed to ultraviolet or visible light, respectively. In addition, many printing inks, such as those used in currency, have fluorescent security features that are not easily duplicated by counterfeiters. Collectively, these techniques are called "luminescent techniques," and they avail themselves of both absorbance and fluorescence characteristics. To observe infrared fluorescence, the analyst illuminates the document with visible radiation, and the induced fluorescence is detected by means of filters and IR-sensitive film or video equipment. The effect is to convert IR emission to a visual equivalent. The excitation of visible fluorescence by UV light is analogous, except that the visible emissions can be observed without conversion. Currency notes often incorporate single fibers with exact fluorescent properties as an added security measure. UV and, particularly, IR characteristics are useful in differentiating inks with similar colors, as well as in examining charred documents and obliterations by using another ink or correction fluids.

Exhibit A: Examination of Questioned Documents in the Terrorist Age

In October 2001, a person or persons sent anthrax through the mail, resulting in seven deaths, thousands of exposures, and major disruptions. The anthrax powder was contained in an envelope along with a handwritten letter. The envelope and letter were invaluable physical evidence, but analysis had to wait months while methods were developed to open and sterilize the evidence before traditional forensic examinations such as ink analysis could even begin.

12.1.3 SOLUBILITY TESTS AND THIN-LAYER CHROMATOGRAPHY

Solubility tests were once a mainstay of forensic ink and paint analysis, but are now used less frequently as instrumental and microspectrophotometric techniques have improved. TLC remains widely used in ink analysis and, by definition, incorporates solubility testing. If the ink won't dissolve in the mobile phase, it won't leave the origin or participate in selective partitioning. For paints, solubility testing incorporates organic solvents and acids, whereas ink solubility testing relies principally on organic solvents. With paints, solubility testing is of limited use unless layers are isolated from one another; however, inks are easily tested in this manner, as long as sufficient sample is available. Table 12.1 summarizes the solvents employed in solubility testing. One interesting addition to solvent and spot testing is the use of the diphenylamine reagent discussed previously for gunshot residue. Older nitrocellulose lacquers produce a positive result with this reagent.

Applying the Science 12.1 Dyes in Drugs

The dyes used in the preparation of illicit pills can be incorporated into drug analysis. In a recent study, researchers used capillary electrophoresis to evaluate 14 dyes as part of a drug-profiling application that included Bayesian statistical analysis. The study, conducted in Europe, focused on dyes developed for use in foodstuffs. Many of these dyes, which are acidic and water soluble, are available in the United States and Canada. In the study, LOQs were in the range of ~0.008–0.06 ppm and LOD was reported at ~0.008 ppm. Calibration curves (an internal standard method) had about two orders of magnitude of linearity. Detection was achieved with UV at 255 nm, although different wavelengths were used in some cases to optimize the response for a particular dye.

The analysis consisted of three stages, beginning with SPE of the dyes from pills, using a polyamide solid phase. Thin-layer chromatography was utilized to screen the dyes via two solvent systems and solid supports (silica gel and cellulose), followed by confirmation by CE coupled to a diode array detector. The authors reported that the 14 dyes could be unambiguously identified with these parameters.

Source: Goldmann, T., et al., "Analysis of Dyes in Illicit Pills (Amphetamine and Derivatives)," *Journal of Forensic Sciences,* 49 **2004.**

If a colorant can be solubilized, it can be evaluated by means of TLC. This technique is commonly employed for ink analysis but not for paints. A 1982 report described the use of TLC in isolating pigments in house paint, followed by IR identification of separated spots,[3] but this is one of few such reports and TLC is infrequently used this way. However, for inks, TLC is an accepted and widely used discriminatory tool that is applicable to a variety of pens and toners.[4,5,6] The ASTM guide for ink analysis (E 1422) recommends pyridine as a solvent for glycol-based ballpoint inks and an ethanol–water (1:1) combination for nonballpoint inks. The stationary phase is typically silica gel and the solvent systems are based on ethanol and water. There are still many inks in which the colorants can be separated with nothing more than water and filter paper. Dyes in textiles can be similarly examined,[6] a topic discussed in Chapter 14.

12.1.4 SPECTROSCOPY AND MICROSPECTROPHOTOMETRY

Spectroscopy and, particularly, microspectrophotometry are the most versatile tools for the analysis of colorants, inks, and paints. Visible spectroscopy and colorimetry are used to define color, assign color space coordinates (usually with CIELAB), and differentiate among colorants with similar appearance, but different visible spectra. IR spectroscopy is useful in characterizing colorants, binders, and coatings, whereas Raman spectroscopy is used for inks and paints. Microspectrophotometry has significantly reduced the need for large sample sizes, lessened destruction of samples, and made it much easier to examine layers without physically separating them. Extensive and growing forensic databases are continually increasing the utility of FTIR in colorant analysis.

Microspectrophotometry in the visible range is used to compare pigments and dyes, to evaluate pigment mixtures, and to compare samples with similar color. Visible spectra are information poor relative to IR spectra and are not amenable to library searches. However, differences in spectra are useful in classifying and discriminating similarly perceived color and in identifying mixtures of colorants.[7] Homogeneity and preparation of the sample are paramount to interpretation. Aging and weathering, addressed in Section 11.7, are also important considerations in comparing visible spectra of paint samples. As an example, a recent review reported that, within the same sample layer, distances between replicate spectra plotted in CIELAB space ranged from 1.3 units for a 10-year-old green paint to 7.2 years in a 10-year-old yellow paint.[7] Differences between cars using the same finishing colors were in this same range.

Table 12.1 Solubility Testing of Solvents	
Paints	**Inks**
Acetic acid	Acetone
Acetic acid anhydride	Acetonitrile
Acetone	Aniline
Benzene	Bleach
Chloroform	Butanol
Dichloroethane	Chlorobenzene
Ethanol	Chloroform
Ethyl acetate	Cyclohexane
Hexane(s)	Dimethylformamide
Methanol	DMSO
Methyl ethyl ketone (MEK)	Ethanol (pure and 50%)
Methylene chloride	Ethyl acetate
Nitric acid	Ethyl ether
Pyridine	Hexane
Sodium hydroxide	MEK
Sulfuric acid	Methanol
Toluene	Methylene chloride
Xylene(s)	NaCl(sat'd)
	Na_2SO_3
	Sodium hydroxide 5%
	Petroleum ether
	Phenoxyethanol
	Propanol
	Propylene glycol
	Pyridine
	Tetrahydrofuran
	Water

Source: Wilson, J. D., et al., "Differentiation of Black Gel Inks Using Optical and Chemical Techniques," *Journal of Forensic Sciences* 49 (2004).

FTIR is particularly valuable in classifying the binders used in paints as shown in Figure 12.3.[1,8] Flowcharts are useful in interpreting absorbance band patterns and relating them to types of resin. Binders and pigments are also amenable to flowchart analysis. Since paints are mixtures, the entire absorption spectrum is of interest, not just the fingerprint region. The analysis of pigments in paint by FTIR and MSP have been studied in detail, and a large amount of information is available in the literature. Early studies used diffuse reflectance infrared Fourier transform spectroscopy (DRIFTS) techniques,[9] but they were supplanted by MSP in the 1990s. Starting in 1996,[10–16] Suzuki and Marshall published a comprehensive series of articles addressing pigments and binders in automobile paints. The work was supplemented with elemental analysis using XRF. A recent interlaboratory report demonstrated that, by 2001, practices and procedures using FTIR and micro-FTIR were reproducible and intercomparable among the testing laboratories.[17] The samples analyzed were a black base-coat and clearcoat layer system selected because the pigment was carbon black, an IR-inactive compound. This experimental design highlighted the use of IR applied to binders, without the complication of pigments adding to the signal. The binders were acrylics with other components present. As illustrated in Figure 12.4, three of the samples showed consistent and indistinguishable IR spectra; however,

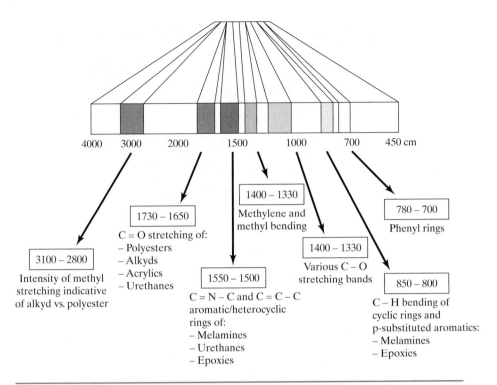

▲ Figure 12.3 *IR absorbance bands that correlate to functional groups common in resins, binders, and vehicles.*

pyrolysis GC successfully differentiated them (Figure 12.5). This example illustrates the value (often, the necessity) of multiple analytical techniques in paint and ink analysis.

Raman spectroscopy and microspectroscopy are also used to characterize colorants and paints. With paints, one significant advantage of Raman spectroscopy is that binders and resins show minimal interference, allowing for characterization of the pigment.[12] Many spectral features are sharper in Raman spectra than in IR spectroscopy,[12] and the combination of the two kinds of spectroscopy provides significantly more information than does either one alone. In general, IR spectra of inorganic pigments such as TiO_2 have broad peaks, whereas the corresponding Raman spectra have narrow peaks.[12] Figure 12.6 illustrates the value of the combined technique for characterizing a white finish using TiO_2, which, as noted previously, has two useful crystal forms. The Raman spectra differentiate these two forms, whereas the IR spectra do not, owing to their broad absorbance peaks.

Ink analysis and related analyses of questioned documents have come to rely heavily on IR spectroscopy. As with paints, applications evolved from traditional IR through DRIFTS techniques and now employ principally MSP.[19–22] Inks are analyzed in situ or on sampling substrates such as KBr plates. Like paints, inks produce IR spectra representative of mixtures; unlike paints, inks rarely have a layered structure. Regardless, spectra of inks do contain information that is useful for classification. For example, a study of 108 inks demonstrated that distinctive absorption bands could be rationalized on the basis of ink composition and then employed to divide the test population into two groups.[22] As shown in Figure 12.7, one group contained C=C stretching characteristic of an epoxy resin and features associated with triarylmethane dyes, as shown in

a.

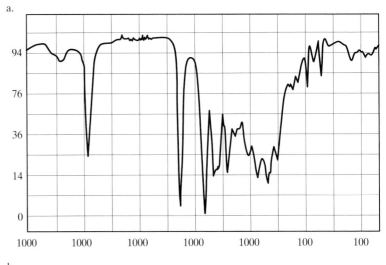

b.

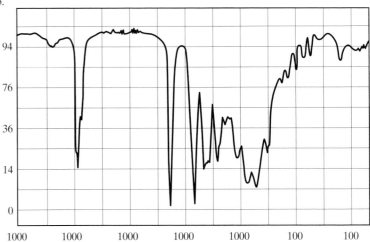

c.

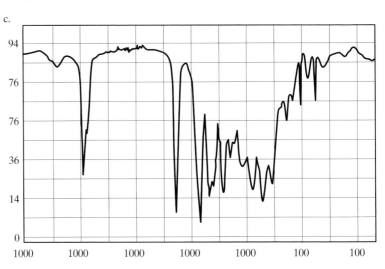

▶ **Figure 12.4** *IR absorbance spectra of three similar clearcoat resins. These spectra are indistinguishable but addition of a second analytical technique as shown in the next figure, can facilitate discrimination. Reproduced with permission from Ryland, S. G., et al., "Discrimination of the 1990s Original Automobile Paint Systems: A Collaborative Study of Black Nonmetallic Base Coat/Clear Coat Finishes Using Infrared Spectroscopy." Journal of Forensic Sciences 46 (2001), 31–45. Copyright 2001 ASTM International.*

Table 11.5. A second group of inks had spectral features consistent with an alkyd resin. Note that this is the same general approach described for paint, and similar considerations apply to the IR analysis of toners used in laser printers and copiers.[19,23–29]

a.

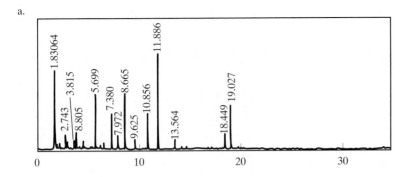

b.

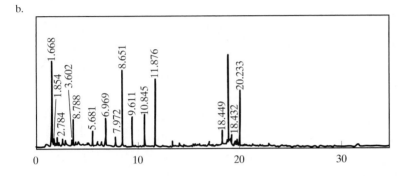

c.

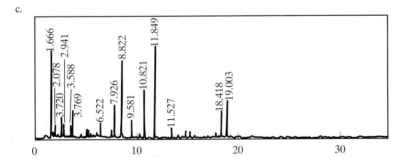

◀ **Figure 12.5** *Pyrolysis GC analysis of the three resins shown in Figure 12.4. Reproduced with permission from Ryland, S. G., et al., "Discrimination of the 1990s Original Automobile Paint Systems: A Collaborative Study of of Black Nonmetallic Base Coat/Clear Coat Finishes Using Infrared Spectroscopy."* Journal of Forensic Sciences *46 (2001), 31–45. Copyright 2001 ASTM International. Copyright 2001 ASTM International.*

One of the interesting aspects of toner particulates is the difficulty in sample preparation, since toner is a waxy solid before it is bonded to a paper substrate. Heat affixing to a metallic substrate such as foil has been used, along with KBr salt plates. Using heat to affix toner to paper was found not to be an issue, except in isolated cases.[25,27] As with inks, toners could be grouped on the basis of the polymer resins they contain,[29] such as acrylates, methacrylates, polystyrene, and epoxides and corresponding spectral features.

12.1.5 Mass Spectrometry, GCMS, and HPLC

Mass spectrometry can be applied to inks and paints as instrumentation allows. Routine GCMS, as described for drug analysis and toxicology, is limited to volatile and chromatographically suitable components of inks and paints such as solvents. In addition, volatile components dissipate over time as they dry and cure. As the tables in the last chapter show, many dye and pigment molecules are large enough that typical solvent extraction GCMS is impractical or only of limited use.[27] With gel-pen ink, GCMS has been reported to be useful in identifying solvents and other volatiles in samples up to six months old.[30] Volatiles identified included glycerin (the largest single component), triethylene

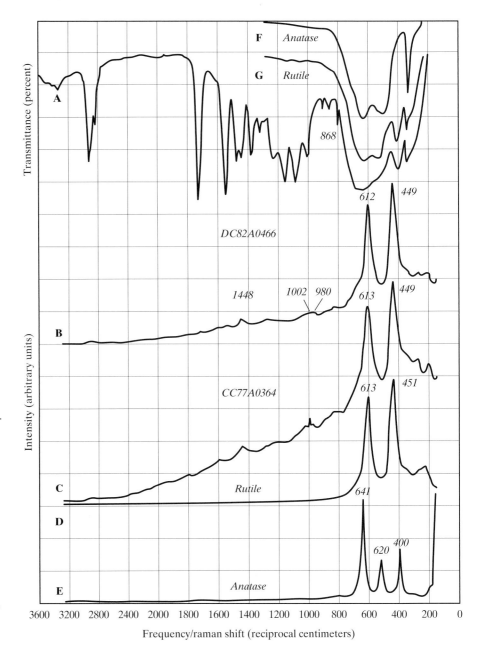

▶ **Figure 12.6** *IR and Raman spectra of a white coating. Note that the Raman spectra differentiate the Rutile and Anatase crystal forms whereas IR data cannot. Reproduced with permission from Suzuki, E. M., and M. Carrabba, "In Situ Identification and Analysis of Automotive Paint Pigments Using Line Segment Excitation Raman Spectroscopy: I: Inorganic Topcoat Pigments," Journal of Forensic Sciences 46 (2001), 1053–1069.*

glycol, pentaethylene glycol, and triethanolamine, compounds extracted from the substrate through the use of ethanol.

Mass spectrometry using alternative ionization and sample preparation methods are employed in ink and paint analysis. The oldest of these techniques is based on pyrolysis of the sample (typically, a paint) prior to its introduction into the GC. Detectors for PyGC are MS and FID. Pyrolysis patterns can be examined in the same way accelerant patterns are (Chapter 10), but increasingly, GCMS is preferred over FID. Pyrolysis is, by definition, destructive, but the sample size is reasonably small, and recently a micropyrolysis GCMS has been developed and applied to photocopier toners and paint.[31] A laser is focused on the sample through a microscope, and the pyrolysis vapor product is directed into the GCMS system. The pattern of the pyrolyzates and chemical composition

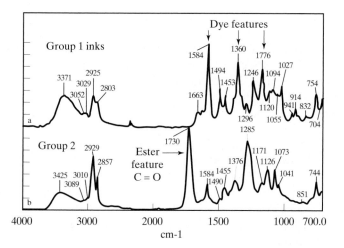

◀ **Figure 12.7** *IR spectra illustrating features used to divide sample inks into two populations. Reproduced with permission from Wang, F., et al.,* "*Systematic Analysis of Bulk Blue Ballpoint Pen Ink by FTIR Spectrometry,*" *Journal of Forensic Sciences 46 (2001), 1093–1097. Copyright 2001 ASTM International.*

allowed for clear delineation among paint and toner samples. One significant advantage of the system was its ability to directly sample toner applied on paper with only one pyrolysis product—chlorobenzene—attributed to the paper matrix. The mass range scanned went up to 550 amu. Because pyrolysis does not directly reveal chemical components of the mixtures, potential disadvantages and limitations include sampling homogeneity, standardization, and reproducibility of heating profiles and the resulting patterns.

Laser ionization without pyrolysis has been applied to paints and inks.[32–34] Briefly, in desorption–ionization methods, a laser is used to volatilize and ionize a sample prior to its direct introduction into an MS. The latter is a usually a magnetic-sector or time-of-flight type providing enhanced mass resolution over typical benchtop quadrupole designs. Several ionization variants are included in this category, including matrix-assisted laser desorption and ionization, or MALDI. As shown in Figure 12.8, for MALDI, the sample is embedded in a matrix consisting of inorganic crystals. These compounds absorb the laser energy and ionize, and transfer charge to the sample, yielding positive and negative ions. Fast atom bombardment (FAB) achieves desorption and ionization. The advantage of laser desorption and ionization is that inks and paints can be analyzed as discrete samples or in situ. The disadvantage is that all desorbed and ionized species are introduced into the mass spectrometer simultaneously, rather than sequentially with a chromatographic inlet. Some discrimination is inherent in the method, since pigments and dyes are composed of larger molecules than solvents, but the mass spectrum remains a composite of multiple components. Another variant is

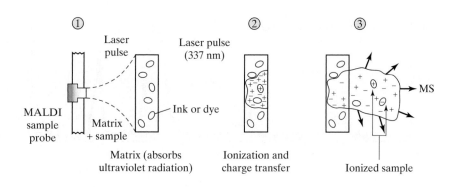

◀ **Figure 12.8** *Formation of ions in matrix-assisted laser desorption and ionization (MALDI).*

more selective: Laser desorption, or LD, uses a tuned laser operating in this instance at 337 nm.[34] Only compounds that absorb this wavelength are ionized.

A study by Balko and Allison addressed the characterization of security dyes—compounds used to stain currency and persons who take it in events such as bank robberies.[32] Figure 12.9 illustrates the identification of two cationic red dyes on currency and cotton fabric and shows no interference from dyes and pigments found in the currency. The cationic structure was deduced from the observation that no negative ions were produced when the dyes ionized. In Figure 12.10, the mass spectrum of a green pigment in currency (Pigment Green 7) is shown and illustrates the high mass range of this technique, as well as the ability to obtain natural-isotope ratios. The compound in question could not be analyzed with traditional solvent extraction GCMS, given its size, poor chromatographic performance, and low volatility.

Because many dyes and pigments are not amenable to GC, HPLC methods have been explored as an alternative.[35,36] This makes sense in light of the relationship of HPLC to TLC, still a staple of colorant analysis. However, the lack of specificity in a detector system has been a limitation, and consequently, HPLC has been used in the same way as pyrolysis GC and peak or pattern matching.

12.1.6 ELEMENTAL ANALYSIS

Pigments are well suited to examination by elemental analysis techniques such as XRF (for elemental identification), XRD (for identifying structure), and SEM.[37–39] XRF provides elemental analysis in conjunction with SEM imaging and can identify the metallic constituents of pigments such as those listed in Table 11.3. XRD can reveal information about crystal structure and is useful for detecting very small amounts of inorganic colorants. XRD is capable of differentiating crystal forms of pigments, such as the two common forms of titanium dioxide (rutile and anatase).[1] SEM and XRF offer the ability to focus easily on individual layers and particles and obtain elemental ratios. Other elemental analysis procedures, such as ICP-MS and AES, have not been widely used for colorant analysis to date.

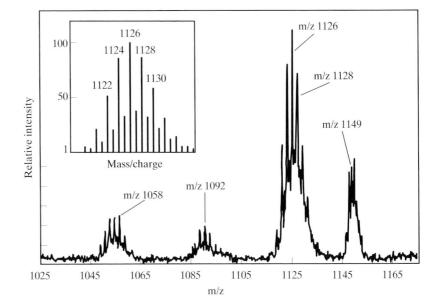

▶ **Figure 12.9** *LDMS spectrum. Reproduced with permission from Balko, L., and J. Allison, "The Direct Detection and Identification of Staining Dyes from Security Inks in the Presence of Other Colorants, on Currency and Fabrics, by Laser Desorption Mass Spectrometry,"* Journal of Forensic Sciences *48 (2003). Copyright 2003 ASTM International.*

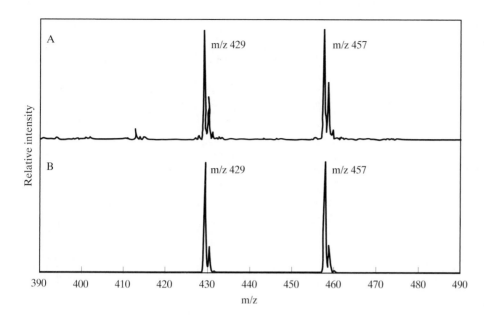

12.2 AGING AND DATING

Ink in a pen and paint in a can are chemically distinct from ink applied to paper and paint applied to a car. In forensic casework, the latter is typically of more interest. Paper and inks age in chemically predictable ways, although the time frame of the decay is dependent on many factors. The age of ink or paint in terms of when it was applied to the substrate can provide invaluable investigatory information, as well as inclusive or exclusive evidentiary information.

The aging process is illustrated in Figure 12.11 and is similar for paints and inks. When the solution or emulsion is applied to the substrate, solvent evaporation commences, in concert with film formation, which occurs by oxidation, polymerization, or cross-linkage. Materials diffuse across and into the substrate during film formation. Once formed, the protective film is subject to degradation by exposure to UV light, moisture, temperature extremes, and other environmental factors. Colorants may fade, and primer layers can crack and peel away from a surface.

The time frame over which aging is thought to have occurred is an important consideration in the analysis. Synthetic colorants were not well developed or widespread until after 1900, so paints and inks produced before that time cannot contain synthetic colorants or vehicles. Similarly, ancient colorants were relatively crude, often containing particulates that were not as uniformly ground as their modern counterparts. Certain crystal forms were not available as well, making optical microscopy one of the most valuable tools for detecting counterfeit art and historical forgeries.

A second and straightforward tool of dating is the use of **taggants**, such as those which were used in inks. A taggant is a material, typically fluorescent, that is added to ink formulations by manufacturers. For a short period (approximately 1970–1994), taggants were added to many inks in the United States, and as recently as 2002, new efforts were being made as part of a collaborative effort between companies and the U.S. Secret Service, which maintains a large reference collection of about 8000 inks, domestic and foreign.[40] The collection dates back to the 1920s.

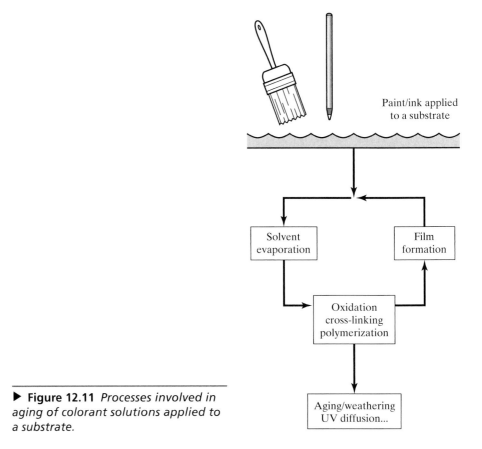

Paint/ink applied
to a substrate

Solvent
evaporation

Film
formation

Oxidation
cross-linking
polymerization

Aging/weathering
UV diffusion...

▶ **Figure 12.11** *Processes involved in aging of colorant solutions applied to a substrate.*

For time frames of days to years, chemical analysis has proven valuable in estimating relative ages with techniques such as HPLC, MS, UV/VIS, and IR spectroscopy targeting components and processes across the drying process. Solvent evaporation is generally the least useful analytical angle, whereas film formation and aging due to UV light the most useful for dating and aging studies. In the late 1980s, investigators proposed a solvent extraction technique for aging based on the idea that the older an ink is, the drier it is and thus the harder it is to extract.[41–43] In this scheme, samples are extracted from substrate and the relative concentration of extracted dyes is used to evaluate the relative age of the writing. Investigators have also identified 2-phenoxyethanol as a volatile compound that could be useful for dating inks, given that the evaporation rate should allow for detection over roughly two years and that a high percentage of commercial inks appear to contain that compound.[40] GCMS was used in this instance to isolate and identify the compound.

Investigations of UV aging and **photodegradation** are logical choices for estimating relative ages of colorants and coatings. To combat degradation, coatings and inks may contain compounds that absorb UV radiation or compounds that scavenge free radicals which form as a result of UV absorbance. These compounds protect the layers beneath, but are subject to degradation as a result. Thus, UV spectra are useful for weathering studies,[44] but have not been widely used in forensic chemistry to date.

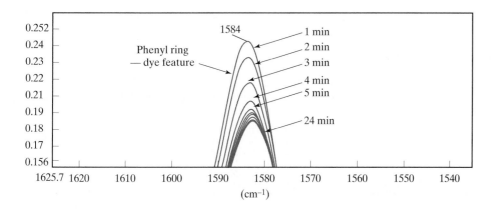

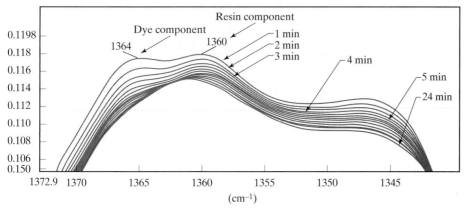

◀ **Figure 12.12** *Decrease in peak intensity as a function of heating time meant to mimic aging. Reproduced with permission from Wang, F., et al., "Systematic Analysis of Bulk Blue Ballpoint Pen Ink by FTIR Spectrometry,"* Journal of Forensic Sciences *46 (2001), 1093–1097. Copyright 2001 ASTM International.*

One of the challenges of dating inks is generating reliable standards. Because it is unusual to have an old (months to decades) ink sample that can be definitively linked to an unassailable source, artificial aging is required. By definition, this type of aging does not necessarily match gradual aging. Regardless, such studies are useful and the casework is relevant. One study illustrates interactions in aging between the colorant (in this case, a triarylmethane dye) and the binder medium.[21] Figure 12.12 illustrates heat-accelerated aging and shows spectral peaks associated with the phenyl structure of the dye decreasing over time. A peak associated with the epoxy resin decreased as well, but at a slower rate than the dye features. The authors concluded that the dye initially broke down quickly, but slowed as a protective film of cross-linked epoxy formed over it.

Degradation of components found in inks and similar products is characterized by the breakdown of larger molecules to small molecules, a phenomenon that is useful in chromatographic and mass spectral analyses. UV aging has been used to stimulate the aging and degradation of dyes in inks analyzed with laser desorption mass spectrometry (LCMS).[34] Degradation toward smaller compounds was clear and dramatic, as shown in Figure 12.13. Similar results are seen in an HPLC analysis in which the pigment crystal violet showed characteristic degradation products after a few months of natural aging. In this case (shown in Figure 12.14), the change in peak height was used to create a degradation curve for approximate dating.

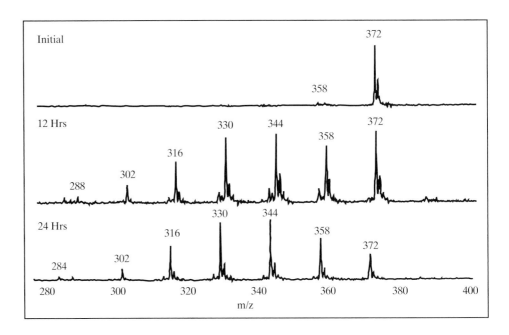

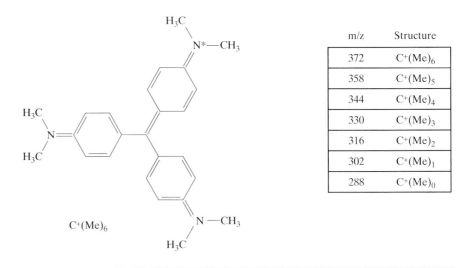

m/z	Structure
372	$C^+(Me)_6$
358	$C^+(Me)_5$
344	$C^+(Me)_4$
330	$C^+(Me)_3$
316	$C^+(Me)_2$
302	$C^+(Me)_1$
288	$C^+(Me)_0$

▲ **Figure 12.13** *LDMS spectra of dye exposed to UV radiation. Reproduced with permission from Grim, D. M., et al., "Evaluation of Desorption/Ionization Mass Spectrometric Methods in the Forensic Applications of the Analysis of Inks on Paper,"* Journal of Forensic Sciences 46 (2001), 1411–1420. Copyright 2001 ASTM International.

SUMMARY

These two chapters conclude our discussion of colorants and some of the primary types of physical evidence that incorporate them. We are not entirely done with colorants however; they will surface again in Chapter 14 in our discussion of fibers. Before that however, we will next explore the fundamental chemistry of another broad category of physical evidence, that based on polymers.

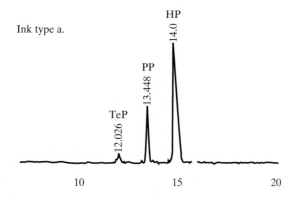

Ink type a.

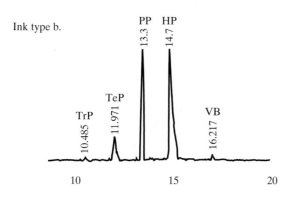

Ink type b.

◀ **Figure 12.14** *HPLC chromatogram of ballpoint pen ink types a) and b) from January to August and September to December, respectively. The ink types are distinguishable by the different concentration ratios of crystal violet (HP, at 14.8 min) and its degradation products (methyl violet: PP, at 13.4; TeP, at 12.0; and TrP, at 10.5 min) as well as by the ingredient Victoria blue (VB, at 16.9 min) that is only present in ink type b). Reproduced with permission from Hofer, R., "Dating of Ballpoint Pen Ink,"* Journal of Forensic Sciences *49 (2004), 1353–1357.*

KEY TERMS AND CONCEPTS

Alternative lighting	**PDQ database**	**Rutile**
Anatase	**Photodegradation**	**Taggant**
MALDI		

PROBLEMS

From the chapter

1. Why are pigments typically more difficult than dyes to analyze with chromatographic techniques such as TLC?

2. How does the complementary relationship between FTIR and Raman spectroscopy enhance the analysis of inks and paints?

3. List and discuss some of the caveats and limitations of artificial aging studies such as those discussed and shown in Figure 12.12.

Integrative

1. Which dye molecules shown in the previous chapter-would be amenable to typical GCMS methods and which would not? Why?

2. In fire debris analysis, weathering is manifest by an increase in chromatographic peaks with relatively higher molecular weights, whereas in ink evidence, weathering is manifest by a shift to lower molecular weights. Why?

Food for thought

1. Why are the solvents used in inks and paints usually of less forensic interest than the binders and colorants?

FURTHER READING

Bentley, J., and G. P. A. Turner. *Introduction to Paint Chemistry and Principles of Paint Technology*, 4th Ed. London: Chapman and Hall, 1998.

Ellen, D. *The Scientific Examination of Documents*. London: Taylor and Francis, Ltd., 1997.

Green, F. J. *The Sigma–Aldrich Handbook of Stains, Dyes, and Indicators*. Milwaukee: Sigma Aldrich Chemical Company, **1990**.

Laden, P., ed. *Chemistry and Technology of Water Based Inks*. London: Blackie Academic and Professional/Chapman and Hall, 1997.

Lubs, H. A., ed. *The Chemistry of Dyes and Pigments*. New York: Reinhold Publishing Corporation, **1955**.

Nassau, K. *The Physics and Chemistry of Color: The Fifteen Causes of Color*, 2d ed. New York: John Wiley and Sons, 2001.

Nickell, J. *Detecting Forgery: Forensic Investigation of Documents*. Lexington, KY: University of Kentucky Press, 1996.

Ryland, S. G. "Infrared Microscopy of Paints." *Practical Spectroscopy* 19 (1995), 163–243. This chapter has an excellent introductory portion that covers (pun intended) paint thoroughly, but concisely, and includes several useful tables.

REFERENCES

1. Thornton, J. "Ch. 8: Forensic Paint Examination," in R. Saferstein, ed., *Forensic Science Handbook, Volume II* 2d ed. Upper Saddle River, NJ: Prentice Hall, 2002.

2. Petraco, N., and T. Kubic. "Ch. 10: Paint Examination," in N. Petraco and T. Kubic, *Color Atlas of Microscopy for Criminalists, Chemists, and Conservators*. Boca Raton, FL: CRC Press, 2004.

3. Home, J. M., et al. "The Discrimination of Modern Household Paints Using Thin Layer Chromatography." *Journal of the Forensic Science Society* 22 (1982), 147–154.

4. Tandon, G., Jasuja, O. P., and V. N. Sehgal. "Thin Layer Chromatography Analysis of Photocopy Toners." *Forensic Science International* 73 (1995), 149–156.

5. "Standard Guide for Test Methods for Forensic Writing Ink Comparison," in *ASTM Standard E 1422-01* ASTM International, 2004.

6. "Standard Guide for Forensic Examination of Non-Reactive Dyes in Textile Fibers by Thin-Layer Chromatography," in *ASTM Standard E 2227-02* ASTM International, 2004.

7. Cousins, D. R. "The Use of Microspectrophotometry in the Examination of Paints." *Forensic Science Reviews* 1 (1989), 1–141.

8. Ryland, S. G. "Infrared Microscopy of Paints." *Practical Spectroscopy* 19 (1995), 163–243.

9. Suzuki, E. M., and G. WR. "Forensic Science Applications of Diffuse Reflectance Infrared Spectroscopy (DRIFTS) I." *Journal of Forensic Sciences* 31 (1986), 931–952.

10. Suzuki, E. M. "Infrared Spectra of US Automobile Original Topcoats (1974–1989): I. Differentiation and Identification Based on Acrylonitrile and Ferrocyanide CN Stretching Absorptions." *Journal of Forensic Sciences* 41 (1996), 376–392.

11. Suzuki, E. M. "Infrared Spectra of US Automobile Original Topcoats (1974–1989): II. Identification of Some Topcoat Inorganic Pigments Using an Extended Range Fourier Transform Spectrometer." *Journal of Forensic Sciences* 41 (1996), 393–406.

12. Suzuki, E. M., and M. Carrabba. "In-Situ Identification and Analysis of Automotive Paint Pigments Using Line Segment Excitation Raman Spectroscopy: I. Inorganic Topcoat Pigments." *Journal of Forensic Sciences* 46 (2001), 1053–1069.

13. Suzuki, E. M., and W. P. Marshall. "Infrared Spectra of U.S. Automobile Original Topcoats (1974–1989): III. In Situ Identification of Some Organic Pigments Used in Yellow, Orange, Red, and Brown Nonmetallic and Brown Metallic Finishes—Benzimidazolones." *Journal of Forensic Sciences* 42 (1997), 619–648.

14. Suzuki, E. M., and W. P. Marshall. "Infrared Spectra of U.S. Automobile Original Topcoats (1974–1989): V. Identification of Organic Pigments Used in Red Nonmetallic and Brown Nonmetallic and Metallic Monocoats—DPP Red BO and Thioindigo Bordeaux." *Journal of Forensic Sciences* 42 (1997), 619–648.

15. Suzuki, E. M., and W. P. Marshall. "Infrared Spectra of U.S. Automobile Original Topcoats (1974–1989): VI. Identification and Analysis of Yellow Organic Automotive Paint Pigments—Isoindolinonoe Yellow 3R, Isoindoline Yellow, Anthrapyrimidine Yellow, and Miscellaneous Yellows." *Journal of Forensic Sciences* 44 (1997), 1151–1175.

16. Suzuki, E. M., and W. P. Marshall. "Infrared Spectra of U.S. Automobile Original Topcoats (1974–1989): V. In Situ Identification of Some Organic Pigments Used in Yellow, Orange, Red, and Brown Nonmetallic and Brown Metallic Finishes—Benzimidazolones." *Journal of Forensic Sciences* 43 (1998), 514–542.

17. Ryland, S. G., et al. "Discrimination of the 1990s Original Automobile Paint Systems: A Collaborative Study of Black Nonmetallic Base Coat/Clear Coat Finishes Using Infrared Spectroscopy." *Journal of Forensic Sciences* 46 (2001), 31–45.

18. Massonnet, G., and W. Stoecklein. *Identification of Organic Pigments in Coatings: Applications to Red Automotive Topcoats. Part III: Raman Spectroscopy (NIR FT-Raman).* Lausanne, Switzerland: European Academy of Forensic Sciences, 1997.

19. Merrill, R. A., and E. G. Bartick. "Analysis of Ballpoint Pen Inks by Diffuse Reflectance Infrared Spectroscopy." *Journal of Forensic Sciences* 37 (1992), 528–541.

20. Trzcinska, B. M. "Writing Materials Examination in Criminalistics Research by FTIR Spectroscopy." *Journal of Molecular Structure* 294 (1993), 259–262.

21. Wang, F., et al. "Systematic Analysis of Bulk Blue Ballpoint Pen Ink by FTIR Spectrometry." *Journal of Forensic Sciences* 46 (2001), 1093–1097.

22. Andrasko, J. "A Simple Method for Sampling Photocopy Toners for Examination by Microreflectance FTIR." *Journal of Forensic Sciences* 39 (1994), 226–230.

23. Bartick, E. G., et al. "Forensic Discrimination of Photocopy Toners by FTIR Reflectance Spectroscopy," in J. A. de Haseth *Fourier Transform Spectroscopy: 11th International Conference.* Athens, GA: University of Georgia, 1998.

24. Mazzella, W. D., et al. "Classification and Identification of Photocopying Toners by DRIFTS: I: Preliminary Results." *Journal of Forensic Sciences* 36 (1991), 449–465.

25. Mazzella, W. D., et al. "Classification and Identification of Photocopying Toners by DRIFTS: I: Final Report." *Journal of Forensic Sciences* 36 (1991), 820–837.

26. Mizrachi, M., et al. "Classification and Identification of Color Photocopiers by FTIR and GC/MS." *Journal of Forensic Sciences* 43 (1998), 353–361.

27. Sarin, R. K., et al. "Forensic Examination of Forged Colour Xerox Documents by Micro-RAS FTIR Spectroscopy." *International Journal of Forensic Document Examination* 5 (1999), 265–269.

28. Tandon, G., et al. "The Characterization of Photocopy Toners Using FTIR." *International Journal of Forensic Document Examination* 3 (1997), 119–126.

29. Wilson, J. D., et al. "Differentiation of Black Gel Inks Using Optical and Chemical Techniques." *Journal of Forensic Sciences* 49 (2004).

30. Armitage, S., et al. "The Analysis of Forensic Samples Using Laser Micro-Pyrolysis Gas Chromatography Mass Spectrometry." *Journal of Forensic Sciences* 46 (2001), 1043–1052.

31. Balko, L., and J. Allison. "The Direct Detection and Identification of Staining Dyes from Security Inks in the Presence of Other Colorants, on Currency and Fabrics, by Laser Desorption Mass Spectrometry." *Journal of Forensic Sciences* 48 (2003), 1172–1178.

32. Dunn, J. D., et al. "Photodegradation and Laser Desorption Mass Spectrometry for the Characterization of Dyes Used in Red Pen Inks." *Journal of Forensic Sciences* 48 (2003), 652–657.

33. Grim, D. M., et al. "Evaluation of Desorption/Ionization Mass Spectrometric Methods in the Forensic Applications of the Analysis of Inks on Paper." *Journal of Forensic Sciences* 46 (2001), 1411–1420.

34. Kher, A. A., et al. "Evaluation of Principal Component Analysis with HPLC and Photodiode Array Detection for the Forensic Differentiation of Ballpoint Pen Inks." *Journal of Forensic Sciences* 46 (2001), 878–883.

35. Andrasko, J. "HPLC Analysis of Ballpoint Pen Inks Stored at Different Light Conditions." *Journal of Forensic Sciences* 46 (2001), 21–30.

36. Curry, C. J., et al. "Pigment Analysis in the Forensic Examination of Paints: I. Pigment Analysis by X-Ray Powder Diffraction." *Journal of the Forensic Science Society* 22 (1982), 173–177.

37. Govaert, F., and M. Bernard. "Discriminating Red Spray Paints by Optical Microscopy, Fourier Transform Infrared Spectroscopy, and X-ray Fluorescence." *Forensic Science International* 140 (2004), 61–70.

38. Vogt, C., et al. "Investigation of Ball Point Pen Inks by Capillary Electrophoresis (CE) with UV/Vis Absorbance and Laser Induced Fluorescence Detection and Particle Induced X-Ray Emission (PIXE)." *Journal of Forensic Sciences* 44 (1999), 819–831.

39. LaPorte, G. M., et al. "The Identification of 2-Phenoxyethanol in Ballpoint Inks Using Gas Chromatography/Mass Spectrometry—Relevance to Ink Dating." *Journal of Forensic Sciences* 49 (2004), 155–159.

40. Brunelle, R. L., et al. "Determining the Relative Age of Ballpoint Inks Using a Single-Solvent Extraction Technique." *Journal of Forensic Sciences* 32 (1987), 1511–1521.

41. Brunelle, R. L., and H. Lee. "Determining the Relative Age of Ballpoint Ink Using a Single-Solvent Extraction, Mass-Independent Approach." *Journal of Forensic Sciences* 34 (1989), 1166–1182.

42. Cantu, A. A., and R. S. Prough. "On the Relative Aging of Ink—the Solvent Extraction Technique." *Journal of Forensic Sciences* 32 (1987), 1151–1174.

43. Stoecklein, W., and H. Fujiwara. *The Examination of UV-Absorbers in 2-Coat Metallic and Non-metallic Automotive Paints.* Paper presented at first meeting of the European Academy of Forensic Sciences, Lausanne, Switzerland, September 1997.

44. Hofer, R. "Dating of Ballpoint Pen Ink." *Journal of Forensic Sciences* 49 (2004), 1353–1357.

CHAPTER

13

The Chemistry of Polymers

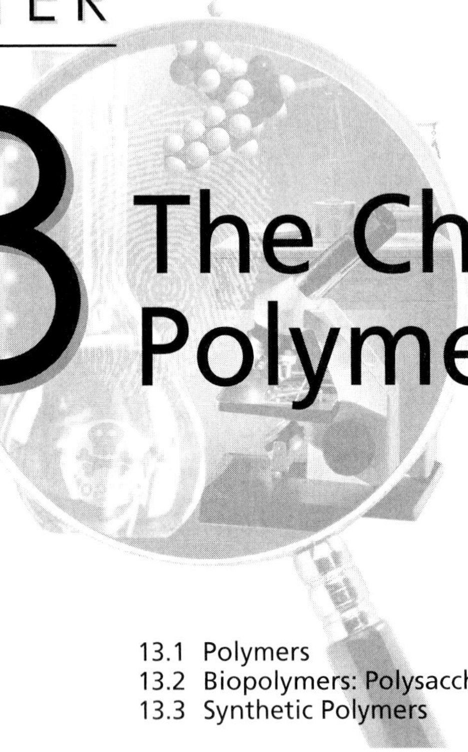

13.1 Polymers
13.2 Biopolymers: Polysaccharides
13.3 Synthetic Polymers

OVERVIEW AND ORIENTATION

These last two chapters have it all: Chemistry, analysis, and statistics. They are great chapters to finish with, because polymer evidence integrates nearly every niche of forensic chemistry. Polymers are a prominent form of physical evidence, as was already mentioned in the previous chapter's discussion concerning binders in paints. Polymers are evidence in their own right, as in adhesive tapes, or as the substrate for colorants—for example, in paper and fibers. Thus, we can think of the previous chapter as describing the coatings and toppings placed on substrates described in the pages to follow. The common theme is polymers, biological and synthetic.

13.1 POLYMERS

Polymers can be classified in different ways. From the forensic perspective, a reasonable starting point is to divide polymers into biologically derived polymers (**biopolymers**) and synthetic organic polymers. Biopolymers are extracted from natural sources such as plants or animals. Even though proteins and DNA are biopolymers of unquestioned importance in forensic science, their analysis resides in the context of forensic biology. The biopolymer we will concentrate on is **cellulose**, the base material in paper and cotton fibers. Historically and chemically, semisynthetic polymers fall between naturally derived and synthetic polymers. **Rayon** and **cellophane** are made from regenerated

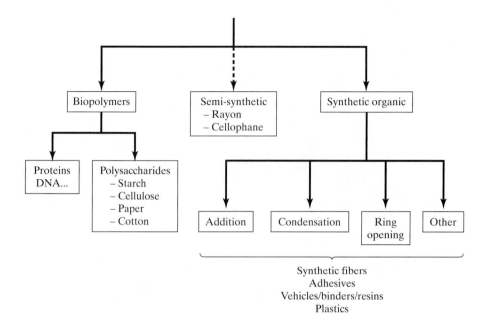

cellulose and were among the first synthetics made, introduced in the late 1800s. Nitrocellulose, or guncotton, one of these regenerated materials, was discussed in Chapter 10. Semisynthetics bridge the gap between the naturally derived materials and synthetic polymers that emerged in the 1930s.

Polymers are composed of linked **monomer** units. The monomers may be all the same or different (making **copolymers**) and with many different types of linkages, as shown in Figure 13.2. The monomers may be small and simple, as in PVC, or complex, as in nylon. Polymeric solids have characteristics that lie between the extremes of an ordered crystal (a crystalline substance) or an **amorphous** solid possessing little or no organized structure (*a-morphus*, "without morphology"). Glass is an example of an amorphous solid that lacks internal organization. Polymers with repeating units and some degree of order are "**pseudocrystalline**," a characteristic that is crucial to understanding the behavior of fibers and other similar materials studied by means of polarized light microscopy (Section 5.1). Copolymers come in a variety of configurations, including random, block, and grafted types, as shown in Figure 13.3. Finally, polymer strands can be connected and interconnected in various ways, as illustrated in Figure 13.4. Descriptors can be combined, as in the case of a cross-linked random copolymer. The chemical characteristics of the monomers, together with their crystalline nature, linkages, and organization, give a polymer its chemical and physical properties.

For materials of forensic interest, such as coatings, paints, and fibers, the degree of crystallinity is important in determining the thermal response of the polymer (Figure 13.5). A polymer with a more amorphous character is a solid similar to glass at lower temperatures. A transition to a more rubbery solid occurs at the **glass transition temperature** (T_g). This temperature is not the melting point of the polymer, but rather marks a temperature at which the tension in

Historical Evidence 13.1—The Rubber Meets the Road

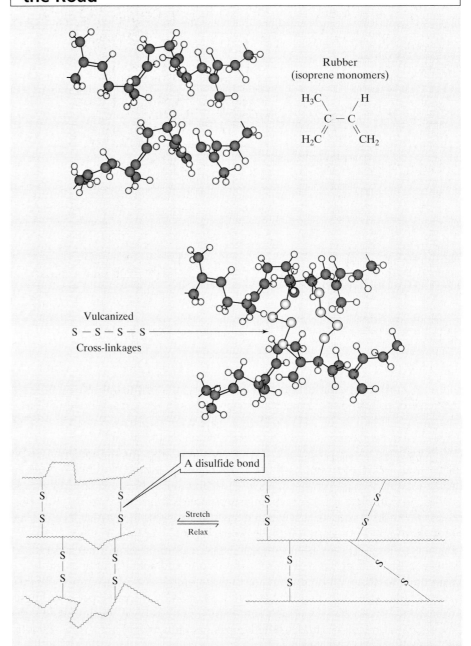

Rubber
(isoprene monomers)

Vulcanized
S — S — S — S
Cross-linkages

A disulfide bond

Stretch

Relax

The first useful polymerization reactions were conducted in the late 1840s. One important raw material in early work was rubber, which comes from the exudates of a tree. The vulcanization of rubber (a reaction with sulfur that produced a sulfurous volcano-like smell) was one of the first reactions studied. This reaction not only creates cross-linkages in rubber that improve its performance in materials such as raincoats, but also imparts flexibility and memory so that stretched rubber (i.e., stretched within limits) will return to its original shape when the force is released. The discoverer of vulcanization was a man named Charles Goodyear, who was not a chemist, but an inventor. Interestingly, he did not found the Goodyear Company, which is the largest maker of tires in the world and a leading manufacturer of polymeric materials such as resins and adhesives. Goodyear Tire and Rubber Company was founded in 1898, 38 years after Charles Goodyear died several thousand dollars in debt.

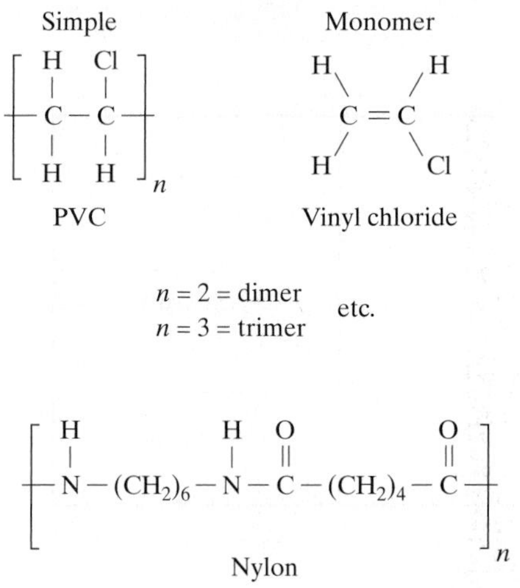

Simple

$$\left[\begin{array}{ccc} & H & Cl \\ & | & | \\ -C & - & C- \\ & | & | \\ & H & H \end{array} \right]_n$$

PVC

Monomer

$$\begin{array}{ccc} H & & H \\ \diagdown & & \diagup \\ & C = C & \\ \diagup & & \diagdown \\ H & & Cl \end{array}$$

Vinyl chloride

$n = 2 = $ dimer
$n = 3 = $ trimer   etc.

$$\left[\begin{array}{c} H \\ | \\ -N-(CH_2)_6-N-C-(CH_2)_4-C- \\ \end{array} \right]_n$$

Nylon

◀ **Figure 13.2** *Polymers are composed of monomers in chains, with n indicating a number of repeating units. Vinyl chloride is an example of a simple monomer that polymerizes to form polyvinylchloride, or PVC. The monomer of nylon is more complex.*

Random

$X-Y-Y-Y-X-X-Y-X-Y...$

Block

$X-X-X-Y-Y-Y$

Alternating

$X-Y-X-Y$

Graft

$$\begin{array}{c} Y \\ | \\ Y \\ | \\ X-X-X-X-X-X-X \end{array}$$

◀ **Figure 13.3** *Possible arrangements in copolymers.*

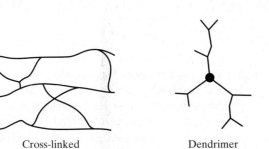

Linear

Branched

Cross-linked

Dendrimer

Tri-star

◀ **Figure 13.4** *Modes of linkages in polymers.*

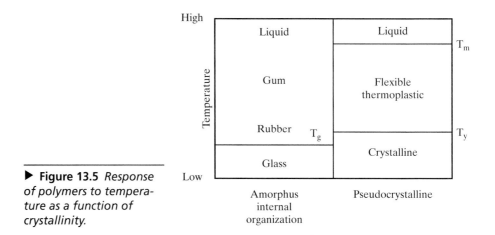

▶ **Figure 13.5** *Response of polymers to temperature as a function of crystallinity.*

the polymer backbone lessens sufficiently to impart flexibility, but not flow.[1] The polymer's softness increases with temperature, with no further distinctive phase transitions. In a more crystalline polymer, a distinct melting point exists, as does a distinct liquid phase. Collectively, these changes with temperature are referred to as **thermoplastic behavior**.

Polymers frequently contain additives to alter their characteristics. One common additive is a **plasticizer**—a material that softens a plastic and reduces its rigidity. A tough coating would be desirable to protect a layer of paint, but if the coating is too rigid, it will be prone to cracking. Consider the paint job on a car. The layers of coating sit atop metal that expands and contracts with temperature. If the paint layers cannot flex, they will crack. Similarly, polymers used in tubing, such as that from a Bunsen burner to a gas outlet, need to be flexible, while polymers used to hold carbonated beverages have to be rigid and strong enough to contain elevated pressures. Phthalates are a common group of plasticizers, and there are also antiplasticizers. However, the first polymeric group we will consider is one that initially has no additives: the biopolymers based on **polysaccharides** found in plants.

13.2 BIOPOLYMERS: POLYSACCHARIDES

Aside from proteins, another important class of biopolymers in forensic science are the polysaccharides. These polymers consist of carbohydrate monomers such as glucose. Sugars are classified as carbohydrates, and the formula of simple sugars such as glucose $(C_6H_{12}O_6)$ can be expressed as "hydrated carbon," or $C_6(H_2O)_6$. The simplest polysaccharides are dimers (disaccharides), many of which are familiar. Table sugar is a disaccharide consisting of fructose linked to glucose. Saccharide monomers such as glucose exist in open-ring and closed-ring conformations, with the closed ring preferred. When glucose forms a ring (the hemiacetal form), carbon 1 (Figures 13.6 and 13.7) is converted to a chiral center yielding two diastereoisomers. This carbon is referred to as the **anomeric** carbon, and in the case of glucose, there are two anomers: the α-D-glucopyranose and the β-D-glucopyranose. The term **pyranose**, used to describe a six-membered ring structure, is nomenclature derived from the structure of pyran (Figure 13.7).

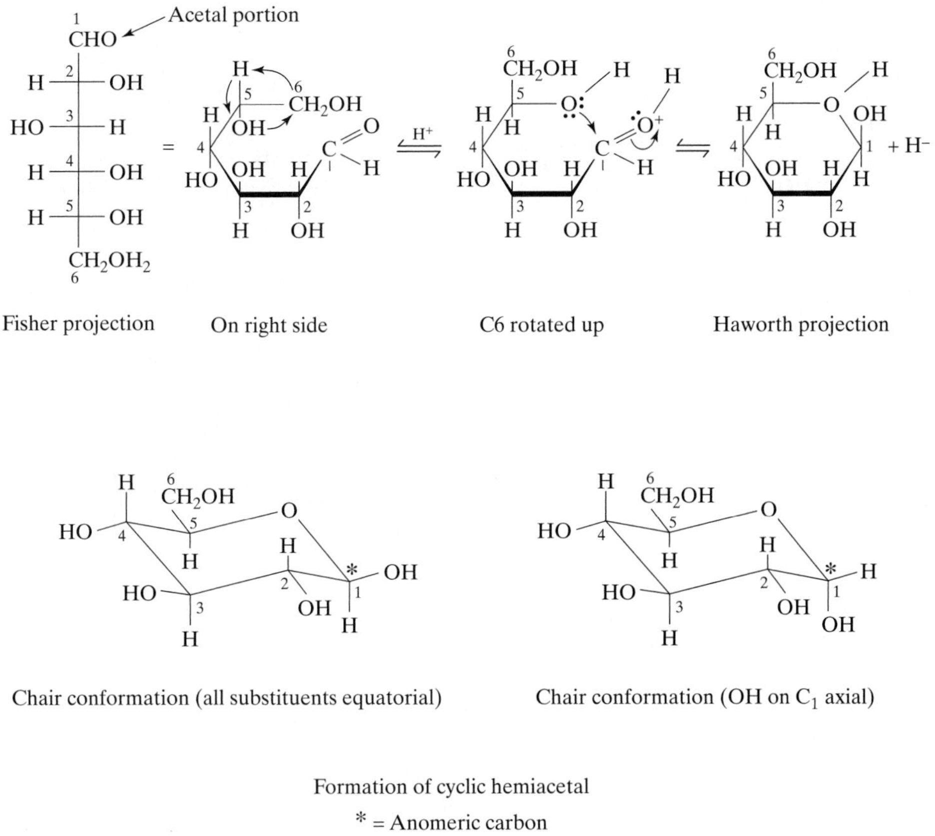

Fisher projection — On right side — C6 rotated up — Haworth projection

Chair conformation (all substituents equatorial) — Chair conformation (OH on C_1 axial)

Formation of cyclic hemiacetal

* = Anomeric carbon

▲ **Figure 13.6** *Different views and forms of glucose. The asterisk (*) indicates the anomeric carbon. The ring form is the monomer found in glucose polymers such as starch.*

The existence of an anomeric carbon on a monosaccharide implies that dimers, trimers, and polymers linked through this carbon assume different geometries. Disaccharides form when two sugars link and water is lost (Figure 13.8). The resulting structure depends on how the anomeric carbons are involved and how they interact. The three possibilities are shown in Figure 13.9. Sucrose results from a linkage formed between the anomeric carbon of glucose and the anomeric carbon of fructose.

Exhibit A: Sides and Tides

Polysaccharide is a generic term for a polymer composed of sugar monomers. This category is further broken down into disaccharides (two sugars), trisaccharides, and other polymer units consisting of ten or fewer units. Collectively, these smaller polymers are called oligosaccharides. When the polymer chain exceeds ten monomers in length, the term *polysaccharide* is used. In biochemistry, analogous nomenclature is used. A nucleotide unit consists of a ribose molecule linked to a phosphate group and base unit (adenine, guanine, etc.). DNA and RNA are polymers consisting of nucleotides. The term *oligonucleotide* is used to describe smaller nucleotide polymer units.

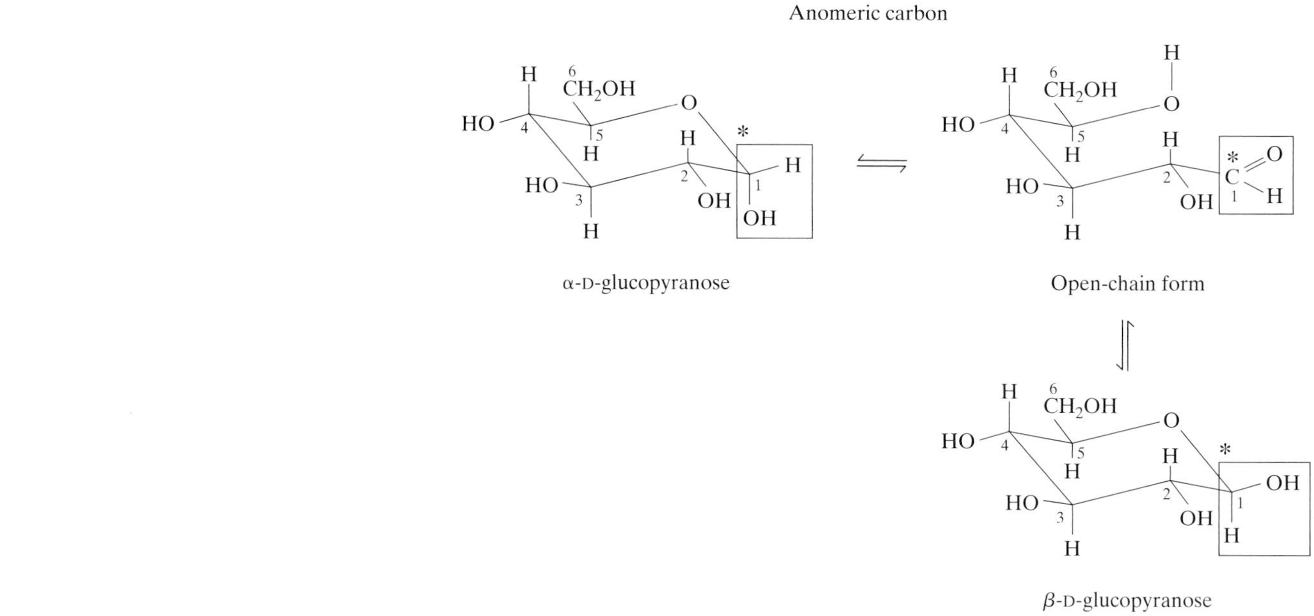

Anomeric carbon

α-D-glucopyranose   Open-chain form

β-D-glucopyranose

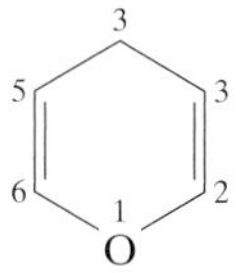

Pyran

▲ **Figure 13.7** *Formation of the ring converts the C1 to an asymmetric carbon, leading to a pair of diastereoisomers.*

There are four categories of saccharide-based biopolymers that are of interest to forensic chemists and forensic toxicologists, as shown in Figure 13.10. The first is **chitin**, the tough material found in the exoskeletons of insects and arthropods. The monomer is an amide formed from the replacement of a carbon in glucose with an amide group. Chitin (Figure 13.11) is the polymer that results from β-1,4′ linkages of the monomer. Because the carbonyl group forms strong hydrogen bonds with the N—H hydrogens, chitin is a strong but rigid polymer. Consequently, an insect must shed its exoskeleton periodically to grow. Forensic entomotoxicologists examine insects found associated with cadavers in an effort to identify characteristic metabolites of drugs or poisons. To do so, digestion of the chitins is required.

The remaining categories of biopolymers are based on glucose or are closely related to glucose structures. Glucose polymers are formed via different linkages, leading to a family of glucose-based polysaccharides, as shown in Figure 13.12. These polymers are also referred to as **vegetable fibers** or **anhydroglu-cose polymers**. **Starches** are glucose polymers that are used by organisms to store energy. Starches are differentiated from each other on the basis of how the chains connect and branch. Animals store excess glucose in the form of **glycogen**, a highly branched form of starch. To access a glucose unit, it has to be on the end of the polymer chain, so this design is an efficient way to store energy in a rapidly accessible form. The other components of starch are **amylose** and **amylopectin**. Amylose makes up about 20% of starch and is a linear glucose

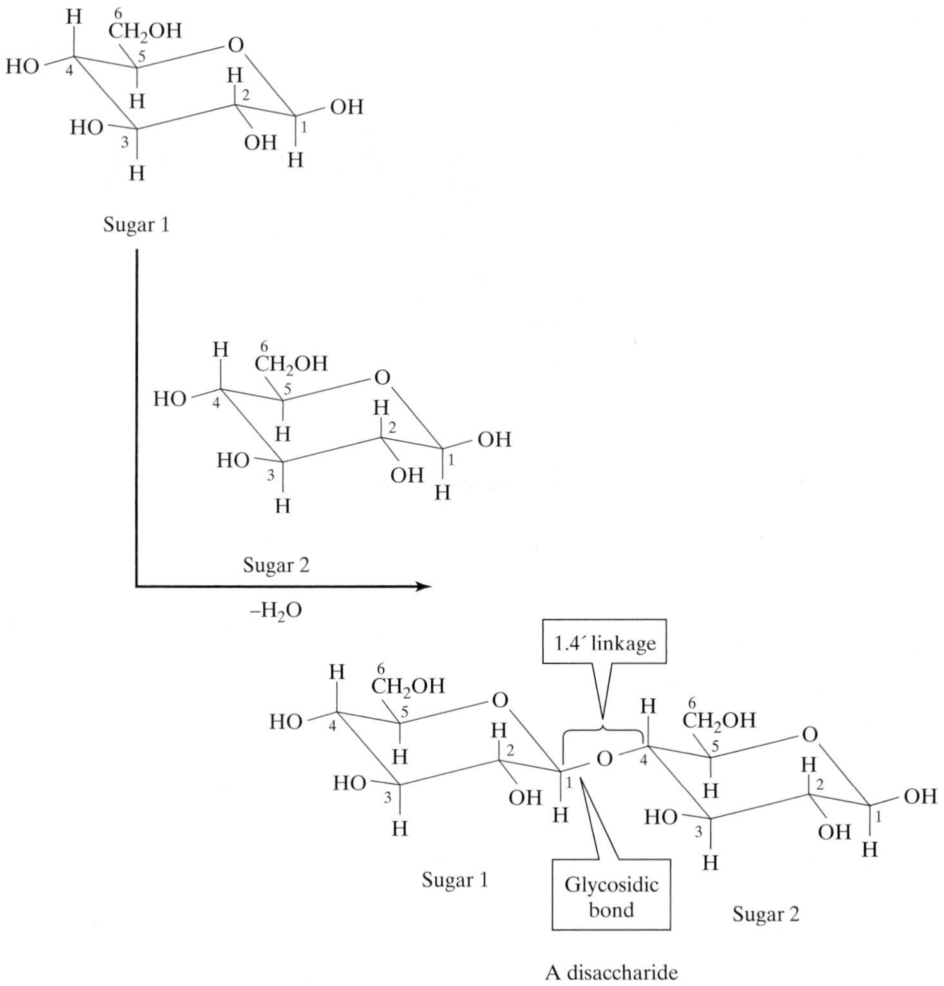

Sugar 1

Sugar 2

$-H_2O$

1,4′ linkage

Sugar 1

Glycosidic bond

Sugar 2

A disaccharide

▲ **Figure 13.8** *Formation of a disaccharide results in loss of water and the formation of a linkage. The type of linkage is important in determining the physical and chemical characteristics of the dimer.*

polymer. The monomers are linked by α-1,4′ bonds, which allow the chain to form a helix.[†] The other component of starch is insoluble amylopectin, which is also based on glucose monomers, but this time linked by both α-1,4′ and α-1, 6′ bonds, as shown in Figures 13.13 and 13.14, respectively. The branching is found approximately every 6–12 monomer units, and the overall size of amylopectin may reach a million glucose monomers.

Example Problem 13.1

Forensic biologists make extensive use of starch gels to perform electrophoretic separations. Explain how starch forms a gel matrix.

Answer: The helical structure affords the opportunity for strong intermolecular hydrogen bonds to form with water within the helix, causing it to swell and form a semirigid structure. When a starch gel dries, it forms a flimsy, thin film.

[†]The starch–iodine complex used as an indicator in titration reactions is formed when I_2 resides inside the helix.

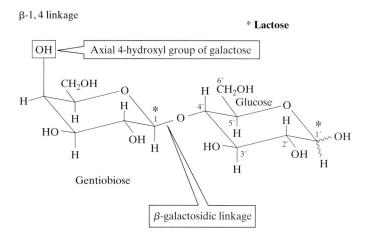

▶ **Figure 13.9** *Different link-ages possible in disaccharides and polysaccharides in general.*

Cellulose is structurally similar to amylose and is a linear chain of glucose molecules. The difference is in the linkage. Cellulose is composed of β-1,4' linkages, rather than the α-1,4' type found in amylose. This seemingly small alteration results in significant differences in the chemical and physical properties of cellulose compared with amylose and is a common theme that will be seen throughout the discussion of polymers. The linkage in cellulose allows for hydrogen bonding, as shown in Figure 13.15 and imparts a strength and rigidity to cellulose that is lacking in amylose. Cellulose is insoluble in water and is

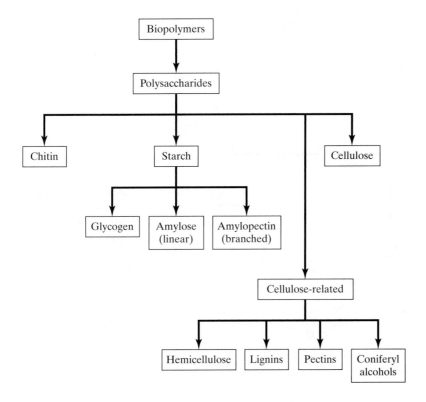

◀ **Figure 13.10** *Biopolymers.*

used in plants as structural support in the form of microfibrils. Although cellulose is a glucose polymer many animals, including humans, are not able to digest it because they lack the enzyme β-glucosidase necessary to break the linkages.

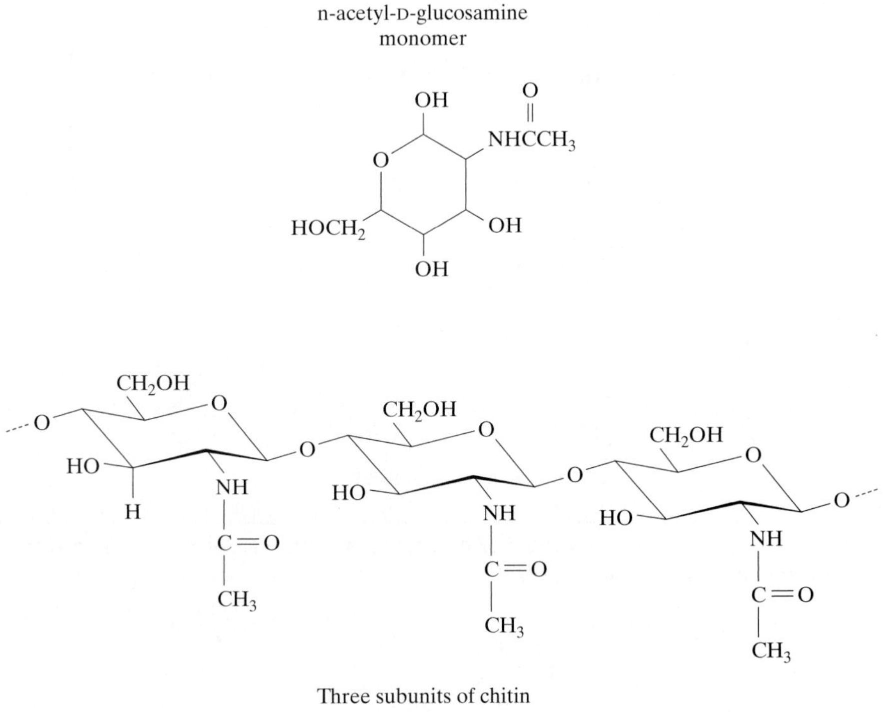

n-acetyl-D-glucosamine
monomer

Three subunits of chitin

◀ **Figure 13.11** *The monomer and structure of chitin.*

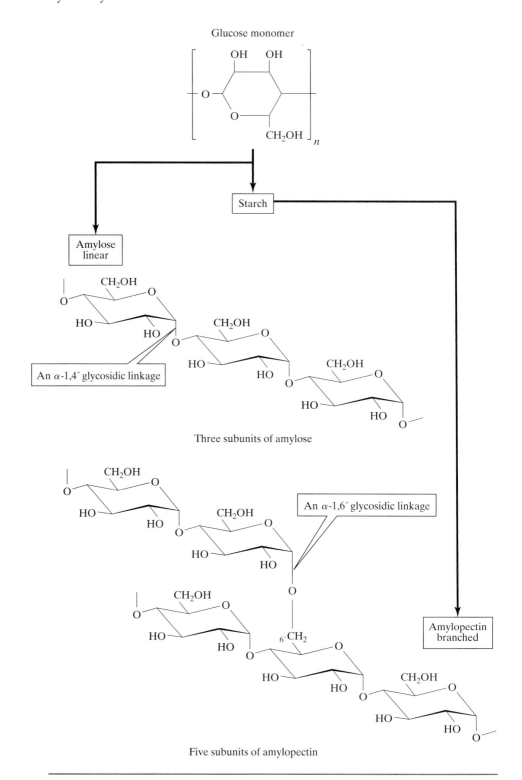

▲ **Figure 13.12** *Starch is composed of two types of glucose polymers that differ only on the basis of their linkages.*

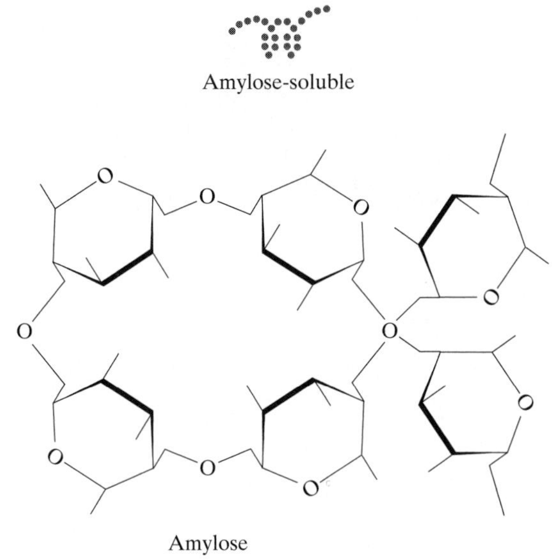

Amylose-soluble

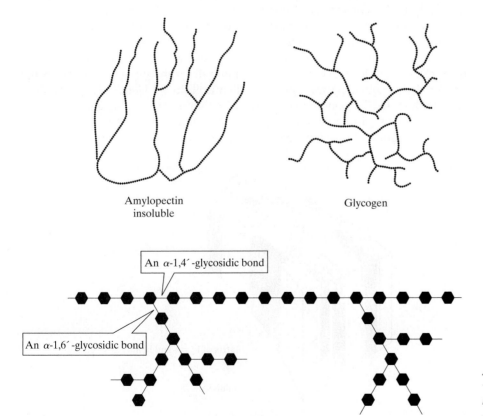

Amylose

◀ **Figure 13.13** *Amylose is linear, and curls into a helix in water.*

Cellulose is closely related to other biopolymers found in wood and plants. Together, these compounds are the raw materials used in a number of products encountered in forensic chemistry. For example, paper is made from wood chips derived from soft or hard woods, plants, or recycled paper stocks. Of interest in paper production are the polysaccharides found in wood—**lignin, hemicellulose**, and cellulose, all classified as part of the **lignocellulose** complex found in biomass such as wood. The lignocellulose compounds impart strength and

Amylopectin
insoluble

Glycogen

An α-1,4'-glycosidic bond

An α-1,6'-glycosidic bond

◀ **Figure 13.14** *Amylopectin is branched, but not as branched as glycogen.*

Cellulose

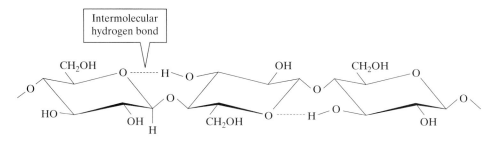

β-glucosidic linkage

Intermolecular
hydrogen bond

▲ **Figure 13.15** *Cellulose forms linear chains strengthened by hydrogen bonds.*

varying degrees of rigidity to plants. For example, a tree that stands several feet tall needs a different support framework than do mosses and grass, which are of little use in modern paper production. The organization of fibrils, structures in plants that contain lignocellulose compounds, is shown in Figure 13.16.

Typical wood samples contain approximately 40% cellulose,[2,3] and cotton is nearly 90%. Cellulose has a pseudocrystalline structure in the form of fibrils that are bonded together by the lignin and hemicellulose.[4] Hemicellulose is also a saccharide-based biopolymer composed of subunits of glucose, galactose, mannose, and xylose, to name a few.[5] The most common subunit is the xylans,[5] as shown in Figure 13.17. Hemicelluloses constitute approximately 25% of wood

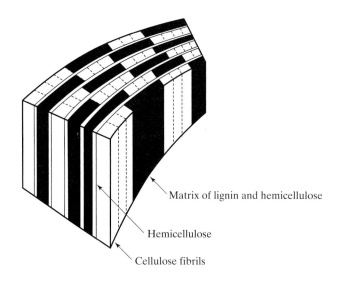

Matrix of lignin and hemicellulose

Hemicellulose

Cellulose fibrils

▶ **Figure 13.16** *The structure of a fibril in plants.*

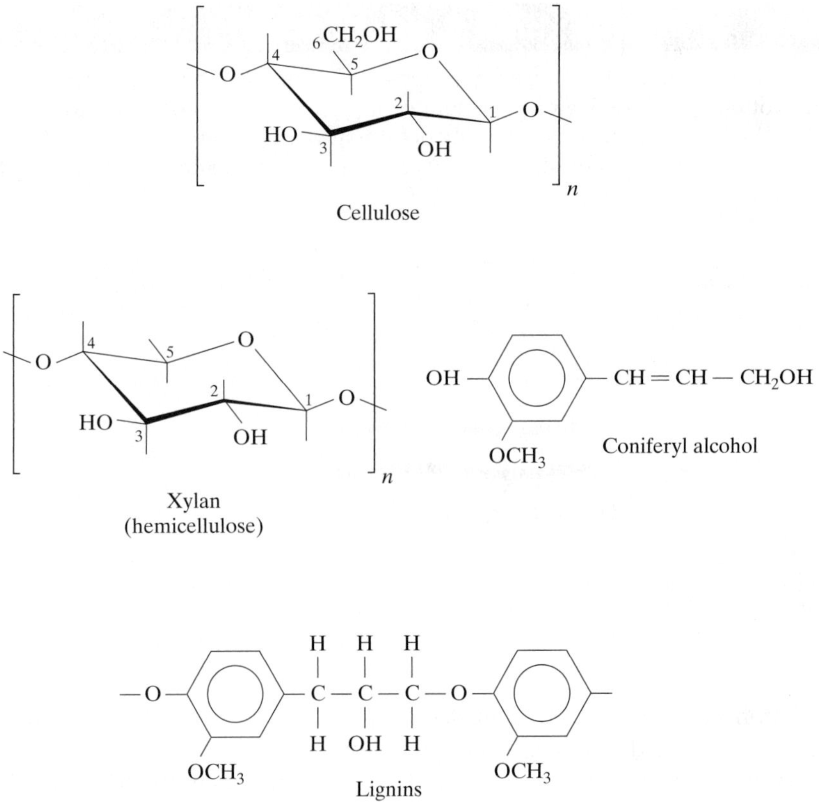

Cellulose

Xylan
(hemicellulose)

Coniferyl alcohol

Lignins

◀ **Figure 13.17** *Biopolymers related to starch. Hemicellulose is composed of xylan and other monomers. Coniferyl alcohols and lignins are important monomers in other structural polymers extracted from wood.*

solids.[2,3] Lignins are the most complex of the lignocellulose compounds and the least well characterized. When a plant decomposes, lignins produce humic and fulvic acids; lignins are also a precursor of peat and coal.[6] Lignins are a family of related biopolymers based on phenylpropyl units which are linked by strong C—C bonds that are resistant to many degradation pathways.[7] When extracted, lignins have a gluelike consistency—not surprising in light of their function.

13.2.1 NATURAL FIBERS

Cotton fibers are the most prevalent of the natural fibers encountered in forensic laboratories. Other natural fibers include kapok, hemp, silk, and animal hairs, the last two of which will not be addressed here. Cotton is classified as a **seed fiber**. The cotton plant is a shrub that grows to height of a few feet and produces pink flowers that fall off and leave behind a seed pod called a *boll*. The cellulose fibers grow inside until the boll breaks open when it is ready for harvesting. The raw cotton fibers are yellowish to white and up to 2" long. The seeds are removed by a cotton gin, and the baled fibers are shipped for processing such as raking and spinning into yards or fabrics.[8] Because cotton is so common, cotton fibers are typically not very useful as evidence,[9] although there are always exceptions.

Exhibit B: Fireproofing Cotton

Cotton clothing is popular because it is comfortable to wear and easy to work with. However, it is highly flammable and thus is not recommended for use in applications such as children's sleepwear. One method of increasing the fire resistance of cotton apparel has been recently proposed. Researchers dissolved the cellulose from cotton and added montmorillonite clay particles before reconstituting the fibers. When heated, these treated fibers form a char layer on the surface that prevents oxygen from penetrating, thereby impeding combustion by depriving the process of the oxidant.

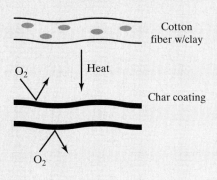

Source: Goho, A., "Textiles," *Science News* 165 (2004), 253.

Cotton fibers are easily identified by polarizing light microscopy and appear as thin, twisted ribbons. Although cotton lacks a uniform crystalline structure, cellulose has ordered regions that will interact with polarized light. However, these regions are randomly located, so cotton lacks distinctive extinctions or birefringence, also called incomplete extinction. Given the ease of identification with optical techniques, there is little reason for further instrumental analysis, unless other classifications are possible on the basis of dyes or other treatments. The —OH groups in cellulose are often targeted as sites for interaction, as illustrated in Figure 13.18.[10] The analytical approach used in these examinations is discussed in the next chapter.

13.2.2 REGENERATED AND REFORMULATED CELLULOSE: SEMISYNTHETICS

The first manufactured fibers were regenerated forms of cellulose classified as semisynthetics. Cotton is a versatile fiber, but because the fibers are short, cotton yarns and fabrics consist of these shorter fibers spun together rather than single contiguous fibers; as a result, cotton is not a strong fiber.

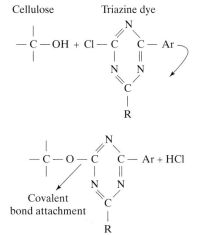

▲ **Figure 13.18** *The covalent attachment of a dye molecule to cellulose via the —OH functional group. The dye molecule in this example has an active halogen site.*

▶ **Figure 13.19** *Generic process for regeneration of cellulose.*

$$ROH + NaOH + CS_2 \longrightarrow \left[RO-\overset{\overset{\displaystyle S}{\|}}{C}-S^- \right] Na^+ + H_2O$$

Cellulose   Cellulose xanthate
                                    (viscose)

$$\left[RO-\overset{\overset{\displaystyle S}{\|}}{C}-S^- \right] Na^+ + H_2SO_4 \xrightarrow[H_2O]{} ROH + CS_2$$

Extruded into   Sulfate salt   Rayon
   solution   (Regenerated cellulose)

However, the —OH functionality of cellulose provides a chemical handle that is exploited for the generation of contiguous cellulose fibers. In the simplest process, raw materials such as wood are treated with a strong base, which promotes the partial oxidation of the cellulose and decreases the degree of polymerization by about a factor of three.[9] Carbon disulfide is then added to create cellulose xanthate, a thick, viscous solution that can be extruded through an orifice as a single long fiber. The extruded fiber enters a coagulating solution containing sulfuric acid and sulfate salts.[9] The outer surface forms first and then shrinks and wrinkles as the inner cellulose re-forms. The surface is much smoother than that of cotton fibers. The regenerated material is highly reflective and appears shiny if it is not treated with delustering agents. The characteristic sheen is the origin of the name "**rayon**," referring to the shine as giving off rays of light. In addition to being made into fibers, the viscous solution can also be cast as a thin film, producing cellophane.

Both cotton and rayon are cellulose, but because of the extrusion process, their properties are significantly different. Even though rayon exists as a long fiber, the degree of polymerization of rayon is about ten times lower than that of cotton cellulose. Rayon has less of a crystalline nature than cotton, with predictable consequences based on Figure 13.5. Because of these properties and the silky sheen (luster) of rayon, it is used for undergarments and other delicate items. One variant of rayon is **hollow viscose**, made by adding Na_2CO_3 to the extruded solution. When hollow viscose is placed in the acidic coagulation bath, any Na_2CO_3 trapped inside the fibers is converted to CO_2, producing a void in the structure. There are a number of other production modifications in use that result in rayon with yet other chemical and physical properties.

Historical Evidence 13.2—Dyes, Drugs, and Now, Polymers

Previous Historical Evidence boxes have pointed out the linked history of drugs and dyes, which emerged in the late 1800s as bulk products. Polymers can now be added to that list. Rayon was first synthesized in 1865, but the first moldable polymer was introduced a decade earlier. Celluloid, a polymer made from nitrocellulose and camphor, was created as a substitute for ivory. Celluloid worked well and was used in applications such as billiard balls. Unfortunately, nitrocellulose (guncotton) is flammable and explosive, leading to predictable problems in pool halls. Celluloid was also used for making films, another inherently dangerous process, given film's proximity to hot projection bulbs. Eventually, cellulose acetate replaced celluloid in this role. Meanwhile, rayon was discovered by accident, as are so many breakthrough products. Frenchman Louis Chardonnet was working with nitrocellulose during an effort to find a replacement for silk. He spilled some nitrocellulose on a tabletop and, when he wiped it up, noticed filaments forming. Cellulose acetates were pursued by two Swiss brothers, Henry and Camille Dreyfus, who went on to form the Celenase Chemical Company, named after their flagship product. The name was derived from the comfortable wearing characteristics of their cellulose acetate–based fabrics. The Dreyfus brothers began work in 1904 by making a synthetic dye, but decided that the polymer industry had more promise. The company remains a primary supplier of many polymeric materials and precursors.

The hydroxyl groups of cellulose can be esterified with the use of acetic anhydride to produce a group of semisynthetic **cellulose acetate** fibers. (See Figures 8.10 and 8.11 for a review of the use of acetic anhydride to esterify —OH groups—in this case, morphine.) The chemical treatment of the raw wood pulp begins with soaking in acetic acid, followed by acetic anhydride. In any cellulose monomer unit (Figure 13.15), there are three —OH groups that are vulnerable to esterification, and when it occurs, the product is a tri-acetate. Unlike rayon, the polymer is dried and ground up before being re-constituted in solvent and extruded.

Example Problem 13.2

Cellulose acetate is another regenerated polymer based on cellulose. It is made by treating cellulose with acetic anhydride (seen previously in the conversion of morphine to heroin) and pyridine. Show this reaction.

Answer:

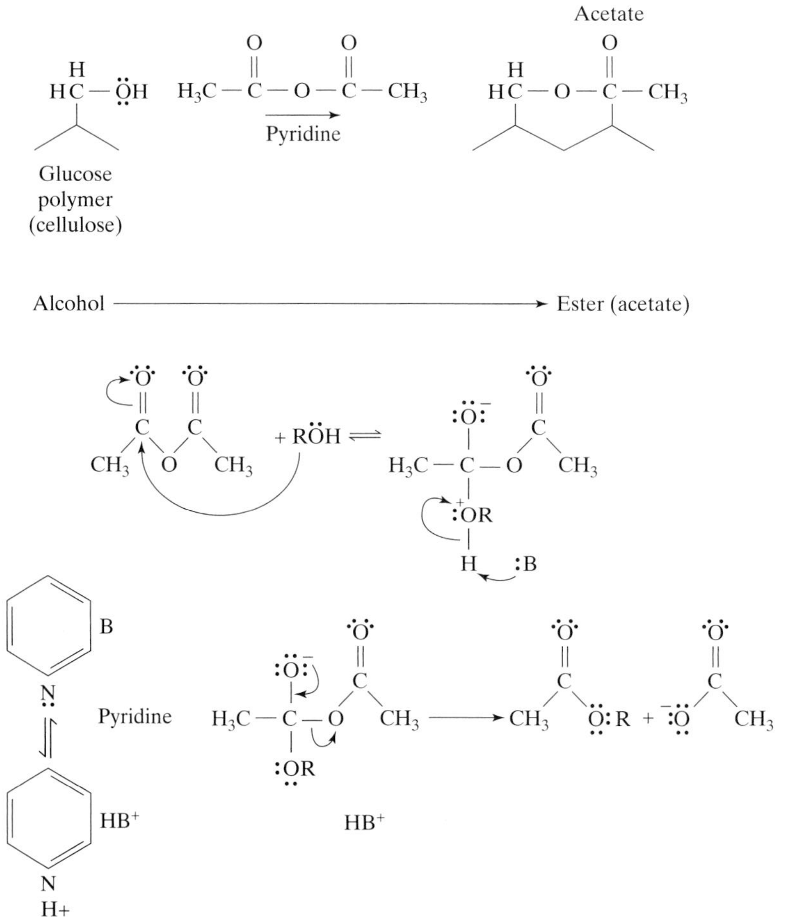

13.2.3 Paper

Paper is made from wood pulp which consists of fibers that are processed ("**beaten**") to incorporate water into the matrix. The generic steps are shown in Figure 13.20. Dewatering removes much of the moisture and allows hydrogen bonds to form between fibers, the interaction that gives paper mechanical strength. Chemical additives are introduced at several points in the process. Paper manufacturing is an example of mass production, and as a result, the batch-to-batch variation is small by design. From a forensic perspective, this small variation affords few opportunities to individualize paper, but assigning class characteristics is feasible.

The paper production cycle starts with wood chips or other ground-up starting material. Once reduced in size, the chips are moved to the pulping stage, where lignins are broken down and the fibrils are separated. Pulping is typically accomplished by treating raw pulp with NaOH and Na_2S at alkaline pH.[11] The process is referred to as the Kraft process or **Kraft pulping**, but there are many alternative names for it. Once the lignin is broken down, the pulp that remains is a brownish color that can be bleached by oxidizing agents to a whiter color and to remove additional lignin.[12] Chlorine gas was once the bleaching agent of choice, but environmental concerns have led to the development of alternatives such as ClO_2 and H_2O_2. One consequence of bleaching is the conversion of some of the end groups of cellulose to carboxylic or lactone forms.[2] (Lactones were discussed previously in Chapter 7 in the context of the drug GHB, which has a lactone form GBL.)

The beating stage serves several purposes. Large fiber structures are broken down mechanically, resulting in a roughened surface and internal changes in the fibers. These changes increase the potential for hydrogen bonding and create a matrix of fibers that can hold water and other materials. Fibers also become more flexible with beating. Approximately 35% of the lignin component

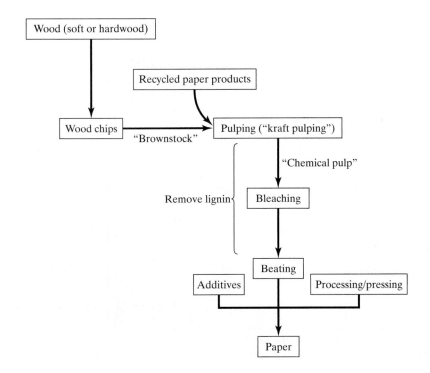

◀ **Figure 13.20** *A generic outline of paper production.*

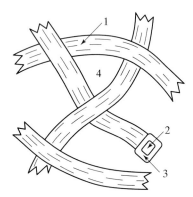

▲ **Figure 13.21** *Places where water can interact with cellulose fibers: (1) on the surface; (2) internally; (3) within the wall of the fiber; (4) within spaces between fibers.*

is typically dissolved during beating. Hemicelluloses are also degraded to a comparable extent.[12] Although paper is dry to the touch, the fiber matrix is capable of holding significant quantities of water via ion–dipole and dipole–dipole interactions. The sites within the fiber matrix that can interact with water are shown in Figure 13.21; Figure 13.22 illustrates routes of water penetration into paper fibers.

The beating stage is important for facilitating the associations of water and encouraging fibers to swell. Fillers can be added at this stage to fill voids in the fiber matrix and to give paper its desired physical characteristics and appearance. Additives include starches, binding agents, fibrous components, finishing agents, whiteners, cotton fibers, and colorants (dyes). Fillers range from clay materials such as kaolin (hydrated aluminum silicate) to $CaCO_3$ and TiO_2. Fillers have many functions, including altering the feel of paper, modifying its weight, and changing its optical properties such as reflectivity (gloss) and absorbance. Cotton is often an ingredient in paper because it is high in cellulose, but low in lignin. In general, the higher the quality of the paper, the higher is the cotton or "rag" content. Fine writing papers are high in cotton content and have a thickness, strength, texture, and feel different from paper used for copiers, printers, and other mechanical printing applications. Some papers are treated with buffers to prevent gradual acidification of the medium; the cover page of this book indicates that the book is printed on acid-free paper. As a method of preservation, this technique ensures that the book will survive at least long enough for a bedraggled student to sell it back in reasonable shape at semester's end. The wet strength of paper—particularly products such as paper bags and cardboard—can be increased by the addition of binders and agents that increase the strength of the attractive forces between fibers.

Once the pulp has been treated and lignin broken down, the preparation process involves combining the remaining ingredients, mixing them, and diluting the mixture into a thin slurry, which is poured over screens that capture the

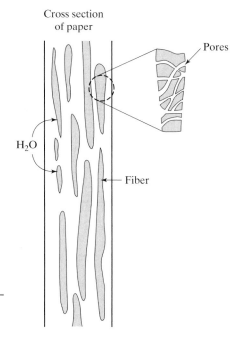

▶ **Figure 13.22** *Ways for water to interact with, and be absorbed by, paper.*

fibers as they are shaken. The fibers form a network held together by hydrogen bonds. Since excess water will disrupt hydrogen bonding between fibers, a heating and pressing stage follows, but not all of the water is removed. Coatings can also be added as required. A watermark may be placed in the paper at this stage. A watermark is a thinner area of the paper that is emblazoned with a manufacturer's characteristic mark that is visible when the paper is held to the light. Cutting is part of the process as well. Thus, in addition to chemical characteristics, striations and toolmarks may be useful in classifying papers. Figure 13.23 illustrates typical fiber matrix geometry in the final sheet of paper. The paper surface or the matrix itself can absorb water, which then moves through voids and fiber pores therein. Not surprisingly, excess water causes paper to lose strength because of the disruption of the hydrogen-bond matrix holding the fibers together. Finally, a number of ionizable groups exist in paper and are important for processing and paper chemistry. All of these ionizable groups, summarized in Table 13.1, form anions.

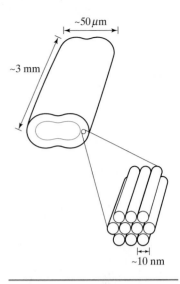

▲ **Figure 13.23** *A processed cellulose fiber in paper, showing approximate sizes and the geometry of packed fibrils.*

Table 13.1 Anionic Groups in Paper	
Chemical group	**Approximate pK_a**
Phenolic	7–8
Carboxylic	4–5
Alcoholic	13.5–15
Hemiacetal*	12

*Recall from organic chemistry that a hemiacetal is formed when an alcohol is added to an aldehyde. For example, the addition of methanol to acetaldehyde results in formation of a compound with an —OH and an —OCH_3 group bound to what was the carbonyl carbon.
Source: Eklund, D., and T. Linstrom, *Paper Chemistry: An Introduction* (Grankulla, Finland: DT Paper Science, 1991).

Dyes and pigments can be incorporated into paper in many ways, including impregnation and surface treatments. Solubility is an important concern, as is the mechanism of binding. Other materials that are part of the papermaking process are foam- and slime-control agents, required to prevent problems with the machinery used to manufacture the paper.

13.3 SYNTHETIC POLYMERS

The cellulose fibers in paper are the starting material for regenerated fibers such as rayon and cellulose acetate, which, together, form the historical bridge from biopolymers to completely synthetic fibers. Synthetic rubber was created in Germany in 1917, but from the forensic perspective, a much more important advance was the synthesis of **nylon** (specifically, nylon 6,6) in 1935. The discovery of nylon is credited to Dr. Wallace Carothers, who worked at DuPont Chemical Corp. Initially, his work had been with esters and phenols, but he became interested in amides for possible use in the then-infant world of polymer science. What would become known as nylon was developed in 1935 and commercialized in 1939, initially for women's hosiery. World War II jump-started the polymer industry, and many advances quickly followed. The emphasis here will be on fibers, with later sections in the chapter examining other applications of synthetic polymers.

Historical Evidence 13.3—Teflon®

In a repeat of a theme seen in many scientific discoveries, one of DuPont Chemical's most famous and profitable polymers was discovered by accident. Teflon®, a fluoropolymer best known for use in cookware, is highly resistant to most solvents and acids and is used in analytical chemistry in applications such as soil and acid digestion. Teflon® was accidentally made for the first time by DuPont chemist Roy Plunkett in 1938. Plunkett had been working with refrigerants based on chlorofluorocarbons when he returned to the lab one morning to find a waxy solid in a container where none should have been. Thus was Teflon® born.

As a first-pass chemical classification, synthetic polymers can be categorized by how they are produced. The two major categories (Figure 13.24) are **chain growth** and **addition**, with **ring-opening** polymers sometimes placed in a separate category. Polydimethylsiloxane (PDMS) and related silanes utilized in chromatography are generated by ring-opening reactions. Addition polymers are also called **condensation polymers**, due to the loss of chemical species such as a water molecule. Chain-growth polymers react and link via an active site. Regardless of their chemical mechanisms, polymerization reactions usually require the presence of an initiator, which can be a chemical or energy such as thermal or light energy. The initiator may also be a catalyst, but this is not always the case. Recall that a catalyst speeds a reaction by lowering its activation energy and that the catalyst is not destroyed in the process. It may be inert or regenerated, but it is not consumed. An initiator usually is consumed during polymerization, although a few initiators are also catalysts.

13.3.1 CHAIN-GROWTH POLYMERS

Chain-growth polymers grow by reactions occurring at an active site on the monomer or existing chain. Polymerization occurs via free radicals, anions, or

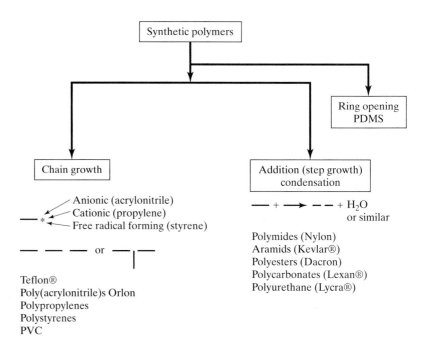

▶ **Figure 13.24** *One approach to the categorization of synthetic polymers.*

cations generated by the initiator. Many monomers are capable of different mechanisms; styrene polymerizes by all three routes.

Free-radical reactions were discussed in the context of combustion in Chapter 9, and the same principles apply here. Radical reactions start with the formation of the radicals by initiators such as peroxides. As shown in Figure 13.25, radicals react with monomers to create more radicals that combine with monomers. The process continues until the chain reaction is stopped by one of three mechanisms, all of which involve the combination of two radicals. Monomers capable of free-radical polymerization include styrene, vinyl chloride, and methyl methacrylate. Chemical initiators include hydrogen and other peroxides and potassium persulfate. Most initiators have weak O—O bonds that cleave **homolytically** (i.e., an electron pair splits in half) to form radicals, as in peroxides.

When radicals drive polymerization, branching can occur anywhere that a radical attacks hydrogen. The type and degree of the branching alter physical properties of the polymer. As shown in Figure 13.26, polyethylene is a chain-growth

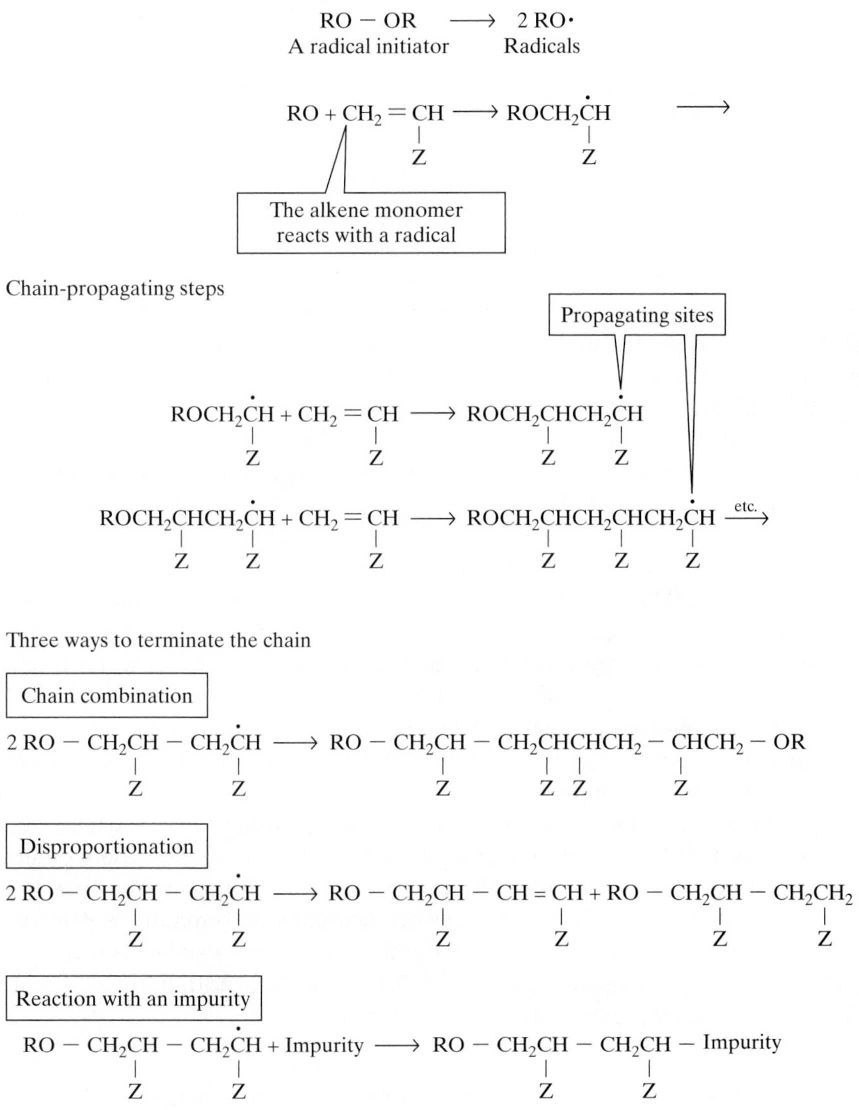

$$RO - OR \longrightarrow 2\,RO\cdot$$

A radical initiator   Radicals

$$RO + CH_2 = \overset{|}{\underset{Z}{CH}} \longrightarrow ROCH_2\overset{\cdot}{\underset{Z}{CH}} \longrightarrow$$

The alkene monomer reacts with a radical

Chain-propagating steps

Propagating sites

$$ROCH_2\overset{\cdot}{\underset{Z}{CH}} + CH_2 = \overset{|}{\underset{Z}{CH}} \longrightarrow ROCH_2\overset{|}{\underset{Z}{CH}}CH_2\overset{\cdot}{\underset{Z}{CH}}$$

$$ROCH_2\overset{|}{\underset{Z}{CH}}CH_2\overset{\cdot}{\underset{Z}{CH}} + CH_2 = \overset{|}{\underset{Z}{CH}} \longrightarrow ROCH_2\overset{|}{\underset{Z}{CH}}CH_2\overset{|}{\underset{Z}{CH}}CH_2\overset{\cdot}{\underset{Z}{CH}} \xrightarrow{\text{etc.}}$$

Three ways to terminate the chain

Chain combination

$$2\,RO - \overset{|}{\underset{Z}{CH_2CH}} - CH_2\overset{\cdot}{\underset{Z}{CH}} \longrightarrow RO - \overset{|}{\underset{Z}{CH_2CH}} - CH_2\overset{|}{\underset{Z}{CH}}\overset{|}{\underset{Z}{CH}}CH_2 - \overset{|}{\underset{Z}{CH}}CH_2 - OR$$

Disproportionation

$$2\,RO - \overset{|}{\underset{Z}{CH_2CH}} - CH_2\overset{\cdot}{\underset{Z}{CH}} \longrightarrow RO - \overset{|}{\underset{Z}{CH_2CH}} - CH = \overset{|}{\underset{Z}{CH}} + RO - \overset{|}{\underset{Z}{CH_2CH}} - CH_2\overset{|}{\underset{Z}{CH_2}}$$

Reaction with an impurity

$$RO - \overset{|}{\underset{Z}{CH_2CH}} - CH_2\overset{\cdot}{\underset{Z}{CH}} + \text{Impurity} \longrightarrow RO - \overset{|}{\underset{Z}{CH_2CH}} - CH_2\overset{|}{\underset{Z}{CH}} - \text{Impurity}$$

◀ **Figure 13.25** *Polymerization via free radicals. Peroxides are common initiators, due to their tendency to cleave homolytically to form radicals.*

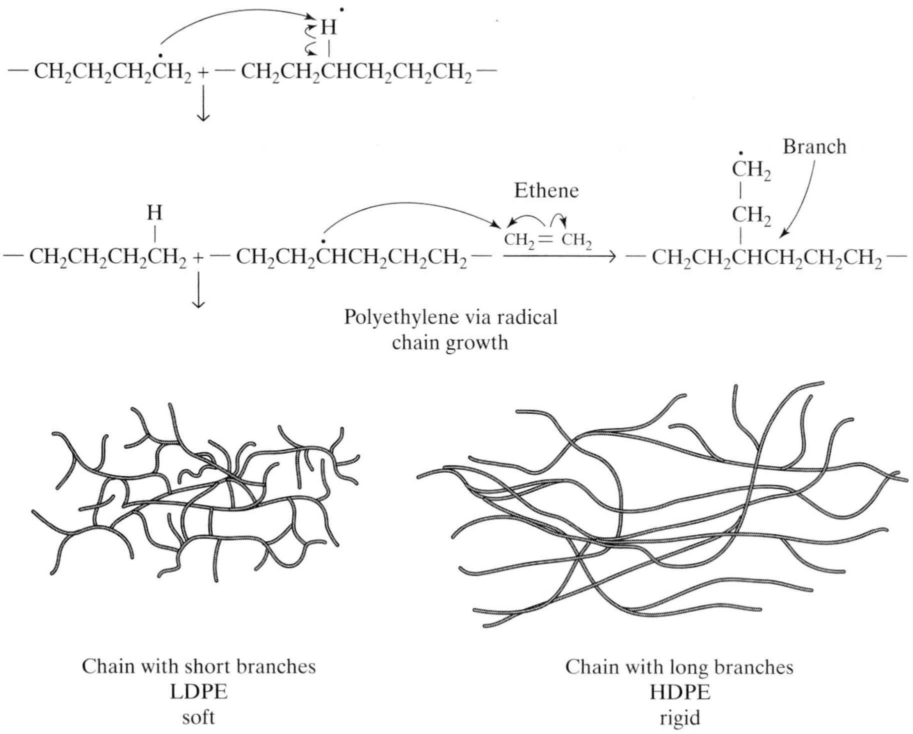

Polyethylene via radical
chain growth

Chain with short branches
LDPE
soft

Chain with long branches
HDPE
rigid

▶ **Figure 13.26** *Branching and its effects on polyethylene.*

polymer that is formed by a free-radical mechanism. Reaction conditions can be controlled such that chains with numerous short branches result, yielding low-density polyethylene (LDPE, recycle symbol 4). The density is low because the branching is not conducive to tight packing, as are long strands. As a result, LDPE is a softer, pliable material with relatively low strength. It is used in grocery sacks and trash bags. When the branches are long, the chains pack more efficiently and produce high-density polyethylene (HDPE, recycle symbol 2), a rigid material that retains a molded shape. HDPE is used in food containers, shampoo bottles, and the like. Some of the polymers that are formed by chain growth are shown in Table 13.2.

Cationic polymerization begins when an electrophilic initiator attacks a nucleophilic (electron-rich) monomer, resulting in the formation of a cation such as a carbocation. The initiator is also called a catalyst and is usually a Lewis acid,[†] such as BF_3. The carbocation is attacked by another monomer, lengthening the chain and propagating the reaction, which terminates when the cation is neutralized. Three examples of cationic polymerization are shown in Figure 13.27. Anionic polymerization, illustrated in Figure 13.28, involves monomers with electron-withdrawing groups such as $C{=}O$, and the reaction mixtures are often highly colored due to conjugation.[18] The nucleophilic catalyst adds to the double bond in the monomer to form a carbanion that propagates the reaction until it terminates. Unlike the cationic case, in which proton loss and the formation of double bonds quenches the reaction, there is no such possibility here. Reactions with water or CO_2 are possible, as are reactions with materials purposely added to "kill" the reaction. Anionic polymerizations can also be **"living" polymerizations** for this reason. Unless a quenching agent is added, the carbanions will keep polymerizing until the monomer is gone.

[†]Recall that a Lewis acid accepts electrons, whereas a Lewis base donates them.

Table 13.2 Chain-Growth Polymers

Monomer	Repeating unit	Polymer name
$CH_2 = CH_2$	$-CH_2-CH_2-$	polyethylene
$CH_2 = CH_2$ $\|$ Cl	$-CH_2-CH-$ $\|$ Cl	poly(vinyl chloride)
$CH_2 = CH-CH_3$	$-CH_2-CH-$ $\|$ CH_3	polypropylene
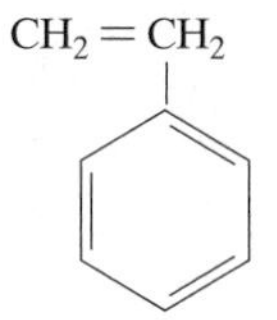 $CH_2 = CH_2$ (phenyl ring)	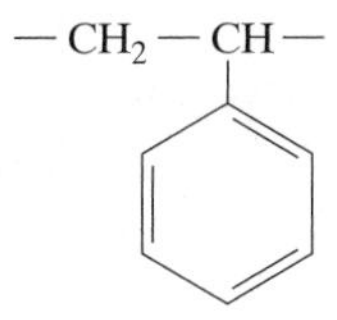 $-CH_2-CH-$ (phenyl ring)	polystyrene
$CF_2 = CF_2$	$-CF_2-CF_2-$	poly(tetrafluoroethylene) Teflon®
$CH_2 = CH$ $\|$ $C \equiv CH$	$-CH_2-CH-$ $\|$ $C \equiv N$	poly(acrylonitrile) Orlon®, Acrilan®
$CH_2 = C - CH_3$ $\|$ $COCH_3$ $\|\|$ O	CH_3 $\|$ $-CH_2 = C-$ $\|$ $COCH_3$ $\|\|$ O	poly(methyl methacrylate) Plexiglas®, Lucite®
$CH_2 = CH$ $\|$ $OCCH_3$ $\|\|$ O	$-CH_2-CH-$ $\|$ $OCCH_3$ $\|\|$ O	poly(vinyl acetate)
CH_3 $\|$ $nCH_2 = C$ $\|$ CH_3	$\left(\begin{array}{c} CH_3 \\ \| \\ CH_2 = C \\ \| \\ CH_3 \end{array}\right)_n$	Polyisobutylene (butyl rubber)
CH_3 $\|$ $C = CH_2$ $\|$ $nCH_2 = CH$	$\left(\begin{array}{c} CH_2 \quad CH_2 \\ \| \quad\quad \| \\ CH = C \\ \| \\ CH_3 \end{array}\right)_n$	cis-1,4-Polyisoprene (natural rubber)
$CH = CH_2$ $\|$ $nCH_2 = CH$	$\left(\begin{array}{c} CH - CH_2 \\ \|\| \\ CH_2 - CH \end{array}\right)_n$	trans-1,4-Polybutadiene

Table 13.2 (Continued)

Monomer	Repeating unit	Polymer name

$$n\text{CH}_2=\overset{\overset{\displaystyle \text{Cl}}{|}}{\underset{\underset{\displaystyle \text{CH}}{|}}{\text{C}}}=\text{CH}_2$$

(repeating unit)

$$\left(\begin{array}{c}\text{Cl}\\|\\ \text{CH}-\text{CH}_2\\\|\\ \text{CH}_2-\text{CH}\end{array}\right)_n$$

trans-1,4-Polychloroprene (Neoprene rubber)

$$n\text{CH}_2=\text{O}$$ $$(\text{CH}_2-\text{O})_n$$ Polyformaldehyde (polyoxymethylene, Delrin)

Chain-initiating steps

Propylene

Catatoninc polymerization

$$\text{BF}_3 + \text{CH}_2=\overset{\overset{\displaystyle \text{CH}_3}{|}}{\underset{\underset{\displaystyle \text{CH}_3}{|}}{\text{C}}} \longrightarrow F_3\bar{B}-\text{CH}_2\overset{+}{\underset{\underset{\displaystyle \text{CH}_3}{|}}{\text{C}}}{}^{\nearrow \text{CH}_3}$$

The alkene monomer reacts with an electrophile

Initiator (catalyst)

Chain-propagating steps

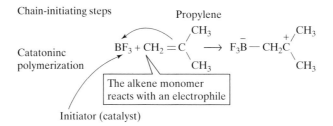

Propagating sites

Three ways to terminate the chain

Loss of a proton

$$F_3\bar{B}-\text{CH}_2\text{C}-\text{CH}_2\text{C}-\text{CH}_2\overset{+}{\text{C}} \longrightarrow F_3\bar{B}-\text{CH}_2\text{C}-\text{CH}_2\text{C}-\text{CH}=\text{C} + \text{H}^+$$

Reaction with a nucleophile

$$F_3\bar{B}-\text{CH}_2\text{C}-\text{CH}_2\text{C}-\text{CH}_2\overset{+}{\text{C}} \xrightarrow{\text{Nu}} F_3\bar{B}-\text{CH}_2\text{C}-\text{CH}_2\text{C}-\text{CH}_2\text{C}-\text{Nu}$$

Chain-transfer reaction with the solvent

$$F_3\bar{B}-\text{CH}_2\text{C}-\text{CH}_2\text{C}-\text{CH}_2\overset{+}{\text{C}} \xrightarrow{\text{XY}} F_3\bar{B}-\text{CH}_2\text{C}-\text{CH}_2\text{C}-\text{CH}_2\text{C}-\text{X} + \text{Y}^+$$

▶ **Figure 13.27** *Cationic polymerization. The initiator is an electrophilic compound.*

Anionic polymerization

Chain-initiating step

Acrylonitrile

$$\ddot{\text{Bu}} + \text{Li}^+ + \text{CH}_2 = \text{CH} \longrightarrow \text{Bu} - \text{CH}_2\ddot{\text{CH}}$$
$$\quad\quad\quad\quad\quad\quad | \quad\quad\quad\quad\quad\quad |$$
$$\quad\quad\quad\quad\quad\quad \text{C} \equiv \text{N} \quad\quad\quad\quad\quad \text{C} \equiv \text{N}$$

The alkene monomer reacts with a nucleophile

Chain-propagating step

Propagating sites

$$\text{Bu} - \text{CH}_2\ddot{\text{CH}} + \text{CH}_2 = \text{CH} \longrightarrow \text{Bu} - \text{CH}_2\text{CH} - \text{CH}_2\ddot{\text{CH}}$$
$$\quad\quad\quad | \quad\quad\quad\quad | \quad\quad\quad\quad\quad\quad | \quad\quad\quad\quad |$$
$$\quad\quad\quad \text{C} \equiv \text{N} \quad\quad \text{C} \equiv \text{N} \quad\quad\quad\quad \text{C} \equiv \text{N} \quad\quad \text{C} \equiv \text{N}$$

$$\text{Bu} - \text{CH}_2\text{CH} - \text{CH}_2\ddot{\text{CH}} + \text{CH}_2 = \text{CH} \longrightarrow \text{Bu} - \text{CH}_2\text{CH} - \text{CH}_2\text{CH} - \text{CH}_2\ddot{\text{CH}}$$
$$\quad\quad | \quad\quad\quad\quad | \quad\quad\quad\quad | \quad\quad\quad\quad\quad\quad | \quad\quad\quad\quad | \quad\quad\quad\quad |$$
$$\quad\quad \text{C} \equiv \text{N} \quad \text{C} \equiv \text{N} \quad\quad \text{C} \equiv \text{N} \quad\quad\quad\quad \text{C} \equiv \text{N} \quad \text{C} \equiv \text{N} \quad \text{C} \equiv \text{N}$$

Termination

$$\text{H}_2\text{O} \nearrow \sim\!\!\sim\!\!\sim - \overset{|}{\underset{|}{\text{C}}} - \text{H} + \text{MOH}$$

$$\sim\!\!\sim\!\!\sim - \overset{|}{\underset{|}{\text{C}}} - \text{M}^{\oplus} \qquad\qquad\qquad \text{M}^+ = \text{Counter ion}$$

$$\text{CO}_2 \searrow \sim\!\!\sim\!\!\sim - \overset{|}{\underset{|}{\text{C}}} - \text{COOH} + \text{MCl}$$

◀ **Figure 13.28** *Anionic polymerization. The initiator is a nucleophilic compound such as the butyl lithium shown in this example.*

Example Problem 13.3

What types of monomers would be best suited for polymerization via a cationic process?

Answer: Monomers that stabilize the positive charge. The most stable carbocations are tertiary and the least stable are primary, so a branched monomer or a monomer that contains stabilizing groups or one that can form stabilizing resonance structures is best suited to cationic polymerization.

Chain-growth polymers can be made from ringed monomers and ring-opening reactions. Epoxides, described briefly in the context of inks are common in ring-opening polymerizations, which proceed via cationic or anionic mechanisms, depending on the initiator (Figure 13.29). Monomers can also be activated by electromagnetic energy, such as the formation of radicals via photolytic and electrolytic methods.

Exhibit C: Super Glue

Methyl methacrylate, the monomer used in super glue, polymerizes by an anionic mechanism. Its structure is typical of such monomers and consists of two electron-withdrawing groups that facilitate reactions with relatively weak nucleophiles such as the —OH groups found in cellulose through the formation of a strong polymer

Exhibit C: (Continued)

network, super glue will bind any two surfaces, such as paper, that contain initiator groups. Another common adhesive, epoxy, that works on a different principle is described near the end of the chapter.

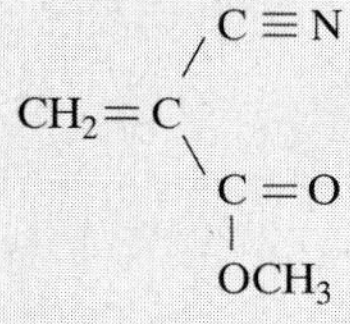

$$CH_2=C \begin{array}{l} C\equiv N \\ \\ C=O \\ | \\ OCH_3 \end{array}$$

Methyl α-cyanoacrylate

$$-CH_2\overset{\overset{\displaystyle C\equiv N}{|}}{C}-CH_2\overset{\overset{\displaystyle C\equiv N}{|}}{C}-CH_2\overset{\overset{\displaystyle C\equiv N}{|}}{C}-CH_2-\overset{\overset{\displaystyle C\equiv N}{|}}{C}-CH_2-\overset{\overset{\displaystyle C\equiv N}{|}}{C}-CH_2\overset{\overset{\displaystyle C\equiv N}{|}}{C}-$$
$$\begin{array}{cccccc} C=O & C=O & C=O & C=O & C=O & C=O \\ | & | & | & | & | & | \\ OCH_3 & OCH_3 & OCH_3 & OCH_3 & {}_nOCH_3 & OCH_3 \end{array}$$

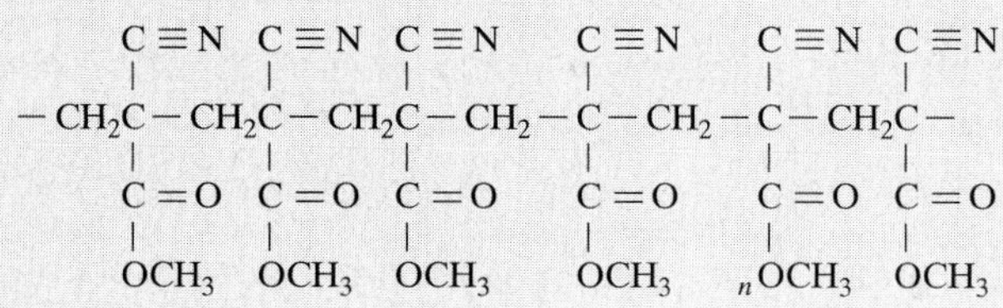

Super glue

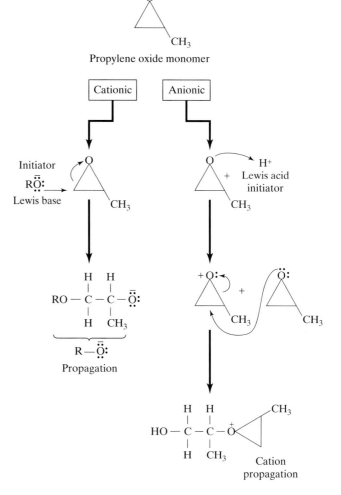

Propylene oxide monomer

Cationic | Anionic

Initiator RÖ: Lewis base

Propagation

Cation propagation

▶ **Figure 13.29** *An example of polymerization based on ring opening.*

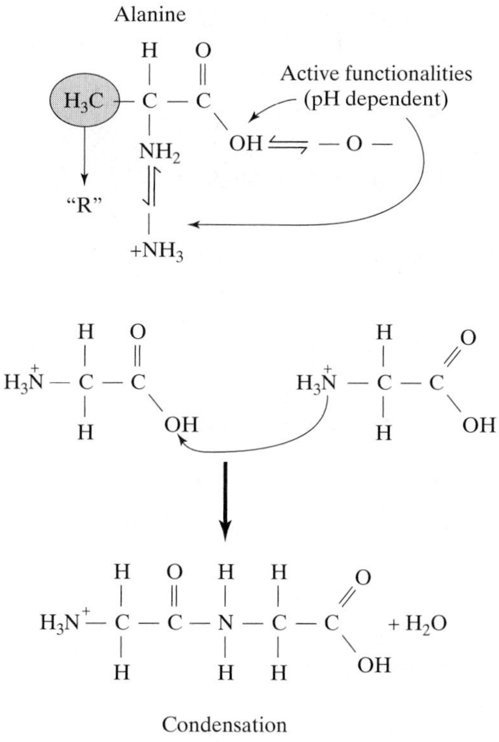

Alanine

◀ **Figure 13.30** *Amino acids such as alanine have dual functionality with pH-dependent activity. Most step growth monomers are also bifunctional. A peptide bond forms by a condensation reaction between the amino group of one monomer and the carboxyl group of another.*

Condensation

13.3.2 STEP-GROWTH POLYMERS

Monomers that polymerize by step-growth methods must have two active functional groups within their molecules. A familiar example is the combination of amino acids to form proteins (biopolymers) by a step-growth condensation mechanism shown in Figure 13.30. Amino acids have a carboxylic group and an amine group that will be ionized, depending on the pH. This is the same pattern that was discussed relative to drug chemistry, wherein the same functionalities (amines and acid) are central. To form a dimer, the protonated amino group reacts with the protonated carboxylic acid group (acidic conditions), and water is lost—hence the term "condensation." There are no initiators in step-growth polymers, and there is no chain reaction.

The first completely synthetic polymer, nylon, is a polyamide that forms by step growth and condensation. Nylon 6 is a **homopolymer** made from 6-aminohexanoic acid, whereas Nylon 66 is a copolymer. Kevlar® is closely related to nylon and is classified as an aramid because of the presence of

---

Example Problem 13.4

Will a different pattern be observed for changes in the molecular weight of the polymer over time for chain-growth versus addition polymers?

Answer: Yes. When an initiator is added to a chain-growth mixture, many monomers are activated, each becoming an active site to which other monomers will quickly add. Consequently, the molecular weight of the mixture jumps quickly. In contrast, step-growth polymers grow steadily, adding successively to the end of the chain. The molecular weight of the mixture increases gradually.

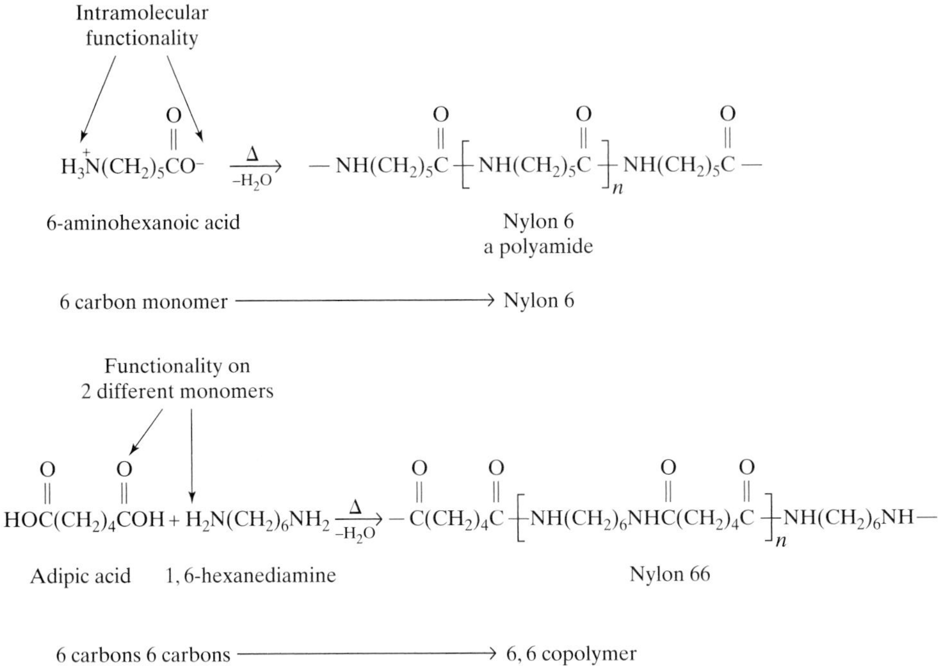

▲ **Figure 13.31** *Nylon 6, a homopolymer made from a bifunctional monomer, and nylon 66, a copolymer made from monomers with different functionalities. The condensation reaction that forms nylon 66 has many similarities to the reaction whereby amino acids combine to form peptides, as shown in Figure 13.32.*

aromatic rings. Kevlar's strength derives from a strong network of hydrogen bonds, as shown in Figure 13.32. Other condensation polymers are named on the basis of the type of linkages formed. Polyesters are held together by ester linkages, while polycarbonates are linked through carboxylate groups. Polyurethanes are interesting in that the step-growth process does not result in the loss of a small molecule. Some common step-growth polymers are shown in Table 13.3.

The last entry in Table 13.3, Melmac®, is representative of a large and forensically important class of formaldehyde-based polymers that includes phenol–formaldehyde, formaldehyde–melamine (triamino-s-triazine), and phenol–urea formulations. Melamine, shown in Figure 13.33, is one example. One of the earliest moldable polymers was Bakelite® and the associated group of "Bakelite®" resins[19] synthesized in 1872. As shown in Figure 13.34, the initial reaction of phenol and formaldehyde generates prepolymers called resols that polymerize under heating and acidic conditions.[19] The form of the polymer depends in part on the temperature. Polymers made with urea and formaldehyde form tough, clear resins, as do melamine–formaldehyde combinations. Melamine resins are used as topcoats in automotive paint applications.

13.3.3 Physical and Chemical Properties

Before delving into the world of synthetic fibers, we need a few more generalizations and descriptions concerning polymers in general. As noted in the polyethylene example (Figure 13.26), the chemical structure and bonding within a polymer dictate its physical properties. Kevlar® is strong enough to protect against bullet wounds because of cross-linkages of hydrogen bonds. Another way to engineer

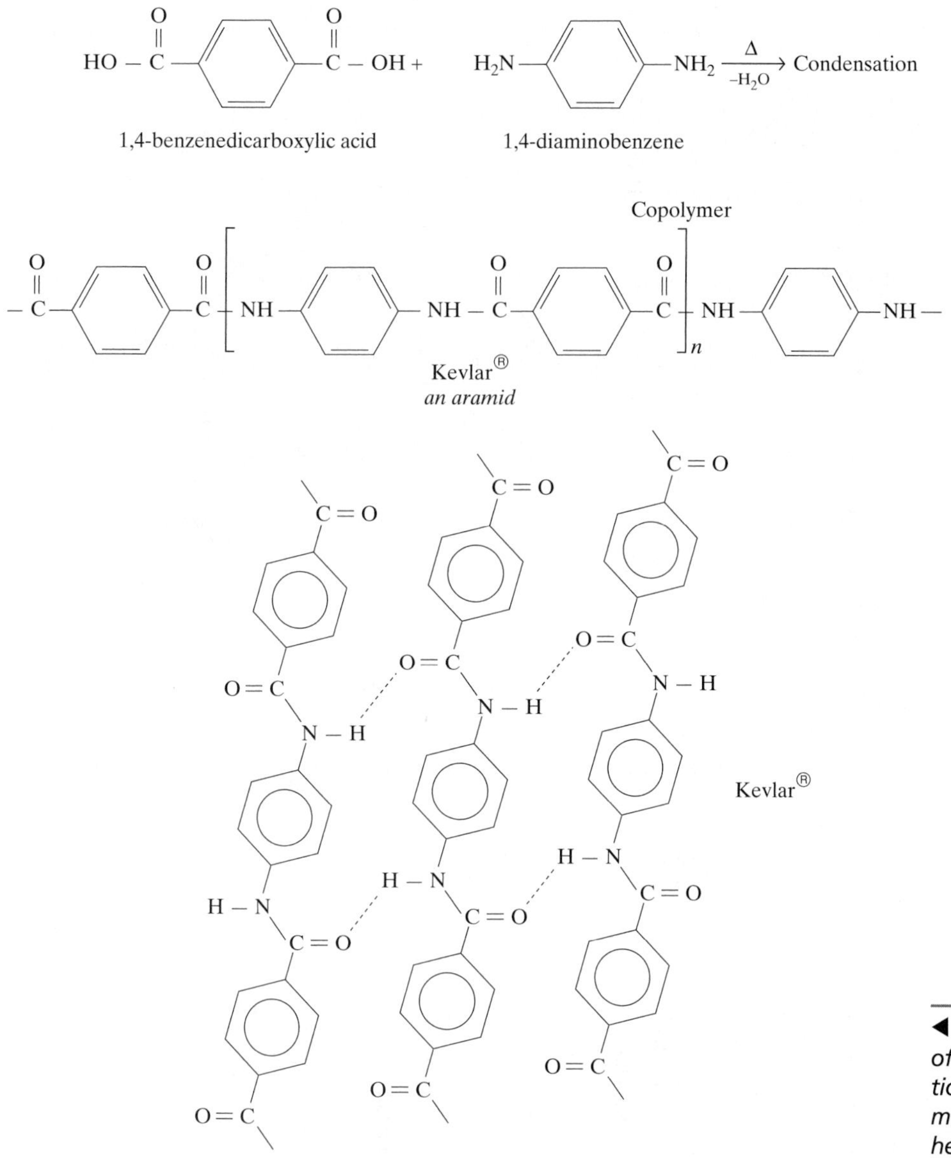

◀ **Figure 13.32** *The formation of Kevlar®, similar to the formation of nylon 6,6. Kevlar can be molded into shapes such as helmets.*

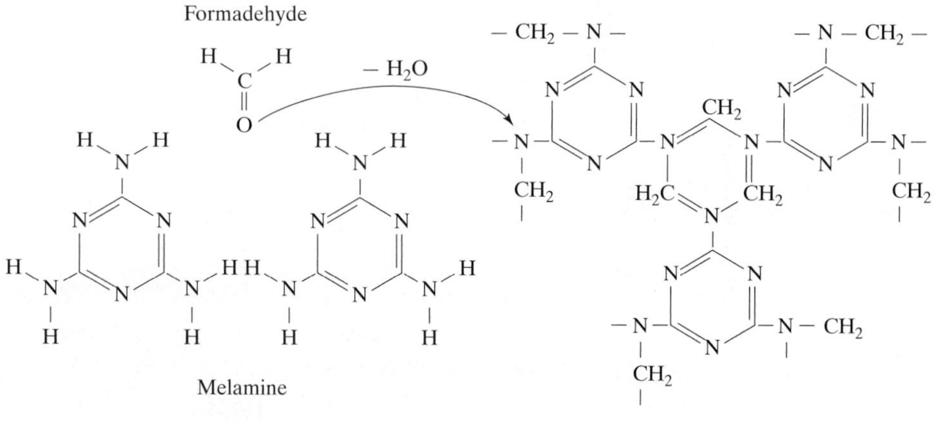

▲ **Figure 13.33** *Melamine, a formaldehyde-based condensation polymer.*

Table 13.3 Step Growth Polymers

Monomer 1	Monomer 2	Lost	Polymer
 Phosgene	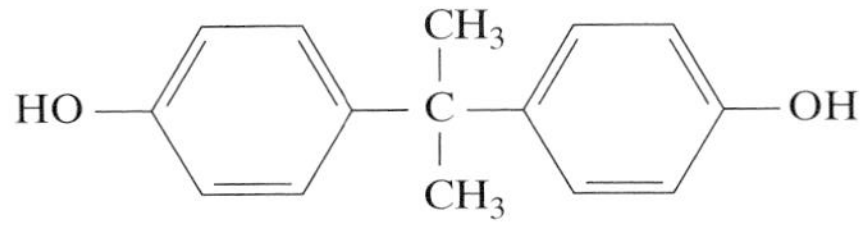 Bisphenol A	HCl	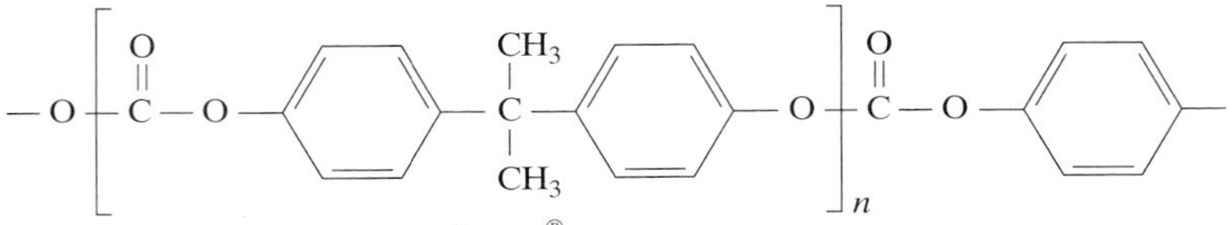 Lexan® — A polycarbonate
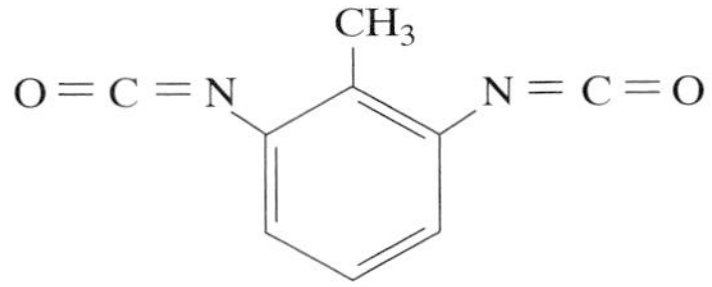 Toluene-2,6-diisocyanate	HOCH₂CH₂OH — Ethylene glycol	None	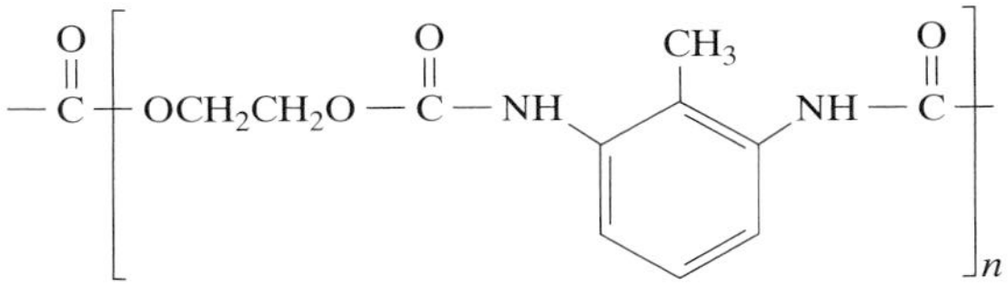 A polyurethane
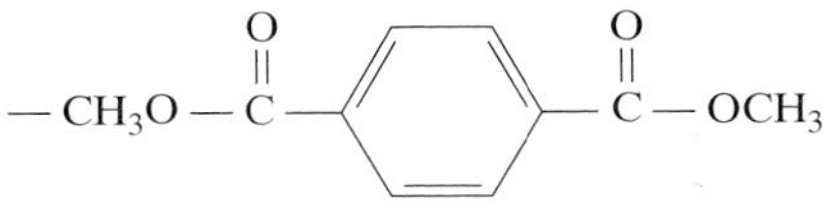 Dimethyl terephthalate	HOCH₂CH₂OH — 1,2-ethanediol ethylene glycol	CH₃OH	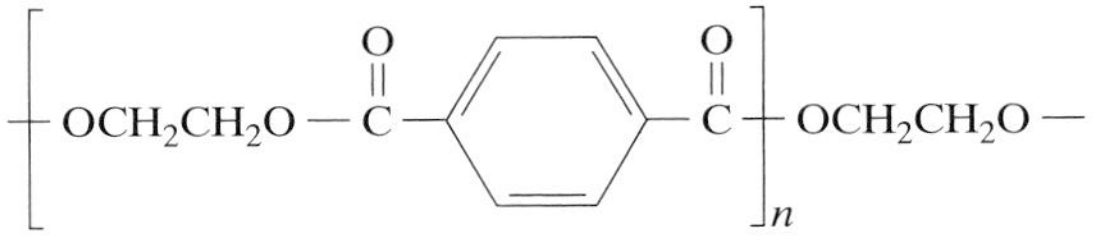 Poly(ethylene terephthalate) Dacron® a polyester
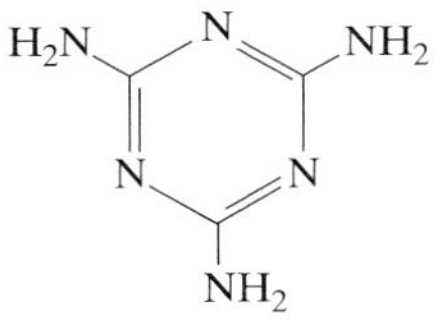 Melamine	H₂C=O — Formaldehyde	H₂O	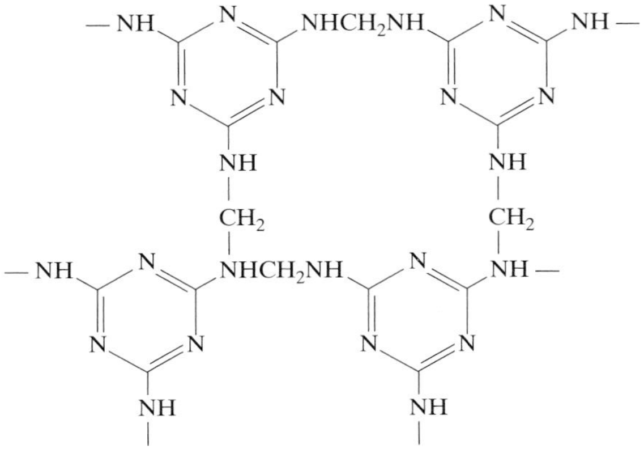 Melmac®

558

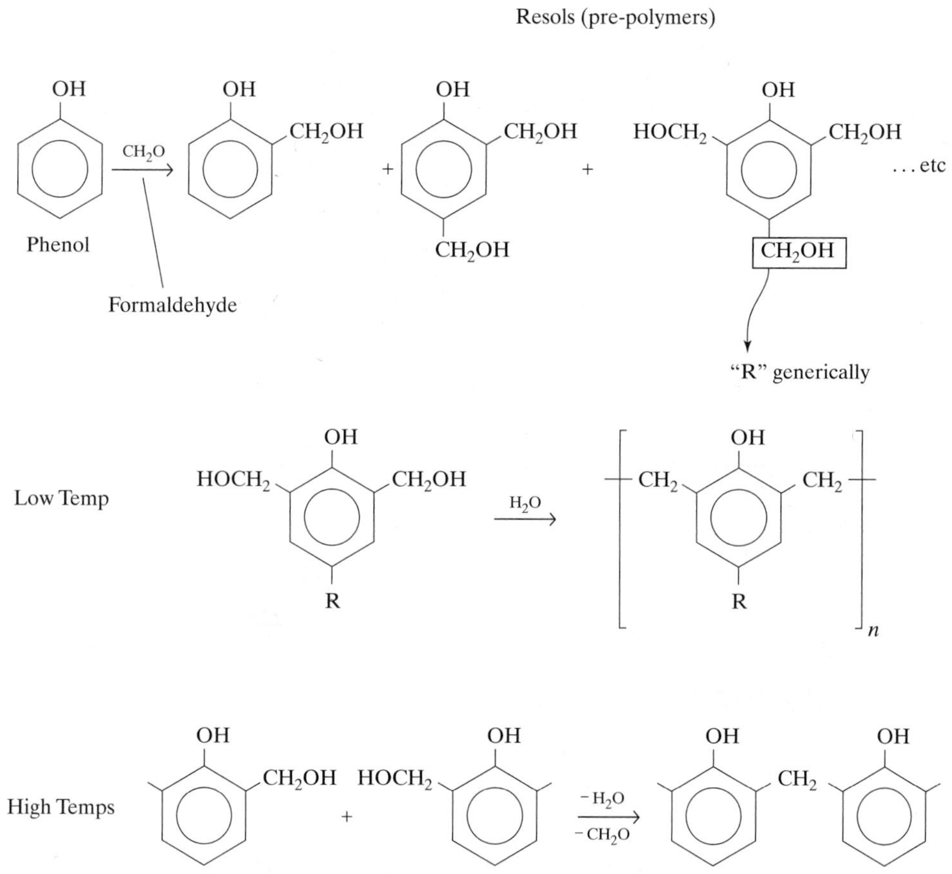

Resols (pre-polymers)

▲ **Figure 13.34** *The formation of formaldehyde–phenol polymers.*

strength is to organize polymer chains such that all the strands are parallel in what is called an **oriented polymer**. Most polymers have some degree of order, due either to chemical synthesis or physical processing such as drawing into strands. Figure 13.35 illustrates a polymer with ordered and random regions, a common occurrence. The more ordered a polymer, the denser it becomes, since chains can be lined up and packed tightly together. Increasing order also increases strength and heat resistance.

The behavior of polymers when heated is an important characteristic for manufacturing and applications. **Thermoplastics** are polymers with a mixture of ordered and random regions. At lower temperatures, the polymer is solid and holds its shape, but as it is warmed, the disordered regions facilitate motion and allow the polymer to be molded and shaped. Numerous consumer items are made of thermosetting plastic. **Thermosetting** polymers also respond to heat, but once they assume a shape, they cannot be heated and reshaped, because the heat promotes cross-linkages that are essentially irreversible. Thermosetting resins are used as topcoats in cars and form strong protective coats. However, the coatings lack flexibility and are prone to cracking and brittleness.

Elastomers are another large group of polymers classified by their ability to stretch (within limits) and return to their original shape. Rubber is an example of an elastomer. As described in Historical Evidence 13.1, rubber was one of the first raw materials used in early polymer research. Because of its elasticity, untreated rubber flows when hot and becomes brittle when cold. It also will pull completely apart with little applied force. All of these properties are undesirable for

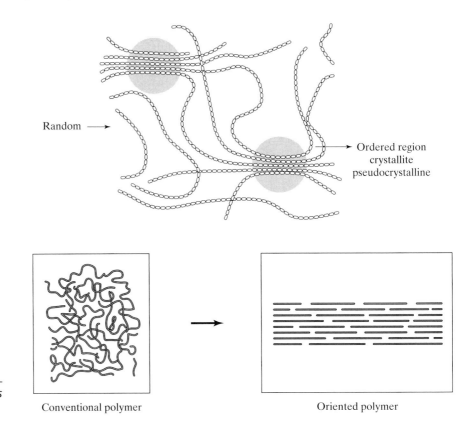

Random ⟶

Ordered region
crystallite
pseudocrystalline

Conventional polymer

Oriented polymer

▶ **Figure 13.35** *Ordered regions and crystallinity in polymers.*

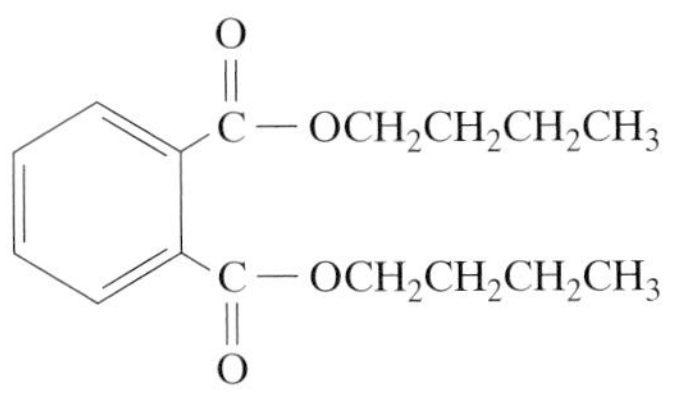

Dibutyl phthalate
a plasticizer

▲ **Figure 13.36**

applications such as rainwear and tires. When Goodyear vulcanized rubber, he introduced disulfide linkages into the polymer that stiffened the material to a certain extent, but preserved some flexibility and moldability.

Finally, many polymers tend to be hard and brittle. When these properties are undesirable, plasticizers are added to increase softness and pliability. Most such polymers are phthalates, and with the advent of mass-produced plastics, they have become ubiquitous. "New-car smell" results from the volatilization of plasticizers from synthetic upholstery and similar materials; when enough of the plasticizer is gone, the material becomes brittle and can crack. Plasticizers have recently been identified for further study as a possible health concern for children, who tend to put soft plastic toys in their mouth.

13.3.4 PROCESSING AND FABRICATION

When a raw polymer is shaped, molded, or drawn into a configuration such as a film or fiber, properties and characteristics are added or altered. From the forensic perspective, these characteristics may play a central role in the study of polymer evidence above and beyond a purely chemical analysis. For example, plastic garbage bags are made from films of polymer cast on rollers, which leave distinctive striations in the bag. Suppose body parts are found in a plastic garbage bag dumped in a remote location and that a suspect is identified. The striation pattern on the bag containing the evidence may be sufficient to link the bag to a roll of garbage bags at the suspect's home. Such a physical match is simple, often definitive, and made on the basis of knowledge of how polymer products are produced. Three common methods of converting raw polymer to product are by film casting, drawing into fibers, and molding. The processes are illustrated in Figures 13.37 and 13.38.

Solution casting (films)
"cold" methods

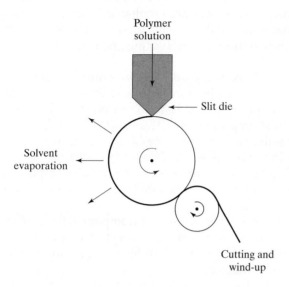

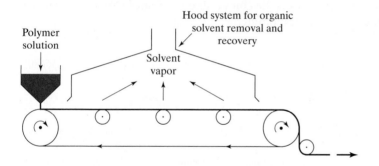

� ◀ **Figure 13.37** *Methods of casting liquid polymer into a film. The polymer solidifies as the solvent evaporates.*

Solution casting films
(heated) melt-extrusion

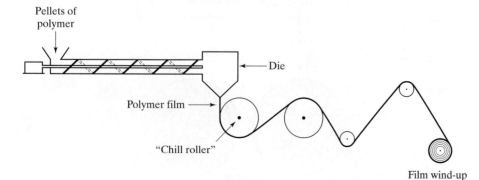

◀ **Figure 13.38** *Melt extrusion film casting involves melting the polymer.*

Thin films are made by casting techniques. **Solution casting** is as the name implies: dissolving the polymer in a solvent system and pouring it onto a surface from which the dried or cured polymer sheet is removed. On an industrial scale, systems of rollers and presses are employed in methods analogous to those used to make paper. Depending on the nature of the polymer, the film is cast from solution (cold methods) or by heating, melting, and casting (hot, or **melt, extrusion** methods).

Hot and cold methods are also used to create synthetic fibers. A strand of fiber is a single filament that can be combined or spun with other filaments to create the final fiber product. The process from raw polymer to final product is called **spinning**, as illustrated in Figures 13.39 and 13.40. The cross-sectional shape of the strands is dictated by the shape of the orifice through which is it extruded. As shown in Figure 13.39, extruded fibers are spun together into a filament (bundle of fibers) that can be cut into smaller staple fibers with lengths on the order of centimeters or less that may be further processed into textile materials.[20]

A recent development in fiber processing is **bicomponent fibers** (Figure 13.41). As the name suggests, these are fibers that consist of two different polymer types within the filament itself. Bicomponent fibers are engineered for specific applications and take advantage of the characteristics of each. Two designs are used: side-by-side and sheath–core. The sheath–core designs can be quite exotic, with a letter or other branding identifier embedded down the length of the fiber. The polymers must be compatible for manufacturing, as are, for example, polypropylene and polyethylene.

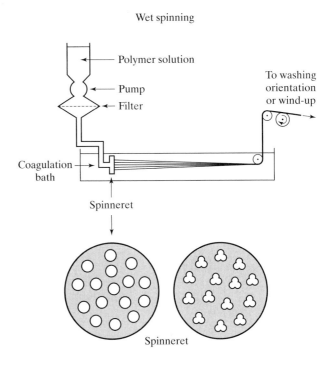

▶ **Figure 13.39** *Wet spinning of fibers is similar to cold casting of films, except that the fibers are extruded through a spinneret, which dictates the cross-sectional shape of the strands.*

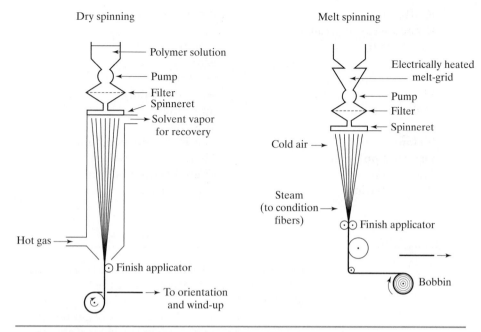

▲ **Figure 13.40** *Dry and melt spinning methods of fiber extrusion.*

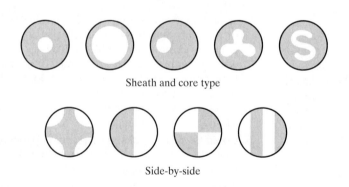

◄ **Figure 13.41** *Examples of possible combinations in bicomponent fibers.*

SUMMARY

We now understand the basics of polymer composition and synthesis and are ready to move into the forensic analysis of such evidence, focusing on paper, fibers, and other polymeric materials. Cellulose makes up a large part of these materials as a component of papers, cotton, and regenerated fibers such as rayon. In addition, much of what we have discussed here helps round out our understanding of coatings that we investigated in the last chapter. It should come as no surprise that our understanding of forensic chemistry is becoming more inclusive and integrative. It is appropriate that our final chapter should emphasize this.

KEY TERMS AND CONCEPTS

Addition polymerization	**Amylose**	**Bicomponent fibers**
Amorphous	**Anhydroglucose fibers**	**Biopolymer**
Amylopectin	**Beating**	**Cellulose**

Cellulose acetate	Kraft pulping	Pyranose
Chain growth	Kramers–Kronig transform	Pyrolysis
Chitin	Leuco form	Rayon
Condensation polymerization	Lignin	Ring opening
Copolymer	Lignocellulose	Seed fiber
Glass transition temperature	Living polymerization	Solution casting
Glycogen	Melt extrusion	Spinning
Hemicellulose	Nitrocellulose	Starches
Hollow viscose	Nylon	Thermoplastic behavior
Homolytic cleavage	Oriented polymer	Thermoplastic polymers
Homopolymer	Plasticizer	Thermosetting polymers
Interference colors	Polysaccharide	Vegetable fibers

PROBLEMS

From the chapter

1. Why is the term *anhydroglucose* used to describe glucose polymers? What classification of polymer does this place cellulose in?

2. Provide the chemical explanation for why lignin would be expected to contribute to the acidity of paper. What other groups are involved, and how does the bound water in paper (Figures 12.21 and 12.22) contribute?

3. Most papers lose their strength when wet. What is the chemical explanation for this phenomenon?

4. Based on the characteristics of cellulose, what group(s) of dyes would be appropriate for dying cotton and paper, aside from those already discussed? Explain on the basis of intermolecular forces such as ion–ion and ion–dipole forces.

5. In 2002, Cargill Dow introduced a new synthetic fiber labeled PLA and made from lactic acid monomers. What are the characteristics of this fiber? How is it made? How is it similar to cellulose?

6. Kevlar® is relatively easy to identify. Why?

7. Of the three types of dye shown in Figures 12.64, 12.65, and 12.66, which one would likely have the least "black" appearance and why? How could this appearance be exploited in a forensic analysis?

Integrative

1. An older, color-based presumptive test for saliva is based on the presence of the enzyme amylase. This test employs starch gel and iodine in an interesting way. Explain how the test is performed, and discuss its chemical basis and its limitations. How is this test related to material presented in the chapter?

2. Describe and discuss similarities and differences between the helical conformation of amylose and the helical structure of DNA. What fundamental chemical principles and intermolecular forces lead to the respective conformation and structure?

3. Locate a reference that describes sample preparation in entomotoxicology. What approach is used to break down chitin?

4. From your knowledge of the structure of glucose and cellulose, identify which groups are infrared absorbers. Where in the spectrum would most IR spectral features be expected to appear? Locate or obtain an IR spectrum of cellulose, and correlate absorbances to chemical functionality.

5. A question from the previous chapter dealt with the indicator phenolphthalein, which is also used in a common presumptive test for blood. If a typical sheet of office paper is slightly wetted, and a drop of phenolphthalein placed on the surface, what color would the indicator likely assume and why? From the perspective of using it for a presumptive test for blood, is there a possibility of interference?

6. Could the cation exchange capacity of paper be used to characterize the paper? Why or why not? What variables would have to be controlled?

7. A simple TLC experiment can be performed in which water-soluble inks are applied to filter paper and the chromatogram is developed with the use of water as the solvent. Explain what interactions in the paper allow for separation to occur. Examine the various classes of dyes, and predict how each would be expected to behave under these chromatographic conditions.

8. How is the process of dyeing a fiber similar to the processes that occur in chromatography? How is it similar to the movement of ions in solution to the surface of an electrode?

Food for thought

1. Why are whiteboards (Dry-Erase boards) nonporous? For writing on such boards, what type of dyes or pigments and what type of solvents would be best? Justify.

2. Why would a bicomponent fiber be considered to have strong evidentiary value?

FURTHER READING

Allcock, H. R., et al. *Contemporary Polymer Chemistry*, 3d ed. Upper Saddle River, NJ: Prentice Hall, 2003.

Biermann, C. J. *Essentials of Pulping and Papermaking*. San Diego: Academic Press, 1993.

Eklund, D., and T. Linstrom. *Paper Chemistry: An Introduction*. Grankulla, Finland: DT Paper Science, 1991.

Houck, M. "Inter-comparison of Unrelated Fiber Evidence." *Forensic Science International* 135 (2003), 146–149.

SWGMAT. "Forensic Fiber Examination Guidelines." *Forensic Science Communications* (www.fbi.gov/lab/fsc), Volume 1(1) (1999).

Website: www.tappi.org; Technical Association of Paper and Pulping Industry. This website has a wealth of information on paper and pulping.

REFERENCES

1. Allcock, H. R., et al. "Ch. 1: The Scope of Polymer Chemistry," in H. R. Allcock, et al., *Contemporary Polymer Chemistry*, 3d ed. Upper Saddle River, NJ: Prentice Hall, 2003.

2. Eklund, D., and T. Linstrom. *Paper Chemistry: An Introduction*. Grankulla, Finland: DT Paper Science, 1991.

3. Timofei, S., and W. M. Fabian. "Comparative Molecular Field Analysis of Heterocyclic Monoazo Dye–Fiber Affinities." *Journal of Chemical Information and Computer Science* 38 (1998), 1218–1222.

4. Bardet, M., et al. "High-Resolution Solid-State CPMAS NMR Study of Archaeological Woods." *Analytical Chemistry* 74 (2002), 4386–4390.

5. Sun, X. F., et al. "Fractional Isolation and Physico-chemical Characterization of Hemicelluloses by a Two-Stage Treatment." *Journal of Agricultural and Food Chemistry* 50 (2002), 6400–6407.

6. Faulon, J.-L., and P. G. Hatcher. "Is There Any Order in the Structure of Lignin?" *Energy and Fuels* 8 (1994), 402–407.

7. Sun, R.-C., et al. "Fractional and Structural Characterization of Lignins Isolated by Alkali and Alkaline Peroxide from Barley Straw." *Journal of Agricultural and Food Chemistry* 49 (2001), 5322–5330.

8. "Cotton," *Encyclopedia Britannica*. Downloaded December 5, 2004, http://search.eb.com/eb/article?tocid=9026524.

9. David, S. K., and M. T. Mailthorpe. "Classification of Textile Fibres: Production, Structure, and Properties," in J. Robertson and M. Grieve, eds., *Forensic Examination of Fibres*, 2d ed. London: Taylor and Francis, 1999.

10. Allcock, H. R., et al. "Ch. 8: Biological Polymers and Their Reactions," in H. R. Allcock, et al., *Contemporary Polymer Chemistry*, 3d ed. Upper Saddle River, NJ: Prentice Hall, 2003.

11. Mulvaney, S. P., and C. D. Keating. "Raman Spectroscopy." *Analytical Chemistry* 72 (2000), 145R–157R.

12. Bajpoa, P. "Application of Enzymes in the Pulp and Paper Industry." *Biotechnology Progress* 15 (1999), 147–157.

13. Allcock, H. R., et al. "Ch. 4: Ionic and Coordination Polymerization," in H. R. Allcock et al., *Contemporary Polymer Chemistry*, 3d ed. Upper Saddle River, NJ: Prentice Hall, 2003.

14. Allcock, H. R., et al., "Ch. 2: Condensation and Other Step-Type Polymerizations," in H. R. Allcock et al., *Contemporary Polymer Chemistry*, 3d ed. Upper Saddle River, NJ: Prentice Hall, 2003.

15. Petraco, N., and T. Kubic. "Ch. 9: Textile Examination," in N. Petraco and T. Kubic, *Color Atlas and Manual of Microscopy for Criminalists, Chemists, and Conservators*. Boca Raton, FL: CRC Press, 2004.

14

The Forensic Analysis of Paper, Fibers, and Polymers

INTRODUCTION AND OVERVIEW

In the last chapter we studied the chemical details of natural and synthetic polymers; now we conclude our journey through forensic chemistry describing how these compounds are analyzed. It is an ideal place to finish given the complexities of sampling, analysis and interpretation. Nearly every analytical tool we have discussed can be used on polymer evidence, including those that focus on color and colorants. We begin with paper, then move into fibers, and end with a discussion of some of the other types of polymers that may be seen as evidence. Prominent among these are plastic bags and adhesive tapes.

14.1 FORENSIC ANALYSIS OF PAPER

In questioned document cases, the analysis of paper is usually associated with the analysis of ink or other media used to create writing or printing. Chemical analysis of paper by itself utilizes the traditional three types of forensic tools: visual and microscopic examination, organic analysis, and inorganic analysis. Since paper is ubiquitous and mass produced, discrimination is facilitated with quantitative data and statistical classification methods. Still, it is extraordinarily difficult to unequivocally match one paper sample to another. Indeed, this is one of the conundrums of forensic science that is applicable to all types of mass-produced materials. Forensic scientists exploit differences to individualize, whereas mass-produced items are purposely designed to minimize differences. Paper manufacturers strive to achieve consistency among batches so that the paper leaving the plant on Monday is as close as possible to that leaving on Tuesday. When differences are small, the only way to compensate is by the depth and detail of the analysis, but this must be done with minimal destruction of the sample. This concern is particularly acute in questioned document cases, where destroying the paper may be out of the question.

Exhibit A

There are cases in which one fragment of paper can be associated with another. For example, if a ransom note is written on a pad of paper, and the note is carelessly torn out of the pad, it may be possible to physically match the tear marks on the pad to those on the sheet. A fit such as this is called a physical match. Physical matches can also be made between a piece of tape and a roll, a plastic bag and a source roll, and many other kinds of evidence.

Historical Evidence 14.1—Albert Osborne and the Lindbergh Kidnapping

One of the most famous trials of the 20th century was also a pivotal one for forensic science and the discipline of questioned documents. Charles A. Lindbergh became a national and international hero in 1927 after flying the Atlantic alone in the *Spirit of St. Louis.* He later married Anne Morrow, and their first child, a son named Charles Jr., was 20 months old when he was kidnapped around 9:30 P.M. on March 1, 1932. He was taken from his nursery, located on the second floor of the Lindbergh's home in Hopewell, New Jersey. The kidnapper left a homemade ladder at the scene that would later provide critical evidence, but footprints that were also left were not properly documented or preserved. A ransom note, 1 of 14 that would be sent by the kidnapper, demanded $50,000 for the boy's safe return. Mailed notes all had postmarks from the New York City area. The investigation by the New Jersey State Police was headed by Colonel Norman Schwartzkopf, father of the general who would later lead coalition forces to victory in the 1991 Gulf War. The case took many bizarre turns and became the subject of a worldwide media frenzy. An elderly retired teacher named John Condon became the intermediary between Lindbergh and a man who called himself "John," and eventually a ransom of $50,000 was paid, the majority of it in gold certificates, which were used as currency at the time. Serial numbers of the bills were recorded before the money was delivered. Sadly, the body of the child was found a month later in the woods close to the Hopewell home. The cause of death was listed as a skull fracture, most likely the result of an accidental fall from the ladder during the kidnapping. However, given that no forensic pathologist or medical examiner conducted the autopsy, that conclusion has been questioned. It is possible that the kidnapper killed the

Historical Evidence 14.1—(Continued)

boy shortly after the abduction and dumped the body near the home. The kidnapper was never heard from after the ransom was paid.

In 1933, President Roosevelt ordered that all gold certificates be exchanged for standard currency. Law enforcement agents working the case hoped for a break, anticipating that the kidnapper would have to turn in a good portion of the ransom money, most of which had not yet surfaced. That which had been spent was all in the New York City area, allowing the agents to concentrate their efforts there. The break came in September 1934, when an exchange bank received a $20 gold certificate from a man who matched the description of the kidnapper. More importantly, a license plate number had been written on the bill, and the number was quickly traced to a truck belonging to Bruno Richard Hauptmann, who lived in the Bronx. He was arrested, and a subsequent search of his garage uncovered a gun and several thousand dollars of the ransom money gold certificates. Hauptmann at first denied all knowledge of the money, but soon changed his story, claiming that a friend had given him the money. The friend had previously returned to Germany and died there, making it impossible to investigate that claim.

During the time between the kidnapping and murder of the child and Hauptmann's arrest, forensic investigations were undertaken on the physical evidence, including the ransom notes and trace evidence. Also, psychological and psychiatric studies were carried out, and, perhaps most damning for Hauptmann, the ladder was analyzed. Albert S. Osborn, a pioneer in the field of questioned documents, performed an analysis of the handwriting found in the ransom notes and concluded that the handwriting was that of Hauptmann. Even more damning was testimony from Arthur Koehler, a wood expert employed by the Forest Service. He undertook a meticulous evaluation of the ladder, including the wood, techniques used to construct the ladder, and toolmarks found on the wood. Eventually, he was able to trace the lumber used to a lumberyard and mill located in the Bronx. Marks made by planers on the wood in the ladder matched a planer at the yard. A search of the attic above Hauptmann's apartment revealed a missing floorboard. Nail holes and tree-ring patterns from a rail of the ladder lined up perfectly where the floorboard had been. Furthermore, Koehler was able to demonstrate this alignment at the trial, as well as to show how the planer marks from the ladder matched Hauptmann's planer. Hauptmann was convicted, and after a series of appeals and reviews, including one by the Supreme Court, he was executed on April 3, 1936.

Microscopy is a powerful tool for paper analysis and can be used to identify fiber types and particulates. Staining techniques such as Grafs C stain can help differentiate pulping methods and fiber types. Cotton fibers have a distinctive appearance under polarized light and are easily recognized. Fibers can be counted in order to estimate the cotton rag content of the paper. If a coating has been applied to increase the paper's strength or slickness or to add glossiness, the coating can be observed as well. Pulp fibers found in the paper can be identified by the specific source wood (pine, birch, etc.), but such identification requires specialized skills and training. Paper can also be exposed to UV light to see if it fluoresces, a property that is not unusual in papers treated so that they are of high whiteness. The same treatment is used to make white clothing appear brighter and whiter.

Applying the Science 14.1   Novel Use of the Fourier Transform

The Fourier transform has been discussed in the context of FTIR. The mathematical goal of the transform is to detect periodicity in the signal produced by the interferometer. Periodicity refers to a repeating pattern, such as individual scans from 4000–400 cm^{-1}. The periodic table is called "periodic" because patterns such as outer electron configurations are repeated. Forensic researchers in Japan have reported using an FT algorithm to extract periodicity or repeated patterns in the surface of manufactured paper. Such patterns could arise from the wire mesh on which the pulp is dried or from the rollers used to press the paper.

The Japanese experimental design was simple and used a scanner with a modified bulb and transmitted light. The paper to be studied was scanned, and the image was saved as a .TIFF file. As with an FTIR instrument, the source covers all wavelengths of interest simultaneously, but in this case the physical features of the paper, and not an interferometer, generated the interference pattern. The recorded image was a visual record of the interference pattern. Image analysis software was then used to apply a Fourier transform to the image file. In an extension of the experiment, the authors used a modified technique to scan and analyze 130 different copier papers representing 12 brand names and 6 manufacturers. Several different sheets of each type were scanned and averaged to produce the composite images seen here. Mathematical similarity values were calculated from these "spectra," allowing discrimination of 10 brands out of the 12 examined.

◀ *2- dimensional Power Spectrum image of the light transmitted image of paper. A frequency analysis of 2-dimensional fast Fourier transmission has been applied onto the specimens of 256 X 256 pixels of Fig 1.*

Source: Miyata, H., et al., "A Discrimination Method for Paper by Fourier Transform and Cross Correlation," *Journal of Forensic Sciences*, 47 **2002**, 1125–1132. Figure reproduced with permission from this reference, copyright 2002, ASTM International.

The organic characterization of paper has focused on infrared techniques[1,2] and some use of thin-layer chromatography in the case of dyed papers. At a minimum, the cellulose in paper is an infrared absorber; organic and inorganic additives can add detail to a spectrum.[2] In a recent report recounting their success with FTIR using a micro-ATR objective, the authors noted that the scanning time was fast and that the use of a principal component analysis (PCA), coupled to classification algorithms, allowed for most of the papers that were evaluated to be discriminated.[1]

Inorganic analysis with ICP-MS has also been used to discriminate between groups of papers,[3,4] although the techniques were destructive. In one case, the elements Na, Mg, Al, Mn, Sr, Y, Ba, La, and Ce were found sufficient for classification and discrimination.[4] Paper samples were treated in hydrogen peroxide and nitric acid solution and were digested via a microwave-assisted procedure; clear discrimination of two origins for paper exhibits was demonstrated. The results are summarized in Figures 14.1 and 14.2.

Results such as shown in these figures must be interpreted with caution. In examining paper, any differences or similarities noted between known and questioned samples has to be evaluated in light of the answers to questions such as the following:

- How variable are elemental concentrations across a single piece of paper?
- Does it matter where a sample is taken?
- Are replicates essential?
- What is the typical method and instrumental percent RSD for each element?
- What is the expected batch-to-batch variation within a plant?
- What is the expected variation from roll to roll of paper within a single plant?
- How should samples be cleaned and prepared to ensure that elemental concentrations are attributable to the paper matrix and not to handling or some other kind of contamination?

These considerations relate to inter- and intrasample variations that must be characterized before analytical results are interpreted. For example, suppose that a questioned paper and a known paper had different concentrations of three elements, as shown in Table 14.1. There is not enough information in the table to interpret the

Element	LOD ($n = 9$)	Q_1 ($n = 5$)	% RSD	S_1 ($n = 5$)	% RSD	S_1 ($n = 5$)	% RSD	Instrumental Precision (% RSD) ($n = 7$)
Na	84	2300 ± 100	4.3	580 ± 30	5.2	560 ± 30	5.4	1.4
Mg	78	420 ± 30	7.1	400 ± 80	20	420 ± 80	14	1.5
Al	26	178 ± 7	3.9	140 ± 40	29	150 ± 30	20	1.7
Mn	0.7	4.55 ± 0.16	3.5	5.37 ± 0.06	1.1	5.4 ± 0.2	3.7	2.2
Sr	1.4	13.4 ± 0.7	5.2	12.8 ± 1.2	9.4	12.9 ± 0.9	7.0	1.6
Y	0.007	0.102 ± 0.004	3.9	0.199 ± 0.004	2.0	0.203 ± 0.008	3.9	2.4
Ba	0.5	0.86 ± 0.07	8.1	1.1 ± 0.3	27	1.08 ± 0.14	13	1.8
La	0.015	0.049 ± 0.003	6.1	0.233 ± 0.006	2.6	0.238 ± 0.011	4.6	2.7
Ce	0.03	0.047 ± 0.004	8.5	0.429 ± 0.009	2.1	0.441 ± 0.019	4.3	2.7

▲ **Figure 14.1** *Reproduced with permission from Spence, L. D., et al. "Comparison of the Elemental Composition of Office Document Paper: Evidence in a Homicide Case."* Journal of Forensic Sciences *47 (2002), 648–651. Copyright 2002, ASTM International. "Q" = questioned sample and "S" = standard samples.*

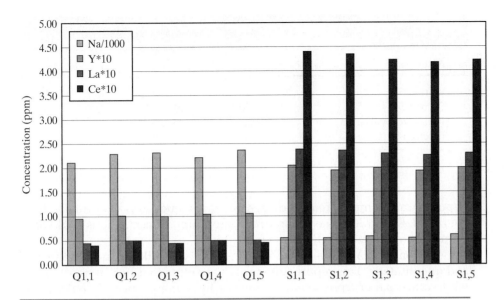

▲ **Figure 14.2** *Reproduced with permission from Spence, L. D., et al. "Comparison of the Elemental Composition of Office Document Paper: Evidence in a Homicide Case."* Journal of Forensic Sciences *47 (2002), 648–651. Copyright 2002, ASTM International.*

Table 14.1	**Hypothetical Paper Analysis (n = 1 for each sample)**		
Sample	Na (μg/g)	Al	Sr
Known (K)	2200	1000	18.2
Questioned (Q)	2450	1040	33.0

findings properly. Because no replicate analyses were performed, uncertainties are unknown, as is intrasample variability. Similarly, no data are provided to indicate the expected batch-to-batch or roll-to-roll variations.

For example, consider the following possibility: The observed variation in elemental concentrations shown in Table 14.1 may exceed the normal roll-to-roll variation within a plant, but not the normal batch-to-batch variation. Thus, the paper could have come from the same plant, but have been produced days or weeks apart. This hypothetical situation illustrates the caveats associated with low- and trace-level analyses of evidence. The lower the concentrations studied, the more likely it is that there will be greater variation. The same phenomenon occurs near the LOQ of a calibration curve. The lower the concentration, the higher will be the %RSD of replicates. Thus, any differences seen in the present paper analysis example must be interpreted in light of a complete understanding of what constitutes normal variations, no matter what the source of those variations. When uncertainties are known and taken into account (Table 14.2), interpretation is reliable and quantifiable. In this example, the strontium concentrations are telling: The variation indicates that the differences observed between the questioned and known samples cannot be attributed to expected variations, even from month to month. Does this mean that the two papers are different? At this point, our

Table 14.2	Hypothetical Paper Analysis Revisited (Uncertainty reported as percent RSD)		
Sample	**Na (μg/g)**	**Al**	**Sr**
K (n = 5)	2200 ($\pm$10%)	1000 ($\pm$10%)	18.2 ($\pm$0.1%)
Q (n = 5)	2450 ($\pm$10%)	1040 ($\pm$10%)	33.0 ($\pm$0.1%)
Roll-to-roll variation	<1%	<1%	<0.1%
Batch-to-batch variation	$\pm$20%	$\pm$3%	<0.1%

hypothetical example breaks down, since many questions would have to be answered. Regardless, the difference in strontium concentrations could be of significant value to investigators.

A second ICPMS analysis illustrates how variability can be addressed and quantitated.[3] This report summarizes attempts to differentiate standard white office paper from several countries by using elemental analysis and simple statistical techniques, such as the *t*-test between means (Section 2.2.3). The authors evaluated a number of important considerations, such as differences between monthly batches and different rolls of paper produced on the same day. The results are summarized in Figures 14.3–14.6. In all elements analyzed, there was no significant difference in elemental concentrations between handled and unhandled paper. When several elements were evaluated, differences were seen between batches on the same day, as illustrated by cluster analysis, but principally between the first batch and all others. Overlaps between batches 2, 3, and 4 are evident. Variations between monthly batches are illustrated by means of cluster analysis and *t*-test results. These data show that the expected variation between batches is greater than that between different rolls produced on the same day. Also, data indicate a change in processing in May compared with the other months. This report is an excellent example of the need for meticulous and complete analytical work. Such background data are indispensable to the evaluation of evidentiary value, be it of paper, fibers, or any other type of evidence, especially mass-produced items.

Like inks, paper ages in predictable ways. The time frame of that decay depends on many factors. Ink aging and dating were discussed in the previous

▶ **Figure 14.3** *From Spence, L. D., et al. "Characterization of Document Paper Using Elemental Compositions Determined by Inductively Coupled Plasma Mass Spectrometry."* Journal of Analytical Atomic Spectroscopy *15 (2000), 813–819. Reproduced by permission of The Royal Society of Chemistry.*

	Concentration in paper/μg g^{-1}		
	Handled	Unhandled	$t_{\text{statistic}}$
Element	(*n* = 5)	(*n* = 5)	(t_{critical} = 3.36)
Na	(2500 $\pm$ 200)	(2540 $\pm$ 110)	0.07
Mg	(800 $\pm$ 40)	(820 $\pm$ 20)	1.07
Al	(1030 $\pm$ 90)	(1050 $\pm$ 110)	0.33
Mn	(11.6 $\pm$ 0.7)	(11.4 $\pm$ 0.3)	0.55
Sr	(30.1 $\pm$ 0.9)	(29.5 $\pm$ 1.1)	0.95
Y	(0.521 $\pm$ 0.009)	(0.52 $\pm$ 0.03)	0.42
Zr	(18 $\pm$ 4)	(19 $\pm$ 4)	0.41
Ba	(3.3 $\pm$ 0.2)	(3.16 $\pm$ 0.14)	1.19
La	(0.64 $\pm$ 0.13)	(0.58 $\pm$ 0.04)	1.08
Ce	(1.07 $\pm$ 0.08)	(1.05 $\pm$ 0.09)	0.46

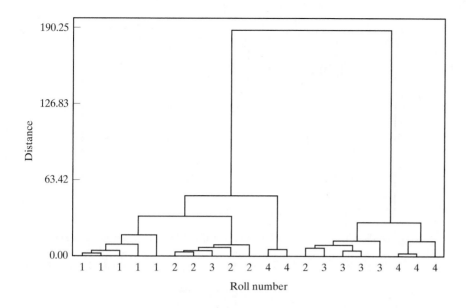

◀ **Figure 14.4** *From Spence, L. D., et al. "Characterization of Document Paper Using Elemental Compositions Determined by Inductively Coupled Plasma Mass Spectrometry."* Journal of Analytical Atomic Spectroscopy *15 (2000), 813–819. Reproduced by permission of The Royal Society of Chemistry.*

chapter. The aging of paper is an even more difficult analytical challenge. Paper ages principally as a result of the acid-driven hydrolytic breakdown of cellulose to glucose[5] that eventually produces yellowing and brittleness in the paper. The presence of additives such as aluminum, a Lewis acid, increases the acidity and further accelerates the process:

$$Al(H_2O)_6{}^{3+}(aq) \longleftrightarrow Al(H_2O)_6{}^{3+}(aq) + H^+(aq) \qquad pK_a \sim 5 \quad (14.1)$$

$$H^+ + cellulose \longrightarrow glucose \qquad (14.2)$$

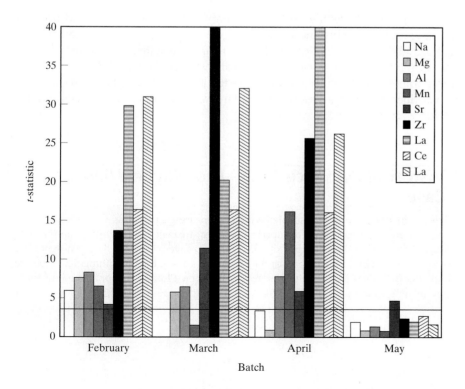

◀ **Figure 14.5** *From Spence, L. D., et al. "Characterization of Document Paper Using Elemental Compositions Determined by Inductively Coupled Plasma Mass Spectrometry."* Journal of Analytical Atomic Spectroscopy *15 (2000), 813–819. Reproduced by permission of The Royal Society of Chemistry.*

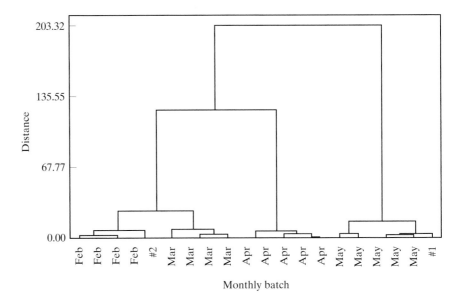

▶ **Figure 14.6** *From Spence, L. D., et al. "Characterization of Document Paper Using Elemental Compositions Determined by Inductively Coupled Plasma Mass Spectrometry."* Journal of Analytical Atomic Spectroscopy *15 (2000), 813–819. Reproduced by permission of The Royal Society of Chemistry.*

Cellulose also degrades via oxidation reactions with the atmosphere, creating more acidic products and perpetuating the cycle.[5] However, while dating papers and treating them to prevent deterioration has been of interest to historians, archaeologists, and conservators, not a great deal of forensic work has been done on dating relatively recent paper items.

14.2 FIBERS AND FORENSIC CHEMICAL ANALYSIS

Fibers—specifically, textile fibers—are common forms of transfer and trace evidence and are arguably the largest category of polymer evidence analyzed in forensic laboratories. Fibers are amenable to analysis with nearly every tool available to the forensic chemist, from optical instruments and PLM to microspectrophotometry and chromatography. As the arsenal of analytical tools available grows, fiber evidence is getting renewed interest from forensic chemists and trace evidence analysts.

Historical Evidence 14.2—The Wayne Williams Case

Starting in 1979, young black males were disappearing in Atlanta, Georgia, and their bodies were later discovered dumped in wooded areas or near highways and streets. Most of the victims died of asphyxiation. The bodies were found with a wealth of fiber evidence which indicated that all of the victims had spent the time immediately before and after their death in the same environment. When a local paper published information relating to the fiber findings, the killer began stripping his victims completely or

Historical Evidence 14.2—(Continued)

down to their undershorts and dumped some of the bodies into the Chattahoochee River. This change of pattern led to Williams's arrest in the early morning hours of May 22, 1981, as his car passed slowly over a bridge being watched by a surveillance team. Subsequent searches of his home and vehicles led to the discovery of the probable sources of the fibers, hair (from a family dog), and, most importantly, the greenish carpet fiber with an unusual cross section. Additional research eventually led to the probable manufacturer of the carpet and allowed the forensic analysts to estimate that this type of carpet would be found in only 1 in approximately 8,000 homes in the Atlanta area. When the particular combinations of fibers were considered, the odds of a random match were even smaller. Williams was tried for two of the murders, with evidence from ten more introduced; however, the suspicion remains that Williams may have killed others. In the absence of any other significant physical evidence, it was the totality of the fiber transfers and the combination of fibers found on the victims which could be linked to Williams that won the conviction.

Applying the Science 14.2   Dyes That Bind

The discussion of paper in this text illustrates the critical role that hydrogen bonding plays in the structure of paper and how such bonds form between cellulose fibers. Cellulose is also the fiber found in cotton. To color cotton fabric and fibers, the dye selected has to be able to associate irreversibly with the fiber. One report described a molecular-modeling study of the mechanism of association that occurs between cellulose and monoazo dyes. The authors based their approach in part on the model of how a drug interacts with a specific binding site, a topic mentioned in Chapter 6. Although the interaction between a dye and a cellulose fiber is less specific, the authors found the model to be a reasonable one. Not surprisingly, their work showed that the binding of the monoazo dyes to the cellulose fiber was dominated by polar interactions, principally of the dipole–dipole and hydrogen-bonding varieties.

Source: Timofei, S., and W. M. Fabian, "Comparative Molecular Field Analysis of Heterocyclic Monoazo Dye–Fiber Affinities," *Journal of Chemical Information and Computer Science* 38 (1998), 1218–1222.

Fibers are first classified as natural or synthetic, with rayon and reprocessed cellulose considered as part of the synthetic group. Natural fibers consist of materials such as wool, cotton, silk, hair (and furs), and mineral fibers such as asbestos. The synthetic fibers constitute the bulk of the categories of fibers that are of forensic interest, and these categories correspond to consumer textiles and fibers. The Federal Trade Commission (www.FTC.gov) has specified the classifications of consumer textile fibers, shown in Table 14.3. Graphical schemes and tree diagrams are also useful for classifying fiber, and an example is shown in Figure 14.7.

Several characteristics of fibers are targeted by forensic analysis. As shown in Figure 14.8, the chemical composition of the fiber is just one of many important characteristics. The diameter and cross section are useful for determining how a fiber is used. For example, carpet fibers are relatively thick and often have hollowed-out cross sections compared with those of fibers used in clothing. Cotton fibers have a characteristic flat ribbon geometry. Fiber color and how it

Table 14.3   Rules and Regulations under the Textile Fiber Productions Identification Act (16 CFR Part 303, § 303.7, Generic Names and Definitions for Manufactured Fibers)

Name	Description	Monomers/structures
Acrylic	"A manufactured fiber in which the fiber-forming substance is any long chain synthetic polymer composed of at least 85 percent by weight of acrylonitrile units"	$(-CH_2-CH-)$ $\quad\quad\quad\; CN$
Modacrylic	"A manufactured fiber in which the fiber-forming substance is any long chain synthetic polymer composed of less than 85 percent but at least 35 percent by weight of acrylonitrile units"	$(-CH_2-CH-)_n$ $\quad\quad\quad\; CN$
Polyester	"A manufactured fiber in which the fiber-forming substance is any long chain synthetic polymer composed of at least 85% by weight of an ester of a substituted aromatic carboxylic acid, including but not restricted to substituted terephthalate units."	$p(-R-O-C-C_4H_4-C-O-)_n$ $\quad\quad\quad\quad\;\; O \quad\quad\quad\; O$ and para substituted hydroxy-benzoate units, $p(-R-O-C_4H_4-C-O-)_n$ $\quad\quad\quad\quad\quad\quad\;\; O$
	"Where the fiber is formed by the interaction of two or more chemically distinct polymers (of which none exceeds 85% by weight), and contains ester groups as the dominant functional unit (at least 85% by weight of the total polymer content of the fiber), and which, if stretched at least 100%, durably and rapidly reverts substantially to its unstretched length when the tension is removed, the term *elasterell-p* may be used as a generic description of the fiber."	
Rayon	"A manufactured fiber composed of regenerated cellulose, as well as manufactured fibers composed of regenerated cellulose in which substituents have replaced not more than 15 percent of the hydrogens of the hydroxyl groups."	
	"Where the fiber is composed of cellulose precipitated from an organic solution in which no substitution of the hydroxyl groups takes place and no chemical intermediates are formed, the term *lyocell* may be used as a generic description of the fiber."	
Acetate	"A manufactured fiber in which the fiber-forming substance is cellulose acetate. Where not less than 92 percent of the hydroxyl groups are acetylated, the term *triacetate* may be used as a generic description of the fiber."	

Table 14.3 (Continued)

Name	Description	Monomers/structures
Saran	"A manufactured fiber in which the fiber-forming substance is any long chain synthetic polymer composed of at least 80 percent by weight of vinylidene chloride units ($-CH_2-CCl_2-$)."	
Azlon	"A manufactured fiber in which the fiber-forming substance is composed of any regenerated naturally occurring proteins."	
Nytril	"A manufactured fiber containing at least 85 percent of a long chain polymer of vinylidene dinitrile ($-CH_2-C(CN)_2-$) where the vinylidene dinitrile content is no less than every other unit in the polymer chain."	
Nylon	"A manufactured fiber in which the fiber-forming substance is a long-chain synthetic polyamide in which less than 85 percent of the amide linkages are attached directly to two aromatic rings."	
Rubber	"A manufactured fiber in which the fiber-forming substance is comprised of natural or synthetic rubber, including the following categories: (1) A manufactured fiber in which the fiber-forming substance is a hydrocarbon such as natural rubber, polyisoprene, polybutadiene, copolymers of dienes and hydrocarbons, or amorphous (noncrystalline) polyolefins." "(2) A manufactured fiber in which the fiber-forming substance is a copolymer of acrylonitrile and a diene (such as butadiene) composed of not more than 50 percent but at least 10 percent by weight of acrylonitrile units. The term *lastrile* may be used as a generic description for fibers falling within this category." "(3) A manufactured fiber in which the fiber-forming substance is a polychloroprene or a copolymer of chloroprene in which at least 35 percent by weight of the fiber-forming substance is composed of chloroprene units."	
Spandex	"A manufactured fiber in which the fiber-forming substance is a long chain synthetic polymer comprised of at least 85 percent of a segmented polyurethane."	
Vinal	"A manufactured fiber in which the fiber-forming substance is any long chain synthetic polymer composed of at least 50 percent by weight of vinyl alcohol units ($-CH_2-CHOH-$), and in which the total of the vinyl alcohol units and any one or more of the various acetal units is at least 85 percent by weight of the fiber."	
Olefin	"A manufactured fiber in which the fiber-forming substance is any long chain synthetic polymer composed of at least 85 percent by weight of ethylene, propylene, or other olefin units, except amorphous (noncrystalline) polyolefins qualifying under paragraph (j)(1) of this section. Where the fiber-forming substance is a cross-linked synthetic polymer, with low but significant crystallinity, composed of at	

Table 14.3 (Continued)

Name	Description	Monomers/structures
	least 95 percent by weight of ethylene and at least one other olefin unit, and the fiber is substantially elastic and heat resistant, the term *lastol* may be used as a generic description of the fiber."	
Vinyon	"A manufactured fiber in which the fiber-forming substance is any long chain synthetic polymer composed of at least 85 percent by weight of vinyl chloride units ($-CH_2-CHCl-$)."	
Metallic	"A manufactured fiber composed of metal, plastic-coated metal, metal-coated plastic, or a core completely covered by metal."	
Glass	"A manufactured fiber in which the fiber-forming substance is glass."	
Anidex	"A manufactured fiber in which the fiber-forming substance is any long chain synthetic polymer composed of at least 50 percent by weight of one or more esters of a monohydric alcohol and acrylic acid, $CH_2=CH-COOH$."	
Novoloid	"A manufactured fiber containing at least 85 percent by weight of a cross-linked novolac. Novolac is an epoxide phenolic formaldehyde resin."	
Aramid	"A manufactured fiber in which the fiber-forming substance is a long-chain synthetic polyamide in which at least 85 percent of the amide linkages are attached directly to two aromatic rings."	$\left[\!\!\begin{array}{c} C-NH \\ \| \\ O \end{array}\!\!\right]$
Sulfar	"A manufactured fiber in which the fiber-forming substance is a long chain synthetic polysulfide in which at least 85% of the sulfide ($-S-$) linkages are attached directly to two (2) aromatic rings."	
PBI	"A manufactured fiber in which the fiber-forming substance is a long chain aromatic polymer having reoccurring imidazole groups as an integral part of the polymer chain."	
Elastoester	"A manufactured fiber in which the fiber-forming substance is a long-chain synthetic polymer composed of at least 50% by weight of aliphatic polyether and at least 35% by weight of polyester, as defined in § 303.7(c)."	
Melamine	"A manufactured fiber in which the fiber-forming substance is a synthetic polymer composed of at least 50% by weight of a cross-linked melamine polymer."	
Fluoropolymer	"A manufactured fiber containing at least 95% of a long-chain polymer synthesized from aliphatic fluorocarbon monomers"	
PLA	"A manufactured fiber in which the fiber-forming substance is composed of at least 85% by weight of lactic acid ester units derived from naturally occurring sugars."	

Source: http://www.fibersource.com/Fiber.html (downloaded December 2004). This is a comprehensive source of information and links for fibers and synthetic materials.

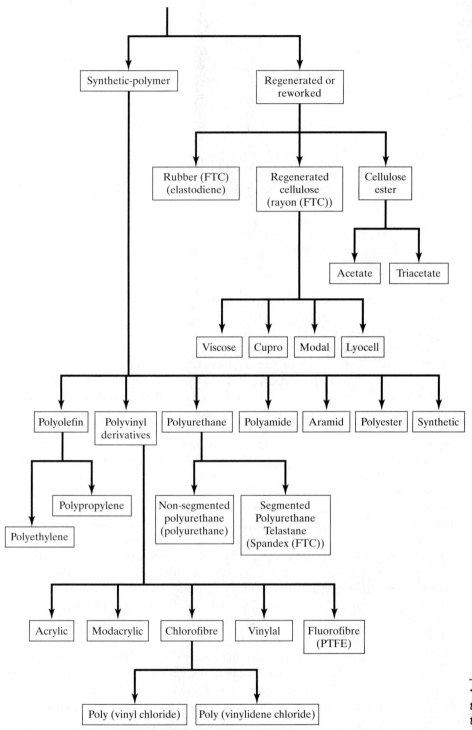

◀ **Figure 14.7** *Example of a tree diagram for the classification of synthetic fibers.*

is applied also constitutes important information. A red fiber colored by a vat dye differs from a red fiber colored with a cationic, surface-attached dye, for example. Many fibers have treated surfaces. Shiny fibers may be treated with delustering agents such as TiO_2. Fibers can be roughened or weathered as well. Because the morphology and appearance of a fiber provide so much information, most forensic analysis of fibers or textiles begins with microscopic study

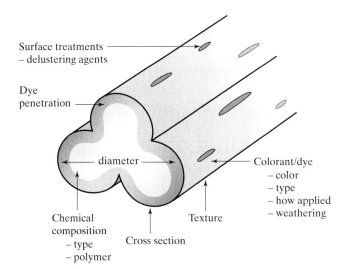

Surface treatments
– delustering agents

Dye
penetration

diameter

Colorant/dye
– color
– type
– how applied
– weathering

Chemical
composition
– type
– polymer

Cross section

Texture

▶ **Figure 14.8** *Analytical "handles" on a fiber.*

and polarizing light microscopy. In many cases, PLM alone is sufficient to chemically identify the fiber and determine its likely use (in clothing, in carpeting, as an automotive interior, etc.).

Among the various guides that provide an overview of fiber analysis are the SWGMAT "Forensic Fiber Examination Guide"[6] and the ASTM "Standard Guide for Microscopic Examination of Textile Fibers."[7] As shown in Figure 14.9, fiber examination begins with microscopy. Beyond PLM, analytical schemes and approaches vary widely. A recent survey[8] compiled lists of techniques used in fiber analysis around the world and reported (not surprisingly) that PLM was used nearly universally.[†] Comparison microscopes are also widely used and consist of two stages linked by an optical bridge. This design, similar to that of the reflecting comparison microscopes used to examine bullets, cartridge casings, and other toolmarks, allows for side-by-side comparisons of different fibers. Fluorescent microscopy is common in Europe, but is used by less than half the responding laboratories in the United States. **Hot-stage microscopy**, employed to determine melting points, is used in about 75% of laboratories, as is FTIR microspectrophotometry. GCMS and pyrolysis GC are also frequently utilized. It is no surprise that nondestructive or minimally destructive instrumental tests are increasingly favored over destructive methods such as solubility testing. However, the most powerful single instrument for fiber analysis remains the microscope.

14.2.1 MICROSCOPY

Optical properties are often sufficient to classify fibers by chemical composition as per Figure 14.9. Skilled examiners can quickly distinguish natural fibers such as cotton, wool, or silk from synthetics. Within the synthetics group, many can be classified on the basis of the following optical and physical properties:[7]

1. *General morphology.* The general appearance of a fiber under magnification provides information on the fiber's surface texture, striations, finishing and damage, and surface particulates. Delustering agents are small particulates (typically, less than a micrometer in size) found on the fiber surface. TiO_2 and a number of other materials may be used for delustering. Fibers may also have void areas and inclusions. If pigments are used for colorants,

[†]This survey raises the question as to why two laboratories did not use PLM.

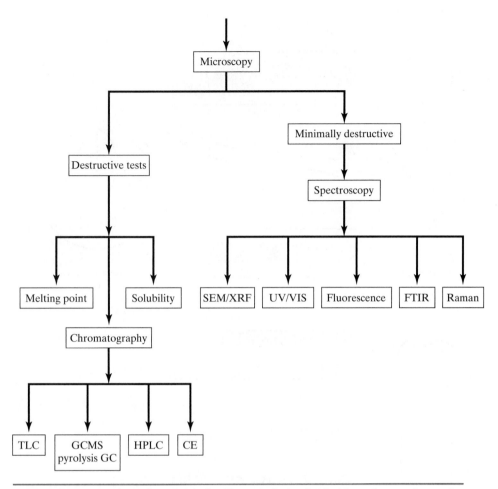

▲ **Figure 14.9** *Analytical methods for fiber analysis, divided into destructive and non- or minimally destructive methods.*

they will be seen as granules, whereas dyes will penetrate the fiber to some degree. Preliminary morphological examinations require that the fiber be in air or mounted in a medium with a refractive index sufficiently different from that of the fiber to provide good contrast and facilitate easy viewing. Bright-field illumination and PLM are both used at this stage.

2. *Cross-section and diameter.* Cross-sectioning of a fiber or fibers is an inherently difficult task, but a necessary one. The cross-sectional shape is another classifier and discriminator that can be added to the chemical class. Figure 14.10 shows some examples of cross sections and how they appear from above. With practice, an analyst can often determine the cross section of a fiber by its appearance from above by the shading and by appearance under plane polarized light. Under bright-field illumination (transmittance), the thicker the fiber, the darker it appears. Under polarized light, retardation (Section 5.1) and thus interference colors correlate with thickness and can be read in a way similar to reading a topographic map, where color can be used to illustrate elevation. The diameter of the fiber is noted with micrometers and calibrated optics, and quantities such as the modification ratio (Figure 14.10) of trilobal fibers can also be calculated.[9]

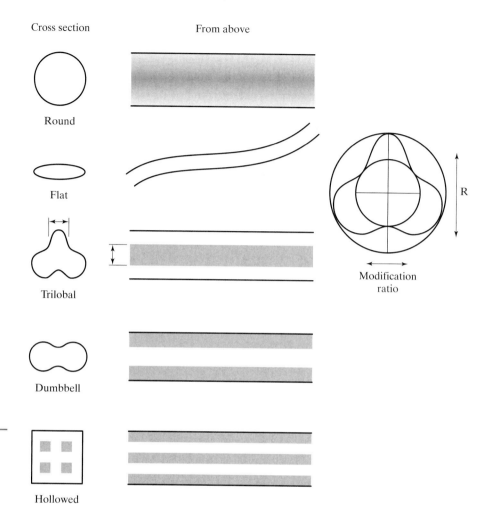

Cross section   From above

Round

Flat

Trilobal

Dumbbell

Hollowed

R

Modification ratio

▶ **Figure 14.10** *Example of fiber cross sections. To the right, the method of measuring the modification ratio is shown.*

3. *Dichroism and pleochroism.* Recall that a dichroic material appears to have two different colors, depending on the orientation of the material. This is the result of different absorbances in the visible range at different orientations. Two-colored materials are dichroic; if there are more than two colors, the material is pleochroic. Pleochroism is observed via a polarizing light microscope, with the polarizer in, but the analyzer out. Rotating a fiber on the stage will show whether it changes color. Recall that this is not the same phenomenon as birefringence, which refers to differences in refractive index as a function of orientation.

4. *Isotropy and anisotropy.* Materials with no repeating crystal structure, such as glass, have only one refractive index and are classified as isotropic. Anisotropic materials show a different refractive index depending on their orientation, and the difference is attributable to the crystalline or pseudocrystalline nature of the substance being observed. Cotton contains cellulosic polymers and ordered regions such as those shown in Figure 13.21–13.23. As a result, cotton has areas in the fiber where interference colors are observed. However, since these areas are dispersed randomly throughout the fiber, there is no consistent pattern. By contrast, most synthetic fibers have a more consistent ordering and will demonstrate a different refractive index, depending on the orientation of the fiber.

The more crystal-like the polymer structure, the more dramatic is the difference. Note, however, that some fibers, such as the nytrils and triacetates, have small or no detectable difference related to orientation, a valuable observation for classification.

5. *Refractive index and birefringence.* The refractive index of a fiber is found by using different mounting media with different indices of refraction. The **Becke line** technique is a simple method that involves placing the fiber in a mounting medium of a known refractive index—for example, 1.525. Under transmission illumination, the image of the fiber is brought into focus and then the objective is slowly raised. A line will appear to move into the medium (fiber or mounting medium) with the higher refractive index. If the sample's RI is greater than 1.525 (in this example) the Becke line will appear to move into the sample. By using different mounting media and repeated experimentation, the RI of the sample can be bracketed into a small range. If the sample is birefringent, the same technique is used, but the RI is observed in two orientations, first with the long axis of the fiber parallel to that of the polarizer ($n_{\parallel}$) and then rotated so that the long axis is perpendicular to the polarizer ($n_{\perp}$). This process is illustrated in Figure 14.11. Birefringence is calculated as follows:

$$\Gamma = n_{\parallel} - n_{\perp} \tag{14.3}$$

The symbol B or Bi is sometimes used in place of gamma.

6. *Sign of elongation.* The sign of elongation of a birefringent material is determined by comparing $n_{\parallel}$ and $n_{\perp}$. If $n_{\parallel}$ is greater than $n_{\perp}$, the sign of elongation is positive ($+$); if the reverse is true, the sign is negative ($-$). **Compensators**, described in the next section, can also be used to determine the sign of elongation.

7. *Interference colors.* The observations described up to now in this list are obtained with the source light polarized, but the analyzer left out of the optical path. Inserting the analyzer provides additional information and confirmation.[†] If the fiber is isotropic, the field will appear black. Anisotropic materials will show interference colors, the pattern of which is used to determine thickness and birefringence. When a fiber is mounted and rotated, it shows maximum contrast at certain rotation angles and it disappears into the black field of view at other rotation angles. The angle at which the fiber is invisible is called the *extinction angle*, and it repeats every 90° of rotation, as shown in Figure 14.12. At the point of maximum contrast (45°), the colors observed in the fiber are called the **interference colors** and should not be confused with the true color of the fiber. A colorless nylon fiber will show vivid interference colors because of the way polarized light interacts with the pseudocrystalline nature of the fiber, not because of the way the fiber absorbs or reflects visible light.

   Figure 14.13 illustrates how interference colors are formed. If polarized light enters a fiber and vibrates in a plane parallel to the light's long axis, the light is unaffected and the field of view remains dark. However, at orientations other than parallel, the polarized light is split into two

---

[†]When the analyzer and polarizer are in the optical path and are oriented at 90° to each other, this is called "crossed polars."

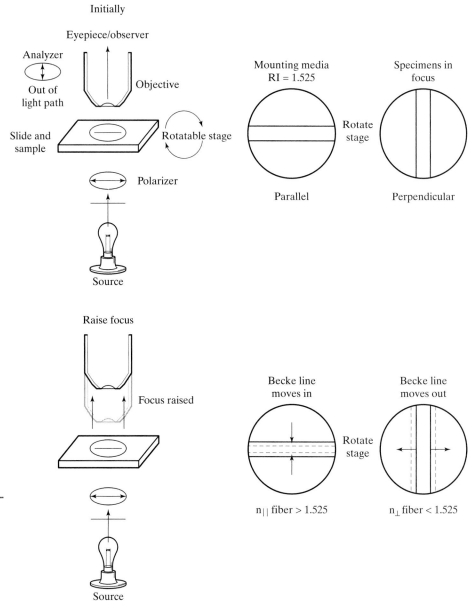

▶ **Figure 14.11** *The Becke line method of determining a material's relative refractive index. When the focus is moved upward, the Becke line moves into the medium with the higher RI.*

components that vibrate perpendicular to each other along the axes. The two components are referred to as Fast (F) and Slow (S). In one direction, the light encounters a higher density of atoms than in the other and thus is slowed to a greater extent than light that encounters a lower density of atoms. In effect, the fiber acts as a beam splitter,[10] and two rays—one fast and one slow—emerge out of phase by a distance R called the **retardation**. When the two rays recombine at the analyzer, they interfere, producing colors that are visible under crossed polars. These colors can be related to crystal structure and to thickness, because the thicker the material, the greater is the retardation.

Recall our discussion of interferometry as related to FTIR in Section 5.2.5. The interferogram is produced by splitting a beam of infrared energy into two components. As the mirror moves back, the distance that one beam travels is farther than the distance traveled by the other beam. In this way,

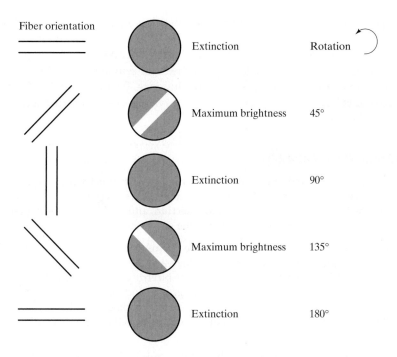

Fiber orientation

Extinction — Rotation

Maximum brightness — 45°

Extinction — 90°

Maximum brightness — 135°

Extinction — 180°

◀ **Figure 14.12** *Anisotropic fiber under crossed polars. When the long axis of the fiber is parallel to the polarizer, the fiber disappears into the black background. Rotated 45°, the fiber shows the brightest interference colors.*

one beam is fast and one slow and an interference pattern results when the two beams recombine. The same principle is at work here; the difference is in how one beam is slowed relative to the other.

Interference colors coupled to fiber diameter can be used to obtain birefringence without resorting to the use of different mounting media. This is accomplished with a **Michel-Levy chart**, shown in the color insert, and microscope accessories called **compensators or wave plates**. Recall that a birefringent material breaks polarized light into a fast and a slow component. The thicker the sample, the greater is the offset. Suppose a fiber is rotated such that interference colors are at their most vivid and

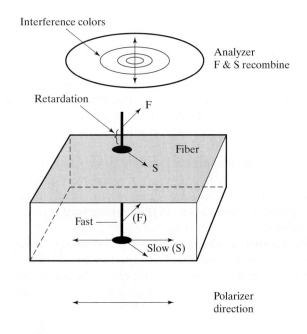

Interference colors

Analyzer
F & S recombine

Retardation

F

Fiber

S

Fast — (F)

Slow (S)

Polarizer direction

◀ **Figure 14.13** *How a pseudocrystalline fiber produces interference colors. The degree of retardation, measured in nm, refers to how far the slow component lags behind the fast component when polarized light emerges from the fiber oriented with the long axis parallel to the polarizer.*

appear as a pinkish red. Using the Michel-Levy chart, we see that this corresponds to a wavelength of 630 nm. If the fiber is circular with a diameter of 50 μm, the birefringence of the fiber is approximately 0.014. Note that the intersection of the thickness and the color wavelength defines the origin of a vector that points to the birefringence. From the Michel-Levy chart, it is clear that any combination of two pieces of information can yield the third.

Example Problem 14.1

A nylon fiber is studied in different mounting media and is found to have a parallel refractive index ($n_\parallel$) of 1.575 and a perpendicular refractive index ($n_\perp$) of 1.525. The fiber is found to have a circular cross section, and under PLM the center of the fiber appears to be a vivid green. What is the diameter of the fiber?

Answer: The two refractive indices provide the information necessary to obtain the birefringence value of 0.050 (the difference between the two). With this information and the Michel-Levy chart, the vector from the birefringence value (on the right y-axis) is retraced until it intersects the vivid green band with a central value of 840 nm. Moving directly across to the left intersects at a thickness of ~20 μm or slightly less. Because the cross section is circular, the thickness is the same as the diameter.

Compensators are used in this context when the difference between fast and slow components is relatively small. On the Michel-Levy chart, there is a large band to the left where the interference colors are whitish and not very informative. A compensator adds a constant offset to the small offset created by the fiber. The labels on the bottom of the chart correspond to fixed offsets that can be added to increase the contrast. A compensator is a crystal that is inserted in the light path after the sample, but before the polarizer. Compensators are labeled by the amount of offset they add. A full wave-plate compensator adds 550 nm, for example, corresponding to the x-axis labels on the Michel-Levy chart. A quarter wave plate would add 137.5 nm. A full wave-plate compensator is also called a first-order red compensator, because of the red color it imparts to the background under crossed polars.

An example of the use of a full wave-plate compensator is presented in Figure 14.14. A fiber with retardation R of 100 nm is observed under crossed polars. The fiber would show a barely distinguishable white interference color. The same would be true of a fiber with an R of 300 nm. A compensator is simply a crystal with a known R value that, when inserted into the light path, provides further separation between the F and S components. In other words, a constant is added to both. In this example, the total retardation for the first fiber shown in Frame A of Figure 14.14 is now 650 nm, corresponding to a purplish pink on the Michel-Levy chart. The second fiber displays green–blue interference colors with a total retardation of 850 nm. Note that the background color when the compensator is in changes from black to magenta, corresponding to the 550-nm offset added by the compensator alone. Compensators with increasing thickness can be progressively inserted until the best contrast is observed; these devices are referred to as *compensation wedges*.

Finally, compensators are useful for determining the sign of elongation. To do so, a birefringent fiber is oriented so that it is 45° off extinction, or at maximum brightness, under crossed polars. The compensator is inserted and the results are observed. If the sign of elongation is positive ($n_\parallel$ is greater than $n_\perp$), the retardation is additive, since the difference between

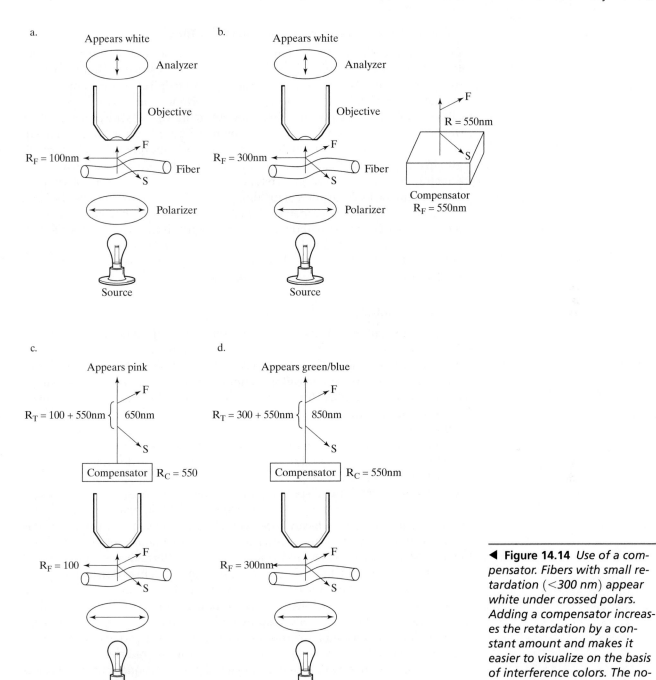

a.

Appears white

Analyzer

Objective

$R_F = 100nm$ F   Fiber   S

Polarizer

Source

b.

Appears white

Analyzer

Objective

$R_F = 300nm$ F   Fiber   S

Polarizer

Source

F   R = 550nm   S

Compensator
$R_F = 550nm$

c.

Appears pink

F

$R_T = 100 + 550nm$ { 650nm

S

Compensator $R_C = 550$

$R_F = 100$ F   S

Source

d.

Appears green/blue

F

$R_T = 300 + 550nm$ { 850nm

S

Compensator $R_C = 550nm$

$R_F = 300nm$ F   S

Source

◀ **Figure 14.14** *Use of a compensator. Fibers with small retardation (<300 nm) appear white under crossed polars. Adding a compensator increases the retardation by a constant amount and makes it easier to visualize on the basis of interference colors. The notation "Rf" refers to retardation factor.*

F and S rays emerging from the fiber add to that of the compensator. If the sign of elongation is negative, the 550-nm offset from the compensator is subtracted from the R of the fiber.

Skillful use of PLM, compensators, and calibrated optics (for measurement) are sufficient to determine the key optical features of a fiber, such as its dimensions, morphology, RI, birefringence, and sign of elongation, without resorting to multiple mountings and repetitive experiments.

14.2.2 MELTING POINTS AND SOLUBILITY TESTING

Melting points of fibers have become easier to determine with the advent of accurately controlled heated microscope stages. Melting is destructive, but with a microscope, the amount of sample that is destroyed is small. The melting point of any substance is correlated with its structure and intermolecular forces. In polymers, melting occurs when the polymer chains are able to move and slide past each other to the point of liquefaction. However, as shown in Figure 13.5, the transition to liquid may not be simple to discern. Fibers that are more amorphous will go through a gumlike stage before truly melting, whereas fibers that are more crystalline will transit through a "gooey" stage. Careful observation, along with control samples, greatly aids in the interpretation of melting points. Also, as shown in Table 14.4, not all synthetic fibers melt at temperatures that are available on a hot-stage accessory. Others char or decompose without moving through a discernible liquid stage. Solubility testing is available for fibers, but as more advanced nondestructive tests become available, it is being used less and less. Common solvents employed are dimethylformamide (DMF), cyclohexanone, and nitromethane.[11]

14.2.3 CHROMATOGRAPHY

As applied to synthetic fibers, chromatographic techniques target the polymer, colorants, or other chemical treatments. Like solubility and melting-point tests, chromatographic analysis is destructive, but it provides significantly more information than those instruments afford. Thin-layer chromatography is used much the same as was described for inks: to evaluate the colorants used in the fiber. Typically, the colorants are extracted inside a capillary tube with the use of solvents dictated by the type of fiber involved.[12] Accordingly, the fiber must first be examined microscopically and classified by type of polymer. If this were not done first, analysts might find themselves inadvertently performing a fiber solubility test. The generic classes of dyes most commonly encountered in fibers and textiles are acid, base, dispersive, and metallized. Others, including indigos and pigmented dyes, are not easily extracted.[12] ASTM Standard E 2227-02 provides a summary of TLC techniques, extraction systems, and solvent systems that are useful with fibers and bulk textiles.[12] Another source of information is the SWGMAT fiber analysis guidelines.[6] A natural alternative to TLC is liquid chromatography (HPLC), which can be coupled to UV/VIS and mass spectrometer detectors.[13] To date, however, this technique has not been widely used, given the cost of the instrumentation and complexity of the analysis. Recently, a microextraction followed by electrospray ionization mass spectrometry was applied to acidic dyes found in nylons. The technique shows promise, but uses instrumentation that is not widely available to forensic laboratories.

Currently, the most widely used chromatographic technique in fiber analysis is **pyrolysis gas chromatography** (Py-GC).[11,14,15] Pyrolysis is forced thermal decomposition in an inert environment, producing decomposition products. An FID detector produces a pattern analogous to the patterns produced by accelerants and used to classify the fiber. More information is provided when a mass spectrometer is the detector. Under pyrolysis, monomers, dimers, and other small polymer fragments, as well as thermal degradation products, may be isolated. A sample pyrogram of a polymer containing styrene and butyl acrylate copolymers is shown in Figure 14.15. Note the presence of monomers, dimers, and trimers correlated with the blocks of styrene (S) and butyl acetate (B). Py-GC-MS has been used to distinguish two poly(methyl methacrylate)s with identical polymer backbones differing only in how they were made; one was synthesized via radical polymerization, the other by anionic polymerization.[16] Py-GC-MS has also been used to identify and

Table 14.4 Optical Properties and Melting Points of Selected Synthetic Fibers

Polymer	Subtype	MP range C	$n_\parallel$	$n_\perp$	Birefringence	Sign of elongation
Acetate	Diacetate	250–260	1.474–1.479	1.473–1.477	0.002–0.005	+
Acetate	Triacetate	288–300	1.469–1.472	1.468–1.472	0.000–0.001	+, −
Acrylonitrile	Acrylic	No melt	1.510–1.520	1.512–1.525	0.001–0.005	−
Acrylonitrile	Modacrylic Verel	No melt	1.538–1.539	1.538–1.539	0.000–0.001	+
Aramid	Kevlar	425	2.050–2.350	1.641–1.646	0.200–0.710	+
Aramid	Nomex	371	1.800–1.900	1.664–1.680	0.120–0.230	+
Azlon		265–275				
Cellulosic	Cupro	No melt	1.548–1.562	1.519–1.528	0.021–0.037	+
Cellulosic	Lyocell	No melt	1.562–1.564	1.520–1.522	0.044	+
Cellulosic	Rayon	No melt	1.541–1.549	1.520–1.521	0.020–0.028	+
Fluorofiber (Teflons)		280–300; some decompose	1.389	1.35	0.039	+
Glass		No melt				Isotropic 1.541–1.552
Novoloid		No melt	1.649	1.649	0.000–0.002	−
Nylon	1	182–186	1.553	1.507	0.046	+
Nylon	6	210–230	1.568–1.583	1.525–1.526	0.049–0.061	+
Nylon	6,6	250–264	1.577–1.582	1.515–1.526	0.056–0.063	+
Nytril		218	1.464–1.480	1.464–1.480		−
Olefin	Polyethylene	120–138	1.568–1.574	1.518–1.522	0.050–0.052	+
Olefin	Polypropylene	160–175	1.520–1.530	1.491–1.496	0.028–0.034	+
Polyester	PBT	221–222	1.688	1.538–1.540	0.148–0.150	+
Polyester	PCDT	282–290	1.632–1.642	1.543–1.542	0.098–0.102	+
Polyester	PET	250–270	1.699–1.710	1.535–1.546	0.147–0.175	+
Saran		150–176	1.599–1.610	1.607–1.618	0.008	−
Vinal			1.540–1.547	1.510–1.522	0.025–0.030	+
Vinyon (chlorofibers)	PVC	No melt	1.527–1.541	1.524–1.536	0.002–0.005	+

Sources: 1. Gaudette, B. R., "The Forensic Aspects of Textile Fiber Examination," in R. Saferstein (ed.), *Forensic Science Handbook, Volume II* (Upper Saddle River, NJ: Prentice Hall, 1988).
2. Palenik, S. J., "Microscopical Examination of Fibres," in J. Robertson and M. C. Grieve, *Forensic Examination of Fibres*, 2d ed. (London: Taylor and Francis, 1999).

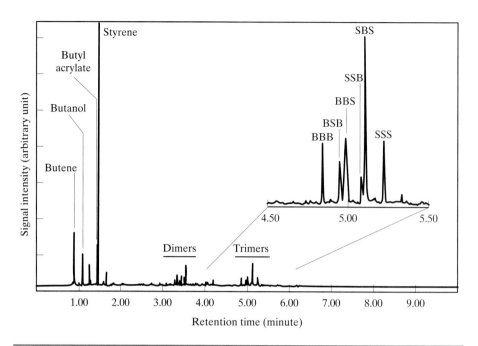

▲ **Figure 14.15** *An example of a pyrogram obtained by pyrolysis GCMS of a copolymer. The insert shows blocks of the copolymer. Reproduced with permission from Wang, F. C.-Y., "Characterization of a Polymeric Chain by Pyrolysis Gas Chromatography and Computer Simulation,"* Macromolecules 33 (2000), 2437–2445. *Copyright 2000 by the American Chemical Society.*

quantitate cross-linking moieties in poly(vinylpyrrolidone).[17] Thus, although pyrolysis techniques provide a variety of information, concerns have been raised over their reproducibility, particularly as regards the conditions of pyrolysis;[12,15] also, the information provided is typically the same as that which can be derived from nondestructive FTIR analysis. As microspectrophotometric techniques continue to improve, it is likely that pyrolysis techniques will be used less frequently.

14.2.4 SPECTROSCOPY AND MICROSPECTROSCOPY

Next to PLM, IR spectroscopy (principally, micro-IR) makes up the most important family of techniques in fiber analysis. As with PLM, IR spectroscopy is minimally destructive or nondestructive and is useful on even the smallest fiber fragments. Microspectrophotometry (MSP) probes the chemical identification of the synthetic fiber, colorants, and other treatments. MSP is indispensable in the comparative analysis of questioned and known fibers, the central task of most forensic fiber analysis cases. The caveat is that such comparisons require knowledge of typical inter- and intrasample variation. Consider, for example, a pair of blue jeans; typically, fibers from along the seams and hems are worn compared with fibers to other portions of the garment. Also, the source from which a sample is obtained will clearly affect any visible spectra and color analysis. Along a single fiber, characteristics of a dye or colorant will vary as well. Such inherent variations must be factored into any conclusions drawn from a comparative analysis, be it of dye or chemical composition.

The three types of MSP used in fiber analysis are visible (and, to a lesser extent, UV), FTIR, and, increasingly, Raman. Fluorescence techniques sometimes also play a role.

UV/VIS: The topic of colorants and color analysis was introduced in the previous chapter; textiles represent one of the most important forensic applications of colorant chemistry and analysis. Colorant analysis and comparison and the use of chromaticity coordinates were discussed in detail in the previous chapter; all are applicable to fibers. The plotting of CIELAB coordinates is useful in comparing colors and shades. Some fibers are metameric, meaning that their color will appear different under different illuminants. Textiles are often designed to have this property. Metameric fibers perceived as being the same color are distinguished by different UV/VIS spectra.

Fibers are colored principally by dyes. Pigments are seen occasionally and appear under the microscope as particulates similar to delusterants, but usually more densely applied than the delustering agents. The dyes used to color fibers vary with the nature of the polymer. Common types of dyes in textiles are reactive, direct, vat, azoic, sulfur, acidic, dispersive, and basic dyes,[18,19] essentially the gamut of dye classes. The chemical interactions that hold dyes to fibers are the typical group of intermolecular forces: hydrogen bonds, van der Waals forces, hydrophobic interactions, and covalent bonding.[20] Reactive dyes bond covalently to the substrate, for example, and there can be more than one type of interaction fixing a dye molecule to a fiber. Dye molecules are transferred to the fiber "phase" by a solvent, either liquid or gas.[20] Further treatments may follow to ensure that the dye will not be soluble in water. A simplified depiction of the dyeing process is shown in Figure 14.16. Note that the only irreversible step in the process is the final step, which immobilizes the dye in the fiber. Depending on the immersion time and other factors, the dye may not penetrate far into the fiber. Finally, one must be cognizant of the fact that the color of a fiber is often the result of a combination of dyes rather than a single dye.

The interesting and challenging aspect of colorant analysis in fibers is often the size of the exhibit, which may be as little as a lone fragment of a single fiber. It is a simple task to obtain a UV/VIS spectrum on a swatch of fabric with an

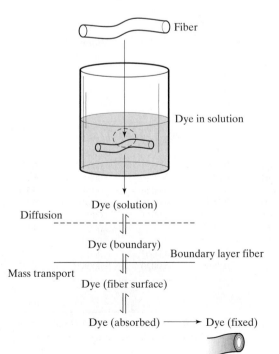

◀ **Figure 14.16** *Processes involved in dyeing. The dye must first reach the fiber surface and then penetrate it to be absorbed. A fixing stage may or may not be used.*

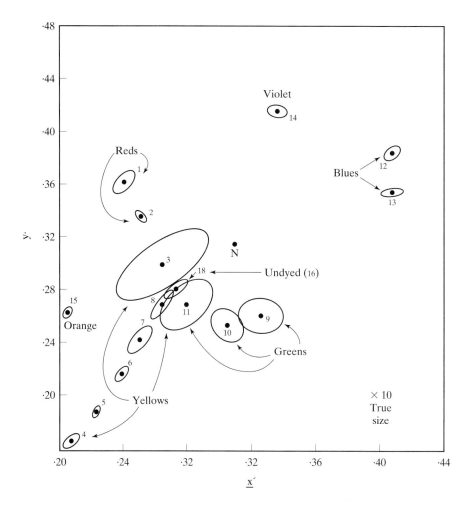

▶ **Figure 14.17** *Example of uncertainty ellipses around the chromaticity coordinates obtained from fibers treated with a single dye. Sample identifiers are found in the next figure. Reproduced with permission from Hartshorne, A. W., and D. K. Laing, "The Definition of Colour for Single Textile Fibers by Microspectrophotometry,"* Forensic Science International *34 (1987), 107–129.*

Identification		Dye conc. %	Mean complementary chromaticity coordinates		Error ellipse		
			x´	*y´*	*Major axis length*	*Minor axis length*	*Angle to X-axis*
1.	Disperse red 302	3.0	0.2426	0.3603	0.0018	0.0009	57.8
2.		1.0	0.2527	0.3357	0.0008	0.0005	−72.1
3.		0.2	0.2651	0.3011	0.0073	0.0031	49.1
4.	Disperse yellow 3	3.0	0.2118	0.1646	0.0012	0.0005	45.1
5.		1.0	0.2258	0.1882	0.0008	0.0003	71.8
6.		0.5	0.2411	0.2172	0.0012	0.0004	60.6
7.		0.2	0.2535	0.2430	0.0025	0.0005	63.2
8.		0.05	0.2651	0.2689	0.0026	0.0003	62.2
9.	Disperse green*	3.0	0.3261	0.2609	0.0026	0.0025	89.9
10.		1.0	0.3053	0.2532	0.0026	0.0011	−66.6
11.		0.2	0.2804	0.2687	0.0046	0.0024	54.2
12.	Disperse blue 3	3.0	0.4059	0.3829	0.0011	0.0006	48.0
13.	Disperse blue 7	3.0	0.4068	0.3537	0.0011	0.0003	14.8
14.	Disperse violet 1	3.0	0.3361	0.4194	0.0013	0.0009	−8.2
15.	Disperse orange 3	3.0	0.2047	0.2592	0.0007	0.0004	57.8
16.	Undyed fiber	—	0.2712	0.2808	0.0020	0.0006	42.7

* Color index generic name unknown

▲ **Figure 14.18** *Identifiers for the previous figure. Reproduced with permission from Hartshorne, A. W., and D. K. Laing, "The Definition of Colour for Single Textile Fibers by Microspectrophotometry,"* Forensic Science International *34 (1987), 107–129.*

easily perceivable color. It is quite another challenge to define the color of a fiber fragment when the color is not discernible to the naked eye. Extracting the dye from the fiber is one approach that has been used,[21] but with the requisite problems of extraction. For example, if dyes are combined to produce a color, the extraction solvent may selectively extract components. Thus, it was clear by the 1980s that the best way to study fiber colorants was in situ using microscopy.[22] Research performed with visible microspectroscopy uncovered interesting and important findings, including the following:[22,23]

- When fibers are dyed with different concentrations of the same dye, the chromaticity coordinates (CIE 1931) are not identical.
- The uncertainty can be plotted in an oval area with an axis that passes through the yellow area of a chromaticity diagram.
- The region of uncertainty varies among types of fiber.
- The region of uncertainty varies with fiber size.
- The minor axis of the ellipse is defined by experimental and instrumental uncertainty.
- The more heavily dyed a fiber is, the smaller is the associated uncertainty ellipse. Undyed fibers have low absorbances closer to the LOD of the instrument, corresponding to larger %RSD values of the absorbances.

Figure 14.17 shows the elliptical regions of uncertainty for the fibers shown in Figure 14.18. The fiber here is a round polyamide type treated with different dispersive dyes. Figure 14.19 shows an example of an error or uncertainty ellipse in more detail. When a fiber is treated with a single colorant, the central axis of the uncertainty ellipse generally points toward the coordinates of the undyed fiber. This observation is attributed to the depth of penetration of the dye varying from fiber to fiber.[23] In other words, the fiber "starts" at the undyed position on the chromaticity diagram. The more of a single dye that is accepted by the fiber, the deeper the color is and the farther the chromaticity coordinates shift away from the undyed fiber color. Taken to the extreme, this line would extend to coordinates of the pure dye. Because different individual fibers have different dye uptake characteristics, some fibers will take on more dye and some less, even when made of the same polymer in the same batch.

Delustering fibers affect the perceived color and thus the chromaticity coordinates. The goal of delustering is to decrease the apparent depth of color and the shine (i.e., saturation and hue). In general, a delusterant causes the perceived color and chromaticity coordinates to shift toward the red region because of selective scattering of the incident light. Also, the less shiny a fiber, the greater is the absorbance, and the greater the absorbance, the smaller is the relative variation between replicative measurements. Thus, compared with untreated fibers, delustered fibers produce uncertainty ellipses with smaller minor axis contributions. Also, in the experiment whose findings are listed a couple of paragraphs ago, when dye was extracted from the fiber and evaluated, the uncertainty ellipses collapsed to points on the chromaticity diagram. As a result, the authors concluded that the long (major) axis of the uncertainty ellipse is attributable to characteristics of the fiber matrix while the minor axis is attributable principally to instrumental error and other, proportionately smaller, errors.[23]

Why are these findings of such importance? Consider a case illustrated in Figure 14.20, in which a single yellow fiber is submitted for examination. This known fiber (K) was recovered from the body of a murder victim. A second fiber, found on the clothing of a suspect, is submitted for comparison (Q, or "questioned" in the figure). Both are analyzed by visible MSP and are found to

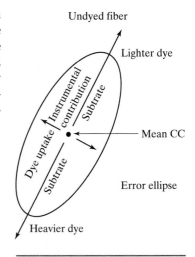

▲ **Figure 14.19** *Uncertainty region defined. The long axis points toward the undyed fiber, and the smaller, minor axis is defined by instrumental and experimental uncertainties.*

Case 1: No overlap   Case 2: Overlap

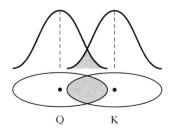

Questioned (Q)   Known (K)   Questioned (Q) Known (K)

Case 3: Significant overlap

Q   K

▶ **Figure 14.20** *Do the ellipses overlap or not?*

have similar chromaticity coordinates. How can this information be interpreted? The situation harkens back to a discussion in Section 2.2.3 dealing with comparing data sets. The fundamental question is a rephrasing of the *t*-test of means: Do the mean values (the error ellipses) overlap or not? If there is overlap, the color is indistinguishable and other factors are needed to classify and perhaps differentiate the fibers. If the ellipses don't overlap, they are distinguishable on the basis of color. Without knowledge of expected inter- or intrasample variation, analytical results cannot be properly interpreted.

Example Problem 14.2

Suppose the ellipses don't overlap. Does this mean that the Q and K fibers have different origins?

Answer: More data are needed (i.e., this is a trick question). Was the fiber found on the victim out in the sun and subject to bleaching? Was the body immersed, so that the fiber weathered and the color faded? If so, the depth of color in the weathered fiber would be less than that of the unweathered fiber, producing an expected alteration of the chromaticity coordinates. This is where the "forensic" part of forensic chemistry comes in: What do the analytical data mean in the context of what is known about the case?

A detailed understanding of such information also facilitates the analysis and interpretation of evidence that at first might seem of little value. Cotton fibers are common types of transfer evidence, given their popularity in clothing and their fragility compared with that of most synthetics. On the basis of this knowledge, black cotton fibers would at first appear to be of limited use, but a recent study shows that this is not necessarily the case.[18] Black is a difficult color to impart with a single dye, since such a molecule would have to absorb equally across the visible spectrum. As of the year 2000, the types of single black dyes used to color cotton are reactive, vat, azoic, sulfur, and direct types[18] (Chapter 11), with the largest proportion being reactive dyes that bond covalently to the cotton (cellulose) through an oxygen atom (—OH group). Because of their covalent bonds with cellulose, reactive dyes are much harder to remove than a dye that is held to the fiber by less powerful intermolecular forces. Vat dyes are usually insoluble in water, but can be converted to a soluble reduced, or "**leuco**," form in basic solution.[24] When the dye solution dries and oxidizes, the original color returns. Direct dyes are those dyes which can be applied directly to cellulose and thus cotton and related cellulose-based fibers such as rayon.

In a study by Grieve et al., UV/VIS microspectrophotometry was shown to be capable of differentiating black cottons on the basis of the type of dye. Some spectra obtained from the study are shown in Figures 14.21, 14.22, and 14.23. The sulfur dyes have smooth, featureless curves in the UV and VIS range, while the reactive dye spectrum shown in Figure 14.22 is comparatively feature-rich in both ranges, including a notable drop in absorbance in the red range. The vat dyes vary more than the sulfur dyes. Thus, even black cotton fibers can be further classified with VIS and UV spectral analysis. However, it is important to note that obtaining a UV spectrum from a fiber is not necessarily nondestructive and should be performed with care. UV light, particularly in the 200–300-nm range, may damage the dye and introduce a spectral artifact.

Regardless of the wavelength range, another experimental condition that must be taken into account in working with MSP is illustrated in Figure 14.24. As with "macrospectroscopy," the source illumination must be focused exclusively on the sample. Light that falls off the sample will, at best, introduce noise and decrease the analytical signal. At worst, it will introduce spectral artifacts. Accordingly, the aperture size and shape must be optimized. With fibers, additional considerations apply as well. If the fiber is pseudocrystalline, then polarization of the source light must be taken into account. If the source illumination is polarized, then the long axis of the fiber should be aligned parallel to the direction of polarization. Although polarization has been discussed exclusively in connection with visible light, any range of wavelengths can be polarized. In some cases, (e.g., with IR microspectroscopy), polarization studies are valuable adjuncts to the analysis, as long as appropriate orientation considerations are accounted for. Finally, as shown in Figure 14.25, the aperture should not be too wide, but rather should cover about one-third of the area of a fiber, assuming a roughly circular cross section.[25] Too narrow an aperture unnecessarily restricts the path length, while too wide an aperture will exceed the curvature of the fiber and introduce stray light. *Fluorescence:* Many fibers will fluoresce under UV excitation, although the signal obtained is usually weak and, to date, this technique has not been widely used.[25] Because UV light is used to stimulate the fluorescence, the technique can also damage the fiber, as described earlier.

FTIR: IR spectroscopy is used to identify the polymer in synthetic fibers and occasionally to evaluate colorants. Micro-IR in transmission, reflection, and ATR modes has become nearly indispensable for fiber analysis, given the quantity of information that is obtainable without destroying the evidence. Working in the IR region with larger wavelengths requires additional sampling considerations, which depend on the type of micro-IR being performed.

Figure 14.26 illustrates the three modes of IR as applied to fiber evidence. The transmission mode is implemented on a fiber placed in the path of the beam, either by suspension across the sampling gap in the stage or with the fiber mounted on a KBr pellet. Adhesive tape is often used to hold the fiber in place. For

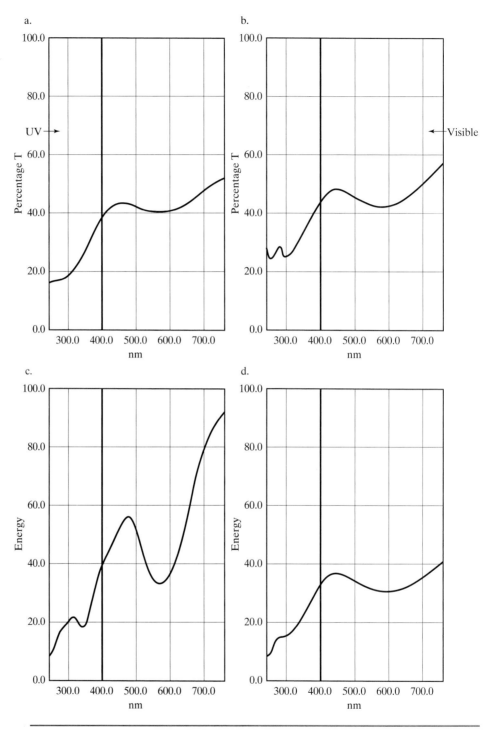

▲ **Figure 14.21** *UV/VIS spectra from sulphur dyes. a) Sulphur Black 1 (James Robinson Sulphur Black BS, b) Sulphur Black SG, c) Sulphur Black QLC, and d) spectrum from Wrangler black jeans fibers. Reproduced with permission from Grieve, M. C., et al., "The evidential value of black cotton fibers,"* Science and Justice *41 (2001), 245–260.*

reflection-mode studies, the fiber is mounted on a reflective surface such as a gold mirror. One advantage of the reflection mode is that the path length is effectively doubled, increasing the sensitivity of the technique. ATR is performed by pressing the ATR crystal (typically, diamond or germanium) into contact with the fiber.

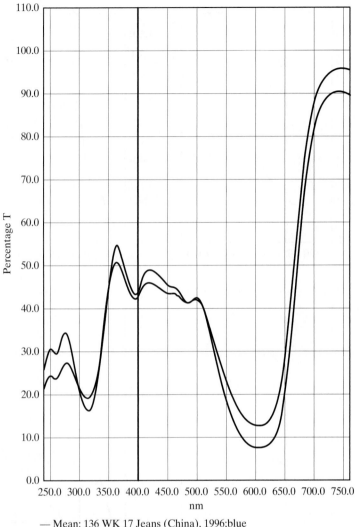

— Mean: 136 WK 17 Jeans (China), 1996;blue
— Mean: Remazol Black B; blue (Reactive Black 5)(upper)

◀ **Figure 14.22** *Reproduced with permission from Grieve, M. C., et al., "The evidential value of black cotton fibers,"* Science and Justice *41 (2001), 245–260.*

Note that in all three applications the fiber is flattened prior to analysis, for reasons depicted in Figure 14.27. If a fiber has a very rough surface, IR energy will be lost due to scattering and diffuse reflectance. Rounded fibers, in addition to being prone to the aperture limitations shown in Figure 14.25, can act as lenses for IR energy, "focusing" energy away from the collector in the worst case.[26] This lost energy is recorded as false absorbance. In less odious cases, the alteration of path length caused by this lens effect changes the band intensities. Flattening fibers alleviates these problems, but can introduce another. A flattened fiber can take on characteristics of a thin film in which internal reflections can occur. As a result, some wavelengths may be held up in the fiber and emerge behind the transmitted wave front. In effect, this creates a second interferogram,[26] as well as interference fringes, in the spectrum, as shown in Figure 14.28. To flatten a fiber, it is usually rolled with a steel roller on a slightly roughened surface, such as the frosted area of a microscope slide,[26,27] or by a hydraulic press with diamond surfaces.[27]

When a fiber is analyzed in the reflective mode, it is often necessary to apply a corrective transformation to the data because most fibers have some degree of

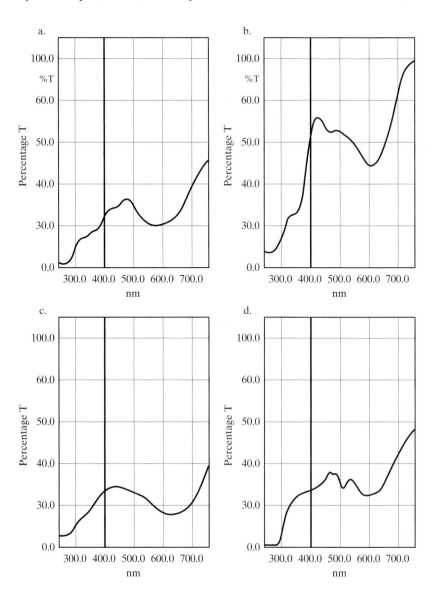

▶ **Figure 14.23** *Four examples of the spectral variety found in Vat dyes. a) Indanthren Direct Black R, b) Indanthren Grey 5607, c) Cibanon Black 2Ba, and d) ICI Solanthrene Black BN. Reproduced with permission from Grieve, M. C., et al., "The evidential value of black cotton fibers,"* Science and Justice *41 (2001), 245–260.*

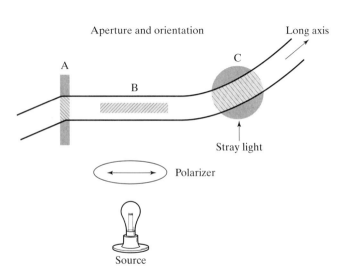

▶ **Figure 14.24** *Setting the aperture in MSP.*

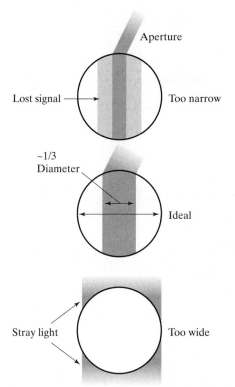

Aperture

Lost signal — → Too narrow

~1/3 Diameter

Ideal

Stray light — Too wide

◀ **Figure 14.25** *Fiber cross section and aperture setting.*

Transmission mode

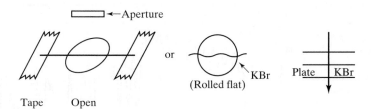

▭ ←Aperture

Tape   Open

or

KBr (Rolled flat)

Plate | KBr

Reflection mode (flattened)

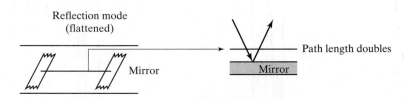

Mirror

Path length doubles

Mirror

ATR (pressed flat)

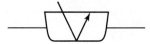

◀ **Figure 14.26** *Three sampling methods in micro-IR.*

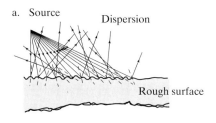

a. Source   Dispersion

Rough surface

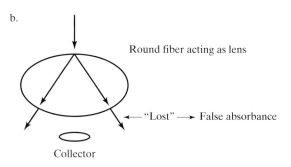

b.

Round fiber acting as lens

"Lost" → False absorbance

Collector

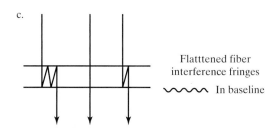

c.

Flatttened fiber interference fringes

〜〜〜 In baseline

▶ **Figure 14.27** *Issues in micro-IR. Too rough a surface or a round fiber can falsely show absorbance. Too flat a specimen may introduce interference fringes.*

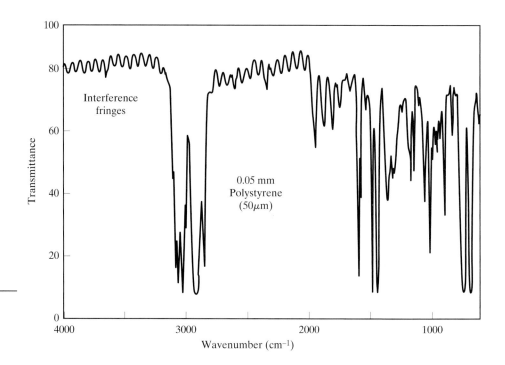

Interference fringes

0.05 mm
Polystyrene
(50μm)

Transmittance

Wavenumber (cm^{-1})

▶ **Figure 14.28** *IR spectrum demonstrating interference fringes—sinusoidal patterns in the baseline.*

crystallinity and thus favor some degree of specular reflection. The resulting dispersion is wavelength dependent and introduces artifacts into spectra that appear as drop-offs associated with peaks, similar in appearance to a first-derivative curve. To compensate for this effect, the **Kramers–Kronig transform** is applied as shown in Figure 14.29. The mathematics is somewhat complex and involves imaginary values and the extinction coefficients of the different wavelengths in the spectra.[28]

The third micro-IR analysis option is ATR with a diamond or germanium crystal. The fiber does not have to be preflattened, since pressure contact is part of the analysis. IR energy will penetrate only a short distance into the fiber, on the orders of a few micrometers.[26] This property can be useful with coated or sheathed bicomponent fibers, because it allows the analyst to subtract the contribution of the surface from a traditional transmission or reflection spectrum, to obtain spectra of both.[26,27] The depth of penetration of the IR radiation into the sample depends on the wavelength, so a correction should be applied to any ATR spectrum before it is compared with transmission spectra.

In the reflection and transmission modes, the thickness of the sample is an important variable and should lie between 10 and 20 μm.[26] Thickness defines the path length, and, as shown in Figure 14.30, it can be too long or too short. Too thin a sample means loss of information for low absorbing groups, while saturation of selected wavenumbers and loss of resolution occur when samples

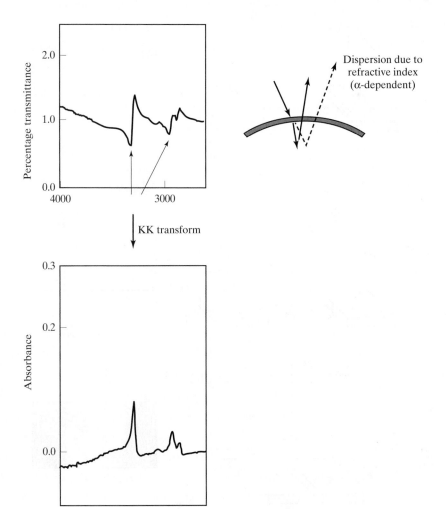

◀ **Figure 14.29** *If a sample has high specular reflectance, characteristic dips appear in the baseline. These features can be removed by the Kramers–Kronig transform.*

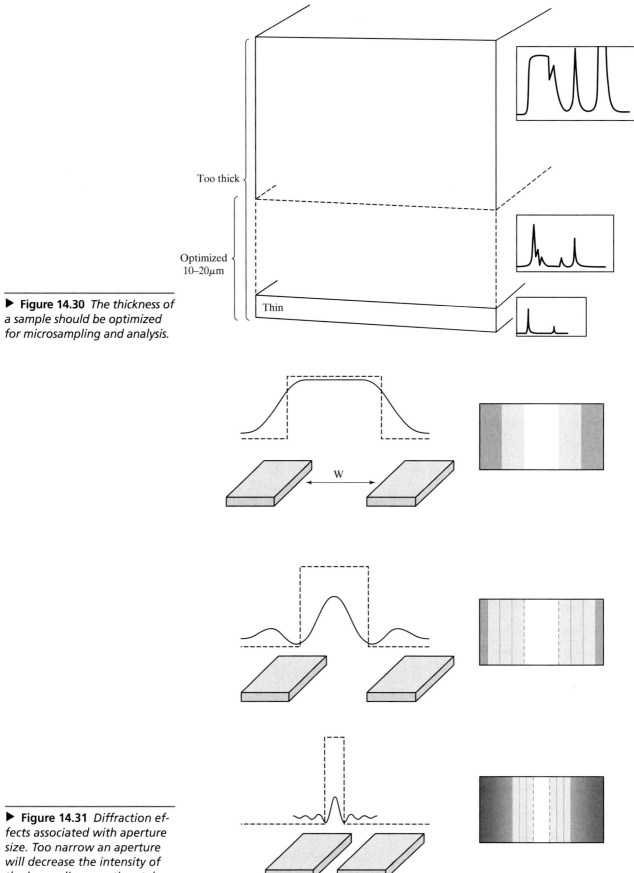

▶ **Figure 14.30** *The thickness of a sample should be optimized for microsampling and analysis.*

Too thick

Optimized
10–20μm

Thin

W

▶ **Figure 14.31** *Diffraction effects associated with aperture size. Too narrow an aperture will decrease the intensity of the beam disproportionately.*

are too thick. As was the case with UV/VIS MSP, aperture size is critical. At IR wavelengths, diffraction effects add to concerns about stray light. Figure 14.31 depicts edge effects that result if the aperture is too wide or too narrow. Wide apertures ($w \gg \lambda$) do not introduce diffraction effects, and the peak energy is seen evenly across the sampling window. As w decreases, diffraction occurs, resulting in a loss of energy from the sampling window. Increasing diffraction leads to decreasing beam power and increases in the signal-to-noise ratio. However, as discussed, the aperture can be too wide as well as too narrow, and the analyst must be cognizant of these issues when he or she seeks to obtain micro-IR spectra. Figure 14.32 is a flowchart summarizing sampling methods and modes.

Having discussed the "how" of obtaining micro-IR data, we can now address the "why" and "what" of the technique. As per Figure 14.7, there are many aspects of a fiber that can be analyzed with IR MSP, starting with, but not limited to, the composition of the polymer. In many cases, PLM is sufficient to classify fibers, but not into subclasses. For example, two common types of nylon—nylon 6 and nylon 6,6—are easily differentiated by their IR spectra, and a number of different acrylic fibers also can be differentiated by micro-IR techniques.[29]

Once a good-quality spectrum has been obtained, the next step is typically a library search to identify the composition of the polymer and subclass of the fiber. The situation is more complex if the fiber is treated or dyed, but such

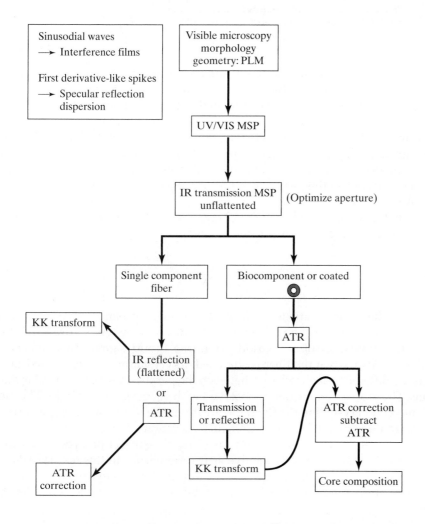

◀ **Figure 14.32** *Flowchart summarizing fiber analysis incorporating PLM, UV/VIS, and IR MSP.*

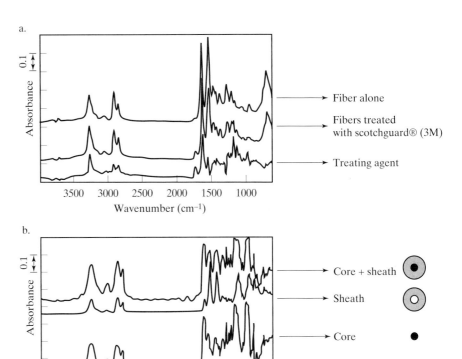

▶ **Figure 14.33** *a): ATR spectra of single nylon carpet fiber untreated (top), treated (middle), and the result of spectral subtraction (bottom). b): Bicomponent fiber transmission spectrum (top), ATR spectrum of Nylon 6 sheath (middle), and difference spectrum of PET core (bottom).Reproduced with permission from Cho, L., et al., "Single Fiber Analysis by Internal Reflection Infrared Microspectroscopy," Journal of Forensic Sciences 46 (2001), 1309–1314. Copyright 2001, ASTM International.*

cases demonstrate the versatility of micro-IR. Figure 14.33 shows two examples.[30] In the top frame, the spectrum of nylon is subtracted from that of a nylon carpet fiber which has been treated with Scotchguard®, an aerosol often sprayed on carpets to increase stain resistance. Scotchguard® is a fluoropolymer with many of the characteristics of Teflon®. Fluoralkyl groups absorb strongly in the highlighted 1400–1000 cm^{-1} regions. The lower frame illustrates the combined use of transmission and ATR sampling methods to obtain a spectrum of the core, in this case polyethylene terephthalate (PET).

A recent extension to IR microscopy is the inclusion of polarized radiation to study the **dichroic ratio**,[31,32] the IR equivalent of birefringence or the sign of elongation. The dichroic ratio is defined as[26]

$$R = \frac{A_{\parallel}}{A_{\perp}} \tag{14.4}$$

To apply the dichroic ratio to an IR spectrum, the absorbances at selected bands are used. An example of how the ratio is applied is shown in Figure 14.34. Note that the orientation of the absorbing nitrile group significantly affects absorbance. Also, when the fiber is stretched, its crystalline nature is maximized, as is the difference in absorbance between the parallel and perpendicular directions. The same phenomenon is observed with visible light and PLM. The more oriented and crystalline the fiber, the greater is the difference in appearance of the fiber in the parallel and perpendicular directions.

Finally, to close the section on micro-IR, the subject of dyes needs to be mentioned. A look at any of the dye structures shown in this text reveals that many possess functional groups that absorb in the infrared region. Note that dyes are present in much lower concentrations than the polymer substrate, but

a.

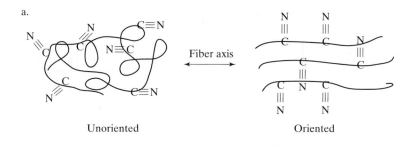

Unoriented   Oriented

b.

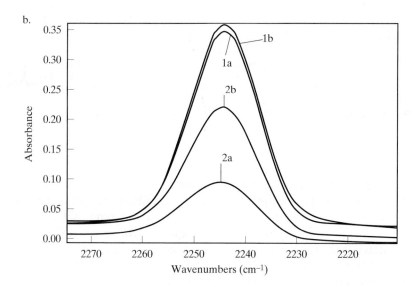

◀ **Figure 14.34** *a) Structure of the polyacrylonitrile shows the nitrile groups oriented 90° to the fiber axis. The left structure shows the fiber before being stretched and the right structure shows the result after stretching. b) Polarized infrared absorption spectra acrylic fiber showing the orientation of the nitrile functional group at 2244 cm⁻¹. Top: perpendicular (1b) and parallel (1a) polarized infrared spectra of a single unstretched fiber. Bottom: perpendicular (2b) and parallel (2a) polarized infrared spectra of a stretched fiber. Reproduced with permission from Cho, L., et al., "Forensic Classification of Polyester Fibers by Infrared Dichroic Ratio Pattern Recognition."* Journal of Forensic Sciences *44 (1999), 283–291. Copyright 1999, ASTM International.*

given the sensitivity of FTIR microscopy, absorbances arising from colorants may be observed on occasion. Identifying and interpreting these minor spectral features is not straightforward[33] and requires that the dye be extracted from the fiber. The important point from the findings discussed in this section is that, in comparing sample fibers with library spectra, minor discrepancies may arise from colorants.[33]

Raman: Micro-Raman spectroscopy is attracting increasing attention in the analysis of fibers, for both their polymeric composition and the colorants used. Raman microscopes are increasingly affordable and simple to operate; the limitations are the inherently weak signals due to scattering and potential destruction of the sample from exposure to the intense visible laser used to induce scattering. Background fluorescence is also a concern, as shown in Figure 14.35.[34] The use of longer wavelengths alleviates, but does not eliminate, this concern. Fiber classes and subclasses have been identified, and Raman microspectroscopy appears promising for dye analysis, as shown in Figure 14.36. As in the case of micro-IR, spectral subtraction is useful in isolating spectral contributions—here, dye and fiber.

14.2.5 ELEMENTAL ANALYSIS

With the exception of SEM and XRF microscopy, this family of analyses has not been used extensively with fibers. In general, fiber analysis does not require the extreme of magnification provided by SEM, nor is elemental analysis of

▶ **Figure 14.35** *a) Raman microprobe spectra of a polypropylene fiber showing fluorescence reduction with longer wavelength excitation light. (A) 632.8 nm excitation; (B) 780 nm excitation. b) Raman microprobe spectra (632.8 nm excitation) of a set of polyester fibers from different manufacturers. (A) Allied (AO196); (B) Firestone Fibers (AO421); (C) Hoechst (AO243); (D) Tolaram (AO333). Reproduced with permission from Keen, I. P., et al., "Characterization of Fibers by Raman Microprobe Spectroscopy." Journal of Forensic Sciences 43 (1998), 82–89. Copyright 1998, ASTM International.*

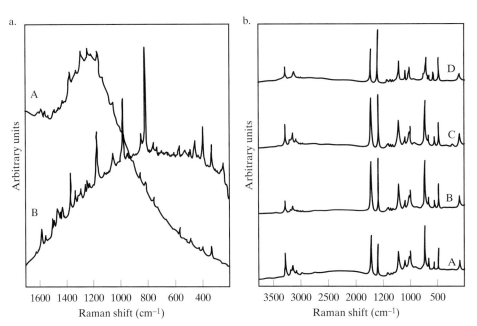

primary concern in what is principally an organic analysis challenge. Inorganics and metals are not commonly associated with fibers and, when present, are usually attributed to contamination, additives, or finishing materials such as delusterants or as residues from manufacturing.[15] One area in which SEM has been somewhat useful is the study of damage to fibers, such as determining whether a fiber has been cut or torn.[35] XRF microscopy is nondestructive and has been used as an adjunct to other types of microscopy and spectroscopy.[36−38] One promising application of XRF is to colorless fibers,[36] which was reported to significantly improve the ability to distinguish such fibers.

▶ **Figure 14.36** *a) Raman microprobe spectra (with 780 nm excitation) of two different red-dyed polyester fibers. Polyester bands are marked with an asterisk. b) Raman microprobe spectra (with 780 nm excitation) of a blue-dyed fiber. (A) Fiber with dye; (B) Fiber only, after solvent extraction of dye; (C) Dye spectrum obtained by computer subtraction of B from A. Reproduced with permission from Keen, I. P., et al. "Characterization of Fibers by Raman Microprobe Spectroscopy." Journal of Forensic Sciences 43 (1998), 82–89. Copyright 1998, ASTM International.*

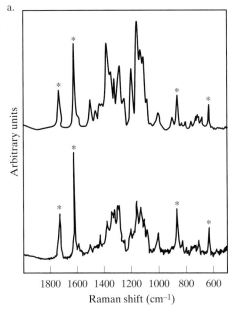
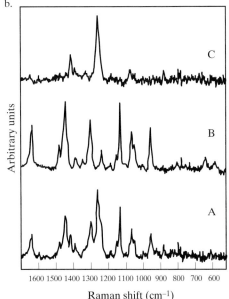

14.2.6 SAMPLING CONSIDERATIONS AND SIGNIFICANCE

So far, the discussion has focused on the wealth of tools available for fiber analysis. However, mention must be made of some of the practical sampling issues that arise. Fibers are ubiquitous and are easily transferred as per Locard's exchange principle. Along with dust, fibers are the most common class of transfer and trace evidence, and this commonality itself creates caveats that affect any fiber analysis. In addition, modern mass-production techniques are purposely designed to manufacture fibers that have minimal variation. This is good for the consumer, but bad for the forensic scientist, given that evidence is classified and distinguished on the basis of differences. Mass-production techniques have made it harder to find those differences which are critical to differentiation.

Cases involving fiber evidence rarely involve one fiber. On the contrary, a case may involve dozens or hundreds of fibers, and sampling methodology becomes critically important. Recall the discussion of sampling in Section 2.2.5 and the observation that is it much easier to critique a bad sampling plan than to design a perfect one. In fiber analysis, analyst experience is central to devising the sampling protocol. Fibers can be collected by means of tape, with a single tape yielding dozens of fibers. Suppose a victim is killed in a carpeted home where a dog lives. The victim is wrapped in a blanket, transported in a car that also has carpet, and dumped in a remote location. This was the situation facing investigators in the Wayne Williams case; in this and similar situations, the importance of judicious and directed sampling can't be overemphasized. Unfortunately, as was made clear in Chapter 2, there is no set formula for achieving that, so it is incumbent on the analyst to make sure that whatever approach is taken is logical, flexible, and defensible. Guidelines exist, but by necessity can remain only guidelines. The Scientific Working Group on Materials Analysis (SWGMAT) suggests probability (random) sampling, "judgment sampling," or bulk sampling, depending on the circumstances.[6]

Continuing with the example of a dumped body, the fibers associated with that body reflect its most recent environment. Unlike a stain, fiber evidence is transitory, and as more time passes since the time of transfer, the more fibers are lost. The body will carry with it evidence of the environment, including the dump site, in which the person spent the last hours of life. Absent unusual treatment, the decay of fibers on a substrate approximates a first-order decay curve.[39] Consequently, fiber evidence is perishable evidence; yet, while any one fiber may not be particularly telling, the combination often is, as it was in the Williams case.

Example Problem 14.3

Suppose research shows that cotton fibers which are transferred to a nylon jacket are lost according to first-order decay and that the half-life is 2 hours when the jacket is subject to normal wear. What percentage of cotton fibers would be expected to remain after 7 hours?

Answer: This problem can be solved with an equation or, here, graphically. Using first-order decay and graphical approximation, we find that about 12% of the fibers will remain. Given the difficulty of replicating all variables, a graphical method is a reasonable approach to obtain what will, at best, be an approximation.

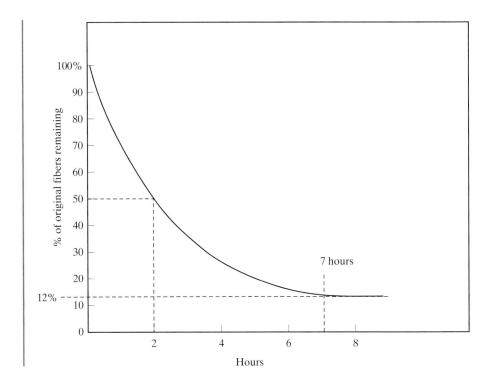

Although it might not be obvious at first, issues raised in the interpretation of fiber evidence are analogous to those encountered in chemical analysis. If cocaine is found in a person's bloodstream, that finding is significant because it is known that cocaine does not normally exist in that environment. Alternatively, cocaine may be a natural component of the blood, but at such low levels (i.e., <LOD) that it is not detectable. Fiber evidence can be considered in the same light: To judge the significance of fibers, it is necessary to know the normal background or baseline level of fibers that would be expected to be found in the environment.

In pursuit of this knowledge, the first important piece of information needed is some idea of what materials are produced annually and in what amounts. In 2002, 36 million metric tons of fibers were produced, of which 94% were synthetic and 6% based on cellulose.[40] The breakdown of synthetic fibers is shown in Figure 14.37. Although fibers are used in many applications besides textiles, this distribution of production would lead to the expectation of finding significant numbers of synthetic fibers, principally polyesters, as part of the environmental baseline. A recent study by Grieve and Biermann evaluated the outdoor fiber environment during summer and obtained results that might at first seem to contradict expectations based on fiber production volumes.[41] The authors found that cellulosic fibers (cotton) were the most common by a wide margin, followed by synthetics. In the synthetic category, nearly half were rayon, and polyesters were third. The apparent disparity between production values and observed values is explainable. First, cotton fibers are less durable than synthetics and therefore more likely to break and be available for transfer. Second, cotton is a favorite fabric for textiles and clothing and hence is found as part of clothing in a much higher percentage than would be extrapolated from production figures alone. Finally, the authors noted that, in summer, cotton is a much more comfortable fabric than most synthetics. Not surprisingly, the most common fiber by color was blue denim.

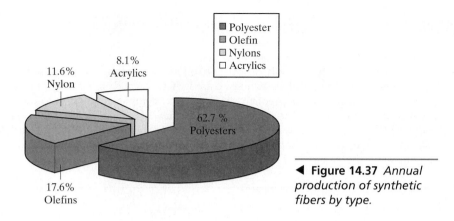

Knowledge of background levels helps the examiner determine which types of fiber likely carry the most evidentiary weight. Typically, such weight is inversely proportional to commonality. Blue denim fibers are common because blue jeans are so common; finding a blue denim fiber on a piece of evidence would ordinarily not be very significant. Synthetics, because of their durability and resistance to transfer, would likely be more important and reflect a more recent contact.[41] Orange and purple fibers would be more significant than white or blue. Finally, longer fibers would be potentially more significant than shorter fibers, which would be easier to transfer. In Grieve and Biermann's study, 65% of the fibers were less than a millimeter in length and only about 7% were longer than 3 mm.

Laboratories and analysts allocate their time and effort to those areas which appear most promising. On the basis of the preceding discussion, it should not be surprising that some types of fiber evidence are deemed too common to be of evidentiary value. A 2001 survey revealed that about half the responding laboratories in the United States and Europe did not routinely examine undyed cotton fibers. Blue denim is not routinely analyzed in 20% of U.S., and nearly 50% of European, laboratories. The decision to analyze or not to analyze a particular kind of fiber is based on knowledge of the background environmental level of the fiber.

14.3 ADHESIVES, TAPE, AND OTHER POLYMER EVIDENCE

Synthetic fibers and textiles are not the only type of polymer evidence analyzed by forensic chemists. All kinds of materials, such as building materials and PVC pipes, may be submitted as exhibits. Among the more frequent types of evidence are adhesives and tapes, most of which are based on or include polymeric substances. Tape is also frequently used to collect evidence; fibers are often collected by adhesion to inside-out rolls of tape. Gunshot residue can also be collected this way. Tapes of the most forensic interest consist of a polymer backing with a pressure-sensitive adhesive coated on one or both sides, as in the case of double-sided tape. Within this group are found cellophane tape (informally, "Scotch tape"), as well as duct, packing, and electrical tape.

Applying the Science 14.3   Ancient Adhesives

Humans have been sticking one thing to another for thousands of years. Ancient adhesives are, not surprisingly, based on materials similar to ancient paints and varnishes, which served to bind pigments to surfaces. Tree saps, as well as surprisingly complex adhesive mixtures containing beeswax and natural resins, have been identified. To analyze residues of interest, archeological chemists have the same tools as forensic chemists and many of the same constraints, such as a preference for nondestructive or minimally destructive techniques. Among the tools used to analyze adhesives are Py-GC-MS and IR, although the latter is problematical, given the complex mixtures encountered. The figure shows the results of a direct pyrolysis-MS analysis of an adhesive found on a ceramic vessel dating back to approximately 800 B.C. and recovered from an archaeological site in France.

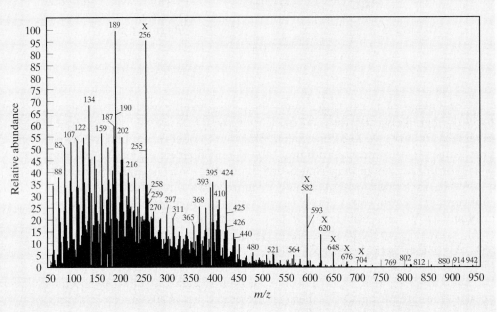

▶ *Mass spectrum obtained by direct inlet electron ionization mass spectrometry on a solid microsample of a brownish residue from the Iron Age site of Grand Aunay characteristic of a mixture of birch bark tar (m/Z 189, 424, and 426) and beeswax. The peaks due to the presence of beeswax are indicated with a cross.*

Source: Regert, M., and C. Rolando, "Identification of Archaeological Adhesives Using Direct Inlet Electron Ionization Mass Spectrometry," *Analytical Chemistry* 74 (2002), 965–975.

Example Problem 14.4

Super glue is used to close wounds and to develop fingerprints on substrates such as aluminum cans. How does this process work?

Answer: The same way that super glue works to bind cellulose with available —OH groups which act as initiators. Recall that proteins are composed of amino acids that have —COOH groups which can act as initiators. Fingerprints contain residual proteins that polymerize into a white plasticky polymer that can be further developed to enhance visualization.

Cellophane is a form of regenerated cellulose that is cast in thin films and is well suited for use in tapes. However, it lacks mechanical strength and is gradually being replaced with materials such as cellulose acetate and polypropylene[42] as backing. Some backings, such as those in duct tape and packing tape (strapping tape), are reinforced with fibers for added strength. Adhesives that are used generally fall into four categories:[42,43] rubber based, acrylic, copolymers of styrene (with butadiene and isoprene), and vinyl ethers. In addition to physical analysis (physical matching, dimensions, etc.), successful discrimination of tapes

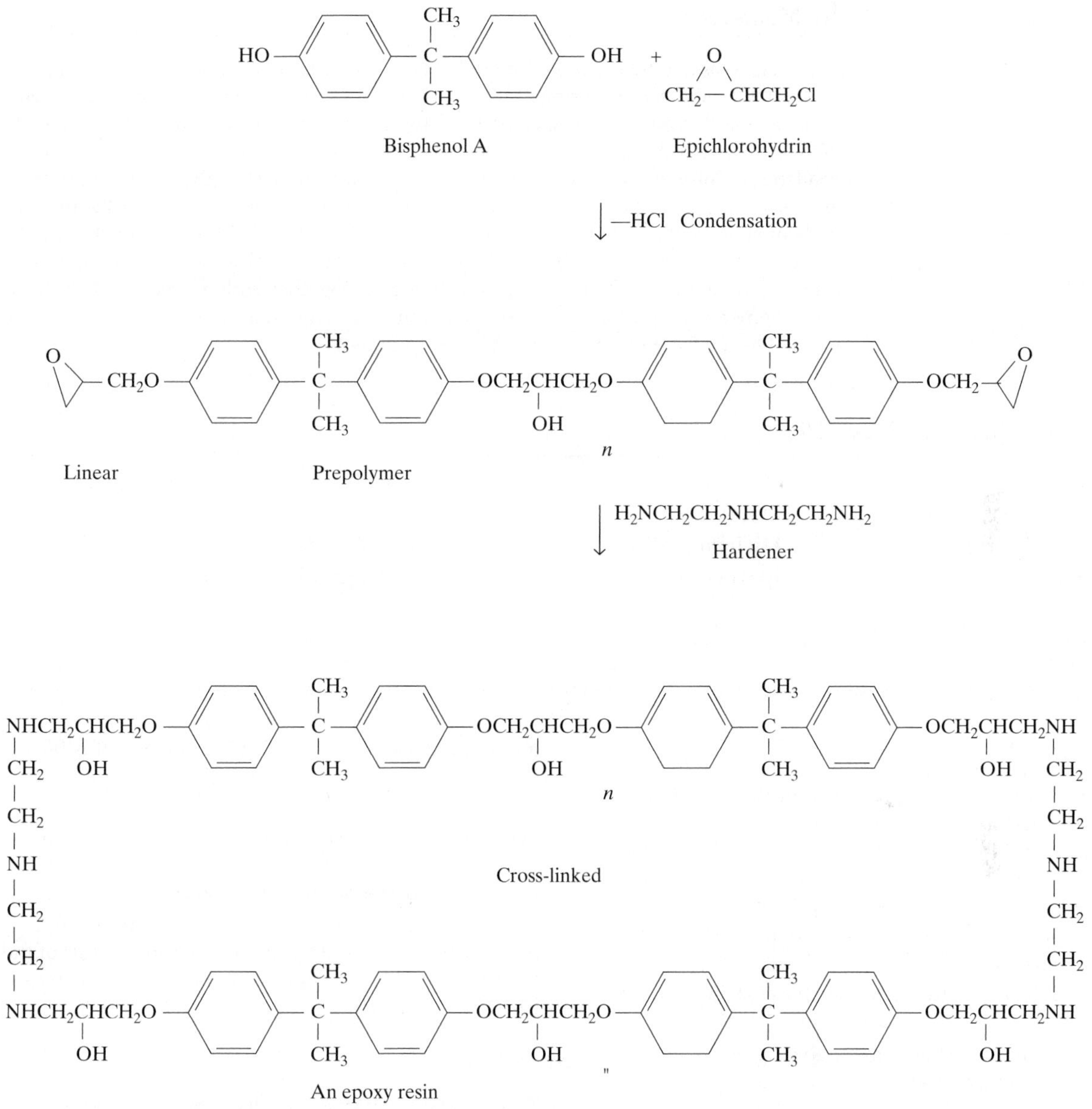

▲ **Figure 14.38** *Epoxy glue consists of a prepolymer that cross-links when mixed with a hardener.*

has been reported with the use of Py-GC-MS coupled to FTIR. The latter can be applied to polymer backing separately from the adhesive-using micro-ATR methods.[44]

Finally, let us mention adhesives in glues, which differ from those in pressure-sensitive tapes in that there is a curing or setting stage which results in a polymerization reaction and a chemical bond to substrates. Exhibit C in Chapter 13 described how cyanoacrylates (super glue) works; another type of polymeric adhesive is epoxy. Epoxy glue (Figure 14.38) is supplied in two tubes: the adhesive and the hardener, which are mixed in equal proportions just before the bond is made. The polymer is made from bisphenol A and epicholorhydrin, an epoxide. When combined with the hardener (an amine compound with a distinctive smell), the polymer cross-links, forming one of the strongest adhesive bonds available.

SUMMARY

This chapter is a good capstone for our study of forensic chemistry. The subject of polymers, fibers, and textiles brings many aspects of forensic chemistry together: organic chemistry and synthesis, dyes, colorants, physical measurements, microscopy, a variety of instrumental techniques, complex sampling considerations, and nontrivial interpretive challenges. Polymer evidence such as tape and paper may skirt the need for chemical analysis altogether if a physical match can be made, but when it cannot, all the modern tools of analytical chemistry and forensic science can be brought to bear to classify the evidence. Improvements in minimally destructive and nondestructive techniques continue, as is the case of micro-Raman spectroscopy. Together with related research, these improvements are likely to increase the amount of evidentiary information that can be obtained even from tiny fiber and polymer fragments.

KEY TERMS AND CONCEPTS

Becke line method
Compensator (wedge)
Crossed polars

Delusterant
Dichroic ratio
Extinction

Hot stage
Michel-Levy chart
Sign of elongation

PROBLEMS

From the chapter

1. Based on the element list presented for the ICP-MS discrimination-of-papers approach, what would be some of the practical problems related to sample preparation? In other words, how can the analyst be confident that the measured concentrations of elements are attributable to the paper matrix and are not incidental or indicative of contaminants?

2. How do delustering treatments such as placing particulates of TiO_2 on a fiber surface decrease shine?

3. A case examination reveals the following fibers and their colors and lengths on a piece of evidence:

Number	Type	Color	Length
1	Viscose rayon	Black	3.1 mm
2	Cotton	White	7.2 mm
3	Cotton	Orange	0.2mm
4	Dacron	Green	5.1 mm
5	Wool	White	<0.2 mm
6	Triacetate	Orange	4.2 mm
7	Polyamide	Red	2 mm

Rank the fibers in order of likely relative evidentiary importance, and justify your answer.

4. A PBT polyester fiber has a symmetrical dumbbell cross section with a maximum thickness of 80 μm and a minimum thickness of 40 μm. Describe how this fiber would appear under crossed polars (maximum interference colors).

5. Suppose you were to observe a nylon fiber under cross polars while the fiber was gradually heated to its melting point. Describe what you would see.

6. If a case involved a single nylon fiber as crucial evidence, what tests would you select for an analysis of the fiber and why? How would your answer change if you had 20 fibers (all similar)?

Integrative

1. Research how paper is recycled, and comment on how the process(es) will affect the chemical characterization of paper. Should there be ways to distinguish recycled from nonrecycled paper? to distinguish among recycled batches? Present your answers in three analytical areas; microscopic/visual, organic, and inorganic analysis.

2. Predict how paper will appear under polarized light. Justify your answer.

3. Show by calculation why aperture size is of more concern in IR than in UV/VIS. If an aperture size of 5×5 μm is used to gather an IR spectrum, will diffraction likely occur? What if this aperture size were used in the visible range?

FURTHER READING

Allcock, H. R., et al. *Contemporary Polymer Chemistry*, 3d ed. Upper Saddle River, NJ: Prentice Hall, 2003.

Biermann, C. J. *Essentials of Pulping and Papermaking*. San Diego: Academic Press, 1993.

Eklund, D., and T. Linstrom. *Paper Chemistry: An Introduction*. Grankulla, Finland: DT Paper Science, 1991.

Houck, M. "Inter-comparison of Unrelated Fiber Evidence." *Forensic Science International* 135 (2003), 146–149.

SWGMAT. "Forensic Fiber Examination Guidelines." *Forensic Science Communications* (www.fbi.gov/lab/fsc), Volume 1(1) (1999).

REFERENCES

1. Kher, A., et al. "Classification of Document Papers by Infrared Spectroscopy and Multivariate Statistical Techniques." *Applied Spectroscopy* 55 (2001), 1192–1198.

2. Andrasko, J. "Microreflectance FTIR Techniques Applied to Materials Encountered in Forensic Examination of Documents." *Journal of Forensic Sciences* 41 (1996), 812–823.

3. Spence, L. D., et al. "Characterization of Document Paper Using Elemental Compositions Determined by Inductively Coupled Plasma Mass Spectrometry." *Journal of Analytical Atomic Spectroscopy* 15 (2000), 813–819.

4. Spence, L. D., et al. "Comparison of the Elemental Composition of Office Document Paper: Evidence in a Homicide Case." *Journal of Forensic Sciences* 47 (2002), 648–651.

5. Giorgi, R., et al. "Nanotechnologies for Conservation of Cultural Heritage: Paper and Canvas Deacidification." *Langmuir* 18 (2002), 8198–8203.

6. SWGMAT. "Forensic Fiber Examination Guidelines." *Forensic Science Communications* (www.fbi.gov/lab/fsc) 1 (1999).

7. "Standard Guide for Microscopic Examination of Textile Fibers," in *ASTM Standard E 2228-02*, ASTM International, 2004.

8. Wiggins, K. G. "Forensic Textile Fiber Examination across the USA and Europe." *Journal of Forensic Sciences* 46 (2001), 1301–1308.

9. Palenik, S. J., and C. Fitzsimons. "Fiber Cross Sections: Part 2, a Simple Method for Sectioning Single Fibers." *The Microscope* 38 (1990), 313–320.

10. Robinson, P. C., and M. W. Davidson. "Nikon Microscopy U: Plane Polarized Light Microscopy." March 7, 2004.

11. Gaudette, B. R. "The Forensic Aspects of Textile Fiber Examination," in R. Saferstein, ed., *Forensic Science Handbook, Volume II*. Upper Saddle River, NJ: Prentice Hall, 1988.

12. "Standard Guide for Forensic Examination of Non-Reactive Dyes in Textile Fibers by Thin-Layer Chromatography," in *ASTM Standard E 2227-02* ASTM International, 2004.

13. Huang, M., et al. "Forensic Identification of Dyes Extracted from Textile Fibers by Liquid Chromatography Mass Spectrometry (LC-MS)." *Journal of Forensic Sciences* 49 (2004), 238–241.

14. Armitage, S., et al. "The Analysis of Forensic Samples Using Laser Micro-Pyrolysis Gas Chromatography Mass Spectrometry." *Journal of Forensic Sciences* 46 (2001), 1043–1052.

15. Challinor, J. M. "Instrumental Methods Used in Fibre Examination," in J. Robertson and M. C. Grieve, eds., *Forensic Examination of Fibres*, 2d ed. London: Taylor and Francies, 1999.

16. Ohtani, H., et al. "Quantification of End Groups in Anionically Polymerized Poly(methyl methacrylate)s by Pyrolysis Gas Chromatography." *Macromolecules* 30 (1997), 2542–2545.

17. Cheng, T. M., and E. G. Malawe. "Identification and Determination of Cross-Linkers in Cross-Linked Poly(vinylpyrrolidone) by Pyrolysis-Gas Chromatography/Mass Spectrometry." *Analytical Chemistry* 71 (1999), 468–475.

18. Grieve, M. C., et al. "The evidential value of black cotton fibers." *Science and Justice* 41 (2001), 245–260.

19. Tuinman, A. A., et al. "Trace Fiber Color Discrimination by Electrospray Ionization Mass Spectrometry: A Tool for the Analysis of Dyes Extracted from Submillimeter Nylon Fibers." *Analytical Chemistry* 75 (2003), 2753–2760.

20. Zollinger, H., "Ch. 11: Application of Dyes," in H. Zollinger, *Color Chemistry: Synthesis, Properties, and Applications of Organic Dyes and Pigments*, 3d ed. Zurich: VHCA/Wiley-VCH, 2003.

21. Paterson, M. D., and R. Cook. "The Production of Colour Coordinates from Microgram Quantities of Textile Fibres. Part I." *Forensic Science International* 15 (1980), 249–258.

22. Laing, D. K., et al. "Colour measurement on a single textile fiber." *Forensic Science International* 30 (1986), 65–77.

23. Hartshorne, A. W., and D. K. Laing. "The Definition of Colour for Single Textile Fibers by Microspectrophotometry." *Forensic Science International* 34 (1987), 107–129.

24. Zollinger, H., "Ch. 8. Carbonyl Dyes and Pigments," in H. Zollinger, *Color Chemistry: Synthesis, Properties, and Applications of Organic Dyes and Pigments*, 3d ed. Zurich: VHCA/Wiley-VCH, 2003.

25. Adolf, F.-P., and J. Dunlop, "Ch. 10: Microspectrophotometry/Colour Measurement," in J. Robertson and M. C. Grieve, eds., *Forensic Examination of Fibres*, 2d ed. London: Taylor and Francis, 1999.

26. Kirkbride, K. P., and M. W. Tungol, "Ch. 8: Infrared Microspectroscopy of Fibres," in J. Robertson and M. C. Grieve, eds., *Forensic Examination of Fibres*, 2d ed. London: Taylor and Francis, 1999.

27. Tungol, M. W., et al. "Forensic Examination of Synthetic Textile Fibers by Microscopic Infrared Spectrometry." *Practical Spectroscopy* 19 (1995), 245.

28. Krishan, K., and S. L. Hill. "FTIR Microsampling Techniques," in J. R. Ferraro, ed., *Practical Fourier Transform Infrared Spectroscopy*. New York: Academic Press, 1989.

29. Grieve, M. C. "Another Look at the Classification of Acrylic Fibres, Using FTIR Microscopy." *Science and Justice* 35 (1995), 179–190.

30. Cho, L., et al. "Single Fiber Analysis by Internal Reflection Infrared Microspectroscopy." *Journal of Forensic Sciences* 46 (2001), 1309–1314.

31. Cho, L., et al. "A New Method for Fiber Comparison Using Polarized Infrared Microspectroscopy." *Journal of Forensic Sciences* 44 (1999), 275–282.

32. Cho, L., et al. "Forensic Classification of Polyester Fibers by Infrared Dichroic Ratio Pattern Recognition." *Journal of Forensic Sciences* 44 (1999), 283–291.

33. Grieve, M. C., et al. "Characteristic dye absoption peaks found in FTIR spectra of coloured acrylic fibres." *Science and Justice* 38 (1998), 27–37.

34. Keen, I. P., et al. "Characterization of Fibers by Raman Microprobe Spectroscopy." *Journal of Forensic Sciences* 43 (1998), 82–89.

35. Pelton, W. "Distinguishing the Cause of Textile Fiber Damage Using the Scanning Electron Microscope (SEM)." *Journal of Forensic Sciences* 40 (1995), 874–883.

36. Cartier, J., et al. "A Study to Investigate the Feasibility of Using X-Ray Fluorescence Microanalysis to Improve Discrimination between Colorless Synthetic Fibers." *Journal of Forensic Sciences* 42 (1997), 1019–1027.

37. Koons, R. D., et al. "Comparison of Individual Carpet Fibers Using Energy Dispersive X-Ray Fluorescence Forensic Analysis of Single Fibers by Raman Spectroscopy." *Journal of Forensic Sciences* 41 (1996), 199–206.

38. Prange, A., et al. "Microanalysis in Forensic Science: Characterization of Single Textile Fibers by Total Reflection X-Ray Fluorescence." *Analytical Sciences: The International Journal of the Japan Society for Analytical Chemistry* 11 (1995), 483.

39. Pounds, C., and K. Smalldon. "The Transfer of Fibres between Clothing Materials and Their Persistence during Wear: Part 1: Fibre Transference." *Journal of the Forensic Science Society* 15 (1975), 29–37.

40. AFMA (2003). American Fiber Manufacturers Association/Fiber Economics Bureau. *Fiber Facts* (December 2004).

41. Grieve, M. C., and T. Biermann. "The Population of Coloured Textile Fibres on Outdoor Surfaces." *Science and Justice* 37 (1997), 231–239.

42. Maynard, P., et al. "Adhesive Tape Analysis: Establishing the Evidential Value of Specific Techniques." *Journal of Forensic Sciences* 46 (2001), 280–287.

43. Sakayanagi, M., et al. "Identification of Pressure-Sensitive Adhesive Polypropylene Tape." *Journal of Forensic Sciences* 48 (2003), 68–76.

44. Merrill, R. A., and E. G. Bartick. "Analysis of Pressure Sensitive Adhesives Tape: I. Evaluation of Infrared Accessory Advances." *Journal of Forensic Sciences* 45 (2000), 93–98.

APPENDIX 1 Alphabetical Glossary of Terms

A

5 Ps A moniker for the 5 most common forms of drugs and physical evidence: pills, powders, plant matter, precursors, and paraphernalia.

Absolute error In any measurement, the difference between the expected (true) value and the experimental value.

Absolute uncertainty In any reading from a device or instrument, the uncertainty associated with it expressed in the units associated with that device (mL, mg, etc.).

Accelerant A solid, liquid, or gas used to start and sustain an intentionally set fire.

Accuracy How close the calculated value is to the true or accepted value.

Achromatic Without color; white, gray, or black.

Active headspace method A sample preparation and pre-concentration procedure in which vapors from a headspace are continually withdrawn and (often) concentrated outside of the original vessel for later analysis. The headspace is continually swept or purged.

Active metabolite A metabolite that is pharmacologically active and possibly toxic.

Addition polymerization Also called *condensation polymerization*; form by a stepwise addition of a monomer to an active site, often (but not always) involving the loss of a small molecule such as water.

Additive color system A color system based on transmission where RGB colors are combined to yield a color, such as on a computer monitor.

Adiabatic combustion A combustion in which Q (heat evolved) is used only to heat the reaction products. It is the basis of some simple combustion models.

Adulterant A material added to dilute a drug that is pharmacologically active. Caffeine and lidocaine are adulterants. The term diluent is often used interchangeably with adulterant and cutting agent, but they are not equivalent.

Adversarial system A system in which opposing arguments are presented to the party that makes the decision (trier of fact).

Alkaloid A basic molecule obtained (or at one time obtained) from a plant. In older literature, a vegetable alkali. Alkaloids are basic due to the presence of an amine group.

Alkyd A group of binders in paints and inks derived from acids and alcohols.

Amine An organic compound or functional group that has a nitrogen but not an oxygen, of the form RNH_2 (primary amine), R_2NH (secondary), R_3N (tertiary).

Amorphous "Without form;" non-crystalline, no repeated structural units. Glass is an amorphous solid.

Amphetamine A synthetic alkaloid and CNS stimulant.

Amylopectin A highly branched and insoluble glucose polymer that is part of starch.

Amylose A linear glucose polymer that is a component of starch.

Anabolic steroids Steroids, natural or synthetic, that encourage muscle growth and purportedly improve athletic performance.

Analgesics Drugs that alleviate pain such as aspirin, acetaminophen, or morphine.

Androgens Male sex hormones.

Angle aperture The angle of the cone of light exiting a sample observed by microscopy.

Anhydroglucose fibers Vegetable fibers; fibers based on glucose polymers.

Anisotropic Materials that have more than one refractive index.

Anomeric carbon A chain terminating carbon in a sugar, bound to a $C{=}O$ that is converted to a chiral center as a result of ring closure.

Antibody A substance produced in an organism in response to the introduction of an antigen.

Anti-Drug Abuse Act (ADA) A federal law passed in 1986 that regulated designer drugs.

Antigen A substance that when introduced into an organism stimulates an immunological response and production of an antibody.

Antiserum A solution of antibodies with a strength reported as the titer.

Anti-Stokes scattering Scattering interactions that start from a virtual excited state; a type of inelastic scattering.

Aperture An opening, often adjustable, that determines how much light or electromagnetic energy passes through; usually designed to limit stray light.

Apparent volume of distribution A calculated quantity in toxicology that is used to express where and how a substance is distributed in the plasma and tissues. V_d depends primarily on the lipophilicity of the drug and the degree of protein binding.

Aryl Another term for a phenyl ring constituent in an organic molecule.

Atomic emission spectroscopy Spectroscopy in which thermal excitation is used to stimulate electronic transitions and photon emission.

Auxochrome A group or substituent on a chromophore that alters the absorption characteristics.

Aza linkage A linkage, such as in a dye molecule of the form —N=.

Aziridine A three-membered ring compound that can be associated with the Emde method of methamphetamine synthesis.

Azo A linkage of the type —N=N—.

Azo linkage A linkage, such as in a dye molecule of the form —N=N—.

B

Bandwidth Generically, the width of a band of electromagnetic energy measured in terms of wavelength. For example, the bandwidth of a monochromatic source such as an HCL is typically 1 nm or less.

Barbiturates A family of drugs based on the barbituric acid skeleton. Once widely abused, the introduction of benzodiazepines has reduced illicit use.

Baseline resolution In a spectrum, chromatogram, or other peak-based output, the situation that occurs when there is some portion of flat baseline in the space separating them.

Batch A group of samples and related QC samples.

Bathochromic shift A shift of absorbance to a higher wavelength.

Bayesian statistics Statistical method that uses likelihood ratios as a part of estimating the probability of certain outcomes.

Bear claw An informal description of the morphology of the cystolythic hairs on the surface of the leaves of the marijuana plant.

Beating A process in paper making in which water is incorporated into the fiber matrix.

Becke line method A method of determining relative refractive index using mounting media of known refractive index and adjustment of focus.

Beer's law $A = \epsilon b c$; the law describing absorption quantitatively and the basis of linear calibration curves in spectroscopy.

Bell curve An informal term for the Gaussian curve derived from the characteristic shape.

Benzodiazepines A group of synthetic alkaloids used to treat anxiety, depression, and related ailments.

Bertrand lens A lens that, when inserted into the optical train of a microscope, allows the viewer to see an image of the filament; used to establish Koehler illumination. A lens that focuses on the rear apeture of the objective lens assembly.

Bias An offset; a repeatable error that is the same magnitude and direction each time.

Bicomponent fibers Fibers that consist of two distinct polymers, such as in a core and sheath design.

Binder Substance used in inks and dyes that bind pigments to the surface; materials that polymerize as they cure.

Binomial distribution A distribution of possible outcomes of an event or events when the outcome of each is binary, as in flipping a coin (heads or tails).

Biopolymer Polymer derived from a natural source such as cellulose or proteins.

Biotransformation The conversion of an ingested xenobiotic substance by biological processes; metabolism is a type of biotransformation.

Birch method A method of making methamphetamine.

Birch reduction A reduction that reduces a benzene ring by removing one double bond.

Birefringence The difference in the refractive indexes of an anisotropic material; can be calculated by subtraction or with a Michel-Levy chart.

Blackbody emitter A theoretical material that emits wavelengths of light that correlate to the temperature of the body.

Blank A sample that contains no analyte of interest.

Bleaching agent A treatment applied to a drug sample to remove tan/brown coloration.

Blind samples QC samples provided to the analysis without a known value.

Boltzmann distribution A function that describes the fraction of atoms in a given excited state as a function of temperature, energy gap, and degeneracy.

Buoyant flame A flame in which the hot gas products and heated air drift up and away from the reaction zone due to density differences generated by heating.

Bulk method An analytical method yielding results from the totality of a sample.

C

Caffeine A xanthine alkaloid sometimes encountered as an adulterant of heroin or related drug samples.

Cahn-Ingold-Prelog convention The most common method used to describe bonding around a chiral atom; uses the R/S notation and assigned priorities.

Caliber The nominal diameter of the barrel of a firearm.

Calibration The process of establishing a link between the output of an instrument or equipment and sample concentration.

Calibration check sample A sample prepared independently of the calibration curve and used to detect problems with the curve.

Capillary electrophoresis/capillary zone electrophoresis Electrophoresis in a capillary tube that exploits electroosmotic flow.

Carbitol Similar to *cellusolve*; a solvent created from glycols and epoxides.

Carbocation A species that contains a carbon atom that carries a positive charge.

Cassegrain lens A focusing device that utilizes highly polished mirrors in lieu of glass lenses.

Cathine An alkaloid and one of the active ingredients in Khat.

Cathinone An alkaloid and one of the active ingredients in Khat.

CBD Cannabidiol, a compound related to THC and found in marijuana.

CBN Cannibinol, a compound related to THC and found in marijuana.

Cellophane Regenerated cellulose cast in a film.

Cellulose A biopolymer consisting of glucose monomers; the fiber of cotton and used in paper.

Cellulose acetate Regenerated cellulose fibers made by treating cellulose with acetic anhydride.

Cellusolve A type of solvent made from glycols and epoxide.

Central nervous system The physiological system consisting of the brain and the spinal cord.

Chain growth polymerization Polymer that grows via a free radical, anion, or cation chain reaction process. Involves the typical generic steps of any free radical reaction: initiation, propagation, and termination.

Chain of custody A cradle-to-grave document that tracks evidence.

Chemical Diversion and Trafficking Act (CDTA) A federal law passed in 1986 designed to limit access to precursor chemicals and pharmaceutical drugs used in clandestine synthesis.

Chemometrics The application of multivariate statistics, data analysis, predictive modeling, and data mining to problems within chemistry.

Chitin A biopolymer that forms the exoskeleton of insects.

Chroma The degree of saturation of a color.

Chromaticity diagram A 2D plot of the chromaticity values x and y derived from the tristimulus values XYZ. A plot of CIE color space.

Chromophore That portion of a molecule that is capable of absorbing light in the UV or visible range. In organic compounds, this is a conjugated system.

CIELAB A mathematical transform applied to chromaticity coordinates to address the asymmetry in a chromaticity diagram.

Circumstantial evidence Evidence that alone proves nothing directly; requires additional inference to prove a fact in dispute.

Civil law Law that deals with disputes between parties.

Classification To assign an exhibit of evidence or other object to a group of like objects based on descriptors such as chemical and physical properties.

Classification Successive categorization of an item into smaller and smaller groups.

Clearance rate The rate at which a drug or other substance is removed or eliminated from the body.

Club drugs Drugs such as MDMA, GHB, LSD, and methamphetamine used by young people and young adults at clubs and parties.

Cluster analysis A technique used to represent relationships within a dataset in two dimensions; identifies similar groups.

Coagulation One process by which film-forming agents in paints and inks create a protective polymer coating; latex paints work this way.

Cobalt thiocyanate A reagent used for a color test for cocaine and related tropane alkaloids.

Coca paste The pasty material that results from crushing and mashing cocoa leaves for purposes of extracting cocaine.

Cocaine A tropane alkaloid and CNS stimulant used medically as a topical anesthetic.

Codeine An opium alkaloid found in the milky latex of opium poppies at ~1–2%.

Color test A test that involves the addition of a reagent or reagents to a sample and if positive, results in production of a color or a color change.

Colorant A substance that can impart or is colored such as dyes or pigments; a substance that absorbs or emits energy in the visible range.

Colorimeter A spectrometer that operates in the VIS range only.

Common source Associating two or more items or exhibit of evidence to one and only one possible source.

Compensator (wedge) A crystal with a known retardation factor; used to distinguish small retardation values.

Competitive assay A category of immunoassay that involves competition by antigens for a limited number of antibody binding sites.

Condensation polymerization See *addition polymerization*.

Condensation reaction An organic reaction in which two separate molecules combine and a water molecule is lost from the combination as a result.

Condenser/condenser lens The assembly in a microscope below the sample stage; focuses the beam into a tight cone of light.

Conjugation (conjugated system) A series of consecutive alternating single and double bonds.

Control chart   A running record of the performance of a device or solution that identifies when performance is no longer within accepted uncertainty ranges.

Controlled Substances Act (CSA)   A federal law first passed in 1970 that placed abused drugs on five schedules based on acceptable medical uses and potential for abuse.

Cook   A slang term for those that manufacture illicit methamphetamine.

Coordination complex   A stable complex formed between a transition metal cation such as copper or cobalt and ligands.

Copolymer   A polymer made of different monomers; nylon is a copolymer.

Correlation coefficient   A value calculated to gauge the goodness of fit of points to a line generated by a linear regression algorithm.

Cracking   Another term for *thermal distillation*; applied to refining crude oil.

Criminal law   Law that deals with crimes committed against society as defined by law and administered by government.

Crossed polars   In PLM, the situation when the analyzer and polarizer are in the light path oriented at 90 degrees to each other.

Cross-reactivity   In immunoassays, the tendency of an antibody to react with antigens other than the target antigen.

Crystal Field Theory (CFT)   A theory that describes bonding in transition metal complexes and explains color and magnetic properties. It is based on electrostatic forces.

Crystal test   A presumptive test performed on a microscope slide in which the color, crystal morphology, and behavior under PLM are used to judge the outcome.

Cutting agent   Substances used to dilute a drug; can be pharmacologically active (adulterant) or inactive (diluent). Caffeine is an adulterant while cornstarch is a diluent.

Cystolith   A nodule of calcium carbonate $CaCO_3$ found in cystolythic hairs.

Cystolithic hair   A fine hair-like structure on the leaves of marijuana informally referred to as "bear claws".

D

Daubert   A court ruling on admissibility that among other things tasked judges with the role of gatekeeper for admissibility of scientific evidence and expert testimony.

Deflagration   Burning or combustion that propagates at less than the speed of sound.

Degressive burning propellant   A propellant that burns from the outside of the granule inward.

Delusterants   Particulates applied to a fiber to decrease the shine or brightness; works by scattering light.

Dependent variable   A variable that has a value derived from or dependent on the value of another.

Depressants   A class of drugs that causes depression of the CNS, resulting in slowed breathing and heart rate and sleepiness, among other symptoms. Alcohol is a depressant.

Depth of field   How far into a sample the field can be viewed and remain in focus.

Deterrent   A material used to treat propellants in order to slow the rate of burn.

Detonation   Explosive combustion driven by pressure and a compressive shockwave.

Detonation wave   A compressive pressure wave (shockwave) that propagates through an explosive and caused combustion.

Diacetylmorphine   See *heroin*.

Diamorphine   See *heroin*.

Diazo coupling   The creation of an azo compound. This is a common way to make dyes and indicators.

Diazoniation   Another term for diazo coupling.

Diazonium salt   The combination of an anion and the cation $R{-}N^+{\equiv}N$.

Dichroic   A material that has two colors due to different absorbances depending on orientation.

Dichroic ratio   The ratio of absorbances at a given wavelength in the parallel and perpendicular directions.

Diffuse reflectance   Reflections in which the angle of reflection is random, such as off an uneven surface; basis of DRIFTS.

Diffusion   Natural spreading of a concentrated band of analyte.

Digestion   A sample preparation technique that attacks and destroys most of the matrix, leaving analytes behind; primarily for inorganics and metals.

Dilli-Koppanyi   A presumptive test used mostly for barbiturates and based on formation of a colored complex with cobalt.

Diluent   A material added to dilute a drug that is pharmacologically inactive. Cornstarch and sugars are diluents. The term diluent is often used interchangeably with adulterant and cutting agent, but they are not equivalent.

Dipole-dipole interactions   Electrostatic attractions or repulsions between partially $(+)$ or $(-)$ regions of two polar molecules.

Direct evidence   Evidence known to a person directly by personal knowledge.

Dispersion   Physical separation of constituent wavelengths by a device such as a prism or grating.

Dissociative anesthetics   Anesthetics that produce what is often described as an "out-of-body" sensation. Includes ketamine and PCP.

Distant precursor   A chemical that can be converted to a controlled substance only after several steps.

Dixon's test   See *Q test*.

Double base powder   Propellant in which the main ingredients are guncotton and nitroglycerin.

Dragendorff test   A color test reagent and TLC developer based on ion pairing with bismuth-iodide complexes.

Dronabinol   Synthetically derived THC.

Drug   A substance that when ingested is capable of inducing a physiological change.

Drug facilitated sexual assault   A sexual assault that involves the use of a predator drug such as rohypnol or ketamine.

Dry extraction   In drug analysis, a simple one-step extraction method in which a solvent is added to a solid sample. Typically, the next step is GCMS analysis of the extract.

Drying oils   Oils that speed the drying and curing of binders in paint and inks; linseed oil is among the best known.

Duplicates   Separate samples taken from the same source; not the result of subdividing one sample.

Duquenois-Levine   A presumptive test for THC, the active ingredient in marijuana.

Dye   A colorant that is soluble in the solvent or vehicle being used.

E

Ecstasy   Another name for the stimulant MDMA.

Effluent   See *eluant*.

Electron impact ionization   Ionization and fragmentation of molecules entering a mass spectrometer achieved by collision with a stream of electrons produced by a heated filament.

Electronic transition   Transition of an atom or ion from the ground to an excited state via electron promotion among atomic orbitals.

Electroosmotic flow   Flow of ions that occurs in a silica capillary tube exploited in capillary electrophoresis.

Electropherogram   Output of CE or MEK analysis.

Electrophoresis   Separation of charged and neutral species based on size-to-charge ratio.

Eluant   The material that exists in a SPE or chromatographic column.

Eluent   The solvent or mobile phase used in SPE or chromatography.

Embalming   The process of preservation of a body that involves removal of the blood and replacement with preservative solution, such as one containing formaldehyde.

Emde method   A type of methamphetamine synthesis.

Enantiomers   Isomers of a compound with a chiral center that are mirror images of each other.

Enantioselectivity   The ability of a sorbent (typically a cyclodextrin) to separate chiral compounds.

Endogenous substance   A substance, compound, element, or material that is naturally present in the body. Arsenic is such as substance, but it is found in very small amounts.

Endorphins   A term derived from endogenous morphine, compounds that mimic the psychological effects of morphine and that can produce a feeling of well-being and euphoria.

Entomotoxicology   The analysis of insects and associated materials found at a death scene for the presence of drugs or poison. The results are used to help reconstruct the cause or contributing factors in a death.

Enzyme linked immunoassay   A heterogeneous immunoassay that is based on an enzyme catalyzed colorimetric reaction.

Enzyme multiplied immunoassay   A heterogeneous immunoassay that is based on an enzyme catalyzed colorimetric reaction.

Ephedra   A grass, herbal supplement, and natural source of ephedrine and pseudoephedrine.

Ephedrine   A natural or semi-synthetic alkaloid that is used as a decongestant and precursor in methamphetamine synthesis.

Equilibrium constant   The ratio of products to reactants raised to the power of the coefficients.

Ergot alkaloid   Alkaloids with an indole structure derived from fungus. LSD is an ergot alkaloid.

Ergotism   Ergot alkaloid poisoning with symptoms such as hallucinations.

Euclidean distance   The distance between two points in data space, be it 2, 3, or more dimensional.

Evanescent wave   In an ATR, a series of reflective absorptive interactions; multiple internal reflections.

Excipients   An inactive or inert ingredient found in commercial drugs and medicines.

Exclusive evidence   Evidence that by itself excludes a person or a possibility.

Exhibit   A piece or individual item of physical evidence.

Exploratory data analysis   Analysis of a data set using statistical and graphical techniques.

Explosion   Combustion that propagates faster than the speed of sound.

Explosive power index   The power of explosives scaled to that of picric acid and expressed as a percentage.

Extenders   Compounds, often pigments such as calcium carbonate, added to inks or paints.

External standard curve   A calibration curve in which the standards are made in simple solvents that may not match the matrix.

Extinction   In PLM, the point at which a birefringent material is not visible.

Extraction   A sample preparation technique that removes the analyte from the matrix.

Eyepiece   See *ocular lens*.

F

Field of view   How large a portion of the sample can be seen in focus at one time.

Film-forming agent   A binder or resin that polymerizes and protects a colorant in a paint or ink.

First order process   A chemical reaction or other process, the speed of which depends only on the concentration of one reactant.

First pass metabolism   Metabolic changes that occur to a drug after absorption in the GI tract but before any pharmacological effect can occur.

Flame ionization detector   A GC detector selective to organic carbon and C-H bonds; based on creation of charged species in the flame.

Flash point   The lowest temperature at which an ignitable mixture is capable of combustion.

Flow cell   A cell used to isolate separated analytes in a flowing system long enough to obtain a spectrochemical measurement with an adequate pathlength.

Fluorescence   Emission of a photon from an excited state; immediate.

Fluorescent polarization immunoassay   A homogenous immunoassay in which the label is a fluorophore.

Focal length   The distance along the optic axis of a lens that covers the distance from the lens to the principal focus.

Focal plane   The plane at which a real image will be focused; the plane is centered about the focal point.

Fourier transform   A mathematical procedure that converts a function from the time domain to the frequency domain; a function that translates an interferogram into a spectrum.

Free radical   A species that has an atom with an unpaired electron.

Frye rule   A rule of admissibility of scientific evidence and expert testimony that relies on general acceptance by the scientific community.

Functional groups   A group of atoms within an organic molecule that are reactive. The functional group in alcohols is —OH for example. Many drug molecules have multiple functional groups.

G

Galvanization   A treatment applied to steel that prevents rust; zinc is used.

Gauge   In a shotgun, the size of the barrel.

Gaussian curve   The graphical depiction of the Gaussian or normal distribution.

Gaussian distribution   A type of distribution that can be assumed by a set of replicate measurements of the same criteria. The data is centered about a mean value and the spread is defined by the standard deviation.

General unknown   An exhibit for which there is no prior knowledge or outward signs that point to its composition. Forensic samples are often treated as general unknowns even if there is some prior knowledge.

Glass transition temperature (T_g) Temperature at which a polymer is transformed to a more rubbery material, but distinct from a melting point.

Glycogen   A highly branched glucose polymer; primary energy storage molecule (glucose based) in animals.

Graphite furnace   An alternative sample holder and thermal excitation source for atomic absorption spectroscopy.

Griess test   A presumptive test used in the analysis of GSR.

Grubbs test   A hypothesis test to identify outliers.

Guncotton   A propellant made by treating cotton with nitric and sulfuric acid.

H

Half-life $(t_{1/2})$ The amount of time for half of the original amount of a substance ingested or existing in the body to be eliminated or converted to another substance.

Hapten   The large protein portion of a drug-protein complex used to stimulate the production of antibodies.

Hashish   The oily resin of the flowering tops of marijuana plants. Hashish has a high concentration of the active ingredient THC.

Headspace   The gas above a solvent or sample into which analytes can volatilize.

Hemicellulose   A saccharide-based biopolymer composed of subunits of glucose, galactose, mannose, and xylose.

Hemp   Marijuana; a term used to describe the plant when it is used to obtain fibers and other products unrelated to illicit drug use.

Henderson-Hasselbalch equation   An equation used to describe buffers and other weak acids; relates pH to pK_a and concentrations of acid and conjugate base.

Henry's Law   The law that relates partial pressure of a substance above a solution to the concentration in the solution; $K_H * P_a = [A]$.

Heroin   Diacetylmorphine; diamorphine. A potent narcotic prepared by acetylation of morphine.

Heterogeneous assay   A category of immunoassay in which the bound and unbound phases must be separated prior to measurement.

High explosive   An explosive that is relatively stable and insensitive to heat and shock.

High spin complex   A complex in which electrons are distributed among the d-orbitals with the maximum number of unpaired electrons.

Hollow cathode lamp   A monochromatic light source used in atomic absorption spectroscopy.

Hollow viscose   A rayon produced such that there is a hollow space inside.

Homogeneous   A substance or sample that is the same no matter what portion is examined.

Homogeneous assay   A category of immunoassay in which the bound and unbound phases do not have to be separated prior to measurement.

Homolytic cleavage   During formation of free radicals, an even splitting of an electron pair, one electron per involved atom.

Homopolymer   A polymer consisting of all the same monomers.

Hot stage   An accessory for a microscope that allows for gradual and accurate heating. Used to determine melting points of fibers as one example.

Hue   The descriptive color such as red, blue, green, etc.

Human performance toxicology   Area of toxicology that concentrates on substances that alter performance, such as alcohol and steroids.

Hybridoma cells   Cells created by a fusion of antibody-producing cells and cancer cells; used to produce monoclonal antibodies.

Hydrocodone   A synthetic or semi-synthetic opiate alkaloid.

Hydromorphone   A synthetic or semi-synthetic opiate alkaloid.

Hydrophilic   "Water loving"; water soluble. Hydrophilic compounds are usually lipophobic.

Hydrophobic   "Water hating"; water insoluble; hydrophobic compounds are usually lipophilic.

Hyphenated instrument   A combination of a separation module with a detector module such as GC-MS (GCMS); hyphen is often omitted.

Hyperchromic shift   An increase in λ_{max} of a chromophore resulting in a more intense color.

Hypergeometric distribution   A distribution of possible outcomes of an event or events when samples are withdrawn or replaced.

Hypochromic shift   A decrease in the λ_{max} of a chromophore resulting in a less intense color.

Hypothesis tests   Statistical tests that compare two quantities, one calculated and one tabulated, to determine the acceptance or rejection of a hypothesis.

Hypsochromic shift   A shift of absorbance to a lower wavelength.

I

Ice   A form of methamphetamine purified by re-crystallization and resembling shaved ice.

Identification   In forensic science, the linking of something unambiguously to one and only one possible source.

Ignition energy   The amount of energy that must be transferred to a fuel/air mixture within flammability limits to cause ignition.

Immediate precursor   A chemical precursor that can be converted to the controlled substance by 1 or 2 simple steps and easily obtainable materials.

Immunoassay   Analytical technique based on antigen-antibody reactions.

Immunogen   The drug-hapten complex that stimulates the production of antibodies.

Immunological reaction   The binding of an antigen to an antibody.

Incendiary device   In arson fires, the device used to supply ignition energy.

Inclusive evidence   Evidence that by itself includes a person or a possibility.

Independent variable   A variable with a value that does not depend on or derive from any other variables.

Indole   A molecule that contains a heterocyclic structure of a benzene ring connected to a 5-membered ring containing a nitrogen.

Inductively coupled plasma   An extremely hot excitation source for elemental analysis via emission or mass spectrometry. A plasma is not a flame and reaches much higher temperatures, so it can excite a significant portion of the ground state atoms.

Inhalants   Volatile substances that are abused by inhalation and that produce effects similar to anesthetics.

Intaglio printing   A process used in making currency that creates ridges and grooves in the printed substrate; an anti-counterfeiting measure.

Interference colors   In PLM, colors observed for a birefringent material under crossed polars away from extinction.

Interferogram   A plot of the distance traveled in an interferometer by the mirror versus retardation; can also be plotted versus time.

Interferometry   Techniques that exploit interference (constructive and destructive) to limit or control the wavelengths of light emitted by a source.

Internal standard curve   A calibration method that involves addition of internal standards to all samples and standards and to which concentration and responses are ratioed.

Intramuscular "Into the muscle;" a method of injection for drug delivery.

Intravenous "Into a vein;" a method of injection or drug delivery.

Ion mobility spectrometry Gas phase separation of ion/molecule clusters at atmospheric pressure; generically gas phase electrophoresis.

Ion pair A tightly bound cation and anion that behave as molecular compound or particle in solution.

Ion-dipole interactions Electrostatic attractions or repulsions between an ion and a partially $(+)$ or $(-)$ region of a polar molecule.

Ion-ion interactions Electrostatic attractions and interactions between two ions.

Ionization center In a large molecule, a site where ionization can occur typically in an acid/base manner.

Isoelectric point (isoelectric pH) The pH at which a molecule with multiple ionization centers is neutral.

Isotope ratio The ratio of a heavier stable natural isotope to a lighter more abundant isotope. Ratios are used in drug profiling.

Isotropic Materials that have the same refractive index regardless of orientation.

K

Ketamine A veterinary anesthetic diverted for abuse as a dissociative anesthetic and club drug.

Khat A leave that is chewed for its stimulant properties much as coca leaves. It is native to the Middle East and Africa.

Knowns Samples with known accepted values.

Koehler illumination In a microscope, the alignment of lamp and lenses that produces optimal and even illumination.

Kraft pulping A pulping process used in paper product conducted at alkaline pH; principle lignin dissolution stage.

Kramers-Kronig Transform A mathematical transform of FTIR data that corrects for specular reflection.

L

Lactone A cyclic ester that can form from an internal condensation between an alcohol functional group and a carboxylic acid functional group.

Laminar flame A flame with defined regions delineated by temperatures and flame color.

Latex The thick, milky liquid that can be extracted from an unripe seed pod of the opium poppy. The consistency is like that of latex paint.

Le Châtelier's Principle When a chemical equilibrium exists, any disturbance of the system will result in the system compensating.

Lean mixture A combustive mixture in which the concentration of oxidant is greater than the stoichiometric ratio.

Least-squared fit A fit of a line or other curve to a set of points that is optimized by minimizing the total distance of all points to the curve. Distances are squared to eliminate potential canceling with some $(+)$ and others $(-)$ relative to the curve.

Leuckart method A synthetic method to make methamphetamine from P2P.

Leuco form A soluble form of a vat dye.

Lewis acid A species that can accept electrons, such as a transition metal cation in a coordination complex.

Lewis base A species that can donate electrons such as nitrogen or oxygen.

Lidocaine An alkaloid related to cocaine used medically as a topical anesthetic; also an adulterant of cocaine and heroin.

Lieberman reagent/test A presumptive test based on nitrous acid. Also spelled as Liebermann.

Ligand A ion or molecule that coordinates with the central metal cation in a coordination complex.

Ligand field theory A theory that is used to describe bonding and interactions in transition metal complexes.

Lignin A family of compounds of related biopolymers based on phenylpropyl units that are linked by strong $C - C$ bonds resistant to many degradation pathways.

Lignocellulose The complex of cellulose-based materials that impart rigidity and structure to plants.

Like dissolves like (LdL) A rule of thumb concerning polarity and solubility. A polar solute will dissolve in a polar solvent but not in a non-polar one.

Lime method A procedure used to extract morphine from opium using lime (calcium hydroxide) to make extract basic.

Linear correlation A relationship between two variables that can be described by a linear equation of the form $y = mx + b$.

Linear dynamic range The concentration range over which a calibration curve demonstrates linear response with concentration. LDR is usually reported in terms of orders of magnitude.

Linear regression The process of creating a straight line and linear equation to describe the relationship between a dependent and independent variable.

Linkage distance In clustering, the distance between two points amalgamated into one cluster, usually expressed as the Euclidean distance.

Lipophilic   Literally, "fat loving"; molecules that are more soluble in fats and oils than in water. The degree of lipophilicity is gauged by the LogP value (octanol/water partition coefficient).

Lipophobic   "Fat hating"; insoluble in nonpolar solvents. Compounds that are lipophobic are usually hydrophilic.

Liquid/liquid extraction (LLE)   Separation and isolation of analytes based on preferential affinity for one solvent over the other; solvents must not be miscible.

Living polymerization   A self-perpetuating anionic or cationic polymerization that is stopped by quenching ("killing").

Log P/K$_{ow}$ The relative solubility of an analyte on octanol; a measure of lipophilicity/hydrophobicity.

Low explosive   An explosive that detonates easily and is sensitive to heat or shock.

Low spin complex   A complex in which electrons are distributed among the d-orbitals with the least number of unpaired electrons.

Lower flammability limit (LFL)   The lowest mixture ratio of fuel and oxidant that will ignite and sustain combustion.

LSD   Lysergic acid diethylamide, an ergot alkaloid and Schedule I hallucinogen.

L'vov platform   A graphite shelf where sample is placed in a graphite furnace used in atomic absorption spectroscopy.

Lysergic acid   Ergot alkaloid and precursor to LSD.

Lysergic acid methylpropylamide (LAMPA)   An isomer of LSD.

M

MAM   Monoacetylmorphine. An intermediate between morphine and heroin in which C3 or C6 is attached to an acetyl group.

Marinol   A commercially produced medicine containing synthetic THC (dronabinol).

Marquis Reagent   A color test reagent that reacts with a variety of controlled substances, principally alkaloids.

Mass spectrometer   A detector that ionizes and fragments molecules and creates a reproducible and usually unique fragmentation pattern that can be used for identification.

Mass transfer   The process of a solute moving in and out of a stationary phase.

Matrix controls   Samples of pristine background material that must be analyzed to facilitate interpretation of analysis.

Matrix mismatch   The situation that arises when the solvent system used to generate a calibration curve does not match the matrix of the sample.

Mayer test   An older and rarely used presumptive test based on mercuric compounds.

Mean (average)   The sum of all values in a population or sample divided by the number of samples or measurements.

Measurable quantity   Legally, similar to a, "useable quantity," but in chemical terms, more akin to the limit of detection (LOD).

Medicine   A mixture of drugs or other physiologically active materials. Aspirin is a drug while a cold preparation is a medicine.

Melt extrusion   A method of casting or making fibers in which raw polymer is heated until liquid and then extruded into a film or fiber.

Mescaline   A tryptamine alkaloid obtained from the peyote cactus.

Metabolites   Products of metabolic reactions and conversions.

Metamerism   Occurs when a colorant takes on a different perceived color based on a change in illumination.

Methamphetamine   A synthetic alkaloid and CNS stimulant.

Methamphetamine Anti-Proliferation Act (MAPA)   A federal law passed in 2000 to address the availability of methamphetamine precursors.

Micelles   Structures formed by surfactants above a critical concentration in water.

Micellular electrokinetic chromatography (MEKC)   Capillary electrophoresis using micelles and selective partitioning to separate neutral species.

Michel-Levy chart   A chart showing interference colors and relating them to birefringence and thickness; shown in the color insert.

Microcrystal tests   Another term for crystal tests; refers to the use of the microscope to study crystal form.

Microspectrophotometry   Use of a microscope in conjunction with a spectrometer.

Minimum ignition temperature   The temperature at which molecules in the environment can transfer sufficient energy to the fuel to overcome E_a and begin the reaction.

Mobile phase   In solid phase extraction or chromatography, the phase that moves over the solid or stationary phase; may be polar, nonpolar, or inert.

Mobility spectrum   Output of an ion mobility spectrometry.

Mode of ingestion   The route or pathway by which a drug or poison enters the body.

Molecular explosive   An explosive that detonates relatively easily when in the pure form.

Molecular orbitals (MO)   An orbital that forms from the overlap and combination of atomic orbitals and that belongs to a molecule; a covalently bonded compound.

Molecular transition   Transition of a molecule (covalently bonded) from the ground to an excited state via electron promotion among molecular orbitals.

Monochromator A device such as a prism, filter, or grating that selectively removes all but a narrow range of electromagnetic energy from an impinging source.

Monoclonal antibody A nearly pure antibody produced by a several step procedure that includes the use of hybridoma cells.

Monomer The base unit of a polymer such as vinyl chloride in PVC.

Morphine The principal active opium alkaloid extracted from the opium poppy found at ~10% levels in the milky latex.

Multidimensional data Data that has more than 3 variables associated with it; data that can not be examined with graphical methods without selecting or reducing the number of variables.

Multivariate statistics/analysis Statistics applied to data with more than one variable.

Munsell Color System A color space based on a catalog of standard colors and a uniform 3D color space.

Muzzle velocity Speed at which a projectile leaves the barrel of a firearm.

N

NA The numerical aperture of a lens; an ability of the lens to collect light. As magnification increases, NA decreases.

Narcotic Analgesic that also acts as a CNS depressant.

Narcotics A class of drugs that relieve pain and encourage sleep. Morphine and heroin are narcotics.

Natural drug/natural product A drug that is derived directly from a plant. THC and morphine are natural products.

Nazi method Another term for the Birch method, a clandestine methamphetamine synthesis.

Nebulizer A device that converts a flowing liquid into a mist, somewhat like a thumb over a garden hose.

Negative control A sample that should produce a negative or no reaction or response in an analytical procedure; part of QA and QC.

Neurotransmitter A compound vital in the process of transmitting a nerve impulse.

Neutral burning propellant A propellant that burns evenly throughout the granule due to pores and holes that expose more surface area.

Nitrocellulose Informally, *guncotton*; made by treating cotton with nitric and sulfuric acids; attaches nitro groups to cellulose.

Nitrogen phosphorus detector A GC detector selective to N- and P-containing compounds; similar in design to an FID and includes an alkali salt.

Nitroprusside A complexed species with the formula $[Fe(CN_5)NO]_2^-$.

Non-competitive assay A category of immunoassay that does not involve competition by antigens for a limited number of antibody binding sites.

Normal phase Separation or chromatography using a nonpolar stationary phase and a polar mobile phase.

Normalization The process of scaling data across a data set such that large variables do not overwhelm small ones.

Noscapine An opiate alkaloid sometimes encountered as an adulterant of heroin or related drug samples.

NSAID Non-steroidal anti-inflammatory drugs such as aspirin that relieve pain by reducing inflammation at the sight of an injury.

Nylon A class of completely synthetic fibers and the first completely synthetic fiber; also a copolymer.

O

Objective lens The lens or lens assembly closest to the sample in optical microscopes.

Ocular lens The lens or lens assembly closest to the viewer's eyes in optical microscopes.

Opiate alkaloids Alkaloids derived from the opium poppy.

Optic axis The imaginary line that runs through the point of a curved lens where the curvature is at a maximum; may or may not be the geometric centerline.

Optical isomers Enantiomers; compounds with chiral atoms that rotate plane polarized light in opposite directions (+/- or d/l).

Oriented polymer A strong polymer in which all the chains are aligned parallel.

Outlier A sample result that appears to be unusually far from the mean in a normal distribution; can be evaluated using significance tests.

Oxidation A gain of oxygen; a loss of hydrogen; or a loss of electrons.

Oxycodone A synthetic or semi-synthetic opiate alkaloid and the active ingredient in Oxycontin®.

Oxycontin A time-released form of oxycodone that is widely abused. Users crush the tablets and get the entire dose at once.

Oxygen balance A measure of the amount of oxygen in a molecule that undergoes combustion. A positive oxygen balance means that all the oxygen needed for complete combustion is available intramolecularly.

P

Papaverine An opiate alkaloid sometimes encountered as an adulterant of heroin or related drug samples.

Paracetamol A term used for acetaminophen outside of the United States.

Paraphernalia Equipment and supplies used in the process of ingesting a drug. Pipes, mirrors, and syringes are examples.

Partitioning A preference or affinity for one physical phase or state over another; the basis of solvent extraction and chromatography.

Passive headspace method A sample preparation procedure in which vapors from a headspace are withdrawn for analysis.

PCP A powerful dissociative anesthetic, easily synthesized and used as a club drug. It is often seized as a liquid.

p-DMAB p-Dimethylaminobenzaldehyde, a color test reagent also called Erlich's reagent. It is particularly valuable for detecting ergot alkaloids such as LSD.

per-Fluorotributylamine (PFTBA) A compound used to standardize the performance of mass spectrometers to insure intercomparability of spectra.

Petroleum distillate A product that is or was at one time derived from crude oil by distillation techniques.

Peyote The dried top of the peyote cactus *Lophophora williamsii* used by Native Americans for religious purposes and abused for the mescaline content. Also called *mescal buttons*.

Pharmacodynamics The study of effects of drugs over time and is concerned with the interaction of the drug with its target.

Pharmacokinetics The study of the movement of the drug and metabolic products through the body; studies the traversal of a drug or foreign substance (xenobiotic) by dividing it into stages of absorption, distribution, metabolism, and elimination.

Pharmacology The study of how drugs behave once ingested; can be broadly divided into pharmacodynamics and pharmacokinetics; includes metabolisms, rates of elimination, etc.

Phenacetin A non-narcotic analgesic sometimes encountered as an adulterant.

Phenethylamines The family of stimulants based on a phenyl ethylamine structure. The family includes amphetamine and methamphetamine.

Phenobarbitone A barbiturate; occasionally encountered as an adulterant of heroin or related drug samples.

Phosphorescence Emission of a photon from an excited state; emission is not immediate but rather delayed.

Photodiode array (PDA) A detector that works by detecting photons dispersed in space; one photodiode per geometrical location.

Pigment A colorant that is insoluble in the solvent; exists as a suspension and not a solution.

pK value The $-\log$ of the quantity of interest such as pH or pK_a

Planar chromatography See *Thin layer chromatography*.

Plasticizer An additive to a polymer, typically a phthalate, that imparts softness and pliability.

Pleochroic A material that has two or more colors due to different absorbances depending on orientation.

Point of origin The location(s) where a fire began.

Polarity Arises from asymmetric electron distribution around a molecule; leads to partially positive and partially negative areas.

Polarizable bonds Chemical bonds that are altered by passage of light; bonds in which the electron clouds can be distorted by scattering interactions.

Polarized light Light that vibrates in a single plane; also called *plane polarized light*.

Polarized light microscopy (PLM) A technique that uses polarizing filters in the optical train of a microscope.

Polyclonal antibody A mix of related antibodies produced when an antigen is introduced into an organism.

Polysaccharide A polymer consisting of sugars such as cellulose.

Population The larger group of possible measurements from which a subset is drawn; has N member.

Positive control A sample that should produce a positive reaction or response in an analytical procedure; part of QA and QC.

Post-mortem (toxicology) Literally "after death;" toxicology that analyzes biological materials collected at autopsy

Power (of a color) A value derived from the location of a color as plotted on a chromaticity diagram.

Precedent That which has gone before; previous rulings and approaches made by courts and supported over time.

Precision Reproducibility of replicate measurements.

Precursors Chemical compounds, including pharmaceuticals that are used as the starting point for clandestine synthesis of controlled substances. A precursor can be immediate (one step from product) or distant (several steps).

Percussive explosive An explosive that is shock-sensitive, such as a primer used in ammunition.

Predator drugs A class of drugs used in drug facilitated sexual assault.

Presumptive test A test used to narrow down the possible identity of a sample or to classify it. Results are not conclusive and a positive result is best phrased as "more likely than not."

Primers Devices used in ammunition to ignite the propellant; consist of low explosives that are shock sensitive (percussive explosives).

Principal component analysis (PCA) A technique used to reduce the dimensionality of data and to reveal groups; works based on creating new linear combinations of variables.

Principal focus The point in space where light rays that have passed through a lens will converge.

Probability sampling The selection of an unbiased subset for sampling a large population such that the subset adequately and appropriately represents the characteristics of the population.

Procaine An alkaloid related to cocaine used medically as a topical anesthetic; also an adulterant of cocaine and heroin.

Product moment correlation coefficient See *correlation coefficient*.

Profiling A thorough organic and inorganic analysis of a drug, diluents, adulterants, contaminants, and in some cases, isotope ratios and DNA profile. The goal is to link a sample to a batch and/or place of origin.

Progressive burning A propellant that burns slowly at first due to a deterrent. Once the deterrent is burned away, the burn speed increases.

Propagation of uncertainty A technique that combines uncertainties from individual steps to obtain an estimate of the uncertainty of a process.

Propellant A powdered combustive fuel used in firearms; typically contains nitroglycerin and guncotton.

Prostaglandin (PG) Fatty acid derivatives found associated with cell membranes that affect many processes, including inflammation.

Provenance Location or place of origin. In drug profiling of natural products, the geographic area where the plant grew.

Pseudocrystalline A material such as a synthetic fiber that has organization and repeating structure but that is not a true crystal.

Pseudoephedrine Also called *pseudofed*, a natural or semi-synthetic alkaloid that is used as a decongestant and precursor in methamphetamine synthesis.

Psilocin/psilocyn An indole amine/tryptamine found in mushrooms *Psilocybe mexicana*.

Psilocybin/psilocybin An indole amine/tryptamine found in mushrooms *Psilocybe mexicana*; converted to psilocin by dephosphorylation.

Purge-and-trap A type of active headspace method in which analytes are trapped and pre-concentrated before being desorbed and analyzed.

Pyranose A 5-membered ring form of a sugar.

Pyrogens Literally, "fire starters;" compounds released by white blood cells in response to injury or infection. Pyrogens act on the hypothalamus and stimulate the release of prostaglandins.

Pyrolysis Decomposition by heat in an inert atmosphere; not combustion.

Pyrolysis (combustion reactions) A high temperature decomposition that occurs in a reducing environment; an inlet for instrumentation and also an element of combustion reactions.

Q

Q test A hypothesis test to identify outliers.

Quadrupole A type of mass filter for a mass spectrometer that uses DC/Rf voltages to control ion trajectories.

Quality assurance (QA) The philosophy and practices used to insure the goodness and reliability of data.

Quality control (QC) Procedures used as part of quality assurance.

Quiescent Quiet, an unstirred solution.

Quinine A compound often encountered as a diluent of heroin samples.

R

Radiation-less transition A transition of an excited state to a lower state that occurs without emission of a photon; a transition in which energy is dissipated typically as heat.

Radioimmunoassay A heterogeneous immunoassay in which the label is a gamma or beta emitter.

Raman spectroscopy A vibration technique based on scattering and polarizable bonds.

Random errors Errors that are not the same, not reproducible, equally plus and minus, and generally small.

Rayleigh scattering Scattering that results in no change in wavelength; elastic scattering.

Rayon A semi-synthetic fiber made from regenerated cellulose.

Real image An image created by a lens that can be projected onto a screen; an image that exists at a plane in space and does not require one to look through a lens to see it.

Reduction A loss of oxygen; a gain of hydrogen; or a gain of electrons.

Reductive amination The chemical conversion required to go from P2P to methamphetamine.

Refluxing Prolonged heating in an enclosed container in which evaporated solvent condenses and is recovered.

Regression line A line describing points that have a linear relationship or correlation.

Relative affinity The comparative affinity of a compound to different phases such as two different solvents; the basis of partitioning, separations, and chromatography.

Relative error In any measurement, the difference between the expected (true) value and the experimental value expressed as a percentage or other unitless way.

Relative uncertainty In any reading from a device or instrument, the uncertainty associated with it expressed in a unitless form such as one-part-per ... or as a percentage.

Reliability The "goodness" of data; measured by accuracy and precision.

Replicates Repeat measurements of the same criteria under similar conditions; multiple samples derived from one larger sample.

Representative sample A sub sample of a larger sample or group that accurately reflects the composition of the whole.

Resins Natural binders used in paints and inks.

Resolving power The ability of a lens or optical train to distinguish two objects; $= 0.6/NA$.

Reversed phase Separation or chromatography using a polar stationary phase and a nonpolar mobile phase.

Rich mixture A combustive mixture in which the concentration of fuel is greater than the stoichiometric ratio.

Ring opening polymerization Polymerization that involves a ring opening such as the opening of an epoxide ring.

'Roid rage An informal term referring to excessively aggressive behavior that can be associated with steroid abuse.

ROYGBIV An acronym for the simple colors of visible light: red (~ 700 nm wavelength), orange, yellow, green, blue indigo, and violet (~ 400 nm).

S

Salicylates Drugs such as aspirin based on the salicylic acid skeleton.

Saltpeter An older name for KNO_3, potassium nitrate.

Sample A subset of a larger population selected for analysis.

Sampling statistics The application of statistical techniques to sampling to insure that the samples are sufficient to adequately represent the larger population or sample.

Scanning electron microscopy (SEM) An imaging technique that uses interaction of a sample with electrons to create an image.

Schiff base A compound of the form $R_2C = NR$.

Seed fiber A natural fiber such as cotton that is derived from the seed pod of a plant.

Semi-synthetic A drug that is derived indirectly from plant matter. Heroin is a semi-synthetic that is made by acetylation of morphine, which is derived from opium.

Sequential In a detector, the process of scanning one-at-a-time through masses or wavelengths.

Sign of elongation The sign of the birefringence; ppositive SE is where the parallel RI exceed the perpendicular under crossed polars.

Significance test See *hypothesis test*.

Significant figures These arise from instrumentation and consist of every digit that is certain plus the first uncertain one.

Simon test See *sodium nitroprusside test*.

Simultaneous In a detector, the ability to detect a range of masses or wavelengths simultaneously rather than by traditional scanning.

Single base powder Propellant in which the main ingredient is guncotton.

Snell's Law An expression that described the angles of refraction of light when it passes through an interface;

$$\frac{\sin i}{\sin r} = \frac{n_2}{n_1}$$

where i = angle of incidence and r = angle of refraction.

Sodium nitroprusside test A presumptive test using the nitroprusside complex and the NO associated with the central iron cation.

Solid phase extraction An extraction in which one of the phases involved in the selective partitioning is bound to a solid support.

Solid phase microextraction Extraction into a solid phase coated on a microfiber. The pre-concentrated analytes are typically introduced directly in the injector port of a GC.

Solubility S, calculated using K_{sp}.

Solution casting A method of making thin polymer films by pouring a solution in a thin film and allowing it to dry or cure.

Solvent extraction Use of a solvent to extract an analyte or analytes from a matrix.

Solvent strength A measure of the ability of a solvent to elute a material in solid phase extractions or chromatography, based on relative polarity.

Specular reflection "Perfect reflection"; angle of reflection = angle of incidence; occurs at a surface where there is a change in the refractive index.

Spikes Analytes purposely added to a sample to gauge recovery and flag potential matrix problems and affects.

Spinning The physical process of converting polymer into a synthetic fiber product.

Spontaneous ignition temperature See *minimum ignition temperature*.

Spot plate A plate, typically in the range of $3 \times 4''$ made of white or black ceramic or glass. Spot plates have depressions in which the sample is placed and color test reagents are added. The design and color helps with interpretation of colors produced.

Spot test Used as a synonym for color and presumptive testing. The name arose from an early method of qualitative analysis in which small spots were applied to paper and the paper rotated to disperse reagent in a radial manner.

Springall Roberts rules One of several sets of rules used to approximate the mixture of products produced in an explosion.

Stabilizer   An organic constituent of propellants.

Stable isotope ratio (SIR)   The ratio of stable isotopes ratios such as $^{13}C/^{12}C$ that are determined by mass spectrometry and that can be incorporated as part of drug profiling of plant-derived substances such as heroin.

Standard addition   A calibration method which uses the sample as the matrix and to which increasing aliquots of the target analyte are added.

Standard deviation   The average deviation of all points in a data set from the mean of that data set.

Standard observer curves   In the CIE colorant space system, three spectral curves that describe the contribution of red, green, and blue light to a perceived color.

Standard operating procedure   A laboratory procedure or analytical method that has been validated and accepted for routine use in a forensic or other laboratory; SOP.

Standards   Analytical solutions used for calibration; ASTM documents describing a standard procedure or method.

Starches   Glucose polymers that store energy; include glycogen, amylopectin, and amylose.

Stationary phase   A solid immobile material to which an active material is bound; the stationary phase in solid phase extraction or chromatography; may be polar or nonpolar.

Stimulants   A class of drugs that stimulates the CNS resulting in elevated heart rate and less of a need for sleep. Methamphetamine is a stimulant.

Stoichiometric ratio   The ratio of fuel to oxidant in a combustion reaction, ϕ. The ratio is critical in determining the heat evolved Q.

Stokes scattering   Scattering interactions that start from the ground state; a type of inelastic scattering.

Subcutaneous   Below the skin surface; a method of injection for drug delivery.

Subtractive color system   A color system based on reflection where colorants absorb or subtract colors; used in color laser printing such as CMY.

Surface absorption-reflection   A process where energy is absorbed to some degree by a substrate before being reflected.

Surface method   An analytical method yielding results from the surface of a sample, typically within a few microns.

Synthetic   A drug that is synthesized in the traditional organic chemistry sense as opposed to extracted from a plant or obtained by simple chemical processing of a plant extract.

Systematic errors   Errors that are the same size and magnitude each time; reproducible errors.

T

Temperature (color)   The temperature of a color refers to how it correlates to light emitted by a blackbody emitter.

Testosterone   A male sex hormone that is produced in the testes. It plays a central role in the development of secondary sex characteristics. It is a steroid hormone derived from cholesterol.

Tetracaine   An alkaloid related to cocaine used medically as a topical anesthetic; also an adulterant of cocaine and heroin.

Tetrahydrocannibinol   The principal active ingredient in marijuana, shorthand for delta-9-tetrahydrocannibinol (Δ^9-THC).

THC   See *tetrahydrocannibinol*.

Thebaine   An opium alkaloid used as a starting point for the manufacture of drugs such as hydrocodone.

Theophylline   A xanthine alkaloid sometimes encountered as an adulterant of heroin or related drug samples.

Theoretical plates   A measure of the efficiency and resolving power of a chromatographic column; based on a distillation model.

Thermal transfer printing   Mechanical printing in which colorant is delivered to a surface by heating of a waxy substrate.

Thermoplastic behavior   Physical changes observed in a polymer as it is heated.

Thermoplastic polymers   Polymers with dispersed ordered and amorphous regions that can be molded by heating.

Thermosetting polymers   Polymers that set with heat but that cannot be reheated and remolded, in contrast to thermoplastic polymers.

Thin layer chromatography (TLC)   Chromatography in which the solid phase is coated on a support such as glass and solvent is drawn up by capillary action.

Thinner   Diluent in a street drug sample.

Three-dimensional data   Data from a hyphenated instrument that produces three dimensions of data such as GCMS or LC-PDA.

Titer   A measure of the relative strength of an antiserum.

TMS   Tetramethylsilane, a derivatizing agent used to alter functional groups such as alcohols in a molecule to improve GC characteristics and performance.

Toner   A waxy particulate mixture used in laser printers and copiers to deliver colorant to a substrate that is then heat-affixed.

Total quality management (TQM)   A cradle-to-grave approach to quality assurance that integrates all aspects inside and outside of a particular organization or lab.

Traceability   The ability to relate a measurement or piece of equipment to an unassailable standard.

Transducer   A device that converts whatever arrives at a detector (photons, ions, etc.) into a electrical signal.

Transition metals   Metals that have electrons in their d-orbitals starting with scandium on the periodic table. The d-orbital structure can be exploited to produce colorful compounds and complexes.

Trier-of-fact In a court or legal proceeding, the person or person that makes the ultimate decisions; can be a judge or jury.

Triple base powder Propellant in which the main ingredients are guncotton, nitroglycerin, and nitroguanidine. Used in high caliber weapons.

Tristimulus values Three values (XYZ) calculated using a spectrum in the visible range, standard illuminate values, and weighting factors; associated with the CIE color space system.

Tropane alkaloid An alkaloid characterized by a bridged structure across a ring. Cocaine is a tropane alkaloid.

Tryptamines A class of amine drugs based on tryptamine, a double ringed structure similar to the neurotransmitter serotonin. Psilocin is a tryptamine.

Type I error An error in which the null hypothesis is incorrectly rejected.

Type II error An error in which the null hypothesis is incorrectly accepted.

U

Uncertainty The range associated with any measurement or result that arises from sample, analyst, procedure, etc.

Univariate Involving a single variable.

Upper flammability limit (UFL) The highest mixture ratio of fuel and oxidant that will ignite and sustain combustion.

Useable quantity An amount of a controlled substance that is deemed as usable; an amount that would evoke a response; an amount worth taking.

V

Valium® The first commercial benzodiazepine.

Value (of a color) The depth of a color analogous to a scale of white (lower value) to black (higher value); also referred to as "lightness".

Van Deemter curve A plot of HETP versus flow rate; describes three contributing factors to band broadening and thus column efficiency.

Variance The square of the standard deviation.

Vegetable fibers Fibers based on cellulose; also called *vegetable fibers*.

Vehicle The solvent used in a paint or ink; the solvent used to suspend a pigment or dissolve a dye. A solvent system used to deliver colorants; typically includes materials that will polymerize as they cure.

Virtual image An image created by a lens that does not exist in a point in space and one that can't be captured on a screen. It exists only when viewed through the lens.

Volume of distribution (V_d) See *Apparent volume of distribution*.

W

Walker Test A presumptive test used in distance determinations and analysis of GSR.

Weathering The loss of lighter components of hydrocarbon mixtures used as accelerants.

Working distance The amount of space available between the stage and the lens of a microscope for sample insertion.

Xanthine alkaloids Alkaloids that include caffeine, theophylline and other compounds found in coffee, tea, and chocolate.

Xenobiotic A substance that is foreign to the body; one that is not normally ingested or that is present but in much smaller quantities than the dosage in question.

X-ray diffraction (XRD) A technique in which electrons analogous to light where the diffraction pattern relates to crystal structure.

z-transform A normalization procedure that expresses a variable in terms of its offset from the mean

$$z = \frac{x_i - \bar{x}}{s}$$

where x_i = point to be normalized.

Abbreviations

A	Absorbance
AA	Angle of acceptance; related to light exiting the condenser and entering the objective lens of a microscope
AA/AAS	Atomic absorption spectrometry
AAFS	American Academy of Forensic Sciences
AATCC	Association of Textile Chemists and Colorists
Ab	Antibody
ABC	American Board of Criminalists
ABFT	American Board of Forensic Toxicologists
ADME	Absorption, distribution, metabolism, and elimination; stages of pharmacokinetics
AES	Atomic emission spectroscopy
Ag	Antigen, can also be the symbol for silver.
ANSI	American National Standards Institute
ASCLD	American Society of Crime Laboratory Directors
ASQ	American Society of Quality
ASTM	American Society for Testing and Materials
ATR	Attenuated total reflectance; a mode of infrared spectroscopy that requires surface contact and internal reflections.
B	Birefringence; also sometimes Bi but not used here to avoid confusion with the element bismuth
Bi	See B
BSTFA	N,O-bis(trimethylsilyl) trifluoroacetamide, a derivatization reagent used prior to chromatographic analysis of liable or low volatility compounds
C	Concentration
CDTA	Chemical Diversion and Trafficking Act
CE	Capillary electrophoresis
CI	Color index
CIE	International Commission on Illumination (color spaces)
CMC	Color Measurement Committee of the Society of Dyes and Colorists
CMY	Cyan magenta yellow; a coloring system used in printing; a subtractive system
CNS	Central nervous system

CRM	Certified reference material from NIST
CSA	Controlled Substances Act
CV	Coefficient of variation; same as %RSD
CZE	Capillary zone electrophoresis
DEA	Drug Enforcement Adminstration (US Department of Justice)
DFSA	Drug facilitated sexual assault
DHS	Dynamic headspace
DP	Degree of polymerization
DPA	Diphenylamine
DRE	Drug recognition expert
DRIFTS	Diffuse reflectance infrared spectroscopy, a mode of infrared spectroscopy
DTGS	A deuterium-triglyceride sulfate detector used in IR
E_a	Energy of activation
EC	Ethyl centralite, an ingredient in propellants
ED_{50}	Effective dose-50; The dose of a drug that generates the desired therapeutic effect in half of the test population
EDA	Exploratory data analysis
EDS	Energy dispersive x-ray fluorescence spectroscopy
ELISA	Enzyme-linked immunoassay
EMIT	Enzyme multiplied immunoassay
EOF	Electroosmotic flow
FID	Flame ionization detector
FIR	Far infrared region of the electromagnetic energy spectrum, wavelengths of 50–10,000 um
FPIA	Fluorescent polarization immunoassay
FTIR	Fourier transform infrared spectroscopy
GBL	The lactone form of GHB
GHB	γ hydroxybutyric acid or γ hydroxybutyrate
GSR	Gunshot residue
HATR	Horizontal attenuated total reflectance
HCL	Hollow cathode lamp, versus HCl for hydrochloric acid
HETP	Height equivalent of a theoretical plate
HMX	A high explosive also known as octogen or cyclotetramethylenetetranitramine
HOMO	Highest occupied molecular orbital
HSDB	Hazardous Substance Database; a database available on-line through the National Library of Medicine Gateway

	that contains information on drugs and other compounds
HSV	Hue-saturation-value; a color description system
ICP	Inductively coupled plasma
IGSR	Inorganic gunshot residue
IMS	Ion mobility spectrometry
IR	Infrared region of the electromagnetic spectrum, wavelengths of 2.5 um–50 um
IRMS	Isotope ratio mass spectrometry
ISO	International Standards Organization
K	Known or known sample
K_a	Acid dissociation constant
K_b	Base dissociation constant
K_D	Distribution coefficient
K_H	Henry's Law constant
K_{sp}	Solubility product constant
K_w	Water dissociation constant, $= 1.0 \times 10^{-14}$
LAMPA	Lysergic acid methylpropylamide
LD_{50}	Lethal dose-50; The dose of a drug that kills half of the test population
LDL	Like dissolves like
LDR	Linear dynamic range
LEL	Lower explosive limit; same as LFL, lower flammability range
LFL	Lower flammability range
LFT	Ligand field theory
LLE	Liquid/liquid extraction such as performed in a separatory funnel or Soxhlet extraction unit
LOD	Limit of detection
LOQ	Limit of quantitation; lowest point on a calibration curve
LSD	Lysergic acid diethylamide
LUMO	Lowest unoccupied molecular orbital
MAM	Monoacetylmorphine
MAOI	Monoxamine oxidase inhibitors
MAPA	Methamphetamine Anti-Proliferation Act
MCT	A mercury-cadmium-tellurium detector used for MSP; requires liquid nitrogen cooling
MDEA	3,4-methylenedioxyethylamphetamine
MDMA	3,4-methylenedioxymethamphetamine, Ecstasy
MEK/MEKC	Micellular electrokinetic chromatography
MIR	Multiple internal reflections
MS	Mass spectrometry
MSP	Microspectrophotometry
MVA	Multivariate analysis
N	Theoretical plates; Number of samples in a large population or parent set
NA	Numerical aperture, a measure of a lens to collect light
NG	Nitroglycerin
NIDA	National Institute on Drug Abuse
NIR	Near infrared region of the electromagnetic spectrum, wavelengths of 770–2500 nm
NIST	National Institute of Standards and Technology
NLM	National Library of Medicine
NPD	Nitrogen-phosphorus detector
NSAID	Non-steroidal anti-inflammatory drugs
OGSR	Organic gunshot residue
OTC	Over-the-counter; drugs and medicines that can be purchased without a prescription
P2P	Phenyl-2-propanone, a methamphetamine precursor
PCA	Principal component analysis
PCP	Phencyclidine. A potent synthetic hallucinogen. Likely derived from the description "PeaCe Pill"
PDA	Photodiode array
PDB	Peedee Belemnite, a calcium carbonate used as a reference material in SIR measurements
PDMS	Polydimethylsiloxane
PDR	Physician's Desk Reference
PFTBA	per-Fluorotributylamine, a compound used to tune mass spectrometers
PG	Prostaglandins
PI	Power index of an explosive relative to picric acid
PLM	Polarized light microscopy
PPA	Phenylpropanolamine
PT	Purge and trap
Py-GC	Pyrolysis gas chromatography
Q	Heat released by a combustion reaction, $-\Delta H$; also a questioned sample.
QA	Quality assurance
QC	Quality control
R	Retardation
RDX	A high explosive also known as hexogen or cyclotrimethylenetrinitramine
Rf	Radiofrequency
RGB	Red-green-blue; additive color system used in computer monitors and other projection systems
RIA	Radioimmunoassay
%RSD	Percent relative standard deviation; same as CV
SAR	Surface absorption-reflection
SAX	Strong anion exchange
SCX	Strong cation exchange
SDC	Society of Dyes and Colourists
SEM	Scanning electron microscope
SIR	Stable isotope ratio
SMOW	Standard mean ocean water, used as a reference material for SIR measurements
SOFT	Society of Forensic Toxicology
SOP	Standard operating procedure
SPE	Solid phase extraction

SPME	Solid phase microextraction	TNT	Trinitrotoluene
SPSE	Solid phase stirbar extraction	TQM	Total quality management
SRM	Standard reference material from NIST	UEL	Lower explosive limit; same as UFL, upper flammability range
SSRI	Selective serotonin re-uptake inhibitors	UFL	Upper flammability range
SWDRUG	Scientific Working Group for the Analysis of Seized Drugs	UV	Ultraviolet region of the electromagnetic spectrum, wavelengths of 200–400 nm
TATB	A high explosive, 1,3,5-triamino-2,4,6-trinitrobenzene	V_d	Apparent volume of distribution
T_g	Glass transition temperature	VIS	Visible region of the electromagnetic spectrum, wavelengths of 400–700 nm
THF	Tetrahydrofuran		
TLC	Thin layer chromatography	WDS	Wavelength dispersive x-ray fluorescence spectroscopy
TMS	Tetramethylsilane, a derivatization reagent used prior to chromatographic analysis of liable or low volatility compounds	XRD	X-ray diffraction
		XRF	X-ray fluorescence

APPENDIX 3

Solvent Properties for SPE and HPL

Properties of solvents for liquid
chromatography including miscibilities

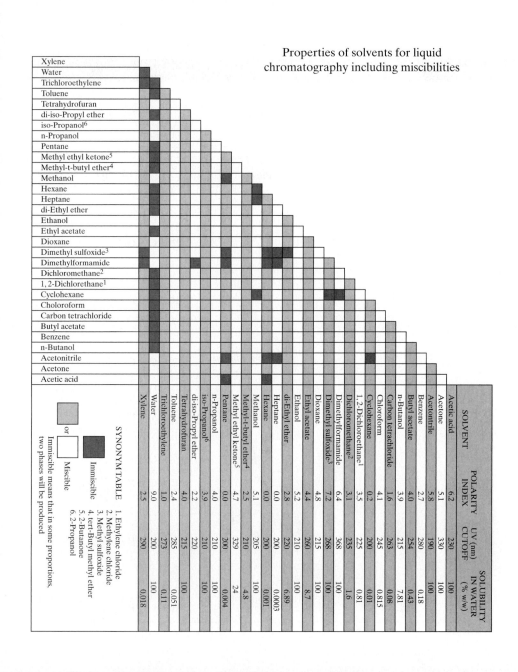

Legend

- Miscible (light gray)
- Immiscible (dark) or (white)

Immiscible means that in some proportions, two phases will be produced

SYNONYM TABLE

1. Ethylene chloride
2. Methylene chloride
3. Methyl sulfoxide
4. tert-Butyl methyl ether
5. 2-Butanone
6. 2-Propanol

SOLVENT	POLARITY INDEX	UV (nm) CUTOFF	SOLUBILITY IN WATER (% w/w)
Xylene	2.5	290	0.018
Water	9.0	200	100
Trichloroethylene	1.0	273	0.11
Toluene	2.4	285	0.051
Tetrahydrofuran	4.0	215	100
di-iso-Propyl ether	2.2	220	0.2
iso-Propanol[6]	3.9	210	100
n-Propanol	4.0	210	100
Pentane	0.0	200	0.004
Methyl ethyl ketone[5]	4.7	329	24
Methyl-t-butyl ether[4]	2.5	210	4.8
Methanol	5.1	205	100
Hexane	0.0	200	0.001
Heptane	0.0	200	0.0003
di-Ethyl ether	2.8	220	6.89
Ethanol	5.2	210	100
Ethyl acetate	4.4	260	8.7
Dioxane	4.8	215	100
Dimethyl sulfoxide[3]	7.2	268	100
Dimethylformamide	6.4	368	100
Dichloromethane[2]	3.1	235	1.6
1,2-Dichlorethane[1]	3.5	225	0.81
Cyclohexane	0.2	200	0.01
Chloroform	4.1	245	0.815
Carbon tetrachloride	1.6	263	0.08
Butyl acetate	4.0	254	0.43
Benzene	2.7	280	0.18
Acetonitrile	5.8	190	100
Acetone	5.1	330	100
Acetic acid	6.2	230	100

Key Organic Chemistry Terms and Reactions

Table A4.1 Common Functional Groups

Alkane	RCH_3	Aniline	$\langle\text{benzene ring}\rangle-NH_2$
Alkene	$C=C$ (Internal) $C=CH_2$ (Terminal)	Phenol	$\langle\text{benzene ring}\rangle-OH$
Alkyne	$RC\equiv CR$ (Internal) $RC\equiv CH$ (Terminal)	Carboxylic acid	$R-\overset{\overset{O}{\|\|}}{C}-OH$
Nitrile	$RC\equiv N$	Acyl chloride	$R-\overset{\overset{O}{\|\|}}{C}-Cl$
Ether	$R-O-R$	Acid anhydride	$R-\overset{\overset{O}{\|\|}}{C}-O-\overset{\overset{O}{\|\|}}{C}-R$
Thiol	RCH_2-SH	Ester	$R-\overset{\overset{O}{\|\|}}{C}-OR$
Sulfide	$R-S-R$	Amide	$R-\overset{\overset{O}{\|\|}}{C}-NH_2 \quad -NHR \quad -NR_2$
Disulfide	$R-S-S-R$	Aldehyde	$R-\overset{\overset{O}{\|\|}}{C}-H$
Epoxide	$\triangle$ (with O at top)	Ketone	$R-\overset{\overset{O}{\|\|}}{C}-R$

Table A4.2   Substitution Notation

	Primary	Secondary	Tertiary
Alkyl halide	$R - CH_2 - X$ $X = F, Cl, Br, or I$	$R - \overset{\overset{\displaystyle R}{\mid}}{CH} - X$	$R - \overset{\overset{\displaystyle R}{\mid}}{\underset{\underset{\displaystyle R}{\mid}}{C}} - X$
Alcohol	$R - CH_2 - OH$	$R - \overset{\overset{\displaystyle R}{\mid}}{CH} - OH$	$R - \overset{\overset{\displaystyle R}{\mid}}{\underset{\underset{\displaystyle R}{\mid}}{C}} - OH$
Amine	$R - NH_2$	$R - \overset{\overset{\displaystyle R}{\mid}}{NH}$	$R - \overset{\overset{\displaystyle R}{\mid}}{\underset{\underset{\displaystyle R}{\mid}}{N}}$

Table A4.3   Mechanisms: S$_N$2: Substitution, Nucleophilic, Bimolecular. The following summarizes the four generic organic reaction mechanisms using alkyl halids (RX) as examples.

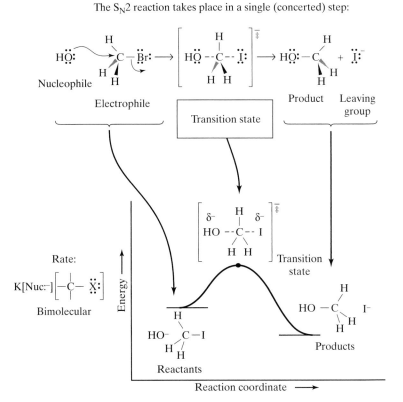

Generic substitution reaction

S$_N$2
The S$_N$2 reaction takes place in a single (concerted) step:

Inversion of configuration in the S$_N$2 reaction

(S)-2-bromobutane   (R)-2-butanol

Backside attack

Source: The information is summarized from Wade, L.G., *Organic Chemistry* (4th ed.), Chapter 6, "Alkyl Halides: Nucleophilic Substitution and Elimination." 2003, Prentice Hall: Upper Saddle River, NJ, pp. 212–271.

Table A4.3 (Continued)

1. A species with a negative charge is a stronger nucleophile than a similar neutral species. In particular, a base is a a stronger nucleophile than its conjugate acid.

$$^{-}{:}\ddot{O}H > H_2\ddot{O}{:} \qquad ^{-}{:}\ddot{S}H > H_2\ddot{S}{:} \qquad ^{-}{:}\ddot{N}H_2 > {:}NH_3$$

2. Nucleophilicity decreases from left to right in the periodic table, following the increase in electronegativity from left to right. The more electronegative elements have more tightly held nonbonding electrons that are less reactive toward forming new bonds.

$$^{-}{:}\ddot{O}H > {:}\ddot{F}{:}^{-} \qquad {:}NH_3 > H_2\ddot{O}{:} \qquad (CH_3CH_2)_3P{:} > (CH_3CH_2)_2\ddot{S}{:}$$

3. Nucleophilicity increases down the periodic table, following the increase in size and polarizability.

$${:}\ddot{I}{:}^{-} > {:}\ddot{Br}{:}^{-} > {:}\ddot{Cl}{:}^{-} > {:}\ddot{F}{:}^{-} \qquad ^{-}{:}\ddot{Se}H > ^{-}{:}\ddot{S}H > ^{-}{:}\ddot{O}H \qquad (CH_3CH_2)_3P{:} > (CH_3CH_2)_3N{:}$$

Weak bases that are common leaving groups

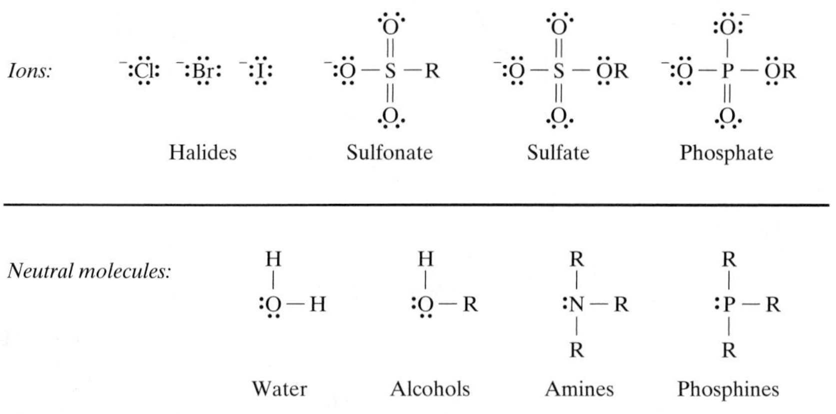

Ions:
Halides
Sulfonate
Sulfate
Phosphate
Neutral molecules:
Water
Alcohols
Amines
Phosphines

Table A4.4 Mechanisms: S_N1: Substitution, Nucleophilic, Unimolecular

Generic substitution reaction

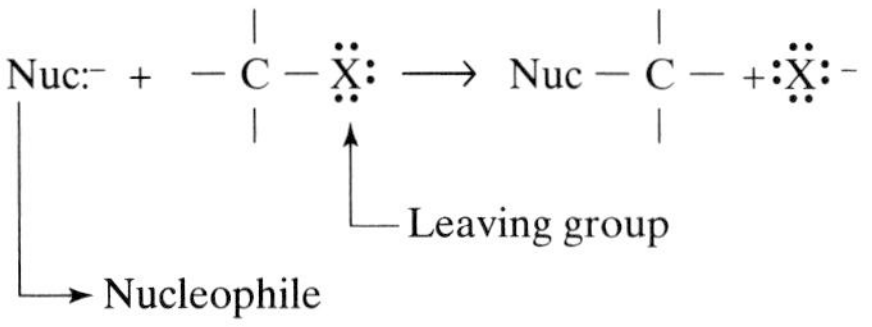

Nuc:⁻ + —C—X: ⟶ Nuc—C— + :X:⁻
Leaving group
Nucleophile

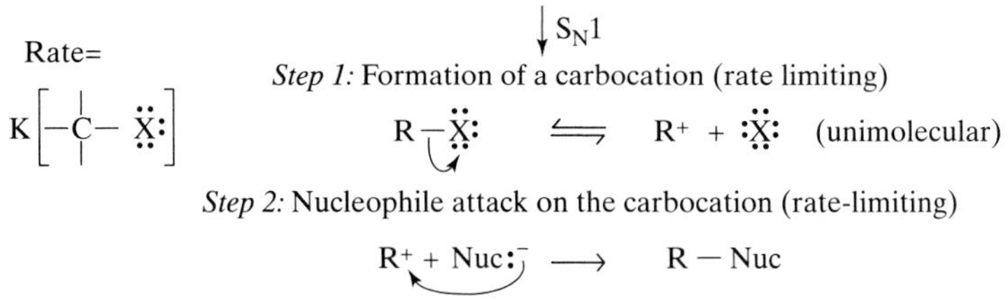

SN1
Rate=
K[—C—X:]
Step 1: Formation of a carbocation (rate limiting)
R—X: ⇌ R+ + :X: (unimolecular)
Step 2: Nucleophile attack on the carbocation (rate-limiting)
R+ + Nuc:⁻ ⟶ R—Nuc

Carbocation
stability
3° > 2° > 1° > CH3 X
Rate-limiting
transition state
Intermediate
‡1
‡2
R+ + X⁻
+ Nuc:⁻
Energy
R—X + Nuc:⁻
R— Nuc: + X⁻
SN1

Not stereospecific
Racemic
mixture
CH3CH2ÖH
From the top
–H+
OCH2CH3
H3C C (S)
(CH3)2CH CH2CH3
Retention of configuration
:Br:⁻
CH3CH2OH
:Br:⁻
H3C C
(CH3)2CH CH2CH3
(S)
H3C C+ — CH2CH3
(CH3)2CH
CH3CH2ÖH
From the bottom
–H+
H3C CH2CH3
(CH3)2CH C
(R)
OCH2CH3
Planar carbocation (achiral)
Inversion of configuration

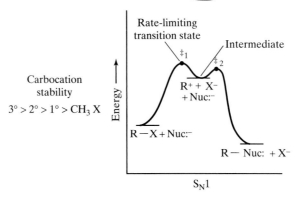

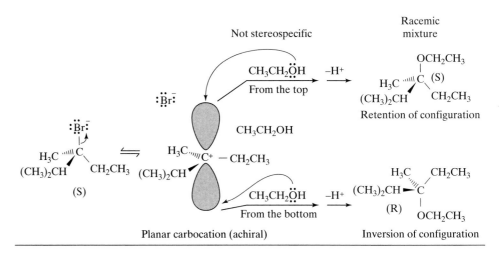

Table A4.5 Elimination Mechanisms: E1 (Elimination, Unimolecular) and E2 (Elimination, Bimolecular)

Elimination reactions

E1

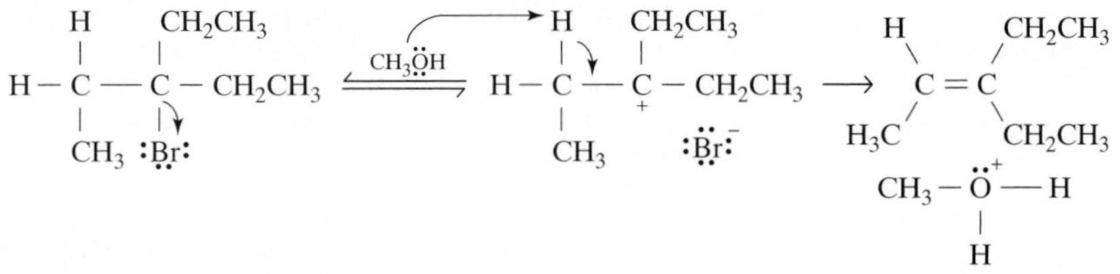

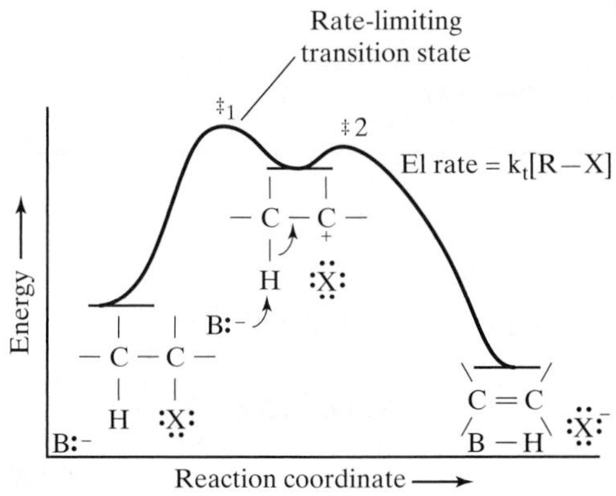

H—C—C—CH₂CH₃ ⇌ H—C—C—CH₂CH₃ ⟶ C=C

Step 1: Formation of a carbocation (rate limiting).

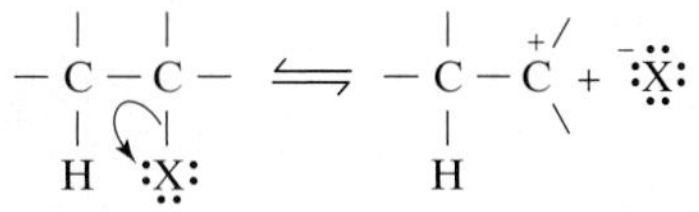

Step 2: A base abstracts a proton (fast).

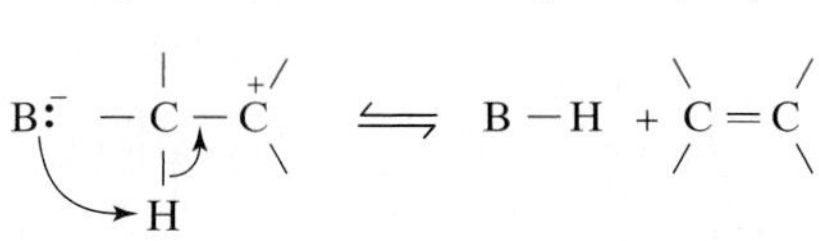

Rate-limiting transition state

E1 rate = $k_t[R{-}X]$

Energy ⟶

Reaction coordinate ⟶

E2

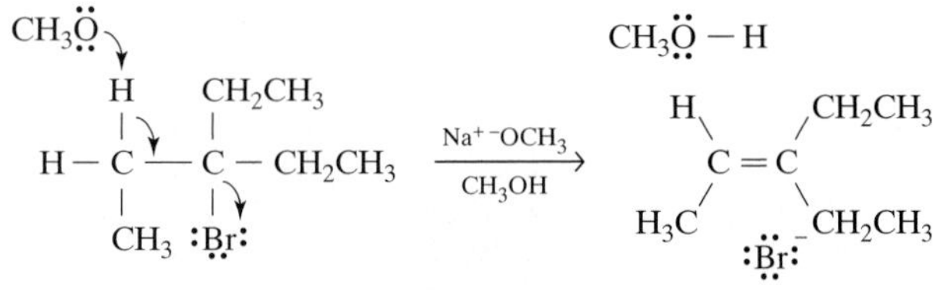

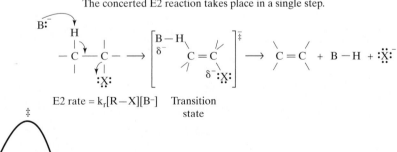

The concerted E2 reaction takes place in a single step.

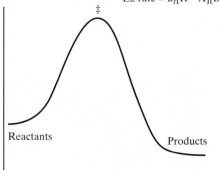

E2 rate = $k_r[R{-}X][B^-]$ Transition state

Reactants

Products

Table A4.6 Summary of Substitution and Elimination Mechanisms

Nucleophillic substitutions — Summary

	S_N1	S_N2
Promoting factors		
Nucleophilic	Weak nucleophiles are OK	Strong nucleophile needed
Substrate (RX)	$3° > 2°$	$CH_3X > 1° > 2°$
Solvent	Good ionizing solvent needed	Wide variety of solvents
Leaving group	Good one required	Good one required
Other	$AgNO_3$ forces ionization	
Characteristics		
Kinetics	First order, $k_t[RX]$	Second order, $k_t[RX][Nuc:^-]$
Steriochemistry	Mixture of inversion and retention	Complete inversion
Rearrangements	Common	Impossible

Eliminations — Summary

	E_1	E_2
Promoting factors		
Base	Weak bases work	Strong base required
Solvent	Good ionizing solvent	Wide variety of solvents
Substrate	$3° > 2°$	$3° > 2° > 1°$
Leaving group	Good one required	Good one required
Characteristics		
Kinetics	First order, $k_t[RX]$	Second order, $k_t[RX][B:^-]$
Orientation	Most highly substituted alkene	Most highly substituted alkene
Stereochemistry	No special geometry	Coplanar transition state required
Rearrangements	Common	Impossible

R/S Naming and Stereochemical Nomenclature

The information provided in this appendix will assist you when working with isomers and compounds containing chiral centers (asymmetric carbons). The types of isomers are summarized below:

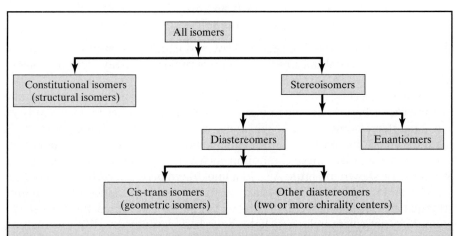

Isomers are different compounds with the same molecular formula.
Constitutional isomers are isomers that differ in the order in which atoms are bonded together. Constitutional isomers are sometimes called **structural isomers** because they have different connections among their atoms.
Stereoisomers are isomers that differ only in the orientation of the atoms in space.
Enantiomers are mirror-image isomers.
Diastereomers are stereoisomers that are not mirror images of each other.
Cis-trans isomers (geometric isomers) are diastereomers that differ in their cis-trans arrangement on a ring or double bond.

◀ **Figure A5.1**

Stereoisomers contain one or more asymmetric carbon or a carbon with four different groups attached to it. The first step in assigning a configuration to an asymmetric carbon is to assign priorities to each attached group.

5.1 CAHN-INGOLD-PRELOG METHOD FOR DETERMINING PRIORITY OF ATTACHED GROUPS

(a) Locate the asymmetric carbon and the 4 atoms directly attached (not the group).

(b) The highest priority is assigned to the atom with the highest atomic number.

(c) If isotopes are involved, the highest priority is assigned to the heaviest isotope.

(d) In the case of a tie, move down the chain until a difference is encountered. An ethyl group would have higher priority than a methyl group because of the bond to a carbon (atomic number 6) versus a bond to a hydrogen (atomic number 1).

(e) If multiple bonds are involved, break them into imaginary single bonds and imaginary atoms.

(f) View the asymmetric carbon with the lowest priority group pointed backward. Imagine or draw an arrow from group 1 to group 3. If the arrow flows clockwise, the configuration is R; if counterclockwise, S.

Fischer projections make it easier to draw and compare stereoisomers. In this convention, horizontal lines represent bonds projecting away from the viewer while vertical lines project toward the viewer.

Fischer projections are particularly useful if a molecule has more than one asymmetric carbon. As shown in Figure A5.4, tartaric acid has two such carbons and three stereoisomers, one of which is a meso compound. Meso compounds are superimposable on their mirror image and do not interact with polarized light. In other words, a meso compound such as (2R,3S)-tartaric acid has a plane of symmetry, shown in Figure A5.5 as a line drawn between carbons 2 and 3.

The table of physical properties illustrates the importance of the atomic arrangements. A racemic mixture of tartaric acid, as well as the meso compounds do not rotate polarized light, have had significantly different melting points than the pair of enantiomers.

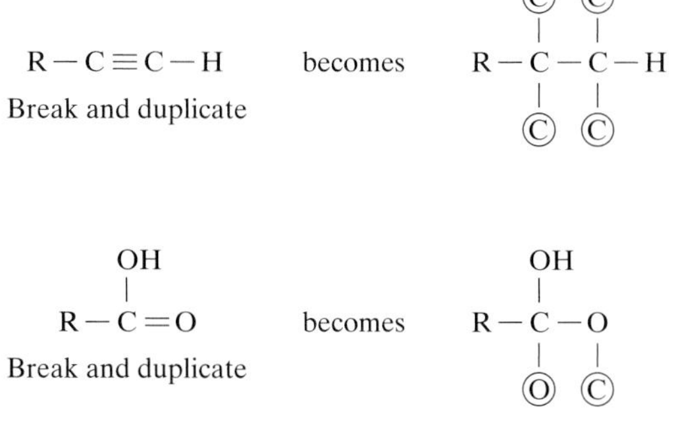

▶ Figure A5.2

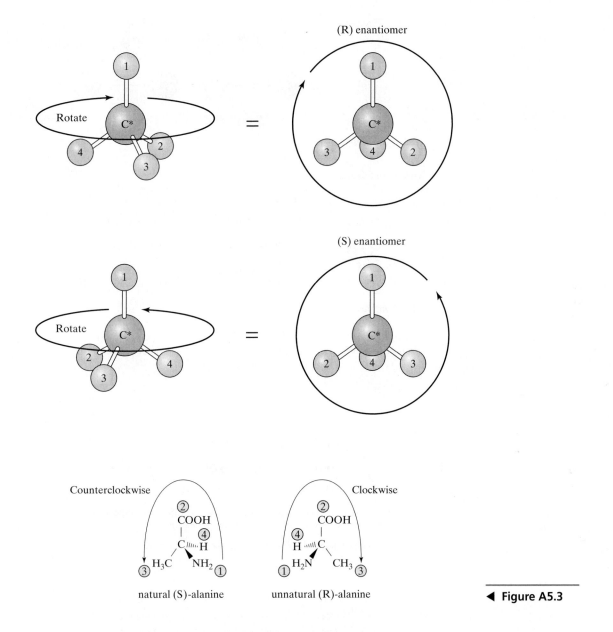

natural (S)-alanine   unnatural (R)-alanine

◀ **Figure A5.3**

5.2 DL NOTATION (FISCHER-ROSANOFF CONVENTION)

This naming system for proteins and carbohydrates (rich in chiral carbons) pre-dates methods capable of establishing the actual molecular configuration. In this system, the D/L notation is derived by comparing Fischer projections of the molecule in question with glyceraldehydes. The molecule is drawn such that the carbonyl is as close to the top as possible. If the –OH is on the right, it is la-beled D as in D-glyceraldehyde. If the –OH is on the left, the carbon is labeled L. Note that DL does not correspond to the direction of rotation of polarized light.[1]

---

[1]Recall that the $+/-$ notation refers to the direction a molecule rotates polarized light. This direc-tion cannot be predicted based on R/S configuration; it must be empirically determined.

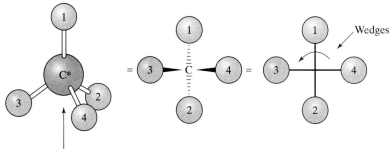

View from this angle

COOH
C^{llllll} CH$_3$
HO   H

View from this angle

= HO►C◄H
COOH
CH$_3$

= HO─┼─H
COOH
CH$_3$

(S)-lactic acid
perpective drawing

(S)-lactic acid
Fischer projection

▶ **Figure A5.4**

HOOC   OH
H ^{lllll}C$-$C◄H
HO   COOH

HOOC   H
H ^{lllll}C$-$C◄OH
HO   COOH

H   COOH
HO ^{lllll}C$-$C◄H
HOOC   OH

(2R, 3S)-tartaric acid
a meso compound

(2R, 3R)-tartaric acid
a pair of enantiomers

(2S, 3S)-tartaric acid

Perspective formulas of the stereoisomer of tartaric acid

COOH
H─┼─OH
H─┼─OH
COOH

COOH
H─┼─OH
HO─┼─H
COOH

COOH
HO─┼─H
H─┼─OH
COOH

(2R, 3S)-tartaric acid
a meso compound

(2R, 3R)-tartaric acid
a pair of enantiomers

(2S, 3S)-tartaric acid

Fischer projections of the stereoisomer of tartaric acid

Physical Properties of the Stereoisomers of Tartaric Acid

	Melting point, °C	$[\alpha]_D^{25\,°C}$	Solubility, g/100 g H$_2$O at 15 °C
(2R, 3R)-(+)-tartaric acid	170	+11.98°	139
(2S, 3S)-(−)-tartaric acid	170	−11.98°	139
(2R, 3S)-tartaric acid	140	0°	125
(±)-tartaric acid	206	0°	139

▶ **Figure A5.5**

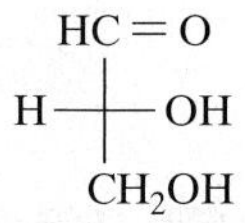

D-glyceraldehyde 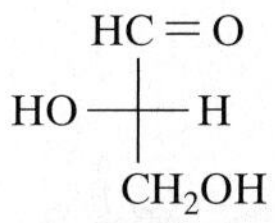 L-glyceraldehyde

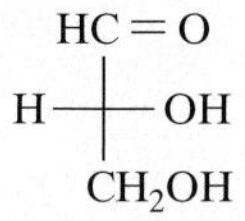

D-(+)-glyceraldehyde 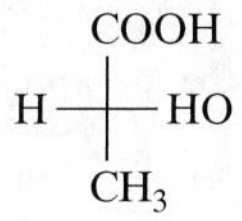 D-(−)-lactic acid

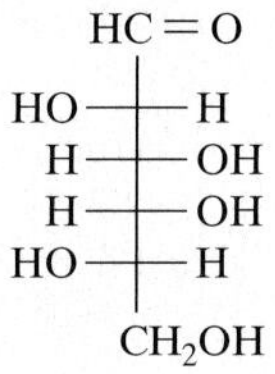

L-galactose

◀ **Figure A5.6**

Thermodynamic Quantities

Substance	ΔH_f° (kJ/mol)	ΔG_f° (kJ/mol)	S° (J/mol-K)
Aluminum			
Al(s)	0	0	28.32
AlCl₃(s)	−705.6	−630.0	109.3
Al₂O₃(s)	−1669.8	−1576.5	51.00
Barium			
Ba(s)	0	0	63.2
BaCO₃(s)	−1216.3	−1137.6	112.1
BaO(s)	−553.5	−525.1	70.42
Carbon			
C(g)	718.4	672.9	158.0
C(s, diamond)	1.88	2.84	2.43
C(s, graphite)	0	0	5.69
CCl₄(g)	−106.7	−64.0	309.4
CCl₄(l)	−139.3	−68.6	214.4
CF₄(g)	−679.9	−635.1	262.3
CH₄(g)	−74.8	−50.8	186.3
C₂H₂(g)	226.77	209.2	200.8
C₂H₄(g)	52.30	68.11	219.4
C₂H₆(g)	−84.68	−32.89	229.5
C₃H₈(g)	−103.85	−23.47	269.9
C₄H₁₀(g)	−124.73	−15.71	310.0
C₄H₁₀(l)	−147.6	−15.0	231.0
C₆H₆(g)	82.9	129.7	269.2
C₆H₆(l)	49.0	124.5	172.8
CH₃OH(g)	−201.2	−161.9	237.6
CH₃OH(l)	−238.6	−166.23	126.8
C₂H₅OH(g)	−235.1	−168.5	282.7
C₂H₅OH(l)	−277.7	−174.76	160.7
C₆H₁₂O₆(s)	−1273.02	−910.4	212.1
CO(g)	−110.5	−137.2	197.9
CO₂(g)	−393.5	−394.4	213.6
HC₂H₃O₂(l)	−487.0	−392.4	159.8
Hydrogen			
H(g)	217.94	203.26	114.60
H⁺(aq)	0	0	0
H⁺(g)	1536.2	1517.0	108.9
H₂(g)	0	0	130.58
Lead			
Pb(s)	0	0	68.85
PbBr₂(s)	−277.4	−260.7	161
PbCO₃(s)	−699.1	−625.5	131.0
Pb(NO₃)₂(aq)	−421.3	−246.9	303.3
Pb(NO₃)₂(s)	−451.9	—	—
PbO(s)	−217.3	−187.9	68.70
Nitrogen			
N(g)	472.7	455.5	153.3
N₂(g)	0	0	191.50
NH₃(aq)	−80.29	−26.50	111.3
NH₃(g)	−46.19	−16.66	192.5
NH₄⁺(aq)	−132.5	−79.31	113.4
N₂H₄(g)	95.40	159.4	238.5
NH₄CN(s)	0.0	—	—
NH₄Cl(s)	−314.4	−203.0	94.6
NH₄NO₃(s)	−365.6	−184.0	151
NO(g)	90.37	86.71	210.62
NO₂(g)	33.84	51.84	240.45
N₂O(g)	81.6	103.59	220.0
N₂O₄(g)	9.66	98.28	304.3
NOCl(g)	52.6	66.3	264
HNO₃(aq)	−206.6	−110.5	146
HNO₃(g)	−134.3	−73.94	266.4

Oxygen

O(g)	247.5	230.1	161.0
$O_2(g)$	0	0	205.0
$O_3(g)$	142.3	163.4	237.6
$OH^-(aq)$	−230.0	−157.3	−10.7
$H_2O(g)$	−241.82	−228.57	188.83
$H_2O(l)$	−285.83	−237.13	69.91
$H_2O_2(g)$	−136.10	−105.48	232.9
$H_2O_2(l)$	−187.8	−120.4	109.6

Potassium

K(g)	89.99	61.17	160.2
K(s)	0	0	64.67

KCl(s)	−435.9	−408.3	82.7
$KClO_3(s)$	−391.2	−289.9	143.0
$KClO_3(aq)$	−349.5	−284.9	265.7
$K_2CO_3(s)$	−1150.18	−1064.58	155.44
$KNO_3(s)$	−492.70	−393.13	132.9
$K_2O(s)$	−363.2	−322.1	94.14
$KO_2(s)$	−284.5	−240.6	122.5
$K_2O_2(s)$	−495.8	−429.8	113.0
KOH(s)	−424.7	−378.9	78.91
KOH(aq)	−482.4	−440.5	91.6

Photo Credits

Chapter 1: Page 9 Courtesy of the National Library of Medicine **Page 10** Mary Evans Picture Library Ltd.

Chapter 5: Page 140 (top) The Granger Collection **Page 140 (bottom)** Science and Society Picture Library **Page 143** National High Magnetic Field Laboratory **Page 145 (top & bottom)** Suzanne Bell **Page 169** Richard During/Getty Images Inc. - Stone Allstock **Page 172** Courtesy of the Beinecke Rare Book and Manuscript Library, Yale University **Page 173** Reprinted with permission from Brown and Clark, *Analysis of Pigmentary Materials on the Vinland Map and Tartar Relation by Raman Microprobe and Spectroscopy*, ACS, 74(15) pp 3658-3661, 2002. Copyright 2002 American Chemical Society. **Page 174** Sheila Terry/Photo Researchers, Inc. **Page 184** Courtesy of Dr. Paul Martin, Criac Technologies

Chapter 6: Page 213 (left) Randy Taylor/Index Stock Imagery, Inc. **Page 213 (right)** Frank La Bua/Pearson Education/PH College **Page 214** © Corbis **Page 215** Picture Desk Inc./Kobal Collection **Page 216** The Coca-Cola Company **Page 220** Courtesy of Aaron Brudenell, Tucson Police Department Laboratory **Page 222** Andy Crawford/Dorling Kindersley Media Library **Page 223** H.F. Farny/CORBIS-NY **Page 226** Courtesy of the Oklahoma State Bureau of Investigation **Page 227 (top)** Courtesy of the Oklahoma State Bureau of Investigation **Page 227 (bottom)** Courtesy of the Oklahoma State Bureau of Investigation **Page 228** Suzanne Bell **Page 241** Suzanne Bell **Page 259** Fra Angelico (1387-1455), "Saint Albertus Magnus," roundel. Detail from the Crucifixion, Museo di S. Marco, Florence, Italy. Scala/Art Resource, NY

Chapter 7: Page 300 (top) Courtesy of the Oklahoma State Bureau of Investigation **Page 300 (bottom)** Courtesy of Aaron Brudenell, Crime Laboratory, Tucson Police Department **Page 301 (top)** Courtesy of the Oklahoma State Bureau of Investigation **Page 301 (bottom)** Courtesy of the Oklahoma State Bureau of Investigation **Page 734** Courtesy of Heather Campbell, Idaho State Patrol Forensic Laboratory **Page 305** Courtesy of the Oklahoma State Bureau of Investigation **Page 306** Courtesy of the Oklahoma State Bureau of Investigation **Page 307 (top)** Courtesy of the Oklahoma

State Bureau of Investigation **Page 307 (bottom)** Courtesy of the Oklahoma State Bureau of Investigation **Page 308 (top)** Courtesy of the Oklahoma State Bureau of Investigation **Page 308 (bottom)** Courtesy of the Oklahoma State Bureau of Investigation **Page 309** Courtesy of the Oklahoma State Bureau of Investigation

Chapter 8: Page 322 Francoise de Mulder/CORBIS-NY **Page 329** Courtesy of the Oklahoma State Bureau of Investigation **Page 336 (left & right)** Courtesy of the Oklahoma State Bureau of Investigation **Page 340** Courtesy of the Oklahoma State Bureau of Investigation **Page 341** Courtesy of the Oklahoma State Bureau of Investigation **Page 349** © Henry Diltz/Corbis **Page 350** Courtesy of the Oklahoma State Bureau of Investigation **Page 357 (top)** Courtesy of the Oklahoma State Bureau of Investigation **Page 357 (bottom)** Courtesy of the Oklahoma State Bureau of Investigation

Chapter 9: Page 410 Courtesy of the Federal Emergency Management Agency (FEMA) **Page 420** Courtesy of the Federal Emergency Management Agency (FEMA) **Page 424** Courtesy of Aaron Brudenell, Firearms Examiner, Tucson Police Department Crime Laboratory **Page 428** Suzanne Bell

Chapter 10: Page 437 Suzanne Bell **Page 447** Reprinted with permission from Lebiedzik, J., and D.L. Johnson, *Handguns and Ammunitions Indicators Extracted from the GSR Analysis*, Journal of Forensic Sciences, 47 (2002), 483-489. Copyright 2002, ASTM International **Page 453** Reprinted with permission from Gowadia et.al., *The Natural Sampling of Airborne Trace Signals from Explosives Concealed upon the Human Body*, Journal of Forensic Sciences, 46(6) (2001), 1324-1331. Copyright 2001, ASTM International

Chapter 11: Page 476 Reprinted with permission from Williams Mazzella, et.al., *A Study to Investigate the Evidential Value of Blue Gel Pen Inks*, Journal of Forensic Sciences, 48(2) (2003), 419-425. Copyright 2003, ASTM International **Page 496** Courtesy of Amy Richmond and Jennifer Wiseman, WVU Department of Chemistry **Page 505** Courtesy of William M. Schenck, Microvision Northwest-Forensic Consulting, Inc.

Index

Page numbers followed by b indicate boxed material; f, figures; n, footnotes; t, tables.

A

AAFS (American Academy of Forensic Sciences), 11
AAS (atomic absorption spectrometry), 173–178
ABC (American Board of Criminalistics), 11
ABFT (American Board of Forensic Toxicology), 11
Absolute error, definition of, 20
Absolute uncertainty, 16
Absorbance, spectroscopy and, 154, 155f
Absorption, 247–249, 249f
Accelerants, in arson and fire investigation, 433–434
Accreditation, of laboratory, 69
Accuracy, definition of, 65
Acetaminophen, structure of, 315f
Acetate fibers, description of, 576t
Acetic anhydride, formation of, 334, 334f
Acetone, characteristics of, 100t
Acetonitrile, characteristics of, 100t
Acetylcodeine, structure of, 330t
Acetylsalicylic acid, structure of, 315f
Achromatic color, 273
Acid-base-neutral extractions, 104–106, 105f, 106f
Acidic drugs, forensic drug analysis of, 296–315
Acids, 267, 268f
Acrylic fibers, description of, 576t
ACS (American Chemical Society), 11
Active headspace methods, of partitioning, 107
Addiction, physical, 223
Addition polymers, 548, 548f
Additive color systems, 473–474, 474f
Adhesives, forensic analysis of, 609–611, 610b, 611f
Adiabatic combustion, 392
Adulterants
    definition of, 228
    in profiling, 236, 238–239
Adversarial system, 3, 4f
AES (atomic emission spectroscopy), 178–179
Affinity, relative, 96

Aging
    of inks and paints, analysis for, 521–524, 522f, 523f, 524f
    of paper, 572–574
Aliquot, 71
Alkaloids
    analysis of, 329–356
    ergot, analysis of, 345–354. *See also* Hallucinogens
    as natural products, 216
    opiate. *See also* Opiate alkaloids
        analysis of, 329–338, 329f, 330–332t, 333f, 334f, 336f
    tropane, 338–345. *See also* Cocaine
    tryptamine, analysis of, 346, 349. *See also* Hallucinogens
    xanthine, analysis of, 354, 356, 356f
Alkyd resins, in paints, 501
Allocaine, structure of, 339t
Alprazolam, structure of, 377t
Alto, in mechanical printing, 497
Alumina A, characteristics of, 110t
Alumina B, characteristics of, 110t
Alumina N, characteristics of, 110t
Alzarin, structure of, 485t
American Academy of Forensic Sciences (AAFS), 11
American Board of Criminalistics (ABC), 11
American Board of Forensic Toxicology (ABFT), 11
American Chemical Society (ACS), 11
American Society for Testing and Materials (ASTM), standards of
    for fire debris analysis, 435t
    for paint and ink analysis, 509
American Society of Crime Laboratory Directors LAB program (ASCLD), 11
Aminopropyl, characteristics of, 110t
Amitriptyline, structure of, 378t
Ammunition, types of, 425f
Amorphous solid, 529, 532f

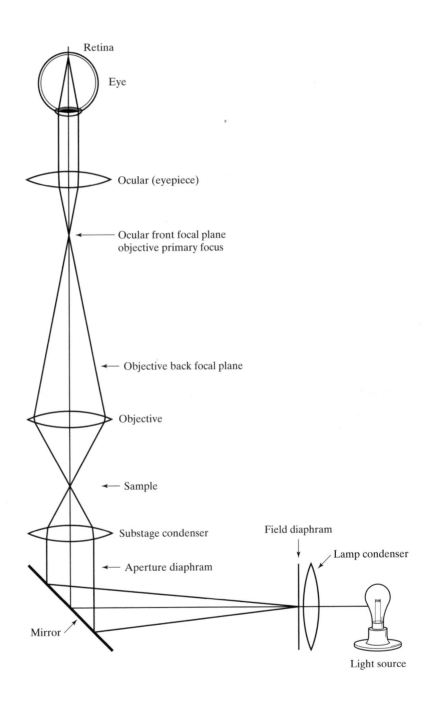

Retina

Eye

Ocular (eyepiece)

Ocular front focal plane
objective primary focus

Objective back focal plane

Objective

Sample

Substage condenser

Field diaphram

Lamp condenser

Aperture diaphram

Mirror

Light source

▶ *Optical path of a generic
light microscope*

Regions of the Infrared Spectrum for Preliminary Analysis

Region	Group	Possible compounds present (or absent)
3700–3100	—OH	Alcohols, aldehydes, carboxylic acids
	—NH	Amides, amines
	$\equiv$C—H	Alkynes
3100–3000	=CH	Aromatic compounds
—	—CH$_2$ or —CH=CH—	Alkenes or unsaturated rings
3000–2800	—CH, —CH$_2$—, —CH$_3$	Aliphatic groups
2800–2600	—CHO	Aldehydes (Fermi doublet)
2700–2400	—POH	Phosphorus compounds
	—SH	Mercaptans and thiols
	—PH	Phosphines
2400–2000	—C$\equiv$N	Nitriles
	—N=N=N	Azides
	—C$\equiv$C—	Alkynes
1870–1650	C=O	Acid halides, aldehydes, amides, amino acids, anhydrides, carboxylic acids, esters, ketones, lactams, lactones, quinones
1650–1550	C=C, C=N, NH	Unsaturated aliphatics, aromatics, unsaturated heterocycles, amides, amines, amino acids
1550–1300	NO$_2$	Nitro compounds
	CH$_3$ and CH$_2$	Alkanes, alkenes, etc.
1300–1000	C—O—C and C—OH	Ethers, alcohols, sugars
	S=O, P=O, C—F	Sulfur, phosphorus, and fluorine compounds
1100–800	Si—O and P—O	Organosilicon and phosphorus compounds
1000–650	=C—H	Alkenes and aromatic compounds
	—NH	Aliphatic amines
800–400	C—halogen	Halogen compounds
	Aromatic rings	Aromatic compounds

Electronic Absorption Data for Isolated Chromophores

Chromophore	Example	Solvent	λ_{max} (nm)	ε (liter mol^{-1} cm^{-1})
C=C	1-Hexene	Heptane	180	12,500
—C$\equiv$C—	1-Butyne	Vapor	172	4,500
⬡	Benzene	Water	254	205
			203.5	7,400
	Toluene	Water	261	225
			206.5	7,000
C=O	Acetaldehyde	Vapor	298	12.5
			182	10,000
	Acetone	Cyclohexane	275	22
			190	1,000
	Camphor	Hexane	295	14
—COOH	Acetic acid	Ethanol	204	41
—COCl	Acetyl chloride	Heptane	240	34
—COOR	Ethyl acetate	Water	204	60
—CONH$_2$	Acetamide	Methanol	205	160
—NO$_2$	Nitromethane	Hexane	279	15.8
			202	4,400
=N=N	Diazomethane	Diethyl ether	417	7
—N=N—	*trans*-Azomethane	Water	343	25
C=N—	C$_2$H$_5$CH—NC$_4$H$_9$	Isooctane	238	200

From J.B. Lambert, H.F. Shurvell, L. Verbit, R.G. Cooks, and G.H. Stout, *Organic Structural Analysis*, Macmillan Publishing, New York, 1976.